...and the skills you need to get there.

The book is full of **Skill Modules** that focus on basic skills that you'll need to develop as you start your small business. Here's a complete listing.

IMPORTANT

HERE IS YOUR REGISTRATION CODE TO ACCESS MCGRAW-HILL PREMIUM CONTENT AND MCGRAW-HILL ONLINE RESOURCES

For key premium online resources you need THIS CODE to gain access. Once the code is entered, you will be able to use the web resources for the length of your course.

Access is provided only if you have purchased a new book.

If the registration code is missing from this book, the registration screen on our website, and within your WebCT or Blackboard course will tell you how to obtain your new code. Your registration code can be used only once to establish access. It is not transferable

To gain access to these online resources

1. **USE** your web browser to go to: **www.mhhe.com/katzesb**
2. **CLICK** on "First Time User"
3. **ENTER** the Registration Code printed on the tear-off bookmark on the right
4. After you have entered your registration code, click on "Register"
5. **FOLLOW** the instructions to setup your personal UserID and Password
6. **WRITE** your UserID and Password down for future reference. Keep it in a safe place.

If your course is using WebCT or Blackboard, you'll be able to use this code to access the McGraw-Hill content within your instructor's online course.
To gain access to the McGraw-Hill content in your instructor's WebCT or Blackboard course simply log into the course with the user ID and Password provided by your instructor. Enter the registration code exactly as it appears to the right when prompted by the system. You will only need to use this code the first time you click on McGraw-Hill content.

These instructions are specifically for student access. Instructors are not required to register via the above instructions.

Thank you, and welcome to your McGraw-Hill/Irwin Online Resources.

Katz / Green
Entrepreneurial Small Business, 1/e
0-07-325603-X
978-0-07-325603-0

UA8M-TDPD-K4AK-9VFA-93U9

REGISTRATION CODE

REGISTRATION CODE

The McGraw-Hill Companies
McGraw-Hill Irwin

Entrepreneurial Small Business

Jerome A. Katz
Saint Louis University

Richard P. Green
University of the Incarnate Word

McGraw-Hill Irwin

Boston Burr Ridge, IL Dubuque, IA Madison, WI New York
San Francisco St. Louis Bangkok Bogotá Caracas Kuala Lumpur
Lisbon London Madrid Mexico City Milan Montreal New Delhi
Santiago Seoul Singapore Sydney Taipei Toronto

The McGraw-Hill Companies

ENTREPRENUERIAL SMALL BUSINESS

Published by McGraw-Hill/Irwin, a business unit of The McGraw-Hill Companies, Inc., 1221 Avenue of the Americas, New York, NY, 10020.

This book is printed on acid-free paper.

2 3 4 5 6 7 8 9 0 VNH/VNH 0 9 8 7 6

ISBN-13: 978-0-07-296798-2

ISBN-10: 0-07-296798-6

Editorial director: *John E. Biernat*
Senior sponsoring editor: *Ryan Blankenship*
Developmental editor: *Sarah Reed*
Developmental editor: *Kirsten Guidero*
Associate marketing manager: *Margaret A. Beamer*
Producer, Media technology: *Damian Moshak*
Senior project manager: *Susanne Riedell*
Senior production supervisor: *Sesha Bolisetty*
Senior designer: *Mary E. Kazak*
Photo research coordinator: *Lori Kramer*
Photo researcher: *Mary Reeg*
Media project manager: *Joyce J. Chappetto*
Senior supplement producer: *Carol Loreth*
Cover design: *Jillian Linder*
Interior design: *Amanda Karanagh*
Typeface: *10.5/12 Sabon*
Compositor: *TechBooks/GTS, York, PA*
Printer: *Von Hoffmann Corporation*

Library of Congress Cataloging-in Publication Data

Katz, Jerome A.
Entrepreneurial small business / Jerome A. Katz, Richard P. Green.
p. cm.
Includes index.
ISBN-13: 978-0-07-296798-2 (alk. paper)
ISBN-10: 0-07-296798-6 (alk. paper)
1. Small business—Management—Textbooks. 2. New business enterprises—Management—Textbooks. 3. Entrepreneurship—Textbooks. I. Green, Richard P. II. Title.
HD62.7.K385 2007
658.02'2–dc22 2005054393

www.mhhe.com

To our parents, who gave us inspiration.

To our children, who gave us motivation.

To our spouses, who gave us dedication.

About the Authors

Jerome A. Katz

Jerome (Jerry) Katz is the Coleman Foundation Chair in Entrepreneurship at the John Cook School of Business, Saint Louis University. Previously he held the Mary Louise Murray Endowed Professorship in Management at the Cook School, and prior to his coming to Saint Louis University he was an Assistant Professor of Management at the Wharton School, University of Pennsylvania. Jerry holds a Ph.D. in organizational psychology from the University of Michigan, and other graduate degrees from Harvard and the University of Memphis.

Throughout the years he has worked in or advised his family's businesses including stints working in the family's discount department store, sporting goods wholesaling, pharmacies, auto parts jobbing, and secondary market wholesaling of frozen food. As a professor he has served as adviser to nearly 200 business plans developed by students at Saint Louis University, whose Entrepreneurship Program (which Jerry leads) has been nationally ranked every year since 1994. Earlier in his career he served as Associate Director for the Missouri State Small Business Development Centers. He has taught, trained or consulted on entrepreneurship education and business development services in Sweden, Switzerland, the United Kingdom, Brazil, Singapore, Israel, Croatia, and the West Bank. His consulting firm, J. A. Katz & Associates, has a client list including the Soros, GE, Kauffman and Coleman Foundations as well as the Jerusalem Institute for Israel Studies, Sweden's Entrepreneurship and Small Business Research Institute, the International Labor Organization (ILO), RISEbusiness, the National Federation of Independent Business, the National Science Foundation, and the Committee of 200.

Inc. Magazine identified him in its 1995 and 2001 issues as one of the world's top small business researchers. He has done research and theorizing on career models of entrepreneurship and entrepreneurship/small business education, as well as collaborating with others on topics as diverse as opportunity recognition (with Connie Marie Gaglio), the properties of emerging organizations (with William Gartner), Internet-based businesses (with Scott Safranski), and international entrepreneurship (with Sumit Kundu).

Jerry edits two book series, *Advances in Entrepreneurship, Firm Emergence and Growth* (with Dean Shepherd and Tom Lumpkin, published by Elsevier) and *Entrepreneurship and the Management of Growing Enterprises* (published by Sage) and has edited over a dozen special issues on small business, entrepreneurship, and entrepreneurship education for journals such as *Entrepreneurship: Theory & Practice,* Academy of Management *Learning & Education, Entrepreneurship & Regional Development,* and *Simulation & Gaming.* He has been a member of the founding editorial boards of *Entrepreneurship: Theory & Practice, Entrepreneurship & Regional Development,* Academy of Management *Learning & Education, International Journal of Entrepreneurship and Small Business,* and the *International Journal of Technoentrepreneurship.* He has also served on the editorial boards of the *Journal of Business Venturing, Journal of Small Business Management,* and the Academy of Management *Executive.*

Following his parents' tradition of civic entrepreneurship, Jerry has served the profession working his way up to become Senior Vice

President for Research and Publications of the International Council for Small Business and eventually Chair of the Entrepreneurship Division of the Academy of Management. He was also one of only a handful of small business or entrepreneurship faculty to be elected to Academy-wide office, serving as a Governor of the Academy of Management from 2000–2003. He developed eWeb, one of the first Web sites dedicated to entrepreneurship education, and he was a winner of top-tier ratings from Anbar, Argus, LookSmart, and Studyweb. Other innovations in small business education in which he was involved included co-developing the *Gateways to Entrepreneurship Research* Conference, as well as the first adjunct teacher's guide and first center director consortia in the field.

For these efforts, he has been a recipient of more than a dozen major professional awards including Babson's Appel Prize for Entrepreneurship Education, the Family Firm Institute's LeVan Award for Interdisciplinary Contributions to Family Business, the Outstanding Lifetime Achievement Award given by the Academy of Management's Entrepreneurship Division, as well as Mentorship Awards from the Entrepreneurship Division of the Academy of Management, and from Saint Louis University's Graduate Student Association. In 2004 he was elected the fiftieth fellow of the U.S. Association for Small Business and Entrepreneurship, and in 2005 he received Saint Louis University's John Cook School of Business Alumni Award for Outstanding Educator.

Richard P. Green

Richard Green is a successful serial entrepreneur who has started, built, and sold several businesses across an extraordinarily wide range of industries. His first business was an electrical sign repair company, which he began while an undergraduate student. Since then, Richard has started two other sign companies, a structural steel business, a manufacturer of stainless steel products, a real estate brokerage, and a tax return preparation service. During the "go-go banking" years, he held controlling interest in a state-chartered bank. More recently, Richard, with his long-time associate Richard Carter, conducted the start-up of Lineas Aereas Azteca (Azteca Airlines). Today the tradition of diversity continues with Richard serving as co-owner with his spouse of a San Antonio bed-and-breakfast, the Adams House, while at the same time serving as Chief Financial Officer of a high-tech start-up, Celldyne Biopharma LLC. As a corporate entrepreneur, Richard has worked on expansion plans for companies as diverse as the Mexican airline Aerolineas Internationales, Minneapolis based Land O'Lakes, Inc., and the Venezuelan dairy, Criozuca, S.A.

Richard brings a similarly diverse set of skills to *ESB,* ranging from a pilot's license (he was a professional pilot, instructor, and check airman for TWA) to a CPA. A late-life Ph.D. (from Saint Louis University), he is currently Associate Professor of Accounting at the University of the Incarnate Word in San Antonio, Texas. His academic achievements are similarly impressive, with papers in the proceedings of NACRA, American Accounting Association Midwest, the American Association for Accounting and Finance, and the International Council for Small Business, as well as journals such as the *Atlantic Economic Journal* and *Simulation & Gaming*. Richard also authored more than three dozen articles in popular magazines on topics ranging from personal computers to financial decision-making. Richard is co-developer (with Jerry) of the measures for financial sophistication in the Panel Study of Entrepreneurial Dynamics, and is senior author of *Investigating Entrepreneurial Opportunities: a Practical Guide for Due Diligence* (Sage). He has received research grants from Pharmacia Corporation and the Kauffman Foundation.

Always active in professional and civic roles, Richard's contributions have ranged from serving as chair of the Airline Pilots Association's grievance committee to serving on the City of San Antonio's Air Transportation Advisory Committee. He is a member of the American Accounting Association, Academy of Management, United States Association for Small Business and Entrepreneurship, North American Case Writers' Association, and the World Association for Case Method Research and Application.

Brief Contents

Preface

This book got its start with a simple question from my mother, "What is the difference between what you teach and what your father did for a living?"

We were sitting *shiva* (which is the ancient Jewish tradition of mourning), in this case after the death of my father, a Polish immigrant to the United States who had been a small business owner for almost 50 years at the time of his death in 2003. When sitting *shiva* the immediate family mostly sits and reflects and prays for a week, so my mother, sister, and I had plenty of time to talk. And talking as we did, the question came up.

I gathered my thoughts for a minute. First off, I realized that throughout his life my father had picked up on my comments about the very rare high-growth, high-tech businesses that came through my class. Somehow he thought that was who I had as my run-of-the-mill student. That was funny to me, because in teaching entrepreneurship for nearly 20 years, fewer than a dozen of the several hundred business plans I worked on involved high-growth, high-tech firms.

But thinking about what my father heard, I realized that I talk about two sets of rules, one for when I have a potentially high-growth business and another for the more conventional businesses that most of my students start and that my own father had mastered three times in his life. The answer to my mother came out this way:

Conventional Small Businesses	**High-Growth Ventures**
Imitation	Novelty
Autonomy	Involve key others
Control as goal	Growth as goal
Financial independence	Wealth
Fund with your own money	Fund with other peoples' money
Cash flow as key	Profits as key
Cash crunch? Tighten belt	Cash crunch? Sell more

The list goes on, and you will have a chance to see it in Chapter 1, but this gives you an idea of the difference. I told my mother that when I am teaching to students who have really big dreams, I try to get them to create businesses that would be innovative, using new technologies or markets. These would be businesses that could grow to be big businesses, creating major wealth for their founders. The founders are in it for the wealth. They expect to go after others' investment in the business and they expect to give away some of their autonomy along with their stock. My father's businesses were imitative, businesses like those already existing. He did the businesses to have a comfortable income and wanted to limit his growth to what he could comfortably control personally. No investors, no one second guessing him. When times got tough, my father would cut his expenses; in a high-growth business that's when it needs to sell more. My father's business was built on his personal reputation, while high-growth firms try to maximize the reputation of the firm or its products.

I kept talking, but as I listened to myself, I realized that I had never seen a book that talked about small business the way I described it. I have students who have started such businesses—in fact the vast majority of my students have started businesses in their own ways much like my father's three firms. I continue to help those alums out with advice, just as I did my father and his business. But in the end, what was important was that they *were* a different kind of business, and I felt that no book really addressed it that way anymore.

That was why I decided to write *this* book, and get Richard to join me in the effort. Why Richard? Because I knew a person with a story like his would make a great co-author for a book like this. His story goes like this:

"When Jerry first asked me if I would be interested in co-authoring a new small business management text, I was a bit reluctant. Where would I create time for such a daunting task?" I asked myself. "But when he described his vision—a text about starting and managing the type of small businesses that we patronize every day—restaurants, beauty salons, plumbing companies, lawn care firms—I became enthusiastic. Yes, I definitely wanted to be part of a project that would deal with the 98 percent of businesses that start small and stay that way, not the 2 percent that become CNNs, Oracles, and Dells.

"In many ways, I exemplify the type of entrepreneur for whom we wrote this book: people who start and operate the many ordinary enterprises with which you do business every day.

"I come, unlike Jerry, from a family of employees. Neither of my grandfathers and none of my many uncles and aunts were ever business owners. My father began working as an employee while he was still in high school, and he continued as an employee until his retirement. I, on the other hand, started my first entrepreneurial enterprise the summer I was 12. I began my first "real" business the summer I was 18. In the years since, I have started several businesses and purchased three. In between businesses I have been, as my father and his father, an employee.

"Not a single business that I have owned has ever been high tech, high growth, or even high innovation. I started every one either because I needed a source of income right then or because I expected to lose my current job very soon and didn't want to live on unemployment. I have been an owner-manager in the electrical sign business, structural steel erection, light manufacturing, consumer electronics retailing, real estate brokerage, construction, farming, and lodging.

"Why so many businesses, you may ask. My mother probably would say that I have a short attention span. However, the real answer is that each time I started a business I took the first opportunity available, not necessarily the best opportunity. And what was the result? Some, such as the Grandview Sign Service Co., went broke (but not before it paid for flying lessons). Signgraphics, Inc. was sold. Paul's Sound Shop was a victim of recession. Real estate brokerage was financially very successful, but I hated the business. When my top producing salesman finally passed his broker's exam, I eagerly made a deal for him to buy the company. I am still actively engaged in construction and in the lodging industry.

"My interest in entrepreneurship as a field of study stems from this varied experience. I asked myself many questions, including, Why did I just make a living in the sign business, while Ted Turner made himself a billionaire from the same beginnings? Why is it that Paul's Sound Shop didn't become a retail behemoth as Best Buy did, although both started about the same time? And am I a success because I made money in several different businesses, or a failure because none became big businesses? This book is largely the result of my search for answers to these questions."

Together, Richard and I crafted our approach for *Entrepreneurial Small Business*, and as we will point up in the business planning chapter, all plans start with a vision.

The ESB Vision

In *Entrepreneurial Small Business*, you will not find a lot on venture capital, and very little on strategic concepts like "first to market." What you *will* find is a lot of coverage of the kinds of businesses most people (and especially most undergraduate and lifelong learning students) really *do* start—small businesses in traditional industries and markets. These businesses are vitally important—we will tell you why we think so in a moment—and helping them survive has long been an art. Today like never before, that art is supplemented by science, and that is where your class—and this book—can help. In *ESB* we try to build a book that can combine the art of small business survival and the science of small business. If you can get the benefit of both *before* you get into your business, you are likely to do better than someone who has to get by with the advice they can catch on the fly as they get started.

Over the past 10 years, there has been a quiet revolution among professors of entrepreneurship and small business. Together they control resources such as entrepreneurship centers, endowed professorships and chairs, and even endowed programs worth more than *one billion dollars.* They dedicate a portion of that to research, and governments around the world contribute even more. Today, more than 40 countries annually survey their people to determine the level of entrepreneurial and small business activity (check www.gemconsortium.org to see the results). Another group called the Panel Study of Entrepreneurial Dynamics (PSED) has been tracking hundreds of people in the process of starting businesses to see what they encounter. Look at http://projects.isr.umich.edu/psed/ to see its results. We have even had the privilege of working together to contribute some of the questions asked in the PSED.

There are more than 50 journals in which professors write about what works and does not work in small firms. What this means is that for most of the topics of concern to small business owners, there are actual results helping define what works and what does not. What is great to see is that much of the new knowledge supports the best practices we have come to know—careful cash management, planning, customer focus, making loans that make financial sense, getting advice from others, and networking, for example—and they continue to make sense in research as in practice.

And sometimes the research helps us improve our thinking. Today we have whole sectors of strategic planning that work on the assumption that your business is entering a crowded industry (like being the eleventh Italian restaurant to open in town). Those sectors of strategic planning focus on how to get established and be noticed by customers already flooded with choices from your competitors. This new knowledge pops up in unexpected, but welcome places—like substituting competencies for personality profiles in deciding who should be successful at becoming an owner—but the point of *ESB* is to get that knowledge and make it available to you, the small business owner of today or tomorrow. You and your business deserve every break you can get, and our economy and society *need* you to survive and succeed.

Why is that so important? That has been the other revolution, and it has proceeded with a bit more fanfare than the academic research one. It turns out that small business is essential for big business, and it is essential for high-technology, high-growth business, and it is essential to our communities. In a world of relentless cost cutting and global competition, big businesses outsource everything but their most critical tasks. Often the best expertise, the best service, or sometimes even the best price exists in small businesses. Whether it is janitorial services or new product development, big businesses increasingly depend on small businesses to get their jobs done.

Small business is essential to our communities in much the same way. If you come from a small town or a neighborhood that gets passed-by by the big chains, you know how important small businesses can be. Without small businesses, there might be *no* places to buy products or needed services. Big business and small communities depend on small business to get the job done.

For high-tech businesses, the same argument can be made, but there is also another issue—that small business *defines* the community in important ways. If you work in IT, biotech, nanotech, medicine, media, or the like, when you finish your day in the lab or cubicle, where do you want to be? In a soulless, interchangeable town or a vibrant and diverse locale? These members of the "creative class," as Richard Florida calls them, are demanding customers. They make their livings from their minds, and those minds crave stimulation, whether at work or at play. A big part of stimulation comes from being diverse, different, *special,* and that is where small businesses come into play. You can go to a dozen different small coffeebars, and each is distinctive. Go to a dozen Starbucks, and they are all pretty much the same. There are times we all crave the expected, but the creative class also often craves the unexpected, and that is much more likely in small businesses than chains and large firms. No high-tech center can survive as a place to live without the excitement and variety a population of small businesses can provide.

The fact is that *every* small business is important, for two reasons: first because we can never be sure which ones are unimportant (if you can believe there could be such a thing), and second, it takes a lot of small businesses to support and enable one billion dollar business.

For us, one of the lessons of the PSED was that while high tech might be the ship folks hope will come in, for it to work that ship needs to be supported by an ocean of small businesses. Billion dollar high-tech companies are rare. Less than one in 100,000 start-ups achieves that billion-dollar level. The irony is that *nobody* knows which of the next 100,000 start-ups is going to be that next billion dollar business. All we can do is try and start as many as possible, knowing the more that get started, the greater the chance of that one breakthrough success.

And the fact is that nearly every big business got its start as a small business. HP really *did* start in a garage, and Wal-Mart started small in rural Arkansas. They are giants today, but some part of their culture got defined in those early days when they were small businesses. When they started, none of their founders *knew* they were going to become billionaires, and neither did their investors, bankers, lawyers, or friends. You start your business, you take your chances, and the rest of us hope you make it.

In the meantime, however, those hundreds of thousands of starts literally help support big business and high-tech businesses. They do this by providing jobs and wages to half the country so people can buy things. They do this by providing products and services to big and high-tech businesses, and they do this by training and preparing the next generation of workers and owners. Small businesses for the past 25 years have been the major source of new jobs created in the United States. While the Fortune 500 have cut their payrolls by millions, the slack created has been filled by small businesses and especially those small businesses that grow to multiple sites or multiple shifts.

When you start on the path to creating your own small business, you make life better for us all. *Entrepreneurial Small Business* is dedicated to giving you the specific help you need to get started and be successful.

The ESB Network

If there is one key lesson of *ESB* it is that "help helps." It turns out that entrepreneurs who get help, whether from consultants, lawyers, industry or trade associations, mentors already in the business, incubators, small business development centers, or (gasp!) even business school professors do substantially better than those who try to get by alone. That is true for us too. As that body of small business knowledge grows, it also grows more specialized. For creating *ESB,* the key question we always asked ourselves was, "What is absolutely necessary for our students to know in order to succeed?" We tried wherever possible to get to the point quickly, and give the points that are essential. To do that across fields ranging from A (accounting) to Z (zoning), we needed help.

To get us pointed in the right direction and help us make informed decisions about what was absolutely important and absolutely right, we depended on our network. Over the years, through work with students pursuing their Ph.D.s at Saint Louis University's John Cook School of Business, and through work with professors at other schools, we developed a network of colleagues, just as you will discover we suggest *you* do.

These colleagues include graduates of the doctoral program who worked with Jerry: Co-author Richard Green, CPA, an expert in accounting and now a professor at the University of the Incarnate Word in San Antonio; Kathy Lund Dean, an expert on ethics, now teaching at Idaho State University, Pocatello; Father Gregory Konz, an expert on women's and ethnic entrepreneurship and co-director of the Kohler Center for Entrepreneurship at Marquette University; and Susan Peters, an expert in marketing, now teaching at California State Polytechnic University—Pomona. We also depended on other professors at Saint Louis University, such as Laurel Boone, JD, an expert in business law, and Scott Safranski, an expert in organizational processes. The members of the network who did not pass through Saint Louis University included Lisa Gundry of DePaul, who is one of the nation's top experts on creativity in business, her protégé Jill Kickul, now the McCandless Chair of Entrepreneurship at Simmons College whose own expertise focuses on marketing and human resource management, and Janice Jackson of Western New England College, who is an expert on minority issues and educational design.

It is common for texts these days to make use of a number of outside experts, but what is unusual about this group is that they have known and written together for most of their professional lives. The ten people mentioned above have authored more than three dozen papers together over the past 15 years in small business, entrepreneurship, and other business disciplines. This group has been instrumental in creating an approach to small business and entrepreneurship that is strongly identified with Saint Louis University's John Cook School of Business and has been part of the reason the school's entrepreneurship program has held one or more national rankings every year since 1994. *ESB* in many ways is the culmination of a view of small business we have been working on for more than a decade.

It makes for a very strong sense of shared vision and a strong shared basis in our common discipline, small business. This extended even to our ancillaries (which is what publishers call the additional materials that go with a textbook), which includes network members such as Susan Peters, who handled the student and instructor guides, and Pamela Williams, who got her doctorate at SLU and now teaches at Culver-Stockton College, who handled getting the PowerPoint slides together.

One other aspect of this group and the co-authors is that by and large they have been entrepreneurs and worked with small businesses. We all consult for small businesses as well as work with them through our schools and classes. Richard has consulted with small, entrepreneurial businesses in Missouri, Texas, Mexico, and Venezuela, Jerry with small businesses in Tennessee, Mississippi, Michigan, Pennsylvania, New Jersey, Missouri, Illinois, Croatia, Israel, the West Bank, and Sweden, and Susan worked with businesses in California, Tibet, Venezuela, Malawi, and Poland. The list goes on, but the point is that a part of the shared vision is rooted in the idea that research is not enough; staying involved with small business is central to being effective in teaching it.

We also want to thank a remarkable group of students, who agreed to share their work with you. Every business plan, industry analysis, marketing plan, and feasibility study you see in this book or on our Web site was authored by a student. This gives you a very realistic idea of what students *can* do using the ideas and approaches in *ESB*. Our thanks go out to our students and alums of the Entrepreneurship Program at Saint Louis University (in alphabetical order): Julia Dalton, Rebecca Ellis, Beatrice Emmanuel, Collin Fischer, Alon Ginzburg, Tim Hayden, Patrick Hughes, James P. Keating, Scott Kettner, Eric McMahon, Plamen Radev, Theresa Resnik, Todd Robben, Kristin Scully, Denis Thein, Tim Tobben, and Dan Watkins. The business plan class where these students did their work has always been co-taught by Jerry and an entrepreneur, and those entrepreneurs left their mark on the plans you see. They included Steve Rull of Hancock Securities, Robert Vitale of the Westgate Group, Rich Pisani of American Marketing Group, and two now retired entrepreneurs—Terry Dougherty and Madonna Laws-Lowell. When Jerry was on sabbatical, the course stayed in-network, being taught by two names you have heard before—Richard Green and Kathy Lund Dean.

As you would expect with our network of colleagues, there is also a host of students at other schools who contributed to the materials you see in *ESB*. These include Shannon Sheehee (California Polytechnic University—Pomona), Yong Xu (California Polytechnic University—Pomona), Mingkit "Jerry" Lai (California Polytechnic University—Pomona), and Laurel Ofstein (DePaul).

One of the unpredictable benefits of starting a project like *ESB* is that you make new collegial relationships along the way. *ESB* gave us the chance to get to know and appreciate the talents of people like Rick Koza of Chadron State College, who did the initial draft of the first SIFE module ever included in a small business text, as well as David Tooch of the University of New Hampshire, who worked on most of the cases at the end of the text. Robert Ledman of Morehouse College also contributed the Saunders case at the book's end. Dr. Jennifer L. D. Shaver helped by running new analyses of the PSED for some of the results we report in *ESB*. Ed Rogoff of City University of New York and Allison Lehr of CUNY's Field Center for Entrepreneurship contributed business plans that their students had done according to the model used in *ESB*.

Keeping with this networking idea, you will see that this book makes extensive use of several strategic partnerships. These include the Global Student Entrepreneur Awards program (www.gsea.org), which celebrates collegiate entrepreneurs, the Panel Study of Entrepreneurial Dynamics, *Entrepreneur* magazine and its affiliates, and even Google, a billion-dollar company which started as a two-person small business.

Some online content for this book is provided by The Biz Info Library (www.bizinfolibrary.org) which contains articles, case studies, best practices from and/or about successful entrepreneurs, how to articles, entrepreneur training materials, and extensive information and data resources specifically developed to assist small businesses. The library is a joint project of the Ewing Marion Kauffman Foundation (www.kauffman.org), the Edward Lowe Foundation (www.edwardlowe.org) and the James J. Hill Reference Library (www.jjhill.org). From examples such as these, we hope you will see the practical value of strategic partnerships, which we talk about in Chapters 2 and 7. The fact is that we can show you more about the world of small business *because* of our partnerships, and that makes the book, and your experience, better. With *ESB* based at McGraw Hill, we have the unique opportunity to build using the remarkable resources of this great publisher, having access to *BusinessWeek* and one of the most extensive collections of text, case, and Web materials in all of academia.

The ESB Package

Professors reading this are probably wondering how all this translates into helping them teach their courses. One way we hope to help is through providing "imitation with a twist," which you will learn more about in Chapter 7. There are many other small-business texts out there, and from an author's perspective, they can be intimidating because so many of them *are* so good. So how can *ESB* expect to get your attention? As you will find as you look through the book, all the major topics you expect to see are present—that's the imitation that is basic to all mature industries (like small business education).

What adds value are those aspects of the book that are distinctive—our "twists." We give the specifics on how to sell, how to negotiate, how to ask for help, and how to handle a crisis, building from the best of research and professional practice. You will see it in small touches in the chapters, such as our discussion of issues such as when you get or use gifts as a way to fund start-ups, or why an LLC should be your default legal form of organization. We tried hard to give students the easiest introduction

possible to the potentially frightening issues of accounting and financial reports. *ESB* is also the first book we know of that has devoted a chapter to the special needs and problems of part-time businesses. It is the first book to embrace not just business plans, but the increasingly popular external projects, such as those sponsored by Students in Free Enterprise (SIFE) or the Small Business Institute (SBI). We include real-life, high-quality *student written* examples of the reports we expect students to work up as they start their business. And all the while we tried to keep the *ESB* vision in the forefront—asking ourselves what the absolutely critical things are for our students to know in order to start their small businesses and succeed in them despite a lot of competition. We have tried whenever possible to focus on providing just what is needed, and what would be relevant for the traditional small businesses our students most often start.

The ESB Role/Goal/Celebration

This book started with a wife and mother's simple question about the difference between the traditional small businesses her husband started and the high-growth ventures she heard about in her son's stories. Today there is a groundswell of converging ideas in business, economic development, job creation, and government showing us that the revitalization of those traditional small businesses is a key component of reviving our economies and communities.

Our students know this. The Kauffman Foundation–sponsored surveys of youth attitudes report the highest rates ever recorded for young people planning to be self-employed. Adults in our neighborhoods know this. Every day over 2,700 new businesses start in the United States, and about 2,695 of them are small businesses. New forms of small business, such as eBay selling, are further swelling the numbers of small businesses in ways that government record-keeping does not yet record. Like those students and adults, *Entrepreneurial Small Business* also knows this revitalization is taking place, and we want *ESB* to help.

For students, we want *Entrepreneurial Small Business* to be your handbook, lightning rod, and motivator. When you read this book, mark it up! If something is important to the way you plan to run your business, dog-ear the page or highlight the material. Write how something applies to your proposed or existing business. If you have not started a journal for business ideas, start using the margins or end pages of this book to hold them. We know from experience there is a simple way to see if a book is really valuable. In college, the *really* valuable book is the one students do not sell at the end of the semester, because they actually see themselves using that book. If you are serious about becoming an entrepreneur and we did *our* job right, then success is measured in books kept and marked up. If you are serious and the book did not do the job for you, let *us* know what we need to do better. We got this far on the wisdom of a network of a lot of students and faculty, and as you go through this semester, you become part of the network, too.

For faculty, our job as educators is not just to know about this small business groundswell, and not just to help make this work, but to *celebrate* this. Academics have the power to legitimize through their acceptance and support, and they have the power to propagate through their contacts with hundreds of students and businesses a year. But most of all, we have the power to excite and to energize, most often through our own energy and support and occasionally even by the new opportunities and vistas we open for our students. You and all of us collectively have an important contribution to make to the revitalization of small business as a key component of the economy, just doing what you do every day.

We, the people behind *ESB,* want to be a part of that effort with you—providing the examples to celebrate, the realities that help prepare our students for what they will face, and most of all the skills, knowledge, and resources that will prove to them that most critical of concepts in life and in small business success—"help helps."

We are the authors behind *Entrepreneurial Small Business.* We want to help. Let us know how we could do so better in the future. And welcome to the network!

Jerome A. Katz
Saint Louis University
katzja@slu.edu
Richard P. Green II
University of the Incarnate Word
greenr@universe.uiwtx.edu

Walkthrough

Entrepreneurial Small Business

FINALLY . . .

a book about the kinds of businesses your students are most likely to start.

Entrepreneurial Small Business provides students with a clear vision of small business as it really is today. It focuses on small businesses that students might actually start versus high-growth firms dependent on venture capital. It presents the *realities* small business owners face every day and strategies for those starting or maintaining a small business.

There are several chapters that emphasize the distinct focus of this book.

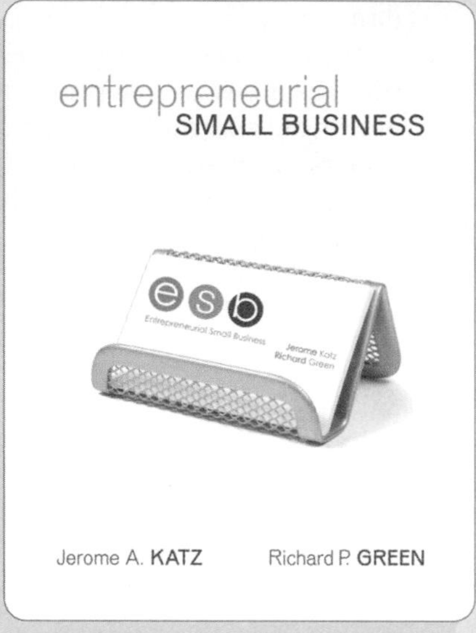

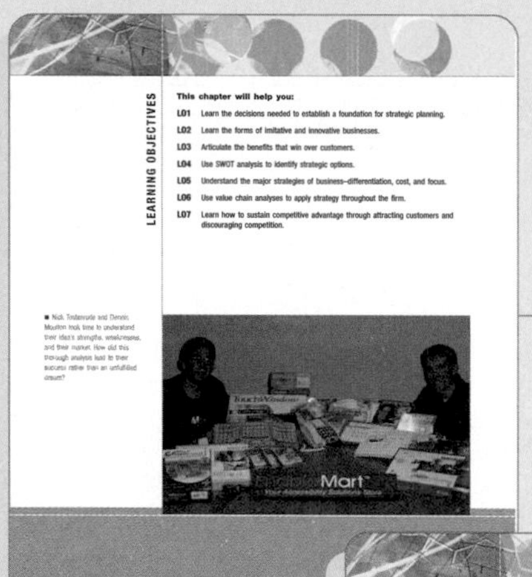

Chapter 7: Small Business Strategies: Imitation with a Twist

Most small businesses go into established lines of business. This text emphasizes the benefits of this strategy.

SMALL BUSINESS REALITY: Almost two-thirds of people starting business today plan to use imitation as their approach.

Chapter 5: Small Business Entry: Paths to Part-Time Entrepreneurship

Part-time businesses are tremendously important as they are a major portion of all current entrepreneurship, and it's the way most people enter into self-employment. This chapter discusses the benefits—and challenges—of part-time entrepreneurship.

SMALL BUSINESS REALITY: 75 percent of those starting a business already work full time for someone else and are pursuing their new business part time.

Chapter 14: Cash: Lifeblood of the Business

All small businesses must understand how to manage the business's cash flow. This chapter focuses on the basics of cash, budgets, shortages, and strategies to deal with cash flow problems.

SMALL BUSINESS REALITY: About 55 percent of small businesses that fail do so because of cash flow problems.

Business Plans

Business plans are a part of every small business course. A business plan may not be necessary to start your business, but it is critical to plan and understand your business in any circumstance.

> 202 PART 1 Entrepreneurs, Ideas, and Plans: The Basis of Small Business
>
> ■ Going up? Each year, Wake Forest University's Babcock Graduate School of Management holds their annual elevator pitch contest. Teams must progress through a rigorous weeding-out process to advance to the semi-finalist stage, where they get the chance to present their pitch to real venture capitalists and experts on a two-minute elevator ride. To read more about this year's contest, visit www.mba.wfu.edu/elevator/index.html
>
> **The Elevator Pitch**
>
> elevator pitch
> A 30-second (100 words or less) action-oriented description of a business designed to sell the idea of the business to another.
>
> An elevator pitch is an action-oriented description of your business that is somewhat longer than a vision statement or tagline. It is designed to open the door to a more in-depth dialogue. Even when it doesn't lead to any specific business, this information about your business should be memorable enough so that the listener can tell others about your business. The idea of the elevator pitch is that you are alone with a prospective customer or investor for the length of an elevator ride, say, around 30 seconds.[19] That comes out to 100 words or less. This description is used in one-on-one business settings and when someone asks for more detail after hearing your concept. In a time when politicians develop sound bites and a good phrase can make a product (Altoids, for example, are "curiously strong"), having a high-quality concept or elevator pitch for your business is more important than ever.[20]
>
> CellTunes: You hear it, you got it! Ever wanted to buy a tune you heard on the radio but missed the name? Well, CellTunes is the instant gratification music ordering service. CellTunes lets you buy the songs you hear on you favorite FM radio, AM radio or internet radio station with a single cell phone call. CellTunes tracks the songs playing on your favorite stations and can download the song to you or to your account at services like iTunes or PressPlay. CellTunes is demonstrating its technology and seeking seed investors. CellTunes makes song ordering faster and easier than ever before—you hear it, you got it!
>
> The above elevator pitch leads with the hook—the frustration people have felt at not being able to recall a song or find it to buy. It follows up with the purpose of the service—helping people obtain the song. Because this pitch is for a new type of service, it gives the listener more details about how it works than may otherwise appear in an elevator pitch. For a familiar type of business, you might talk instead about what makes your firm unique or superior to the competition. The pitch ends with where the business is now—seeking money from seed investors. This is about 100 words and would take about a minute to say. Note that a lot of it sounds like a sales pitch, and that is intentional. Listeners might be customers or investors, but either way, the goal is to sell them on the idea and their need for it. With this background, Skill Module 8.1 explains how to craft an elevator pitch.

Chapter 8 includes practical information helpful to any small business owner, such as

- the elevator pitch–how to quickly get people interested in your business.
- how to write your executive summary–a key component of the business plan.
- Seven types of business plans and what components they should include.
- tips on presenting your plan.

Chapter appendixes contain samples of important business plan components:

Feasibility Plan (after Chapter 4)

Industry Analysis (after Chapter 7)

Resume and Cover Letter (after Chapter 8)

Marketing Plan (after Chapter 12)

Two sample business plans (one long, and one short) are included in the end-of-book appendixes and dozens more are on the text Web site.

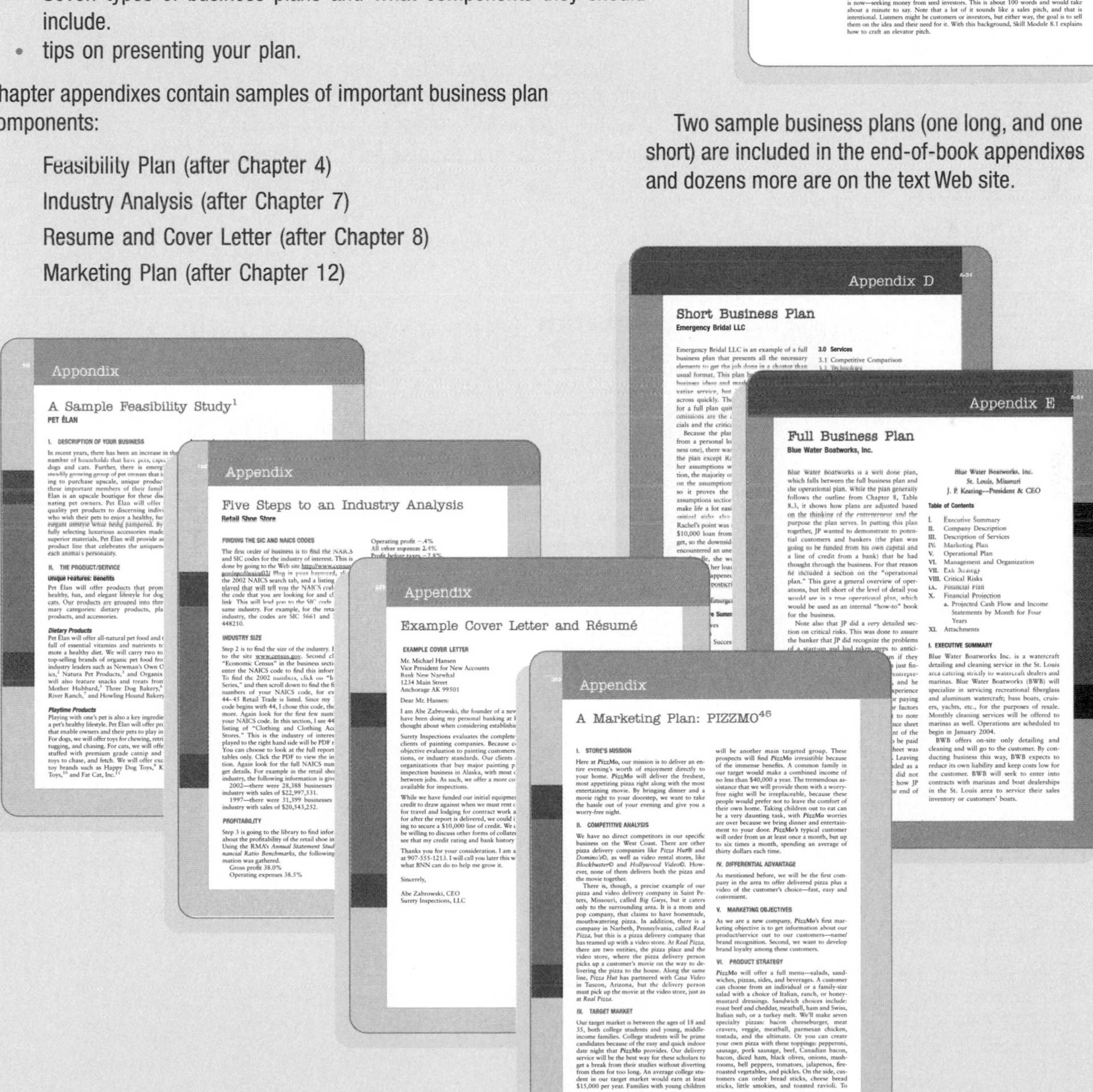

E S B Features

To help students learn more about the benefits of small business ownership, as well as the challenges many small business owners face, ESB is full of practical advice and examples from true small businesses in a variety of industries. Its focus is to give students the tools and knowledge they need to go out and start their small business.

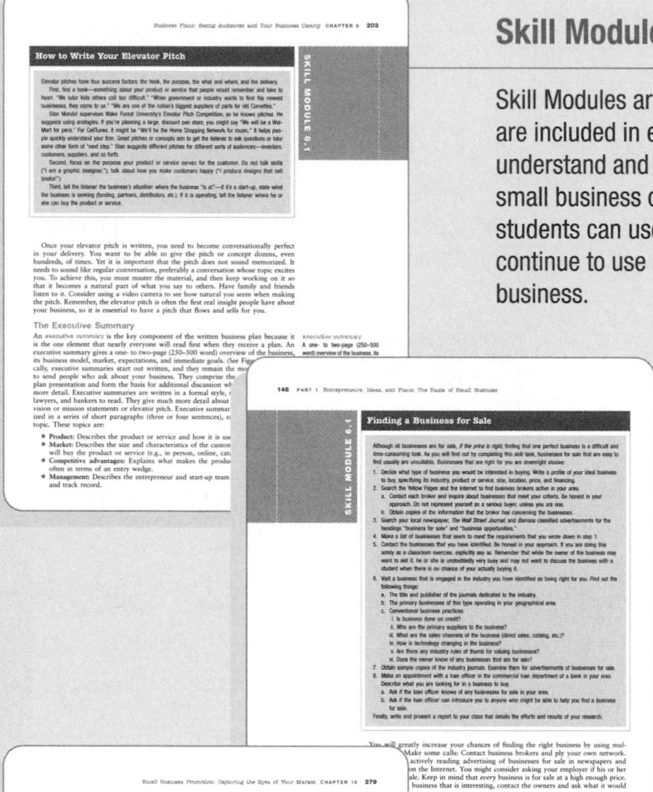

How to Write Your Elevator Pitch

SKILL MODULE 6.1

Finding a Business for Sale

Writing a Press Release

SKILL MODULE 10.3

Skill Modules

Skill Modules are a key component of this text. They are included in every chapter to help students understand and practice critical competencies for small business owners. These are resources that students can use in the course and that they can continue to use as they plan or grow their small business.

Examples include: Competency Self-Assessment, Steps to EBay Success, Building a Customer Base, Sweet and Short Industry Analysis, and The Art of Closing.

See the inside front cover for a full listing of Skill Modules.

Focus on Small Business

Each chapter opens with a vignette that highlights an entrepreneur and an aspect of a small business that relates to the chapter concepts. Discussion questions are included for students to consider as they read the chapter.

CHAPTER 4

Small Business Ideas: Creativity, Opportunity, and Feasibility

Focus on Small Business
Dave Kapell: Poetry in Motion[1]

Dave Kapell was a guitarist and songwriter who played in funk and heavy metal bands in Minneapolis. His bands were popular locally, but he still worked at other jobs doing clerical work for nonprofits and driving a cab. Problem was, he often suffered from writer's block (an especially bad ailment for a lyricist!) and was constantly looking for things to inspire him so that he could write more songs. He happened to see a documentary on the life of David Bowie and learned that Bowie used a technique that Kapell found very intriguing. Following Bowie's suggestion, he began to cut up magazine stories, entries from journals, and even letters from family members and rearrange these small bits of paper to try to spark inspiration for songs. He would often have all these pieces laid out in a room, or across the front seat of his cab. There was just one problem.

Dave suffered from allergy attacks that caused him to sneeze, and when he sneezed, he would send the pieces of paper scattering all over the room or the seat of his car. He thought about gluing them to cardboard backing, but then he would have to put them away and take them out again whenever he wanted to use them. This is when opportunity met need.

Thoughtful Entrepreneur Boxes

These boxes illustrate topics for students who want to explore the more complex issues and practices small businesses encounter.

176 PART 1 Entrepreneurs, Ideas, and Plans: The Basis of Small Business

THE THOUGHTFUL ENTREPRENEUR

Value and Cost Benefits

VALUE BENEFITS

Quality: Offering a quality level others do not. It can be the highest quality, just enough quality to meet the basic need, or a bit more quality than is typical for the price. Offering guarantees and warranties also reflect quality benefits.
Style: Items that are beautiful, fashionable, popular, or otherwise aesthetically pleasing.
Delivery: Sometimes simply offering delivery is enough, but other times you may need to deliver quickly, on schedule, or where others do not.
Service: Examples include the go-the-extra-mile sort, the personalized know-your-customer's-name sort, the we-serve-you-in-one-minute sort, or even the service-after-the-sale sort.
Technology: You can offer state-of-the-art or leading-edge technology, technology that others do not have, or technology that automates or simplifies tasks or that meets industry standards. Offering complementary technology such as voice mail or answering machines to people with telephones also fits in here.
Shopping ease: Providing one-stop shopping; having all of a product line; making ordering, returning, or upgrading easy for the customer are all benefits.
Personalization: This can come in building custom products or services, or personalizing the customer experience.
Assurance: Offering guarantees, warranties, or service that takes the risk out of buying your product or service.
Place: Being conveniently local is one example. Being willing to sell and deliver where others do not is another.
Credit: One key benefit small businesses offer customers can be extending credit where larger firms and chain stores will not.
Brand/reputation: This can come from the products or services that you offer, or from your own firm's reputation.
Belonging: Some products confer value because they make the customer part of a larger group, such as a member of a club or an online gaming community.
Altruism: If your product helps the community, a group, the environment, or the world, it is a benefit.

Cost Benefits

Lower costs: Operating from your home, getting family members to contribute their time for free, or selling something you've already gotten your value out of are all examples of ways small businesses keep their costs low.
Scale savings: Buying in volume usually produces savings, so some firms buy in bulk and sell or repackage in smaller amounts, passing along some of the cost savings.
Scope savings: A multifunction printer has a broad scope—it combines a printer, a scanner, and a fax machine into one box. This is because they can share parts, and this sharing results in lower costs.
Learning: As a firm gets more experience, it can often work with fewer mistakes and greater efficiencies, thereby lowering costs.
Organizational practices: Possibly a small business has automated or professionalized or mastered a product or service to the extent it can do it more cheaply than others.

and influence every part of the strategy process. As we will see later, benefits can be combined to offer themed strategic packages.

Offering the benefits your customers want opens up the possibility of your being able to charge a premium price and make higher profits, since people are willing to pay for value-based benefits they desire. Having cost-based benefits can also increase profits by lowering your cost of doing business, increasing your margin relative to

Small Business Insight Boxes

These boxes include "under the radar" advice from real small business owners and helpful statistics from small businesses around the country.

34 PART 1 Entrepreneurs, Ideas, and Plans: The Basis of Small Business

SMALL BUSINESS INSIGHT

Treating Temps Right

How do you get good employees for a seasonal retail business that traditionally has long hours and relatively low pay? Hold your employees accountable to a code of ethics and model those behaviors. Skeptical? Just ask Phil Jamieson how he manages to get seasonal workers to come back to his New Mexico chili-pepper farming business year after year, and he'll tell you it's because employees know up front what behaviors are expected and because he is responsible for the same code of ethics as his employees. "The short term is different, but the most efficient, best run business truly is the ethical business. Short term, it will cost you money. But in the long term, you never make the wrong decision when you make the ethical decision, and employees see that, no matter how long they work in your business. And that decision will never come back to bite you." Still skeptical? Phil has proudly kept a notebook full of letters he has received from former workers, all of whom were temporary employees. They write to say that they wish their current company was run the way Phil runs his business, and how thankful they are to have worked for Phil.[31]

to stay in business or build on your personal reputation. Only when you treat people fairly, build trust, and act responsibly can you expect your business to be open for many years.

Using the ethics planning process takes time and concentration. Using it also means that you are committed to your business, your customers, your employees, and your community. The payoff is decision making you can be proud of—and decision making that'll get you through tough years, thanks to customer and employee loyalty.

Ethics Planning

LO4 Learn ethics planning, a three-step process to help you make ethical decisions.

Since there is no workable list of "do this" or "don't do this" sort of answers, how does an entrepreneur come to make an ethical decision? Over the years a model has emerged that works in a wide variety of situations and gives you a high likelihood of finding a workable ethical decision while taking all key factors into account. This process, *ethics planning*, is detailed below.

FIGURE 2.1 Three Steps of the Ethical Decision-Making Process

1. Ask the Four Questions.
2. Create options for action.
3. Conduct Ethical Tests.

End of Chapter Materials

End of chapter materials include:

Chapter Summary
An end-of-chapter summary is included, bulleted by chapter objective, to help students review the chapter material and study for tests.

Discussion Questions
Discussion questions are included in each chapter that can be given as assignments or that can be used for in-class discussion. Suggested answers are included in the Instructor's Manual.

Experiential Exercises
The experiential exercises include brief activities students can complete to get more information on the chapter topic, to look for additional resources, and to help build their competencies in a certain aspect of small business ownership.

Mini-Case
A mini-case for each chapter is included as an additional opportunity for the student to apply the lessons of the chapter.

Additional Resources

Cases

A case for each chapter (20 total) is included at the end of the text. These cases offer additional opportunities for students to analyze situations in a carefully crafted case drawn from real-world small businesses, along with discussion questions that can be used in class or as an assignment. The Instructor's Manual provides suggestions on how to use and discuss each of these cases.

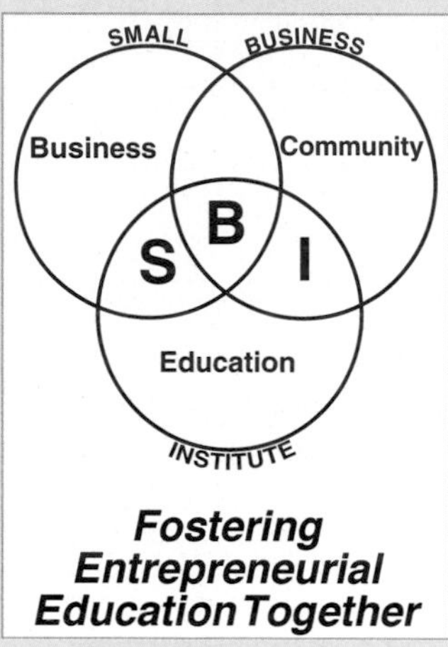

End of Book Appendixes

Consulting to Small Business—SBI and Beyond

Some courses give students the opportunity to work on consulting projects, or "live" cases. The appendix includes key guidelines and information about how to carry out effective fieldwork. Information is included such as meeting with the client, setting objectives, preparing the final report, ethical considerations, and ongoing communication with the client.

SIFE (Students in Free Enterprise)

Increasingly popular external projects, like the ones sponsored by Students in Free Enterprise, are included in the end of book appendixes. The appendix introduces SIFE and illustrates the process for developing and completing a SIFE project.

Other Appendixes

The final three appendixes include a full marketing plan, as well as a short and long business plan example. These serve as excellent resources and examples for students so they can see how a fully executed plan is organized. Additional business plan examples are included on the text Web site, so students can access a variety of plans.

- A Marketing Plan for "Asian Eden"
- Short Business Plan: Emergency Bridal LLC
- Full Business Plan: Blue Water Boatworks, Inc.

The Panel Study of Entrepreneurial Dynamics (PSED)

The PSED was developed to provide accurate information on new small business owners and is now considered by experts to be one of the best small business studies ever done. The PSED team surveyed 871 people who were starting or who had just started a business and surveyed them for 18 months to see how they and their business fared. The resulting survey is a carefully detailed and long-term look at the process of starting a small business. Statistics from the PSED are used throughout *Entrepreneurial Small Business* to help students understand business as it really is.

The Google Search Tool

Throughout the text there are examples of Internet searches that students can try for more information or where they can turn for additional resources. We include Google search bars so students can easily see how to conduct specific and important searches.

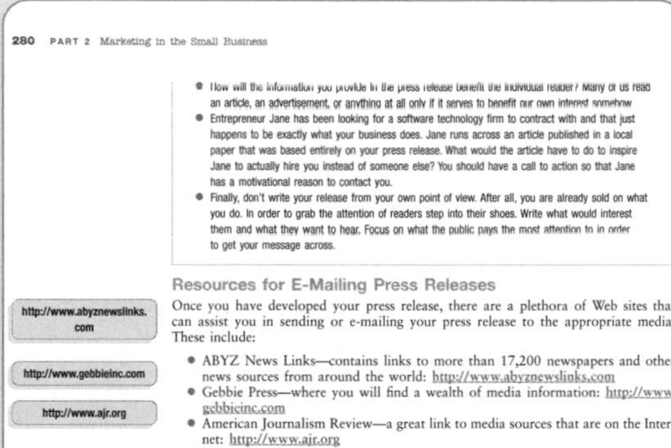

280 PART 2 Marketing in the Small Business

- How will the information you provide in the press release benefit the individual reader? Many of us read an article, an advertisement, or anything at all only if it serves to benefit our own interest somehow
- Entrepreneur Jane has been looking for a software technology firm to contract with and that just happens to be exactly what your business does. Jane runs across an article published in a local paper that was based entirely on your press release. What would the article have to do to inspire Jane to actually hire you instead of someone else? You should have a call to action so that Jane has a motivational reason to contact you.
- Finally, don't write your release from your own point of view. After all, you are already sold on what you do. In order to grab the attention of readers step into their shoes. Write what would interest them and what they want to hear. Focus on what the public pays the most attention to in order to get your message across.

Resources for E-Mailing Press Releases

http://www.abyznewslinks.com

Once you have developed your press release, there are a plethora of Web sites that can assist you in sending or e-mailing your press release to the appropriate media. These include:

http://www.gebbieinc.com

http://www.ajr.org

- ABYZ News Links—contains links to more than 17,200 newspapers and other news sources from around the world: http://www.abyznewslinks.com
- Gebbie Press—where you will find a wealth of media information: http://www.gebbieinc.com
- American Journalism Review—a great link to media sources that are on the Internet: http://www.ajr.org

URL Boxes

Throughout the text, important URLs relevant to small business owners are included. Web sites that may be frequented more often by those starting or maintaining a small business are highlighted in the margins for easy and quick reference.

Supplements for Students and Instructors

Instructor's Manual

The Instructor's Manual includes lecture outlines, chapter summaries, descriptions of the text features, answers to end of chapter materials, additional activities, and references to relevant articles.

Test Bank

The Test Bank includes multiple-choice, true-false, and short answer questions, along with the correct answer and a rationale for the answer. The Test Bank is also available in a computerized version that allows you to add and edit questions.

PowerPoint

Over 800 slides keyed to the text are available in the narrated PowerPoint presentation. Included are figures from the text, lecture outline material, links to relevant information on the Internet, figures that expand concepts in the book, and questions that can be used in class (through CPS—see below). The PowerPoint is available on the Instructor's Resource CD.

Instructor's Resource CD

The IRCD includes the IM, Test Bank, PowerPoint slides, and video clips for your convenience in customizing your lectures.

Videos

Thirteen videos are included, and each of the videos brings important concepts to life by taking viewers on a fieldtrip of sorts to these companies and to hear directly from these entrepreneurs.

Video cases and notes are included for professors in the Instructor's Manual. Some of the videos are also included for students on the OLC, and a wealth of shorter video clips are available on the OLC as well.

Online Learning Center (OLC)

www.mhhe.com/katzesb
The text-specific Web site includes a wealth of information for both students and professors. Professors can access downloadable supplements as well as all of the student material. The Student Edition includes professional resources, interactive exercises, sample business plans, financial worksheets, video clips, key term review, additional chapter quizzes, and links for every chapter.

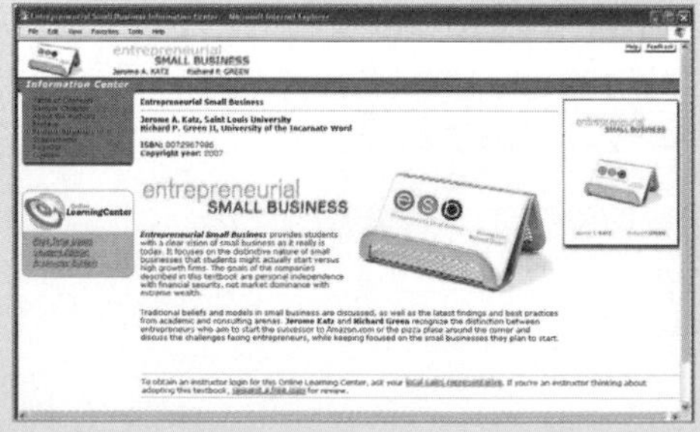

Student Study Guide

The Study Guide contains various ways to review—learning objectives from the chapter, key term exercises, assessment/concept checks, critical thinking exercises, and practice tests (and answers).

CPS (Wireless Classroom Performance System) by eInstruction

If you've ever asked yourself, "How can I measure class participation?" or "How do I encourage class participation?" then CPS might be the product for you. CPS enables you to record responses from students to questions posed in a PowerPoint slide, even record attendance, and offers a variety of reporting features, including easy to export to WebCT or Blackboard grade books. For your students, it's as easy as using buttons on a remote control. Questions can be designed by you, or you can choose from the questions included in the Entrepreneurial Small Business PowerPoint. Ask your local sales representative how to get CPS for your classroom.

Business Plan Writer

The Business Plan Writer software helps you go from concept to completion in three easy steps. First it will help you set up your business by answering questions that help the software customize your plan. Then you will enter basic financial data to generate financial worksheets and statements, and finally you can print your business or marketing plan and even create covers or add your company logo. Over 250 sample business plans and 400 case studies are also included to give you a wide variety of examples as you create your own plan. Talk to your McGraw-Hill/Irwin sales representative if you are interested in packaging this software with your course.

PowerWeb

PowerWeb can help keep your course up to date. PowerWeb provides the easiest way to integrate current real-world content with *Entrepreneurial Small Business*. Articles and essays relevant to small business have been chosen from a wide range of periodicals including *The Wall Street Journal, USA Today, The New York Times, Forbes,* and many others. Now you can access these articles through the text's Online Learning Center (www.mhhe.com/katzesb) and see firsthand what PowerWeb can mean to your course.

Online Courses

If you are interested in educating students online, McGraw-Hill/Irwin offers *Entrepreneurial Small Business* content for complete online courses. We have joined forces with the most popular delivery platforms available, such as WebCT and Blackboard. These platforms have been designed for instructors who want complete control over course content and how it is presented to their students. You can customize the EST Online Learning Center content or author your own course materials—it's entirely up to you. The content of EST is flexible enough to use with any platform currently available (and, it's free). If your department or school is already using a platform, we can certainly help.

Acknowledgments

Even with all the students and faculty mentioned earlier, there are still literally dozens of people who deserve mention for the help they have provided in bringing *Entrepreneurial Small Business* to completion. Perhaps the easiest way to think about them is as those providing inspiration, those providing information, and those providing evaluations. Inspiration for a book like *Entrepreneurial Small Business* comes from many sources. Real-life entrepreneurs like Joe Shaughnessy or Michael McMyne and the other Global Student Entrepreneur Award winners are an enduring source of motivation. There are also professors who, through their academic lives, have served as inspiration to us all about the enduring importance of small business: Frank Hoy (University of Texas—El Paso), Charles Matthews (University of Cincinnati), George Solomon (SBA and George Washington University), as well as three pioneering Coleman Chairs, Gerry Hills (University of Illinois—Chicago), Bob Brockhaus (Saint Louis University), and Gerry Gunderson (Beloit College).

Information is what we hoped would differentiate *ESB* from other books on small business. Getting information that is representative of small businesses and checked for quality was a daunting task made easier by several key sources. The Panel Study of Entrepreneurial Dynamics is the brainchild of Paul Reynolds of Florida International University, but as an endeavor was achieved only through a team effort, and that team—the executive committee of the PSED—was composed of Candida Brush (Babson College), Nancy Carter (St. Thomas), Per Davidsson (Jönköping International Business School and Brisbane Graduate School of Business), William Gartner (Clemson), Patricia Greene (Babson), Kelly Shaver (College of Charleston), and Mary Williams (Widener). Another key source was the surveys of the National Federation of Independent Business, contributed by Denny Dennis of the NFIB Foundation.

ESB also builds from an ongoing series of books and special issues edited or co-edited by Jerome Katz over the years, which includes the research series *Advances in Entrepreneurship, Firm Emergence and Growth* (published by Elsevier), the text-supplement series *Entrepreneurship and the Management of Growing Enterprises* (published by Sage), and special issues of journals such as *Entrepreneurship: Theory & Practice, Entrepreneurship & Regional Development,* Academy of Management *Learning & Education,* and *Simulation & Gaming.* To the dozens of contributors, reviewers and co-editors who made those publications possible and that information available, a collective thanks does not do justice, but is all that is possible. Theresa Welbourne (Michigan), Ron Mitchell (Texas A&M), and Connie Marie Gaglio (San Francisco State) deserve special mention for their unique and repeated contributions to the informational underpinnings of *ESB*. One name that deserves special mention, however, is Dean Shepherd (Indiana) whose work as an author and later as a co-editor of the Elsevier series shaped many of the key ideas of *ESB*.

Evaluation is central to the professional approach, whether in small business or in publishing. One of McGraw-Hill's strengths is its unwavering professionalism in the pursuit of publishing. At first, it is frankly daunting. It seems that *every* detail of *every* aspect of a textbook is subject to review—and that perception turns out to be accurate. Yet it serves a purpose. When McGraw-Hill releases a textbook, it has been reviewed, rewritten, and refined until it is a truly first-class product. It is a time consuming, painstaking, and often underappreciated effort, but it produces textbooks that you have to admire.

At the core of this effort are faculty. These faculty contributed feedback about chapters within the text, the text organization as a whole, and some reviewed the entire manuscript to help us develop the best product available for your small business course. (For those who reviewed the entire text, their affiliation names are listed in boldface; we greatly appreciate their patience and detailed feedback during this extensive process.) For a text as complex and far ranging as *ESB,* a large, diverse, and committed set of faculty offering opinions and reviews is needed, and we were fortunate to have more than 100 dedicated colleagues willing to take time to help make *ESB* better. They have our thanks, and should have yours too, because without them, opening a book like *ESB* would be a game of chance. These faculty include:

David Aiken
Hocking College

Dave Arseneau
Eastern Illinois University

Jay Azriel
Illinois State University

Calvin Bacon
University of Arkansas

Kevin Banning
Auburn University Montgomery

Kenneth Becker
University of Vermont

Verona K. Beguin
Black Hills State University

Harvey Bronstein
Oakland Community College

Phil Bessler
Baldwin-Wallace College

David Borst
Concordia University

Don Bradley
University of Central Arkansas

Steven Bradley
Austin Community College

Mark Brostoff
Indiana University

Ingvild Brown
George Mason University

Rochelle R. Brunson
Alvin Community College

Bob Bryant
Allan Hancock College

Robert J. Calvin
GSB University of Chicago

Martha Carney
College of DuPage

Teresa Campbell
Pima Community College

Kevin Carlson
Montana State University, Northern

Shawn Carraher
Cameron University

Carol Carter
Louisiana State University

Ed Cerny
Horry-Georgetown Technical College

Robert Chelle
University of Dayton

Jewel B. Cherry
Forsyth Technical Community College

Felipe Chia
Harrisburg Area Community College

Rod Christian
Mesa Community College

Michael Cicero
Highline Community College

William Clark
Leeward Community College

Ed Cole
St. Mary's University

Roy Cook
Fort Lewis College

Cory L. Dobbs
South Mountain Community College

Michael Dougherty
MATC

Mike Drafke
College of DuPage

Robert Ericksen
Craven Community College

Michael Fathi
Georgia Southwestern State University

Brian Fink
Danville Area Community College

Dana Fladhammer
Phoenix College

Rusty Freed
Tarleton State University

Leatrice Freer
Pitt Community College

Janice Gates
Western Illinois University

David Gay
College of DuPage

Donald Hardwick
Lexington Community College

Joe Hartnett
St. Charles Community College

Gene Hastings
Portland Community College

Brad D. Hays
North Central State College

Mark Hoelsher
Illinois State University

Edward Huff
Alcorn State University

Fred Hughes
Faulkner University

Ralph Jagodka
Mt. San Antonio College

Rusty Juban
Southeastern Louisiana University

Linda Kice
Delgado Community College,
West Bank Campus

Larry Klatt
Florida Atlantic University, Boca Raton

Mary Beth Klinger
College of Southern Maryland

Vicky Koonce
Craven Community College

William Laing
Anderson College

Ed Langlois
Palm Beach Atlantic University

Les Ledger
Central Texas College

Art Lekacos
SUNY, Stony Brook

Richard Lester
Louisiana Tech University

Paul James Londrigan
Mott Community College

Luigi Lucaccini
University of San Francisco

Leyland Lucas
Morgan State University

Shawna Mahaffey
Delta College

Greg McCann
Stetson University

Joseph McDonnell
SUNY, Stony Brook

Pam McElligott
St. Louis Community College

Norman McElvany
University of Vermont

Angela Mitchell
Wilmington College

Douglas Moesel
University of Missouri-Columbia

Greg Moore
Middle Tennessee State University

John Mullane
Middle Tennessee State University

Terry Noel
California State University, Chico

Don A. Okhomina Sr.
Alabama State University

Gerald Perry
University of Kentucky, Lexington

Fred Pragasm
University of North Florida

William Rech
Bucks Community College

Levi Richard
Citrus College

Kenneth C. Robinson
Kennesaw State University

Mary Ellen Rosetti
Hudson Valley Community College

Tammy Schakett
Columbus State Community College

Duane Schecter
Muskegon Community College

Jim Schroeder
Irvine Valley College

Gerald Segal
Florida Gulf Coast University

Tom Severance
Mira Costa College

Jack Sheeks
Broward Community College

Cynthia Singer
Union County College

Bernard Skown
Stevens Institute of Technology

Bill Snider
Cuesta Community College

Robert Sosna
Menlo College

Stuart Spero
Nebraska Wesleyan University

William Steiden
Jefferson Community College

James Swenson
Minnesota State University

Yvette Swint-Blakely
Lansing Community College

Vanessa Thomas
Chaffey College

Kathleen Voelker
Indiana University Southeast

Charles Wellens
Fitchburg State College

Rebecca White
Northern Kentucky University

Ira Wilsker
Lamar Institute of Technology

A special thanks is due to the nine faculty members who volunteered to provide extensive early feedback about how to best structure the book; their comments and debate greatly helped us to shape this product: Christine Adamow (Miami University), Dave Arseneau (Eastern Illinois University), Don Bradley (University of Central Arkansas), Janice Donaldson (University of North Florida), Cathy Hagan (University of North Florida), Melody Kamerer (Butler County Community College), Terry Noel (California State University, Chico), Fred Pragasm (University of North Florida), and Robert Schuttler (Marian College).

Penultimately, there is the team at McGraw-Hill. We had both written books before, and thought we had some appreciation of the process of book publishing. However, publishing a *textbook* is a far cry from publishing text supplements or research tomes. In those cases, it is usually just words, with an occasional figure. For a textbook, it is figures, pictures, tables, key terms, URLs, cases of all different lengths, examples, discussion questions, experiential exercises, skill-building exercises, footnotes, business plans, manuals, Web site components, *and* words. And like a car assembled at one point where dozens of items miraculously come together, the assembly of a modern textbook is a similar experience.

We were fortunate to have Sarah Reed as our senior development editor—the person who has to check all the elements and bring them together at the end. She has shown tremendous good humor and dedication during what was a remarkably complex two years of work. At the end of the project developmental editor Kirsten Guidero did an outstanding job of shepherding the manuscript through its final phases. The job of a sponsoring editor is that of the corporate entrepreneur or product champion, landing the contract, then assembling the resources to make it happen, and motivating everyone to keep his or her eyes on the timeline, budget, book outline, and, oh, yes, the market. Ryan Blankenship's job often was to commiserate and as often to think up new ways to do things. He never failed us in either role. Meg Beamer was *ESB*'s marketing manager and the person responsible for the selling effort that got *ESB* into your hands. As such, she comes onboard late in the process, but at the critical time for the book's commercial success. In addition, there are people such as Mary Kazak, our designer, Roberta Mantas, our copyeditor, Damian Moshak, our media producer, Lori Kramer, our photo research coordinator, and Susanne Riedell, our project manager, at McGraw-Hill who made all this possible. To each and every one of these fine publishing professionals, we offer our thanks and our promise that it *will* be easier for the second edition.

Similarly, Professor Jim Fisher of Saint Louis University's Emerson Center for Business Ethics deserves special thanks for contributing the videos used for the ethics chapter.

Finally, while the book writing process took almost two years, the process leading to the idea for the book was formed over the past ten years, in classrooms, at meals, at social get-togethers, and over many, many phone calls, e-mails, presentations, and papers. What started as a labor of learning among professors and protégés became a labor of love among colleagues. Often this labor was possible because of time contributed by (or stolen from) families and significant others. The number of meals missed, calls taking over the family phone, late nights spent over the computer, or weekends spent at work over the past ten years are innumerable. What those family members and significant others saw was the passion for discovery and the excitement of finding and telling others about a better way of doing things in small businesses or explaining small business. For all of the network, and especially the authors, that support was the critical enduring ingredient in making *Entrepreneurial Small Business* a reality. For that reason, we want to recognize the enormous emotional and motivational contributions made by: Peter Gundry, Dave Peters, James F. Amrhein, Henry and Florence Guithues, the Jesuits living in Arrupe House at Marquette University, Dan Dean, Nora L. Peterson, Josh Katz, Lauren Katz, and Cheryl Nietfeldt.

Contents

Part One

Entrepreneurs, Ideas, and Plans: The Basis of Small Business

Part Four

Management and Organization in the Small Business

Chapter 18

Chapter 19

PART 1

Entrepreneurs, Ideas, and Plans: The Basis of Small Business

LEARNING OBJECTIVES

This chapter will help you:

LO1 Understand the scope of small business in the United States.

LO2 Learn the differences between small businesses and high-growth ventures.

LO3 Discover the rewards entrepreneurs can achieve through their businesses.

LO4 Be able to dispel key myths about small businesses.

LO5 Identify actions key to becoming a small business owner.

LO6 Understand how small businesses are important to our economy and your community.

■ Aaron McGruder and his creations. How did his passion for becoming a cartoonist help him break into the business? THE BOONDOCKS © 2005 Aaron McGruder. Dist. By UNIVERSAL PRESS SYNDICATE. Reprinted with permission. All rights reserved.

CHAPTER 1

Small Business: Its Opportunities and Rewards

Focus on Small Business: Aaron the Cartoonist[1]

Aaron McGruder loved to draw cartoons. He was born in Chicago, and at age 6 he moved with his family to Columbia, Maryland, near Washington, DC. With the support of his parents, he kept drawing through his teenage years. At age 18 he went to the nearby University of Maryland, sketchbook in hand, and for the next three years he worked on refining his cartoons and completing his major in African American studies.

While in college, he realized he was passionate about becoming a professional cartoonist. He did a research paper in which he identified America's fewer than a dozen professional African American cartoonists. He learned that most professional cartoonists were self-employed, with their work distributed to newspapers by one of the big syndicates. Knowing that breaking into the cartooning business was going to be extremely difficult, he decided that he needed to perfect his cartoons but also establish himself in *the business* of cartooning.

McGruder started publishing his cartoons on a Web site called "The Hitlist Online," in 1996; then in 1997 he had them published in *The Diamondback,* an independent student newspaper at the University of Maryland. Later that

year he was published in *The Source,* a magazine aimed at the urban music scene. While Aaron's cartoons were published, he kept working on his art. This was his form of pilot testing.

He adapted his art. Based on feedback from his readers and editors, Aaron improved his comics. For example, the characters changed a lot from "The Hitlist Online" versions to those seen the following year in *The Diamondback,* and again when his work was syndicated through the United Press Syndicate.

On the business side, he leveraged himself. Aaron convinced a writer at *Editor & Publisher,* the trade paper for the newspaper industry, to build a story from his research paper on African American cartoonists. The story gave him national visibility among the publishers who would be signing the checks for his comic strip.

With his visibility increasing, he networked. McGruder approached the syndicates by mail and in person. He went to the National Association of Black Journalists convention in Chicago in 1997 and met a representative from Universal Press Syndicate (UPS)—the company that picked up the strip.

Perhaps most significantly, he also knew when to get help. When UPS expressed interest, he handed over the negotiations to an attorney (another lesson learned from the research paper), and he was able to keep virtually all the rights to the strip and its characters.

The payoff? You can say he did all right. *The Boondocks* began syndication in 160 papers in 1999, outdoing the previous superstar strips *Doonesbury* and *Calvin and Hobbes.* Aaron is positioned to make more money from these than the typical cartoonist because he made sure he held onto ownership of more of the rights to his strips and characters than cartoonists typically do. He admitted to an income in the "six-figure range" for his first year of syndication, before merchandising or book sales kicked in. Not bad for a one-person firm start-up working from his bedroom in his parents' house in Columbia, Maryland.

DISCUSSION QUESTIONS

1. How did Aaron move what was his passion and hobby into a viable business?
2. What did Aaron do to develop his skills as a cartoonist?
3. What kinds of research did Aaron use to understand the cartooning industry?
4. What kinds of help did Aaron use to develop his business?

LO1
Understand the scope of small business in the United States.

The Role of Help in Starting a Small Business

small business
Involves 1–50 people and has its owner managing the business on a day-to-day basis.

entrepreneur
A person who owns or starts an organization, such as a business.

Aaron's story makes a simple point—you *can* start a **small business**, and knowledge can help. Aaron did it the right way—doing research, planning, networking, and seeking help when he needed it. By reading this book for a class, you too are approaching small business the right way, and it *will* make a difference.

By taking a course in small business or entrepreneurship, you are making a tremendous difference in your chances for success. At any moment, about half the adults in the United States think about owning their own business, but only one person in eleven who thinks about it actually starts a business.[2] Even at that small a rate, there are over 1 million new businesses in the United States each year.[3] There are two hurdles that people need to overcome to move from thinking to achieving. One of these is moving from inaction to action. According to Stanford University professors Gerry Salancik and Bob Sutton,[4] inaction is the natural state of most people, and potential **entrepreneurs** are no exception. Only one person in seven of those who think about starting a business (around 7 percent of the population) make any kind of effort to turn their intentions into reality. Reading a book, or better yet taking a course, goes a long way toward getting you past the first hurdle of inaction.

The second hurdle is taking the *right* actions. You need to find out what you need to do to start a business—and *how* to do what you need to do. Skill Module 1.1 helps you learn more about these key resources. Small business and entrepreneurship classes or consulting advice from experts can help you get what you need. The goal for courses like the one you are taking and textbooks like this one is to get you the information you need to be successful. We know that help helps.

SKILL MODULE 1.1

Ten Key Online Sources for Small Business Knowledge

Twenty years ago entrepreneurs complained about the lack of resources to help them keep up on the latest advances. Today it is totally different! There are literally tens of thousands of resources on the Internet to help small business owners. Sometimes it can be hard to know where to begin.

First off, you need to know about your locality—its economy, its laws, and its entrepreneurs. The Web site **www.bizjournals.com** offers free access to weekly business news from more than 60 metropolitan areas. It also offers information organized according to 46 industry categories at **http://www.bizjournals.com/industries/**. Most local newspapers also offer free online editions, giving you a chance to find out about local businesses and laws that could affect you.

To learn about small businesses in general, there are a lot of sources. The major magazines about small businesses are *Entrepreneur* (**www.entrepreneur.com**) and *Inc.* (**www.incmagazine.com**). Of the two, *Entrepreneur* is more focused on small businesses, while *Inc.* includes more on high-growth firms. All the major business magazines also have specialized sections on small business. Often the online versions have more small business material than do the print editions. The major examples are *BusinessWeek* (**http://www.businessweek.com/smallbiz/index.html**) and *Fortune Small Business* (**www.fsb.com**).

The U.S. Small Business Administration offers a brief annual overview of small business in America. It is called "Small Business by the Numbers" or "Small Business FAQ" and can be found at the SBA Office of Advocacy (**http://www.sba.gov/advo/stats/sbfaq.pdf**).

If you are interested in national laws and policies affecting small business, there are several places to go. The SBA Office of Advocacy (**http://www.sba.gov/advo/**) is one resource. Another is the National Federation of Independent Business (**www.nfib.org**) which tracks laws on the free portion of its Web site. You can find a complete list of small business associations on Google's directory at: **http://directory.google.com/Top/ Business/Small Business/Associations/**.

When you find publication sources you like, you can often register to receive periodic e-mails providing you with the latest information on your favorite topics. It's a great free way to stay on top of the knowledge explosion in small business.

The **Small Business Administration** reports that about two-thirds of new firms with employees survive four years, and for owner-only firms the rate is 50 percent surviving four years.[5] But people who get help do better! More than 81 percent of the clients of **Small Business Development Centers** were still going after five years,[6] and 87 percent of firms getting help in **incubators** were still going at four years.[7] The studies with college students in small business and entrepreneurship classes show similar results for programs in the United States[8] and elsewhere.[9] Small business knowledge means small business success.

In this chapter we introduce you to small business, including the specialized language and knowledge models of small business, and we take a look at people involved

Small Business Administration
A part of the United States government which provides support and advocacy for small businesses.

Small Business Development Center
Offices co-sponsored by states and the federal government that offer free or low-cost help to existing and potential small businesses.

incubator
A facility which offers subsidized space and business advice to companies in their earliest stages of operation.

in small business today. Our goal for this book is to give you the ability to see small business as it really is.

Defining a Small Business

According to the U.S. Small Business Administration, there were 23.7 million small businesses in the United States in 2003.[10] Small business can be defined in different ways. The U.S. government agency that helps people start businesses is the Small Business Administration or SBA. It categorizes a business in the United States as small if it has fewer than 500 employees.[11] The international community uses the term **small and medium enterprise**, or SME, instead of small business. Among SMEs, small enterprises have 1 to 50 people, while medium enterprises have 51 to 500 people. This text focuses on owner-managed small businesses of 1–50 people and places greater emphasis on the lower end of the range.

small and medium enterprise
The international term for small businesses.

US Small Business Administration
www.sba.gov

US SBA Office of Size Standards
www.sba.gov/size/

Our focus is also primarily on independent and owner-managed small business. **Independent** means that the business is owned by an individual or small group rather than existing as part of a larger enterprise or a business whose stock can be bought on an exchange. Owner-management refers to constant or at least daily management of a business by its owner. It is possible to become an absentee owner, who profits from a business but is not involved in its day-to-day operations. This, however, is a different type of business with different problems from those of firms run by an **owner-manager**. Absentee businesses are not the focus of this text.

Small Business Owners and Entrepreneurs

Truly entrepreneurial businesses are characterized by **novelty**, in their products, services, or business models. Small businesses, on the other hand, are **imitative** in nature, with most small firms doing what other firms do, with only slight variations. But when we think about the people who start firms for the first time, the situations they face are situations of novelty. So whether they start the successor to Amazon.com or the pizzeria on the corner, the person who starts a business is living the life of the entrepreneur. We recognize this distinction and address the challenges facing entrepreneurs, while focusing on the small businesses they plan to create or enter.

In *Entrepreneurial Small Business* we use the popular broad definition of *entrepreneur*[12]—anyone who owns a business is an entrepreneur. This, of course, means anyone who is a small business owner is an entrepreneur.[13] It also means that the **self-employed**, anyone who works for himself or herself instead of for others, is also an entrepreneur. According to the Census Bureau, there were about 10 million self-employed people in 2005. Within the population of entrepreneurs, it is sometimes useful to split out certain groups. One of these is **founders**, the people who start a business, whether it is one of their own devising, or a **franchise**, which is a prepackaged business you buy or lease from a franchisor. Another group consists of **buyers**, those who purchase an existing business, or **heirs**, who inherit or are given a stake in the family business. These roles deal with the entry stage of the business from the perspective of the entrepreneur. After entry, another role emerges, that of the owner-manager, the role in which most entrepreneurs spend their working lives. Throughout this text the terms *small business owner*, *entrepreneur*, and *self-employed* are used interchangeably. When founders or buyers or postentry owner-managers are discussed, we specify which one is the focus.

independent small business
A business owned by an individual or small group.

owner-manager
The individual who owns and runs a business.

novelty
Characterized by being different or new.

imitative
Characterized by being like or copying something that already exists.

self-employed
Working for yourself.

founders
People who create or start new businesses.

franchise
A prepackaged business bought, rented, or leased from a company called a *franchisor*.

buyers
People who purchase an existing business.

heir
A person who becomes an owner through inheriting or being given a stake in a family business.

Small Businesses vs. High-Growth Ventures

You've probably heard of Dell Computer's founder Michael Dell. He is a billionaire and famous for the business he built. But did you know that Dell Computers wasn't the first business he started? Before he was 10 years old, Dell started selling collectible stamps through the mail.[14] He typed his catalog one key at a time since he had never

■ Michael Dell is well-known now as the CEO of Dell Computer, a major industry leader in PC production. Before his success, though, Dell spearheaded at least three other much smaller businesses. What factors do you think led to Dell's decision to expand his earlier ventures and eventually to his successful capturing of the PC market?

learned to type, and he made $2,000. His next business was selling newspaper subscriptions by phone from home; he made $18,000 on this venture. His third business was reselling IBM PCs from his dorm room at the University of Texas at a time when IBM was trying to limit sales to official IBM dealers like Sears and IBM's own personal computer stores.[15] It was Michael's fourth business, selling PCs, that led to the Dell Computer we know today.

LO2
Learn the differences between small businesses and high-growth ventures.

Michael Dell's four businesses point up the difference between small businesses and high-growth ventures. Both may be small when they start. However, small businesses are usually intended to remain small, generally a size that the owner feels comfortable controlling personally. For Michael Dell, his stamp, newspaper, and IBM PC businesses were designed to be small-scale operations that he could handle alone. He did everything himself, and he worked when he wanted to. The businesses were fairly conventional, with dozens or even hundreds of competitors all imitating one another.

High-growth ventures start small but are intended to grow rapidly, often requiring a team of partners or managers to handle the growth. When Dell got serious about the upgraded PC business, he created a company and started hiring others to help out. He moved from his dorm room to a commercial location, kept open regular hours, and started thinking about putting together a much bigger operation. That much bigger operation is the Dell Computer known worldwide today. While the computer business as a whole was established, Dell's approach to assembly from highly standardized (and therefore low-cost) parts was fairly revolutionary, as was his use of mail-order and later telephone and Web-based ordering. In his fourth business, Dell led the industry, and others imitated him.

TABLE 1.1 Differences between Small Businesses and High-Growth Ventures

	Small Businesses	High Growth Ventures
Preferred funding source	Owner's own money	Other people's money
When the firm's in trouble	Cut costs	Sell more
What's more important	Sales	Marketing
Personal control preference	Retain autonomy	Involve key others
Focus	Efficiency	Effectiveness
Metastrategy	Imitation	Novelty
External control preference	Control firm	Control market
Grow	When necessary	When possible
Human resources	Personalize	Professionalize
Acceptance	Personal validation	External legitimacy
What limits growth	Loss of control	Market response
Delegation orientation	Delegation is difficult	Delegation is essential

The differences between small businesses and high-growth ventures aren't just semantic. They're fundamental. Table 1.1 shows the differences between small businesses and high-growth ventures.

People starting high-growth ventures need to know how to seek and obtain external financing, particularly venture capital. They also need to know how to dominate the market and grow dramatically and quickly, according to the schedule of investors or as the market will allow. High-growth venture founders would ultimately want to know how to cash out through the sale of an initial public offering of stock or through the sale of the company to a larger company or set of investors.

The knowledge needed for a small business focuses on how to start small, with resources from the owner, family, and friends. A key type of knowledge would be how to grow on the schedule set by and for the purposes of the owner, not outside investors. The key market knowledge for a small business focuses on its immediate marketplace and communities. Knowing about how to achieve maximum flexibility while pursuing a comfortable level of sales, growth, and profit is also part of this outlook. This flexibility might be used to return something to the community, to become totally invested in the product or service, to have time to spend with one's family or on one's self, or some other purpose.

This text focuses on the knowledge you need to be successful in small business, helping you get started the smartest way possible, and managing your business for personal as opposed to investor or financial market satisfaction. Only 1.4 percent of the nearly 23 million businesses in the United States are high-growth ventures.[16] *Entrepreneurial Small Business* focuses on the other 98.6 percent and helping you join them to reap the rewards.

Rewards for Starting a Small Business

LO3
Discover the rewards entrepreneurs can achieve through their businesses.

Why become an entrepreneur? If you said, "For the money," or, "To do things my way," you'd be right, but these are only a few of the reasons behind owning your own firm. We know that people go where they feel they have the best chance of getting the rewards they value most.[17] The kinds of rewards people report are also fairly well

THE THOUGHTFUL ENTREPRENEUR

Paul Reynolds and the PSED[18]

As a sociology professor, Paul Reynolds realized that accurate information about new small business owners was in short supply. Unfortunately, those prospective or new owners are scattered all over the country and are often hard to find. Turning them up would take a major and expensive effort. To get this done, Paul became an entrepreneur in his own right, creating a partnership called the Entrepreneurship Research Consortium which in turn created the Panel Study of Entrepreneurial Dynamics (PSED). This partnership was itself a small business that initially involved nearly 30 different institutions as investors and over 100 academics and policy makers as advisers.[19] Armed with money and expertise, Paul's team developed a technique to find and survey a random sample of people in the United States in order to find those few in the process of starting a business. The resulting survey and sampling was considered by experts to be one of the best small business studies ever done.

The initial sample was of 31,261 people, and among these people, 2,024 (about 6.5 percent) were starting or had just started businesses. To keep the survey costs reasonable, the PSED team surveyed 871 people from those who were starting or had recently started small businesses. It surveyed these people every 18 months to see how they and their businesses fared. It looked at whether the business was operating or growing. It also looked at hiring, financing, exporting and sources of help used. The result is the most careful, detailed, and long-term look anyone has ever taken at the process of starting small businesses. Because of this, statistics from the PSED are used throughout this text to help you understand small business as it really is.[20]

For Paul Reynolds, the PSED led to an even more ambitious undertaking, the annual Global Entrepreneurship Monitor, which surveys small business conditions in over 40 countries (see **www.gemconsortium.org**). For his achievements, in 2004 Paul was awarded small business's equivalent of the Nobel Prize, Sweden's FSF-Nutek International Award for Small Business and Entrepreneurship Research. Paul's example shows how entrepreneurial thinking can solve all kinds of problems.

known based on results reported from the Panel Study of Entrepreneurial Dynamics (see The Thoughtful Entrepreneur Box: Paul Reynolds and the PSED) . The rewards mentioned by people in the process of starting their own firms are listed in Figure 1.1.

Nearly all entrepreneurs talk about three key rewards—flexibility, a livable income, and personal growth. These are covered in more detail below. There are two other rewards—building great wealth and creating products, which entrepreneurs mention more often than working people in general. There are also rewards that entrepreneurs mention *less often* than working people in general. These are social rewards, like the respect or admiration of others, or power over others, and family rewards, like continuing a family tradition in business. Those items are marked with an asterisk (*) in Fig. 1.1. These "go it alone" tendencies are probably a good thing, because they help entrepreneurs keep some distance from others and pursue what they think is right.

The three most popular types of rewards for small business owners are growth, flexibility, and income. **Growth rewards** are what people get from facing and beating or learning from challenges. Self-professed computer nerd Marc Fleury's first venture went under with the dot-com bust.[21] His second business, The JBoss Group, was built around the challenges of going it alone financially while outperforming and outlasting his first venture. JBoss, which sells programming and support services, was successful from day one, and is still going strong. And it is still entirely self-funded.

growth rewards What people get from facing and beating challenges.

income rewards The money made by owning one's own business.

JBOSS Group
http://www.jboss.org

Income rewards refer to the money made from owning your own business. For more than three-quarters of entrepreneurs, this means seeking to match or slightly better the income you had before you started your own business. Only one entrepreneur

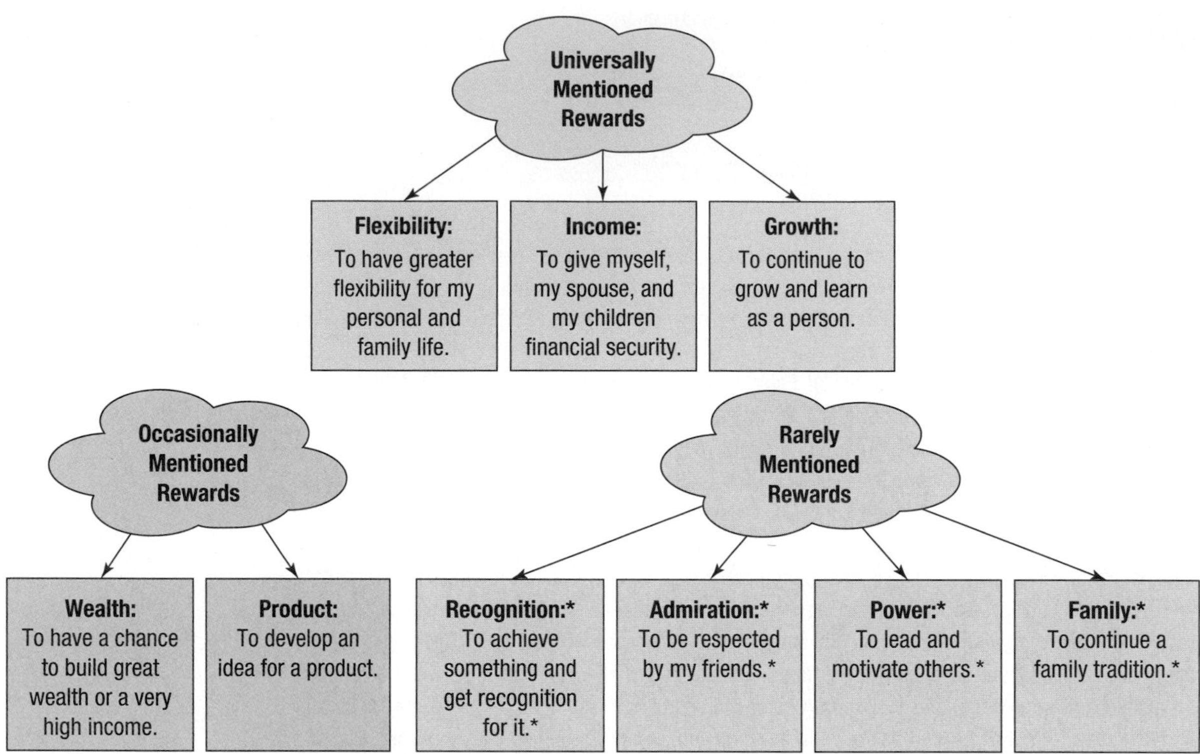

FIGURE 1.1

Rewards New Entrepreneurs Seek Through Small Business[22]

in four says that she or he is seeking high income through her or his business. But entrepreneurs are looking in the right place. More than 75 percent of the millionaires in the United States are entrepreneurs.[23] Two-thirds of the millionaires are business owners, and one-third are self-employed professionals like doctors, lawyers, or therapists.

flexibility rewards
The ability of business owners to structure life in the way that suits their needs best.

Flexibility rewards are perhaps the most rapidly growing type of reward. They refer to the ability of business owners to structure their lives in the way that best suits their needs. When Cyndi Crews was laid off from her work as an Information Technology resources manager of a large corporation, she bought a franchise of Schooley Mitchell Telecom Consultants. Today she advises companies on how to get the most from their telephone systems. She runs the business from her home in Lumberton, Texas, where she is able to set her own work schedule. This ensures her the flexibility she needs to take time off to be with her young son and husband.[24] Another variant of this is pursuing spiritual or religious goals through business. For example, Noah's Ark, a Kosher deli with branches in Teaneck, New Jersey, and New York City closes from 4 p.m. on Friday until 6:30 p.m. or so on Saturday night in observance of the Jewish Sabbath.

LO4
Be able to dispel key myths about small businesses.

http://www.noahsark.net

Myths about Small Businesses

Here is a sobering truth. At any moment about half the people in the United States are thinking about owning their own business, but fewer than one in ten of those people with self-employment ideas actually starts his or her own business.[25] The challenges of small business scare off or derail people. For years potential entrepreneurs have mentioned problems like these:

- There's not enough financing to start businesses.
- You need to make something (or something high tech) if you're going to make money.
- Seventy percent (or 80 percent or 90 percent) of all new businesses fail within two years.

■ Companies like Wells Fargo attempt to attract potential small business owners as clients for their financial services. What are some of the advantages and disadvantages to this traditional way of raising capital? To more innovative options?

Over the past 10 years small business experts in academia and government have studied small business and potential entrepreneurs and learned that a lot of the challenges scaring people away from small business are the stuff of urban legends. Let's look at these three problems with the latest information.

1. **There is not enough financing to start businesses:** For decades when small business owners were asked what the greatest challenge was facing their business, the answer was a lack of financing. So it is only natural for people thinking about starting their own firms to assume that a lack of money will be their greatest challenge. In the PSED, financial problems and difficulty raising capital are reported as problems by the people who are in their earliest stages of starting their firms, but for those farther along in the firm creation process, financial concerns fall behind problems such as finding customers or good employees or the time to get everything done. The word must be getting out. In a recent survey of Small Business Problems and Priorities, financing issues were ranked 66th and 69th.[26] In a 30-nation 2002 Global Entrepreneurship Monitor (GEM) study, Americans reported that financial support was not a problem, but they also reported that they'd like to see even more financial support available.[27] Looking at *Entrepreneur* magazine's 2004 crop of young millionaires (in Small Business Insight Box), you can see an example of the wide variety of techniques used to fund fledgling firms.

SMALL BUSINESS INSIGHT

Financing Tips from *Entrepreneur* Magazine's 2004 Young Millionaires

Every year *Entrepreneur* magazine features a group of new businesses started by people under age 40. Although all the businesses are successful when they make it to the magazine, for the most part their owners had to work hard, sacrifice a lot, and be creative in their tactics to survive long enough to be successful. One place where their creativity is most evident is in the ways they funded their business. Of the fifteen firms listed by *Entrepreneur*, nine firms gave information on how they financed their start-ups. Six of the nine mentioned personal savings and some fairly well-known approaches such as:

- Borrowing from family and friends.
- Getting a line of credit from a bank.
- Getting a bank loan (with SBA loan guarantees, and without).
- Getting venture capital money.
- Getting seed investment money from "angel" investors.
- Getting money from a private placement (a specialized equity offering to professional investors).

But many of these entrepreneurs also mentioned more creative approaches to raising or saving money. Examples these young millionaires gave from their early days included:

- Replacing their car with a cheaper one and putting the extra money in the business.
- Doing the same with a home.
- Taking out a mortgage on their home.
- Consulting on the side to raise money for the start-up.
- Deferring payments to creditors.
- Using credit cards to finance the business.
- Living in the office to save on apartment rent.

Their stories match up reasonably well with the findings from the GEM and other studies. If you start with your own savings and work hard and creatively look for and manage money, you too can finance your business.

2. **You need to make something (or make something high tech) to make money:** If you look at TV and read magazines, you might think that high-tech businesses and manufacturing are the only ways to do well in your own business. But these days service industries represent the single biggest business sector in terms of the number of businesses, the number of people employed, and the amount of revenue generated. Forty million of the 110 million people working in the United States in 2001 worked in service industries.[28] The creation of intellectual property in the forms of reports, artistic works, databases, education, inventions, and computer programs are the major products in America these days, and they are generally created by service firms, not manufacturing ones. For example, Eric Bulock used less than $1,000 to start Passport Express Services, a service business that helps people get their passports renewed within 24 hours rather than the usual six weeks. From his start in 1996, sales have grown to well over the $1 million mark.[29] In their book *The Millionaire Next Door,* Stanley and Danko point out that most self-employed millionaires are in services or professions, not manufacturing.[30]

3. **Seventy percent (or 80 percent or 90 percent) of all new businesses fail within two years:** Overall 50 percent of businesses with employees survive four years or more.[31] That is better than the myth suggests, but it gets even better. For example, getting help helps. At the beginning of this chapter we report on the survival rates for people who get help. For example, 87 percent of incubator-based start-ups are still going after five years.[32] Small Business Development Center clients usually have only half the failure rate of start-ups in general.[33] College graduates who have taken classes in small business or entrepreneurship also have much better chances of starting and growing businesses than business school graduates without such training, and they have much higher rates of success than the general public.[34]

Taking a course like this puts you into the group likely to make it not only for the first two years, but also well beyond. Now let's look at the specific kinds of things you need to know and do to successfully start your own business.

Getting Started Now: Entry Competencies

LO5
Identify actions key to becoming a small business owner.

There are a million things you *could* do to start a business, but which ones are best? Sometimes the answer will come to you in the form of an opportunity or offer, and sometimes you'll need to take the first steps yourself. In order to start a business, you need four elements to come together—boundary, resources, intention, and exchange.[35] This is referred to as the BRIE model, as shown in Figure 1.2.

A business needs the benefits of a *boundary*—something that sets it up as a firm, and sets it off from the buying or selling or bartering we all do occasionally. A boundary can be something as simple as a business name or government registration, a phone or e-mail address dedicated to the business, or a specific location for the firm in a home, commercial space, or even on the Internet. Having a boundary gives you a place to locate and protect the resources you've gathered for the business. *Resources* include the product or service to be offered, informational resources on markets and running a business, financial resources, and human resources such as your own time to devote to the business, or that of others working with you or for you.

Intention is the desire to start a business and is the most frequently occurring element of the BRIE model. Those 50 percent of Americans who think about starting their own business are expressing their intentions. *Exchange* is also needed. This refers to moving resources, goods, or service to others, in exchange for money or other resources. If the firm doesn't exchange with its environment, there is no "business" taking place.

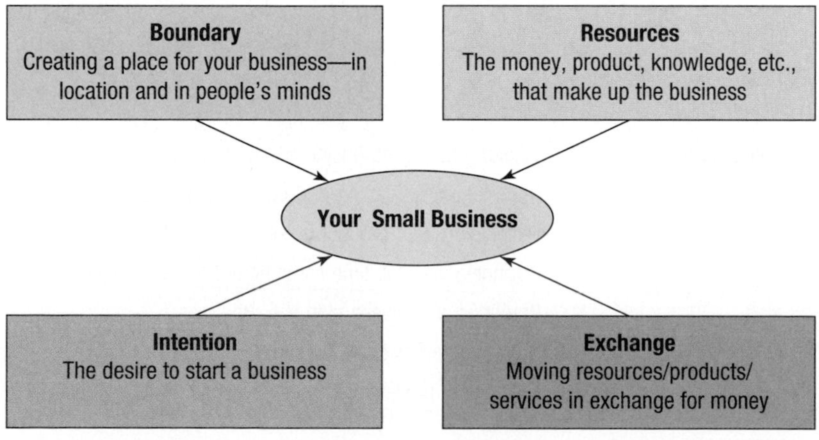

FIGURE 1.2

Four Elements Needed to Get Your Business Started (BRIE)

SKILL MODULE 1.2

BRIE Self-Assessment

The BRIE (boundary-resources-intention-exchange) model is a proven[36] and handy way to think about the activities necessary to get a business started. The complete list of BRIE activities is given in the following table. Look at the BRIE list and check off actions you've taken already. Then write in the first column how many of each BRIE category you've done so far.

BRIE Checklist

Done

Boundary—Creating a Place for Your Business in Space and in People's minds

Number of boundary actions done

- ☐ Opening a bank account for the business (Ch. 14)
- ☐ Registering the business name with the state (Ch.18)
- ☐ Creating business cards and/or stationery
- ☐ Purchasing a domain name (Ch.11)
- ☐ Creating a business Web site (Ch. 11)
- ☐ Obtaining a business telephone line
- ☐ Identifying a place for the business at home or elsewhere (Ch. 11)

Resources—the things that make up the business, like money, products, knowledge, etc.

Number of resource actions done

- ☐ Organizing a start-up team (Ch. 19)
- ☐ Obtaining copyright, patents, trademarks (Ch. 18)
- ☐ Purchasing raw materials, inventory, supplies (Ch. 16)
- ☐ Acquiring major items (equipment, facilities, property) (Ch. 16)
- ☐ Hiring employees and managers (who do not share ownership) (Ch. 19)
- ☐ Participating in classes or workshops on starting a business (If you are taking a small business course, you can check this item.)
- ☐ Participating in programs that help new businesses get established like SIFE, CEO or SBIDA (Appendix II)

Intention—demonstrating a determination to get the business going and for it to be successful

Number of intention actions taken

- ☐ Thinking about the business (Ch. 4 & 6)
- ☐ Undertaking marketing and promotional efforts (Ch. 7 & 10)
- ☐ Developing your product or service (Ch. 4 & 9)
- ☐ Beginning your full-time commitment to the business (> 35 hrs/wk)
- ☐ Preparing a business plan (Ch. 8)
- ☐ Defining market opportunities (Ch. 4 & 12)
- ☐ Developing projected financial statements (Ch. 7 & 14)

Exchange—making investments in and sales from the business

Number of exchange actions done		
	☐	Generating sales revenue (Ch. 10)
	☐	Arranging child care to work on business
	☐	Establishing credit with a supplier (Ch. 15)
	☐	Saving money to invest in the business (Ch. 13)
	☐	Investing money in the business (Ch. 15)
	☐	Seeking funds from financial institutions or others (Ch. 15)
	☐	Seeking funds from spouse or household partner (Ch. 15)
	☐	Seeking funds from current employer (Ch. 15)

The scoring is straightforward. At a minimum you need to have taken at least one action in each of the BRIE categories[37] to successfully start and grow a business. Business survival rates increase with the number of items checked across the different categories.[38] So people who can check three or four items in each BRIE category are more likely to have surviving and growing firms than those who check only one item per category. Having a BRIE category with nothing checked indicates that it is likely that something major is being overlooked, so the business is likely to fail. It is also important to balance BRIE activities. For example, having lots of boundary activities done and only a few exchange ones is likely to lead to an unbalanced approach to business and a lesser chance of survival.

The BRIE model factors outline the activities that need to take place to get a firm going. Skill Module 1.2 is a self-assessment that can help you recognize what important steps you have taken to start your business, and what remains to be done.

The BRIE model can help you deal with one of the biggest hurdles to starting a business. According to the experts, the biggest problem is simply inaction as mentioned earlier. Stanford management professors Gerry Salancik and Bob Sutton[39] say that even when people know taking action would be in their own best interests, most folks tend to procrastinate, sticking with inaction or doing familiar things that have not worked. Salancik and Sutton recommend taking small steps toward a goal as an easy way to start. The BRIE checklist gives you the kind of small steps that can make all the difference. Consider coming back to this checklist periodically to help assess your preparations for business and determine what you still need to do. Taking lots of small steps is a sure way to achieve your goals.

Small Business and the Economy

LO6
Understand how small businesses are important to our economy and your community.

We've talked about why small business is important for the individuals for whom income, growth, and flexibility were among the most important rewards of ownership. But you also need to know that small business is also vitally important to your community and even to our economy. Part of this comes from the new things small businesses contribute to the economy, particularly new jobs and innovations, as well as the basics that small businesses provide for all of us—jobs, taxes, and products or services.

New Jobs

Since the 1970s big business has cut tens of millions of jobs. In the meantime, small business has added tens of millions of jobs. In the latest statistics, small businesses created 75 percent of the 3.4 million new jobs created.[40] When the Census Bureau looked more closely at the figures, it concluded that small business start-ups in the first two years of operation accounted for virtually all the net new jobs in America.[41] Small business *is* the engine of job generation, but it is important for existing jobs, too.

Small businesses employ more than half of all Americans, providing wages, salaries, and the taxes those working people pay the government.[42] Aiming for self-employed occupations like dentistry, building inspection, plumbing, or farming means also choosing to go into small business. It's that way because those occupations are structured that way.[43] The same is true when you decide to go into the family business—the **occupational structure** results in your becoming a small business owner.[44]

occupational structure
The sequence or organization of jobs and careers in the economy.

Small businesses are also a key employer because they are more willing than most large businesses to offer jobs to people with atypical work histories or needs, like people new to the workforce, people with uneven employment histories, and people looking for part-time work. These employment issues are at the core of what makes small business attractive to local and state governments.

Innovations

Small business is a key element of every nation's economy because it offers a very special environment in which the new can come into being. Austrian economist Joseph Schumpeter labeled this process **creative destruction**.[45] It refers to the way that newly created goods, services, or firms can hurt existing goods, services, or firms. For example, when a new restaurant opens in your neighborhood, people flock to it to find out what it's like. This helps the new restaurant, but it also causes the other restaurants in the area to lose business, at least temporarily. One of the most famous examples of creative destruction is the personal computer, which started as a hobby that big business spurned.

creative destruction
The way that newly created goods, services, or firms can hurt existing goods, services, or firms.

In the 1970s there were microcomputers. Radio Shack had thousands of TRS-80s in schools. Another type of computer called an S-100 was used in tech-savvy small businesses. However, there were no computers designed with families in mind. Members of the Silicon Valley's Homebrew Computer Club made these personal computers from scratch in their basements and garages, and showed them off to one another. One member of the club was Steve Wozniak, who worked part time at a Hewlett Packard (HP) lab. Using parts he scrounged from the lab, he built a personal computer on a wooden board. It combined graphics with text (a revolution at the time). Homebrew members went wild over it and assured Steve that it would be a commercial hit. Ever a loyal HP employee, Wozniak offered the machine to his bosses at HP. After all, he built it with HP parts, in his spare time at HP. They rejected the idea, saying that personal computers would never be a success, but they gave Wozniak permission to go ahead on his own. Wozniak showed it to his best friend, Steve Jobs, who called it the Apple computer to make it seem friendly and popular, and together they formed Apple Computer.[46] Apple made the personal computer popular and paved the way for IBM PCs and the personal computer explosion. That explosion redrew the lines of the entire computer industry, but it also created tremendous new wealth, utility, and innovation. Big business often has trouble with innovations that would eat away at existing business, but small businesses are more likely to see new revenues in innovations.

Why do so many innovations come from small business? Remember that most people going into small business mention flexibility as a key reward, such as the flexibility to do the work they think is important. Small business owners are more free of the judgments and social constraints of workers elsewhere.[47] To give you an idea how much more powerful innovation is in small business, the U.S. Small Business Administration reports that among firms that hold one or more patents, small businesses generate 13 to 14 times the number of patents per employee than do big businesses. And the patents produced in those small businesses are twice as likely to be among the top 1 percent of all patents cited by others.[48] That citation is a measure of the importance of the invention. The Small Business Administration compiled a list of major inventions that came from small businesses (see Table 1.2).

TABLE 1.2 The SBA's List of Major Inventions from Small Businesses[49]

Air-conditioning	Heart valve	Prefabricated housing
Air passenger service	Heat sensor	Pressure-sensitive tape
Airplane	Helicopter	Prestressed concrete
Articulated tractor chassis	High-resolution CAT scanner	Programmable computer
Assembly line	High-resolution digital X-ray	Quick-frozen food
Audio tape recorder	High-resolution X-ray microscope	Reading machine
Bakelite	Human growth hormone	Rotary oil drilling bit
Biomagnetic imaging	Hydraulic brake	Safety razor
Biosynthetic insulin	Integrated circuit	Scanner cotton picker
Catalytic petroleum cracking	Kidney stone laser	Six-axis robot arm
Cellophane artificial skin	Large computer	Soft contact lens
Computerized blood pressure	Link trainer	Solid fuel rocket engine
Controller	Microprocessor	Stereoscopic map
Continuous casting	Nuclear magnetic resonance scanner	Strain gauge
Defibrillator	Optical scanner	Strobe lights
DNA fingerprinting	Oral contraceptives	Supercomputer
Double-knit fabric	Outboard engine	Two-armed mobile robot
Electronic spreadsheet	Overnight national delivery	Vacuum tube
Freewing aircraft	Pacemaker	Variable output transformer
FM radio	Personal computer	Vascular lesion laser
Front-end loader	Photo typesetting	Xerography
Geodesic dome	Polaroid camera	X-ray telescope
Gyrocompass	Portable computer	Zipper

In the end, the freedom small business gives owners to pursue and perfect their dream creates the innovations from which we all benefit—not just major inventions like the personal computer, but whole classes of products such as snowboards (21-year-old Dimitrije Milovich in 1969[50]), earmuffs (15-year-old Chester Greenwood in 1858[51]), computer-controlled telephone systems (Krisztina Holly in 1992[52]), date rape drug testing coasters (Brian Glover, 35, and Francisco Guerra, 34, in 2002[53]), and Kitty Litter (Ed Lowe, 27 in 1947[54]) that were developed by innovative small business owners.

New Opportunities

People who own their own business are presented with tremendous opportunities—not only to improve their life and wealth, but also to help them move into and upward in the economy and society of the United States. The opportunities small business offers for getting into the economic mainstream of American life makes it attractive to people who foresee problems fitting into existing businesses—not only people with innovative ideas, but immigrants; people facing unusual schedules, demands, or limitations on their lives; and even people who need a second chance.[55] For many such people, small business *is* the best business opportunity.

Small businesses offer communities another type of opportunity—the opportunity to enjoy goods and services. Imagine a neighborhood or town without a grocery store or a pharmacy. In important ways, the town would not seem like a real community. A small grocery, drugstore, hardware store, or gas station might be able to use its low overhead and capacity to adapt to local needs (e.g., a grocery store stocking a lot of fishing supplies to appeal to visiting fishing enthusiasts) to make a profit where larger chain stores could not.[56] For a small town or a neighborhood to be able to stand on its own, it needs a variety of businesses.[57]

Small businesses provide unexpected opportunities to large businesses and entrepreneurial high-growth firms. High-growth ventures and big businesses are like a giant boat, and where the boat sails, the economy sails along too. But for the boat to work, it has to be supported by deep water. The ocean supporting the boat consists of the tens of millions of small businesses. Without small businesses offering supporting services or offering to subcontract at low cost to the high-growth ventures and big businesses or creating the kinds of communities where creative and entrepreneurial people like to live,[58] those economic boats would lose their buoyancy or profitability and sink like stones. For example, industry giant Procter & Gamble outsourced the making of Ivory and other bar soaps to a small Canadian company, Trillium Health Care Products,[59] saving millions of dollars a year. In addition, big business depends on small business as a source of key ideas for new products. You might think this means high-tech inventions, but there is a lot of money to be made from everyday inventions. Consider the Buffalo hot wings in the Small Business Insight Box below.

SMALL BUSINESS INSIGHT

Success: Mother Teressa and Buffalo Hot Wings[60]

The Anchor Inn looks like a pretty run of the mill neighborhood bar and grill outside downtown Buffalo, New York, but this unassuming place is the home of a major food invention—the Buffalo hot wing. Back in 1964, the owners of the Anchor, Teressa and Frank Bellisimo, started splitting wings in half, broiling (and later frying) them, then covering them in a Tabasco-like sauce (Frank's, but no relation to Frank Bellisimo), and serving them with celery and blue cheese dressing for dipping. These came to be called "Buffalo hot wings" and became a local staple. And Teressa, who came up with the recipe, got the local name "Mother Teressa."

■ Anchor Inn, by all appearances a typical neighborhood bar and grill, is actually the birthplace of a now widely-known and wildly popular food item, the Buffalo Hot Wing.

As Buffalonians emigrated to warmer places, they reported missing the hot wings they grew up with, and so hot wings began to appear in other parts of the country. It was only a matter of time until franchised restaurants grew up around the concept, and today there are chains such as Buffalo Wild Wings, Wing Zone, Wingstop, and Winger's selling thousands of Buffalo hot wings and their variants. Even big business got into the act with the world's largest pizza chain, Domino's, selling its own version of Buffalo hot wings starting in 1992. Other big businesses benefiting from the innovation included big food companies like French's (which own's the Frank's Red Hot Sauce brand), making wing sauce, cooking kits, and recipe books. By 1995 Domino's was selling 10 million wings a week, and Pizza Hut valued the wing business nationally at an estimated $400 million. So it is easy to see how small business innovations become an important source of opportunity for big business growth.

In this chapter we have considered some of the key ideas and myths about small business. We have seen the work of founders of small business that stayed small and those that started small and grew larger. Either way, when small businesses are created, nearly every part of our society benefits—through new jobs, new ideas, and the new opportunities created for individuals, communities, and the economy. The key element in getting small businesses started is helping people who have the intention to start a business take the steps to get it done, and that is what it is hoped this text will help you achieve. If we can help you follow in the model of Aaron McGruder, you are certain to do well. He did.

CHAPTER SUMMARY

LO1 Understand the scope of small business in the United States.

- There were 23.7 million small businesses in the United States in 2003.
- Half of working Americans have thought about self-employment.
- Every year more than 1 million businesses are started in the United States.
- Getting help increases your chances of business survival.
- A small business in the United States has fewer than 500 employees, according to the SBA.
- The focus in this text is on businesses with 1 to 50 people.
- An entrepreneur (alias *self-employed* or owner or owner-manager or founder) is someone who owns a business.
- You can create a new business or buy an existing business or a franchise.

LO2 Learn the differences between small businesses and high-growth ventures.

- Small businesses are different in strategy, structure, and action from high-growth ventures.
- Small businesses are usually intended to remain small, generally a size that the owner feels comfortable controlling personally.
- High-growth ventures start small, but are intended to grow large rapidly, often requiring a team of partners or managers to handle the growth.

- There is a lot of high-quality information on small business available online.
- Only 1.4 percent of businesses are high-growth ventures.

LO3 Discover the rewards entrepreneurs can achieve through their businesses.

- Nearly all people starting small businesses have flexibility, income, and growth as reasons for starting those businesses.
- Small business owners are less motivated by social reasons (recognition, admiration, power, or family) than the general public.

LO4 Be able to dispel key myths about small businesses.

- *Myth 1:* There's not enough financing to start businesses. While we all would like more money, the vast majority of people starting small businesses report finding funding is not a problem.
- *Myth 2:* You need to make something (or something high tech) if you're going to make money. The service economy is growing. Moreover, studies of millionaires show most are in service businesses or professions, not manufacturing.
- *Myth 3:* 70 percent (or 80 percent or 90 percent) of all businesses fail within two years. Around half go at least four years, and, among firms with employees, the survival rates are even higher.

LO5 Identify actions key to becoming a small business owner.

- The BRIE (boundary, resources, intention, exchange) model describes the actions that need to take place for the business to be created in the earliest stage.
- The more BRIE activities that were pursued, the greater the likelihood of the new business surviving.
- The BRIE checklist gives easy-to-perform actions to help move prospective entrepreneurs from inaction to action.

LO6 Understand how small businesses are important to our economy and your community.

- Small businesses are important because they are the major source of new jobs in our economy.
- Small businesses are also the major source of innovations in society.
- Small businesses offer many benefits to localities including employment, taxes, new revenue inflow, support for other businesses, and visibility.
- Small business is also the major source for new opportunities, such as moving up in the economy and society, the opportunity for customers and businesses large and small to obtain needed goods and services.

DISCUSSION QUESTIONS

1. Describe the population of small businesses in America. How many firms are there and how many new firms are started each year?
2. Why do you think half the population says it would *like* to start a small business, but only about one person in seven who expresses an interest actually tries to do so?

3. What are the differences between small businesses and high-growth ventures?
4. Fewer people going into small business mention social or obligational reasons for making their choice than do people from the rest of the population. What do you think this says about people who start small businesses?
5. What do you think will be some of the advantages and disadvantages of starting your own firm versus buying an existing firm?
6. What are some of the franchised firms you deal with regularly? What do you like or dislike about them as a possible business you could own?
7. Describe the BRIE model and how it applies to creating a firm.
8. Why are small businesses better at innovation than large businesses?
9. Why is the presence of small businesses important for large businesses?

EXPERIENTIAL EXERCISES

1. Go through the list of reasons people give for going into self-employment, and identify which of the reasons seem to fit you. Explain why you identify with each reason.
2. Think about the list of reasons people give for becoming self-employed. If you can, interview local entrepreneurs about their reasons and see how your real-life examples fit with the national survey results.
3. Check your state and locality's Web sites for information on programs that support economic development through small business creation and job creation. You can get a start at Firstgov's State Business Supports page: **http://www.firstgov.gov/Business/Business_Resources.shtml.** At the state Web sites, look for "Economic Development" or "Business Supports." Make a list of programs that might be worth looking into as you develop your business idea.
4. Look at the local newspaper's Web site, or the bizjournals.com Web site for the paper in your region. Use the terms "entrepreneur" and "small business owner" to find articles about local entrepreneurs. From this, compile a list of prospective "local small business heroes and heroines" to serve as role models and prospectors for local sources of help.

Mini-Case

SUCHIN PRAPAISILP AND GLOBAL FOODS—"YOU WORK HARD, YOU CAN MAKE IT.[61]"

Small business to the rescue! It had to be a heady day when Suchin Prapaisilp signed an agreement with the city of Kirkwood, Missouri, to open a Global Foods supermarket in 1998. The store had become available again. A&P supermarkets couldn't make it there by the 1970s. National Supermarkets couldn't make it there by the 1990s. And a team of local grocery managers couldn't make it there by 1998, but Chin (as he's known locally) was sure he could. And he was so sure that he convinced Kirkwood's city council to grant him a favorable package to make it happen. The deal was that the store would offer half-traditional American foods for the local community and half-international foods for the regional community.

As satisfying as that moment in the public and industry spotlight was, it was a long road getting there. When he came to America in 1974, 22-year-old Chin's day stretched from 4 a.m. to midnight. He worked for others making donuts, then doing a factory shift. He closed the day as a kitchen helper.

In his off hours he taught dance and even delivered phone books. But his philosophy is, "You work hard, you can make it." Chin and his newly arrived brother Chatchai opened a small grocery store in St. Louis in 1975, and in 1986 opened a bigger grocery that became the anchor for a miniboom of Asian businesses in the neighborhood. This kind of steady growth gave Chin the experience and capital to aim for an opportunity like Global, which would take $2.15 million for the building and improvements. But even with experience and capital, as one of Chin's American employees at Global volunteered, "They took a big gamble opening the store."

The store got a tremendous response, but not exactly as expected. It became the favorite source for exotic ingredients for recipes in the local newspapers, and international customers were regularly coming from as far as 100 miles away to shop Global's well-stocked aisles. But the American products weren't selling as well as expected, and they were taking up space that could be more profitably used for international foods. In the spring of 2000, Chin and Global were doing all right, but Chin knew he could make it better still.

CASE DISCUSSION QUESTIONS

1. What can Suchin do to resolve the problem?
2. Why would Suchin acting on his own to change the grocery be a problem?
3. Was Suchin an entrepreneur? If he was an entrepreneur, what role or roles was he playing—founder, buyer, or owner-manager—at the time he opened Global Foods?

LEARNING OBJECTIVES

This chapter will help you:

LO1 Define *ethics* and *ethical dilemmas* and the relationship between them.

LO2 Find out why ethics are a big part of small business.

LO3 Understand why there aren't any "do this" and "don't do this" types of lists for ethical decisions.

LO4 Learn ethics planning, a three-step process to help you make ethical decisions.

LO5 Learn the techniques of building social capital through legitimacy.

LO6 Learn the basic skills for handling a crisis.

■ Finding a solution to construction problems and delays is one ethical dilemma development companies face regularly. How might the ethical decision-making process for small business owners differ from the processes used by larger companies?

CHAPTER 2

Small Business Ethics: A Key to Long-Term Success

Focus on Small Business: Tobin Real Estate and Development

As Martin Tobin hung up the phone, he felt a headache coming on. Martin and several family members owned Tobin Realty & Development, the community's largest real estate sales and development company. The phone call was from one of the builders Tobin used fairly regularly, and it wasn't good news. The builder, Bob Sarski, had hit a "soft spot" in the soil just before pouring a large new home's concrete foundation. Sandy places in the dirt meant unstable concrete and an unsteady foundation—definitely not what a homeowner wants! Digging out all the sand from a soft spot was an expensive process and really delayed the build.

During the phone call, Sarski told Tobin he couldn't pay for this "extra" work, costing thousands of dollars. Normally, builders pay for all digging costs, including soft spot excavation. But, with the bad economy, Martin knew that Sarski's money was tight. Tobin needed this home built, but if he paid for this problem, what else would the builder ask for? How long would construction be delayed if Tobin didn't pay? Or worse, would Sarski walk off the

job completely and find a new project that provided cash flow? Martin leaned back in his chair, rubbing his temples to try to relieve his headache.[1]

DISCUSSION QUESTIONS

1. Does Tobin have any responsibility toward resolving this problem?
2. What are the main facts to consider when deciding what the right thing to do is?
3. What are the options for resolving this dilemma? How would you rank them?
4. Why is this problem an ethical dilemma?

Why Small Business Ethics Are Different from Big Business Ethics

LO1
Define *ethics* and *ethical dilemmas* and the relationship between them.

Business ethics are always important. With ethics, what may seem like just a decision is really a more complicated *set of decisions* that small business owners have to think about. When people at a big business behave unethically, the way those at Enron did, thousands lose their jobs, others lose their investments, and everyone loses faith. How can it happen? Managers in big businesses report feeling that they think no one will notice what they do.[2] That same thinking *can't* work in small business, because the small business owner most often is the public face of the business. Big businesses are usually national, even global, but small businesses are always local, even when they market halfway across the globe. That is why it is important that small business owners see their decisions, their personal reputation, and their businesses as one thing.

ethics
A system of values that people consider in determining whether actions are right or wrong.

ethical dilemma
A situation that occurs when a person's values are in conflict, making it unclear whether a particular decision is the right thing to do.

But what are ethics, really? **Ethics** are a system of values that people use to determine whether actions are right or wrong. We consider ethics in determining whether a decision we are about to make is good or bad. And, we make judgments about actions—something is good or bad; someone is right or wrong—based upon our own personal ethics. An **ethical dilemma** occurs when a person's values are in conflict, making it unclear whether a decision we're thinking about making is right or not.[3] An ethical dilemma also occurs when there are several different options for a decision we have to make and the best choice isn't clear.

How Ethics and Small Business Go Together

LO2
Find out why ethics are a big part of small business.

Ethics play into five key aspects of nearly all small businesses: community impact, trust, culture, flexibility, and innovation.

Community Impact

Unethical behavior in a small business commonly leads to lower sales and perhaps even bankruptcy. It's often the employees of the small business who suffer first, as they are fired or laid off. This deprives them of their income and deprives other local businesses of the money those employees would spend. It also deprives the local and state government of taxes, around $3,700 per employee per year,[4] and often costs the state or locality money for unemployment benefits or welfare to tide former employees over until they find another job.

How Trust Pays Off

John Bauer understands how trust works in small businesses, and he uses it as a competitive advantage over larger competitors. John's construction company has been in business in the Salt Lake City area for three generations, and John still buys building supplies from the same companies his grandfather did. His major competitors are large, multistate companies, and while he worries about time-consuming paperwork and legal filings when doing builds, the trust John has built with his suppliers allows him to make handshake deals and even buy huge loads of supplies over the phone. His suppliers know that John's good for the money, and the time he saves not having to do paperwork before getting supplies means faster building completion and happier customers. "I get five or six additional projects a year because I build faster and with fewer paperwork snags than any other builder in town. I can't put a price on the trust factor," John says.[5]

Small business owners who make unethical decisions jeopardize the firm's reputation and, worse, its survival. The Council of Better Business Bureaus reports that most of its consumer complaints from around the United States are about small businesses.[6] Studies indicate that customers actively avoid doing business with sellers they perceive as dishonest or unethical.[7] Such consumer perceptions of unfair treatment have a *direct, economic impact on the communities in which the small businesses operate,* because potential customers will choose another company over a business that has a BBB (Better Business Bureau) complaint registered.

Trust

Trust is an essential ingredient to the survival of small firms. **Trust** in this context means fairness in all business transactions in which the firm engages, such as financial transactions, employee matters, regulatory compliance, and complaint resolution.

trust
A feeling of fairness in all business transactions in which the firm engages, such as financial transactions, employee matters, regulatory compliance, and complaint resolution.

In many cases, the business and its owner are seen as one and the same thing, not only by the community, but by the owner as well.[8] The business is really the same as the owner's personal word and credibility.[9] As one small business owner put it, "I *am* the business to my customers. They wouldn't think to separate me from the business. When I make a decision, it is the business making that decision."[10]

Trust in a small business is a double-edged sword. It can be a competitive advantage, as with John Bauer, for business owners who have kept their word over the years and made lasting business relationships. Big businesses often can't compete, because when community members and customers buy from a local business, they know they are dealing with folks who come through on promises. The flip side of having trust as a competitive advantage is the backlash when trust is broken. When small business owners and employees don't treat customers and other stakeholders fairly, there's nowhere to hide. Since small business owners and their businesses are often viewed as the same thing, community members expect personal accountability from small business owners.[11] **Personal accountability** is when people take responsibility for decisions they make and the consequences of those decisions. They don't try to pass the buck. Community members want answers when they think a small business owner makes a questionable decision.

personal accountability
A process in which people take responsibility for decisions they make and the consequences of those decisions.

Trust is the glue of relationships, and once it's broken, it may be impossible to get back. Peter Economy, who writes *1099,* an online column for independent professionals, tells the story of Susan, a business professional who referred an acquaintance to one of her own top clients. The acquaintance was so glad to get work that he promised Susan a "finder's fee" in return for the referral. Once his contract with the client was signed,

SMALL BUSINESS INSIGHT

The Horrors of the Unsatisfied Customer

David and Veronica Sullivan live in a small southwestern U.S. community and have owned several Starlit Dry Cleaners stores for almost 10 years. When customers are unhappy with how their clothes turn out, David tries everything he can to satisfy the customer, including recleaning their clothes free of charge. Usually, customers are happy with this extra attention, but as David notes, not always: "Sometimes a customer won't go away satisfied, no matter what I do. And sometimes people blame Starlit for damaging clothes that they brought in already damaged! Then, it's my word against theirs."

David recalled a customer whose beautiful suede jacket had a spot right on the collar when she picked it up. Even though the counter worker had noted the spot on the cleaning ticket when the jacket was brought in, the customer insisted Starlit had ruined her jacket. The spot remained stubbornly in place, even after several attempts to remove it. David didn't want to send the customer away empty-handed, and agreed to pay for half the jacket's cost. He says, "I thought we had an agreement, and she seemed happy with our paying half the cost. After about a week, she started calling our house, complaining about how we had cheated her and ruined her clothes without fairly paying her! Veronica and I also heard she complained about us to anyone who would listen: in the grocery store, at the vet's, everywhere. Not about the business, but about Veronica and me personally. We still will get customers who bring us something suede and ask if we're sure we can clean it, because they heard about us ruining someone's jacket. It's unbelievable."[12]

though, he refused to pay Susan what he had promised her. The result? No more referrals from Susan and broken trust that won't be regained.[13] Breaking promises, no matter what they are, can be devastating to the relationships that small business owners rely on.

Trust is so important in a small business that even the appearance of unfairness or untrustworthiness can have negative effects. Sometimes, despite a business owner's best efforts, a customer feels he has been treated unfairly. This is when "being the business" can have unexpected consequences.

In small business, reputation is king. Trust is the foundation that makes a solid reputation. As we've seen above, small business owners build trust with many stakeholders, including customers, suppliers, and community members.

Culture

organizational culture
A set of shared beliefs, basic assumptions, or common, accepted ways of dealing with problems and challenges within a company that demonstrate how things get done.

When a small business is being formed, the owner starts to create an **organizational culture** that helps direct the company's operations. A company's culture is a set of shared beliefs or basic assumptions that demonstrate how things get done. Organizational culture also includes common, accepted ways of dealing with problems and challenges within a company.[14] In a small business, there is a lot of flexibility in terms of roles and expected behaviors, especially when the business is first getting started.[15] Business start-up is the best time for owners to communicate an ethical culture that all employees understand. Ethical cultures build trust between owners and employees. If an owner sets up a business culture in which employees are expected to act ethically, then no matter when a new employee joins the company, the culture will help shape a new employee's actions.

A recent study indicates that when key people in a business behave in a consistently ethical way, employees do, too.[16] Edgar Schein, a pioneer in small business research, says that owners shape culture by "walking the talk" every day in their business.[17] Whether they mean to be or not, small business owners are role models for employees every time they step foot in their business. Owners had better make sure they're behaving the same way they want their employees to behave. That modeling is the foundation for business cultures in which ethical behavior is expected. **Modeling** is when small business owners act in ways they want their employees to act. With modeling, employees know what's expected of them and how to act when they're working.

modeling
When small business owners act in ways they want their employees to act.

Schein also says that coaching, rewards, and what the owner pays attention to are very important ways in which employees figure out what's accepted behavior.[18] Patrick Schwartz, cofounder of the advertising agency PSCC, Inc., in Washington, D.C., stressed that **consistency** and **visibility** of ethical behaviors are the keys to building an ethical business culture. Day in and day out, owners have to model the behaviors they want their employees to exhibit. And, they have to behave that way where everyone can see them, including customers, suppliers, and employees. That's consistency and visibility.

consistency
Maintaining the same behavior, attitude, or value over long periods of time.

visibility
Demonstration of a behavior, attitude, or value in ways that are evident to others.

Employees often like working in small businesses for the same reasons owners start them: People who work in small businesses can be more independent and be more "themselves."[19] Because of this, personal values play an important role in decision making.[20] **Personal values** are what you believe is important in life and what you believe is the best way to live your life. Research has identified the "spillover effect,"[21] a consistent link between the way personal and work-related decisions are made. Spillover matters because an owner's values as well as an employee's personal values may conflict with the needs and expectations of the business.

personal values
Attitudes regarding what a person believes is important in life and the best way to live one's life.

Sometimes, what owners think is important in their personal lives may not be in their company's best interest. For example, outside the business, owners might believe that "blood is thicker than water" and that family relationships mean the most to them. Inside the business, though, they might see that nonfamily members make better employees, even though their brother and sister want to be a part of the business. This can create major conflict between personal values and business needs.

Most business dilemmas arise in relationships with customers and employees.[22] Table 2.1 shows the most common stakeholders a small business owner has conflicts with and the reasons why they have problems.

The point of the research is that differences between owners' personal values and what they're expected to do in their business can cause real problems. The more closely personal and business values match, the more smoothly a business will run. Table 2.1 shows that small business owners have the most personal values/business values conflicts when dealing with customers and employees, and the reasons are about what customers and employees think is honest and fair. That's why we emphasize the importance of trust earlier in the chapter. Trust and fairness in small businesses are really important.

An employee's personal ethics are really important to how any small business operates.[23] **Personal ethics** are what you believe is right and wrong and are the beliefs that guide your decisions in your everyday life. As a small business owner, you need to realize that if an employee makes decisions you don't agree with in his personal life, that decision-making pattern will almost definitely follow him or her into your business.

personal ethics
Beliefs about what is right and wrong which guide decisions in everyday life.

Flexibility

As we saw in the first chapter, owners start small businesses because they like independence and have more control over their work. That's great, until an ethical dilemma pops up. **Flexibility** in small business means not having lots of rules, policies, and procedures. It also means that employees probably handle many different jobs. In bigger businesses, there are usually rules for how decisions should be made. But small business owners have to deal with more "first time" situations that they might not have thought about before, especially right after start-up.[24] There's not much consistency in the way small businesses run, at least not at first.

flexibility
The freedom of not having lots of rules, policies, and procedures.

Small businesses don't have lots of rules—by design. Usually, how a problem gets fixed depends on who's fixing it. Not having policies as guides means that employees are not sure how to handle ethical dilemmas. The idea of an owner "walking the talk," as discussed in the last section, works here, too. Generally, a small business employee looks at how the owner makes decisions about ethics and then does the same thing, rather than relying on a policy or rule.

TABLE 2.1 Conflicts between Personal Ethics and Business Expectations

	Never	Sometimes	Mean[a]
In Relations with:			
Customers	24.8%	32.9%	2.403
Employees	25.0%	33.1%	2.304
Peers	34.2%	23.3%	2.048
Suppliers	36.2%	22.1%	2.060
Friends	37.2%	20.0%	1.959
Government and the law	40.8%	24.5%	2.190
Competitors	41.1%	27.4%	2.240
Superiors	43.1%	28.5%	1.979
Family	48.6%	22.3%	1.878
Retailers	50.4%	22.6%	1.854
Wholesalers	52.2%	15.9%	1.739
Potential investors	67.4%	11.9%	1.578
With Regard to:			
Honesty in contracts and agreements	46.3%	17.4%	1.805
Granting pay raises	47.3%	16.2%	1.851
Firings and layoffs	49.3%	13.0%	1.822
Giving of gifts and kickbacks	49.7%	23.1%	1.837
Honesty in internal communications	53.0%	17.4%	1.745
Fairness and discrimination	63.7%	11.0%	1.582
Honesty in promotion decisions	65.8%	9.6%	1.534
Honesty in external communications	66.2%	9.5%	1.568
Price collusion and pricing practices	68.5%	6.8%	1.438

[a]5-point scales (1 = never; 3 = yes, sometimes; 5 = yes, often).

Source: Scott J. Vitell, Erin Baca Dickerson, and Troy A. Festervand. "Ethical Problems, Conflicts and Beliefs of Small Business Professionals," *Journal of Business Ethics,* vol. 28, pp. 15–24, 2000. Chart is on page 17. Reprinted with kind permission of Springer Science and Business Media.

A small business needs to be flexible as it grows and runs into new situations. And a small business generally has fewer resources than a large corporation,[25] which means that small businesses can't hire lots of people to do specific jobs. Needing to be flexible with fewer workers means employees need to wear multiple job "hats"—being able to do different jobs within the company. Not many small business employees have only one specific job and a routine for getting it done. This is usually a short-term issue, most common at start-up. The chance of making a poor decision while learning different jobs is high. Eventually, employees get experienced in the company and get better at decision making. Owners can train employees on how to make the right decisions by looking back at problems the company has faced before and then anticipating similar potential problems.

For instance, one day an owner has to take a business trip and has an employee fill in for him. While he's gone, the employee could have access to petty cash, the bank account, or other money, just as the owner would. This wouldn't be too unusual

■ Flexibility in small businesses means greater freedom to make decisions but also greater responsibilities and a heavier work load in making sure all aspects of the business are staffed. What are some of the risks inherent in such flexible work roles? What are some of the benefits?

in a small business, where employees do lots of different jobs. Everything each small business employee does matters, because small businesses start out with little extra cash resources and often have to be very careful when spending money. Criminal actions and mistakes by employees are a big deal in a small business—a $1,000 theft or mistake is huge if there is only $5,000 in the bank. Small business owners have to be careful about who has access to cash and other resources—this is where flexibility and trust are linked together. Small business owners have to trust their employees to make the right decisions when they are not there, and they should show employees that spending money in the wrong way has a big negative impact on a small business.[26]

Innovation

Small businesses are often the first to try something innovative. **Innovation** is the creation of something new or trying something for the first time. Innovation also suggests that you're not sure how a new idea is going to turn out. Taking advantage of an innovative idea is often the reason small business owners start their businesses in the first place.[27] Sometimes small businesses become very successful at doing new things better than anyone else—and may get into ethical hot water because of it.

innovation
The creation of something new or trying something for the first time.

SMALL BUSINESS INSIGHT

The Bleeding Edge of Innovation

Carl Moore fought the battle of his professional life, and lost—for now. In November 2003, the U.S. Justice Department shut down Moore's company, Rx Depot, which helped Americans buy prescription drugs from Canadian pharmacies for a lot less money than they cost in the United States. This practice is called *reimporting.* Rx Depot and its Canadian subsidiaries helped Americans, mostly seniors on fixed incomes, buy name-brand prescription drugs for up to 60 percent less than they would pay in U.S. pharmacies. American drug companies were furious and said that Rx Depot was breaking the law by reimporting Canadian drugs. The Justice Department went after Moore using another argument: that the safety of the Canadian drugs can't be assured and that Americans should use only U.S. pharmacies.

Rx Depot was on the cutting edge of online prescription services and risked everything by being an industry innovator. Although reimporting is illegal, four states (Minnesota, Wisconsin, North Dakota, and New Hampshire) maintain state-run Web sites to help their state employees buy Canadian and other non-U.S. drugs.[28] At the heart of the issue are seniors who say they can't afford their health-related medicines without using discounters like Rx Depot. They say seniors suffer most from high drug costs and that Rx Depot was, literally, a lifesaving business.

Moore says his service fills a need better than anyone else has been able to, a common reason why small businesses become very successful. Was Rx Depot a risky business? Was Moore putting senior citizens in danger? Moore believes the Canadian drugs are as safe as the drugs sold in the United States and that the fight is about huge lost profits for powerful U.S. drug firms. According to Moore, charging U.S. citizens much more money for the same, safe drugs is unethical. Rx Depot's innovation has redefined a whole industry.[29] With the addition of a drug benefit for Medicare in 2006, lawmakers are considering legalizing reimporting as well as other measures to make prescriptions more affordable—moves the big pharmaceutical companies are fighting each step of the way. Carl Moore's innovation put him at the forefront of a major ethical debate and, for now at least, cost him his company.[30]

It's important to remember that since small businesses often find a niche of customers that big business has forgotten, it's easy for that small business to become a target if it becomes successful. Big businesses have the resources to fight smaller upstart firms that threaten their profits and the ways they do business. Small business owners should be prepared for this and should think about where they stand on ethical issues, like Carl Moore did.

■ RxDepot owner Carl Moore found himself on the losing end of the recent battle over reimporting prescription drugs to the States. What are some resources you can think of that would help small-business owners like Moore to continue producing innovative products and services while managing questions of ethical practices?

Small businesses have unique characteristics that make ethics and ethical decision making high-stakes issues. The ideas of community impact, trust, culture, flexibility, and innovation as they relate to small business often mean good decisions are harder to make. Each decision in a small firm matters, and you can't afford to leave it to chance that you and your employees will make the right decisions without some training. The rest of this chapter is devoted to just that: helping you learn how to craft ethical decisions to sustain and grow your business.

Making Ethical Decisions

LO3
Understand why there aren't any "do this" and "don't do this" types of lists for ethical decisions.

It would be great to make a list that says, "Do this" or "Don't do this" to simplify your making ethical decisions. The problem is that most ethical dilemmas don't lend themselves to an easy "match the ethic" approach. Consider Tobin Realty's situation discussed at the beginning of this chapter. The builder's contract says he pays for all digging costs in construction, so legally, Tobin doesn't *have* to pay for the extra digging. But if Tobin refuses to pay, what might happen? The builder might delay building the home or stop altogether and work instead on a project that provides badly needed cash. Tobin's home buyer will be upset because of delays in construction, and Tobin's excellent service reputation could be damaged. Tobin has used this builder before with good results—and good builders are hard to find. Going to court costs money and time and would really damage the builder's reputation around town.

In Tobin's case, doing what's best for Martin and his family's business conflicts with what's best for the customer, Tobin's reputation, and the builder—all members of a small community. Finding the right answer is complicated.

Ethics decisions are among the toughest a small business owner can make, because the stakes are so high—your reputation, your relationships, and even your firm are at risk—and the potential for hurting someone else is real. There aren't lists with right answers, but there are ways to improve your thinking through ethical dilemmas with ethics planning.

ethics planning
A process used to better consider issues of right and wrong.

first principles
Basic ideas about what constitutes right behavior.

Ethics planning is a three-step process that will help you make better, more ethical decisions. The first step is asking yourself some questions so that you can separate the important issues about your dilemma from the issues that don't matter. Then ethics planning helps you determine possible actions that would resolve your problem. Last, ethics planning lets you think through the potential solution you've chosen to see if you're okay with what might happen once you put your decision into effect. This last step includes thinking about ethical **first principles**, which are the ground-floor ideas about what ethical behavior is, such as:

- It's wrong to steal.
- It's wrong to lie.
- Treat others as you want to be treated.

Just as you think through a marketing plan or a financial projection, you can use the ethics planning approach to think through the options for ethical action. The important thing to remember is that action is important. This chapter gives you some tools that make ethical dilemmas easier to understand, but none of that matters if you don't *act* on your decisions and make ethics a key part of your company's decision making.

You need to ask yourself whether you have a short-term or a long-term orientation in your small business. How long do you want to stay in business? Do you see yourself passing the business down to your kids or other relatives? Do you want to build equity in a business to sell it years from now? Or do you want to go into business, make a "quick hit," make as much money as possible, and then close your doors?

If you want the quick hit, stop reading this chapter now. You won't have much need for ethical decision making. Ethics grows more important the longer you plan

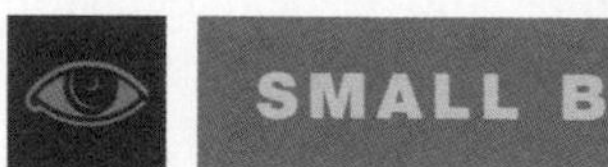

Treating Temps Right

How do you get good employees for a seasonal retail business that traditionally has long hours and relatively low pay? Hold your employees accountable to a code of ethics and model those behaviors. Skeptical? Just ask Phil Jamieson how he manages to get seasonal workers to come back to his New Mexico chili-pepper farming business year after year, and he'll tell you it's because employees know up front what behaviors are expected and because he is responsible for the same code of ethics as his employees. "The short term is different, but the most efficient, best run business truly is the ethical business. Short term, it will cost you money. But in the long term, you never make the wrong decision when you make the ethical decision, and employees see that, no matter how long they work in your business. And that decision will never come back to bite you." Still skeptical? Phil has proudly kept a notebook full of letters he has received from former workers, all of whom were temporary employees. They write to say that they wish their current company was run the way Phil runs his business, and how thankful they are to have worked for Phil.[31]

to stay in business or build on your personal reputation. Only when you treat people fairly, build trust, and act responsibly can you expect your business to be open for many years.

Using the ethics planning process takes time and concentration. Using it also means that you are committed to your business, your customers, your employees, and your community. The payoff is decision making you can be proud of—and decision making that'll get you through tough years, thanks to customer and employee loyalty.

Ethics Planning

LO4
Learn ethics planning, a three-step process to help you make ethical decisions.

Since there is no workable list of "do this" or "don't do this" sort of answers, how *does* an entrepreneur come to make an ethical decision? Over the years a model has emerged that works in a wide variety of situations and gives you a high likelihood of finding a workable ethical decision while taking all key factors into account. This process, *ethics planning*, is detailed below.

FIGURE 2.1

Three Steps of the Ethical Decision-Making Process

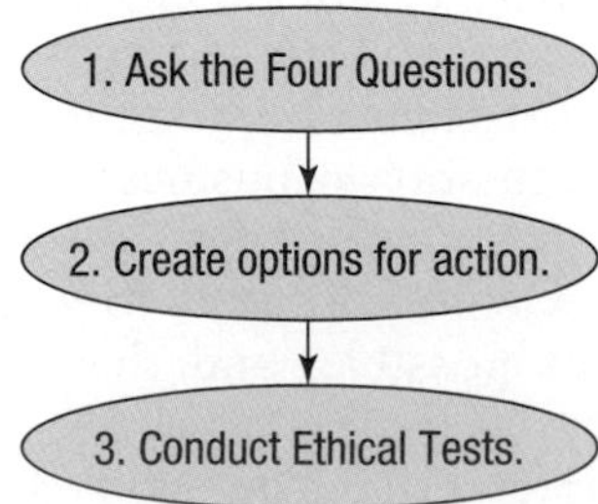

TABLE 2.2 The Four Questions

Focus	Ask Yourself the Four Questions	Determine a Weighting	What to think about
Outcomes of decisions and planned courses of action are important.	*Who will be hurt?*	*How badly will others be hurt?* How long will the harm last?	What is the balance between benefits and harms? Is it right to hurt one group of people to benefit another? Are the benefits big enough to justify the harm?
Balancing consequences, both good and bad, is the key to making the right decisions.	*Who will benefit?*	*How much will others benefit?* To what extent is the benefit concentrated in a small group of people?	
Duties and responsibilities as a key decision maker in your company are important. Balancing obligations to your business and to your community is the key to making the right decisions.	*What do you owe others?*	*Is there anything you owe other people* because of your role as a business owner or decision maker?	What are you obligated to do because of your ability to affect other people's lives? What is fair to expect other people to do for you? Should you make a certain decision based on a long-standing relationship, historical precedent, or your role as a business owner?
	What do others owe you?	*Is there anything you can expect from others* because of your role as a business owner or decision maker?	

Step One: The Four Questions

When you're faced with an ethical decision and you're not sure what to do, the first step is to think about the dilemma asking yourself the following four questions[32]:

1. Who will be hurt, and how badly?
2. Who will benefit, and how much?
3. What do you owe others, if anything?
4. What do others owe you, if anything?

The Four Questions, and their answers, help you figure out important facts about the situation. This step also helps you figure out what's *not* important about your situation, which helps make the problem clearer. Table 2.2 summarizes the Four Questions and what they help you decide.

Look more closely at the Four Questions. What are they really asking you to think about? The first two, about who'll be hurt and who'll gain from the decision, focus on the *outcomes* of actions. Often in an ethical dilemma, the resolution will benefit some people while making other people's situation worse. Is the balance fair? Will some people gain enough to make it okay that others will lose?

When you think about the first two questions and the *outcomes* of your decisions, it's important to try to quantify the answers to help you add the right weighting (refer to Table 2.2). When you think about "how long?" "how much?" or "how badly?" it will help to have some numbers, even if they are relative.

The last two questions, about what you owe others and what they owe you, focus on **obligations** of people who make decisions. The idea is that business owners and

obligations
The social force which impels people who make decisions or have responsibilities to act ethically because the actions they take could affect many other people.

THE THOUGHTFUL ENTREPRENEUR

Thinking through an Ethical Dilemma

You need to buy office supplies. Do you go to Wal-Mart or the local office supply store, a small business like yours? Wal-Mart will cost less, but Wal-Mart's pricing has been putting small businesses out of business all over the country. Small local stores can't compete with Wal-Mart on price.

If you go to Wal-Mart, the local office supply business will be hurt by losing your business, and Wal-Mart will benefit. Over time, if you always choose Wal-Mart, you can add up your office supplies expenditures and see how much you might have spent at your local store. Do you think that amount would matter to the local store's bottom line? Do you think that amount matters to Wal-Mart's bottom line? As a fellow small business owner, do you owe the local business your office supplies dollars? Does it owe you more competitive prices, so the gap between Wal-Mart and it isn't so big?

A Four-Question analysis isn't easy. There aren't right answers from a list. Buying office supplies may not seem like a big ethical question, but this scenario presents a situation that does have ethical implications, especially since you probably will know other small business owners in your community. Would it matter if you knew the office supplies store owner? Would it matter if the local office supplies store owner knew you had gone to Wal-Mart?

managers have responsibilities to act ethically because the actions they take affect many other people.

It's important to remember that the Four Questions are not mutually exclusive, meaning that you can be struggling with more than one at the same time.

The example above gives one situation in which asking yourself the Four Questions helps bring ethical issues to your attention. The local office supplies store owner could be hurt if you use Wal-Mart (Question 1), and, depending on how much you buy in office supplies, it could hurt the owner's business a lot. Wal-Mart benefits from your business (Question 2), but probably not by as much, since Wal-Mart sold about $250 billion worth of goods last year.[33] Some people believe small business owners should buy from one another as a show of support (Question 3), even if prices are higher than in chain stores. Maybe you think the local store owner should offer you a discount if you agree to buy from him or her (Question 4) rather than from Wal-Mart. Do you think it's right to ask for such a discount, knowing it will cut into some badly needed profits? As we said, ethical dilemmas aren't easy.

When you're done asking yourself the Four Questions, you'll have a list of people, groups, or other businesses that are important to your particular situation. Write them down. You can even use a chart similar to the one in Table 2.2 to organize your thoughts. The next step is about forming possible action plans to resolve your dilemma.

distributive view
An ethical overview which involves thinking of problem solving as a win-lose issue. Compare to the integrative view.

integrative view
An ethical overview which involves considering what is best for everyone involved in a situation. (Compare to the distributive view.)

Step Two: Creating Options for Action

After asking yourself the Four Questions, you should be able to see the important issues and people in your decision—who or what matters and who or what doesn't. There are two ways for you to think about what actions you're going to take. One is called the distributive view and the other is called the integrative view.[34] Having a **distributive view** means that you think of problem solving as a win-lose issue. You're interested in the best decision for yourself and your business, and what happens to the other person involved is much less important than what happens to you. The problem with the distributive view occurs when you have a short-term perspective on problem solving, and you do not consider what may happen down the road to your reputation or small business.

Having an **integrative view**, on the other hand, means that you're interested in what's best for everyone involved in a situation. Helping the other people who have

TABLE 2.3 Distributive vs. Integrative View

Distributive	Integrative	What Is Affected
I do what's best for me, no matter what happens to others.	I do what's best for everyone involved, as much as possible.	Who wins
I come up with a solution and sell it to the other person(s).	All people involved get together to figure out what to do.	Who comes up with the solutions
This is a short-term relationship.	This is a long-term relationship.	How long relationships last
I am a lone ranger—and need to do what's best only for my company.	Decisions are made knowing I have to see people in my community every day. I feel like I'm an important part of my community.	How I fit in with my community

a stake in this situation (using the Four Questions) is as important to you as helping yourself. And you think keeping good relationships is important in the long run.

Table 2.3 shows the differences between having a distributive view and an integrative view.[35]

Since we know that community relationships are important to small business owners, the integrative view is the best way to think about your options in resolving ethical dilemmas. Figure 2.2 shows how the integrative view works.

FIGURE 2.2

Creating Options for Action

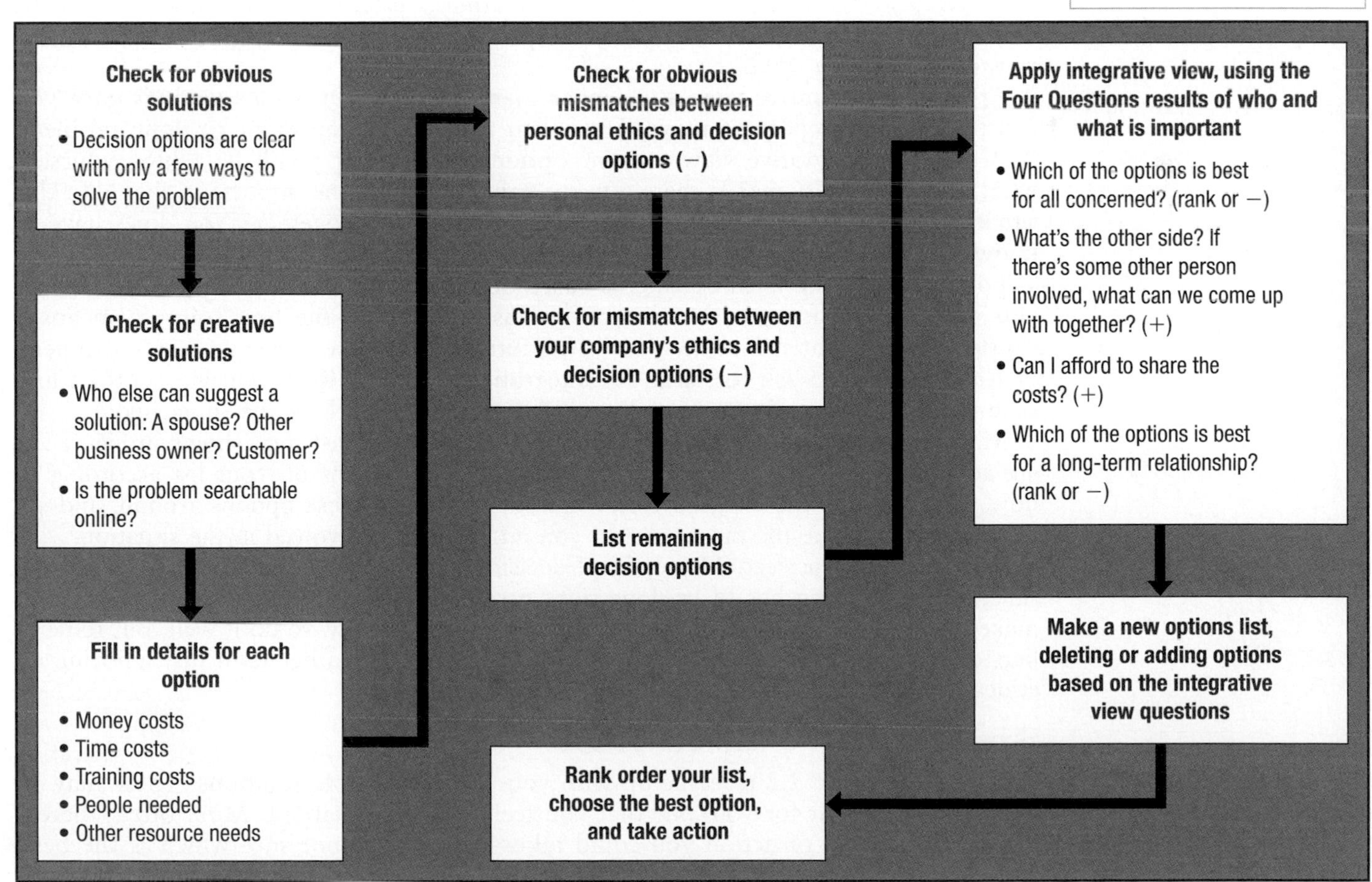

Let's go through how to use Figure 2.2.

Check for obvious solutions. There will be some possible ways to resolve the problems that naturally pop up right away, simply because of the nature of the situation. In the Tobin situation, for example, many of the obvious solutions will revolve around money: Who pays for the extra digging costs? When you're trying to find the best decision option, it's not a good idea to stop at the obvious solutions. The next step is to check around for some options you can't think of alone.

Check for creative solutions. Ask a friend, your spouse or partner, another business owner you know, or maybe even a customer whether they've ever run across anything like what you're facing. You'd be surprised at how often other people struggle with doing what's right, and many times they're willing to share their stories. Another way to find creative solutions is to turn to the Internet for help. There are many Web sites, including discussion forums, devoted to small businesses. Try http://eweb.slu.edu/Default.htm as a first source of information and help online.

Fill in details for each option. Different options will cost you different things: Some cost more money than others; some take more time than money. List each option. Then next to it, list what it will take for you to be able to choose that option. Once you do that, you'll find that certain options cost too much for them to be real possibilities—decide on your limits, see which options are over those limits, cross them off your list, and move on.

Check for mismatches. There are two possibilities for mismatch here. The first is that some of your decision options will go against your personal ethics, or what you believe is right and wrong. The minus sign in Figure 2.2 means that you'll probably eliminate some of your options at this step—certain decisions just don't fit *you*. The second possible mismatch is that some of your decision options will go against your company's ethics, or what you believe are good and bad ways to do business. A company's ethics include how the company wants to be seen by others. There's a minus sign here, too, because just as with personal ethics, certain decisions just won't fit the way you want to do business. Cross off your list any mismatches, and *list all your remaining decision options.*

Apply the integrative view. Remember that your Four-Questions analysis gave you a list of what's important to your problem and who's important to your problem. Applying the integrative view to your options means that you'll be asking yourself, what's best for everyone? Is there a way I can work with the important people in this situation so that we can come up with creative solutions together? You don't have to know everything or know every option yourself. Let other people help you.

Lots of times an ethical decision is based on money costs. The integrative view asks you if you can afford to share costs, because sometimes the best solution means a short-term cost that will repay you in the future with more business, new customers, or a favor you can ask for later. An integrative view is a long-term view. Ethics and time orientation are discussed earlier in the chapter—it's the same thing here.

Make a new list, rank order the options, and choose. The last steps shown in Figure 2.2 are adding, crossing off, and ranking all the different options on your list according to how you answered the integrative view questions. Shuffle those options around, and see what seems to make the most sense to you and to others involved in the situation.

No decision is perfect. Most ethical decisions are made when you're squeezed for time, and something has to be done right now. Practicing the steps in Figure 2.2 will make that process easier for you, and it's worth learning how to do it well. But remember to make the decision in the first place and act on it, rather than just ignoring an ethical dilemma.

Step Three: The Ethical Tests

You've used Figure 2.2 to come up with your list of possible solutions. There may be one that stands out for you, one that you feel pretty good about. More often, there'll be several courses of action you could take—and you're not sure which is the best.

We talk about four major ways of looking at ethical solutions in this section. These are "big picture" ways of seeing if what you're about to do is something you can defend—to yourself and others. Can you make the decision and still hold your head up? We'll see. And what about legality?

Ethics and legality are not at all the same concepts. Generally speaking, think of legality as the "lowest common denominator" for acceptable actions. Many times, a decision you're struggling with will be clear from a legal perspective. Think again about Tobin's situation. You need to make sure your decision falls within legal guidelines. Even though small businesses might not have many of the same rules and regulations as big business, ethics is one area where they do. The Federal Sentencing Guidelines, passed in 1991, have been given new life since all the corporate scandals like Enron happened. And they apply to every U.S. business, whether large or small, public or private.[36] The guidelines want you to, "Promote an organizational culture that encourages ethical conduct and a commitment to compliance with the law."[37] But how do you accomplish this?

The Ethical Tests will help. With the Ethical Tests, you won't ask yourself whether your potential solution is legal or not. Ethics are harder than legality. Being ethical requires a higher standard, because you're asking different questions. Sure, law is concerned about people being hurt and about obligation, but we can tell you that you'll be faced with situations in which a decision will be legal but it won't be your best ethical choice of action. Legal decisions often won't fit the integrative view.

Ethics aren't about politics. Ethics aren't about completing a business transaction and walking away. Ethics are concerned with community, long-term business prosperity, and caring about the people you know. Don't rely on the legal system to help you with those kinds of issues.

You're ready now to apply your list of possible solutions to the four Ethical Tests, and see which stick.

Is my solution the best thing for the most people? You may have seen this idea called **utilitarianism**. Basically, it means that the action resulting in the greatest good for the greatest number of people is the right action to take. This idea has a strong community focus. One of the most important aspects of it is that you have to consider how your actions will affect other people.

utilitarianism
An ethical model that supports seeking the greatest good for the greatest number of people.

Utilitarianism also has a long-term focus, so it works well with the integrative view. It's not about what's fun or quick in the short term but asks you to think about peoples' best interests down the road. If your solution means that many people will benefit from your actions, with acceptable costs to you, it's probably a good solution.

What if everyone did what I want to do? What kind of world would it be? Those questions in a nutshell are the idea of **universalism**, a code of right and wrong that everyone can see and follow. You may have read about universalism in philosophy class, since it's the brainchild of the German philosopher Immanuel Kant. You may have also heard it expanded by mothers everywhere.

universalism
An ethical model that suggests that there is a code of right and wrong that everyone can see and follow.

What would make a good standard that everyone had to follow? That's the idea behind universalism. You get your ideas of right and wrong from your upbringing. Family, religion, education, and community are the major sources. From these sources, there are ideas of right and wrong in which everyone seems to believe and that could become the expected standard of behavior. Some professions, like accountants or doctors, have codes of ethics that all members of that profession need to follow. You can find these by searching Google using the term "code of ethics."

Applying universalism is fairly straightforward—your solution is okay if you can imagine everyone following it the same way.

Am I treating others the way I would want to be treated? You've probably heard of this one before. It's the **Golden Rule**, and almost every major religious tradition in the world has some version of it. The Golden Rule means you'd be okay if someone treated you the way you would treat others when following your solution. Dumping

Golden Rule
An ethical model which suggests you treat others in the manner you wish to be treated.

toxic waste in someone's pond would be acceptable behavior if he or she could dump toxic waste in your pond. An unlikely example, but the point is that you need to think how you'd feel if someone took the same action you're thinking about taking *to you*.

The Golden Rule can be one of the easiest ways to think about ethical dilemmas and potential solutions. It's a simple question: *Would I want to be treated in the way I am thinking about treating someone else?*

billboard principle
An ethical model that asks whether someone would be comfortable having his or her decision and name advertised on a billboard for the public to see.

What if my decision were advertised on a billboard? You've wrestled with the whole process of the rest of the Four Questions, and you've followed Figure 2.2 to the letter, but you still can't decide whether what you plan to do is ethical. Here's the last thing we can offer you for help—the **billboard principle**. As the name implies, this asks whether you'd be comfortable having your decision (with your name, of course) advertised on a billboard for everyone you know to see. Picture it in your mind!

Would you be proud to see your potential course of action up there in giant letters? Would you be ashamed? Would others think worse of you if they knew what you had done to resolve your ethical dilemma? Those questions are the heart of the billboard principle.

So Now What?

After running your list of solutions through the four tests in the prior section, were you able to cross any off the list? You probably have. The Ethical Tests won't automatically give you the best solution to your dilemma, but they're where the rubber hits the road. If your potential solution can't pass at least a couple of these tests, you need to rethink what you're about to do.

Ethics aren't easy, and making ethical decisions isn't a skill you pick up quickly or easily. Our goal with this section of the chapter is to give you some tools that you can use to examine your problem with, and come to decisions you can be proud of. Ethical decision making forms the foundation for everything about a small business, but to leverage the benefits of taking the ethical road, it is important to also take other organizational steps to let others know yours is an ethical organization—one with whom they would like to do business. The ways of doing that depend on building social capital, which is detailed next.

Ethics and Small Business Success: The Creation of Social Capital

L05
Learn the techniques of building social capital through legitimacy.

social capital
Characteristics of a business, like trust, consistency, and networks, that represent potential social obligations which are an asset of the firm or entrepreneur.

Why make ethical decisions? For some, it may be a matter of personal choice or religious command.[38] Simply put, ethical businesses last longer, make more money, and face fewer legal hardships than firms that don't make ethical decisions.[39] It is true that in the short term, unethical behavior can lead to higher profits than can ethical behavior, but if you are in business for the long term, there is only one way to go.

A key benefit of ethical action is that it builds the social capital of a firm.[40] **Social capital** includes characteristics of a business, like trust, consistency, and networks, that help make business operations smooth and efficient. Small businesses high in social capital are more trusted, checked up on less, treated more fairly by regulators, and given the benefit of the doubt when problems occur.[41] Social capital links directly to the idea of trust discussed earlier in the chapter. It means building "capital" in your firm by treating others, including customers, community members, and employees, fairly and honestly. It is capital in the same sense that cash or land can be. You can accumulate it or spend it, and the more of it you have, the greater the value of your firm. Social capital is the major component of what accountants call "good will," and you can find it on a business's balance sheet.

TABLE 2.4 People-Based Legitimacy Indicators

People	More Legitimate	Less Legitimate
Goodwill	Having well-known or well-regarded owners, employees, supporters, or spokespeople	Lacking well-known or well-regarded owners, employees, supporters, or spokespeople
Public recognition	Firm, owner, or employees receive awards (e.g., "Small Business of the Year") or make notable achievements outside the business (e.g., president of the PTA or BBB)	Little or no public recognition
Product/service name recognition	Selling brand name merchandise or services	Nonbrand name
Business network membership	Membership in trade (e.g., National Restaurant Association) and business (e.g., BBB, NFIB, Chamber of Commerce) organizations	No memberships
Organizational size	Having employees	Only yourself
Attire	Wearing uniforms or business attire	Casual attire

There are two ways to build social capital, by building your firm's legitimacy and by creating a social network of people and institutions who think well of you. Let us consider each.

Legitimacy

legitimacy
The belief that a firm is worthy of consideration or doing business with because of the impressions or opinions of customers, suppliers, investors, or competitors.

Legitimacy means that a firm is worthy of consideration or doing business with because of the impressions or opinions of customers, suppliers, investors, or competitors.[42] Gaining legitimacy is one of the top challenges facing new small businesses, but it can be especially difficult for entrepreneurs seen as "different"—women, minorities, home-based businesses, businesses started by young people, entrepreneurs introducing a new technology, or people new to the area or industry. Achieving legitimacy is also a major goal of all new businesses or of existing businesses that have gone through a significant change, like getting new owners or changing their product lines. Achieving legitimacy means building trust among customers and other key groups.

There are three general forms of legitimacy that you can develop—based on your people, based on your product, and based on your organization.[43] Each is discussed below.

Remember that often the owner *is* the business in many peoples' minds. So, he or she is the most important element of social capital to customers and supporters of a business, such as bankers, lawyers, and suppliers. Having people in the organization—an owner, employees, or even media spokespeople—whom customers know and respect increases the firm's legitimacy. Making sure the people of your business always work in the best, friendliest, and most professional way also helps make the sale possible. Some of the major examples of people-based legitimacy are given in Table 2.4.

Also, many small business owners think that the most important source of legitimacy comes from an understanding of the product or service offered.[44] If customers do not understand it, the company is unlikely to get any customer attention because customers may not trust it. Fortunately, most small businesses offer products or services

TABLE 2.5 Product-Based Legitimacy Indicators

Product	More Legitimate	Less Legitimate
Customer assurance	Publicly stated guarantees, bonding, try-before-you-buy policies, return policies, etc.	None stated or given
Experiential supports	Documentation, demonstration offered	None offered
Customer service	Providing customer service live or online	No customer service
Quality standards	Meets or exceeds industry standards for quality	Fails to meet industry standards for quality
Certifications	ISO, Baldridge Award, minority or women-owned business, professional licensing	None or self-certified
Testimonials	Present testimonials from customers satisfied with the product	No information from users
Intellectual property	Has trademarks, service marks, patents or copyrights	None
Industry leadership	Setting technological or service standards adopted by competitors	Common technologies or services
Media product/service visibility	Interviews, articles, placements, or columns in print or electronic media about the product	Little or no attention in print or electronic media about the product

Baldridge Award
The Malcolm Baldridge National Quality Award is given by the US Government to businesses and nonprofit organizations that have been judged outstanding in seven measures of quality leadership; strategic planning; customer and market focus; measurement, analysis, and knowledge management; human resource focus; process management; and results (see http://www.quality.nist.gov).

ISO
Stands for the International Standards Organization, and refers to certification for having met a standard of quality that is consistently evaluated around the world (see http://www.iso.org).

with which customers are already familiar (what we will call an "imitative strategy" in Chapter 7). The goal then becomes making sure the customer knows about the details of the product, its competitive advantage, how to use it, and has the assurance that it will be high quality and backed up by the firm. Table 2.5 describes many forms of product-based legitimacy.

If the customer understands the product, the final key legitimacy factor is promoting knowledge about the organization itself. This might focus on telling about the history or visibility the firm already enjoys. It might come from published information that makes sure your firm looks like a substantial and professional business. Whatever gives customers confidence in the quality and survivability of the firm helps the selling process and in turn increases the all-important trust factor. Table 2.6 gives the key factors for organizational legitimacy.

Across these three types of legitimacy indicators, there are 29 characteristics, and few small businesses incorporate all these elements. Most of the time the small business owner will pick two or three legitimacy-building features from each of the product, organizational, and people indicator listings and then work to implement them. Once implemented, they should be locked in. Part of legitimacy and building trust comes from the consistency of a firm's actions over time. Repeating one legitimacy characteristic daily does more to build your social capital than changing the legitimacy characteristics stressed by the firm in hopes of finding the perfect mix of characteristics.[45]

TABLE 2.6 Organization-Based Legitimacy Indicators

Product	More Legitimate	Less Legitimate
Media organization visibility	Interviews, articles, or columns in print or electronic media about the organization	Little or no attention in print or electronic media about the organization
History	In operation for a long time	New
Time commitment	Full time	Part time
Hours of operation	9–5, 9–9, 24/7	1–5, 6–9
Days of operations	M–F, 7 days a week	One day, weekends only
Phone line	Dedicated to business	Shared with home
Phone answering	Human answered	Answering machine, voice mail
Legal form	Corporation, partnership, or LLC	Sole proprietorship
Physical setting	Commercial site like a store, office building, or mall	Home-based business; a business with no physical location; a business run out of a post office mailbox
Public listings	Yellow Pages, Dun & Bradstreet Business Profile, Business directories	White pages or none
Internet identity	Uses business name **katz@sb2020.com**	Uses generic name **katz@yahoo.com**
Graphic design (business cards, stationery, Web sites, etc.)	Professionally done	Personally done
Partnering	Partners with known businesses	Partners with unknown businesses or no partnering
Dealer network membership	Being an authorized dealer or agent	Unauthorized, gray, or black market dealer or agent

Social Networking

The other basis for building social capital is through building a social network. A **social network** is the entrepreneur's relationships and contacts with others.[46] Social networking is a way to work trust, reciprocity, and long-term relationships into your day-to-day business operations. It's a way to build your company's expertise by convincing others to share their skills and knowledge with your firm. The most successful owners are those who recognize that others have the expertise needed and establish relationships that give them the benefits of that expertise. In many of the stories of small business owners in this book you will see how success hinges on getting others to help you. You might be new to your business, industry, or locality, but, with the right expertise, your business can improve its chances of succeeding. The key is building a network of people who trust you and are willing to help you,[47] and who can depend on you for help and advice in return. Through this mutuality, social networking helps build long-lasting relationships.

social network
The entrepreneur's set of relationships and contacts with individuals and institutions.

Reputation is important to successful social networking. In the beginning of this chapter we talk about how ethical businesses have positive community impact, increase trust, and create a culture that enables people to make good decisions.

FIGURE 2.3

Sources for Network Connections

Family: Start here, and ask your parents, grandparents, and extended family. Include in-laws.

Friends and neighbors: Include your friends, and friends of friends.

Kids: Think about the people you've met through your children at their school and in their extracurricular activities.

Bank: You probably have a bank account, possibly several. Get to know your bankers and ask them for introductions or referrals.

Customer contacts: You are a customer, patient, or client to doctors, dentists, insurance agents, lawyers, and small business owners of all sorts. They know you and because they're in business, they may have the kind of contacts you need.

School: Think about students, faculty, and support organizations where you or your family have gone to school. Many colleges have alumni offices and entrepreneurship or small business development centers, and these can put you in touch with helpful others.

Hobbies: Hobbies often bring together people with diverse backgrounds. That makes them a great place for finding different sorts of contacts.

Business associations: Most communities have some form of a chamber of commerce. Most industries and professions have associations. People join these in order to network. Ask the officers of the chamber of commerce or the association for referrals. Be willing to assist others who ask for your help.

Other organizations: Religious, civic, community, and political organizations often publish member lists. Go over these to see if you recall people who have the business ties or expertise you need.

Work: Consider co-workers, bosses, customers, suppliers, and folks in other firms with whom you deal. Note that work contacts can be problematic. Check company rules or expectations first. Many firms consider such contacts a conflict of interest.

Small business support organizations: There are always organizations dedicated to small business such as the National Federation of Independent Business, National Small Business United, the National Association for the Self-Employed. You can get lists of these by searching Google's directory for "small business associations" as shown. Many of these organizations have local chapters, and all encourage members to contact and help one another.

Social networking helps all those aspects of small business by building your reputation as giving the most expert business goods or services and as being an important community resource. Social networking can help your long-term reputation as a business owner by showing others who you are[48]—a consistently top-notch community player.

You probably already know many of the people who can help you build a social network. Figure 2.3 gives a list of the most popular places to look for network contacts.

What kind of help do entrepreneurs seek from their social network? The PSED provides some insight as to the type of help people starting their own business seek out and these results are shown in Figure 2.4. Information is the number one type of help, followed by introductions to others. In the PSED, most prospective and early stage entrepreneurs reported having one or two people in their helping network, and they typically reported around 3 contacts a month across their whole network of folks providing help.[49]

Knowing whom and what to ask is only part of the story. The other part involves building the relationships and encouraging others to help you. One of the key parts of social networking is actually seeking the help or advice of others. Asking for help

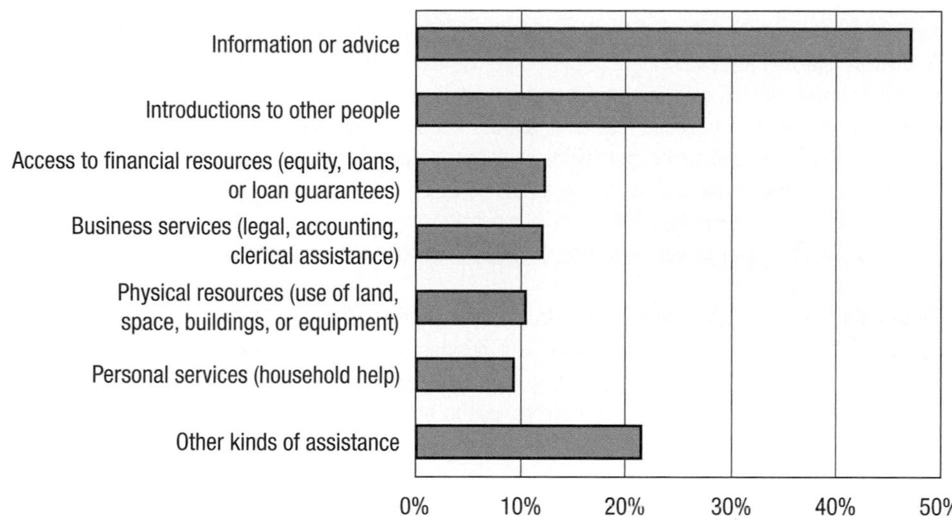

FIGURE 2.4

Types of Help Sought from the PSED

Source: Adapted from: H. E. Aldrich and N. M. Carter, (2004). Social Networks, In Gartner, William B., Shaver, Kelly G. Carter, Nancy M. and Reynolds, Paul D. (Eds.) (2004). *Handbook of Entrepreneurial Dynamics: The Process of Business Creation.* Thousand Oaks, CA: Sage, Table 29.1, page 331.

well is a skill. A little advance thinking and preparation can dramatically produce positive results. Skill Module 2.1 gives you one of the most successful methods for asking others for help.

Asking for Help

SKILL MODULE 2.1

The best people to ask for help are often the people who are the busiest. Knowing this, some small business owners shy away from imposing. In reality, there is no substitute for expertise, and getting it from others is one of the most efficient and effective ways to do it. Building on the ideas of Paula Caproni[50] here is an eight-step approach to asking others for help:

- **Request from people you trust:** Either ask people who already know you, or establish a relationship with the people you want to ask before seeking help from them. This can be as little as a few minutes of talk to find common ground or common friends at a chamber of commerce reception, but it is an important foundation for the relationship.
- **Ask for specific behavior:** Your request is more likely to fit someone's schedule if it is specific and something that has a definite end. So, asking, "How can I get an introduction to someone in purchasing at BigCorp?" is more likely to get a positive response than, "What can I do to sell more?"
- **Do not be defensive:** When explaining what you need, do not blame others for your needing help. And when asked questions by potential helpers, do not get upset or accusatory. Often they need to know what you have tried, how you did it, and how it worked out. They also often need to know what you are capable of doing, or what expertise you bring to the situation. Give concise answers and show your willingness to answer more. After all, they need the information to help you.
- **Do not overreact or underreact:** Think of your regular conversations with good customers or friends. That kind of give and take and that kind of emotional level is what a good asking-for-help exchange sounds like. While being brief is good—after all, time is money—if you sound like you are holding back or are unwilling to talk, it does not help build the relationship. On the other hand, going overboard with praise and information can come across as phony or irritating. Think of regular conversations, and try to emulate them here.
- **Summarize what was said to ensure understanding:** When your conversation is nearing the end, repeat what you understood as the advice. It is fine to put it in your own words. The goal here is for you and the person helping you to know that each of you understood the other. If you are going to try the advice on your own, you want to be certain you understand what to do, how to do it, and maybe even why to do it that way. Summarizing is a great way to confirm all that and show how attentive you have been.

- **Explain what you are going to do about feedback:** People you approach as experts often take part of their satisfaction from knowing that their expertise has made a difference—especially in your business, but at least in your thinking. If you can tell such people how you will use their help, it can provide them with an immediate reward. If you are not sure what action you will take, be honest about this, but also point to the new things you have learned or discovered from the help they offered.
- **Thank the person for the input:** This is in part providing an immediate payout to the person helping you, but also laying a foundation for future contact. Provide a simple thanks and mention how you hope to return the favor or help someday. A good handshake and a smile, and you are ready to get back to business.
- **Follow through:** It is always a good idea to inform any person who tried to help you about how your efforts came out. Tell them how you solved your business problem in general terms. If their help was used, mention this. Thank them for their help (whether you used it or not). Finish with a mention of your appreciation of their help and your willingness to help them in the future.

mutuality
The action of each person helping another.

networking
Interacting with others in order to build relationships useful to a business.

Remember, social networking is an ethical issue about how you'll conduct business every day. It means asking for help when you need it, respecting the other person's time and expertise, and most importantly being willing to reciprocate if asked. **Mutuality** is the idea and action of each person helping the other. Part of building social capital with social networking comes from the help people in the network can provide one another. Why help? Reasons may be making a new friend or making a friendship stronger, creating a relationship that can lead to future business or friendship, having a chance to demonstrate expertise, incurring a debt for future repayment, or even just wanting to help others. Helping others means you understand the idea of positive community impact, trust and relationships—critical success factors in building an ethical business.

Building social capital through social networking involves giving information, letting people know they belong, and providing social support and approval. You have to take the time to build and keep up your relationships with others in your network. This is called **networking**, which means small business owners interacting with others in order to build relationships useful to the business. Key skills for effective small business networking are given in Skill Module 2.2.

SKILL MODULE 2.2

Networking Skills[51]

Networking is a skill like any other. In business you often know the kind of situation you are about to go into or are likely to face. Knowing this, you can take several steps to prepare yourself to socialize with others as a basis for establishing a business relationship. Here are the steps you can take to prepare:

- **Know who you are:** Craft a 30-second spot about yourself and your firm, and practice it until it sounds like a natural expression of your interests. This is often called an *elevator pitch,* and Chapter 8 (Business Plans) gives details on putting together a winning one.
- **Know whom you want and why:** Once you know who will be attending an event (from your buddy, looking at the materials for the event, or going through the member list of the sponsoring organization), start putting together a list of names of people and organizations you want to make contact with. Make sure you keep track of why you are looking for particular people. When you are at the event, walk around the room to see who is there from the list, or ask the organizers of the event if the people you seek are around.
- **Buddy up:** When you know you are going to a particular event, check around to find a friend or business associate (a customer, supplier, lawyer, insurance agent, banker, etc.) who has attended a similar event before. Ask if you can go with him or her, and ask about the people and firms likely to be there.

- **Bone up on small talk:** What do you say after hello? A good place to start is to give your elevator pitch and close with why you were looking forward to meeting the person. If you think your business can help the other person's, talk about that. If the other person wants to limit the conversation to social topics, go with that. To help with chitchat in those situations, make sure you look at the local newspaper (sports section included) on the day of the event, and take a look at *The Wall Street Journal* or *USA Today* front page if you can.
- **Do not forget why you're there:** People tend to gather in groups of like-minded folks. This can mean that all the golf players are together talking strokes, but it can be deadly if it means that all the women entrepreneurs are gathered together and not networking with the male businesspeople. If you are at a networking event and you start feeling comfortable, check to make sure it is not because you have actually stopped networking.
- **Make the connection:** The key to making networking work is to make the personal connection. Businesspeople *expect* to be approached by others at events. Do not be shy. Just walk up and say hello. If necessary, ask a friend or an event organizer to make the introduction, but, however you do it, meet the people.
- **Follow up**: After you meet someone at a networking event, periodically keep up the contact through e-mails, phone, mail, or personal contact. If you can offer help or information, that is the best reason to stay in touch.

Most entrepreneurs who recognize the value of networking develop some means of keeping track of their contacts. Using paper-and-pencil contact managers such as those from Rolodex or Franklin Covey, computer software such as Microsoft Outlook (which is a part of MS Office), or specialized contact management software such as ACT! or Goldmine, or online services,[52] that you can quickly find using a Google search. The goal is to make sure you keep track of your social and business contacts. The best approaches help you identify whom you need to contact to keep relationships fresh. This is because networking is one of the key skills for *all* business owners, female and male, minority and majority, high tech and no tech. Because in the end, business is all about making the sale and the sale depends on making a connection with customers, and that connection is what networking is all about.

Rolodex Equipment and Software - www.Rolodex.com

ACT! Software - www.act.com

Goldmine Software - http://www.frontrange.com/ProductsSolutions/subcategory.aspx?id=808.ccid=15&cp=911

Handling a Crisis

LO6
Learn the basic skills for handling a crisis.

While some ethical challenges come slowly and give the small business owner a chance to think about how to choose, all businesses sooner or later face some sort of crisis. A crisis is a situation that poses a major problem for the business or its people, in which the survival of the business is at stake, and immediate action is necessary.[53] For owners, knowing what to do during a crisis is a very specialized and very emotionally demanding form of ethical decision making. Small business owners are optimists about their businesses, and it can be wrenching when something goes wrong. When the crisis is in full swing, knowing what to do is critical. The gold standard for crisis leadership comes from Norman Augustine,[54] former president of Lockheed Martin—a Fortune 500 company. Although originally given for large businesses, the six steps to follow can be readily adapted to small ones.[55] The steps are:

1. Admit you're in trouble—quickly. It is better to say, "If there is a problem, I will find it and fix it," than to delay an admission until fact finding is done.
2. Get to the scene as soon as possible. Your job? Show caring and accountability.
3. Communicate facts you know (and those you don't) to employees, customers, and suppliers.
4. Have one person serve as the firm's spokesperson. It is best if it can be the owner, but an articulate employee, family member, or outside professional (e.g., lawyer) can stand in.

5. Separate crisis management from the everyday management of the firm. If you are doing both, try to take time to do each separately. Delegate as much as possible of the everyday management to employees or family while you are concentrating on dealing with the crisis.
6. Deal with the crisis quickly. Take steps to solve the problem, and make the process of dealing with the problem as open as possible.

Managing crisis is a difficult but necessary skill. Obviously, anticipating problems and avoiding them or handling them before they become major is a better approach, but only one business in ten has a disaster or crisis plan.[56] The challenge to small business owners is figuring out what those problems might be. Small businesses that build legitimacy and take good care of their social network build social capital and trust among the people and institutions around them. Being a good social network member and a legitimate organization gives you a chance to display and demonstrate your ethical approach to business, and it helps others feel good about putting their faith, and their dollars, in your business, even in times of crisis.

Ethics in its many forms are a key requirement for any entrepreneur in small business. Ethical action makes it possible for others to believe in a small business, especially when it is starting up and has little in the way of a track record. For established small businesses, ethical action is essential to building and maintaining goodwill. And the skills of applying ethics—whether ethical decision making, network building and maintenance, building legitimacy, seeking help, or handling a crisis—are among the most important skills any small business owner can master. In the end, a small business without an ethical foundation or the skills of ethical business practice is a firm not long for this world. In small business, ethical action is not an option—it is a necessity, and it is one that can help your business in a variety of ways.

CHAPTER SUMMARY

LO1 Define *ethics* and *ethical dilemmas* and the relationship between them.

- *Ethics* is a system of values that people use to determine whether actions are right or wrong.
- An ethical dilemma occurs when a person's values are in conflict, making it unclear whether a decision being considered is the right thing to do.
- Ethics guides our decisions, mostly without us even knowing, until a situation arises in which we can't see a clear best way to go. That's a dilemma that needs to be resolved.

LO2 Find out why ethics are a big part of small business.

- Ethics are important in five key aspects of small businesses: community impact, trust, culture, flexibility, and innovation.
- Because small businesses form the majority of businesses in the United States, they are an important part of any community. People avoid doing business with companies they perceive to be unethical, so unethical decision making jeopardizes a small business's very survival.

- Trusting the small business owner is key, because the owner and the business are often the "same" in peoples' eyes.
- Owners set the culture for their small business, and employees watch owners to know how to act. If owners act unethically, so will their employees.
- Small businesses don't have lots of policies and rules, so owners and employees don't have clear-cut guidelines for how to resolve ethical dilemmas.
- Small businesses are usually the ones that come up with innovations, thus putting them in potentially risky ethical situations.

LO3 Understand why there aren't any "do this" and "don't do this" types of lists for ethical decisions.

- There are too many important and varied factors for small businesses to make lists like that.
- Relationships, reputations, and family dynamics are some of the reasons small business ethics decisions can be more complicated than those in larger businesses.
- Ethics aren't like law, where it's "one size fits all."

LO4 Learn ethics planning, a three-step process to help you make ethical decisions.

- The Four Questions (creating action options) and the Ethical Tests form ethics planning.
- The Four Questions help you figure out how to deal with important people and apply information for your decision.
- Creating action options helps you build a list of realistic possibilities to help you resolve your problem.
- The Ethical Tests are a "big picture" way to understand your possible options and to help you pick out the best one.
- Owners' decision making becomes the model for the way all employees will make decisions, so it's worth spending time to make sure those decisions are the best ones available.
- Word-of-mouth is key to small business success and growth, and even the perception of unethical treatment can lead to lost sales.

LO5 Learn the techniques of building social capital through legitimacy.

- Social capital is built from legitimacy and social networking.
- Legitimacy is others' acceptance of the people, products, and organization of the small business.
- Social networking involves building relationships with others through mutual contact and help.

LO6 Learn the basic skills for handling a crisis.

- Crises are problems that risk a business's existence and require immediate action.
- There are six suggestions for handling a crisis.
- Being honest and open is a big part of handling crises.

DISCUSSION QUESTIONS

1. Why is ethical action important to small businesses? Give at least three reasons.
2. How can the owner of a start-up business help promote an ethical organizational culture?
3. Why is flexibility important to the survival of a small business? Is it all right for ethics to be flexible in a small firm?
4. What are the three steps in ethics planning?
5. How does your time orientation as an owner make a difference in ethical decision making?
6. What are the Four Questions of ethical decision making?
7. What are the four major Ethical Tests?
8. What are the three general forms of legitimacy? Give two examples of ways to build legitimacy in each general form.
9. Why is a social network important for a small business?
10. What are the six steps of handling a crisis?

EXPERIENTIAL EXERCISES

http://ethics.iit.edu

1. When talking about codes of ethics, you were encouraged to do a Google search. One of the sites that may have turned up is the Center for the Study of Ethics in Professions at the Illinois Institute of Technology. Check out the site's collection of Codes of Ethics. Select one in an area that matches your small business interests (e.g., business, management, real estate, service, etc.) and look at one of the codes for that area. What do you need to do to prepare yourself to understand and follow that code when you enter your business?
2. Your instructor will show you one or more video clips of role plays and ask you questions about what you think was going on and how you might handle the situation using the ideas presented in this chapter.
3. You can complete and discuss the self-assessment below.

Is your behavior ethical?

Part I.

For this exercise, you will be using the same set of statements twice. The first time you answer them, focus on your own behavior and the frequency with which you use it for each question. On the line before the question number, place number 1–4 that represents how often you did, do, or would do the behavior if you had the chance. These numbers will allow you to determine your level of ethics. You can be honest without fear of having to tell others in class of your score. *Sharing ethics scores is not part of the exercise.* The scale is:

Frequently 1 2 3 4 Never

The second time you use the same statements, focus on other people in an organization that you work for or have worked for. Place an O on the line after the number if you observed someone exhibiting this behavior. Also place an R on the line if you reported this behavior either within the organization or externally to some other person or organization. As you read the statements, state how often you ***did*** the behavior in the past, if you ***do*** the behavior now, or if you ***would do*** the behavior if you had the chance.

1–4		O-R	
			College
____	1.	____	Cheating on homework assignments.
____	2.	____	Cheating on exams.
____	3.	____	Turning in papers as your own work that were completed by someone else.
____	4.	____	Helping someone do any of the above.
			Job
____	5.	____	Lying to others to get what you want or stay out of trouble.
____	6.	____	Coming to work late and getting paid for it.
____	7.	____	Leaving work early and getting paid for it.
____	8.	____	Taking long breaks or lunches and getting paid for it.
____	9.	____	Calling in sick to get a day off, when you are not sick.
____	10.	____	Socializing rather than doing the work that should be done.
____	11.	____	Doing personal work on company time.
____	12.	____	Using the organization's phone to make personal calls.
____	13.	____	Using the organization's computer and Internet access for personal use.
____	14.	____	Using the company copier for personal use.
____	15.	____	Using the company car for personal use.
____	16.	____	Mailing personal things through the company mail.
____	17.	____	Taking home company supplies and keeping them, or taking home company tools or equipment without permission for personal use and then returning them.
____	18.	____	Giving company supplies or merchandise to friends or allowing them to take them without saying anything.
____	19.	____	Putting in for reimbursement for meals and travel or other expenses that weren't actually eaten or taken.
____	20.	____	Taking a spouse or friends out to eat and charging it to the company's expense account.
____	21.	____	Taking a spouse or friend on business trips and charging the expense to the company.
____	22.	____	Accepting gifts from customers or suppliers in exchange for giving them business.
____	23.	____	Being pressured, or pressuring others, to sign documents containing false information.
____	24.	____	Being pressured, or pressuring others, to sign documents you haven't read, knowing they may contain information or decisions that might be considered not in your or their best interest.
____	25.	____	If you were to give this assessment to a person you work with whom you don't get along with very well, would she or he agree with your answers? Use a scale of 1–4 on the line before number 25 and skip the line after the number for O or R.

Note to students: This self-assessment is not meant to be a precise measure of your ethical behavior. It is designed to get you thinking about ethics and your behavior and that of others from an ethical perspective. It is also designed to help you see situations in which you might have to think twice about your decision, because there is an ethical part to it. There is no right or wrong score. Another ethical issue of this exercise is your honesty when rating how often you might do these things—how honest were you?

Scoring: To determine your score, add the numbers 1–4. Your total will be between 25 and 100. Place the number here ____________ and on the continuum below that represents your score. The lower your score, the more you need to be thinking about the types of behavior you are doing in your organization.

Needs some thought 25——30——40——50——60——70——80——90——100 A role model

Discussion Questions:

1. For the college items 1–4, who is harmed and who benefits from these behaviors?
2. For job items 5–24, select the three (circle their numbers) that you consider the most severe unethical behavior. Who is harmed and who benefits from these behaviors? Would it matter if they were in a small business or a big company? Why?
3. If you observed unethical behavior but didn't report it, why not? If you did report it, why? What was the result? Was it worth it to you to report the behavior?
4. As a small business manager, you know unethical behavior can threaten the company's existence. If you know some of the employees are stealing from the company, would you tell the owner? Why or why not?
5. If you were a small business owner and you caught your employee, who is also your friend, doing any of the three behaviors you circled in Question 2 (most severe), what would you do?

Application:

1. What did I learn from this exercise?
2. How might I use this self-understanding in the future if I own my own or manage a small business?
3. As a small business owner, what can I do to prevent unethical behavior?

Mini-Case

THE GIFT[57]

You have recently been hired as the purchasing manager at CDI Electronics, a small electronics research firm. You've been getting settled in your new position and becoming acquainted with the other 26 CDI employees. You've also started getting to know the vendors with whom CDI does business.

It's late November and the holidays are approaching. In your mail for the day is a small package containing an expensive watch from one of CDI's main vendors. Your first reaction is to send the watch back because accepting expensive gifts from vendors clearly violates all the company policies you've ever seen in larger companies you've worked in. It is a very fine watch with your name engraved on the back, along with the vendor's logo.

Before you get a chance to return the watch, Jim Fitzpatrick, an employee who's been with CDI since its beginning 12 years ago, approaches you about the situation. Apparently, everyone at CDI except for Joe Balsam, the founder and current CEO, received similar watches. According to Jim, this vendor sends some type of gift each holiday season, and CDI employees look forward to receiving the gift. He goes on to say that while everyone enjoys the gifts and is most appreciative, no preferential treatment is given to the vendor, nor is any expected.

Jim is concerned. He and the other CDI employees have noticed that your watch has just been sitting on your desk for the past two days. Employees are wondering why and what you may be thinking.

They're concerned that if you make an issue of the gift, there will be trouble over gifts accepted in past years, because no one knows how Joe Balsam might react if he knew. Joe is apparently unaware of the annual gifts.

After Jim leaves your office, you sit and think about your options. The easiest solution would be to accept the gift as others have done in the past. Or you could go to Joe for guidance and cover yourself that way. There is a risk, though, that bringing it to Joe's attention would cause him to crack down on the practice if he doesn't like it. You haven't known Joe for very long, and you're really not sure if he'll go along with the gifts or not.

CASE DISCUSSION QUESTIONS

1. What is the important decision you're faced with, and why is it an ethical dilemma?
2. Is this a situation that matters in the short term or the long term? Why?
3. What does a Four Questions analysis tell you?
4. The case tells you some of the obvious solutions or courses of action. What are some of the creative solutions you can come up with?
5. Using Figure 2.2, recommend your "best" ethical course of action, and see if it passes any or all of the four Ethical Tests. What do the four tests tell you about your possible decision?
6. Defend the course of action you've decided to take to a small group of your classmates.

WHOLE GROUP DISCUSSION QUESTIONS

1. How did your individual answers differ from your group's answers? Were your answers generally the ones the group decided to adopt? Why or why not?
2. Did your group members help you think about aspects of the decision you didn't think of yourself? How might you change your ethical decision-making process because of what your group said?

LEARNING OBJECTIVES

This chapter will help you:

LO1 Learn about entrepreneurial personality types.

LO2 Learn the competencies of the successful entrepreneur.

LO3 Discover the types of career paths entrepreneurs pursue.

LO4 Understand the challenges of family business owners.

LO5 Recognize the special nature of entrepreneurial teams.

LO6 Gain insight into the challenges women and minority business owners face.

LO7 Understand the situation of people who become business owners later in life.

■ New advances in technology and communications are helping entrepreneurs like Laura Tidwell fulfill their career goals while also balancing their family life priorities. In addition to learning how to take advantage of these resources, what other entrepreneurial skills and qualities enabled Laura to grow her business into what it is today?

CHAPTER

3

Small Business Entrepreneurs: Characteristics and Competencies

Focus on Small Business: Internet Entrepreneur Laura Tidwell[1]

In 1990 at the age of 16, Laura Tidwell entered Brigham Young University as a communications major specializing in advertising. Laura did not stay in school long enough to earn her college degree, but she remained very much interested in the field of advertising. At 18, she found herself divorced, broke, and the single mother of a toddler. Yet Laura was determined to have a career in advertising—one that would allow her to stay at home, earn a decent living, and raise her daughter.

While socializing at a club in 1994, one of her dance partners told Laura that he wrote Web pages for a living. Never having heard of such a job, she asked, "Web, as in spiders?" Although he initially laughed at her response, he did take the time to explain his job. She suddenly realized that the Web was the answer to her dream. That night, she decided to become the owner of a home-based Internet advertising company.

Laura lacked expertise and funding, but she had a goal and the determination and self-confidence to make it a reality. Laura learned the business every way she could using Web-related sources, but she focused on developing contacts at Internet trade shows and through industry associations. She realized she needed even more expertise and started working for people in the industry, at first for free and then in a paying job with an Internet start-up company. By 1996, the then 22-year-old Laura thought she had learned enough, knew enough people in the industry, and saved enough money to step out on her own. She quit her job and started her own Internet advertising business, Advantage Advertising.

Operating out of the one-bedroom apartment she shared with her daughter in Troy, Alabama, Laura began with only one small business client. Seeking big name clients that would prove her firm's credibility, she bravely made an offer to representatives of Encyclopedia Britannica and the Thomas Register she met at a trade show. She would handle their online advertising purchases, such as banner ads, free of charge for a period of time. In return they would become her clients if they were satisfied with the quality of her service. Intrigued, they gave her a chance, and she quickly proved her worth, making these large companies her first major clients. Laura then had the visibility and credibility she needed to attract additional clients, and she has enjoyed a thriving, profitable, growing business ever since.

DISCUSSION QUESTIONS

1. Why did Laura Tidwell decide to become an entrepreneur?
2. What skills did she develop to become a successful entrepreneur?
3. What opportunities did Laura find and pursue?

The Entrepreneurial Personality

L01
Learn about entrepreneurial personality types.

Entrepreneurs like Laura Tidwell have always fascinated people. All the great explorers were entrepreneurs—Marco Polo, Columbus, and Magellan. Each explored to find new opportunities for trade and wealth—or at least that is what they told their royal backers! The classic entrepreneur was a loner, often socially isolated, a hard worker, a fast learner, and a risk taker seeking wealth. This view lasted from the seventeenth century until the later half of the twentieth century.[2] Even today, the classic entrepreneurial personality fits like a glove some famous business founders. Think of Bill Gates of Microsoft or the late Sam Walton of Wal-Mart. They certainly fit the profile, as do literally millions of other self-employed people.

There were more than 15.3 million self-employed people in 2003,[3] and one profile is unlikely to fit them all. When researchers began to look more closely, they discovered a number of entrepreneurial personalities kept cropping up (these are summarized in Figure 3.1). For example, the first new profile was for the small business owner.[4] Like classic entrepreneurs, small business owners typically are hard workers, often alone and socially isolated. But unlike the classic entrepreneurs, small business owners are actually risk-averse, which makes them slower to decide and learn than classic entrepreneurs. These small business owners are also looking to make a living income, not to build great wealth.

Other profiles emerged. Another departure from the classic entrepreneur was the idea person,[5] like J. J. Rosen (see Small Business Insight Box on page 58). Idea people are hard working and socially isolated, but often find other outsiders to work with. Idea people are not particularly driven by great wealth, but they are driven by having their idea achieve greatness, and they can be great risk takers and learners while trying to make that idea come alive.

FIGURE 3.1

History and Types of Entrepreneurial Personalities

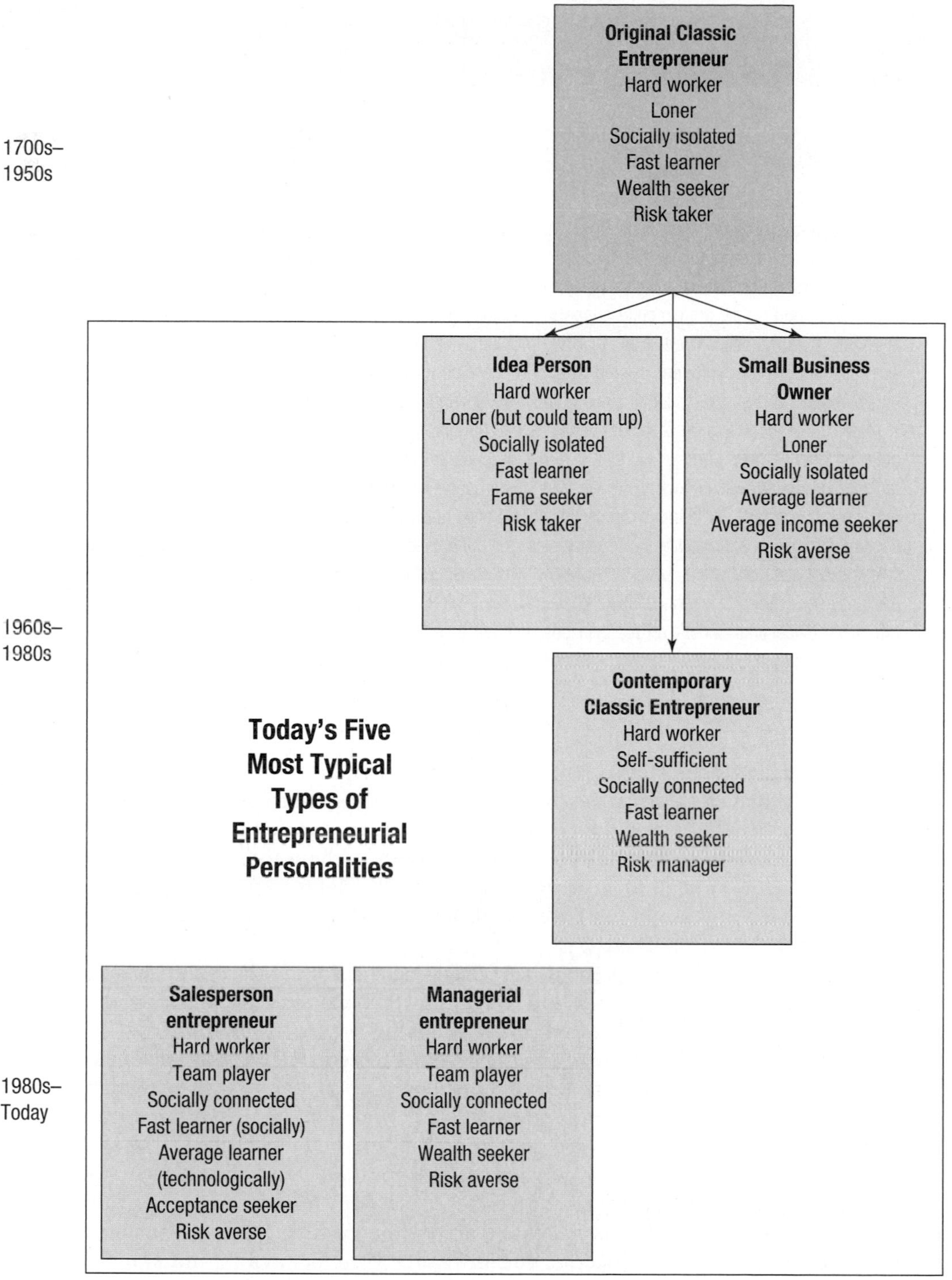

There are personality types that have emerged that are very different from the classic entrepreneur. One variant is the managerial entrepreneur.[6] Often a refugee from big business, these folks are socially very adept and connected. They are comfortable with people and power, and are interested in creating wealth. However, they are often very risk-averse, preferring to build wealth through careful planning and action. They are often big on learning, but slow on acting. For example, Catarina Norman and Malin Leschly, who were previously investment bankers, are now the co-owners of Flicka, a Scandinavian clothing and design boutique based in San Francisco. When they started in September 2004, Flicka had five employees, but also had human resources, legal, and finance departments.[7]

SMALL BUSINESS INSIGHT

J. J. Rosen and Atiba Software and Consulting[8]

After graduating from Vanderbilt University in 1992 as a psychology major, J. J. Rosen landed his first job as a child-support coordinator for the Tennessee District Attorney General Conference, an administrative branch of the state's court system. As he closely observed the work processes, he soon realized that much of the work performed by the state's child-support collection agencies could be done more efficiently and effectively if it were computerized. There were just two problems—many of these agencies had no computers, and no specialized computer software existed to handle the type of functions needed by the organizations. J. J. set out to resolve this problem, fulfill a need, and take advantage of this potential business opportunity.

Here J. J. faced his third problem—while he had an idea for software, he did not know how to write a computer program. Driven to make his idea a reality, J. J. taught himself this skill. A few months later he had mastered programming well enough to create child-support services software that could track child-support payments and collection efforts. With this product, the Atiba Software and Consulting Company was born as a part-time venture. Promoting his software as a better idea and offering very low prices to get an initial customer base, he sold the software statewide. Soon his business was growing through word-of-mouth advertising, and he landed his first major client, Andersen Consulting, within a year of starting. Only then did J. J. quit his job in the district attorney's office and embark on his own business full time. Today Atiba is housed in a small four-room office and has 17 employees, most of whom work onsite with clients. For J. J., the idea drove the business.

Another variant is the salesperson.[9] As all entrepreneurs, this type works hard, and is very socially driven. Sales types build and maintain extensive networks within and outside their firms. They use their networks to minimize risk, and they may be more concerned with their social standing and acceptance than their personal wealth. In many ways Laura Tidwell is a great example of the salesperson. A quick master of social situations, she was slower to learn about business or technology—a pattern typical of salespeople entrepreneurs.

Today even the classic entrepreneur has seen some revision.[10] Hard working, fast learning, and wealth seeking still hold, but we know that classic entrepreneurs do not see themselves as risk takers. They often report knowing ways to minimize risk, ways that give them the competitive advantage they need to succeed. Rather than a loner, modern classic entrepreneurs work hard to be self-sufficient, able to stand on their own, and even stand up to nay-sayers, yet they are ready to work with others to achieve success.

Even with these five profiles—the contemporary classic entrepreneur, the small business owner, the idea person, the managerial entrepreneur, and the salesperson—there are still dozens of profiles that can describe people who have been successful at starting their own business. That is because part of the beauty of small business is that there are so many routes to success, and in reality your behaviors and skills are more important than the personality characteristics buried in your psyche. Successful individual entrepreneurship builds on competency more than personality.

LO2
Learn the competencies of the successful entrepreneur.

Entrepreneurial Competencies

All the entrepreneurial personality types include hard work, but there are other specific types of business-related expertise—called **competencies**—that appear repeatedly in successful entrepreneurs around the world.[11] While there could be as many competencies as there are personality types, theories, like the BRIE (boundary/resources/intention/exchange) model introduced in Chapter 1, help us focus on those few competencies that are essential to successfully starting and running a business.

competencies
Forms of business-related expertise.

Competency Self-Assessment

SKILL MODULE 3.1

In this exercise, rank your skill or competency at different types of business activities. The goal is to see where you feel you have strengths and on which competencies you need to work. For each skill, think of a person or a company that does a really good job at that activity. Then compare your own performance to it using one of four levels of competency: *needs development* means that you still have to learn the skill; *needs refinement* means that you have the rudiments of the skill, but still need to practice it and carefully check your performance; *competent* means you can perform the activity consistently and without mistakes; *excellent* means you perform the activity as well as your role model, or nearly so. The categories of competencies are built from those listed in the text.

		Level of Competency			
Skill	Role Model	Needs Development	Needs Refinement	Competent	Excellent
Basic Business Functions					
Sales					
Operations (production)					
Accounting					
Finance					
Human resources					
Industry Specific Knowledge					
Industry expertise					
Industry skill					
Market knowledge					
Ability to diagnose					
Ability to see opportunities					
Resource Competencies					
Business information					
Business financing					
Space for the business					
Raw materials					
Support people					
Determination Competencies					
Business as primary focus					
Willingness to act					
Opportunity Competencies					
Found profitable idea					

Idea is distinctive					
Idea is hard to copy					

Entrepreneurs often find it useful to copy this list and ask people who know them well to fill it in with them in mind. Good examples can include business consultants or bankers, people who have worked with you, or even family members. Comparing what others see to what you see in yourself can help you put in perspective which skills need further development or better demonstration to others. In big business, such an approach is called "360 degree feedback," but it can also be applied in small businesses.

The competency suggested by boundary relates to the organizational and business processes of a firm. This type of expertise can be called *basic business competency*.[12] There are certain fundamental activities that all businesses must perform, which are called the **key business functions**, and include sales, operations (also called *production*), accounting, finance, and human resources. Getting organized and registered—which creates the boundary—is an example of an operations activity. There is also **industry-specific knowledge**. A restaurant really is different from a mechanics' shop or a computer store or a portrait studio. Each requires you to understand a particular industry and market, and each requires a very particular kind of skill. This was a large part of the reason that Laura Tidwell, in the example at the start of this chapter, worked for others before going off on her own.

key business functions
Activities common to all businesses such as sales, operations (also called *production*), accounting, finance, and human resources.

industry-specific knowledge
Activities, knowledge, and skills specific to businesses in a particular industry.

Some of these skills focus on knowing your new business and its context (Chapters 5 and 6), having the kind of skills that fit the business, being able to diagnose your business's health (Chapters 8, 12, 13, 17, and 18), and being able to see future business opportunities while doing your everyday work (Chapters 4, 7, and 20).

Resources lead to specific **resource competencies**.[13] For even the smallest part-time business, the entrepreneur needs to find or gain access to resources such as time, information, financing, space for the business, raw materials, and a variety of people (advisers, suppliers, service providers, customers). For J. J. Rosen of Atiba Software, getting the computer programming knowledge was critical. Knowing the best place to get raw materials or set up your operation, finding better information than your competition on your market, or having enough financing to ride out downturns in sales are examples of resources that could give you an advantage. You'll learn more about gathering resources in Chapter 5 (Small Business Entry: Paths to Part-Time Entrepreneurship), Chapter 11 (Small Business Location: Place and Layout Selection), Chapter 14 (Cash: Lifeblood of the Business), Chapter 15 (Small Business Finance: Using Equity, Debt, and Gifts), and Chapter 19 (Human Resource Management: Small Business Considerations).

resource competencies
The ability or skill of the entrepreneur at finding expendable components necessary to the operation of the business such as time, information, location, financing, raw materials, and expertise.

Intention reflects your determination to start your business and make it a success. These determination-driven skills can be called **determination competencies**[14] and are demonstrated by your focusing on your business over other choices and being ready to find out about and do what it takes to pursue opportunities that will help get the business going. Virtually all the entrepreneurs we have mentioned in this chapter—Gates, Walton, Tidwell, and Rosen—displayed tremendous determination to do the work and stick with the business through thick and thin. Many of these willingness competencies are essential to deciding if a business is feasible for you, a topic that is covered in Chapter 4 for the time before you start a business and in Chapter 20 for businesses already in operation.

determination competencies
Skills identified with the energy and focus needed to bring a business into existence.

Exchange deals with the actual process of exploiting the opportunity for profit—which is a fancy way of saying "making sales." The competencies that make this work are called **opportunity competencies**,[15] which include identifying an opportunity, a product, or service idea that is likely to lead you to a profit and is ideally distinctive to your firm and, you hope, hard for others to copy. For Bill Gates and J. J. Rosen,

opportunity competencies
Skills necessary to identify and exploit elements of the business environment that can lead to a profitable and sustainable business.

■ Look carefully at this photo of a Common Dog vehicle. How do the descriptions of product services, contact information, and endorsement slogans all demonstrate Common Dog's grasp of opportunity competencies?

the opportunity each found was for creating software that would make life and work easier. You'll learn more about the opportunity process and protecting opportunities through strategic planning in Chapter 4 and Chapter 7.

Research suggests that people can learn what they need to know to have adequate levels of expertise in all four competency areas. In fact, students who go through formal training or classes often score higher on the expertise tests than people running businesses.[16] In addition to training or classes, you can get consulting assistance from public or private sources, or you can even buy expertise in package form by adopting industry standard techniques. You can use state-of-the-art services or you can franchise.

The presence and absence of certain skills makes a tremendous difference in distinguishing those who start businesses from those who don't. But for those businesses that do get started, the amount of expertise is what distinguishes the more successful from the less successful firms. The concern about expertise leads to thinking about the level of professionalization you choose to use in your firm.

Professionalization

Professionalization refers to the extent to which a firm meets or exceeds the standard business practices for that industry. A **standard business practice** is one that has been widely adopted within an industry or occupation. Standard business practice examples include being asked if you want to supersize your order at a fast-food restaurant, showing only part of your credit card number on receipts, or using steel wire instead of elastic in inexpensive bracelets.

professionalization
The extent to which a firm meets or exceeds the standard business practices for its industry.

standard business practice
A business action that has been widely adopted within an industry or occupation.

There are three levels of professionalization: expert, specialized, and minimalized.[17] **Expert** businesses are those in which all the major functions of the firm follow standard business practices of the industry. They inspire the highest levels of trust among customers. Consider doctors' offices. Doctors have to be up-to-date on the latest in medical practices, medications, and treatment options. Insurance providers expect your doctor to keep records in a standard format and to bill you and the insurance company using only certain "best practice" techniques. The state even gets into the act, requiring the office to be cleaned using expert techniques designed to protect the cleaning crew as well as the patients from the risk of accidental infection, by making sure the hazardous wastes are handled correctly. In short, nearly every function of your doctor's office has been developed to represent procedures based on a high level of expertise.

expert business professionalization
A situation that occurs when all the major functions of a firm are conducted according to the standard business practices of its industry.

There are three other situations in which expert professionalization is common for small businesses. One relates to subcontractors and suppliers to big businesses, such as Wal-Mart, GM, or Boeing. Here the big firms require subcontractors to meet hundreds of corporate-dictated procedures intended to ensure high professionalization. Likewise, franchises such as McDonald's or Play It Again Sports specify most of the procedures for the business's operation. Finally, small businesses pursuing international quality certifications such as ISO 9000 have to literally write a book on how they ensure consistency and professionalism in every aspect of their firm.[18] Some businesses opt for an expert level of presentation as part of their strategy. For example, The Granite Rock Company of Watsonville, California, has won a Malcolm Baldridge Quality Award for its quality focus. For example, as a check on its quality, any customer who feels an order was not exactly right or was lacking in quality can "short" Granite Rock. That means he or she can pay less than the amount on the invoice. How does the customer know this? The offer is at the bottom of every invoice.[19]

www.graniterock.com

specialized business professionalization
A situation that occurs when businesses have founders or owners who are passionate about one or two of the key business functions, such as sales, operations, accounting, finance, or human resources.

Specialized businesses have founders or owners who are passionate about one or two of the key business functions, such as sales, operations (also called *production*), accounting, finance, or human resources. A restaurant owner might be passionate about cooking, part of the production function. That favored functional area receives the major share of the owner's care and concern.[20] Often that part of the business is consciously designed to meet or exceed the standards of the industry. For example, a restaurant might work toward getting high ratings from travel guides and local restaurant critics, or a local deejay might obtain and advertise a state-of-the-art portable sound system. Specialized firms tend to generate moderate levels of trust among customers.

minimalized business professionalization
A situation that occurs when the entrepreneur does nearly everything in the simplest way possible.

At a **minimalized** level of professionalization, the entrepreneur does nearly everything in the simplest way possible. Typically, there is no systematic accounting; money is simply put in a pocket or cash box. Sales are all personal, and little or no marketing or advertising is done. Record keeping will vary between nonexistent and haphazard. At this extreme, we find street vendors; some vendors at farmers markets, swap meets, and art fairs; and other very part-time businesses. Gaining trust is hardest for minimalized businesses.

It is also true that businesses can change over time: A business that starts as a minimalized firm can mature into a specialized or even an expert firm. For example, the Zildjian Company started in 1623 as a one-person business when a Turkish alchemist named Avedis discovered a way to make an alloy essential to making cymbals. Avedis received the name Zildjian from the Turkish sultan for his skill (the word means *cymbal smith*). The company operated in much the same way for hundreds of years. Then the company moved to the United States in 1929, when the American heir to the business took over. This American Avedis Zildjian had started and grown his own candy store by focusing on manufacturing and marketing.[21] The American Avedis applied the same sort of expertise to the cymbal making operations and made Zildjian not only a world leader in cymbal making, but also one of the oldest professionalized business firms in the world.[22]

Entrepreneurial Careers

L03
Discover the types of career paths entrepreneurs pursue.

When we combine personality characteristics, competencies, professionalization levels, and the actual types of businesses entrepreneurs pursue over their working life, we are looking at their careers. A **career** is a lifelong series of jobs or occupations,[23] and small business owners have careers, just like everyone else who works. Only the careers of small business owners often look a bit different. There are five typical career paths for entrepreneurs (see Figure 3.2):[24]

career
A lifelong series of jobs or occupations.

- **Habitual entrepreneurs** are owners for a lifetime, sometimes in one business, sometimes across several firms (which usually get closed down, not sold). The owner's career goal is personal satisfaction first, income second. Usually these entrepreneurs have no succession plan and intend to keep working until they can no longer continue. As they get older, they may scale down their ventures, but they continue to work in their business. Imagine the small business version of Steve Jobs—who founded Apple, then NeXT Computers, and finally Pixar before coming back to Apple.

- **Growth entrepreneurs** are also lifetime owners. Their goal is major success, and if they top out with one business, they'll start another growth-oriented company, often before they exit from the first one. They typically keep doing this until they can no longer work—in part because there is always more to achieve. When they do retire, they tend to want to micromanage their successors. This is the small business version of Bill Gates. Even though he is no longer the CEO of Microsoft, most people believe he is still pulling the strings at the company.
- **Harvest entrepreneurs** are owners with an exit plan. Their goal is to work first in order to play later. They are interested in giving their firms strong balance sheets, sizable market shares, proprietary products or processes, and capable teams to take over from them. They may start several companies, but they build one company at a time, harvest it, enjoy the proceeds, and *then* start another. As they age, the unspoken exit strategy is to let the time between deals drag out. Harvest entrepreneurs are often wealthy, but largely unknown. Consider Jim Clark. He was a contemporary of Gates and Jobs, founder of Silicon Graphics, Netscape, Healtheon/WebMD, and myCFO.com. He built a business, sold it, and waited until another promising prospect came along, but few know of him. The small business version of harvest entrepreneurs is even less visible.

■ Jim Clark is an example of a harvest entrepreneur. Which form of the various entrepreneurial careers appeals to you most? Why?

- **Spiral, or helical, entrepreneurs** alternate periods of growth and stability which are determined by personal or family needs. They are driven by a need to balance family and business, being successful at each. A typical spiral strategy is to slow down when children are young and push for growth when the children are older. Imagine what Laura Tidwell's business will look like when her daughter leaves home for college. A helical entrepreneur's typical endgame strategy, like that of the habitual entrepreneur, involves scaling down the business.
- **Occasional entrepreneurs** are people who generally have another job that is their primary one. They are often fascinated by entrepreneurship and pursue it periodically. They are the classic part-time entrepreneurs, who might work on a seasonal basis (e.g., doing taxes or making Christmas wreaths).

Central to the career perspective is the idea of how the owner's work and life change as he or she gets older. Recognizing the type of career path you favor can help you better define what will make you happy in work, and what to expect as you mature in your business.

FIGURE 3.2

The Five Career Paths of Entrepreneurs

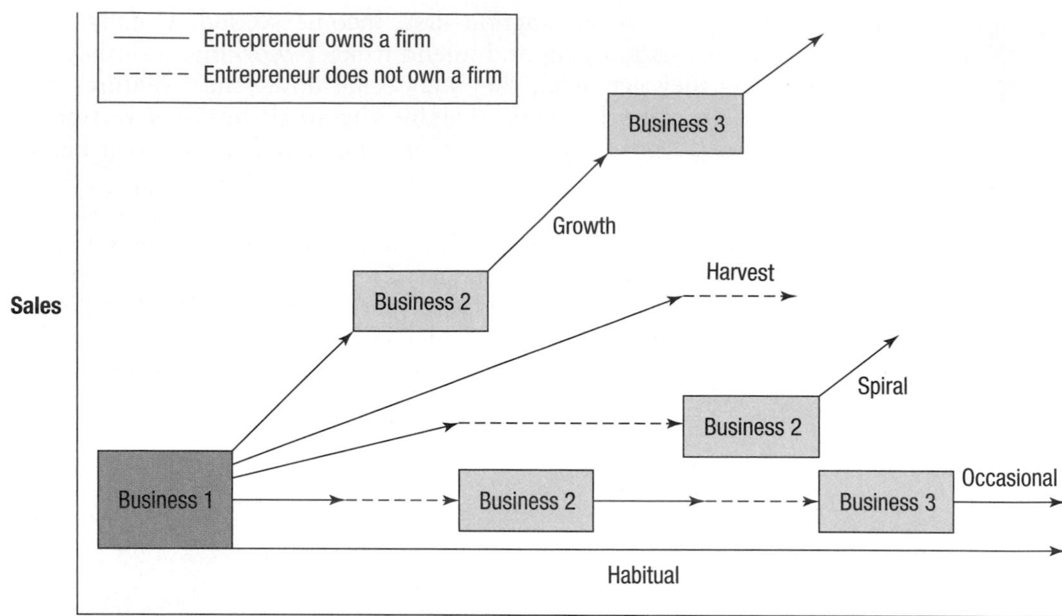

What Makes a Difference in Entrepreneurial Efforts

No personality type works equally well in all situations. Imagine a daring, risk-taking sort like James Bond living the life of a suburban husband and father. The same is true for entrepreneurs. Success in starting and running a business is a function of the personality of the entrepreneurs, the skills they have (or learn or hire from others), and the particular type of situation they face.[25] Over the years, certain specific kinds of situations crop up again and again, and each requires specific additional behaviors from entrepreneurs in order for them to be successful. Five types of entrepreneurs face special challenges: family business owners, team entrepreneurs, women entrepreneurs, minority entrepreneurs, and second career entrepreneurs.

Family Businesses

LO4
Understand the challenges of family business owners.

We think that the U.S. economy is built on an array of very large, publicly held companies—General Motors, Boeing, IBM, Bank of America, Exxon, and others—but this is only part of the picture. Many of America's largest companies—Anheuser-Bush, Wrigley, Hallmark, Dell, Motorola, Nordstrom, Campbell Soup—fully one-third of the S&P 500 companies, are family owned and managed.[26] Small and large, they make up over half the businesses in the United States and were the creators of well over half the new jobs in the United States in the latter half of the 1990s.[27] But our interests are in those small businesses that are also family businesses, and those represent 39 percent of American businesses, or about 10.8 million firms. Defined as firms with a majority family ownership and direct daily family involvement, **family business** is a major economic force, employing 58 percent of America's total workforce.[28]

family business
A firm in which one family owns a majority stake and is involved in the daily management of the business.

Small, family-owned businesses have many advantages. If the business is managed at the top by a group of tight-knit family members, communication-based integration can be more effective, and decision making can be easier and quicker.[29] A strong family bond can become a strong business culture, enabling members to make effective, coordinated decisions with little or no formal communication. Family members already

SMALL BUSINESS INSIGHT

Two Routes to the Family Business[30]

Ross's Teal Lake Lodge and Teal Wing Golf Club is a family-owned business. Victoria Ross began helping wait tables at the Hayward, Wisconsin, resort when she was only 6 years old. By the time she was 18, she had moved into management positions. Having already earned her bachelor's degree in business administration, she is now working on her master's in global tourism. At 25, Ross is ready to take over the family business.

Jamee Enstrom Simons took a different track to management of her family's business, Enstrom's Almond Toffee. She began working in the company when still a child, hand dipping chocolates after school. Jamee eventually became a registered nurse, but when her parents expressed interest in selling the company, she and her husband bought it in 1993. Under her leadership, sales revenues for Enstrom's Almond Toffee reached $10 million in 2001.

Ross and Simons both gained the confidence and skills they needed to succeed as small business owners from their early experiences in the families' businesses.

have developed strong relationships and interact on a regular basis both in and outside the workplace. Families are a major source of funds and personnel for new small businesses,[31] providing a support network made up of people the entrepreneur knows and trusts. Family businesses are also a self-perpetuating source for future small businesses. Many new entrepreneurs have been raised in families in which one or both parents or other relatives owned a family business,[32] as you can see in the examples of the Ross and Enstrom families above. As children of family business owners, these individuals learned how business works by observing their family at work. They gained early experiences that helped them develop the skills, competencies, and self-confidence that contributed to later decisions to become entrepreneurs and to their ability to succeed.[33] In fact, most entrepreneurs come from families of entrepreneurs.

There are two challenges typical to family businesses—role conflict and succession.[34] **Role conflict** describes the kind of problem that arises when people have multiple responsibilities, such as parent and boss, and each makes different demands on them.[35] As a boss, you might want your daughter to stay at the store and work, while as a parent you might want your daughter to take time off to be with her own children. Role conflict is at its worst when people fail to recognize it. Often, reminding yourself and others that you face multiple, conflicting roles helps them understand the types of choices that must be made and the kinds of decisions that are most important.[36] For family business, the most effective approach for avoiding role conflict is to keep family issues out of the family business, as you can see in the case of Boyd Coffee (see Small Business Insight box on the next page). Whenever possible, try and make decisions based on business necessities. When making a decision from a family perspective, broaden it to apply equally to nonfamily as well as family members. For example, if family members in the business can take off for their children's graduations, so should employees who are not part of the family.[37]

role conflict
The kind of problem that arises when people have multiple responsibilities, such as parent and boss, and the different responsibilities make different demands on them.

Thirty-nine percent of U.S. family-owned businesses are expected to face the retirement or semiretirement of their CEO within the next five years. This statistic grows in importance if you factor in the idea that only one-third of family-owned businesses survive beyond the first generation.[38] Part of the problem can be an entrepreneur, like Rudy Boyd, who has difficulty letting go. Problems can arise when the owner cannot come to grips with retirement or envision someone else running the company.[39] Owners often resist giving up control and undermine—consciously or unconsciously—potential

SMALL BUSINESS INSIGHT

Boyd Coffee[40]

Boyd Coffee, started in 1900 in Portland, Oregon, had survived its first transition from founder P. D. Boyd to heir Rudy Boyd. Rudy's sons, David and Dick Boyd, grew up working in the family business. In 1975, Rudy officially retired, but he refused to leave the business. Even though David, the eldest son, became the CEO, Rudy stayed on as chairman of the board, and for many years he remained an active and influential presence around the company—often to the irritation of son David. A few years after Rudy's "retirement," the board of directors of Boyd Coffee—Rudy, his wife Ellen, David, and Dick, then president—voted 3–0 (with David abstaining) to remove David as CEO and name Dick the new CEO.

David and Dick believed the management change was based solely on members of the family taking sides in the David/Rudy conflict, rather than on sound business judgment. With the loss of the CEO position, David also wondered whether he had originally received the job because he had earned it through hard work and demonstrated ability or simply because of his name and family position as the eldest. Although after the awkward switch the brothers continued to work together for many years, their personal and professional relationships deteriorated to the point where they seldom communicated. The tension and lack of coordinated effort between the two inevitably led to the financial decline and instability of Boyd Coffee. Finally, in 1997, David threatened to dissolve the company. Only when faced with such a drastic possibility did the brothers begin the slow and difficult process of reconciliation.

With the assistance and guidance of outside advisers and consultants, the brothers have now made succession planning their top priority. They have established a family trust that allows younger family members the opportunity to leave home and develop their business skills and networks independently. The brothers also have encouraged their children to gain work experience outside the family business before deciding whether they want to return to work for the company, something the brothers never got to do.

successors.[41] This is a problem because top managers at family firms tend to stay in their positions much longer than those at nonfamily firms. One study found that CEOs of family firms had an average tenure of 17 years as opposed to just 8 years for CEOs in other businesses.[42]

succession
The process of intergenerational transfer of a business.

When the current owners are ready to think about what follows them, we get into **succession**—the process of intergenerational transfer of a business. Often the lack of a clear succession plan is the death knell for those family firms facing their first intergenerational transition.[43] If the founder dies, becomes seriously ill, or is incapacitated before he or she can groom a successor, the new family leader may be suddenly thrust into the role before coming up to speed on vital company information and developing needed skills. Also, in the absence of a succession plan, private and public dissension among various factions of the family becomes more likely, negatively affecting operations within the firm, and may eventually cause the business to fail.[44]

As is true of so many things in a successful small business, the answer lies in taking a professional approach to the problem. In this case the professional approach involves crafting a succession plan like the one created by Boyd Coffee after Dick became president. Succession plans deal with the people who will take over, what roles they will fill, and what supports (such as training, outside assistance, voting power, resources control) they will receive.[45] Problems arise when there are no successors available within the family. One study found that only 5 percent of all entrepreneurs were able to rely on family members to take over.[46] Sometimes none of the children have an interest in the family business. The opposite problem arises in situations like that at Boyd Coffee when several family members believe they should take over the top spot and vie for the position to the detriment of both family and business. Problems like the Boyd Coffee competition remind us that it is important to plan how disputes will get resolved. Expect those disputes. The owners of a family also tend to be especially passionate about their enterprise, because they have a huge economic incentive to pay very close attention.[47]

One way to maximize communication in the succession process is to create a family council. A family council includes family members with immediate interests in the business (spouse, sisters and brothers, older children, etc.). The focus of council meetings is the business-family relationship. The meetings can also be a good forum for grappling with issues like role expectations, commitment, and personal responsibility.[48]

An advisory board, or a formal board of directors, can also contribute important skills and strategic direction. At Helzberg Diamonds, Barnett Helzberg Jr. set up a board to confront planning issues and to "help bring order (read *professionalization*) to the seat-of-the-pants decision making" at the firm. The board was critical to succession planning at Helzberg when trusted board members convinced Mr. Helzberg that he needed to step aside as president. He brought in someone else who had the skills to lead day-to-day operations while keeping the chairmanship himself.[49]

The key difference between a family council and a board of directors is that the function of the family council is to keep the family involved while the board is focused on running the business. The board includes significant nonfamily membership.[50] Careful use of a family council can also help by keeping family members involved in an appropriate way, allowing you more room to maintain a different balance with your board of directors.[51]

In addition, a good plan, like the one Boyd Coffee developed, also talks about the handling of the assets of the company in order to minimize the tax burden on the family and the firm and provide a suitable income for the former owner and his or her household. Because of the legal, tax, accounting, and leader development complexities, succession planning is best done with the advice of experts.[52] For family councils and boards of advisers, it is often helpful to get professional advice at the start, and then continue on your own. One organization that tracks experts in family business is the Family Firm Institute.

Family Firm Institute – www.ffi.org

One special situation of the family business is the case of a married couple who jointly own and manage their business.[53] You only need to consider the divorce rate in general to realize that marriage and business can be a volatile mixture. The problems of a lack of agreement, difficulty keeping business and family issues separate, and how to handle endings[54] are very much in evidence in couples' businesses, and the solutions are very much the same—being clear about responsibilities, trying to maintain boundaries between work and home, having outside advisers to help sort out thorny issues, and planning for how the firm might end or change.[55]

Entrepreneurial Teams

LO5
Recognize the special nature of entrepreneurial teams.

Family firms represent a special case of the most popular form of small business leadership, the entrepreneurial team. The majority of new small business start-ups involve teams of two or more entrepreneurs. Shown in Figure 3.3, in the Panel Study of Entrepreneurial Dynamics, 52% of all start-ups consisted of teams, while 48% were solo entrepreneurs.

Where do these teams come from? For more than half of the teams (53%), they are spouses or life partners working together. Working with family members other than spouses accounts for another 18% of the teams, with only 15% of teams composed of unrelated business associates.[56] Those teams of unrelated business associates represent over 150,000 new businesses a year, with all forms of entrepreneurial teams accounting for about 600,000 new firms a year.[57]

When a couple jointly own and manage their business, the particular strength of the firm comes from knowing and trusting one another. There is also a financial flexibility that comes from two people in one family running a business. Two unrelated people working in a business would each expect to take some funds out of the business

FIGURE 3.3

Number of Owners Involved in Start-ups from the Panel Study of Entrepreneurial Dynamics

Adapted from Howard E. Aldrich, Nancy M. Carter, and Martin Ruef (2004). Teams, In Gartner, William B., Shaver, Kelly G. Carter, Nancy M. and Reynolds, Paul D. (Eds.)(2004). *Handbook of Entrepreneurial Dynamics: the Process of Business Creation.* Thousand Oaks, CA: Sage, Table 27.1, page 307.

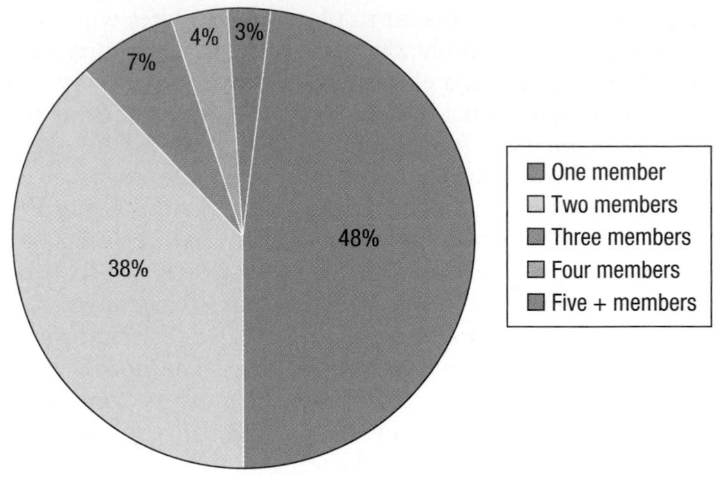

to live on, but for two people living together, it becomes possible for the two to live on one income taken from a business. This can leave more funds in the business during the crucial early times.

Teams of unconnected individuals face additional problems over those of working couples. Two team members might put different amounts of money and time into the business, but expect identical returns. This problem of equity needs to be handled for everyone at the start of a team endeavor.[58] Identifying outcomes for best-case, worst-case, and most likely scenarios for the business can help clarify contributions and returns before problems arise. Teams also face conflict over shared goals and how to make decisions, especially when the team is evenly split on choices.[59] Legal solutions to setting up partnerships are discussed in Chapter 19, and the solutions mentioned above for couples—being clear about responsibilities, trying to maintain boundaries between work and home, having outside advisers to help sort out thorny issues, as well as planning for how the firm might end or change[60]—work just as well for teams composed of unrelated individuals as they do for couple based teams.

Women and Minorities in Small Business

LO6
Gain insight into the challenges women and minority business owners face.

Women-owned businesses are one of the fastest growing sectors of all U.S. businesses.[61] Between 1997 and 2004, the number of private businesses with at least 50 percent female ownership increased by 17 percent, while the rate for firms overall was 9 percent.[62] Around 30 percent of all businesses are majority owned by women, with another 18 percent equally owned by women and men.[63]

In part, this growth represents the actions of a new group of women starting businesses. Most women starting businesses 10 or more years ago lacked managerial experience and generally had worked in the more traditional "female" occupations such as office administration, retail sales, or teaching. Today, women entrepreneurs are more likely to match male entrepreneurs in terms of managerial or scientific/technical experience related to their entrepreneurial enterprise.[64]

Representing approximately 11 percent of all U.S. businesses, the number of minority-owned firms has likewise grown explosively in recent years.[65] While the total number of U.S. businesses edged up by only 7 percent between 1992 and 1997, minority-owned businesses witnessed a remarkable 30 percent growth rate. During this period, the number of Native American or Alaskan native-owned businesses swelled by the most incredible 84 percent, especially notable since their population increased by only 6.5 percent.

During that same time period, the number of African American-owned businesses climbed by 26 percent, Hispanic-owned businesses by 30 percent, and Asian or Pacific Islander-owned businesses by 30 percent.[66]

What are the reasons for such phenomenal growth in the number of minority entrepreneurs? The establishment of both public and private funding and networking initiatives have helped to level the business playing field for minority entrepreneurs by offering information, advice, and funding access. Another explanation lies in the growth of racial and ethnic groups within the U.S. population, a trend that is expected to continue. The two fastest growing minority groups (Hispanics and Asians) represent the largest segments of minority business owners. Hispanics represent 40 percent of all ethnic business owners, Asians 30 percent, and African Americans 27 percent.[67]

■ Women- and minority-owned businesses are rapidly increasing, due to unprecedented educational and financial opportunities now available. What are some of the challenges you perceive still facing minority and women entrepreneurs today? Can you think of any resources these entrepreneurs may be able to tap into which traditional entrepreneurs lack?

Despite the growth in the number of women and minority entrepreneurs, both groups still face the challenge of access. Access refers to the simplest form of discrimination—often women- or minority-owned firms are simply excluded from the opportunities offered to firms owned by white males. This can result from the way that networks built from interpersonal relations in business exclude women and minorities. When business relationships build from shared hobbies, sports, or even college ties, social situations that are all male or largely white outside of work can lead to unintegrated business networks.

Access problems for women- and minority-owned small businesses crop up most often as discrimination in financing.[68] This means that they may not be given the same access to funds[69] or contracting opportunities[70] that white male-owned firms are given. For example, a national survey of small business finances found that minority business loan applicants were denied at twice the rate of whites, even though application rates did not vary by race.[71] The same study found that Asian and Hispanic business owners pay higher interest rates on their loans. These differences in loan denial rates and in interest rates occurred even when all business-related differences were considered.

National Minority Supply and Diversity Council— http://www.nmsdc.org/

Women's Business Enterprise National Council—http://www.wbenc.org/

There are two solutions for access-based challenges. One solution is institutional, when minority- and women-owned small businesses pursue dedicated contracting funds, known as **set-asides**, among big companies and government agencies. The good news is that governments at all levels have special contracting opportunities for small businesses that are owned and operated by minorities or women. For example, the U.S. government spent nearly $7 billion on set-aside based contracts with women-owned businesses in 2002.[72] Big companies and those with government contracts also have similar programs. In 2002, those companies spent $72 billion on minority set-aside purchases.[73] Qualification for set-asides requires certification as a business owned and operated by a woman or a minority (or both).[74] For corporations, certification is handled by organizations that are not affiliated with the government or big business, such as the National Minority Supply and Diversity Council or the Women's Business Enterprise National Council. **Certification** consists of proving that the business is truly owned and operated by a woman or minority. A similar process is used by the U.S. government, with the Small Business Administration certifying firms for the SBA's 8(a) Business Development Program, whose details are online at the SBA site.

set-asides
Government contracting funds which are earmarked for particular kinds of firms, such as small businesses, minority-owned firms, women-owned firms, and the like.

certification
An examination based acknowledgement that the firm is owned and operated as specified.

U.S. Small Business Administration's 8(a) Business Development Program—http://www.sba.gov/8abd/

Certification is not for every women- or minority-owned small business. For example, the SBA 8(a) and most corporate certification programs require a business to be in operation at least two years. As is true for any program involving government or big business, the small business needs to put more energy and resources into record keeping than it might otherwise do, especially businesses that opt for minimalized or specialized levels of professionalization. For those businesses that qualify, certification provides a ready means of access to opportunity and to networks of businesses and government agencies which can be leveraged to gain access to other sectors of business.

The second approach to solving problems of access is personal and involves making extra efforts to network. As discussed in Chapter 2, building a social network is central to business success. For minority-owned and women-owned businesses, networking is especially important because such firms need to network even more than other types of firms. While networking with other minority-owned or women-owned firms will feel comfortable, and lead to business within that group, the real gains in business require networking in more diverse and potentially less comfortable situations, such as industry and trade associations, chambers of commerce, and the like. Success comes from the number of different types of contacts one makes, and for a minority- or woman-owned business, this requires having business contacts from other races, genders, ages, and sectors.

Second Career Entrepreneurs

LO7
Understand the situation of people who become business owners later in life.

late career entrepreneurs
(also known as *second career entrepreneurs*) People who begin their businesses after having retired or resigned from work in corporations at age 50 or later.

A special group of entrepreneurs are called second career or **late career entrepreneurs**—people who begin their businesses after having retired or resigned from work in corporations at age 50 or later. Whether these individuals start their business as part of a postretirement career plan or after early retirement has forced them to reevaluate their lives, a late career as a business owner has become a necessity for them.[75]

As increasing numbers of corporations merge, downsize, reorganize, and/or close altogether, many firms are offering attractive retirement packages to encourage employees to voluntarily leave the organization.[76] Workers are opting to accept generous offers to retire early (between ages 50 and 64). People's decisions of whether to return to work depend on their individual level of wealth (retirement income and savings), their health, and their work experience, as well as general economic conditions.[77]

About a third of the retirees who return to work decide to become self-employed.[78] Those who do face three challenges—adjusting to the entrepreneurial life, reestablishing self-confidence, and keeping personal finances out of the business.

Working for others for most of their life, late career entrepreneurs are likely to have gotten used to having many of the daily chores of running a business done for them. Even for former managers, the mechanics of getting the location cleaned or the payroll checks written may have been things they could take for granted. As entrepreneurs, they have to do these things themselves or arrange to have them done. All entrepreneurs get used to a do-it-yourself approach, and this is a challenge for everyone, but it can be especially trying for late career entrepreneurs, who may have hoped that life would get easier rather than harder later in their careers.

The key for managing the demanding life of the entrepreneur is to get advice from people in your line of business, or from consultants (which can include the free consulting available through Small Business Development Centers or SCORE) about the basic activities of the small business. Make sure you have all the demanding aspects of running a business covered. Pick one or two that are particularly hard or onerous and consider subcontracting those out in order to keep the early stage of the business manageable.

The second challenge comes from a loss of confidence.[79] The stigma attached to older workers' departure from their former job can make a tremendous difference in their level of confidence. Being given early retirement can be seen as a company's effort

SMALL BUSINESS INSIGHT

Donna Herrle[80]

Imagine getting an invitation to a wine and cheese party for a new business, where the owner shows a "before" picture of herself in her corporate garb and an "after" picture of her in her home office, wearing pajamas and slippers, with the adage "change is good" over them both. That is what Donna Herrle, 51, sent to business acquaintances, friends, former co-workers, and family when she started her Pittsburgh graphic design business, Drawing Conclusions. A graphic designer and former sales manager of design and print services, she was out on her own after being laid off from corporate America in 2002. That layoff had set off alarm bells for Donna, who feared the loss of security a regular paycheck had brought her. At loose ends after the layoff, she also wondered what she should, or could, do.

Her turnaround and focus on starting Drawing Conclusions came about from talking to everyone she knew. She was surprised at how many others had been in or were facing the same situation, and the advice she got helped her make her own transition to self-employment. The advice she received again and again was to plan the business carefully and keep networking, and the work would come.

And the work came. One client brought a project to the wine and cheese party, based on Donna's graphically impressive invitation. Five more projects came in within 10 days of the party. Within a year she had over 50 clients and gross sales in six figures.

to replace expensive (if capable) older talent with junior people who work for less. But being laid off or downsized suggests that the person was expendable at best, deadwood at worst. The difference in labeling makes a difference in the late career entrepreneur's self-confidence.

When there are self-confidence issues, the first solution is to take some time to get over the shock to self-image. Counseling, whether job or psychological, can also help tremendously. When the person is ready, the solution often involves redefining one's life. The goal is to describe life in ways that help the individual take control over it. A layoff becomes an indication that it was time to move on. A downsizing becomes something that occurs to those best able to land on their feet. In taking control over the past, it can become easier to assert control over the present and future.

The second self-confidence solution comes from networking. Entrepreneurs as a group are an energetic and optimistic group. Just talking to people you know, as Donna Herrle did (see Small Business Insight Box above), or joining local entrepreneur organizations, such as the chamber of commerce or the local chapter of a trade or professional organization, can expose you to people full of energy and ideas. This is contagious, and as you hear the stories of perseverance and overcoming challenges that abound among entrepreneurs, the possibilities for a successful entrepreneurial life seem to become more realistic.

The third problem is keeping personal finances out of the business.[81] Often when individuals are laid off or given early retirement, they can receive lump-sum financial settlements. Frequently, people intending to become late career entrepreneurs plan to use a substantial portion of these funds to start the new business. Sometimes this happens because late career entrepreneurs see their personal funds as "easy money," funds that can be obtained quickly and without a lot of hassles. The problem is that many people who take the easy money are also taking the easy way out. They fail to carefully consider how they will invest the money in the business, and how it will be used. Taking the easy way out can often mean late career entrepreneurs underprepare for the rigors of business, and they are risking their retirement nest egg.

For late career entrepreneurs, the solution is to treat their own money as objectively as possible. Invest it only if you can make a strong case that the investment in the business is going to produce reasonable returns. Treat your own money as an outsider's investment. Do a business plan and consider seeking outside funding from friends and family to help keep you honest about the chances for the business.

This chapter starts with the idea that while no single explanation can really cover all 15.3 million self-employed people in the United States, there *are* aspects of the entrepreneurial life that apply to many. Some of these are general ideas, such as the entrepreneurial career or the competencies needed to be successful in small business. There are also types of entrepreneurs that describe many, but not all, self-employed people. Whether we look at attitudinal or behavioral types like the classic entrepreneur or small business owner, or if we look at demographical groups such as women entrepreneurs, the more we know about people pursuing entrepreneurship, the better it is for identifying important issues in their business and personal lives. Every entrepreneur's story is uniquely his or her own, but across millions of entrepreneurs, there are some similarities, and these help make it easier to think about the entrepreneurial process and get the right kind of help to entrepreneurs.

CHAPTER SUMMARY

LO1 Learn about entrepreneurial personality types:

- From the 1700s to the 1950s people thought there was only one type of entrepreneurial personality.
- Since the 1960s five distinct types of entrepreneurial personalities have been found: small business owners, idea people, the managerial entrepreneur, the salesperson, and the contemporary classic entrepreneur.

LO2 Learn the competencies of the successful entrepreneur:

- Forms of business-related expertise are called *competencies.*
- To be successful, an entrepreneur needs competency in the basic business functions (e.g., sales, operations, etc.), industry-specific knowledge, resource competencies, determination competencies, and opportunity competencies.
- Professionalization describes the extent to which a firm meets or exceeds the standard business practices for that industry. Professionalization can be minimalized, specialized or expert.

LO3 Discover the types of career paths entrepreneurs pursue:

- A career is a lifelong series of jobs or occupations.
- The five typical career paths for entrepreneurs are habitual, growth, harvest, spiral (or helical), and occasional.

LO4 Understand the challenges of family business owners:

- Family businesses are one of the major forms of small business.
- The major challenges facing the family business are role conflict and succession.

- Both challenges can be met through careful planning.
- Married couples and even nonfamily partnerships face many of the same problems and solutions.

LO5 Recognize the special nature of entrepreneurial teams:

- The majority of businesses are started by teams.
- Spouses or life partners are the most common form of team.
- Couple teams can benefit from trust and financial flexibility.
- Typical problems include lack of agreement, separating work and family issues, and handling endings.
- Similar problems also crop up in non-spouse teams.

LO6 Gain insight into the challenges women and minority business owners face:

- Women-owned and minority-owned businesses are growing at rates faster than other types of businesses.
- The major challenge facing these businesses is gaining access to opportunity.
- Access is achieved through networking and set-asides.

LO7 Understand the situation of people who become business owners later in life:

- Late career entrepreneurship happens when a person is laid off, downsized, or given early retirement.
- The challenges facing late career entrepreneurs come from having to do everything themselves, loss of confidence, and using too much of their personal money too soon in the business.
- Having to do everything can be handled by identifying the tasks to be done ahead of time. Loss of confidence can be dealt with through taking time to heal and by networking with enthusiastic entrepreneurs. Late career entrepreneurs should use their own money only when it makes sense for the business, usually proven through a business plan.

DISCUSSION QUESTIONS

1. What are the different types of entrepreneurial personality?
2. Why is it important to recognize that there is more than one type of entrepreneurial personality?
3. An entrepreneur started a business from scratch and grew it to a multimillion-dollar operation. After about 10 years he sold his business and bought a boat in order to take a round-the-world cruise. What type of career path do you think he was following? Why?
4. Could someone with good industry-specific knowledge but low competency in basic business skills be successful as an entrepreneur in that industry? Why or why not?
5. When does it make sense to create a business using a minimalized approach to professionalization? Why is that so?
6. What are the strengths and weaknesses of a team?
7. What is the major challenge facing women- and minority-owned firms? How can this be solved?
8. What makes the situation of late career entrepreneurs problematic? What can they do to smooth their way?

EXPERIENTIAL EXERCISES

1. Which of the entrepreneurial personality types fits you the best? Be ready to explain why.
2. Which entrepreneurial competencies do you possess? Be ready to provide examples and explain why you made these choices. You can use the result of Skill Module 3.1 to aid you in this.
3. Pick small businesses with which others in the class are familiar and analyze what level of professionalization they display. Be ready to explain the basis for your classification.
4. Select a local family business owner or female or minority entrepreneur whom you admire, and research the person's business and professional background. Interview this person if possible. What particular challenges were faced? What competencies were used to overcome them?

Mini-Case

ELAINE MARTIN, MARCON, INC.

Elaine Martin entered the construction business in 1985. She and her husband were in danger of losing the family farm, because he was injured and unable to work. Crop prices were too low to pay the bills, and their renter was able to pay only half his rent. Martin had no experience and no connections in the construction business. But her background in farming had taught her how to build fences. Martin noticed that construction sites needed fences, so she and her sister-in-law borrowed $25,000 from her mother to form a company.

The first three years were very difficult. The company had revenues of only $13,000 the first year. Contractors were reluctant to believe that a woman knew enough about construction to be trusted with a job. Martin finally convinced one contractor to take a chance on her. She worked in the field all day. At night, she was busy researching ways to build better fences. Her hard work and research paid off. Martin became known as an innovator and a problem solver. By the second year, her business grossed $200,000.

Martin applied to the Idaho Department of Transportation to be certified as a woman-owned business so she could take advantage of the department's special programs for women- and minority-owned businesses. Officials within the department refused to certify her, because they did not believe she was truly the owner. By the end of 1987, Martin's company was over $50,000 in debt and in danger of bankruptcy.

In 1988, Martin reorganized her company and began producing highway guardrails. That same year, the owner of a local guardrail construction company whom Martin knew from trade association meetings decided to retire. Martin ran the company for one year to prove she could do it. In 1989, she bought the company with the original owner providing the financing. The previous owner's brother became a partner, owning 49 percent of the company. The new company earned $1.2 million in 1990 and was earning double that amount by 1992. Martin became the sole owner of the company in 1996. MarCon now earns over $3 million annually. Martin was named the 2002 Idaho Small Business Person of the Year by the Small Business Administration.

CASE DISCUSSION QUESTIONS

1. What type of entrepreneurial personality do you think Martin displayed?
2. In starting her fence business, name two entrepreneurial competencies that Martin possessed.
3. How did networking pay off for Martin's business?
4. How did Martin handle the resource competencies when she took over the guardrail manufacturing company?

LEARNING OBJECTIVES

This chapter will help you:

LO1 Learn the sources of opportunity entrepreneurs draw on to get business ideas.

LO2 Track the traditional ways opportunities are screened for business potential.

LO3 Understand how creativity methods can help business owners recognize new opportunities.

LO4 Understand the five pitfalls that hinder innovation.

LO5 Identify strategies for innovation in your business.

LO6 Learn how to conduct a comprehensive feasibility study for your business ideas.

LO7 Understand the value of building a creative culture in your business.

■ Dave Kapell's company, Magnetic Poetry, was formed through several intriguing circumstances which were marked by creativity, opportunity, and feasibility. How did Dave's later business practices continue to promote creative, feasible opportunities? What kind of entrepreneurial company is Magnetic Poetry?

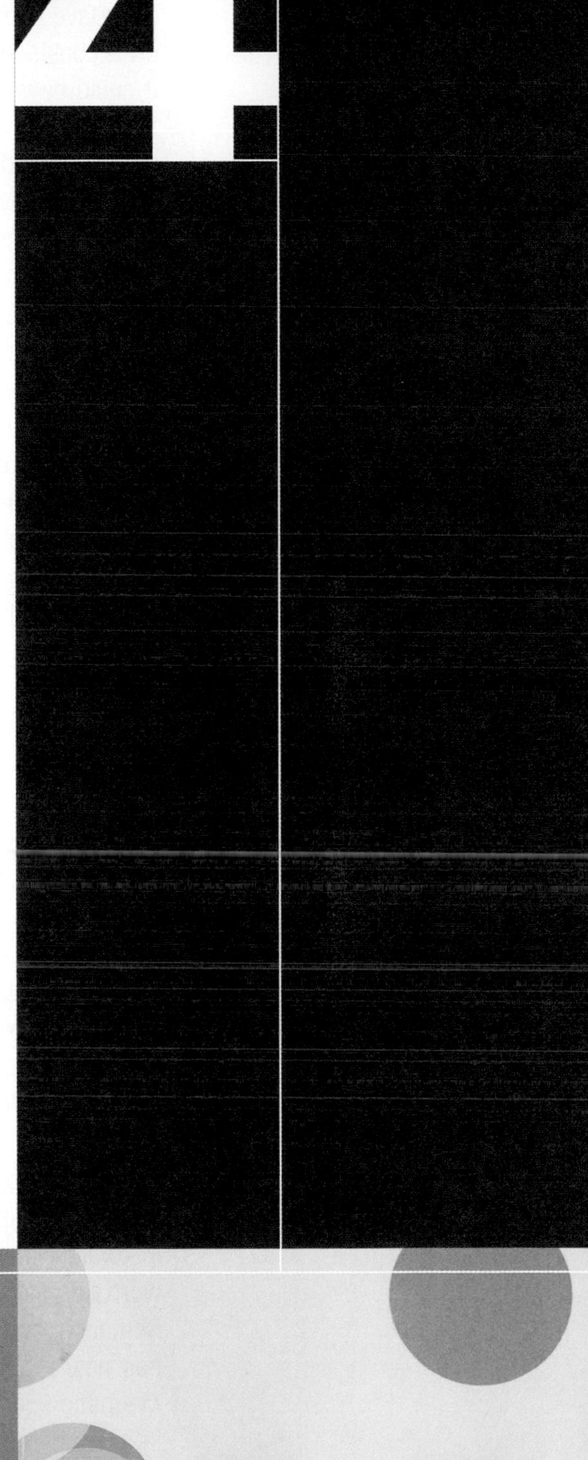

Small Business Ideas: Creativity, Opportunity, and Feasibility

Focus on Small Business: Dave Kapell: Poetry in Motion[1]

Dave Kapell was a guitarist and songwriter who played in funk and heavy metal bands in Minneapolis. His bands were popular locally, but he still worked at other jobs doing clerical work for nonprofits and driving a cab. Problem was, he often suffered from writer's block (an especially bad ailment for a lyricist!) and was constantly looking for things to inspire him so that he could write more songs. He happened to see a documentary on the life of David Bowie and learned that Bowie used a technique that Kapell found very intriguing. Following Bowie's suggestion, he began to cut up magazine stories, entries from journals, and even letters from family members and rearrange these small bits of paper to try to spark inspiration for songs. He would often have all these pieces laid out in a room, or across the front seat of his cab. There was just one problem.

Dave suffered from allergy attacks that caused him to sneeze, and when he sneezed, he would send the pieces of paper scattering all over the room or the seat of his car. He thought about gluing them to cardboard backing, but then he would have to put them away and take them out again whenever he wanted to use them. This is when opportunity met need.

One of Dave's roommates was an employee at a pizza restaurant, and the restaurant had a batch of refrigerator magnets it had intended to give to customers as advertising. But the magnets were misprinted and could not be used. Dave's friend brought these magnets home, and Dave came up with the idea of gluing the words to them. He then put the word magnets on a cookie sheet and kept them there so that he wouldn't have to put them away every day. It could have ended there. After all, Dave had solved the problem of the disrupted word collection. But one day someone in the house wanted to actually use the cookie sheets for what they were intended for—bake cookies! Now Dave had the problem of what to do with the magnets, so he casually put them on the refrigerator.

As Dave's roommates and friends came through the kitchen, Dave noticed that they all stopped by the fridge and played with the magnets—rearranging the words the magnets were holding to the fridge into phrases that were funny and bizarre. Dave would say that, while he never intended to start a business, this was a lightbulb experience. His friends started asking for sets of these words, and Dave saw an opportunity. He recalled, "I told everyone that I could make a kit for seven bucks, and I was earning seven dollars an hour in my job at the time and my student loans were coming due, so I made up a bunch of kits. I took 100 kits to my first craft show, and I figured that would be enough for the whole weekend. They sold out in three hours. I knew I was on to something."[2]

That was 1993, the year Dave's company, Magnetic Poetry, was born. As the idea took off, Dave realized he could no longer make the kits himself. He saved $5,000 from craft fairs and began visiting local screen-printing and die shops in Minneapolis. He paid for 1,000 prototype sets. But the road was not smooth yet. Dave knew next to nothing about distribution. He also learned that retailers are not interested in amateur packaging, and Dave's kit looked like a cardboard jewelry box. Pam Jones, a manager of a local art museum gift shop, gave Dave lots of tips on product presentation. In three weeks, he developed a clear plastic package that Jones thought would fit on her gift shop's shelves. By the end of that first day, she sold the 12 kits Dave gave her. The new packaging was attractive to retailers such as Borders Bookstores, gift shops in the Guggenheim and Whitney museums in New York City, and Signals catalogs. By 1994, Dave's kits were selling in the Museum Company in the eastern part of the United States, and at the San Francisco Museum of Modern Art on the West Coast.

As time went on, Dave decided to do his own manufacturing, since he felt he wasn't getting quick enough turnaround from his manufacturer. He went back to Murray Condon, who had helped him with his prototypes, and the two formed a separate company called Screen D'or Graphics, Inc. Kapell funded the company with the goal of a three-day order-to-delivery turnaround. He now had a number of employees in production, sales, administration, inventory control, and shipping and was looking for other opportunities for his kits, such as introducing them in foreign languages. Today, the Magnetic Poetry product line features over 100 products. Its word kits include everything from the Shakespearean, Artist, and Genius kits to the Dog Lover, Romance, and College kits. (The Original kit remains wildly popular, too.) Magnetic Poetry also has new products that go beyond the magnetic word tile genre, including Sidewalk Poet, the Magnetic Poetry 2002 Calendar, and Magnetic Poetry: The Game, a new board game packaged in a refrigerator shaped storage tin.

Polished versions of the hand-glued magnets that once decorated Dave's refrigerator door in his Minneapolis home now can be found on millions of such doors and metal surfaces across the country. Since Dave Kapell invented Magnetic Poetry in 1993, more than 3 million kits have been sold. Magnetic Poetry, a cultural phenomenon, has appeared in the movies *Conspiracy Theory, City of Angels,* and *Notting Hill,* as well as on Jerry Seinfeld's refrigerator on the TV show *Seinfeld.*[3]

DISCUSSION QUESTIONS

1. How did Dave Kapell discover that his idea would be a good business opportunity?
2. How did Dave evaluate whether or not his idea for Magnetic Poetry was successful?
3. What other opportunities might there be for Magnetic Poetry in the future?

The Source of Business Ideas

L01
Learn the sources of opportunity entrepreneurs draw on to get business ideas.

Do you recall seeing a new product or service in a store, or maybe hearing about an idea on radio or television, and thinking, "Now, why didn't I think of that?" In fact, most of the ideas that are turned into new businesses, or result in "new and improved" products and services, come from information and observations that we are surrounded by every day. Does it seem to you that successful business owners must possess unusual powers of observation or use top-secret strategies unknown to anybody else when seeking ideas for new businesses or **innovations** to their existing businesses? It's far more likely that these people have learned to pay attention to the cues that are around them and to ask many questions of things that most people take for granted, such as the way Dave Kapell did when making Magnetic Poetry. This search and capture of new ideas that lead to business opportunities is called **opportunity recognition**. Researchers in the field of entrepreneurship and small business believe that opportunity recognition behavior is the most basic and important entrepreneurial behavior.[4]

innovation
Implementation of a creative idea or opportunity leading to profitable and effective outcomes.

opportunity recognition
Searching and capturing new ideas that lead to business opportunities. This process often involves creative thinking that leads to discovery of new and useful ideas.

The exact reasons why entrepreneurs seem to be better able to find ideas that work are unclear. The notion of **entrepreneurial alertness** is one that has captured the attention of scholars in the field. This phrase means that entrepreneurs have a special set of observational and thinking skills that help them identify good opportunities. Some scholars have suggested that entrepreneurs are able to notice things that have been overlooked, without actually launching a formal search for opportunities.[5] Others suggest that we also consider the motivations of entrepreneurs to search for new ideas.[6] For example, if an owner of a fast-food restaurant notices that customers are asking for substitutions of healthier ingredients to the food items, she may be motivated to contact her suppliers to ask about obtaining new ingredients and to change the menu and increase the healthy offerings on the menu to keep customers satisfied, possibly bringing in more customers.

entrepreneurial alertness
A special set of observational and thinking skills that help entrepreneurs identify good opportunities; the ability to notice things that have been overlooked, without actually launching a formal search for opportunities, and the motivation to look for opportunities.

Ideas for new businesses come from a great variety of sources. A person who desires to start a business may begin searching for opportunities that exist in the marketplace, perhaps as a way to use skills and knowledge that he or she has acquired in college or in work experience. In the nationwide Panel Study of Entrepreneurial Dynamics,[7] a sample of 480 entrepreneurs were asked whether the business idea or the decision to start some kind of business came first:

TABLE 4.1 What Came First for New Businesses

Business idea	37%
Decision to start a business	42%
Idea and decision were simultaneous	21%

Source: Adapted from: G. E. Hills and R. P. Singh, "Opportunity Recognition." In *Handbook of Entrepreneurial Dynamics: The Process of Business Creation*, ed. W. B. Gartner, K. G. Shaver, N. M. Carter, and P. D. Reynolds. Thousand Oaks, CA: Sage, 2004. Table 24.1, page 266.

But regardless of whether the idea came first or the decision to start a business came first, we now examine the factors that lead small business owners to their business idea.

Work Experience

Many successful business owners spent years working for a company and gained valuable experience about how things might be done differently. Sometimes the idea grows out of listening to customer complaints.

You can use your own work and personal experiences to think of ideas for doing things differently. Sometimes the best business ideas come from your own frustration or from not finding exactly what you are looking for as a consumer. Anita Roddick, founder of the The Body Shop International PLC, whose 1,900 skin and body care retail stores are in 50 countries spanning 25 languages and 12 time zones,[8] got the idea for her business because she was very frustrated at having to spend a lot of money on moisturizer in fancy bottles from the big name cosmetics companies. Her idea was to give customers an inexpensive, good quality product made from natural ingredients in a recyclable bottle.

A Similar Business

Even if you don't have years of work experience in an industry or market, you might see a business in an area that intrigues you because you like certain products, or you

SMALL BUSINESS INSIGHT

Cleaning Up through Innovation

Russell Kendzior of Bedford, Texas, worked as a floor-covering salesman in the late 1980s. He heard customers complain that their floors were slippery right after they were purchased. He did some digging around and even commissioned chemists to develop a soap-free floor-cleaning product. He spent $5,000 of his own money, quit his job, and finally developed his own product. He gave away some product to friends who owned McDonald's locations, and before long it was the top-selling floor cleaner at McDonald's restaurants in the Dallas area. He ended up licensing his product, Traction Plus, which permitted him to think about other opportunities. Now, companies that bought his license manufacture and distribute wet-floor signs and floor-safety shoes. Traction Plus is a $20 million company, and its products include chemicals and footwear. Kendzior also developed and now runs the National Floor Safety Institute. He protects his ideas carefully. His soap-free formula is manufactured in several places, so no one knows exactly what is in it. Even Johnson Wax could not match Traction Plus because of Kendzior's vast experience. He describes himself as a resistant virus: "We're very resistant, very strong, but a very small company. I don't want to be Johnson Wax. I think they want to be me."[9]

Russ Kendzior's success sends an important message about looking for business opportunities that emerge through experience, including the frustrations of customers, which in this case was floor safety. Finding a new way to solve people's problems can be an excellent source of ideas for business.

learn that there is a growing market for this business and you think of a way to expand on the opportunity. The mini-case at the end of this chapter introduces Amy Nye Wolf, who founded AltiTUNES, a chain of 26 music stores located in airports around the country. She got the idea for the business while traveling through Heathrow Airport in London while a college student.

Hobby or Personal Interest

Many people find a way to turn their hobbies into successful businesses. David and Tom Gardner, the founders of Motley Fool, didn't start out wanting to write an online investment advice newsletter and Web site. They were avid players of a dice baseball game in high school called Strat-O-Matic, and they had a league in their town outside Washington, DC, where they grew up. Tom recalled, "It was a numbers game, and we kept lots of stats. There were so many different variables, just like the stock market and just like businesses have. And it was also a people thing, which is a big part of running a business, because all the fun of it was making trades with your competitors."[10]

Chance Happening, or Serendipity

If it is true that successful business owners are alert to what goes on around them and pay attention to things most people miss, then it is no surprise to learn that another popular source for business ideas comes from the chance happening. Whether you think of it as being in the right place at the right time, as luck, or as being observant to the cues around you, many businesses have been formed as a result of the unexpected. In the early 1980s, Rangaswamy Srinivasan worked for IBM, where he worked with lasers and organic plastics. He happened to come upon his "great idea" while at the Thanksgiving table, where he wondered how effective a laser might be in slicing a turkey leg. His experiments contributed to the development of laser eye surgery, an idea that came to him by observing the environment around him. In 2002 he was inducted into the Inventors Hall of Fame.[11]

Family and Friends

Ideas can come to you through your conversations with your family and friends. If you are open to their suggestions, a great business idea can result. Joan Ecker, founder of The Fat Hat Factory, a $1.7 million clothing company, got the idea for making a shapeable "fat" hat when a friend told her he would visit her at her new home in Vermont only if she provided him with a warm hat.[12]

Education and Expertise

As we saw earlier in the chapter, some small business owners decide first that they want to own a business and then go about searching for a viable idea for that business. Often, would-be entrepreneurs look to their own skills and talents for business ideas. Consulting companies are a very popular example of this approach to business ideas. Many owners of consulting companies took their own skills and launched businesses by selling those skills to other companies or individuals who needed them. Some of these consultants were laid off or voluntarily left large employers to consult with clients because they felt their talents would be more significantly recognized and rewarded in their own businesses.

In the Panel Study of Entrepreneurial Dynamics, 480 entrepreneurs were asked, "What led to your business idea?" Figure 4.1 presents the results of this question. Work experience in a particular industry or market was the most frequently mentioned source of ideas, followed by discussion with family and friends.

FIGURE 4.1

What Led to Your Business Idea? [13]

Source: Adapted from: G. E. Hills and R. P. Singh, "Opportunity Recognition." In *Handbook of Entrepreneurial Dynamics: The Process of Business Creation,* ed. W. B. Gartner, K. G. Shaver, N. M. Carter, and P. D. Reynolds. Thousand Oaks, CA: Sage, 2004. Table 24.4, page 268.

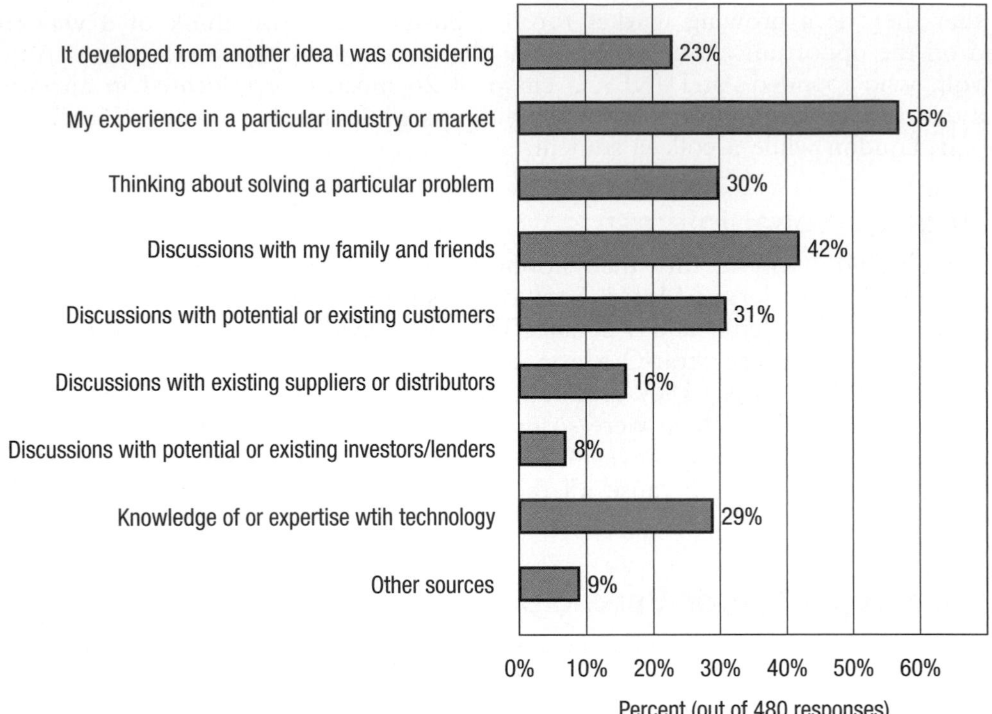

Technology Transfer

www.ipp.nasa.gov

www.dtic.mil/matris/t2/orgt2.html

http://iridium.nttc.edu

www.autm.net

One powerful but rarely used source of ideas are universities and government agencies. Both develop a tremendous range of new technologies or refinements of existing technologies, *but never do anything with them!* Major universities and government agencies, like NASA and the Departments of Agriculture and Defense, all offer technological inventions for free to small businesses to develop. There are even government programs to help fund such efforts. A good place to start are government technology commercialization sites such as NASA's (www.ipp.nasa.gov), the Department of Defense's site at (http://www.dtic.mil/matris/t2/orgt2.html), or the Byrd National Technology Transfer Center Web site at (http://iridium.nttc.edu). If you have a university nearby which has government funded research, you can contact their technology transfer office and find out about inventions available for commercialization in your own backyard, or check out the Web site of the Association of University Technology Managers www.autm.net.

SMALL BUSINESS INSIGHT

Royal Touch Salon Plus: A Cut Above the Rest[14]

Chiquita Miller-Nolan already was in business when she entered Kingwood College in the fall of 2002. She had won first place in the regional Global Student Entrepreneur Awards as a freshman for her business, Royal Touch Salon Plus. Started in 1997, it was the first African-American-owned salon in Atascocita, a surburb of Humble, just northeast of Houston. She grew the salon from 950 square feet to 1,600 square feet, consistently donated 30 percent of profits to nonprofit organizations, and donated food, clothing, and toys to help needy families. For all these reasons, Chiquita was the winner of the Global Student Entrepreneur Award for her region in 2003. How did Chiquita get the idea for her business? She recalls, "At the time I opened my business I had been a stylist for 10 years. I worked in the Houston/Humble, Texas, area for about two years before I opened my own salon. You've heard it said, 'Necessity is the mother of invention'? Well, honestly there were needs that I endeavored to meet. I needed more options such as flexibility and control concerning my career since I am a mother. At the time I was a stylist for JC Penney. I loved the security that the company gave me, yet for the first time it wasn't enough. I needed a different type of security and Penney's couldn't give me what I needed."

"I was a skilled hairstylist in *all* hair types, and that was and is something that's rare for this area. My goal then became to open a full-service salon that could treat *all* hair types, black, white, Asian, Hispanic, Indian, etc., men, women, and children. The next thing I planned was to have a play area so that mothers like myself could bring their children with them. On Mother's Day, Valentine's Day, Easter, and special days we set out breakfast croissants, doughnuts, and juice to show our appreciation."

What does Chiquita advise other business owners who are looking for an opportunity?

"Seek to fulfill a need, not just be another of the same thing that already exists. Get feedback from those you survey, don't just count on a paper survey. Not all the time do things work out that look good on paper. Talk to people and get the heartbeat of the area."

■ The Global Student Entrepreneur Award, sponsored by Saint Louis University, draws student contestants from eight global regions. Visit www.gsea.org for more details on this year's application process, information on past winners, and access to entrepreneurial resources.

Assessing Viability

LO2
Track the traditional ways opportunities are screened for business potential.

In the previous section we examine various ways you can search for your business idea or for ideas that improve existing products, services, or business processes. Is every good idea a viable business opportunity? Definitely not. The marketplace is replete with examples of bad business ideas that seemed great in concept but were poor in execution—witness the dot.com bubble that burst recently. The business world learned—in some cases very harshly—that not every idea is evaluated properly or deserves to evolve into a business. So although you may feel strongly that an idea is the *right* idea for you to invest some time and effort in, there are many more steps you need to take before opening your door. Here we use the word *idea* to broadly mean a new or improved product, service, or process. We begin with some fundamental questions. Later in this chapter you will learn how to conduct a comprehensive feasibility analysis for your idea, a formal approach to assessing whether your idea is sound and could lead to a viable business. For now we offer a simple approach to help you start quickly assessing the **viability** of opportunities.

viability
The preliminary assessment of the potential for a business to be created or, once created, to survive.

Here are four main questions to ask yourself. They reflect each of four primary areas you should consider when evaluating an idea or opportunity: revenue-generating ability, people, resources, and information.

1. **How viable is the idea?** Will what you are planning to sell generate actual revenues? One of the mistakes would-be entrepreneurs make is to assume that everyone will love the idea and that people will be standing in line to buy it once the business opens.
2. **Who are the people behind the idea?** If a great idea with high market potential also has a person or team behind it that is a good fit, the idea is much more likely to be successful than it would be without that person or team. While your skills and talents might have led you to discover the idea, do you have what it takes to turn this idea into a business?
3. **What resources are needed to take the idea and sell it to the customer?** Beyond the start-up dollars that will be needed to buy any raw materials to make the product or develop the service, what information, relationships, and degree of effort will be needed to turn it into reality?

SMALL BUSINESS INSIGHT

Falling in Love with the Idea

Have you ever thought of an idea that was good—great, actually—and then found yourself amazed that nobody else had ever thought of it? Did you think, "Hey, maybe I could do this since no one else has come up with a way to do it?" Then you find yourself getting more and more excited about the prospect of starting this really great business with your amazing idea? If so, you are in good company. Many people who went on to start successful businesses found that during the early stages of preparing to go into or grow their businesses, their so-called "great idea" really wasn't so great after all. Tim Knox owns a software company, Digital Graphiti, and he recounts such an experience: "We came up with what we thought was an amazing piece of software—a piece of software so amazing, in fact, that we just knew that all of humankind would sit up and take notice, then line up to write us checks. After hundreds of hours and thousands of dollars spent developing the product and finally bringing it to market, we were amazed to find that the only people who thought the software was amazing was us. We made humankind yawn . . . quite an amazing accomplishment."[15]

The pitfall of idea infatuation happened to Lisa Thomas and Gary Erickson, who now own a successful energy bar company called Clifbar. Before they introduced the energy bars, they had an idea to sell a dessert they really liked called Choclava. They were selling more traditional baked goods and thought they knew what tasted good. After all, as Lisa described, "We made what we liked." The Choclava was a chocolate version of baklava that Erickson had created. Thomas said, "We thought we had it made. We were going to be on the cover of *Gourmet* magazine." They put their efforts into Choclava, which required layering phyllo dough, a dough that is very challenging to work with, and chopping walnuts and blending premium chocolate into the mixture. It wasn't easy to produce, but they were inspired. In the end they couldn't sell it. "People are either hot or cold on baklava," acknowledges Erickson. In retrospect, he adds, "We're probably lucky. Phyllo is incredibly hard to work with."[16]

4. **What do you need to know about the industry and market for the idea?** Even if you have done some preliminary research on industry and market trends and forecasts, you should consider what you don't yet know (about competition or about customers' preferences) that could affect the way your idea is turned into a business.

From Ideas to Opportunities Through Creativity

LO3
Understand how creativity methods can help business owners recognize new opportunities.

You might have a viable business opportunity, but is it the best one to pursue? Are you sure you have the right approach for making the most of the opportunity? Very often the first good idea an entrepreneur has is not necessarily the best one they will have. Before committing yourself to one viable idea, it is a good practice to take some time and see if you can take that viable opportunity and innovate on it to create an even better—more profitable, more distinctive, harder to copy—opportunity.

Why worry about being innovative in your approach? Consider the ease with which you can get data over the Internet on industries and markets, such as your competition, and how small business research and how-to articles are at your fingertips with many journals and magazines available over the Web. Of course, everybody else who is thinking about starting a business similar to yours has this same information at his or her fingertips also. There are, however, some very creative methods you can use to help you generate ideas and opportunities that take you beyond what everybody else already knows. This is what can give you the innovative edge in business ownership, whether you are looking for ideas that are just a little bit different from the competition, or a world apart from what everybody else is doing or not even doing yet. These strategies are discussed later in the chapter.

Figure 4.2 provides one tool you can use to help you identify new opportunities. It is based on the work of Alex Osborne, a pioneer in the field of **creativity**, who first coined the word, *brainstorming*. The tool is known as **SCAMPER**, and it is an acronym for a set of cues that trigger new ideas for your business.

S – Substitute

C – Combine

A – Adapt

M – Magnify or modify

P – Put to other uses

E – Eliminate

R – Rearrange

FIGURE 4.2

Using SCAMPER to Recognize Business Opportunities[17]

creativity
A process producing an idea or opportunity that is novel and useful, frequently derived from making connections among distinct ideas or opportunities.

SCAMPER
A creativity tool that provides cues to trigger breakthrough thinking. The letters stand for substitute, combine, adapt, modify, put to other uses, eliminate, and rearrange.

Substitute: Think of what you might substitute for something else to form a new idea. A feature that allows your customers to order directly from a Web site rather than visiting your store or ordering by mail is an example of substitution. Sometimes solutions derived through SCAMPER cues are very "way out" and lead people to some creative ideas for solving annoying problems. One city in the Netherlands, for example, was experiencing a growing litter problem (not unlike your own town or city, no doubt), and the civic leaders tried all the usual ways of fixing the problem: They increased the number of trash bins around the city, they posted signs reminding people not to litter, and they fined people for littering. Nothing seemed to help. Then they got a breakthrough idea: a tiny recording device was installed inside trash bins, and every time someone pushed the lid to deposit litter, a joke would play from the recorder! Not surprisingly, it was not too long before the litter problem declined.

Idea Trigger: What opportunities can you think of that come as a result of substituting or replacing something that already exists?

Combine: Think of possible combinations you can make that result in something entirely different. Not long ago, if you wanted to buy a book, you went to a store that typically carried only books, and if you wanted to buy a cup of coffee you went to a coffee shop, and if you wanted to hear music you went to a club or theater. Today, you can have all three under one roof at many establishments, including big ones such as Borders and Barnes & Noble, but also some smaller businesses such as Tattered Cover Book Store in Denver, Colorado. Also, when you buy gasoline at the service station, you most likely can pick up some groceries along with basic auto supplies, and maybe even CDs or videotapes.

Idea Trigger: What separate products, services, or whole businesses can you put together to create another distinct business?

Adapt: Think about what could be adapted from products or services that already exist. Many successful businesses are founded on the concept of adaptation. It's a popular innovation strategy that can be just as effective, and much more likely in the real world, than business opportunities that are the result of **radical innovations** such as inventions. You may remember the original Book-of-the-Month club that sent members a different book every month. What adaptations can you find? How about beer-of-the-month, pasta-of-the-month, and many other variations? Did you know that one day a manufacturer of toilet tissue received a shipment of paper that was too thick to use? The manufacturer could have thrown it out, but instead it improvised, and paper towels were introduced! Sometimes adaptations occur when entrepreneurs try their best to work with scarce resources.

radical innovation strategy
Rejecting existing ideas, and presenting a way to do things differently.

Idea Trigger: What could you adapt from other industries or fields to your business?

Magnify or modify: Taking an existing product and changing its appearance or adding more features or more hours your store is open or making its advertising more dramatic are some ways you could magnify or modify your idea. Washington Mutual is a financial services company that is currently opening branches all over Chicago, among other cities. All along the expressways are billboards proclaiming this in some very dramatic and humorous ways, poking fun at the traditional fees that banks and other financial service companies charge for checking accounts, for example. It has also launched a series of hilarious TV ads, including the famous "money shrub" which depicts scientists attempting to grow money on plants in the laboratory. Unfortunately, while they do manage to produce a large tree with money growing on its branches, the tree suddenly grabs the scientist and hurls him all around the laboratory. The scene reminds viewers of Audrey II in Little Shop of Horrors. The announcer notes that while not everything is ready for the market, did you hear about the new credit card? Clearly, such messages are remembered by potential customers, and the effect is to make the business stick out among its competitors. There is much a small business can do to create memorable images and advertising for itself, and it does not need expensive television ads to do it. M also can cue you to "minimize" something. The microchip industry was born, for example, when someone asked the question, "What if we shrunk them?"

Idea Trigger: What could I make more noticeable or dramatic, or different in some way from my competitors? It need not be in the product itself, but it could be the way you advertise or treat the customer during the transaction that becomes memorable.

Put to other uses: Think of ways you could generate a high number of opportunities for your product or service beyond what it is traditionally used for. A few years ago, Arm & Hammer Baking Soda was known as a product customers used by the teaspoonful every few weeks when they baked a batch of cookies or a cake. The problem for Arm & Hammer was that it wasn't selling a lot of boxes of the stuff since it tended to sit in people's kitchen cupboards for years. At 59 cents a box, that doesn't bring tremendous sales revenues. One day, the company brought together a group of employees and gave them the challenge to think of all the uses for baking soda (besides baking) that they could. Ideas took off, and today the company produces an entire line of baking soda–related products that bring a handsome return in profits. Can you think of some? (Hint: washing clothes, refrigerators that smell, a product cats use, etc.)

Antoine Fuerchtwanger sold frankfurters at the Chicago Exposition over 100 years ago, and his customers complained that they burnt their fingers when holding them. Fuerchtwanger tried gloves, but customers kept walking off with them. Finally, he took some rolls that a baker had made, cut them in half down the middle, and placed the frankfurters inside them. Hotdogs met buns, and today it's hard to imagine one without the other.

Idea Trigger: Suppose you learned that all the traditional uses for your product had disappeared and that you have trailer truckloads out back with tons of product. What other uses might there be? Aim for quantity, and allow outrageous ideas to flow along with more mundane ones. Who knows what new applications you may find.

Eliminate: Search for opportunities that arise when you get rid of something or stop doing something. What products or services emerged when these questions were asked: What if people didn't have to leave their houses to go grocery shopping? What if you could buy something (or do bank transactions) without leaving your car?

Idea Trigger: What could I get rid of or reduce that would eliminate something my customer has to do, and as a result give the customer more than he or she expected?

Rearrange or reverse: One of the best examples of this technique is shown in the opening vignette to this chapter. Magnetic Poetry is a product that by definition is about rearranging things to inspire ideas. Other examples include using reverse psychology or paradox to challenge old ways of thinking, for example, using stimulants to calm hyperactive children.

Idea Trigger: What can you rearrange or reorder in the way your product or service appears, or the way businesses in your industry usually look or are decorated or located?

SCAMPER is a very effective method for helping business owners and their employees come up with alternative solutions and opportunities. The method works because it helps you to step outside the usual way you look at opportunities or try to solve problems. It offers cues that push you outside your traditional areas of expertise, to consider what interesting new forms might be out there that you could try. We know that highly creative individuals are people who usually ask lots of questions. Creative business owners similarly question and challenge the way things appear, to see if they can find a new way of doing things. When you see a highly innovative business, don't think that there is something especially magical or lucky about the entrepreneur or the situation. It's more likely that the person or team behind the business is simply persistent about asking questions. Following are several recommendations to help you put yourself and your business in an innovative frame of mind.

■ When you're looking for ways to change your business, consider getting out of your comfort zone for innovation. Get together with a group of professionals to discuss trends in your industry and how they are affecting your business. Do you have other recommendations for challenging the way things are being done and coming up with creative new techniques?

Get into an Innovative Frame of Mind

Regardless of whether you feel your business needs a subtle change or a drastic one, building "change-ability" into a core business is possible if you actually practice change.[18] Here are some techniques you can try as you practice the business of innovation:

- Read magazines or trade journals outside your area.
- Invite someone you never included before to a meeting at which you are solving a problem or searching for a new opportunity. Try a supplier or a friend who works in a different field.
- Have a "scan the environment" day in which you discuss trends and happenings that could impact your business.
- Try a mini-internship. Ask a colleague or friend if you can spend a week at his or her business to see what you can learn that may be applicable to yours.
- Instead of trying to simply sell your product or service to customers, put yourself in their shoes and ask them what frustrates them most or what problems they cannot seem to solve that relate to your business.
- Redesign your work environment. Get a room with a view.[19] This doesn't have to cost a bundle in remodeling or even redecorating costs. Try to bring in some items from nature and add color and inspirational objects or quotations.

SKILL MODULE 4.1

The Creative Process

The creative process in individuals, teams, and organizations has been studied intensively for over 75 years. It is concerned with the way in which creativity actually happens. Much of what we know about creativity comes from understanding the process that highly creative people go through when they get their ideas. Artists, scientists, composers, poets, and inventors have attempted to describe their creative moments. Graham Wallas[20] developed one of the early descriptions of the creative process, and it is still widely used today to guide the creative process in business. This research suggests that creative thought includes four stages:

1. Preparation—exploring the problem or opportunity in all directions.
2. Incubation—thinking about the problem or opportunity in a "not-conscious" way, putting it on the back burner, so to speak.
3. Illumination—the lightbulb comes on, and ideas begin to flow.
4. Verification—testing of the idea and reducing it to its most exact form.[21]

This process is very useful when you want to explore a business problem, such as why you lost a customer, or when you want to identify further opportunities for your business, such as new markets or features for your product line. If you can pinpoint what stage of the creative process you are in, you can guide yourself through to an innovative solution by looking at things from different perspectives and allowing the issue to simmer in the background for a bit. This technique has worked for many famous creative people—from Leonardo da Vinci to Albert Einstein.

Avoid Pitfalls

L04
Understand the five pitfalls that hinder innovation.

In your quest for new business ideas, from time to time you may catch yourself rejecting ideas or jumping on the first good idea you get because you are excited and there is no time to lose.

There are five major pitfalls[22] that business owners can become victim to when trying to become more innovative. See if you recognize the ones that apply to you and your business, so that you can sidestep them at every opportunity:

1. **Identifying the wrong problem:** When a problem doesn't stay solved or an opportunity doesn't pan out as expected, it could be that the wrong problem was defined. For example, a synthetic-fiber producer brought a group of employees together to help find ways to reduce the manufacturing costs of a particular product. After spending a few days brainstorming and finding that the problem was not leading them to any interesting or useful solutions, the employees turned the problem around and began developing ways to increase the sales of a highly profitable part of the product line. How were they able to change their focus in this way? They simply examined the problem within the broader context of profitabilty (instead of costs) and discovered that the real problem was low profits.
2. **Judging ideas too quickly:** At many business meetings when someone suggests a new idea or approach, often the first reaction you hear is, "We've tried that before and it didn't work," "The boss will never go for it," "It's not in the budget," or the frequently heard, "Yes, but . . . " People tend to judge ideas prematurely, before they take the time to ask, "What's right about this idea?" or "How could this idea be made better?"
3. **Stopping with the first good idea:** The first good idea you come up with is rarely the best. That's because it was the easiest to think of, and so there is little doubt that your competitors have already thought of it, too. The very best ideas come a little later, after the ideas that are on the top of your mind come out. Using a tool such as SCAMPER, for example, encourages you to explore things more deeply than just rattling off the first thing you can think of and then doing that.
4. **Failing to get the "bandits on the train" and ask for support:** Imagine you are on a train in the American West in the late 1800s. At the time, bandits often placed dynamite on the tracks to hold up the train. How can you keep that from happening? One way is to get the bandits on your train. In modern business terms, this means figuring out whose support you must have or who could derail your project and then involving them early in the project. If you need an employee's involvement or a supplier's agreement, get them on board early to avoid failure later.
5. **Obeying rules that don't exist:** We sometimes put obstacles in front of ourselves because we think we can't do something, when in fact there is no reason we can't. Are you assuming that as the business owner you need to do all the work, or make all the sales calls, or solve everybody's problems (including your employees' or partners' problems)? Before you assume that you do, challenge the assumption.

Types of Innovations Small Businesses Develop

L05
Identify strategies for innovation in your business.

Companies may find it easier to mimic the strategies of other firms because of the expense and intense effort required to make decisions based on a radical innovation strategy. In addition customers may view a new company as more legitimate if it imitates established practices in the industry.[23] This is the idea behind several of the methods for product-based legitimacy described in Chapter 2. It is also central to the idea of pursuing an **imitative strategy**, which is covered in detail in Chapter 7.

imitative strategy
An overall strategic approach in which the entrepreneur does more or less what others are already doing.

But mimicking others is not the only strategy that an entrepreneur can pursue. Gaglio and Katz[24] offer a model for thinking about the business implications of opportunities. Called the *opportunity identification process* (see Figure 4.3), it has the

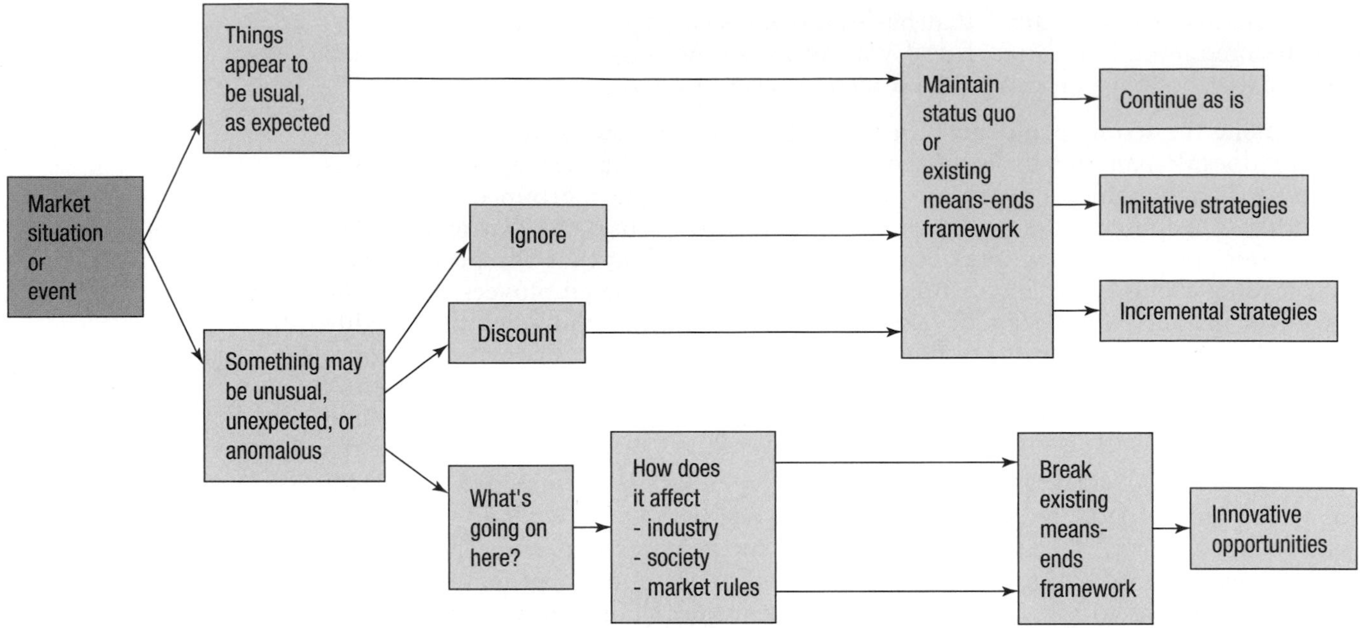

FIGURE 4.3

Opportunity Identification Process

Source: Adapted from: C. M. Gaglio and J. A. Katz, "The Psychological Basis of Opportunity Identification: Entrepreneurial Alertness," *Small Business Economics, 16*, no. 2, (March 2001), p. 99.

entrepreneur assess whether the situation faced is one that is the same as it has been traditionally or if it is changing. Strategies that involve doing the same thing, or mimicking others, or pursuing an **incremental strategy** make a lot of sense when the business is continuing on a fairly steady course. Sometimes during these periods of stability, trying innovative ideas might help win more business from rivals, and "shake up" the industry, perhaps giving the innovator an advantage. During times of great change—whether from technological, political, economic, or cultural change—the potential for steady business declines, and the attractiveness of innovations increases. At times of great change, people become more willing to try extreme new ideas, so it becomes a great time to introduce extremely innovative ideas.

incremental strategy
Taking an idea and offering a way to do something slightly better than it is done presently.

One unusual ability found in the entrepreneurs studied by Gaglio and Katz was that many of them can come up with new ideas given nearly any combination of resources. Sitting at an airport, entrepreneurs begin to look where lines are forming and wonder how to make money off that. Others can be given some everyday items and in a few minutes they are thinking up ways to combine them to make a profit. Their use of the opportunity identification process tells us that being creative can become a way of life.

LO6
Learn how to conduct a comprehensive feasibility study for your business ideas.

Make Sure an Idea Is Feasible

feasibility
The extent to which an idea is viable and realistic and the extent to which you are aware of internal (to your business) and external (industry, market, and regulatory environment) forces that could affect your business.

Before you implement a business idea, you should test the idea for its **feasibility**, which means the extent to which the idea is viable and realistic and the extent to which you are aware of internal (to your business) and external (industry, market, and regulatory environment) forces that could affect your business. In this section, we examine the major criteria that will help you determine the feasibility of your business opportunity. Before we examine an outline for conducting a feasibility study, let's take a look at the results of a study in which entrepreneurs revealed what matters most to their business, with respect to the economic and community context in which their businesses are located.[25] The entrepreneurs were asked, on a scale of 1 (very confident) to 5 (very unconfident) how certain they were that the new business would be able to accomplish the following:

TABLE 4.2 What Start-Up Entrepreneurs Feel Confident About

Comply with local/state federal regulations	1.64
Keep up with technological advances	1.84
Attract customers	1.85
Obtain raw materials	1.95
Deal with distributors	1.95
Compete with other firms	2.10
Attract employees	2.29
Obtain working capital	2.70
Obtain start-up capital	2.84
Obtain a bank's help	3.15
Obtain venture capitalists' help	3.41

Source: Adapted from C. H. Matthews and S. E. Human, "The economic and community context for entrepreneurship." In *Handbook of Entrepreneurial Dynamics: the process of business creation,* ed. W. B. Gartner, K. G. Shaver, N. M. Carter, and P. D. Reynolds. Thousand Oaks, CA: Sage, 2004. Table 36.1, page 424.

Feasibility studies consist of careful investigation of four primary areas: the product/service, the industry and market, financial projections (profitability), and the plan for future action. Within each of these areas you will examine the strengths and weaknesses (advantages and disadvantages) of your business opportunity. Figure 4.4 is an outline of a feasibility study,[26] and we will look more closely at each of the areas that will help you decide whether your idea or opportunity can be a viable business or not.

FIGURE 4.4

The Feasibility Study Outline

Guidelines for Completing Your Study

I. Description of Your Business

What business are you *really* in? Describe your product or service in the most concise way you can, and think beyond the characteristics of the product or service to the *experience* that you hope the customer receives from buying the product or service.

II. The Product/Service

- **Unique Features: Benefits**

What are the unique features of the product or service? How do these features meet your customers' needs or preferences? What are the benefits of this product or service compared to the competition? Describe your product or service very simply, and use photos or drawings to illustrate how it works.

- **Unique Features: Limitations**

What are the specific shortcomings of the product or service? Can it become obsolete soon? Is it perishable, difficult to use or install, or are there legal restrictions? An honest assessment of your product or service is extremely important during this analysis. You do yourself no favor by being in denial, or failing to see the disadvantages *before* you go into business. Noting them now will help you prepare solutions or ways to minimize these issues.

- **Stage of Development**

Is the product still in the idea stage, or is there a model or working prototype available? Have any samples been manufactured? If it is still in the idea or prototype stage, what is the time frame for getting it ready for production?

- **Legal Restrictions and Rights**

List any patents, copyrights, trademarks, or licenses that apply to your product or service. If you are entering into a franchise agreement, partnerships, distributorships, etc., these should be discussed in this section. Seek the assistance of patent attorneys or intellectual copyright specialists for assistance. Also list the government regulations you must adhere to, such as FDA, EOA, OSHA, IRS, Secretary of State, etc., and research zoning restrictions carefully. If you will be home-based and your clients will be coming to your house, will this be impacted by your neighborhood's zoning restrictions?

- **Insurance Requirements**

Research the liability of your product or service and consult an insurance specialist to be sure you are protected adequately. This will depend on the nature of your business. A flower shop that sells floral arrangements is in a different liability situation than a pet grooming business, for example. If you have employees, you will need insurance to protect them from harm also, along with any insurance benefits you want to provide your staff.

- **Trends Related to the Product or Service**

How will you keep your finger on the pulse of change in your product or service area? What trends are likely to occur in the way the product is used, or what features it offers, for example?

- **Production or Service Delivery Costs**

Will you be producing or sub-contracting out the manufacturing or delivery of your product or service? List all the costs, including labor, supplies, shipping, repairs, etc.

III. The Industry and Market

- **Current Industry**

Describe the industry as specifically as you can. There are some excellent sources in your college or public library that can help you determine the size of the industry, location of the industry (local, regional, national or global), and average sales and profitability for the industry. For example, the Risk Management Association provides industry-specific data based on the SIC (Standard Industry Classification Code) that can tell you what the average revenues are for a particular industry, and what profits you might expect to earn.

- **Market Potential for this Industry**

Is the industry in a period of decline, stability, or growth? What is the market demand likely to be for the next 1 to 3 years? Talk to people in the industry as well as potential customers for their ideas about where the industry might be headed. Consider how technology or the global economy might affect the market potential for the business. Research trends in the industry.

- **The Competition**

Who are your primary competitors, and what are their distinct advantages and disadvantages? Consider not only your direct competitors, but also your indirect ones who might be selling a substitute for your product or service or bundling your product with something else they provide.

- **Your Customers**

Who are your customers? Demographic information tells you all about your customers' personal characteristics, such as where they live, how much household income they have, and how many children they have. You can find very specific information in your library or on-line using zip codes for communities. What are your customers' preferences, values, attitudes that relate to your business? How will you find out what your customers think or intend to buy? How can you find out what problems they have, what they need, or what they want that they don't know yet! Use your creativity to learn as much as you can about your potential customers. If you have more than one target market, do this for each market segment. It's important to note the different benefits and limitations for each customer group.

- **Market Penetration**

How will you reach your target customers? What forms of distribution or selling will you use? How will your potential customers become aware of your business? How will you advertise?

IV. Financial Projections

- **Pricing**

How much will you charge for your product or service? Do a break-even analysis, and list all the assumptions behind your pricing.

- **Sales Revenue Forecast**

How much of your product or service will you expect to sell? What will your gross revenues be? What percentage of market share do you think you will reach in one year? Three years?

- **Cost Forecast**

What does it cost to produce, distribute, deliver, etc., your product or service? If you plan to manufacture goods, consider the cost of raw materials, labor, and delivery of goods. If you plan to retail or wholesale goods and services, consider mark-up, inventory costs, and freight. Refer to the RMA (Risk Management Association) studies for more information to help you compute these costs. See www.rmahq.org.

- **Gross Profit**

What are your sales minus cost of goods sold? Do this for each product or service and compare to industry averages.

- **Operating Expenses**

What marketing expenses (advertising, etc.), administrative (clerical and management), and general expenses do you expect to incur? Be sure to state your assumptions about these figures.

- **Profitability**

What is your expected net profit? After you have derived your gross profit above, subtract other expenses you expect to incur, such as rent, insurance, and salaries. This will help you determine your net profit.

V. Future Action Plan

- **Start-up Capital**

How much money do you need to start the business? In addition to the cost of goods sold that you calculated and your marketing and administrative expenses, what additional costs do you have, such as renting space, utility expenses, and salaries?

- **Sources of Start-up Capital**

Where can you obtain the money you need to start the business? Consider all the sources available to you, such as personal savings, family and friends, bank loans, investors, etc.

- **Further Information Needed**

What are you uncertain about? Whom could you ask? Where can you find this information? Your analysis is incomplete if you haven't considered what it is you don't yet know.

- **Writing a Business Plan**

The feasibility analysis will help you get started writing your business plan. You will have the information you need to address the competitive advantages and disadvantages of your business and the strategies you will use to meet your goals.

- **Support Needed**

List the individuals or groups you could consult for advice. Consider developing an advisory board consisting of people with experience in your industry and professionals from other industries who might be expert marketers, for example. Do you have an attorney, accountant, Web site designer, etc., who could help you when needed? Make a list of all the supporting actors your business may need in the future.

Ways to Keep On Being Creative

LO7
Understand the value of building a creative culture in your business.

Once you have generated your business idea and evaluated it and determined whether or not it is feasible, you have completed the opportunity identification and evaluation process. But this process never really ends. Even after you are well on your way into business and even after your business is successful and you have met your initial goals, the nature of entrepreneurs and small business is that you will always be on the lookout for new opportunities. Successful business owners never rest on their laurels and assume that, since they have achieved success, it will always be there. One of the pitfalls small business owners can fall into is to fail to build a company culture—a way of thinking and behaving—that encourages new ideas and embraces change. This is especially important if you employ or plan to employ other people. There is nothing as discouraging as working for someone who feels there is nothing new you can possibly contribute to the business. And you would be surprised to learn how many business owners have this mentality. Here are some ways you can avoid this and build a company that is "idea prone." You will find that you can attract more creative employees and get more useful ideas out of them that affect your business's bottom line by following the recommendations given in Skill Module 4.2.

Innovation is at the heart of entrepreneurship, because every time people start a business or become the owner of one, it is a new start and often a new experience for them. Some businesses are themselves built on new ideas or new twists on existing ideas. For

SKILL MODULE 4.2

Great Ideas for Making Idea-Prone Companies

1. Give yourself and your employees time to think of ideas. While it can seem that there is never enough time to get everything done and deadlines are always looming, you can't afford not to take the time to come up with new ideas. Allow even just a few minutes every day to discover what your customers or employees are thinking and what problems or frustrations they may be experiencing. Ask your employees what they are working on, where there may be problems, and what ideas they have for solving them.
2. Positively reinforce ideas[27]—avoid the automatic no. As discussed earlier, don't rush to judge ideas. It's the process of coming up with ideas that needs to be reinforced, not whether the idea is good or not. Evaluation can come later.
3. Look to unlikely sources of opportunities. You never know where creativity and innovation will emerge. Think beyond your age group, socioeconomic status, and education.
4. Get a room with a view. Give your employees—and yourself—varied experiences. Get away from the office, go visit customers, allow employees to learn one another's jobs, and so on. It enables people to get a different perspective, and it is when we can change our routine that breakthrough ideas often can be discovered.

An innovative company does not automatically develop out of an innovative business idea. You have to deliberately set your expectations and communicate them to your employees. Remember that recognition is fuel—it fans the fires of creativity and helps your business reach potentials that you may never have anticipated. Einstein said, "Creativity is contagious . . . pass it on." As the business owner, you are in a unique position to make sure that people's brains don't stop at your company's door.

these kinds of situations, taking some time before committing your money to think about which ideas make the most sense as a profit-maker can save a lot of grief later on. That is where the opportunity identification process and the assessment of viability and feasibility come in to play. It is also true that one of the greatest challenges facing a business is getting control over the process of change—knowing when and how to change and try something new. Sometimes even thinking in new ways can be difficult, and that is when techniques like SCAMPER can make all the difference. The point is that while many people think innovation is a bolt from the blue, unpredictable and uncontrollable, in reality it is anything but that. That is good news, because it means that one of the most powerful techniques for building your business is under your control.

CHAPTER SUMMARY

L01 Learn the sources of opportunity entrepreneurs draw on to get business ideas.

- Opportunity recognition is one of the most basic entrepreneurial behaviors.
- Entrepreneurial alertness means that entrepreneurs have a special set of observational and thinking skills that help them identify good opportunities.
- A plurality of entrepreneurs studied knew they wanted to start a business and were very motivated to find business ideas.
- Ideas for new businesses come from a great variety of sources. These include work experience, seeing a similar business, hobbies or personal interests, a chance happening, discussions with family and friends, and education and experience.

LO2 Track the traditional ways opportunities are screened for business potential.

- In assessing the potential value of your business idea, there are four major areas to consider:
  - What is the viability or the ability of your idea to actually generate revenues?
  - Who are the people behind your idea?
  - What resources do you need?
  - What information do you need to know about industries and markets for your idea?
- Avoid the pitfall of idea infatuation. If no one else has ever tried the idea, is there a reason why?

LO3 Understand how creativity methods can help business owners recognize new opportunities.

- Creative methods help you identify opportunities beyond what everybody else already knows.
- SCAMPER is a tool you can use to trigger new opportunities for your business.
- Use techniques to help you get into an innovative frame of mind. Read outside your area, invite a "wild card" to a business meeting, have a "scan the environment" day, arrange a mini-internship, solve your customer's problem rather than selling a product, redesign your work environment to stimulate your innovative skills.
- The creative process has four stages: preparation, incubation, illumination, and verification.

LO4 Understand the five pitfalls that hinder innovation.

- Identifying the wrong problem.
- Judging ideas and opportunities too soon.
- Stopping with the first good idea.
- Failing to get support.
- Obeying rules that don't exist.

LO5 Identify strategies for innovation in your business.

- There are three innovative strategies small business owners can select:
  - Imitative strategies take an idea that somebody else has already discovered and build a business around that idea.
  - Incremental strategies take an idea and offer a way to do something better than it is done now.
  - Radical innovation strategies reject existing ideas and present a way to do things differently.

LO6 Learn how to conduct a comprehensive feasibility study for your business ideas.

- Conduct an analysis to determine whether or not your business idea is feasible.
- Describe your business idea concisely, including the experience you wish to sell to potential customers, as well as details about your product or service.
- List the unique benefits and limitations of your product or service, at what stage of development it is now (idea or prototype), any proprietary restrictions and obligations, insurance needs, product or service trends, and any production costs.

- Describe your industry, including its size and trends. Provide the market potential for your product or service, the strengths and weaknesses of your competition, who your customers are, what their needs and preferences are, and how they will find you.
- Compute financial projections. Provide sales revenues, cost forecasts, gross profits, operating expenses, and net profit.
- Write a future action plan. Determine the start-up capital you need and where you can raise it. Consider any further information you need, and begin writing a business plan. Decide where you can find additional support, such as from attorneys, accountants, and other business advisers.

LO7 Understand the value of building a creative culture in your business.

- Build a company culture that values new ideas and embraces change.
- Create slack time to enable employees to think of new ideas.
- Positively reinforce ideas others bring to you.
- Look to unlikely sources of opportunities.
- Get a room with a view and establish an environment that stimulates innovation.

DISCUSSION QUESTIONS

1. How do entrepreneurs recognize new ideas for their business?
2. What are some common ways you can search for new business opportunities?
3. How can entrepreneurs evaluate the merit of a new idea?
4. How are creative methods for opportunity recognition different from traditional ways of searching for ideas?
5. What should you watch out for as you are searching for new opportunities?
6. What are the differences between imitation, incremental, and radical innovation strategies? How can you assess which one is right for your business?
7. What should a good feasibility study contain? What questions can it help you answer to determine if your business idea is a sound one?
8. How can entrepreneurs ensure that their business stays innovative and fresh? Why do you think some small businesses lose their creative edge as the business grows?

EXPERIENTIAL EXERCISES

1. As you go on errands or walk around your campus, notice all the things that you could improve. Make a list of things that frustrate you or things that could be made even better. Does your list surprise you in terms of how much you noticed?
2. List 15 new uses for a popular product or service. Try paper clips, or coffee mugs, or home delivery. Use SCAMPER to generate new uses and make connections to other uses.

3. Interview a local business owner and ask how he or she thought of the idea behind the business. How does the business develop new ideas now?
4. Do some research on innovative companies in your area. What sets them apart? How are they designed to take advantage of the innovativeness of their staffs?
5. Next time you are working on a problem or looking for new ideas (your major in college? Where to move on campus? What do to this weekend?), go to a museum, a park, or anywhere outside the ordinary places you frequent. Were any new ideas suggested to you?
6. Keep a journal in which you can record your ideas as they come. Sometimes we get breakthrough ideas while our brain is incubating as we sleep. By the time we wake up in the morning we have lost them, so keep your journal near your bed.
7. Pick a business idea and research its industry and market. What did you learn? What are some creative questions you might ask about contemporary trends in this business? How could you find out the answers?

Mini-Case

AltiTUNES: FROM IMITATION TO CONTINUOUS INNOVATION[28]

Amy Nye Wolf had completed a backpacking tour across Europe in the mid-1980s when she saw a store selling music at London's Heathrow Airport. Wolf recalled that she was tired of the music she had and was very happy to see it. She purchased some music, and returned to the States excited to have found the store. At that time retail outlets in American airports consisted of food service restaurants and newsstands.

It wasn't until five years later, after Wolf had completed college and worked as an investment banker for Merrill Lynch, that she decided to go into business for herself. She never forgot the music store at Heathrow, and Wolf founded AltiTunes Partners LP, now a chain of music stores with 28 locations. All but one are in airports (one is called Train Tunes, and it is located inside Grand Central Station in New York). AltITUNES' five year mission is to become the leading brand for small format, extraordinary location, music and electronics retailing with an expanding network of domestic and international locations.

Plans include at least 10 more airport locations. Over the next five years, AltiTUNES will expand to other extraordinary locations such as hospitals, hotels, and travel plazas. Its latest innovation is that shoppers can carry a PDA-sized device that lets them scan any CD they pick off the shelf and hear selections of music. The EARport™ is another innovation at AltiTUNES that features a series of interactive listening stations that are programmed to preview music and help customers decide on their music selections. The EARport features individual stations (which are each sponsored by a record label or distributor), as well as a top 100 station. All are equipped with headphones so as not to disturb other customers. Members of AltiTUNES's retail staff match the music they play to the audience, which varies at each specific location and at different times of the day. Amy Nye Wolf's success sprang from an idea she saw while traveling, and she found a way to take what somebody else had done and move it to the next level.

CASE DISCUSSION QUESTIONS

1. How did Amy Nye Wolf discover her business opportunity?
2. How did she evaluate whether it was a good opportunity or not?
3. What did she copy from the store in Heathrow?
4. What innovations did Wolf add to AltiTUNES to make her idea unique?
5. How do you think Wolf and her staff continue to identify new opportunities for AltiTUNES?

A Sample Feasibility Study[1]

PET ÉLAN

I. DESCRIPTION OF YOUR BUSINESS

In recent years, there has been an increase in the number of households that have pets, especially dogs and cats. Further, there is emerging a steadily growing group of pet owners that is willing to purchase upscale, unique products for these important members of their family. Pet Élan is an upscale boutique for these discriminating pet owners. Pet Élan will offer high-quality pet products to discerning individuals who wish their pets to enjoy a healthy, fun, and elegant lifestyle while being pampered. By carefully selecting luxurious accessories made with superior materials, Pet Élan will provide an elite product line that celebrates the uniqueness of each animal's personality.

II. THE PRODUCT/SERVICE

Unique Features: Benefits

Pet Élan will offer products that promote a healthy, fun, and elegant lifestyle for dogs and cats. Our products are grouped into three primary categories: dietary products, playtime products, and accessories.

Dietary Products

Pet Élan will offer all-natural pet food and treats, full of essential vitamins and nutrients to promote a healthy diet. We will carry two to three top-selling brands of organic pet food from the industry leaders such as Newman's Own Organics,[2] Natura Pet Products,[3] and Organix.[4] We will also feature snacks and treats from Old Mother Hubbard,[5] Three Dog Bakery,[6] Flint River Ranch,[7] and Howling Hound Bakery.[8]

Playtime Products

Playing with one's pet is also a key ingredient for a pet's healthy lifestyle. Pet Élan will offer products that enable owners and their pets to play in style. For dogs, we will offer toys for chewing, retrieving, tugging, and chasing. For cats, we will offer toys stuffed with premium grade catnip and other toys to chase and fetch. We will offer exclusive toy brands such as Happy Dog Toys,[9] KONG Toys,[10] and Fat Cat, Inc.[11]

Accessories

Pet Élan will make walking or traveling with a dog or cat an extension of the owner's unique style with leashes, collars, and travel bags that make a statement. We will also offer pet home accessories including food and water bowls, pet furniture and pillows, and pet clothing made from fine fabrics such as silk, suede, and faux fur.

Unlike other pet stores, Pet Élan will target clientele who demand top quality in pet couture. To fulfill this demand, Pet Élan will order pet clothing and accessories from the trendiest brands such as Woof: The Small Dog Company,[12] Dogz Togz,[13] and Ruff Ruff and Meow.[14]

Unique Features: Limitations

One of the largest threats to the luxury pet accessory industry is the presence of online stores. Pet Élan will compete with these online retailers, as well as other local pet stores. Consumers have the opportunity to comparison shop on the Internet, so Pet Élan will need to carefully determine the pricing strategy for each line of accessories to remain competitive. However, it is likely that pet owners will want to sample and view unique products we carry and will be willing to come to our store for its one-of-a-kind shopping experience—and bring their pets with them.

The rise of larger chain pet stores, like PETCO and PETsMART, has made it much easier for pet owners to satisfy all their pet needs in one place. These stores are now offering pet apparel, pet furniture, and natural pet food. Pet Élan will offer a higher quality, but more expensive, product mix that may overlap with these stores in some areas. To counter this, Pet Élan will showcase the products we carry that cannot be obtained at the larger retailers.

Competitive Advantage

Pet Élan's competitive advantage is quality and the ability to provide customers with the feeling that pampering their pets is an integral part of a healthy, fun, and contemporary lifestyle. Pet Élan must establish this reputation through *high quality products* and *selective advertising* and through *exceptional customer service*.

Stage of Development

Pet Élan is currently in the idea stage. This feasibility study is the first step in exploring the market potential for a luxury pet store. The current time frame for introducing Pet Élan is one year. Pet Élan has set the following milestones to accomplish prior to launch:

- Complete feasibility study: month 1.
- Begin and complete business plan: months 2–4.
- Pursue start-up capital: months 5–6.
- Receive start-up capital: month 7.
- Identify store location and secure appropriate permits: months 7–8.
- Plan and order inventory: month 9.
- Receive inventory and set up store: months 10–11.
- Store launch: month 12.

Legal Restrictions and Rights

Pet Élan will operate as a Sub-Chapter S Corporation to ensure limited personal liability and for tax advantages. Pet Élan will have one owner, who will have day-to-day responsibility for running the business. The corporation will receive all income generated by the business and pay the owner a salary and/or reinvest in the store. A board of directors will be appointed by the owner.

Insurance Requirements

Although business insurance may not be *required,* Pet Élan will purchase insurance to protect the corporation's assets and to benefit employees:

- Property insurance will cover the business in the event of damage or loss to the business property. The insurance will need to cover the store location's fixtures, cash registers/computers and any other equipment, any store furniture such as display tables and shelving, as well as inventory and supplies.
- Liability insurance will protect the business against the unfortunate situation of a customer or employee being injured on the property and suing.[15]

As an employer, Pet Élan will also need to secure additional insurance for:

- **Workers' compensation insurance:** The Workers' Compensation and Workers' Occupational Diseases Acts require employers to provide insurance for accidental deaths, injuries, and occupational diseases of employees arising in the course of employment. Temporary workers who normally do not receive company benefits are still provided workers' compensation. The Illinois Workers' Compensation Act requires all employers to post a notice in the workplace that explains workers' rights and lists the name and address of the workers' compensation carrier.
- **Unemployment insurance:** Since Pet Élan will most likely employ one or more workers in each of 20 or more calendar weeks, the business will be required to make unemployment insurance contributions to the Illinois Department of Employment Security.[16]

Trends Related to the Product or Service

Several studies show that pet ownership is at an all-time high and that people are taking better care of their pets and spending more money on them than previously. Surveys conducted every two years by the American Pet Products Manufacturers Association, Inc. (APPMA) show that 63.4 million households have a pet, compared to 52.6 million households a decade ago.[17] Pet Élan will cater to the increasing number of customers that consider their pets a full-fledged member of the family.

Trends in Customer Demographics

The demographics of the typical customers of the pet industry have been shifting over recent years from married with children, to younger, cohabitating couples who are waiting longer for marriage, as well as married baby boomers looking to fill their empty nests, and single households composed of divorcees and seniors looking for companionship. In fact, only one-third of all pet owners today are married with children.[18]

Trends in Pet Products

The pet products industry is booming. The upscale pet services industry was named as a hot market by *Entrepreneur* magazine in its annual prediction of the hottest business ideas for both 2004 and 2005.[19] The APPMA also cites luxury, natural, and hygiene products as the top three amongst its top ten trends in pet gifts.[20] In fact, the APPMA further notes that high-tech and high-end products such as luxury doghouses are showing the most growth.[21]

Similar to the human food industry, pet food trends are moving toward more organic and natural products. The Organic Trade Association reported that organic pet food sales are up by 63 percent from last year and are growing at almost three times the rate of human organic food sales.[22]

III. THE INDUSTRY AND MARKET

Current Industry

Americans spent a total of $34.4 billion on pet food, care, and supplies in 2004, and the industry is estimated to increase to $35.9 billion in 2005. Sixty-five percent of this estimated total was spent on food and supplies alone (*supplies also included medicine*).[23]

This growing industry is made up of a diverse customer base. Although families have been the traditional focal point of pet-related businesses, only one-third of all pet owners today are married with children.[24] Pet Élan plans to not only target this traditional market, but also to reach out to newer niche markets such as seniors, young unmarried, and middle-aged couples who are married but have no children.

Thirty-nine percent of Americans between the ages of 55 and 64 own a pet.[25] One of the largest percentages of pet owners is 18- to 34-year-old married Americans without children (52 percent). Of this group, 36 percent own a dog and 26 percent own a cat. In addition, this group is 33 percent more likely than the average American to own more than one pet.[26] Finally, 52 percent of married 35- and 54-year-olds without children have a pet and 31 percent have two or more.

Market Potential for This Industry

One out of three U.S. households owns a dog or cat,[27] and over 80 percent of pet owners purchased at least one accessory for their pet during the past year.[28] In 2003, MarketResearch.com predicted that the pet supplies industry would be an $8 billion market by 2007.[29] Business Communications Co. projects that the pet services industry as a whole (including pet food, pet services, and pet supplies) will grow to $36.3 billion by 2008.[30]

Despite this promising growth and if the economy continues to contract, customers may have less disposable income. The percentage they intended to spend on their cat or dog may be diverted for necessity purchases. However, according to pet industry analyst Julia Dvorko, "Owners tend to pamper their pets even when they have to cut back on [household] spending. After all, even during economic downturns, people give gifts to family members and buy special treats for their children."[31]

The Competition

Pet Élan plans to open in the 60657 zip code area of Chicago, Illinois, locally known as Lakeview. There are 22 pet-related businesses in this zip code: nine are veterinarians, three are pet sitting/walking services, three are pet grooming services, three large chain pet stores (one PETsMart, two PETCO), two combination pet grooming/accessories stores, a combination boarding/training store, a pet adoption/accessories store, and one boutique called "Sam & Willy's: A Bow Meow Boutique."

While not competing directly in the 60657 area code market, national companies including Paul Mitchell, Omaha Steaks, Origins, Harley Davidson, and Old Navy are now offering lines of pet products ranging from dog shampoo, pet attire, and name-brand toys to gourmet treats and food.[32] Although these companies have recognizable brand identities, they do not specialize in the pet retail market. They do not carry a full line of pet products as Pet Élan will, and they cater more to impulse buyers rather than discerning pet owners.

The following table compares the strengths and weaknesses of a subset of the competitor pet stores in the 60657 area code, as well as online retailers, and highlights the differentiating features of Pet Élan.

Customers

According to the APPMA, 62 percent of households in the United States own a pet, and 46 percent of households own more than one pet. Also, as mentioned earlier, dogs or cats are found in at least one out of three households (in the United States).[33] Data collected on dog owners show that they are likely to be married high school graduates who own their homes. As income increases, the percentage of households with a dog increases as well.[34] In fact, 75 percent of the households with dogs have a combined income of greater than $35,000. This is consistent with the specific market profile of the clientele Pet Élan plans to target in the 60657 zip code.

Competitive Analysis of Pet Stores

Competitor Pet Stores in Zip Code	Strengths	Weaknesses	Differentiating Features of Pet Élan
Area pet grooming/ accessories stores	• Customers whose pets are being groomed can browse while they wait for their pets	• Limited selection • Pet grooming is core competency, not selling accessories	• Core competency and primary focus of store are on selecting and selling luxury pet products and accessories
PETCO[35]	• Well-established brand identity • All-in-one brick-and-mortar stores • Wide selection of basic pet necessities • Online shopping	• Does not sell pet food because of high shipping costs • Limited number of brands in pet clothing and accessories • Inexperienced sales associates	• Caters to discerning pet and owner tastes by providing high-end pet products and accessories • Store owner builds personal relationships with customers based on knowledgeable service that focuses on their individual preferences and pet's personality
PETsMart[36]	• Well-established brand identity • All-in-one brick-and-mortar stores • Wide selection of basic pet necessities • Online shopping	• Sells pet food online, but consumer faces high shipping costs • More pet clothing and accessories brands than PETCO but not high-end brands • Inexperienced sales associates	• Caters to discerning pet and owner tastes by providing high-end pet products and accessories • Store owner builds personal relationships with customers based on knowledgeable service that focuses on their individual preferences and pet's personality
Omaha Steaks[37]	• Customers may add on pet treats as an impulse when shopping for themselves or for gifts	• Limited selection—only offers one variety of pet treats	• Pet Élan will offer a wider variety of pet treats (all organic)
Old Navy/Harley Davidson[38]	• Recognizable brand • Can target impulse buyers who are making other purchases	• Products are not currently available on Web site • Very specific target audiences	• Pet Élan will target customers that look for the latest pet couture by focusing on brands made exclusively for pets
Sam & Willy's: A Bow Meow Boutique[39]	• Provides accessories and gifts to pets and their owners in a boutique setting • Provides variety of organic pet food brands	• Static Web site • Sponsor local animal shelters but doesn't have social entrepreneurial mission	• Web site will provide tips and trends for hip pet owners • Five percent of pretax profits will go to a local no-kill animal shelter

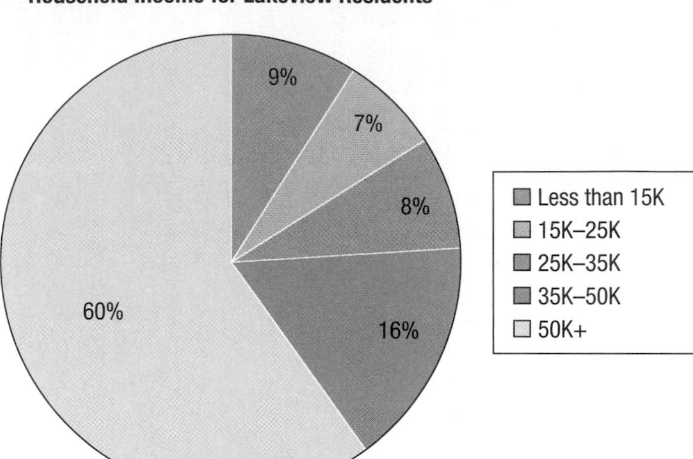

Seventy-six percent of Lakeview households have a combined income of $35,000 or more (see chart).[40]

Additionally, 30 percent of Lakeview residents own their homes, and 94 percent of residents over age 25 are high school graduates. The average family size is 2.56 with 7,523 residents below the age of 16 and 7,706 senior residents (65+). The median household income is $63,695.[41] Of the approximately 49,534 employed residents 16 years and older in the 60657 zip code area (as of the 2000 census), 64 percent are in "management, professional, and related occupations."[42]

Market Penetration

Pet Élan will serve customers in a boutique setting where pets are welcome to browse along with their owners. The store will operate with a social entrepreneurial mission and will donate 5 percent of pretax profits to a local no-kill animal shelter. Consistent with this socially responsible mission, Pet Élan will work with other area pet-related businesses to form a network of highly qualified veterinarians, as well as well-established boarding, grooming, in-home sitting, and training service providers. By connecting Pet Élan customers with reliable service providers, Pet Élan will also benefit from the reciprocal referrals from these service providers.

Pet Élan will also maintain a Web site, but initially only to provide the location and hours of operation. As the business grows, the Web site could include tips and trends information for current and future consumers to keep up with the latest in pet fashion accessories. Pet Élan will seek assistance from a local college or Small Business Development Center for the Web site and market research assistance.

When the Pet Élan storefront opens, we plan to advertise by hosting a series of pet fashion shows, combined with an adoption event with local pet shelters. The events will raise awareness among clientele and would help a good cause. Until Pet Élan breaks even, the store will rely on the advertising and public relations from partnering with other service providers to draw customers into the store.

IV. FINANCIAL PROJECTIONS

Pricing

Pet Élan will price the merchandise it intends to sell using cost-plus pricing. The base cost will be the wholesale cost of the pet product, and the markup component will be the profit Pet Élan will make on each product. For purposes of this feasibility study, Pet Élan will assume a 54 percent margin on goods sold. Because Pet Élan will be selling luxury products and because the target clientele is customers with a large percentage of disposable income, we will work to maximize the profit from each item sold.

The store will also follow a price skimming strategy, meaning it will set relatively high prices on the newest luxury products when they are first released, and then lower the price over time. By maintaining a wide selection of the newest fashions and accessories for cats and dogs, Pet Élan will be able to charge a higher price for newly released items, reducing prices as the trend becomes more mainstream.

The social entrepreneurial mission is to donate 5 percent of pretax profits to a local no-kill animal shelter, and this amount will be donated quarterly based on pretax profits from that quarter. Pet Élan made the following assumptions in putting together the sales revenue forecast for the first three years of operations:

- Pet Élan will sign a three-year rental agreement for a 2,000 square-foot storefront location. The rental property will be priced at $35 per square foot, with an additional real estate tax of $9.50 per square foot per annum.
- Pet Élan will be open for business six days a week (Monday through Saturday) from ten o'clock in the morning until seven o'clock in the evening. The store will be closed on Sunday.
- It is estimated that the average Pet Élan customer will spend $18 per visit and will visit the store, on average, two times per month.
- Pet Élan will contribute 5 percent of pre tax profits to a local no-kill animal shelter on a quarterly basis. This contribution has been accounted for in the pretax net profit (loss) forecast.

Based on these assumptions and a break-even analysis, Pet Élan's break-even sales will be $263,699, or $21,975 per month. This was calculated by determining the total fixed costs in the first year and by dividing it by a gross margin expressed as a percentage of sales.

Sales Revenue Forecast

Pet Élan forecasts gross revenues during year one of operations to be $296,740. The gross revenues for year two and year three are predicted to increase to $404,448 and $458,304, respectively.

Cost Forecast

Pet Élan will maintain an inventory of products in each of the three primary areas of focus mentioned earlier: dietary products, playtime products, and accessories. As products are purchased, Pet Élan will reorder monthly to maintain a sufficient inventory to serve its customers' needs. Pet Élan has estimated that initial inventory will cost $20,000. The wholesale cost of inventory for the first year is estimated to be $147,000. As the customer base grows, Pet Élan will need to have a significantly higher amount of inventory on hand to support increased demand. The future cost of inventory is forecast to be $186,880 for year two and $211,730 for year three.

Gross Margin

The gross margin (sales minus cost of goods sold) for Pet Élan during the first three years of operation is estimated to be $159,620, $217,568, and $246,574 respectively.

Operating Expenses

There are several operational costs associated with running a pet store like Pet Élan, and these are also accounted for in the budget forecast for the first three years of operation. These operational expenses include items such as rent, utilities, advertising costs, and professional services assistance. These operational costs are summarized in total operating expenses and are forecast to be $147,907 for year one, $190,881 for year two, and $201,744 for year three.

The owner will be the primary employee of Pet Élan for the first three months of operation. Beginning in the fourth month of operation, Pet Élan will hire one full-time sales associate. As the business grows, Pet Élan anticipates hiring a second full-time sales associate during the second year of operation. The full-time sales associates will assist the owner with customer service and other retail functions. Pet Élan will pay the sales associate approximately $12.25 per hour (or $25,500 per year) for the work.[43]

Profitability

The expected net profit of Pet Élan for the first year of operation is $10,660. This profit is expected to grow significantly in the future two years as some of the initial start-up costs are defrayed and the customer base becomes larger. In year two the net profit is forecast to be $25,345, and in year three it is estimated to be $42,589.

V. FUTURE ACTION PLAN

Start-up Capital

To start the business, Pet Élan will need to have enough start-up capital to cover leasing costs to secure the storefront location. The start-up capital will also need to cover insurance and operating expenses including appropriate licensing, store utilities, and professional services such as legal and accounting assistance. Initial inventory, as well as retail equipment needs (such as a cash register) will require a large initial investment. These needs will be funded through the start-up capital that Pet Élan secures prior to opening. The amount needed is estimated to be $70,000.

Sources of Start-up Capital

The start-up capital of $70,000 is composed of 45 percent (or $31,500) of the owner's personal savings, 25 percent (or $17,500) of a bank loan, in addition to two equity investors (one family member of the owner and one local veterinarian), each with a 15 percent stake (or $10,500) in the company.

Further Information Needed

To ensure the successful opening of Pet Élan, we must have a deeper understanding of the customer needs in the area. Conducting market research in the 60657 zip code area, using techniques such as surveys and/or focus groups of customers in Pet Élan's target market, could assess these needs. Pet Élan should also begin to approach other pet service providers in the area to explore potential partnership opportunities that could help raise awareness about both Pet Élan and the partnering business. This would also allow the owner of Pet Élan to form a network within the local pet products and services industry.

Writing a Business Plan

Pet Élan's next step is to create a business plan to further explore the business model of Pet Élan from an objective point of view. By identifying strengths and weaknesses, opportunities and threats for Pet Élan as compared to other market competitors, the company will have a much better chance of reaching the business and financial objectives outlined in this feasibility study. The business plan will also provide vital information about the business to potential investors and allow them to evaluate the viability of Pet Élan's business model.

Support Needed

Pet Élan will seek guidance from a local Small Business Development Center. Pet Élan will review the initial draft of the business plan with a volunteer from the Service Corps of Retired Executives (SCORE), which is associated with the Small Business Association, to learn from his or her experience. Pet Élan will also form an advisory board made up of small business owners and members of the pet retail industry.

FINANCIALS–SUMMARY

	Year 1	Year 2	Year 3
Revenue	$296,740	$404,448	$458,304
Cost of Goods Sold	137,120	186,880	211,730
Gross margin	159,620	217,568	246,574
Operating expenses	$147,907	$190,881	$201,744
Net profit (loss) pretax	$ 11,713	$ 26,687	$ 44,830
Net profit (loss) pretax and post contribution (5%)	$ 10,660	$ 25,345	$ 42,589

FINANCIALS—YEAR 1

	Month 1 September	Month 2 October	Month 3 November	Month 4 December	Month 5 January	Month 6 February
Sales	**$11,620**	**$16,900**	**$20,060**	**$27,460**	**$20,060**	**$21,120**
Less Cost of Goods Sold	$ 5,370	$ 7,810	$ 9,270	$12,690	$ 9,270	$ 9,760
Gross Margin	**$ 6,250**	**$ 9,090**	**$10,790**	**$14,770**	**$10,790**	**$11,360**
Operating Expenses						
Utilities	185	160	165	180	200	200
Salaries	2,500	2,500	2,500	2,500	2,500	2,500
Labor	—	—	—	2,125	2,125	2,125
Payroll Taxes and Benefits	313	313	313	578	578	578
Advertising	300	300	300	300	300	300
Website	20	20	20	20	20	20
Office Supplies	150	75	50	50	50	50
Insurance	250	250	250	400	400	400
Maintenance and Cleaning	50	50	50	50	50	50
Legal and Accounting	350	350	350	350	350	350
Licenses	300	—	—	—	—	—
Bags, Paper, etc.	150	150	200	250	250	250
Telephone	85	85	85	85	85	85
Miscellaneous	200	200	200	200	200	200
Rent	5,833	5,833	5,833	5,833	5,833	5,833
Total Operating Expenses (Fixed Costs):	**10,686**	**10,286**	**10,316**	**12,921**	**12,941**	**12,941**
Gross Profit (Loss)	**(4,436)**	**(1,196)**	**475**	**1,849**	**(2,151)**	**(1,581)**
Contribution to Charity (5% of net):	—	—	***24***	***92***	—	—
Net Profit (Loss) Pre-Tax:	***(4,436)***	***(1,196)***	***451***	***1,756***	***(2,151)***	***(1,581)***

First year fixed costs (FC)	$ 147,910
Contribution Margin Ratio (CMR) ((sales - cogs)/sales)	53.8%
Annual breakeven sales (FC / CMR)	$ 274,970
Average monthly breakeven sales	$ 22,910

Month 7 March	Month 8 April	Month 9 May	Month 10 June	Month 11 July	Month 12 August	Total
$24,290	**$26,400**	**$28,510**	**$31,680**	**$35,900**	**$32,740**	**$296,740**
$11,220	$12,200	$13,170	$14,640	$16,590	$15,130	$137,120
$13,070	**$14,200**	**$15,340**	**$17,040**	**$19,310**	**$17,610**	**$159,620**
180	170	165	185	185	185	2,160
2,500	2,500	2,500	2,500	2,500	2,500	30,000
2,125	2,125	2,125	2,125	2,125	2,125	19,125
578	578	578	578	578	578	6,141
300	300	300	300	300	300	3,600
20	20	20	20	20	20	240
50	50	50	50	50	50	725
400	400	400	400	400	400	4,350
50	50	50	50	50	50	600
350	350	350	350	350	350	4,200
—	—	—	—	—	—	300
300	300	300	300	300	300	3,050
85	85	85	85	85	85	1,020
200	200	200	200	200	200	2,400
5,833	5,833	5,833	5,833	5,833	5,833	69,996
12,971	**12,961**	**12,956**	**12,976**	**12,976**	**12,976**	**147,907**
99	**1,239**	**2,384**	**4,064**	**6,334**	**4,634**	**11,713**
5	***62***	***119***	***203***	***317***	***232***	***1,054***
94	***1,177***	***2,265***	***3,861***	***6,017***	***4,402***	***$ 10,660***

FINANCIALS—YEAR 2

	September	October	November	December	January	February
Sales:	**$31,680**	**$33,790**	**$35,900**	**$35,900**	**$29,570**	**$32,740**
Less Cost of Goods Sold	$14,640	$15,610	$16,590	$16,590	$13,660	$15,130
Gross Margin	**$17,040**	**$18,180**	**$19,310**	**$19,310**	**$15,910**	**$17,610**
Operating Expenses						
Utilities	195	170	175	190	210	210
Salaries	2,500	2,500	2,500	2,500	2,500	2,500
Labor	4,250	4,250	4,250	4,250	4,250	4,250
Payroll Taxes and Benefits	844	844	844	844	844	844
Advertising	400	400	400	400	400	400
Website	30	30	30	30	30	30
Office Supplies	100	100	100	100	100	100
Insurance	550	550	550	550	550	550
Maintenance and Cleaning	60	60	60	60	60	60
Legal and Accounting	400	400	400	400	400	400
Licenses	300	—	—	—	—	—
Bags, Paper, etc.	400	400	400	400	400	400
Telephone	100	100	100	100	100	100
Miscellaneous	225	225	225	225	225	225
Rent	5,833	5,833	5,833	5,833	5,833	5,833
Total Operating Expenses:	**16,187**	**15,862**	**15,867**	**15,882**	**15,902**	**15,902**
Gross Profit (Loss)	**853**	**2,318**	**3,443**	**3,428**	**8**	**1,708**
Contribution to Charity (5% of net):	43	116	172	171	0	85
Net Profit (Loss) Pre-Tax:	**811**	**2,202**	**3,271**	**3,257**	**8**	**1,623**

March	April	May	June	July	August	Total
$31,680	$32,740	$34,850	$35,900	$33,790	$35,900	$404,448
$14,640	$15,130	$16,100	$16,590	$15,610	$16,590	$186,880
$17,040	**$17,610**	**$18,750**	**$19,310**	**$18,180**	**$19,310**	**$217,568**
190	180	175	195	195	195	2,280
2,500	2,500	2,500	2,500	2,500	2,500	30,000
4,250	4,250	4,250	4,250	4,250	4,250	51,000
844	844	844	844	844	844	10,125
400	400	400	400	400	400	4,800
30	30	30	30	30	30	360
100	100	100	100	100	100	1,200
550	550	550	550	550	550	6,600
60	60	60	60	60	60	720
400	400	400	400	400	400	4,800
—	—	—	—	—	—	300
400	400	400	400	400	400	4,800
100	100	100	100	100	100	1,200
225	225	225	225	225	225	2,700
5,833	5,833	5,833	5,833	5,833	5,833	69,996
15,882	**15,872**	**15,867**	**15,887**	**15,887**	**15,887**	**190,881**
1,158	**1,738**	**2,883**	**3,423**	**2,293**	**3,423**	**26,687**
58	87	144	171	115	171	1,334
1,100	**1,651**	**2,739**	**3,252**	**2,179**	**3,252**	**$ 25,345**

FINANCIALS—YEAR 3

	September	October	November	December	January	February
Total Sales:	**$35,904**	**$33,792**	**$38,016**	**$42,240**	**$33,792**	**$35,904**
Cost of Goods Sold:	$16,590	$15,610	$17,560	$19,510	$15,610	$16,590
Gross Margin	**$19,314**	**$18,182**	**$20,456**	**$22,730**	**$18,182**	**$19,314**
Operating Expenses						
Utilities	205	180	185	200	220	220
Salaries	2,750	2,750	2,750	2,750	2,750	2,750
Variable Labor	4,674	4,674	4,674	4,674	4,674	4,674
Payroll Taxes and Benefits	928	928	928	928	928	928
Advertising	400	400	400	400	400	400
Website	32	32	32	32	32	32
Office Supplies	120	120	120	120	120	120
Insurance	570	570	570	570	570	570
Maintenance and Cleaning	70	70	70	70	70	70
Legal and Accounting	440	440	440	440	440	440
Licenses	300	—	—	—	—	—
Bags, Paper, etc.	420	420	420	420	420	420
Telephone	125	125	125	125	125	125
Miscellaneous	225	225	225	225	225	225
Rent	5,833	5,833	5,833	5,833	5,833	5,833
Total Operating Expenses:	**17,092**	**16,767**	**16,772**	**16,787**	**16,807**	**16,807**
Net Profit (Loss) Pre-Tax:	**2,222**	**1,415**	**3,684**	**5,943**	**1,375**	**2,507**
Contribution (5%)	111	71	184	297	69	125
Final Net Profit (Loss) Pre-Tax:	**2,111**	**1,344**	**3,500**	**5,646**	**1,306**	**2,382**

March	April	May	June	July	August	Total
$38,016	**$40,128**	**$40,128**	**$40,128**	**$40,128**	**$40,128**	**$458,304**
$17,560	$18,540	$18,540	$18,540	$18,540	$18,540	$211,730
$20,456	**$21,588**	**$21,588**	**$21,588**	**$21,588**	**$21,588**	**$246,574**
200	190	185	205	205	205	2,400
2,750	2,750	2,750	2,750	2,750	2,750	33,000
4,674	4,674	4,674	4,674	4,674	4,674	56,088
928	928	928	928	928	928	11,136
400	400	400	400	400	400	4,800
32	32	32	32	32	32	384
120	120	120	120	120	120	1,440
570	570	570	570	570	570	6,840
70	70	70	70	70	70	840
440	440	440	440	440	440	5,280
—	—	—	—	—	—	300
420	420	420	420	420	420	5,040
125	125	125	125	125	125	1,500
225	225	225	225	225	225	2,700
5,833	5,833	5,833	5,833	5,833	5,833	69,996
16,787	**16,777**	**16,772**	**16,792**	**16,792**	**16,792**	**201,744**
3,669	**4,811**	**4,816**	**4,796**	**4,796**	**4,796**	**44,830**
183	241	241	240	240	240	2,242
3,486	**4,570**	**4,575**	**4,556**	**4,556**	**4,556**	**$ 42,589**

INITIAL CALCULATIONS

Cost Assumptions First Year of Operations

Fixed Costs (FC)		**Monthly**	**Annually**
Lease payment ($35 / sq. foot)		$ 5,833	$ 70,000
Utilities		200	2,400
Insurance		833	10,000
Salary of Owner		2,500	30,000
Salary of Sales Assistant		2,125	25,500
Advertising		200	2,400
General supplies		300	3,600
Professional Services		667	8,000
Miscellaneous Expenses		417	5,000
Website		20	240
Total		13,095	157,140
Variable Costs (VC)		**Monthly**	**Annually**
Cost of Goods Sold		11,427	137,120
Total		28,250	339,000
Break-Even Amount		**Monthly**	**Annually**
Contribution margin ratio (CMR)		53.8%	53.8%
Breakeven (FC \ CMR)		$ 24,340	$292,082
	Daily	**Monthly**	**Annually**
Breakeven number of customers	45	1,352	486,803

Assumptions:

Rental location will be 2,000 square feet

Average customer spends $18 per visit and comes to the store on average twice per month.

One Time Startup Costs	
Licensing & permits	$ 300
Decorating	$ 800
Signage	$ 5,000
Beginning Inventory	$40,000
Fixtures and Equipment	$ 6,000
Professional fees (accountant, attorney)	$ 5,000
Total	$57,100

LEARNING OBJECTIVES

This chapter will help you:

LO1 Know when and why part-time entrepreneurship makes sense.

LO2 Learn the four major paths to part-time entrepreneurship.

LO3 Understand what it takes to be successful in part-time entrepreneurship.

LO4 Learn how to optimize your delegation within the firm.

LO5 Learn the benefits of bootstrapping.

LO6 Learn the ethical challenges of part-time entrepreneurship.

LO7 Find out about the challenges of moving from part-time to full-time entrepreneurship.

■ Dan Murza stumbled into entrepreneurship when he successfully sold a sports jersey for a 1000% profit. Aided by his involvement with the online auction center eBay.com and fueled by his creative problem-solving strategies, Murza's business has grown past his beginning part-time venture into something larger. What are some of the advantages to a small business owner of starting an enterprise in part-time work?

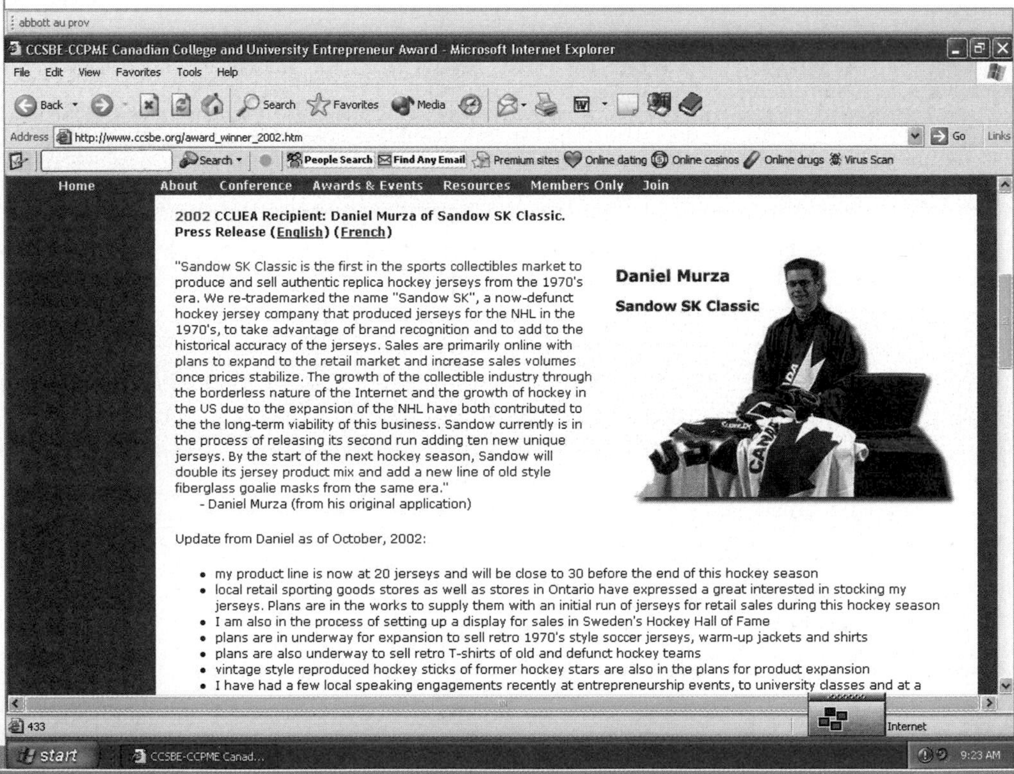

CHAPTER 5

Small Business Entry: Paths to Part-Time Entrepreneurship

Focus on Small Business: Dan Murza[1]

Dan was a sophomore at the University of Saskatoon when he got hooked on eBay.com, the giant online auction site. At the time, the New York Giants had made it to the Super Bowl, and Dan had one of the team's old jerseys in mint condition. Borrowing his grandfather's Polaroid camera, he took a couple of shots and scanned them. Putting the pictures and a description of the jersey on eBay during Super Bowl week, he made a 1,000 percent profit over his original purchase price. This launched his part-time business.

With no more inventory and no money to buy inventory, Dan needed to think creatively. Dan's solution was to convince the manager of a local hockey equipment store to let him buy jerseys at wholesale and resell them on eBay. Aware of his precarious financial situation, Dan also asked permission to pay the store after his eBay customer paid him. This way he had no out-of-pocket expenses. Dan kept up his part-time business on eBay throughout college, juggling classes, friends, and the rest of his life.

Dan moved from part-time to full-time business when he started Sandow SK Classic, a company that would sell recreations of historic hockey jerseys.

He subcontracted the manufacturing of the jerseys, and the clothing companies would have to be paid up front. To get that money, Dan was going to need outside investors, and that meant it was time to do a business plan.

DISCUSSION QUESTIONS

1. Would you call Dan's first foray into small business planned or happenstance? Why?
2. What was the problem Dan faced in getting inventory to sell? How did he handle it?
3. How did Dan's business grow over the years?
4. What are likely to be some of the problems Dan faces as he takes his business full time?

Why Part-Time Businesses Are Important

LO1
Know when and why part-time entrepreneurship makes sense.

While Dan Murza's success might be better than average, his story is repeated millions of times a year. Dan's first business developed as a spur of the moment activity. The simplicity of starting a part-time business on eBay made it fast and easy to do. Much of what Dan did in that first business laid the groundwork for Sandow SK Classic, a business that utilized a business plan, outside investors, and considerable preparation.

The difference in Dan's first and second firms is the difference between part-time and full-time entrepreneurship. Working at your business 35 hours a week or less is called **part-time self-employment**. Working part time means that the entrepreneur can do other work, such as have a job in another company, go to school, or take care of family. For people working more than 35 hours a week, the term is **full-time self-employment**. Working full-time means that the majority of one's time is spent on the business.

part-time self-employment
Working for yourself for 35 or fewer hours a week.

full-time self-employment
Working for yourself for more than 35 hours a week.

When you enter business, you make a choice about pursuing a full-time or part-time approach. Full-time approaches include buying or inheriting existing businesses, franchising, or opening a new full-time business. Those approaches are discussed in Chapter 6.

This chapter considers part-time approaches to business. Part-time businesses are tremendously important for two reasons. First, part-time self-employment is the way most people start in entrepreneurship. In the Panel Study of Entrepreneurial Dynamics (PSED), about three-quarters of those starting a business already work full time for someone else, and so are pursuing their new business part time.[2] Virtually every business started by winners of the Global Student Entrepreneur Awards started out as a part-time business. Famous businesses like Apple, Dell, Microsoft, Mary Kay Cosmetics, the Ford Modeling Agency, or even Lionel Trains started out as part-time firms.[3] The ease and low cost of entry and exit of part-time entrepreneurship means that people can try their hand at a variety of different businesses without major risk. These part-time self-employment opportunities are important because they let entrepreneurs learn about different aspects of the business without necessarily betting all they own on each effort.

Second, part-time self-employment is a major portion of all current entrepreneurship. Of the 23.7 million small businesses in the United States in 2003, around half were part-time businesses,[4] and that statistic understates the real numbers. Because of this ease and low cost, there is tremendous **volatility** as individuals jump in and out of self-employment quickly and frequently. This changing situation means that government counts of business owners or self-employed people are often at their worst tracking the smallest, newest, and least established of firms.[5] For example, teenagers earning less than $1,400 a year from work such as babysitting or lawn mowing do not have to report their income. Folks who sell occasionally through garage sales or

volatility
The frequency of business starts and stops.

online at auction sites such as eBay may simply list additional income without specifying the source of the income as a business they own. These examples come in under the radar of government, but represent millions of people. For example, there are more than 6 million people selling online through product and service auction sites, few of whom are tracked by the government.[6]

When to Consider Part-Time Entrepreneurship

These days, the conventional wisdom is that if you are serious about starting a business, you ought to start a business full time and prepare for it by doing a business plan. That makes a lot of sense, since a business plan enables you to look at every aspect of your business. Business plans are also important if you intend to ask others for expertise or financial investments. However, running a business full time can be a major commitment and is not always the best way to go about becoming an entrepreneur.

There are three situations in which it might make better sense to undertake a part-time business first. One of these is when you are new to business and need to *gain basic experience*. If you have not been involved in pricing, buying, and selling, learning how to do such things makes a lot of sense before launching the business of your dreams. You might want to obtain other types of experience before starting a full-scale business or writing a business plan. These can include experience in the industry, in the line of business, in the locality of the specific market you plan to serve, in managing cash, or in managing yourself in self-employment.

A second type of situation is one in which you *lack resources* to pursue a full-scale business or create a business plan. Time is probably the ultimate resource, and starting a business can tax it heavily. Estimates suggest that a business plan may take anywhere from 50 to 200 hours or more if you are new to business and working on your own.[7] Starting a full-time business can absorb 70 hours a week or more in its early stages. You might not be able to commit the time to work that way, and pursuing a precursor makes a lot of sense. It also makes sense if you are missing other resources. Think about Dan Murza. He lacked a resource—inventory. By pursuing a small-scale business online through eBay, he was able to match his business scale to the resources available.

The third type of situation is *a narrow window of opportunity*. Dan saw this when the New York Giants were in the Super Bowl. He identified a time when interest would be high, and his Giants jersey would be a hot property. He had to act fast, and that meant going the part-time route. Part-time businesses can generally be created quickly, and they offer a concrete example of a business to customers, suppliers, and others. When there is not enough time to do a business plan or get the entire business going, pursuing a part-time business to capture the attention of others makes a lot of sense. (See Fig. 5.1.)

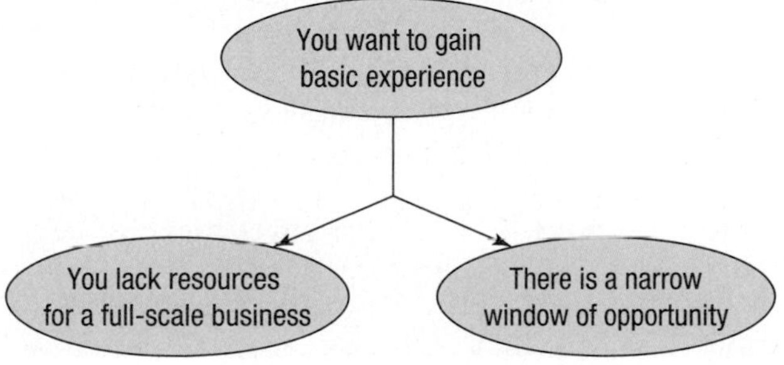

FIGURE 5.1

When to Consider a Part-Time Business

What Kinds of Part-Time Entrepreneurship Exist?

LO2
Learn the four major paths to part-time entrepreneurship.

Fundamentally, part-time entrepreneurs sell products and services. Some provide these personally; others resell products or services produced by others. The forms their businesses take tend to fall into four major categories—*stands, homes, consignment,* and *mail order*. Each of these is discussed below, along with the key success factors and risks for that type of business.

Stand Retail

Stand retailing—the roadside, flea-market, farmers' market, or craft fair business—is one of the most ancient forms of small business. It is mentioned in the Bible, and marketplaces full of stands have been found in virtually all archeological digs. Today stands tend to be either semipermanent ones that remain in one place and are built to be sturdy, like a farmer's roadside stand, or movable ones that can be quickly assembled and disassembled for use in farmers' markets, flea markets, and craft fairs. To get started inexpensively, people often start selling from the back of their cars or using a folding table or blanket laid out with wares.

The advantages of stand businesses is that you can start with little investment. Stands can be a box or ground cloth. They also do not require a lot of investment in inventory. There are a variety of locations where a stand can be set up, such as flea markets. Stands can also be quickly established and easily ended as a business. Stands vary widely in the products they sell. The disadvantages of stands are the variable income they provide, the difficulty of making sure your stand and business meet legal requirements such as compliance with registering, licensing, and zoning (for help with this look at the section on "Exchange: Dealing with Others" later in the chapter), the problem of knowing how to price goods, and building up a customer base for your stand.

While stands can be among the least expensive ways to set up a shop, a high-end version exists too. It is the mall cart, if it is on wheels, or kiosk, when it is in a fixed location. Carts and kiosks cost between $2,000 and $10,000,[8] although carts can be rented from many malls. Carts and kiosks are often among the most expensive locations in the mall in terms of rent per square foot. A cart in a high-end mall like the

■ This part-time business worker has his finger on the pulse of a niche market, capitalizing on the limitations experienced by boaters who are hungry for a sweet snack. His signs and position on a floating deck create visibility and boost market desire for his products. His stand allows him to easily take down and set up shop elsewhere as he perceives needs.

Mall of America in Bloomington, Minnesota, can go for $2,300 or 15 percent of sales a month in rent.[9] Costs include rent (usually a percentage of sales with a base monthly rental), mall member fees, and cart design costs. On the other hand, carts can be rented for specific periods (holiday seasons, weekends). The advantage of carts and kiosks is that your products can be seen by more than 100,000 people a week as they walk through the mall. One idea to minimize rents is to consider placing your cart or kiosk away from the high-traffic locations, but near specific stores where your most likely customers would come from, for example, putting a trading card kiosk near a mall arcade or sporting goods store.[10]

The key success factor for a stand is having a location where there is enough foot or vehicle traffic to sustain the business. High traffic concentrations are why flea markets, farmers markets, and craft fairs are popular locales for stands. However, even in these, locations will have traffic levels that vary. Try to locate on or near a major walkway, or near the food, entertainment, or major vendor areas to get the most traffic. Always make sure to keep your documentation (e.g., vendor's permits, licenses, tax numbers, etc.) handy for checks by police and venue officials.

The other success factor is inventory. You might be selling products you make yourself. If you are looking for others' products to sell, there are a host of sources. Always start with what you know. If you have seen someone's work and think it would sell, ask if you can be an agent or reseller. You can go online to search for products or services to resell at the Industrial Resource Network, or at Thomas Register's online site, which has a print version available in many libraries. You can also do a search online for the manufacturers of particular products.[11]

http://powersourcing.com

www.thomasregister.com

Home Retail

Another major approach to part-time retailing builds from homes—the party and door-to-door model. One home-venue approach is the shopping party. In these, the retailer arranges a get-together at someone's home where participants can socialize and get acquainted with the retailer and the products. Pioneered by cosmetics firms, most notably Avon and Mary Kay, it is a widely used technique with dozens of franchised sales operations using it today. One example is Sheila di Matteo who created Parties Victorian, where hostesses throw a party with a Victorian theme, and attendees can purchase Victorian themed goods and reproductions for their homes and parties. Originally, Sheila's friends recognized her skill at finding Victorian looking products, and asked her to buy goods for them. Sheila turned this into a part-time business and later began franchising it.[12]

The advantages of home businesses are the speed and ease of setup, the low cost of getting started, and the ability to do the work away from your home and employer, thus minimizing potential conflicts. The disadvantages come from always working "on the road," lacking a base from which you can organize and work, having a highly variable income, and finding ways for customers to get in touch with you (although cell phones and e-mail have made a major difference).

You can arrange sales parties without selling a franchised product. One of the ways to make arrangements with minimal setup is to have the party at someone else's home. This person in return gets a portion of the proceeds in product discounts, products, or cash. You and the host work up a guest list, and the arrangements for refreshments and participation presents are agreed to in the early stages of the negotiation.

Picking hosts with good contacts and a pleasant home is the key factor in party success. Often the opportunity for repeat customers and customers hosting later parties presents itself, and it's a great way to keep sales growing.

In door-to-door selling, the retailer goes to the home to demonstrate and sell the product. Matching the product to the community is a key factor. For example, it is hard to find good prospects for buyers of seeds if you are working an apartment community. Think about the income and lifestyle of the community with respect to your product.

■ Pampered Chef is an example of a home retail business which grows its clientele by hosting demonstration parties. If you were a home retail business worker, what are some of the ways you would get your message out to the market? What priorities involved in home retail are unique to this type of business?

The fundamental success factor in door-to-door selling is closing the sale. *Closing* means getting the customer to agree to buy. Amazingly, asking the customer to buy is often all that is needed. If the answer is no, the natural comeback is to ask customers what they need to know or have in order to buy. If they tell you something they need, your job becomes trying to meet that need. Meanwhile you continue to ask if they are ready to buy. Only if you cannot meet a need do you give up and go to the next customer.[13]

network marketing
An approach to selling in which the salesperson recruits customers to become distributors of the product or service to others.

Another variation on the home model is **network marketing** efforts, also called multilevel marketing or MLM. These are organized through a parent organization; agents sell in part using in-home parties and person-to-person sales. The added twist is that current salespeople are invited to recruit additional new salespeople. The recruiter gets a commission from the sales made by his or her recruits. Everything mentioned above also applies in network marketing, with the added need to carefully check into the parent organization and the terms of the recruiting. The extra caution is necessary because illegal pyramid schemes are often made to look like legal MLMs. For example, where the fees paid by newly recruited network members are paid directly to more senior network members, there is a good chance you are seeing an illegal pyramid scheme. You can check with the Federal Trade Commission (www.ftc.gov) and the Better Business Bureau (www.bbb.org).[14]

www.ftc.gov

www.bbb.org

Consignment Stores and Auctions

consignment shops
Retail stores in which customers can come and buy products placed in the shops by a wide variety of sellers.

auction
A business setting in which products consigned from multiple sellers are available for bidding by customers.

One popular way to sell is to give your product to someone else to sell. This can be done through consignment shops or auctions. **Consignment shops** are retail stores in which customers can come and buy products placed in the shops by a wide variety of sellers. The shop's owner handles the sale and gets a portion of the money from the sale in return (typically around 50 percent).

Auctions are a variation of the consignment shop. For auctions, customers are told where and when they can bid. Typically, in bricks-and-mortar auctions (auctions at specific physical locations), there is a chance to check out the merchandise before the bidding starts, while online auctions offer pictures and descriptions. Making the most of online auctions takes a special approach, which is detailed in Skill Module 5.1. The advice comes from Pamela Williams, a professor at Culver-Stockton College and the founder of Highlandgear.com—a sporting goods company that got started on eBay (with her living room as the warehouse) and eventually grew to be an eBay Power Seller and a full-time business with a warehouse in Quincy, Illinois.

Steps to eBay Success

List it, watch it sell, and collect your money. If only selling on eBay were really that simple. To sell on eBay requires a little skill, access to a few simple tools, and a little luck. The process for selling in a standard eBay auction can be broken down into a few simple required steps and some optional steps, which may help increase your selling success.

Step 1: Register for a seller's account. eBay members can sign up for a seller's account by providing credit card and bank account information or choosing the ID verification process, which helps eBay confirm that you are who you say you are and that you live and bank where you say you do.

Step 2: Create your auction. To do this you will need to create a short title and a complete description and fill in a few eBay blanks such as method of payment, shipping fees, etc. In this crucial step, a few things are important to remember:

a. Use key search words in the title to draw buyers in. It is especially useful to use the brand name or a unique product name. Think in terms of the key words you would use if you were searching for the product.

b. Give as much information as possible in the description, including product condition, flaws, paperwork included, original product packaging, etc.

c. To really succeed, especially if you are new to eBay, a digital photograph is necessary. It provides proof of the product and its condition, and buyers trust what they see.

d. Create a professional-looking auction with a word processor or Web design program. Fancy flashing animation is not necessary, but a professional auction look is. Even using a product such as Microsoft Word to center and boldface titles, create paragraphs, add font colors, and add graphics will help. You are not trying to show off graphics skills but to boost your legitimacy.

Step 3: Answer your e-mails. Potential buyers will ask lots of questions. Timely answers will help improve your standing. Buyers want to be able to trust you, and your friendly and quick response will help build that trust.

Step 4: When the auction is over, collect your money and mail the merchandise. Send the buyer an e-mail reminding him or her of how much is owed, the method of payment, and where to send the money. If you do not receive payment, don't be shy. In the sellers' section of eBay there are helpful hints about contacting bidders and filing nonpaying bidder notices. Most of the time collecting payment is not difficult, but if you run enough auctions, you will find some buyers who won't pay.

eBay has been called "the perfect marketplace," providing a place on the Internet that connects gigantic numbers of buyers and sellers worldwide in an open market. eBay does not guarantee that a buyer will receive a particular item or that the seller will receive the payment. With that in mind, eBay is an open community and the majority of the time the transactions are good.

The advantage of consignment approaches is that they permit full-time sales with only a part-time involvement from you, low setup cost, a low risk level, and the flexibility that comes from the variety of consignment stores and auctions available to you. The disadvantages include little effort being put forth to sell your product, high potential for competing offerings, long amount of time before payouts, and low profitability because of seller fees. Consignment shops are popular for used products such as antiques, collectibles, and clothing. In-person auctions are more common for large ticket items such as cars and antiques, while online auctions such as eBay.com offer almost everything.

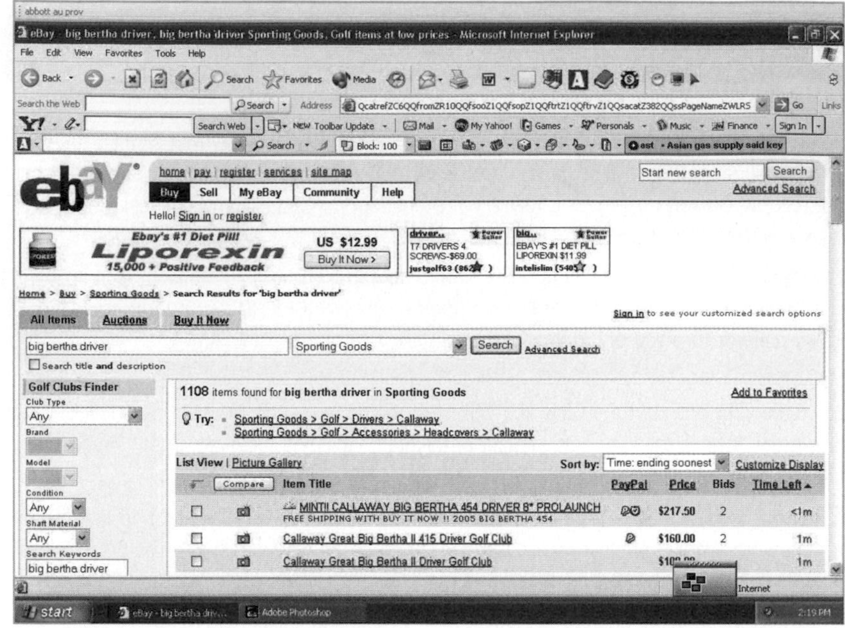

■ eBay.com, the online auction house where people like Dan Murza and Pamela Williams have gotten businesses off the ground, was itself originally a small business. By offering geographically dispersed sellers and buyers an unprecedented opportunity to search for and bid on an incredible variety of items, ranging from wedding dresses to cars, eBay has truly revolutionized the way people shop.

The primary success factor to look for in a consignment shop or auction is a location that gets good numbers of the kind of customers you think would be interested in your product. You can learn this best by visiting at busy times (e.g., Saturdays and Sundays) and slow ones (e.g., midweek). The best shops and auctions advertise locally. You also should look for the condition of the location itself and the quality and condition of the other merchandise. Also, check if the firm has computerized inventory checking. It helps customers find goods and helps you keep better track of fast and slow sellers.

If you can check with other consignees, that is usually best, but also be sure to check with the local Better Business Bureau about the business and its track record. As with everything, it is better to do some comparison shopping to make sure the consignment store or auction you have chosen is the best one for your goods.

Mail Order and Catalog Sales

Imagine that you have goods or services to sell but little time to spend on selling. Your product or service is one that people would recognize and understand how to use. Now also imagine that the customers are scattered across the city, country, or world. That is the situation for which mail order and catalog sales is made.

The advantages of mail order and catalog sales include the ability to sell on your schedule, low costs for getting started (especially if you place your goods in others' catalogs or online), the ability to get by without major inventory investments, and the potential for selling to large markets. The challenges include preparation before selling, the need for writing and photography skills, the need to find the right market for your offering, and a way to get customers' attention.

Mail order sales are typically made from ads placed in newspapers or magazines. Despite the name, orders these days might be taken online or by phone as well as by mail. Marketing is key to successful mail order sales. One part is preparing an ad that does a good job of answering the customers' questions and entices them to buy. The other key element is placing the ad in newspapers or magazines in which your target market is likely to see it. These are discussed in Skill Module 5.2.

Everyone is familiar with catalogs. They offer customers a description and often a picture of the product and tell the customer how to order it by mail, phone, or online. Catalogs are usually targeted at particular types of consumers and focus on particular types of products.

Making Mail-Order Ads Work[15]

SKILL MODULE 5.2

WRITING AD COPY

1. **Headlines are key:** Focus on the customer's needs, benefits, problems, or goals. Keep the headline short—five words or less. Scan the mail order ads of your newspaper or magazines to see what attracts your attention, and check the headlines of your competitors. Unless your company name is famous, its name should not go in the headline.
2. **Put the payoff up front:** If the customer doesn't see the payoff to them for using your product in the first sentence or two, they will give up and look elsewhere.
3. **Offer incentives:** In the body of your ad, consider putting in a discount ("Save 20% if you mention this ad!") or coupon to spur customers to action. Put an end date on the offer to move them along. A variation of this is to register customers in a drawing for a prize. This helps keep promotion costs down.
4. **Visuals:** While adding pictures can be prohibitively expensive, check out lower-cost options such as different font styles or sizes to make your ad distinctive. Sometimes line drawings are possible, and they are usually less expensive than photos.

PLACING ADS

1. **Newspaper ads:** You can always place classified ads, but for ongoing sales, you will want to use column ads in the regular sections of the paper. Think about what section of the paper is the one most likely to be read by your customers. Also, think in terms of what days of the week make sense. If the big auto motive ads are in the Wednesday paper, that may be when you want to advertise your car repair service.
2. **Finding magazines:** In order to find the appropriate magazines in which to place your ads, consider the following: Oxbridge Communications offers an online database of 75,000 magazines and newspapers you can search by keyword or title. At your library, you can find hard copy magazine directories from Burelle and Bacon.
3. **Get the media kit:** Contact the magazine or newspaper of interest and ask for its media kit. These kits tell you about the types of ads, placement options, and costs. They're a great way to get an understanding of the basics of the ad business.
4. **Monitor**: Put a code in every ad, and ask customers for the code in their orders. That way you can track which ads work best for you.

You can start a catalog of your own. Depending on the size and quality of the catalog, costs for print versions start at around 50 cents each and can rapidly go up to $2, $5, or more. Typically, the number of catalogs you will have to order is 5,000 at a minimum. Online catalogs are a less expensive approach. Creating and disseminating a catalog online saves you the cost of printing and mailing. Generally, Web-hosting services offer shopping baskets that are in fact online catalog-making programs.

However, most part-time entrepreneurs typically try to get their products into existing catalogs. Here the catalog firms function as your first customer; you want to convince them to carry your product. You can find catalogs through the Oxbridge online site or from print directories in the reference section of your local library.

When you have found the catalogs, try to obtain copies and check to see how your product would fit. Once you've identified your target catalogs, the key person you will be trying to find (by phone, mail, or online at the Web site) is called a *buyer*. For the bigger catalogs, there will be several buyers, each specializing in a few product areas. Buyers usually require pictures of the product, and some will want to see the actual product. Buyers are used to buying based on preproduction models and prototypes. This works well with part-time entrepreneurs trying to maintain a microinventory. A **microinventory** is a set of goods or services that consists of only one or a few items.[16] Microinventories are the small business's answer to **just-in-time inventory** methods in big business. In microinventories, you try to buy your product or prepare your service only after you get an order. For this to work, you need a stable, consistent, and secure source of inventory supply.

microinventory
A set of goods or services that consists of only one or a few items.

just-in-time inventory
Having just enough product on your shelves to meet the immediate purchases. This usually requires frequent shipment from your supplier.

When possible, try to talk to the buyers by phone first to make sure your product would fit their needs. Entrepreneurs typically send buyers a packet with ad copy and pictures of the product. It often helps to provide different versions of the ad copy and different pictures to maximize the chance buyers see something they like. If possible (or if asked), send a sample product.

Catalog sales, like most business-to-business sales, are rarely immediately successful. Be prepared to come back repeatedly to catalogs that best fit your product or market. Persistence shows you are serious about the business.

Also, think about local wholesalers. The phone book or business directory at the library can point you to wholesalers who supply local businesses with products. If you know a business your product would fit, you can ask the owner who the wholesaler is and build on that. The materials developed for the catalogs work in terms of introducing your product to wholesalers, too. The product description and photo for a catalog can quickly be made into an offering circular that you send to wholesalers to test their interest.

Success Factors for Part-Time Businesses

LO3
Understand what it takes to be successful in part-time entrepreneurship.

Research indicates that most service and retail firms typically start out as a hobby.[17] There are many different ways to start a part-time business. Consider for example the way Courtney Hennessey got CodiJewelry going. The BRIE model introduced in Chapter 1 can point out many of the key factors you need to think about. Intention is usually

SMALL BUSINESS INSIGHT

Courtney Hennessey and CodiJewelry

Courtney Hennessey of CodiJewelry.com did not intend to go into the jewelry business. It just grew. During Christmas break of her junior year at Saint Louis University, Courtney decided to make stretchy crystal bracelets for her friends as holiday presents. When she left the bead store, she had another problem—she had spent $400 on beads and string, and she needed to make the money back before her father found out. Courtney became a walking ad for her bracelets and sold them throughout the holiday, including at a family wake. Eventually the business grew to have in-person and online retail sales as well as wholesaling to stores, including Neiman-Marcus. Eventually Courtney won a Global Student Entrepreneur Award for innovative thinking.

■ Courtney Hennessey, the founder of CodiJewelry.com, began her small business part-time out of the necessity to recover her Christmas gift-making costs. Like many others highlighted in this chapter, her part-time business afforded her the chance to earn a reasonable profit while carrying on with her other life priorities.

where part-time businesses start in the BRIE process, and we talked about key resources—such as inventory or competencies—earlier. Let's go further to address the other two other aspects of the model for part-time businesses: boundary and exchange.

Boundary: Separating and Balancing Business and Home

Time is central to balancing home and business. It is important to organize a business around a schedule that makes sense for you. Internet-based businesses let you work any time that is convenient for you. For Courtney, having time during Christmas break was critical. Operating on weekends at roadside stands or at flea markets or farmers' markets is the best way to structure time that is convenient for you and your customers.

Either way, time management is the crucial skill for juggling your part-time business and the rest of your life. The key device for managing time is the to-do list. To be effective, the list needs to be with you at all times. You can get by with a small notepad, or can go for preprinted organizers, such as those from Day-Timer or Franklin Covey. You can even go electronic, using a personal digital assistant like a Palm PDA. Today many cell phones come with calendar and to-do list capabilities built in.

When using a to-do list, be sure to list the key information such as due dates and contact information if it applies. Most entrepreneurs find that it also helps to prioritize the list. One of the simplest ways to do this is 1-2-3 ordering. Those activities that are absolutely essential to your business or life are coded 1. Those that are current but of lesser importance or that can be rescheduled if necessary are assigned a 2. Activities that you want to do when you have some extra time or that have due dates far in the future get coded as 3. Typically, owners keep a to-do list of 6 to 20 items per week, and they reprioritize on a daily basis.[18]

For people with a part-time business, the to-do list includes items from business and personal life. For students, tests are probably a 1 priority. For parents, children's extracurricular activities are also 1s. Often family and personal lives make demands that put business and the rest of life in conflict.

Having some general rules to help sort out these conflicting demands helps. Fred Kiesner, an entrepreneurship professor at Loyola Marymount College suggests six key ideas:[19]

1. Do not waste time complaining; do something about a problem.
2. Do not aim for perfection; "good enough" really is good enough.
3. Do not dwell on the past; just plan to do better next time.
4. Minimize your time spent in meetings, or schedule meetings to be short.
5. Schedule and protect quality time with your family.
6. Schedule and protect some time for yourself to have fun.

The majority of part-time businesses are based in the home. The business takes space, uses resources the family also uses, and generally places stress on the household. Keeping a clean boundary, like an area known as the "business corner," helps make sure that family and business are protected from each other.

Exchange: Dealing with Others

There are two key groups outside your business with whom you must deal—government and customers. Even part-time businesses have to deal with government, and three issues pop up repeatedly: registration or licensing, taxes, and zoning. For businesses run from a home or commercial venue like a fair or consignment shop, most states and localities require some form of **registration**, but the requirements vary so it is important to check. The U.S. government has a Web page with links to state registration information at http://www.business.gov/regions/states/. Click on your state or territory, and then on "Starting a Business" and look at the section on "Licenses and Permits."[20] It is also important to check whether your business needs special **licensing**. For example, home-based beauticians need state licensing, and in many states home-based day-care providers need to get special registration and, in some cases, licensing.

registration
Information provided to the government concerning the existence of, name of, nature of, and contact information for your business.

licensing
Documented permission from the government to run your business.

http://www.sba.gov/hotlist/license.html

Even when you do not have to register a business, you need to keep track of your sales in order to pay your income taxes later. Although taxes are discussed in Chapter 13, it is useful to mention here that you want to keep track of your costs, too, because if you itemize your deductions on Schedule C, you can deduct your costs from your income (and a lower income means lower taxes). In many states and localities, you must also pay sales taxes, and these often need to be kept in a separate bank account and tracked as well. Often, flea markets and craft fairs include temporary local tax numbers in the booth rentals, but it is important to check.

zoning
Government specifications for acceptable use of land and buildings in particular areas.

Zoning restrictions can be an unexpected problem for home-based part-time businesses. Localities sometimes prohibit using homes for commercial purposes. Commercial use can be defined as storage or having customers at the house. Even neighborhoods can have similar restrictions in the covenants people agree to when they buy their homes. The only way to know for sure is to check.

Customers are central to making sales, and for part-time businesses, keeping customers is especially important, since few part-time businesses can afford to find and sell to new customers all the time. Successful part-time selling depends on developing and leveraging a solid customer base. The list in Chapter 2 called "Sources for Network Connections" is a good place to start building your customer base too.

Pricing and Costing

Because exchange is the way businesses make profits, it is important to price your goods or services to make profits likely. Folks working part time can be prone to underestimate their costs. Using things found around the house or neighborhood or not adequately considering the cost of the time you contribute are typically what lead to underestimating the cost of a product or service. Taking some time to think through the real cost is of your product or service is critical to your success. Central to figuring the real cost is recognizing that your own time has value. When you price your product or service to pay yourself what you could get working part time for someone else, then you have achieved a real milestone on the road to growing your business.

Pricing is also often seen as a challenge by part-time businesses. Even if the business is part time, that does not mean the prices have to be cut-rate. One good way to get an idea of realistic pricing is to price competitors' offerings. Doing some window-shopping in person, via catalog, or on the Internet is the classic way. Once you know the kind of price your product or service can get and once you know your costs, then you are in a great position to know the kind of profit it's possible to make in your business.

What Are the Challenges of Being an Entrepreneur Part Time?

LO4
Learn how to optimize your delegation within the firm.

Five aspects of part-time entrepreneurship are very different from full-time business. Two of these, deciding how professional you want your business to be and gaining legitimacy and trust among customers, are discussed in Chapter 2. Three other key aspects remain: determining what you are able to delegate, the special ethical challenge that comes from juggling part-time entrepreneurship and other work, and the challenge you face when you try to move from part-time to full-time entrepreneurship.

Delegation and Outsourcing

For part-time entrepreneurs, time is the ultimate resource. While the most successful entrepreneurs in high-growth ventures are those who learn to get and leverage other people's money (OPM), for entrepreneurs in part-time businesses the key is leveraging other people's time (OPT). There are two major ways to do this—delegation and outsourcing. **Delegation** happens when you assign work to those over whom you have power, usually people you employ or those volunteering to help you out. When you employ outsiders who are not your employees to handle all or part of a functional area of your business, it is known as **outsourcing**.

delegation
The assignment of work to others over whom you have power.

outsourcing
Contracting with people or companies outside your business to do work for your business.

Delegation makes sense in two situations. The first is when others can do things better than you. For example, an entrepreneur who is a wizard at sales may be totally lost doing the books. The second is when you want your business to operate when you are not present, or operate in two places at once. If you have two people working in a store, you could be selling to two customers at once. Done well, delegation frees the owner to pursue those things that make the biggest difference in the business—key sales, strategic thinking, negotiating, or inventing. It is a powerful concept, and there are several tips that can help make any delegation effort more successful.[21]

- Start delegation with simple tasks to get you and your employee used to the process.
- Match the task to the person with the best skills and attitude for it.
- Be specific about what outcomes you want from their work.
- Solicit questions from your employees about the delegated work.
- Attach a motivating outcome to the delegated work—a chance to learn new skills or demonstrate leadership, increased visibility, or an opportunity to see more of the business or its customers.
- Allow time for the employees to learn the task and correct the inevitable early mistakes.
- Give employees feedback about their performance soon after they start.
- Hope for perfection in performance, but be satisfied with good enough.
- Once delegated, do not take responsibilities back. When problems arise, remedy them, rethink your approach, and retrain the employee.

Delegation is not for everyone and every situation. It makes the most sense when you have people who are good at their jobs and trustworthy, but with some additional steps, delegation can work in less than optimal situations. Even with these tips, being able to delegate depends on the owner's ability to trust others and on the quality of the people to whom the owner can delegate. Table 5.1 shows four approaches to delegation, depending on the mix of owner's trust and employee quality. When delegation is essential but it is hard to trust employees, checking up on an unpredictable schedule helps keep the employees on their toes and provides maximum assurance to the owner. When trust is high but employees lack skills, the owner should allow time to train them

TABLE 5.1 Delegation Approaches for Small Business Owners

	Low Trust	High Trust
Low-Quality Employees	Do not delegate	Train, delegate, monitor less often as employee gains experience
High-Quality Employees	Delegate, monitor irregularly to ensure performance	Delegate and check at the end

TABLE 5.2 What Do Small Businesses Outsource?[22]

Legal issues, 78%	**Sales**
MIS	Advertising and marketing, 37%
Web site hosting, 70%	Finding new customers, 29%
Computer technical support, 57%	Public relations, 21%
Web site design, 55%	Customer service, 6%
Database management, 18%	**HRM**
Accounting and Financial	Payroll, 26%
Accounts receivables, 50%	Recruiting and hiring, 20%
Financial advice and management, 48%	Training, 16%
Bookkeeping and accounting, 30%	
Collections, 27%	

Source: Dun & Bradstreet (2002).

and monitor their work—frequently at first, but less often as they prove they know their jobs.

As noted earlier, when you employ outsiders who are not your employees to handle all or part of a functional area of your business, it is known as outsourcing. The most popular types of outsourcing among small businesses are shown in Table 5.2.

In the nineteenth and twentieth centuries, the idea behind automation was to save time. If you can get a computer program or another company to do work instead of you, you save time, and that is good. Table 5.2 shows that the most technical aspects of a business—issues such as law, computers, or financial records—are the areas in which outsourcing is most likely to occur. This provides some insight into how to think about outsourcing. In areas in which expertise is hard to come by, changes frequently, or is an important support to the functioning of the firm, it makes sense to outsource. The other key idea for outsourcing is to never outsource what *defines your distinctive competence*, what you think makes your business unique. Consider the example of Gourmet Gatherings on the next page.

Gourmet Gatherings' "symphony" suggests the kind of careful involvement and oversight needed to make outsourcing work. Activities that are central to the strategy of the business, like cooking and running the cooking groups for Gourmet Gatherings, stay inside the firm. Activities that are not strategically critical are outsourced, especially when they can be done better or more cheaply by outside firms.

LO5
Learn the benefits of bootstrapping

Making Do When You Are Starting Out

bootstrapping
Using low-cost or free techniques to minimize your cost of doing business.

undercapitalization
Not having enough money available to the business to cover shortfalls in sales or profits.

Bootstrapping—finding a low-cost or no-cost way to do something—is a popular approach for all businesses and essential for part-time firms. It is especially important for firms early in their lives because one of the major threats to the survival of firms is **undercapitalization**.[23] Running out of money before the business is self-supporting is a major threat. This can come from a shortage of cash in the business or even from a shortage of cash in the owner's personal life, since for small businesses starting out the two are often drawing from the same resources.[24] The key ideas of bootstrapping are simple:[25]

- Do without as long as you can.
- Cut your personal and business expenses to the bone (e.g., no salary, work from home).

SMALL BUSINESS INSIGHT

Gourmet Gatherings[26]

Bibby Gignilliat has bounced from job to job. She was a programmer, bookseller, travel agent, bike tour guide leader, public relations representative, and marketing manager before she started as a cook teaching for HomeChef and later on San Francisco television. Her prior skills equipped her for a special project, using cooking as part of a team building exercise for a group of lawyers, and later for a group of 40 business-people. This led to the idea for Gourmet Gatherings, which provides culinary entertainment "designed to inspire conviviality, camaraderie and confidence in people who appreciate good food."

Armed with a strong network of contacts, Bibby partnered with longtime friend Shannan Bishop (their fathers were partners in a brokerage business). Bibby's varied experience had an interesting side effect—she knew all the kinds of work she did not want to do. So she and Shannan outsourced every function of the business except the recipes, menus, and leading the gatherings. Their financial, marketing, legal, and Web work were all outsourced. They describe their role as "conducting a symphony of specialists" and argue that they could never have grown if they had to do everything themselves. Besides, it was the cooking that was fun, not the bookkeeping.

- If you need something, see if you can get it for free (like help from SCORE or former professors), borrow it, barter your time for it, or rent it before you buy it.
- If you need to buy outside services, consider offering **equity** instead, but be stingy with this.
- Before you buy, see if you can substitute a lower-cost alternative (e.g., a printing calculator and lock box instead of a cash register).
- If you buy, buy used or at a deep discount, and always ask if you can stretch out your payments to minimize cash flow.
- If you need money, borrow it from yourself first, then from family, then friends, and after that banks, credit card advances, and finally, credit companies, in that order.
- If mortgage rates are low, consider first or second mortgages to put money into the business, if you are comfortable risking your house.
- To minimize debt, use a cash card like American Express, which requires repayment in 30 days, instead of a credit card.
- When you use a credit card, limit purchases and keep your credit balance as clear as possible.
- And always, always keep track of your cash!

equity
Ownership of a portion of a business.

One key to making bootstrapping work is leveraging low costs with free expertise. One way to do this is to set up an advisory board. Andy and Chad Baker, founders of the CashCard Coupon Company, recognized the value of seeking advisers and were surprised at how easy it could be to find experts interested in helping a fledgling business.

The Baker brothers were able to obtain lots of help from advisers while keeping their business small. There are many people from whom you can get free expertise for your part-time business, such as: bankers, insurance agents, trade and professional association officers, former or retired entrepreneurs, and public business development organizations such as your local SCORE or Small Business Development Center. In Chapter 2, Skill Module 2.1 gives you the specifics for successfully getting others to help you.

SMALL BUSINESS INSIGHT

CashCard Coupon Company[27]

Andy and Chad Baker operate a business called the CashCard Coupon Company. Initially selling advertising to businesses in Bloomington, Indiana, the company manufactures distinctive signs predominantly for restaurants and bars. Just after starting their business, they sold some products to Rodney Wasserstrom, a Columbus, Ohio, businessman, but their delivery times were very slow. Because they were feeling bad about their service to him, Andy and Chad sent him an explanatory letter along with free coupons to a trade show—not realizing that Mr. Wasserstrom was owner of a nearly $250 million business in Ohio. Getting a huge kick out of the letter, Wasserstrom became both a great customer and a mentor with unparalleled marketing experience. Since that time the Bakers have received mentoring help from others—in one case two brothers that they read about in an article in *Inc.* magazine. Having gone to the same college as these brothers, the Bakers had an immediate connection. The Bakers note that they "always seek out the best people in a given field when [they] get involved in that field." They note that if "you are not aware of anyone to advise you, just contact your local Chamber of Commerce or pick up a newspaper. We have found that simply sending a letter explaining that you are interested in some advice normally elicits an 'I would be happy to meet with you' response."

Ethics and Part-Time Small Business

LO6
Learn the ethical challenges of part-time entrepreneurship.

It is impossible to gain legitimacy for your small business if your ethics are in question. There are two situations in which part-time entrepreneurs are particularly at risk: moonlighting and aggrandizing.

Moonlighting

Often, the most successful small businesses build from the business expertise and personal contacts of the entrepreneur. However, managing this without offending your current employer, or getting into legal or contractual trouble, is not easy. Working on your own part time after your regular job is called **moonlighting**, and it poses particular risks.

moonlighting
Working on your own part time after your regular job.

The major concerns are conflict of interest, cannibalizing sales, and poisoning the well. Conflict of interest crops up when people do work for their part-time business while they are at their full-time job, blurring the boundary between them. **Conflicts of interest** happen when what is best for your part-time business is different from what is best for your full-time employer or when people cannot be sure which of the two firms you represent. The key is to keep your full-time and part-time jobs clearly separate. For example, do not contact customers of your part-time business when you are at your full-time job.

conflict of interest
A situation in which a person faces two or more competing standards or goals.

Cannibalizing means taking business away from your employer. This can come from your taking sales away from your employer or taking working hours away to do your own business. This is a real problem if your part-time business is similar to your full-time occupation, for example, if you are a painter for a building contractor in your day job and do similar sorts of painting as your part-time moonlighting enterprise. In such cases, the usual course is to get your employer's approval at the start. This, however, may be easiest to get when the kinds of work you are doing, or the kind of clients you have, are *not* like those at your day job. In fact, it is often possible to get your boss to refer customers to you when they

cannibalizing
Taking business away from your employer.

fit your type of schedule, pricing, or type of work a little better than that of the bigger enterprise.

Poisoning the well refers to creating a negative impression among your employers' customers. If you use your business contacts through your day job as the basis for your part-time self-employment, you will inevitably find some customers who do not want to hear your sales pitch. If, because of this, they tell your employer they are less likely to buy from him or her, your part-time business has hurt the full-time one. The traditional work-around for this is to develop a separate customer list without names from your full-time job and then wait for your employers' customers to ask you about this other business they hear you've started.

poisoning the well
Creating a negative impression among your employers' customers.

Aggrandizing

For a part-time small business, achieving legitimacy and business respect can become a driving force. Occasionally, the entrepreneur sees an opportunity that is possible, but a stretch. If it looks like a stretch to the customers, the entrepreneur may start thinking about making the firm seem bigger, more substantial, or more capable than it really is. This misleading impression, called **aggrandizing**, can spell the death of a firm if discovered at an inconvenient time. As discussed below, this was the lesson Jeremy Barbera encountered in the early days of his business.

aggrandizing
Attempting to make your business or yourself seem more accomplished or grander than reality.

Jeremy Barbera "got away with it." He lied quickly and easily, no one checked up on his firm, and he was able to meet his obligations. However, if his aggrandizing had been exposed before he could prove himself, he would have lost all credibility. Jeremy says that an entrepreneur has to take risks to get ahead. When Jeremy started his firm, checking up on a firm required time-consuming investigations or credit reports, so Jeremy's risk was perhaps not so great. Today, with credit reports and business directories available online in seconds, the potential for being found out is much higher, and the risk is greater.

The most typical form of aggrandizement is implying that a firm is a full-time one when it is only part time. Recall from Chapter 2 that it is hard for a part-time firm

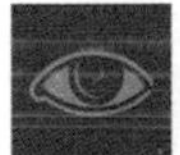

SMALL BUSINESS INSIGHT

Metro Services Group Inc.[28]

Trained as a physicist and employed by NASA, Jeremy Barbera started Metro Services Group as a part-time business on his kitchen table with his "partner," his mutt Luka. Of the $900 he invested in the business, $200 went to rent a Madison Avenue mailing address at a local incubator to help his business look more professional. Selling direct-marketing services to financial and entertainment firms, Barbera was a one-person operation, but he consistently stretched the truth. For example, he used "we" and "us" when talking about the firm. He would promise a prospective client to have his secretary type up the proposal and courier it over before 5 p.m., but it was Jeremy who did both.

This once came close to backfiring. Jeremy had delivered the proposal in the afternoon, dressed as a delivery person, and reappeared the next morning for the follow-up meeting with the CEO, this time attired in suit and tie. An alert security guard informed the CEO's office that the delivery man claims to have a meeting with the CEO. Jeremy told the guard and CEO that the delivery man was his brother, down on his luck. Jeremy's favorite line was, "It all depends on the light you portray yourselves in." Jeremy made MSGI look bigger than it was until it landed its first contract—with American Express.

to achieve the legitimacy of a full-time firm, and there can be a strong temptation to make the firm sound like it is a regular nine-to-five business. Remember that in the end, however, the biggest risk is that of losing the trust of your current and potential customers. In a small business, especially a part-time one, the owner *is* the business. If you cannot trust the owner, you cannot trust the firm.

Moving from Part-Time to Full-Time Entrepreneurship

LO7
Find out about the challenges of moving from part-time to full-time entrepreneurship.

Some people start their businesses part time with hopes of moving to full-time operations when the time is right. For them, landing a major contract or sale may be the financial and marketing indicator of the right time. Others start part time and want to stay that way, and they can face challenges when they achieve success. The strains of producing goods or services for a voracious market can make staying part-time difficult.

In deciding whether to make the move to full time, the key question is usually financial. If you are already employed full time somewhere else, the move to full-time entrepreneurship means taking a close look at your financial situation. Can you afford to go on your own? This means having enough to cover personal and family expenses (typically for six months), as well as business expenses. There may also be new costs, as you scramble to replace employer-provided health insurance.

The way to determine the financial situation of a business is through crafting a business plan such as the one you will learn about in Chapter 8. Having a business plan helps you work out all the major details of the business and how you plan to organize it as you are growing it. For example, Nancy Bombace of Mill Valley, California, took the time to do a business plan before taking her part-time honeymoon registry service, HoneyLuna, full time. By doing the plan, she learned she needed to keep her full-time job and run HoneyLuna on the side to make ends meet.[29] In addition, bankers, lawyers, big corporate customers, consultants, and potential investors will ask you for your business plan, so it makes sense to do one to show you have done your homework in starting a full-time business.

There are several ideas to keep in mind to help in this transition. First, it often makes sense to wait until there is a solid income likely for the business before moving over to full time. Second, make use of any transition services your former employer offers, such as COBRA health coverage (look at http://www.dol.gov/dol/topic/health-plans/cobra.htm to get information on this from the U.S. government). Third, recognize that initially at least you will spend nearly all your time running and marketing the business, so it makes sense to change over when your family and personal obligations are at their lowest and support from family and friends is at its highest.

http://www.dol.gov/dol/topic/health-plans/cobra.htm

Often people move into full-time entrepreneurship by building their part-time work to longer hours, until they have, in effect, two full-time jobs. Done this way, sleep, family, and personal time take a hit, but as a financially secure way to operate, the two jobs approach is great when done for short periods.[30]

Like the work of Nancy Bombace, Jeremy Barbera, Pamela Williams, Sheila di Matteo, Courtney Hennessey, or Dan Murza, part-time entrepreneurship is around you all the time. Millions of people are working at part-time businesses of their own. Whether in retail or wholesale, selling service or products, they or their wares are in our stores and our markets, on our streets, and in our homes. Part-time entrepreneurship is important because it gives people a chance to learn the ropes in business and to test out their ideas. It also is often the only way people can engage in entrepreneurship amid their other responsibilities. Part-time entrepreneurship is important as a test bed for starting full-time, larger firms and as a means of self-reliance and self-expression. However, as long as a few minutes online or simply saying, "I can do that for you" to a neighbor is all it takes to start a part-time business, it will remain an option that lots of potential entrepreneurs are certain not to overlook.

CHAPTER SUMMARY

LO1 Know when and why part-time entrepreneurship makes sense.

- It makes sense when you need to gain basic experience.
- It makes sense when you lack the resources for a full-time business.
- It makes sense when you face a narrow window of opportunity.

LO2 Learn the four major paths to part-time entrepreneurship.

- Stand businesses include roadside stands, flea markets, farmers' markets, and fairs.
- Key issues for stands are location, where traffic is high, and having adequate inventory.
- Home businesses include shopping parties, door-to-door selling, and network marketing.
- Key issues for home businesses include having a good hostess for shopping parties, or a solid technique for closing sales in door-to-door selling.
- Consignment stores and auction-based businesses include online auctions such as eBay.
- Key issues are location and traffic for consignment shops and Internet auction sites.
- Mail order and catalog sales vary widely in costs and markets covered.
- Key issues are writing ad copy that sells and placing it in the right publication.

LO3 Understand what it takes to be successful in part-time entrepreneurship.

- Use the BRIE model to help identify key boundary and exchange issues.
- *Boundary*—you need to manage your time carefully and keep business and home separate.
- *Exchange*—you will need to register with the government, pay your taxes, and comply with zoning regulations. You will also need to keep careful track of your costs including the cost of your own time.

LO4 Learn how to optimize your delegation within the firm.

- Delegation is getting others to do your work. It can help an entrepreneur to get more done.
- Managing the delegated work and the people performing it is a key challenge for the entrepreneur.
- Outsourcing is paying experts to take on the functional tasks of your business.
- You may outsource to experts anything but the tasks that make your firm unique.

LO5 Learn the benefits of bootstrapping.

- Bootstrapping means making do with little or no money.
- Keep your costs down, do without, borrow instead of buy, buy used or at a discount, and check out the other bootstrapping techniques listed.
- Bootstrap expertise by creating an advisory board.

LO6 Learn the ethical challenges of part-time entrepreneurship.

- The two ethical challenges of part-time businesses are moonlighting and aggrandizing.
- Moonlighting can result in cannibalizing sales from your employer or poisoning the well by making your employer's customers angry.
- Aggrandizing can happen when a part-time firm tries to present itself as a full-time one or a bigger one than it really is.

LO7 Find out about the challenges of moving from part-time to full-time entrepreneurship.

- The key challenges of moving to full-time self-employment are mainly financial.
- Do a business plan to assess your financial situation in the new business.
- When you make the move, do it when support from your family and previous employer are at their strongest.
- Consider increasing part-time work hours until you are working at two full-time jobs, and then quit to devote your full time to your firm.

DISCUSSION QUESTIONS

1. What are the three situations in which it might make more sense to go into business part time rather than full time?
2. There are four major categories of part-time business—*stands, homes, consignment*, and *mail order*. Describe each of these briefly and give at least one of the critical success factors for that category of business.
3. What are the differences between party and door-to-door retailing?
4. How do creating your own catalog and placing your product in an existing catalog differ? When does each approach make the most sense?
5. When managing your time using a to-do list, how do you go about prioritizing the list? Why?
6. What kinds of tasks do small businesses most often outsource? Why do you think they are popular tasks to give to others?
7. Of the two ethical problems prevalent to part-time small businesses (moonlighting and aggrandizing), which do you think is the biggest problem for entrepreneurs? Why?

EXPERIENTIAL EXERCISES

1. Search for craft and art fairs in your area using Google Local (**http://local.google.com**). Enter "fairs" in the box under "What" and your target city and state (like "Chicago, IL") under "Where." When you look at the results, try the links for category searches like "Carnivals, Fairs & Exhibitions" to get a narrower set.

2. Check the kind of licensing you need for a part-time business in your state. Go to **www.business.gov** and click on "Region" where it says "ACCESS ADDITIONAL INFORMATION BY: Region." Then pick your state or territory, and from the listing for your state click on "Starting A Business." In the section on "Licensing & Permits" you can find the information you need to know.
3. Research pricing your product or service electronically. Go to eBay.com (if you are selling a product) or eLance.com (if you are selling a service), and enter the term for your product or service. From the resulting list, note the offerings that most closely match yours and check the prices posted. If possible, look for recent sales or contracts for your offering to see what people paid for the goods or services.
4. Create your own first-pass customer base. List family members; friends; people you know from religious, fraternal, civic, and school organizations; and people who provide you goods and services. Look at the list again and select five people who you think are most likely to know the kind of person you would imagine would make your best customer.
5. Create a to-do list for the upcoming week using the technique described in the chapter. Prioritize your tasks using the 1-2-3 method, and use the list for a week. Ask yourself if you felt having the list helped you remember better what you had to do and if it helped you better decide what to do and when to do it.

Mini-Case

Edith Zrabowski works as a forms clerk for a large health insurer. In her 22 years on the job, she has learned about all the ways medical reimbursement forms can get messed up. In her full-time job, when she sees such a problem, she flags the problem form, and it gets sent to a claims specialist for resolution.

One summer evening, Edith was at her apartment community's swimming pool talking with neighbors. One woman started to complain about problems getting reimbursed from their health insurance company—fortunately a competitor of Edith's employer. The amount at stake was several hundred dollars, and she was at her wits' end. Edith offered to look at the forms and see if she could advise on what was wrong. The neighbor asked how much Edith would charge. Without much thought, Edith decided on $25, to be paid only if Edith could resolve the situation.

It turned out that the problem was quickly spotted and easily fixed. The neighbor cheerfully paid Edith the $25 and spread the word about a medical forms magician in the apartment community. Soon Edith's customers included elderly neighbors with Medicare problems, a small business owner with claim form trouble, and families at odds with insurance firms, including her employer. When she saw her employer's form, she realized she was suddenly walking on thin ice.

CASE DISCUSSION QUESTIONS

1. What was the conflict of interest Edith faced?
2. What method did Edith use to set prices? Is there a better way she could have done this?
3. When Edith started taking her second and subsequent clients, what steps should she have taken around boundary and exchange issues?

LEARNING OBJECTIVES

This chapter will help you:

LO1 Describe five ways that people get into small business management.

LO2 Learn the rewards and pitfalls of starting a new business.

LO3 Understand the opportunities and pitfalls of purchasing an existing business.

LO4 Explain four methods for purchasing an existing business.

LO5 Learn about the approach and reasons for buying a franchise.

LO6 Understand the problems of management succession in a family-owned business.

LO7 Describe how hired managers become owners of small businesses.

■ Success as a small-business owner may require multiple start-up attempts, as Rebecca Mathias found out with her company, Mothers Work. Strategy and perseverance are essential to growing your business from being just an outlet for your needs, hobbies, or interests to becoming a vital force in its market. What are some other examples of products and services you can think of that have also harnessed a founder's particular focus into a profitable company?

Small Business Entry: Paths to Full-Time Entrepreneurship

Focus on Small Business: Mothers Work

Rebecca Mathias, pregnant with her first child, faced a quandary. She was an active civil engineer and needed stylish maternity clothes to wear to work. Despite the innumerable stores and specialty shops of Philadelphia, where she lived and worked, Rebecca could not find anything appropriate.

"Everything was pink flowers, frilly, really inexpensive." Rebecca stated, "I couldn't wear that to work. The good-quality clothes didn't exist, and they didn't have clothes to wear out, because you were expected to just stay at home."[1]

The situation left her with few choices. She could continue to work, wearing frilly, inappropriate clothes. Or she could quit work, as she believed was expected of pregnant women. Or she could . . . ?

Rebecca Mathias, showing great entrepreneurial spirit, chose the third alternative. She neither settled for wearing inappropriate clothing nor for quitting the work that she liked doing. Rather, she decided to start a business that she could operate from her home. She went to a clothing wholesaler on Seventh Avenue in New York City and purchased $10,000 worth of executive style maternity clothing. Rebecca then proceeded to go into business, not from her garage, but from her hall closet. She sent out thousands of catalogs. The net result of this was a loss of $6,500 and a closet full of maternity clothes she no longer needed.

Faced with a problem, Rebecca recognized an opportunity.

She proceeded to call the people who had requested catalogs but had not subsequently placed an order. She asked each woman what it was she needed that Rebecca's catalog did not offer. The replies led Rebecca to begin having clothes made to her own exacting specifications. Armed with seed money from a small business investment company,[2] Rebecca franchised her line of executive maternity clothing. Today, her company, Mothers Work, has over 1,000 stores and over $500 million in annual sales. The company designs and distributes three lines of clothing—A pea in the pod, mini maternity, and motherhood maternity, employing about 5,000 people.

home-based business
A business that is operated from the owner's home.

Rebecca succeeded in building her **home-based business** into the primary supplier of maternity clothes in the United States because she followed the first rules of entrepreneurship: consider problems to be opportunities, find a customer need and fill it, and, most importantly, do not ever, ever give up.

DISCUSSION QUESTIONS

1. What prompted Rebecca to develop her business?
2. What was the difference between her first and second tries in the business?
3. In what other ways could Rebecca have organized her business?

The Five Paths to Business Ownership

LO1
Describe five ways that people get into small business management.

There may be "50 ways to leave your lover,"[3] as the song states, but there are only five ways to get into small business management:

- You may start a new business.
- You may buy an existing business.
- You may **franchise** a business.
- You may inherit a business.
- You may be hired to be the professional manager of a small business.

franchise
A legal agreement that allows a business to be operated using the name and business procedures of another firm.

start-up
A new business that is started from scratch.

Although everyone gets into business by one of these five paths, the specific details of going into business are unique to each person. **Start-ups** may be deliberate, well planned, and financed. On the other hand, many start-up businesses "just happen." Often a compelling hobby slowly morphs into a profitable business, or a chance occurrence leads to a new business venture. Purchases of existing businesses may occur in any number of ways, from cash purchases to "earn-outs" in which the business is bought over a period of time with money earned from the business. Franchises may range from "turnkey," in which every part of setting up the business is handled by professionals, to those in which the only thing that is franchised is the right to use the business name. Some business managers work their way to the top from a beginning part-time employee position. Other professional managers are recruited to become the chief executive. It is common for hired management to use leveraged **buyouts** or employee stock option plans to purchase the

buyout
The purchase of substantially all of an existing business.

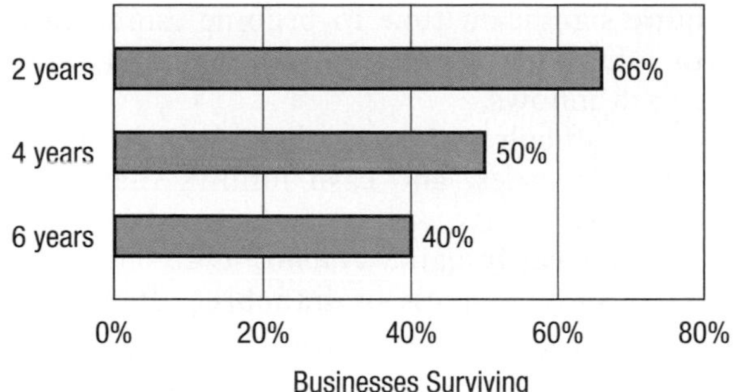

FIGURE 6.1

Survival Rate of Start-up Businesses

firms for which they work. This chapter examines the details of these paths of entry into small business: start-ups, purchasing, franchising, inheritance, and professional management.

Starting a New Business

LO2
Learn the rewards and pitfalls of starting a new business.

Starting a new business is at once the most risky path into business and the path that promises the greatest rewards for success. The success rate of start-up businesses is a matter of some controversy. As we note in Chapter 1, while the Small Business Administration (SBA) reports that 66 percent of new employers survive two years or more, 50 percent survive at least four years, and 40 percent survive more than six years,[4] those businesses that get help last much longer. Eighty-seven percent of start-ups that begin in business incubators are still in operation five years later,[5] and the survival rates for students from entrepreneurship programs and entrepreneurs seeking help from Small Business Development Centers are about twice that of businesses in general.[6] Even for those who get help in starting their business, one must admire the courage and optimism of a person who chooses to start a new business (see Figure 6.1). Despite the rather high failure rate, creating a start-up is not, as some maintain, a triumph of hope over reality. Many businesses that end do so not because they failed, but because the owner took advantage of a better opportunity.[7] The rewards, both financial and personal, of starting a successful new business can be most impressive.

Advantages of Start-ups

There are many reasons that people choose to start a new business rather than purchasing an existing business, franchising, or being an employee:

- A start-up begins with a "clean slate." There are no existing employee problems, debts, lawsuits, contracts, or other legal commitments that must be satisfied.
- A start-up provides the owner with the opportunity to use the most up-to-date technologies. There are no "legacy" locations, buildings, equipment, or software that can hamper productivity.
- A start-up can provide new, unique products or services that are not available from existing businesses or franchises. Existing businesses and franchises exist because of their success in providing proven products and services.
- A start-up can be kept small deliberately to limit the magnitude of possible losses. A purchased business or franchise requires immediate and constant cash flows to meet ongoing obligations.

cash flows
The receipt and spending of cash.

Disadvantages of Start-ups

Offsetting the advantages of starting a new business are several disadvantages:

- A start-up business has no initial name recognition. An existing business or franchise has invested in developing its market. The brand rights can guarantee immediate acceptance of the business.

- A start-up will require significant time to become established and provide positive cash flows. An established business or franchise has built-in customers to provide immediate cash inflows.
- A start-up can be very difficult to finance. Established businesses and franchises provide immediate **assets**, sales, and cash inflows that can be used to obtain financing for the business.
- A start-up usually cannot easily gain **revolving credit** from suppliers and financial institutions. An existing business or franchise often has lines of credit that transfer with the business.
- A start-up may not have experienced managers and workers. Established businesses and franchises provide experienced workforces, training, and management support.

asset
Something the business owns that is expected to have economic value in the future.

revolving credit
A credit agreement that allows the borrower to pay all or part of the balance at any time; as the loan balance is paid off, it becomes available to be borrowed again.

Creating a New Business

The first step in creating a start-up business is to determine what the business is to be. The vast majority of start-up businesses are "me-too" enterprises. Often the business idea is simply to create another occurrence of a common business: a beauty shop, a restaurant, a bar or lounge, a rock band, a sign company, plumbing service, yard care, and so on. Starting a copycat business provides some protection from business

SMALL BUSINESS INSIGHT

Amy's In-Home Child Care Service

Amy Conti had no intention of going into the babysitting business. She was a straight A student at the University of the Incarnate Word, majoring in business administration. In addition to maintaining her academic standing, Amy worked full time in her father's financial management business, and she also was very active in extracurricular activities. As one teacher said of her, "Amy is the current president of most things, and the past president of everything!" She really had no time for so mundane a job as watching small children.

However, Amy was constantly receiving pleading calls from mothers for whom she had babysat during her high school years. Having once again yielded to a desperate mother's need for a sitter, Amy decided that there must be a better way. Once her "little darlin'" for the evening was asleep, Amy began plying the phone. She called young women whom she believed would be acceptable to her clients as substitutes for her own services. Within a couple of days, Amy was in business for herself.

Amy didn't recruit just any girl who was willing, however. Sitters had to be 18 years old, or older, and had to have successfully completed both Red Cross advanced first aid and CPR classes. She accompanied every sitter on at least her first engagement, observing how the sitter got along with both the parents and the child.

Another innovation was the standby sitter. She kept at least two girls on "standby" over every weekend, ready to dash to a client's house should the scheduled sitter have a car, boyfriend, or other problem that caused her to have to cancel at short notice. The standbys were paid for either the actual engagement that they covered, or $40 if they were not called out on an actual sitting job.

"It's the standbys that have really made my service unique," Amy said. "I can guarantee a parent that we will have someone, no matter what. Of course, every now and then I have to go myself to make good on that promise. But you know, if I didn't like babysitting, I wouldn't have done this in the first place."

So, is it worth Amy's time to run a sitting service, on top of all the other things that she does?

"It depends on how you look at it, " said Amy. "On a monthly basis, I probably only make about a thousand dollars or so. On the other hand, I'm making well over a hundred dollars an hour for the time that I put in. It sure beats flippin' burgers."

failure. It is not necessary to define the business to the market because everyone knows what a beauty shop, restaurant, or lounge provides.

On the other hand, this type of start-up can be very difficult to differentiate from other similar businesses. Often, the only competitive advantage may be the location of the start-up. This is why owners of common businesses go to so much effort to try to make a difference between their business and other, essentially identical firms. An example is how Morton's of Chicago and the Ruth's Chris steak houses operate. Careful sampling of the firm's steaks reveals no significant difference in price, quality, tenderness, size, or taste. The restaurants have similar menus and wine lists. Each, however, has distinctive interior decorating and presentation of their meals. Morton's brings a selection of huge uncooked steaks to each table for patrons to make their choices. The cooked steaks are served on oversized china plates. Ruth's Chris provides equally large steaks, selected from a printed menu, served on plates that are heated to a high temperature to create the trademark "sizzle."

Amy is an example of an accidental business start-up. She did not set out to create a new business model. However, her strict standards and ability to pay for standby sitters has made her service unique. The high reliability of her service and the confidence that parents have in the abilities of her sitters have made a business that is usually considered to be a part-time thing for the girl next door into a professional and profitable business for its founder.

The specific concept that leads to a start-up business usually comes from the experience of the person starting the business. Two-thirds of all start-ups are based on ideas from prior work experience, hobbies, and family businesses.[8] These businesses are generally more likely to succeed than are businesses based on ideas from other sources. Research into the indicators of successful start-ups shows that one of the best predictors of success is the level of experience of the **founders**. Random events, suggestions from friends and associates, and specific education courses are the sources of only a relative few start-up ideas.

founder
The person or people who start a new business.

Increasing the Chance of Start-up Success

The probability of creating a successful start-up is increased greatly when the founder has certain attributes and when the founder takes certain actions. Doing the following things has been shown to be the most effective route to success (see Figure 6.2).

- **Start business in a business incubator:** A business incubator is an organization that provides financial, technical, and managerial help to start-up businesses. Most incubators are associated with economic development agencies and are integrated into the community. Incubators provide access to angel investors, public grants for seed money, and technology support.

Business incubators are created to strengthen the local economy by helping create jobs through the establishment of successful small businesses. But incubators do much

FIGURE 6.2

Top 12 Indicators of Start-up Success

1. Starting the business in a business incubator.
2. Taking part in a mentoring program.
3. Having a detailed start-up budget.
4. Producing a product or service for which there is a proven demand.
5. Securing outside investment.
6. Starting with more than one founder.
7. Having experience managing small firms.
8. Having industry experience.
9. Having previous experience in creating a start-up business.
10. Choosing a business that produces high margins.
11. Starting the business with established customers.
12. Building trust in your "story."

■ Keep your business's products and services out of NewProductWorks' failed product museum by testing the demand for your ideas before attempting to implement them. What are some ways and means available to small business owners that can help determine market needs for new products?

more than just create new jobs. They aid in the commercialization of new technologies, the revitalization of distressed neighborhoods, and the creation of wealth. The best incubators provide inexpensive office space with full-time on-site managers who can assist the entrepreneur in many ways. Incubator participants share common office services, such as telephone answering, and production and copying of documents. Perhaps most important, incubators provide legitimacy by furnishing the business with a location and with established business processes.

- **Take part in a mentoring program:** Successful business owners and corporate executives do well by doing good. They can, by helping others, in a way repay the many people who helped them achieve success. Executive volunteers contribute their time and energy to assisting start-up and struggling small businesses as a public service. Because of their experience, mentors can help you avoid mistakes and make good business decisions.
- **Have a detailed start-up budget:** The start-up phase is usually the most difficult time you will have in business. You are required to make myriad decisions concerning location, product, target market, promotion, sales, and all the facets of starting and operating a business. And you must juggle all these demands while simultaneously seeing that you have enough cash. A detailed start-up budget provides a road map for necessary spending during the start-up phase, when cash inflows are likely to be small or nonexistent. Companies that carefully plan their start-up activities and avoid any unnecessary spending are much more likely to succeed.
- **Produce a product or service for which there is a proven demand:** It is an unfortunate fact that most new products and services fail to gain acceptance. NewProductWorks of Ann Arbor, Michigan, maintains a "failed product museum" that contains samples of over 73,000 items, all of which were commercial failures. During the dot-com bubble of 1998–2001, many businesses started with novel and completely untested products and services. Examples are Beenz.com, which was started to facilitate Internet transactions; webvan.com and yourgrocer.com, both of which sold groceries online for home delivery; and estamp.com, which offered online purchasing of U.S. postage, to be printed on the user's printer. All four of these businesses failed to gain success with their products. Only estamp.com is still currently in business.

  Large corporations, such as Procter & Gamble or Sony, spend millions of dollars annually testing the market acceptance of new products. Despite their huge resources and years of experience, they regularly introduce products that fail. (Are you old enough to remember "New Coke"?) Your start-up business will not have either the experience or the resources to absorb the loss from product failure. By producing a product or service for which there is a proven demand, the risk of product failure can be reduced or eliminated.

- **Secure outside investment:** Securing outside investment accomplishes two things: First, the process of obtaining investment funds means that your business will be critically examined by outsiders who have no vested interest in your idea, product, or service. Second, the fact that you were able to convince outsiders to invest in your business indicates a level of belief in the business and you that provides legitimacy.
- **Start with more than one founder:** Starting with more than one founder provides the business with more experience, skills, and resources than can be furnished by a single individual. Having more founders in the business also provides an opportunity for synergy, in which the business results are greater than the sum of the input. Multiple founders can also provide a forum for examining ideas, evaluating information, and making good business decisions.

synergy
A combination in which the whole is greater than the sum of its component parts.

- **Have experience managing small firms:** Managing a small business requires attention very much like that displayed by a person spinning plates on sticks. As a performer must move quickly from plate to plate, many demands of small business management require that you have the ability to quickly move from task to task, without allowing any task to ultimately go uncompleted.

  The process can be overwhelming for inexperienced managers. Those entrepreneurs who have experience in small business management are more likely to be able to meet the many simultaneous demands of guiding a successful start-up than would a person new to small business.
- **Have industry experience:** Each industry has its own peculiarities. Only through experience can you learn the methods, sources, and markets for any specific one. Even simple tasks, such as buying necessary material, can be nearly impossible without industry knowledge.

  For example, suppose that you plan to start a quality steak house, similar to Ruth's Chris or Morton's of Chicago. Where do you buy prime beef of the required cut and quality? How do you cook the meat? Or, consider making high-tech, lightweight bicycles. Where can you buy titanium tubing? What does it cost? What do you need to cut, shape, and weld it? How will you sell the bikes? Are bicycles sold through wholesalers? Are they sold directly to bicycle shops? Or maybe you want to start a sign company to make sand-blasted signs. Where will you buy the resist material to protect the wood you don't want blasted away?

  The less you know about something, the easier it appears to be. A true expert makes a task seem effortless. Watching Tiger Woods play golf might lead you to believe that it is an incredibly easy game. Just stand up, hit the ball, and watch it fly to the green. Sure it's easy: So why do fewer than 2 percent of golfers ever make a course par? The same is true of business. Business people such as Michael Dell, Scott McNealy, and Warren Buffet make the process of succeeding in business seem effortless. But if you have been in the business, you know better. Being experienced won't make your start-up easy, but at least you have firsthand knowledge of how your industry works that will make your task easier.
- **Have previous experience in creating a start-up business:** "Nothing succeeds like success." In the 150 years since Dumas made this famous statement, it has come to be an unquestioned part of our language. It is just succinct enough, just truthful enough to seem like a universal truth. For entrepreneurs, it is fortunate that the statement is also not completely true. Although one may learn from successes, most learners acquire expertise through a process of repetition, which only occasionally results in successes. One study of entrepreneurs who had successfully created a start-up business found that on average an entrepreneur suffered three start-up failures before achieving success. Thus it is more nearly correct to state that no entrepreneur succeeds without having prior experience in failing.

- **Choose a business that produces high margins:** High margins, the amount by which sales prices exceed product costs, provide a buffer for lots of mistakes. The single greatest hurdle to a successful start-up is obtaining and maintaining sufficient cash to support both operations and growth. When margins are high, loss of any one sale or customer has an immediate effect. However, the problem of replacing the lost margin is much easier if you have to make only one or two sales or get one or two new customers to make up for the lost business.
- **Start the business with established customers:** When you start with established customers, you know that you will immediately have cash inflows. There are basically three ways that you can go about obtaining committed customers prior to start-up: (1) You can start your new business as a "spin-off" from your current employer's business. (2) You can start a business to specifically go into competition with your employer. (3) Or, you can start a business to subcontract services to your employer or to other established businesses.

spin-off
A business that is created by separating part of an operating business into a separate entity.

(1) Creating a spin-off is a regular business practice that is done by businesses of all sizes and at all stages of development. Some spin-offs are created to get rid of "noncore" activities. By disposing of the noncore activity, the parent firm reduces capital requirements and provides a tighter focus for management on the remaining businesses. Other spin-offs are created when the parent lacks either the interest or the resources to pursue the opportunity. By being spun off, the start-up can gain access to resources other than those of the parent.

(2) Going into competition with your current employer is also a common practice. Of course, this almost always results in resentments and often ends in lawsuits over issues of trade secrets, rights to intellectual property, and abridgment of contractual provisions. You will have to make difficult ethical decisions. From a legal point of view, the contract between employer and employee is satisfied when all wages and other benefits have been paid in return for you accomplishing the tasks for which you were hired. Absent a specific contract providing otherwise, neither party, employer nor employee, is obligated beyond this exchange. However, not so easily answered are the questions (1) Is it ethical to use your employment to build relationships with customers that subsequently can be used to start a new business? and (2) Is it ethical for you to use knowledge and skill received through training and education furnished by your employer to go into business competing with your employer?

(3) Subcontracting services to an existing business is somewhere between doing a spin-off and starting a competing business. Services that are often contracted include sales, janitorial services, accounting, research, and product development. It is a common, accepted practice for the contractual relationship to be created prior to starting a business.

- **Build trust in your "story":** Building trust is essential to the success of all start-ups. You must be able to convince suppliers, employees, and, most importantly, customers that the business is now successful and will be in the future. Not only is there an understandable reluctance for people to be associated with a potential "loser," but customers, vendors, and employees all take risks by doing business with an unknown and unproven start-up.

Suppliers are often reluctant to deal with start-ups, even if you make your purchases in cash. Most new businesses are small compared to established businesses in the same industry. There is a good reason why you, as the owner of a new business, would prefer to make numerous orders of small quantities of the goods and services you need. Doing so reduces cash flow requirements and reduces the risk of your being stuck with old or obsolete inventory. For the vendor, however, accepting your frequent small orders greatly increases the cost of providing goods and services to you. Most vendors, especially wholesalers, work on very small margins. The cost of accepting and filling numerous orders for a new customer may well make such business unprofitable. It is, therefore, essential that the vendor believes in your eventual success and that you will become a valuable customer in the future.

Employees take on significant risks when they go to work for a start-up business. Not only may the start-up fail, but frequently the cash flow problems of start-ups cause payments for wages to be late or missed entirely. This is one reason why so many start-ups offer stock options and stock bonuses to employees. The start-up doesn't have enough cash to pay high wages right now, but if it's successful, employees will share the rewards in the future.

Customers can similarly be at risk when purchasing from a start-up business. In the event that the start-up fails, there is no recourse for warranty problems, for maintenance, or for upgrades to the product. This risk is especially acute when the product or service of the start-up affects the core business of its customers. For example, the San Antonio Bed & Breakfast Association contracted with a start-up business to develop and maintain a Web-based availability and reservation service for the association's members. The start-up failed during the dot-com bust of 2001. When problems with the system subsequently developed, there was no one to fix them. The system was complex and the source code incomprehensible. As a result, the association lost a core service that provided value to its members.

The issue of building trust in your story is a catch 22. If customers, vendors, and employees do not have trust in the entrepreneur and in the business, quite simply, there is no business. However, there must be a business, or you don't need customers, vendors, and employees. There are several ways for a start-up business to build trust and legitimacy, and these are detailed in Chapter 2. Specific examples for the kinds of businesses discussed in this chapter include obtaining a performance bond that will pay vendors and customers if your business fails. Restaurants, lodging establishments, barbers, beauty shops, and other businesses that deal with issues of cleanliness as a business requirement can obtain licenses and join industry groups that perform inspections. Displaying licenses and certificates of inspection provides assurance that you are at least meeting minimum standards. Manufacturing businesses and construction businesses may hire engineers to certify design and construction details. Warranty service can be contracted to an independent company that specializes in providing such services. Rigorously maintaining business procedures that ensure on-time delivery of products and services and on-time payment of bills, wages, and loan payments will, in time, result in the start-up being trusted.

Many businesses have been successfully created which lacked one or more of these indicators. It is also true that many start-up businesses have failed, despite having all these characteristics. No one knows what makes the difference between such successes and failures. Some have speculated that the one indispensable trait of people who create successful businesses is determination to make the business work.

Special Strategies for Starting from Scratch

Having a business based at home is one way to reduce the cash flow requirements of a start-up business. By using space in your home, you can avoid the cost of renting office, production, and storage space. Often, no additional insurance is required above ordinary homeowner's coverage. Because of the proximity of the business to the living area, no time is spent commuting between home and office.

Placing a business in your home is not a new idea. Until about 50 years ago, it was common for doctors, dentists, lawyers, and other professionals to operate their practices from their homes. Many a grocer, general merchandiser, or innkeeper lived in quarters either attached to or on the floor above the business space. From around 1950 to 1990, home-based businesses largely fell out of favor. This was in part because home businesses came to be regarded as somehow less than "real" businesses. Also,

■ Increasing numbers of the United States workforce are opting to work from home, in a variety of roles and capacities. What are some of the advantages you see to making your business home-based? What are some of the disadvantages, and how could a small-business owner work to overcome these potential setbacks?

negative news stories about multilevel sales organizations, such as Nutrilite, Amway, and Shaklee, further reduced the perception of the legitimacy of home-based businesses.

This changed in the early 1990s. The recession of 1991 resulted in thousands of service workers and professionals being laid off, or put on shortened hours. Many started to work from their homes. Some simply continued to do the work from which they had been downsized, either as part-time e-commuters or as independent contractors. Others set up businesses as consultants, technical writers, financial planners, analysts, and similar kinds of jobs that are not sensitive to the location of the business. The U.S. Small Business Administration estimates that 53 percent of all businesses are home-based, putting the number at around 12 million firms.[9]

Partnering is simply the process of two or more entities agreeing to work together for a common goal. Working with a partner can reduce the risks of start-up in several ways. In an ideal situation, the partner or partners have different talents, experience, and assets that complement those of the business founder. Partners may provide capital, equipment, advice, or specific services. A partner may be "silent," that is, not actively involved in the planning and operations of the start-up, or a partner may take an active role. Partners may be individuals, organizations, or other existing businesses. Because of the contributions of the partner, the founder of the start-up may either (1) reduce the amount of personal investment in time and money required to make the business succeed, or (2) "leverage" the contributions of the partner to provide faster growth and higher returns on the investment made in the start-up.

Individuals who have special competencies can be brought into the business as partners, stockholders, employees, or advisers. In order for any business to grow beyond the size necessary to simply provide a living for the owner, other individuals must eventually be brought into the business to share the many tasks of operating a business. In the book, *Good to Great*, Jim Collins asserts that those firms which make the transition from being merely "*good*" businesses to being "*great*" businesses do so by "first getting the *right* people."[10]

SMALL BUSINESS INSIGHT

Julia Dalton and UltimateKeychains.com

While Julia Dalton was a business student at Saint Louis University, she did an internship at a local Internet e-commerce provider, MonsterCommerce. One of the subsidiaries of MonsterCommerce was a Web site that sold keychains, UltimateKeychains.com. MonsterCommerce received the firm when business got bad and UltimateKeychain's founder defaulted on his bills to MonsterCommerce. Julia was assigned the business as one of her projects. The owners of MonsterCommerce, and now UltimateKeychains, had bigger fish to fry.

Julia realized that the business could be turned around. She asked what it would take to buy UltimateKeychains, and her bosses actually gave her the business for free. Julia restocked the inventory, updated the Web site, and began to make money almost immediately. She still kept working at MonsterCommerce and continued to bounce ideas off of her bosses to keep UltimateKeychains on top of its game. For her work, Julia won Saint Louis University's campuswide 2005 Global Student Entrepreneur Award.

Your current employer may provide assistance if your new venture is not going to be a direct competitor. Often, a new product or service idea arises from the work being done in the current employment of the start-up founder, as in the case of UltimateKeychains.com. The employer may, however, have no interest in pursuing the opportunity. In such cases, the start-up may well proceed with the employer's active support.

Buying an Existing Business

The second most common way to enter small business management is to purchase an existing business. Buying an existing business has important advantages over creating a start-up. However, purchasing a business has its own, unique set of risks.

LO3
Understand the opportunities and pitfalls of purchasing an existing business.

Advantages of Purchasing an Existing Business

There are some advantages to buying an existing business:

- Established customers provide immediate sales and cash inflows. Because the business is already successful, it has proven that there is sufficient demand for its products and services to operate profitably.
- Business processes are already in place in an existing, operating business. This eliminates the need to hire employees, find vendors, set up accounting systems, and establish production processes.
- Purchasing a business often requires less cash outlay than does creating a start-up. The seller will often provide financing that makes it possible for you to buy the business.

Disadvantages of Purchasing an Existing Business

Disadvantages to buying an existing business include:

- Finding a successful business for sale that is appropriate for your experience, skills, and education is difficult and time-consuming.
- It is very difficult to determine what a small business is worth. The value of a small business can never be known with certainty. You must rely on analyses, comparisons, and estimates.
- Existing managers and employees may resist change. It can be very difficult to convince employees to adapt to new business methods, procedures, and processes that can provide increased profits.
- The reputation of the business may be a hindrance to future success. Sellers are usually reluctant to tell you about problems that the business has. Business owners are especially sensitive about discussing past disputes and lawsuits with vendors and customers.
- The business may be declining because of changes in technology.
- The facilities and equipment may be obsolete or in need of major repair.

Finding a Business to Buy

The first problem you must solve is finding a business for sale. Of course, you aren't looking for just any business. You are looking for one that is right for your own experience, education, and skills. The things that make a business appropriate for you are like those things that help create a successful start-up. The business should be in an industry in which you have experience. It should be producing a product or providing service that is in demand and that has high margins. Perhaps, most importantly, it should have adequate financing available so you can continue operations and make the business grow.

SKILL MODULE 6.1

Finding a Business for Sale

Although all businesses are for sale, *if the price is right*, finding that one perfect business is a difficult and time-consuming task. As you will find out by completing this skill task, businesses for sale that are easy to find usually are unsuitable. Businesses that are right for you are downright elusive:

1. Decide what type of business you would be interested in buying. Write a profile of your ideal business to buy, specifying its industry, product or service, size, location, price, and financing.
2. Search the Yellow Pages and the Internet to find business brokers active in your area.
   a. Contact each broker and inquire about businesses that meet your criteria. Be honest in your approach. Do not represent yourself as a serious buyer, unless you are one.
   b. Obtain copies of the information that the broker has concerning the businesses.
3. Search your local newspaper, *The Wall Street Journal*, and *Barrons* classified advertisements for the headings "business for sale" and "business opportunities."
4. Make a list of businesses that seem to meet the requirements that you wrote down in step 1.
5. Contact the businesses that you have identified. Be honest in your approach. If you are doing this solely as a classroom exercise, explicitly say so. Remember that while the owner of the business may want to sell it, he or she is undoubtedly very busy and may not want to discuss the business with a student when there is no chance of your actually buying it.
6. Visit a business that is engaged in the industry you have identified as being right for you. Find out the following things:
   a. The title and publisher of the journals dedicated to the industry.
   b. The primary businesses of this type operating in your geographical area.
   c. Conventional business practices:
      i. Is business done on credit?
      ii. Who are the primary suppliers to the business?
      iii. What are the sales channels of the business (direct sales, catalog, etc.)?
      iv. How is technology changing in the business?
      v. Are there any industry rules of thumb for valuing businesses?
      vi. Does the owner know of any businesses that are for sale?
7. Obtain sample copies of the industry journals. Examine them for advertisements of businesses for sale.
8. Make an appointment with a loan officer in the commercial loan department of a bank in your area. Describe what you are looking for in a business to buy.
   a. Ask if the loan officer knows of any businesses for sale in your area.
   b. Ask if the loan officer can introduce you to anyone who might be able to help you find a business for sale.

Finally, write and present a report to your class that details the efforts and results of your research.

You will greatly increase your chances of finding the right business by using multiple sources. Make some calls: Contact business brokers and ply your own network. You should be actively reading advertising of businesses for sale in newspapers and magazines and on the Internet. You might consider asking your employer if his or her business is for sale. Keep in mind that *every* business is for sale at a high enough price. If you hear of a business that is interesting, contact the owners and ask what it would take to buy it.

Brokers advertise and facilitate the sale of businesses for a fee, most usually a percentage of the ultimate selling price. Most states have laws that require brokers to work solely for the interest of the seller and to obtain the highest selling price possible. This creates a conflict of interest between the broker and you. The broker is trying to get the highest price. You're trying to get the lowest.

The quality of broker services ranges from excellent to outright rip-offs. Only a few states have any education or licensing requirements, although some, such as Illinois, do require business brokers to register by filing a simple form. Accusations of misrepresentation and fraud by brokers are common in the business press.

Networking is an excellent way to find businesses for sale. While most businesses are for sale at any time, for competitive reasons most owners do not want to say so explicitly. Because customers, vendors, and employees are likely to feel threatened, openly advertising a business for sale can lead to the loss of revenue, credit from vendors, and key employees. For these reasons, it is common for businesses owners to make their intention to sell known only to trusted confidants in the industry and in the community. Attorneys, bankers, accountants, and insurance agents all will provide you with information only if they know that they can trust your discretion. You can usually get solid leads just by telling other business people that you're interested in buying a business.

There is a trade journal for every industry that exists. People in the mortuary business bone up with *Embalmer* and *American Funeral Director*. The replacement window industry looks through *Fenestration*. The electric sign industry is energized by *Signs of the Times*. The folks who process dead and decomposing animals into useable products digest *Render* magazine. The construction industry digs *Rock and Dirt*. No matter what type of business you might be considering, there is a magazine for it. They all have advertisements of businesses for sale. You can find out how to locate trade journals by trying out Skill Module 7.2 "Finding Your Trade and Industry Association" in Chapter 7.

The Internet also has numerous sites that advertise businesses for sale. A search using Google™ with the key word "business" and the phrase "for sale" resulted in over *38 million* pages listed. None of the advertisements that were inspected during the research for this book provided the name or the exact location of the advertised business. Rather, the sites have various ways you can obtain additional information. Some provide a link by which you can request more information. A very few listed phone numbers you can call. Others require becoming a member and paying a fee for access.

Your current employer is probably a ready source of information about businesses for sale in your industry. Most managers of small businesses are members of formal and informal groups of businesspeople, for example, the Chamber of Commerce, Rotary, Kiwanis, and other groups that have meetings and provide resources. Also, your employer probably has information about competitors and vendors in the area. Don't forget the example of UltimateKeychains.com—your employer just might be interested in selling his or her business, as well.

Investigating Entrepreneurial Opportunities: Performing Due Diligence

Suppose you've actually found a business you'd like to buy. Your job has just begun. Finding an appropriate business is merely the first, and easiest, step in the process. Buying a business is a lot like getting married—it is easy to get into, but if it turns out bad, it's very hard to get out. Now that you've found that "perfect" business, you must make an exhaustive investigation to tell if it is really suitable. Unlike residential real estate, which is highly regulated in the United States, sellers of businesses are not legally required to make disclosures of impairments or deficiencies. If you are outside the United States, your laws may be different. For example, in Canada, sales of businesses for a price less than $200,000 are tightly regulated. Sales for amounts greater than $200,000 are not regulated at all. As in the United States, it is *your* responsibility to fully investigate the business and to come to your own independent evaluation of its value.

due diligence The process of investigating a business to determine its value.

Due diligence is the process of investigating to determine the full and complete implications of buying a business. During the process of due diligence every aspect of the business is examined in exacting detail. Nothing is taken for granted. No statement is accepted without evidence. Evidence is, itself, substantiated with sources external to the company. Properly performing due diligence minimizes the risk of failure and maximizes the probability of success by identifying the strengths and weaknesses of the business.

When a business is acquired, there is a clear order of steps that should be followed:

1. Conduct extensive interviews with the sellers of the business.
2. Study the financial reports and other records of the business.
3. Make a personal examination of the site (or sites) of the business.
4. Interview customers and suppliers of the business.
5. Develop a detailed business plan for the acquisition.
6. Negotiate an appropriate price for the business, based upon the business plan projections.
7. Obtain sufficient capital to purchase and operate the business.

The first five steps together make up the process of due diligence.[11]

caveat emptor
Latin: let the buyer beware.

A basic tenet of business law is "**caveat emptor**," or "let the buyer beware." This does not mean that a seller can freely lie to you about the business. Deliberate misrepresentations can lead to lawsuits and may be prosecuted as fraud. However, except for specific representations by the seller, you are responsible for understanding the condition and the facts of the business. It's kind of a "don't ask—don't tell." If you don't ask the right questions, the seller has no obligation to tell you the right answers. Thus, as the buyer, you must determine how the business is currently being operated, and you must substantiate (or disprove) representations made by the seller regarding the existence and value of assets, liabilities, financial performance, and the condition of the business.

Due diligence has two primary goals. *First*, you are attempting to find any wrongdoing: (1) fraud committed by the owners or managers; (2) misrepresentations of the sellers, such as improperly recognized revenues or expenses; and (3) missing information, including pending or threatened litigation, technological obsolescence of equipment, processes, product, or service, and unpaid taxes. *Second*, you are trying to find any inefficiencies, unnoticed opportunities, waste, and mismanagement. The first goal is information that greatly affects the value of the business and the advisability of purchasing it. The second goal is how you, as a new owner, can make changes to increase its value. Both goals can give you a negotiating advantage.

The first information that you get is usually a set of financial statements. There are four reasons why this is so: (1) the seller usually has financial statements available and incurs little added cost in providing them, (2) you, as a business person, are most likely familiar with financial statements and can extract useful information from them, (3) financial statements are accepted as representative of the business by bankers and investors, and (4) financial statements are considered to be indicators of future business results.

Financial statements should include (1) a balance sheet, (2) an income statement, and (3) a statement of cash flows. You should also examine the federal and state tax returns for at least the last five years. Information forms for partnerships, corporations, or limited liability companies should be examined also. Any financial statement prepared by or for the seller must be treated with skepticism. Some financial statements that you see will have been subjected to rigorous examination by professionals outside the business; some will have been dashed off by the owner at midnight on April 15. To be believable, the statements must be substantiated by external sources.

When you examine the income statement, you should focus on corroborating the amount and timing of revenues and expenses. Be aware that the income statements of small businesses are commonly misstated. To avoid taxes, owners often charge personal expenses to the business, such as cars, country club memberships, travel, and even home office expenses. On the other hand, when preparing to sell the business, owners are motivated to overstate revenues and understate expenses to show the highest profit.

Balance sheet items that are likely to be misstated are intangibles, that is, things that have no physical existence, but rather are legal rights and obligations. Intangibles include accounts receivable, patents, licenses, and liabilities. Assets claimed on the balance sheet must be examined to ensure that they exist and that the stated value is reasonable. Because liabilities are legal requirements to give up economic value in the future, such as debts for borrowed money or merchandise purchased on account, your risk is that there will be liabilities that are not disclosed. Your problem is that you are attempting to prove the absence of something. Once the examination is complete, you should adjust the amounts, contents, and format of the statements to reflect what you have discovered through due diligence.

During due diligence you should also try to answer many nonfinancial questions. Why is the business for sale? Who are key employees? What is the extent of obsolescence of equipment and key technologies? What are the prospects for the firm's products and services? What opportunities can the firm reasonably expect to have in the near future?

Determining the Value of the Business

After you have completed a thorough and exacting investigation, you need to analyze all the information you have gathered in depth. This is the time to consult with your business, financial, and legal advisers. The purpose of these discussions is to arrive at an estimate of the value of the business. Outside advisers are impartial—unlike you, they haven't invested money and time in the process. While you are likely to see only the good things about the business, they probably will clearly see the bad. Together, you can arrive at a value for the business and determine the suitability of the business and the availability of adequate financing. Then, and only then, should you make a decision to actually attempt to buy the business. If you do it this way, due diligence will greatly increase the chances that your business will succeed.

It is very difficult to place a value on a small business. The most theoretically rigorous method of valuing an ongoing business, using **discounted cash flows**, is based upon estimates of future cash outflows and inflows, given the change in ownership. Making such estimates is highly problematical. Because of these difficulties, it is common to use other, less rigorous methods to place a value on a business, such as comparable sales or various multiples and ratios of financial statement items.

discounted cash flows
Cash flows that have been reduced in value because they are to be received in the future.

Discounted cash flow methodology is based on the concept that the longer you have to wait to receive money, the less valuable it is right now. It is detailed in Chapter 15, Small Business Finance: Using Equity, Debt, and Gifts. In practice, cash flow valuation comprises (1) estimating the amount and timing of future cash flows, and (2) dividing each cash flow by some required rate of return compounded by the time that will pass before the cash flow is received. The sum of the resultant quotients is the value of the business.

The application of discounted cash flows to business valuation is similar to having an annuity. An annuity consists of some amount of money which is invested to earn interest. The interest that is earned and a portion of the capital invested is then paid to the holder of the annuity in a series of equal cash payments. In a similar way, when one buys a business, an investment is made. The business then should provide a return sufficient to repay the investment and also provide a return on that investment.

The use of discounted future earnings explicitly recognizes that the value of a business is its future earnings, not its past earnings. You need only look at the many, many failed businesses to understand this concept. For example, what was the value of Osborne Computers, Inc., at the time it went public? Osborne, the first manufacturer of what is now called laptop computers, at one time had a market value of hundreds of millions of dollars. However, the company never made a profit. Today, there is no Osborne Computers. Had future earnings been accurately forecast, the company would have had zero value. The same was true of many dot-com firms.

The primary disadvantage of discounted cash flow methods is that they provide the appearance of certainty, when in fact, they are no more than educated guesses. The process of determining the net present value of an investment opportunity requires (1) estimating the cash that must be invested, (2) estimating the cash that will be returned, (3) estimating the periods in the future in which cash inflows will occur, and (4) estimating the cost of capital to the buyer. Then the estimated rate is raised to an estimated power and used to divide an estimated amount of cash to be received at an estimated time in the future. This calculation can be carried to any number of decimal places, thus providing the illusion of accuracy. The buyer of a business should always remember two things: First, the word *estimate* is simply a Latinate word with the same meaning as the English word *guess*; second, it is better to be approximately right than to be precisely wrong.

book value
The difference between the original acquisition cost and the amount of accumulated depreciation.

Asset valuation methodology is based on the assumption that a business is worth the value of its assets minus the value of any liabilities. There are numerous ways to estimate the value of a firm's assets. One may use **book value**, that is, the original acquisition cost of the asset, less depreciation to date. The major problems with book value are that: (1) the original cost of an asset might bear no relation its current value—for example, a computer bought five years ago may be worth next to nothing now, (2) depreciation is an arbitrary, although systematic, method of transferring asset value to expense, so it can transfer values at the wrong time, for example a new car is depreciated over 5 years, where in fact it loses 40% of its value when you drive it off the lot, and (3) internally developed assets, such as patents, trademarks, and trade secrets do not have book value. This can be a major deficiency of the method. Consider The Coca-Cola Company. Its single greatest asset is its rights to the names, "Coca-Cola" and "Coke." However, if you examine the annual statement of the company, you will discover that no value for this right is shown in the balance sheet. To address such problems, one may adjust the value of assets that are obviously worth more or less than book value in a process called *modified book value*.

net realizable value
The amount for which an asset will sell, less the costs of selling.

replacement value
The cost to acquire an essentially identical asset.

A second asset valuation methodology is to estimate the current value of the assets without reference to book values. Two approaches are commonly used: (1) net realizable value and (2) replacement value. **Net realizable value** is an estimate of the amount for which an asset would sell, less the costs of selling the asset. If you were selling a building, the cost of selling would be the money spent on the real estate agent, advertising, and preparing the building for display. **Replacement value** is an estimate of what an essentially identical asset would cost to be acquired and readied for service. Net realizable value is usually significantly less than the replacement value of any specific asset. The major problems with estimating current values are that (1) the estimate does not consider the value of an ongoing firm over the value of its identifiable assets; for example, the value of a band staying together as opposed to having the band sell off its rights to its music (hits and flops), and (2) it is very difficult and time consuming to separately identify and estimate the values of all the assets of a business—imagine a hardware store with tens of thousands of items.

Comparable sales of other firms in the same industry are commonly used to estimate the value of a business. This method has two major problems. First, no two firms are exactly alike. Second, there are often no recent sales to use for comparison.

earnings multiple
The ratio of the value of a firm to its annual earnings.

Businesses are never identical. At the minimum they occupy different locations. At the other extreme, they may be different in all measurable aspects: location, size, gross sales, profitability, condition of markets, and physical assets. To deal with dissimilarity among businesses, you must use some type of ratio as a measure. The most common ratio is **earnings multiple**, which is firm value divided by actual or expected annual earnings. To use this metric, you have to calculate it for both the business you are considering and for businesses that have been recently sold. You then compare the earnings multiple of the business you are considering to that of recent sales, using the latter as a benchmark.

For example, consider the purchase of a small inn or a bed & breakfast. By examining readily available data, such as county property tax rolls and state lodging tax records, you can easily obtain the selling prices and reported earnings of inns that have sold in the last year. For example, you might find that similar inns have recently sold for an average of $600,000. If the average reported five-year income for the inns was $85,000, then the earnings multiple equals 7.06 ($600,000/$85,000). To determine the comparative sales value of the inn being considered, it is only necessary to multiply the average of the prior five years earnings by the multiple 7.06. If the inn you are considering has reported average income of $68,000, the value would be $480,000.

The process of applying comparative sales to determine the value of a business is more difficult than this discussion and example make it appear. In many industries, unlike the lodging industry, sales of businesses are rare, and often, when a sale is made, the purchase price and income are not disclosed. Also, you should adjust the financial statement amounts to reflect the likely business results under your ownership. This means removing any personal expenses of the sellers that are being charged to the business and any expenses that are unlikely to recur. You also should consider the riskiness of the business. For these reasons, when possible, you should determine a range of earnings multiples and not a single number.

Industry **heuristics** are simply rules of thumb that are commonly used to estimate firm value in relation to some easily observable characteristic of the business. Industry heuristics are similar to comparable sales in that they represent the combined experience of people active in the industry. For example, in the bed and breakfast and small inn industry, three heuristics are often used to estimate the value of an operating inn. The first is that an inn should sell for approximately $100,000 per rental room. This implies that an inn that has 6 rental rooms should be worth about $600,000 and that an inn with 12 rental rooms should be worth about $1,200,000. The second is that an inn should sell for approximately four times its annual gross revenue. Thus, an inn priced at $600,000 should be grossing about $150,000 per year. The third, called *income capitalization*, looks very much like a discounted cash flow. To calculate the metric, the net income of the inn, excluding depreciation, interest, and owner draws, is divided by the best return that the buyer could expect to obtain in other investments. For example, if the inn is producing a net income of $66,000 and the buyers' cost of capital is 11 percent, then the estimated value would be $600,000 ($66,000/0.11).

heuristic
For a common-sense rule, a rule-of-thumb.

Industry heuristics can be amazingly accurate. In a recent survey of 300 inns, the Professional Association of Innkeepers International found that the average selling prices of inns between 2000 and 2002 was $99,300 per guest room. The average gross revenue multiplier was 4.3, and the average income capitalization was 12.1 percent.[12] Similar heuristics exist for nearly all industries, usually through the group's trade association, which you'll learn how to find in the next chapter.

Structuring the Deal

LO4
Explain four methods for purchasing an existing business.

A buyer and seller get together to negotiate the final price for a business. The buyer should have performed the due diligence procedure and be confident about the assessment of the condition and value of the business. Along the way you, as the buyer, should have decided on the absolute highest price that you would be willing to pay. That highest price is called your **point of indifference**[13] in the negotiation process. The term comes from the idea that once that price is reached, you should be indifferent as to whether or not a deal is made.

point of indifference
The price at which a buyer is indifferent about buying or not buying the business.

Of course, you'll open negotiations with a price substantially lower than your point of indifference. The purpose of opening low is twofold: (1) you want to make the purchase at the lowest price possible, and (2) you recognize that the seller assumes that any opening offer is less than what you are actually willing to pay. A low opening bid allows both parties room to reach a compromise satisfactory to both.

In addition to negotiating for price, you also negotiate about the terms of the sale. When you are buying a business, everything is negotiable, not just the price. In fact, the terms of the acquisition, such as seller financing, payment periods, noncompete agreements, and the exact details of what is being acquired all interact to affect the price that you are willing to pay and that the seller will accept. There are four basic ways that a business may be bought: (1) you may buy out the seller's interest in the business, (2) you may **buy in**, by acquiring some, but not all of the ownership, (3) you may *buy only the key assets* of the business such as the inventory or equipment of the business, and not the business itself, and (4) you may **take over** a public business by buying a controlling interest of its stock.

buy-in
The purchase of substantially less than 100 percent of a business.

takeover
Seizing of control of a business by purchasing its stock to be able to select the board of directors.

Buyouts

Buyouts are restricted to businesses that have a formal legal form of organization, including corporations, limited liability companies, and some partnerships. Legal business organizations are artificial entities that exist separately from the owners. Buyouts are accomplished through purchasing the ownership interest in the entity. Technically, partnerships and sole proprietorships do not exist separately from the owners and thus cannot be purchased. Rather, the assets of the business must be purchased and the liabilities assumed in a process called *key resource acquisition* or *bulk asset sale*. The subsequent business is considered to be a new entity different from the selling entity. In practice, partnerships can continue in existence despite a change in ownership. Sole proprietorships cannot.

The primary advantage to a buyout is simplicity. The seller must only transfer his or her stock to the purchaser to complete the transaction. The business continues as an entity, owning its assets and maintaining responsibility for its liabilities. The primary disadvantage to a buyout is that all liabilities are transferred, including potential lawsuits that arise from actions and transactions that took place prior to the change in ownership. This has, as in the case of the widespread class-action suits concerning asbestos, led to bankruptcy for the purchaser.

A buyout may take place all at once, with all stock being transferred at a single point in time. Sometimes buyouts are made with ownership being transferred over some agreed upon time range. Buyouts made by employees are examples of changes of ownership over time. Employee buyouts were made legal in 1974 when employee stock ownership plan regulations were codified into law. An employee buyout occurs when the owners of a company sell a majority of stock to the employees through an employee stock option plan (**ESOP**) as was provided in the 1974 legislation. ESOPs are complicated transactions that require highly skilled professionals to implement them.

ESOP
Employee stock option plan: a method for employees to purchase the business for which they work.

Buy-ins

A buy-in results when someone acquires only a part of the ownership of an existing business. Any amount of ownership may be considered a buy-in, as long as less than 100 percent of the ownership is transferred. Buy-ins can be made in any form of business. Technically, if one buys into a sole proprietorship, it becomes a partnership. Corporations and limited liability companies may continue without a change of the form of entity.

There are two advantages to making a buy-in: (1) a buy-in allows the purchaser to leverage inside knowledge, and (2) it aids in keeping key employees. The seller and the managers of a successful business, by definition, have experience in operating that business profitably. The buyer, no matter how expert, does not have the same depth of knowledge of the business being purchased. One great threat to the buyer of a business is that employees who are key to its operations will leave the business. Keeping the current owner as an active participant of the business reassures employees that large changes are not likely to occur.

The disadvantages of a buy-in are the same as the advantages: the prior owner and management remain with the business. This often causes friction when the new owner wishes to make changes, and the old owner and managers do not.

Key Resource Acquisitions

Key resource acquisitions, also called *bulk asset purchases,* are the only way a sole proprietorship may be purchased. This technique may also be used with any other form of business. As the name implies, key resource acquisitions comprise purchasing only the assets of the business. Most usually, the seller will keep any cash and receivables and will retain responsibility for some short-term liabilities such as notes payable.

As we saw earlier, the most difficult issue in purchasing a business using this method is assigning a value to the **intangible assets**, such as the value of the business name, the value of having an ongoing business, the value of established relationships, and so forth. The value of the business in excess of the value of the identifiable assets is called *goodwill.* You should attempt to recognize a minimum amount of goodwill. One advantage of business ownership is the ability to shelter income by using noncash deductions to reduce income taxes. Prior to 2002, a business could reduce income taxes by deducting goodwill over a period of years. However, businesses purchased after December 15, 2002, are now prohibited from deducting for goodwill.[14] Thus the more of the business's value that is recognized as goodwill, the less income can be sheltered from income tax.

intangible assets
Things of value that have no physical existence, for example, patents and trade secrets.

Key resource allocation provides one important advantage. Because only the assets are acquired, the subsequent business, regardless of its legal form, is not responsible for any of the acts or transactions made prior to purchasing the business. Although this does not completely relieve the successor business from all prior liabilities, it does protect it from action concerning any noncollateralized liabilities, such as a line of credit or a personal loan of the seller.

Takeovers

Takeovers are possible only of businesses that have stock which is freely transferable without the permission of management or other owners. In other words, only corporations and certain partnerships can, under any circumstance, be acquired in a takeover process. A takeover comprises purchasing enough of the target business's stock to gain control of the board of directors of the business. In a takeover, the buyer (often called a *raider*) seizes control of the business without the permission of all owners. Sometimes, only a few owners are involved, as takeovers can often be accomplished by purchasing or even borrowing a relatively small percentage of outstanding stock.

Takeovers are hostile events. There is the threat that current management will be replaced. Occasionally, the raider will explicitly state that the intention of the takeover is to sell off portions of the business, or even to liquidate it completely. In these circumstances, current management is likely to make strenuous efforts to prevent the takeover from occurring.

Because of the requirement that stock be freely transferable, only a few small businesses are vulnerable to hostile takeovers. Accomplishing a takeover of a small business is likely to result in the loss of key employees and the resentment and resistance of those employees who remain. As a result of these limitations and problems, takeovers are usually done on medium to large businesses. Only very rarely does anyone acquire a small business through a hostile takeover.

Franchising a Business

What Is Franchising?

LO5
Learn about the approach and reasons for buying a franchise.

Franchising is a legal agreement that allows one business to be operated using the name and business procedures of another. The most ubiquitous franchise, worldwide, is McDonald's, which has over 30,000 restaurants in more than 100 countries. Approximately 73 percent of McDonald's restaurants are owned by independent businesspeople who operate them in a franchise relationship. The remainder are *company stores*, that is, stores that are owned and operated by the McDonald's Corporation.[15]

■ Franchising a business, such as Auntie Anne's or McDonald's, may be the right avenue for starting your own business if you want to lower some of the risks involved in small business. Franchising gives owners the opportunity to cash in on an already developed, market-tested product. However, drawbacks include less creative control and greater reliance upon your parent company's financial status. Does franchising appeal to you? Why or why not?

Most franchisors are large businesses, most franchisees small: McDonald's Corporation is a large business; McDonald's franchisees are small businesses.

Franchises are agreements between two entities, (1) the franchisor who sets conditions and standards and who grants operating permissions, and (2) the franchisee, who pays a fee for the rights, and who agrees to abide by the conditions and standards. The value of a franchise is determined by (1) the rights granted and (2) the cash flow potential to the franchisee. Each of these factors can be highly variable from one franchise to another.

There are three basic forms of franchising:

trade name franchising
An agreement that provides to the franchisee only the rights to use the franchisor's trade name and/or trademarks.

product distribution franchising
An agreement that provides specific brand name products which are resold by the franchisee in a specified territory.

business format franchising
An agreement that provides a complete business format, including trade name, operational procedures, marketing and products or services to sell.

1. **Trade name franchising** is an agreement that provides only the rights to use the franchisor's trade name and/or trademarks. Two examples of this are TrueValu Hardware and B. F. Goodrich tires.
2. **Product distribution franchising** provides the franchisee with specific brand named products, which are resold by the franchisee in a specified territory. Two examples of this type of franchising are Snap-on Tools and Archway Cookies.
3. **Business format franchising** is exemplified by the McDonald's Corporation. A McDonald's franchise includes the right to use McDonald's many trade names, specifications of the product to be sold, operating methods, marketing plan, and national advertising. Franchisees pay to the franchisor both an up-front fee to obtain the franchise rights and a percentage of gross sales.

In addition to the above, some franchisors, such as Subway (sandwich shops), sell *master franchises* that require opening multiple stores within a specified area. Subway describes these franchisees as being "development agents." Master franchisees are required to open a minimum number of stores within a specified time period, which they may do by selling *subfranchises* within the development area.

Advantages of Franchising

The advantage of franchising is that the franchisee receives the benefit of a proven successful business model. For example, McDonald's specifies every aspect of the business, from the temperature to which burgers are to be cooked, to the time that they may be kept before being sold, to the number of fries in a "Super Size."

As a franchisee you also receive training and management support. For example, should you become a McDonald's franchisee, you would be required to spend a minimum of two weeks at "Hamburger University" in Oak Brook, Illinois, before being allowed to begin business. McDonald's then sends an experienced manager to assist you during the start-up phase of your new business. Additionally, most franchisors require attendance at annual meetings at which regular training is provided concerning operations, techniques, products, and new promotions. Franchisors commonly furnish proprietary computer programs for sales registers and accounting. Marketing, product placement, advertising, and promotion are all controlled and directed from the franchisor's headquarters.

Franchising has proven less risky than either starting a new business or acquiring an operating business. The fees that franchisors charge are the price you pay to reduce your risk of failure.

Disadvantages of Franchising

One disadvantage of franchising is that you give up control of marketing and operations. Most franchisors have strict contractual requirements that severely restrict what you may do. The franchisor often sets policies as detailed as at what time you have to open and at what time you must close. Franchisors may require that you buy inventory and supplies from specific, designated vendors. If you are allowed to buy from local suppliers and contractors, your purchases are tightly controlled by written policies and contract provisions. For example, the building in which a McDonald's franchisee operates must be built to the parent company's exacting standards, including design, decor, construction methods, equipment, and signage. You will be regularly inspected to ensure that you are meeting all contract standards. If you consistently fail to meet standards, the franchisor has the right to take your business from you.

Another disadvantage of franchising is that your success is determined to a large extent by the success of the franchise itself. Many have gone out of business, leaving franchisees without access to supplies and services. Even the mighty McDonald's Corporation has recently suffered declining sales and reduced profits for both company-owned stores and franchisees.

Franchise Opportunities

There are more franchises available than you can count. Unlike finding a small business to buy, finding a franchise is easy. Every issue of *Entrepreneur* Magazine contains the advertisements of dozens of franchisors eager to sell their franchises to you. If you don't find one you like in *Entrepreneur*, the Internet contains thousands of resources for identifying franchise opportunities. A Google™ search of the Web using the terms "franchise opportunity" returned 788,000 pages. Several of the highest listed pages were the sites of services that offer information concerning franchises of all types. Some offer free services. Some charge a fee for information.

Among the 788,000 sites listed by Google are two U.S. government agencies, the Federal Trade Commission (FTC) and the Small Business Administration (SBA), a British government site, Business Link (http://www.businesslink.gov.uk), and an Australian site, Smallbusiness.gov.au, (http://www.smallbusiness.gov.au). Similar government sources are available around the world.

http://www.ftc.gov/bcp/franchise

Franchising's industry association, the International Franchise Association (IFA) (http://www.franchise.org) maintains a Web site that contains a database of over 800 franchises. The companies listed range from old familiars such as 7-11 stores to the really obscure such as Jet-black and Pop-A-Lock®.

http://www.businesslink.gov.uk

Once you've identified a potential franchise, you should perform due diligence, just as if you were buying an operating business. What you are most interested in with

http://www.smallbusiness.gov.au

THE THOUGHTFUL ENTREPRENEUR

When Your Franchisor Goes Broke[16]

Burt Benepal had just received a most unwelcome call. A business colleague reported that American Hospitality Concepts, Inc., had just declared bankruptcy. This news was delivered Friday the thirteenth, 2004, just before Benepal was to have opened his first-ever Ground Round Grill and Bar restaurant.

Because of the filing, American Hospitality had ordered all company-owned stores closed immediately. Timing could not have been worse for a restaurant. The announcement was delivered just as the Friday evening rush began. Diners were sent home with half-eaten meals in doggie bags. Over 3,000 employees were dismissed without any notice or severance pay. Their final paychecks bounced when they attempted to cash them.

Because he was a franchisee, Benepal did not necessarily have to stop work on his restaurant. However, he was under no illusion about the magnitude of the task facing him if he were to stay in business. He already had committed to a capital investment of $1 million. Would customers come to a restaurant that was involved in a bankruptcy?

"What should I do," he wondered.

In the subsequent weeks, struggling to stay in business, the franchisees organized. They formed a co-op, renegotiated contracts with suppliers, and even introduced a new lo-carb menu to capitalize on the Atkins Diet fad. Soon they realized that they were not so bad off. They no longer had to pay royalties or toe the line to meet franchisor requirements. Soon they developed a plan to buy Ground Round out of bankruptcy. On July 7, 2004, their offer to the bankruptcy court was accepted. The franchisees were now the proud owners of Ground Round Grill and Bar, Inc.

What about Burt Benepal?

He finally opened his restaurant in Richmond, California. He opened five months later than he had planned, but at least it was open and successful. Benepal stated that he expected his first full year of sales to be almost $2 million. He was actively searching for a location for his next Ground Round to be opened in 2005. He has plans to open five more before the end of 2006.

In many ways, Benepal was incredibly fortunate. Often when franchisors go bankrupt, franchisees soon follow. Even in the Ground Round case, not all franchisees fared so well. Mike Metz, owner of three Ground Round restaurants in Pennsylvania, had a sales decrease of 20 percent. According to attorney Craig Tractenberg, several franchisees were forced into involuntary bankruptcy. Similar stories of failed franchisors abound. Have you ever heard of Aurthur Treacher's Fish and Chips, Griffs Hamburgers, 50 Flavors in a Tub, Spud Nuts, or Minnie Pearl's Fried Chicken? Probably not, but they represent just a tiny fraction of the scores of failed franchisors who not only went out of business but who took hundreds of franchisees along, as well.

http://www.franchise.org

franchises is the stability, integrity, and financial performance of the franchisor. You really should interview current franchisees, and you should talk to competing franchisors and their franchisees. If you buy a franchise, you will invest thousands of hours and thousands of dollars. Be sure that it is really an opportunity for you and not just for the franchisor.

Legal Considerations

Before you sign on the dotted line, you should personally study two key documents you always receive from a franchisor—the uniform franchise offering circular (UFOC) and the franchise agreement. The UFOC is a standard document franchises use to explain their operations, requirements, and costs to potential franchisees. You can get a guide to help interpret the UFOC at the Federal Trade Commission site. The franchise agreement is the specific contract signed, often incorporating the information included in the UFOC. Both documents are complex. To make sure you have all your bases covered, it is important to get the opinion of an experienced franchise lawyer. You want to know several things, including (1) if and how you can transfer the franchise license to someone else, (2) how you may terminate the contract, (3) how the franchisor may terminate the contract, and (4) what disclosures you are required to make.

http://www.ftc.gov/bcp/franchise/netdiscl.htm

If the contract restricts or prohibits you from transferring the franchise to another or if it requires that you achieve unrealistic results to be able to renew, an unscrupulous franchisor has an opportunity to take over your successful business at a bargain price. Your blood, sweat, tears, and life savings will have gone for naught.

The contract must specify the conditions under which it may be terminated. There have been lawsuits and allegations of fraud against some franchisors because of contract provisions that prohibit the franchisee from terminating the contract, but give the franchisor permission to cancel with specifying cause or giving advance notice. If you can't terminate the contract in the case that the franchisor goes bankrupt, most likely you will also be forced out of business.

Franchising has a long history of unscrupulous and fraudulent operations. Because of the many abuses, the U.S. government and the governments of all 50 states have passed regulatory legislation for franchisors. The minimum disclosure standards that a franchisor must meet are specified by Rule 436 of the Federal Trade Commission. Despite this law, however, abuses and frauds are still being perpetrated. In fact, the third item listed on the SBA's Hot List site is a document that details how to avoid being victimized by scam artists. In college terms, do your homework—know what the opportunity is and who the franchisors are. As is true of purchasing an operating business, caveat emptor.

Inheriting a Business

LO6
Understand the problems of management succession in a family-owned business.

Unless your parents or grandparents are small business owners, you might think that this section does not apply to you. However, someday you may well find yourself on the other end of the inheritance process: You may be the founder who wishes to pass your business to your heirs. Whether you are inheriting a business or bequeathing a business, you face the same problems of passing ownership. Only your point of view changes.

Family Businesses Succession

One of the most difficult things that you will ever have to do is make a successful ownership transition. Turning over management authority is not easy for most founders, nor is it easy for the heir of the founder. However, if the firm is to prosper, you've got to find a way to do it. Research shows that family-owned businesses usually fail after the death or retirement of the founder. Less than 30 percent are successfully transferred to a second generation. Less than 13 percent succeed long enough to be inherited by the third.[17] Family businesses that successfully make the transition do so by taking specific actions to organize the business and ensure that it can run profitably when the founder is gone.

Obtaining Professional Management

To make the transition, you will have to establish a formal management structure. You will have to develop a comprehensive business plan that states clear goals and objectives. Most difficult, you must be able to clearly see the strengths and weaknesses of family members who will remain in the business.[18] You must then hire professional managers to run those functions that family members cannot. Once successors have been selected, they must be educated in all parts of the family business in order for them to develop experience and skills.

Whether you are the founder or the successor, you face an overwhelming task. The founder must impart his or her unique knowledge, skill, and experience that have made the business successful. The successor must learn all these things. While this is happening, the founder and successor will have to work closely together.[19] Always there will be issues of who is in charge. No matter the skills and experience of the successor, as long as the founder is active in the business, many people will automatically turn to him or her for decisions.

Succession Issues for the Founder

To ensure that your business survives after you're gone, you must be proactive in bringing selected family members into the business as soon as you can.[20] You should write out your specific decisions and desires concerning who inherits what and then personally inform everyone who is affected by your decisions. You must also explicitly state the reasons for selecting any one family member. All too often the heir not selected challenges the succession after the founder dies. When this happens, the business often fails, and only the lawyers win.[21]

Succession Issues for the Successor

To ensure that the business thrives after you've taken over, you must be able to gain the loyalty of other family members, professional managers, and employees. You will be walking a fine line between acceding to the wishes of the founder and making changes that all dynamic business require. When changes are necessary, you should take the time to involve as many of those affected as possible in the decision process. It is important that you neither allow the business to become fossilized—a monument to the founder—nor present yourself in such way that you are perceived as an "upstart," determined to erase all signs of the founder.

Ownership Transfer

Regardless of whether you are the founder or the successor, you certainly do not want to wait until the founder dies to pass ownership. If you are the founder, once you're dead, your desires become irrelevant. If you are the successor, once the founder is dead, there is no authority figure who can help with issues of control and strategy. Rather than waiting for the founder to die, you should assist in completing a comprehensive estate planning process while the founder is still healthy and in charge.[22] In most cases, a gradual transfer of ownership is preferable to a single inheritance.[23] This strategy may not be appropriate, however, if there are multiple heirs. Of greatest importance is determining who gets voting stock. If the heirs who are not involved in management receive voting stock, issues of who is in control can arise because of jealousy and intrafamily rivalries.

Family Firm Institute – www.ffi.org

There is no easy answer to these issues. In fact, the transfer of ownership is highly complex and is unique to each family business. The larger and more successful your business is, the more complex and difficult the problem becomes. Using experts in law, accounting, and business can help identify the potential problems and help organize solutions. For family business succession plans, using specialists is essential. For family business experts, the major professional association is the Family Firm Institute. There are several organizations for business brokers; you can find them in the Google directory by entering "business broker association." In any case, it always pays to ask other entrepreneurs and advisers such as lawyers and accountants if they have recommendations and personal experience with these experts. Involving specialists also sends a clear message to creditors and suppliers that both old and new owners are determined to make a success of the transition.

Professional Management of Small Business

LO7
Describe how hired managers become owners of small businesses.

As small businesses grow, the requirements of managing them increase proportionately. If your business grows large enough, no matter how experienced or talented you are, eventually the demands of managing will become too great for you to handle alone. At this point, one of two things happens: (1) the business starts to decline, or (2) professional managers are hired to share the management load.

In the terms of small business, professional management is not an issue of education, titles, or credentials. A professional manager of a small business is one who has the experience and skills to use a systematic approach to analyzing and solving business problems.

These kinds of people are not easy to find. You may have to look to other businesses in your industry for experienced managers who are seeking new challenges and opportunities. You may find such people working for your vendors or your customers. In an ideal world these people would already be working among your employees, people who, because of their individual drive, personality, and skills, have learned your business quickly, and have taken on responsibility and authority.

Employee managers of small firms are often would-be entrepreneurs. The set of management skills needed to be an effective manager of small business is very similar, if not identical, to the set needed to be an effective business founder or owner. Because of this, it is common for a manager to become an owner—either of your business or of a competing business. Entry into ownership is accomplished through all the ways discussed in this chapter, including leaving employment to start up a new business, buying out or buying into an existing business, or contracting a franchise relationship.

There are only five paths of entry into small business management, although the details of how any one person gets started are unique. You may start a business, buy a business, franchise a business, inherit a business, or be employed as a manager in a business. Getting into business, for all its difficulties and problems, is however, the easiest part of small business management. Making the business successful and finding a graceful and appropriate way to get out is the true challenge, and that is what we look at in later chapters.

CHAPTER SUMMARY

LO1 Describe five ways that people get into small business management.

- You may start a new business.
- You may buy an existing business.
- You may franchise a business.
- You may inherit a business.
- You may be hired to be the professional manager of a small business.

LO2 Learn the rewards and pitfalls of starting a new business.

- **Advantages:** A start-up begins with a clean slate and provides the owner with the opportunity to use the most up-to-date technologies and new unique products or services. It can be deliberately kept small to limit possible losses.

- **Disadvantages:** A start-up business has no initial name recognition, will require significant time to become established, can be very difficult to finance, cannot easily gain credit, and may not have experienced managers and workers.
- There are 12 methods for increasing start-up success.
- Starting a new business from scratch can be made easier by using methods to reduce initial capital requirements and to gain access to business and industry experience, such as starting a business in your home to reduce start-up costs, having a partner to share capital, and making an alliance with your current employer to gain access to industry sources.

LO3 Understand the opportunities and pitfalls of purchasing an existing business.

- **Advantages:** Established customers provide immediate sales and cash inflows, business processes are already in place in an existing business, and purchasing a business often requires less cash outlay than does creating a start-up.
- **Disadvantages:** It is very difficult to determine the value of a small business, existing managers and employees may resist change, the reputation of the business may be a hindrance to future success, the business may be declining because of changes in technology, or the facilities of the business may be obsolete or in need of major repair.
- There are multiple sources to help find businesses for sale, such as business brokers, networking in the industry of interest, advertising of businesses for sale, and your current employer's business.
- You must do an exhaustive investigation to determine a business's suitability and value.

LO4 Explain four methods for purchasing an existing business.

- Buyouts are restricted to businesses that have a formal legal form of organization, including corporations, limited liability companies, and partnerships.
- A buy-in involves acquiring only a part of the ownership of an existing business.
- Key resource acquisitions, also called bulk asset purchases, are the only manner in which a sole proprietorship may be purchased.
- A takeover involves purchasing enough of the target business's stock to gain control of the board of directors of the business.

LO5 Learn about the approach and reasons for buying a franchise.

- Franchising is a legal agreement that allows a business to be operated using the name and business procedures of another firm.
- There are three basic forms of franchising: trade name, product distribution, and business format.
- Master franchises require opening multiple stores within a specified area.
- **Advantages:** the benefit of a proven successful business model, training and management support, and less risk than in starting a new business or acquiring an operating business.
- **Disadvantages:** little control of business marketing and operations, and success determined to a large extent by the success of the franchisor.

LO6 Understand the problems of management succession in a family-owned business.

- Family-owned businesses tend to fail after the death or retirement of the founder.
- Those family businesses that make the transition from the founder to the next generation take specific actions to organize the business.

LO7 **Describe how hired managers become owners of small businesses.**

- Entry into ownership by employee managers may be accomplished in three ways: leaving employment to start up a new business, buying out or buying into a business, or contracting a franchise relationship.

DISCUSSION QUESTIONS

1. What is the best way to get into business? Why do you think so?
2. If you were able to enter into any small business that you desired, what things would you look for in the business?
3. Suppose you had arranged enough capital so that you could either buy into an existing Outback Steak House or could start your own independent steak house restaurant. What are the advantages and disadvantages of each alternative? Which would you prefer and why?
4. Suppose that you have developed an idea for a new business service. You have limited capital and you do not want to drop out of college. How might you successfully start up a new business using your idea?
5. One evening when you went to pick up your child at the KinderKare, the owner mentioned to you that she would like to sell the business. You have always wanted to run a day care facility and would like to try to buy her business. What facts should you consider in making this decision?
6. After discussing the KinderKare purchase with your banker, you decide to make a determined effort to purchase the business. To make a good decision, what information must you have, and how will you get it?
7. Based on the information you developed, you have decided that the maximum value of the KinderKare, including the building and lot is $350,000. You have $35,000 that you inherited from your favorite great aunt. Your parents have promised to invest $25,000. Based on the $70,000 that you have available, the bank has promised to make you an SBA guaranteed loan of $70,000. What are your options if you wish to pursue this opportunity?
8. You took a job bagging coffee for a business that purchases directly from Guatemalan farmers, thereby getting the coffee at a bargain price, while still paying the farmers above market for the coffee. Working with all that caffeine has you charged up about going into business for yourself. The owner is only 60 years old, but he has told you that he'd like to slow down. He has offered to sell you all or part of the business. What things should you consider in making a decision about what to do?

EXPERIENTIAL EXERCISES

1. Using the resources of your library, find the name and address of an active business broker in your area. Arrange an interview with the broker. Write a report detailing what methods the broker uses to place a value on a business for sale.
2. Find out how the owner of the business where you are employed got into business.
3. Visit the Small Business Administration Web site franchising page at **http:///www.sba.gov/starting_business/startup/franchise.html**. Using the links on that site, find a franchise business that you believe might be successful, were you to buy it. Contact the franchisor, explain your interest, and find out the specifics of the franchise opportunity. Report your findings to your class.

Mini-Case

TOO HOT TO HOLD

Gwendolyn Bonnefille, a single mother, is barely scraping by. Although she earns a fair salary working in the accounts receivable department of a local business, she has to pay for child care for her two children, Samantha who is 5 and Merlin who is 3. While surfing the Web, under a listing titled "businesses that can be moved," she found for sale a business that makes a great hot-sauce called Caterwauling Coyote, with the slogan, "You'll howl at the moon!" The sauce is made in the kitchen of the owner, bottled, labeled, and then delivered to gift and specialty shops in south Texas. The equipment to make the sauce is commercial quality and appears to be in good condition.

The business financial statements and the owner's 1040 C business tax returns do not agree. The financial statements show that in the most recent year the business earned $60,000 on sales of $200,000. The 1040 C shows a profit of only $10,000, and a zero tax liability because of deducting losses suffered in prior years. The sellers are asking $240,000 for the business. They are willing to finance $190,000 at 10 percent for 15 years.

When Gwendolyn sat down with the owner, Sylvester Gatos, he attempted to explain the discrepancy between the accounting and the tax returns.

"You see," Sly said, "there are two things. First, some of the expenses on the schedule C aren't really business expenses, if you know what I mean. Second, when we did the income statement, we took out depreciation, interest, property tax, and the money that we used from the business because a buyer will not have those expenses."

CASE DISCUSSION QUESTIONS

1. What do you think about Sly's explanation of the differences between his income statement and his 1040 Schedule C?
2. Suppose that the income statement is reasonably accurate. What do you think about the purchase price?
3. What information should Gwendolyn obtain before making a decision to purchase the business?

LEARNING OBJECTIVES

This chapter will help you:

LO1 Learn the decisions needed to establish a foundation for strategic planning.

LO2 Learn the forms of imitative and innovative businesses.

LO3 Articulate the benefits that win over customers.

LO4 Use SWOT analysis to identify strategic options.

LO5 Understand the major strategies of business–differentiation, cost, and focus.

LO6 Use value chain analyses to apply strategy throughout the firm.

LO7 Learn how to sustain competitive advantage through attracting customers and discouraging competition.

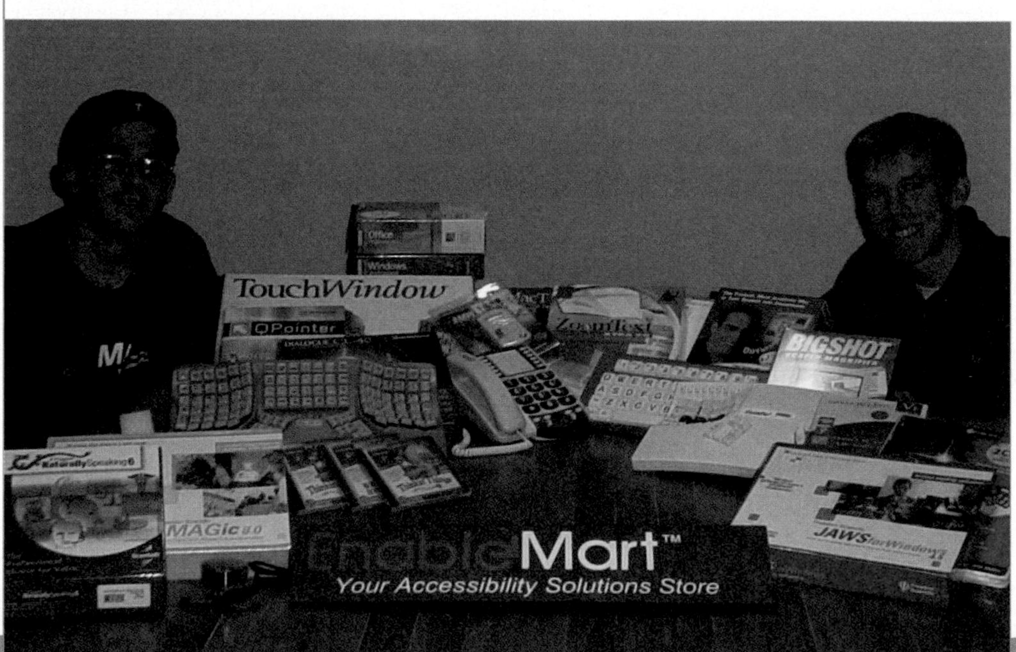

■ Nick Tostenrude and Dennis Moulton took time to understand their idea's strengths, weaknesses, and their market. How did this thorough analysis lead to their success rather than an unfulfilled dream?

Small Business Strategies: Imitation with a Twist

Focus on Small Business: Mindnautilus.Com[1]

Nick Tostenrude was attending the University of Portland when he met Dennis Moulton in 1999. The two got to talking, and it turned out both wanted to get into business for themselves. Dennis offered an idea from his father—PC- and Internet-based programs to help the cognitive functioning of people recovering from traumatic brain injury. While Dennis's father developed the software on the Apple II years before, its functionality was limited by the less capable hardware and software of that early computer. Dennis and Nick thought they would try again, with state-of-the-art technology. They incorporated in March 2000.

The fundamental idea made sense. Doing an industry analysis, they discovered some interesting opportunities. Most of the substitutes for their proposed product involved the person going to a hospital, rehabilitation center, or health professional's office for therapy. The alternative was working at home, but books were hard to use, and videotapes offered limited interaction. Research also showed a market of 54 million people with disabilities in the United States.

There were also some threats in the market. Numerous small mom-and-pop companies offered one or two products, but none had taken the market by storm, due largely to poor marketing, mostly confined to one locality. Another major market hurdle was that many people with traumatic brain injury did not have personal computers equipped with special features, like keypads, pointing devices, and screen enlargers. Without this equipment, even the best cognition software would be unusable. By far the biggest threat was technological. While Dennis's father had developed the software years earlier, creating software that met the demands of a market increasingly sophisticated about therapies and personal computer software was turning out to be a real challenge.

Mindnautilus looked like a promising idea, but one that would require three or four years of expensive research, development, programming, and debugging before any sales could be made. Neither Nick nor Dennis had the deep pockets it would take to fund the research and development effort. The problem was to find a strategy that would leverage what they could do now and use it to build toward their dream.

They knew there was a large market of potential consumers. They also knew there was a pool of firms making assistive devices and software for the market, but for the most part these firms had weak marketing and hence weak sales. Nick and Dennis realized that the Internet was the perfect way to sell these products to a market of families with one or more members with disabilities. Fortunately, the software for creating online stores was easy to master and inexpensive. So they started Enablemart.com, an online store specializing in selling assistive devices and software for people with disabilities. Sales of the Enablemart store would provide cashflow to support development of the program, Mindnautilus.

Today the business has customers in all 50 states and in over 20 foreign countries. The firm's expertise is great enough that it has done contract work for Microsoft and Goodwill Industries. The firm gives 10 percent of its pretax profits to charitable causes nominated by its customers. All these together led the firm to its receipt of a 2002 Global Collegiate Entrepreneur Award for the Pacific Northwest region. It also happened that Nick graduated from the University of Portland in 2002 with his bachelor's degree in electrical engineering. How did Nick describe the secret to his success? A superior strategist to the end, he said, "Find a niche."

DISCUSSION QUESTIONS

1. What were the strengths Mindnautilus possessed? What were the weaknesses it faced?
2. What could Mindnautilus do better than its competition?
3. What kind of strategy did Nick and Dennis plan for Mindnautilus?
4. Do you think Dennis and Nick could have predicted they would start Enablemart when they started Mindnautilus? Why or why not?

Strategy in the Small Business

LO1
Learn the decisions needed as a foundation for strategic planning.

Strategy is the idea and actions that explain how a firm will make its profit. Whether you know it or not, all small businesses have a strategy. The strategy may be a blueprint for planning or a standard to compare actions against. Either way, strategy defines for you, your customers, and your competition how your business operates.

Good strategy leads to greater chances for survival and higher profits for a small business. What makes a strategy good is its fit to the particulars of your business and the resources you can bring to it. In this chapter, we consider how strategy can be created and applied to help your business be its best.

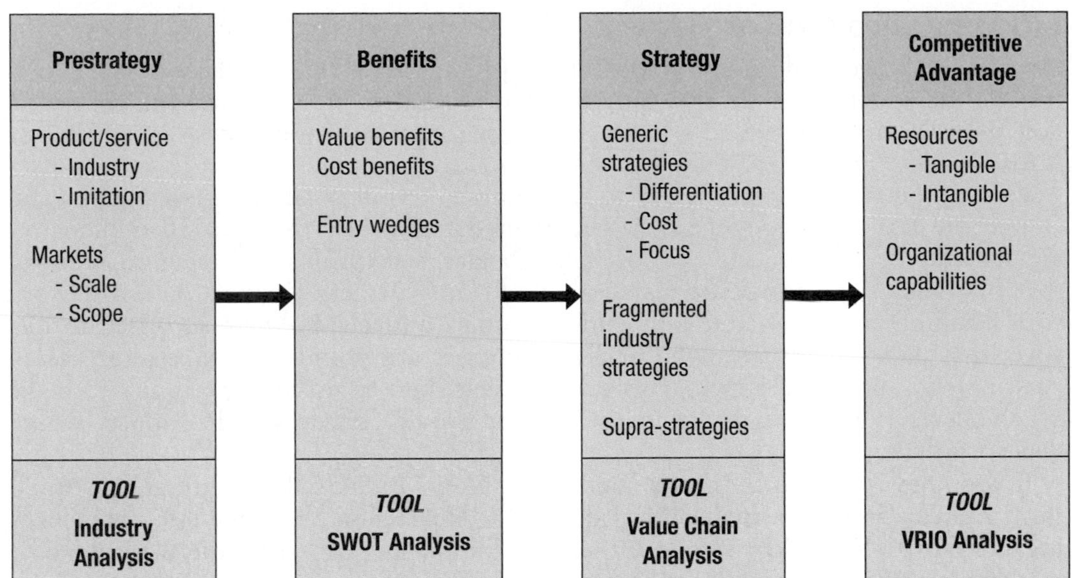

FIGURE 7.1

The Small Business Strategy Process

Strategy in small business is special because most small businesses are more imitative than innovative. If you are opening a home day care center, a machine shop, an Italian restaurant, or an online collectible figurine store, these types of businesses already exist. You can find examples, books, and often even magazines to study, as well as trade and professional associations to join. There are special strategies that aim to help imitative businesses be successful.

Getting to the useful strategies is a four-step process. Figure 7.1 shows the strategic planning process for small businesses. The first stage involves the prestrategy decisions you make which define your firm and your approach to it. Typically, these ideas are shown in a tool called an *industry analysis*. The second stage considers the benefits you want to offer your customers, and this information is tied to a SWOT (strength, weakness, opportunity, and threat) analysis. The third stage is where you select a strategy, which is usually applied to the firm through a value chain analysis. The final stage is where you work to ensure your firm's competitive advantage, using a VRIO (value, rareness, imitability, organization) analysis.

As you can see in Figure 7.1, strategy builds on four key decisions you make about your firm. These may be made formally or informally in your opportunity analysis or feasibility analysis. These decisions are:

1. The product or service you've chosen (also known as the industry).
2. The scope of the market you plan to serve, which can range from local to global.
3. The scale of the market for your product or service, whether it is a mass market or a niche market.
4. The decision to go for a firm that imitates existing businesses or one that seeks to be innovative.

Prestrategy: The First Step of Strategic Planning

The goal in the first stage of strategic planning involves deciding on the product or service you intend to offer and the general nature of your intended market, which is defined by how broadly you want to sell and how big a locality you want to cover. Each of these topics is covered next.

Industry: Product or Service

industry
The general name for the line of product or service being sold, or the firms in that line of business.

Industry is the general name for the line of product or service being sold. Examples include the restaurant industry, the computer consulting industry, and the collectible doll industry. In addition to a name, industries have numeric codes, called SIC or NAICS codes,[2] which are discussed below.

Picking the right industry is key to the success of your small business. Stanley and Danko, in *The Millionaire Next Door*, point out that two-thirds of all millionaires are self-employed. They say that the key to being successful is selecting an industry that offers good potential for making a profit and attractive opportunities to work with a minimum of risk and competition. Stanley and Danko were surprised to discover that most millionaires who owned businesses are in industries like scrap metal, coal mining, and dry cleaning. This suggests that there is much opportunity to make a good, even a great, living in industries that provide services and products we all depend on every day.

If you know the industry's code number (see Skill Module 7.1 to find out how to do this), you can find out a tremendous amount of information about the industry. This is because most information is coded using the industry number. From the work done by marketing researchers Stanley and Danko[3] as well as BizMiner.com and others, we know there are between 15,000 and 30,000 different industries in the United States.

There are two major classification systems that code industries: the new NAICS (North American industry classification system) and the better-known standard industrial classification system, or SIC.[4] SIC codes have four digits; NAICS have six. NAICS covers more industries and more of the newer types of industries. Skill Module 7.1 gives you help in finding the NAICS and SIC codes for the industry for your business.

SKILL MODULE 7.1

Finding Your Firm's Industry

Finding the NAICS and SIC codes for your industry is essential to tracking down information about the line of business you want to pursue. Most libraries have reference works that you can read to find your industry such as the *Standard Industrial Classification Manual, 1987* (NTIS, 1987) and the *North American Industry Classification System: United States, 2002* (NTIS, 2002).

It's easier to search online. Go to **http://www.census.gov/epcd/naics02/** and find the text box that says "enter keyword." Enter the name of your industry. If you are not sure of the exact name, you can try using a part of the name. For example, you could enter *comp* in the box and get computers and compact disks. For today's example, think about opening a hamburger and fries sort of restaurant to compete with McDonald's. Enter *restaurant* and click on the *2002 NAICS search* button. The results give almost a dozen possibilities including "Restaurant, fast food," "Restaurant, full service," and even related industries like "Restaurant Associations."

"Restaurant, fast food" is the key. Its NAICS code is 722211, officially known as "Limited-Service Restaurants." The SIC code is 5812.

To see what you can do with it, go to **www.census.gov** and click on "Economic Census," which is in the business section. There is another text box where you can enter an NAICS code. Its label is "industry statistics sampler." Enter 722211 and click on the *NAICS search* button. The result on screen will give you a link to the statistics. Click on the hot link, and you'll find yourself looking at the results from the economic census. You can find out how many fast food restaurants there are nationally or in your state. You can find out how much revenue they had and how many people were employed by them. You can figure averages for per-store sales and employment to get an idea of how well these restaurants do.

For example let's use the 2001 data. Texas has 13,068 fast food restaurants (establishments), employing 248,779 people. So the average restaurant employed 19 people. Those 13,068 restaurants spent $2,616,550,000 in payroll in 2001, or $200,225 per fast food place. That works out to around $10,538 in wages or salaries for each employee on average. Now you know a bit about the going rates for workers and the kind of money you'll need to budget.

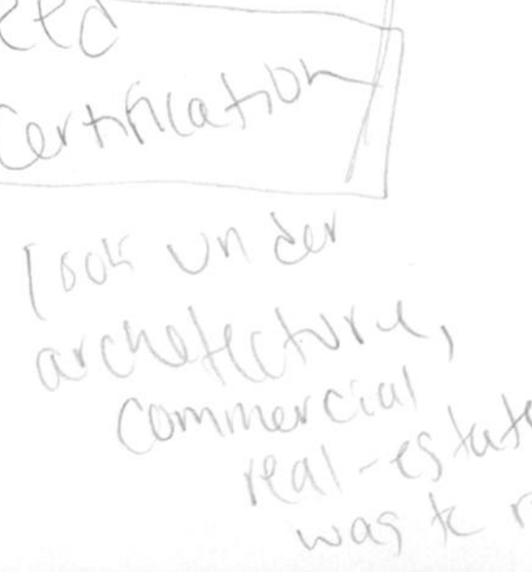

Armed with the NAICS or SIC codes, you can go to library sources such as the *Standard and Poor's Industry Surveys* or online sources such as Wetfeet.com **http://www.wetfeet.com/asp/industries_atoz.asp** (which is free) or BizMiner **www.bizminer.com** (which charges for reports) to find more detailed information about the industry you're thinking of entering.

Government, as well as **trade and professional associations**, gathers and reports industry data by SIC or NAICS codes. A trade association or professional association is a group of people in the same industry who band together to gather and share information, as well as present and represent the industry to the public and government. Trade associations are truly important sources when you are going into business. For example, you might be starting a traditional laundromat (called "coin-operated laundries & drycleaners" and given an NAICS code of 81231, SIC 7215). A trade association can offer a lot of help. Enter "laundry, association" into Google.com and you get directed to the Coin Laundry Association, the trade group for this industry. Like many associations, the CLA offers free information to people thinking about entering the industry—things like industry profiles and analyses.

trade association (also known as professional association)
A group of people in the same industry who band together to gather and share information and present and represent the industry to the public and government.

www.coinlaundry.org

Finding Your Trade or Professional Association

SKILL MODULE 7.2

Following are five ways to find the trade or professional association for your industry:

You can use the Google approach we tried for laundromats. Enter the name of the product or service. If it takes multiple words, like "child care," put the phrase in quotation marks. Add a comma and the word *association.* For this example, Google turns up groups such as the National Child Care Association and the National Association for Family Child Care.

If that does not work, the American Society of Association Executives Gateway has a searchable online directory of nearly 7,000 trade and professional associations.

An industry portal is a Web site with capabilities for multiple groups like current members, potential members, media, and policy makers. Portals offer multiple services like disseminating documents, chat rooms, discussion groups, registration services, databases, and the like. Polson Enterprises maintains one of the most extensive industry portals pages on the Internet.

Most public and university libraries have Gale Publishing's *Directory of Associations,* which lists tens of thousands of trade and professional groups.

One other way to find associations is by looking up the magazines that target specific industries and professions (called **trade magazines**), since many are published by trade and professional associations. The best online search source is Oxbridge Communications which has over 75,000 newsletters, catalogs, and other publications in its database. Printed directories of publications by Bacon Publishing or Burrelle can be found on many libraries' reference shelves.

www.nccanet.org

www.nafcc.org

http://info.asaenet.org/gateway/OnlineAssocSlist.html

http://www.virtualpet.com/industry/mfg/mfg.htm

The green trade association

The key to finding information about industries is knowing how to check the information, and NAICS and SIC codes are essential to that. It is also important to know that there are no "safe" industries. In much the same way that families and societies are living things—things that are born, mature, and can die—industries can be considered living too. Ten years ago, coffee shops were a dead industry in most of the country. However, today, with Starbucks, Panera Bread, Seattle's Best, and a host of independent coffee shops blanketing the country, the industry has revived through franchises, company-owned stores, and innovative independents.

trade magazines
The magazines that target specific industries and professions.

www.mediafinder.com

Markets

market
The business term for the population of customers for your product or service.

scale
A characteristic of a market that describes the size of the market—a mass market or a niche market.

scope
A characteristic of a market that defines the geographic range covered by the market—from local to global.

mass market
A customer group that involves large portions of the population.

niche market
A narrowly defined segment of the population that is likely to share interests or concerns.

www.simplyshe.com

A **market** is the business term for the population of customers for your product or service. If you know your market inside and out, you are likely to know much of the key information for how to be successful in your line of business. There are two market decisions you need to make early in the process of going into business. One of these is the **scale** of the market, which is the size of the market—whether you plan to aim for a mass market or a niche market. The other is the **scope** of the market, which defines the geographic range covered by the market—from local to global.

Scale: Mass or Niche

When you think about the market for your product or service, you typically have two choices. A **mass market** is a market that involves large portions of the population—all men, all women, all teens, all elderly, all families, all manufacturers, all restaurants. Mass markets are broad, and a mass-market approach targets the entire market.

A **niche market** is a narrowly defined segment of the population that is likely to share interests or concerns—25–34 year-old women, families with twins, Boy Scouts, Italian restaurants, manufacturers in your city. Niche markets are specific and narrow, and in a niche market approach, you try to target only customers in the niche.

Most industries have both mass and niche markets. For example, the greeting card industry has mass-market giants like Hallmark and American Greetings, which advertise nationally on TV (a sure sign of a mass marketer). However, the industry is also full of niche markets. For example, Maria Peevey and Lisa Bicker started SimplyShe with greeting cards targeting women going through trying life experiences such as breaking up, motherhood, or weddings. Having identified their niche and its needs, they market their cards through specialty fashion boutiques such as Henri Bendel, as well as online.[5]

Scope: Local to Global

Market scope is related to market scale. Market scope refers to the geography of your target market. It can be local (like a neighborhood or a city), regional (e.g., a metropolitan area or a state), national, international (usually meaning two to a few countries), or global (meaning everywhere). Owners of the businesses studied in the PSED[6] were asked how much of their business they thought would come from each of the geographic categories. Overall, they estimated that 58 percent of sales would be local (within 20 miles), 30 percent would be regional (from 21–100 miles), 22 percent would be national (from 100 miles out to the rest of the United States), and only 4 percent would be international (outside the United States).

Market scope is important for two reasons. First, knowing your market scope helps you decide where to focus your sales and advertising efforts. The second benefit is that knowing your target market gives you a way to determine which potential competitors you need to worry about most, namely those also in your market scope.

Imitation and Innovation

LO2
Learn the forms of imitative and innovative businesses.

imitative strategy
An overall strategic approach in which the entrepreneur does more or less what others are already doing.

The choice between imitation and innovation is truly important and often overlooked. Businesses, especially new firms, can do more or less what others are already doing—an **imitative strategy**—or they can start doing something that is very different from what others do—an **innovative strategy**. Imitation is the classic small business strategy. We know from the PSED that almost two-thirds of people starting businesses today plan to use imitation as their approach.[7]

There are several advantages to using an imitative strategy.[8] You benefit from being able to buy existing technologies, such as industrial grade washing machines for a laundromat, Web servers for a hosting service, or calligraphy pens for greeting card publishing. Architects, builders, real estate agents, zoning boards, equipment manufacturers, equipment servicing companies, and banks are more likely to understand the industry and what is expected. Because of this, they can give you firm estimates of costs and schedules. With imitative approaches, there is also the possibility to buy existing businesses.

Perhaps the key benefit of an imitative strategy comes from your customers. Chances are they already know about the kind of product or service you are offering. This means your marketing efforts can focus on the benefits you offer instead of explaining the product itself.

innovative strategy An overall strategic approach in which a firm seeks to do something that is very different from what others in the industry are doing.

When you elect an innovative strategy, you have the benefit of making your business precisely fit your own ideas and preferences. Take the example of snowboards. When Dimitrije Milovich built the first modern snowboard in 1969, he not only had to have the product available for purchase, but he also had to inform the customers that such a product existed and how it could be used. With highly innovative businesses, there is often not much opportunity to sell the business, and the owner spends a lot of energy in creating the processes and markets as well as informing suppliers, resellers, and investors about the new product or service.

In practice, most firms use imitation plus or minus one **degree of similarity**. Imitation minus one degree of similarity would be the business equivalent of cloning. It is franchising, first discussed in Chapter 6, in which you purchase a precise and complete copy of an existing business from the franchisor. Imitation itself involves patterning a business on existing firms and processes. Your imitation is not likely to match the precision or completeness of copying seen in franchising, since you are unlikely to have all the information about the model businesses or processes. You may also adapt your business to fit local situations or your current situation. You might pattern your new Italian restaurant after the Olive Garden, but you end up buying your equipment and food from different sources and add local favorites, such as toasted ravioli in St. Louis, barbeque pizza in Memphis, or deep-dish pizza in Chicago. This approach is called **parallel competition**.

degree of similarity The extent to which a product or service is like another.

Imitation plus one degree of similarity is where you look at existing businesses and pattern yourself after them, with the exception of one or two key areas in which you seek to do things in a new, and hopefully better, way. This is called **incremental innovation** and is second only to parallel competition in frequency. You have seen it in the fast-food business where Burger King told customers "have it your way." This approach was bettered by Wendy's, which offered custom-built hamburgers that were, in addition, "hot and juicy." Hardees moved into the fray with supersized custom burgers. Each company makes custom-built hamburgers, but each added a small innovation to differentiate it from its competition. Small businesses do the same thing, whether they are offering haircuts or golf clubs.

parallel competition An imitative business that competes locally with others in the same industry.

incremental innovation An overall strategic approach in which a firm patterns itself on other firms, with the exception of one or two key areas.

The last stage is **pure innovation**, which results in a new product or service. These situations are rare. Typically with a new product or service, you also have a unique setting. For example, Philadelphia chef Joseph Poon was one of the early developers of a food style called *Asian Fusion*, which combined Asian food with contemporary American and nouvelle cuisine elements. His restaurant reflected the Asian Fusion theme with light woods, simple lines, and oriental details. Other Asian Fusion restaurants, such as Roy's of Seattle or the E&O Trading Company in San Jose, California,[9] added different wines, beers, and liquors, and even new types of mixed drinks developed to complement the food. After all this, the Asian Fusion chefs had to convince diners to try these new combinations of flavors.

pure innovation The process of creating new products or services, which results in a previously unseen product or service.

www.josephpoon.com

Tool: Industry Analysis

Armed with the concepts and preliminary information about the product/service and the market, you are ready to do a preliminary industry analysis. **Industry analysis (IA)** is a research process that provides the entrepreneur with key information about the industry, such as its current situation and trends. Most entrepreneurs initially do an IA to find out what the profits are in an industry in order to better estimate possible financial returns. Taking this one step further, finding out how those profits are generated

industry analysis (IA) A research process that provides the entrepreneur with key information about the industry, such as its current situation and trends.

■ Chef Joseph Poon, of Philadelphia Chinatown, showcases Asian Fusion cooking, an innovation he helped to spearhead. What kinds of ethical challenges might a pure innovation product or service pose to a small business owner?

often makes the difference between success and failure. Armed with this information, the entrepreneur can tell if the industry is growing, stable, or in decline and what the degree of competition is. Skill Module 7.3 provides a how-to description for gathering the five key types of information needed to perform an industry analysis. It also explains how the information is useful.

SKILL MODULE 7.3

Short and Sweet Industry Analysis

The basics of industry analysis (IA) consist of knowing five pieces of information.

1. **SIC/NAICS number and description (online):** Getting this information is detailed in Skill Module 7.1. It is important to know to search for other information about the firm.
2. **Industry size over time (online):** Getting this information is detailed in Skill Module 7.1 for 2001 data, but you can also get earlier years. These numbers tell you the overall trend (growing, stable, declining) and the degree of fragmentation of the industry (how many firms are in the industry, and how much of the market the largest firms have). Fragmented industries—in which the largest four firms control 40 percent or less of the sales[10]—are more likely to have active small business populations.
3. **Profitability:** This is key data. Getting it online free is usually not possible. You can pay for online reports at the Risk Management Association (RMA) or BizMiner Web sites, or you can check if your school or local library has a copy of the RMA's *Annual Statement Studies: Financial Ratio Benchmarks.* The key numbers are in the "Income Data" section in percentage form. Find the size of your firm above the "Number of Statements" number (for start-up businesses, the smallest size is often the best place to start). Then look down the column for the "Gross Profit," "Net Profit," and "Profit Before Taxes" numbers. **Gross profit** is what is left after deducting the cost of goods

gross profit
Funds left over after deducting the cost of goods sold.

sold. Net profit is what is left after deducting the operating expenses of the business. Profit before taxes represents the amount of money the owner or owners take out of the firm annually. When the business can sustain it, owners tend to put their salaries in the operating expense category. However, if the firm cannot afford the owner's salary, the only income is the profit before taxes.

4. **How profits are made (interview or articles):** Armed with the information from above, you can look for the last piece of the puzzle—how profits are made. There are usually four activities to evaluate. One is what can be done to generate more sales. Second is a judgment of whether it is possible to charge a premium for a product or service. Third is how to keep the cost of goods or services below the industry's average. Fourth is looking at ways to keep operating expenses below industry averages. Small businesses may use one or more of these approaches. Finding out which get used and the specifics of how they are used generally requires either talking to people in the industry or checking out the industry press. Skill Module 7.2 talks about where to find the trade and professional press for particular industries. If you go the interview route, you can talk to people at companies in the industry. Among the owners most willing to talk are those who have been officers in trade and professional associations or owners of businesses who would not see you as competition, such as owners in other cities. Many people have also found chat rooms, like those at **http://groups.google.com** or discussion boards (via **www.boardreader.com**), to be useful in finding people and comments. Whenever possible, try to get at least five different sources to make sure you know what is really going on.
5. **Target market competitor concentration (directory checking):** By looking at the listings for local and commercial directories (and companies' Web sites), you can get an idea of the market scope and scale of the businesses with whom you'll be competing. By getting the number that matches your firm in scale and scope, you can get a clear idea of the concentration of competitors in your segment of the industry—and whom you will need to keep an eye on.

net profit
The amount of money left after operating expenses are deducted from the business.

profit before taxes
The amount of profit earned by a business before calculating the amount of income tax owed.

Armed with the information from your industry analysis, you are in a better position to decide if the industry meets your needs for income (which comes from profits and operating revenues), financial growth (depending on the trend of the industry as a whole), and competitive challenge (depending on the number and concentration of competitors). It can also help you determine if you have or can get the expertise needed to run a profitable business (comparing how profits are made to how you would run your business if you started now). If the IA outcomes do not look promising, there are thousands of other industries to try, and it is time to think about what you can offer to attract customers to *your* business.

Benefits: The Second Step of Strategic Planning

LO3
Articulate the benefits that win over customers.

The key strategic decision you make is deciding what benefits you plan to offer your customer. Benefits are characteristics of a product or service that the target customer would consider worthwhile, such as low cost or high quality. Benefits can focus on value added to the product or service or on the cost of the product or service.

benefits
Characteristics of a product or service that the target customer would consider worthwhile.

Value and Cost Benefits

Value benefits can include quality, style, delivery, service, technology, ease of shopping, personalization, assurance, place, brand or reputation, belonging, or even altruism. *Cost benefits* can come from lower costs, from savings brought on by scale or scope, or even from greater efficiencies resulting from thorough learning or superior organizational practices.[11] You can get more detail on these in The Thoughtful Entrepreneur.

Benefits are central to how you appeal to your target customer base. Picking benefits customers find attractive makes your firm attractive to them. Picking customer-desired benefits that your competitors do not offer is a powerful way to make your firm stand out from the competition. Benefits drive your firm's offering to its customers

THE THOUGHTFUL ENTREPRENEUR

Value and Cost Benefits

VALUE BENEFITS

Quality: Offering a quality level others do not. It can be the highest quality, just enough quality to meet the basic need, or a bit more quality than is typical for the price. Offering guarantees and warranties also reflects quality benefits.

Style: Items that are beautiful, fashionable, popular, or otherwise aesthetically pleasing.

Delivery: Sometimes simply offering delivery is enough, but other times you may need to deliver quickly, on schedule, or where others do not.

Service: Examples include the go-the-extra-mile sort, the personalized know-your-customer's-name sort, the we-serve-you-in-one-minute sort, or even the service-after-the-sale sort.

Technology: You can offer state-of-the-art or leading-edge technology, technology that others do not have, or technology that automates or simplifies tasks or that meets industry standards. Offering complementary technology such as voice mail or answering machines to people with telephones also fits in here.

Shopping ease: Providing one-stop shopping; having all of a product line; making ordering, returning, or upgrading easy for the customer are all benefits.

Personalization: This can come in building custom products or services, or personalizing the customer experience.

Assurance: Offering guarantees, warranties, or service that takes the risk out of buying your product or service.

Place: Being conveniently local is one example. Being willing to sell and deliver where others do not is another.

Credit: One key benefit small businesses offer customers can be extending credit where larger firms and chain stores will not.

Brand/reputation: This can come from the products or services that you offer, or from your own firm's reputation.

Belonging: Some products confer value because they make the customer part of a larger group, such as a member of a club or an online gaming community.

Altruism: If your product helps the community, a group, the environment, or the world, it is a benefit.

COST BENEFITS

Lower costs: Operating from your home, getting family members to contribute their time for free, or selling something you've already gotten your value out of are all examples of ways small businesses keep their costs low.

Scale savings: Buying in volume usually produces savings, so some firms buy in bulk and sell or repackage in smaller amounts, passing along some of the cost savings.

Scope savings: A multifunction printer has a broad scope—it combines a printer, a scanner, and a fax machine into one box. This is because they can share parts, and this sharing results in lower costs.

Learning: As a firm gets more experience, it can often work with fewer mistakes and greater efficiencies, thereby lowering costs.

Organizational practices: Possibly a small business has automated or professionalized or mastered a product or service to the extent it can do it more cheaply than others.

and influence every part of the strategy process. As we will see later, benefits can be combined to offer themed strategic packages.

Offering the benefits your customers want opens up the possibility of your being able to charge a premium price and make higher profits, since people are willing to pay for value-based benefits they desire. Having cost-based benefits can also increase profits by lowering your cost of doing business, increasing your margin relative to your competition's. Therefore, it is easy to see how benefits help you select a strategy that improves your firm's profitability.

Leveraging Opportunities during Entry

How can the owner of a small business decide where to focus attention? Entrepreneurship professor Karl Vesper suggests that success depends on picking the right **entry wedge** to get into the market.[12] An **entry wedge** is an opportunity that makes it possible for a new business to gain a foothold in a market. Vesper suggests seven wedges specific to small businesses pursuing an imitation strategy.

entry wedge
An opportunity that makes it possible for a new business to gain a foothold in a market.

awayirs.com

- **Supply shortages:** Supply shortages occur when a new product is in demand. The target audience is leading-edge buyers who are willing to pay a premium to be the first to have the product. This is a short-term market and one that changes rapidly. The key benefits are delivery, shopping ease, and style.
- **Unutilized resources:** Unutilized resources can be a physical resource like gravel in a farm field or even entire inner cities (see Small Business Insight: Initiative for a Competitive Inner City). It can also be a human resource. Tax Resources, Inc., got started in 1988 by people experienced in dealing with the IRS in order to advise taxpayers on legal strategies to minimize their taxes or handle audits.[13] The key benefits are lower costs, scale savings, or organizational practices.
- **Customer contracting:** Customer contracting occurs when a customer, most often a business, is willing to sign a contract with a small business to ensure a product or service. Because big businesses frequently downsize, they have ongoing needs to outsource work. Former employees are often the preferred source for independent subcontractors. (See http://www.entrepreneur.com/ Your Business/ YB SegArticle/0,4621,297205,00.html for example, if needed). The key benefits are quality, delivery, technology, shopping ease, brand/reputation, and assurance. Style and personalization are often factors too.
- **Second sourcing:** Second sourcing seeks out customers who are already being serviced by another firm. The strategy is to offer customers a second place to obtain goods or services. Often the advantage the small business offers is being locally based. Second sourcing provides the customer with greater certainty of supplies or services, and at its best provides a competitive pressure to keep both suppliers providing the best service and prices. Like customer contracting, the key benefits are quality, delivery, technology, shopping ease, brand/reputation, and assurance.
- **Market relinquishment:** Market relinquishment occurs when business firms leave a market. Since the 9/11 terrorist attacks, the major American airlines have dramatically scaled back their service. For small commuter airlines, these market

SMALL BUSINESS INSIGHT

Initiative for a Competitive Inner City

The inner city of Buffalo, New York, is an unlikely place to find a growing construction company. It is an economically depressed, gritty, urban center still on the long road to revitalization. Some folks, however, see a lot of potential in it. Sundra Ryce graduated from Buffalo State in 1996, and started SLR Construction Services Company. She knew the industry from working in her father's construction firm. She chose the inner city because it put her close to her clients in government and helped keep costs low. One of the few woman and minority certified construction firms in the United States; SLR was able to land major contracts with the Veterans Administration. Her drive led SLR to become number four on a national list of most accomplished inner city businesses[14] in 2003 when she was 28 years old.

■ Market relinquishment, such as the scaling back of services by several major airlines in the United States since September 11, 2001, is one of the ways big businesses create opportunities for smaller companies. How does market relinquishment play into the other entry wedges available to small businesses?

relinquishments have been opportunities to expand and provide ongoing service to smaller airports. Key benefits are place, shopping ease, quality, delivery, and service.

- **Favored purchasing:** Favored purchasing occurs because government agencies, government-sponsored commercial contracts, and many big businesses have policies that provide for set-asides or quotas for purchases from small businesses. You can find out more at the SBA's online government contracting site. Key benefits are quality, delivery, service, assurance, place, and belonging.
- **Government rules:** Rule changes by the government can help small firms compete. For example, when the Environmental Protection Agency let small construction firms out of some of the water pollution treatment requirements that large firms must face, it gave the small businesses a savings of $1.5 billion, which made them more competitive. The Regulatory Flexibility Act of 1980 drives many of these rule changes in government.[15] Key benefits here are technology, service, personalization, lower costs, and organizational practices.

http://www.sba.gov/GC/

Tool: SWOT Analysis

LO4
Use SWOT analysis to identify strategic options.

SWOT stands for strength, weakness, opportunity, and threat. *Strengths* are characteristics of the business or team that give it an advantage over others in the industry. *Weaknesses* are characteristics that place the firm at a disadvantage relative to others. *Opportunities* are chances to make greater sales or profits in the environment, and *threats* are elements in the environment that could cause trouble for the business.

SWOT analysis is a strategic planning tool that looks critically at these factors. It is probably the best-known strategic planning tool. It is used to organize and perform an analysis of your company's current and future resources and situations. It provides one of the best ways to organize your thinking about how to pursue the benefits you have identified as important to your customers.

In a SWOT analysis, you gather information from yourself and others who know you, your company, the market, and the industry. Talking to potential customers is also a positive in SWOT analyses. The questions are simply the SWOT topics: "What do you see as the opportunities and threats in the market or industry?" and "What do you see as the strengths and weaknesses of my firm?" You can obtain this information from formal or informal interviews, as well as from brainstorming sessions. **Brainstorming** is a group discussion in which people are asked to give their ideas and thoughts about a topic. In a brainstorming session there is one special rule—nobody can criticize or put down an idea. The only types of questions that can be asked are to clarify what someone meant.

brainstorming
A group discussion in which criticism is suspended in order to generate the maximum number of ideas.

SKILL MODULE 7.4

The Mechanics of a SWOT Analysis

Take the responses from the sources and put them into a SWOT table like the one shown in Figure 7.2. To analyze the ideas listed in the SWOT table, start with opportunities. Identify the opportunities that seem strongest. Compare these to your strengths, looking for matches. For example, if there is an opportunity for "more postsale support" in a computer store and one of your strengths is "great at explaining computers," you would be well-positioned to move on the opportunity.

Similarly, you compare threats to your weaknesses. A typical threat is "insufficient capital" for a start-up. Then if you see "lack of capital" as one of your firm's weaknesses, you know where you need to put in extra effort. It also makes sense to do a cross-comparison, such as strengths to threats and weaknesses to opportunities. This can point the way to solving problems. For example, in the lack of capital problem, having a strength such as "a large support network" might offer a way to look for the missing start-up capital. Along the same lines, strong opportunities can offset weaknesses. For example, a lack of experience with a product is less of a weakness when the product is new and demand for it is very high.

FIGURE 7.2

Typical SWOT Topics

Strengths	Weaknesses
Customers ready to buy Contracts for products or service Adequate financial backing Specialized knowledge Strong support network Trade secrets, secret recipes Patents, trademarks, copyrights Brand or personal recognition Location or facility advantages Superior product/service or processes Superior staff Prior self-employment experience Prior managerial experience Prior sales experience Prior experience in the industry Prior experience in the locality Prior experience in the market	Customers not ready to buy Inadequate financial backing Easy-to-copy business Weak or no support network Undistinctive product, service, or brand Location or facility disadvantages Inadequate staff Lack of self-employment experience Lack of managerial experience Lack of sales experience Lack of experience in the industry Lack of experience in the locality Lack of experience in the market
Opportunities (from entry wedges)	**Threats**
Supply shortages Unutilized resources Customer contracting Second sourcing Market relinquishment Favored purchasing Rule changes by government Technology creating new products/services New markets opening up	Economic downturn Oversupply Competitive pressures Supplier/customer pressures Major supplier/customer loss Missed window of opportunity Negative government regulations or actions Obsolescence from market or technology change

Look again at the chapter's opening story about Mindnautilus.com. You will see some of the key results of the SWOT analysis that Nick and Dennis conducted. They found opportunities, such as the large market size and the lack of marketing among competitors. They also found threats to their business plan in the need for PCs to be equipped with assistive devices before the Mindnautilus software would work. Another major threat was the time and money it would take to get the software operational.

FIGURE 7.3

Strategic Suggestions from SWOT Analysis Combinations

Outside the Firm	Strengths	Weaknesses
Threats	**Fight**	**Flee**
Opportunities	**Flaunt**	**Fix**

Inside the Firm

strategic direction
The conceptualization of how a business might best move in response to the findings of a SWOT analysis—Flaunt, Fix, Fight or Flee.

For them, the SWOT analysis made clear the challenges facing the company, before they had committed their funds or lives to it.

At the end of a SWOT analysis, you have to make a decision about the **strategic direction** of the business. The options are generally described as: flaunt, fix, fight, or flee. You make the decision based on which pair of relations are the strongest. Where strengths match opportunities, you have the winning combination and you should flaunt and focus your efforts. Where a weakness gets in the way of pursuing an opportunity, you need to fix it to clear the way. Where your firm faces a threat, the best approach is to fight it with your strengths. When you see a threat that is made worse by a weakness in your firm, the best strategy is often to flee, trying to keep the weakness from exacerbating the threat. For Mindnautilus.com, the SWOT seemed to suggest to either flee in the short term or get ready for a long-term fix. Think about what you would recommend. It comes up at the end of the chapter.

The final stage of SWOT analysis is to match it against the benefits sought by your market. Central to making this work is having your benefits come up in the opportunities you and others see for the industry and market. If not, you need to rethink the benefits based on what the SWOT analysis uncovered. Your strengths should match or support the benefits, and your weaknesses should not get in the way of delivering the desired benefits. Threats that can challenge or limit the delivery of benefits to customers become a major hurdle that needs to be overcome before starting the business.

L05
Understand the major strategies of business—differentiation, cost, and focus.

Strategy Selection

generic strategies
Three widely applicable classic strategies for businesses of all types—differentiation, cost, and focus.

differentiation strategy
A type of generic strategy aimed at clarifying how one product is unlike another in a mass market.

cost strategy
A generic strategy aimed at mass markets in which a firm offers a combination of cost benefits that appeals to the customer.

focus strategy
A generic strategy that targets a portion of the market, called a *segment* or *niche*.

There are three classic strategies for businesses of all types—differentiation, cost, and focus. Because they are so widely applicable, they are called **generic strategies**. **Differentiation strategies** are aimed at mass markets—situations in which nearly everyone might buy your product or service. With this strategy, you try to show how your firm offers some combination of value benefits that is different from and better for the customer than those offered by competitors.

Relatively few small businesses use differentiation strategies, because it is hard for small businesses to have the resources to pursue mass markets. It happens most often when a small business offers a mass-market product or service locally. For example, a gas station offers a mass-market service, but its sales are naturally limited to a particular location. This business reality sets boundaries for where the firm competes, which helps target advertising and pricing.

Cost strategies are also aimed at mass markets. In a cost strategy, you try to show how your firm offers a combination of cost benefits that appeal to the customer. Small businesses in a variety of industries make use of mass-market cost strategies. Typically, this comes when the small business can pursue a very low cost operation. For example, one gravel supplier in Memphis, Tennessee, was the undisputed low-cost provider. His secret? A farmer by trade, he discovered gravel under one of his farm fields. He sold directly to the users, cutting out intermediaries and their costs.

Focus strategies target a portion of the market, called a *segment* or *niche*. Instead of selling mass-market gravel for everyone, a focus strategy might target people seeking decorative gravel. For example, Scott Stone Company in Mebane, North Carolina, offers eleven different types of gravel that differ in color, stone size, and durability.

Craftsmanship: Specialized product, localized business operations, high levels of craftsmanship (vs. competitors with scale economies).

Customization: Short delivery times, custom features, short production runs, high quality (vs. products that are mass produced).

Super-support: Extensive, intensive, and personalized after-sales service.

Serving the underserved/interstices: Targeting markets forgotten by larger competitors.

Elite: High-quality products with high prices, backed up by high expenditures for advertising and R&D (vs. mass-market products).

Single-mindedness: Developing and demonstrating exceptional expertise in one product or service (vs. competitors with broad approaches or product lines).

Comprehensiveness: Offering one-stop shopping with complete inventory, immediate delivery, knowledgeable staff, and the major supporting services in one location.

FIGURE 7.4

Seven Small Business Supra-Strategies

By ensuring the quality and consistency of the gravel and knowing which types work best in specialized settings, such as oriental gardens or waterscapes, Scott Stone offers customers products and expertise not readily available elsewhere.

www.scottstone.com

A focus strategy can use aspects of differentiation or cost approaches that are reformulated for the niche market. You identify a focus strategy by figuring out what benefits your market most wants. This can be done by asking customers outright, through surveys, or by looking at what is working among your competitors locally or in more advanced markets. Often you will find that your market seems to want several benefits at once.

Building from this, strategy researchers Dean Shepherd and Mark Shanley identify seven classic benefit combinations which they call *supra-strategies*:[16] craftsmanship, customization, super-support, interstices, specialization, elite, and single-mindedness. The details about these are given in Figure 7.4.

Harvard strategy professor Michael Porter offers strategies for small businesses in industries in which virtually all firms have small market shares. Examples of these **highly fragmented industries** are given in Figure 7.5. Some of Porter's suggestions follow

highly fragmented industries
Collections of similar businesses in which virtually all firms have small market shares.

In the list below, the most fragmented lines of business in each industrial sector are given by name and NAICS* number. The percentage represents how much of the industry's sales are made by the top 50 firms.

Wholesale Trade
4218201 Farm machinery & equipment-farm dealers, 9.9%*
421830 Industrial machinery & equipment whsle, 15.4%

Manufacturing
332710 Machine shops, 8.7%
311811 Retail bakeries, 11.4%

Professional, Scientific, and Technical Services
541410 Interior design services, 10.9%
541613 Marketing consulting services, 21.9%

Accommodation and Foodservices
722410 Drinking places (alcoholic beverages), 3.4%

Arts, Entertainment and Recreation
713910 Golf courses & country clubs, 9.2%

Retail Trade
441110 New car dealers, 6.0%
453110 Florists, 6.8%

* NAICS code and industry name, 50 largest businesses in the industry in the United States.

FIGURE 7.5

Highly Fragmented Industries List

the seven Shepherd and Shanley supra-strategies, but Porter also offers four cost-driven strategies for small businesses worth a mention on their own.

Porter's first addition to the supra-strategies is to use *formula facilities* where you benefit from buying a prepackaged business. Franchises like McDonald's are the extreme example of this. However, there are also companies such as Sysco that can equip your restaurant with everything you need from equipment to food to menus. There is also usually an opportunity for a *bare bones* or *no-frills* provider. Being able to keep prices super low by cutting back on decor, hours, or employees always appeals to part of the market. Wal-Mart started this way, and chains like Weekends Only built on the idea, but in most cities, the truly low prices are found in small businesses that make a point of having even fewer frills than the national chains.

www.sysco.com

The way you run your business can also make a big difference in keeping costs low. Porter talks about backward integration. What this means is *cutting out the intermediary*. For example, when farmers start roadside stands or sell their food at a farmers' market, they can sell at lower prices and still make more money by eliminating wholesalers' and retailers' mark-ups.[17] The same approach will work wherever a product or service gets resold. The other type of efficiency comes when you can *tightly manage decentralization*. Once you know how to efficiently run one type of business, it often becomes easier to open related firms. The Menlove family mastered the auto business in southern Utah with a Dodge dealership started in 1962. Family members opened a Toyota dealership in 1986, and a Mitsubishi-Subaru dealership in 2002. Each one is highly rated in customer satisfaction and sales volume.[18] Part of the underlying reason is their ability to transplant the skills they mastered in the first dealership.

Tool: Value Chain Analysis

LO6
Use value chain analyses to apply strategy throughout the firm.

Offering the right benefits can make all the difference in your success. Many say that the best way to find out the right benefits for your market is to ask customers in that market. The key questions are what benefits do they see getting from the product or service they currently use, and what kinds of benefits would they like to have. Their answers become your target list of benefits.

Let's say that the key benefit your prospective customers say they want is the easiest shopping experience possible when buying collectible figurines. In designing your business, you can use a value chain analysis to make sure the benefits get applied throughout your firm. Michael Porter, the Harvard strategy professor mentioned above, also popularized value chain analysis. The **value chain** is the collection of processes and activities a small business conducts to design, produce, market, deliver, and support its product or service. The chain (see Figure 7.6) follows the production sequence: inbound logistics, operations, outbound logistics, marketing and sales, and service. The four areas that affect all of the organization are also considered: infrastructure, human resources, technology, and procurement. These are detailed in Table 7.1.

value chain
A collection of processes and activities a small business conducts to design, produce, market, deliver, and support its product or service.

FIGURE 7.6

Porter's Value Chain for Small Businesses

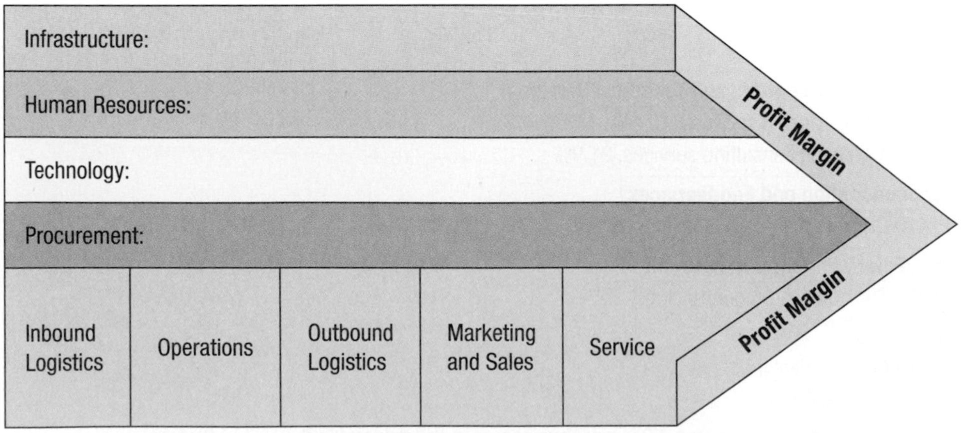

TABLE 7.1 Value Chain Analysis for Two Kinds of Businesses

	Collectible Gift Shop (NAICS 45322, SIC 5947)	Machine Shop (NAICS 332710, SIC 3599)
Intended Supra-Strategy: Underlying Benefit	**Comprehensiveness: Ease of Shopping**	**Single-Mindedness: Delivery**
Organizationwide Factors		
Infrastructure includes your location and the physical internal parts of the firm, like its computer system, offices, or sales area.	Lots of display space for inventory. Attractive sales area. Aisles wide enough to accommodate wheelchairs or walkers.	Space for major equipment and supplies onsite.
Human resources include your employees and their skills, the benefits you offer, and the working conditions they face.	Salespeople are collectors; offer employee discounts. Accommodate flexible scheduling.	Offer comparable benefits. Have industry leading overtime package to ensure delivery as promised.
Technology includes using training and technology to improve your products, services, processes, and people.	Keep inventory up to date and online. Tie register into inventory. Send staff to trade shows and provide subscriptions to trade magazines at store.	Get equipment needed to ensure delivery on schedule. Keep training to improve estimation.
Procurement includes your raw materials and how you obtain them.	Go to shows to buy. Keep complete stock of brand name lines. Participate in online procurement and auction services.	Keep multiple sources to ensure supplies arrive quickly when needed. Set up accounts with delivery and courier services.
Product/Service Sequence		
Inbound logistics focus on getting raw materials to where your firm can work on them.	Get new stock out as soon as it arrives.	Build procurement time into estimates. Double-check inventory or delivery time.
Operations are the processes that actually create the firm's products or services.	Have the most complete stock of collectible lines in the area. Deliver when out-of stock items arrive.	Once started, ensure no interruptions on project, and provide support as needed.
Outbound logistics focus on getting the finished product or service out to the customer.	Wrap all gifts over $10 in bubble-pack. Daily UPS/FedEx pickups with online tracking enabled.	Provide for rush delivery when needed. Provide delivery tracking.
Sales and marketing involve promotions such as discounts or loyalty programs, advertising, word-of-mouth campaigns, media reports, but most often the personal relationship between your firm and your customers.	Announce new stock in store windows, online, and via e-mails. Use color posters and displays. Participate in mail catalog distribution programs. Traveling show for nursing homes, working moms, and Girl Scouts.	Advertise rock-solid delivery schedules, percentage within schedule, stories of extraordinary efforts to deliver on time. Aim for time-sensitive customers.
Service involves everything after the sale, including repairs and replacements, upgrades, and customer support.	Greet all customers upon entry. Ask all customers if they need help. Answer questions. Have return, repurchase, and upgrade programs. Arrange for standing orders by series.	Keep customers informed of progress, especially when time is a critical factor. Check on delivery tracking. Call for follow-up on delivery and satisfaction.

Two outcomes are evaluated for each of these components. One is what each of these elements can add to the profit margin of the firm. In the case of the collectible figurine store, this becomes how can every function in the business make the shopper's ease of use the greatest possible. The other is how each component contributes to the strategy of the firm; for example, how can marketing and sales help the rest of the firm make the shopping experience easier. Table 7.1 shows a value chain analysis looking at the strategic contributions for two very different kinds of businesses—a collectible gift shop pursuing an ease of shopping benefit and a machine shop pursuing a delivery strategy.

The idea in a value chain analysis is to think through the different parts of the business with an eye toward getting the most bang for the buck from each part of the firm when pursuing your supra-strategy. Not every part of the firm can make a contribution to every type of supra-strategy, but using the value chain analysis can help people understand the overall goal of the business better as well as how their portion of the business contributes to the whole operation.

Competitive Advantage

LO7

Learn how to sustain competitive advantage through attracting customers and discouraging competition.

competitive advantage

The particular way a firm implements customer benefits that keeps the firm ahead of other firms in the industry or market.

To secure success, there is a step you need to take past picking and implementing the right strategy. It is the step of securing competitive advantage. **Competitive advantage** is the particular way you implement your customer benefits that keeps your firm ahead of other firms in your industry or market. Competitive advantage is your firm's edge in meeting and beating the competition.

It can be harder than it looks. Why? In part because most small businesses face a lot more forms of competition than they initially realize. Strategy guru Porter identifies five different threats of competition for any business. Imagine you plan to start a gourmet Asian fusion restaurant in the Philadelphia suburb of Wynnewood.

The first place we all look at are *existing firms* in your industry. Pretty much all the other gourmet restaurants and Asian-themed restaurants in the vicinity pose the threat of rivalry. Since Asian fusion food is still a new trend, another potential competitive threat will be *potential entrants*, other Asian fusion restaurants that open after yours. If you think about why people come to a restaurant, you realize that there is a very broad threat of *substitutes* with which you compete. The gourmet food take-outs at the local markets and food delivery services are obvious examples, but what about substitutes for a couple looking at your restaurant as a night's entertainment? You could be competing with movies, plays, bars, and clubs for that couple's entertainment dollars.

Part of what makes your restaurant special is the type of food you obtain. The *suppliers* of those unique foods are in a position to threaten bargaining for higher prices or premiums for giving you exclusive access to those foods. Similarly, your customers or *buyers* can also threaten you by bargaining for lower prices. This might be for catered dinners, or coupons, or through a frequent diner or early diner program, or even by corporate rates for repeat business customers.

The goal in finding a competitive advantage is to give you some protection against the many competitive threats your firm faces. Competitive advantage takes you from meeting the competition to hopefully beating it. The keys to this lie in the resources and the organizational capabilities available to your firm, as well as your ability to fight the competition.

resource

Any asset, capability, organizational process, information, or knowledge that contributes to the firm's performance.

tangible resources

Assets of a firm that can be easily and concretely identified.

intangible resources

Capabilities, organizational processes, information, or knowledge of a firm that are not clearly evident.

Resources: What You Bring to the Firm

A **resource** is any asset, capability, organizational process, information, or knowledge that contributes to the firm's performance. Strategy theorist Jay Barney suggests that resources fall into two types: **tangible resources**, which are those that are easily identified, and **intangible resources**, which are those typically informational and expertise-based practices and routines that are not clearly evident. Specific examples of these are given in Figure 7.7.

FIGURE 7.7

Resource Examples

Tangible

- *Financial:* Cash and cash equivalents (savings, stocks, bonds, accounts receivable), ability to raise money, credit lines.
- *Physical:* Land, buildings, equipment, tools.
- *Technological:* Trade secrets, recipes, patents, trademarks, brand names, superior technology, superior expertise.
- *Organizational:* Financial controls, cash controls, planning systems, development procedures, R&D efforts, monitoring customers/competitors/markets, use of insurance and protective or security systems.

Intangible

- *Human:* Employee experience, skill, expertise, morale, work ethic, loyalty, relations with customers/suppliers/community.
- *Innovation/Creativity:* Willingness to take risks, experimentation, problem-solving techniques, brainstorming.
- *Reputation:* Trust, legitimacy, goodwill, brand reputation, name recognition, firm reputation.

Organizational Capabilities

Related to resources are **organizational capabilities**, which are the abilities, skills, and competencies used by the firm to make profits from tangible and intangible resources. There are two types of competencies: **Transformational competencies** happen when the firm can make its product or service better in value or more efficient in cost than those of other firms. A famous example is chili at Wendy's. The meat in the chili comes from hamburgers that were cooked but unsold. Every bowl of chili Wendy's sells gives it a profit edge over its competition.

Combinational competencies come from combining tangible and intangible resources in ways superior to the competition's. The Vermont Teddy Bear Company's Bear-Gram is an example of this (see below).

organizational capabilities
The abilities, skills, and competencies used by the firm to make profits from tangible and intangible resources.

transformational competencies
The abilities of a firm to make its product or service in a way that enhances value or efficiency compared to other firms.

combinational competencies
Organizational capabilities that come from combining tangible and intangible resources in ways superior to the competition.

SMALL BUSINESS INSIGHT

Early Years of the Vermont Teddy Bear Company[19]

While playing with teddy bears with his young son, John Sortino was surprised to find that none was made in the United States. He also thought the quality of the foreign-made bears was not as good as the teddy bears he recalled from his youth. Seeing an opportunity, he started making teddy bears by hand at home. From 1981 to 1983, he mostly sold the bears when friends asked about them. With his bear-making skills established, he thought he would try a little more proactive an approach. He opened a peddler's cart at the open air market in nearby Burlington, Vermont. It took four days to sell the first bear, and after a year, he had sold only 200. It did not become his full-time work until 1984.

Although most of the bears were being sold by department stores, the key moment came when a customer bought a bear from Sortino and asked to have it shipped back to her home. It got Sortino thinking about how he could sell to a larger market if he repositioned his business as a direct response gift delivery business—one that just happened to specialize in custom, high-quality teddy bears. He called these direct-delivered bears Bear-Grams.

Starting in 1985, he advertised heavily on radio, directing customers to a toll-free ordering number. The Bear-Grams were specially packaged with air holes and instructions not to turn the box upside down. When he started using New York radio stations in 1990, sales skyrocketed. The combination of product, a novel delivery approach, and a targeted ad campaign proved a hit. While other teddy bear companies exist, Vermont Teddy Bear's combination of organizational capabilities continues to sustain its competitive advantage.

valuable resource
An asset, capability, organizational process, information, or knowledge that lets a firm take advantage of opportunities or lock out competitors.

rare resource
An asset, capability, organizational process, information, or knowledge that is not generally available to competitors.

difficult to imitate
A resource characteristic which enhances value through offering uniqueness to the buyer.

http://www.driftwoodfurniture.ca

Ohio State University strategy professor Jay Barney offers advice on what makes a resource especially useful.[20] A resource that lets you take advantage of opportunities or lock out your competitors is considered a **valuable resource**. An example would be an exclusive contract to provide a product or service to your local government. It is great if it is a **rare resource**—not generally available to your competitors. Having the first stall by the main entrance at the local flea market or mall is an example of a rare resource.

If a resource is **difficult to imitate**, it helps secure your advantage. That is why resources such as secret recipes are so important to advertise on the one hand and protect on the other. Other factors that make a resource difficult to imitate are things like physical uniqueness (having that entryway stall at the flea market), hard-to-copy combinations of organizational and human resources, and even maintaining causal uncertainty on what makes your product or service unique. For example, Maxwell Newhouse created Ocean Interior when he pioneered producing contemporary furniture from driftwood. His daughter Nicole now turns out the furniture from their location in Cultus Lake, British Columbia. While conventional woods, even high-quality ones, are easy enough to come by, using driftwood makes their furniture very distinctive and hard to imitate.

Discouraging Competitors

Sometimes the best offense in competitive advantage comes from building a superior defense. There are two classic ways to do this. One is locking in customers. Anything you can do that increases customer loyalty aids your competitive advantage. For example, the Vermont Teddy Bear Company has its PreFURD Member program that offers customers Furballs—coupons and discounts via e-mail. The program has gotten over 500,000 customers to register and receive promotional e-mails from the company.[21]

The other defensive strategy involves inhibiting or retarding imitation. This often involves leveraging government or legal processes. A popular way involves protecting key information with patents or trademarks. Snowboard binding inventor Jeff Sand pursued patent infringement cases against overseas competitors. These did not work as well as he wanted, but he found another government action he could leverage. After the 9/11 attacks, government drastically cut back on imports. Capitalizing on this, Sand was able to get the government to block imports of his major overseas competitor.[22]

Tool: VRIO Analysis

A resource or organizational capability that gives your firm a competitive advantage also gives you a chance to make above-average profits. So finding such resources makes a lot of sense. The ultimate test for competitive advantage in resources is VRIO analysis.[23] This analysis uses strategy professor Jay Barney's model for competitive advantage as the basis for analysis. It has you asking questions about the value, rareness, imitabilty, and organization (VRIO) of the resource. Skill Module 7.5 walks you through the questions in a VRIO analysis.

SKILL MODULE 7.5

The VRIO Analysis

Think of the resources that make a particular product or service that you offer or plan to offer. In order to determine if you can charge above-average prices (and make above-average products), you want to be honestly able to answer yes to tests 1–3, before you answer test 4.

Test 1—Value: Does the resource help you increase sales or decrease costs? For example, using the Internet to log sales rather than using paper forms can be a major cost savings for personnel database management costs or can generate savings from multiple sources (e.g., billing, shipping, support) by being able to use the same database.

Test 2—Rareness: Is the resource rare enough that it lets you charge more than competitors who lack the resource? If you have locked up the sauce recipe from this year's national barbeque championship, few will be able to compete, and there are always aficionados who are willing to pay to be the first to try out the newest winner.

Test 3—Imitabilty: Can the competition imitate the resource? For example, can it hire people with the expertise that gives your firm its advantage? You might see your advantage as your knowledge of the local market, but what happens if a new player hires a salesperson with local market knowledge? Your advantage could be matched quickly.

Test 4—Organization: (Asked only if the resource passes tests 1, 2, and 3) Can the firm make use of the resource to increase sales or decrease costs? Many firms might have the *ability* to lock in rare resources or use the Internet to save money, but they often fail to act on these opportunities. Sometimes it is a fear of the new or the time and trouble it involves to change; sometimes they feel they are doing well enough without gaining a competitive advantage; and sometimes it's just the cost of doing something new. So to gain a competitive advantage, the willingness to commit the organization to it becomes the key empowering resource.

Often tangible resources fail one or more of the first three tests. Locations can be matched, and being tangible makes resources easier to see and copy. Most of the time what survives a VRIO analysis are intangible resources (like expertise, reputation, or creativity) and organizational capabilities (like the particular combination of location, selection, and customer service you offer).

Resources and capabilities that clear all four VRIO tests represent a key component of your firm used to achieve superior profits and survivability. When these resources and capabilities are always being used by the organization to do its main work, it is called **core competency**. Large businesses have no more than five or six core competencies. Even the most successful small businesses often have only one or two. Your firm can survive without mastering a core competence when there is little or no competition from firms in your industry and locality, new entrants, or substitutes. If competition heats up, you need some sort of competitive advantage to survive, and it's best if the advantage is one of your core competencies.

core competency
The main work of a firm in a particular line of business.

Life Cycle and Business Strategy

Another popular technique is to match your strategy to the life cycle stage of your industry.[24] The **industry life cycle** describes the stages an industry goes through from its birth to its ending. There are five stages: introduction, growth, maturity, decline, and death.

The **introduction stage** is when the product or service is being invented and initially developed. At first the entrepreneurs in the industry are working to come up with a version of the product or service that receives a major endorsement from customers, moving it from a hobby to a regular purchase. This is a time for niche strategies because the initial customer segment contains buyers who are likely to be pioneers and early adopters. **Pioneers** are eager to be the first to try or have something new and are willing to spend extra time making it work—like early users of cell phones, digital cameras, or personal computers. Pioneers often had to play with the hardware and software to make it work.

Early adopters are highly influential. Their purchases define a product or service as cool, hot, or desirable. For the firm, having one of those few products or services around which early adopters coalesce is the key goal. Typically, early adopters want products and services that are stable, but they are willing to risk making a choice that might have to be abandoned later. Since the product or service is new, it is a time for innovators, and a differentiation strategy makes sense to set off your approach from your competitors. The entrepreneur's goal at this stage is to master the technology in

industry life cycle
The stages an industry goes through from its birth to its ending. There are five stages: introduction, growth, maturity, decline, and death.

introduction stage
The life cycle stage in which the product or service is being invented and initially developed.

pioneers
A customer adoption segment characterized by customers most willing to be the first to try or have something new.

early adopters
A customer adoption segment that purchases after pioneers.

a decisive way—making expertise the key resource. This fits with the supra-strategies of single-mindedness and super-support.

growth stage
An industry life cycle stage in which customer purchases increase at a dramatic rate.

customer segment
A group or subgroup of potential purchasers that can be approached in a coherent manner.

early majority
Customer adoption segment that purchases after early adopters, and whose demand creates a mass market.

The **growth stage** takes place when customers begin to notice the product or service and buy significantly more of it. Often there is a proliferation of companies providing the product or service, and tremendous variation in the offerings. Sales are booming, and this opens up the possibility of a mass market. The **customer segment** here is called the **early majority**. People in this segment tend to popularize the trends identified by the early adopters, and their demand creates a mass market. Typically, a differentiation approach focusing on different features is a large part of the appeal, so there is still time for an innovative approach. The growth stage fits well with the supra-strategies of craftsmanship, customization, and elite.

maturity stage
The third life cycle stage, marked by a stabilization of demand, with firms in the industry moving to stabilize or improve profits through cost strategies.

late majority
A customer adoption segment describing people who wait until the technology has stabilized and the costs have begun to drop.

The third stage is called the **maturity stage** and is marked by a stabilization of demand, with firms in the industry moving to stabilize or improve profits through cost strategies. By this time, the key customer segment is the **late majority** in the mass market—people who wait until the technology has stabilized and the costs have begun to drop. They are often sensitive to particular touchstone prices, called *price points*. For example, when cell phones were included free with service, it signaled to late adopters that it was time to buy. For personal computers, when the price point dropped below $1,000, sales to the late majority grew. Making a profit in this market usually comes from being more successful with cost strategies than your competitors. This usually means taking an imitative approach. The goal for the firm in this stage is to get as much market share as possible, even in a fragmented industry. The supra-strategies that work best here are single-mindedness applied to cost savings, and comprehensiveness in product or service offering, such as offering the broadest array of sewing supplies, cigars, or wooden toys, making one-stop shopping possible.

decline stage
A life cycle stage in which sales and profits of the firm begin a falling trend.

laggard
A customer adoption segment that holds off buying new products or services until either they are forced to or prices reach rock-bottom.

When sales and profits actually start to fall, it is a sign that the industry is in its **decline stage**. This stage sees cost strategies and low-cost pricing proliferate as companies scramble to survive in a dwindling market. The customer segment here is the **laggards**, who do not change either until they are forced to or until prices reach rock-bottom. Laggards tend to be completely price-driven, and making a profit depends on a cost strategy, one that works hard to imitate competitors but that ekes out a bit better efficiencies or economies than others do. Another chance for small businesses in declining industries is a focus strategy that comes when larger firms abandon customers by dropping products and services. Often, small businesses can serve these markets more efficiently than can large firms. The supra-strategies for declining industries are typically serving the underserved from cost-efficient smaller firms, and customization for laggards who need a slightly adapted product. Table 7.2 provides a summary of the industry life cycle approach to strategy.

retrenchment
An organizational life cycle stage in which established firms must find new approaches to improve the business and its chances for survival.

You may notice the column for retrenchment in Table 7.2. Sometimes between decline and death, an enterprising manager or entrepreneur finds a way to revitalize an industry, referred to as a **retrenchment**. Yamaha did this in the 1970s and 1980s with musical instruments, an industry long thought to be in decline and populated almost entirely by small businesses. In the appliance sales industry, the advent of big box stores like Best Buy or Circuit City got new profits out of an industry thought to be teetering between maturity and decline. Retrenchments often involve finding new cost efficiencies for mass-market sales, which is frequently a particular problem for small businesses. However, there have been notable exceptions like Airport Appliance and Kitchens in Hayward, California, or Goedekers Superstore in St. Louis, Missouri, where family-owned businesses imitate big box retailers and their pricing, but differentiate with services keyed to their local markets.

http://www.airportappliance.com, http://www.goedekers.com

From all this, you can see that strategy represents the way by which an entrepreneur plots a path to success. For strategy to work, it needs to draw on most of the elements discussed in the chapter. When Nick and Dennis were putting together the idea for Mindnautilus.com, they were trying to strategize the right way. You know by now that they did an industry analysis and worked out their SWOT analysis.

TABLE 7.2 Industry Life Cycle Approach to Small Business Strategy

	Introduction	Growth	Maturity	Decline	Retrenchment
Market Scope	Niche	Mass	Mass	Niche	Mass via consolidation
Optimal Strategy	Differentiation	Differentiation	Cost	Cost; focus	Cost
Imitation/Innovation	Innovation	Innovation	Imitation	Imitation	Innovation
Customer Segment	Pioneers and early adopters	Early majority	Late majority	Laggards	Late adopters and laggards
Organizational Goal	Master technology	Product and service leadership (being "the one")	Market share	Serve remaining markets	New efficiencies
Supra-Strategy	Single-mindedness; super-support	Craftsmanship; customization; elite	Single-mindedness (cost); comprehensiveness	Serving the underserved; customization	

Unfortunately, their SWOT led them to see that Mindnautilus faced significant threats, and at that time, the partners lacked the strengths, especially financial strength, to overcome the threats. This suggests that they should *flee* if they have to decide in the short term, or *fix* if they can set up for the long term.

Long term or short, every small business has a strategy, and successful small businesses have strategies that fit their industry, market, and resources. Strategy is one of those areas in which you can take charge and think through the options available to you and your firm. For all the ideas on which strategy touches, in the end there are some straightforward ways to help you decide on strategies, such as industry, SWOT, VRIO, and value chain analyses. These analysis techniques can help you narrow down your choices to a model of strategy that can help you succeeed. For the vast majority of small businesses, the most powerful technique is to pursue an imitative strategy. By following the industry standard practices, with only one or two innovations to differentiate your firm from others, you can gain many of the benefits of established businesses and industries and still benefit from the power of innovation along smaller lines, which can make a real difference for your customers. For many owners, strategy *is* the grand game of business, but it is a game in which winning can make a major difference in the success of your firm.

CHAPTER SUMMARY

LO1 Learn the decisions needed to establish a foundation for strategic planning.

- Strategy is the idea and actions that explain how the firm will make its profit.
- Strategic planning for small business is a four-step process.
- Rely on trade and professional associations for information on your industry.
- Choose whether your firm will focus on a mass or niche market.

LO2 Learn the forms of imitative and innovative businesses.

- Imitation is the classic strategy of small businesses.
- An imitative approach lets you build on existing products, services, and markets.
- An innovative approach lets you build a business in your own unique way.

LO3 Articulate the benefits that win over customers.

- Benefits are desirable characteristics of a product or service.
- Benefits can target values, such as quality or style, as well as cost.
- Situations and benefits can help clarify entry wedges that can offer exceptional profits.

LO4 Use SWOT analysis to identify strategic options.

- SWOT stands for strength, weakness, opportunity, and threat.
- SWOT analysis links benefits to the specifics of your firm's situation.
- SWOT analyses lead to the choice of one of four strategic directions: flaunt, fix, fight, or flee.

LO5 Understand the major strategies of business—differentiation, cost, and focus.

- There are three generic business strategies—differentiation, cost, and focus.
- Most small businesses use a focus strategy, targeting a niche by combining cost or differentiation approaches.
- Particular combinations of benefits are called supra-strategies.

LO6 Use value chain analyses to apply strategy throughout the firm.

- The value chain is the collection of processes and activities a small business performs to design, produce, market, deliver, and support its product or service.
- Getting a value chain to focus on delivering customer benefits is a powerful way to organize a firm.

LO7 Learn how to sustain competitive advantage through attracting customers and discouraging competition.

- Competitive advantage is your firm's edge in meeting and beating the competition.
- Competitive advantage works best when it involves resources that are valuable, rare, and difficult to imitate.
- Evaluate resources using a VRIO (value, rareness, imitability, organization) analysis.
- Business and market life cycles also help identify the kind of strategies most likely to work for a firm at a given time.

DISCUSSION QUESTIONS

1. What are the four steps of the strategic planning process in small business?
2. How can industry and trade associations help the small business get started and develop its strategy?
3. What is the difference between a mass market and a niche market? Which is more likely to be something a small business can pursue?
4. What are the differences between innovative and imitative strategies? Which is more likely to be something a small business can pursue?
5. What are the two general kinds of benefits of each type of strategy?
6. How does the SWOT analysis relate to the selection of a strategic direction of the business?
7. What are the three generic strategies of business? Give one example of a firm pursuing each type of generic strategy.
8. What is the competitive advantage of a business, and how does it lead to success?
9. In the life cycle of an industry, how can you tell when it has left the introductory stage and entered the growth stage?

EXPERIENTIAL EXERCISES

1. Find the trade or professional association for the kind of business you plan to pursue.
2. Look at local hamburger restaurants. How do they pursue imitative strategies, and where do they offer their innovations?
3. Pick five online businesses in the same industry. From their Web sites, see if you can identify what *they* think is their competitive advantage. Do you agree with their assessment? Why or why not?
4. Think of the life cycle of an industry. Give examples of industries that are at the different stages, and be ready to defend your classification.

Mini-Case

Fitchburg was a small town whose proudest moment came about when Active Air, a national airline, started service to the town. In the eyes of the business community, having daily commercial air service was a sign that its town "had arrived." It was therefore a blow to the community's self-esteem when Active Air cut service back because of its larger financial woes. The city leaders found this ironic, since they knew from the head of the airport that the Active Air flight was running at 80 percent daily capacity, which was a profitable load for a plane.

Another person who observed this was Ed Tangier, who owned several small airplanes, including a 12-seater. He would not have been able to compete with Active Air, with its 24-hour reservation lines, relationships with other carriers, and national advertising. But when Active Air dropped its service to and from Fitchburg, a new opportunity opened up to fly the 12-seater daily, replacing the Active Air service.

CASE DISCUSSION QUESTIONS

1. What is the entry wedge that Ed was going to pursue?
2. What kind of benefits do you think would make the most sense for him to offer his customers?
3. Does he have any resources that would let him charge a premium price?

Appendix

Five Steps to an Industry Analysis

Retail Shoe Store

FINDING THE SIC AND NAICS CODES

The first order of business is to find the NAICS and SIC codes for the industry of interest. This is done by going to the Web site http://www.census.gov/epcd/naics02/ Plug in your keyword, click the 2002 NAICS search tab, and a listing is displayed that will tell you the NAICS code. Find the code that you are looking for and click the link. This will lead you to the SIC code for the same industry. For example, for the retail shoe industry, the codes are SIC 5661 and NAICS 448210.

INDUSTRY SIZE

Step 2 is to find the size of the industry. First go to the site www.census.gov. Second click on "Economic Census" in the business section and enter the NAICS code to find this information. To find the 2002 numbers, click on "Industry Series," and then scroll down to find the first few numbers of your NAICS code, for example, 44–45 Retail Trade is listed. Since my NAICS code begins with 44, I chose this code, then click more. Again look for the first few numbers of your NAICS code. In this section, I see 448 for a listing of "Clothing and Clothing Accessory Stores." This is the industry of interest. Displayed to the right hand side will be PDF reports. You can choose to look at the full report or the tables only. Click the PDF to view the information. Again look for the full NAICS number to get details. For example in the retail shoe store industry, the following information is given.

2002—there were 28,388 businesses in this industry with sales of $22,997,531.

1997—there were 31,399 businesses in this industry with sales of $20,543,252.

PROFITABILITY

Step 3 is going to the library to find information about the profitability of the retail shoe industry. Using the RMA's *Annual Statement Studies: Financial Ratio Benchmarks,* the following information was gathered.

Gross profit 38.0%
Operating expenses 38.5%
Operating profit −.4%
All other expenses 2.4%
Profit before taxes −2.8%

WAYS TO MAKE PROFITS

Information about making profits can be found by looking at trade articles and information or doing actual-interviews. The following information came from two sources: One source is a trade site, National Shoe Retail Association (http://www.nsra.org/brightideas.pdf), and the other is from the home business site www.PowerHomeBiz.com. The questions mentioned in skill module 3 yield the following answers:

- First is the question, What can be done to generate more sales?
  - Excellent service
  - Courteous and well-trained staff
  - Diversity in product selection
  - Competitive pricing
  - Functional store design
  - Location, location, location (more heavily populated cities have greater demands for shoes)
- Second is a judgment of whether it is possible to charge a premium for a product or service.
  - Depends on the market that you are catering to. If it is high end, then your target customer has the means to spend more money on more expensive (name brand) shoes. Also, if the store is located where families have higher discretionary income, the demand for brand name shoes will be higher.
- Third is how to keep the cost of goods or services below the industry's average.
  - Put adequate stock control in place to reduce inventory costs and increase stock turns. Loss prevention is critical in any retail establishment, as theft and shrinkage represent lost dollars for the retailer. Have systematized procedures for doing physical counts of your inventory as well as clear policies on

employee theft. It is also important to choose styles that are hot to the consumer to avoid inventory costs.
   - Another cost saving tactic is to use "start ship" and "in store" completion dates on all orders. Start negotiating on everything received past completion date.
- Fourth is looking at ways to keep operating expenses below industry averages.
   - Always check your freight expenses against the freight charge on the packing slip. It is usually different. Charge the difference back to the vendor.
   - Join forces with other same brand concept stores for savings on your direct mail advertising. In direct mail, the higher the quantity printed, the lower the cost per unit. There are additional savings to be realized in the cost of mailing if all pieces are sent from the same location. Savings can be substantial.
   - Use co-op dollars to reduce costs. Use some of your co-op dollars to co-brand with suppliers on things like business cards, shopping bags, and so on.
   - If you're doing a profit and loss statement monthly, consider doing it quarterly. Chances are you are simply putting it in a file anyway and are not adjusting the operating budget that often. This can trim the accounting bill considerably.
   - Negotiating better terms and rates with your bankers and other service providers can really save on fees. For example, go to other banks to get competitive rates and then renegotiate with your bank or change banks. For a bank, this applies to bank transaction fees as well as interest and credit terms.
   - Bid or get multiple estimates for things like construction/repair projects, insurance, contract services (i.e., refuse removal), and so forth.

COMPETITOR CONCENTRATION

The last step is using a directory provider to find out how many competitors there are in an area. Using Yahoo's online yellow pages directory, there are 200 retail shoe establishments in the St. Louis metropolitan area.

ANALYSIS

Overview

It seems as though the retail shoe industry is shrinking. From 1997 to 2002 the industry decreased by 10 percent. Using the information from the Industry Size section, we can determine that although the number of stores has declined, the sales have increased and gone from an average of $654 per store to $810. The retail shoe industry is very competitive, and it is important for hopefuls to be able to distinguish themselves in a mature market.

Profitability

The gross profit for this industry looks very good compared to other similar businesses. At 38 percent an owner could make a good living from this type of business, depending on the sales. Operating profit and profit before taxes are negative, so it is important for those thinking of going into this industry to differentiate and focus on customer service and added value. Also, an owner should do everything possible to cut the cost of goods sold and expenses, or profits may not be realized.

Differentiation and Cost

There are several ways to differentiate in the retail shoe business. There are many different categories for retail shoes. An owner could choose to focus on men's or women's shoes, kids shoes, or athletic shoes or include all these categories in one store. Then within these categories, there is low end, one price and discount, mass designer, and high end. Again, the shoe business is very competitive, so it is important to choose an image and stick to this image to establish and build a reputation with customers.

Once the image is established, there are six areas that must be covered to be successful and maintain a foothold in the industry. They are as follows:

- Excellent service—many a customer is won over by receiving great service.
- Courteous, honest, and well-trained staff.
- Diversity in product selection—offer a wide range of shoes appropriate for the surrounding environment. For example, if the location is near a beach, be sure to

include plenty of sandals, thongs, and flip-flops in the inventory.

- Competitive pricing—be competitive with other stores in the area to maintain a loyal customer base.
- Functional store design so that customers may move around with ease.
- Location, location, location—locations in or near heavily populated cities tend to have higher sales.

Incorporating these elements well, along with a differentiating image, will cause an owner to have strong placement and be able to compete effectively in the industry. It would seem that with a solid business plan, a marketing edge, and great location, a retail shoe business could be very viable and rewarding.

Bibliography

"Bright Ideas" From National Shoe Retailers Association's February 2005 Conference http://www.nsra.org/brightideas.pdf.

Jenny Fulbright, *Starting a Shoe Retail Store,* n.d. www.PowerHomeBiz.com/vol136/Shoe.htm, July, 2005.

Annual Statement Studies: Financial Ratio Benchmarks, Pennsylvania: Risk Management Association, 2004. U.S. Census, NAICS page, http://www.census.gov/epcd/naics02/.

Source: This industry analysis was written by Beatrice Emmanuel of Saint Louis University under the direction of Professor Jerome Katz.

LEARNING OBJECTIVES

This chapter will help you:

LO1 Understand why and when to develop a business plan.

LO2 Know how to tell the business plan story.

LO3 Learn the major sections of the classic business plan.

LO4 Focus business plan sections to meet specific needs.

LO5 Identify the major risks to business plan success.

LO6 Master presenting your business plan to others.

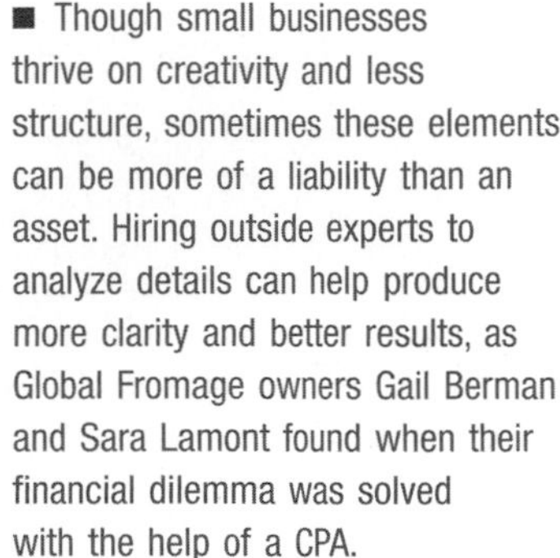

■ Though small businesses thrive on creativity and less structure, sometimes these elements can be more of a liability than an asset. Hiring outside experts to analyze details can help produce more clarity and better results, as Global Fromage owners Gail Berman and Sara Lamont found when their financial dilemma was solved with the help of a CPA.

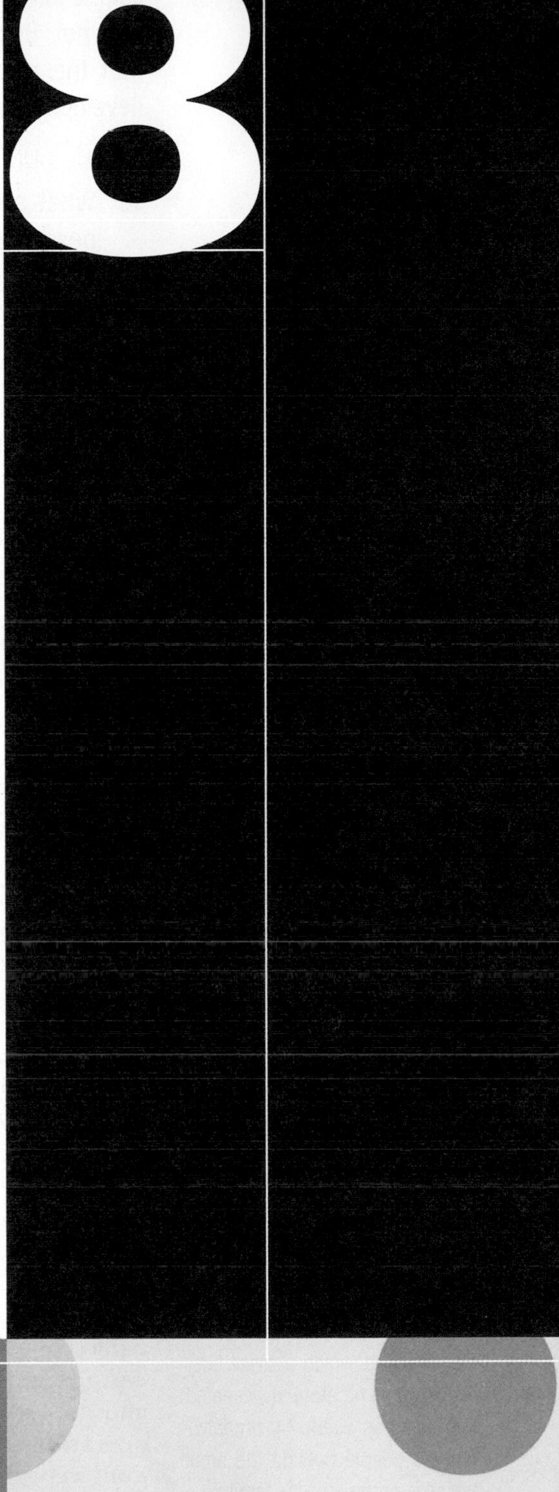

Business Plans: Seeing Audiences and Your Business Clearly

Focus on Small Business: Global Fromage

Gail Berman and Sara Lamont started Global Fromage, a specialty cheese shop in Kansas City's Westport, a revitalized entertainment and shopping district. Through discussion, they settled on a general plan for the company:

- Their products would be gourmet and specialty cheeses to be sold at a premium price.
- Their target market was to be people like themselves in the 20–50 year-old age range with middle to upper incomes.
- The Berman and Lamont families put up the nearly $100,000 it would take to secure a lease and pay for improvements and the initial inventory.

The shop had a steady flow of sales, but when it came time to pay bills at the end of the month, Global Fromage always seemed to come up short. Gail and Sara didn't know what the problem was. A CPA (certified public accountant) friend they hired quickly found the problem. Gail and Sara's "premium" pricing technique was simple. For any cheese they bought, they sold it for twice the price they paid for it. This seemed as if it should be enough, but in fact it was not. Because they never worked out the costs of running their business, they didn't know that the markup should have been closer to 200 than 100 percent. Armed with financials developed by the CPA, Gail and Sara repriced their cheeses and began to show a profit.

DISCUSSION QUESTIONS

1. What are the reasons you think Gail and Sara would have given for *not* doing a business plan?
2. What are the kinds of business costs that Gail and Sara are likely to have missed?
3. Since they got the money to start up from their families, who would have been the audience for the business plan?
4. Do you think it makes sense to create a business plan for a business *after* it starts? Why or why not?
5. Gail and Sara used a CPA to find the problem. Where else could they have turned for help?

Business Plan Background

L01
Understand why and when to develop a business plan.

Gail and Sara had a good idea, a good sense of their market, and a good location. They were great salespeople, and yet they were not making a profit. The reason was that they did not plan their business all the way through. When you are serious about your business or when a lot of money of your own or someone else's is at stake, creating a business plan is perhaps the most critical activity you can undertake. The plan is important, but what is even more important is the understanding you get from the planning process. This chapter will help you understand the thinking behind business plans and how to make and present your own.

business plan
A document designed to detail the *major* characteristics of a firm—its product or service, its industry, its market, its manner of operating (production, marketing, management), and its financial outcomes with an emphasis on the firm's *present* and *future.*

A **business plan** is a document designed to detail the *major* characteristics of a firm—its product or service, its industry, its market, its manner of operating (production, marketing, management), and its financial outcomes with an emphasis on the firm's *present* and *future.*

external legitimacy
The extent to which a small business is taken for granted, accepted, or treated as viable by organizations or people outside the small business or the owner's family.

There are two circumstances under which creating a business plan is absolutely necessary. One is when outsiders expect it. This is called **external legitimacy**. Creating a business plan is the acknowledged best way to build external legitimacy for your firm. When you are seeking outside support—whether financial or expert—you do a business plan to signal your professionalism and how serious you are about the business. Investors, whether they are venture capitalists, informal investors (called *angels*), bankers, or your two great aunts, are going to expect to see a business plan before considering investing in your business. In addition, many small business consultants and government agencies want to see your business plan in order to understand your operations, goals, and level of understanding.[1] If you are pursuing a partnership or joint venture with a larger firm, people there will expect to see a business plan before they even consider partnering. In these situations, a plan is the only way you are going to get the attention of outsiders. The kinds of benefits these different groups look for in a plan are given in Table 8.1.

internal understanding
The extent to which employees, investors, and family members involved in the business know the business's purposes and operations.

The other circumstance under which a business plan is needed is for **internal understanding**. This is when you want to get all the aspects of the business clear in your mind and the minds of others in the business, such as your partners or your key employees. When you want everyone to understand the business in the same way, a business plan can make a tremendous difference. For example, the La Terrasse

TABLE 8.1 Concerns of Different Business Plan Audiences[2]

Audience	Concerns
Family and friend investors	Amounts and Schedules for returns Stability of firm Funds use Your investment
Silent Partners/Angel Investors	Growth rate Market Business team Amounts and schedules for returns
Joint venture partners	Fit between the firms Competitive advantage Benefits Intellectual property protection R&D
Bankers	Cash flow and cash cycle Asset/collateral base Long-term prospects
Government agencies and institutions	Compliance with regulations and laws Monitoring compliance
Potential customers	Service/product quality Benefits Competitive advantage Responsiveness to customers
Key employees	Stability of firm Growth (as applies to increased opportunities within the firm) Long-term prospects

Restaurant in Philadelphia has long had an extensive business plan. It talks about the history and vision of the restaurant and includes a detailed operational plan covering everything from table layouts to techniques for minimizing waste. For new hires, the plan offers insight and specific information on the La Terrasse way of doing things. Business plans can also be used as a way of establishing a baseline against which a firm can measure its performance.

Is a business plan absolutely essential? If you are seeking a banker, investor, or partner, yes. Generally if you need outside support to get a business going, those you are seeking support from will want to see a business plan—and you will want to make sure the plan addresses their concerns.

Also, if you are trying to start or run your business in a professional or ambitious way, a business plan is vitally important. It is true that some of the most famous entrepreneurial firms—Apple, Microsoft, Dell, Holiday Inns—started without business plans. On the other hand, there are a lot more famous firms that started from the business plan—Amazon, eBay, Mrs. Fields, Red Hat, Xerox, and Federal Express to name a few.[3] When *Inc.* magazine polled 500 owners of high-performing small businesses, 54 percent had a plan and 41 percent did not.[4] Typically, the higher-performing firms in any industry (measured in profits) tend to be those who engage in planning.[5]

It is important to know that research suggests that firms without a business plan are more likely to close down than firms with plans.[6] While having a business plan does not guarantee higher profits,[7] it is essential to qualify to be considered by business professionals for investments, loans, or credit lines. For example, Apple and Microsoft drafted business plans when they wanted to go for venture capital funds.[8]

These days, more start-up businesses are doing business plans than in the past, which increases the importance of your doing one to stay competitive and look as legitimate as the other competing start-ups.[9] In your head or on paper, sooner or later most businesses need to do a plan.

The Business Plan Story: Starting Small and Building Up[10]

LO2
Know how to tell the business plan story.

Business plans are a type of story. In a business plan, you tell the reader about a future place—your business. Every business plan is a bit like fiction. The best fictional stories are based on what exists now, as a good business plan should be. The business plan tells a story that starts in the here and now and builds believably toward a better future.

Good storytellers know that you make the story fit the audience's time. Sometimes you have only a moment to get the story of your business across; sometimes you have hours. Entrepreneurs need to have a variety of versions of their business's story available.

Figure 8.1 shows the range of presentations entrepreneurs may create when planning to go into business. When you have only a moment to talk, your vision statement or a tagline you've developed is the way to go.[11] When you have more time to talk about your business, longer and longer presentations are possible. These range from the 2-sentence concept all the way to the 40-page business plan. The five types of

FIGURE 8.1

Business Plan Levels of Involvement

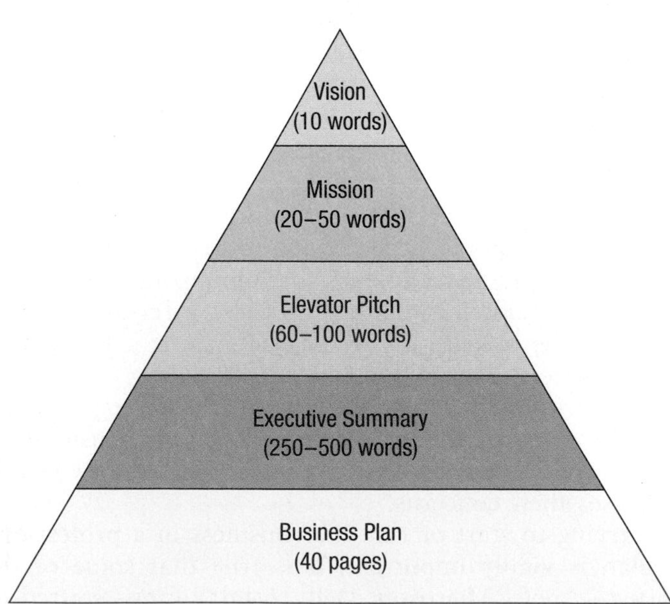

business planning presentations are (1) vision statements, (2) mission statements, (3) elevator pitches, (4) executive summaries, and (5) business plans. We tell you how to do each below.

The Vision Statement

A firm's vision statement is perhaps its most important single idea.[12] The **vision statement** is a very simple 5–10 word sentence or **tagline** that expresses the fundamental idea or goal of the firm. As strategy professors Greg Dess and Tom Lumpkin suggest, a vision statement is supposed to be inspiring, overarching, and long term.[13] When Bill Gates and Paul Allen started Microsoft as teenagers, their vision was "a computer on every desk—running Microsoft software."[14] At the time, personal computers were being constructed by hobbyists and even lacked keyboards! So you can easily see how visionary their vision statement was.

vision statement
A very simple 5–10 word sentence or tagline that expresses the fundamental idea or goal of the firm.

tagline
(also known as a slogan) A memorable catchphrase that captures the key idea of a business, its service, product, or customer.

Taglines or slogans are a good way to present vision statements, because a good tagline is brief and memorable. The tagline can also serve as the company's vision statement.[15] Some examples of good taglines encompassing the firm's vision statement are:

- Kelliher/Samets/Volk Advertising (Burlington, Vermont): Creating wow ideas for clients who want to soar.
- Book Passage (Corte Madera, California): The Bay Area's Liveliest Bookstore.
- Cook's Cake Decorating & Candy Supplies (West Allis, Wisconsin): No one should ever go without a decorated birthday cake.
- Crum Electric Supply (Casper, Wyoming): Plug into Quality—People, Products, Service.
- Progressive Insulation & Windows (Chatsworth, California): Total Living Comfort.

The Mission Statement

The mission statement is closely related to the firm's vision statement. The **mission statement** takes the vision statement's description of the firm's goal and adds the competitive advantage information developed as part of the firm's strategy. For example, the Excalibur Seasoning Company says its mission is "to provide you, as a customer, with the highest quality products and service available in the seasoning industry."[16] Typically a mission statement talks in terms of what will make a difference for the customer or the industry. It rarely discusses profits, but it often mentions the entry wedge that follows from the firm's strategy[17] discussed in Chapter 7. A few more examples of mission statements from small firms are:

mission statement
A paragraph that describes the firm's goals and competitive advantages.

- BabyGenie.com (Fort Lauderdale, Florida): The mission of BabyGenie.com is to become one of the best online resources for young mothers and repeat parents.
- Bob Victor's (Topeka, Kansas): Our GOAL is to serve YOU, the custom picture framing and professional portrait photography industries, with molding manufactured from carefully selected American solid hardwood.
- D.A. Kadan Co., Inc. (Waxhaw, North Carolina): Our mission is to maintain a high standard of excellence in developing genuine, far reaching, and mutually beneficial relationships with physicians. We achieve this through the delivery of a wide range of quality medical equipment at reasonable prices.
- Fantastic Gift Baskets (Raleigh, North Carolina): The family at Fantastic Gift Baskets puts the same care and love into designing our gourmet gift baskets as you would . . . if you had the time![18]

Mission statements can get long. Since they are usually oriented toward those inside the firm or to formal investors, mission statements tend to cover everything that is truly important. This might include the major competitive advantages of the firm, its position in the industry, and its attitudes toward customers, competitors, and the environment.

■ Going up? Each year, Wake Forest University's Babcock Graduate School of Management holds its annual elevator pitch contest. Teams must progress through a rigorous weeding-out process to advance to the semifinalist stage, where they get the chance to present their pitch to real venture capitalists and experts on a two-minute elevator ride. To read more about this year's contest, visit www.mba.wfu.edu/elevator/index.html.

The Elevator Pitch

elevator pitch
A 30-second (100 words or less) action-oriented description of a business designed to sell the idea of the business to another.

An **elevator pitch** is an action-oriented description of your business that is somewhat longer than a vision statement or tagline. It is designed to open the door to a more in-depth dialogue. Even when it doesn't lead to any specific business, this information about your business should be memorable enough so that the listener can tell others about your business. The idea of the elevator pitch is that you are alone with a prospective customer or investor for the length of an elevator ride, say, around 30 seconds.[19] That comes out to 100 words or less. This description is used in one-on-one business settings and when someone asks for more detail after hearing your concept. In a time when politicians develop sound bites and a good phrase can make a product (Altoids, for example, are "curiously strong"), having a high-quality concept or elevator pitch for your business is more important than ever.[20]

> CellTunes: You hear it, you got it! Ever wanted to buy a tune you heard on the radio but missed the name? Well, CellTunes is the instant gratification music ordering service. CellTunes lets you buy the songs you hear on your favorite FM radio, AM radio, or Internet radio station with a single cell phone call. CellTunes tracks the songs playing on your favorite stations and can download the song to you or to your account at services like iTunes or PressPlay. CellTunes is demonstrating its technology and seeking seed investors. CellTunes makes song ordering faster and easier than ever before—you hear it, you got it!

The above elevator pitch leads with the hook—the frustration people have felt at not being able to recall a song or find it to buy. It follows up with the purpose of the service—helping people obtain the song. Because this pitch is for a new type of service, it gives the listener more details about how it works than may otherwise appear in an elevator pitch. For a familiar type of business, you might talk instead about what makes your firm unique or superior to the competition. The pitch ends with where the business is now—seeking money from seed investors. This is about 100 words and would take about a minute to say. Note that a lot of it sounds like a sales pitch, and that is intentional. Listeners might be customers or investors, but either way, the goal is to sell them on the idea and their need for it. With this background, Skill Module 8.1 explains how to craft an elevator pitch.

How to Write Your Elevator Pitch

Elevator pitches have four success factors: the hook, the purpose, the what and where, and the delivery.

First, find a hook—something about your product or service that people would remember and take to heart. "We tutor kids others call too difficult." "When government or industry wants to find the newest businesses, they come to us." "We are one of the nation's biggest suppliers of parts for old Corvettes."

Stan Mandel supervises Wake Forest University's Elevator Pitch Competition, so he knows pitches. He suggests using analogies. If you're planning a large, discount pen store, you might say "We will be a Wal-Mart for pens." For CellTunes, it might be "We'll be the Home Shopping Network for music." It helps people quickly understand your firm. Great pitches or concepts aim to get the listener to ask questions or take some other form of "next step." Stan suggests different pitches for different sorts of audiences—investors, customers, suppliers, and so forth.

Second, focus on the purpose your product or service serves for the customer. Do not talk skills ("I am a graphic designer."); talk about how you make customers happy ("I produce designs that sell books!").

Third, tell the listener the business's situation: where the business "is at"—if it's a start-up, state what the business is seeking (funding, partners, distributors, etc.). If it is operating, tell the listener where he or she can buy the product or service.

SKILL MODULE 8.1

Once your elevator pitch is written, you need to become conversationally perfect in your delivery. You want to be able to give the pitch or concept dozens, even hundreds, of times. Yet it is important that the pitch does not sound memorized. It needs to sound like regular conversation, preferably a conversation whose topic excites you. To achieve this, you must master the material, and then keep working on it so that it becomes a natural part of what you say to others. Have family and friends listen to it. Consider using a video camera to see how natural you seem when making the pitch. Remember, the elevator pitch is often the first real insight people have about your business, so it is essential to have a pitch that flows and sells for you.

The Executive Summary

An **executive summary** is the key component of the written business plan because it is the one element that nearly everyone will read first when they receive a plan. An executive summary gives a one- to two-page (250–500 word) overview of the business, its business model, market, expectations, and immediate goals. (See Figure 8.2.) Typically, executive summaries start out written, and they remain the most popular item to send people who ask about your business. They comprise the core of a business plan presentation and form the basis for additional discussion when someone asks for more detail. Executive summaries are written in a formal style, suitable for investors, lawyers, and bankers to read. They give much more detail about the business than the vision or mission statements or elevator pitch. Executive summaries are usually organized in a series of short paragraphs (three or four sentences), each with a particular topic. These topics are:

executive summary
A one- to two-page (250–500 word) overview of the business, its business model, market, expectations, and immediate goals. It is typically put at the start of a business plan and is the most popular summary form for a business plan.

- **Product:** Describes the product or service and how it is used.
- **Market:** Describes the size and characteristics of the customer group and how it will buy the product or service (e.g., in person, online, catalog).
- **Competitive advantages:** Explains what makes the product or service unique, often in terms of an entry wedge.
- **Management:** Describes the entrepreneur and start-up team in terms of expertise and track record.

FIGURE 8.2

Executive Summary for Pizzeria Fresco

Pizzeria Fresco is a pizzeria dedicated to the idea of delicious "healthy pizza." Compared to the majority of existing pizzerias today, Pizzeria Fresco's idea and target are highly unique. A niche market opportunity exists in the fast food pizzeria business, serving consumers who are health conscious and interested in reasonably priced gourmet-style pizza. Existing pizzerias offer the "typical" slice of pizza or a pizza pie that has tomato sauce, mozzarella cheese and perhaps a choice of toppings such as pepperoni, mushrooms, or sausage. Specialty restaurants that do offer gourmet style pizza (i.e., pan pizza, brick oven pizza) charge a much higher price than that of fast food pizzerias.

Pizzeria Fresco proposes to fill this niche in the Greenwich Village New York City area, by establishing a fast food pizzeria operation offering this "unique" style pizza as an alternative to the "traditional" pizza, at comparable prices. Pizzeria Fresco's competitive advantage will lie in the style of the pizza it offers customers—prepared in the authentic northern Italian style—with a gourmet flair and incorporating health-oriented ingredients.

Pizzeria Fresco will be located in a premium retail/storefront space on University Place in the Washington Square/Union Square area of New York City's West Village.

Anthony Pandolfini, who will leave his current job, will operate the business. Mr. Pandolfini has five years' experience in operating a pizza business, with an additional six years in the hospitality industry. Jennifer Lee will assist on a part-time basis while she maintains her current employment.

Pizzeria Fresco seeks a five-year SBA loan for $100,000 to lease and renovate retail space, purchase equipment and supplies, support its marketing program, and maintain sufficient cash reserves to provide adequate working capital to expand its gourmet pizzeria business. The owners will contribute $93,372 of equity to start the business. This sum will finance this new company through the start-up phase into a profitable and growing business.

- **Business:** Describes the current stage of the business and when major milestones of starting, sales, or profitability will be met.
- **Finances:** Describes the deal being offered investors and the schedule for payouts.

The order for the topics in an executive summary is not fixed, although most experienced readers will be looking for the same items—markets, advantages, and management. The summary is probably the single most important written part of the business plan for two reasons. First, it is the single most widely distributed written description of the business. Second, all readers of a business plan typically start with the executive summary of the plan, and then go on to the section of the plan where they can best apply their expertise. For example, accountants typically go to the financial projections after they've read the executive summary.

It also is typical to include the key numbers for the business, such as industry size, customer base, number of employees, or projected sales. However it is important to make sure that the numbers can be supported by a trustworthy source. Examples of such sources include the government, industry associations, and major commercial sources such as Dun & Bradstreet, the Risk Management Association, or Bizminer. The sources may be included in the executive summary or made available to readers in footnotes.

The Classic Business Plan

L03
Learn the major sections of the classic business plan.

The business plan remains the standard for describing the business in detail. The business plan takes all the elements introduced so far and includes them in a complete description of the major elements of the business. The nine parts of the full business plan are detailed below and outlined in Table 8.2. The full (or classic) business plan contains a maximum of 25 single-spaced pages of text and 15 pages of financials and appendixes.[21] Plans for any business whose product or service is new, even revolutionary, or in which the entrepreneur is new to the industry, are the ones that really

TABLE 8.2 Business Plans Outline[22]

1. Cover letter (1 p., but is separate from plan)
2. Title page (1 p.)
3. Table of contents (1 p.)
4. Executive summary (1–2 pp.)
5. The company
    - 5a. Company description (1–2 pp.)
        - 5a1. Vision statement
        - 5a2. Mission statement
        - 5a3. Objectives (optional)
        - 5a4. Company background
    - 5b. Product/service and industry (1–8 pp.)
        - 5b1. Product/service description
        - 5b2. Industry description
6. The market
    - 6a. Market and target customer (1–3 pp.)
    - 6b. Competition and competitive advantage (1–2 pp.)
    - 6c. Marketing strategy (1–3 pp.)
        - 6c1. Overall strategy
        - 6c2. Sales plan
        - 6c3. Competitive plan
        - 6c4. Research and development or growth plan
7. The organization
    - 7a. Legal and organizational structures (1/2–1 p.)
    - 7b. Key personnel (1/2–3 pp.)
    - 7c. Related service providers (1/2–1 p.)
    - 7d. Location (1/2 p.)
8. The financials
    - 8a. Critical risks (1 p.)
    - 8b. The deal (1 p., if needed)
    - 8c. Income statement (2 pp.)
    - 8d. Cash flow projection (2 pp.)
    - 8e. Balance sheet (1 p.)
    - 8f. Start-up costs (1 p., if needed)
    - 8g. Assumptions (1 p.)
    - 8h. Schedule (1 p.)
9. The appendixes (optional)
    - 9a. Owner's résumé
    - 9b. Examples of other popular appendixes: Product or service pictures or specifications; customer/investor contracts; marketing studies or pilot sales efforts; industry reports; price lists; floor plans; advertising copy; customer or spokesperson testimonials; letters of opinion.

need these 25 pages. However, recall from our discussion of strategy that most small businesses are more imitative than innovative. When you are going into an imitative business, your business plan can be shortened considerably. Where the type of business is well established, such as a dry cleaner or word processing service, the market is well defined and well known, and the entrepreneur comes to the business with experience in the industry, the amount of necessary description drops dramatically. In such cases, these simple business plans may require only 10 pages of text.[23] Even so, the financial section remains its usual length, although the appendixes may be sparse.

Table 8.2 summarizes the classic business plan in outline form, and page budgets are given for each content section. The shorter lengths are the typical page budgets for simple business plans, while the longer lengths are typical for full business plans.

Cover Letter

cover letter
A one-page document on business stationery (also called *letterhead*) that introduces the business plan and the business owner to the recipient and indicates why the recipient is being asked to read the plan.

When you send a business plan to someone, it is a good business practice to include a cover letter. A **cover letter** is a one-page document on business stationery (also called *letterhead*) that introduces the business plan and owner and indicates why the recipient is being asked to read the plan. It is typically the first written material someone sees about your business, so it needs to look and sound just right. The specifics of writing a cover letter are provided in Skill Module 8.2, and an example of a cover letter is given in the appendix to the chapter.

SKILL MODULE 8.2

How to Write a Cover Letter

We all know that first impressions are important. For business plans, the first impression is made by the cover letter, so having a good one-page letter is vital. Fortunately, writing a good cover letter is easy.

Step 1: Get the stationery. Since the cover letter shows off your firm, the paper it appears on is important. These days, you can print high-quality stationery from a color printer, using templates that come in word processing programs. For a more distinctive template, you can buy ready-made ones from companies like TemplateZone.com or from your local office supplies or computer store. You can also make a template on your own. Stationery should be heavier (at least 20-pound weight) paper. Printed on this should be your firm's name, address, phone and fax numbers, e-mail and Web addresses, and the firm's logo if it has one. Great stationery should be simple and eye-catching and leave a lot of space for your letters.

Step 2: Get all the recipient's address information. Find out the proper name, title, and address of the person to whom you are sending the plan. Call or e-mail this person's office to get the right information if you are not sure.

Step 3: Draft your letter. There is a classic format for cover letters.

a. **Salutation:** "Dear Mr. Monroe," "Dear Ms. Craft," or "Dear Dr. Jones" is how cover letters typically start. If you have a long-standing personal relationship with the reader, you can start informally, like "Dear Chris."

b. **First paragraph:** Here you introduce yourself and your business ("I am Edward Blankenship, owner of PROmote Advertising"). You explain how you got the recipient's name ("Brigit Hawkins at Security Bank suggested I contact you." Or "I am contacting you in your role as president of the Northside Investment Group.").

c. **Second paragraph:** Here you explain your company in a little greater detail. Typically this will be a variation of your vision statement in the first sentence ("PROmote specializes in increasing sales of small-lot professional and technical books through market expansion."). The next sentence describes the product or service in a sales-oriented manner ("PROmote's expertise gets books into specialty bookstores, online bookstores, and professional and trade association booklists for new sales.").

The third sentence points up your competitive advantage, or what makes your product, service, or firm special ("PROmote is the only company in the industry that targets small-lot professional books on behalf of the authors, helping them increase sales.").

d. **Third paragraph:** Here you describe the current situation of the company and explain what you are seeking from the recipient ("PROmote is in start-up phase, having completed its pilot tests and secured its first customers. PROmote is currently seeking a $20,000 line of credit. I would appreciate your consideration of the attached business plan."). The typical requests are for investment, lines of credit, partnering or joint ventures, sales, or feedback on those areas of the plan in which the recipient is expert.

e. **Fourth paragraph:** In closing, you thank the recipient for his or her consideration, let the reader know you are available to answer any questions, and close with a mention of your future action, such as a promise to contact the recipient within a week.

f. **Signature block:** Typically you sign off with "Sincerely," and your name the way it appears in the business plan.

Step 4: Proofread. A cover letter with misspellings or grammatical errors sends the worst possible first impression. If the cover letter has problems, imagine what the plan must look like!

Step 5: Package and send. Print or type mailing labels for the recipients' addresses and your return address. Send the plan, with the cover letter clipped to the cover, in a 9- by 11-inch envelope. Make sure you put enough postage on it.

Title Page

The title page typically contains the following information:

- Company name (usually in large type, with a logo if you have one).
- Contact information (owner names, company address, telephone and fax numbers, e-mail and Web site addresses).
- Date this version of the plan was completed.
- Proprietary statement to protect your ideas: For example, "*This document contains confidential and proprietary information belonging exclusively to [your company's name goes here]. Do not copy, fax, reproduce, or distribute without permission.*" Often on the line following this statement is a copy number unique to each copy of the plan. This helps you keep tabs on individual copies.

There are three other possible items to include on the title page. One might be a securities disclaimer. If you are using a business plan to seek individual investors, it is important to state the following on the title page: "*This is a business plan. It does not imply an offering of securities.*" Typically this comes after or as part of the proprietary statement. The disclaimer is needed to comply with Securities and Exchange Commission (SEC) rulings. Another item to include is the name of the person who prepared the business plan, if it is someone other than the owner. The third possible item for inclusion is a notice of copyright for the plan or trademark for your brand name or logo, if you choose to pursue those forms of intellectual property protection. You can learn more about those in Chapter 18.

Table of Contents

The table of contents typically puts the major section headings (e.g., executive summary, company, market, etc.) in boldface type and the sections underneath each in regular type. Page numbers are given for every component, including financial statements and appendixes. Remember to put page numbers on every page of the business plan, even the financials.

Executive Summary

Many entrepreneurs write the one- to two-page executive summary first, using it as a guide, and then write the rest of the plan. (We discussed the executive summary earlier in this chapter.)

The Company

The first section of a business plan tells the story of your company. Ideally it should sell the reader on the company and the ideas and people behind it. It usually consists of two subsections—one that provides an overall description of the business and another focusing on its product or service.

Company Description (1–2 pp.)

Typically the first two subsections are the vision statement and mission statement of the business, which were discussed earlier. If you have specific goals or objectives for your business (e.g., "Third year sales of $50,000," "Picked-up by a major national chain by year 2"), they go in a subsection after the mission statement.

The next subsection is typically labeled "Company Background," or you can use the name of the business (PROmote Advertising, for example). This section gives a brief description of the business—its age and location, as well as the markets it serves or plans to serve. The firm's current status (start-up, seed stage, ongoing, expansion, and so on) is covered, and the most recent milestone achieved is often mentioned (received initial investments, finalized product design, tested a prototype, completed market testing, made first sales, and so on). For an existing business, the history of the business is briefly covered here.

The last part of the company background describes the business's competitive advantage and the way that it goes about making its profits and achieving its mission—its business model. These are the ideas covered in Chapter 7 on strategy. This is where the plan gets a chance to sell the key ideas about the firm's approach to business. The language should be upbeat and positive, and where there are numbers that support the operation of the business model, such as a 25 percent profit margin, 98 percent customer satisfaction, or double-digit growth, those should be included.

Product/Service and Industry (1–8 pp.)

The goal of this section is to describe your firm's product or service in order to help the reader understand what you are selling and how it could help your target customers. The best descriptions entice the reader to want to buy the product or service or get involved in the company that sells it. These descriptions often include pictures or graphics that help readers visualize the product or service. It is also common to explain how the customer uses the product or service or how it fulfills some need or desire or solves a problem for the customer. Often the descriptions explain how the firm is able to deliver value benefits to the customer (quality, style, delivery, service, technology, ease, personalization, assurance, place, credit, brand/reputation, belonging, and altruism), as discussed in Chapter 7.[24] If the product or service has protection through a **proprietary technology** or from patent, trademark, or copyright, you mention it here.

proprietary technology
A product or service or an aspect of one that is kept as a trade secret or is protected legally using patent, copyright, trademark, or service mark.

Every product or service is part of an industry, and here is where you talk about it. Industry descriptions typically include the key information identified in the industry analysis, also discussed in Chapter 7. This includes the industry's SIC and NAICS codes, the size of the industry (in number of firms and sales), and some indication of the historical trend of growth, stability, or decline (how much it is growing, how long it has remained stable, or by how much sales overall is it declining over time). Industry profit margins are an important part of this section, as is how profits are typically made. Then you point up what your firm's projected or achieved profit margins are, and how your business model helps make this possible.

The Market

The market section talks about your customers—who they are and what they are like, who else is pursuing them, and how you plan to get or keep your customers. The market section builds on material you may have developed in the feasibility analysis (see Chapter 4), the industry analysis (Chapter 7), and the marketing plan (see Chapter 12).

Market and Target Customer (1–3 pp.)

The market refers to the total population of people or firms to whom you plan to sell. Markets are usually described in terms of their size (both in numbers of customers and size of sales) and scope (local, regional, national, international, global). The major ways the market is organized are also covered. Professional, trade, or industry associations, special-interest clubs, major national gatherings, and media dedicated to the market (e.g., *Restaurant Business* magazine for restaurant owners, or *Simple Scrapbooks* magazine for people who are into scrapbooks) are all relevant.

The target customer section focuses attention on the individual who would buy your product or service. Target customers are described in terms of demographics (such as age, gender, education, income, experience), their relation to the product or service (will they use it themselves, gift it, resell it, etc.), how often they buy (once a day, once a week, twice a month, every three years, once in a lifetime, etc.), their past experience with your kind of product or service (new user, prior user of competitor's product, prior user of your product), and what they are looking for when buying your product or service. What they are looking for should be based on discussions with potential customers, and it hopefully matches closely with the value benefits your product offers. Providing a comparison of the two is often a good idea.

It is very common to have multiple target audiences. When this is the case, you should provide a separate description of each one. It often helps to give each target group a specific name when you refer to them in the rest of the business plan. For scrapbookers, the target audiences have names like "kiddies," "moms," "grandmoms," "hobbyists," and "historians." Since your marketing plan can differ dramatically among the different groups—imagine how to sell to "kiddies" and "historians"—you want to have an easy way to differentiate them.

Competition and Competitive Advantage (1–2 pp.)

Consider doing this section with one page of text and a one-page table. The table identifies the major competitors for your market by name and location. Other columns mention the competing product or service, its market share, price, competitive strength, and competitive weakness. The accompanying page of text talks about your firm's competitive advantage—what makes your product or service or firm unique—and how your competitive advantage gives you an opportunity to win sales from these firms. Often this information is based on material gathered from the industry analysis (see Chapter 7).

Marketing Strategy (1–3 pp.)

A good marketing strategy section focuses on three ideas: (1) The overall strategy your firm pursues in the market, (2) the sales plan that shows the specific ways you apply strategy to secure sales from your customers, and (3) the longer-term competitive plan that shows how you protect your firm from efforts of the competition to unseat you. Much of the specifics are built from the ideas you develop in the marketing chapters of the book, Chapters 9 through 12.

The overall strategy subsection discusses your generic strategy (differentiation, cost, focus) as well as any supra-strategies (craftsmanship, customization, etc.) or fragmented industry strategies (no-frills, formula facilities, etc.) you pursue. Explain here how each is used in your firm and in your sales efforts.

The sales plan addresses the day-to-day specifics of how sales are achieved. It builds on the value benefits being sought by your customers and shows how these are turned into promotional efforts, pricing and incentive programs, distribution techniques, and location. Most of all, it emphasizes the way you or your employees go about selling. Examples of advertising materials, displays, coupons, or the like are useful and typically mentioned here, but details are put in an appendix. The proof that your approach is working comes from sales made using these approaches, so the strongest sales plans talk positively about the results of pilot tests, **preselling** efforts, or conventional sales already made. Being able to name customers (especially repeat customers) really builds up this section.

preselling
Involves introducing your product to potential customers and taking orders for later delivery.

Over the longer term, even with a clear competitive advantage, a sound strategy, and a good sales plan, your competitors are not likely to give up the market. They will fight back. When they do that, trying to match your sales plan features or competitive advantage, what are you keeping in reserve to help you fight back? Here is where you want to have several additional strategies that play against weaknesses in the competition, or further improve your product or service. These can include protections through patents and intellectual property protection or relationships with powerful partners. You may have contracts that tie customers to you long term, but most often advantages come from bringing out improved versions of your product or service before the competition introduces its own improved product or service.

Having these improvements ready requires some preparation on your part. In a business, this is often called **research and development** (alias R&D) or the *growth plan*. Most business plans add a section on R&D or growth here to explain how they are working to maintain an in-depth competitive advantage, with one or more additional generations of products or services ready to be used, or quickly brought to market, in order to keep the competition one generation behind your firm in meeting customer needs. Growth plans often talk about longer-term partnerships to be sought, new markets to be pursued, or ways to leverage the firm's assets, for example through licensing or franchising.

research and development
(often abbreviated R&D)—The part of a business (and a business plan) that is focused on creating new products or services and preparing new technologies, ideas, products, or services for the firm's market.

The Organization

In this section you lay out the components and supports for the firm itself. So far you have covered the product and the customer. The goal for this section is to convince the reader that the business will be successful because it has access to high-quality people both within the firm and within the larger business community, and the organization itself is structured to make the best use of those people.

Legal and Organization Structures (1/2–1 p.)

This subsection describes the legal form of the business (LLC, LLP, sole proprietorship, etc.) and where it is formally registered (topics discussed in Chapter 18). It also describes the organizational structure of the firm. Often for big businesses these are drawn using organizational charts. For small businesses with an owner-manager and an employee or two, it is easier to just give the description in words. The typical format for this is to start from the top, with the highest-level manager, giving his or her title and major duties, as described in the human resource management chapter (Chapter 19). Successive sentences describe the positions and duties of workers at each level below. This section should make clear how many employees there are and whether they are full time or part time, permanent or seasonal, family or nonfamily. If you have schedules for seasonal hiring and if you have standards for hiring, they get mentioned in this section.

Key Personnel (1/2–3 pp.)

By now you have sold people on your vision, mission, product, service, competitive advantage, and even your sales approach. It is now time to sell the most important single element in the business plan—you! In any business and any business plan, everything hinges on the quality of the entrepreneur behind it. If we do not have confidence in the entrepreneur, there is no way to have confidence in the other parts of the plan. The goal for the key personnel subsection is to inspire that confidence in your reader.

Who are your key personnel? Any owners or senior managers count, as do people who will be handling key aspects of the business. For example, a salesperson with an extensive customer base would be a key employee, as would an employee who is locally famous for a skill the business will use. Often businesses have a circle of outsiders involved. This might include a local media personality who will be promoting your business, or the inventor or holder of a patent or trademark you are using, or the owner of a key outside venture partner.

While you might put in the résumés of one or two key people if you have the space, typically the key personnel are described in a half- to one-page description. Simply put, the goal is to impress the reader. What is impressive? Accomplishments, and the closer these are to the business, the better. Having been successful in the business in this industry in another firm or in your own firm (if this plan is for an existing business rather than a start-up) is the best proof. Having been successful in another line of business is a good second choice. Having experience in sales is always useful, as is experience managing projects or people.

Whenever possible talk about accomplishments rather than just experience. Achieving some mark of distinction, such as being a store's top salesperson, is best, followed by years of experience in some aspect of business, followed by education. Sometimes giving the specifics of the accomplishment does the job, even if no award was given. For example, being able to say, "In my five years at Hobbyco, my sales increased an average of 50 percent a year" shows your sales abilities are improving, which is good.

When looking for accomplishments, do not limit yourself to business. Particularly for students and stay-at-home spouses, there are often organizational accomplishments that are relevant. Activities undertaken or managed for schools, churches, social organizations, civic organizations, or community groups are often important indicators of expertise. For example, managing a team during a fund-raising event may help prove your skills in people management and making quick decisions.

Related Service Providers (1/2–1 p.)

These days, small businesses are rarely alone, and the quality of the professionals surrounding you tells people a lot about how good you might be. Taking a paragraph or two to identify your bank and banker, your attorney and legal firm, accountant or bookkeeper, and other consultants can help show that you have high-quality supports. If you have major relationships established with well-known suppliers or customers, list these here also. If you have a board of directors, members can be mentioned here or under key personnel. If you have a board of advisers made up of people who are not owners, they would be listed here.

Location (1/2 p.)

The other major organizational asset of a business is its location. This is given here, along with a description of the facility that focuses on how it meets the strategic and sales goals of the business. Also mention whether you own, lease, or rent the property. If you have investments in the property, either in terms of ownership or improvements made to it, mention those too. If there are plans to expand the facilities, mention them.

The Financials

There are two parts to the financial section of a business plan. When you are using a plan to find investors, the financials section starts with two subsections—one on critical risks and one on the deal being offered investors. For all types of business plans, a set of financial reports or projections is expected. For either approach, it is always important to develop the financials in the most conservative way possible—never overstate your sales or profits, always explain the assumptions you are making, and provide (or be ready to give) the source for every number you include. It is usually better to include fewer numbers, but ones you understand inside-out rather than having lots of numbers, but knowing only in a general way how you arrived at them.

Critical risks are discussed in more detail below. The deal subsection typically talks about how much money is needed and how the funds will be used. This subsection goes on to address any prior or existing investments and the current ownership situation. Then it explains the equity being offered to investors, giving the price and the kinds of assurances offered (e.g., seats on the board of directors, buy/sell agreements, etc.). Here the plan details how investors will be able to sell or redeem their equity in order to harvest their investment and exit the business. The best plans explain how investors will be assured that management will be responsive to investor concerns. Typically the critical risks and the deal will each take about one page each.

The financial statements expected include: (1) income statements (also called a P&L for profit and loss) and its assumptions, (2) cash flow and its assumptions, and (3) balance sheet and its assumptions. For start-up businesses, it is also common to include a listing of the expenses incurred in the start-up process.

For an existing business, the financials section reports the last two years of actual data, and then offers three-year projections for the income, cash flow, and balance sheet. For a start-up business, the tradition is to offer three years of data projections. If you will take three or more years to show a profit, it makes sense to give projections for five years. In either case, income and cash flow are given monthly for the first year, quarterly for the second year, and annually for the third and any later years. Think in terms of a layout described in Figure 8.3.

Note that each of the financial statements also includes its assumptions. Included as endnotes, the assumptions are often considered to be the most important part of the financials. Assumptions explain how the computations are made, which items are included or excluded, and whether there are any special considerations underlying the particular numbers. For example, key assumptions include how sales are computed, which items are expensed versus depreciated, and how inventory and business valuations are made.

A schedule of the major milestones or benchmarks the company plans to achieve is often included in the financials section, typically after the assumptions page. If significant milestones or benchmarks have already been achieved, these can top off the schedule, so readers can see how the firm has progressed.

FIGURE 8.3

Financials Layout for a Typical Business Plan

Page 1: Critical assumptions.

Page 2: The deal (if the plan is going to investors).

Page 3: Income statement for year 1, by month. Assumptions marked as endnotes.

Page 4: Income statement for year 2 by quarter and year 3 (and later if needed) by year. Assumptions marked as endnotes.

Page 5: Cash flow statement for year 1, by month. Assumptions marked as endnotes.

Page 6: Cash flow statement for year 2 by quarter and year 3 (and later if needed) by year. Assumptions marked as endnotes.

Page 7: Balance sheet for years 1–3 (or 1–5) by year. Assumptions marked as endnotes.

Page 8: Start-up cost budget. Assumptions marked as endnotes.

Page 9: Assumptions (endnote) page for financial statements.

The Appendixes

With approximately nine pages used for financials, you have up to six pages left for appendixes. The most popular appendix is a one-page version of the owner's résumé (an example of a résumé for a student starting a business is given in the appendix at the end of this chapter). There are several other useful appendixes, listed below. The ones you select depend on what you are trying to highlight in your business plan. They can include:

- Product or service pictures or specifications (important when you stress features or style, or when your product or service is not familiar to readers).
- Copies of signed contracts, letters of intent or commitment, or contingency contracts from customers or investors (useful to show acceptance).
- Results of marketing studies or pilot sales efforts (useful for showing market acceptance).
- Industry reports (if there is significant information not included in the plan).
- Price lists for products or services.
- Floor plans of the location, if it is central to the business (e.g., a manufacturing facility or restaurant).
- Advertising copy, such ads, logos, catalog pages, brochures, sales letters, or press releases.
- Customer or spokesperson testimonials.
- Letters of opinion from intellectual property attorneys on prospects for patent or trademark protection or from manufacturers or consulting engineers about the viability of production processes for the product.

If readers want to know more about something that is not in the plan, they can ask you for the additional information. So do not worry too much about the many possible appendixes you cannot include. The goal of appendixes is to provide supporting information that helps detail or support the key selling points of your plan.

At this point, the writing of the classic business plan is done, but there is still work to be done assembling it. Plans are typically delivered as an 8-1/2- by 11-inch document, which has been carefully and repeatedly checked to eliminate spelling and grammar mistakes. It has been checked to make sure all pages are included and cleanly printed. While your own copy of the plan might be kept in a loose-leaf binder to make insertions and deletions easy, the copies you give out should be spiral bound (so they lay flat when opened). Covers should be sturdy to protect the plan from the inevitable coffee stains of business. Cover letters are typically clipped to the cover, rather than included in the plan itself, so the reader opens the plan to see the title page.

Focusing Your Business Plan

To be successful in telling the firm's story, a business plan needs to match the needs of the reader. Businesses face four situations in which reader needs are specific enough and distinct enough that it makes sense to write the plan with particular emphases in mind.

LO4
Focus business plan sections to meet specific needs.

- **Plans for a pioneering business:** When your product or service is truly new to everyone, it is considered a pioneering business. With a pioneering business, your greatest problems are: (1) helping people understand how it works, (2) showing them how they would use it, (3) estimating how many people would want it, and (4) estimating how much they would be willing to pay for it. Anything you can do to help readers experience and understand the product or service helps demystify it. Plan on a detailed explanation of the product or service and how it works. Make sure you explain the benefits customers would receive, and talk about the customer's personal experience in trying out, buying, and using the product. The value of preselling, pilot tests, or test marketing cannot be stressed

pioneering business
A firm whose product or service is new to the industry or is itself creating a new industry.

test marketing
Selling your product or service in a limited area, for a limited time.

enough. If 100 people tried the product and 10 bought it, you have a powerful proof of concept. Pioneering products also face a hurdle around manufacturing—can they be manufactured at a cost that leaves a chance for profit? Letters from manufacturers or consulting engineers confirming the viability and production costs of your product go a long way to alleviating fears in this area. Also, if your product is a minor variation on a product already made (for example, a consumer version of an existing industrial product), play this point up, since it means fewer problems are likely for your specific product.

new entrant business
A firm whose product or service is established elsewhere and is new to this market.

- **Plans for a new entrant business:** When your product or service already exists but your *firm* is the first of its kind in your market, it is considered a **new entrant business**. As such it is always harder to prove that your product or service will work. Just imagine trying to explain the idea of a $5 cup of coffee to people who had never heard of Starbucks! In response, help make the product or service seem more familiar by detailing how it is used by customers, and give more background on how the product or service has done in other markets, especially markets similar to yours. Also emphasize existing operations in your industry analysis. Seeing that it has worked elsewhere takes much of the mystery out of the question of whether it would work where you plan to market it.
- **Plans for an existing business:** Occasionally, entrepreneurs start a business before they write a plan for it. When writing a plan for an existing business, you have the benefit of knowing the history, the existing market, and the financial track record of the firm. These form a foundation for the plan, so the projections about future markets, sales, and profits should clearly build on these historical facts. It can make sense to gather information on existing customers to help clearly define the market, and often suppliers and trade associations can provide more in-depth information on market shares and competitors. Existing firms have assets to protect, such as the customer list, the firm's name, and any intellectual properties it has developed (e.g., a patented way of performing work, a trademark, a copyrighted report, a recipe protected as a trade secret). Showing how you plan to protect and perhaps even make additional profits from your intellectual property (e.g., through licensing patents or trademarks) strengthens the plan, as does talking about new ideas for increasing sales, which typically appears in the research and development section.
- **Plans for a business with significant government involvement:** Some businesses depend on government approvals to go forward. Examples include salvage yards, garbage dumps, companies using toxic chemicals, nursing homes, service stations, and even in many places, day care centers. When government gets involved in a major way, for example, having to approve the business license, zoning, or environmental impact, delays are inevitable. You need to build a plan that anticipates delays and either works around the parts of the business requiring approvals or is able to go into a type of sleep mode, using as few resources as possible until approval arrives. Working around approvals usually hinges on selling services or products that are part of the business but do not require specific approval. For someone starting a service station, it may be possible to do minor car repairs such as oil changes, detailing, or tune-ups at the customer's home or workplace. This helps spread word, build a customer base, improve skills, and keep cash flowing until approval for the service station comes.

Once you have written the complete business plan, you are positioned to create special-purpose versions of the plan to meet the needs of a wide variety of people important to your business. Usually these special-purpose plans use a subset of the total plan. In addition to the full business plan described above, there are five other special-purpose types of plan:[25]

- If you intend to send your plan to professional funding sources such as private banks, investment clubs, or venture capital firms, it is common to send what is called a *mini-plan* or a **screening plan**. The idea is to give the basic overview of the firm and a detailed look at the financials. This is because funding sources typically start their decision process with clear ideas about the industry and the profit levels they want to pursue. Screening plans usually consist of the cover letter, title page, executive summary, and financials sections of the business plan. The only time any appendixes would be included is when it is important to prove the viability of contracts, intellectual property protection, or the product's ability to be manufactured. A screening plan can also be a useful way to get into the planning process. Michael McMyne won one of the Global Student Entrepreneur Awards for his consulting business. When he started, all he used was his executive summary and the financials.[26]
- You may find that the business plan has a lot of information you would like to share with potential customers or suppliers, but you do not want them to see your financials. One variant of the traditional business plan is called the informational plan. **Informational plans** typically consist of company and organization sections. The cover letter, title page, executive summary, and table of contents are typically revised to reflect the differences. Relevant appendixes might also be included, such as detailed product descriptions or price lists.
- A special form of informational plan posted on the Internet is the **proof-of-concept Web site**. This kind of site is designed to solicit information on customer interest. They are particularly useful for demonstrating a technology or service that is new or novel (see Small Business Insight: VividSky), or to reach a market that is very widely spread out, making conventional promotional techniques too expensive. The goal is to inform customers and partners about the firm and the product, so proof-of-concept Web sites consist of the vision and mission statements, the product/service description, and often an animated or interactive demonstration of the product or service. Short biographies of the key personnel replace résumés, and the site may also have price or product lists or testimonials. The site itself tracks information about the viewers. Visitors are asked for feedback on the concept and are offered the chance to be kept up to date as the product nears the market.
- In seeking a marketing or joint venture partner or a key employee, you need to provide more of an idea about your market and approach to it. In the early stages of finding a partner, however, it is usually too soon to share your detailed financial information. As a result, a **key employee/partner plan** (also called a *summary plan*, *concept plan*, or *idea plan*) can be drawn up to include all the materials of an informational plan, plus the market section and critical risks subsection of the regular business plan.
- An **invention plan** focuses on the market and operationalization of a new invention. Inventions are typically licensed to others, so the organization section

screening plan
Also called a *mini-plan*, gives the basic overview of the firm and a detailed look at the financials.

informational plans
Give potential customers or suppliers information about the company and its product or service.

proof-of-concept Web site
An Internet-based type of business plan providing information or demonstration of a product or service designed to solicit information on customer interest.

key employee/partner plan
Provides information on the company, product/service, market, and critical risks to prospective business or marketing partners or to prospective key employees.

invention plan
A business plan that provides information to potential licensees. Invention plans focus on the details of an invention, including intellectual property rights.

VividSky and SkyBox

Tim Hayden developed a wireless PDA (personal digital assistant) designed to be rented to spectators at sporting events. Called SkyBox, the PDA would be manufactured and sold to sports stadiums and teams through his company, VividSky. SkyBox would let the fans at a game see all the video feeds and statistics for the game. It would also offer interactive food and drink ordering, live chats, and directions to seats, restrooms, and exits. The PDA was a lot more advanced than those most people were used to, and Tim needed a way to help people understand the technology and the value it added to the spectator's experience in the stadium. To do this, he created a proof-of-concept Web site at **www.vividskyco.com** that provides visitors with an interactive demonstration of the SkyBox system using Macromedia Flash. While there were several competing systems in development, the SkyBox demonstration was unique, giving SkyBox an edge over rivals. The Web site also became the basis for an interactive CD sent to stadium and team owners, creating even more recognition for the SkyBox system.

simply describes the inventor and any business the inventor runs, to provide background. The product or service being invented is given a very detailed description, with diagrams or pictures to help the licensee understand it. While the plan helps to explain the market and competition to the prospective licensee, the marketing strategy is not typically included. Legal issues tend to focus on intellectual property protection (e.g., patents, trademarks, etc.) instead of on the legal form of organization, and the financials are limited to the prospective deal and risks, since the invention does not come with a firm that creates sales.

- There is only one type of plan that actually adds material to a full business plan. **Operational plans** are designed to be used as working documents within a business. So in addition to all the material typically included in a full business plan, an operational plan includes detailed specifications of the major techniques, methods, recipes, formula, and sources used by the firm to do its work.

operational plan
Business plans designed to be used internally for management purposes.

Table 8.3 provides an easy way to compare the different types of special-purpose plans and the components they take from the full business plan. Even though the table shows the business plan sections and subsections usually included, it is important to keep the specifics of your business and your readers in mind. If sections of the business plan seem inappropriate for your type of business or for the specific readers who will see the plan, it makes sense to leave them out. The business plan is first and foremost a sales document, and tailoring the plan's "pitch" to the specifics of your business and the readership is always a smart move.

Addressing Critical Risks in a Plan

LO5
Identify the major risks to business plan success.

Every business faces risks in the real world, so every business plan needs to spend some time addressing them. The exact issues raised by business experts, bankers, lawyers, and investors are often specific to your plan, but the themes they consider in assessing risks are actually quite common. Knowing these risk themes, you can go through your business plan, identify the risks, and determine how you want to handle them, the way Dan Watkins of DigitalFirst Productions did (see Small Business Insight Box).

TABLE 8.3 Types of Business Plans

Business Plan Sections	Full Business Plan	Operational Plan	Invention Plan	Key Employee/ Partner Plans	Informational Plans	Proof-of-Concept Web Site	Screening Plans
1. Cover letter	X	X	X	M	M		M
2. Title page	X	X	X	M	M		M
3. Table of contents	X	X	X	M	M		
4. Executive summary	X	X	X	X	M		X
5. The company	X	X	M	X	X		
5a. Company description	X	X	M	X	X	X	
5a1. Vision statement	X	X		X	X	X	
5a2. Mission statement	X	X		X	X	X	
5a3. Objectives (optional)	X	X		X	X		
5a4. Company background	X	X	M	X	X	X	
5b. Product/service and industry	X	X	X	X	X	X	
5b1. Product/service description	X	X	X	X	X	X	
5b2. Industry description	X	X	X	X	X		
6. The Market	X	X	X	X			
6a. Market and target customer	X	X	X	X			
6b. Competition and competitive advantage	X	X	X	X			
6c. Marketing strategy	X	X		X			
6c1. Overall strategy	X	X		X			
6c2. Sales plan	X	X		X			
6c3. Competitive plan	X	X		X			
6c4. R&D/growth plan	X	X	X	X			

(continued on next page)

X = Included; M = Included in modified form; O = Optionally included

TABLE 8.3 Types of Business Plans (Continued)

Business Plan Sections	Full Business Plan	Operational Plan	Invention Plan	Key Employee/ Partner Plans	Informational Plans	Proof-of-Concept Web Site	Screening Plans
7. The organization	X	X		X	X		
7a. Legal and organizational structures	X	X	M	X	X		
7b. Key personnel	X	X	X	X	X		
7c. Related service providers	X	X	X	X	X		
7d. Location	X	X		X	X		
8. The financials	X	X					X
8a. Critical risks	X	X	X	X			X
8b. The deal	X	X	X				
8c. Income statement	X	X					X
8d. Cash flow projection	X	X					X
8e. Balance sheet	X	X					X
8f. Start-up budget	0	0					
8g. Assumptions	X	X	M				X
8h. Schedule	X	X	X				X
9. The appendixes	X	X					
9a. Owner's résumé	X	X		0	0	M	0
9b. Other popular appendixes	X	X		0	0	0	0
10. Detailed specifications of work	0	X					

X = Included; M = Included in modified form; 0 = Optionally included

SMALL BUSINESS INSIGHT

Analyzing Risks at DigitalFirst Productions

Award winning photographer Dan Watkins of DigitalFirst Productions (www.digitalfirstproductions.com) started two businesses in the last decade—one succeeded, and one failed. In that first business, sales never seemed to take off, and the financial health of the business was not as clearly known as it should have been. Dan feels the major difference between the two was the presence of what he called "a good solid business plan" for the second business. Dan argues that a thorough business plan can turn great ideas into reality because it forces you, the prospective entrepreneur, to take a close 360-degree look at your business ideas. For Dan the plan became a basis for evaluation as his business grew, with detailed sections on the market, how to sell to them, and the financial projections those sales should generate. He knew he was getting the hang of business when the second business venture became profitable in the exact year, quarter, and month that his original business plan had forecast it would. The one element of the plan Dan credits with the most importance was the critical risks section. Dan claims, "If I hadn't considered some of the potential pitfalls associated with my original business ideas, my business venture probably wouldn't have been successful or profitable at all." For Dan, the plan made all the difference, and the critical risks section made the plan.

There are six **risks** that are common threats to businesses. These situations can cause investors, bankers, and other readers to evaluate a plan negatively.[27] Each of the risks can be handled, but the best test is to have people in your target audiences give you feedback on your plan.

risks
The parts of a business or business plan that expose the firm to any kind of loss—profits, sales, reputation, assets, customers, and so on.

1. **Overstated numbers:** Key numbers in your business plan that seem too good to be true, or are just large to begin with, tend to get a lot of attention—most of it negative. Sales or profits that are too optimistic, salaries that are too high for a firm of its age, and profitability are the three most likely culprits. For salaries, it makes sense in start-up firms for owners to take out the minimum, with additional income derived from profits, if and when you get them. For sales and profits, always give the most likely number, not the most optimistic. Profits depend on your being able to meet sales projections and keep within your costs, so if either one is off, profits will be too. Sales depend on conversion rates (see below).
2. **Uncertain sales (especially conversion rates):** The *conversion rate* is the percentage of people who buy out of the total population of people you approach. It is also called the *hit rate*. The best test of the conversion rate is through test marketing or preselling. Test marketing is selling your product or service in a limited area, for a limited time. Often in test marketing efforts, you give buyers incentives in return for information that helps you profile your actual target customer. Preselling involves introducing your product to potential customers and taking orders for later delivery. In either case, the key information is the number of customers approached and the percent who bought. Knowing the conversion rate, a reader then takes your projected market size, applies the conversion rate (probably something like 50–75 percent of the claimed rate "just to play it safe"), and then estimates what the total sales might be.
3. **Overlooked competition:** You are supposed to be *the* expert on your product or service and part of that involves knowing every competitor. For example, a student was developing a wireless cell phone headset. At the time, the student claimed there were no competitors, but most people familiar with the industry knew there were several wireless headsets using the increasingly well-known Bluetooth wireless protocol. Switching protocols would be a matter of a few

weeks for the existing manufacturers, so the competition facing the student was much greater than he thought, and the plan kept getting rejected. You need to know about your immediate competitors, as well as substitutes and potential competitors if you are going to prove your long-term vision for the company.

4. **Experience deficits:** A lot of the success in business comes from experience. In any business, one critical risk is not knowing as much as your competition does. Four types of experience—in the line of business, in the industry, in the locality, and in managing—are the most important.[28] Successful firms invariably possess (or develop) all four types. Some you should be able to supply. If there is any experience lacking, you need to get it yourself or hire it through partners, employees, or consultants working with you.
5. **Inadequate cushion:** According to the *Dun & Bradstreet Failure Record,* the single most common reason for business closure is a lack of financial resources. In short, the firm ran out of money. Customers who take too long to pay, unexpected expenses, accidents, and mistakes can be deadly to a firm if it does not have enough money saved for such rainy days. Having enough cash to survive three months goes a long way to avoiding this risk.
6. **Inadequate payback:** It is always important to think about what the reader of the plan is expecting. For bankers, it is the payback of the loan or line of credit, so cash flows and collateral issues are important. For investors, growth rates and profit margins are important because those determine their earnings. For key employees, knowing the firm's operation and prospects helps them visualize their future in the firm. When the plan does not clearly specify the key paybacks to readers, it fails to sell them on the idea.

www.score.org
www.sba.gov/sbdc
http://www.ibisassoc.co.uk/analysis_new_business.htm
www.businessekg.org

Ideally, you should have a circle of advisers who can review the plan and help identify the critical risks and your coverage of them. This circle might include successful entrepreneurs you know, lawyers, or accountants. Other good sources include the free consultants from the Service Corps of Retired Executives (SCORE), available via www.score.org or your local Small Business Development Center (www.sba.gov/sbdc). There are even Web sites that make it possible for you to get a preliminary analysis of your plan. One of the most complete is Ibis Associates checklist at http://www.ibisassoc.co.uk/analysis_new_business.htm. To get a quick check of your major financial measures, you can use the Kauffman Foundation's Business EKG Web site (www.businessekg.org). The key is to get as much feedback as possible before sending it out in hopes of money, sales, or people.

Presenting Your Plan

LO6
Master presenting your business plan to others.

When it works, a written business plan is the way to get on the schedule of someone who can provide the money, the expertise, or the markets you seek. In such cases, the written plan is followed by a chance for you to make a formal presentation of your plan and answer questions about it. The business plan presentation, like the plan itself, has a very clear tradition about how it is supposed to be done. Knowing this tradition can help you quickly learn what is expected when presenting a plan to others.

A business plan presentation usually lasts 10–15 minutes, followed by 15 or more minutes for questions. Usually the presentation provides an overview of key points of the business plan—a chance to sell your ideas and, most of all, a chance to sell yourself.

A major part of any business plan presentation is a chance for the listener to form an opinion about you as an entrepreneur. The key things an influential person looks for in you are: (1) your passion for the business, (2) your expertise about the business and the plan, (3) how professional you are in your work, and (4) how easy it would be to work with you. How do you show these?

- **Passion for the business:** When presenting, do not read. Think of yourself as telling a story—a fascinating story—about your business. Help listeners understand why you are excited about the business, proud of it, and ready to stake your reputation and assets on it. Learn your presentation so well that it comes out as an often-repeated, beloved story, not as a prepared statement.

- **Expertise about the business and the plan:** Practice answering questions about the plan. Expect really tough questions. Assume people do not trust your assumptions when they first read them. Be ready to explain where you get your assumptions, your numbers, and your ideas. Be ready to mention sources. Be ready with comparisons to competitors and their offerings. Know how every number in the plan came about and what it means. For example, it is not uncommon for a banker to ask, "In your cash flow statement for April in the first year, you say you will be spending $1,140 on sales promotion expenses. How did you get that number—and isn't it a bit high?" It is better to have less material and know it backwards and forwards than to have material in the plan you do not totally understand.
- **How professional you are in your work:** Your plan should look professionally done. It should be neat and orderly, with perfect spelling and grammar. When you present it, you should be in business suit or dress, clean and pressed. Carry copies of your presentation slides to give the listeners. And have copies of your slides on acetates and on disk so that you can present no matter what technology is available. Have business cards ready, and bring a couple extra copies of the plan in case someone unexpected comes to the presentation. Meet all those attending the presentation with a smile and a firm handshake. Give them your card and take theirs if they offer one in return. Make sure you know the names of all the people in the room, and their position, so if there is a part of the plan you think might be of interest to them, you can mention it.
- **How easy it would be to work with you:** Typically when you are presenting a business plan, you are doing it with the goal of establishing an ongoing relationship with the listener. All relationships carry an element of liking. It is easier to see yourself establishing a relationship with someone you like than with someone you do not like. Part of the goal in the presentation is to get the listeners to like you. How? The techniques are simple—use eye contact, use peoples' names, remember what they might be interested in or in what they have shown an interest before, smile, and above all, be honest. When they ask tough questions, try not to get nervous, upset, angry, or defensive. If you do not have the answer, tell them so honestly, make a note about their question and name, and tell the person you will get back to him or her with the answer. Recognize that tough questions are the listeners' way of making sure they—and you—are protected from risks.

Typically the presentation follows the content of the business plan. For different audiences, for example, potential partners or customers, you delete slides—just as you delete sections in the business plans for partnering or customer information plans.

Business, and the understanding of business you get from business plan writing, changes. Sometimes it changes quickly as you achieve new things or learn new things (including errors that crept into the plan you just finished). This means that parts of your plan may change from week to week. You handle this by creating handouts with the new information. These can be mailed to people reading your plan, or handed to them at the presentation. Both approaches are common. If there are detailed parts of your plan that you have left out, such as a market survey or a detailed cost breakdown, it makes a lot of sense to make copies to use as handouts during a presentation or question-and-answer period.

Dwight Eisenhower was not only the 34th U.S. President, but he was the general who planned the most daring effort in all of World War II, the D-Day landing. A master planner, Eisenhower said, "I have always found that plans are useless, but planning is indispensable." The best way to think about the business plan is as a way to get yourself to think through your entire business. Some parts will be so easy that you can instantly know how everything works. Things in the business you imitate from others are classic examples. For other aspects of the business, planning may become the way

THE THOUGHTFUL ENTREPRENEUR

The Seven Slides of Classic Business Plan Presentations

While 15 minutes sounds like a lot of time to talk, when summarizing a 40-page business plan, the time can go very quickly. From watching winning presentations in business plan competitions and in the real world, it is clear that a superior business plan presentation is usually built around seven slides.

1. **Introductory slide:** Has your firm's name and the names of the owners and presenters. While showing this slide, you thank your listeners for the opportunity to present and explain the purpose of the business plan (e.g., financial, partnering). Introduce your firm by name, as well as yourself and any other people from your firm that you have brought with you. (1 minute)
2. **Product/service slide:** This slide demonstrates the product or service in terms of the benefit it provides customers or the problem it solves. Often a picture is included. Your talk describes the product or service in detail. The slide also gives the size of the target or overall market. Although you mention this, spend more time showing how the market has already accepted your product/service or ones like it. (3–4 minutes)
3. **People slide:** Investors invest in people as much as in ideas. This slide presents the key people with the one or two skills they have that are most persuasive in proving their expertise or their contributions to the business. If you have partnerships or alliances with names the listeners would know and respect, these can be included (often as corporate logos) and briefly mentioned. (1 minute)
4. **Strategy slide:** This focuses on a one or two line explanation of your strategy as it relates to your making profits (your overall strategy). The slide also has one or two lines explaining how you plan to make the majority of your sales (your sales strategy). For both, think about specifics rather than general jargon. Saying, "We will get business because we offer faster service than anyone else," for your strategy sounds more persuasive than, "We leverage time-sensitivity in a manner superior to our competitors." (2–3 minutes)
5. **Risk slide:** Admit to the two or three greatest risks or challenges facing your firm, and for each, explain how you are preventing, insuring, repairing, or monitoring the situations. Your goal here is to head off the most threatening questions by showing you are working on the problems. (1–2 minutes)
6. **Financial slide:** Here you give the sales, breakeven, and profit projections for the firm for the period covered in the plan. Mention the worst-case scenario projections, but explain why you think the numbers on the screen are the most likely ones. (1–2 minutes)
7. **Summary slide:** This gives a one-to-two line summary of the firm in a positive, upbeat manner ("PROmote Advertising's quality service and large potential market will lead to excellent sales and profits"). Give this line in your most confident and sales-oriented manner and mention that you believe you have shown this in today's presentation. Include a line on the slide with the request from the listener ("Loan of $25,000," "Line of Credit of $100,000," "Investment of $50,000"). In covering this, explain briefly what the money's use will be. There is also a line on the slide for what is offered in return (savings moved to a bank, pledged securities, stock in the firm for investors). You conclude with a repeat of thanks, and then ask for questions. (2 minutes)

you get a handle on the complexities and risks you face.[29] Some results of the planning process you will write down. Other parts will be kept in your head, ready to be used or amended as circumstances require. Many of the parts of the plan will quickly become outdated or need to be changed or adapted as the business is in operation.[30] In fact, the Eisenhower quote makes sense in another way too—business planning is a process you continue throughout your firm's life. Plans, once done, get revisited. Sometimes this is done formally, but more often you informally compare reality with the plan.

However you approach it, the idea of business planning is a powerful one, helping you imagine and then realize the business the way you want it to be. The techniques that contribute to creating a business plan—forming vision and mission statements, elevator pitches, financials, and marketing plans—can be used as stand-alone activities that help you meet the many demands you face as an aspiring entrepreneur. Whether you become an avid business planner or not, the process of business planning goes a long way to helping firms survive and prosper.

CHAPTER SUMMARY

LO1 Understand why and when to develop a business plan.

- Plans are done for external legitimacy and/or internal understanding.
- Plans are sometimes essential, and are often linked to improved firm survival.
- Different audiences seek different goals when reading business plans.

LO2 Know how to tell the business plan story.

- The business plan is a story you write about your firm.
- The story gets told in different ways and lengths, from vision statements, to elevator pitches, to executive summaries, to full business plans.

LO3 Learn the major sections of the classic business plan.

- The full business plan gives the complete story of the firm and its major elements: the company's product/service, market, competition, marketing strategy, organization, key personnel, service providers, location, and financials.
- It is a maximum of 25 pages long, with up to 15 pages of supporting material.
- Plans for simple businesses can be shorter than those for innovative types of firms.

LO4 Focus business plan sections to meet specific needs.

- A full business plan is often modified for special circumstances the firm faces, such as pioneering technology, new markets, or established operations.
- Parts of a full business plan are often combined to create shorter plans for particular audiences such as investors, partners, or others.

LO5 Identify the major risks to business plan success.

- All business plans face risks; part of the role of the business plan is to explain how the firm will handle these risks.
- The risks come from numbers or assertions that are not adequately explained or supported.

LO6 Master presenting your business plan to others.

- Most business plans are presented to others using a seven-slide show.
- Listeners check presentations for the presenter's passion, expertise, professionalism, and potential as a colleague.

DISCUSSION QUESTIONS

1. What are the reasons to write a business plan?
2. Imagine you were presenting your plan to a consultant who specializes in your industry. Your goal is to get her help. Using the ideas in Table 8.1, what kinds of issues do you think would be of interest to her as she reads your plan?
3. You are going to attend an after-work gathering sponsored by your local chamber of commerce. Which of the types of short business plan presentations (vision statement, mission statement, elevator pitch, executive summary) will you prepare for use, and when will you use them?
4. What is the most important part of a business plan in general? Considering the way you plan to use your business plan, what will be the most important part of it?
5. What are the differences in a business plan for a start-up pizza business and for an existing pizza business?
6. Students know people, including some who might invest in your business. What kind of business plan (e.g., informational, screening, key employee, full) would you give to other students?
7. For a business plan being put together by a student in his late teens or early 20s, what are the most likely risks?
8. Passion is clearly important in the business plan presentation. How can you display your passion for the business during the presentation?
9. What can you do to make the business plan easy to read and understand?

EXPERIENTIAL EXERCISES

1. **Evaluating a Business Plan** The goal of this exercise is to help you get used to scoring business plans the way bankers and investors do in the real world. Most financial professionals have checklists and scoring sheets that convert their accumulated wisdom into the factors that make a difference. Knowing how this scoring works can help entrepreneurs to bulletproof their plan, identifying problems before outsiders see them.

   One of the best business plan scoring systems is available to everyone for free on the Web. It comes from France's Ibis Associates. Originally built from a test of 57 firms, today it has been refined and is used on thousands of businesses, mostly from the United States and Western Europe.

   a. Go to Ibis Associates New Business Plan analysis page at **http://www.ibisassoc.co.uk/analysis_new_business.htm.**
   b. Print out the checklist and familiarize yourself with it.

c. Now read through the Blue Water Boatworks business plan included in the text. When you see something that relates to the scoring checklist, mark it.

d. After reading the plan, fill in 'no' for those items missing.

e. Go to the Web site and fill in the questionnaire for the Bluewater Boatworks Plan, and check the score received.

f. Be ready to discuss your findings (and defend your scoring) in class. Give some thought to what could be done better in the plan to achieve a higher score.

Your score will vary from those of others in the class. You will find that some of the difference comes from how closely people read the plan and the checklist. But there will be times when everyone will agree on what was read, but disagree on the meaning or score. That happens in business too. That is why it is important to try your plan out repeatedly. Just because one person or firm or bank said no does not mean that every one will see it or score it the same way. (Scoring site used with permission of **alan.west@ntlworld.com** for Ibis Associates, January 25, 2004.)

2. **Business Plan Archives** See if you can find a plan for your business at one of the business plan archive sites, because there is no shortage of business plans available for review on the Internet. For example, **www.businessplanarchive.org** provides plans from the dot-com boom and bust, including some plans of businesses still operating today. The commercial site behind Business Plan Pro offers a number of example business plans on its site, **http://www.bplans.com/sp/businessplans.cfm**. This is the site the SBA refers people to when they seek example plans. The key academic archive comes from the Moot Corp competition, which pits MBA students against one another in an international competition. Their archive is at **http://www.businessplans.org/businessplans.html**, although the site is sponsored by another commercial company, Business Resource Software. One review of business plan sites on the Web can be found at **http://eweb.slu.edu/bpsites.htm**.

Mini-Case

LOFT IN SPACE[31]

A student at the University of Nebraska—Lincoln (UNL), Michael Cain, built a loft for his dorm room bed. Others asked him to build one for them, and he started to think about making a business out of it. He had put together his marketing plan in his head and had even begun to think about operational details that would help make his business more efficient. He knew he needed to get some sort of official approval, since his business would be on campus. So he started checking with university officials about setting his business up, but it was here that he started hitting problems, such as:

- He could not run the business out of his dorm room.
- He couldn't use his UNL telephone or e-mail account for the business.
- His firm needed a 1 million dollar liability policy to work on campus.

He needed to be able to address these problems and make sure the solutions would leave him with a profitable business.

CASE DISCUSSION QUESTIONS

1. If he was going to build a business plan to present to the university administrators, what type of plan should he develop (following the types mentioned in Table 8.4)?
2. What parts of the plan should he make sure are included?
3. What solutions would you suggest for his three problems?

Example Cover Letter and Résumé

EXAMPLE COVER LETTER

Mr. Michael Hansen
Vice President for New Accounts
Bank New Narwhal
1234 Main Street
Anchorage, AK 99501

Dear Mr. Hansen:

I am Abe Zabrowski, the founder of a new painting inspection company, Surety Inspections, LLC. I have been doing my personal banking at BNN for several years, and so you were the first people I thought about when considering establishing a business line of credit.

Surety Inspections evaluates the completeness and quality of commercial painting projects for the clients of painting companies. Because commercial painting is difficult to evaluate, we offer an objective evaluation to painting customers to make sure everything was done according to specifications, or industry standards. Our clients are industrial plants, commercial firms, and government organizations that buy major painting projects. We are the only full-time professional painting inspection business in Alaska, with most of our competition consisting of painting firms that work between jobs. As such, we offer a more consistent and higher-quality evaluation, and we are always available for inspections.

While we have funded our initial equipment and operations, it is possible that we will need a line of credit to draw against when we must rent or buy equipment specific to particular contracts, or to pay for travel and lodging for contract work away from Anchorage. Since work in our industry is paid for after the report is delivered, we could incur costs early in a project and need credit. We are looking to secure a $10,000 line of credit. We can offer the firm's equipment as collateral, and we would be willing to discuss other forms of collateral or conditions that would make this workable. You will see that my credit rating and bank history are very solid.

Thank you for your consideration. I am available to answer any questions you have. Please call me at 907-555-1213. I will call you later this week to schedule an appointment to discuss my business and what BNN can do to help me grow it.

Sincerely,

Abe Zabrowski, CEO
Surety Inspections, LLC

EXAMPLE RÉSUMÉ[32]

DANIELLE SHERWOOD

123 University Drive
St. Louis, Missouri 63101
(314) 555-XXXX
dsherwood@ggg.com

SKILLS

- Able to plan and organize self, others, and operations.
- Exceptional sales ability.
- Capable leader and team member.
- Excellent presentation and communications skills.

EDUCATION

Saint Louis University, St. Louis, MO, May 2005
Bachelor of Science in Entrepreneurship, Minor in Marketing, GPA: 3.6/4.0

WORK EXPERIENCE

Owner, CardinalAngelSales, St. Louis, MO, 2004–Present

- eBay Gold level reseller specializing in St. Louis Cardinals memorabilia and logo wear.
- Grew sales to over $15,000 in year one, with a 99.8 percent customer approval rating.

Student Intern, Saint Louis University, St. Louis, MO, 2003–Present

- Partner with program director in writing and editing brochures and advertisements on leadership.
- Trained 10 new student employees and facilitated orientation on job duties.
- Generated new ideas to update department's Web site.

Sales Associate, May Company, St. Louis, MO, 2001–2003

- Sold merchandise to clients, increasing monthly sales by 25 percent.
- Resolved customer complaints and problems in a positive manner.
- Implemented customer service questionnaire which helped improve buyer satisfaction.

Sales Consultant, J. C. Penney Co. Inc., St. Louis, MO, 1999–2001

- Made suggestions and sold clothing items to customers.
- Developed customer service procedures and training program for staff.
- Assisted in training new employees on store procedures.

HONORS/ACTIVITIES

Collegiate Entrepreneurs Organization

- Vice President, Membership (2004–present)
- Textfile Shift Manager (2003–2004)

Alpha Delta Pi

- President (2003–Present)
- Philanthropic Chairperson (2002–2003)

Marketing in the Small Business

PART

LEARNING OBJECTIVES

This chapter will help you:

LO1 Know the characteristics of goods and services.

LO2 Define the total product.

LO3 Learn the stages of new product development.

LO4 Learn the product life cycle.

LO5 Understand the concepts of price with variable costs, fixed costs, and breakeven.

LO6 Understand price elasticities, pricing psychology, and other price influencers and their impact on pricing.

LO7 Understand different pricing strategies.

■ How has the pricing strategy most likely changed for Beyond Fleece as the company has expanded? What might be the future challenges in terms of pricing and continuing to deliver customized products to its customers?

CHAPTER 9

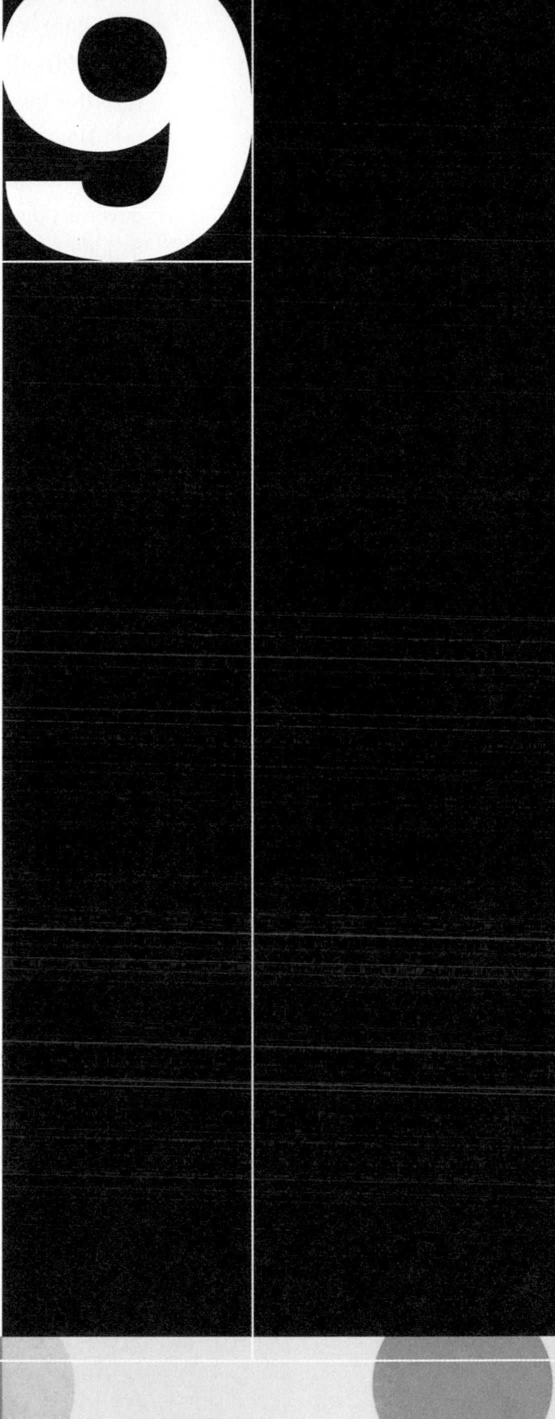

Small Business Marketing: Product and Pricing Strategies

Focus on Small Business: Scott the Seamstress[1]

Scott Jones was a junior at the University of Oregon when he discovered that he had a problem. Eugene, Oregon, is cold and wet much of the year and Jones wanted a fleece jacket like those he saw popping up all over campus, but he couldn't afford one. So Jones went to the campus Craft Center, bought a pattern and two yards of fleece, and sewed his own. At that time, Jones said, "I didn't know the seams had to line up. . . . The whole thing was pretty mismatched, but everybody seemed to like it. All my friends were saying, 'Hey, I want one, too.' So I kept making them."

With that, Beyond Fleece was born. Beyond Fleece began in 1996 in Jones's room where he would sew every morning from 5:00 a.m. until 8:00 a.m. before his morning classes. Jones experimented with various patterns from the Craft Center, and each jacket was custom-made for his individual customer. At first pricing was pretty easy. Scott needed to cover the costs of his materials plus a little extra for mistakes and enough profit to be worth the time he put in.

After graduation in 1998, Beyond Fleece's first Web site www.beyondfleece.com went live, and Jones began to sew full time while he

www.beyondfleece.com

coached in the University of Oregon's rowing program. The Web site began generating hundreds of orders, each one still individually customized, and Jones became a busy man. After he finished 20–40 jackets, Jones would load them into a large backpack and set off on his bike to ride the five miles to the embroidery shop.

Now Beyond Fleece offers dozens of basic pants, jackets, vests, and pullovers in fleece for both male and female weekend warriors. Jones allows customers to customize the product by offering several options. For example, the Classic Women's Jacket offers 5 colors and 16 feature options including armpit zippers, internal and external pockets, a hood, reinforced elbows, and thumb loops. Jones puts his target market between the ages of 25 and 45, estimates that about 70 percent are male, and says that they have to be comfortable buying online. Most orders come from the colder climates of the East Coast, although, ironically, he has noticed many from Texas and Georgia.

Jones expects to top $500,000 in sales in 2003 and $1 million in 2004. Pricing his product now means covering overhead, including equipment such as laser cutting tables and computerized sewing machines. Also, as the popularity of his product has grown and customer loyalty has increased, he doesn't have to be the cheapest product around.

DISCUSSION QUESTIONS

1. How would you describe the pricing approaches used by Beyond Fleece when it started and as it grew?
2. As Beyond Fleece continues to grow, Jones will face several challenges. First and foremost, how can he continue to offer a unique, customizable product while he produces hundreds of garments?
3. Is he producing too many products to have them viewed as customized anymore? If they're not customized, will consumers continue to pay higher prices?
4. If Beyond Fleece ceases to be viewed as a provider of custom clothing, how will the business's prices be affected?

Product

Goods Versus Services

LO1
Know the characteristics of goods and services.

A *product,* in general terms, is anything that is offered to the market to satisfy consumer wants, needs, and demands. This can include goods (like Beyond Fleece's clothing, a car, a can of green beans, a CD), services (haircut, divorce), people (political candidates, celebrities), and ideas (a political platform, an environmental message). Usually, we tend to group items as either goods or services; however, these two classifications are not discrete categories, as we see shortly for Beyond Fleece. There are elements of both goods and services in nearly every offering (see Figure 9.1). Knowing and understanding the particular blend of goods and services in your particular offering helps you to find its differential advantage and to communicate it better to customers.

We differentiate goods from services in several ways. These differences provide a whole set of potential problems for services that goods manufacturers do not have to face—or at least, do not have to face to the same extreme:

FIGURE 9.1

Goods-Services Mix

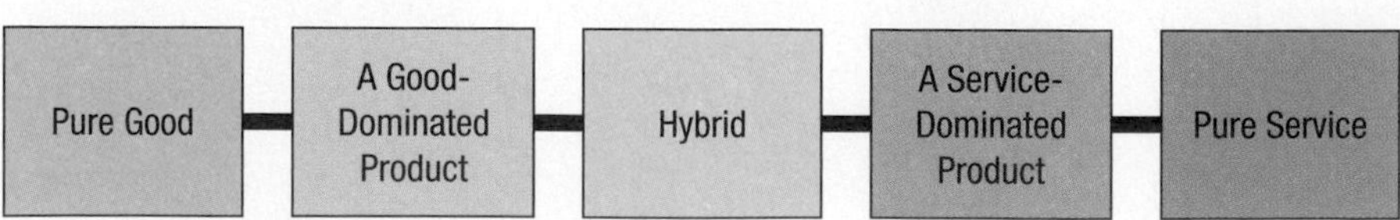

- **Tangibility:** Goods are tangible, while services are intangible. Goods are physical, solid items that can be touched, seen, held, tasted, and/or moved, while services cannot. Services often try to make their product more tangible in their advertising efforts as consumers are more comfortable with something they can see. For instance, Allstate insurance uses the image of "good hands," while Prudential has its rock. If you are trying to strengthen the idea that your service is fast, you could use a race car, a cheetah, or other symbols representing speed. For representing exclusiveness and high quality, certain colors are indicative of this. (Think of gold and silver versus hot pink.)

tangibility
An item's capability of being touched, seen, tasted, or felt.

- **Inseparability:** Services are inseparable from consumption, that is, they are produced and consumed at the same time. When you get a haircut, the production of the haircut by the hair stylist happens at the same time as you "consume" the product (get your hair cut). A good, on the other hand, can be produced anytime (within limitations) from a bottle of wine purchased years after production to the fast food hamburger prepared when you place your order. If you have several employees, you will want to make sure that they all are capable of producing a similar level of service; your pizza shouldn't be good only on the nights you make it.

inseparability
A quality of a service in which the service being done cannot be disconnected from the provider of the service.

- **Heterogeneity:** Services are *heterogeneous;* the quality of a service is dependent on the company and person performing the service, as well as on particular circumstances at the time of the performance of the service. The quality of your haircut depends on which shop you visit and which stylist you use, and may even vary day to day depending on the mood of the stylist, how busy the worker has been, whether you are the first or last client of the day, and so on. While goods can have a degree of heterogeneity, getting and keeping a manufacturing process under control can greatly reduce the difference between products, as well as the range of differences. Similar to inseparability, service firms try to reduce this variability through various methods including employee training. Franchises often have identical—or nearly identical—store layouts, employee uniforms, services offered, prices, and the like in order to reduce heterogeneity among franchisees. Automating parts of the service (for example, ATMs at banks) also reduces inconsistency.

heterogeneity
A quality of a service in which each time it is provided it will be slightly different from the previous time.

- **Perishability:** Goods can be stored for later use. In other words, if a store does not sell the red sweater today, it can sell it tomorrow or next week. Services are perishable. A haircut cannot be stored in a warehouse and then sold later. A plane with empty seats on a particular flight cannot use those seats at a later date. To combat this, service companies try to encourage consumers to use off-peak time services usually by offering better prices or other incentives (for cell phones, unlimited minutes after 5 p.m., for example).

perishability
A service exhibits perishability in that if it is not used when offered, it cannot be saved for later use.

Facing Intangibility and Perishability

SKILL MODULE 9.1

1. Brainstorm a list of service industries. Divide these services into groups of three to four and distribute them to different groups of students.
2. Each group of students should first consider companies they know. They should list examples of how these companies address intangibility and perishability. (Inseparability and heterogeneity may be more difficult to see from an outsider's viewpoint, but when possible, should also be considered.)
3. Pretend your group is planning to start a business in one or more of these service areas.
   a. Design a logo, sign, the building look, and so on to address some of the intangibles.
   b. What new and different ideas can you come up with to address perishablity?
   c. How might heterogeneity and inseparability be addressed?
4. Each group should share its ideas with others in the class.

Does Beyond Fleece sell a good or a service? Surely the jacket you receive is a good, but what of the ability to customize it? Is that a part of the good or an accompanying service? What about returning a product that doesn't meet your needs? What if someone wants to buy a gift certificate but doesn't know the recipient's size or color preference? Beyond Fleece's Web site has a FAQ section (frequently asked questions); isn't that a service? Many business owners believe they offer either a good or a service to their customers; however, nearly all really offer a combination.

Goods-Dominated Products, Hybrid Products, and Service-Dominated Products

Hybrid products are a balanced combination of good and service. A hybrid product has approximately equal portions of tangible and intangible components. Portions of the hybrid product will be inseparable, perishable, and heterogeneous. A good example is a meal at a restaurant. Why do you choose a particular restaurant? Is it for the food offered or for the atmosphere? Is it the good desserts or the fast service? If a restaurant has empty tables on Monday night, it cannot use these on Tuesday. However, the steaks not served on Monday can be cooked and served on Tuesday. If the server had a fight with his girlfriend, he may not notice that your water glass isn't refilled or that you have no silverware, while the last time you visited, he was extremely attentive and detail-oriented. On the other hand, the table, chairs, dishes, and such probably are identical to what you used before.

Other products are goods- or service-dominated. A house is a goods-dominated product, but why do identical houses sell for different prices? Often it's being in the right school district or climate, having the "right" address, the home warranty offered, and other service features. Your haircut is strongly service-oriented, but I'll bet your stylist uses shampoo and perhaps other styling products—goods.

The Total Product Approach

LO2
Define the total product.

There are very few items that can be considered a pure good or a pure service. Perhaps it would be helpful to view a product as a bundle of goods and services. Figure 9.2 illustrates this concept, which we discuss below.

core product
The very basic description of what a product is—a bar of soap, a house-cleaning service.

augmented product
Core product plus features that tend to differentiate it from the competition.

The **core product** is fairly easy to define. When someone asks you what your company does, the core product is your answer (at least, the short version). When you decided to start a business, you had an idea that you wanted to clean houses or make birdhouses or sell sports equipment. That's your core product component.

An **augmented product** has features that differentiate it from the competition but are still closely related to the core product. This includes brand names, quality levels, packaging, and specific features of your product. This is the somewhat longer answer to "what do you do?" "I run the Happy Housekeeper, a housekeeping business in the greater Chicago area." "I design custom-made birdhouses that are exact replicas of historical buildings." "I sell secondhand sports equipment on consignment by mail

FIGURE 9.2

Total Product Concept

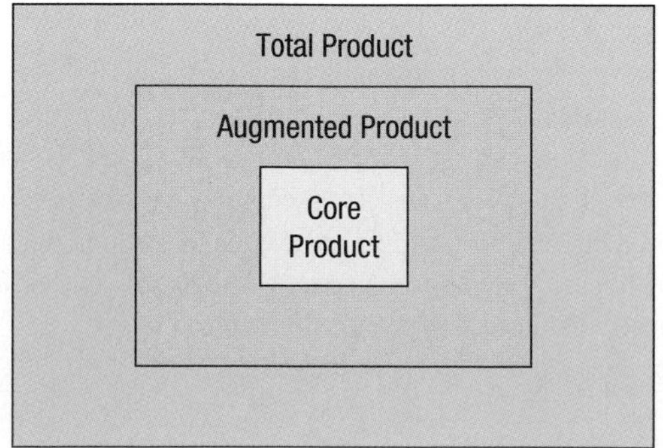

order and the Internet." When you decide to go into business, you consider what makes you different from the competition and what the particular strengths and weaknesses of your product are. These may not be totally visible to an outsider at first, but they are relatively easy to define.

The **total product** includes the entire bundle of product and services that you offer. This is the hardest of the three for a small business owner to define because there are often components that you are unaware of or that change with time. Things that fall into this category often include delivery, installation, warranty, repair, spare parts, instructions, and training—additional services that are not a part of your core product. When discussing strategy in Chapter 7, we talk about value and cost benefits, and these often help define the total product. For example, a hair stylist might also offer manicure and pedicure services or makeup consultation.

total product
The entire bundle of products, services, and meanings of your offering; includes extras like service, warranty, or delivery, as well as what the product means to the customer.

If you are the custom birdhouse designer, you have probably already considered whether you will offer to deliver and install the birdhouse for a set price. What about repairs? How much will you do for free, and what will you do at an extra cost? If the homeowner has a birdhouse that's a replica of his house and he remodels, are you willing to remodel his birdhouse? This one you might not think about until the first time it comes up.

In addition, the legal, cultural, and economic environment may force you into making changes you hadn't thought necessary. If more and more of your Happy Housekeeper customers do not speak English as a first language, are you willing to hire bilingual house cleaners? If the economy suffers, will you offer a more basic "no frills" service in order to keep a customer? If the state enacts particular laws involving disposal of certain household cleaning products, will you counter with special environmentally friendly products or use your ability to handle and dispose of these products as a marketing tool?

Why is this important for you as a small business owner? First of all, your product means more to a consumer than just the core component. If a car is just for transportation, why do people want to drive Mercedeses, Jaguars, and other luxury cars? These cars have a value for the customer beyond simple transportation. Coke doesn't sell just a soft drink. It sells refreshment and sociability; look at the ads. Sure, a housekeeper will clean your house, but this will give the consumer additional leisure time, might be a status symbol, and probably has other meanings for your customers. Merry Maids sends its personnel to your house in distinctive vans with the company's name plastered all over it; when your neighbors see that in your driveway, they know that you are important/rich/busy enough to be able to afford this service.

Second, as a small business owner, chances are that you don't have access to endless supplies of money. Why waste your time and money designing features for your product or service that your **target market** doesn't want? If you are in a small Midwest town, offering bilingual housekeepers just may not make sense—and such a service would be more expensive to provide; in Los Angeles, Phoenix, Dallas, and other major metropolitan areas, this might be a marketing niche worth pursuing. By analyzing your target market, you can get inside your customers' heads and figure out the most cost-effective value and cost benefit "bundle" to give them.

target market
The group of people on which a marketer focuses promotion and sales efforts.

Last, when you're designing the rest of your marketing plan, knowing what your product really "means" to consumers will help you set an appropriate price (would driving a BMW mean as much if it cost only $10,000?), design effective advertising ("we give you valuable free time" versus "we clean your house"), and select the distribution chain that will successfully carry out some of your service components (delivery, installation, repairs, instructions, etc.).

Branding

Your brand sets the product personality and helps separate it from competitors.[2] For some small firms the brand name and the company name may be the same—especially if you are a service (Speedy Dry Cleaning) or have a limited product line (e.g., Beyond Fleece). There are certain guidelines for coming up with a company or brand name, but there are many exceptions. Here are some things to keep in mind:

- The first thought for many entrepreneurs is to name the firm after themselves. While that is not necessarily a problem, it is also not very clear to potential customers what it is that you do. What is the Smith Company? What products can I find at Brown's Emporium? Consider adding another descriptive word to your name—Smith Machining Company will attract a whole different clientele from Smith Beauty Supply. This isn't usually a problem with a product because we usually add the product category: Smith Dishwashing Detergent.
- Another issue with using your name concerns how to handle the name if you decide to sell the company. The new buyer of Smith Machining Company will be tired of explaining that there is no longer any Mr. or Ms. Smith with the business. If you decide later to reenter the business (or any business), your name is now on someone else's business; while "Smith" is common enough, customers may wonder why Mr. John Cuttlebrink doesn't work at John Cuttlebrink Machining Company. In addition, should the new owners have a bad reputation, it's your name that will be smeared.
- Is your name appropriate? If your name is Payne, you might not want to use it for a dental clinic. How many other firms are using the same name (with or without additional descriptors), and will that cause confusion? (City or place names can get overused as well.) Maybe you are the only Srivhantinivasthian in the phone book, but will your customers remember your name or be able to spell or pronounce it? Maybe you should consider a nickname or a first name, or forget vanity for now and go with something else.
- Be careful about infringing on trademarks. Even names relatively close can cause you trouble. Dr. Peter wouldn't work for a soft drink, but it could be used for other products.
- Something that describes your firm or product and is easy to remember is ideal. While plain old "Discount Furniture" certainly fills that bill, "Cheap Seats" is a little more catchy and memorable. Be careful, though: This technique isn't appropriate for every type of business. "Divorce Depot" or "Bankruptcy Barn" probably won't convince potential clients that you're a serious, competent attorney.
- Creative spellings are eye-catching, but don't go overboard; "Myk's Otto Groj" is certainly different, but Mike's customers won't have an easy time finding him in the phone book or on the Internet when they need their cars repaired. Product brand names, too, are often evocative of the benefits they offer—Vaseline Intensive Care—but they may also be simple names—Dove, Zest, and so on. The same guidelines about being relatively easy to spell (not too creative) and to pronounce apply here as well.
- Beware of selecting a name that's too narrow to allow your firm to grow. "Just Jams and Jelly" might work right now, but what happens when you expand into candy, juices, pies, and the like?

Of course, many firms use one name for their company and a separate brand name for their products. Procter and Gamble doesn't use its company name on a single item. Kraft uses its name on some products (cheese, for example) and not others (Jell-O). The nice thing about separating your company name from your brand name is that if you have a product that doesn't take off—or fails catastrophically—you can drop that product line with minimal impact to the company image. Dropping New Coke was a bigger problem for Coca-Cola than dropping the Edsel was for Ford Motor Company. The same basic rules apply here as well: catchy, easy to spell and pronounce, and descriptive are usually the best options.[3]

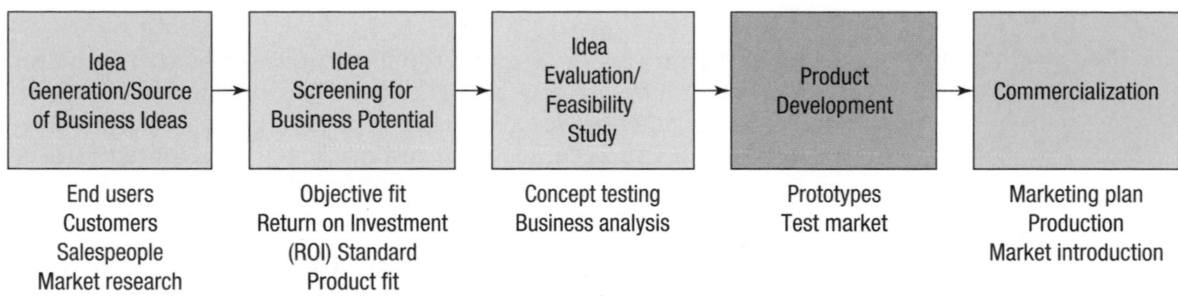

FIGURE 9.3

Stages of New Product Development

New Product Development Process

Before a product is introduced, it needs to go through the development process illustrated in Figure 9.3 above. This process may take a few hours for simple products that are similar to existing products (commonly referred to as **me-too products**) or may take years and years of preparation and testing, such as introducing a new pharmaceutical product. For me-too products, steps may even be skipped.

Regardless of the pace you are able to move at, this is a necessary process; the U.S. Patent Office issues about 100,000 patents a year, but only about 0.1 percent of those are profitable.[4] This process will make you less likely to end up in the 99.9 percent category; at least you can stop before you get too much invested.[5]

The first three steps are covered in Chapter 4; let's review them briefly.

LO3
Learn the stages of new product development.

me-too products
Products essentially similar to something already on the market.

Idea Generation[6]

Behind every great product is a great idea. The difficult question is where do you get the ideas? The traditional first idea generator—and often what gets an entrepreneur started—is something they need or want themselves and either can't find or can't find the way they want it. The new way to find opportunities is through the use of the SCAMPER approach as discussed in Chapter 4. Skill Module 9.2 provides you with an example of how to implement a simple SCAMPER application.

SKILL MODULE 9.2

Creating Your Idea Notebook

There are many products and services out there that we use regularly and often think that there's got to be a better way. Even with products and services we like, we can often think of improvements that we'd like to see:

1. Make a list of about 10 products or services you believe could be improved.
2. Specify exactly what it is about each one of them that you do not like.
3. Select three or four of them and think of ways that would "fix" the "defect." (Assume you have relatively unlimited money and technology.) Use the SCAMPER approach.
4. Talk to several friends and brainstorm to see if they have similar opinions about the product or service. Ask their opinion of your solutions and if they have any other ideas.
5. Add all these to your "idea" notebook—and who knows?

Many new products or services are "invented" because someone was unhappy with the available alternatives. Sometimes the technology isn't there yet; sometimes the solutions are too expensive to implement or make the product too expensive. Others are just waiting for someone to do something.

Idea Screening

Idea screening is the process of selecting the most promising ideas to be further evaluated for feasibility. There are four things that should be considered in the screening process: (1) the idea's potential for generating revenues, (2) whether you have the right people to make the idea succeed, (3) what resources will be required to bring the idea to successful completion, and (4) what information you must have about the product, market, and industry to be able to make the idea successful.

Idea Evaluation

Idea evaluation is an exhaustive process of specifying the details of each idea's technological feasibility, its cost, how it can be marketed, and its market potential. Additionally, you should consider how the idea fits with the mission and goals of your business.

A basic tool for idea evaluation is to create a checklist of important factors to be considered for all ideas. Figure 9.4 is an illustration of such an evaluation grid. The ideas are listed across the top of the grid, and the important factors are listed vertically. Each idea is given a numerical score for each of the factors. The scores are totaled and the idea with the greatest score is further considered for product development.

This simple example can be expanded as you need for your actual business. The feasibility analysis discussed in Chapter 4 provides several additional factors that should be considered when evaluating ideas.

Product Development

Concepts that survive to this stage are ready for formal development. The first versions are called *prototypes* and are used in further consumer testing.

If you are just starting out (rather than adding a product to your product line), you may need to get a prototype made. Prototypes can be expensive, but there are a few shortcuts you can try. Study the manufacturing process necessary to make your product and see if you can't come up with a simplified "desktop" version. This is especially useful if you may need to go through several iterations to debug your process. Jorge Lahens did just this to prototype a fragrance tab that hooks onto dog collars. He used Thomas Register (http://www.thomasregister.com/) to find companies dealing with scented plastics and learned all he could from them. He

http://www.thomasregister.com/

FIGURE 9.4

Idea Checklist

Factor	Scale	Idea 1	Idea 2	Idea 3	Idea 4
Technologically feasible	Go/No Go	Go	No Go	Go	Go
High customer need	1–10	5		5	9
Potential competition (reverse scale: 1 is undesirable)	1–6	1		6	2
Fit with existing products	1–6	1		5	6
Potential ROI (return on investment)	1–10	3		6	5
Total		10		22	22

perused *Inventor's Digest* (www.inventorsdigest.com) and found information about how to set up a small scale manufacturing model for just a few hundred dollars. Other sources of information include local inventor's clubs; *The Inventor's Resource Guide,* available for about $10 from the United Inventor's Association, lists clubs (www.uiausa.org).[7] Some manufacturers may be interested in developing your prototypes in exchange for a portion of your business.[8] Try the Job Shop Technology Web site (www.jobshoptechnology.com) to find local services, or try posting a request for a bid on eLance (www.elanceonline.com).

www.inventorsdigest.com

www.uiausa.org

www.jobshoptechnology.com

www.elanceonline.com

Once the prototype is developed and tested, the product is ready for test marketing. Test marketing involves selling the prototype in either a real or simulated market environment. Standard test marketing introduces the product and the marketing strategy in the actual environment. Small businesses, for financial reasons, primarily choose smaller local markets and conduct fewer tests than their larger counterparts. While test marketing can reduce the potential for failure and can identify weaknesses in the product, advertising, price, or distribution method, there are also opportunities for astute competitors to "steal" your ideas and launch before you do.

Simulated test markets re-create the market environment. Traditionally, a store would be physically created and products placed on the shelves to duplicate the environment in which the product would be sold. Potential consumers would then be brought in to shop, and the success of the product, advertising, and pricing strategy is then evaluated. Consumers can also be contacted at a later time and asked about their intent to repurchase the product, what their feelings are about the brand/product, and even if they recall seeing your product. More recently, simulated test markets have also been computer-generated. While this is relatively safe from competitive interference, the biggest problem with simulations is that they are artificial and do not always reflect actual buying behavior. Also, for small businesses, simulations may be expensive—especially the traditional method.

Depending on your product, giving samples to friends and family may be a convenient option for getting test market type of feedback. They are less likely to tell your competitor, but they may try to spare your feelings if they don't like your product. If appropriate for your product and if you are patient, you could pass out samples to friends and family and then wait to see if they come back asking for more; that's a sure sign they liked it. Then see if they'll pay you the next time they want a replacement. You may also be able to find (or belong to) a group that is willing to try your product and report back to you about how it works.[9] Sometimes nonprofit groups (a church's Ladies Aid, Friends of the Library, or something similar) might be willing to be a test market in order to gain a small donation toward one of their causes. Maybe the product would be appropriate for use at one of their activities, such as trying out your environmentally friendly detergent at a series of church suppers. Be sure to select one that represents your target market as much as possible.

With a service idea, this stage is necessarily different. If you are already in a similar business, you can offer your new idea as a supplemental service—for example, in St. Charles, Illinois, McDonald's restaurants are now testing an automated self-serve kiosk.[10] A customer can try this new system or stick with what is familiar—the waitperson at the counter. If the customer starts with the automated system and runs into problems or difficulties, the old system is right there beside the new. The customer can get help from the counter staff, but better yet for the business, this same staff can be asking questions about what the customers like or don't like about the new system, how likely they are to try it, what other features they would like to see, and the like.

If you're not in business—or if you are in a very different business—prototyping and test marketing services are very difficult. Simulations work in some cases. Focus groups and concept testing work in others.

SMALL BUSINESS INSIGHT

The Story of Kryptonite[11]

How do you build a strong brand on a small budget? The 25-employee Kryptonite Lock Company **(http://www.kryptonitelock.com/)** has found the answer and now owns more than 60 percent of the North American bike lock market.

Back in 1972, Michael Zane founded Kryptonite and created a unique "U-shaped" lock which changed the face of bicycle locks forever. By mid-1972, Kryptonite was so convinced of its product's superiority that it began offering the first antitheft guarantee to protect against bike theft caused by lock failure.

In the early 1980s, the U-shaped locks were gaining acceptance as a strong security measure. Additionally with its commitment to creating high-quality products, Kryptonite rose to become the leader of bike security technology. Competitors then began to aggressively target the company and captured the low-end market. Kryptonite's response was to introduce the lower-cost KryptoLok in 1988, again increasing market share. The KryptoLok helped to offer a wider range of products at different price points.

■ Kryptonite's rise from idea stage to its current status of multi-million dollar market leader is a story of consistently innovative product development, competitive pricing, and creative marketing. How does Kryptonite's story reflect product development and pricing?

In 1989, with the increased popularity of mountain bikes, Kryptonite introduced the ATB (all-terrain bike) model, further diversifying its product offerings. In 1992, the Evolution 2000 was introduced with a stronger Kryptonite steel.

In 1994, in response to a new method New York City thieves were using to break locks, the New York Lock was introduced with a flurry of hype. Zane locked up his own bike on the streets of New York and sat in a surveillance van for 48 hours with a *New York Post* reporter. Together they watched as several would-be thieves tried unsuccessfully to steal his bike.

Now known for product innovation and attention to customer needs, Kryptonite continues to add new products. In addition to bike locks, Kryptonite offers a complete line of security devices for motorcycles, sporting goods, skis, and snowboards, and it sells these products in over 50 countries. Attention to detail and to changing customer needs has earned Kryptonite the reputation as the number 1 bike lock brand in the world. Not bad for a bearded kid who started with only a VW van and a big idea.

Commercialization

Commercialization is the process of making the new product available to consumers. By the time of commercialization, many weaker ideas have dropped out of consideration, but still only about 60 percent of all new product launches are successful.[12] There are very high costs associated with commercialization. A small business may need to rent or purchase manufacturing space and equipment. Large companies may spend between $10 million and $200 million for advertising, promotion, and other marketing efforts during the first year of a product's introduction.[13] A small business, especially a young one, cannot afford to spend that much money. That does not mean, however, that a small business cannot compete. (See Small Business Insight: The Story of Kryptonite.)

Smaller firms generally introduce their products city by city or region by region in a gradual fashion until their potential market is covered—a limited rollout. Mistakes made in earlier markets can be addressed before rolling out to additional markets.

Limited rollouts also have the problem of allowing competitors to anticipate your movement into their markets and to counterattack.

If you're great on ideas, but really don't want to get into the day-to-day details of manufacturing your products, there are many contract manufacturers who will do it for you. If the product isn't really a good fit for what you are currently doing, you may want to have someone else handle all the marketing and distribution as well. There are companies, like Inventor's Universe (www.inventorsuniverse.com), that are always looking for products with wide consumer appeal to add to their already diverse line.[14]

www.inventorsuniverse.com

Do a little research. Is your product/service really new or is it a me-to? Has it truly never been done before? As we saw in the strategy chapter, most small businesses are based on imitative strategies. Maybe someone tried this a dozen years ago and couldn't make it work. Is now a better time for the product? If nobody's ever done it before, could it be that the market just isn't big enough to support it or that there really isn't a need for the product?[15,16]

Let's sidetrack for a minute: there are very few new products out there. When television first came out, that was a truly new product. Color TV, HDTV, plasma TV, and on and on, are really "me-to" products, but with a significant improvement over the old one. DVD players are merely a better system than VHS, which is really only a peripheral device for your TV—not truly a new product. The Innovation Index[17] shows that since 1990, innovative products ran well under 10 percent of all new products introduced—and the index includes as innovative things such as reaching an unmet market, repositioning of a product, or even creative new uses. The point is that you can do—and probably will do—a me-too product, but it better have something unique about it that separates it from everything out there or you won't even get it on the store shelves.[18]

The product introduction cycle for me-too products is greatly reduced. If you are introducing a me-too product, most of the testing has already been done and public acceptance is pretty much assured. Your me-too product though will have a differential advantage over your competition—otherwise, why would you introduce it?—and this advantage may be the only thing you need to test. Customers are familiar with the product category, and some of them may already have been thinking about what they'd like to see different about the product or service. Much of the up-front testing can simply be polling existing users of the product and suggesting to them what you might see as an improvement. "I see you are using XYZ; what if I was able to sell you the same thing, but deliver and install it (or add or change features, etc.)?" Open-ended questions (If you could change one thing about XYZ, what would it be?) might confirm your potential improvement, might point out other new ideas, and won't necessarily tip off the competition as to what you are planning to do.

Product Life Cycle[19]

LO4
Learn the product life cycle.

Every product, service, and even industry goes through a life cycle. The standard product life cycle (Figure 9.5) has four stages. (Services are a bit different, and we talk about them later in the chapter.) In each section we examine sales, profits, marketing, and competition.

Stage 1—Introduction

Once the product is introduced, sales slowly take off and then begin to grow. It takes time for consumers to become aware of new products and then to seek out the product for purchase. During this time it is very important for a small business not only to get information out about the product, but also to build brand awareness and recognition and to get the consumer to try it. Many times this can be an educational process for the consumers: What is this product and how do I use it?

In addressing consumer concerns, your advertising should speak to the *relative advantage* your product has over other products the consumer may have been using

FIGURE 9.5

The Product Life Cycle

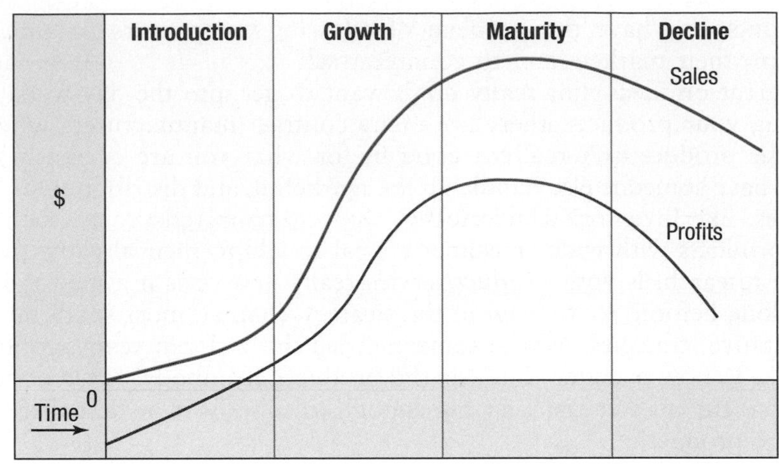

to date. Ads tell us that this new headache medicine works faster than others or that using our service instead of doing it yourself will give you valuable free time. For more elaborate products or real innovations, consumers will want to know how *compatible* it is with what they're used to and how *difficult* it will be for them *to learn* to use it. Does it feel familiar or is it jarring? A new flavor of soft drink is one thing, but how difficult will it be to learn a new software program even if it promises to save considerable time and money in the long run?

Consumers like to be able to try things out, to prove that they work, especially if they are really new. A product sample or the ability to test something (a test drive for a car, playing around with a new computer system at the dealer, listening to music on a new CD player) helps them see if they'll like it and can also address some of their concerns about how difficult it would be for them to learn how to use it. For certain products, the ability to be able to rent before buying is also a way to establish *trial-ability* of a new product. For certain products, *observability* or the publicity value of the product is also important. Certain items can be status symbols, and we want people to see that we're driving a new hybrid vehicle, wearing the latest designer fashions, or drinking designer beverages. In some cases we want to be the first on the block to own a new high-definition TV or a hybrid car. These wants can be integrated into our advertising, and our salespeople can be trained to remind potential customers of these features.[20]

In addition to convincing the customers that they can't live without your product, during this stage a company will also need to market to any middlemen it chooses to use. To convince a retailer to carry your product, you may need to grant special price discounts, help with advertising expenses, or pay a *slotting fee* (a fee to get shelf space). You can offer to make more frequent deliveries (so that middlemen don't have to use as much shelf or warehouse space) or to place your goods with them on consignment. These marketing costs often run double to what you'll pay for your consumer advertising.

If you are introducing a me-too product, it's not so much of an educational process for your customers or middlemen, but more one of convincing them why your product is preferable. Customers know how and why to eat at a restaurant, but why should they select yours? Better or different menu? Better prices? Better atmosphere? Great service? Are you the only one in this particular location or the only one open these hours? Even if you are in a nearly duplicative situation, figure out what makes you different. Let's say that you opened the second Chinese restaurant on a block because people were standing in line at your competitor's place. You even offer a similar menu and similar prices (not recommended). At least, you can advertise immediate seating. Likewise, with middlemen: They are already carrying six toothpaste brands, so why should they add your all-natural, herbal brand? Deeper price concessions, consignment sales, and such will work, but often the best way of getting their interest is to show established sales through direct marketing. (More about that in Chapter 10.)

During the introduction stage, as sales slowly grow, these heavy introductory marketing expenses will keep profits suppressed. Profits are generally only seen toward the end of this stage. Competition in the introduction stage is generally low.

It should be noted that not all products survive the introduction phase of the product life cycle. Some products may take too long to begin making a profit because of high marketing expenses. Other products simply never catch on with consumers and never sell enough to cover their costs. Products that are successful move on to the growth stage.

Stage 2—Growth

During the growth stage acceptance of the product increases rapidly, and sales and profits grow at higher rates than at any other part of the product life cycle. Consumers are aware of your products and know how it will make their lives better. Products nearly fly off the shelf. During this stage, advertising and promotion are much less critical than in the introduction stage, but keeping up with production and ensuring good distribution become more critical. Marketing goals in this time are to maximize your market share—competition is out there, and you want your product to be the consumer's first choice—and to maximize penetration—get into *all* the markets nationally (or internationally). Prices tend to drop as production becomes more efficient and competition increases.

This is a very critical time for a small firm. Established firms will notice the growth in sales and will develop competitive products in order to compete aggressively. This is the time for small businesses to stress their uniqueness in the advertising they do. Many firms associated with the Internet are in the growth stage—Napster and other music downloading companies, for example. Consumers are well aware of these products/services and what they will do for them, and they have attracted a lot of competition.

Stage 3—Maturity

Once the rapid growth begins to slow down, the product enters the *maturity stage*. During this stage sales will level off and start to decline, and profits follow suit. By now, there are few new users for the product; it has gained general acceptance among most of the potential market. At this point, competition becomes fierce. Most gains in market share are made by stealing customers from competitors. Now you'll focus on defending the market share you have. Weaker competitors will start to leave the market, and you'll have opportunities to take their "leftover" customers. EBay's core business—auctions—may be in the early stages of maturity. There were a number of Internet auction sites a few years ago, and now eBay is one of the few survivors.

Price competition starts to rise, and manufacturers need to find ways to cut costs or introduce new features to keep or gain market share. Something as simple as coming out with a new flavor or color may spark customer interest and keep or gain market share, but this is the time that it is critical to have new ideas in the pipeline and to get them ready for commercialization. Adding services to the core product can help; now you offer delivery and installation if you hadn't before or online shopping convenience. EBay has added its version of an Internet mall and has half.com where books, videos, DVDs, and other products are sold for a fixed price. Some of eBay's chief competitors in the Internet used book market, for example, ABEBooks (www.abebooks.com), now use half.com as one of their outlets for their products.

www.half.com

www.abebooks.com

Advertisements taper off and become reminder ads. (See Chapter 10.) Promotions become an important marketing tool—coupons, rebates, multipacks, and so on. Companies begin to seek out new markets, maybe going international or targeting a different demographic. Rembrandt toothpaste repositioned its product from being a smoker's toothpaste to a low-abrasion, whitening toothpaste for kids.[21] EBay added a business-to-business auction Web site and has set up or purchased auction sites around the world. Advertising will often suggest new uses for the product. (Look at Chex cereals' advertising, which now often suggests Chex as a party mix, rather than as a breakfast food.) Who else could use your product or service who isn't using it now? Fancy sit-down restaurants might offer catering or carry-out. What other uses might customers have for your product? If you can't think of some, ask your customers; they've probably already experimented. What services could you add that would appeal to more customers? Why do you think beauty salons started selling products and offering manicures, tanning, and other related services? This helps them keep their market share in a market that is mature.

A product can stay in the maturity stage for a long period of time. While the technology of the product may be older, the product is comfortable for the consumer. A quality product that inspires brand loyalty, such as Murphy's Oil Soap, can remain in the maturity stage for decades.

Stage 4—Decline

Once a product begins its permanent decline, this decline can be slow or fast, steady or unsteady. This decline may come from the introduction of a new technology such as music CDs replacing vinyl records, or color televisions replacing black and white. The decline may also be caused by a shift in consumer preferences, such as bell-bottom jeans going out of style.

Whatever the reason for the decline, the characteristics of the decline stage remain the same. Both sales and profits fall during this stage. Advertising and promotion expenses are usually nearly eliminated at this point. Companies pare back their product lines and don't market to less profitable segments in order to cut costs and squeeze as much profit out of the final stage as possible. Tab, a popular diet soda in the early 1980s, is now available in only certain locations with highly loyal consumers, such as Cincinnati, New York, Atlanta, Phoenix, and Houston.[22]

Beauty salons hit a period of decline in the late '60s and early '70s as the bouffant hairstyles gave way to long and straight hair. Up to the present, few women go to a salon for their weekly wash and set, as they did all those years ago. The market hasn't totally died and probably won't as people will likely always cut their hair. Many salons did die, and those that survived did so by expanding the types of products and services they provide—selling hair care products, providing make-up, tanning, or manicure services, offering day spas, and providing other related activities.

■ What has contributed to the decline of Tab soda? Can you identify other products that may be entering their decline stage? How is the company reacting?

Service Life Cycle

While services do in fact go through the same four stages—introduction, growth, maturity, and decline—it can be somewhat easier to extend the life cycle and to virtually eliminate the decline stage of a service. Primarily, this is because services are often much easier to change "on the run." You can add and remove items from menus, change service levels, add additional services, and otherwise modify your service bundle much quicker than those who are manufacturing products. For example, you can go with a low-carb menu to accommodate the Atkins and South Beach diet fad, just about as fast as you can have new menus printed. You can hire a manicurist and add that service to your hair salon as fast as you can get her paperwork processed and a station set up. You can attend a seminar or course to learn about adding new skills and offer that service to your accounting or legal clients. All these changes can be done relatively quickly, and, if they don't work out well, they can be removed just as quickly.

If you set up a service business and never change what you are doing, your service will go through all four stages and react as discussed above. By being more fluid than product manufacturers and being able to react more quickly, services, in effect, are starting new life cycles with each tweaking of their existing offering. Their curves will

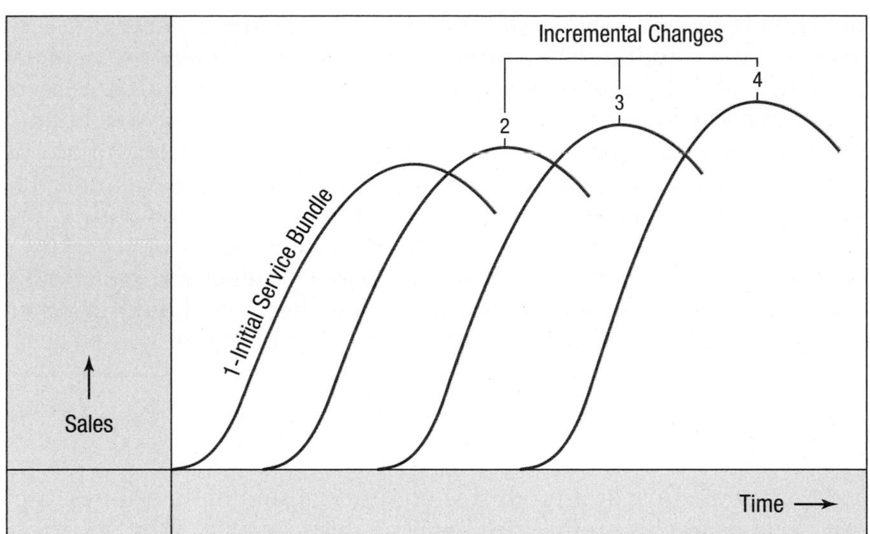

FIGURE 9.6

Service Life Cycle

look more like those in Figure 9.6, where curve 1 is the initial service bundle and curves 2–4 represent the incremental changes. This diagram shows the old and new ways overlapping for a time period—for instance, adding new items to a menu, but not removing the older ones right away. In some cases, though, adding a new service may terminate an older one (switching from an Italian menu to a Chinese menu). In other cases, the new service is on top of all existing services—no impact on existing services—like adding a manicurist to your beauty salon.

Similar to products, new services will take a little time to attract customers, and initial advertising efforts will be to educate your clients as to the benefits of this service (or, perhaps, that you now offer this service). As sales seem to level off, continue to remind your customers that you offer the service and why it's better than that of your competition. Eventually, as sales drop off, eliminate the service totally or perform it only for those "old time" customers who ask for it.

Using the Product Life Cycle[23]

The product life cycle shows the typical way a product moves through the four stages. Marketers who can identify product stages can use this information to tailor their marketing program to take advantage of the unique situations in each stage and to increase profitability. Changes may need to be made in distribution, pricing, advertising and promotion. Furthermore, they may consider ways of lowering production costs (perhaps, off-shore manufacturing) and decide when to eliminate a product and make sure new replacement items are proceeding through the development cycle in a timely manner. Thus awareness of the product life cycle can establish trigger points for marketing changes, product changes, and, eventually, product deletions.

Part of the difficulty in using the product life cycle is that the curves are never as smooth as they appear in Figure 9.5. Rather they are full of peaks and valleys, approximately following the general shape illustrated. When sales fall is it a signal that the product has reached maturity or is it just a temporary setback because of economic conditions, the seasonality of the product, or a new competitor with better prices? A marketer must weigh many things before trying to decide what phase a product is in. Moreover, products often experience a "revival" as new generations discover them. Brands such as Oxydol, Fanta, Breck, and Ovaltine, after near extinction, are experiencing new popularity.[24] Tattoo shops, a service that was nearly extinct, have started a new life cycle as styles have changed.

Additionally, how long will it take to move through a particular stage? This varies by product type and marketing environment. Certain products have built-in life cycles;

cars introduce new models every year, and clothing fashions change by season. Fads have extremely short product lives; products such as Pet Rocks or Tickle-Me-Elmo have a popularity that lasts only a few months at most. Right after September 11, 2001, many entrepreneurs got into the security business; whether it was building bomb shelters, selling gas masks, or providing entire "siege kits." A year later, no one had heard of most of these; they were fads, growing out of the immediate fear and uncertainty of those days. Other products—like Murphy's Oil Soap mentioned earlier, or Morton Salt, or Coca-Cola—have lasted for decades and show no signs of stopping.

The bottom line is that you must be aware of the product life cycle and consider where your product might be and what that means, but you should understand that the determination can be imperfect and somewhat unpredictable.

Pricing

LO5
Understand the concept of price with variable costs, fixed costs, and breakeven.

What exactly is a *price*? Just as a product is not just the sum of its features, a price isn't just the cost of the item plus profit. Price implies value or worth. Why do you pay more for Coke than a store brand cola? Why are prices higher on clothing carrying certain designer labels than others? In order to properly set a price on your product or service, you need to take a little time to understand the psychology behind consumer decisions.[25]

Pricing Basics[26]

Let's look at pricing basics. To be sure, you do have to cover your costs and make a reasonable profit or you won't be in business for long. To do this, you have to have a handle on some of the basic costing terms.

fixed costs
Those costs that remain constant regardless of the quantity, for example, rent.

variable costs
Those costs that change with each unit produced, for example, raw materials.

The cost of your product is the sum of **fixed costs** and **variable costs**. Variable costs are the expenses tied directly to the production of one item. For example, if you manufacture desks, you have expenses for all the pieces—wood, nails, glue, drawer pulls and slides, stain or varnish, and the like. Let's estimate these at $200. You also have the cost of the time it takes to manufacture that item; if it takes six hours and your labor costs $20 per hour, you'll have $120 worth of labor as a variable cost.

You will usually have some amount of waste or scrap in a production process. For example, you may bend about 1 nail in 20. You may damage one drawer slide for about every 30 desks. Varnish dries out or gets spilled. Your wood will have an occasional flaw. Depending on your skill level, the quality of your raw materials, the product you are making, how well your manufacturing process is controlled, the quality of the tools you use and other variables, this scrap or waste factor may run from less than 1 percent to as much as 10 percent of your material cost. (Over 10 percent and you should be looking seriously for ways to eliminate waste.) Let's say that your desk-building venture averages about 3 percent scrap or $6. This is another variable cost.

Expendables are often variable costs. *Expendables,* also called indirect materials, are products used in manufacturing that part of the finished product. You may need $2 worth of sandpaper to sand each desk. The sandpaper is not part of the desk, but once you use it up in making the first desk, it is not available for the second desk.

Other operations might have packaging and labels, testing, outside operations, or other variable costs. Generally services are based on an hourly rate multiplied by the typical number of hours needed to perform the service. Services might also include items like mileage (for delivery or site-based services), government fees (for certain legal services), and other variable costs. The key to variable costs is that the more you do, the higher your total costs are.

For our example, you now have $328 dollars of variable costs ($200 materials + $120 labor + $6 scrap + $2 sandpaper). So if you sold this desk for $330 dollars, you'd make a profit, right? Well, no. You still must take into account fixed costs.

Fixed costs are those that cannot be (or are extremely difficult to be) assigned to a specific item manufactured. For desk-making, you may be renting a small building. You

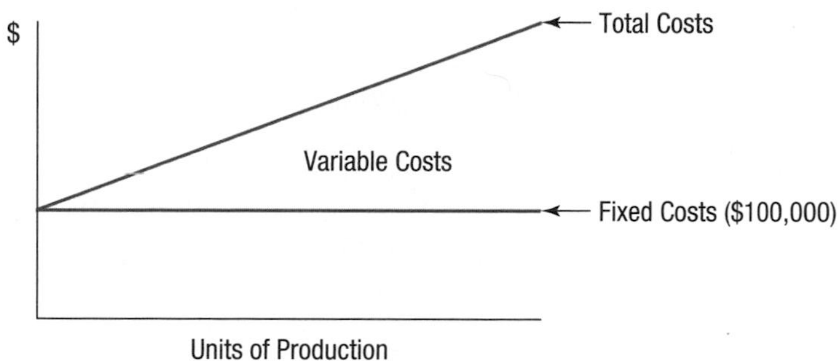

FIGURE 9.7

Total Costs

had to purchase equipment—hammers, screwdrivers, sanders, and so on. You'll need to pay for utilities to heat or cool the building, and for lighting and ventilation. You'll have all the paperwork expenses of running a manufacturing operation. You'll have legal fees and accounting fees. You may have hired a secretary or office manager or salesperson. You may pay for security, cleaning, or other services. None of these items is directly connected to the manufacturing of a certain item, but you couldn't do business without them.

Additionally, fixed costs are paid whether you make one product, one million products, or nothing. If you hire an office manager, he or she will want to get paid whether you sell anything or not. The electric company and your accountant don't care what your sales are doing; they expect to be paid regardless.

Generally, both fixed and variable costs tend to be averaged over a year. For example, you may bend every other nail on building one desk but none on a second desk. You do not adjust your scrap rate higher on one product and lower on another, but you look at the average over time. Your legal fees might be paid only once a year, but you won't load up your fixed costs for that particular week. There are some accounting exceptions to this, but as a rule of thumb for estimating costs, breakeven, and such, looking at averages is not only perfectly acceptable, but about the only reasonable way to handle the situation. Other costs, such as marketing, may be variable or fixed. Each company's situation must be reviewed separately, and your accountant can help you figure out what goes where.

Going back to our example, let's say that your fixed costs amount to $100,000 per year. If you make only one desk, you will need to charge $100,328 just to cover expenses. That's probably not going to happen. If you build 10 desks, you'll need $10,328 each [($328 × 10 + $100,000)/10]. Those desks are good, but not that good. What if you sell 100 desks this year? Your variable costs go up to $32,800, but your fixed costs (of course) are still $100,000, for a total of $132,800. If you divide this over the 100 desks you'll sell, you'll see that your total cost per desk is $1,328. At that cost, you can make a reasonable amount of profit—maybe sell them for a price of $1,499 each—and your business is launched.

Look at that last paragraph once more. It seems a little obvious, but there are some key points here:

- Fixed costs plus variable costs equal your total cost.
- While fixed costs remain constant, variable costs increase constantly and evenly based on the number of units manufactured.
- The more desks you make, the less your fixed costs *per item* become. In our example, at one desk, the entire fixed cost of $100,000 needs to be applied to that desk. At 10 desks, your fixed cost per desk drops to $10,000, and at 100 desks, it is a mere $1,000 per desk. This truism has a name and is called *economies of scale.*

Graphically, the relationship between variables, fixed, and total costs is represented in Figure 9.7.

One last important concept is **breakeven**.[27] The idea behind breakeven is to find the number of products (or services) you must sell at a particular price in order to cover

breakeven
The point at which total costs equal total sales.

FIGURE 9.8

Breakeven Point

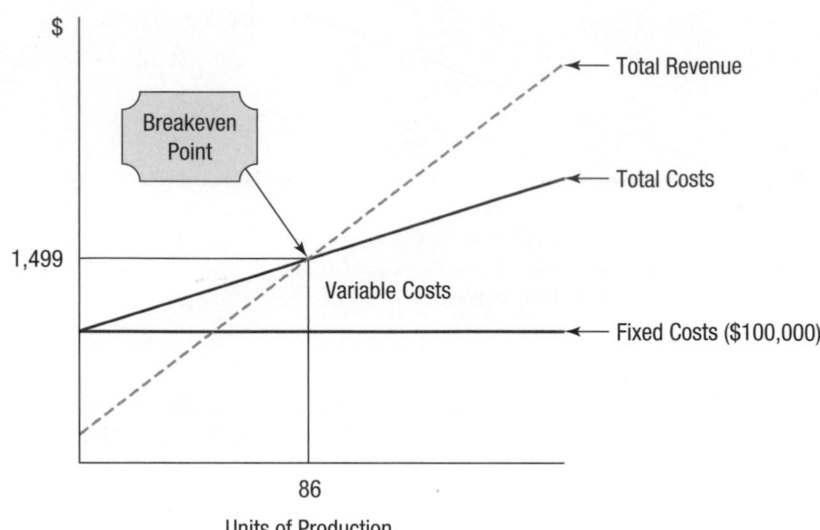

your total costs. At this point, you haven't made any money, but you are no longer losing any money. You can see why this would be an important number to know.

In the example above, how many desks priced at $1,499 would you need to sell in order to cover your $100,000 fixed costs and the $328 per desk variable cost? Mathematically, this would look something like this, where x stands for the breakeven:

$$\$328x + \$100{,}000 = \$1{,}499x$$

If you solve for x, you'll find that you need to make 86 desks to reach breakeven. Figure 9.8 shows how this would look graphically. Breakeven is where the total revenue equals the total cost.

What if you could sell the desks for $1,999? Then you'd need to make only 60 desks. You can also work the equation the other way. Let's say that your market research shows that your probable market share is 50 desks. What price would you need to get in order to break even? That's a $2,328 per desk selling price. Can you get $2,328? (Actually, you'll need to get more than that; $2,328 is only your breakeven price, and you probably want a nice profit.) This depends on a lot of things—how much you can change your price without turning your customers away (technically known as *price elasticity of demand*), how customers react to prices (known in marketing circles as *pricing psychology*), and other price influencers—which we cover in the next sections.

As a rule, in calculating breakeven, many small firms look at a best case, a worst case, and a most realistic case—sort of a midpoint. The difference in these cases might mean adjusting costs of materials, fixed costs, selling prices, market sizes, or a combination of all four. Try to base your increases and reductions on logical reasons. For example, raising your market share by 10 percent might be acceptable; raising it by 200 percent probably is not. By doing adequate market research, you will have an idea of how large your market is.

Analyze your time as well to make sure there is adequate time; just because the market might support 1,000 desks, doesn't mean you'll have the time to make them. If you hire help, you can make more, but your costs will go up. Also allow yourself time for other activities—marketing, vacation and holidays, a small business seminar, and so forth.[28] In the example above, a desk took six hours to build; that's about one a day allowing for time to order materials and other daily business activities. If you assume you'll be able to make three desks a week—using the other time for other activities—and you work 50 weeks a year, you'll have time to make 150 desks. This number can go back into your formula, and you can recalculate your breakeven price ($995). (Remember to balance your capacity against the market size and your reasonable share of that market.)

Using Your Breakeven Point

SKILL MODULE 9.3

Sarah has always made lovely baby quilts as gifts for family and friends. When Sarah was expecting her first child, she decided to leave her middle manager position and turn her hobby into a business. She realized that she needed a dedicated and organized workplace and proper equipment, so she set up a spare bedroom with a cutting table and cabinets to organize her supplies. These, along with a new sewing machine that she really thought would help, cost her $3,000. She purchased high-quality quilting squares, rulers, cutters, and miscellaneous other tools she needed for another $200. All other supplies—pins, needles, clamps, and so on—she already had on hand. After careful calculation, she estimated the material, quilt batting, and thread she used cost about $30 a quilt. There is very little scrap as pieces not used in one quilt can be saved for another, so she opted not to include a scrap rate:

1. For the first year, all Sarah wants to do is to make enough money to cover all her fixed and variable costs. She thinks that she can produce two quilts a month and still have plenty of time to enjoy her new baby. At what price must she sell the two quilts a month in order to break even?
2. Sarah finds that comparable quilts are being sold on consignment at a local baby furniture store for $180 each. The store takes a 25 percent commission on each sale. If Sarah decides to match the competition's price and sell through this store, how many quilts does she need to make in order to break even?
3. Sarah didn't realize that a new baby would take so much time. She finds that she's able to make only about three quilts every two months. She is able to find an online supply house that allows her to cut her material costs to $25 per quilt. Under these new assumptions, what price does she need to charge in order to break even in one year? If she chooses to continue to sell on consignment at the prices mentioned above, how many months will it be before she breaks even?

Retailing

Retailing is a slightly different story. This goes as well for the part of the business of manufacturers who purchase and resell certain items for the convenience of their customers (the desk maker may sell furniture polish) and services not primarily retail (the hair salon may sell shampoo and other styling aids). Since the number of items resold and their individual prices are quite numerous, it's much more typical to use a technique called *mark-up*. Mark-up is the difference between the selling and buying price and should be enough to cover all fixed costs (generally termed *overhead* in retailing). The mark-up percent can be based on the cost of the product or on the final selling price and, although the first one is generally used more often, it doesn't matter which you use as long as you are consistent. Let's illustrate:

A T-shirt sells for $10. It cost the retailer $8 to purchase. The mark-up is $2.
Mark-up on sales = mark-up/selling price = 2/10, or 20%
Mark-up on cost = mark-up/cost = 2/8, or 25%

While the actual mark-up is $2, the percentage of mark-up is 20 percent or 25 percent depending upon what it is based.

How do you know what amount your mark-up should be? You can estimate the total cost of running your operation including profit and divide this by your estimated sales. If my overhead will run $100,000, I want $50,000 profit, and I estimate the cost of goods at $300,000 per year, then I need to have a mark-up on cost of 50 percent [($100,000 + $50,000)/$300,000].

LO6
Understand price elasticities, pricing psychology, and other price influencers and their impact on pricing.

Price Elasticity

To determine the impact of a price change—and to set the change appropriately—you need to know if your product is elastic or inelastic. An **inelastic product** is something

inelastic product
Product for which there are few substitutes and for which a change in price makes very little difference in quantity purchased.

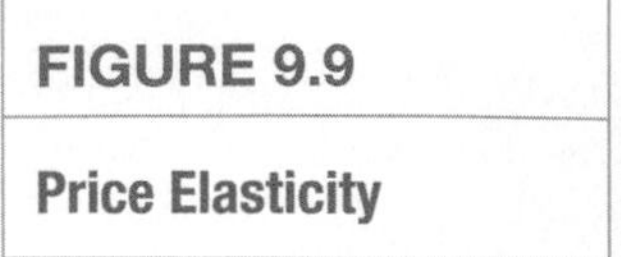
FIGURE 9.9

Price Elasticity

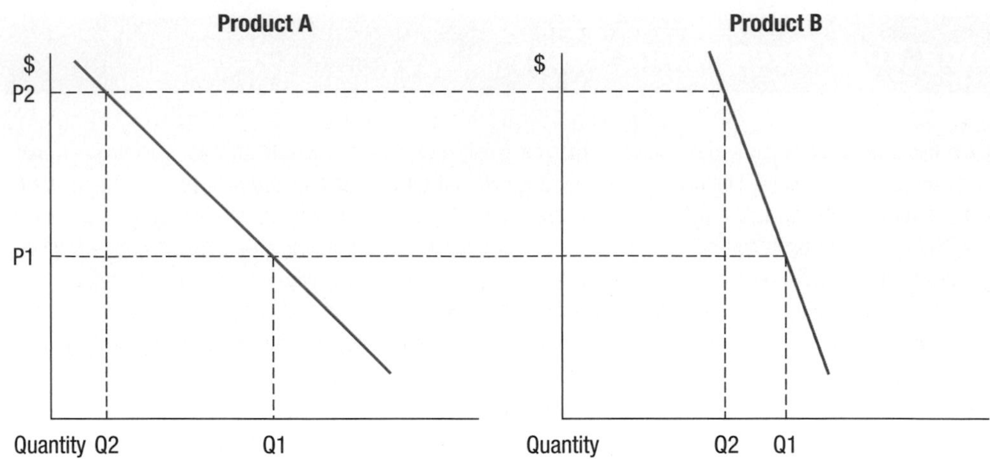

people cannot, or will not, do, without—gasoline, heating oil—or for which there are few substitutes—if you have to go to Paris, your only real option is flying, and there are not many airlines to choose from. Inelastic products are fairly protected from economic downturns. **Elastic products** have lots of substitutes, or are not necessities. A candy bar is not a necessity, and if one brand raises its price, there are lots of other brands; if all candy prices go up, you can switch to fruit or chips or something else.

elastic product
Product for which there are any number of substitutes and for which a change in price makes a difference in quantity purchased.

Figure 9.9 shows two price elasticity curves for two different products. Product A represents something like a sandwich—something that has lots of substitutes. Product B is something like a gallon of gasoline; you can't really use something else in your car. To begin with, we set our price for both products at P1 and, in each case, sold the same number of products, Q1. Later we raised our price for both products to P2. You'll notice that we sold about the same quantity of product B (gallons of gasoline) but considerably less of product A (sandwiches). We call Product A *elastic,* meaning that a price change will have a large impact on the quantity sold. Product B is *inelastic,* meaning that a significant price change has little impact on the quantity sold.

Elasticity curves aren't quite as smooth as they appear in the illustration. Often they may be inelastic over certain ranges of prices and then become more elastic beyond a certain point. Here's an example: Let's say you want to buy a new pair of jeans, and you think you'll pay about $30 for them. You find a pair you really like. Would you pay $32 for them? How about $35? Maybe $40 or $50? For most people, $32 or $35 would hardly make them think twice (unless $30 was all the money they had). It's possible that $40 and even $50 might be justifiable if the jeans are exactly what you're looking for. Jeans would tend to be an elastic product, but the quantity sold might not change at all between $30 and $35, might only slightly drop off at $40, and then become much more elastic beyond $50. Even elastic products have "sticky" places, where price changes don't cause changes in quantities sold.

Pricing Psychology

When you shop for products, you look at a price and make a judgment as to whether this is a fair price or too low or too high. Where you shop and under what circumstances you shop can also influence this judgment. We expect different prices at different places. We expect to pay more for emergency plumbing repairs or for certain conveniences. If your needs change, your willingness to pay changes. A submarine sandwich has little value to you if you have just completed a five-course meal, but if you haven't eaten in two days, you might pay almost anything for it. (Even though it is exactly the same sandwich.)

Consumers have what are known as internal and external reference prices. Basically these are expectations about what a price should be, based on their own knowledge (**internal reference pricing**) or from gathering information from outside sources (**external reference pricing**). External reference prices may come from looking at competitive ads, researching on the Internet, visiting several stores, or asking friends. Consumers will also pick up on external clues. If the product is sold at Wal-Mart, they will expect to pay less than if it's sold at an upscale department store (expectations based on where it is bought). A Rolex watch sold by a street vendor in Beijing should cost less than a Rolex at Tiffany's in New York City (expectations based on perception of the likely quality and authenticity). You'd expect lower prices at a "going out of business" sale than at a "back to school sale" (perception of motivation of the seller—how eager he or she is to sell).

internal reference price
A consumer's mental image of what a product's price should be.

external reference price
An estimation of what a price should be based on information external to a consumer, such as advice, advertisements, or comparison shopping.

Consumers' internal reference price may be based on the last time they purchased something, recollections of what they might have read or heard in the past, their understanding of how much it would cost to make it (it's made in China, so it should be inexpensive; it's gold-plated, so it'll cost more), or their perception of the value the product has. If the last time you went to the movies you paid $4 for a ticket and today you find out it costs $10, you might just wait for the video to come out. (You're forgetting that the last time you went to the movies was 10 years ago.)

Perception of value varies from person to person. For example, if you can clean your apartment in two hours and figure your time is worth $10 an hour, you won't want to pay someone else $30 to do it for you. On the other hand, if it takes you four hours or if you figure your time is worth $20 per hour, then $30 sounds like a good deal. It doesn't need to be purely financially motivated either. If you find cleaning relaxing and a break from your regular job while other people rank it as their absolute least favorite thing to do, they are willing to pay something, while you may be willing to pay nothing at all. Skills may be involved; some people might be able to figure their taxes themselves; others may find any math involving more than three digits beyond their capabilities.

Expectations of future prices may be internal or external. The newspaper says interest rates are going up; consumers may decide to pay a bit more to get their new house now while rates are low. You're going to the Bahamas next November; you'll wait for the end of the season sales to buy your vacation clothes because you remember end of the season sales from past experience.

Consumers also have a price range of acceptability. Any price within this range is really okay with them. How wide the range is varies by product, by consumer, and by situation. This price range of acceptability tends to be the inelastic parts—the "sticky" parts—of the elasticity curves, like the $30–$35 range in the jeans example above.

Setting a price somewhat above the competitive midpoint has a psychological impact on buyers.[29] If three sweaters appear to be identical but are priced at $30, $40, and $50 dollars, you are likely to feel that the more expensive one is of higher quality.[30]

Pricing Psychology

SKILL MODULE 9.4

Customers often view pricing as a proxy for quality, especially when it is difficult for them to truly evaluate the products:

1. Tell your friends that you are conducting a taste test and provide three samples of the same product in containers marked A, B, and C. (Choose products for which brands are not easily visually detected, such as pasta, soft drinks, etc.)
2. Predetermine three price points: one that is about average for the product, one that is relatively high compared to the competition, and one that would reflect the "discount" brand price.
3. As your friends sample each of the three, give them some data about the product. Include exactly the same data about each—in a different order—except for the suggested retail price. (For example, soft

drink A might be sugar-free, vitamin-fortified, cola-based, only one calorie, manufactured in the United States, and available locally for 50 cents. Sample B sells for 75 cents and is cola-based, and is manufactured in the United States as well. It has only one calorie and is sugar-free and vitamin-fortified. Sample C is an American, cola-based, vitamin-fortified, soft drink with no calories. It retails for $1.00 and is sugar-free as well.)

4. Allow your friends to taste each product once, and do not permit them to go back and resample. Between samples, provide a sip of water or a cracker to remove any lingering taste—anything to separate the three samples slightly.
5. After tasting all three, ask them to discuss each one of them, stating what they did or did not like about the product.
6. If done in a classroom setting, provide a score sheet for each student to rate the product.
7. Often you will find that the more expensive product's characteristics are rated higher.

Note: This test often works with similar results on other "quality indicators" such as the store where something is purchased—the item bought at Wal-Mart versus an upscale department store—or country of origin—products from a country with a good reputation versus a less-developed country (e.g., wine from France or Bulgaria).

How you define your product really determines your competitive advantage and affects your price. When you get right down to it, there are really only two competitive advantages: your product or service must be better (quality, features, distribution, etc.) or cheaper. Being better is sustainable, but someone else can always match or beat your price.[31]

Customers who are attracted to low prices will not be loyal and will switch as soon as something cheaper comes along.[32] Customers will always pay more for a product or service that stands out from the crowd. Treehouse Cuts Salons is a children's hair salon that has chairs designed as Barbie jeeps and other kid-friendly items such as televisions or Sony PlayStations at each chair. The salon charges about 30 percent more than the competition, but parents are willing to spend the money to make their child's haircutting experience more pleasant.[33] Consumers perceive Treehouse Cuts as a better value—regardless of the actual price.

Price Setting[34]

We've learned how to determine our product costs, and we've briefly explored pricing psychology, but how do we use this information to set our price? Figuring your costs is the first step, because it helps you set your bottom line. As discussed earlier, if you know your market size and your costs, you can come up with a breakeven price. In the desk-building example above, $2,328 was your breakeven price (if the market could absorb only 50 desks); if you drop below that, you can't cover your costs. While you might settle for breakeven for the short term, it's very rare that this is good enough long term. If your market research has established that custom desks like the ones you're making go for $2,000, you need to head back to the drawing board. If you find out that they go for $3,500–$6,000, then it sounds like you have a viable product.

return pricing
A price that is set so as to achieve a certain profit level.

Breakeven is a good first step in setting your price. It will show you where you need to be to cover your costs—your absolute minimum. Realistically you'll want some profits to reinvest into the firm. Setting prices by figuring in desired profits is called **return pricing** or return on investment pricing.[35] In this case you need to estimate what that might be and rework your breakeven. Let's say you want $100,000 in annual profits. You can add desired profit to total costs and compute the required level of sales. Use the number of desks that you expect to sell in a year, and solve for price. Using the 50-desk market from above, your equation would look something like this:

$$(\$328 \times 50) + \$100,000 + \$100,000 = 50x$$

Your sales price to achieve the desired profit is $4,328. Is that reasonable? Keep in mind what you have learned about elasticities: There's a big difference in price between your original breakeven price and your return price. Can you still sell 50 desks at that price, or, when you get over the $4,000 figure, will that drop down to 45 (or fewer) desks? What is your competition doing? What is the perceived value of your desks, that is, do the customers think your desks are worth over $4,000 each?

Return pricing will give you another figure to consider, but, as alluded to above, pricing cannot be conceived in a vacuum. Breakeven and return pricing are great mathematical models, but the numbers they give you are worthless without considering both your internal situation and the external environment. Basically, there are seven things that influence the prices you set for your products: costs, your company's objectives, your marketing strategy, the channels of distribution you use, the customer, the competition, and legal and regulatory issues. Costs (breakeven and return costing) and the customer (pricing psychology) have been covered; let's look at the others.

Your Company Objectives[36]

For most small businesses, the early years are survival years, and the tendency is to sell your product for whatever you can get for it. Sure, you'd like $5,000 per desk, but if someone offers you $3,000, well, at least it'll help you to meet this week's payroll. While it may be a fact of life at certain times, it shouldn't be your firm's pricing objective.

More commonly firms set prices to maximize profits or to increase market share. Increasing market share usually means pricing toward the low end of the competition in order to take market share from the competition. This strategy becomes more popular as a product reaches the maturity phase of the product life cycle. However, this shouldn't be an objective for a small business for several reasons.[37] Bigger, better-established companies have deep pockets, and often more geographic diversity, and larger product lines than you do. They can match or undercut your price in a heartbeat—even sell below cost because they're supported by sales of other products or in other regions.[38] Another reason why a small firm shouldn't try to compete on price is that it probably won't be working at full capacity for some time. Your building rent is the same whether you are producing at top speed or working only a few hours a week. If you cut your prices too low, you won't be able to cover costs during your nonproductive times. When you are up to full speed, you could drop your prices, or you might find other ways to please your customers, such as including free delivery or other services, and leave your price alone.[39, 40]

Maximizing profits is a much better option for the small firm. This doesn't mean that you have to have the most expensive product out there unless you're worth it, but it does mean that you should be well above the average price.[41] First, this simply adds to your profit. Let's revisit the jeans example. If it costs you $28 to make a pair of jeans and they sell for $30 a pair, you make a $2 profit. If you sell them for $32, you make a $4 profit. Did you notice? Your profit doubled. We've already established that at prices between $30 and $35 there is virtually no difference in quantity sold. Why wouldn't you sell at a little higher price and make more money?

Studies have also shown that companies that compete on product innovation and high quality achieve higher growth than those that try to compete on price. Firms that compete on price even tend to experience negative growth.[42] Another study of 1,000 firms shows that a 1 percent price increase converted to a 12 percent increase in profitability, all else being the same.[43] There are times and places to compete on price, but exhaust all other strategies first.

One more example: J. David Allen, now the director of a large entrepreneurship center, once owned a company that sold dominoes. He barely sold any at $3 per box. Then, he added a design for the Texas Sesquicentennial and couldn't keep them on the shelf at $19.95.[44] The product cost roughly the same—adding the design had minimal impact—but look at the difference in the profit. Be different, be better, but don't be too cheap. And remember: it's always easier to lower prices than it is to raise them.[45]

Marketing Strategy

Your price must be consistent with the rest of your marketing strategy. If you are advertising high quality or prestige but price your product lower than the competition, your customers will be confused at best, or at worst simply not believe your ads. If you're trying to get into Wal-Mart, you don't want to have Rodeo Drive prices. If you package in a plain cardboard box, you're hinting at a different price point from a silk-lined, leather case. If you are making custom desks, they had better be higher priced than the pressed board, assemble-it-yourself ones you find at the discount stores. Consistency is key.

Channels of Distribution

Everyone who handles your product will be expecting to make something from it. If you are using a traditional retailer, your product may go through several middlemen (see Chapter 11 for more information) before getting on the shelf. The end price to your customer might be four times from what *you* got. This is called *price escalation.* You need to make sure that once all those involved get their cut, your product is still priced correctly to reach your target market. If the distribution costs price you out of the market, you may want to sell direct. (More information is available in Chapter 11 on this subject.)

Competition

We've talked a bit about pricing in relation to your competition, but you can't just look at the competition's price ranges and pick something at, oh, about 75 percent of maximum. Just as yours is, your competitor's products are a "bundle of satisfactions." How does their product bundle match up to yours? You may make athletic shoes just as good as Nike's, but you don't provide the prestige of the Nike logo (at least not to start). What other "extras" do customers get from your competition—additional service, brand recognition, prestige, bragging rights, comfort of knowing a big company will back up their product, and others? These intangible things are hard to price, but you need to really think about how your product or service matches up to theirs.[46]

Dan and Russell Schlueter sell pet products, including Ultra Pearls and Crystal Clear Litter Pearls. This cat litter offers a significant benefit over ordinary litters. About 4 pounds of the Schlueters' product lasts as long as 28 pounds of other litters. Competing brands sold 14-pound bags for $6 to $7, but the Schlueters priced their 4-pound bag at $14 to $16. Their 4-pound bag lasts a month—the same as two bags of the other litter. Still, they're at a premium to the competition. Which would you rather carry from the store—28 pounds of the old stuff or 4 pounds of Ultra Pearls? Add some awards from *Cat Fancy* magazine and PetSmart Outstanding Technology Achievement Award and in less than five years, they have a $10 million plus business.[47]

■ Ultra Pearls, sold by Dan and Russell Schlueter, offer the ultimate in cat litter control. How does the Schlueter pricing strategy reinforce their product's known benefits?

Legal and Regulatory Issues

There's a plethora of items that can fall under legal and regulatory issues. There are laws, for example, against price fixing and other collusion among competitors. The government sometimes establishes "acceptable" prices or price minimums or maximums—especially if you are selling to the government. Some forms of price discrimination are illegal.[48] It's okay to lower your prices during happy hour (effectively discriminating against those who work during that time period), but you can't charge different prices to customers of different races. You can offer a senior citizen's discount, but you can't charge a "skinny person" premium. In most states, you must collect sales tax for retail purchases. Usually however you are not required to do so for mail order and Internet sales. Sometimes there are special taxes or fees that must be collected, such as deposits or hazardous waste handling fees. Talk to your accountant and your attorney about specific rules pertaining to your product or service.[49]

Pricing Strategies[50]

We have discussed all the "externalities" that can affect your price. These set the limits for what you are able to do with your pricing strategies. For example, if the government has set a price maximum, you may not be able to use a skimming or premium price strategy—strategies that mean setting prices relatively high compared to the competition. If you have determined that the price range of acceptability for a large pizza is between $8 and $15 and your costs determine that you need to charge $20, then the premium pricing route—with creating the correct mindset through other parts of the marketing mix—is almost imperative.

LO7
Understand different pricing strategies.

To reiterate, it's almost always a bad idea for a small firm to try to compete on price. Competing on price may lead to a price war in which you just don't have the staying power of a big firm. Lower prices are "throwing away" profit you really need. They can signal your customers that your product isn't as high quality as your competitors'. There are, however, plenty of strategies available to small businesses that you can use as successfully as the larger firms.[51]

Skimming[52]

Skimming is charging the highest price the market will bear. This technique is usually only possible if you are absolutely the first product or service of your type in the market, and only if it's something people really want. Companies sometimes use this strategy in order to recoup research and development costs or heavy marketing expenses. If your product or service is truly innovative and at the beginning of the product life cycle (no/or little competition)—for instance, plasma television—and if you can convince customers to try it through effective advertising, then skimming may be an option. This method will attract competition, so it's not a long-term strategy.

skimming
Setting a price at the highest level the market will bear, usually because there is no competition at the time.

Prestige or Premium Pricing[53]

Just as setting your prices low signals low quality, having a high price can signal great quality and an item that is prestigious to own.[54] When a consumer has difficulty assessing the quality of the item—for example, the first time he or she purchases a product in that category—price is used as a proxy for quality. Similarly with prestige. Consider average computer buyers: Do they really understand RAM and ROM and gigabytes and all those other terms or do they have the vague impression that "bigger is better"? The same goes for the price; that more expensive computer just *has* to be better than the less expensive, no-name brand. (If you needed a root canal, would you rather go to a dentist who says it'll cost several hundreds of dollars or one who states he or she can do it for $49?) Certainly most everyone would agree that a Toyota Corolla is a good-quality automobile, but if you ask people to what kind of car they aspire to own, you'll hear Jaguar, BMW, Mercedes. It's a prestige thing determined partly by a higher price tag.

Generally **prestige pricing** is for an item considered a status symbol, such as a Rolex watch or a Mercedes automobile. **Premium pricing** is used for non-status symbol types of products, such as toothpaste, shampoo, or laundry detergent. The idea behind both is the same.

prestige or premium pricing
Setting a price above that of the competition so as to indicate a higher quality or that a product is a status symbol.

A few warnings. If you are going to go for the high-end market, remember what we say about marketing mix consistency: Make sure your product, packaging, advertising, distribution—in short, everything—matches your price. If your product or service quality isn't appropriate, you'll not only not get a second chance, but you'll generate a lot of bad word of mouth as well. Also you may not want to be the very highest out there; a Lamborghini and a Jaguar are both prestigious cars, but the Jaguar market is much larger. Figure 9.10 shows a couple of ads that demonstrate a good use of prestige and premium pricing.

FIGURE 9.10

Prestige/Premium Pricing Ads[55]

Odd-Even Pricing[56]

odd-even pricing
Setting a price that ends in the number 5, 7, or 9.

Odd-even pricing simply means setting a price that ends with a 9, 7, or 5. For example, don't charge $100; charge $99.99 (or $99.97 or $99.95). Numbers that are multiples of 10 are a psychological hurdle for consumers. Therefore, $9.99 seems much cheaper than $10, and the difference between $9.99 and $10 feels greater than the difference between $9.99 and $9.98. Consumers will set price limits in their minds; they'll want to spend under a thousand for a new computer. They may spend $999, before taxes and other extras are added on, and they'll feel that they've succeeded in meeting their budget—and will brag to their friends that they were able to buy "all this for under a grand."[57] Does odd-even pricing work? A recent study showed that when an identical dress was priced at $34, $39, and $44, a third more dresses were sold at $39 than at either of the other two prices.[58]

Partitioned Pricing

partitioned pricing
Setting the price for a base item and then charging extra for each additional component.

Partitioned pricing is alluded to in the computer example above—setting a base price and charging extra for all other components. You set the price for the main component—a computer for $999—but just about everything else you need is extra. You need a printer? That's another $100. How about cables to connect the printer to the computer? That's $29.95. Did you realize you could increase your computer's memory, add a read/write CD burner, or a DVD player? They cost more, of course. Extended warranty? $79.95. Don't you want to scan photos, add a digital camera, and upgrade to a flat screen monitor? What about some ink cartridges for that new printer? And several different kinds of paper? Don't forget to check out our excellent selection of software on your way up to the checkout. That $999 computer may end up costing twice that much (or more) before the consumer gets out the door.

Partitioned pricing works because once consumers make a decision that a certain product is the one they want, they are very reluctant to change their mind. It's sort of like saying that they made a bad decision or decided too quickly. They don't want to look stupid or cheap or settle for something less than they really "deserve." A number of products are sold that way: shipping, extended warranties, installation, training, additional services, and the like are not often included in the final price.

Captive Pricing

captive pricing
Setting the price for an item relatively low and then charging much higher prices for the expendables it uses.

For certain products and services, **captive pricing** works well. In captive pricing, you sell something, usually a base system, at a relatively low price, but the expendables it uses are relatively expensive. Computer printers are usually priced low for the technology—sometimes even thrown in for free when you buy a computer—but the cost of the replacement ink cartridges is high. By the time you purchase three or four, you've spent more money for them than the price of the printer. For services, something you can offer a low price for, such as first time membership to a health club, can be a candidate for captive pricing. Any extra classes, sauna, massage, and the like can be higher priced and more profitable. Although it's true that customers could get a massage elsewhere, they have already purchased this membership and it's convenient.

Price Lining

Price lining is an attempt to appeal to several different markets. In this situation, you might have three models of your product or service price to appeal to the high-, mid-, and low-end market. You might have a computer with all the bells and whistles priced at or near the top of the competitive price range, a bare-bones, stripped down version priced at or near the bottom, and a third model at a midrange price with midrange features. This way you appeal to customers with different budgets and different needs. Even if it's a product without a lot of features to add or remove, price lining can work. Next time you are at the store, find all the Procter and Gamble or Unilever products in the shampoo or laundry detergent aisle; they'll have products at every price point with different brand names. For example, Unilever manufactures both Suave hair care products at the low price end and Helene Curtis products at the high price end. Procter and Gamble has Gain (low price) and Cheer (high price) laundry detergents. Figure 9.11 shows an ad that is an example of price lining, although the prices are only implied.

price lining
The practice of setting (usually) three price points: good quality, better quality, best quality.

Price-Lowering Techniques[59]

Even though all-out price competition is not usually the best strategy for smaller businesses, there are times when a company needs to reduce its prices in order to attract more business, smooth service cycles, build loyalty, move excess inventories, alleviate

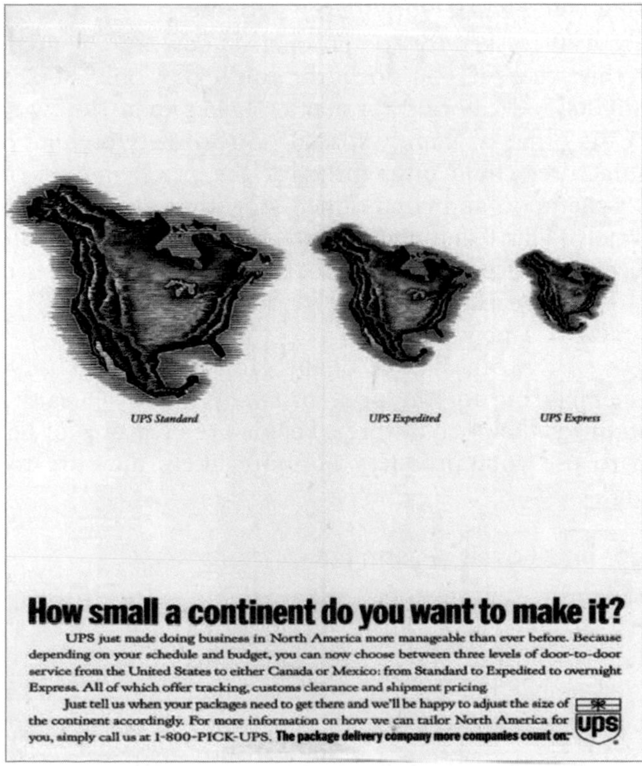

FIGURE 9.11

Price Lining by UPS

temporary cash flow problems, and the like. The following techniques can be used without starting price wars, or reducing the quality perception of your product or service.

Periodic and Random Discounting

periodic or random discounting
Sales conducted at either predictable or nonpredictable intervals.

These are simply sales. **Periodic discounting** refers to sales that happen on some regular cycle, such as once a month, once a year, or whenever. Christmas cards are half-price December 26. Midsummer usually means clearance sales on summer clothes, and by August there's the back-to-school sale on everything you need for school. While some products are notably seasonal, **random discounting**—running a sale without a definite pattern or cycle—is a better option. If customers know that something is going to go on sale soon, they may wait for that sale. Sales shouldn't be too frequent because consumers begin to realize if they stock up in this sales period, they can probably wait until the next sales period. A recent study shows that even just the word "sale" can drive up demand by 50 percent without any actual price change.[60]

Off-Peak Pricing

off-peak pricing
Charging lower prices at certain times to encourage customers to come during slack periods.

The technique of off-peak pricing is particularly appropriate for services. Services have busy periods and slow periods. Sometimes you can schedule your personnel to meet the variation in business, but your building, equipment, and the like are still sitting idle (losing money or at least not making any). Wouldn't it be great if you could level out this variation? **Off-peak pricing** helps. This is Happy Hour to attract business in the late afternoon or early evening slump just before the dinner crowd arrives. This is like having "Taco Tuesday" at On the Border Mexican Restaurant where tacos are $1 on Tuesdays because this day is traditionally a slow day for restaurants. Dry cleaners offer midweek specials. Movie tickets are cheaper for afternoon matinees.

Sort of a reverse concept is charging more for peak periods. Veterinarians and beauticians offer better rates to those with appointments than walk-ins so they can schedule customers more evenly. After hours or weekend services are sometimes priced at a higher rate. These are also ways of smoothing service to customers or trying to get them to come when you want them.

Bundling or Multiple-Packs or Bonus-Packs Pricing

bundling
Combining two or more products in one unit and pricing it less than if the units were sold separately.

This works equally well for services or products. Let's say a haircut is $25 and coloring is $50. For this week, if you do both, you'll pay only $60. The beauty salon has "**bundled**" haircuts and coloring for a price lower than the two would cost separately. Treehouse Cuts offers a "family-special" price for two children's and one adult haircut.[61] A manufacturer could offer three for the price of two, or bundle complementary products—shampoo and conditioner—together at a price less expensive than buying each separately. This technique is particularly effective for promoting the sales of a second product or service that might not be doing as well or is newly introduced. (Remember what we said earlier about new products? "Trialability" is important to get a customer to accept a new product.)

multiple or bonus pack
Combining more than one unit of the same product and pricing it lower than if each unit were sold separately.

Multiple or bonus packs can also be of the same product or service. For example, buy a three-year membership for the price of two years at a health club, or buy five bottles of hand lotion for the price of three. People are creatures of habit, and the more you can get them to use your product, the more likely they are to internalize it—it becomes their brand.

Coupons, Rebates, and Loyalty Programs

These three methods also reduce prices and promote sales. Most coupons are delivered in newspapers (80 percent),[62] but magazines, mail, on package, Internet, and in person are all other ways of delivery. The higher the value of the coupon, the more likely it is to be redeemed. But even so, coupon redemption runs only 2 percent in the United States. About 64 percent of all Americans are willing to switch brands if

Mardi Gras Café

"BREA MALL" "SANTA ANA" Main Place

FREQUENT DINNER CARD

Purchase of Mardi Gras Bowl or Cajun Combo Required

1	2	3	4	5	Free soft drink with Bowl or Combo Purchase
6	7	8	9	10	Free Two-Entrees Combo on this visit

Expiration Date: August 31, 2006

Not valid with other discounts or promotion items.

Card must be completely stamped and used before expiration date.

FIGURE 9.12

Typical Loyalty Program

they have a coupon.[63] Coupons are a great way to get people to try new products as well (reduces the risk). Even if coupons aren't redeemed, they serve an advertising purpose. Consumers see them and their brain registers a lower price. Even if they forget to clip the coupon or use it, their subconscious remembers the product favorably.

Rebates are also great tools for small businesses because the redemption rate for these is extremely low. People lose their sales receipts, destroy the necessary packaging, just forget to send them in, or fail to send in everything correctly, but they'll remember that there was a rebate and think favorably about the product. Seeing that there is a rebate is an incentive to buy something, even something they might not be in the market for at this time.[64]

Loyalty programs are especially good for getting customers to return to your business. Most often, these take the form of a card (see Figure 9.12) on which each purchase is stamped, and when a certain number of purchases or visits have occurred, the customer gets a free service, a discount, or a gift. Again, people may lose their cards, forget to bring them in, forget to get them stamped, never quite make enough purchases, or otherwise fail to redeem their cards. Their minds, though, hold the perception that they are getting a good deal. If that's not a good enough incentive for you, how about the fact that 45 percent of all consumers spend more money in stores with loyalty programs?[65]

Referral Discounts

Referral discounts are a great way to build business during the start-up phase or during slumps. A customer who refers someone else who uses the service or buys the product gets a discount on future business. Word-of-mouth is one of the least expensive methods of advertising your business. Especially for services, the recommendation of a friend or relative is often a deciding factor in a purchase or in trying a new service. Some of the people your customers tell will fail to buy from you, but they may pass the word along as well. "I've never tried this place, but my sister recommended it."

referral discount
A discount given to a customer who refers a friend to the business.

Pricing Strategy Wrap-Up

The great thing about all these price reduction strategies is that the customer recognizes them for what they are, a temporary reduction in price, and they won't tarnish your product image. Competition may match a sale or offer a coupon or other promotion to match or counteract your offering, but it's not as aggressive an action as a price war. Consumers also feel smart about buying something at a better price. Even if your prices are higher than the competition's and you offer a sale that brings you in line with its pricing, customers are still likely to buy from you—all else being equal—and feel they got a great deal.[66]

There are a number of other pricing strategies and price reduction strategies that haven't been discussed here. These are some of the more common ones and ones more popular with small businesses. Table 9.1 summarizes the ones we have covered here and others. If you are interested in learning more, you can consult a marketing or pricing textbook. Pricing possibilities are limited only by imagination, and we see new ideas crop up all the time. For example, we are now seeing cases in which the customer sets the price, such as on Amazon.com (with their auction bidding) or Priceline.com (where customers offer what they wish to pay, and suppliers can opt to take their bid).[67]

As a wrap-up here are a few pricing statistics to consider. Ellen Rohr, the financial management expert at *Entrepreneur* magazine, estimates that 99 out of 100 small businesses in financial difficulties have set their prices too low.[68] And when it's all said and done, depending on the product, only 15 to 35 percent of consumers decide on a product using price as the number one factor. Nearly 80 percent cannot accurately recall the price on something they purchased a week ago.[69]

The marketing effort in small businesses starts with the idea for the product or service and builds from there to include the key benefits that customers will want, the price they are willing to pay, and also some larger issues such as innovativeness and where the product or service is in terms of its life cycle. Together, these issues can help you craft a pricing strategy that can lead you to success. Even if your product or service is imitative, your profits do not need to be. The secret is in understanding the market, the cost of doing business, and the prices your customers are willing to pay.

Table 9.1 Pricing Strategies

Pricing Technique	Description	Example
Secondary market pricing	One price for the primary market and a different one for secondary markets	Computer priced at $2,000 for U.S. business markets and at $1,500 in Mexico
Periodic discounting	Patterned or systematic price reduction	Holiday sale, back-to-school sale
Random discounting	Nonsystematic price reduction	Sales without a discernable pattern
Price skimming	Charging the absolute highest possible price due to inelastic demand	Prices of plasma television
Off-peak pricing	Lower prices during off-peak periods in order to smoothe customers	Happy hours or late night specials at restaurants
Loss leaders	Selling a name brand at or near cost in order to attract traffic to a retailer	Toys R Us selling Pampers at cost and locating them at the back of the store, hoping a customer might pick up other items while in the store
Price discrimination	Charging different prices to different groups, usually to attract a different demographic	Senior citizens' discounts
Penetration pricing	Setting a low price in order to get market share	A later entrant into the market may set prices below all competition in order to steal market share
Limit pricing	Extremely low penetration price to discourage competitors from entering a market	Instead of skimming, the first on the market may price just above cost until it feels the competition has given up on the market

Price signaling	Setting a high price on a product in order to imply high quality or similar quality to a competitor	If I set my price the same as Levi's jeans, people will assume they are the same quality
Going rate	At or near industry average	Competitors price from $5–10 and your price is $7.50
Captive pricing	Selling one item at a very low price (even below cost) when there are necessary supplies that you can sell for a high price	Low-price ink-jet printers, but high-priced replacement ink cartridges
Bait pricing	Advertising an inexpensive product and placing it near better, more expensive models. The idea is to get the consumer to buy up. Sometimes the product will be intentionally ugly—unpopular color, etc.	The ad shows a $300 computer, but to see it you have to walk by all the other computers that have many more features, better quality, etc.
Reference pricing	Two similar products displayed side-by-side in ad or at the store but at different prices. Implies the same product but at a better price	Wal-Mart brand aspirin next to Bayer, but at half the price
Everyday low Price	Implying that the price stated is always low and it's always a good deal	The Wal-Mart strategy; even when its prices are higher than the competition's, the consumers feel that they are not
Odd-even pricing	Ending a price with a 9, 7, or 5	This book is $69.99
Customary pricing	Prices based on tradition; it's very difficult to raise above this limit	Penny gumball machines, 50-cent candy bars
Prestige/premium pricing	Setting a high price to imply that this product is a status symbol and/or of much better quality than others	Pricing of luxury cars, the best perfumes
Professional pricing	Fees set by doctors, lawyers, and other similar professionals that tend to be uniform in a geographic region	Lasik eye surgery runs about $499 at all eye doctors
Product line pricing	Selling products at different price points to attract the low-, mid-, and high-end customers	Marriott hotels are high priced, but the Marriott Courtyards are moderate priced
Bundling/bonus pack/Multipack	Putting two or more of the same or different products or services together and selling for a price somewhat under the products individual prices	An oil change is $49 and tire rotation is $69, but if you do them both, it will only cost $99
Partitioned pricing	Pricing each piece separately; the consumer gets "hooked" on the core component and then pays extra for everything else needed	The computer is only $699, but the printer is another $100 and cables are $30 and the modem is . . .
Coupons/rebates	Temporary price-reduction strategies	This coupon is worth $1 off my next visit
Loyalty programs	A reward given to repeat customers	If I buy nine sandwiches, the tenth one is free
Referral discounts	A reward to customers who encourage others to buy from you	If one of your friends signs up at our health club, you'll get one month free

CHAPTER SUMMARY

LO1 Know the characteristics of goods and services.

- Goods differ from services in tangibility, inseparability, perishability, and heterogeneity.
- Very few true goods or service exist; most products fall somewhere along a goods/service continuum and have components of each.

LO2 Define the total product.

- A product is a bundle of services and goods and has three basic levels: core, augmented, and total product.
- Understanding the total product allows you to concentrate on the features and aspects important to the customer and to coordinate your other marketing activities.

LO3 Learn the stages of new product development.

- The stages include idea generation, idea screening, idea evaluation, product development, and commercialization.
- During the product development phase, prototypes can be developed in order to do additional screening, and test markets or test market simulations can be run.
- The last stage, commercialization, involves developing the final marketing plan, getting the product into production, and the start of sales.
- "Me-toos" are products similar to competitive products that need a much-abbreviated new product development cycle. In this case, only the aspects that are different from competition need to be tested.

LO4 Learn the product life cycle.

- Like the Industry Life Cycle, the stages of the Product Life Cycle include introduction, growth, maturity, and decline.
- From a marketing viewpoint, the different stages tell us about the competition, and how to focus the individual elements of the marketing plan—product, price, promotion, and distribution.
- As services are usually more able to make incremental changes almost continually, the service life cycle is more typified by a series of mini-product life cycles.

LO5 Understand the concept of price with variable costs, fixed costs, and breakeven.

- The price of a product is more complex than just the costs of its manufacturing and includes the value placed on the product by the customer.
- Variable costs are those costs that change directly with the quantity of a product made, while fixed costs stay constant regardless of the quantity produced.
- Breakeven is determined when the sales revenue of a number of products equals the total cost, or:

  (Sales price)(Quantity sold) = (Variable Costs/item)(Quantity sold) + Fixed Costs

  Using this equation, a business may solve for breakeven quantity or breakeven sales price.

- In retailing, rather than breakeven, a mark-up system is used where each product is marked up a percentage based on cost or sales price.

LO6 Understand price elasticities, pricing psychology, and other price influences and their impact on pricing.

- Products tend to be price elastic or inelastic, that is, the quantity sold may vary considerably due to changes in price (elastic) or not (inelastic).
- Consumer psychology has an impact on pricing as well. Through a number of ways, consumers get ideas about what is an acceptable price and what is not.
- In addition to costs and consumers, price setting is influenced by five other factors: Company objectives, marketing strategy, channels of distribution, competition, and legal and regulatory restrictions.

LO7 Understand different pricing strategies.

- Firms may use a variety of different pricing strategies. Some of the more common ones include: skimming, prestige or premium pricing, odd-even pricing, partitioned pricing, captive pricing, and price lining.
- Dropped prices are hard to raise. Rather than dropping prices, firms should consider using periodic or random discounting, off-peak pricing, bundling, coupons, rebates, and referral discounts.

DISCUSSION QUESTIONS

1. A college education comes pretty close to being a true service. Discuss the four main characteristics of service—intangibility, inseparability, perishability, and heterogeneity—as they pertain to a college education.
2. What is the core component, the augmented product, and the total product sold at your college or university? How does it differ from your institution to others in the area?
3. List all the products/services you have seen lately that are promoted as new, different, improved, or otherwise changed from what has been available before. What percentage of these are actually me-too products? Identify the differential advantages these companies believe they have over the competition.
4. You manufacture fresh Italian meals sold in grocery stores. Which of the following costs are fixed and which are variable? Cost of printing the price list, cost of pasta, the chef's salary, cost of foil trays and plastic lids used to package the product, cost of delivery to the stores, and cost of running a newspaper ad.
5. You handcraft decorative floral wreaths that you sell at craft fairs. You make them at home, so there's no rent, but you did buy a worktable and some tools, amounting to $800. The wreath frame, ribbons, and dried flowers you use cost $25 for each wreath. The craft fair runs one weekend a month, and the cost to rent a booth is $100. Other similar wreaths sell for $50 to $75. What is your breakeven quantity if your price is $50 per wreath? What is it if your price is $75?
6. Continuing with the example above, you realize that you are devoting 20 hours per month to operate the booth at the craft fair, plus two hours for each wreath you make. Because you are working

full time, you figure you have about only 40 hours a month to devote to this project. Do you have enough time to make your breakeven quantity of wreaths? At what price could you sell the wreaths to achieve breakeven at your maximum production rate?

7. After doing some marketing research, you have discovered that the local market for decorative wreaths is around 300 a year. There are five other booths selling decorative wreaths at the craft fair, and that seems to be the only source in this market for this product. If you assume that all the products are roughly the same quality and no producer has any discernable competitive advantage, your market share should be about equal to everyone else's. Should you sell your product? What if one of your competitors has a booth near the entry of the craft fair and gets half the market, where the rest is divided among the remaining competitors? What is your decision then?

8. While displaying at the craft fair, a representative of a mail order catalog company wants to put your product in the catalog. It will pay you $40 and mark the product up to $55 for the catalog. It estimates that your market share could be substantial and should be dependent only on your production output. You decide to quit your real job and devote all your time to making wreaths, but you want to match your current $50,000 salary. You really don't want to work more than 40 hours per week in actual wreath manufacturing (assume all paperwork, material purchasing, and such takes place beyond those 40 hours). You want four weeks a year for vacation, holidays, and sick days or personal days. Taking into consideration time constraints, the price you will get from the catalog company, and your revised costs, does this make sense?

9. Describe a situation in which you have been influenced by consumer buying psychology towards considering a price too high or a real bargain.

10. Think of two products in the same product category—one high priced and one low priced. How do the other parts of the marketing mix—the product itself, the advertising message, and the distribution—support or detract from the message the price tag gives?

EXPERIENTIAL EXERCISES

1. At this time, you are fairly experienced with college education. What could you suggest could be done in order to reduce intangibility, inseparability, perishability, and heterogeneity of this service?

2. BMW automobiles call themselves "the ultimate driving machine." The advertising tagline attempts to capture the total product package—what driving a BMW means to its owners. Review other advertising and come up with a list of five other products that do the same thing. What do their products mean to their consumers?

3. With a group of friends, brainstorm a list of ideas for a service you could provide for your college professors. Design an idea checklist to evaluate this list.

4. Select a service you know. Brainstorm a list of potential incremental changes—whether technologically feasible or not—that might extend the product life cycle for it over the next several years.

5. Set up several selling scenarios for the same product displaying different cues about the value of a product (e.g., where it's sold, whether it's on sale), the motivation of the seller, prices of competitive products (external reference price), and other possibilities appropriate for your product. Ask several people what they would pay under the circumstance you've set up.

6. For one week collect all the coupons you find in newspapers, magazines, mail, and so on. What percentage are for products or services or brands that you would really buy? Typically, how

many coupons do you actually use in a week? Pull all the coupons for one product category and visit a store. Are there other brands of that same product that do not have coupons? Is the store engaging in any other methods to attract customers—rebates, sales, contests, multipacks, and so on?

Mini-Case

YAK MILK[70]

Dongzhou Gongbu saw a golden opportunity, only he wasn't quite sure what to do with it at first. A native Tibetan, he had worked in the Chinese government for a number of years and had witnessed the difficulties the Chinese government was facing feeding its people. While China is quite a large country, over 60 percent of its landmass is unsuitable for agriculture. Those areas that are suitable are also where China's huge population lives, further reducing available land. Dongzhou remembered the vast Tibetan plateau dotted with yak, the only animal suited to the severe climate found there and knew there had to be a solution.

Yak are "low maintenance" animals needing no feed that they can't gather themselves and living on the open range herded by nomadic Tibetans. While yak are milk producers, the quantities produced are much less than that produced by dairy cattle. In addition, because of its remoteness, bringing milk from the plateau to the population centers is an expensive proposition. A quick look at the prices on existing milk products and yak milk cost structure showed that yak milk just couldn't compete, because it would need to be about 50 percent more expensive than cow's milk.

Dongzhou didn't let this stop him, though. He consulted a specialist and found that yak milk was higher in certain nutrients than cow's milk. In addition, the Tibetan plateau is well respected in China for being pollution-free. Dongzhou capitalized on these features plus the fact that the yak was truly organically raised and revered in Chinese mythology. He positioned his product not as just another milk but as an extremely healthy alternative to other products—almost a nutritional drink—and priced it at a premium level.

CASE DISCUSSION QUESTIONS

1. How did Dongzhou Gongbu "discover" his new product?
2. What was his "total product"?
3. How did this help him with his pricing strategy?
4. How might he use this in advertising?
5. Can you think of another product that is basically the same as the competition and has been positioned much differently in order to command a higher price?

LEARNING OBJECTIVES

This chapter will help you:

LO1 Understand how to assess your value proposition.

LO2 Segment and further define your target audience.

LO3 Recognize the different approaches and methods you can use to convey your promotional message.

LO4 Learn the key skills involved in personal selling, especially closing the sale.

LO5 Differentiate public relations from advertising and know how to write a press release.

LO6 Know what "news" is and how to leverage the press to generate publicity.

■ Addie Swartz's lifestyle brand, Beacon Street Girls, is aimed at two market audiences. What challenges are posed to this small business by its double-pronged approach? How might this approach work to Swartz's advantage?

Small Business Promotion: Capturing the Eyes of Your Market

Focus on Small Business: Addie Swartz and Accessories for Girls Who Are "Between Toys and Boys"[1]

As Addie Swartz's two daughters approached the pivotal "tween" years, she—like many mothers—struggled to find something to help her girls bridge the gap between Barbie and Britney. Frustration stoked her entrepreneurial spirit, and the Beacon Street Girls, a new lifestyle brand for girls ages 9 to 13, was born.

NO DOLLS OR ICONS

The Beacon Street Girls invites tweens into a rich and exciting contemporary world in which values matter, friendships are everything, and community service is important.

In promoting the brand, Swartz comments that all of Beacon Street Girls marketing initiatives need to understand and speak to two audiences: tween girls and their parents/older gift-buying relatives. Their goals are to:

- Build awareness among stakeholders.

- Create interest and desire in tweens to engage with the brand and share with their peers.
- Drive customers into the stores to seek and purchase Beacon Street Girls products.
- Encourage tweens and their parents to come to the Web site.

Marketing programs are aimed to promote retailer presence, push to the Web, and leverage the tween consumer to promote the brand via Web-based viral marketing programs. In describing her market further, Swartz divides the market into two segments, the primary and secondary. The primary market consists of girls ages 9–13 years, with the "sweet spot" being the older, 11–12-year-old tween. These girls are entering middle school, a time of new friendships, body changes, and growing up experiences. They are media-savvy, looking for fun and possibilities, admiring of teenagers, but still want to be kids. They are in the early stages of navigating the often rocky waters of adolescence and desperately want to fit in. The secondary market consists of their mothers, fathers, aunts, uncles, and grandmothers who seek positive role models and messages for their daughters/relatives.

www.beaconstreetgirls.com

DISCUSSION QUESTIONS

1. What are some ways that Beacon Street Girls can promote its brand in order to meet the company's goals?
2. What ways can Beacon Street Girls market to the tween girls?
3. How can it also reach the parents of the tweens? In what ways is the marketing message different or the same?
4. How can Addie Swartz continually develop and promote the brand that has meaningful, value-driven tween girl properties that are also relevant, cool, and realistic?

LO1
Understand how to assess your value proposition.

The Need for Promotion

You've experienced your business "light bulb" idea for a terrific new product or service. You've organized an office complete with desk, phone, and computer, and you may possibly even have a small storefront or service vehicle. By all accounts, you are in business. Now ask yourself this: Does your target market know you exist?

In order for customers to purchase your goods and services, you must first go to them. You need to advertise and actively promote your business before you can expect inquiries into what you have to offer. While there are a handful of promotional means that are standard for all business ventures, entrepreneurs' limit to promotions is their own creativity.

The Basics: Crafting Your Value Proposition

Prior to putting together any marketing plan, prior to developing any advertisement, and prior to calling the press or distributing a press release, you first need to know what you want to say, and who, specifically, is the target of that messaging. To establish this messaging, the first thing you need to do is establish your unique selling points—otherwise known as your **value proposition**. This is directly related to developing your small business strategy as discussed in Chapter 7. In that chapter, you had the opportunity to learn the benefits that win customers and how to sustain your competitive advantage. You can think of defining your value proposition along the same categories of value and cost benefits of quality, style, delivery, service, technology, shopping ease, place, and scale and scope. For each of the categories mentioned in

value proposition
Small business owners' unique selling points that will be used to differentiate their products and/or services from those of the competition.

Chapter 7, think about how your company, product, or service is different from anyone else's. Under each category, answer a few questions as objectively as you can:

- Why would someone want your product or service? What need does it fill? List the benefits and the problems it solves. In what way does it improve the life of the user?
- Would you personally buy this product? Why or why not? The "why nots" may give you an insight into potential weaknesses or categories of differentiation that you need to work on.

From there, you can then start to determine who will most benefit from your product or service. Begin with these questions:

- Who, in your opinion, is most likely to buy it? Be as specific as you can. How old are they? Male or female? Where do they live? Where do they work? These people are your primary target market. It doesn't mean that you don't have second- or third-tier markets.
- How does your primary target market currently go about buying existing products or services of this type? What are its sources of information? Word-of-mouth? Trade publications? Yellow Pages? The Internet?[2]

By answering these questions, you can start to further develop the value of your product and ways you can find and communicate with your customers. Once you know who needs your product or service, you can begin to craft your value and message directly to where your market would look to find information related to your small business. Skill Module 10.1 will help you develop a value proposition.

SKILL MODULE 10.1

Developing a Value Proposition

Choose one small retail business (e.g., children's clothing store, pet store, independently owned beauty salon, restaurant, etc.). Using promotional and advertising material, level of service, in-store displays, location, and any other information available (Web site), create a value proposition for that business. The goal of this value proposition is to create and occupy a space inside the target customer's head. Create a value proposition for your chosen small retail business by replacing the text in parentheses below as it reflects the product, market, and strategy.

- **For** (target customer)
- **Who** (statement of the need or opportunity)
- **The** (retail business name) **is a** (product or service category)
- **That** (statement of key benefit—that is, compelling reason to buy/purchase)
- **Unlike** (primary competitive alternative)
- **Our business** (statement of primary differentiation)
- **Is available** (where)

Now place the answers in paragraph format to arrive at the overall value proposition. Feel free to share your perception of the proposition with the actual small business owner.

Segmenting Your Market

LO2
Segment and further define your target audience.

Many entrepreneurs have trouble answering the question, "Who is your target market?" Most entrepreneurs assume that everyone is their target market. Why should an entrepreneur care who buys their product, as long as it's sold? If pressed, the entrepreneurs can usually tell you who is most likely to buy their product or service and why. When they can tell you this, they have targeted their market. Although targeting and market segmentation are more fully discussed in Chapter 12, there are some concepts that are important to know in order to understand promotion.

Segmentation is the process of dividing the market into smaller portions of people who have certain common characteristics. Your **target market** is the segment or segments you select on which to concentrate your marketing efforts. A marketer can chose more than one target market, but it is customary for a smaller business to concentrate its efforts on one target market at the beginning and consider second ones later. Marketers use information on the target market's wants and needs in order to tailor the product or service, as well as its price, distribution, and promotion.[3]

Dividing the market into different segments can be done in a number of ways. Some of the more typical ways include geographically (in a certain city or neighborhood), demographically (income, age, religion, ethnicity, and many others), or by the benefits sought (clothing that is practical, stylish, for a particular sport, etc.). Most companies will use several ways of segmenting to come up with their final target market. For example, the Beacon Street Girls products were segmented by sex (girls) and age (9–13). In addition, the fact that they were into values and community service would be a form of benefit segmentation. Beacon Street Girls also had primary and secondary target markets—the girls and their parents and other gift givers.

Let's start with an example: you run a day care center. Who is your market? For starters, it is small children, or at least, the parents of small children. You have segmented by life cycle position; that is, you have eliminated children, teenagers, senior citizens, and parents of older children. But this really does not eliminate very many potential customers. How else could you limit your potential customers? Driving distance, say 15 miles, is a popular limit since parents are unlikely to want to drive too far. Income, or disposable income, is also a key segmentation device. Families need to be rich enough to afford your service but not so rich as to hire nannies. Other segmentation ideas include schedule (parents who work evenings and nights) or children's hobbies (e.g., offering soccer or music lessons). The more accurately you define your segment, the closer you come to defining your target market.

■ What are the benefits to both your primary and secondary market customers if you open a bilingual day care center in the middle of a largely Hispanic neighborhood? How would you promote to both of these markets?

Using our example from above, let's say that you are located in a town with a large Hispanic population (Phoenix) and all of your day care workers are fluent in Spanish. Your day care center is located in a middle-class, Hispanic area where most households are dual income parents with several children. Your research has shown only a couple of nearby competitors and none of them have the bilingual staff that you have. This opens up the opportunity for the business approach you have in mind, targeting a bilingual day care center for the Hispanic parents needing day care. A potential secondary market might be non-Hispanic families who desire their children to be fluent in Spanish—a market that could be considered at another time.

With the target market defined, it becomes easier to determine what information customers need in order to make a decision to buy your service. The Juarez family (as we imagine our typical customer) needs to find a day care center for little Tomas, who speaks a mix of English and Spanish. Good news! At your center he is not likely to be misunderstood. Other benefits include being able to leave instructions in English or Spanish or having children get a mix of both cultures, such as holiday and birthday celebrations, stories that are read, decorating colors, the day care center's name, and such. These are things that an entrepreneur could use to make this day care center "perfect" for a bilingual clientele.

Promotion includes getting the message out to the target market so that they can make decisions about your product or service. When advertising, your day care center will want to mention the language abilities and other benefits likely to be important to the target market. In order to catch the eye of the audience, the advertising might make use of Hispanic music, a Hispanic model/spokesperson, or symbols that will resonate with the Hispanic culture. (In the Phoenix area, perhaps a Mexican flag would work well.) It is likely to run ads in Spanish or at least partially in Spanish. It is likely to use local Spanish television, radio, or newspapers depending on its budget and the ability of these media to reach the target market. It may send out mailers in the local area and other predominately Hispanic neighborhoods.[4] Parents who visited the day care center would likely hear a sales pitch that was directed to cares and concerns of this target market.

Consider, for a moment, promotion for the secondary market mentioned earlier: the non-Hispanic parents that wanted their children to be fluent in Spanish. Now the ads are likely to be in English. They are likely to run in different media. Mailings would go out to other areas. The sales pitch that the prospective parents would hear would likely be much different.

LO3

Recognize the different approaches and methods you can use to convey your promotional message.

Conveying Your Message

Once you can determine through market research which audience would care about your value proposition and message, you can begin work on how you may want to convey the message. Some of these messages will be an "overall" message that can be used in general communications, like advertisements, brochures, and Web sites. The rest of the messaging should be used for tactical public relations activities, such as press releases, content for contributed articles and case studies, and discussion points with the press. If used consistently, these messages will ensure the development of a solid business identity, as seen in the opening vignette of the Beacon Street Girls' communication messages to both the tween and parent markets.

advertising
Advertising is often used to support the corporate identity and value propositions that are established through public relations efforts. Part of conveying your message to your customers, advertising outlets include newspapers, magazines, billboards, television, and Internet banner ads, to name a few.

To start initially, you can use your value propositions for each identified market to help you develop a succinct message that will make your business clear to potential clients and customers. Try to think of three key words that would describe your business to anyone. What three words capture the essence of what you do and why you exist? Great example: Mary Kay's mantra is "Enriching women's lives." Put your company

succinct message
Your key point in as few and as memorable words as possible.

business cards
A 2- × 3½-inch cardboard card with your personal and company contact information; the key way of leaving information about yourself.

business stationery
A standard 8½ × 11-inch page of blank paper typically imprinted with your company's name and contact information.

brochure
A sales document, typically consisting of multiple panels (when folded) or multiple pages, describing your business or specific products or services.

flyers
A sales document to be posted or handed out, typically printed on a 8½ × 11-inch sheet of colored paper (or printed in color on white stock to increase visibility).

name and a short tag line on **business cards** and **stationery**. Hand out your cards to potential customers, give extras to friends and family for distribution, and post them on bulletin boards where potential clients may see them. Use your stationery whenever you correspond with clients to reinforce your company's message. **Brochures** and **flyers** are other important methods of promotion and ways to advertise your business. Brochure contents range from information about your company to specific product features and benefits. It may be appropriate to place all this information in one brochure or to create a family of brochures for individual products. Individual businesses and budgets may guide your decision. Flyers are usually single sheets printed front and back and used for inexpensive distribution. Flyers are frequently used to announce a sale, open house, or other limited-time event. One of the most inexpensive ways to design a brochure or flyer is to buy preprinted paper from your local office supply store (e.g., Staples, Office Direct, or Office Max; all also have an Internet Web site from which to order directly). Many of the latest office productivity tools for your computer already have embedded templates that can guide and assist you in customizing your own brochures and flyers (e.g., Microsoft Office templates).

Again, post flyers wherever your potential clients congregate, and use brochures and flyers for mail or e-mail campaigns. Also keep a stack in your briefcase for those chance meetings with people interested in your business. If you have a storefront or a company vehicle, make sure your company name and contact information is prominently displayed and adequately represents your business's image. Along these lines, give-away items like pens, key chains, or industry-specific novelties with your business information are also great ways to build awareness among potential clients. When conveying your message, consideration should be given to the following guidelines to help you communicate and promote your business:

- **Design and layout:** Is the material visually appealing and attractive? Does it invite the individual to open it or read further about your business? Do the layout components and design complement the message?
- **Formatting components of design and layout:** Do you have a good balance of text and white (or empty) space? Are the fonts, colors, graphics, illustrations, photos, and charts readable?
- **Written message:** Is the information accurate? Are the sentences simple and clearly written? Is the text grammatically correct? Does it spark the individual's curiosity? Does it communicate the benefits of your small business? Does the message ask the reader to respond? Does it tell the reader how to contact your business?
- **Management issues:** What is the specific marketing goal for this marketing piece? Who is the intended customer? Does the production cost fit within your budget? Does it complement your other marketing materials?

Publicity

press kits
Another vehicle to use for promotional purposes, press kits should include product or service brochures, press releases with the latest news about your company (new product, media mentions, etc.), biographies on you and key employees, and photos or digital images of products or services, if appropriate.

Press kits about your business are great vehicles for promotion. Other than your business cards and stationery, your press kit should include product or service brochures, press releases with the latest news about your company (new product, media mentions, etc.), biographies on you and key employees, and photos or digital images of products or services, if appropriate. You could also write articles on your own company and pitch the idea as a story to a newspaper or magazine. Whenever you run across a new media outlet appropriate to your clientele, add it to your media list. We will have an opportunity to explore further the use of press releases and ways to create an effective one later in the chapter.

Web Sites

Potential clients and customers may search for your business's services on the Internet. New small businesses may find a Web site useful as a cost-effective way of gaining new clients and keeping current customers. Your business's Web site should be

SMALL BUSINESS INSIGHT

A Web Strategy Runs Through It[5]

A business Web site doesn't win awards because it has cool features and bells and whistles that are part of many Web sites. It has to work for both the customers and the company. Recently rated as one of the top sites according to *Inc.* magazine, that's what really distinguishes the Web site of AO Rafting (**www.aorafting.com**). Established by a schoolteacher nearly 40 years ago, the company All-Outdoors Whitewater Rafting or AO Rafting is a multigenerational family business. It's a regional company in a seasonal business, with about $2 million in annual revenues and fewer than 20 permanent employees year round. However, during its eight-month annual season, AO Rafting employs more than 100 people including some 75 part-time guides. Based in Walnut Creek and Lotus, California, right by the mother lode that drew the forty-niners out west for the Gold Rush, this business seems isolated, deep in canyon country. Yet, it has built a Web presence that puts to shame a lot of other small businesses that may be more tech-savvy and have greater resources. Prospective customers can tour the Klamath and Tuolumne rivers through the site's virtual tours. They can also plan trips right on the site, check the availability of tours, make reservations, access real-time information on water conditions, refer the company to friends, and find discounts on trips. The site has virtually replaced almost all the traditional marketing and promotion that All-Outdoors Whitewater Rafting used to do.

www.aorafting.com

easy to read and understand by anyone visiting the site, and it should be possible for important information to be found within one to two clicks. Too much information may confuse visitors, and inappropriate graphics and "bells and whistles" may discourage repeat visitors. Effective sites include links for subscribing to e-newsletters, feedback forms, online press kits, and contact information, along with business and product descriptions. A company's Web site needs unique **keyword and description tags** for each screen in order to obtain a prominent listing on search engines.

keyword and description tags
Terms included in the hidden portion of a Web page (called the document head) which are used by search engines such as Yahoo! and Google to describe your Web site and evaluate its focus and category placement.

Professional Web developers and search engine specialists are able to analyze sites for their effectiveness in reaching target audiences and can help small business owners develop the site to best suit their needs.

Network Advertising: Referrals and Word-of-Mouth

When it comes to promoting a small business that is just starting out, spreading the news by word-of-mouth is the fastest way to build a client base. Whether a potential customer meets the owner directly or hears of the business secondhand, a connectedness is established that cannot be matched by advertising or other marketing methods. Entrepreneurs should make use of every opportunity to meet potential clients and expose them to their products or services. Ways to get face to face with new customers are by joining local or regional business networking groups and becoming involved in local business organizations like the Chamber of Commerce or trade groups. Secondhand exposure in the form of referrals from current customers also goes a long way in spreading the word about a new business. Business owners who are confident they have met or exceeded their clients' expectations should not be shy about asking them to pass on their name to others. Depending on the nature and type of business, business owners can offer discounts or incentives to customers who successfully bring in new clients.

THE THOUGHTFUL ENTREPRENEUR

Overcoming Stumbling Blocks to Spreading Word of Your Business[6]

The ability to connect with future customers and other small business owners is necessary to success in any business, small or large. Business events present opportunities to interact with others on a personal level and to develop profitable relationships. However, along the way, there may be several roadblocks that may influence your own way of talking about your small business to others.

- **Fear of talking to strangers:** To get past your discomfort in talking to strangers, set a goal for yourself before you attend any event. Decide how many new contacts you want to make or how many strangers you want to meet. In some cases, you may specifically target individuals whom you'd like to know. Next, come up with some icebreakers or conversation starters. Have questions prepared that you can ask anyone you meet at the event. You may want to inquire about other people's businesses, their connection to the sponsoring organization, or their opinion of the venue.
- **No formal introduction:** It is much easier to make a new contact when there is someone else to handle the introduction and pave the way. However, at many events, there may not be someone else there to give you that formal introduction. One way to overcome this is to, of course, walk up to people you don't know, introduce yourself, and start a conversation. You can do this if you have prepared your self-introduction in advance, and you do not need to introduce yourself the same way on every occasion. Perhaps it is your first time attending a business meeting. In that case, you might want to say so as part of your introduction. Let people know who you are and why you are there, and give them a reason to inquire more abut you.
- **Fear of being perceived as too pushy or aggressive:** You may think that you will turn people off if you are assertive and that if they want to talk to you, they will make the first move. If this is your line of thinking, you will find yourself spending your time alone at the reception or meeting and leaving without one new connection. Being open, friendly, and interested will not turn other individuals off. You may not come across as overly aggressive if you seek out the "approachable" people. These are the ones who are speaking in groups of three or more or standing alone. Two people talking to each other are not always approachable since they may be having a private conversation and you would be interrupting.

Whatever your stumbling blocks, face them before the next event and devise a personal strategy for getting past them. When you do, you will find yourself connecting with confidence and courtesy on every occasion, and the results will be reflected in sales for your small business.

If you ask most service providers how they get business, the answer is usually referrals or word-of-mouth.[7] Carter Prescott, head of New York-based Carter Communications, which provides high-level writing and speaking services for Fortune 500 clients, doesn't even have a listed phone number. "I've never needed one," she says. "It's better to have people call you on their own, rather than soliciting calls anyway. You get a better client that way." She only gets calls when a current client gives her number to a potential client.

Although this may be true, you still have to work to generate referrals. Even the most loyal customers aren't likely to think about generating business for you—they have other concerns. You may try many of these methods to build your word-of-mouth business and develop your client prospect list:

1. Offer incentives for referrals that turn into business. They can be in the form of discounts on future business, free estimates or samples, or just plain cash. Even a small offer will catch people's attention.
2. Create a referral form, and send it to clients or customers with your invoice for services rendered. If you've done a good job, the time to leverage yourself is upon completion of the project.
3. Ask for referrals from prospects who have turned you down. This gives them a graceful exit from a potentially unpleasant task. The only secret, as with any request, is to time it appropriately so that you offer people a natural, unforced opening to help you.
4. Tap your suppliers for leads by reminding them that when your business grows, theirs does, too. Spark this exchange by giving leads to your suppliers.

LO4
Learn the key skills involved in personal selling, especially closing the sale.

One cold call to a dealer can start *word-of-mouth advertising*[8] and get your product into stores. Lynn Gordon, proprietor of French Meadow Bakery in Minneapolis, Minnesota, started her bread-making business in her kitchen, producing 40 loaves a week for local co-ops. One day she made a cold call to a local gourmet shop, which started a word-of-mouth snowball. As luck would have it, the buyer was on a special diet, and Gordon's bread was just what she was looking for. Soon other grocery stores signed up. Meanwhile, customers sent loaves to friends around the country, who called to order more.

Under pressure from stores, distributors started asking for French Meadow bread. Next, Diane Sawyer and the *60 Minutes* crew showed up to do a story about the Women's Economic Development Corp., a program for women entrepreneurs in which Gordon was involved. Sawyer highlighted Gordon and her gourmet bread on the show. Then the state helped subsidize a trip to the International Fancy Food & Confection Show in Chicago, where 300 stores placed orders. Will Steger, the tundra explorer, ordered Gordon's bread for the international trip he was leading across the Antarctic. Even Neiman Marcus bought French Meadow bread to include in a $5,000 Ultimate Cocktail Buffet. As a result of that first cold call, Gordon moved her operation into a 13,500-square-foot storefront bakery in Minneapolis, where she eventually employed 15 people.

■ Entrepreneurs are, in a sense, always selling their company/product/service. Being skilled in personal selling is important for many reasons. What elements of the process of personal selling are you confident in? Are there elements you think you need to practice?

The Importance of Personal Selling

Entrepreneurs just starting out with their small businesses must wear many hats—president, CEO, marketing director, and in some cases, general contractor. However, it has often been said that no hat bears as much responsibility as salesperson. With each personal interaction, business owners represent their business and effectively have the opportunity to gain new customers. Learning about the **process of personal selling** may result in new business from your direct contacts and also from their referrals.

process of personal selling
The process of selling your products and service; includes prospect and evaluate, prepare, present, and the close.

Personal selling is an important technique for the small business owner for a number of reasons:

1. You can craft your product or service message to answer a customer's specific questions and needs. Compared to the uniform and general messages of marketing materials, personal selling offers the customer more information, thereby increasing the chance of completing a sale.
2. You can gain information on how you can make your product or service better, or adjust it to better meet customers' needs. You may also find that your potential and current customers have found new ways to use your product, thus opening up new potential markets.
3. You can gain personal information about your potential customer, especially relating to communication preferences. One-on-one interactions give you a feel for how people like to be treated and how they best process information.
4. You can direct your focus on the most promising potential sales, and cultivate them with personal attention.

The Process of Personal Selling[9]

While selling may be thought of as an art, there is a general formula for generating interest in your product or service:

1. **Prospect and evaluate:** Gather prospective customer names through sales records, referrals, newspapers, classified ads, and even the phone book if that is appropriate. Wherever you believe your customers can be found, search out their contact information. To save time, analyze your prospect list and determine if there are any reasons that may prevent some people from becoming customers. For example, your unlicensed prospect might not want to buy a car from your dealership.
2. **Prepare:** Review the prospect list and gather as much information as possible on a person or a company's key decision maker. If appropriate, check credit history, speak with the person who had given the referral, find out about the person's business. You will more easily meet people's needs and answer their questions if you do this.
3. **Present:** When designing and giving a presentation, remember AIDA:
   - Hold the prospect's *attention.* As much as 80 percent of sales success is a direct result of a good opening statement or headline. This is your first impression—it's critical. And it should be crafted with care. What you say here determines whether your prospect is going to listen eagerly or shut the door in your face. A key benefit helps. "We've just received our largest shipment of coffee mugs ever. Check them out before you leave us today!"
   - Stimulate *interest.* This next step is designed to generate increasing interest from the prospect. This must be done by quickly establishing a relationship. Individuals don't do business with individuals they don't trust. Demonstrate that you have a solution to the problem or need. Show prospects how they might benefit by allowing you to go into further detail about the solution that you have for them.
   - Stir up *desire* in the product, leading to the potential customer taking the appropriate *action.* This step is simple yet often overlooked. You need to ask the prospect to take action now (or you lose a sale). You must be proactive by asking for the order. Give prospects an incentive to act now. There are many tools to move people to immediate action. It may be a special price, a free add-on, or any number of incentives. "All you need to do is sign here, and we'll get started on it right away. And since you are a first-time customer, I'd like to give you a 20 percent discount if you buy today."

A good presentation must be able to change at any point in order to meet the needs of potential customers and should highlight how your product is the best product to meet your clients' needs. Encourage questions and be prepared to answer every one to your customers' satisfaction. They will not be ready to make the buying decision if questions still linger.

4. **The Close:** Beyond stimulating interest, ask prospects to buy your product! Don't assume they will jump in at the end of your presentation and write a check. Be prepared to close the deal using any of a number of techniques:
   - **Trial close** ("Which credit card would you like to use to pay for that?")
   - **Assumptive close** ("I'll just need your credit card for payment.")
   - **Urgency close** ("This rate will end at the end of the day.")

The Art of Closing[10]

SKILL MODULE 10.2

Consider the closing advice from entrepreneur Barbara Corcoran, chairman of The Corcoran Group, a $2.5 billion New York City real estate firm. Corcoran says guidelines that helped make her one of the nation's top realtors can be applied by salespeople across the board. Here are a few of her tips:

- **Restate the need.** Ask what clients' requirements are, then reword them—including needs they hadn't thought of or couldn't articulate. As mentioned in her book, *Use What You've Got,* tie those needs to your product or service.
- **"When would you want it?"** You should ask this early on. The answers will help gauge customers' urgency levels and the effectiveness of your strategy.
- **Get feedback.** "Ask customers what they like and dislike about everything you show them," she says. Their responses will help guide you to the close.
- **Forewarn customers about buyer's remorse.** If you're selling big-ticket items that include out-clauses or money back guarantees, inoculate clients against buyers' remorse by reinforcing their need for the product and sharing other buyers' positive experiences.
- **Practice.** "Role-playing puts your inhibitions to rest and results in a well-prepared, confident delivery," says Corcoran, who started her firm with just $1,000.
- **Ask to be last in line.** "When you know you'll be competing in a beauty lineup, ask for last position. You don't want to hear, 'We still have a few other people to meet' after you've made your presentation. If you're in last position, your competitors are out of the way." Then you can gently ask about offers they made and then counter or top them, she suggests.
- **Take your assistant along.** You may discount this, but customers "respond well to someone important enough to have help," Corcoran says. The attention of two people shows that the client is important as well.
- **If your buyer gets cold feet, unfurl more benefits.** Recapping the pluses, and perhaps throwing in related benefits, can reaffirm the decision to buy.
- **Play your hand.** Don't focus on a single element such as price. Use everything in your arsenal—"delivery, date, financing terms, warranties, and extras," she says.
- **Weigh the angles before you start.** If you're bidding or negotiating, you'll be able to overcome objections before they become an issue.
- **Don't rush.** "Buyers change their mind when pushed to buy before they're really ready," Corcoran says.
- **Don't outbid yourself when bidding on a project.** Your first low bid could become the ceiling.
- **Counter with care.** When closing in on a final counteroffer, use delaying tactics. "When you reply, 'I'll try to have an answer for you in an hour,' you build anticipation" and the lesser the chance it will be quickly tossed off with another counter, Corcoran says.
- **When in doubt, get more facts.** Squelched deals usually result from careless haste, not prudent review.
- **Scope the bottom line.** To overbid a rival, ask, "What number will make this deal happen? Without knowing the number, you're only shadow-boxing," she says.

5. **Follow Up:** If you closed on the sale, what your customer needs now is service. Follow up the sale to see if the order went smoothly or if further assistance is needed; it helps you track your success and learn where there's room for improvement. A follow-up call will:

- Give the customer short-term satisfaction.
- Stimulate referrals.
- Encourage repurchasing.
- Prevent **cognitive dissonance**.

cognitive dissonance
Doubt that occurs after a purchase has been made. An inconsistency between experience and belief.

The important objective of follow-up is to make your customer feel at ease. Do this by staying with the clients for a few minutes postsale and get to know them. Ongoing correspondence (e.g., sending follow-up and greeting cards) may be useful for the business. Building relationships over time is an investment in building your sales.[11]

Press and Public Relations

LO5
Differentiate public relations from advertising and know how to write a press release.

public relations
Activities used to establish and promote a favorable opinion by the public.

One issue in marketing that is often discussed is the difference between **public relations** and advertising, and when to use one versus the other. Unless you are Coca-Cola or Microsoft, full-blown advertising campaigns are not where early-stage companies typically look to invest their limited marketing dollars. In short, advertising is often used to support the corporate identity and value propositions that are established through public relations efforts. And, with a product like software or hardware, for example, things like product reviews and other third-party endorsements become much more valuable than an advertisement, in which the company can control the messages used.

For example, how many times have you been in line at the grocery store and gotten into a random conversation with a stranger about a particular brand of food? You don't know this person, yet you take his or her recommendation that the Sara Lee pound cake is the best brand on the market and buy three on your way out of the store. Did you really need those pound cakes? And are you sure they truly *are* the best on the market? Probably not. But that is the power of third-party endorsement. And in many ways that is how public relations works.

Advertising, on the other hand, is in the same marketing family as public relations but often plays a much different role. As seen earlier with advertising, companies specifically choose their messages and are able to have total control over their image, unlike public relations. Advertising is great for targeting a consumer market and for getting the attention of other niche audiences, but, as a whole, public relations is effective in helping to build the foundation, and, after that has been laid, advertising acts as a supportive maintenance program. One of the ways to jump start your public relation campaign is to learn how to develop a press release.

The Basics of a Press Release[12]

press release
A written announcement intended to draw news media attention to a specific event.

One of the most critical lessons that entrepreneurs need to learn is that writing **press releases** is about formulating and developing a persuasive communication within the framework of a traditional news story format. Many editors will quickly look away from press and media releases that make outlandish promotional promises—"everyone wins," "the best ever," and "one-of-a-kind." Instead, put yourself in the reporter's shoes. That is, press releases *must* follow journalistic style in order to be given any kind of consideration. How do you accomplish this? Below are some guidelines and suggestions of how to structure your own press release:

- Start with the *headline:* In ten words or less you will need to grab the attention of the editor. In essence, the headline should summarize the information in the press release, but in a way that is exciting and dynamic. Think of it as a billboard along a highway. You have just a few words to make your release stand out from among the many others the editors receive at any given time or day.

- Second, open with your summary lead (the *opening paragraph*): This first paragraph is critical since it must explain the "five Ws and one H" of the story—*the who, what, when, where, why,* and *how.* This paragraph must summarize the press release, with the following paragraphs providing the detail. This opening paragraph should also contain the important hook—the one thing that gets your audience interested in reading more. Keep in mind that the hook has to be relevant to your audience as well as to the news media. It is a factual statement that is neither a devious promotion nor a hard sell.
- Third, start the *body* of the press release: The body of the press release should be written with the most important information and quotes first. One strategy is to use the *inverted pyramid technique.* To do so, start the news release with the most important part of your story. You should clearly state the "who, what, where, when, why, and how" of your story in the first paragraph. Follow this with the second most important information and end with the details. If editors need to cut your story to fit space restraints, they can edit from the end without losing critical information.
- Finally, the *closing paragraph:* In this last paragraph, include the critical contact information, such as your name, phone number, and e-mail address.

Writing a Press Release

SKILL MODULE 10.3

Start by going to **http://www.pressbox.co.uk/Sports/index.html** This Web site has thousands of press releases that are submitted to the pressbox newswire and directory every day. It also has several categories of press releases ranging from arts, business, sports, and technology. Pick one of your favorite categories and start reviewing several of the newly posted press releases, some good, and some needing improvement. Your task is to find one that is less appealing and probably would have a difficult time catching the editor's eye. Given the information provided in the press release along with any additional information (Web site address, additional contacts), rewrite the press release so that it would capture the attention of the media. Again, consider how the information provided in the press release benefits the individual reader. Using all the recommendations mentioned, make sure you get the five Ws and one H of the story—*the who, what, when, where, why,* and *how.* When you're finished, take the original press release and your revised one to one of your classmates. Have him or her critique both and ask which of the two he or she believes would grab the attention of the press and other readers.

http://www.pressbox.co.uk/Sports/index.html

- Simply ask yourself how meaningful your topic would be to a large audience. The more people who would be interested, the better chance you have at getting your story covered in the local or national media.
- Write your press release about an event that doesn't happen every day. There are press releases that have been written to announce someone's promotion in a small to midsize company. However, and the fact of the matter is, individuals are out there finding jobs and getting promoted every day of the week. If you can find something uncommon having to do with your announcement, focus on that. It will certainly capture a reader's interest for a longer period of time and have a greater chance of being picked up by the press.
- Even if you have found something to write your release about that would be interesting and meaningful to a majority of people, you might want to consider whether or not the topic will promote your business. After all, writing the press release was intended to gain publicity.

FIGURE 10.1

Secrets of Successful Press Releases

Successful press releases do not just "happen." They usually offer one or more of the proven techniques given here for getting the reader's attention.

- How will the information you provide in the press release benefit the individual reader? Many of us read an article, an advertisement, or anything at all only if it serves to benefit our own interest somehow.
- Entrepreneur Jane has been looking for a software technology firm to contract with and that just happens to be exactly what your business does. Jane runs across an article published in a local paper that was based entirely on your press release. What would the article have to do to inspire Jane to actually hire you instead of someone else? You should have a call to action so that Jane has a motivational reason to contact you.
- Finally, don't write your release from your own point of view. After all, you are already sold on what you do. In order to grab the attention of readers step into their shoes. Write what would interest them and what they want to hear. Focus on what the public pays the most attention to in order to get your message across.

Resources for E-Mailing Press Releases[13]

http://www.abyznewslinks.com

http://www.gebbieinc.com

http://www.ajr.org

Once you have developed your press release, there are a plethora of Web sites that can assist you in sending or e-mailing your press release to the appropriate media. These include:

- ABYZ News Links—contains links to more than 17,200 newspapers and other news sources from around the world: http://www.abyznewslinks.com
- Gebbie Press—where you will find a wealth of media information: http://www.gebbieinc.com
- American Journalism Review—a great link to media sources that are on the Internet: http://www.ajr.org

FIGURE 10.2

Sample Press Release

Source: Reprinted with permission of 8minuteDating.com.

■ 8minuteDating.com, the pioneer in offering speed dating services, started small and now reaches over 60,000 customers in 55 major cities. What elements of their Cupid Party press release illustrate how 8minute successfully attracts and relates to its market audience?

Draft release: Jan. 23

Contact:	Chris Perkett	Tom Jaffee
	PerkettPR, Inc.	8minuteDating.com
	781-555-5852	617-555-7764, x201
	chris@perkettpr.com	tom@8minutedating.com

8minuteDating.com Hosts "Biggest Dating Event in History" on February 11

8minuteDating.com Cupid Parties provide singles in 47 cities across the U.S. and Canada with a unique alternative for Valentine's Day

Boston, Mass. — Jan. 27, 2003 — 8minuteDating.com, the world leader in round robin dating, today announced it will be holding the largest recorded dating event in history on Tuesday, February 11. The "8minuteDating.com Cupid Party" will be held in 47 cities at 59 venues across the U.S. and Canada, providing singles with a fun new way to enjoy the Valentine holiday, as well as the opportunity to meet someone. The marquee event will be held at the Hard Rock Café on 57th Street in New York City.

Single people often dread Valentine's Day because they want something fun to do that offers the possibility of making a romantic connection. The 8minuteDating.com Cupid Parties are not only a great party, but using the automated 8minuteDating.com matching system, participants are likely to get a date in time for Valentine's Day.

"Today's singles are busier than ever and they need help meeting people to date," said Tom Jaffee, CEO and founder, 8minuteDating.com. "8minuteDating is the 'bar scene made better' because participants get to meet like-minded people every eight minutes, rather than staying clustered with their friends in a smoky bar. It's a fun party, and we expect about 60 percent of the participants to find a date in time for Valentine's Day."

Appealing to America's 82 million singles of diverse ages, ethnicities and sexual orientations, 8minuteDating.com provides a fast, fun, safe and comfortable way to meet people for dating, friendship or business. 8minuteDating.com is the first and the largest company to bring together the best of today's most popular dating services, combining the ease of the Internet with the opportunity to meet a room full of like-minded people, face-to-face, before committing to a lengthy one-on-one date.

How does it work?

— An equal number of single men and women gather at a restaurant or other venue.

— Each person has eight one-on-one dates that last eight minutes each.

— To keep the conversations comfortable for everyone, participants do not ask anyone for their last name, for their phone number or for a date.

— An intermission enables participants to meet everyone at the event, in addition to their pre-determined eight dates.

— After the event, participants log on to www.8minuteDating.com and enter the names of the people they want to meet again, whether it's for dating, friendship or business.

— Whenever two people enter each other's names in the same category, 8minuteDating.com automatically sends the contact information to both people so they can set up another date.

Guaranteed Success

More than 99 percent of 8minuteDating.com attendees report that they enjoyed their evening of 8minuteDating. Of that number, 81 percent had a "very good" or "excellent" time. An overwhelming 96 percent of attendees say they would attend another 8minuteDating.com event, and 95 percent recommend 8minuteDating.com to others. Most importantly, more than 90 percent of participants meet someone who they want to see again. In fact, the company guarantees that if a participant does not meet someone who they want to see again, their next event is free.

Cupid Party Information

For information regarding the nearest 8minuteDating.com Cupid Party, please visit www.8minutedating.com.

About 8minuteDating.com

8minuteDating.com, part of Match Events Inc., is the world leader in round robin dating. 8minuteDating.com's mission is to create a fast, fun, safe and comfortable way for singles of all ages, religions, ethnicities, sexual orientations and other special interests to meet for dating, friendship or business. Match Events, Inc. was founded in 2001 by Tom Jaffee, a successful high tech entrepreneur. The company is headquartered in Boston, Mass., and can be reached online at www.8minutedating.com.

LO6
Know what "news" is and how to leverage the press to generate publicity.

newsworthy events
To garner serious attention from the media and the public, a news story needs to deliver certain essentials that will hold their attention and keep your news in their thoughts. It should have public recognition, importance, and interest.

public recognition
Being recognized or acknowledged by large numbers of people, similar to "fame."

issue recognition
A concept in public recognition which alludes to the extent to which the public is familiar with the issue or problem at hand.

trendiness
A concept in public recognition which alludes to the fit of the topic to current fashion or public interest.

famous faces
A concept in public recognition which alludes to connections of your event or firm to individuals the general public would recognize.

proximity
A concept in public recognition which alludes to the impact level of the issue being discussed.

public importance
(1) Things that are considered important to large numbers of otherwise unrelated people, (2) things that are of civic importance, as opposed to private or corporate entities.

power
A concept in public importance which alludes to potential shifts in control or influence.

currency
A concept in public importance which alludes to the degree to which the issue is immediate in its impact.

What Is Newsworthy?[14]

Press releases are meant to draw the attention of the public to something that's new and **newsworthy** which could be a range of things, from products and people to services and solutions. To further garner serious attention from the media and the public, a news story needs to deliver certain essentials that will hold readers' attention, and keep your news in their thoughts. It should have public recognition, public importance, and public interest.

Public recognition includes **issue recognition** (Have you solved a problem that is an at-large issue? If your problem is not familiar to the public, people need to be familiarized with it before they understand your news), **trendiness** (Is your news a low-carb diet or a Cabbage Patch Kid? That is, will you be able to ride the wave of fashion or will you be just another in a long and dated line of related stories?), **famous faces** (If the news is connected to one or more recognizable people or organizations, the public will already feel a connection to the story.), and **proximity** (News is sure to attract attention if it can potentially affect a number of people. The more people it will affect, the further your story will spread.). **Public importance** includes **power** (Does your news represent a power struggle or shift? Power affects the community, and the farther its potential reach, the more newsworthy the event.) and **currency** (Your event will have its greatest importance while the issues are current. Will your news be connected to other recent events?). Finally, **public interest** includes a **good story** (Does your news present a good conflict and resolution? Nothing grabs attention and memory better than a good story.), **human interest** (A character with whom the public can relate helps generate interest and attention. Can you pull human interest into your news? The human interest story line helps connect the news to the audience with emotion.), **visuals** (graphics—action, photography, and so on—draw attention to the piece, making another connection between viewer and the news. Are there interesting visuals in the piece?), and **cultural resonance** (Broad cultural themes expose the event or news to a wider audience. Does the event or campaign speak to a wide demographic range? Is it meant to?).

Even though something is "new," it might not have enough of the three "essentials" above to grab the attention you had hoped. For example, hiring nonexecutives doesn't hold importance for the media. Even new products aren't newsworthy unless they are something new and innovative on the market.

Leveraging the Press and Generating Publicity

How do you further leverage the press to grow your business? The press can be extremely valuable in helping businesses of all sizes succeed and gain market share by generating a high level of exposure to a wide audience. As discussed above, the first challenge is to develop that unique story or angle, but once that is done the next task is to find the appropriate person at specific press outlets that would be interested in this news. All reporters or editors have their own beat, so it's imperative that you do your research before approaching them to find out what kinds of stories they typically write, what trends might be interesting to the audiences they write for, and whether or not they just did a similar story last week.

For a small business, mentions in the "corporate notes" sections of the daily and local business papers are a good way to start. These are great places to list new client acquisitions, project completions with substantial results, and new hires—all reflective of a solid, growing company. Consumers and companies want to buy goods and services from a company that has demonstrated it's going to be around in a few years, not one that has an interesting idea but can't properly articulate why the idea is good.

Three Ways to Generate Publicity[15]

Even though it may be the latest innovation on the market, a newsworthy product, event, or service always benefits from well-planned publicity. Aside from advertising, there are several tools that can help your news gather a piece of the limelight.

1. Write or provide materials:
    - Offer exclusive articles, photos, or columns to publications that are read by your target audience.
    - Offer (through a national service) ready-to-reproduce, typeset feature stories to smaller newspapers (**mat releases**, color pages).
    - Not-for-profit organizations can produce public service announcements for broadcast, print, and other media.
    - Produce and distribute video or audio news releases for the broadcast media.
    - Produce your own program or short feature for the broadcast media. Depending on distribution rights, this might also be used as a video brochure or for other groups.
    - Include your products as props for films and TV shows (consider whether the show's message would help or hinder your product's image).
2. Conduct interviews:
    - Appear on local TV talk shows or radio call-in shows.
    - Hire a professional spokesperson to make appearances and talk about your product or service.
    - Take your message to the media on a multicity media tour.
3. Stage events:
    - Educate the media on your news by holding a seminar or program in your community.
    - Let the media come to you—offer your facilities as TV, movies, or commercial sets.
    - Become involved in charitable events that will earn recognition for your organization.
    - Offer your products as prizes at events, and make sure the media know of the event.
    - Sponsor or financially support awards for media coverage of an industry, issue, or event.[16]

Figure 10.3 offers some additional ideas for generating news for your business.

Having a great product or service does not do you or your business any good if potential customers do not know about it. Getting the word out about your business and its offerings is the purpose of promotion in small business. The avenues for getting the word out are fairly well known—current or potential customers, the press, and

public interest
(1) Things that are generally considered to be beneficial to large numbers of people, (2) civic causes and benefits, as opposed to private and corporate benefits.

good story
A concept in public interest which alludes to an incident with good triumphing.

human interest
A concept in public interest which alludes to a character to whom the public can relate.

visuals
A concept in public interest which alludes to the graphic interest held by an event.

cultural resonance
A concept in public interest which alludes to events with a broad appeal within the market or population.

mat release
A news release that is typeset and thus may be photographically reproduced for inclusion in a newspaper.

■ Vermont Teddy Bear Company, whose products are pictured, promotes their merchandise primarily through radio spots. What marketing and promotion research and factors do you think have motivated their choice to focus on radio advertising as their main avenue of generating publicity?

FIGURE 10.3

Top 10 Ideas for Generating News for Your Organization[17]

Many of these techniques and methods for generating news about your small business are cost-effective and can place your business in a positive light the next time you promote your business—not only to your primary market but to new customers who may have a future need for your particular product or service.

1. **Tie in with news events of the day.** Perhaps your product or service can address a current news event. Offer your news through press releases as a solution or to provide further information.
2. **Issue a report.** Release findings on a topic related to your organization and its products or services. Gather the information yourself, or hire a research firm. One example could be a report on teen smoking released by a cancer research organization.
3. **Arrange for a testimonial.** Make sure your organization receives the attention it deserves through testimonials of satisfied clients. Knowing someone has been satisfied with your organization has even more weight when that testimonial comes from a public figure.
4. **Announce an appointment.** When new colleagues with impressive backgrounds are hired at an organization or new appointments have been made, be sure the media and your clients are aware. New appointments in many cases mean new direction from individuals with expertise.
5. **Issue a summary of facts.** Announce facts about or related to your products, services, or events to draw attention to their usefulness. For example, issue facts about heart disease, and then announce how your medication can address these concerns.
6. **Present an award.** Honoring people and other organizations benefits everyone. Recognize an expert or volunteer in your field or a local hero, and continue to do so through the years.
7. **Hold or sponsor a contest.** This could draw upon many of the above ideas and add some fun as well. For example, an insurance company could sponsor "Fire Safety Week" and offer prizes to children for the best poster relating to fire safety. This will have even more of an impact if educational seminars are held in conjunction with the event.
8. **Stage a special event.** Be sure it's related to your organization and reflects a positive image. This could be a "gala" fund-raiser for your nonprofit, or an all-day concert for your radio station.
9. **Organize a tour.** This could be a tour of your facilities or other places related to your news or event. Couple this with brief educational seminars at the locations for added value. Media, especially from the trade, are sure to cover the event.
10. **Tie in to a well-known week or day.** Can you relate your news, organization, or event to a well-known local or national event, like a community summer festival or a national fund-raising event? Doing so could bring attention to your involvement and associate your organization with the popular event for those attending.

these days the Internet—but because everyone knows those avenues, crafting and distributing a message that people will notice and respond to amid all the ads they face is an ever-increasing challenge. This chapter focuses on preparing you with the basic skills of press and public relations, as well as advice on what makes promotion efforts pay off. Armed with these ideas, you *can* make your business stand out and be noticed. The other key role of this chapter is to discuss the specifics of selling—how to get started and how to close sales. In the end, sales are everything, because everything in business depends on sales. If you can master promotion and selling, your business will have gone much of the way toward eventual success.

CHAPTER SUMMARY

L01 Understand how to assess your value proposition.

- Craft your value proposition to present your firm's unique selling points.
- Tailor your value proposition to the needs of your intended customers.

LO2 Segment and further define your target audience.

- Aim for a narrow segment (or portion) of the market.
- Develop a profile of the needs of your target market.
- Match your product or service and promotion to your target market's needs.

LO3 Recognize the different approaches and methods you can use to convey your promotional message.

- Follow the basic methods for conveying your message.
- The basic methods include:
  - Business cards, brochures, flyers, and signage.
  - Advertising in the media outlets.
  - Publicity and press kits.
  - Web site.
  - Network advertising.
  - Referrals and word-of-mouth.
  - Methods to build your word-of-mouth business.
  - Developing of your client prospect list.

LO4 Learn the key skills involved in personal selling, especially closing the sale.

- Recognize the importance of personal selling.
- Key process of personal selling includes prospect and evaluate, prepare, and present.
- The art of closing the sale includes:
  - Restate the need. "When would you want it?"
  - Get feedback. Forewarn customers about buyer's remorse.
  - Practice.
  - Ask to be last in line. Take your assistant along.
  - If your buyer gets cold feet, unfurl more benefits.
  - Play your hand.
  - Weigh the angles before you start. Don't outbid yourself when bidding on a project—counter with care.
  - Scope the bottom line.
  - Follow up the sale (in order to stimulate referrals, encourage repurchasing, and prevent cognitive dissonance).

LO5 Differentiate public relations from advertising and know how to write a press release.

- Recognize the key differences between public relations and advertising and know when to use one or the another.
- Public relations can be of great value to the small business.

- The structure of press release includes:
  - Headline.
  - Opening paragraph.
  - Body.
  - Closing paragraph.
- Make your press release draw attention and catch the eye of the average reader.
- Make use of the resources for e-mailing press releases.

LO6 Know what "news" is and how to leverage the press to generate publicity.

- The essentials of determining what news is include:
  - Public recognition.
  - Importance.
  - Interest.
- There are three ways to generate publicity coverage:
  - Write or provide materials.
  - Conduct interviews.
  - Stage events.
- Top 10 ideas for generating news for your small business include:
  - Tie in with news events of the day.
  - Issue a report.
  - Arrange for a testimonial.
  - Announce an appointment.
  - Issue a summary of facts.
  - Present an award.
  - Hold or sponsor a contest.
  - Stage a special event.
  - Organize a tour.
  - Tie in to a well-known week or day.

DISCUSSION QUESTIONS

1. What are some ways that you see small business owners promote their products or services? Provide examples of your perception of their value proposition to each of the markets they are currently targeting. In your opinion, how effective do you think some of their messages are?
2. What are some ways that you could use secondary research to better understand the various segments of your market and to develop your promotional materials?

3. In your opinion, what do you think is the most effective and efficient way for small business owners to promote and market their products or services? Why?

4. How have you seen the use of referrals and word-of-mouth advertising work to the benefit of a small business owner? Provide examples. How have these methods worked in reverse (to the disadvantage of the owner, but possibly to the benefit of the competition)?

5. Recall the last time you purchased a product or service from a small firm. Did it use any of the techniques or skills involved in personal selling? How did the salesperson close the sale with you?

6. If you were consulting for a small firm, what advice would you give to the owner on how to write a press release? What specific tips would you give him or her on ways that they could generate publicity for the business?

EXPERIENTIAL EXERCISES

1. Collect promotional materials from a small business in your area. These can include coupons, loyalty programs, special tie-ins, special events, advertisements, or any other promotional materials. Using these materials, answer the following questions:

- What is the owner trying to achieve with these promotions? What are the goals and objectives of each? If you take the various promotions as a portfolio, what overall goal do they have?
- What incentives (for the customer) are embedded in the promotion materials?
- What business image or business characteristics do these promotions convey or imply?
- Assuming limited funds, how would you improve the promotions for this business? Be sure to tie your ideas to specific goals.

2. Compare the promotional materials from two competitive (small) businesses. What are the goals and objectives of the promotions? How well do you think they fulfill these objectives?

3. Visit three independently owned small retail establishments in the same industry or business. Ask the manager of each business the following questions. What target market(s) does your store appeal to? How are the target markets different? If I were a member of your target market, why would I shop at your store? What new information from your research about the industry can the owners use to improve and enhance what they are currently offering? Or how are they promoting their business based on the latest trends within the industry?

4. Read your local newspaper for information about a small business that you think stems from a publicity effort (e.g., new location or management, product line shift or expansion, special events, or promotions). Compare the information in the article to Web site information and to business advertisements for the same business. What are the differences and similarities? Advantages and disadvantages (for the business and for the customer)?

5. Imagine that you own a small independent bookstore. You are holding a special reading and book signing by a well-known author:

    a. Describe what your goal(s) might be in arranging this event.

    b. Write a press release for the event.

    c. What other events might support the same goal(s)?

    d. Describe how you might use this information in crafting a newspaper advertisement for the store.

    e. Compare the press release, the ad, and any other events arranged in terms of overall promotional strategy for the store.

Mini-Case

MAKING A FASHION STATEMENT: ENTREPRENEUR FOCUSES ON RAISING PROFITS, AWARENESS[18]

Michelle Moran's business plan was, "Do well by persuading shoppers to do good." And the plan is about to be tested. Her two clothing lines, imparted with the lofty mission of educating women about breast cancer and heart disease and raising money for nonprofit groups fighting the illnesses, appear this month at Saks Fifth Avenue in Boston and nearly 50 area T. J. Maxx stores.

"My goal is to use fashion as a vehicle to help women," Moran, 38, said. "Not just as a promotion, but every day." Her aim may sound better-suited for a nonprofit venture than a money-making entity. But Moran's Allston company, Clothes for a Cause, is decidedly for profit. Founded in 1996, the company first turned a profit in 2001. In 2003, it generated millions of dollars in revenues. Because the company is private, however, Moran does not disclose its financial details. Moran commits as much as 10 percent of all her wholesale sales, or roughly 5 percent of the retail price, to a cause. So far, that hasn't translated into huge sums. The American Heart Association expects to raise at least $16,500 from the sales of the Red Dress Collection at the Saks Boston store. The Big Bam!, a nonprofit dedicated to providing mammograms and breast cancer treatment for uninsured women, is expecting its first check for $7,300 from sales of the Pink Ribbon Collection.

"I think the potential for this project is massive," said Janice Bonadio, the president and founder of The Big Bam! The move to imbue Clothes for a Cause with a social conscience is as much about smart business, as it is about doing good. Fashion goliaths such as Jones Apparel Group, Ralph Lauren, and Tommy Hilfiger dominate department stores, while small clothing makers fight for slivers of space on the store floor. At a time when retailers are struggling to offer something different from their rivals and consumers are increasingly concerned about corporate responsibility, Moran's social mission gives her an edge over the thousands of other small clothing makers knocking on retailers' doors. "It opened the door," said Bill Lynch, Saks's senior vice president of merchandising. "Whether we decide to buy her clothes ultimately depends on the product."

Though few companies go as far as Moran in promising to donate a percentage of all sales to nonprofit causes, corporate marketing in the name of philanthropy is on the rise. Corporate sponsorship of nonprofits reached $922 million in 2003, up from $125 million in 1990, according to *IEG Sponsorship Report,* a Chicago newsletter that tracks corporate partnerships with nonprofit groups. Saks donates 2 percent of all sales during a four-day stretch in September to nonprofit groups as part of its "Fashion Targets Breast Cancer" campaign. Companies like Target Corp. are moving beyond annual promotions to link their brands with broader charitable commitments. Through its Take Charge of Education program, Target donates 1 percent of sales made at its stores with a Target Visa or Target Guest Card, giving about $2 million a week to the nation's schools. In perhaps the most extreme example, actor Paul Newman's firm, Newman's Own, donates 100 percent of its profits to educational and charitable organizations and has raised more than $150 million for nonprofits since 1982.

T. J. Maxx plans to support Clothes for a Cause's Pink Ribbon Collection with plenty of signage in its stores. The line features ready-to-wear walking and running suits, cotton polo shirts, and capri pants in colors from aqua to black, and bears just a hint of the pink ribbon in its designs. Down the line, T. J. Maxx will also feature the Red Dress Collection at its Marshalls stores. Shoppers can expect to see both collections in the fall on a major shopping network, though Moran can't disclose which one. "It's nice to know the money goes somewhere to help people," said Fran Marroni, as she perused the Red Dress Collection at Saks with her sister Anne Marroni and their friend Patti Abrams. "It makes you feel good about shopping."

Tags attached to the pieces at Saks give information about heart disease and stroke. Pamphlets on a nearby table provide more information about heart health. Anne Marroni bought a $278 red silk jacket, and Abrams said she'd likely return for the collection's $190 halter dress.

Research shows that one-time or annual promotions do boost sales. More comprehensive efforts can improve a company's image. But the social good remains secondary behind more typical considerations, including price, quality, and store location, said Mark Feldman, executive vice president at Cone Inc., a marketing firm that specializes in cause branding. "That said, in a time when it is harder than ever before to differentiate yourself from rivals with similar brands and products, cause-related marketing is rapidly becoming a cost of doing business," Feldman said. As companies team up with nonprofits to further their commercial interests, however, nonprofit executives are wary of being exploited. Janice Bonadio, of The Big Bam!, said she receives a stack of 20 proposals each month from retailers seeking her permission to use the group's name or logo in connection with some promotion. In most cases, she said, she turns them down because the companies offer little to nothing in return for using Big Bam!'s name.

"The dominant perspective among charities is that some money is better than nothing," said Peter Frumkin, an associate professor of public policy at Harvard University's John F. Kennedy School of Government. For charities, however, there's more to gain than money. The Red Dress Collection furthers the mission of the American Heart Association to raise awareness about heart disease and about the organization, said Heather Maloney, spokeswoman for the association's Boston division. The group sent e-mails to 15,000 volunteers, donors, and invitees to its annual gala event, letting them know where they can find the red dresses.

"This is one more way to reach out to a new group of women," Maloney said. On a recent evening at Saks, three 20-something friends browsed through the Red Dress Collection. They stopped at the nearby table to flip through the heart health pamphlet. Tean Wong, a 27-year-old fashion school graduate, said the idea was smart. But she thought the collection should include shoes, makeup, and a broader range of styles. She and her friends found the Red Dress Collection a bit mature for their tastes. No sale. But Moran still sees it as a small victory.

"If a woman gets the information, even if she doesn't buy anything, well, I think we've achieved something," she said.

CASE DISCUSSION QUESTIONS

1. In order to maintain profits and still contribute 5 percent of the retail price to a cause, what promotional strategies will Moran have to come up with to stay competitive with the big retail giants?
2. What is the primary target market segment for the Red Dress Collection, and how will Moran make this clear to her audience? Would offering several lines of clothing be cost-beneficial for this company?
3. Identify some events or organizations where Moran can potentially create a business relationship. Does Clothes for a Cause effectively utilize the media? How can it do this better?
4. What characteristics about the Red Dress Collection would motivate someone to purchase the clothing? (Think along the lines of developing a value proposition.)

LEARNING OBJECTIVES

This chapter will help you:

LO1 Recognize the different types of direct marketing and their pros and cons.

LO2 Master using the Internet as a distribution channel.

LO3 Learn how to do nondirect distribution.

LO4 Differentiate the types of international strategies.

LO5 Identify the factors to consider in selecting your business location.

LO6 Set up your home-based business location.

LO7 Know what to look for in evaluating a potential site layout.

LO8 Understand the pros and cons of buying, building, or leasing.

■ Steve Niewulis's original marketing efforts focused on major sports stores. When that wasn't successful, he altered the way he marketed his product. Can you think of other methods which he might have employed to create interest in his product?

Small Business Distribution and Location

Focus on Small Business: Steve Niewulis and Tap It!

Steve Niewulis, a minor league baseball player, came up with a solution to a problem all baseball players have—keeping the baseball bat handle dry between pitches. He invented Just Tap It!, a rosin bag attached to a wristband so a player could dry the bat handle between pitches. While it seemed like the perfect product for all the major sports stores, the stores were not interested because they prefer to buy from companies with several products in their product lines. Undeterred, he began attending trade shows and association meetings for high school coaches, tennis association meetings, and other similar venues. He was able to set up a booth displaying his product for just a few hundred dollars, and he created interest, recognition, and sales. At one show, he met up with Baseball Express, a catalog that targets high school, college, and minor league teams. Since he already had orders and customers using the product, he was able to show Baseball Express that this was a product it should carry. Niewulis's company, Tap It! now sells thousands of units to not only baseball players, but also to other sports, such as basketball, tennis, golf, and rock climbing.[1]

DISCUSSION QUESTIONS

1. Niewulis's original intent was to market to major sports stores. How would you describe the market he finally targeted? Is there a commonality?
2. What other methods could Niewulis use to get this product to his customers?
3. Would this method have worked as well had the product been something like baked goods? Or mural painting? What methods would work better for these sorts of products?

Distribution[2]

LO1
Recognize the different types of direct marketing and their pros and cons.

Other chapters have answered a lot of the "who," "what," "how," and "why" questions about small business; this chapter deals primarily with the "where." There are two basic "where" questions to be considered. The first one is, "Where are my customers?" In answering this question, you are primarily interested in figuring out how to get your product or service to them so that they have the opportunity to buy it. *Distribution* is the process of getting your product to the customer. The second question is, "Where should I be?" This question can be closely tied to the first—if your business is a restaurant, you need to be exactly where the customers are. Other businesses can be located at a distance from their customers—and often find advantages in doing so.

There are a variety of channels that may be used to get to the consumer. Some of the more prevalent ones are displayed in Figure 11.1. The last two are referred to as *direct marketing* or *direct selling*, and they work equally well for manufacturers of goods and for services. We start with those.

manufacturer
The entity which produces a product or service to be sold.

Direct Marketing

For many entrepreneurs—and larger firms as well—direct marketing is the way to go. It can be as simple as the child who sets up a lemonade stand in front of her or his home, or as complex as a four-color printed catalog with a mass mailing. Direct mailing can be relatively inexpensive. It also provides more control over where your product or service goes, the information that gets passed along to the consumer, how the product is used, and final pricing. There are about as many forms of direct marketing as there are entrepreneurial ideas, and some of the more common ones are discussed below.

word-of-mouth
A means of spreading information about your business through the comments friends and customers make to other potential customers.

Word-of-Mouth[3]

This is a great way to get customers and is usually the first technique an entrepreneur uses. Word-of-mouth[4] is discussed in detail in Chapter 10.

FIGURE 11.1

Typical Distribution Channels

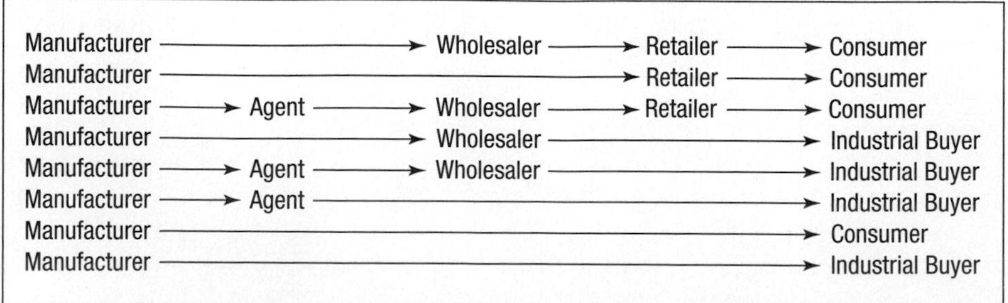

■ 1154 Lill Studio began as a direct sale-based business, offering their custom-made handbags at parties, open houses, and direct appointments before branching out into stores and an online center. Building a strong customer base with the agility of direct selling helped owner Jen Velarde grow 1154 Lill into a successful business that truly taps into its market.

Direct Sales

direct sales Methods of going directly to your customer in order to sell your product. Vending machines, door-to-door salespeople, leasing space at a craft fair, farmers' markets, party sales, and most industrial sales are methods of direct selling.

Direct sales (industrial, door-to-door, party sales, vending) can take several forms. This is the primary way of selling to businesses. A salesperson (often you) contacts industries, churches, schools—whatever type of business is likely to use your product or service—directly. The sales person meets with the decision maker, presents the product, and hopefully makes a sale.

The lemonade stand mentioned above is also a form of direct sales, albeit a little less professional than you may want to be. A more polished approach is a booth at a local fair, cultural event, flea market, craft fair (all of which are discussed in Chapter 5), trade show, or association event. The cost of leasing space can be less than $100 for a local flea market to quite expensive for national trade shows. For a flea market, a simple card table may be appropriate, while the cost of a professional booth at a major trade show could easily be $100,000. The key here is to pick the event most likely to attract your target market and least likely to make a serious dent in your pocketbook. Start small and move up as you get more sales revenues.

Some of the other techniques discussed in Chapter 5 that are also direct sales methods include door-to-door sales (remember the Avon lady?), party sales (think Tupperware or Amway), and vending machines. For products that need demonstrations or detailed explanations, door-to-door selling allows you to show consumers how your product works in their home. Part of the success of home sales is that it is hard for consumers to say no after the salesperson has spent some time in their home—it's just not hospitable. This method is made more difficult these days with dual-income families, because evenings are usually the only time to catch people. Consumers are often reluctant to invite strangers into their home, but you might be able to at least introduce yourself and leave behind information about your product or service. Avon used to sell predominately through door-to-door sales but has branched out into Internet, mail order, and mall kiosks sales in order to combat declining door-to-door sales for the reasons just mentioned.

Vending machines aren't appropriate for every product, but they do offer the flexibility of having your product available around the clock and at convenient locations for your customers. Vending machines are typical for less expensive, convenience products. The key to success is volume achieved with machines located everywhere. People are willing to pay extra in order to have the product readily available. Compare the price of a can of your favorite beverage from a vending machine to what you would pay in the grocery store. The disadvantages of vending machines are their high maintenance and vulnerability to vandalism.

Party sales usually require a range of similar items to be sold, and this kind of selling is not appropriate for every product. Typically, a host or hostess invites a number of friends and family members to his or her house, while a company representative (you, at first) demonstrates the product. Samples of the products as well as catalogs are available for all the guests to browse through, and orders are taken at the party for later delivery. Typical party sales products include everything from laundry aids to makeup to lingerie to cookware to housewares. Two of the disadvantages are the sanctity of the home and the reluctance of people to open up their homes to strangers (salespeople). As these parties take several hours of a salesperson's time and can usually be held only in the evening, one person is limited to how many parties (sales) a week he or she can handle. Generally, the successful companies using this method have hundreds of salespeople who earn a percentage of each sale they make. Many entrepreneurial firms have grown tremendously from a party sales approach—Mary Kay, Amway, Pampered Chef, and others.

direct mail
A method of selling in which catalogs, brochures, letters, videos, and other pieces of marketing materials are mailed directly to customers from which they can mail, call, or e-mail an order. Direct faxing and direct e-mailing are more modern forms of direct mail.

Direct Mail[5]

Direct mail is another form of selling introduced in Chapter 5 because it is so easy for part-time entrepreneurs. Direct mail can take many forms—postcards, catalogs, videos, sales letters, brochures, leaflets, CD-ROMs, and many others. Customers do not see direct mail as a form of home invasion (as they often do with door-to-door sales or telemarketing); they can read it at their leisure, and they have something they can set aside until they need it. It can be done inexpensively—a single folded sheet of paper, a label, and a stamp—or much more elaborately—a video catalog, for example.

www.pcslist.com

www.focus-usa-1.com

www.practicalmarketing.net

www.google.com/dirhp

Getting the addresses is a major hurdle for this form of marketing. There are many companies that will sell you a list of addresses (even a list already typed on labels), and these are often available for virtually any target market you may choose. The cost of these lists can vary, but current rates are about $60 to $75 per thousand names. Try PCS Mailing List Company (www.pcslist.com), Focus USA (www.focus-usa-1.com), or Practical Marketing (www.practicalmarketing.net) or do an Internet search for direct mail lists. You can find a complete listing of mailing list companies using the Google Directory (www.google.com/dirhp) as illustrated here. Also, professional organizations and clubs sometimes will sell their mailing lists for a relatively modest fee.

There are also low-budget ways of getting a mailing list. Often membership rosters are distributed to members of certain organizations: If such an organization meets your target market, you can have the list for the price of membership. One caution, though: Sometimes members are expressly forbidden to use these lists in any commercial way. If it truly is a product or service that a number of these members are likely to want and if it is a one-time "soft sell" mailing, you're probably okay.

Two other direct mail sorts of activities are worth mentioning: direct faxing and e-mail. Particularly for business sales, direct faxing can be a way of reaching potential clients. Fax numbers can be obtained in the same way as mailing lists. Unfortunately, frequently faxes are of relatively poor quality, and often the person receiving the fax is not a decision maker.

Anyone who has an e-mail account is subject to this form of direct mail, commonly known as *spam*. E-mail addresses can be purchased just as can regular addresses from the same companies. There is also inexpensive software (see www.emailsmartz.com, for example, or do a search for "email marketing software") that can easily generate millions of possible addresses. E-mail is one of the least expensive forms of direct mail, and the cost per recipient is, by far, the lowest. There is now a nationwide "can spam" law that overrides the 35 different state rules direct marketers had to consider previously. However, in some cases state laws are more stringent and must be followed as well. For example, in California, the e-mail must state "ADV" in the subject line. Most of the requirements of the national law are fairly straightforward:

- Don't in any way falsely misrepresent who you are, where the e-mail is from, or that the e-mail is anything other than a sales pitch.
- Randomly generated e-mail addresses or harvested e-mail addresses are not to be used.
- All e-mails should allow recipients the opportunity to "opt out" of receiving further e-mail correspondence from you—and you must obey their wishes on this.[6]

Spam is a hot topic, and legislation changes are likely, so be sure to check on current rules. "Opt-in" e-mail, where recipients allow you to e-mail them, is legal and much more acceptable to the potential client.

Telemarketing

We have all received telephone calls from salespeople (or worse yet, recorded messages) wanting to sell us everything from aluminum siding to vacations. While most consumers find this method particularly annoying, **telemarketing** still remains a viable form of direct marketing because it works. It is, however, the most expensive form of direct marketing. Currently, many states have adopted "do-not-call" lists, and there is a national do-not-call list as well. The Direct Marketing Association maintains a comprehensive listing of national and state do-not-call lists (See http://www.the-dma.org/government/donotcalllists.shtml). These are currently facing some legal challenges, and the present situation should be checked out before you consider a telemarketing campaign. Target market telephone lists may be purchased from the same companies as mail or e-mail addresses—theoretically cleansed of all do-not-call registrants—or random dialers (computers that use random number tables to generate possible phone numbers) may be used.

telemarketing
Contact via telephone for the express purpose of selling a product or service. Telemarketing can either be inbound (customer calls company) or outbound (company calls customer).

http://www.the-dma.org/government/donotcalllists.shtml

Inbound telemarketing is a different story. Here, the customer calls the manufacturer or service provider. This may be in response to a direct mail piece, direct response advertising, or other methods. A major consideration for the entrepreneur is handling the phone lines. Your California customer calling at 8 p.m. reaches your home in Connecticut at midnight. This is where an answering machine with a message stating working hours (located far from your bedroom or with the sound turned off) is a necessity.

If inbound telemarketing is your primary way of doing business and if there are enough calls (and profit) to warrant it, there are firms that will answer these calls for you. (See the search screen to see how to find these firms in Google.) Generally these firms can take orders or send on additional information; more technical problems or special situations will require your personal attention. The cost varies, again, based on the amount of service and volume of calls. These centers can also provide services in several languages if this is critical for your firm.

Direct Response Advertising

In **direct response advertising**, you place an ad somewhere—magazine, newspaper, radio, billboard, or television, for example—that includes a phone number, e-mail address, or snail-mail address and wait for the orders to come in. (Placing a Web site in the ad is technically part of Internet marketing, which we get to in a moment.) This can be as simple as a classified ad in the newspaper or as elaborate as a half-hour infomercial—and the costs associated vary as much as the type of ads. (See Table 11.1.)

direct response advertising
Placing an advertisement in a magazine or newspaper, on television or radio, or in any other media. The ad contains an order blank with a phone number and e-mail or regular mail address with the intent of having the customer place an immediate order.

The pros and cons of your media choice are just about what you'd expect. Television can be expensive, but it attracts a large audience and is a good way to demonstrate

TABLE 11.1 Cost per 1,000 for Various Forms of Direct Response Advertising[7]

Media	Billboard	Transit Shelter	Radio—30-Second Spot	Magazine Newsweekly, 4-Color Page	Newspaper Daily, 1/3 Black and White Page	Television, 30-Second Prime-Time Spot
Men 18+	$2.61	$2.07	$8.75–$10.45	$10.30	$22.05	$22.55–$30.80
Women 18+	$3.28	$2.60	$7.75–$9.65	$10.30	$21.15	$18.10–$24.31

what your product is capable of doing. Try cable channels for the cheapest rates. Many stations offer discounted advertising for small businesses. This might not amount to much more than an announcer reading your ad over the credits of the local news, but it's a starting point.

Some of the home shopping networks may be appropriate if your product meets their criteria. These networks publish their standards on their Web sites and may offer days for inventors to demonstrate their products to studio personnel—a chance to sell your concept. Products that work well are those that have a wide appeal and have advantages that are easy to demonstrate.

A magazine allows for very specific targeting—a hobby, sporting interest, a certain age, or other demographic group—and often offers classified type ads (less expensive) or multipage, full color ads (much more expensive). Newspapers allow geographic segmentation; that is, they are a great source if you want to attract people in a specific geographic region (think restaurant, day care center, and the like). Newspaper ads are generally the cheapest from of direct response advertising.

Magazines are also very appropriate places for direct response advertising for business-to-business selling. Virtually every industry, trade, and profession has a magazine dedicated to it. Finding the correct one and placing your direct response ads will give you high contact with your target market. Try *Gale's Directory of Publications and Broadcast Media* or the *Encyclopedia of Associations* probably at your library for lists of industry trade magazines and trade associations. You can also refer back to Skill Module 7.2 in Chapter 7, "Finding Your Trade or Professional Association," for some help along these lines.

Radio ads provide both geographic and demographic segmentation; if you do custom designed cowboy boots or train horses, a radio ad on the local country western

SMALL BUSINESS INSIGHT

Floppy Sprinkler USA[8]

www.floppysprinkler.com

www.qvc.com

Jeff Pettit, the founder of Floppy Sprinkler USA, LLC (**www.floppysprinkler.com**) used television to get the word out about his unique water sprinkler called Rain on Demand. The idea was so different from traditional water sprinklers that a demonstration seemed the logical way to convince customers of the product's worth. Pettit found information for submitting ideas on the QVC Web site (**www.qvc.com**) and got his opportunity. His company started in 2000, reached sales of $250,000 by 2002, and expects sales to quadruple in 2003. He was also able to use his QVC leverage to position his product in garden centers and hardware stores.

station might be just the right place. On the other hand, radio audiences are generally highly distracted; people listen to the radio while driving, or doing housework or other tasks and might not be able to drop everything to write down your phone number. Billboards reach local people but do not permit a lot of details. Other possibilities include signs in buses and cabs or at bus stops.

For a start in direct response advertising, consider a classified type ad—no pictures, limited graphics (if any), and relatively low cost. If your target market is a specific geographic region, newspapers might work best. If it is specific to a hobby, job, sport, or other interest, try a magazine catering to that interest. If the budget allows, try a quarter- or half-page ad with some color or modest graphics. Magazines will sell you an eighth or sixteenth of a page ad.

■ Guerilla marketing, as in the photo, attracts potential customer attention while helping small businesses keep marketing costs down. Which guerilla options seem most effective to you and why? Do you see any ethical concerns with guerilla marketing techniques?

Guerilla Marketing[9]

Guerilla marketing is a relatively new concept in marketing, but the start-up company's best friend. Guerilla marketing is a term for unusual and nearly free advertising. While it can be simply advertising—stating why your product or service is great—it's extremely effective as direct response advertising when you add your phone number, address, Web site, or other contact information. Guerilla marketing includes everything from placing flyers under windshield wipers of cars to waving signs at passing cars to hanging information on doorknobs to placing business cards on bulletin boards at the grocery store. For the cost of copying and a bit of shoe leather, you can get your message out to a lot of potential customers. Then, again, if you aren't interested in delivering the message yourself (How valuable is your time?), there are many companies that will do this for you. CIPS Marketing Group (www.cipsmarketing.com), owned by the *Los Angeles Times,* will distribute a newspaper "ride-along" advertisement, doorknob hangers, flyers, or product samples to selected target neighborhoods for as little as $35 to $130 per thousand. It will even design and print your advertisements for you for an extra fee.

guerilla marketing
The use of creative and relatively inexpensive ways to reach your customer. Examples include doorknob hangers, flyers under windshield wipers, T-shirts, balloons, and messages written on sidewalks.

The key here is to catch the customer's attention. Susan P., moving into a new house in a new subdivision, became part of the target market for landscapers, house cleaners, blinds and drapery manufacturers, pool installers, satellite television installers, painters, decorators, local restaurants and merchants, and a plethora of other such small businesses. Daily there were several pieces of advertising trying to get her attention. A few—very few—are slick four-color brochures or in-mail catalogs and coupons. The majority are low budget or homemade. What attracts her attention? "Coupons are a good bet; I'll try out a restaurant or neighborhood merchant if I get a discount or free dessert or some other gift. Others that catch my eye are those that are different. For example, a landscaper left his business card—just like several dozen before and after him—but his was in a small plastic sandwich bag with a few samples of decorative gravel and bark." It cost him only the time to make these, but this was much more appealing than just sticking a business card in my door. In another case, a decorator printed her ad on a wallpaper sample—colorful and different![10]

Find unusual and unique places to display your products. Can you wear your own creations? Can you pass out samples of your homemade fudge to your bridge club? Give your product as gifts, along with your business card or other contact information, and encourage the recipients to pass along that information to anyone who asks. One popular recent idea is paying college students to wear T-shirts with a message on them, such as LivingAdSpace.com.

www.livingadspace.com

Multichannel Marketing

The term **multichannel marketing** refers to using several outlets for contacting your customers. If you include in your classified ad your phone number, your Web site, and your e-mail address, then you are a multichannel marketer. One customer may pick up the phone. Others will e-mail or browse your Web site. This simply allows your customers to contact you in the way they feel most comfortable. Having your phone number, Web

multichannel marketing
The use of several different channels to reach your customers, for example, a Web site, direct mail, and traditional retailing.

SMALL BUSINESS INSIGHT

Courtney Hennessey Revisited—Guerilla Guru[11]

We met Courtney Hennessey of Codi Jewelry (**www.codijewelry.com**) the first time in the chapter on part-time self-employment. While Courtney might not have realized that she was a guerilla marketing expert, her experience speaks for itself. Her first products were stretchy bead bracelets, and she generated interest by wearing them around town. People would ask about them, and she'd take orders. If they didn't place an immediate order, she had business cards to pass out "for future reference." She gave out business cards with all her sales, too, so her customers could pass them along to people who commented on their new jewelry. One of these cards ended up with a Neiman Marcus associate, which resulted in several trunk shows at the store, where she was allowed to present her merchandise directly to the jewelry buyers. One of her more unusual marketplaces—and possibly a marketing first—was her great aunt's wake where she brought samples of her jewelry and walked away with $800 in orders. During a vacation in the Bahamas, she happened to be eating at the same restaurant as Regis Philbin of *Live with Regis and Kelly,* and worked up the courage to approach him with her story and samples of her jewelry for his wife, daughters, and co-host Kelly. Regis presented the necklace to Kelly during the show, telling the story about Codi Jewelry, resulting in well over 100,000 hits on her Web site the next week. None of these "marketing ploys" cost her very much, but all were incredibly successful at generating publicity for her firm and getting resulting orders.

site address, and e-mail address on your packaging ensure that your customer can find you again should a retail outlet decide not to carry your product any longer.[12]

Internet[13]

LO2
Master using the Internet as a distribution channel.

Internet as a distribution tool for the small business is so powerful that we're devoting a section to it here, and we have talked about it throughout the book. The Internet can be a very cost-effective and efficient way to contact your customers. With the Internet, a small, one-person operation can compete with a billion dollar a year multinational. At a minimum, a small business should have an e-mail account. This could be your personal account, but to make your life simpler, use a separate account, and include your business name in the e-mail address. Having Beachcombershoes@gmail.com (which is a free e-mail service from Google) is good, and having info@beachcombershoes.com is even better. Most Internet service providers will allow you to have more than one account at no extra charge, but make sure your account is large enough to handle the volume. For some services, you will have to pay a little extra to increase the size of your mailbox, but it is worth it.

Most small businesses need to have a Web site regardless of whether or not they use it for actual sales. First of all, potential customers will use it to find you. Second, if they've heard about you from something other than the Internet, they will use your site to find out more information about you and to decide if they want to actually contact you. Letrah International, a firm specializing in international consulting for design and engineering projects, knew it should have a Web site, but it was a low priority and was worked on only when something else did not come up. Dave Peters, the firm's vice president, asked a firm in the United Arab Emirates if there was anything he could do to help convince the firm to accept Letrah's bid. The firm expressed concern that Letrah was not a real company, because it didn't have a Web site, and "everybody knew real U.S. firms had Web sites." The Web site was running the following day.[14]

www.letrah.com

Last, many small businesses are finding that Web sites are a great way of not only providing information to their customers, but also serve as "electronic catalogs."

Web site software now makes it easy for most people to design their own site. There are also a lot of people who can do it for you as well, from your "techno-geek" teenage nephew who will do it for the cost of the latest computer game to firms that will not only design but also maintain your Web site for you—at a cost, of course. Ibuilder (www.imall.com) offers tools specifically for building and hosting your retail Web site, including e-mail, online banking and other financial services, and advanced customer service and marketing tools. There's a $99 activation fee, and the most basic service is under $10 per month. The more tools and services you need and the larger the catalogs you post, the more you will end up paying. It is worth doing some serious comparison shopping for hosting services. Conduct a Google search for "cheap hosting" and "free shopping cart" (a *shopping cart* is the electronic version of a catalog with an ordering system) to find a large number of possibilities. Many offer do-it-yourself software to make designing Web sites and shopping carts easy.

There are volumes and volumes written about what things to consider when building your Web site. Certainly, you want an address that is easy to remember and that ties into your company name or product. Creative spellings are catchy but not remembered very well. Probably the best thing to do is surf the Internet pretending you are a customer. The things that drive you crazy—slow-loading graphics, extreme color combinations, too many layers of screens to get to what you want—will also drive your customers crazy.

Once you've got your Web site up and running and it is a masterpiece in design, how do you get your customers to find it? The first way is multichannel marketing, mentioned above. Have your Web site listed on your business cards and every piece of paper, advertising, and the like that you do. The second and equally important way is to get linked to other Web pages. If you were in the target market for your product, what Web pages would you visit? Figure out what these are and establish mutual links. Scan chat rooms and other electronic message boards to see if people are looking for your type of product or service and post your Web site. Discover what sorts of electronic newsletters they might read and get a mention in them.[15]

Searching online is how about 85 percent of Internet users find Web sites, and users will seldom go beyond the first couple of pages of a search.[16,17] Search engines offer **sponsored links** (guaranteeing you a particular placement on the first page of a search) at very low cost. A Yahoo sponsored link is 16 cents per click. With paid search engine listings, you pay to have your URL come up when the searcher enters certain words—words that you "buy" from the various search engines.[18] Therein lies the problem: Which words do you choose? If you are a bookstore, the word "books" might come to mind, but that's true for lots and lots of other bookstores, publishers, and others. Maybe "first editions" is more appropriate, if that is indeed what you sell. On the other hand, if you have something somewhat more unusual like yo-yos, buying "yo-yo" is likely to get you on a page with limited competition.[19] Watch for jargon; think of what the average searcher might enter. You may like to think of yourself as a prestidigitator, but most people will call you a magician. Your Web page designer will understand where to place the keywords you select and can help you get listed on the major search engines such as Google, AOL Netfind, Hotbot, Alta Vista, Infoseek, Lycos, Microsoft Network, Excite, and Webcrawler.[20] If you want to learn more about this, the term you enter in Google is "**keyword optimization**." You can also search for the more general approach called "**search engine optimization**."

Electronic malls are great places to get your product mentioned as are e-tailers mentioned later.[21] The Internet Mall (www.internetmall.com) lists nineteen major categories

sponsored link
A form of paid advertising that gets your company's Web site at the top of a search list.

keyword optimization
The selection of words that describe a Web site ad that results in the site being displayed toward the beginning of a search engine's (e.g., Google, Yahoo!, etc.) listing for that term.

search engine optimization
A general approach to Web site design intended to result in the site being displayed toward the beginning of a search engine's (e.g., Google, Yahoo!, etc.) listing for that term.

electronic malls
A group of companies—usually with a common target market—selling via the Internet through a specific site.

from art and computer hardware to jewelry and music, and most categories list several subcategories. It offers various pricing strategies ranging from under $10 per month up to $100, depending on the number of services you want or need. The basic service features include the ability to build your Web site and import your catalog, as well as a secure shopping cart and some reports. Additional levels include more sophisticated reporting, the ability to create coupons, search engine submissions, tax and shipping calculators, order confirmations, and the ability to list on eBay from this site.

If you're concerned about being lost among all the categories, subcategories, and clients of The Internet Mall, there are other malls that specialize in a particular target clientele. The Mommy Mall (www.mommy-mall.com) specializes in shops catering to the needs of the mother with younger children. It states that its clientele are married women, over 25, with an average of two children. It lists 26 major categories (called *shops*) including ones you expect like maternity, babies, and toys and games and some you may not expect, such as business supplies, computers, and bridal. The number of retailers within each category is a much more manageable number thereby increasing the likelihood of a visit to your site. To list in The Mommy Mall the current subscription rate is $100 per year for a three- to five-line description of your site in two appropriate shops, links to your site (which you build yourself), and some promotion.

Following are some cautions about choosing an e-mall:

1. Read the agreements very carefully, and make sure you understand exactly what is offered and not offered for the fee you are charged.
2. Avoid e-malls that require exclusive listings. The name of the game is to get to as many people as possible.
3. What exactly is meant by promotional assistance? Does this simply mean a spam e-mail message on occasion?
4. What about search engine help? Will it perform real search engine optimization so that you show up on the first page of a search? Many people will not look beyond the first page.

eBay

We discuss eBay in Chapter 5 as an example of a consignment store, but eBay (www.ebay.com) can also be thought of as the megamall of e-malls.[22] There are thousands upon thousands of sites in the eBay mall. For example, under the major category of collectibles, under the subcategory of advertising, there are 150 pages of listings with 25 listings per page. It's easy to feel overwhelmed. On the other hand, eBay is a well-known name and often one of the first stops for **consumers**. eBay offers a rather sophisticated search engine to help buyers find products in your store, and you have the option of your listings appearing in the auctions several different ways as well. Other nice-to-have perks include being able to use eBay's logo on your business cards, envelopes, and letterhead. Basic service is under $10 per month and includes a variety of reports, cross promotions, and help with just about everything you need to get going. Higher levels of service can run up to $500 per month and the increased services are mostly in the advertising area. You can get up to speed on the basics of getting started on eBay by checking out Chapter 5's Skill Module 5.1: Steps to eBay Success.

consumer
A private individual or household who is the end-user of (the entity that "consumes") a product or service.

People who have set up eBay stores strongly suggest using the auction feature; after all that is what most people think of when they go to the site. Sherry Chase of Fancy That! started an eBay store as a means of getting rid of excess merchandise from her store. She had tried her own Web site with virtually no luck at first. She found that eBay sales exceeded her expectations. She also found that by auctioning items and including her link in the auction description she got people to her eBay store.[23]

eBay auctions themselves are legendary. On any day 12 million items are available with nearly 2 million new postings a day.[24] There are 150 new items for sale listed every minute, and 500 bids placed during that same minute. There are 69 million eBay users who spend $59 million a day.[25] The eBay method means you pay a fee for posting your product and a sales fee based on the final bid price when the item sells. You have the option of setting a bottom offer you will accept, a reserve price (if the bidding does not exceed the price, the sale will not go through), the number of days the auction will run (out of several choices), and can include pictures of the product and links to morc data (like your Web site). eBay allows you a bit of anonymity—all buyers and sellers have screen names. E-mail addresses and limited personal information are only given out in certain circumstance. (Obviously, if you are a successful bidder, the seller needs to know to whom and where to send the merchandise.) eBay sellers may take checks, money orders, or credit cards, or accept payments through PayPal, eBay's own electronic payment system, reducing sellers risk. eBay also allows buyers and sellers to post feedback about their transactions which produces a score that's displayed by the buyer and sellers' screen name and allows others to get a feel for how reputable a certain buyer or seller is. This feedback is also available for the public to read. (See Thoughtful Entrepreneur box below for more tips.)

THE THOUGHTFUL ENTREPRENEUR

Tips for Selling on eBay[26]

1. Use detailed descriptions so that the buyer isn't expecting something different from what you are selling.
2. A picture is worth a thousand words. Make sure the photo is not too dark or too light. Does it adequately display your product? Check out backgrounds, too. They can detract from the subject and might even show things you'd rather not display on the Internet. And don't use huge slow-to-download files.
3. Watch out for misspellings and typos. Experienced eBay buyers use the search engine to find specific things and it won't find your misspelling. Besides, it doesn't look very professional.
4. Be honest and factual. Don't say, "slight damage." Instead state that there is an eight-inch chip on the upper right-hand corner and a faint scratch along one side. The buyer can make an informed decision, and there are no surprises.
5. If buyers have a question, they'll e-mail you. Respond as soon as possible, at least within 24 hours. Don't post auction items just prior to going on vacation.
6. Be honest and up-front about shipping. It is acceptable to charge for postage and a reasonable amount for shipping materials. If you are using recycled boxes, don't charge for them. Some sellers like to use a flat fee for all shipping charges (e.g., $5.00 per paperback book). Experienced eBay buyers will know that for regular U.S. media mail, that price is way out of line. If you're the only one selling that item, they may pay, but if there are a dozen others, they'll shop around or reflect their concerns in the top bid they place.
7. Customer service is very important. You want positive feedback. Dissatisfied buyers may either leave negative feedback or leave no feedback at all on your transaction.
8. Since most buyers are somewhat reluctant about buying from a seller with no feedback, try buying for a while; your feedback rating will grow, and since there is no differentiation between buyer and seller feedback, this puts you in a better position as a seller.
9. Ship promptly. Package well. Notify your buyers when things have been shipped. If you need to wait for a check to clear and you'll be gone a few days during that time, let them know. Most buyers are prepared to be reasonable if they know what's going on.
10. Leave feedback for your buyers, too. First of all, it helps them when making further purchases. Second, if you expect feedback yourself, do it for them. If they see you've posted positive feedback, they are more likely to do so themselves.
11. See what the competition is doing to see if you even want to try eBay auctions. If your product (or something fairly similar) is selling on eBay for less than you need to make your profit goals, find another way to get to your customers.

There are restrictions on the types of products that may be sold—for example, anything that is considered fraudulent, illegal, or harmful, as well as anything that infringes on patent or trademark rules. eBay does enforce this policy. For more detailed information about doing business on eBay, check the Web site www.ebay.com or look at one of the numerous books about eBay, like *eBay for Dummies.*

You can't argue with eBay success stories. Nona Cunane does about $400,000 a year through eBay with designer women's clothing. Adam Ginsberg does nearly $15 million selling billiard tables only on eBay.[27] eBay is also successful for business-to-business selling. Farmer Joel Holstad purchased a tractor, a combine, and a cherry picker for about half of what he expected to pay. Check out eBay's business Web site at www.eBaybusiness.com.[28]

Other Internet Options

Amazon.com (www.amazon.com) offers a variety of selling options. The fees vary depending on the services you choose. High-volume sellers can become Pro Merchants for $39.99 per month. Single items may be sold for a flat 99 cents fee plus a small commission. Their zShops are a basic e-mall and are cross-linked to the Amazon.com catalog. Amazon also allows you to conduct auctions.

Similar options are available for business-to-business transactions and services. Elance (www.elanceonline.com) offers service providers the opportunity to bid on potential projects ranging from Web design to business plans, accounting to translation, training to CAD projects, in a reverse auction format.[29] (In a *reverse auction,* the low bid gets the business.) Businesses post projects, review bids, use the message boards to keep up-to-date, and can even pay online, all for a small fee Elance collects once the provider is paid. Service providers are able to post information about their expertise and experience as well. Cheri Rychlee Tracy was looking for a Web designer. Local companies wanted between $1,500 and $7,500. She was able to find a freelance designer on Elance from the Ukraine for $750.[30] Similar sites include Contracted Work (www.contractedwork.com), FreelancersDirect.com (www.freelancersdirect.com), Get A Freelancer (www.getafreelancer.com), All Freelance (www.allfreelance.com), Freelance Seek (www.freelanceseek.com), and Ariba (www.ariba.com). Several business-to-business e-malls exist such as Business.com (www.business.com) and B2B Today (www.b2btoday.com). B2Bquote (www.b2bquote.com) combines a business-to-business mall with reverse auction features, allowing the B2B firm both options.

Distribution Issues for Direct Marketing

Even when your shippers pay postage, you'll need to know where to go to find the information you need to add that to the amount the seller pays. You'll need a decent postage scale and rate tables. These tables can be downloaded from UPS (www.ups.com), Federal Express (www.fedex.com), or the U.S. Postal Service (www.usps.com). *Tip:* Charge a shipping and handling fee that includes postage as well as packaging materials. Most catalogs have a shipping and handling fee based on the dollar amount of the order. These companies also offer tracking software that can be downloaded and installed on your computer to track your shipments.

fulfillment center
A company that will warehouse your products and fill your customers' orders for you.

retailer
A middleman business which sells to consumers or end-users of a product (typically in single or small quantities).

Another option to consider, especially if you are doing quantity shipping, is to use a **fulfillment center**. These centers will warehouse your products, pack and ship them, and send an automated e-mail to your customers to let them know your product is on its way. Other services include credit card processing, supplying inventory levels to your Web site, reordering products, offering call center services, and handling returns.[31] Fees vary, but they should be less than 10 percent of sales plus freight costs. Distributors are a good idea if you want to offer a whole line of products that you don't have to buy or warehouse. In this case, the distributor services several **retailers** or e-tailers.[32]

How do you find these fulfillment centers or distributors? A good staring place includes http://www.clearcommerce.com/eguide. There are also several companies that

THE THOUGHTFUL ENTREPRENEUR

Best Practices: AtYourOffice.com[33]

AtYourOffice (**www.atyouroffice.com**) was founded by Tom Graham in January 1998. It has the largest selection on the Internet and a best price guarantee. It offers free next business day shipping, and it has "fanatical" customer service. It specializes in the small office/home office market, a market that Graham felt was underserved. His company is able to offer low prices because it is a virtual company. Graham's staff is made up of only three full-time employees. The company has no inventory, but is able to sell over 27,000 office products thanks to his partnerships.

According to the Web site, "They offer Internet tools and services that large Fortune 500 business have come to rely on. The difference . . . is that we offer this up at a cost any business can afford. Through a network of alliances and sister companies, we have woven together a comprehensive and sophisticated network of award winning Internet-based productivity and collaboration tools."

How did AtYourOffice do this? For example, AtYourOffice.com partnered with a distributor that had over 40 distribution centers throughout the United States. Later the company partnered with AtYourBusiness.com to offer a comprehensive package of employee management products and services to support small businesses.

As well as office products and service, AtYourOffice.com also "distributes" information through its extensive links including relevant information from sources such as Dun & Bradstreet, Lexis-Nexis and more.

www.atyouroffice.com

http://www.arlingtonvirginiausa.com/econ/econmews-jan2000.html

http://www.directmag.com/marketing_office_open_business/

exist specifically for Internet sales businesses, such as Shipper.com for larger businesses and ifulfill.com for those companies with fewer than 50 products.[34]

Nondirect Distribution

In Figure 11.1 at the beginning of this chapter you saw **wholesaler**, retailer, and **agent**. Since then, others such as distributors, which along with a dozen or so not mentioned above, are commonly referred to as middlemen. **Middlemen**—frequently small businesses themselves—provide the service of getting the product to the end consumer, including such functions as inventory control, advertising and promotion, delivery and warranty services, to name a few. For these services, they take a percentage of the profit. As a result, the final price the end user must pay is often four (or more) times the manufacturing cost.

LO3
Learn how to do nondirect distribution.

wholesaler
A middleman business which buys (typically in large quantities) and sells (typically in smaller quantities) to businesses rather than consumers.

agent
A middleman business which represents a manufacturer's product or service to other business-to-business middleman firms.

middleman
Any firm that assists in getting your product to your end customer—distributors, retailers, and so forth.

How do you find out which distribution channel is correct for your product? One suggestion is to start at the end and work your way up by asking each link from whom they buy.[35] At that point, you can determine other wholesalers or distributors that carry similar products and begin interviewing them to find the best fit for your product and target market. Another way to locate possible distributors is to attend trade shows. The Manufacturers' Agents National Association publishes a *Directory of Manufacturers' Sales Agencies,* available in many libraries.

Unfortunately for the entrepreneur, many distributors and wholesalers are not interested in taking on a start-up product. They are concerned about an unproven source and market, setup charges, and a multitude of other possible problems. On the other hand, talking to distributors—especially in product development stages—may often give you ideas on what to do and what not to do.

One way to get a distributor interested in trying your product is to be able to prove that it does sell. In this case, you may have to convince a single retailer to give the product a try. Getting your product into a catalog may also convince a distributor that it's a product worth taking, but how do you get into that catalog? One way is by showing your product at trade shows and gaining sales and recognition. This is the route

that Steve Niewulis from the chapter's opening vignette used. Sources for finding trade shows include the quarterly magazine, *Job Shop Technology,* or the Web site http://www.tscentral.com. You can also search using Google.

Another way to get into a catalog is to find one that carries the type of product you have and for about the price you'll want to charge. Call for their guidelines for submitting new products and follow the information you get carefully. If you aren't already receiving such a catalog, you can check out resources such as the *National Directory of Catalogs* or *The Catalog of Catalogs V: The Complete Mail-Order Directory* in your local library. Some will charge you a fee for warehousing your product, while others will simply pass the orders along to you.[36]

Virtually every industry, sport, hobby, or interest has its own trade shows and events. Regional events are usually a better place for the entrepreneur because you have lower expenses and less competition. Hit the library or Internet to find them, and be sure to have all the answers about cost, delivery, product advantages, and the like.

e-tailer
An electronic retailer; a store that exists only on the Internet.

If catalog sales do not feel right and retailers do not seem interested in your product, an **e-tailer**[37] might be willing to take a chance. Because of e-tailers' low overhead and unlimited shelf space, they can afford to take a chance on an unknown firm or product. Sometimes, they will carry inventory, but often they just pass the orders on to you for fulfillment. You can find potential sites by doing an Internet search, such as the one shown in the Google search bar. Sometimes they will post information on how to submit product ideas, while other times be prepared to dig for phone numbers and names. Craig Winchell, the inventor of Conscience, an interactive board game for teaching children right and wrong, tried the American International Toy Fair, a trade show, with disappointing results. He found that EToys was willing to take a chance. EToys' (www.etoys.com) initial order was six games in 1998; in 1999, Winchell shipped close to 10,000 units.[38]

International Strategies

LO4
Differentiate the types of international strategies.

When you are struggling to get through that first year of business, international sales are about the last thing on your mind. The U.S. Department of Commerce, however, indicates that large companies account for only about 4 percent of all exporters, meaning the other 96 percent of the exporters in 2000 were small businesses.[39]

Entrepreneurs typically fall into three categories. There are those who realistically will never go international (for example, a restaurant owner or dry cleaner working from a single site). There are those who intentionally start international businesses[40] (for example, import-export businesses), such as Peter P., the director of procurement for a Russian trading company, who saw a trading opportunity with the opening up of Eastern Europe and the former Soviet Union. Educated in the United States, he is of Ukrainian descent and speaks both Russian and Ukrainian.[41] Last, there are those who think international business might be something they'll do someday way off in the future. This section is primarily for the last two categories.

born international
A new firm that opens a Web site immediately, thus being exposed to customers from around the world.

Thanks to the Internet, once a company has a Web site, it is essentially an international business, a whole new breed of firms known as **born internationals**.[42] Potential foreign customers see the Web site and before you know it—or before you are prepared—the first international order rolls in. Even "Web site–free" companies aren't exempt. A foreign visitor comes across your products and sees a need for it in his or her country, and here comes that order.

Some international orders aren't all that difficult to handle. If the order is small enough, if the product or service is not highly regulated domestically, and if the country is one with which the United States has rather liberal trade such as Canada, the order processing may offer few or no headaches. The customer may use a credit card or international money order, and the product ships in the mail without much more effort than figuring the extra postage. That's okay for the occasional order, but more complex situations will require more time and effort on the part of the entrepreneur. The ideal situation is to consider and prepare an international strategy before it becomes a hit-and-miss method that is too cumbersome or before serious and costly mistakes are made.

Entrepreneurs have available to them the same options as large companies including wholly owned subsidiaries, joint ventures, licensing, franchising, and exporting. For most, though, an export strategy is sufficient and is all that is covered in this section. It's usually inexpensive, quick to start, easy to change, and less risky than other ventures. It has the additional advantage of allowing the entrepreneur the opportunity to learn about doing business abroad in case the company reaches the point of moving further. For U.S. entrepreneurs, the U.S. government offers detailed and useful help for exporters, including seminars and other training, export assistance, Web sites and reports, financing, insurance, and legal and collection assistance.

Exporting[43]

Putting together an export strategy involves answering three questions:

1. Are we ready?
2. Where should we go?
3. Whom do we contact over there?

There are many sources for assistance in answering these questions, and many good ones are free or almost free. One excellent resource is the U.S. Commerce Department's report entitled, "A Basic Guide to Exporting" that can be found at www.unzco.com/basicguide/index.htm.

Question 1: Are you ready to export? Exporting requires a different kind of thinking and preparation from selling locally or even nationally. Are you going to target one country, a region, or the whole world? Do you know what customers want? Do you know what the import requirements are? What aspects will you handle, and which ones will you contract out? Are you ready for the costs and headaches of exporting? To see how you are coming along, you can check your readiness online at the U.S. government's exporting site http://www.export.gov/, which provides extensive exporting basics, including a "readiness test" at http://www.fas.usda.gov/agexport/exporttest.asp.

Consider your product as well. Will your U.S. designed product fit an international lifestyle or needs? Clothing sizes are different—both in how they are numbered and what the sizes mean. A woman's medium in the United States is an XXL in mainland China. Electrical currents are different, as are various other safety and product standards, and the United States is one of only two countries that's not on the metric system.[44]

There are several ways you can export. One is to use online services such as eBay. Approximately one-fifth of eBay's sales are out of country.[45] If you're handling your international business this way, a lot of the rest of this section isn't really for you until you want or need to change methods. Another is to work from personal contacts gained through school, travel, or family. Most exporting small businesses start with countries where they have had personal experience or support.[46] These two methods are called **direct exporting**, since you are selling *directly* to foreign buyers or distributors.

If you want to use outside experts, there are three middlemen who can help. With **indirect exporting**, you use agents, export management companies, or export trading companies as intermediaries to handle most of the exporting process. Direct exporters can also get help from freight forwarders. **Freight forwarders** are specialists in export-related activities including tariff schedules, shipping, insurance, packing, transportation arrangements, customs clearing, and other export details. (By the way, many agents, export management companies, export trading companies, and freight forwarders are themselves small businesses. They know exactly what problems you've

direct exporting
Exporting using no middlemen.

indirect exporting
Exporting using middlemen such as agents, export management companies, or export trading companies.

freight forwarders
Firms specializing in arranging international shipments—packaging, transportation, and paperwork.

faced and are much easier to approach than some megacompany.) The Small Business Administration's Export Assistance Center can help you find one.

Question 2: Where should we go? The United Nations has 191 member countries in the world; chances are not all of them are right for your product. Even if your product should have wide appeal, it makes good sense to pick one or two as first markets. One of the safest bets is to consider countries that are similar to the United States—Canada, United Kingdom, Australia, for example. In those countries, you have few language issues, the culture is pretty close, the governments and economies are stable, and the people there are likely to want or need about the same kinds of products as people in the United States do. Should you decide to go further afield, those are the same sorts of things you want to look for—language and culture issues, government and legal situations, economic situations, and peoples' wants and needs. Here's a good time to use those personal contacts mentioned earlier; if they live there, they are likely to be able to tell you if the product makes sense or not.

International marketing research isn't cheap and can be difficult to do. Contacts are a valuable resource. Additionally, the U.S. government can give a lot of free or low-cost assistance. See Table 11.2 below for a list of some of the major ones.

Question 3: Whom do we contact over there? You may already have international contacts through school, friends, travel, or other methods. If so, you're ahead of the game. Even if they cannot help you with specific questions, they probably know someone who can. On the other hand, if you do not have any contacts, a lot of the government services you have already used can provide lists of potential middlemen or end users. In addition to the free services available, U.S. Commercial Services (www. export.gov) provides a number of levels of fee-based customized services. For $50 per year, BuyUSA.com through the U.S. Department of Commerce will post your firm in an international database and search for and contact qualified international buyers.

Other good ways to make international contacts are to participate in trade shows and trade missions. In a trade mission, a U.S. government official takes a small group

TABLE 11.2 Government Sources of Export Assistance

Agency	Web Site	Assistance Offered
Small Business Association	www.sba.gov	U.S. Export Assistance Centers offer help in virtually all areas of exporting, much for free or at very low costs.
U.S. Department of Commerce	www.export.gov	U.S. government's main exporting site with extensive exporting basics.
	www.unzco.com/basicguide/	This extensive guide is available for downloading and contains virtually everything a beginning exporter needs to know. Includes copies of most paperwork and how to fill it out.
Regional U.S. Department of Commerce offices		Offer export seminars on various topics; many are free or under $50.
Ex-Im Bank	www.exim.gov	Offers seminars on export financing.
Bureau of Industry and Security	www.bxa.doc.gov	Offers seminars on export licensing and compliance issues.
International Trade Administration	www.ita.doc.gov	Has detailed information about U.S. trading partners.
U.S. State Department	www.stat-usa.gov	Has detailed country reports and industry-specific information, some free and some for a price.
State and local governments		Often offer convenient seminars and other export assistance programs.

of business owners to different foreign countries in order to help establish relationships and promote exporting. There are not a lot of these missions, and they are usually specific to a particular type of business and region of the world, so they are not always appropriate. At an international trade fair, similar to domestic trade fairs, you have a booth displaying your products or services and the opportunity for exposure to thousands of potential clients. Again, some fairs are industry-specific, while others are more general. The U.S. government often has a U.S. pavilion featuring export-oriented companies. These companies often have the opportunity to tie into other U.S. government services such as meeting with local U.S. embassy officials, prearranged meetings with qualified customers, market research information, trade barrier information, transportation and customs information, and assistance and access to U.S. trade show experts. Even if you can't exhibit in the fair, attending the fair may give you a chance to meet the sort of people you need to know.

The U.S. government through www.export.gov also provides such services as printed and video catalogs, online databases, and personalized (fee-based) contact services. The U.S. Commercial Service will also assist a company in arranging private promotional activities, including exhibitions, press releases, and receptions when appropriate.

Still another way is to look for foreign companies with a resident representative in the United States, a type of private importing agent. Often these representatives are interested in bringing U.S. products back to their home countries and will already have a good idea if your product is right, and how to promote and distribute it.[47] To find these resident representatives, try the Google search shown here.

The next step is to export your products. But there are a few other things to consider first. Pricing becomes complicated as you need to cover transportation, the additional documents you may need, possible tariffs (taxes on incoming goods), potential currency valuation changes, the cost of converting currencies, and the additional packaging necessary to ship abroad. The importer usually covers foreign taxes, tariffs, additional shipping charges, port handling fees, and the like, but this must be carefully spelled out in your contracts in order to avoid potential differences of opinion.

Shipping documentation and other paperwork are very specific to the product and the country to which it is going. The International Trade Administration (www.trade.gov/td/tic) provides extensive information about tariffs, taxes, specific country information, and other general exporting information. The U.S. Country Commercial guides also provide some assistance in this area, as do some country government Web sites. The Bureau of Export Administration (www.bxa.doc.gov) provides information about when export licensing is necessary and also information on exporting of politically sensitive products. In addition, companies such as NetShip (www.netship.com) have arisen specifically to handle shipping and documentation issues for e-commerce.[48]

There are a variety of payment procedures available. The easiest for you is to require up-front cash payment prior to shipment (or credit card if appropriate). This eliminates your risk, but puts the customer at risk. Providing credit to your customers reverses the risk, and puts it all on you. Both of these are possible methods of receiving payments, but less often used. More typical methods include **letters of credit** or **documentary drafts**. In both cases, the payment procedure now includes four parties—you, your customer, and both of your banks—and payments are made upon proper presentation of certain documents, including the letter of credit or draft, bills of lading, and other paperwork. Although the system is somewhat complex, it provides a lower level of risk for all parties than cash in advance or an open account. You can find assistance here at your current bank.

letter of credit
A document issued by a bank that guarantees a buyer's payment for a specified period of time upon compliance with specified terms.

documentary draft
A draft which can be exercised only when presented with specified shipping documents.

Financing and insurance become important because of the length of time it may take for international payments to be processed and the risk of default, as well as the difficulty of recovery in case of default in international transactions. The Small Business

Administration (www.sba.gov), the Ex-Im Bank (www.exim.gov), and the Overseas Private Investment Corporation (www.opic.gov) provide loans and insurance to cover exporting. In some cases, these loans may also be used to finance trade show participation, to translate brochures and catalogs for international distribution, to renovate or expand existing facilities necessary to produce products for export, to set up lines of credit for potential customers, to provide export working capital, and to provide funding for developing an export program.

Last is the consideration of conflict resolution. Although the possibility exists for pirating, product misuse, and other unfortunate occurrences, the primary areas for conflict resolution include nonpayment and contract default issues. There is no universal court of law that can handle these situations. The U.S. Department of Commerce can provide advice and offer reputable local counsel, but only for sizeable losses, typically several thousand dollars or more. The U.S. Council of the International Chamber of Commerce (www.iccwbo.org) provides international arbitration services and offers some other suggestions, but arbitration, too, is costly and probably not worthwhile unless the loss is significant. This difficulty in international dispute resolution underscores the need to carefully select partners and to do a thorough job of prescreening. This is an area in which various government agencies can help you. The U.S. Commerce Department, for example, prequalifies potential customers in many cases prior to recommending them; you should check the particular program specifics to verify. Ex-Im Bank provides credit information on potential customers and, as mentioned earlier, many agencies provide insurance for export payments.

Importing

Importing strategy is similar to exporting, but with the buyers and sellers reversed. Instead of customers to buy your products, you are looking for sources to sell products to you (which, of course, you'll eventually resell). If you have the opportunity to travel abroad, look for products that are selling well in the country you're visiting and aren't available in the United States or products that are considerably cheaper than similar ones found in the United States (labor and manufacturing costs are often cheaper in other countries than the United States). Trade mission and domestic and international trade shows are also good sources. If you can't travel, ask your international contacts for this information. Next, find out who manufactures them and write the manufacturer a letter, introducing yourself and your company and the potential you see in your market for its product. You're selling yourself, so be sure to tell the producer why you are the best person or company to be representing the product (i.e., experience in that product or in importing, contacts and distribution systems already in place, familiarity with the market, etc.). International mail can be painfully slow, so a fax or e-mail letter is probably best. Also, avoid slang terms (e.g. "your product is da bomb!") and idiomatic expressions (like "break the ice") that are likely to be misunderstood. Since English is rapidly becoming the language of business, a translation is usually not necessary. Follow up with a phone call or visit in which you can pitch the specifics of your marketing plan for the product.[49] One way to conduct international calls for free is to register for Skype, an Internet service which lets you use a broadband connected computer to call other Skype users for free. If you and the overseas company both use Skype, having long conversations to get an understanding of each other will not pose a financial problem. Along the same lines, it is worthwhile these days to check to find out whether an overseas company has video capabilities. Video cameras for PCs are inexpensive, and videoconferencing services are often available on campuses or at commercial locations such as FedEx Kinko's for low costs.

www.skype.com

http://www.fedex.com/us/officeprint/storesvcs/technology/videoconf.html?link=4

With importing, many of the paperwork and insurance details will be your source's responsibility. Import buying works the same way as export selling, that is, the same sorts of paperwork and procedures are followed only in reverse.

Concluding Thoughts on International Business

One of the major mistakes commonly made by U.S. business people (entrepreneurs or major companies) is being insensitive to cultural differences. You're likely to make some mistakes, but take time to learn at least the basics about the culture you're dealing with to avoid the biggest errors. Travel guides and U.S. government country reports often offer brief cultural assistance as do books such as *Kiss, Bow or Shake Hands* and a plethora of "doing business in ____" guides.[50]

Although international business might seem a little daunting with all the paperwork and regulations, small businesses just like yours do it everyday. There's a lot of free or very inexpensive help out there; make use of it.

Location

LO5
Identify the factors to consider in selecting your business location.

When you ask real estate agents the best three things to look for in a house, they will tell you, "Location, location, location." The same holds true in your business. What location—in particular, *good* location—means for your business is highly dependent on what your business is, the amount of money you can afford to budget for it, your particular business philosophy, and the marketing niche you are seeking. Let's start with some general information about location, then move onto specific issues for services (including retailing) and manufacturing businesses. We then discuss some specific choices such as site selection and layout and the buy, build, or lease option.

The first choice, and often only choice, for many entrepreneurs is their hometown because it offers convenience and a familiar setting, and it eliminates a lot of possible family issues. There may also be valid business reasons for this choice: The local banker knows you and is more likely to loan you money; you know your market—the potential customers in the area—and understand their wants and needs; you have seen an unmet need that you can fill; and, for many entrepreneurs, friends and family (usually local) are often the first customers and are great at spreading the word about your business. (Remember that word-of-mouth mentioned above is often the first method of getting to your customers.)

There may also be some compelling reasons to consider a different location. What are the business laws like in your area? Local zoning ordinances specify what sorts of businesses are allowed and not allowed in specific locations.[51] Certain types of businesses—usually those deemed hazardous or that produce foul odors—may be banned or severely restricted. State and local pollution standards, worker's compensation, wage rates, and other such legislation might increase the cost of doing business to the point that other locations become much more favorable. State and local taxes in particular vary considerably from state to state. For example, Wyoming has no personal or corporate income tax, while California has relatively high rates. On the other hand, certain locations often offer attractive incentives for new businesses ranging from tax credits to low-interest loans, from favorable business laws to business incubators (discussed later).

http://www.eda.gov/Resources/StateLinks.xml

http://www.uschamber.com/chambers/directory/default.htm

Most of this information can be found on the Internet. Try the state or city business development office (a good place to start is the Economic Development Administration's state list at http://www.eda.gov/Resources/StateLinks.xml) or the local Chambers of Commerce (look in the phone book or at http://www.uschamber.com/chambers/directory/default.htm to find your local Chamber affiliate). There is also information by state available for your state at www.business.gov/regions/states/, and the Small Business Administration offers links to state-based resources at http://www.sba.gov/sbdc/sbdcnear.html. *Site Selection Magazine*'s Web site (www.siteselection.com) has a number of tools that can help you find the right location. Many of these require being a registered user, but registration is free.

www.business.gov/regions/states/

http://www.sba.gov/sbdc/sbdcnear.html

www.siteselection.com

Other reasons to consider other locations are tied to your customer. Your hometown may not be the best place for you to find your target market customers. Are you close to the people who will use your product or service? Other considerations include population growth or decline (especially in your target sector), income levels, and predicted increases or decreases in income. Is the location expanding economically or slowly dying? Perhaps the best source for this information is the US Census Bureau. State and local municipality business development offices may also carry such information, but they are likely to be slanted toward attracting new businesses.

Also consider the type of business you are planning. Do you need skilled labor? If so, what areas will provide you with the necessary employees? Do you need to be near raw materials or particular methods of transportation? These issues will help determine your choices. Where are your competitors? Certain industries tend to be clustered in certain regions where they can make efficient use of services and employees. Think of California's Silicon Valley or the financial district of New York City.

Doing business in your hometown may be perfectly appropriate; however, the cost of moving a company—whether across town or across the country—can be very expensive. It pays to plan ahead.

Service Firms

There are three typical locations for services: at the client's location, at a mutually accessible location, and at your firm's location. Traditionally, services may have been tied to one or another of these, but marketing niches have been carved out by people daring to be different. Typically dry cleaning and restaurant dining are services provided at a place accessible to both parties, but some dry cleaners now offer pick up and delivery from the client's home, and not only pizza restaurants offer delivery these days. Thanks to the Internet, video rental like Netflix.com and other services are handled electronically, and the customer and service provider may never meet face to face. Whatever innovative niche you select, there are a few things to keep in mind.

At the Client's Location

Typically, these services include things such as house or office cleaning, pest control, remodeling, lawn and gardening services, carpet cleaning, and similar services which must be performed at the client's location. Business headquarters can be a home office with enough room to store and maintain any necessary equipment used in the service. Reliable transportation, preferably modified to organize and store tools efficiently, is imperative. More importantly, the range of your client's locations must be planned to prevent transportation times from being unmanageable. For example, facing a one-hour drive to a client's location might mean you have tied up two hours in commuting. If you cannot charge for travel and do not have other clients nearby, it means you have two hours in which you cannot make any money that day.

If you've done your homework carefully, you already know the geographic area(s) most likely to use your service. Certain services may be organized into a rotating schedule. For example, a house cleaning service may clean a certain set of neighborhoods on Monday, different set on Tuesday, and so on. In other cases, more remote clients may be charged a transportation fee. In some cases, a mileage fee may be appropriate for your business (delivery services, for example).

As the firm grows, it may outgrow its home-based headquarters. As your clients seldom, if ever, visit you, you have more latitude in where you can be located and the ability to seek out low-cost space (see site selection section below). Reasonable distance to the clients and adequate storage room for your expanded fleet and equipment are key to choosing a site.

Mutually Accessible Location

Services using this approach often have too much specialized equipment to be readily transported and a need for at least some client involvement. Barbershops, dentist offices, video rental stores, and restaurants are services typically located at a site that is extremely convenient for the client and reasonably so for the owner and employees.

■ Finding a truly convenient space is one of the challenges to placing one's business in a mutually accessible location. In the example pictured, the owners offer an expanded product line in order to attract passers-by on a busy downtown street. Locating several different kinds of related items in one street front store gives customers the ability to shop for several needs at one time and place.

Even though your service may be traditionally located in a mutually accessible area, consider what you might do to make it home-based. Your watch repair shop might generate clientele by being located in a shopping center, but will the added sales be offset by the high cost of rent, utilities, insurance, and other payments? Can you offer pick-up and delivery and do the work at home? Your restaurant idea might work as a catering service. Instead of a specialized clothing shop, why not try mail order or Internet-based sales?

Remote Location

In this type of service, face-to-face meetings with the client are infrequent. Typical services that meet this criterion include medical transcription, data processing, fulfillment centers, and some consulting work. These services generally are ideal for home-based

SMALL BUSINESS INSIGHT

Lindzey Patterson and Home Cooking

Lindzey Patterson had a real passion for cooking. Even as she was finishing her degree at Saint Louis University, she was planning her next classes at a local cooking school. Her idea was to offer cooking classes in the client's own kitchen. Her business could operate from a van equipped with her cooking equipment and refrigerators for storing food. Reservations could be handled by cell phone. This way, Lindzey had taken a business usually based in a mutually accessible location and made it into a business conducted at the customer's location. In doing so she was able to minimize her costs and personalize her service, called Home Cooking.

businesses. Certain services, for example, fulfillment centers, generally take more space—at the minimum, an attic, garage, or basement. The biggest advantage of these sorts of businesses is that they can be located anywhere in the world. U.S. hospitals, for example, use medical transcription services located in India. One such company, Infoflow/TSVI, operates from a U.S. sales base (which makes handling calls from U.S. hospitals easier) with transcription being done in India, managed there by a co-owner, who is a cousin and long-time friend of one of the two American owners (www.infoflowtranscription.com).[52] Other than perhaps some initial sales meetings, all business is transacted via phone, fax, electronic exchanges, or mail.

www.infoflowtranscription.com

Manufacturers

What if you are selling a product and not a service? What are your considerations about location now? Where you make the product is really dependent on the product. Some products that do not require a lot of specialized or bulky equipment can be produced at home unless zoning ordinances forbid it. In addition to whatever office space is needed, adequate work space is also required. The basement, a garage, or a home workshop may be adequate for some time. As business expands and as you add employees, it will become awkward if not illegal to continue production at home.

Some products require bulky and specialized equipment, utility demands atypical of homes, or sizable warehousing requirements and are never suitable for home businesses. Certain production characteristics—for example, use of hazardous materials and materials with strong odors or noisy operations—may make a home-based business undesirable. Many cities have zoning ordinances prohibiting manufacturing in residential areas. When you start to hire employees, providing the amenities they will expect or that are required by law will usually require moving the business from your home.

Contract manufacturing might be a better option, at least for a while. In this case, a firm with the capabilities to produce your product is contracted to manufacture it for you, usually for a flat per unit fee and a possible setup charge. Some firms will also assist in marketing and sales as well. Trade magazines in your field often list ads for contract manufacturers. An interesting possibility here is to use **sheltered workshops** to perform light manufacturing or assembly sorts of businesses. These workshops exist in nearly every state and offer very competitive pricing, often including tax benefits for the business.

contract manufacturing
An existing firm with the correct manufacturing capabilities makes your product for you.

sheltered workshop
A nonprofit organization or institution that provides business services by using handicapped or rehabilitated workers.

Site Selection

Once you have determined the general location of your business, you need to determine the exact location for your operation. What you should look for falls into three main categories: home-based businesses, high customer contact (e.g., retail), and low customer contact (e.g., manufacturing). Each has certain criteria to be considered.

High Customer Contact Businesses

Businesses with high customer contact include such diverse operations as medical or legal offices, restaurants, retail establishments, dry cleaners, and other businesses that are highly dependent on being convenient to the customer. For these operations, there are three critical site selection considerations: traffic, customer ease, and competition.[53]

First of all, you want a site that is convenient to your target market and to enough of the customers to make you profitable. If you are considering a franchise, many will offer site criteria to help you make your selection. If you are going it alone, consider the population density of the area and how many of the people in the area meet your target market criteria. The U.S. Census Bureau Web site can be a good starting place for free information. If plowing through the Census Bureau Web site doesn't get you what you want, several commercial services including ESRI will sell you data about the population in a particular zip code for several hundred dollars. More detailed and

www.esri.com

specific commercial information is also available and can range in price from several thousand dollars to over $100,000 and is probably not an option for most entrepreneurs.[54] Again, the Web site of *Site Selection Magazine* (www.siteselection.com) mentioned above has tools and additional articles that can help.

SKILL MODULE 11.1

Using the U.S. Census Bureau Web Site

The U.S. government through its Census Bureau Web site (**www.census.gov**) offers so much information free for the taking that it is sometimes difficult to decide what to use and how to get it. While daunting at first glance, the Web site is relatively easy to use and presents quite a bit of data useful to the entrepreneur. Let's say that you are thinking about opening a housecleaning service, a home-based business in the community of Upland, California. Before you open this business, you'd like to know if there would be enough customers interested in using this service within a reasonable geographic area. You've decided that the likely target market would be households with incomes in excess of $100,000, probably managers or other professionals who would like to have someone else do the housework.

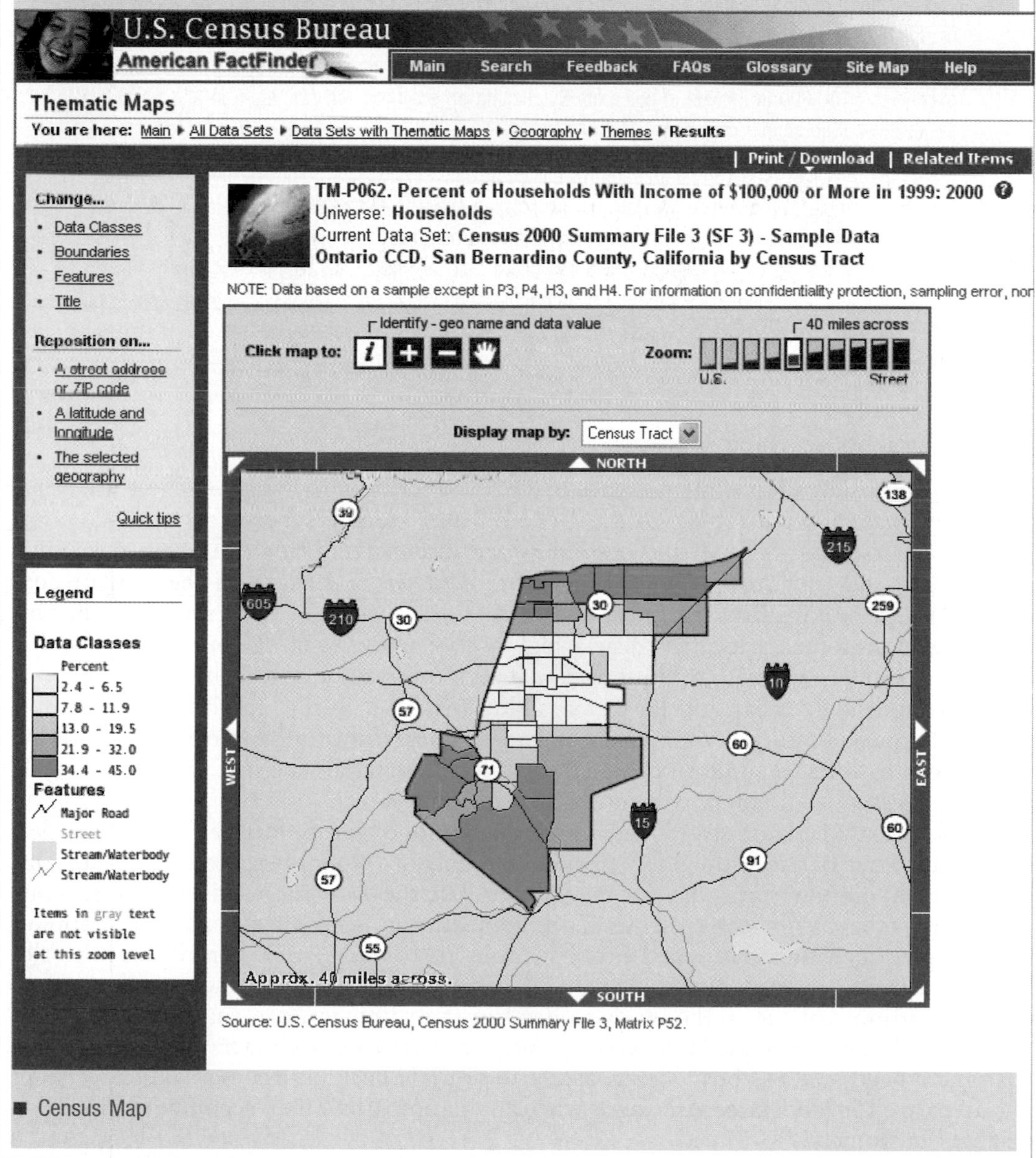

■ Census Map

- **Step 1:** Go to the Web site (**www.census.gov**) and look for and select the link (along the left side) called "American Fact Finder."
- **Step 2:** There's a lot of information on this page that could be useful, but look for the heading "Getting Detailed Data" and the line that reads, "Expert user? Go directly to *Data Sets.*" You're now an expert user, so click the Data Sets link.
- **Step 3:** This page gives you a list of data sets you might want and a brief description of what you might find. For the purpose of this exercise, let's use "Census 2000 Summary File 3 (SF 3)—Sample Data." When you select this file, a menu comes down on the right side of the screen, giving several choices on how to examine these data. A map would be nice so that we could see exactly the areas in which we are likely to find our customers, so select "Thematic Maps."
- **Step 4:** This brings you to a series of screens that helps you select the exact geographic area that you want. Upland is located in the state of California, in San Bernardino County. Since San Bernardino County is so huge, we want to concentrate on the county subdivision of Ontario. The first screen has a pull down menu to let you select the size of the region you want. Choose "County Subdivision." Subsequent screens will have menus listing the state, county, and county subdivision. After selecting "Ontario CCD," click on "Next."
- **Step 5:** Now you have a screen listing the possible maps that could be generated. By scrolling down, you will find both "Percentage of Employed Civilian Persons 16 and over in Management, Professional or Related" and "Percentage of Households with income of $100,000 or more in 1999–2000." Let's select the second one, which brings up a color-coded map showing us by percent the households exceeding $100,000 in income in our area. By clicking on the map, we can zoom in and get down to street level. (See screen capture.)

Depending on what data you need, some of the other options in step 3 might be better. "Detailed Tables," for example, will give you list data in many cases down to the block level. Data are available also by home ownership, ethnic group, commute time, and hundreds of other options.

If you look at the top of the Web page you will find a "You are here" line. By clicking any of these, you can back up one or more steps for different searches. In addition, at the bottom of the page, you'll find the option of entering a street address, which will reposition the map. Enter your home address. How does it compare with Upland?

traffic generators
Other businesses that bring customers (generate traffic) to the area.

Another consideration is the presence of **traffic generators** in the area. These are other businesses that draw customers to the area and may include supermarkets, office complexes, schools, and malls. If the customers are drawn there, for example, to grocery shop, might they not stop at your video store next door? Reflect on the type of customer you are seeking and the likelihood of these businesses in attracting them. If you want a teen customer, a location near a high school works well. If you are looking for evening clientele, offices that close at five aren't the right traffic generators for you. Drive around likely areas and locate possible sites. Visit during the hours you anticipate to be peak times for your business and evaluate foot and car traffic.[55] Look at the crowds or lines in similar businesses and decide whether there is room for you. If most businesses seem empty, you probably will be too.

Intersections of major streets offer high automobile traffic, but because of divided roads and other barriers, they may not make it easy for your customers to get to you. Businesses along interstates have high visibility, but the frontage roads can be so convoluted that the clients seek easier-to-get-to competitors. Even some malls and shopping centers have such tortuous access problems that customers avoid them when possible. Sometimes entry is easy, but getting out is difficult. For example, no signals for left turns when most of the traffic needs to head in that direction can turn off customers.

Parking is also an issue. Is it conveniently located to your place of business? Do customers need to cross busy streets to get to you? Is parking free or paid? Are parking areas well lit and safe? Are there wheelchair ramps or other accommodations for disabled customers?

SMALL BUSINESS INSIGHT

Steak-Out Restaurant[56]

Mark Dukes thought he'd found the perfect location for a restaurant that specialized in the delivery of burgers, chicken, and steaks when he found a location in the middle of the University of Tennessee in Knoxville. Students are always hungry and love delivery. However, during school breaks there are no orders—and also no employees. In addition, there was no parking at his location on campus. After seven years of struggling, Mr. Dukes moved his failing franchise off-campus to a free-standing building with a parking lot. His sales are up 100 percent. He still delivers to students, but he now gets a lot of community business, and a family order averages $30 compared to the student order of $7 or $8.

Customers have strong ideas about how far they should have to drive for things. These vary somewhat from major metropolitan areas to more rural towns and from one region of the United States to another. Generally convenience stores, fast food restaurants, and gas stations need to be close to consumers. Grocery stores and banks can be somewhat farther away, but not much. Discount stores and midscale restaurants can be even farther away, while specialty stores, upscale restaurants, and malls can be relatively remote. Where does your business fit? How far are customers willing to drive to get to you?

Malls are great traffic generators, but space at malls is costly. If it is appropriate for your product, you might consider a kiosk or cart in the mall as a way of testing the market and location without making a large investment.[57] Neighborhood shopping centers (those anchored by a supermarket, drugstore, or major retailer) or strip centers (shopping centers without major anchors) are more modestly priced, but lack the drawing power of malls.[58]

Generally, competition in the area can draw away valuable clients, but this is not true in every case. Many cities have a restaurant row, an antique district, or an automobile mile (as well as other business types) where many competitors cluster. Clients

■ Chicago's jewelry row is an example of clustered competitors whose proximity to each other gives customers added convenience and more options. What are some reasons you can think of that illustrate how clustering helps bring more interest and business to an entire area?

wish to comparison shop or have choices and are drawn to areas where they can see several similar businesses at one time. Locating far from these will mean that you are free from competition, but this benefit may easily be offset by the cost of attracting customers to a different place. Additionally, you can capitalize on competitive advertisements that bring potential customers to the area. Your competitor's high-budget TV ad might get customers to the neighborhood, but the "sale" sign in your window may get them to stop at your place instead.

Another instance when you want to be near competitors is when your business provides a strong contrast to the competition in the area. Do you offer better assistance, additional services, unique advantages, or other benefits that can easily be seen by customers? They may be drawn to the area by a well-known competitor's name, but they may select your establishment instead because of what you offer that differentiates you.

Low Customer Contact Businesses

Generally low customer contact businesses are manufacturing businesses, the headquarters of client location-based services, or remote location services. Customer access is relatively unimportant. More critical are access for your employees, reasonable cost, and the space necessary to do your business. Certain manufacturing operations will need adequate utilities and specialized transportation too.

Unless you plan to use some of this space as a high-traffic showroom, commercial space in a business park or light industrial park might be appropriate. These parks are located near major transportation routes, often have rail spurs, and are designed for industrial utilities; that is, they have adequate electricity, gas, water, waste water treatment, and the like. Frequently, support businesses will be located in or near the park such as warehousing, shipping firms, copy centers, and office supply stores. Industrial or business park space tends to be cheaper in smaller cities and rural towns than in major metropolitan areas. If distribution to customers can be arranged, these locations are certainly cost-effective.

Some major metropolitan areas offer *empowerment zones*. These zones, often in economically depressed areas, offer businesses low-cost space and tax advantages for locating there. For more information, see www.ezec.gov or www.siteselection.com.

www.ezec.gov

www.siteselection.com

A third possibility is a business incubator. The National Business Incubator Association (www.nbia.org) shows over 850 business incubators in the United States sponsored by government, universities, or private investment groups. These business incubators are specifically designed for the entrepreneur, and, in addition to relatively low cost space, they offer a multitude of small business support services. These services range from copy machines, faxes, and conference rooms to accounting, finance, and consulting services. Since the building is populated by other entrepreneurs, it's a great place to talk to others who might have had some of the same problems or to brainstorm new ideas. Most incubators require a stake in your company in exchange for their assistance—maybe as much as 50 percent—and often have quite a bit to say about how you run your business. Opinion is mixed on how much real help a company can get; just like all businesses, there are better and worse incubators, so do your homework.[59]

www.nbia.org

General Comments on Site Selection

How do you go about finding potential sites? Looking for "for sale" and "for rent" signs is a start, but not all space will be advertised that way. Just as a good real estate agent can warn you about the proposed freeway project going through the backyard of the house you are considering or let you know about houses not yet listed but likely to be, an experienced real estate broker will also be able to assist you in your search for your business location. Many have relationships with landlords that can work to your benefit. They are also likely to have at least some of the market statistics you may need to help you decide if the location is right for your business.[60] Level with them about what you can spend. You have your business plan and know the cost per square foot you can afford and be profitable. If you are looking at property more expensive than that, you'll need to cut corners elsewhere.[61]

Home-Based Businesses[62]

LO6
Set up your home-based business location.

As we note in Chapter 5, whether a home-based business is a starting point or appropriate for the life of your firm, there are certain things that will help you keep your sanity. First and foremost is the location of your home-based business. While the dining room table may be infrequently used, is it the best place for your work? While anything can work, the following suggestions come from home-based entrepreneurs and are likely to make your life a lot easier.

First, check with the city for zoning restrictions. If you have a neighborhood association, it may also have restrictions above and beyond the city. Generally a home-office type of business with no client visits is acceptable, but you may need to apply for a variance. Check with your local municipality.

Choose a work location inside your home that is away from distractions and family traffic. Privacy is important; you don't want to be on the phone with a client and have your children running through your office. Your bedroom is generally a bad idea; how can you sleep if you're thinking about business? Consider a guest bedroom, the attic, the basement, or even a large closet. Be realistic about the amount of space you'll need for your equipment. While a window may provide natural light and relieve cabin fever, your workspace might be better without a window if you find things going on outside to be interesting and distracting. A door serves two purposes: It ensures privacy, and it allows you to "shut off" your business at the end of the day. Even the most considerate spouse and children have trouble walking by without at least saying, "Hi." Before finalizing your decision, spend a day or two in the location you've chosen to check out noise, traffic patterns, lighting needs, and distractions.

Once you've chosen your location, you'll need equipment. You'll need a comfortable, usable desk and chair and adequate lighting. Consider the tasks you'll perform most frequently and check out the ergonomic options that will serve you the best. Although you can store files in cardboard boxes, an inexpensive filing cabinet would be so much simpler. Think about the layout of the furniture for access to proper lighting, phone jacks, and electrical outlets. You may need to supplement some or all of these.

Tools typically include a telephone, high-capacity Internet service (like cable or DSL), a business e-mail account, a high-speed desktop computer and appropriate software, a fax machine, and a copier. These days many multiple purpose equipment is available. Printers can double as copiers and scanners. Your computer can retrieve faxes for you. These items reduce the amount of space you'll need. Consider the layout of the equipment and how you'll use each piece. You don't want to reach around your computer monitor to pick up the telephone or race across the room to catch printer pages.

You'll want to have a separate business telephone line with an answering machine or service so that you can get those important calls after hours. Consider a second phone line if you are limited to a modem-based Internet connection. Ideally, this space and its tools will be used only for your home-based office. In addition, totally separate space and equipment make tax deduction preparation much simpler.

Although not specifically related to site selection, here are some other important things to remember. It's easy to work long hours without a break when the office is just down the hall. With the refrigerator conveniently located and work replacing exercise, many entrepreneurs have discovered unexpected weight gains. You need mental and physical health breaks. Limit your work hours to something reasonable.

On the other hand, it's also too easy to get distracted with all the little household items that should get done. What's a minute or two to run a load of laundry? If I schedule my dentist appointments in the middle of the day, I avoid traffic. These things will suck up a lot more time than you think, and you'll find you need the after dinner hours to catch up. Consider getting outside help for some of these jobs. How much do you charge an hour? Isn't a housekeeper or lawn service cheaper? There is a lot of conventional wisdom that has accumulated to help guide decision making for people thinking about a home-based business. Figure 11.2 summarizes the most important, offering 20 questions to ask yourself as you think about setting up a home-based business.

FIGURE 11.2

Twenty Questions to Ask before Planning Your Home Office[63]

1. Do you want clients or visitors traipsing through your home to get to your office?
2. Do you want your family trooping through—or even past—your office?
3. Are you doing mostly desk work?
4. Do you need space to sort, store, and ship materials?
5. Are you producing and assembling a product?
6. Do you want or need to keep your work in progress on hand and available for tweaking at a moment's notice?
7. Does noise or activity easily distract you?
8. How much and what kind of sound can you tolerate while working?
9. Do you work more efficiently when you can see and touch reference materials?
10. Do you wilt in the absence of natural light?
11. Do you need a desktop computer, or would a notebook do as well?
12. Are you left- or right-handed?
13. Do you need a separate entrance to maintain clients' privacy or your own sanity?
14. Is your work life completely separate from or fairly integrated with the rest of your life?
15. Do you need help maintaining healthy boundaries around your work?
16. Is your work something in which your family can participate?
17. Will you be adding more equipment in the near future?
18. Does listening to music boost your creativity?
19. Do you need space to hold meetings?
20. Does your town or city have special zoning requirements for home-based businesses?

Watch out for family, friends, and visitors who don't understand home-based businesses. Set the ground rules early and stick with them. The Peters were both running home-based businesses. Their working-outside-the-home siblings didn't understand why they couldn't drop off their ill or vacationing children so that they "wouldn't miss work."[64] You'll be asked to do extra school or sports carpools, wait for service people, or other such things because of your at-home status. Practice saying no until it becomes comfortable and automatic, and don't feel embarrassed or guilty when you do. When houseguests come to call, set the expectations upfront about when you will and will not be available and the parts of your house that are strictly off limits.

When does a home-based business outgrow the home? For some companies, the answer is never. Some entrepreneurs opt for charging higher prices for their goods or services or limiting their sales so as not to outgrow the space available; being a home-based business is just too important to them to change. Others reinvest their profits into additions to their homes to accommodate their business growth or to upgrade to a roomier house with the extra space they need. Some die-hard home-based entrepreneurs faced with this decision have found creative ways of housing their staff and other operations in an outside office while continuing to telecommute as much as possible.[65]

More typically, a business will find the need for meeting rooms and employee accommodations or zoning restrictions will force the change. In other cases, family situations just aren't favorable to a home-based business. Some entrepreneurs find they aren't cut out for the solitude of working by themselves or find household chores, family, or other distractions disturb them too easily. These home-based businesses are now facing the same situation as high-customer contact or—more likely—low-customer contact businesses discussed above.

Layout

LO7
Know what to look for in evaluating a potential site layout.

Since so much of this is particular to the type of business you are in, what you'll read below is a general guide. Check out competitors or similar types of businesses to see what you like and don't like, what seems to work well, and what seems to cause a lot of problems. In addition, certain categories—restaurants and retailing, for example—have numerous books from college textbooks to do-it-yourself books, like the "For Dummies" series. Try your local library or bookstore.

The layout of a potential site must be considered carefully. Is the building setup appropriately for your use? A restaurant will have different needs from a retail area or a manufacturing plant. The amount of area allocated to the "front room" (e.g., eating or retail areas) versus "back room" (storage, kitchen, warehouse, and office areas) needs to be adequate for the purpose of your business. If you are operating a restaurant or retail operation, how important is space in the front room? A coffee shop or fast food restaurant squeezes in more customers per square foot than a gourmet restaurant. Do you need specialized areas, such as a kitchen or laboratory that are expensive to retrofit into existing buildings? Is there adequate storage area? How much dock space is appropriate for your business? A manufacturing firm usually needs more dock space and storage than a retailer or a restaurant, while a service company may need very little of either. Retail operations need display windows, while manufacturers do not. For restaurants or other services, this need varies. Is there room for expansion should the business grow? Remember: Moving can be expensive. A good strategy is to rough out the desired layout of your operation on graph paper to get a basic idea of the square footage needed and how it should look. What exactly you want may not be out there, but you'll be able to see what's close and what's impossible to live with.

Consider the amenities that are already there. Carpeting may be appropriate for a retail area and perhaps the office or dining area of a restaurant, but not appropriate for manufacturing or cooking areas. What about the walls? What sort of ceilings and lighting is appropriate? Again, a visit to the competition will help you decide what works and what doesn't, as well as where you want to be different.

Check the exterior, too. Is the building attractive and inviting? Are the sidewalks and landscaped areas in decent shape? Is parking adequate, well lit, and safe? Is employee parking separate from customer parking? What about handicap accessibility? The 1990 Americans with Disabilities Act (ADA) specifies that businesses (with few exceptions) must accommodate persons with disabilities. Many buildings have been brought up to code, and all new construction should meet the requirements of this act, but keep your eyes open.

Once the building has been selected, how you lay out the interior also needs to be considered. While retailers, restaurants, offices, and manufacturers all have different layout needs and considerations, two facts hold true: (1) layouts need to be designed so as to eliminate unnecessary and excessive employee movement, and (2) the layout says something about who you are to your customers, employees, and visitors. In retailing, this last factor is called *atmospherics*. While the opportunities for variation are limitless, let's consider the major types of retail and manufacturing layouts as well as what atmospherics might mean to a business.

Traditionally, manufacturing processes are laid out in one of two formats: production line layout and process layout displayed in Figure 11.3. In the production line

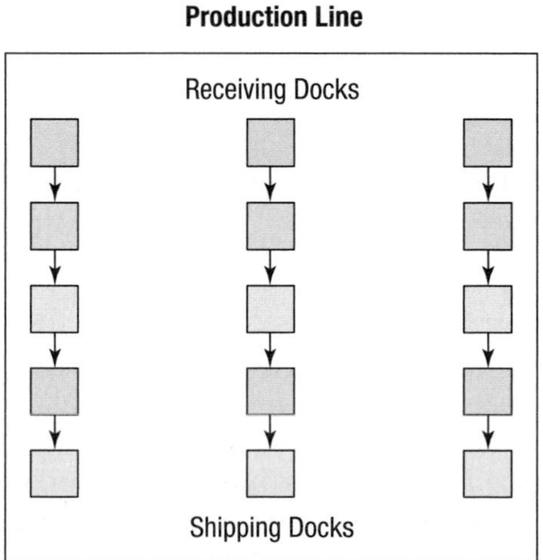

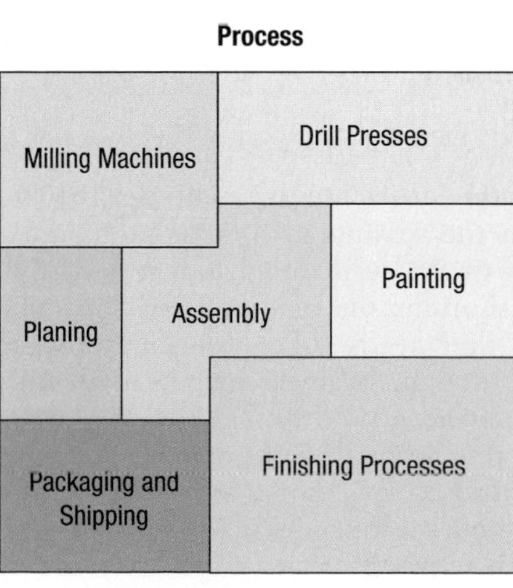

FIGURE 11.3

Typical Manufacturing Layouts

FIGURE 11.4

Typical Retail Layouts

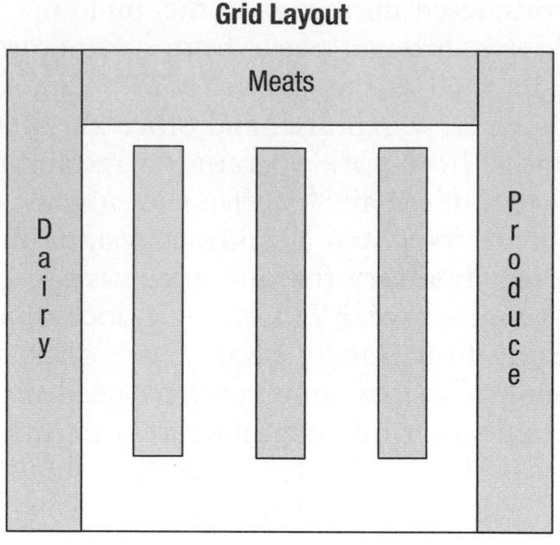

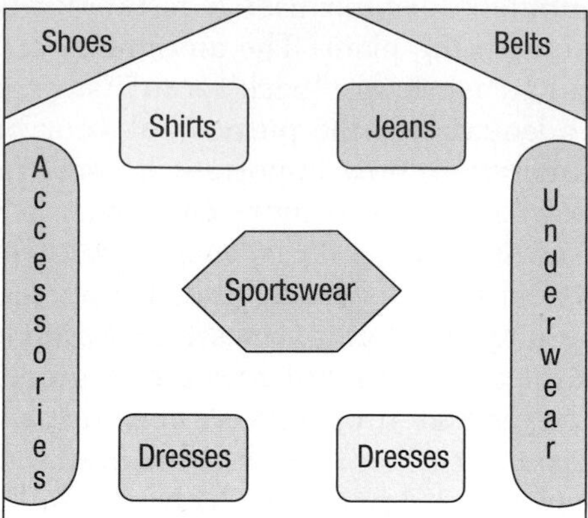

layout, material flows in on one side of the operation and continues to the other end of the operation. Most assembly manufacturing is done this way, often with conveyors moving subassemblies from one station to another. Although a rather rigid flow, it works well for mass production and high-volume manufacturing. The second method, process layout, groups similar machines/or functions together, not unlike a typical machine shop. This format is much more appropriate for lower-volume, flexible manufacturing.

There are also two traditional layouts for retail operations, which are shown in Figure 11.4. The first one, the grid layout, has aisles running from the front of the store to the back like the typical grocery, discount, or convenience store. It's a very efficient and organized layout although it lacks some visual impact. The second layout, the free-form layout, alleviates this problem. In this layout, the store is laid out in sections with aisles that angle or meander through the store. This is the layout more typically found in upscale department stores, clothing stores, and the like.

Atmospherics include all the ambiance items that might be considered in your business. An upscale women's clothing store is likely to have wider aisles, deep carpeting, soft "elevator music," indirect lighting, and, perhaps, a lightly perfumed aroma. These are appropriate atmospherics for the target market. A shop catering to edgy teen fashions may be done in black and chrome with loud rock or alternative music and strobe or black lights. Both of these send a message about whom the store is likely to appeal to. Restaurants use atmospherics, too. Compare a family restaurant to a gourmet restaurant to an ethnic restaurant. Services and the office and public areas of manufacturing firms do this as well in their choice of colors, furniture styles, and background music.[66]

Build, Buy, or Lease[67]

LO8
Understand the pros and cons of buying, building, or leasing.

Ultimately, there are three choices available to the business: build, buy, or lease. Building has the advantage of having the perfect layout in the perfect location and the street appeal of a new building, but it is costly and slow. Buying something already in existence shortens the time and may be somewhat cheaper, but any remodeling or retrofitting that needs to be done may overshadow any time or money savings. In both cases, though, business owners have an asset that they can leverage, as well as the depreciation tax advantage. They have the flexibility to make the changes they need and know what the long-term costs will be.

Renting is, of course, an option with a considerably lower initial cash outlay, and it is often the only feasible choice for new businesses. Rent expenses are deductible business expenses. One of the main downsides of renting is that you are usually limited in the renovations you can do. Another one is that rents tend to get higher with each renewal contract, and your landlord may choose not to extend a lease, forcing you to move before you are ready to do so.

The issues of location and distribution are decisions that business owners make only occasionally. Many businesses operate from the same location for their entire existence. Distribution decisions may come up more often. For example, a business started on eBay develops its own Web site and then grows into a store in the city's commercial center. Regardless of how often these decisions are made, they are central to the success of the small business, because placing a business in the right location and equipping it with the right channels of distribution are essential to finding and connecting with customers. Done right, managing the issues of location and distribution can turn an average firm into a major success.

CHAPTER SUMMARY

LO1 Recognize the different types of direct marketing and their pros and cons.

- Word of mouth is a good starting point and is low cost but is not controllable and is limited in reach.
- Direct sales fall into four main categories:
  - Most business-to-business sales are conducted by the personal contact of a salesperson calling on the potential customer.
  - Door-to-door sales are becoming less popular with the small amount of time to find people at home and privacy issues. On the other hand, they are particularly effective for product demonstration.
  - Party sales also face some time limitations, but are popular ways of selling products from detergents to personal care products and from housewares to lingerie.
  - Vending machines provide 24 hour a day convenience for certain types of products.
- Direct mail encompasses catalogs, flyers, letters, videos, and anything else that can be mailed.
  - Address lists—even lists on labels—can be purchased to match particular demographic or geographic targets.
  - Direct faxing and direct e-mailing are variations on this. Unsolicited e-mail, known as spam, is subject to restrictions from the national CAN-SPAM law and local and state legislation.
- Telemarketing has two forms:
  - Outbound telemarketing is when the company calls the customer. It is severely restricted by "do not call" lists and other legislation.
  - Inbound telemarketing is when the customer calls the company; this is often in response to a piece of direct response advertising.
- Direct response advertising is any ad that prompts the consumer to make contact with the company by phone, mail, or e-mail.
  - In addition to straight-out direct advertising spots, television offers opportunities to reach customers through home shopping networks.
  - Magazines offer targeted audiences and four-color printing opportunities as well as less expensive classified types of ads.

    - Radio direct response advertising is possible, but audiences are highly distracted and frequently unable to immediately respond or write down telephone numbers or addresses.
- Guerilla marketing is a term used to describe extremely low-cost or free alternative marketing. It covers things such as doorknob hangers or flyers stuck under windshield wipers.
- Multichannel marketing refers to giving your customers multiple ways of contacting you—phone, Web site or mail-in order forms, for example.

LO2 Master using the Internet as a distribution channel.

- E-mail is the simplest Internet direct marketing tool. A potential customer may e-mail an order or request for more information.
- Many firms find Web sites advantageous because they offer potential customers opportunities to find out more about your firm and to place orders. Web sites give firms credibility.
    - Some Internet service providers offer free tools to help you design your Web site. Web site designers range from well-qualified nonprofessionals to expensive, top-of-the-line firms.
    - Get information about your Web site to your customers by including it on all your advertisements, placing links on related sites, visiting chat rooms, and joining search engines.
- E-malls are groups of Internet stores gathered into one site for customer convenience. Many offer tools to help manage your Web-based business for a fee.
- eBay is the most well known e-commerce Web site and has auction as well as e-mall capabilities. Although known for its consumer business, eBay has a business-to-business auction and an e-mall as well.
- Business-to-business services can use eLance and similar reverse auction sites to find potential customers and bid on projects. Business-to-business e-malls are also available.
- Direct selling distribution issues include:
    - Federal Express, UPS, and the U.S. Postal Service offer shipping software and services for small businesses.
    - For larger shippers, fulfillment centers or distribution center partners may provide better services.

LO3 Learn how to do nondirect distribution.

- Nondirect distribution requires using wholesalers, distributors, or retailers as well as other middlemen.
- The appropriate channel may be discovered by tracing similar products back to their sources.
- Getting distributors interested may mean starting with direct sales through catalogs or trade shows to establish your product, demand, and reputation.
- E-tailers—Internet stores—may be willing to take on unknown suppliers and products because they have low overhead.

LO4 Differentiate the types of international strategies.

- Entrepreneurs generally fall into three categories in using international strategies: some will always remain local; some are founded specifically to be international; and most believe that international business might be right for them some day, but do not worry about it until that day comes.

- Small businesses have the same options as large businesses in the international area (licensing, joint ventures, etc.) but most will start with—and may always stay with—an exporting strategy.
- Exporting has four main steps:
  - Determining whether you're ready to export. This includes knowing if your product is appropriate, understanding whether you have the expertise or need outside help, and deciding exactly how you prefer to export.
  - Determining where to export. This step helps select the market or markets best suited for your product.
  - Determining whom to contact. This step explores ways to find appropriate contact people internationally.
  - Determining how to begin. Considerations at this stage include:
    - Shipping documents and paperwork.
    - Payment procedures.
    - Financing and insurance.
    - Conflict resolution.
- Importing: While many of the steps are similar to those for exporting, it is important to know how to find potential products to import and how to make the initial contacts.

LO5 Identify the factors to consider in selecting your business location.

- While most entrepreneurs assume they'll operate in their hometown, this isn't always the best location for their businesses.
  - Key consideration 1: What's the best business climate for your operation?
  - Key consideration 2: Where's the best location for getting to your customer?
  - Key consideration 3: Where's the best location for access to the raw materials, labor, and other factors necessary to conduct your business?
- Service firms may perform work at the client's location, at a mutually accessible location, or be remotely located and have limited customer interface.
- Manufacturers may be home-based, but most will be located away from the home. Contract manufacturing is a low-cost way to get started.
- Site selection choices include home-based, high customer contact locations, and low customer contact locations.
- High customer contact considerations include:
  - Traffic:
    - Where is your best-sized target market?
    - What are traffic generators, and which ones are appropriate for you to use?
  - Customer ease: Consider traffic barriers, parking, and distance from the customer.
  - Competition:
    - Competition clusters are typical in some locations and for some types of business.
    - Having a noticeable differential advantage may make you look good compared to the competition.

- Low customer contact considerations include:
  - Business or light industrial parks provide lower-cost space and nearby amenities.
  - Empowerment zones, available in some areas, may also provide tax breaks.
  - Business incubators are an option that is good for networking with other entrepreneurs, generally at the cost of a portion of your equity.

LO6 Set up your home-based business location.

- Determine how much space you'll need and where your work area should be located.
- Consider the tools you'll need—which ones and how and where they'll be stored.
- Establish rules for working at home—for yourself and your family.
- Determine when you outgrow a home-based business.

LO7 Know what to look for in evaluating a potential site layout.

- The first consideration is the physical layout of the building. Is it large enough and laid out appropriately for your business?
- Second, consider the amenities. Remodeling is possible, but expensive.
- Last, take into account the exterior of the building. Does it have street appeal?
- Manufacturing typically is laid out in one of two ways: production line or process layout.
- Retailing also has two primary layouts: grid or free form.
- Atmospherics tell customers a lot about your business and the type of customers you are likely to service.

LO8 Understand the pros and cons of buying, building, or leasing.

- Buying offers you complete control of your facility and tax advantages, but it comes at a high cost with limited flexibility should you need to move. Remodeling costs, should the building not be exactly right for your business, may add considerably to your overall costs.
- Building offers some of the same advantages and disadvantages of buying; however, you are able to design the building perfectly to your specifications. Customers are likely to be attracted to new buildings and tend to feel that a company in a new building must be successful.
- Leasing is the low-cost option and still has some tax advantages, albeit different ones. Leasing allows you the flexibility of moving at any time, but subjects you to increasing rents and landlords who don't renew leases.

DISCUSSION QUESTIONS

1. Some of the most innovative start-ups have been firms that have dared to buck tradition in their distribution choices, like Netflix.com which distributes rental videos through the mail from its Web site. Select four small businesses and come up with unique distribution systems for them. Beyond the differential advantage, what other advantages might this give a firm?

2. If you were to start a home-based business today, where in your house would you put it? What problems do you foresee, and how might you deal with them? What would happen if your spouse or another family member decided to start a home-based business, too?
3. What would be good traffic generators for a fast food restaurant? For an office supply shop? For a tattoo parlor?
4. What competitive clusters can you identify in your hometown or school location?
5. What products could be sold in vending machines that currently are not? What about party sales?
6. The chapter mentioned several unique guerilla marketing pieces that stood out from the rest—the landscaper who used a plastic sandwich bag of decorative stones with his business card and the decorator whose ad was on a wallpaper scrap. Come up with two or three innovative ways of presenting your message.
7. What direct response ads can you recall seeing or hearing lately? Which ones were more effective? Why?
8. Have you ever used eBay? As a buyer or a seller? What were your experiences?
9. What are the disadvantages of selling by auction? Of selling by reverse auction?
10. Pick a hobby or sport you enjoy. If you had developed a product related to that hobby or sport, what are likely groups, associations, or other organizations that have meetings which might be a good place to set up a sales booth?
11. In browsing the Internet, you have found Web sites that you liked and ones that you didn't—not the content necessarily, but the ease of use and other design issues. What were things that you found particularly annoying? What things did you like?
12. Assume you have developed innovative new business software and want to sell it internationally. Without doing any research, come up with a list of likely countries. Why did you choose the ones you did? If the product had been a nutrition bar or soft drink, would the list be different? Why?

EXPERIENTIAL EXERCISES

1. Select a product or service and pretend you are able to start that business anywhere in the United States. Using the Skills Module in the chapter, find a location different from your hometown or school location that would be appropriate to situate your business. What criteria did you use to make your selection?
2. Choose a business that you might someday like to start. Try one of the direct marketing address providers' Web sites listed in the chapter and locate a list that you feel would be appropriate to reach your market. Which list did you select and why? What would it cost?
3. Select a major high customer contact business category (restaurant, retail, dry cleaning, beauty salon, etc.)—and visit two or more different providers. What do you see in their store layout that seems to work well and what suggestions do you have for things that might work better?
4. Visit two stores, one where you belong to the target market and one where you do not. Make a list of all the atmospherics you detect and explain how they appeal to the target market.
5. Select a specific product and find it on eBay. Watch the auction to see what the product sells for. Is this better or worse than you expected? Is the product also available in any of the eBay e-mall stores? How is it priced there?
6. Keep a list of direct marketing you experience for a week. Which messages did you find particularly appealing? Why? Which ones were you more likely to ignore?

Mini-Case

AUCTION DROP[68]

Randy Adams had a garage full of stuff too good to throw away. It was so bad that his car would no longer fit. His wife suggested selling on eBay, but Adams wasn't sure it was worth the effort. He'd have to take digital photos of everything, post auctions, wait for bids, arrange shipments, hope payments came in, and hopefully eventually get rid of everything. Also, as a new "eBayer," he had no feedback from previous sales, something that can make or break a seller as buyers are sometimes reluctant to use untested sellers.

Of course, if he had these problems, so would a lot of other people. This sounded like an entrepreneurial opportunity to Adams, and he started Auction Drop (www.auctiondrop.com) in San Carlos, California, in March of 2003. For a percentage of the selling fee, Auction Drop will do all the work for you—photos, posting, monitoring, packaging and shipping, and payment collection. It sells 92 percent of everything it has listed compared to the typical eBay 50 percent average. If your item isn't sold, Auction Drop will ship it back to you or donate it to charity and provide a tax receipt for you.

Auction Drop isn't the only company doing this. IsoldIt (www.i-soldit.com), Quik-Drop (www.quick-drop.com), Auction Wagon (www.auctionwagon.com), Door to Door Auctions, (www.doortodoor. com) and PictureItSold (www.pictureitsold.net) offer similar services.

Is it working? In less than one year, Auction Drop had five stores with plans for 15 to 20 more. In June, 2004, the company completed an agreement with The UPS Stores that provides more than 3,800 sites, worldwide. It has sold at least 10,000 items and has generated revenues in excess of $1 million. A couple of months ago, Adams sold all his garage treasures through Auction Drop and now has a place to park and a happy wife.

CASE DISCUSSION QUESTIONS

1. If you were starting a similar service, where would you locate? What sort of building would you want?
2. What other possible spin-off businesses could be generated from eBay's success?
3. How could these businesses let eBay users know they are available?

LEARNING OBJECTIVES

This chapter will help you:

LO1 Understand the importance of a marketing plan.

LO2 Recognize the major methods for conducting market research.

LO3 Use sales forecasting methods.

LO4 Find or create a product's differential advantage.

LO5 Identify the critical components of a marketing plan.

■ Kwok-Foon Lai knew the food in his restaurant would be liked. What other market considerations did he take into account when opening his restaurant?

Marketing Plans: Saying How You'll Get Sales

Focus on Small Business: Kwok-Foon Lai and the Kwok Kee Restaurant

The problems of small business marketing are universal. For example, whenever the Lais would serve their family's porridge recipe, their Hong Kong friends raved about it. If all their friends liked it, it seemed reasonable that others would too, and the idea for Kwok Kee, a porridge restaurant founded in 1968, was born. Porridge is an everyday food—almost the Chinese version of fast food—and Kwok-Foon Lai needed a way to be different from the restaurants already out there. He knew that good-tasting food alone would not be the key to success, so he systematically considered his options. Lai decided to stay in the local area—Yuen Long, a small city now one of the "satellite cities" of Hong Kong. There were several good reasons for this. First, it was convenient for him. Second, although the nearby Mongkok district of Hong Kong was a popular location for restaurants, Lai knew that the rent expense would drive up his prices. He selected a location on a major street near a large complex of apartments and across from a park. This way, he was in a place where his competition was not, but yet a place with a lot of foot traffic. Also, because his costs were much lower than the competition's, he was able to keep his prices very low. Extensive advertising was beyond his budget, so he used word-of-mouth and backed this up with exceptional customer service. If customers thought the serving size was a bit small, Mrs. Lai would give them more. If a loyal customer was short on cash, she would say with a smile, "Pay when you come to eat next time."[1]

DISCUSSION QUESTIONS

1. A success is more than having the right product or service. What other things did Kwok-Foon Lai consider?
2. What kind of generic strategy did he use, and how did he implement it in his planning for the restaurant?
3. How did choices in one area of the marketing plan impact other areas of the plan?

The Importance of Having a Marketing Plan

LO1
Understand the importance of a marketing plan.[2]

marketing plan
A systematic written plan of all phases of marketing for a business, including information on the product, price, distribution, and promotion strategy, as well as a clear identification of the target market and competition.

You've got your idea for a new business, whether product or service, and you know it's a great idea and you'll be successful beyond your wildest dreams, but to convince a bank or private investor to loan you money or a store or distributor to carry your product, you'll need more than just "gut instinct." Even if you plan to use only your own personal savings and direct marketing, you're going to need some way to determine whether you are accomplishing your goals, something to make sure you're on the right path. At the absolute minimum, a **marketing plan** will help you articulate what it is that you are going to do.[3,4]

In 2001, 32,025 new domestic products were introduced.[5] If history holds, about 25,000 of these will fail.[6] A few were simply bad products, but the majority were good. Why did they fail? They were at the wrong place at the wrong time and were sold at the wrong price or to the wrong people. Sometimes failure is the result of external factors beyond a company's control—economic recessions, bad weather, or unexpected legal changes—but many are the result of the entrepreneurs not giving enough thought to how they'll sell their product. You wouldn't take a trip without a map or directions, so why would you start your business without the same consideration?[7,8]

The marketing plan is the basic tool for this. This plan examines your current situation, including what your existing competition is doing, and states how you define your product or service, to whom you will sell it, at what price, with what advertising, and how you will get it to your customers. By systematically considering these issues, you can plan for most contingencies and greatly reduce your risk of failure. Creating the marketing plan is the first step in putting together your business plan.

Market Research

LO2
Recognize the major methods for conducting market research.[9]

marketing research
Systematic collection and interpretation of data to support future marketing decisions.

While gut instinct, mentioned above, has its place, there is nothing like specific numbers and hard facts to give entrepreneurs confidence that a plan will actually work. Getting these facts is market research. **Marketing research** can verify the size of the potential market. It can show what the competitors are doing correctly or what their weaknesses are. It can also reveal where potential customers are likely to shop, likely to see advertisements (as well as how they feel about different sources and types of advertisements), and what they consider a reasonable price. You may believe that your product or service has some tremendous advantages over the competition, but marketing research might show you that the customers really aren't willing to switch providers, do not think your features are worth the extra cost, or do not even like these features at all. Without this sort of information, you cannot put together a coherent business plan.[10] Marketing research is where and how you get the facts to support your plan and the proof that what you are planning to do has a reasonably good chance of succeeding.

Research falls into two major categories. **Primary research** is research gathered to answer a specific marketing question. **Secondary research**, which is covered in Chapter 10, is research already gathered for some other reason than your specific question, but can be just as useful. The skills module in Chapter 11 on using U.S. census data is a good example of using secondary data.

primary data
Information collected to solve a problem at hand or answer current questions.

secondary data
Information already collected for some other purpose than the current problem or questions.

As you saw in Chapter 10, secondary research is often free and quick; there is no need to design questions and gather information yourself. Problems with secondary data include that the data may not be timely and you don't always know why the data were gathered and whether they were gathered correctly (biases). Sometimes it is hard to find the exact details you need. Secondary data are always a good starting point and will at least tell you if you are in the ballpark.

Primary data are specific to the problem you are solving. You decide what you need to know and how to get that information. This information is extremely current, but it will take somewhat more time and money to gather it. There are marketing research firms that could do this for you, but the cost—usually several tens of thousands of dollars—tends to put it out of reach for small businesses. A much more reasonable option is an online survey. (See Table 12.1 for some cost comparisons.) Of course, an online survey works only if your target audience is likely to be online and if the questions you want answered are suitable. (Try doing an online taste test, for instance.) Companies such as Zoomerang (www.zoomerang.com), Vista (www.vanguardsw.com/vista), and Web Surveyor (www.websurveyor.com) will help you do professional work. Their prices vary from $195 per month for Vista's program (up to 1,000 responses) to Zoomerang's $599 per year (up to 10,000 responses) and offer assistance in designing your survey and getting it out to respondents. They even offer the opportunity to do very small free surveys. Also check out your local Small Business Administration office or the local SCORE (www.score.org); they can suggest local research companies that might be more reasonable and are used to working with small businesses.

There are volumes written on how to write good questions and how to gather and analyze data scientifically. If you are expecting people to invest huge sums of money in your business, your data had better be accurate and correctly gathered. In order to accomplish this, study a good marketing research text or hire outside help. Most small businesses don't need to be quite so formal; potential investors will let you know where they need more information and what they want to see. For help in designing your questionnaire and collecting and analyzing data, the Small Business Administration office,

TABLE 12.1 Cost Comparisons for Various Survey Methods[11]

	Mail	Phone	Online
Setup	$40,000	$6,000	$1,500
Invitations	34,800	66,667	500
Processing	38,560	72,000	0
Total	$103,360	$144,667	$2,000
Cost/response	$4.31	$6.03	$0.08

(Based on 12 surveys with 2,000 responses each.)

SCORE, or a marketing professor will often be good sources for free or relatively inexpensive help. Many community colleges, technical colleges, and university marketing classes are often looking for projects for their students to do as part of the course. They may not only write the questions, but also gather the data and help analyze them for you. Of course, this is somewhat dependent on your time frame fitting the quarter or semester. In other words, classes may not be a good source if you need the information this week. Many of these schools will also have marketing clubs whose members would love to do a project for a modest donation—well supervised by their adviser.

ethnographic research
Data gathered by simple observation—seeing what consumers do, rather than asking them.

focus group
A form of data gathering from a small group led by a moderator.

There are a number of methods for gathering data. One category consists of observation methods. For example, I could go to the local grocery store and watch people shop. I could make lists of the products they choose and the time they spend making decisions.[12] This is called **ethnographic research** and has its place. For example, if I was considering opening a restaurant in a particular location, I could stand in front of the location and count foot and automobile traffic. I could visit a competitive restaurant and observe what people ordered, how long they stayed, and the time of day they visited. I could listen to the customers' comments about what they like or don't like.[13]

Another method is the **focus group**, which is a small group (8 to 20 people) that is asked to meet to discuss a series of questions about a particular product or service. A skilled researcher, who can make sure the questions are asked the right way and the data are systematically collected, conducts these meetings. Because participants are paid for their time, this can be an expensive prospect for many small businesses.[14] On the other hand, gathering a few friends and neighbors over for dinner and quizzing them on their ideas about your product may be just as productive, if not quite so formal. (See Skill Module 12.1 for a brief explanation of how to conduct a focus group.) This more informal approach is also a good way to test your questions to make sure your audience understands exactly what you are asking. This is especially important with close-ended questions, because there may be alternatives you hadn't considered or ambiguities you hadn't noticed. (This is sort of like the yes/no question, "Have you stopped spanking your children?" How do you answer that if you *never* spanked them?)

SKILL MODULE 12.1

How to Conduct a Focus Group

Focus groups are one of the most widely used techniques for getting information, especially at early stages, when you may not know everything you need to know about your product, service, or market. While it is probably best to have professionals run your focus group, you can do a passable job on your own if you follow these steps:

1. **Background:** Take a look at a book on how to conduct a focus group to familiarize yourself with the technique. Some examples are books like *Focus Groups: A Practical Guide for Applied Research* by Richard A. Krueger and Mary Anne Casey (Thousand Oaks, CA: Sage Publications, Inc., 2000), or the brief guide from the Australian Museum Audience Research Center (**www.amonline.net.au/amarc/pdf/research/focusgps.pdf**).
2. **Questions:** Determine the three things you'd like to know about how potential customers think about their purchases or your product or service. Aim for open-ended questions.
3. **Moderator:** To help people feel at ease, it is better to get someone other than you to moderate the focus group. If you have a friend with experience, that's great. If not, a friend who works as a salesperson, especially the sort who travels, has many of the needed skills, such as getting people to explain their reservations, dealing with a variety of customer reactions, and thinking on his or her feet. You can also check with the local university to see if there are students or professors with experience whom you can hire.
4. **Location:** Get a location that is comfortable and offers few distractions. In order to hear what is going on, buy or borrow a child's in-room monitor, so you can listen from a distance to the focus group as it happens. Get a tape recorder to keep all the comments.

5. **Participants:** Think in terms of friends and friends of friends. Look for people who like to talk and are likely buyers of your product or service or who are already using a competitor's product or service. Offering dinner and perhaps a small gift or a drawing for a larger gift is suitable for this kind of setting.
6. **Scheduling:** Aim for a two-hour block of time. Take a break after around 60–75 minutes so you can talk to the moderator if you need to adjust the questions or probe for answers. Greet the participants as they arrive and leave, and be ready to answer their questions. It is a nice touch to come in and answer participant questions at the end of the session, if you can do it graciously and without sounding defensive.

Analysis: Have an adviser or mentor listen to the tape separately from you, and discuss what he or she noticed and what you did. Where possible, build a poll of responses to see how many people felt one way or another. Be on the lookout for concerns or problems people raised.

A more typical data-gathering tool is the **survey**—some form of questionnaire. The questions may be written, asked in person or asked on the telephone. In person tends to be the most expensive method, with telephone coming in second, and mail the least expensive. On the other hand, mail has the lowest return rate and does not allow for much flexibility. In person, you can ask for clarification, have people expand on their answer, or even change the next question based on the response. Internet surveys, mentioned earlier, are gaining in popularity and have the advantage of being able to collect data from a large geographic area inexpensively. By using multiple screens of questions, respondents can select the screen they will see based on their responses to an earlier question (known in Internet survey terms as *branching*). For example, if a respondent is currently not using a particular product, the next questions he or she sees may go after the reasons for not using it. If respondents do currently use the product, the next questions may ask about their current provider.[15]

survey
A data-collection method using a questionnaire—in person, on phone, on paper, or on the Internet.

Having a set of predetermined written questions has certain advantages whether responses are oral or in writing. If you ask the same questions to each respondent, you can accurately compare answers and even statistically analyze these answers. You can come up with an average answer or compare answers between two (or more) specific groups (and conduct more complex statistical analysis, if the situation warrants it).

For example, suppose you ask people to rate your product on a scale of 1 to 10. The average rating might be 6.5 with 10 being high. This is nice information to know, but what could you find out by reexamining the data? What is the range of answers? If it is 5 to 8, you know that most people have similar feelings about your product—better than average but not perfect, with those at the 8 level being relatively pleased. It might take just a few tweaks of your product to move that average up to 7.5 or higher.

What if the range was from 1 to 10? Now you have people who love your product and others who hate it. It would likely take tremendous changes to convert those 1s to higher scores, and those changes might end up alienating the 10s. You now have a whole different scenario from when the range was small. What if you subdivided the answers based on some demographic value? For example, maybe you could sort by sex, age, wealth, or race. If we subdivide our answers into male and female, for example, we might find out that the average male response was 3.4, while the average female response was 7.8. If our product were a new skin lotion with a floral fragrance, we would expect women to like it better than men. If we thought the fragrance was neutral (and we should have asked this in our questionnaire), maybe we want to revise the scent or simply focus on the target market that likes it, the women.

scalar questions
Questions that are answered by some sort of scale; for example, "On a scale of 1 to 5, how do you like this book?"

dichotomous questions
Questions that have only two possible choices; for example, "Have you shopped here before?"

categorical questions
Questions that are answered by selecting the proper category; for example, "What is your ethnicity? White, African American, Hispanic, Asian, American Indian, Other."

There are two major types of questions used in surveys: open- and close-ended questions. One frequent type of close-ended question—the **scalar question**—is illustrated above: "On a scale of 1 to 5, how would you rate XYZ?" **Dichotomous questions** are those with two choices—sex, employed or not, and so on. **Categorical questions** give you several predetermined groups from which to choose—for example, age levels

open-ended questions
Questions that allow respondents to express themselves as they choose; for example, "What do you like about this book?"

(under 20, 20 to 29, 30 to 39, etc.). **Open-ended questions** allow the interviewees to answer any way they wish. Instead of asking, "Do you like XYZ?" (a question that can be answered, "yes," or "no,"), you could ask, "What are the advantages of XYZ?"

With close-ended questions, which can be answered only in certain ways, it is much easier to compare groups and to statistically analyze. However, they can limit the information you get. Let's say that your research shows that many people are concerned with the quality of their lawn service. What does this mean? One woman may believe that the trimming isn't as accurate as she would like, while a man is upset because the service ruined his in-ground sprinkler system. A simple 1–5 scalar, close-ended question wouldn't capture this information. Open-ended questions—"What do you dislike about your current lawn service?"—would.[16]

Open-ended questions, which can be answered in many ways, can help you find new niches and perfect your product or service before you introduce it. Stephanie Kellar (www.lashpro.com) had an idea for a new eyelash curler. She posted open-ended questions on a Usenet newsgroup called alt.fashion. In just a few months, she had collected information from over 100 people with minimal effort. She also used this venue to find people willing to test her new product in the development phase.[17]

As Stephanie Kellar found out, polling a group of consumers with common interests on the Internet is an inexpensive way to do marketing research and to find potential new customers for both test markets and the real thing. To find Usenet groups appropriate for your product or service, try Google, or more specifically, Google's group search at http://groups.google.com.

Open-ended questions provide data that are more difficult to tabulate; they take considerably more time to ask and evaluate, and answers can be difficult to compare. For example, if you asked, "How often would you use this product?" you might get answers such as "some of the time," "two or three times a month," or "whenever I have guests." Are those answers the same? If not, which one reflects a heavier user? In this case, a categorical question (once a month, 2–3 times a month, 4–5 times a month, etc.) would be easier to interpret. Open-ended questions are best for gathering preliminary information, when samples are small and when there are data that are difficult to get any other way. You can get a feel for the strengths and weaknesses of each type of question from Skill Module 12.2.

SKILL MODULE 12.2

Open- and Close-Ended Questions

With a partner, design two questionnaires about a service business you are considering—dry cleaning, restaurant, and so on.

1. One questionnaire should have only open-ended questions, while the other one should ask similar things using closed-ended questions.
2. Each of you should submit your questions (orally or in writing) to 10 people (different sets of people).
3. Compare your results. What are the pros and cons of each set of data?

Last, you need to recognize that there is no such thing as perfect information. People say one thing and do another. They may like your product but consider it a luxury item that they may or may not purchase. Things are constantly changing, and no one can understand all the interrelationships and how they might affect a business. There are always more questions that could be asked, and more data that could be collected. Look for support for your ideas, but understand that the best you will have is a good, educated guess.

SMALL BUSINESS INSIGHT

GrandKids[18]

Irene Viento thought she had done things right. She decided to start a retail outlet, GrandKids, to target grandparents—especially those who had money to buy extra special things for their grandchildren. Viento had experience with this target group, being a grandmother herself. She studied the demographics of Pelham, New York, her hometown, and relying on school data and information from an advertising circular company, she estimated that there were about 10,000 families in the area. Although there were 10 direct competitors within eight miles, there were none in Pelham, an upscale New York City suburb. She found a location just outside of town and started her business in 1994, but she had to close her doors by 1997. Basically, her research was flawed: Pelham had only slightly more than 3,200 families and the largest age group was in the 22–49 range—not the grandparents Viento needed. She also didn't know whether her potential customers were willing to drive to her out-of-town location, and if they were, wouldn't they be just as apt to visit her competitors?

Sales Forecasting[19]

LO3
Use sales forecasting methods.

One of the most important pieces of the marketing plan—and of the business plan—is knowing what your sales will be. This determines your profitability and, ultimately, whether you will stay in business or not. Often companies base sales forecasts on historical sales, but since you're new, you can't do that. Just as with marketing research, there are costly mathematical or computer-generated models that can be used. There are also much simpler ways of coming up with a reasonably good estimate.

Some products or services are tied to others. For example, if your company lays sod for new lawns, you can estimate the total market by looking at projected new homes being built in your geographic area. From there, you'll need to calculate what percentage of that market you can get. In other words, what's the competition like, and how do you measure up? If the market is underserved and all the competition is relatively equal in terms of size, product, price, service, and such, you might be able to divide the total market by the number of competitors, and maybe deduct a percentage "just to be safe" since you are relatively new. For example, perhaps the three existing firms will cover 85 percent of the business, and you'll only get 15 percent the first year. On the other hand, if you, or your competitor, offer unique products or services or have other advantages (or disadvantages), these can factor in. Using the same example, if you are the only firm offering in-ground sprinkler installation as well, you may be able to capture a larger portion of the market, or maybe most of a subsection of the market, in this case perhaps the more expensive homes.

Other products are not tied as neatly to others. If you are opening a restaurant, looking at the number of people who eat out in your particular geographic area just won't cut it. Some folks eat only fast food. Others don't like Chinese cuisine. Some go out only for breakfast. As a result, there are many different types of restaurant customers.

This is a good situation for some marketing research. You could conduct traffic counts during the hours you'll be open. You could stop a number of people to ask them how often they eat out and what type of restaurant they are likely to choose (and whether they think they'd like to try yours—a little word-of-mouth advertising). You could stop by your competition and see how long the waiting lists are or pick up a menu and see what prices they are charging. From these items you can get an idea of how many customers you might get.[20] This is certainly "softer" than the first method of estimating and is slightly more subject to error (both overestimation and underestimation). However, for most products this is the best information you can get.

This is also the time to verify that the potential market you've identified meets your capacity. If your restaurant will serve only 120 people over the hours you are open and the potential market is 300, you need to use your capacity figure, *not* your potential market figure. (You may also want to consider a larger space, more tables, more hours, more staff, or other ways of handling this unexpected extra market, if not immediately, at least for the future.) On the other hand, if your potential market is only 50, is that enough to be profitable? (Or can you lease a smaller, less expensive place or cut costs elsewhere to make your business profitable?)

Once you have figured out the number of customers, the next step is to estimate the average amount of sales per customer. This is usually a little easier; if your lunch prices range from $10 to $15, you could select the average price, or, more conservatively, assume everyone will eat the least expensive meal.

If you are selling a product, see what competitive products are going for in the market. Using traditional retailers and distributors nearly always quadruples the price you set "at the factory." You know what your costs will be and you know what profit you need; does this price the product beyond the competition? If so, can you find a way to convince your customers of your extra value, to cut your costs in production, or to use a different distribution channel? (More about that is covered in the other marketing chapters.) Are your prices below that of the competition? While this doesn't sound like it could be a problem, it might be a signal for you to double-check all your assumptions to make sure you didn't miss an important step. (Also, lower prices sometimes cause customers to doubt the quality; you expect more from a $10 T-shirt than from a $2 one.)

bot
A web-based program that uses artificial intelligence techniques to automate tasks such as searches.

If you are selling online, a search will bring up competitive products. Or use some of the pricing **bots** such as Froogle (www.froogle.com, a Google affiliate) and Mysimon (www.mysimon.com) for products, or Elance (www.elance.com) and Smarterwork (www.smarterwork.com) for services to come up with the best prices. Depending on your product, there are even specialized price bots; if you deal in books, try www.bestbookbuys.com. (For other products, try an Internet search of "your product price bot." eBay is also a good place to check out what the competition is charging. If your prices seem too high or too low, rethink how you calculated your costs, your product, and your method of distribution, or determine how you can create enough value for your customer to choose you over the competitive products out there.

In many cases, the best sales forecast you can come up with is another educated guess. Consider the assumptions you made and try to justify why you made them. Try to anticipate questions that you will be asked and consider your answers beforehand. In some cases you may want to look at several levels of sales forecast—an optimistic, average, and pessimistic view.[21]

Differential Advantage

LO4
Find or create a product's differential advantage.

differential advantage
The characteristic that separates one company from another in product, price, promotion, and/or distribution.

What makes your product or service different from the competition? In marketing terms, this is called a **differential advantage**, or what strategists call a *competitive advantage*, as discussed in Chapter 7.[22,23] When you first envisioned your product or service, chances are that you had a reason for thinking it would succeed in the marketplace. It could be that you found a target market that wasn't being served or was underserved. More commonly, though, this differential advantage is the result of something we do differently in one area of the four Ps—product, price, place, and promotion. Perhaps there is something different about your product or service, maybe something you identified when you analyzed your competition.[24]

Let's say your Census Bureau research identified a large Chinese population in the area, most who still speak Cantonese at home (true for areas in or near Los Angeles

SMALL BUSINESS INSIGHT

Ruth Fertel and Ruth's Chris Steak House[25]

Steak houses have been around forever, and steak house franchises come and go. So one can forgive the "experts" who didn't back Ruth's Chris Steak House when it started franchising in 1977. Of course, Ruth Fertel, founder and owner until her death in 2002, had been going against "good" advice since she mortgaged her house and purchased her first restaurant against the advice of her lawyer and banker. Ruth's Chris Steak House differentiated itself by using only the finest ingredients, serving gourmet steaks in an upscale setting, with a good bottle of wine available. Currently, the restaurant has over 80 locations and is patronized by those appreciating the ambience and great food.

and other parts of the country). It could be that few of these people use housecleaning services because of real or perceived language problems. Maybe you have Cantonese language skills and can use this to your advantage. Or maybe as a result of rapid new home construction in the area, there are not enough housecleaning services to take care of all the new potential clients. Possibly your research will show people who work evenings and would rather have their houses cleaned then, while they are at work, while most services clean during the days. These would be examples of an underserved or unserved market.

Alternatively, you could create a differential advantage with one of the parts of the marketing mix. (These are the entry wedges discussed in Chapter 7.) Here are some ideas for differentiating based on your product:

- Instead of simply cleaning the house, your service will do grocery shopping, drop off dry cleaning, and run other errands for customers.
- You will provide a homemade meal that can be popped in the microwave once the client returns from their busy day.
- You will offer specialized cleaning services—window cleaning or carpet shampooing.

The possibilities are limited only by your imagination and the customer's perception that you can fill a need.

Your differential advantage could be in pricing. While the lowest prices may attract customers, they are also subject to retaliation by bigger, better-established companies and are usually not a good idea for start-up companies.[26] However, if your cost structure is lower, you may succeed this way. But if your cost structure is not lower, you will not be able to compete in pricing. The key is not necessarily to be cheaper than your competition, but to be different from your competition. For example if the housecleaning services in your area price by the size of house (typical in the industry), you might price by the jobs to be done. Dusting will cost so much, and vacuuming another price; washing dishes is a certain price, while changing bed linens is another. A customer may choose to have your service only vacuum and do laundry.

Why do people pay more to shop at some stores, drive certain cars, or purchase certain brands? While there are differences in products and services, often the differences cannot be justified by the costs. What we have in this case is *prestige pricing*. With prestige pricing, people will pay more for a particular name brand because of the perceived benefits of driving a Jaguar car or wearing Tommy Hilfiger clothing. If you are able to create a prestige image in your customer's mind, you can charge much higher prices than the going rate. As a matter of fact, unlike other firms, prestige firms often lose customers by lowering prices because the product is perceived to be not quite so good. If you offer a custom product or extra service, you may be able to claim this pricing strategy and use it as a differential advantage.

Place is another area in which your firm may have a differential advantage. While a housecleaning service is somewhat limited as to "place" decisions, other product and service firms have carved market niches for themselves by their place decisions. In the computer industry, Dell—by direct marketing—and Gateway—by its stores carrying only Gateway products—bucked tradition by doing something different. (This attempt at differentiation had mixed results as the Gateway stores proved to be too expensive and needed to be closed.) Smaller operations have done the same—dry cleaners with pick up and delivery services, mobile dental offices, renting videos via the Internet (www.Netflix.com) and mail, and many others.

Promotion, too, can create a differential advantage, although more likely it will be the means by which you convey this advantage to your customers. Creative advertising can woo clients from existing competition or encourage clients not currently buying a product or service to try it. By careful targeting, your promotions will appeal to the wants and needs of your potential customers. A money-back guarantee or free first time consultation encourages customers to try new companies. Discounts for client referrals can grow your business through word-of-mouth. Your housecleaning service could offer free carpet cleaning for a one-year commitment. You could offer a "friends and family" discount of 10 percent off the regular cleaning price for up to five new friends or family members who sign up for your services, plus a discounted cleaning to the original client for each successful referral.

In the vignette at the beginning of the chapter, Kwok-Foon Lai used differential advantages in several areas. He started with a better-than-average porridge and combined it with outstanding customer service (product differential advantage). He was able to keep his costs low and pass these savings on to his customers (price advantage). He selected a location away from his competition, arguably an area that was underserved (place advantage). His word-of-mouth strategy may have been a slow way to get started, but it kept his costs down and helped his pricing strategy (promotion advantage). As time passed, however, his excellent reputation passed on by word-of-mouth kept his customers coming back years after they had moved away from the area.[27]

SKILL MODULE 12.3

Determining Differential Advantage

1. Select a product category with which you are relatively familiar.
2. List at least 5 competitors in the category.
3. Carefully consider the competitors' products and any advertising they have done. What seems to be their differential advantage? Analyze them using the four Ps.

The Marketing Plan

LO5
Identify the critical components of a marketing plan.

The components of a marketing plan are fairly straightforward.[28] First you discuss your target market—the people who will be buying your product. Second, you explain your current situation vis-à-vis your competition. In the third section, detail your marketing strategy and objectives. Finally, you explicitly address the 4 Ps: product, promotion, price, and place.[29] Let's discuss each of these components in detail.

Target Market

Marketing professionals like to talk about **market segmentation.** Segmenting is simply a way to divide the total market—everyone in the world, essentially—into manageable pieces that have some common characteristics. Although you could divide by virtually any method imaginable (by middle initial, month of birth, number of cavities, last book read, etc.), marketers look for segments that are likely to have similar needs and buying behavior. *Geographic segmentation* is one method frequently used. Many businesses, large or small, choose to operate in one country, while even the biggest multinationals choose a manageable number of countries.[30] People who live in cities often have different needs from those in rural areas. People who live in Minnesota have different needs from those in Arizona, particularly in the winter. New Yorkers have different preferences from Los Angelinos. Many service industries have no choice but to segment geographically; if your car wash is located in Phoenix, you aren't going to attract too many customers from outside the city.

market segmentation
The process of dividing the market into groups that have somewhat homogeneous needs for a product or service.

Demographic segmentation is also a valuable way to divide the total market. Teenagers have different needs from toddlers, as do other age groups. Where and how people shop and what they buy varies because of income, ethnicity, sex, education level, marital status, and virtually any demographic variable you choose. Life cycle position—unmarried, married without children, married with small children, married with teenage children, empty nesters, retirees, and so on—also determines the types of products a person may be interested in buying.

■ If this photo were used in an advertisement, what markets might it be targeting? What types of products or companies might try to appeal to so many market segments?

Benefit segmentation divides customers into groups based on what benefits they seek when making product or service decisions. For example, one customer buys a certain brand of toothpaste because it is a cavity fighter. Another customer wants the toothpaste that gives him fresher breath. A third may be looking for whitening power, while a fourth may want something that fights plaque. Many cars are segmented this way—speed, safety, capacity, and the like. Frequently used categories include those shoppers interested in a good value versus those more interested in reputation and prestige—think of Wal-Mart shoppers versus those frequenting designer dress shops.

Another category for segmenting has to do with an individual's personality. Adventure seekers buy different products (or for different reasons) than more timid people. Hobbies, sports interests, religion, cultural interests, and similar individual factors can determine the likelihood of people purchasing certain products. For example, you are unlikely to purchase Showgard mounts unless you are a philatelist or Salomon SNS Pilot Equipe Skate bindings unless you are a Nordic skier.

Identifying Target Market Segments

Marketers select their target market (or markets) first and then design their advertisements to attract and appeal to these customers. While there are "universal" advertisements, more effective ones are those that tempt a specific audience. Here's how you can identify your target market:

1. Go to the library and browse through several magazines. Choose several that appeal to very different audiences, for example, different ethnic groups (*Latina, Ebony*), different age groups (*My Generation, Seventeen*), different hobbies or sports (*Skiing, American Philatelist, Opera Today*), different income levels (*Forbes, Rosie*), different sexes - or sexual orientations (*GQ, Ladies Home Journal, Out, Girlfriend*), different life stages (*Bride's, Pregnancy, My Generation*), and the like.
2. Review the ads and look for clues that would cause you to believe that the ad is focused at a particular group.

3. Show several of these ads—without identifying the magazine—and see if your classmates can determine the possible target market. (Figure 12-1 shows a couple of examples.)

FIGURE 12.1

Target Market Ads

These Bridgestone ads are aimed at targeting two different markets. Can you identify which market(s) each ad is geared toward? Is each ad successful in meeting its market's needs? Why or why not?

A target market is the population segment or segments that are likely to buy your product or service. If you design dresses, you'll want to focus your efforts on women; if they are expensive, custom-designed, evening gowns, you'll want to narrow that focus to wealthier women (demographics, benefits) and those who engage in activities requiring the wearing of evening gowns (hobby, cultural interest).

undifferentiated strategy A marketing strategy that uses no segmentation; assumes that all consumers have virtually identical needs and can be reached by the same marketing mix.

Generally, marketers choose one of three targeting strategies: undifferentiated, differentiated, and concentrated. An **undifferentiated strategy** is useful when there is really no difference in the reasons why customers buy your products, that is, when it makes no sense to try to segment or target a particular market. Imagine selling bottled water at an outdoor fair on a hot summer day. Folks don't care what brand of water it is, and they are unlikely to go someplace specific for the water. Being at the right place with any reasonable product will get the job done. A lot of entrepreneurs are prone to fall into this trap ("My market is everybody!"), but as you can tell from the example, it is a rare situation in which an undifferentiated strategy works. While it may be true that you have a product that everyone wants, we can find different ways of promoting, distributing, or pricing the product that often attracts different segments. Even for water, someone could say theirs is colder, their bottles are bigger, their price lower, and so forth.

differentiated strategy A marketing strategy in which a marketer selects two or more distinct groups of consumers and designs specific marketing mixes to meet their needs.

A **differentiated strategy** is used when there is more than one market segment likely to need a product or service. By slight differences in how we make the product, promote it, distribute it, or price it, we can appeal to different markets. For example, both women and men use razors, but the color of the razor, the brand name, and product shape and how it is advertised (who uses it and how) are different.

A **concentrated strategy** is used when a firm chooses one particular segment on which to focus all its efforts. Entrepreneurs often are able to locate a particular niche that the larger companies ignore, and by focusing their efforts on them, are able to do extremely well. For example, Dale Bathum was tired of playing golf in shoes that just didn't fit, so in 1996 he formed Bite Footwear to make fashionable yet comfortable golf shoes (concentrated strategy). In later years, he expanded his product line into other shoes—hiking, fishing, running—and added a women's line as well (differentiated strategy).[31]

concentrated strategy A marketing strategy in which a marketer selects one specific group of consumers and designs a marketing mix specifically for that group.

Why bother with targeting? The main reason is so that you don't waste a lot of effort and money. Once you know who your target market is, you can determine their purchasing behavior. You can find out where people in that group shop, where they are likely to see your advertisements (e.g., what television shows they watch, what magazines they read, what Web sites they visit, etc.), what prices they expect, what messages are likely to appeal to them—in short, everything you need to know to successfully market to them. If you are trying to sell handmade baby clothes, you could buy a banner ad on the CNN Web site, but one on the Mommy Mall Web site is less likely to be wasted on nonpurchasers. It's just logical to be where your potential customers are.[32]

In Chapter 11, you had the opportunity to do a skills module using U.S. census data to locate potential areas for a housecleaning service. Continuing with this scenario, we decided that certain areas in western San Bernardino County had a concentrated population of individuals earning above $100,000 annually. This same area tends to have high numbers of professionals—perhaps too busy to do their own housework. People living in this area would be a likely target market. Using the census data, we could find out more demographic information about them that might be helpful in putting together our marketing plan. For example, looking at their ethnic background or the languages spoken at home might give us some clues for how we will want to do our advertising. The key is to be as specific as we can be about who these people are.

We can also start identifying the best ways of reaching these potential clients. Are there supermarkets, car washes, dry cleaners, or other businesses in the area where it might be appropriate to post notices? Is there a local magazine or newspaper that reaches a majority of those people? For example, in this area, there is a monthly magazine called *Foothill Communities* that contains local news and business ads. The *Los Angeles Times* newspaper provides a weekly local community supplement. A little research would lead us to find out that a majority of the people in this area commute to Los Angeles daily for their jobs. Perhaps a billboard along a major freeway could target geographically. We may be able to find local community events where we can distribute information (guerilla marketing) or we may be able to capitalize on local issues or news for our advertising.

While defining your target market is important, it also pays to think about secondary target markets.[33] These are customers who might be interested in using your product or service, but are not whom you probably start out targeting. You need to at least consider who they are and how you might respond to them, and certainly keep them in mind for future expansion. For example, what will you do if a company calls your housecleaning company and asks if you'll clean its offices? Roy "Bud" Davis, one of the co-founders of Bert and Bud's Vintage Coffins (www.vintagecoffins.com), builds custom coffins designed to be works of art that make a statement about the person who will be buried in them. His target market is wealthier people over age 55 who have "an independent streak, a sense of humor about their mortality, and the practicality to plan ahead." He found secondary target markets in Civil War reenactors who want authentic looking recreations of historical caskets, heavy metal music fans who use them as beds, and pet owners looking for a way to remember a special pet.[34]

Current Situation

The second step in creating your marketing plan is to examine your current situation. If you are an ongoing business, this means examining what you have done over the past year and how effective these actions were. Ongoing and new businesses also need to reflect on the political, economic, cultural, and other external environments and consider how they may affect the business. For example, are you located in a high-population growth area? Then it may be reasonable to expect your business to grow (if the growth is in your target market). Is the unemployment rate growing? Good news if you are an employment service, but bad news for many other services. Ask yourself, "What's going on and how might that affect my business?" What are the challenges you'll face this next year? What unique attributes does your business have to combat these challenges?

Often a SWOT analysis (see Chapter 7) is a good tool for organizing this material. What things do you do very well and what things do you do less well (strengths and weaknesses)? What "gaps" are there in market coverage—specific markets not covered, new technologies not exploited, features competitors ignore, and so on—that you can fill (opportunities)? How could your competition, new laws, the economic environment, or other outside forces negatively affect your business (threats)?

direct competition
Other companies that make a similar product or provide a similar service; for example, direct competition for Coca-Cola includes all other soft drink providers.

indirect competition
Companies that provide alternatives that are dissimilar to your product/service that consumers might choose to meet a similar need; for example, indirect competition for Coca-Cola includes any other company providing items to quench thirst.

Probably the key component in your situational analysis will be to consider your competition. Certainly, you will need to consider **direct competition**, those providing the same product or service. But **indirect competition**, what people use if they do not purchase the product or service category, is also important. In other words, if you are going to clean houses, what other housecleaning services (direct competitors) are doing business in the area? Also, if potential clients do not purchase housecleaning services, what is their alternative? In this case, the indirect competition would be cleaning themselves, having their children or other family members do it, or simply ignoring the dust and cobwebs—an extreme alternative, to be sure. Watching for ads, checking the Yellow Pages, and asking people in the area are all good ways to gather this information for your housecleaning business. Figure 12.2 shows a questionnaire that could be used to do this. Some of the items will be more or less important depending on your particular business, and there will probably be additional questions you will need to add.

Identifying competition does two things for us. First, we can get an idea of how crowded the market is. The Census Bureau tells us how many potential households are out there. An informal poll of residents in the area can give us an idea of what percentage might use a housecleaning service. For a rough estimate, we could simply divide the households who use cleaning services by the number of competitors we've identified and come up with an idea of the number of clients per service. If we add our company to the mix, will the resulting number of clients per service be enough to be profitable? (This is exactly some of the same information needed for your sales forecast discussed earlier.)

The second piece of information identifying competition gives us is a chance to find out what its strengths and weaknesses are. Weaknesses in particular can identify opportunities for our company to excel. Are competitors ignoring certain sectors of the market? Are their clients 100 percent happy with them? If not, what aren't they doing that you could? Are they late to their appointments? Do they cancel too frequently because they are understaffed and an employee illness means that something doesn't get done? What prices do they charge, and do the clients feel they are getting their money's worth?

The Four Ps

Your written marketing plan will contain detailed information about your product or service, how you will promote and price it, as well as how you will get it to the customer

FIGURE 12.2

Competitive Analysis[35]

	Competitor A	Competitor B	Competitor C
Where is your competitor located?			
What are your competitor's annual sales?			
Who are the major managers and members of the board?			
Is the company owned or in partnership with any other corporations?			
What are the competitor's strengths?			
What are the competitor's weaknesses?			
What is the company's product line?			
How do the products compare to yours, in terms of functionality, appearance, and any other criteria?			
What is the price structure?			
What are the company's marketing activities?			
What are the company's supply sources for products?			
What are the strengths and weaknesses of its sales literature?			
Is the company expanding or cutting back?			

(the "place" part of the four Ps). In defining your target market, you have already determined likely courses of action in these areas. For your marketing plan, though, you will be more specific.

In defining your product, you need to describe all the details. What features does it have? Are any of these options? Does it come in different sizes, flavors, or colors? What service elements do you include with the product (for example, delivery, setup, training, warranty, etc.)? If you are providing a service, again, what specific tasks will you do? Will you sell this as a bundled service (e.g., complete housecleaning), or will you sell it in units (e.g., vacuuming separate from windows, cleaning bathrooms, washing windows, etc.)? What short-term (next few years) improvements or changes do you foresee?

An example or photo of your product or service is a great visual aid in helping you sell your plan. If you are a restaurant, have a sample menu, photos of some prepared food, and a photo of the building you'd like to lease. If you write business plans for other companies, a sample table of contents might be adequate. Blueprints, color chips, sketches, and fabric samples are other things that could be included. In addition, the cost structure (e.g., materials, labor, overhead) needs to be included. If the marketing plan is part of an entire business plan, cost details can be left for the financial section, but the total should be identified here.

Price will be determined by your cost structure. In addition to identifying the actual price you will be asking, include information about additional expenses the customer may incur (for example, shipping or installation). Why do you consider this amount of profit to be appropriate? How does your price compare to that of the competition? If it is higher or lower, how do you explain or justify this?

In advertising, for example, you may have determined that a print ad is a good method for reaching your target market; now you will want to consider in which magazines to place the ads (e.g., a hobby magazine, a local magazine, etc.), and what their cost will be. What tools will you use (flyers, Internet, print ads in magazine or newspapers, television or radio, banners and posters, etc.)? How will you schedule your advertising efforts (weekly radio spot, daily newspaper ad, twice a year distribution of flyers, etc.)? What are the various costs of these and how successful are they at reaching your target audience? (In other words, consider costs versus benefits.) What is your advertising budget?

Identify what your message should contain—slogans, promises, photos, and so on. A rough mock-up of a print piece or a script of a radio or television ad should be included, explaining how you feel these will resonate with your target market.

Are you using any promotional tools (e.g., coupons, referral discounts, sales, giveaways, etc.)? If so, what are they? How much will they cost? How often will you do this?

The distribution system of your product or service can vary considerably depending on what you are doing. For example, if you are doing some sort of mail order sales, will you be taking the boxes to the local post office or to UPS or some other shipper? Will you go daily or weekly or on some other schedule? Will you be using a fulfillment center? What will your costs be for shipping boxes, packaging materials, and the like?

If your product or service will be in a store or other building or space you lease, what will this cost you? Why did you choose this place (e.g., traffic counts and other indicators that it is a good spot for your particular business)? If it's the Internet, are you going with eBay, other e-malls, or on your own? Why? What sort of hit rates do you expect?

This is a partial list of the questions that should be answered in writing this part of the marketing plan. What you include will be specific to the type of business you are planning. How do you figure all this out? A very useful tool to consider is called the *filtering process*.[36] Put yourself in the shoes of your prospective customer and consider that you are searching for something to solve the problem your particular product or service will solve. What are the steps you would take to find a solution? Would you first look in the phone book? Then you'll want to make sure you have a Yellow Pages listing. Would you ask friends? Now you may wish to consider some sort of referral bonus to customers who recommend you. What sorts of information would you want to know about the company, product, or service before you made your decision? These may be things to put in your ad (e.g., address and hours of operation) or, for more complicated items, things that should be addressed in your sales pitch (like more detailed information on technical aspects of your product, why you are better than the competition, or specifics about your guarantee). What are the features customers are likely to want (and how will they know you have them)? Where would they likely shop? How far would they drive to get your product or service? Since you are now the expert on your product or service, you might be a little too close to the process and this, too, might be a good place to do a little marketing research by identifying a few potential customers and asking them these questions.

The Written Plan

Your written marketing plan will include the specific details about your target market you consider useful as well as information about your present and near future situation including competitors. The plan will also identify your differential advantage and how this will be conveyed through your product or service, your pricing, your place (your way of getting your product/service to your customers), and your promotion. For a new company, this provides your justification for going into the market. If there aren't enough customers out there to make a reasonable profit or if you have no clearly defined method of finding them, you'll have trouble convincing anyone to loan you money. For an ongoing establishment this is your action plan for the near future, usually the next year.

In addition to the sections mentioned above, the written plan may include financial projections (if not part of an entire business plan). The plan will also include your budget for doing the things you plan to do, the schedule of when you'll do them, and how you will evaluate your progress. This last item will include measurements against your objectives and will include things like matching monthly sales projections and goals against actual sales and similar evaluations. Indicate what you'll measure and when you'll measure it.

Since your marketing plan is essentially your action plan, write it as such. List the major overall goals you have for your company and then the specific tactics you need to achieve them. Make your goals simple, concrete, and measurable. For example, if you plan to open a housekeeping service in western San Bernardino County, your goal or objective could be to have 100 customers within six months (determined from the sales forecasting you did earlier). How are you going to achieve that? What specific tactics will you use? Perhaps, you'll advertise in XYZ local magazine and in ABC newspaper. You'll distribute 1,000 flyers door-to-door or place them under the windshield wipers of cars in grocery store parking lots (where legal and permitted). A shared mail program (those envelopes containing ads or coupons from a number of sources) can print and deliver coupons to 10,000 houses for under $500. Break down and outline the costs for doing each of these activities. Set a time schedule.[37]

What should the written plan look like? There are nearly as many formats as there are companies writing marketing plans. There are software packages that help you work through the plan step by step and will create a high-quality, professional-looking plan, such as Marketing Plan Pro (www.marketingplanpro.com) by Palo Alto software. Even the basic version comes with about 70 sample marketing plans, the idea being that they can serve as templates for whatever business you may be planning. (Check out the Web site for a free sample marketing plan.)

Another consideration is whether the marketing plan is to be part of a business plan or whether it is to stand alone. In the first case, there are a number of items that will be covered in the other part of the business plan and do not need to be duplicated. For example, the financial section of the business plan will include balance sheets, income statements, and such and do not need to be duplicated, but only referred to in the marketing plan section. For a stand-alone marketing plan, at least a summary version of these would need to be included.

Table 12.2 is a suggested layout of things to be included.[38] Two types of marketing plans are considered—a full stand-alone marketing plan and the marketing section of the business plan, like those described in Chapter 8. You'll notice that the categories for the marketing analysis follow the same elements outlined in Table 8.4 in Chapter 8, which gives the different types of plans and the sections of each. Here we add the details of how the four Ps fit into the sections of the marketing analysis and plan.

What's Next?

The marketing plan has been discussed almost as though it's a one-time process, and it's not. It's the basic building block for your business plan and your road map to what you want to do, but it shouldn't be set in concrete.[39] Successful businesses are constantly tweaking their marketing plan to accommodate necessary adjustments found during evaluation and control reviews, or to reflect new research, changes in

TABLE 12.2 Marketing Plan Outline

	Stand-alone Marketing Plan	Marketing Section of a Business Plan
1. Table of contents	X	
2. Executive summary	X	
3. Company description, mission, focus, structure	X	
4. Situation analysis	X	
a. Company SWOT analysis	X	
b. Product/service SWOT analysis	X	(in Competition section)
c. Competitive analysis	X	(in Competition section)
d. Customer analysis	X	(in Competition section)
5. Marketing analysis	X	X
a. Market and target customer	X	X
b. Differential/competitive advantage	X	X
c. Marketing objectives	X	X
d. Overall marketing strategy (the sales plan)	X	X
i. Product strategy and Description	X	X
ii. Pricing strategy	X	X
iii. Promotion strategy	X	X
iv. Place/distribution strategy	X	X
v. Contingency plans	X	X
(1) Reaction to competitors	X	X
(2) R&D/growth plans	X	X
6. Financial data and projections	X	
7. Implementation plan or schedule	X	X
8. Evaluation and control	X	
9. Appendixes	X	

the environment, changes in competition, new target markets, new opportunities in promotion, new anything.[40] In addition, on a regular basis (at least once a year),[41] you should take the time to decide what you want to accomplish next—increase sales, introduce a new product, move into a new market, and the like—and revise your marketing plan to reflect this next step. Caryl Felicetta started her business, The Argyle Studio, an advertising and graphic design firm, without a marketing plan. After a year of haphazard growth, she and her partner did their first systematic review and marketing plan. With this plan, their business grew by 100 percent the next year and has averaged about 50 percent growth each year after that.[42]

If you are uncomfortable with the prospect of doing a marketing plan yourself, there's low-cost help for you available in a number of ways. First, try the Small Business Administration (www.sba.gov) or the Service Corps of Retired Executives (SCORE) (www.score.org) for advice. *Entrepreneur* magazine (www.entrepreneur.com) has examples and a number of worksheets you can use to help you gather and organize your information. Last, contact a local community, technical, or four-year college (small business or entrepreneurship department if they have one, otherwise, the marketing department) or campus club in those areas and offer your company as a class project.[43] (A small donation to the class or club should be considered.)

CHAPTER SUMMARY

LO1 Understand the importance of a marketing plan.

- The marketing plan helps you articulate how you are going to sell your product or service.
- The marketing plan is a necessary piece of the business plan.
- The plan examines your current situation and competition and specifically identifies what you will do with your product, pricing, promotion, and distribution.

LO2 Recognize the major methods for conducting market research.

- Secondary research is data already gathered for some other purpose than the question you are trying to answer.
  - Internet, libraries, newspapers, and magazines offer free data; data are also for sale and can range from relatively inexpensive to very expensive.
  - While using secondary data is quick and often free, it may not give you exactly what you need.
- Primary data is that which you gather to answer your current questions.
  - Primary data can be gathered through observation, focus groups, or questionnaires.
  - Questionnaires can be administered via mail, phone, Internet, or in person and can consist of close-ended or open-ended questions.

LO3 Use sales forecasting methods.

- If your product or service is a component of another product or tied directly to another product or service, your estimated sales can be calculated as a portion of this known number.
- Most products and services, however, will require "softer" estimates such as traffic counts or questionnaire results.
- This sales forecast is critical to and must be checked against your capacity.

LO4 Find or create a product's differential advantage.

- A differential advantage is that which sets you apart from the competition.
- The differential advantage can be in your product, promotion, distribution, or pricing.

LO5 Identify the critical components of a marketing plan.

- Who is your target market?
  - Typically, markets are divided by demographic, life style, or personality traits.

    - The target market is the group that is likely to buy your product or service and that has distinct purchasing behaviors.
    - Secondary target markets should also be considered.
- What is your current situation?
    - Ongoing businesses must reflect over the recent year and how effective their actions were.
    - All businesses must consider likely changes in political, economic, cultural, and other external environments and how these may affect the business.
    - Direct and indirect competition must be identified and its actions and likely actions analyzed.
- What are your specific plans for your product, promotion, pricing, and distribution?
- The marketing plan needs to be written, but the format can vary depending on who is going to use it.
- The plan should be revised regularly—whenever something significant occurs to change a piece of it or at least once a year.

DISCUSSION QUESTIONS

1. Consider that you are planning to open a self-service car wash in town. What sorts of secondary data might be helpful in creating your marketing plan?
2. What sorts of primary data could you collect using observation for your car wash?
3. Create a questionnaire that could be used to gather data for your car wash. Use both closed- and open-ended questions.
4. With your classmates, make a list of products or services that are or could be tied to other products or services. To which products or services are they tied? How could this be used to predict sales?
5. With your classmates, make a list of several products or services unlikely to be tied to other products or services. How might you estimate sales with these?
6. Is it ethical to pose as a customer in order to gather data from a competitor? What sort of behaviors do you believe to be ethical and justifiable, and which ones cross the line?
7. Going back to our car wash example, list all the ways you could differentiate your product, price, promotion, and distribution from the competition.
8. How could you segment your car wash market? Brainstorm as many different ways as possible. (Remember that some of the most successful businesses are those that have found unique ways to segment and reach a particular market.)
9. Use the filtering process and consider the steps you would take in trying to resolve the dirty car problem. What does this tell you about the product, price, promotion, and location of your potential new business?

EXPERIENTIAL EXERCISES

1. Visit your school's library or your local public library and investigate the reference section. Make a list of resources that might be useful if you were opening a new dry cleaning business.

2. Revisit the U.S. Census Bureau Web site (www.census.gov) and list secondary data that might be useful in opening your dry cleaning business.

3. Select a local shopping mall to do some observation and primary data collecting. (Try a food court or bench in a waiting area where you can be comfortable and unobtrusive.) Make a list of the sorts of observational data you could collect.

4. Select an item from your list in question 3 and collect data for 15 minutes. What does your information tell you, and how could you use it?

5. Assume your dry cleaning business is a service that you've found the average person will use once a month in your area. You also discovered that customers want to drive less than three miles for dry cleaning. Get a map of your city and select a street corner at random. (We'll assume that you will be able to build your dry cleaners there.) Use the Census Web site to estimate the population in your three-mile radius. Consult the phone book to find other dry cleaners within that radius. Assuming you will evenly split the customers, what would be your market share?

6. Make a list of the competitors of the company for which you work. What are their strengths and weaknesses? Are you aiming at the same target market(s)?

7. Using the competitors identified in question 6 (or choosing a different product or service), attempt to identify the target marketing they have selected. (Good ways of doing this is by identifying advertising or distribution aimed at particular groups.) Do any of them have secondary markets?

8. Interview someone at the company where you work. What kind of marketing plan does the company have (formal, informal, detailed, etc.)? How often is it reviewed?

Mini-Case

INFOGLIDE[44]

David Wheeler got into business in order to ease his anger about his father's murder and in an attempt to see justice done. A computer database expert, he designed a program that would sift through crime reports in an effort to link and pinpoint criminals. The first trial of the product connected several seemingly unrelated crimes and located a suspect.

In 1991, Wheeler formed InfoGlide, Inc., to sell this software program to law enforcement agencies throughout the country. While the agencies found it a valuable tool and indeed used it to investigate successfully a number of crimes, as government agencies, few could afford it. Wheeler had a product that just didn't have a market.

In 1996, after struggling for several years to attract venture capitalists, InfoGlide reexamined all possible and potential markets. It discovered that hundreds of millions of dollars a year were lost because of insurance frauds—frauds that could be linked with Wheeler's software just as police cases were. InfoGlide immediately retargeted its product and revamped its marketing plan, and by 1998 had raised $5 million in venture capital. Today, the company has 38 employees and is worth $100 million.

CASE DISCUSSION QUESTIONS

1. In selecting a new target market, InfoGlide would have had to adjust all parts of the marketing plan as well. What changes could you envision in the product, the price, the promotion strategy, and the distribution?

2. Can you identify other markets that could benefit from the basic concept of Wheeler's software? What changes might need to be made for these markets?

3. Researchers call this process *transmigration,* changing a company so it can enter a peripheral or related industry. Select a firm you know and brainstorm several transmigrations it could make.

A Marketing Plan: PizzMo[45]

I. STORE'S MISSION

Here at *PizzMo,* our mission is to deliver an entire evening's worth of enjoyment directly to your home. *PizzMo* will deliver the freshest, most appetizing pizza right along with the most entertaining movie. By bringing dinner and a movie right to your doorstep, we want to take the hassle out of your evening and give you a worry-free night.

II. COMPETITIVE ANALYSIS

We have no direct competitors in our specific business on the West Coast. There are other pizza delivery companies like *Pizza Hut*® and *Domino's*©, as well as video rental stores, like *Blockbuster*© and *Hollywood Video*©. However, none of them deliver both the pizza and the movie together.

There is, though, a precise example of our pizza and video delivery company in Saint Peters, Missouri, called *Big Guys,* but it caters only to the surrounding area. It is a mom and pop company, that claims to have homemade, mouthwatering pizza. In addition, there is a company in Narbeth, Pennsylvania, called *Real Pizza,* but this is a pizza delivery company that has teamed up with a video store. At *Real Pizza,* there are two entities, the pizza place and the video store, where the pizza delivery person picks up a customer's movie on the way to delivering the pizza to the house. Along the same line, *Pizza Hut* has partnered with *Casa Video* in Tuscon, Arizona, but the delivery person must pick up the movie at the video store, just as at *Real Pizza.*

III. TARGET MARKET

Our target market is between the ages of 18 and 35, both college students and young, middle-income families. College students will be prime candidates because of the easy and quick indoor date night that *PizzMo* provides. Our delivery service will be the best way for these scholars to get a break from their studies without diverting from them for too long. An average college student in our target market would earn at least $15,000 per year. Families with young children will be another main targeted group. These prospects will find *PizzMo* irresistible because of the immense benefits. A common family in our target would make a combined income of no less than $40,000 a year. The tremendous assistance that we will provide them with a worry-free night will be irreplaceable, because these people would prefer not to leave the comfort of their own home. Taking children out to eat can be a very daunting task; with *PizzMo,* worries are over because we bring dinner and entertainment to your door. *PizzMo's* typical customer will order from us at least once a month, but up to six times a month, spending an average of thirty dollars each time.

IV. DIFFERENTIAL ADVANTAGE

As mentioned before, we will be the first company in the area to offer delivered pizza plus a video of the customer's choice—fast, easy and convenient.

V. MARKETING OBJECTIVES

As we are a new company, *PizzMo*'s first marketing objective is to get information about our product/service out to our customers—name/brand recognition. Second, we want to develop brand loyalty among these customers.

VI. PRODUCT STRATEGY

PizzMo will offer a full menu—salads, sandwiches, pizzas, sides, and beverages. A customer can choose from an individual or a family-size salad with a choice of Italian, ranch, or honey-mustard dressings. Sandwich choices include: roast beef and cheddar, meatball, ham and Swiss, Italian sub, or a turkey melt. We'll make seven specialty pizzas: bacon cheeseburger, meat cravers, veggie, meatball, parmesan chicken, tostada, and the ultimate. Or you can create your own pizza with these toppings: pepperoni, sausage, pork sausage, beef, Canadian bacon, bacon, diced ham, black olives, onions, mushrooms, bell peppers, tomatoes, jalapenos, fire-roasted vegetables, and pickles. On the side, customers can order bread sticks, cheese bread sticks, little smokies, and toasted ravioli. To drink, we'll offer Coke® and Pepsi® products, in addition to bottled water.

PizzMo will carry only DVD rentals, which will be stored in the bookcase behind the front desk in alphabetical order. ***PizzMo*** will carry popular new releases from the last month. When we retain a DVD past this point, we will offer the copies for sale on our Web site at a discounted rate. People can purchase the previously viewed DVDs on our Web site and receive them with a delivered pizza, pick them up at their leisure inside the store, or pay for shipping. Delivered DVD rentals will be due seven days from the day rented, and customers will be given a self-addressed stamped envelope with which to return the DVDs.

VII. PRICING STRATEGY

At ***PizzMo*** our pricing strategy will be very similar to *Big Guys,* our "model," in order to establish a family restaurant feel and an honest appeal to our customers. However, ***PizzMo*** wants to lead the market with a low-price strategy in an attempt to secure loyal customers with our wholesome values, and we also want to appeal to cost-efficient buyers. We will set up a pricing orientation with roughly 65% of our products in the inexpensive range, which consists of items under $9, and 35% in the medium-priced range of $10 to $15. There will be no items priced over $15; however, buying any combination of products will lead to a higher overall price. In addition, customers will be able to build their own pizzas, which could easily go over $15 if many toppings were added. In these instances, the price will be less of a factor and will be second to the amazing quality of the pizza. We will also carry the usual breadsticks, chicken wings/fingers, salads, sandwiches, and other Italian foods and will price these comparable to our competition.

VIII. PROMOTION STRATEGY

In our advertising and promotional scheme, our goal is to get the word out about our delicious pizza, fast and friendly service, and reliability. We will attempt to do this using minimal, but effective advertising that really reaches our target market and transforms them into loyal customers. One of our big campaigns will be to use mailers with coupons attached as well as an offer for a free small pizza with no strings attached. The free pizzas will only require identifying proof that the person is the same as the name on the mailer. We hope that by offering a sample of our delicious pizza in combination with a coupon, we will create a repeat purchase that will turn into a lasting relationship. Since 85% of all pizza consumers use some form of coupons, ***PizzMo*** hopes to acquire many of its original customers through the use of this technique. We will also use electronic coupons on our Web site that customers can print directly and redeem with their purchase. Since these types of coupons typically have a higher redemption rate, ***PizzMo*** hopes to reach people who will adopt us as their pizza and entertainment company of choice.

In order to help our customers create a bond with us, ***PizzMo*** will use advertising techniques that are more personal, but that also reach a large audience. Radio will be one of our main sources of advertisement aside from the mailers. We will use fun and energetic stories that catch the listener's attention and create a picture in their mind, as well as evoke a remembrance of the taste and smell of their last ***PizzMo*** experience. Finally there will be a catchy jingle to end the commercial and reinforce the advertisement, leaving an imprint on the listener's mind. These radio commercials will air primarily before lunchtime and during evening rush hour. We hope to pattern our radio commercials after *In-N-Out* burger chain, which has become a hugely brand loyal, hometown establishment that has no need for a large advertising budget. Instead, most of its profits go back into the company with benefits to its employees and quality products.

Catchy billboard ads will also be used by ***PizzMo*** to reach motorists who are trying to plan their evening. These will be placed primarily near colleges and universities, as well as near a few main freeways (perhaps the 10, 405, 605, 60, etc.). The advertisements will not be overly distracting, but will aim customers in the direction of our Web site by either suggesting free pizza, as in the mailers mentioned above, or promoting the unique and hassle-free service, without saying too much. Ideally, we would like to keep the people guessing, so that they are forced to look at the Web site and would be more likely to buy as a result.

Our costs associated with promotions and advertising are represented in the following table.

Advertising Costs

Promotion Type	Total Expense
Mailers w/coupons	$5,000
Radio	$10,000
Billboards	$5,000
TOTAL	**$20,000**

IX. LOCATION STRATEGY

Our main focus as a start-up organization will be to direct our business to the West Coast, until success allows us to expand to the entire country. We will begin in areas like California, Oregon, and Washington, with quick expansion to Arizona and Nevada. These states place a somewhat high dependency on the personal automobile and so in this case, we feel that ***PizzMo*** will be of ideal service. For that reason, we plan on utilizing our delivery attribute as our prime promotion in hopes of maximizing profits in these areas.

PizzMo will most likely be located in strip malls and will need relatively small square footage to perform daily operations. One of the prime locations found for the first of our stores is a small shop centrally located among other storefronts in Pasadena. The property is up for sale at $20,000 for 1,500 square feet, which should be the perfect size as a start-up. The address is 1704 E. Washington Boulevard and is located in a strip center along with a salon and a liquor store. The prior tenant was a cell phone business, so there will be additional funds required to transform the location into a kitchen-friendly retail outlet. However, the location is one of the most optimum found because of its proximity to a large residential area. The neighborhood has many young families, as well as college students, who are our precise target market. The median household income of the area is $72,889, and the average household size is 2.99 people. The area of Pasadena is 69.4% families and has an average of $28,140 in retail expenses and another $2,577 in entertainment expenses. This is an affluent area, whose residents fit ***PizzMo's*** target market to a T with 57% working in a white-collar job and 38.9% with a college education or better.

The retail configuration of the area around the Pasadena storefront includes a beauty salon, jewelry store, insurance and auto leasing establishment, a nail salon, laundry, delicatessen, wholesale tobacco store, and a preschool. There are a few small restaurants several blocks away, but since ***PizzMo*** is a delivery business, these are not direct competitors. We understand that sometimes people want to go out to eat, but ***PizzMo*** caters to those evenings when the same people want to stay in and have a pleasant experience in their own home. Most of the other stores in this area are family-owned, which may help ***PizzMo*** since we too will be this type of retail outlet. We are hoping that the community welcomes us into the neighborhood with open arms and that the surrounding homeowners enjoy our honest offerings.

X. CONTINGENCY PLANS

There are a lot of pizza places out there, and certainly anyone could add the ability to offer videos along with their pizza. This is perhaps our biggest threat. We hope to "stay under the radar" of the larger pizza chains at first and develop customer loyalty so that our customers will not switch when someone else offers a better deal. In addition, as we are delivery only, we can locate in low-rent areas and should always be able to compete on price.

While we will offer many pizzas similar to our competition, ***PizzMo*** also intends to experiment with local flavors and preferences. We will accumulate information about the "make your own" pizzas to see if there are some local favorites we can add to the menu, things that the large chains usually do not do.

As mentioned above, we will concentrate on the West Coast states at first and gradually expand. The first stores will be in the Los Angeles area and will be located similarly to the Pasadena store. As we move into other areas, we hope to franchise our operation, which allows us to use our local partner's knowledge of the area.

XI. TIME FRAME

Securing the lease, forming the company, and all the related paperwork can be done in the first month. Equipment will be ordered and remodeling started immediately afterwards, along with designing the Web site, packaging materials, and promotional materials and ordering DVDs. About one month before the store opens, advertising and promotion will begin and the Web site will be activated. We expect to be in business within five months.

Cash, Accounting, and Finance in the Small Business

PART

LEARNING OBJECTIVES

This chapter will help you:

LO1 Review the basic concepts of accounting.

LO2 Understand the requirements for a small business accounting system.

LO3 Be comfortable with the content and format of common financial statements.

LO4 Understand how accounting information can help you manage your business effectively.

LO5 Learn how to craft budgets for your business.

LO6 Gain understanding of how people make decisions.

■ Tracy and Brad Butler of Acropolis Computers, pictured here, learned the power of careful accounting practices when their consultant uncovered thousands of dollars of lost income due to poor pricing strategies. Armed with these facts, Acropolis Computers began to grow steadily into a more solid business. Investigate some accounting strategies for yourself by visiting your local Small Business Development Center, checking out additional government resources online, or doing some research at university entrepreneurial centers.

Small Business Accounting: Projecting and Evaluating Performance

Focus on Small Business: Tracy and Brad Butler and Acropolis Computers[1]

After three years of hard work, Tracy and Brad Butler still did not seem to be making very much money. The reason for this was not obvious to the brothers. Sales were growing. The business was regularly working on the computers of between 600 and 700 loyal customers. Customers were satisfied, and it showed in their high rate of referrals.

At a loss as to what they were doing incorrectly, the brothers engaged a consultant to analyze their business processes. What the consultant showed them changed the way they ran their business.

The brothers, engineers by education, were masters of the computer but novices at accounting. They simply did not understand the relationship among costs, revenues, and profits. For example, they charged customers only what Acropolis paid for the parts, without any markup to pay for the time Acropolis spent ordering, storing, and carrying the part in inventory. When they went to a client's home to do repairs, they did not charge a service fee for their travel time or for the wear and tear on their truck. Although they charged for labor by the hour, if the labor was only a few minutes, they gave it away for free. Those lost minutes alone accounted for a $40,000 shortfall in income annually.

"We were actually losing $200 a job," Tracy said.

The process of pricing out their real costs, and then mapping those costs to the work they did for clients, helped Acropolis Computers finally become profitable—even after paying off the consultant's eventual bill for $27,000!

But that was just the start.

"Only 4 percent of our revenue was coming from individuals, but they were a large number of people: 600 to 700," Tracy said.

Once they understood the nature of the costs of their business, the brothers trimmed it drastically, moving away from serving individuals and focusing instead on providing service to businesses with between 15 and 150 employees. As the nature of their business changed, they changed its name to Acropolis Technology Group, moving from the basement to commercial locations in Wood River, Illinois, and Creve Coeur, Missouri.

"The success we have enjoyed has come directly from understanding the relationships among Revenue, Gross Margin, Overhead, and Burdened Labor rates," Tracy Butler said.

Acropolis has been ranked for the last three years by *CRN Magazine* in their yearly Fast Growth list. In 2004, they grossed over $3.1 million in sales.

Success came, but only after they got their numbers under control.

DISCUSSION QUESTIONS

1. What is the nature of the ". . . relationship between costs, revenues, and profits . . ." that Tracy and Brad Butler did not understand?
2. What do you infer about Acropolis' accounting system during the years leading up to this crisis?
3. Why was it important for Acropolis to begin marking up the price of computer parts over their cost?
4. How is it possible for a business to succeed by deliberately getting rid of loyal customers?

LO1
Review the basic concepts of accounting.

managerial accounting
Accounting methods that are specifically intended to be used by managers for planning, directing, and controlling a business.

tax accounting
An accounting approach based on specific accounting requirements set by governmental taxing agencies.

financial accounting
A formal, rule-based set of accounting principles and procedures intended for use by outside owners, investors, banks, and regulators.

Why Accounting Matters to Small Business

The way many people think of it, what makes a business businesslike is its focus on making money, and in the end, the only way an owner knows or can prove to others that money is being made is through keeping careful accounting records. Accountants themselves think of five reasons why accounting is important to a small business:

- It proves what your business did financially.
- It shows how much your business is worth.
- Banks, creditors, development agencies, and investors require it.
- It provides easy-to-understand plans for business operations.
- You can't know how your business is doing without it.

There are three types of accounting, managerial accounting, which is used by managers for planning and control, tax accounting, which is used for calculating and reporting taxes, and financial accounting, which is used by banks and outside investors.

Managerial accounting is forward-looking and attempts to predict the results of management decisions.

Tax accounting is used to produce tax returns and schedules. Tax accounting is important for avoiding penalties for noncompliance and for minimizing how much money you have to pay in taxes.

Financial accounting is a formal, rule-based system intended primarily for absentee owners, bankers, investors, and regulators.

Basic Accounting Concepts

Accounting is a logical system based on a small number of concepts that determine accounting procedures. The most basic accounting concepts are (1) business entity, (2) going concern, (3) the accounting equation, (4) costs and expenses, and (5) information usefulness.[2]

Business Entity Concept

Where does your business stop and you personally begin? Part of what makes a business businesslike or professional is for it to show an existence that is separate and different from yours. This is the business entity concept. When you have a corporation, this is legally true. So following these ideas, we do accounting for your business, recording its transactions separately from your personal ones. One goal of small business accounting is to exclude any of the owner's personal financial information from the business accounting records.

Going Concern

Because your business is separate from you, it can continue to exist, even if you sell it to someone else. Because a business exists, it is expected to continue to exist, which is what makes it a going concern. Accounting therefore assumes that this year's business results will affect next year's, and that the intent of the business is to make money over time. You can have an unprofitable year or two, but the goal over the long term is to make a profit and keep going.

Accounting Equation

The accounting equation is simply an expression of the common sense statement that your net worth is whatever is left over after all of your debts are paid. Expressed as an equation, this is:

value of what you own − the debts you owe = your net worth

The accounting equation simply inserts accounting terms, and moves "the debts you owe" to the other side of the equals sign so that it looks like this:

assets = liabilities + owners' equity

An asset is anything that you own that has value. A liability is something you owe to someone else, such as a loan or an account payable. Owners' equity is what (if anything) is left over after you pay your debts. If what you owe is more than what you own, then you are bankrupt.

What Is a Cost? What Is an Expense?

It is a fact of life that you must give up things to get what you want. Sometimes you give up money; sometimes you give up time. Have you ever considered what it costs to go to college? Not only are you paying money for tuition, but because you are in this class, you are not doing other desirable things. You could be using the time to earn a wage. You could be using the time for entertainment or relaxation. The cost of college is the value of the money you pay plus the value of the other activities that

business entity concept
The concept that a business has an existence separate from that of its owners.

going concern
The accounting concept that a business is expected to continue in existence for the foreseeable future.

accounting equation
The statement that assets equal liabilities plus owner's equity (assets = liabilities + owners' equity).

liabilities
Legal obligations to give up things of value in the future.

owners' equity
The difference between assets and liabilities of a business.

bankrupt
The financial state of having more debt than assets, such that net worth is negative.

opportunity cost
The value of an economic activity or event that is foregone in order to be able to undertake a different, specific activity or event.

cost
The value given up to obtain something that you want.

expense
A decrease in owners' equity caused by consuming your product or service.

you give up to attend class. Thus, going to college has both a financial cost and an **opportunity cost**.

Costs are real changes in what you own. **Expenses**, on the other hand, are simply entries made in your accounting system to record your use of goods and services in the conduct of your business. Sometimes costs and expenses are the same thing. Often, they are quite different. It is important for you to be able to distinguish between costs and expenses because failure to do so can lead to making bad financial decisions.

For example, consider the purchase of a power saw for your desk-making business, discussed in Chapter 9. At the time the saw is put into service, your business incurs a cost equal to the sum of the saw's purchase price, shipping, installation, setup, and testing, a total of $5,500. No amount of this cost, however, is recognized as an expense. Instead, the cost of the saw is recorded as an asset. As the saw is used to make desks, a portion of the asset value of the saw is subtracted from revenue. Over the time that the saw is used in production, its cost will be recognized as an expense called *depreciation*.

Remember that managerial accounting is focused on predicting the future, so it uses expenses only for budgeting and planning purpose. Other managerial accounting activities, such as decision making, focus instead on costs, and *cash flows* (money received and money paid out). On the other hand, financial accounting systems, which are used for those formal reports to bankers and government, *never* recognize opportunity costs. They are totally focused on just those things that result in money being received and money being spent.

Information Usefulness

There are only two reasons to do accounting: first, to produce information that is useful to you for managing your business, second, to meet legal or contractual requirements. To be useful, information must be accurate and relevant.[3] You can ensure that your accounting information is accurate by using a computerized accounting program, as discussed in the following section. Relevance of information must be evaluated for each decision as it is made. If having the information helps you make a smarter decision, a faster decision, or a decision you feel more comfortable about, then the information was relevant.

The following skill module illustrates the issues discussed in this section.

SKILL MODULE 13.1

Why Does Accounting Matter?

Think back to the example in Chapter 9 of manufacturing desks. Your variable and fixed costs are as follows:

Variable costs:	
Materials	200
Labor: 6 hours @ $20	120
Scrap	6
Sandpaper	2
Variable cost of one desk	$328
Fixed costs	$100,000

Suppose that you are currently using a power table saw that you originally bought used for $200. Because the purchase price was small, you treated (or as accountants say, *recognized*) the entire $200 cost of the saw as a business expense in the year it was purchased.

The Bosch representative is trying to sell you a new power saw. The purchase price is $4,000, and the costs of shipping, installation, and testing will be $1,500. The representative has shown you how the new saw, because of its improved material-handling capability, will save 30 minutes of labor time on each desk manufactured.

You have spoken with your accountant and she told you that for tax purposes the saw will have to be depreciated in five years. The amount of **depreciation** expense you will recognize will be the following:

Year	Depreciation
1	$ 1,100
2	1,760
3	1,056
4	634
5	634
6	317

1. What is the cost of buying the new saw?
2. How will your expenses change if you buy the saw?
3. How will your annual fixed costs change if you buy the saw?
4. If you expect to make and sell 150 desks per year, should you buy the saw?
5. Suppose that your accountant called and said that the saw could be depreciated for seven years, deducting an equal amount each year, called straight line depreciation, or $786 for the first six years and $784 in the last year. Would this change your decision of whether to buy the saw?
6. Under what conditions is the amount of depreciation expense relevant to deciding whether to buy the saw?

depreciation
Regular and systematic reduction in income that transfers asset value to expense over time

LO2
Understand the requirements for a small business accounting system.

The primary reason to acquire and use a computerized accounting system in your business is to ensure the accuracy of your accounting information. However, computerized systems provide huge benefits at a very low cost. They are designed to be used by business managers who are not professional accountants. As such, they have built-in automatic error checking, data entry screens that look like the business forms that you currently use, and most important, automatic production of financial statements and reports that are useful for managing your business.

The most commonly used small business systems are Quickbooks, Peachtree, SimplyAccounting, One-write, and Great Plains. All these systems automatically produce financial reports that meet legal requirements for content and format. Although, as with any computer program, you will have to invest some time in learning to use it effectively, each of these accounting programs is very user-friendly. Its use can be mastered in a very short time, a matter of a few hours. Most community colleges offer night and weekend classes in Quickbooks and Peachtree, and you may have (or have even taken) similar courses at your school. There are also numerous online sites that offer tutorials. Each program itself includes a tutorial, help files, and a printed manual to help you master its use.

http://quickbooks.intuit.com/

http://www.peachtree.com/

http://www.simplyaccounting.com/

http://www.peachtree.com/onewrite/

http://www.microsoft.com/businesssolutions/greatplains/default.mspx

To ensure that your accounting information is accurate, reliable, and useful, the accounting system that you choose should easily and efficiently accomplish the following tasks:

- Provide a simple, easy-to-understand user interface.
- Have an exhaustive context-sensitive help function.
- Produce an income statement that clearly lists revenues and expenses by appropriate categories for your industry and type of business.
- Produce a classified balance sheet that clearly shows the financial position of your business.
- Facilitate the development of a cash budget.
- Facilitate the task of developing operating and investment budgets.
- Produce financial statements in approved formats to be furnished to outside investors, bankers, and regulators.

- Produce multiple-year comparison financial statements for management use.
- Provide a method for you to define and produce custom reports to meet your management needs.
- Be able to export financial data in a form that can be used by your accountant and can be imported into tax preparation and spreadsheet programs.
- Maintain an internal "audit trail" that records all entries and changes to the accounting system in order to facilitate the identification and correction of errors.
- Enforce security measures to reduce the opportunity for employee misuse or fraud.
- Have provisions that will either allow the program to grow with your business or to easily export its data into programs that can handle larger businesses.

Setting Up an Accounting System

Your specific accounting needs are largely determined by the industry you're in and by the size of your business. The smallest businesses often need little in the way of accounting records beyond an accurate check register. As businesses become larger, the difficulty of any one person being able to remember all its details increases exponentially. When a business is large enough to have one or more employees, formal record keeping is a must.

Regardless of your business's size, the one essential element of an accounting system is *cash accounting* that is accurate, easy to use, and tracks all checks written and all deposits made.

As your business grows the following accounting functions will become important to your success:

- *Accounts payable* records to track what you owe and to make timely payments in order to capture prompt pay discounts and to maintain a good credit rating for your business.
- *Payroll* records to ensure that payroll and employment taxes are kept current.
- *Fixed asset* accounting that automatically calculates and accumulates depreciation.
- *Inventory* accounting that facilitates maintaining the appropriate levels of inventory and aids in calculation of appropriate stocking and reorder levels.
- *Credit card sales* function to enable reconciling your sales records with the amount of discount and charge backs taken by your credit card provider.
- *Accounts receivable* records if you provide credit to your customers. Accurate and timely accounts receivable records are essential for making decisions concerning the extension of credit. Accurate records also help produce accurate billing of customers, and thus help to maintain good customer relations.
- *Insurance register* to ease the problems of keeping necessary insurance coverage current and in force.
- *Investments* records if your business keeps surplus cash invested in securities.
- *Leasehold* records if your business has made improvements to leased property or equipment.

The actual task of setting up a computerized accounting system for your business is quite easy. All the small business accounting systems listed above include all the functions that you are likely to need. Additionally, each program has a method to establish a set of records that is appropriate for your specific business. Should you have a business that is unique, setting up a set of records from scratch takes less than an hour. Quickbooks and Peachtree include an "interview" function that will guide you through the setup process by furnishing a series of questions and prompts.

www.score.org

Often in such situations, you can get help for free from your local Small Business Development Center or SCORE (the Service Corps of Retired Executives). Alternatively, for a small fee (generally $200 to $1,000) many CPAs (certified public accountant) will set up any of these accounting programs for your specific needs. You can find CPAs in your phone book (hard copy or online) or even through Google searches for a CPA directory like the one in the Google search bar. As when you choose any other professional (like doctors or lawyers), it makes sense to check with others about a professional before making a major commitment.

Financial Reports

LO3
Be comfortable with the content and format of common financial statements.

The final output of a computer system is a set of **financial statements** and reports. Although there is certainly room for you to customize financial reports in many ways, the overall content and form of financial statements have been made standard by long usage. Bankers and investors are familiar and comfortable with standard financial statements. When you apply for a loan or seek equity investment, you will be expected to present financial information in the format and containing the information that is standard for your industry.

financial statements
Formal summaries of the content of an accounting system's records of transactions.

There is not enough space in this book to detail the many small differences that are used among different industries. Therefore, we present the most common formats. When you are familiar with them, you will find that you can easily understand and adapt them to the differences unique to your industry.

There are five common financial statements:

- Income statement
- Statement of retained earnings
- Statement of owners' equity
- Balance sheet
- Cash flow statement[4]

To the uninitiated these financial statements can see almost alien, but in reality each type is similar in concept and operation to financial records we use in everyday life. Think of your checking account. You put money in and write checks to take money out. That is the income statement. The exact amount you have in the account at any moment depends on the deposits credited to your account (which can take anything from minutes to days, depending on how you made the deposit and the speed of your bank) and which checks have been handled by the bank. Figuring that exact amount (which people often do with their check register) is the idea behind the statement of cash flow. The monthly bank statement gives you the check and deposit information as well as any fees the bank charged you or interest it paid your account. That parallels the statement of **retained earnings**. When you do your taxes for the year you look at your equity and liabilities and eventually pay taxes on the growth in your assets over the year. In effect your annual tax return is a variation on the idea of a balance sheet.

retained earnings
The sum of all profits and losses, less all dividends paid since the beginning of the business.

The important thing about these financial statements is that they **articulate**, that is, information flows from the income statement through the statement of retained earnings, the statement of owners' equity to the balance sheet. Information from the income statement and the balance sheet flows to the cash flow statement. (see Figure 13.1.)

articulate
The concept that information flows from the income statement through the statements of retained earnings and owners' equity to the balance sheet.

FIGURE 13.1

Flow of Information in Financial Statements

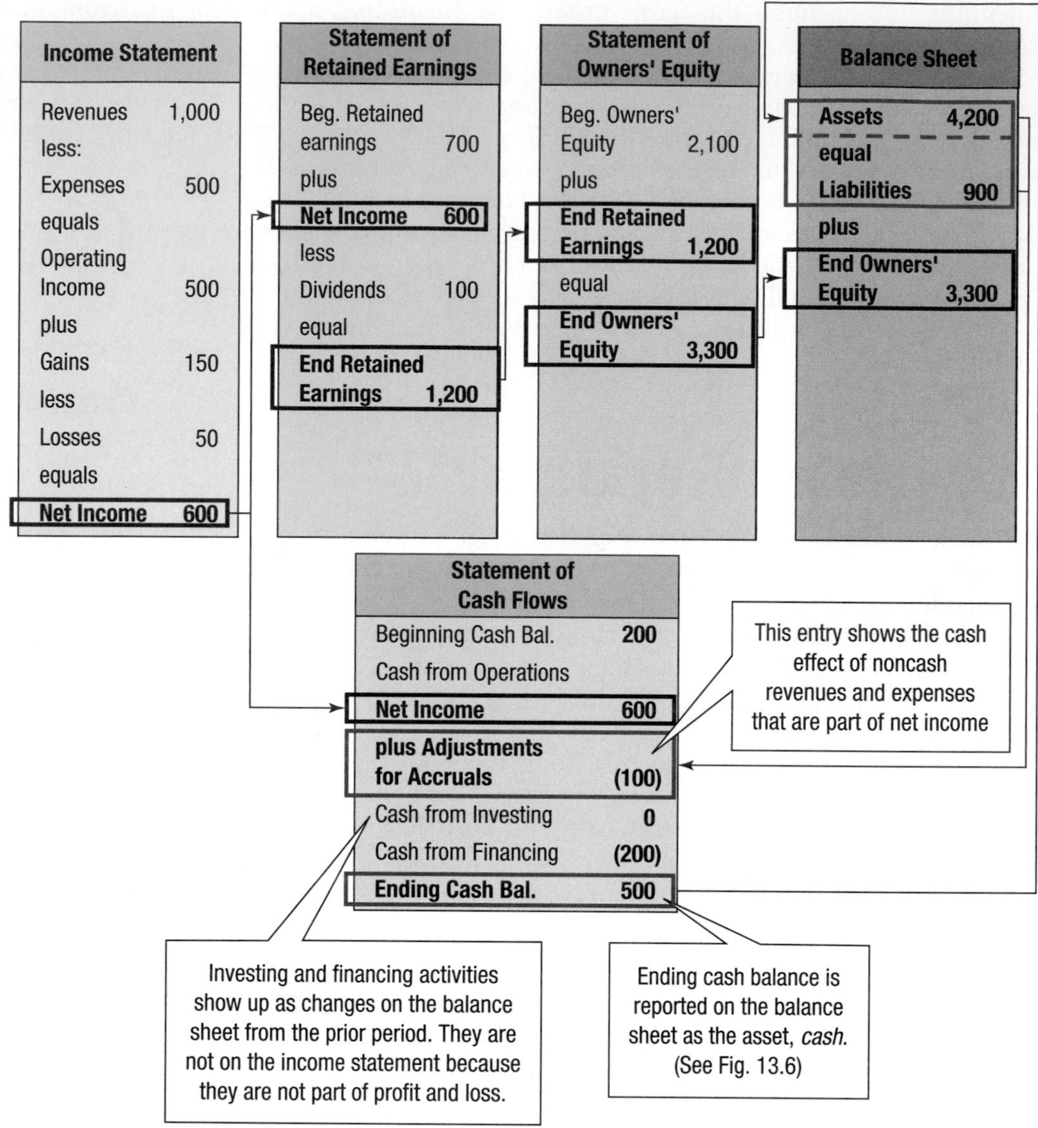

Income Statement

income statement
A statement that lists revenues and expenses and shows the amount of profit a business makes for a specified period of time.

The **income statement** is the primary source of information about a business' profitability. The income statement shows the amount of revenues earned minus its expenses which equals net income:

revenues − expenses = net income

All income statements follow the same simple general format. Reading from the top down, the income statement presents answers to the questions shown in Figure 13.2.

The usefulness of the income statement for managing a small business is related to the amount of detail available in the statement. There are two formats for income statements, (1) a *single-step* format, illustrated in Figure 13.3A, which provides little detail—it simply lists all revenues and gains together, then lists all expenses and losses together and (2) a *multiple-step* format, illustrated in Figure 13.3B, which lists revenues from operations separately from other income and gains.

Most owners and managers of small businesses prefer the multiple-step format because of its greater detail. Notice that in Figure 13.3B operating income of $105,800 is reported separately from the nonoperating gains and income from leasing. The two most commonly used computerized accounting systems for small

Question	Income Statement Content
How much revenue did the business produce?	Sales
	−
What did it cost to produce its product?	Cost of goods sold
	=
	Gross margin
	−
How much did the business use in its continuing operations?	Operating expenses
	=
	Operating income
	−
What costs did the business have for financing?	Interest expense
	=
	Net income before tax
	−
How much tax must the business pay?	Income tax
	=
How much profit did the business make?	Net Income

FIGURE 13.2

Organization of the Income Statement

businesses, QuickBooks and Peachtree, by default produce income statements in the multiple-step format.

Difficulties in Understanding the Income Statement

There are two typical difficulties that arise in understanding and interpreting the income statements. First, there are disagreements about what exactly should be reported as revenue. The second problem arises from disputes over *when* to recognize revenues.[5]

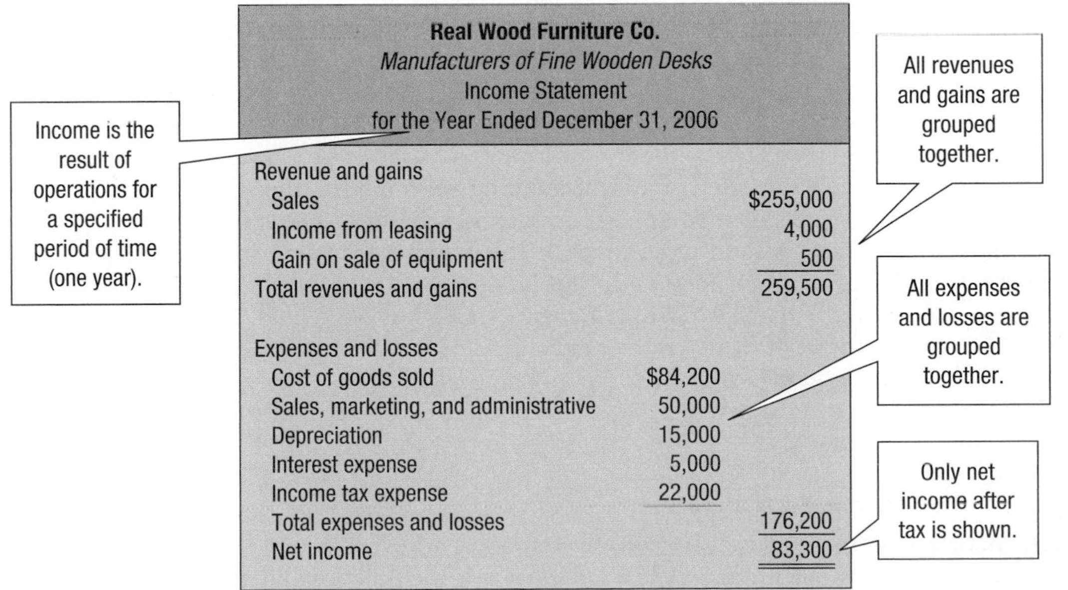

Real Wood Furniture Co.
Manufacturers of Fine Wooden Desks
Income Statement
for the Year Ended December 31, 2006

Revenue and gains		
Sales		$255,000
Income from leasing		4,000
Gain on sale of equipment		500
Total revenues and gains		259,500
Expenses and losses		
Cost of goods sold	$84,200	
Sales, marketing, and administrative	50,000	
Depreciation	15,000	
Interest expense	5,000	
Income tax expense	22,000	
Total expenses and losses		176,200
Net income		83,300

FIGURE 13.3A

Typical Single-Step Format Income Statement

FIGURE 13.3B

Typical Multiple-Step Income Statement

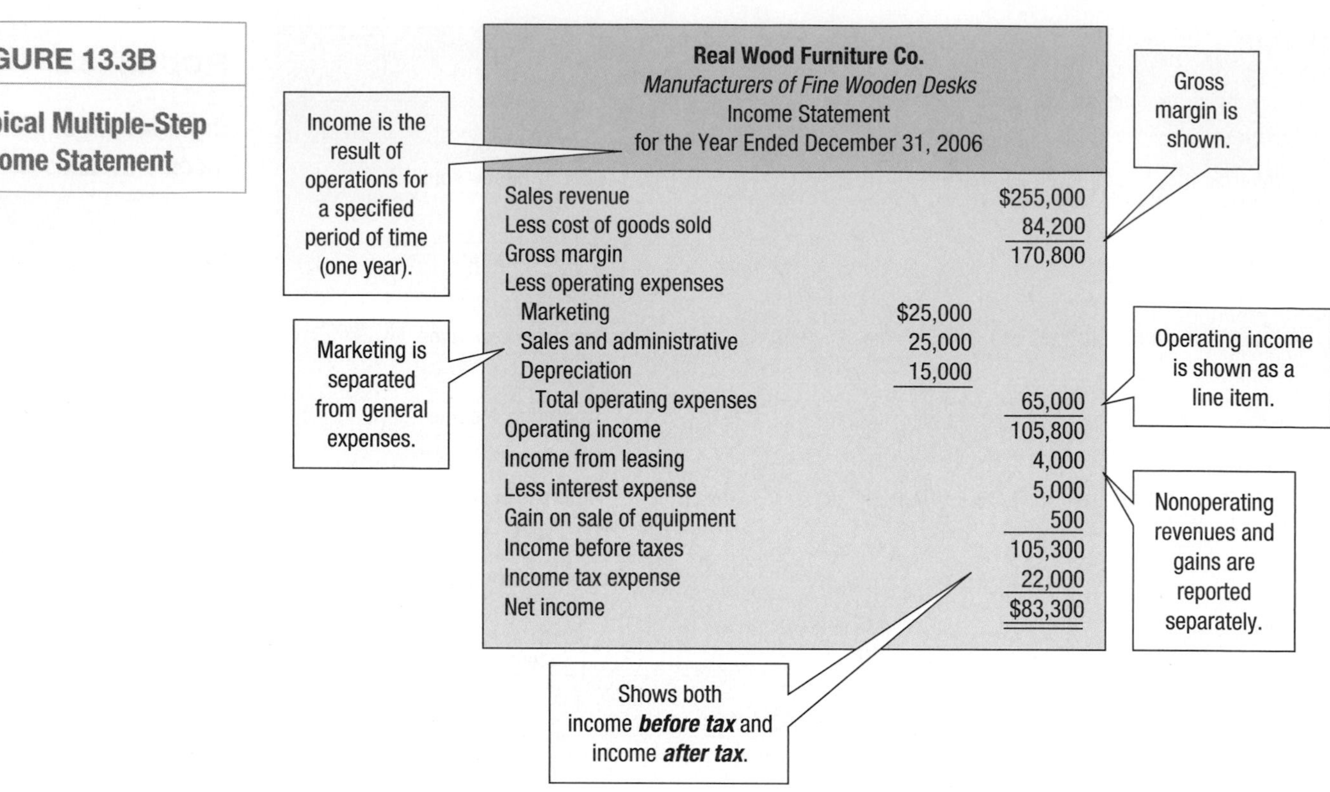

Real Wood Furniture Co.
Manufacturers of Fine Wooden Desks
Income Statement
for the Year Ended December 31, 2006

Sales revenue		$255,000
Less cost of goods sold		84,200
Gross margin		170,800
Less operating expenses		
Marketing	$25,000	
Sales and administrative	25,000	
Depreciation	15,000	
Total operating expenses		65,000
Operating income		105,800
Income from leasing		4,000
Less interest expense		5,000
Gain on sale of equipment		500
Income before taxes		105,300
Income tax expense		22,000
Net income		$83,300

Let us consider what revenue is first. Suppose your business is a water park that is open for only 120 days between June and September. In the late fall you run a promotion to sell season tickets as holiday gifts. Through this promotion, you sell for cash $200,000 worth of season tickets. Have you realized a revenue? The accounting answer is no. To be recognized as revenue, the earnings process must be complete. In the case of a water park that means that even though you have $200,000 in your bank account, you cannot count it as revenue until the holders of season passes use them to visit the park. In fact, the amount of the season passes would be shown on your balance sheet as a liability—you owe the pass holders either access to the park or their money back.

Similar problems arise in determining the amounts and timing of gains, losses, and expenses. Suppose your business sells motor scooters. Customers who buy one will expect to receive a warranty. If they have a problem within the warranty period, they will expect that the scooter will be promptly repaired or replaced. So how much expense should you recognize for warranty? And when should you recognize it? When you sell it, or when it comes back for repair? The amount of warranty cost and the timing of returns are not known at the time of sale. Regardless, accounting rules require that the amount of warranty be estimated and taken as an expense at the time the scooter is sold.

Despite the difficulties and limitations of the income statement, it provides valuable information. Most small businesses do not have any difficulty deciding how much and when revenues and expenses occur. In many small businesses, all sales to customers are made either for cash or as credit card transactions that are essentially the same as cash. Subscriptions and warranties are not an issue. So in many cases, the income statement of a small business is a reliable report of just how well the business is doing in producing profits.

Use of the Income Statement

The income statement is used by you, by lenders, and by investors to analyze the effectiveness of business operations. *Operating income* is the most used item on the statement.

It represents just how well management achieved sales and controlled costs to produce profits. Lenders use operating income as a measure of how much debt a business can support. Interest is deductible for determining income tax, therefore net income before tax is available to make interest payments. Equity investors similarly look to operating income as an indication of future sales, so operating income becomes a favorite indicator of the value of their investment.

Balance Sheet

The balance sheet, also called the *Statement of Financial Position,* presents a "snapshot" of the financial holdings and liabilities at the close of business on a specified date. The balance sheet explicitly details the accounting equation for your business. The balance sheet follows a simple basic format. Assets are detailed and their value summed. Then either directly below or to the right of the asset detail, liabilities and owners' equity are detailed and summed. By definition, the sum of the value of the assets must equal the sum of liabilities and equity—in other words, it has to balance. The balance sheet provides answers to the questions shown in Figure 13.4.

balance sheet
A statement of what a business owns (assets), what it owes to others (liabilities), and how much value the owners have invested in it.

The usefulness of the balance sheet is determined by the detail it includes. As shown in Figure 13.4, the minimum level of detail is to report both assets and liabilities in two categories: current, which will either produce or use cash within a year, and long term, which will convert to cash over a period of time greater than one year. However, your balance sheet may be made in greater detail if there is a need to do so. A common practice is to present multiyear balance sheets to facilitate analysis, as is shown in Figure 13.5.

Use of the Balance Sheet

The information in the balance is used to determine the liquidity, financial flexibility, and financial strength of the business, which are detailed below. These measures of a business's financial position are used by owners, lenders, and equity investors in making financial and investment decisions.

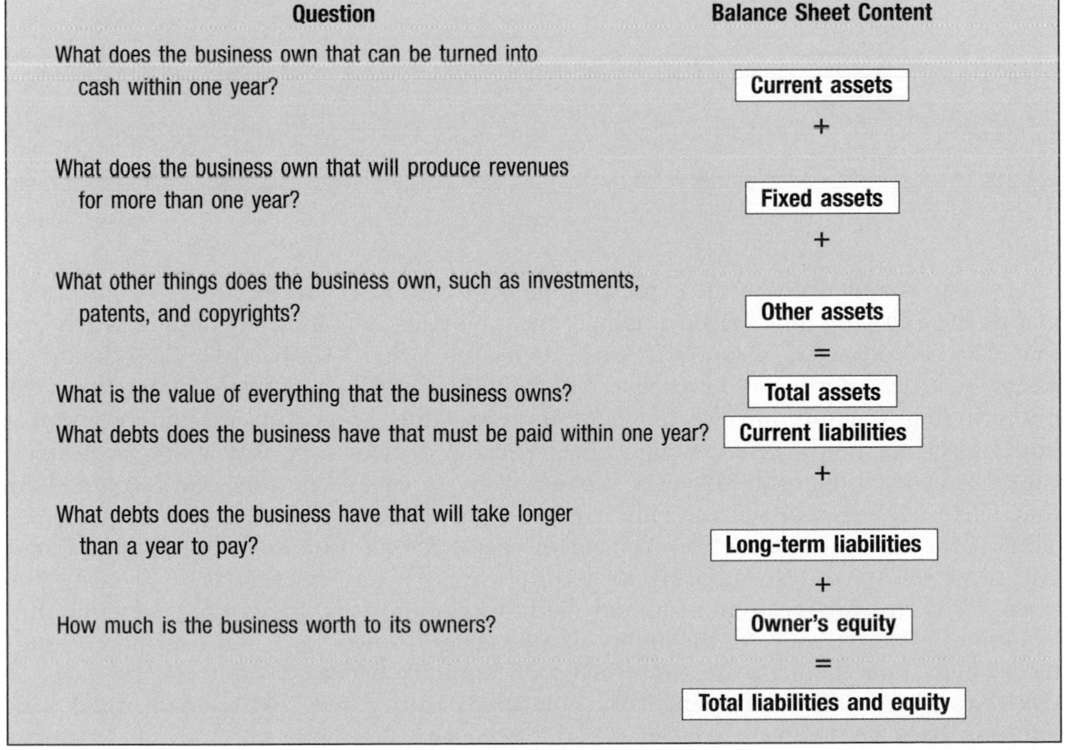

FIGURE 13.4

Organization of the Balance Sheet

FIGURE 13.5

Typical Balance Sheet

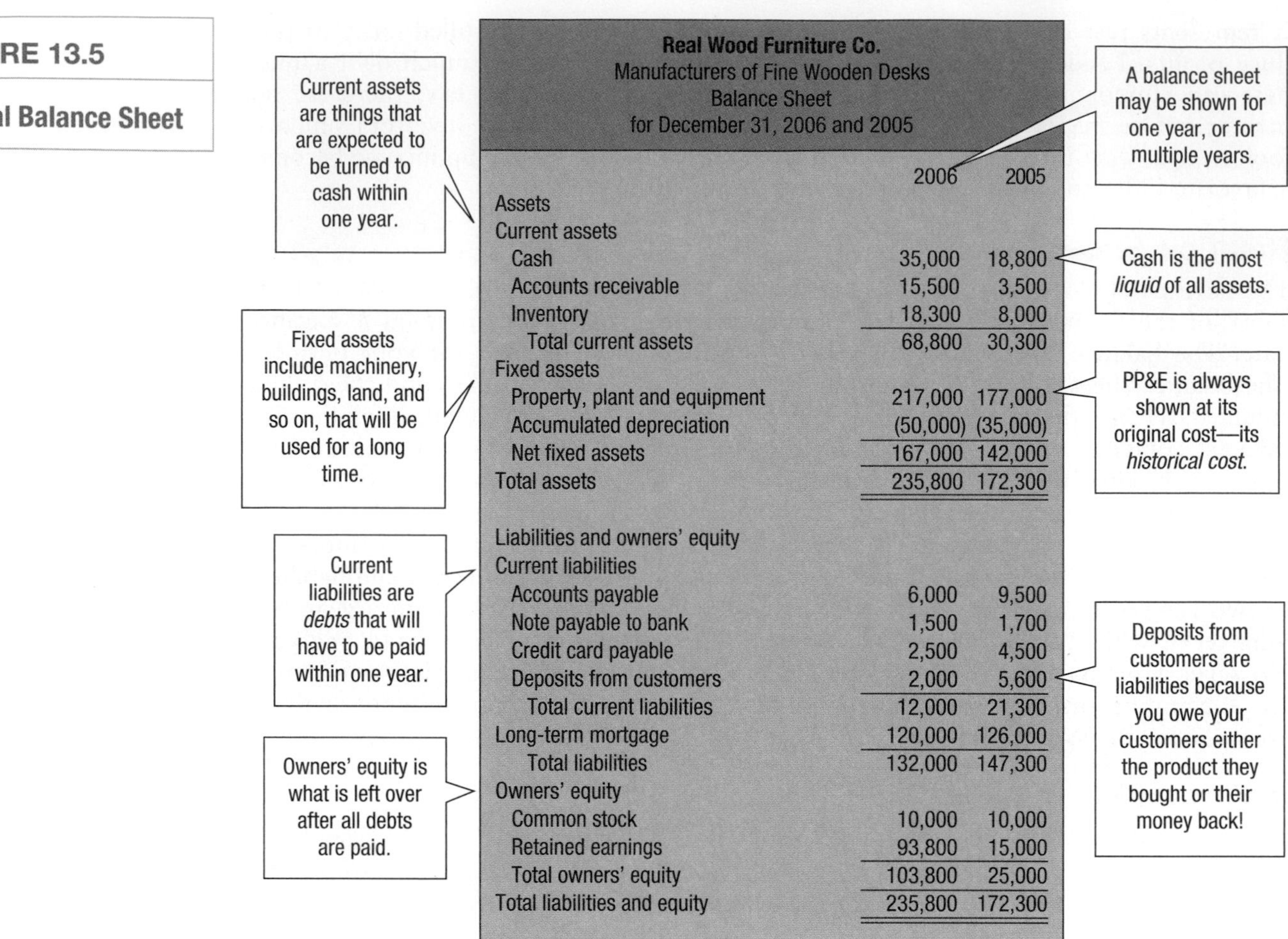

Real Wood Furniture Co.
Manufacturers of Fine Wooden Desks
Balance Sheet
for December 31, 2006 and 2005

	2006	2005
Assets		
Current assets		
Cash	35,000	18,800
Accounts receivable	15,500	3,500
Inventory	18,300	8,000
Total current assets	68,800	30,300
Fixed assets		
Property, plant and equipment	217,000	177,000
Accumulated depreciation	(50,000)	(35,000)
Net fixed assets	167,000	142,000
Total assets	235,800	172,300
Liabilities and owners' equity		
Current liabilities		
Accounts payable	6,000	9,500
Note payable to bank	1,500	1,700
Credit card payable	2,500	4,500
Deposits from customers	2,000	5,600
Total current liabilities	12,000	21,300
Long-term mortgage	120,000	126,000
Total liabilities	132,000	147,300
Owners' equity		
Common stock	10,000	10,000
Retained earnings	93,800	15,000
Total owners' equity	103,800	25,000
Total liabilities and equity	235,800	172,300

liquidity
A measure of how quickly a company can raise money through internal sources by converting assets to cash.

Liquidity is a measure of the expected time before an asset can be converted into cash, and of the expected time before a liability must be paid. A completely liquid asset is one that can be converted instantly to cash, at its full value.[6] Cash is the most liquid of assets, as it does not have to be converted. An illiquid asset *cannot* be sold quickly without suffering a significant discount from its true value. Specialized machinery is not a liquid asset. Certainly, given enough time, specialized machinery that is not technologically obsolete can be sold. However, it is not likely to be sold quickly, and is quite likely that when sold, it will sell for only a portion of its true value as a productive asset. Think of a hot rod automobile. You might spend $20,000 or more building it. But if you must sell it, you are unlikely to get more than a tiny fraction of your cost. The same is true for any custom asset, and the more illiquid it is, the greater the discount.

Liquidity is a measure of the ability of a business to meet both short-term and long-term obligations. Lenders are concerned with liquidity because it indicates the level of risk that a loan will not be repaid as contracted. Equity investors are concerned with liquidity because it affects a business's ability to pay dividends.

The most common ratio used to estimate liquidity is the current ratio. The current ratio is calculated by dividing the value of current assets (those assets expected to be converted to cash within one year) by the value of current liabilities (those liabilities that must be paid within one year). The rule of thumb for evaluating current ratio is that the minimum acceptable ratio is 2.0, and higher is better. The calculation and use of financial ratios are discussed in detail in Chapter 15.

current ratio
The value of current assets divided by current liabilities.

Financial flexibility is an indicator of the business's ability to manage cash flows so that the company has the financial ability to respond appropriately if an unexpected opportunity or problem arises. There are no accepted financial ratios that are indicators of financial flexibility. Financial flexibility is a matter of judgment, usually based on experience. What owners, managers, bankers, and investors look for to help indicate levels of financial flexibility include (1) the ability to sell nonoperating assets, (2) the ability to obtain loans or to sell additional stock, and (3) the ability to increase efficiency and to lower costs of operation.[7] You can see that what is similar across the three indicators is the business's ability to rapidly and efficiently raise additional capital.

financial flexibility
A business's ability to manage cash flows in such a manner that the company can respond appropriately to unexpected opportunities and needs.

The financial strength of the business is also a matter of informed judgment. The balance sheet provides information about the nature of the assets and liabilities of the business. In evaluating financial strength, more cash and cash equivalents indicate higher strength. Current assets that comprise cash, short-term investments, and accounts receivable are more indicative of strength than are inventories and prepaid expenses. In fact, excessive amounts of inventory in the current assets are indicative of management problems and financial weakness. For example, a large inventory may indicate lagging sales or products that have become obsolete or fallen out of favor with customers—all indicators of out-of-touch management. Long-term assets that are relatively new, low current liabilities, low long-term debt, and fully funded retirement plans for employees are all indicative of financial strength.

financial strength
The ability of a business to survive adverse financial events.

Problems in Interpreting Balance Sheet Information

For all its usefulness to the owners and managers of businesses, the balance sheet has several limitations. First, all values listed in a balance sheet are *historical* values—the cost of the asset when it was acquired. In the case of long-lived assets, such as land, buildings, and equipment, the value recorded in the accounting records can be widely different from the asset's current value. Given even a small level of inflation, the original cost of such assets is likely to be a much smaller number of dollars than its current value. On the other hand, cash is always current. This means that ratios such as return on assets (current income/net average asset value) have a current value as numerator and a denominator that, at best, is measured in older dollars of greater purchasing power. At the extreme, the true value of the asset may have changed without regard to any effect of inflation. Value can change greatly, especially in the case of land and buildings, as population density, demographics, highway access, and development change.

Think of it this way. Ed bought a 2,000-square-foot warehouse in 1995 for $40,000. That is the amount he carries on the balance sheet as part of his assets. But a nearby 2,000-square-foot warehouse sold in 2005 for $80,000. Ed's warehouse probably has a similar value, but he continues to report what he paid in 1995, in effect understating the value on the balance sheet. If Ed made $100,000 profit in 2005, what is his *real* return on assets? Using the original value, it is:

$100,000/$40,000 = 2.5

That looks like a very good return, but in reality Ed could probably sell the building for around $80,000, so the value of his assets is higher than he shows. Using the current value of the warehouse, the return on assets is:

$100,000/$80,000 = 1.25

Looked at this way, Ed's profits are not nearly as impressive. Maybe he would do better selling the warehouse and buying a less expensive warehouse farther out. This shows the problem of asset valuation over time.

Second, even a well-done balance sheet might not completely reflect the business. This can happen for several reasons. For example, every balance sheet typically contains one or more estimated amounts, such as estimated loss from uncollectible accounts receivable, estimated warranty cost, accumulated depreciation, depletion, amortization, and income taxes. Sometimes these estimates can be significantly wrong, such as when an unexpected product defect appears. At other times, there may be estimated values on a balance sheet that are not really very relevant to the running of a small business, such as internally developed assets and deferred tax assets or liabilities.

Finally, certain assets and liabilities are omitted from the balance sheet. Assets that are not listed include the value of licenses, established business with vendors, established customers, organizational knowledge and expertise, employee loyalty and morale, and research and development. When such assets represent a major strength of your company, the balance sheet will underreport your firm's financial strength.

Liabilities that are not shown on the balance sheet include such items as certain types of long-term leases and hazardous waste cleanup required by law. As was so clearly illustrated in the Enron debacle, these *off-balance sheet items* can obscure the actual financial position of a business to the point of making the balance sheet fraudulent. For most small businesses, however, the amount of off-balance sheet items is small. Their absence does not materially affect the interpretation and use of the balance sheet.

SKILL MODULE 13.2

Applying for a Loan

You are going to apply for a loan for your business. Your banker told you that you will need to bring him a set of financial statements that show your business income, your business's financial position (balance sheet), and your cash flows for the year to date. To complete this task, you have collected the following information from your accounting records, which you keep manually in a three-ring binder.

Use the information to make a balance sheet in the format shown in Figure 13.5. (You can complete only the current year balance sheet.)

Account	Balance
Accounts payable	2,500
Accounts receivable	5,000
Building and equipment	112,000
Note to bank	27,500
Customer deposits	3,000
Cash	15,000
Accumulated depreciation	35,000
Paid in capital	50,000
Retained earnings	14,000

1. What is the amount of current and long-term assets that you have?
2. Can you pledge the retained earnings of $14,000 as collateral for the new loan? Why or why not?
3. Calculate the current ratio. Using the rule of thumb given in the text, is this a good or bad ratio?
4. Why would the current ratio matter to your banker?

Cash Flow Statement

You compute the cash flow statement in order to see the sources and uses of cash by the business. Cash flow statements can be either direct statements or indirect statements. The direct statement is developed solely from the cash records of the business (only those things bought and sold) and does not make any reconciliation to the income statement. The indirect statement of cash flows starts with net income, and adjusts the accruals and deferrals to provide cash flow information that can be easily reconciled to the other financial statements. Most owners, lenders, and investors prefer the indirect method because it explicitly links net income and the balance sheet to cash flows.

cash flow statement A statement of the sources and uses of cash in a business for a specific period of time.

There are six items that must be reported in an indirect statement of cash flows:

1. Cash flows from operating activities.
2. Cash flows from investing activities.
3. Cash flows from financing activities.
4. Net effect of foreign exchange rates.
5. Net change in cash balance during the period.
6. Noncash investing and financing activities.

Common cash inflows (receipts) and outflows (payments) are shown in Figure 13.6.

Operating activities include all the functions that are performed to create your product or service. Thus the receipt of cash from customers is an operating activity. Funds received from obtaining a loan at a bank is not an operating activity; rather it is a financing activity.

operating activities Activities involved in producing and selling goods and services.

Investing activities include the acquisition and disposal of property, plant, equipment, and investment securities of other firms. The outflows are the cash investments made by the business to acquire noncash assets. Investing outflows arise from the sale or disposal of noncash assets acquired from prior investments.

investing activities The purchase and sale of land, buildings, equipment, and securities; also the process of borrowing and repaying money.

FIGURE 13.6

Typical Cash Inflows and Outflows on the Cash Flow Statement

Inflows	Outflows
Cash Flows from Operating Activities	
1. Cash received from customers	1. Cash paid to purchase inventory
2. Interest received on accounts receivable	2. Salaries and wages
3. Dividends received on investments in other firms	3. Cash paid for rent, utilities, royalities, and license fees
4. Cash refunds from vendors	4. Income taxes, duties, and fines
5. All interest received from loans to other entities	5. All interest paid on liabilities
Cash Flows from Investing Activities	
1. Disposal of property, plant, and equipment	1. Acquisition of property, plant and equipment
2. Disposal of investment securities	2. Acquisition of investment securities
3. Receipt of the capital amount of loans made to customers and vendors	3. Loans made to other entities
	4. Acquisition of assets other than inventories
Cash Flows from Financing Activities	
1. Cash received from owners of the business	1. Cash paid to owners as dividends and draws
2. Cash received from borrowing	2. Cash paid to acquire the firm's own stock
	3. Repayment of the principal of borrowed funds

financing activities
Activities through which cash is obtained from and paid to owners and investors.

Financing activities are those actions taken by management to finance the operations of the business. Thus cash inflows come only from investments by owners and from money borrowed through notes, mortgages, and bonds. Cash outflows from financing activities comprise capital repaid to owners and repayment of the principal amount of borrowings.

Net effect of foreign exchange rates is becoming ever more important to small businesses. The Internet has opened foreign trade to businesses of all sizes. Exchange rates often vary rapidly, affecting the value of contracts and sales made in currencies other than the currency of the home nation of the business.

Net change in cash balance simply reconciles the net increase or decrease with the beginning cash balance and the ending cash balance.

Noncash investing and financing comprise transactions in which an exchange of value other than cash takes place. An example of a noncash transaction is when a debt is settled by issuing stock to the creditor. These types of transactions are rarely made by small businesses. A more common transaction for small businesses is a barter transaction, which is discussed in detail in Chapter 14.

Uses of Financial Accounting

LO4
Understand how accounting information can help you manage your business effectively.

Although financial accounting is not specifically designed for management purposes, it can be a highly valuable aid in decision making. Financial and business managers are familiar with the format, content, and interpretation of financial statements. Obtaining loans, answering Internal Revenue inquiries, and satisfying the reporting requirements of regulatory agencies are all made easier when an appropriate set of financial statements is provided.

As the accounting scandals of recent years have made evident, the existence of financial accounting statements, even when audited by major accounting firms, does not guarantee that the representations of management are complete, accurate, or even true. In this respect, financial accounting is much like a lock on the door. A lock will keep honest people honest. Crooks will pick the lock, jimmy a window, or find another entry to commit burglary. Similarly, a business manager who is determined to commit fraud might be inconvenienced by accounting standards, but will find some way to do the crime.

Thinking about the lock idea, if you have locked something, doesn't it just make sense to double-check that the lock is in fact locked? Doing that just shows a healthy skepticism. Similarly for owners and managers of small businesses, all representations by owners, managers, employees, and providers of business outsourcing should be examined with an attitude of informed professional skepticism. It is just a healthy attitude to have.

Reporting to Outsiders

The greatest value of financial accounting for small business owners and managers is reporting the results of operations and the financial condition of the business to entities outside the business. Outsiders can include absentee owners,[8] creditors and lenders, unions, and taxing and regulatory agencies. Each of these groups has some interest in the conduct of the business. Each has either or both legal rights and political power to enforce honest disclosure of your business's finances. You are less likely to be accused of misrepresentation if your disclosures comply with accepted accounting principles.

Record Keeping

The primary criteria for a small business's record keeping system are: (1) simplicity of use, (2) accuracy of detail, (3) timeliness of reports, (4) understandability to the manager of the business, and (5) security of data. An appropriate accounting system keeps records of the details of financial transactions that facilitate the task of corroborating the conduct of the business. The most convincing evidence that can be provided to outsiders is a set of complete and accurate records that can be substantiated by third-party sources.

Taxation

Current Internal Revenue Service (IRS) regulations require that employers withhold federal income, social security (FICA), and Medicare taxes from the wages of each employee. Employers must also pay the federal unemployment tax (FUTA). The amount withheld, and the employer's share of taxes, must be paid to the IRS regularly, on a schedule determined by the amount of withholding. At the year's end, each employer is required to submit summaries of each employee's total earnings and withholdings for the year and to report the information to the IRS and to each employee on a Form W-2. This process can be automated by using one of the small business computerized accounting systems mentioned earlier.

Similarly, businesses need to pay taxes each year, and having the financial records makes the task dramatically easier. In fact many of the computerized accounting packages have tax modules or are designed to feed information to tax programs such as Intuit's TurboTax or H&R Block's TaxCut.

Control of Receivables

Accounts receivable—money owed your business by customers—is often the key to survival. An appropriate record-keeping system provides detailed reports of amounts due from customers including purchases, payments, and current contact information. The key in controlling receivables is to have them *aged,* by sorting them into groups of those that are 30, 60, 90, and over 90 days past due. If you don't receive payment when due, you should take immediate and appropriate action to collect it. Often businesses step up collection efforts when the receivables are more than 30 days overdue, with many businesses treating receivables more than 90 days old as delinquent. In such cases the owners may refer the account to a collection agency or even factor the account, selling it (at a substantial discount) to a company that will take aggressive actions to collect the entire amount owed and keep all the money it obtains.

Analysis of Business Operations

Your accounting records contain information that can be easily used for analysis of the results and state of your business. Experience in your business provides a benchmark to which all items may be compared. Those items that appear unrealistic—either too high or too low—should be carefully examined. The examination should attempt to answer the following:

- What are the appropriate levels of sales and expenses?
- Why do certain expenses appear too high or too low?
- Can any expenses be reduced or eliminated?
- Are profits appropriate for your investment, risk, time, and effort?

Uses of Managerial Accounting

Managerial accounting—the forward looking form of accounting—is one of the three types of accounting, along with tax and financial. Mastering certain managerial accounting techniques will make you a better small business manager.[9] The techniques of managerial accounting will help you become more accurate at forecasting profits, planning operations, and conserving scarce resources. Managerial accounting information and reports are used in the conduct of all managerial functions: planning, organizing, staffing, directing, and controlling.

No one starts or buys a business for the purpose of losing money. Rather, you go into business for the express purpose of making profits and creating wealth.[10] It is unfortunate that, as business failure statistics show, a significant number of small business owners do not achieve this basic goal. One of the underlying causes of financial failure of small businesses is the lack of a coherent plan to produce the profits necessary for continued existence and growth.[11]

Accounting data contain the information necessary to create detailed plans of how to make a desired level of profit. The problem is coaxing the information out of the data.

The process of profit planning comprises creating a *model* of the business which will allow you to test various situations, assumptions, and occurrences without risking financial loss. If the model "crashes," simply reset it and try again.[12] Models can be as simple as a schedule of expected profits at differing levels of sales, or as complex as a full, interactive computerized simulation of the business and the economy.

The Business Plan and the Budget Process

LO5
Learn how to craft budgets for your business.

The most common model used for small businesses planning is the familiar business plan, like those described in Chapter 8. Looked at the managerial accounting way, a business plan specifies the amounts and types of inputs required to achieve a set of desired outcomes. It is based on assumptions concerning how costs will change in response to changes in the business operations, how risks can be controlled, and what opportunities can be taken. The financial projections in your business plan are a form of a budget which can easily be expanded to be useful for day-to-day management of your business. In fact, the budgeting techniques we show here use exactly the same estimates and calculations as you must make to create pro forma financial statements for a business plan. The budgets here, however, have the advantage of being comprised of a series of small, easy-to-understand schedules. When they are linked and printed as a single set of financial statements, they are identical to the familiar business plan pro forma statements.

pro forma
Latin for "in the form of" when used to describe financial statements, indicates estimated or hypothetical information.

Planning/Budgeting

Strategic planning, as discussed in Chapter 7, results in statements that are expressed in broad terms. For example, your strategic marketing position may be a price strategy, a luxury strategy, or a value strategy. However, if your broad strategic goals are to be achieved, you must take specific tactical steps. Budgeting is the process through which strategy is mapped into a series of tactical and operational actions.[13]

The process of achieving your strategic goals requires complex activities, cooperation among the people in your business, and the use of significant valuable resources. You will be better able to direct all this if you have a documented quantitative plan of action for your business. Such a plan is called a budget.

budget
A financial plan for the future, based on a single level of operations; a quantitative expression of the use of resources necessary to achieve a business's strategic goals.

Once a budget has been prepared, it becomes a standard against which performance can be measured.[14] Your budget establishes resource restraints within which your managers and employees must operate. Your budget becomes the basis for controlling activities and the use of resources. By constantly comparing actual performance to budgeted amounts, determining the causes of the inevitable differences, taking necessary corrective action, and providing feedback concerning performance, you may ensure that you attain your business goals.

Despite the many benefits to comprehensive budgeting, few small business owners consistently budget.[15] Those who do create budgets often set them aside in the rush of business activities.[16]

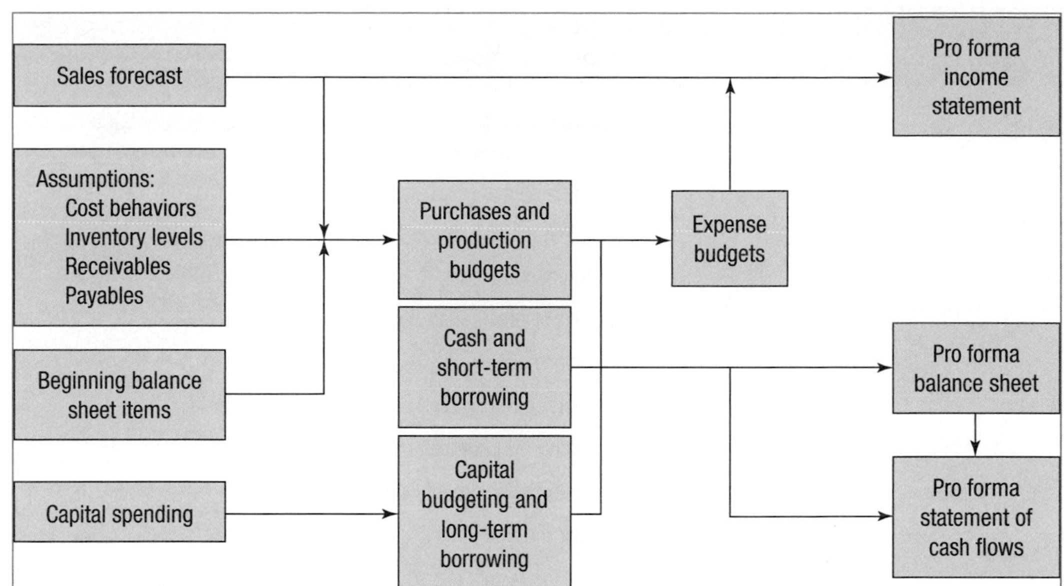

FIGURE 13.7

Budgeting Relationships

Let's face it, budgeting is seen by many entrepreneurs as a tedious and difficult job. We are going to try to convince you otherwise. In fact, business planning is a *simple* process of applying your knowledge of your business to make estimates of future operations and results. In many ways it is little more than an expanded application of the break-even analysis that is discussed in Chapter 9. However, business planning uses more detail than break-even analysis, and thus provides a basis for analyzing, directing, and controlling your day-to-day business operations at the level of detail that is most effective for you.

The first step in budgeting (as in any other method of business planning) is to make a forecast of your future sales. From the sales forecast, and from your knowledge of cost behaviors, collections, payments, and expenses, a complete business plan will be developed. Although this sounds daunting, in practice, you can adjust the level of detail you need to provide a comprehensive budget that is both compact and understandable (see Figure 13.7).

You may create as many or as few supplemental budgets and schedules as you need to model your business. The budgets and schedules that you will find most useful are listed in Table 13.1.

Completing a Master Budget

To illustrate how simple it is to create a master budget, consider the following information. Languid Lizard, Inc. is a manufacturer of folding aluminum lawn chairs. The entire business is located in a single leased building in a light industrial park. The entire process of making and packaging one chair requires 12 minutes of direct labor. Production workers have a total cost of employment of $12 per hour. The machinery has a practical limit of 1,000 chairs per day, which exceeds the maximum budgeted production level. The process of making a chair begins with cutting square aluminum tubing to the appropriate length. The tubing is then bent on an automatic machine, and the parts are hand assembled. The chair frames are then moved to an area of the factory where webbing is attached to form the seat and back. The chairs are then placed into boxes and moved to a warehousing area from which they are shipped to customers. The business tries to have an ending inventory of 10 percent of the next quarter's sales.

TABLE 13.1 Useful Budgets and Schedules

Budget for a Manufacturing Business	Budget for a Retail or Wholesale Business
1. Sales budget	1. Sales budget
2. Schedule of budgeted cash collections	2. Schedule of budgeted cash collections
3. Production budget	3. Purchases budget
4. Direct materials budget	4. Cost of goods sold budget
5. Direct labor budget	5. Labor budget
6. Manufacturing overhead budget	6. Overhead budget
7. Cost of goods manufactured and sold budget	7. Selling and administrative budget
8. Selling and administrative expense budget	8. Cash disbursements budget
9. Cash disbursements budget	9. Cash budget
10. Cash budget	10. Pro forma income statement
11. Pro forma income statement	11. Pro forma balance sheet
12. Pro forma balance sheet	

The master budget for the coming year contains the budgets and schedules for a manufacturing business, shown above, and is detailed in the following pages.

Sales Budget

The first step in preparing a master budget is to prepare a sales budget. The sales budget shows the projected future level of sales in units multiplied by the sales price per unit.

SCHEDULE 1

LANGUID LIZARD, INC.

Sales Budget
For the Year Ending December 31, 2006

	Quarter				
	1st	2nd	3rd	4th	year
Sales in units	4,000	12,000	9,000	3,000	28,000
Unit sales price	$16	$16	$16	$16	$16
Total sales revenue	$64,000	$192,000	$144,000	$48,000	$448,000

Production Budget

The production budget shows the number of units that are expected to be produced during the budget period. The specific number of units to be produced in each period is a function of how many units are on hand at the beginning of the period, how many are projected to be sold, and the desired number of units to be held in inventory at the end of the period. Examine the column for the second quarter of the period. Sales are predicted to be 12,000 units. Management wishes to have 10 percent of the next quarter's sales on hand at the end of the quarter: 900 units. Thus, 12,900 units are needed to meet the demands of sales and ending inventory. However, management plans to start the quarter with 1,200 units in stock. Thus, only 11,700 units must be produced during the second quarter. This simple formula is used over and over to produce most of the schedules of a master budget: the number needed = the number to be used + desired ending number − predicted beginning number. The formula is often presented in accounting format shown in Figure 13.8.

Number used
\+ Ending balance
= Number available
− Beginning balance
= Number needed

FIGURE 13.8

Formula for Master Budget

SCHEDULE 2

LANGUID LIZARD, INC.

Production Budget
For the Year Ending December 31, 2006

	Quarter				
	1st	2nd	3rd	4th	year
Sales in units	4,000	12,000	9,000	3,000	28,000
Plus desired ending inventory	1,200	900	300	500	500
Total units required	5,200	12,900	9,300	3,500	28,500
Less desired beginning inventory	400	1,200	900	300	400
Units to be produced	4,800	11,700	8,400	3,200	28,100

Note: sales for 1st quarter of 2007 are estimated at 5,000 units

Direct Material Budget

Once you know how many units you will make, it is simple to estimate the amount of material you will need to make them. In this example, only the calculations for aluminum tubing are shown. The calculation for webbing, fasteners, and boxes is done in exactly the same manner. It is normal to budget for each required material in a reiterative process.

SCHEDULE 3

LANGUID LIZARD, INC.

Purchases Budget
For the Year Ending December 31, 2006

	Quarter				
	1st	2nd	3rd	4th	year
Units to be produced	4,800	11,700	8,400	3,200	28,100
Aluminum tubing per unit	25	25	25	25	25
Tubing required for production	120,000	292,500	210,000	80,000	702,500
Plus desired ending inventory	29,250	21,000	8,000	15,250	15,250
Total tubing required	149,250	313,500	218,000	95,250	717,750
Less desired beginning inventory	12,000	29,250	21,000	8,000	12,000
Material to be purchased	137,250	284,250	197,000	87,250	705,750
Cost per linear foot	0.15	0.15	0.15	0.15	0.15
Total cost of tubing to be purchased	$20,588	$42,638	$29,550	$13,088	$105,863
Total cost of webbing*	14,410	38,672	26,973	9,677	89,731
Total cost of fasteners*	4,503	12,085	8,429	3,024	28,041
Total cost of boxes*	2,252	6,043	4,215	1,512	14,021
Total cost of direct material purchases	$39,500	$99,437	$69,166	$27,300	$237,655

Note: Production for 1st quarter of 2007 is estimated at 6,100 units

**Cost of webbing, fasteners, and boxes is calculated in the same manner as cost of aluminum tubing.*

See Web site for more details.

Each chair requires 25 linear feet of aluminum tubing that costs $0.15 per foot, and 40 linear feet of nylon webbing that costs $0.08 per foot. All other components, including screws, washers, and fasteners cost $1.00 per chair. The box into which a finished chair is placed costs $0.50. Notice that the sample budget is based upon having ending inventories of 10 percent of the following quarter's needs. This is done for simplification.

Direct Labor Budget

The direct labor budget shows both the amount and cost of labor needed to meet required production. Here we assume that labor can be easily increased or decreased as production levels change. In practice, this is very difficult to achieve, as most workers want to have jobs that provide steady, full-time employment. When a business maintains stable employment despite changes in production levels, labor is not a variable cost. However, labor can easily be modeled as a fixed cost to better fit the actual practice of your business.

SCHEDULE 4
LANGUID LIZARD, INC.
Direct Labor
For the Year Ending December 31, 2006

	Quarter				
	1st	2nd	3rd	4th	year
Units to be produced	4,800	11,700	8,400	3,200	28,100
Direct labor required per unit (tenths of hour)	0.1	0.1	0.1	0.1	0.1
Direct labor required for production	480	1,170	840	320	2,810
Labor cost per hour	$12	$12	$12	$12	$12
Total labor cost	$5,760	$14,040	$10,080	$3,840	$33,720

Manufacturing Overhead Budget

Traditionally, all overhead costs have been treated as fixed, not changing with changes in production. It is becoming more common for managers to use *activity-based* cost estimates for overhead. As was discussed above, many costs that do not vary in proportion to production levels do vary in response to changes in other business activities. If the cost behaviors are known, they can easily be included in the budget process.

For simplicity, the example given here assumes that overhead costs are fixed with respect to production.

SCHEDULE 5
LANGUID LIZARD, INC.
Manufacturing Overhead
For the Year Ending December 31, 2006

	Quarter				
	1st	2nd	3rd	4th	year
Factory lease	$3,300	$3,300	$3,300	$3,300	$13,200
Insurance	1,000	1,000	1,000	1,000	4,000
Maintenance	500	500	500	500	2,000
Utilities	800	800	800	800	3,200
Total manufacturing overhead	$5,600	$5,600	$5,600	$5,600	$22,400

Selling, General, and Administrative Expense (SG&A) Budget

The SG&A budget illustrated here in Schedule 6 contains both costs that change with production and costs that do not. As is discussed above, this is a more real assumption than the common treatment of SG&A costs as being fixed. It is assumed that advertising and freight is a variable cost in respect to sales. Sales cost is mixed: The salesperson receives a salary and a commission based on gross sales.

SCHEDULE 6

LANGUID LIZARD, INC.

Selling, General, and Administrative
For the Year Ending December 31, 2006

	Quarter				
	1st	2nd	3rd	4th	year
Sales in units	4,000	12,000	9,000	3,000	28,000
Commissions (2% of gross sales)	$1,280	$3,840	$2,880	$960	$8,960
Freight out	400	1,200	900	300	2,800
Advertising	6,400	19,200	14,400	4,800	44,800
Sales salaries	7,500	7,500	7,500	7,500	30,000
Clerical wages	6,000	6,000	6,000	6,000	24,000
Total expenses	$21,580	$37,740	$31,680	$19,560	$110,560

Cost of Goods Manufactured and Sold

The cost of goods manufactured and sold combines the cost of materials, labor, and manufacturing overhead. The value of product in ending finished goods inventory is subtracted, providing the cost of goods sold.

SCHEDULE 7

LANGUID LIZARD, INC.

Cost of Goods Manufactured and Sold
For the Year Ending December 31, 2006

Direct materials used	
Beginning direct materials inventory	$3,798
Plus purchases	237,655
Direct materials available	$241,453
Less ending inventory	4,151

Direct material used	$237,301
Direct labor	33,720
Manufacturing overhead	22,400
Total manufacturing costs	$293,421
Plus beginning work in process	0
Less ending work in process	0
Total cost of goods manufactured	$293,421
Plus beginning finished goods inventory	4,083
Total value of goods available for sale	$297,504
Less ending finished goods inventory	5,615
Total cost of goods sold	$291,889

Note: the manufacturing cycle is so short (12 min) that there is no significant work in process.

Budgeted Income Statement

The budgets that have been completed to this point are combined into pro forma financial statements, the first of which is a budgeted income statement. It is common to create the budgeted income statement in only a fiscal year format as is done here. While the income statement could be produced in quarters, or even months, that level of detail is usually not very helpful. The entire budgeted income statement is based on the assumption that all budgeted items, sales, production, purchasing, labor, overhead, and SG&A

SCHEDULE 8
LANGUID LIZARD, INC.
Budgeted Income Statement
For the Year Ending December 31, 2006

Sales revenue		$448,000
Less cost of goods sold		291,889
Gross margin		$156,111
Other expenses:		
Selling, general, and administrative	$110,560	
Interest expense	6,016	
Total other expenses		$116,576
Net income before provision for income tax		$39,535

Note: interest expense comes from the cash budget, prepared in Chapter 14.

will be incurred exactly as planned in the supporting budgets. During the year, comparisons of actual results are made to the budgeted items. If the budget is met, then the projected profit will be realized.

The cost of goods sold is the sum of direct materials, direct labor, and manufacturing overhead applied to the product that was sold. It may be included in the income statement or calculated as a separate schedule, as is done here. Interest expense on the budgeted income statement is calculated on the cash budget, which is included in Chapter 14.

Completing a Comprehensive Budget

The final processes to be accomplished to produce a complete master budget are (1) budgeted cash receipts, (2) budgeted cash payments, (3) a cash budget, and (4) a budgeted balance sheet.

The management of cash is so important to a small business that it deserves a chapter to itself. Therefore, the discussion of cash and cash budgeting is included in the next chapter.

SKILL MODULE 13.3

Preparing a Master Budget

Go to the McGraw-Hill Web site for this textbook (**www.mhhe.com/katzesb**) and download the Excel Budget Template for Languid Lizard. Using the information in the downloaded spreadsheet, complete a monthly master budget, following the examples shown in this chapter.

Controlling

Managerial accounting, primarily through the budget process, provides information that allows managers to determine how well the business is doing in attaining its goals. This is done by comparing actual results to budgeted results. The difference between actual and budget is called a **variance**. Management can determine where the business is not meeting goals through examining a report of variances.

variance
The difference between an actual and budgeted revenue or cost.

Variances should be evaluated to determine the significance of a particular variance. Small variances from budget are expected to occur, as the budget is a collection of estimates. No business manager, in fact, no person, no computer, is capable of making estimates that are exactly what future results will be. For this reason, it is customary for management to determine a range of acceptable variances. Individual variances that fall within the predetermined acceptable range are ignored. Variances that exceed the acceptable range are examined in detail, with the manager tracing the activities that drive the cost to determine the cause of the variance and appropriate methods to deal with it.

variance analysis
The process of determining the effect of price and quantity changes on revenues and expenses.

Variance analysis is a topic that is simple in concept but complex in execution. At the most basic level, variances occur because of one of two events: (1) Prices are different from what was estimated, or (2) Quantities are different from what was estimated. Thus variances can be reduced to determine the amount of variance caused by price changes and the amount of variance caused by changes in volume.[17] The specifics of variance analyses are detailed in the Thoughtful Entrepreneur box.

THE THOUGHTFUL ENTREPRENEUR

Performing Variance Analyses

Suppose that you operate a business that produces aluminum window frames for the replacement window industry. You have used all your expertise to budget the next year's operation of your business. Based on prior years' results, the current state of the economy, and projections for the replacement window industry, you developed the following budget items:

Materials to produce one window frame	Budget
aluminum extrusions 16 ft @ 1.20 per ft	$19.20
sheet aluminum 25 sq in @ $ 0.08	2.00
screws 22 @ .06 each	1.32

For the past month, you estimated total production to be 6,000 window units. You actually produced 5,800 window frames. You used 93,960 feet of extrusion that cost $109,933 in total. As a manager, how would you answer the questions, "How did the price of aluminum affect us?" and "Did we use the extrusions efficiently?"

Logically, the answer to the first question can be found by answering the question, "What would I have paid for the aluminum I actually used if the price had been what I expected?" The difference between that and what you actually paid is the difference caused by price changes.

The second question, "Did we use the material efficiently?" can be answered by asking, "How much material should I have used to make the number of window units that were actually completed?" The difference between what you should have used and actually did use multiplied by the price you expected to pay for aluminum is the difference resulting from efficiency.

These questions are answered by variance analysis, which uses the information mentioned above to produce quantitative results. The equations that make up variance analysis are given in Figure 13.9. Figure 13.10 shows how the calculations are made.

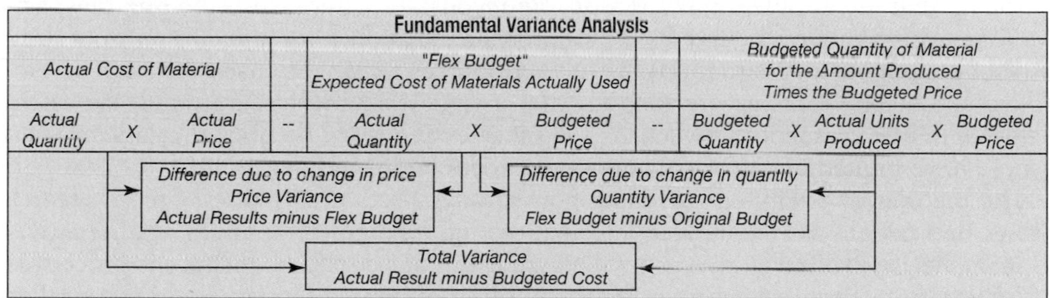

FIGURE 13.9

Fundamental Variance Analysis

Variance Analysis Example

Actual Cost of Material				"Flex Budget" Expected Cost of Materials Actually Used				Budgeted Quantity of Material for the Amount Produced Times the Budgeted Price			
93,960 ft.	X	$109,933 / 93,960 ft.	--	93,960 ft.	X	$1.20	--	16 ft. X 5,800 units	X	$1.20	
93,960 ft.	X	$1.17	--	93,960	X	$1.20	--	92,800 ft.	X	$1.20	
109,933			--	112,752			--	111,360			

Price Variance
$2,819 favorable

Quantity Variance
$1,392 unfavorable

Total Variance
$1,427 favorable

FIGURE 13.10

Variance Analysis Example

favorable/unfavorable variance
A label applied to variances to indicate their effect upon the income statement; favorable variances would result in profits being greater than budgeted, all other things being equal; unfavorable variances would result in profits being less than budgeted, all other things being equal.

Thus we can see that the actual cost of material was $2,819 less than the expected cost for the amount actually used. This is called a **favorable price variance**. On the other hand, the cost of the amount of materials actually used is greater than the budgeted cost of materials to make 5,800 window frames. This is called an **unfavorable quantity variance**. The terms *favorable* and *unfavorable* are determined by the variance's effect on profits, all other things being as budgeted. Paying 3 cents a foot less for extrusions than was budgeted would cause a greater profit than budgeted, if all other budget items were exactly correct. Conversely, using more extrusions to make 5,800 window frames than was budgeted for that level of output would cause a decrease from budgeted profit.

Note that although the variances are labeled as favorable or unfavorable depending on the direction of the variance from budget, no value judgment can be made from the label. A favorable price variance could be a bad event for the company; if, for example, the reason for the lower price was lower quality of materials that would prevent the business from attaining its strategic goals. Additionally, managers must use judgment to determine if the variance is worth the effort to investigate. For example, the price of aluminum extrusions is set by the world price for aluminum. It is not likely that any amount of investigating would result in determining a way to get a lower price. On the other hand, using 0.2 feet more of material than was budgeted might indicate that cutting tools are out of adjustment or that worker efficiency is not as great as expected. Management could reasonably expect to find the cause and to devise a way to improve the use of this resource.

Decision Making

LO6
Gain understanding of how people make decisions.

Managers have five primary functions in a business: planning, organizing, staffing, directing, and controlling the combined efforts of the firm. Each of these functions requires making decisions, both large and small. The primary purpose of managerial accounting is to support good decision making.

To use accounting information for decision making, you need to have some understanding of the processes by which people make decisions.

All current theories of decision making are based on the belief that people are rational, that is, people think, reason, and consider alternatives before they act. Although this assumption may be a bit optimistic, it applies (or *should* apply) to decision making in business situations. The assumption of rationality itself comes in several "flavors." At one extreme are theories that assume that the human mind has essentially unlimited reasoning powers. At the other extreme are theories that assume that people have limited abilities to obtain and process information.

The theories of unlimited reasoning powers have been largely discredited. Research shows that people use incomplete information and incomplete analyses of alternatives to make decisions. Today, it is generally assumed that people are inefficient processors of information. Theories based on the assumption of limited human abilities are called *bounded rationality models.*[18] One implication of the assumption that people are limited in their ability to use information is that the more information available to be included into the decision process, the less efficient that process will be.

Thus to make good decisions we need (1) good information, (2) efficient ways to condense information so it is understandable, and (3) methods to help compare alternatives.

Managerial accounting is both a source of information that is used in decision making and a methodology to reduce the complexity of the information used to make a decision. By definition, managerial accounting deals with only financial information. By limiting the information being considered to financial concerns, the complexity of the alternatives is reduced. Managerial accounting further reduces information complexity by evaluating information for relevance to the decision to be made. For financial purposes, any decision that was made in the past cannot be changed and is therefore irrelevant to any decision to be made today. Information that is the same for two or more alternatives cannot be used to choose between them. For these reasons, managerial accounting decision support is based solely upon the differences in expected financial outcomes among identified alternatives.

Examining some of the common management decisions that can be aided by the use of accounting information and procedures will illustrate these concepts.

Investments are a constant management problem. To reduce the difficulty of choosing from among investment alternatives, managerial accounting has developed two basic methodologies to reduce the magnitude and complexity of the information that must be considered in making an appropriate decision.

The first of these simplification methods is called *differential revenues and expenses.* This methodology comprises estimating the *changes* in revenues and expenses from current operating results that will occur if each alternative is taken. The decision rule that is applied is to accept the investment that produces the greatest profit.

The second simplification method is called *net present value analysis* (NPV). NPV analyses are based on the concept that a dollar to be received right now has more utility (value) than does a dollar to be received at some time in the future. To perform NPV analyses, only cash flows are considered. The decision rule is to accept the largest positive NPV. The theory and application of NPV is covered in detail in Chapter 17.

Outsourcing requires that a decision be made whether the business should make a component of its own product or purchase the component from another business. As is done in investment decisions, accounting information relevant to the decision is reduced to differential revenues and costs, or to cash flows. Depending upon the methodology chosen, either the differential profits (losses) or the net present value of each alternative is calculated. Once the information is developed, decision rules are applied.[19]

A simple example of an outsourcing decision is the provision of salad for a local restaurant. Suppose that the restaurant is a barbeque that serves cole slaw as its only salad. The restaurant may either make the slaw on premises at a cost of $2.87 per pound or purchase it from a wholesaler at $2.40 per pound. Should you make the slaw or purchase the slaw? A superficial examination of the problem would indicate that purchasing it is less expensive. Examining only the differential costs offers a very different conclusion (see Figure 13.11).

FIGURE 13.11

Using Differential Costs to Make an Outsourcing Decision: Make or Buy?

Current Costs to Make Slaw on Premises

Pounds of slaw served per month	900
Materials per pound	$0.87
Direct labor per pound (2.4 hrs @ $10 per 30 lbs.)	0.80
Variable overhead per pound	0.20
Allocated fixed costs per pound	1.00
Total cost per pound	$2.87

Differential Costs between Alternatives

	Alternatives	
	Make	Buy
Materials	$0.87	–0–
Direct labor	0.80	–0–
Variable overhead	0.20	–0–
Purchase price	–0–	2.40
Total	$ 1.87	$2.40

The difference arises from the fact that fixed costs will not change if the decision is made to purchase the slaw. By definition, fixed costs are costs that do not change with changes in output (here output is slaw). As a result, the amount of fixed cost allocated to making slaw is irrelevant to the decision. If you have trouble understanding this, simply put a line for fixed cost into the decision criteria above. Put the allocated amount of $1.00 in the columns for making and buying the slaw. Add the columns and see if your decision would change.

Accounting is useful for managers of small businesses, for record keeping, for reporting to absentee owners and other stakeholders, for substantiating assertions made to regulators and taxing agencies, for support of the five functions of management, and for decision making. Accounting information is a financial model of the operations of the business and provides a wealth of useful reports, analyses, and measures that are valuable to the management of small businesses. Accounting is a rich source of information. It is not, however, the only source of information needed by managers.

CHAPTER SUMMARY

L01 Review the basic concepts of accounting.

- Accounting matters to small businesses because:
  - Accounting proves what your business did financially.
  - Accounting shows how much your business is worth.
  - Banks, creditors, development agencies, and investors require accounting statements.
  - Accounting provides easy-to-understand plans for business operations.
  - Accounting provides information about how your business is doing.
- There are three types of accounting:
  - Managerial accounting attempts to predict the results of management decisions.
  - Tax accounting is used to produce tax returns and schedules.
  - Financial accounting is a formal, rule-based system intended primarily for absentee owners, bankers, investors, and regulators.
- Accounting is based on a few basic concepts:
  - A business is believed to have an existence that is separate and different from the owner's (business entity concept).
  - Because a business exists, it is expected to continue to exist (going concern).
  - The accounting equation is simply an expression of the common sense statement that your net worth is whatever is left over after all your debts are paid.
- To use accounting effectively for management purposes, you must understand the difference between costs and expenses:
  - Costs are real changes in the value of what you own.

- Expenses are simply entries made in your accounting system to record your use of goods and services in the conduct of your business.

- There are only two reasons to do accounting:
  - To produce information that is useful to you for managing your business.
  - To meet legal or contractual requirements.

LO2 Understand the requirements for a small business accounting system.

- The primary reason to acquire and use a computerized accounting system in your business is to ensure the accuracy of your accounting information.
- Your accounting system should easily and efficiently accomplish the following tasks:
  - Provide a simple, easy-to-understand user interface.
  - Have an exhaustive context-sensitive help function.
  - Produce financial statements in the format used by your industry and type of business.
  - Facilitate the development of a cash budget.
  - Facilitate the task of developing operating and investment budgets.
  - Provide a method for you to define and produce custom reports to meet your management needs.
  - Be able to export financial data in a form that can be used by your accountant and can be imported into tax preparation and spreadsheet programs.
  - Maintain an internal "audit trail" that records all entries and changes to the accounting system in order to facilitate the identification and correction of errors.
  - Have provisions that will either allow the program to grow with your business or to easily export its data into programs that can handle larger businesses.
- Your specific accounting needs are determined by the industry you are in and by the size of your business.
- When a business is large enough to have one or more employees, formal record keeping is a must.
- Essential elements of an accounting system are:
  - *Cash accounting* that is accurate, easy to use, and tracks all checks written and all deposits made.
  - *Accounts payable* records to track what you owe and to make timely payments in order to capture prompt pay discounts and to maintain a good credit rating for your business.
  - *Payroll* records to ensure that payroll and employment taxes are kept current.
  - *Fixed asset* accounting that automatically calculates and accumulates depreciation.
  - *Inventory* accounting to facilitate managing inventory.
  - *Credit card sales* function to enable reconciling your sales records to those of your credit card provider.
  - *Accounts receivable* records if you provide credit to your customers.
  - *Insurance register* to ease the problems of keeping necessary insurance coverage current and in force.

- *Investments* records if your business keeps surplus cash invested in securities.
- *Leasehold* records if your business has made improvements to leased property or equipment.

LO3 Be comfortable with the content and format of common financial statements.

- The final output of an accounting computer system is a set of five financial statements and reports.
  - Income statement.
  - Statement of retained earnings.
  - Statement of owners' equity.
  - Balance sheet.
  - Cash flow statement.
- It is common for these statements to be presented as only three separate documents by combining the statements of retained earnings and owner's equity into the equity section of the balance sheet.
- The income statement is the primary source of information about a business's profitability.
- The primary difficulties in understanding and interpreting the income statement arise from two causes:
  - Disagreements about what should be reported as revenue.
  - Disputes over when to recognize revenues.
- The income statement is used in the following ways:
  - The income statement is used to analyze the effectiveness of business operations.
  - Lenders use operating income as a measure of how much debt a business can support.
  - Equity investors similarly look to operating income as an indication of future sales and thus the value of their investment.
- The balance sheet presents a snap-shot of the financial holdings and liabilities at the close of business on a specified date.
- The balance sheet is used in the following ways:
  - The balance sheet is used to determine the liquidity, financial flexibility, and financial strength of the business.
  - These measures are used by owners, lenders, and equity investors in making financial and investment decisions.
- The following are problems in interpreting balance sheet information:
  - All values listed in a balance sheet are *historical* values—the cost of the asset when it was acquired.
  - A balance sheet contains several estimated amounts.
  - Certain assets and liabilities are omitted from the balance sheet.
- The purpose of the cash flow statement is to disclose the sources and uses of cash by the business.
- There are two primary formats of cash flow statement:
  - The direct statement is developed solely from the cash records of the business and does not make any reconciliation to the income statement.
  - The indirect statement of cash flows starts with net income and adjusts the accruals and deferrals to provide cash flow information that can be easily reconciled to the other financial statements.

LO4 Understand how accounting information can help you manage your business effectively.

- Financial accounting is useful for decision making.
- Financial and business managers are familiar with the format, content, and interpretation of financial statements.
- Obtaining loans, answering Internal Revenue inquiries, and satisfying the reporting requirements of regulatory agencies are all made easier when an appropriate set of financial statements is provided.
- Financial accounting is used for reporting to outsiders.
- Uses of managerial accounting include:
    - By mastering managerial accounting techniques, you will become more accurate at forecasting profits, planning operations, and conserving scarce resources.
    - Managerial accounting information and reports are used in the conduct of all the managerial functions of planning, organizing, staffing, directing, and controlling.
- Accounting data contain the information necessary to create detailed plans of how to achieve a desired level of profit.
- The process of profit planning comprises creating a model of the business which will allow you to test various situations, assumptions, and occurrences, without risking financial loss.
- The most common model used for small businesses planning is the familiar business plan.
    - The financial projections in your business plan are a form of a budget which can easily be expanded to be useful for the day-to-day management of your business.

LO5 Learn how to craft budgets for your business.

- Budgeting is the process through which strategy is mapped into a series of tactical and operational actions.
- Once a budget has been prepared, it becomes a standard against which performance can be measured.
- Business planning is a *simple* process of applying your knowledge of your business to make estimates of future operations and results.
- The most common budget schedules are:
    - The sales budget which shows the projected future level of sales in units multiplied by the sales price per unit.
    - The production budget which shows the number of units that are expected to be produced during the budget period.
    - The direct material budget is an estimate of the amount of material you will need to make your product.
    - The direct labor budget shows both the amount and cost of labor needed to meet required production.
    - The manufacturing overhead budget details both fixed and variable overhead costs.
    - Selling, general, and administrative expense (SG&A) budget.
    - The cost of goods manufactured and sold budget combines the cost of materials, labor, and manufacturing overhead.

- These budget schedules are combined into pro forma financial statements.
- The final processes to be accomplished to produce a complete master budget are to produce:
    - Budgeted cash receipts.
    - Budgeted cash payments.
    - A cash budget.
    - A budgeted balance sheet.
- The difference between actual results and budgeted amounts is called a *variance.*
- Variances occur because either actual prices or volume is different from what was budgeted.
- To understand the effect of price changes, you must answer the following questions:
    - What would I have paid for the amount I actually used, if the price had been what I expected?
    - How much material should I have used to make the number of units that were actually completed?

LO6 Gain understanding of how people make decisions.

- The five primary functions in a business—planning, organizing, staffing, directing, and controlling—are combined as input for decision making.
- To make good decisions we need:
    - Good information.
    - Efficient methods to condense information so it is understandable.
    - Methods to facilitate comparing alternatives.
- Managerial accounting is both a source of information that is used in decision making and a methodology to reduce the complexity of the information used to make a decision.
- Common management decisions that can be aided by the use of accounting information and procedures include investments and outsourcing.
- Managerial accounting uses two primary simplification methods to handle information: differential revenues and expenses and net present value analysis (NPV).

DISCUSSION QUESTIONS

1. Which of the three types of accounting is most important to small business? Which is the least? Why do you think so?
2. How does the accounting equation relate to the balance sheet?
3. How are costs and expenses different?
4. Why should you, as a business owner, care about the distinction between costs and expenses?
5. Explain what is meant by "opportunity cost." Provide some examples of opportunity costs.
6. Defend the statement, "The function of accounting is to produce information that is useful for decision making."

7. What are the three most important characteristics of a small business computer accounting system? Why do you think these are the most important?
8. What are the three most important functions (think cash, accounts payable, owners' equity, etc.) that a computerized accounting system should have? Why are they the most important?
9. Which financial report is most important for managing a small business? Why?
10. You can sell your product (have revenues) without receiving any money. You can receive money (customer deposits) without having any revenue. Because revenue, expenses, and cash are so different, why should a small business owner care about the income statement?
11. Why would a small business ever need an accounting system more complicated than a simple checkbook register?
12. A budget is a collection of estimates—a big word that means the same thing as "guess." If you are guessing what future results will be, what value can a budget really have?
13. How are budgets related to business plans, as described in Chapter 8?
14. Is there any advantage to making a series of budget schedules, rather than just producing a pro forma income statement and balance sheet? What are the advantages, if any?

EXPERIENTIAL EXERCISES

1. Assume that you have decided to purchase a computerized small business accounting system. Visit the Web site of each of the accounting systems named in this chapter. From the information there determine:
   a. The price of the accounting system.
   b. The minimum computer requirements for the program.
   c. The availability and cost of training to learn to use the program.
   d. The availability of trained accountants and consultants in your geographic area who can be retained to assist you in setting up and using the program.
2. Choose an industry in which you would like to own a small business. Use the Internet, the university library, and the public library to find the names and addresses of industry trade associations. Examine the Web sites of the trade associations for availability of financial statistics of your industry. Examine governmental agency sites, such as those of the Department of Commerce, Department of the Treasury, Securities and Exchange Commission, and the Small Business Administration, for benchmark statistics.
3. Choose a public business that is in the same industry as the business you would like to own. Go to the company's Web site and find "investor relations." Download a copy of the business's most recent annual report. Examine the financial statements in the annual report. Make a list of the ways in which their content and format differ from the examples in this text.
4. Either by yourself or in a group of other students, select a business that you could reasonably expect to be able to start and run right now. (This could be as simple as a T-shirt company.) Using the techniques learned in exercises 2 and 3, above, develop a set of estimates of (a) sales, (b) variable cost of product or service and (c) the amount of other costs (rent, electricity, transportation, etc.) that you would expect to incur. Using these estimates, create a set of budget schedules through the schedule of cost of goods manufactured and sold.
5. Go to either the Quickbooks or the Peachtree Web site. Download and install a demonstration copy of its accounting program. Using either of the budget schedules you developed in exercise 4, or the

Languid Lizard example from the text, set up the program to do accounting as if this were a real business.

6. Do a Google search on the terms "accounting system" and "small business." Follow the Google returns to the Web sites of the companies (other than the ones named in the text) that you can find that sell computerized accounting systems. Examine the site to determine if its program would be suitable under the criteria specified in the text.

Mini-Case

PHIONIA'S FINICKY FELINE GOURMET CAT DINNERS

Phionia Phelps has developed a gourmet cat food. Not only is this food eagerly eaten by the most finicky felines, but it is specially formulated to prevent the many health problems of aging cats. Phionia has been making the food on her kitchen range and selling it at $250 per case only to close acquaintances who are also cat lovers. One of her wealthy acquaintances has now offered to invest in her business if Phionia will begin selling the product through her Web site. However, the investor wants Phionia to produce a budget for the first six months of operation.

Based on her experience to date, Fionia predicts the following sales in cases:

Nov	Dec	Jan	Feb	Mar	Apr	May	Jun	Jul	Aug
4,300	4,600	5,000	5,500	6100	6,800	7,000	7,200	7,400	7,500

Each case of Finicky Feline Gourmet Cat Dinner requires 5 pounds of prime lamb meat, 10 pounds of short grain Chinese rice, 2 pounds of wild caught Alaskan salmon, and 1 pound of secret vitamins and supplements. Phionia plans to maintain end-of-month inventories equal to 10 percent of the next month's projected sales, to meet expected sales growth. All the ingredients inventories are to be maintained at 5 percent of the production needs for the next month, but not to exceed 1,000 pounds of any one ingredient. January will begin with all inventories at the projected levels.

Phionia has the following price quotes good for the following year:

Item	$ per pound
Lamb	$15.00
Rice	1.20
Salmon	24.00
Vitamins	45.00

The production process requires direct labor at two skill levels, (1) ingredient preparation, $18 per hour and (2) cooking and canning, $24 per hour. Two workers are willing to work part days if there is not enough demand for them to work full time. It takes one hour to process one batch. Because of preparation and cleanup time, only six batches can be produced per day. Each batch produces enough food to fill 100 cases. Manufacturing overhead is $6,000 fixed per month plus $15 per case.

CASE DISCUSSION QUESTIONS

1. Prepare the following budgets for the period, January through June:
   a. Sales budget in dollars.
   b. Production budget in units.
   c. Direct materials purchases budget in pounds.
   d. Direct materials purchases budget in dollars.
   e. Direct manufacturing labor budget in dollars.
2. Comment on the viability of this business and the advisability of the investor making a $50,000 investment to get it started.

LEARNING OBJECTIVES

This chapter will help you:

LO1 Know the importance of managing your business's money.

LO2 Understand the concepts of money, cash, and cash equivalents.

LO3 Understand the basics of managing cash flow.

LO4 Be able to reconcile bank and company book balances.

LO5 Be prepared to develop a cash budget.

LO6 Have strategies for preventing and coping with cash flow problems.

LO7 Learn strategies for coping with cash shortages.

■ Be Our Guest learned the hard way how much a crippled cash flow can hamper a business. Faced with several different options, they eventually expanded their credit line in order to handle the annual peaks and declines of the party supply business. Which route would you have chosen, and why?

Cash: Lifeblood of the Business

Focus on Small Business: Stephen Lizio, Al Lovata, and Simone Williamson of Be Our Guest, Inc.

Stephen Lizio, Al Lovata, and Simone Williamson had run out of financing options. Their firm, Be Our Guest, Inc., of Boston, Massachusetts, had a long-term loan with a principal balance of $315,000 and at $140,000 had also maxed out their revolving credit line. This came about in a year that had seen sales increase by a remarkable 22 percent, but their sky-high debt made it clear that too many customers owed Be Our Guest too much. There were bills to pay, but no money with which to pay them.

Be Our Guest, Inc., rents party supplies. Its business is highly seasonal, with peaks in June, as many weddings occur, and in November–December during the holiday party season. During the rest of the year, especially in the first quarter, revenues are always less than expenses. The instant cash flow problem facing Be Our Guest came about because of a busy December, with high sales and therefore high receivables. Now, facing January bills themselves, many customers were not paying on time. Although the owners expected all the customers to pay eventually, right now Be Our Guest was scraping for cash for daily operations.

The owners had few alternatives available to fix the current problem. Having maxed out their bank credit, additional bank borrowing was not available. The firm could borrow against the receivables, but this was not an attractive option. Many of the receivables accounts were past due, so lenders would loan no more than 70 percent of the amount to be collected from customers. Also, the past due accounts would mean paying the lender more than the customary 5 percent fee, on top of a sky-high 20 percent annual interest rate. Another way would be for the owners to cut what they were paying to themselves, leaving more money to pay the creditors, but that was the last thing they wanted to do, since technically the business had enough money—their marketable assets far exceeded liabilities. It was just that Be Our Guest didn't have enough cash.

"What should we do now?" they asked themselves.

For a time, they did nothing. They continued to scrape by on the cash flow that could be generated, while cutting back on every expense and payout they could. By the midsummer party season, the problem had again resolved itself. Given some financial breathing room, the owners took several steps to find a permanent solution to the seasonal peaks of cash inflows. First, with their financials once again strong and a year of increased sales to show, they arranged for a $40,000 increase in the line of credit to a total of $200,000.[1] Then, in the following year, based on continuing improved results, the line of credit was refinanced, converting it into long-term debt. This reduced the interest rate, resulting in an immediate reduction in cash outflows.

http://www.beourguestpartyrental.com

The business (http://www.beourguestpartyrental.com) is successful and growing today. It still encounters peaks of business in June and December, but it has developed methods to ensure that cash will be available when needed.[2]

DISCUSSION QUESTIONS

1. Why did the current amount of debt limit how much the business could borrow to solve the current cash crunch?
2. Why does the fact that some customers are late paying in January make using the receivables for collateral so expensive?
3. Should the owners have reduced payments to themselves to be able to pay more to vendors and suppliers?
4. How is it that a business could "have enough money," but still not be able to pay its bills?

The Importance of Money Management

LO1
Know the importance of managing your business's money.

Have you ever considered the question, "What is money?"

Certainly you have thought about money. It is a rare small business person who does not think about money—making money, investing money, spending money, having enough money. In fact, money can seem so important to business that sometimes people make the error of believing that money is all that business is about. Of course, as you have already learned in the earlier chapters, business is about many important things, of which money is only one.

But this still leaves the question, "What is this *'money,'* and why is it so important?"

Throughout this book, terms that refer to money are tossed about: money, cash, cash equivalents, profits, and banking, to name a few. Have you given any consideration to what these terms mean? How are they alike? How are they different? How are they related to each other? The differences are important because in the end money in its different forms represents the lifeblood of the business, and knowing which form to use, and when to use it, can make the difference between boom and bankruptcy.

In this chapter, the meaning of these terms and how they are important to managing small businesses is discussed. If you are like most people, this chapter will contain some surprises. Things that you think you know are going to turn out to be false. Things you might think are trivial will turn out to be of great importance. It is part of what makes cash and money fascinating.

Money In/Money Out—Just How Important Is It?

A recent poll conducted by the National Federation of Independent Business (NFIB Foundation) found that almost two-thirds of small businesses experience money problems (see Figure 14.1). Businesses either do not have enough money, or if they have money, they cannot get to it when it is needed. Nearly one-fifth of small business managers reported that cash flow—*how much* and *when* money will come into and go out of the business—is a continuing problem, one they face daily. The owners reported that the three primary causes of cash flow problems were (1) difficulty collecting money due from customers, (2) seasonal variation in sales, and (3) unexpected decreases in sales.[3] Approximately 55 percent of small businesses that fail do so because of cash flow problems with an immediate impact, not because of lack of profitability.[4]

Cash flow management is a problem for small businesses because of the difficulty of matching the *timing* of the *receipt of cash* to the *timing* of the need to *expend cash*. Figure 14.2 illustrates the flow of money into and out of your business as you buy what you need and sell your product or your service. This repeating flow of money is called the cash-to-cash cycle or the operating cycle of your business.

When you start a new business, you put in some money. You then buy all the things necessary to run the business, such as materials, supplies, rent, and labor. Some of these you purchase for cash. Other things you may buy on credit, creating payables, which you will have to pay next month. You then use labor to convert materials and supplies into your product or service, which you sell to your customers. Your customers then either pay you immediately, or agree to pay you soon. The promises of your customers to pay are receivables, which you will collect in the future. The money

cash-to-cash cycle
The time that is required for a business to acquire resources, convert them into product, sell the product, and receive cash from the sale.

operating cycle
See cash to cash cycle.

payables
Amounts owed to vendors for merchandise or services purchased on credit (see receivables).

receivables
Amounts that are owed to a business for merchandise that was sold on credit (see payables).

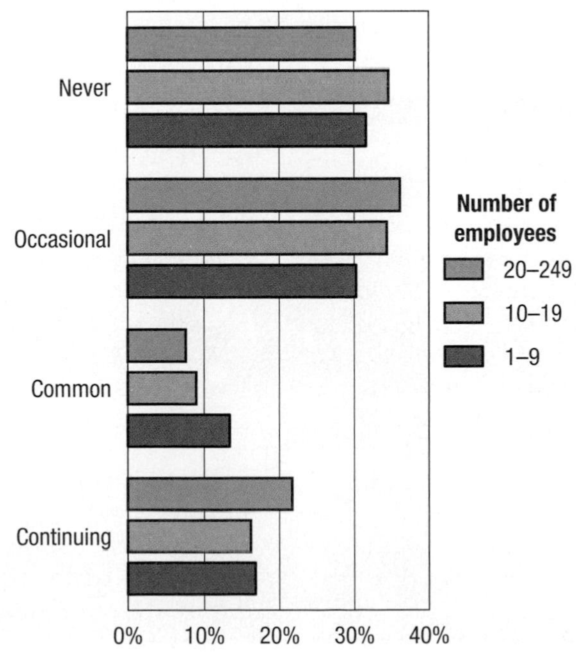

FIGURE 14.1

Percentage of Small Businesses that Experience Cash Shortages by Number of Employees

FIGURE 14.2

The Cash-to-Cash Cycle

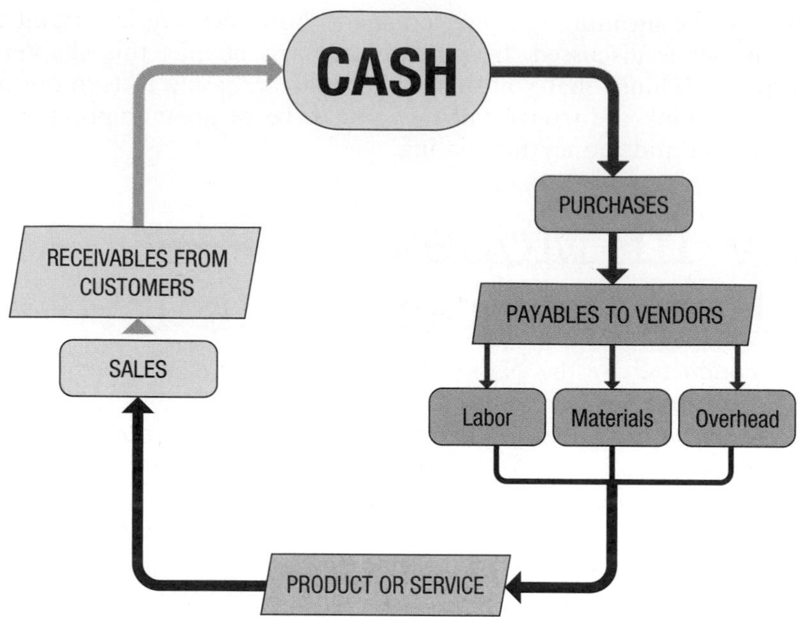

you collect will then be used to buy the things necessary to run your business, and thus the cycle repeats.

The time that it takes to complete this cycle can be as short as a few hours or as long as several years, dependent upon the type of business you are in. The ubiquitous pushcart vendors of hot dogs in New York City purchase inventory on credit every morning. They sell their product for cash during the day. Each evening they pay for the merchandise sold that day. The cash-to-cash cycle of a pushcart vendor is only a few hours. Construction projects, on the other hand, can easily take years to complete. A contractor will borrow money to begin construction. That money is paid out across the time that it takes to complete the project. The contractor, however, receives from his customer either a single payment upon completion or a few payments as prespecified completion targets are met.

Many small businesses experience difficulty or even failure because of (1) the mismatch in time between receiving cash and spending cash and (2) the mismatch between the size of payments received and the size of payments that must be made. In some

■ Push cart vendors, such as the ones pictured here, enjoy a very short cash-to-cash cycle, due to the nature of their business. Each day, their receipt of cash from sales enables them to then expend cash back to their suppliers for exactly what has been sold. Though small in scope, the simplicity of their business set-up allows for the immediate assessment of their profitability. Does this kind of a set-up appeal to you?

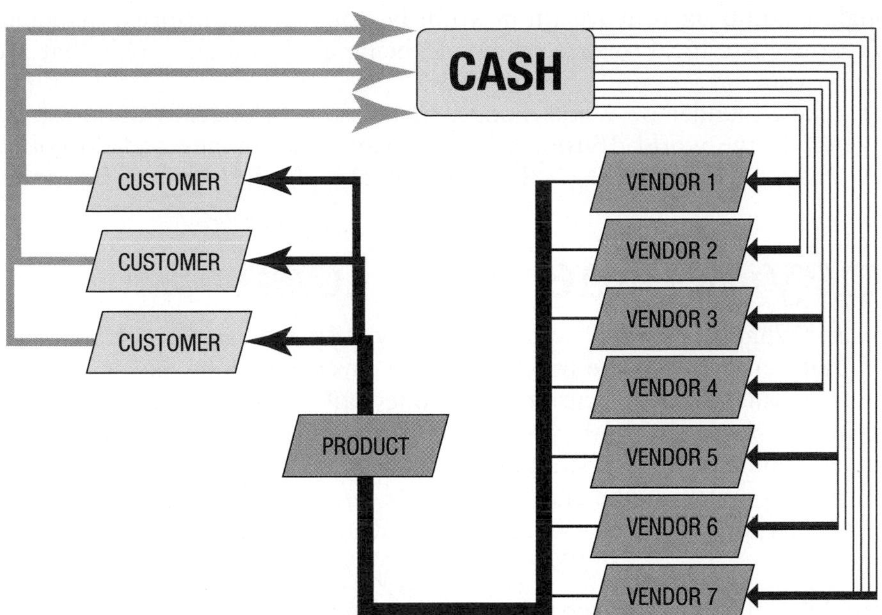

FIGURE 14.3

Cash-to-Cash Cycle

Many vendors, few customers.

businesses, such as restaurants, cash comes into the business in a reasonably dependable pattern that is affected by the state of the economy, the season, the day of the week, and the weather. Expenses, on the other hand, tend to occur less frequently but in larger amounts, as suppliers are paid monthly, and employees are paid weekly. Other businesses, such as construction firms, plumbing contractors, ski resorts, and equipment manufacturers, have cash receipts that tend to occur irregularly but in large amounts. However, the cash payment needs of these businesses are relatively smaller amounts paid consistently from month to month. (See Figures 14.3 and 14.4.)

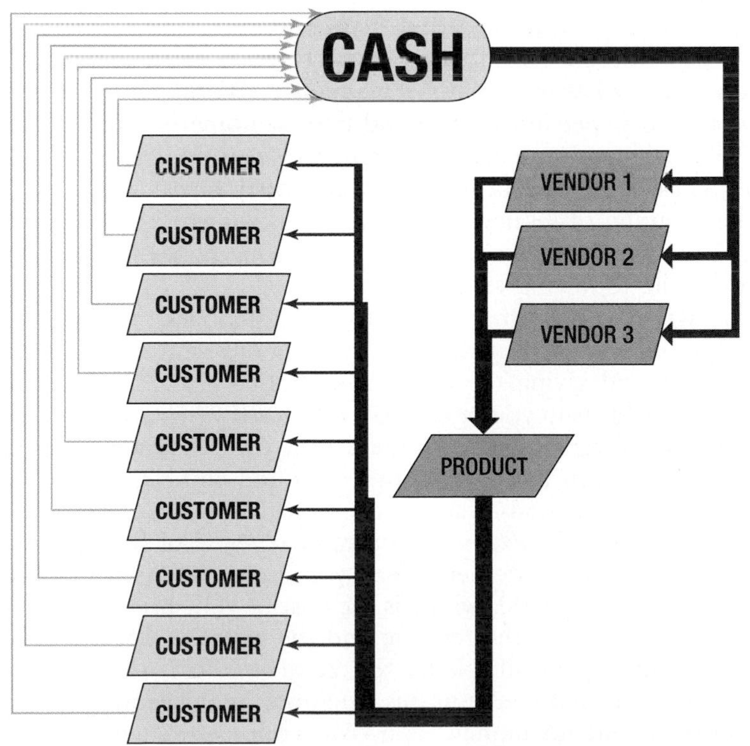

FIGURE 14.4

Cash-to-Cash Cycle

Few vendors, many customers.

Although maximizing your wealth may not be your highest priority, managing your business's money is critical to succeeding and being able to attain goals that are more important to you.

John Mackey, founder of Whole Foods, Inc., said, "Business is the most transformative agency in the world. [Business leaders] can make money and do good. . . . I always wanted to make money. . . . To be sustainable, business has to be profitable."[5]

Money as the Key Idea

LO2
Understand the concepts of money, cash, and cash equivalents.

Ask people, "What is money?" and most likely they talk about currency—the bills and coins that you use to make purchases. That answer is right, but it tells only part of the story, because while all currency is money, all money is not currency.

Today we use many electronic and plastic forms of money: debit cards, online bill payments, electronic bank drafts, and wire transfers. These forms of money make an important point—money in the end is a form of *information.* Money is a very special type of information. The U.S. Dallas Federal Reserve Bank provides the following definition:

> Money is a medium of exchange accepted by the community, meaning it's what people buy things with and sell things for. Money provides a standard for measuring value, so that the worth of different goods and services can be compared. And lastly, money is a store of value that can be saved for later purchases.[6]

money
An accepted medium of exchange.

This definition gives us the two purposes of **money**: (1) to make exchanges and (2) to keep track of wealth or value. More importantly, it also defines the essence of money. In the Federal Reserve's qualifying phrase, "accepted by the community," what makes money "*money,*" is the *belief* users have about the information contained in the money. This information (and belief in it) reflects the two purposes above as well as a third purpose—wealth accumulation as in saving money. Money can even be used for quantifying the value of nonmonetary assets, such as when juries make awards for pain and suffering.

Money is a special type of information that contains value in which people believe. When people lose these beliefs, money ceases to exist, as it once did in the United States following the Civil War and in Germany after World War I[7] when people used their nearly worthless paper money to build fires at home (see picture on next page). Ask yourself, "Can I use Confederate currency to pay my bills?" The answer is an unqualified no, because no one believes in that money anymore.

Knowing the meaning of money is important so that you can recognize where you have money in your business. For example, are profits money? You might think so at first, but consider the following example.

Suppose you own a business that details used automobiles to prepare them for sale. You complete work on a car, removing dings, rubbing out scratches, shampooing the carpets and upholstery, and giving the car a hand-buffed wax job. You promised your brother-in-law that for his help you would pay him $100 when you received payment for the work. When you delivered the car to the dealer, you presented an invoice for $500.

How much profit do you have? How much money do you have?

As is discussed in the previous chapter, profit is simply the difference between two accounting items, revenue and expense. You have revenue of $500, because the work is finished and you trust the customer to pay you in the ordinary practice of business. You also have an expense of $100, which is the cost of your brother-in-law's help. Your **profit** is the difference between the revenue and the expense, $500 − $100 = $400.

profit
The difference between revenue and expense.

But you have no money, at all. Nada, zip, zero!

Suppose for a moment that you're in this situation. Your heating and air-conditioning company has profits, but no money. You owe your equipment wholesaler for last month's purchases. As a result, you cannot get the air conditioner unit needed to finish a job right now.

"Sorry," the credit manager said, "but we just can't extend any more credit until you bring your account up to date."

What are you going to do? If you don't pay what you owe, you cannot get equipment. If you cannot get equipment, you cannot stay in business. If you do not stay in business, you cannot pay what you owe. You are in a classic "catch-22!"[8]

You're in a bind, certainly, but now is not the point to give up. You have several options to help you deal with this problem. Think about your situation. You have profits that are not money, but they are information about money. You have information that shows the amount of revenue and expense your business generates. You also have information for (1) an asset—your customer's promise to pay you for your work and (2) a liability—your promise to pay your vendors.

Your problem is that information about money to come is not the same thing as the money itself. In the first example, you cannot use your customer's promise of payment to purchase groceries at a supermarket, any more than your brother-in-law can spend your promise of payment to him at the local tavern. You will receive money if and when your customer pays you. You will give up money if and when you pay your brother-in-law.

■ People in 1920s Germany lost their faith in the value of paper money so much that they used it as fuel for their home furnaces. What are some of the factors you think caused such a widespread loss of belief in money's values? What might cause something similar to happen today?

The identical situation exists for your heating and air-conditioning company. You have promises to pay from customers, and you have made promises to pay your vendors. The promises of your customers, your receivables, can be quickly turned into money by using them as collateral to obtain a loan from your banker or a factor. If you don't want to borrow, you can call your customers and offer a discount if they will pay up right now. One way or the other, you can turn profits into money, given enough time.

Remember: a profit on your accounting spreadsheet or in your account book is *not* money in your hand. Money is a medium of exchange, store of value, and measure of wealth. Until backed by the actual money, profits in your account books are none of these things.

Cash and Cash Equivalents

To this point we've been throwing around the terms *money* and *cash* as if everyone knows just what they are; just how they differ. Although we have carefully defined the meaning of money, we have not done so for cash.

cash
Money that is immediately available to be spent.

Cash is money, but it's only one form of money, a subcategory of money that is immediately available to be spent. Not all money is "spendable." For example, think of certificates of deposit. Although you may well have a lot of money in CDs, you

cash equivalents
Assets that may be quickly converted to cash.

currency
The bills and coins printed by governments to represent money.

demand deposits
Money held in checking and savings accounts.

marketable securities
Stocks and bonds that are traded on an open market.

commercial paper
Notes issued by credit-worthy corporations.

short-term debt
Any debt that must be paid in less than one year from the date of the financial statement on which it is reported.

bearer
Any person or business entity who possesses a security.

may have very little cash because your money is tied up in the CDs and would take time to convert into cash. Cash is composed of the three forms of money that can be immediately used to make payments: currency, demand deposits, and traveler's checks.

Businesses, on the other hand, use a concept called **cash equivalents** to measure how much money is available to be spent. Cash equivalents are assets that may be turned into cash in a slightly longer time, from a few hours to a few days, such as marketable securities, commercial paper, and debt investments that mature in less than three months. Businesses use cash equivalents because they provide a better measure of the resources available to pay current bills than is provided by cash alone.

Currency is the most common form of cash: bills and coins that represent money. In December 2003, the Federal Reserve Bank of St. Louis reported that the supply of currency in circulation was $663 billion, or approximately $2,300 of currency for each individual living in the United States.

Demand deposits make up most of the noncurrency cash. Demand deposits are accounts that let you withdraw (what bankers call demand) any amount of the balance immediately, without any advance notice to the institution: That is, owners may withdraw money on demand by using a check, draft, currency, or electronic transfer. Checking accounts and savings accounts are the two most common forms of demand deposit accounts.

Marketable securities are made up of stocks and bonds for which there is an active auction market, such as the NASDAQ or the New York Stock Exchange. Marketable securities represent either ownership or debt of publicly held firms and government issued debt, in the form of bonds, notes, and bills.

Commercial paper and **short-term debt** are two forms of short-term financing (30 days to 1 year) whereby a company with good credit can issue a note for cash to another company. Commercial paper is issued to be paid to the **bearer** of the note, and thus is fully transferable. Short-term debt is expected to be collected in less than a year, but it can be sold to other investors at any time.

Managing Cash Flow

LO3
Understand the basics of managing cash flow.

Suppliers, vendors, employees, and lenders all demand payment in cash. Because of this, a small business must have access to cash to be able to remain viable. Cash can come from only three sources: (1) Cash can be obtained by selling the products and services of the business and collecting cash from customers. This is called *cash flow from operations.* (2) Cash can be obtained from investments the business has made, such as stocks, bonds, land, buildings, or equipment. This is *cash flow from investing.* (3) Finally, a business may obtain cash through financing. Financing may be in the form of cash donated to the business in return for ownership or in the form of money borrowed from other entities.

Just as many businesses have failed by failing to manage cash, many businesses have credited their success to good cash management. Baby Einstein is a case in point. Because of the careful cash management of the founders, Julie and Bill Clark, Baby Einstein was able to grow to a $25 million company without once using outside investment.

The starting point in understanding cash management is understanding how banks, and especially your own bank account, work. This is because the vast majority of small businesses depend on banks to store cash, handle checks and credit cards, and finance their debt through credit.[9] You can see how much debt the banks support in Figure 14.5, page 402.

Company and Bank Cash Balances

Because most cash is held as bank deposits, understanding how banks actually work is essential. For example, money you have deposited today may not be immediately available to you. Money that you have spent by writing a check may well remain in your bank account for days after you have made payment. The first step in managing your cash flows is to understand how the bank's idea of your business's cash flow and your own view of the business's cash flow differ.

SMALL BUSINESS INSIGHT

The Baby Einstein Company[10]

When Julie and Bill Clark started The Baby Einstein Company to produce videos for infants, they made a conscious decision to fund the business using only their own resources. They had been involved in an earlier business that produced educational software.

"I struggled through the experience of dealing with a venture capitalist. Julie lived through it with me and wanted to avoid a repeat experience at all costs," Bill said.

They started the business in their home with an initial capital of $10,000 from their savings. Their determination not to use bank debt, private placements, or venture capital meant that they had to have strict control of cash. They had to budget carefully and conduct constant oversight to prevent spending from exceeding cash receipts.

To conserve cash, marketing was initially conducted by word-of-mouth. As the company grew, the product line was gradually extended to include discovery cards and audio CDs.

How well did they succeed? By setting conservative revenue projections and carefully monitoring cash flows, Baby Einstein was able to grow rapidly, financed solely with internally generated cash. By the fourth year of the company's existence, annual sales were approximately $17 million.

In November 2001, the Clarks sold The Baby Einstein Company to Disney. Their one splurge has been to buy a share in a business jet. "We want the kids to see the world," Julie said.

■ Julie Clark of Baby Einstein knows what it means to strictly manage cash flow. By adhering to conservative revenue projections and rigorously monitoring their cash intake and outtake, she and husband Bill got to experience first-hand both the substantial growth of their company and the eventual personal pay-off it granted them.

Let us start with the company. The **company book balance** is the name given to the sum of the company's internal accounting record of all transactions that affect cash. This account (usually called the *cash account*) includes records of all inflows of cash, such as cash from sales, receipts on receivables, checks received from customers, and deposits made directly to the bank through electronic transfers. The cash account also includes records of all outflows of cash, such as checks written to pay for wages, salaries, inventory, services, taxes, and so on. The difference between inflows of cash

company book balance The sum of cash inflows and cash outflows recorded in the firm's accounting records.

FIGURE 14.5

Sources of Credit and Debt for Small Businesses

Share of outstanding debt for all small firms, by supplier of credit, 1998. (Total value = $700 billion)

Source: U.S. Small Business Administration, Office of Advocacy from data provided by the Federal Reserve Board's 1998 SSBF. Table 1.5a. http://www.sba.gov/advo/stats/ssbf_98.pdf, page 14.

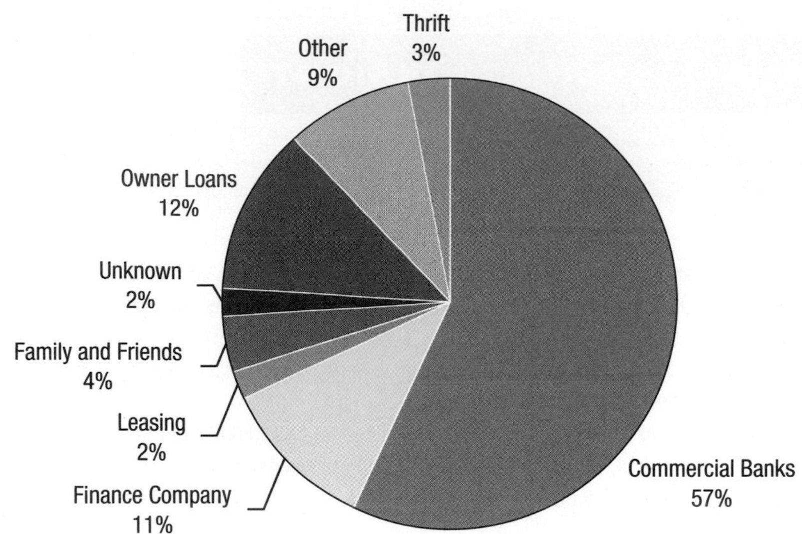

and outflows of cash is called either *company book balance*, or simply, *book balance*. Book balance usually does not reflect the actual amount of cash that is available to the firm at any specific time, because the actual cash amount depends on which checks have cleared or been cashed.

bank ledger balance
The sum of deposits and withdrawals recorded in a bank's accounting records.

Now let us consider the bank's side. The **bank ledger balance** is the name given to the bank's accounting system for all recognized transactions that affect the account, including deposits, electronic transfers, service fees, and checks presented to the bank for payment. However, just as a company book balance may differ significantly from the actual value of cash of the firm, a bank ledger balance may vary significantly from the actual value of cash that the bank is holding for the depositor because of delays in collecting deposits and delays in making cash transfers.

bank available balance
The sum of money that has actually been received and paid out of a depositor's account.

The key measure is called the **bank available balance**, which is the actual cash value of the account and can vary significantly from the ledger balance. The bank available balance is the amount of money that has been received from or on behalf of the customer less all amounts of money that have actually been paid out of the depositor's account by the bank. Bank policies, such as how long checks are held, or when new deposits are added to your account, determine a great deal of the difference between the two balances.

clearinghouse
An entity that processes checks and electronic fund transfers for banks and other financial organizations.

Deposits of cash, electronic transfers, and cash withdrawals result in immediate changes in the available balance because money has been received or disbursed by the bank. Checks, drafts, and automated **clearinghouse** payments result in receipts or disbursements of money only after some delay. The delay can range from as little as a single day up to several days in the event of a check paid across national boundaries. (See Figure 14.6.)

overdraft
A negative balance in a depositor's bank account.

Banks differ in how the ledger balance and available balance are used. Some banks will allow established customers to **overdraft** their accounts by paying a check when the available balance is not sufficient to cover the check amount, but the ledger balance is. Other banks will not allow an account to be overdrafted and will return any check unpaid, if payment of the check would cause a negative available balance (in everyday terms, have less than zero in your bank account). For your own peace of mind and the financial health of your firm, make sure you know your bank's policy about this.

float
Delays in the movement of money among depositors and banks.

Float is the term used to describe the delay in movement of money among depositors and banks. There are two primary causes of float: (1) delays in transferring money among banks due to internal procedures, called *availability float,* and (2) delays in delivering checks from the writer of the check to the recipient's bank, called *processing float.*

Availability float is costly for banks, as the money tied up in float is not earning interest. Banks have reduced the float to as few as two days by transferring an electronic

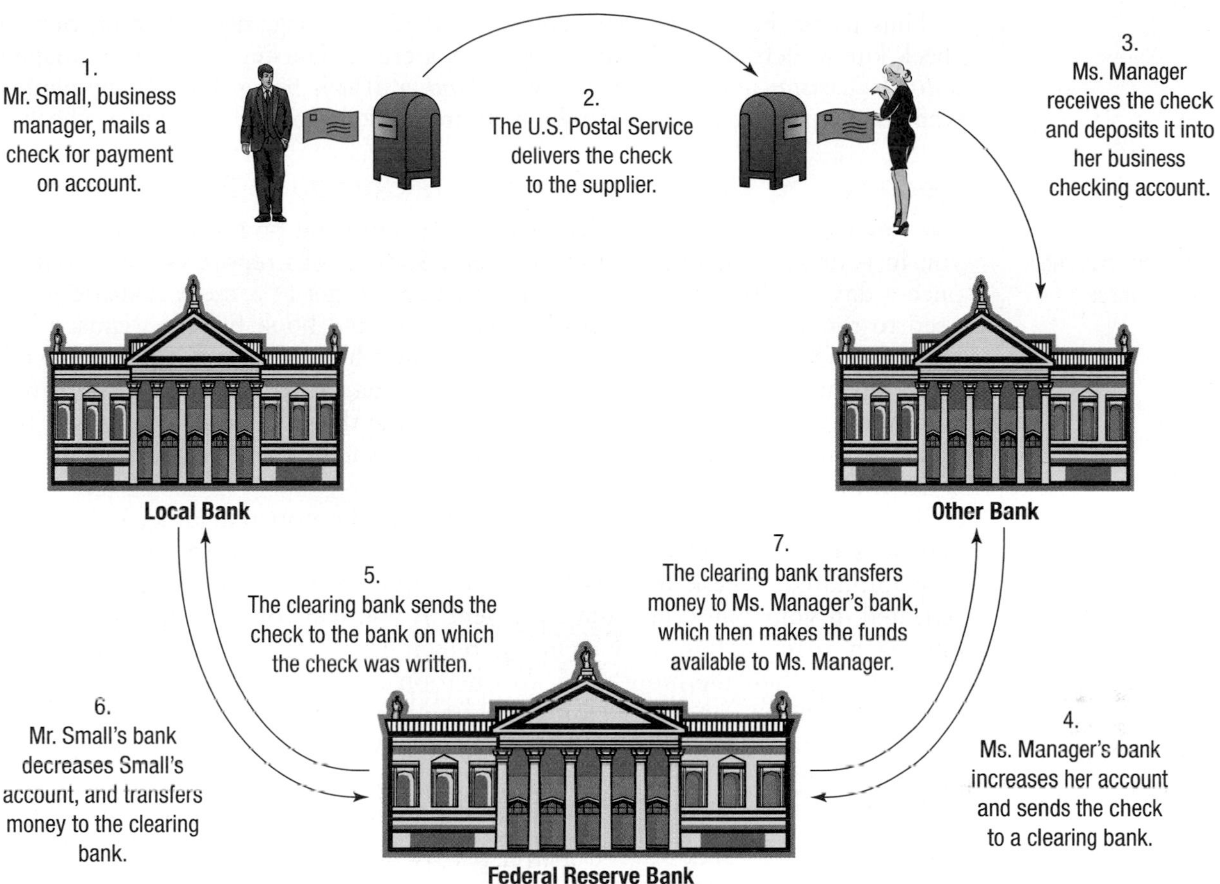

FIGURE 14.6

How Checks Get Cleared

image of the check. The banking system is currently phasing in an electronic check clearing system that will soon reduce availability float to less than one day.

Processing float is the time required to move checks among payers, payees, and banks. Processing float is what individuals refer to when they say, "The check is in the mail."

Business managers can, and often do, use float as a cash management tool. Paying by check rather than by credit card or electronic transfer is one way to increase float. Another is to write a check that you know will require an overdraft, if your bank will let you do such things. To be able to do so effectively, you must understand both the nature of float and how to measure the amount of cash availability resulting from the effect of float. It is likely, given the current efforts to reduce float to the minimum, that float will become less useful in the near future. However, as of now, using float is a common and accepted tool for cash management.

Float can also be used as a technique to manage cash crises. One must be careful, however, not to get involved in **check kiting**. Check kiting is the process of deliberately using the float of the banking system as a financing source. This is accomplished by maintaining multiple bank accounts, usually in different business names. To kite, you write a check on one bank, and deposit it into a second. Before the check can clear, you write a check from a third bank to the first bank, to cover the first check. By reiteratively depositing checks from one bank to another, you can effectively create money that can be used for other purposes.

check kiting
The practice of writing checks when there is not enough money on deposit to cover them.

Check kiting, itself, is not illegal. As a matter of fact, many businesses deliberately set up systems with the assistance of their banks, to capture the value of the float, in essence operating a constant kite. On the other hand, many thousands of business owners and managers have gone to federal prisons when check kites failed. At issue is the *intent* of the person running the kite. If your intent is to defraud, your actions constitute a felony.

Thus using the float is considered a valid cash management method, but creating a check kite to defraud the banking system is a crime. The key here is to manage the float *with the assistance and support of your banker.* If it is being done so the bankers know what is happening, when, and why, you are unlikely to face charges of check kiting.

Reconciling Bank Balances with Company Book Balances

L04
Be able to reconcile bank and company book balances.

reconciling
An accounting process that identifies the causes of all differences between book and bank balances.

The key to managing your daily cash flow is knowing how much cash is available to you in your bank account at that moment. Some banks report available balances only once a day, so that amount can be misleading. To get at a more realistic number, you need to **reconcile** the differences between bank and book balances caused by float to know how much cash is currently available and how much will soon be available for your business needs. Most small business managers concentrate their attention on maintaining a positive book balance and assume that this means there will be an adequate available balance. However, when this assumption is not correct, it often leads to cash flow crises.

If you want to be able to manage your cash flow in real time, it is important to choose a bank that gives you online access to account information that is continuously updated. Check to make sure how quickly transactions get posted and are reflected in your online account statement. If you feel you can afford a more leisurely approach to cash flow management, remember that day-old information is much more timely than the month-old information furnished by a traditional bank statement. A manager can, with a bit of effort, use yesterday's bank transactions and the current business book information to estimate cash availability and demands with reasonable accuracy.

The process of reconciling bank balance and book balances is quite simple. There are only two reasons why the balances differ:

1. The bank knows information about your account that you cannot know until the bank tells you.
2. You know information about your account that the bank cannot know, because relevant transactions have not yet reached the bank.

Information that the bank knows about your account that you do not know includes (1) the amount of service charges taken from your account, (2) the amount of any direct payments made to your account by your customers, (3) the amount of any interest received or charged, (4) and the amount of any checks that were returned because of **nonsufficient funds** (NSF).

nonsufficient funds
A situation that occurs when a check is returned to a depositor because the writer of the check did not have a bank available balance equal to or greater than the amount of the check.

Information that you know about your account that the bank does not know includes (1) the number and value of checks that you have written and mailed but that have not been received by the bank and (2) deposits that you have mailed or made after bank closing.

The process of reconciling the bank and book balances is, therefore, a two-step process:

1. Add (subtract) to the bank balance those things that you know about your account that the bank does not know.
2. Add (subtract) to your book balance those things that the bank knows about your account that you do not know until you receive the bank statement.

When this is done the *corrected* bank balance and the *corrected* book balance will be identical. The appendix to this chapter presents a complete example of performing a bank reconciliation.

Accepting payments by credit card causes significant differences between the bank and book balances for three reasons:

- Your business will record the gross amount of each credit card sale, while the credit card service provider will deposit to your account the sale amount less the credit card service fee.

- Your business will show the amount of the sale deposited on the date of the sale, while the service provider will take up to three working days to actually make the deposit to your account.
- Credit card clearing services also will reduce the amount deposited, or will **charge back** the amount, removing it from the business's account in the event of fraud or customer challenge.

charge back
A reduction in the bank account of a merchant by a credit card company.

Similar patterns of the timing and the amounts of various deposits, fees, and transfers exist for other electronic transactions. A bank may accept payment, charge a handling fee, and deposit only the net amount, or it may deposit the gross amount and show a separate charge for handling fees. Regardless, the use of electronic payment systems, of all types, creates significant differences between bank and book balances.

Why go to all this trouble? Because reconciling differences in the bank and book balances serves four purposes:

- Reconciliation gives you a way to estimate the bank's available balance for the purpose of managing your cash flows.
- Regular reconciliation of bank and book balances identifies any mistakes that were made by either the bank or by your own bookkeeper—and those mistakes happen.
- Performing a reconciliation checks the accuracy of both the bank and business records, providing an accurate statement of the value of cash held by the business.
- A reconciliation lets you know about items on the bank statement that would not otherwise be included in the business's accounting records.

Planning Cash Needs (Budgeting)

LO5
Be prepared to develop a cash budget.

For a lot of people, any sort of accounting or financial form is scary, and probably that starts with budgets. But despite what you may think, "budget" is *not* a four-letter word. Budgets happen, whether you make one formally and intentionally or informally and haphazardly. The question before all prospective small business owners is whether they are going to take control over their budget or run around in the financial dark.

Budgets are the essential starting point for all financial and accounting considerations in a small business. The key financial statements necessary for every business plan build from basic budgeting ideas, and every bank loan is built from a budget—for a home loan, a car loan, or a business loan. Budgets are the basic building blocks for all modern accounting and finance.

For small businesses, the key budget is the **cash budget**. Simply put, the cash budget identifies when, how, and why cash is expected to come into the business, and when, how, and why it is expected to leave. The quality of those expectations is important. Making more realistic or accurate estimates about expected incomes and expenses means that the budget becomes a more useful tool for understanding and managing your cash flow and financial situation.

cash budget
A cash budget identifies when, how, and why cash is expected to come into the business, and when, how, and why it is expected to leave.

All business budgeting begins with a forecast of sales. As is discussed in Chapters 12 and 13, there are several methods that are used to make sales forecasts. We illustrated the process of creating a cash flow budget for the first quarter of the year using the predicted sales of Languid Lizard, Inc., in Chapter 13. The sales forecast is shown in Table 14.1.

Forecasting Sales Receipts

For many small businesses, the sales forecast *is* the cash receipts forecast. Businesses such as barbershops, muffler repair shops, restaurants, and all kinds of retail merchandisers do not provide credit to customers. All sales are made either in cash or by credit card. Despite this, this type of business *can* have cash flow problems created when sales are insufficient to cover required payments. Each type of business has a

TABLE 14.1 **Sales Forecast**

LANGUID LIZARD, INC.

	Quarter 1			
	January	**February**	**March**	**Quarter Total**
Sales in units	1,000	1,200	1,800	4,000
Unit sales price	$16	$16	$16	$16
Total sales revenue	$16,000	$19,200	$28,800	$64,000

different pattern of sales and cash receipts. Some businesses, whose customers make heavy use of credit cards, can face serious cash drains as a result (see Thoughtful Entrepreneur: The Business Costs of Using Credit Cards). Many business have either relatively few large sales events or highly seasonal sales that complicate forecasting cash inflows. Examples include:

- Retailing
- House builders
- Custom electric sign shops
- Machine shops
- Providers of custom software
- Real estate brokers
- Consultants
- Ski resorts
- Water parks
- All businesses that depend upon tourism

THE THOUGHTFUL ENTREPRENEUR

The Business Costs Of Using Credit Cards

Credit card use fees quickly add up to material amounts. Consider a successful restaurant that grosses approximately $80,000 per month, with an average per-customer ticket of $20. If 90 percent of customers pay with a credit card, 3,600 credit card charges will be made in a month ($80,000/$20 × 0.9). Assume that the credit card company charges 20 cents per transaction plus 2 percent of the amount charged. The credit card fee for the month will equal $2,160 (3,600 transactions × 0.20) + (80,000 × .9 × .02). The restaurant will also pay the 2 percent fee on any tips that are added to the bill. If the average tip added is 15 percent, then the added fee on tips charged per month will be another $216. Thus the restaurant will average paying an amount greater than $28,000 in credit card fees per year.

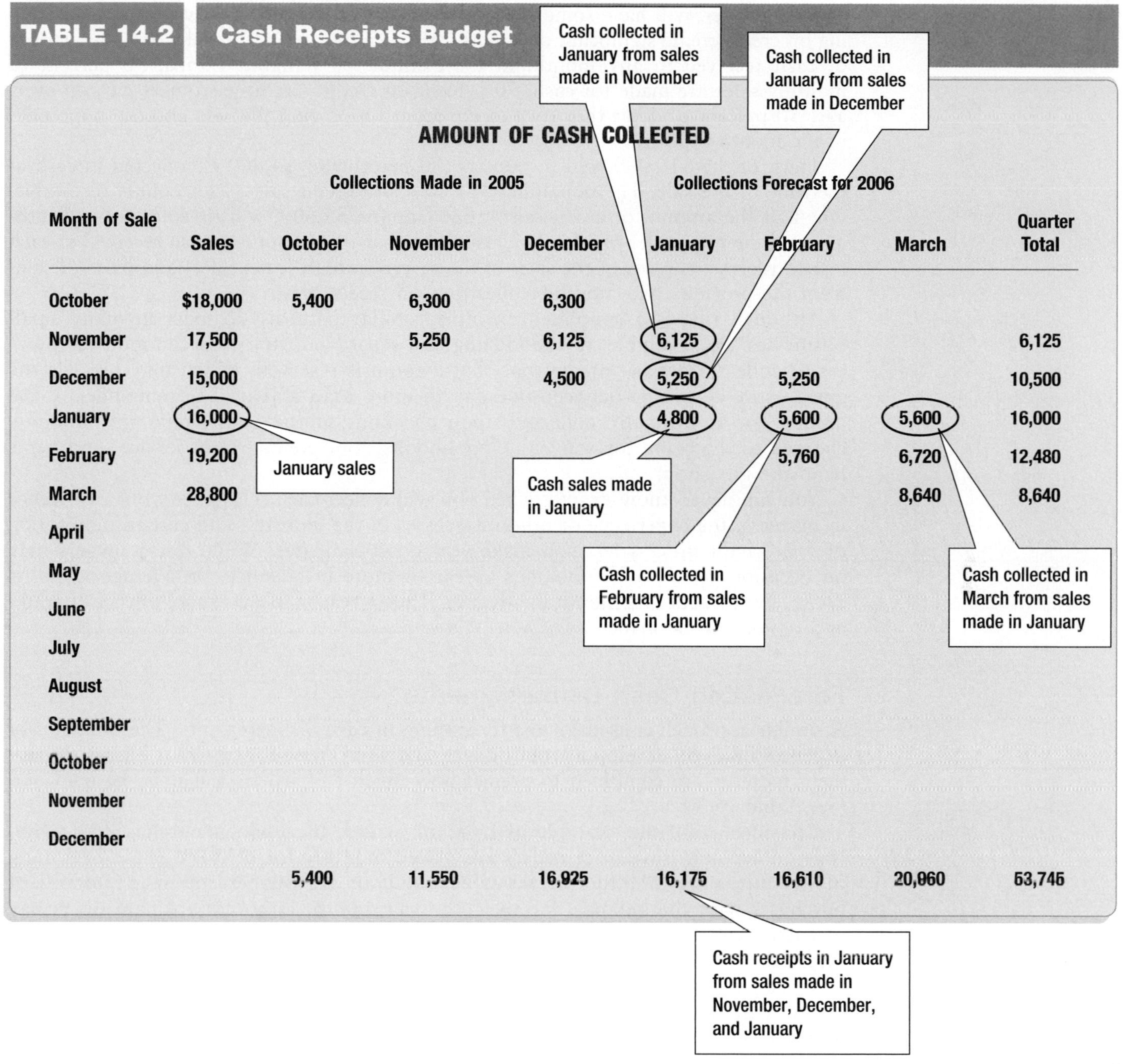

TABLE 14.2 Cash Receipts Budget

AMOUNT OF CASH COLLECTED

		Collections Made in 2005			Collections Forecast for 2006			
Month of Sale	**Sales**	**October**	**November**	**December**	**January**	**February**	**March**	**Quarter Total**
October	$18,000	5,400	6,300	6,300				
November	17,500		5,250	6,125	6,125			6,125
December	15,000			4,500	5,250	5,250		10,500
January	16,000				4,800	5,600	5,600	16,000
February	19,200					5,760	6,720	12,480
March	28,800						8,640	8,640
April								
May								
June								
July								
August								
September								
October								
November								
December								
		5,400	11,550	16,925	16,175	16,610	20,960	53,745

If your business offers credit to customers, you must also know the pattern of collections to be able to forecast cash inflows. Languid Lizard, Inc., provides customers with financing terms, collecting cash over a three-month period. Thirty percent is collected at the time the sale is made, and the remaining 70 percent is collected across the next two months. So let us consider the cash situation in a January. Languid Lizard's cash comes from three sources: 30 percent of January's sales, 35 percent of the prior December's sales, and 35 percent of the prior November's sales. Table 14.2 presents this pattern in tabular form. Notice that January, February, and March each show cash collected from sales in the prior two months.

If you provide credit to your customers, you will always wait some period of time for some of your money—that's what providing credit means, after all. You also, sooner or later, will have some customer who never pays. These two facts about selling on credit create significant differences between the amount of sales and the amount of cash received in any month. In the example of Languid Lizard, 30 percent of monthly sales are made for cash; 70 percent on credit. Credit customers pay, on average, 50 percent of what they owe in the month following the sale and the remainder in the month following.

Thus, of the $16,000 sold in January, 30 percent, or $4,800 is collected in cash at the time of the sale. The remaining $11,200 is in credit sales, as accounts receivable. One-half the amount of credit sales from January, $5,600, will be collected in February, and the remainder in March. This means that the amount of cash received in each month represents parts of the sales of the current month (cash sales) and parts of sales from the previous two months (collections on receivables).

Although this is a simplified example, similar patterns do exist in many small businesses. For example, in the lodging and resort industry, it is common for owners to collect a deposit at the time that a room is reserved, which may precede the guest's stay anywhere between one day to more than a year. The remainder of the money due is normally collected upon checkout of the guest, plus any amounts charged to the room for souvenirs, cookbooks, food items, room service, and items from the gift shop.

You can never know exactly when you will collect cash. However, your experience in business, the experience of other businesses in the industry, and careful monitoring of your credit process lets you make very good estimates. While resort owners may on occasion get advance bookings a year or more in advance, on average, deposits are received about one month in advance. Thus a reasonable estimate of their amount and timing can be made.

Forecasting Cash Disbursements

A similar approach is used for the forecasting of cash disbursements. The estimates of expenses that you develop in your budget, and your knowledge of your business's payment patterns are combined to predict how much and when cash must be paid out. (See Table 14.3.)

Consider again the example of Languid Lizard, Inc., which purchases all materials on account. Inventory orders are placed monthly for delivery at the beginning of the following month. The terms of purchase are 60 percent in the month of purchase, with the balance due the following month. Laborers are paid on Friday of each week for the prior week's work. All other expenses are paid as bills are received.

What are some of the other expenses? Languid Lizard, Inc., has a standing line of credit with the bank. The line of credit allows Languid Lizard to borrow up to $10,000. Draws against the account must be made in $100 increments. Interest is charged at an annual rate of 8 percent. All interest due must be paid at the end of each month. The amount of principal borrowed may be repaid in any amount.

The business also has a capital loan, made on July 1, 2003. A principal payment in the amount of $1,353 will be due on March 31, 2006. Interest for each month, January, February, and March, is $518. The company has a policy of keeping at least a $5,000 ending cash balance for each month.

With the cash receipts and cash disbursements budgets complete, we need to know only how much money we will have on the first day of the year to put together a cash budget for the first quarter. The amount of cash we will have at the beginning of the year is simply the amount of cash we had at the end of the year. We can get this number from either of two sources: (1) the balance of our cash account after the year-end reconciliation is complete or (2) the amount of cash shown on our year-end balance sheet. For this example, we assume that the beginning cash balance is $17,000. (See Table 14.4.)

TABLE 14.3 Cash Disbursements

CASH DISBURSEMENT BUDGET

	January	February	March	Quarter Total
Purchases in prior month (40%)	3,000	3,320	4,499	10,819
Purchases in current month (60%)	4,980	6,748	10,789	22,517
Labor cost previous month (25%)	300	306	378	984
Labor cost current month (75%)	918	1,134	1,773	3,825
Manufacturing overhead	1,867	1,867	1,867	5,601
Selling, general and administrative	6,520	6,924	8,136	21,580
Interest	518	518	518	1,554
Repayment of principal			1,353	1,353
	18,103	20,817	29,312	68,232

Notice that Languid Lizard's cash budget (Table 14.4) begins with a high cash balance in January, which is forecast to be mostly used up by the end of March. Management has set a goal of having no less than $5,000 cash balance at the end of each month of the year. The prediction of a balance of only $2,513 therefore presents a problem. A strategy to handle the expected shortage of cash must be developed. In this example, the obvious strategy is to borrow from the line of credit. The cash shortage will be more than recovered in the next quarter because cash receipts rebound with the spring season sales.

Planning Cash Needs

SKILL MODULE 14.1

1. How would sales for custom electric sign shops, machine shops, providers of custom software, real estate brokers, and consultants vary with (a) changes in the economy and (b) season of the year?
2. Use the spreadsheet, ComprehensiveBudget.xls, from the E.S.B. Web site, **http://www.mhhe.com/katzesb**, to complete the following tasks:

   a. Complete the cash collection forecast for Languid Lizard, Inc., for the current year.
   b. Complete the cash disbursement forecast for Languid Lizard, Inc., for the current year.
   c. Complete the cash budget for Languid Lizard, Inc., for the current year.
   d. Complete annual (i) income statement, (ii) statement of retained earnings, (iii) balance sheet, including statement of owners' equity.

   (Note: all needed data and step-by-step instructions are included in the spreadsheet.)

TABLE 14.4 Cash Budget

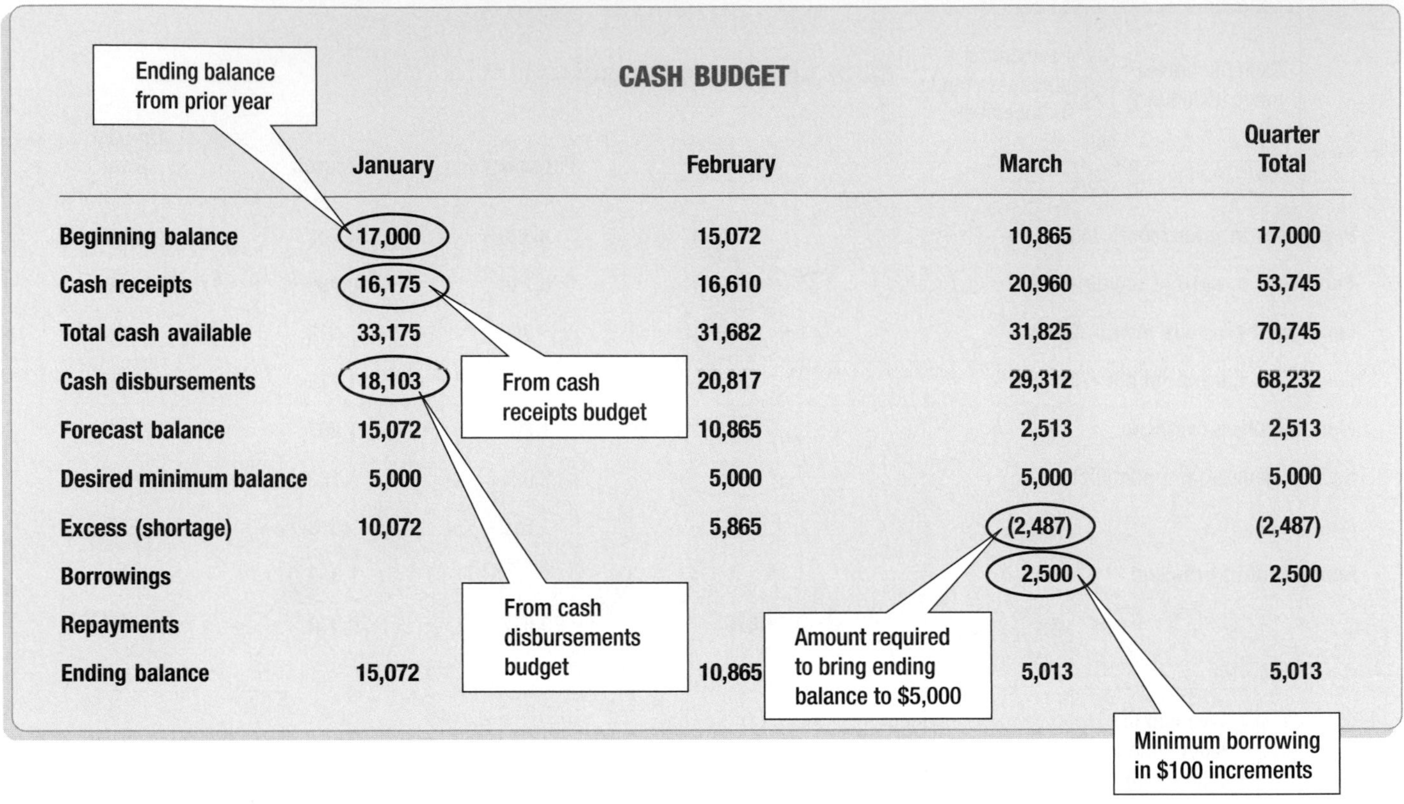

CASH BUDGET

	January	February	March	Quarter Total
Beginning balance	17,000	15,072	10,865	17,000
Cash receipts	16,175	16,610	20,960	53,745
Total cash available	33,175	31,682	31,825	70,745
Cash disbursements	18,103	20,817	29,312	68,232
Forecast balance	15,072	10,865	2,513	2,513
Desired minimum balance	5,000	5,000	5,000	5,000
Excess (shortage)	10,072	5,865	(2,487)	(2,487)
Borrowings			2,500	2,500
Repayments				
Ending balance	15,072	10,865	5,013	5,013

The Comprehensive Budget—the Pro Forma Balance Sheet

As we say above, no matter how daunting, you will budget, one way or another. The budgeting process presented here is specifically designed to feed directly into your business plan. The final step in this part of business planning is to put everything together to create a complete set of pro forma financial statements that you can use for raising money, for evaluating your operations, and for managing your business. All the budgets from Chapter 13 *and* the cash budget developed here are combined at this point to make the comprehensive budget. (Comprehensive budgets are also often referred to as "*master budgets.*")

comprehensive budget
Comprehensive budgets, also often referred to as *master budgets.*

cash receipts budget
A schedule of the amounts and timings of the receipt of cash into a business.

cost of goods sold budget
A schedule of the expected amounts of direct materials, direct labor, and manufacturing overhead that is included in products sold during the accounting period.

With the cash budget in hand, it becomes a simple matter to prepare a pro forma balance sheet in order to project the business's financial position at the end of the planning period. As is shown in Table 14.4, the ending cash balance for Languid Lizard is forecast to be $5,013. Other figures are taken from specific budget items in Chapters 13 and 14:

- The cash receipts budget provides the forecast accounts receivable.
- The ending inventories of raw materials and finished goods are calculated in the cost of goods sold budget.
- The value of fixed assets is the beginning value plus any investments made, less depreciation expense.

TABLE 14.5 Balance Sheet

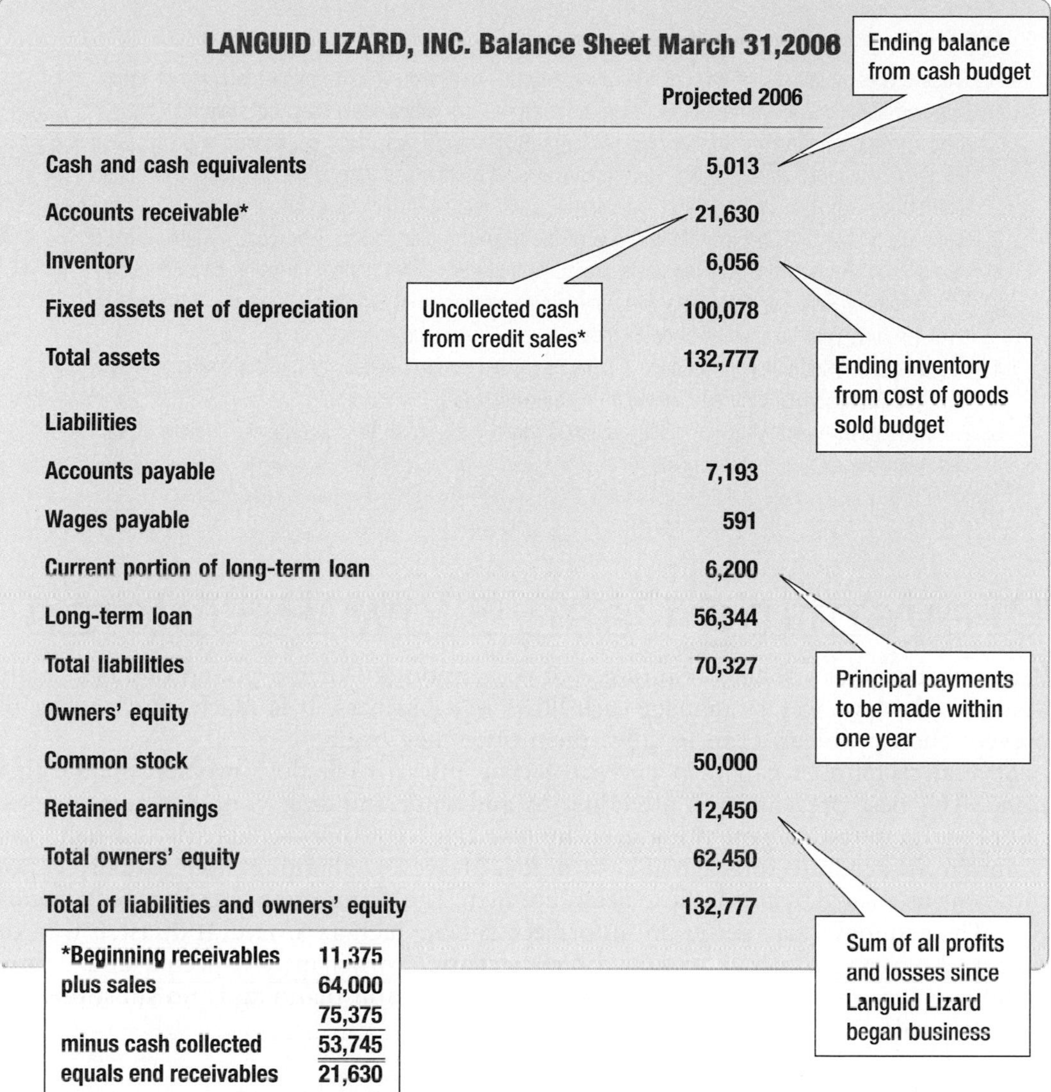

LANGUID LIZARD, INC. Balance Sheet March 31,2006

	Projected 2006
Cash and cash equivalents	5,013
Accounts receivable*	21,630
Inventory	6,056
Fixed assets net of depreciation	100,078
Total assets	132,777
Liabilities	
Accounts payable	7,193
Wages payable	591
Current portion of long-term loan	6,200
Long-term loan	56,344
Total liabilities	70,327
Owners' equity	
Common stock	50,000
Retained earnings	12,450
Total owners' equity	62,450
Total of liabilities and owners' equity	132,777

*Beginning receivables	11,375
plus sales	64,000
	75,375
minus cash collected	53,745
equals end receivables	21,630

- Accounts payable comprises 40 percent of March's purchases of inventory.
- Wages payable is the amount due for labor used in the last week of the quarter.
- The next quarter's payment on the principal of the capital loan will total $1,386 which is shown as part of the current portion of the long-term loan. The beginning balance of the loan, less the payments to be made in the current year, is the long-term balance shown.
- The net profit (or loss) is summed with retained earnings, completing the balance sheet preparation.

The spreadsheets used to prepare the budget examples are available on the Web site for this textbook, www.mhhe.com/katzesb. They may be used as models to develop other planning spreadsheets appropriate for businesses other than manufacturing. (See Table 14.5.)

SKILL MODULE 14.2

A Comprehensive Budget

Choose a business that you are interested in owning.

1. Prepare a complete list of the costs of operating this business. To determine the costs of your selected business, examine sources such as *Entrepreneur* magazine's start-up manuals (**http://www.smallbizbooks.com/cgi-bin/SmallBizBooks/index.html**) or perform a Google search on the term "business startup guide" for other books, manuals, and Web sites. You may also obtain cost information from the Internal Revenue Service, audit guides, franchisors, and industry organizations.
2. Place each cost that you identify into one of the following categories: fixed cost, variable cost, or mixed cost. (Remember: variable costs are costs that vary with changes in sales or production.)
3. From industry sources, determine what the customary payment terms are from vendors and what terms, if any, your business will be expected to provide to customers.
4. Use this cost information to produce a comprehensive budget, based on the ComprehensiveBudget.xls from the McGraw-Hill Web site, **www.mhhe.com/katzesb**.
5. From the cash budget that you have prepared, identify any cash flow shortages. Prepare a plan to deal with the expected shortages.

http://www.smallbizbooks.com/cgi-bin/SmallBizBooks/index.html

Preventing Cash Flow Problems

LO6
Have strategies for preventing and coping with cash flow problems.

Benjamin Franklin's adage, "An ounce of prevention is worth a pound of cure," truly describes the best way to manage cash flows in a business. It is much, much easier to prevent such problems than to solve them once they begin.

Several techniques can help prevent getting into a cash flow problem in the first place. The best prevention is attending to and understanding your business's operations—its patterns of generating cash inflows and outflows—which should help you maintain an accurate forecast of cash needs. However, planning alone usually is not sufficient to ensure that cash flow needs are met. The assumptions made may be incorrect. The economy may suffer an unforeseen shock, such as a natural disaster, war, or energy shortages. Fashions and preferences change, often in unexpected and unpredictable ways. As airline pilots often point out, "Careful planning is no substitute for full fuel tanks."

Techniques to Increase Cash Inflows

There are several simple methods that can be used to increase the amount of cash flows while simultaneously reducing the effects of irregular or seasonal patterns of receipts. Five proven techniques are:

- Taking deposits and progress payments.
- Offering discounts for prompt payment.
- Asking for your money.
- Taking on noncore paying projects.
- Factoring receivables.

deposits and progress payments
Cash payments received before product is completed or delivered.

Deposits and progress payments can greatly smooth the receipt of cash in businesses which otherwise have highly variable levels of cash flows. For example, many businesses that involve summer activities, such as water parks, are open as few as 100 days per year. However, many costs, such as rent, taxes, maintenance, security, and utilities, continue year-round. These types of businesses often choose to obtain cash flow during the closed season by selling season tickets or other forms of advance purchase.[11] Progress payments are payments that are received from your customer as you achieve predetermined goals in a lengthy project. Progress payments are very

TABLE 14.6 Effect of Prompt Payment Discounts on Gross Margin

Gross sales amount	$100.00
Less cost of goods sold	78.00
Gross margin	22.00
Less prompt pay discount of 2 percent	2.00
Net margin	$20.00
Percentage reduction in margin ($2/$22)	9.1%

common in the construction industry where individual projects may take years to complete.

Requiring deposits is advisable in many kinds of businesses in which the process to fulfill a contract with a customer requires significant amounts of time or additional capital. Examples of this type of business are building contractors, consultants, and manufacturers of custom machinery.

discounts for prompt payment A reduction in sales price provided to credit customers for paying outstanding amounts in a timely manner.

Discounts for prompt payment will often motivate your customers to make payments in a timely manner. It is common for wholesale suppliers to offer their customers terms of a 2 percent discount for payment within 5 to 10 working days. You must carefully balance the cost of providing the discount with the cost of obtaining needed cash from other sources.[12] The cost of a discount for prompt payment is deceiving. Consider that you are operating a wholesale distributorship of plumbing supplies, with an average margin on sales of 22 percent, and you provide a 2 percent discount for prompt payment. A customer purchases $100 of supplies on account. What is the effect on your profitability? Your profit margin will decline from $22 to $20, a decline in gross margin of 9.1 percent. (See Table 14.6.)

Asking for your money is at once the most simple and the most effective way to obtain payment from customers.[13] Surprisingly, many owners and managers of small businesses are loath to call customers and request that they pay what they owe. However, you will find that few, if any, businesspeople will be offended by a polite phone call requesting payment. This is especially true of the owners and managers of small businesses who have encountered cash flow difficulties themselves. Very often, a request for prompt payment will be honored, if possible. Of course, there is an implied obligation that, if at some time in the future the customers encounter cash flow problems, you will also be understanding and cooperative, helping them through their own rough spot.

noncore projects Revenue-producing tasks and activities related to, but not part of, the primary strategy of a business.

Taking on **noncore projects** can often provide desperately needed cash during slow business periods. Possibilities are limited only by your imagination. Signgraphics, Inc., of Kansas City, Missouri, during slow times in early spring, often will send a crane truck and operator to hoist air-conditioning and other equipment onto the roofs of buildings. Bill Millers' Barbecue of San Antonio, Texas, for a fee, deep-fries whole turkeys for customers during the slow restaurant periods immediately preceding Thanksgiving and Christmas. Rowan Oak House B&B, in Salisbury, North Carolina, as do many bed and breakfasts, during its slow seasons, sells "murder mystery weekends" that include lodging, breakfast, dinner, and a role-playing mystery game, complete with costumes and props.

factoring receivables Borrowing money secured by a firm's accounts receivable.

Factoring receivables should be considered only if other, less expensive methods to increase cash flows have not been sufficient.[14] Factoring is a method of borrowing against receivables. The factor will usually lend between 75 percent and 80 percent of the amount of uncollected receivables. As the receivables are collected, the factor

THE THOUGHTFUL ENTREPRENEUR

Dangers of Taking on Noncore Business Projects

There are several caveats to be considered in taking on noncore projects:

- First, any noncore project should be such that it can be completed in a reasonable time.
- Second, the project should be clearly specified, with clearly defined outcomes or stopping points.
- Third, no noncore project should be taken solely for the purpose of "churning dollars."

Noncore projects can sometimes provide desperately needed cash. However, the time for such projects is taken from time that otherwise would be used for your core business. When the environment for the core business improves, noncore projects can become very costly distractions.

Specifying outcomes and stopping points prevents making noncore projects into permanent business, which then competes for limited resources with the core business.

It is always tempting, when faced with a need for cash, to offer deep discounts to gain cash inflows. This is counterproductive, however, for two reasons: (1) discounting in either your core or in an associated business devalues your product or service, which will limit the price that can be charged when conditions improve, and (2) accepting business that does not provide an adequate margin reduces profitability for the entire year, which can negatively affect your ability to arrange financing and investment when business conditions improve and additional funding is needed for growth.

deducts a proportional principal amount and remits the remainder, less its fee, typically 5 percent of the gross receivables, to the business.[15]

To factor your receivables, your customers must have good credit ratings. Your credit rating is irrelevant because it is the customers who pay the factor, not you. To provide for losses on uncollectible accounts, some factors either hold back some of the remittances or charge back any uncollected amounts at the end of a specified contract period.

THE THOUGHTFUL ENTREPRENEUR

Effect of Borrowing against Your Receivables

Although it is tempting to use your receivables to obtain immediate cash, doing so is quite expensive. Suppose for example, your business has $100,000 in accounts receivable. If you factor these receivables, you will obtain an immediate $75,000. Now suppose a customer who owes $10,000 pays the full amount. The factor will deduct 75 percent in repayment plus 5 percent of the gross payment amount. You will receive the remaining $2,000:

Customer payment	$10,000
Repayment to factor	(7,500)
5% factor fee	(500)
Balance received	2,000

If your factored receivables are all collected within 90 days, you will have paid $5,000 to receive $75,000 immediately plus $20,000 over three months, a total of $95,000. On an annual basis, this is essentially the same as paying 22 percent interest.

Techniques to Decrease Cash Outflows

Decreasing cash outflows is as important as increasing cash inflows. Regardless of how much money you're making, conserving cash is essential. All companies have certain costs that cannot be avoided and cannot be financed. Examples of unavoidable cash payments include payroll, rent, utilities, and withholding taxes. If you do not have enough cash to pay your employees, keep the door open, the lights burning, and the tax collector at bay, the business will fail, no matter its potential or paper profits. As with cash inflows there are two factors of cash outflows that must be controlled: (1) the amount of cash being paid out and (2) the timing of cash being paid out.

Controlling the amount of cash being paid out is primarily a function of making good purchasing decisions and avoiding waste. By purchasing in the appropriate quantities with the appropriate quality at the appropriate times, the need to make cash payments can be aligned with the receipt of cash, to the extent that the nature of the business allows.

Every business that maintains inventory has an optimal level that minimizes the total cost of (1) carrying inventory, (2) processing orders, and (3) losing sales due to being out of stock. The optimum level of many other business resources can similarly be determined. Setting reasonable standards and carefully monitoring usage and stocking levels reduce the amount of cash required for these essential business resources while maximizing revenues. The determination of optimum stocking levels is fully discussed in the appendix of Chapter 17.

Waste also affects cash outflow. Resources that are wasted represent cash that was paid out with no economic benefit. Almost any resource can be wasted. You can waste the time of your employees by requiring procedures such as record keeping and reporting that are not useful for management. You can waste primary materials by inefficient cutting and by allowing materials to spoil, break, or be stolen. You can waste rent by maintaining space that does not produce revenue. The list of potential waste is endless.

Most of us become so accustomed to our ways of doing business that we often do not recognize waste when we see it. For years, restaurants paid people to haul away old cooking oils and grease. If there was no one to haul the oil, it was often dumped onto gravel parking lots or poured into solid waste dumps. The oil was indeed *scrap*—it had no further economic use in the restaurant. The oil was not *waste*, however, until it was poured out. There was an economically valuable use for the oil in making cosmetics, animal feed, paint, and chemicals. Today, the waste oil from restaurants and commercial food manufacturers is so valuable that not only is there an active market for waste oil, but organized bandits often steal the oil at night. Oil that once was considered trash is today a significant source of revenue.

It takes insight into your particular business to determine what constitutes waste.[16] Suppose you have a sizable store of the leftovers from cutting plywood to make your product. It is certain that the plywood pieces are scrap. But are they waste? To determine if these odd pieces of wood are waste, you need to find out (1) if there is a cutting pattern that will reduce the amount of leftover wood; (2) if you cannot reduce the amount of scrap, if there an economically valuable use for it; and (3) what it is costing you to keep the scrap pieces on hand. You may find that the wood is scrap, but the waste is the space that it occupies—space that you could otherwise put to productive use.

In addition to making wise purchasing decisions and avoiding waste of resources, there are several strategies that will provide savings in cash outflows, including:[17]

- Trade discounts.
- Noncash employee incentives.
- Use of temporary agencies.
- Consignment.
- Barter.

- Control of the timing of paying out cash.
- Negotiation of terms with suppliers.
- Timing of purchases.
- Gaming of the payment process.

Some of these should be familiar, because they are mentioned in the discussion of bootstrapping in Chapter 5, where bootstrapping is introduced as a way to make possible a part-time business operating on a very limited budget; but the ideas of bootstrapping as we can see below also apply to more established kinds of small businesses.

trade discounts
Percentage discounts from gross invoice amounts provided to encourage prompt payment.

Trade discounts are given by suppliers and vendors to encourage customers to make timely payments on account. In effect, you are borrowing from the vendor at the discount rate for the number of days that you may wait to pay after the cutoff date for receiving the discount. The rule of thumb for trade discounts is that you should always capture discounts of 1 percent or greater, if the billing period is less than 30 days.

If the supplier provides payment terms exceeding 30 days, then you must perform a quick analysis to determine whether taking the discount or delaying payment provides the greater value. To decide whether to take the discount, compare the annual effective interest rate of the discount to your cost of borrowing from other sources. Then choose the one with the lower annual effective rate.

noncash incentives
Rewards that do not require payment of cash, such as stock options, compensating time off, or added vacation days.

Noncash incentives for employees is the most widely used technique to reduce the amount of cash that must be paid out of the business. The most common such incentive is to grant stock options, which give the employee the right to purchase company stock at a fixed price in the future. The hope of the employee is that the stock will go up significantly in price and, that upon either selling or exercising the option, the employee will realize large gains. Other noncash incentives include autonomy, a chance to be creative, flexible hours, telecommuting, praise, training, career opportunities, the chance to work with (or learn about) advanced technology, responsibility, benefits packages (health, vacation, retirement, etc.), a supportive or protective culture, and even small prizes and awards.[18]

THE THOUGHTFUL ENTREPRENEUR

Should I Take a Supplier's Discount for Payment?

Assume that Languid Lizard, Inc., can borrow from the bank at 11 percent. The supplier of aluminum tubing provides credit terms at a 1 percent discount, if paid within 10 days of the receipt of the invoice, and the full amount must be paid in 30 days. To see if the heuristic ("take any discount of 1 percent or greater when the payment period is 30 or fewer days") holds in this case, calculate the annual effective interest rate:

Annual effective rate = (discount/100% − discount) × (365/(payment period − discount period)

AER = [1%/(100% − discount)] × [365/(30 − 10)]
AER = (.01/.99) × [365/(20)]
AER = 0.01010101 × 18.25
AER = 18.43%

Yes, indeed, the heuristic holds. 18.25% is much greater than is 11%. Languid Lizard should pay within 10 days, taking the 1 percent discount on the goods.

Suppose, however, that the vendor's terms were 1 percent discount if paid in 10 days, due in full in 45 days after receipt. If you do the same arithmetic, the result is 10.53%. With the more generous terms, it is better for Languid Lizard to delay payment to the full 45 days.

Use of temporary agencies is another way to reduce the cost of employees. If you do not need a full-time, permanent employee, agencies can provide educated, trained, and skilled workers who will work only as much as you need. It is common today for small businesses to contract with agencies to provide all sorts of temporary employees, from unskilled labor to a chief executive officer.

Consignment is the practice of accepting goods for resale without taking ownership for them and without being responsible to pay prior to their being sold. Consignment sales are the norm in the operation of art galleries. Living artists usually make an exclusive contract with a specific gallery to display their works. When a piece of art is sold, either by the gallery or by the artist, the gallery arranges for receipt of payment, delivery of the art, and guarantee of the provenance of the art, in return for a percentage of the sales price.

consignment
The practice of accepting goods for resale, without taking ownership of them and without being responsible to pay prior to their being sold.

Lisa Fittipaldi (www.lisafittipaldi.com) provides an example of this type of arrangement. Lisa, who is completely blind, is a painter who produces remarkable, lifelike representational art. Her phenomenal visual memory allows her to work on several paintings at once, moving with assurance from one to another. Lisa has a contract with Gallery SOCO, of Austin, Texas, to display and promote her art, which she provides on consignment to the gallery.

www.lisafittipaldi.com

Other industries that use consignment sales include the distributors of salty snacks (potato chips, corn chips, peanuts, etc.), specialty food items, used furniture and antiques, sporting goods, and used automobiles. The advantage of receiving goods on consignment is that they remain the property of the consigner and do not have to be paid for until sold, thus matching cash receipts with cash disbursement.

Barter is the practice of trading goods and services without the use of money. For example, an accountant may trade accounting services to a sign company in return for the sign company manufacturing and installing a sign at the accountant's place of business. Barter alleviates the need for cash by trading good for good, service for service, or service for good. Barter is legal in the United States and is widely practiced among small businesses.[19] Although money is not used in the transaction, the legislature, the IRS, and the courts have consistently ruled that barter is a taxable transaction, except in case of trades of "like-kind" goods or services. In other words, you may trade real estate for real estate, or machinery for machinery without creating a taxable transaction. However, if you trade your airplane for real estate or if you use any amount of money in the trade, the transaction is subject to tax.

barter
The practice of trading goods and services without the use of money.

Because of the provision for tax-free treatment of like-kind trades, barter transactions are susceptible to misuse to avoid paying taxes. As a result, the rules for reporting barter transactions are restrictive and quite complex. Misuse of barter is usually considered fraud by the IRS and can lead to criminal penalties.

There are numerous services, organizations and Web sites that facilitate barter transactions. For example, the Open Directory Project, http://dmoz.org/Business/International Business and Trade/Barter/, lists over 60 online barter clubs, organizations, brokers, exchanges, and for-profit companies that support barter, using the Internet. The Google directory, http://directory.google.com/Top/Business/International Business and Trade/Barter/, returns 33 similar references. There are even trade associations for the barter industry such as the International Reciprocal Trade Association (www.irta.com) or the National Association of Trade Exchanges (www.nate.org).

www.irta.com

www.nate.org

Controlling the timing of paying out cash can be accomplished through a number of methods. The strategy is not to unnecessarily delay paying, but to arrange payment schedules in such a way that due dates match the times when cash is available.

Negotiating terms with suppliers is a common, acceptable method for controlling when payment must be made for goods and services. For example, many building contractors who build single-family houses expect to complete and sell a house in a 90-day period. Most builders negotiate with primary suppliers such as lumberyards and plumbing wholesalers to finance the materials needed to build a house. The suppliers are protected by having a lien on the house that must be paid before title of the house can be passed to the buyer.

Similar arrangements are made to finance many types of long-term projects, as well. Often the winning bidder on a large project will make the major suppliers subcontractors who agree to accept payment when the general contractor is paid.

timing purchases
A method of controlling the timing of cash outflows that is invisible to suppliers and vendors.

Timing purchases is a method of controlling the timing of cash outflows that is invisible to suppliers and vendors. Your specific reason for placing any certain order on any certain day is not apparent. However, knowledge of the payment policies of suppliers can provide considerable leeway in when bills must be paid following delivery of goods. For example, it is common for wholesale suppliers to have payment terms that define an on-time payment as being any payment made on or before the tenth day of the month following purchase. Knowing this term, you can gain additional time to pay by delaying purchase until the first day of the month. This provides up to 41 days before payment must be made without being classified as late. Were you to purchase on the last day of the month, you would have only 10 days to make a timely payment.

gaming the payment process
Using methods to appear to be paying bills on time, when in fact payment is being delayed or avoided.

Gaming the payment process is a common, if a bit underhanded, method of controlling cash outflows. Methods range from simply not paying a bill when it is due to sending checks that you've "forgotten" to sign to sending checks in payment and then stopping payment after the payment has been recorded, but the check has not yet cleared. Very few business owners and managers are proud of taking such measures, but most will, if promised confidentiality, admit to having done one or another in times of cash crises.

Gaming payments can be quite costly, however. You may well get away with any one of these strategies with any single vendor one time. The more often you game payment, the more certain it becomes that your business credit rating and reputation will suffer as a result. Being consistently late in payment, regardless of gaming strategies, will cause a decrease in your business's credit worthiness. It is not uncommon for suppliers and vendors to refuse to do business with customers who regularly attempt to game the process.

Controlling Cash Shortages

LO7
Learn strategies for coping with cash shortages.

No matter how well you plan or how well you manage your business, sooner or later you will experience a significant cash shortage. Causes of cash shortages range from the obvious, a customer fails to make an expected payment or goes out of business without paying at all, to the obscure—an economic shock, such as a plant closing, natural disaster, or political turmoil like an oil embargo or war. During a time of economic shock, you may not attain your sales goals, *and* you may not be able to collect from customers as they suffer from the same bad economy. However, many, if not all, your bills go on, demanding payments that you no longer have the money to make.

growth trap
A financial crisis that is caused by a business growing faster than it can be financed.

Another often overlooked cause of cash shortages is a surplus of good news: Your business has proven to be wildly successful, and sales are growing at an exponential rate. This situation is often referred to as the **growth trap**.[20] Because of increased sales, you need more labor, more materials for your product, more factory space, and more warehouse space to store completed products until they can be shipped to your customers. All this growth requires money, and lots of it. However, as discussed above, sales take time to convert into money. The product must be made and shipped before any customer will pay. If you are offering credit to customers, you will have to wait even longer to receive that payment. You are in a "trap" made by growth: Growing will produce more money, but right now you need money to grow.

There are numerous strategies to handle cash shortfalls, including laying off employees, slowing payments for purchases, stepping up collection efforts, selling investment securities, or using your own money. A survey of small business owners (see Figure 14.7) found that there are at least eight strategies employed by small businesses for handling money shortages. These are, in the order of their frequency of use:

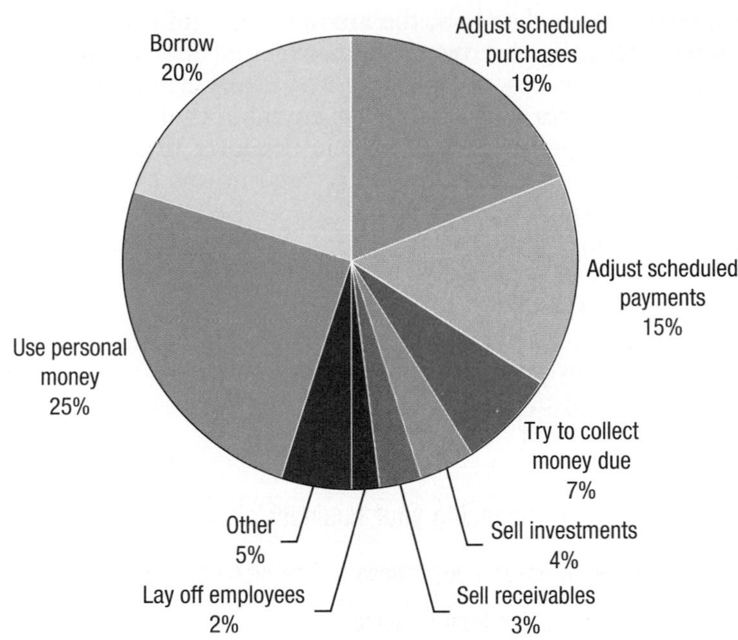

FIGURE 14.7

Eight Top Strategies for Handling Cash Shortages

Strategies for Small Business Managers to Handle Cash Shortfalls

1. Use personal money.
2. Borrow.
3. Adjust scheduled purchases.
4. Adjust scheduled payments.
5. Try to collect money due.
6. Sell investments.
7. Sell receivables.
8. Lay off employees.

Of the strategies employed, the three most common, in order of use, are (1) use personal money, (2) borrow, and (3) adjust scheduled purchases. Together, these three strategies were used by over 60 percent of the respondents to the survey.

In Review

Managing cash flows is at the same time the most important and most difficult task faced by owners and managers of small businesses. What makes it so difficult is the constant juggling act between the timing of cash coming into the business and cash going out of the business.

You now have the basics of understanding what constitutes money, cash, revenue, and profit. You know that they are related, but very different concepts. Money and cash are economic realities that are essential for business operation. Revenues and profits are solely accounting concepts that are used primarily as tools to measure business activities.

Revenue and expenses are used to predict the amounts and timings of cash inflows and outflows primarily through the budgeting process, which starts with forecasting sales and ends in a cash budget.

Since most small businesses depend on their bank checking accounts as a money management tool, the most basic money management skill becomes a bank reconciliation. The best way to go about this is to reconcile the bank balance for items that you know about but are unknown to the bank, and adjust your book balance for those items that are reported by the bank, such as their fees. When done accurately, this type of reconciliation results in the bank and book balances reporting the identical "true" cash position of the firm as of the date of the bank statement.

There are numerous ways that both the amounts and timings of cash flows can be managed, to some extent, by the owner or manager of a small business. Some cash management techniques are very inexpensive and really a matter of common sense, such as not wasting resources and not buying anything that is not absolutely needed for the business. Other techniques incur costs in the form of interest expense and use of management time. All of the techniques discussed in this chapter are used daily by small business managers across the world.

CHAPTER SUMMARY

LO1 Know the importance of managing your business's money.

- Almost two-thirds of small businesses experience money problems because of:
  - Difficulty collecting money due from customers.
  - Seasonal variation in sales.
  - Unexpected decreases in sales.
- The cash-to-cash or operating cycle is the time it takes for a business to obtain resources, produce and sell its product, and collect cash from sales:
  - The cycle can be as short as a few hours or as long as several years, depending upon the type of business.
- Many small businesses experience difficulty or failure, because of:
  - The mismatch in time between receiving cash and spending cash.
  - The mismatch between the size of payments received and the size of payments that must be made.

LO2 Understand the concepts of money, cash, and cash equivalents.

- Money is special type of information with three primary purposes—making exchanges, keeping track of wealth or value, and storing wealth for future use.
  - What makes money "*money,*" is the *belief* users have about the information contained in the money.
  - Profit is not money. Rather profits are information about money derived from the difference between two accounting items, revenue and expense.
- Cash is composed of the three forms of money that can be immediately used to make payments: currency, demand deposits, and traveler's checks.
- Cash equivalents are assets that may be turned into cash in a few hours to a few days. Cash equivalents include marketable securities, commercial paper, and debt investments that mature in less than three months.
- Currency is the most common form of cash and is composed of bills and coins that represent money.
- Demand deposits, which include checking accounts, savings accounts, and traveler's checks, are the second most common form of cash.
- Marketable securities are made up of stocks and bonds for which there is an active auction market.

LO3 Understand the basics of managing cash flow.

- Cash can come from only three sources:
  - Operations which comprise selling the products and services and collecting cash from customers.
  - Investing, which comprises buying and selling stocks, bonds, land, buildings, or equipment.
  - Financing which is either cash donated to the business in return for ownership or money borrowed from other entities.
- The starting point in understanding cash management is understanding how banks work, because small businesses depend on banks to store cash, handle checks and credit cards, and obtain financing:
  - Money you have deposited today may not be immediately available to you because deposits, checks, and electronic transfers take time to complete.
  - Bank available balance is the amount of money that has been received into the account, less all amounts of money that have been paid out of account by the bank.
  - *Float* is the term used to describe the delay in movement of money among depositors and banks. Business managers often use float as a cash management tool.

LO4 Be able to reconcile bank and company book balances.

- Reconciling the differences between bank and book balances caused by float lets you know how much cash is currently available and how much will soon be available.
- The process of reconciling bank balance and book balance is quite simple.
  - Add (subtract) to the bank balance those things that you know about your account that the bank does not know.
  - Add (subtract) to your book balance those things that the bank knows about your account that you do not know until reported by the bank.
- Accepting payments by credit card causes significant differences between the bank and book balances for three reasons:
  - Credit card service providers deposit the sale amount less the credit card service fee.
  - The service provider will take up to three working days to make a deposit to your account.
  - Credit card clearing services reduce the amount deposited in the event of fraud or customer challenge.

LO5 Be prepared to develop a cash budget.

- A cash budget identifies when, how, and why cash is expected to come into the business, and when, how, and why it is expected to leave:
  - For businesses that make sales by cash or by credit card, the sales forecast *is* the cash receipts forecast.
  - If you provide credit to your customers, you will always wait some period of time for some of your money. You also, sooner or later, will have some customer who never pays.
- Cash receipts and cash disbursements budgets are used to put together a cash budget.
- All budgets are combined at this point to make the *comprehensive budget.*

LO6 Have strategies for preventing and coping with cash flow problems.

- The best way to prevent cash flow problems is to pay attention to and understand your business's operations and patterns of cash flows.
- Five proven techniques to even out cash flows are:
  - Taking deposits and progress payments.
  - Offering discounts for prompt payment.
  - Asking for your money.
  - Taking on noncore paying projects.
  - Factoring receivables.
- Controlling the amount of cash being paid out is primarily a function of making good purchasing decisions and avoiding waste.

LO7 Learn strategies for coping with cash shortages.

- No matter how well you plan or how well you manage your business, sooner or later you will experience a significant cash shortage.
- Causes of cash shortages include a customer failing to pay or going out of business, and economic shocks, such as a natural disaster or war.
- The growth trap causes cash flow problems when the rate of growth is faster than the operating cycle.
- The three most common ways to handle cash shortages are (1) using personal money, (2) borrowing, and (3) adjusting scheduled purchases.

DISCUSSION QUESTIONS

1. Why is it important to plan for the amounts and timing of cash inflows and outflows?
2. What is money, and how does it differ from profits?
3. What are the primary purposes of money?
4. How do the economic and accounting definitions of cash differ?
5. What are the relationships among planning, budgeting, and forecasting?
6. Discuss five methods commonly used to increase cash inflows.
7. Discuss four methods to decrease cash outflows.
8. The text calls the practice of gaming the payment process, "underhanded." What is your opinion of this common practice? Does it have any ethical implications?
9. What is the difference between writing a nonsufficient funds check and conducting a check kite? What are the legal and ethical considerations of each of these activities?
10. How does using the float as a cash management method differ from deliberately writing NSF checks and from conducting a check kite?

EXPERIENTIAL EXERCISES

1. Make an appointment with a loan officer at your bank who handles small businesses. Conduct an interview to find out the following:

a. Will the bank lend to small businesses, using receivables for collateral?

b. Does the bank ever factor receivables or act as a collection agent for receivables?

c. Present the example of the air-conditioning company from this chapter. Ask what help from the bank would be available in such a situation.

Write a report of your findings.

2. Form a group from your classmates who completed exercise 1, above. Collect your findings into a chart. Compare and contrast bank offerings. Present your findings to your class with a recommendation of which banks in your area offer the best small business support.

3. Do a Google search, using the name of your city and "online banking" as illustrated. Examine the sites returned to determine:

a. How often is the account balance updated online?

b. Are monthly account statements available on line?

c. How far back (one month, two months, one year) can you retrieve statements and transactions?

d. Can you electronically transfer funds among your accounts?

e. Can you electronically pay bills?

f. Can you download bank account information into your small business computerized accounting system? If so, which systems are supported?

g. What is the cost of online banking?

Make a chart of your findings and report to your class.

4. Do a telephone survey of banks in your area. Ask:

a. Do they use electronic check clearing?

b. If they use a clearing bank to manually clear checks, ask what bank they use.

c. Ask what the average period of float is for the bank.

d. Ask what the bank's policy is for nonsufficient funds: Does it pay to the limit of ledger balance or to available balance?

e. What other provisions does the bank make to help small businesses avoid having checks returned NSF?

f. When does the bank make available funds from deposited checks?

Write a report of your findings and present it to your class.

5. Form a group from your classmates who completed exercise 4, above. Collect your findings into a chart. Compare and contrast bank offerings. Present your findings to your class with a recommendation of which banks in your area offer the best overdraft protection to small businesses.

6. Use the resources of your library and the Internet to identify five credit card processing providers. Contact each and determine the following:
   a. The cost of equipment to be able to accept credit card charges.
   b. The transaction cost, if any.
   c. The amount of discount charged for:
      i. Physically swiped card charges.
      ii. Charges accepted over the telephone.
      iii. Online charges taken on the Internet.
   d. How long does it take between accepting a credit card for payment and receiving the cash in your bank account?

   Report your finding to your class.
7. Assume that you are preparing to open a new business. You need both an on-location sign and professional accounting services. Do a Web search and examine your local telephone book to find (a) a sign company and (b) an accountant who is willing to provide its product and services in a barter transaction for the product or service of your business.

Mini-Case

BULLTUFF STOCK TRAILERS, INC.

Hal Carrier, of Bulltuff Stock Trailers, Inc., has asked you for help. In the last four months, he has had several checks written to suppliers that were refused by his bank because of nonsufficient funds. Now his main supplier, Alcoa Aluminum Supply Co., has cut off credit.

"We're sorry, Hal," Alcoa's credit officer said, "but we simply cannot keep accepting your checks. Every time one bounces, it costs us at least $100 combined in processing fees and our internal accounting. You simply will have to pay cash or bring a cashier's check for future purchases."

Hal simply cannot understand why his checks keep bouncing. "We've plenty of sales," he said, "and our customers pay pretty much as agreed. Right now, I have only one customer who is as much as 60 days past due. My accountant, Brill Yant, assures me that our cash balance never goes negative. So why are my checks bouncing?"

To try to understand Hal' s problem and to advise him how to correct it, you have collected the following information about Hal's business:

1. Cash sales are 10 percent of total sales.
2. Credit card sales are 10 percent of total sales and are collected the week following the sale. The credit card provider deducts 2.5 percent of the gross amount of each credit card sale. (For example, on a $100 sale, $2.50 is deducted.)
3. Sales on account are 80 percent of all sales. All credit sales are to dealers. Terms for dealers are "30-30-30," that is, three equal payments made in each of the three months following the sale. Payments are considered late if they're not received by the tenth of the month in which they are due.
4. Direct materials, primarily aluminum, are 60 percent of the cost of building a trailer. Before credit was cut off, Bulltuff paid 30 percent on delivery and the remainder in 30 days. Now it must pay cash on delivery.
5. Total cost of direct labor is 15 percent of the cost of building a trailer. Workers are paid each Friday for work performed the previous week. Withholding and employment taxes are paid each Friday, also.
6. All other costs combined are treated as fixed costs, and total $1 million per year.
7. Bulltuff leases its building and equipment and has no depreciation.

8. Sales for the year were originally projected to be $2,450,000. However, given the current growth in sales, Hal now estimates that sales will be $5,000,000.

9. Sales for the first four months of the year have been:

January	$208,000
February	261,000
March	293,000
April	328,000

CASE DISCUSSION QUESTIONS

1. What is causing Hal's cash flow problems?

2. Develop a plan to address the problems.

Appendix

Completing a Bank Reconciliation

One very useful skill you can have for managing cash in your business is being able to quickly and accurately reconcile your own cash records with your bank's records.

Carefully examine the copy of Languid Lizard's December bank statement on the next page.

Of special interest are the amounts that are highlighted with the red labels. These are amounts added to and subtracted from the account directly by the bank. Languid Lizard's owner has no way of knowing these transactions have occurred, except to be informed of them by the bank. These amounts are one of the two reasons that the bank balance and Languid Lizard's book balance differ.

Now take a look at Languid Lizard's cash records: Notice five things: (1) According to Lizard's accounting records, there is a cash balance of $42,038.19. Compare this with the bank balance of only $34,220.22. This is an $8,000 difference. (2) Lizard made a deposit of $7,233.99 which the bank has not yet recorded. This may be because the deposit and the bank statement were both made on December 31. Normally, deposits made after 3:00 p.m. will not be recorded by the bank until the next work day. A deposit made at 3:01 p.m. on Friday will not show up as an addition to your bank account until the bank updates accounts *after 3:00 P.M. on the following Monday.* (3) Lizard has received a check from a customer that has been recorded in the company's books, but has not yet been taken to the bank for deposit. (4) Lizard has written two checks to suppliers that have not yet cashed them. (5) None of the items flagged in red that were added and subtracted by the bank show up in Lizard's books in any way.

No wonder that the bank and Lizard have very different opinions of how much money Languid Lizard has.

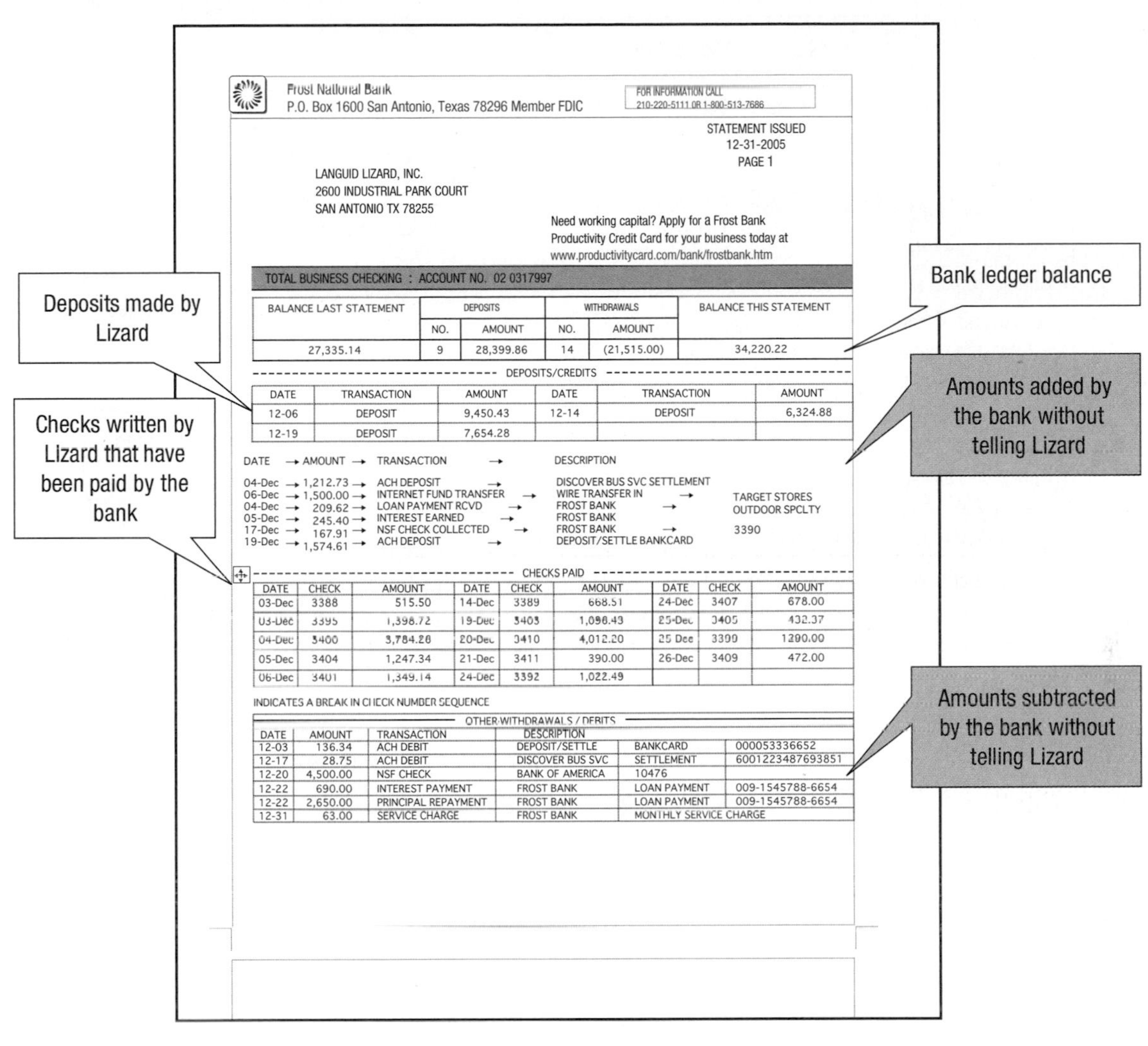

Frost National Bank
P.O. Box 1600 San Antonio, Texas 78296 Member FDIC

FOR INFORMATION CALL
210-220-5111 OR 1-800-513-7686

STATEMENT ISSUED
12-31-2005
PAGE 1

LANGUID LIZARD, INC.
2600 INDUSTRIAL PARK COURT
SAN ANTONIO TX 78255

Need working capital? Apply for a Frost Bank Productivity Credit Card for your business today at www.productivitycard.com/bank/frostbank.htm

TOTAL BUSINESS CHECKING : ACCOUNT NO. 02 0317997

BALANCE LAST STATEMENT	DEPOSITS		WITHDRAWALS		BALANCE THIS STATEMENT
	NO.	AMOUNT	NO.	AMOUNT	
27,335.14	9	28,399.86	14	(21,515.00)	34,220.22

DEPOSITS/CREDITS

DATE	TRANSACTION	AMOUNT	DATE	TRANSACTION	AMOUNT
12-06	DEPOSIT	9,450.43	12-14	DEPOSIT	6,324.88
12-19	DEPOSIT	7,654.28			

DATE →	AMOUNT →	TRANSACTION →	DESCRIPTION	
04-Dec →	1,212.73 →	ACH DEPOSIT →	DISCOVER BUS SVC SETTLEMENT	
06-Dec →	1,500.00 →	INTERNET FUND TRANSFER →	WIRE TRANSFER IN →	TARGET STORES
04-Dec →	209.62 →	LOAN PAYMENT RCVD →	FROST BANK →	OUTDOOR SPCLTY
05-Dec →	245.40 →	INTEREST EARNED →	FROST BANK	
17-Dec →	167.91 →	NSF CHECK COLLECTED →	FROST BANK →	3390
19-Dec →	1,574.61 →	ACH DEPOSIT →	DEPOSIT/SETTLE BANKCARD	

CHECKS PAID

DATE	CHECK	AMOUNT	DATE	CHECK	AMOUNT	DATE	CHECK	AMOUNT
03-Dec	3388	515.50	14-Dec	3389	668.51	24-Dec	3407	678.00
03-Dec	3395	1,398.72	19-Dec	3403	1,098.43	25-Dec	3405	432.37
04-Dec	3400	3,784.26	20-Dec	3410	4,012.20	25 Dec	3390	1290.00
05-Dec	3404	1,247.34	21-Dec	3411	390.00	26-Dec	3409	472.00
06-Dec	3401	1,349.14	24-Dec	3392	1,022.49			

INDICATES A BREAK IN CHECK NUMBER SEQUENCE

OTHER WITHDRAWALS / DEBITS

DATE	AMOUNT	TRANSACTION	DESCRIPTION		
12-03	136.34	ACH DEBIT	DEPOSIT/SETTLE	BANKCARD	000053336652
12-17	28.75	ACH DEBIT	DISCOVER BUS SVC	SETTLEMENT	6001223487693851
12-20	4,500.00	NSF CHECK	BANK OF AMERICA	10476	
12-22	690.00	INTEREST PAYMENT	FROST BANK	LOAN PAYMENT	009-1545788-6654
12-22	2,650.00	PRINCIPAL REPAYMENT	FROST BANK	LOAN PAYMENT	009-1545788-6654
12-31	63.00	SERVICE CHARGE	FROST BANK	MONTHLY SERVICE CHARGE	

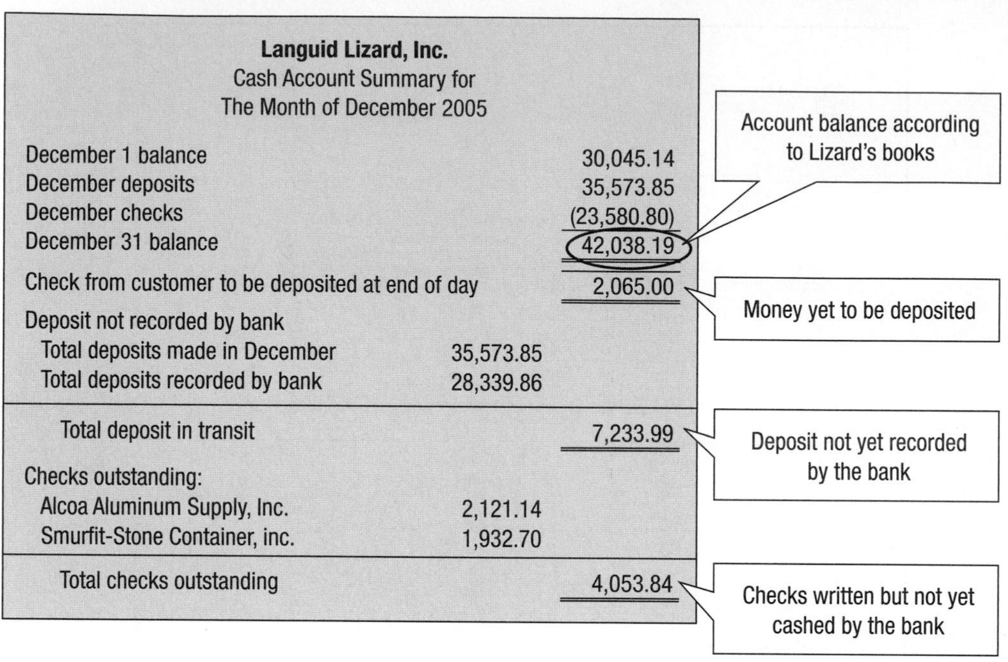

Languid Lizard, Inc.
Cash Account Summary for
The Month of December 2005

December 1 balance		30,045.14
December deposits		35,573.85
December checks		(23,580.80)
December 31 balance		42,038.19
Check from customer to be deposited at end of day		2,065.00
Deposit not recorded by bank		
Total deposits made in December	35,573.85	
Total deposits recorded by bank	28,339.86	
Total deposit in transit		7,233.99
Checks outstanding:		
Alcoa Aluminum Supply, Inc.	2,121.14	
Smurfit-Stone Container, inc.	1,932.70	
Total checks outstanding		4,053.84

Fixing these differences is incredibly simple. We are going to do two little tasks. (1) We are going to add and subtract from the bank's balance those transactions Lizard has done that the bank currently knows nothing about. (2) We are going to add to and subtract from Lizard's balance those things the bank has done, that until now Lizard knew nothing about. When we are done, the *adjusted* bank balance and the *adjusted* book balance will be identical. This process is detailed on the next page:

We start on the bank balance by (A) entering the balance shown on the bank statement into our reconciliation worksheet. To the bank balance we add (B) the things Lizard added that the bank can't know—the undeposited check and the deposit which has not yet been recorded by the bank. Finally, we subtract (C) the checks written by Languid Lizard that have not yet gotten to the bank for payment.

We finish up on the book balance by (D) adding the items that the bank added, but Languid Lizard did not know until it received the monthly bank statement—deposits from the credit card provider, wire transfers in, collections on notes, interest earned, bad check collected, and a check that was incorrectly entered into Lizard's books. Then we subtract from Languid Lizard's balance (E) those things the bank subtracted that Lizard could not know—a bad check from a customer, charges made by the credit card provider, a payment on borrowed money taken directly from the account, and the bank service charge.

To complete the reconciliation, add each of the bank adjustments and the book adjustments, and as predicted, the resulting balances are identical.

Now Lizard's owner simply enters the adjustments into the accounting records. This brings the recorded book balance to $39,465.37, which is the amount of money the business really has.

This one business function, tracking and managing cash, is itself enough reason to buy and use a computerized accounting system. Although such systems cannot make reconciliations automatically, they have very powerful and very easy-to-use built-in functions to complete this important business task. With just a little bit of attention, you can always *know* just how much money your business has.

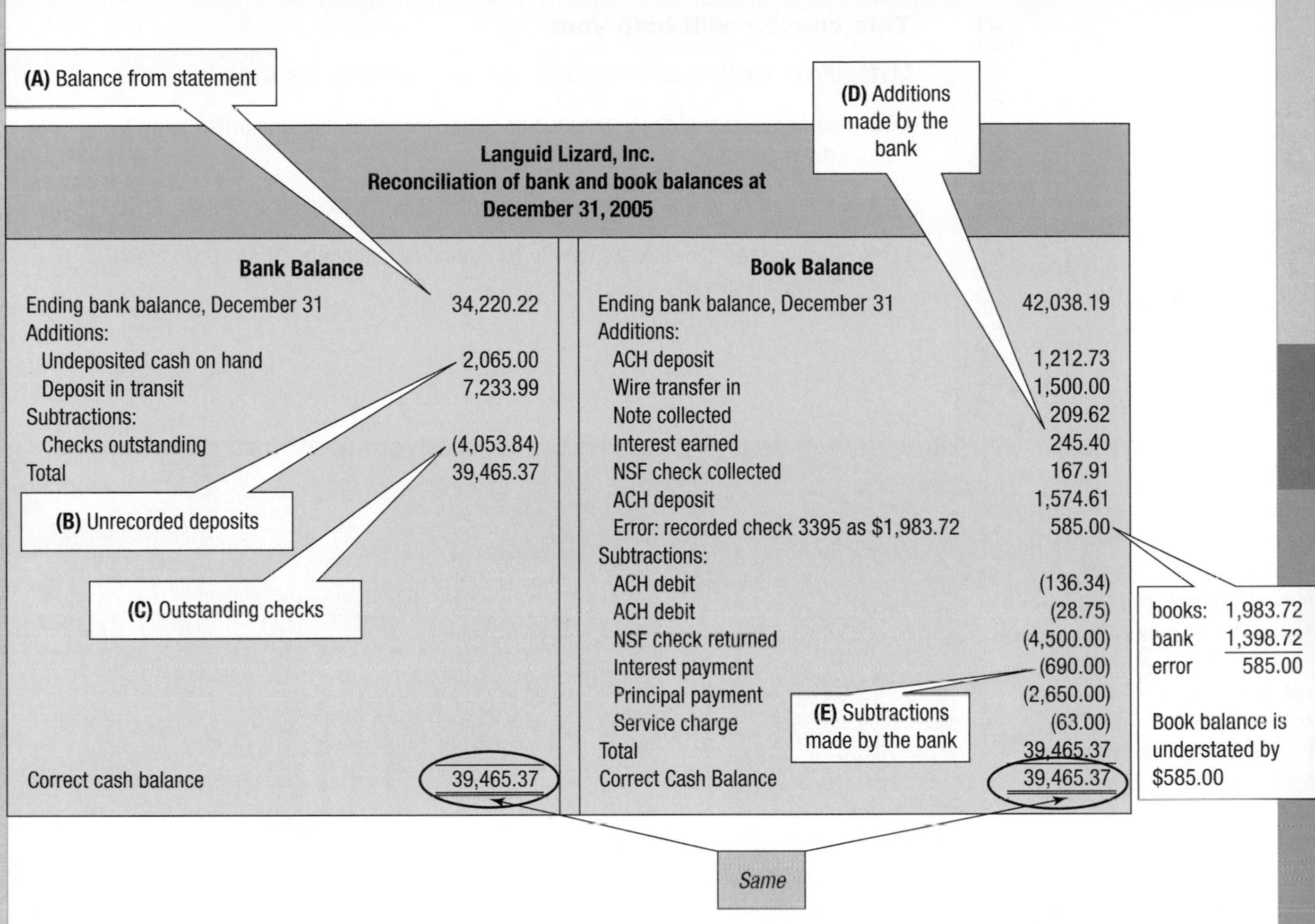
(A) Balance from statement
(D) Additions made by the bank
Languid Lizard, Inc.
Reconciliation of bank and book balances at
December 31, 2005
Bank Balance
Ending bank balance, December 31 34,220.22
Additions:
Undeposited cash on hand 2,065.00
Deposit in transit 7,233.99
Subtractions:
Checks outstanding (4,053.84)
Total 39,465.37
(B) Unrecorded deposits
(C) Outstanding checks
Correct cash balance 39,465.37
Book Balance
Ending bank balance, December 31 42,038.19
Additions:
ACH deposit 1,212.73
Wire transfer in 1,500.00
Note collected 209.62
Interest earned 245.40
NSF check collected 167.91
ACH deposit 1,574.61
Error: recorded check 3395 as $1,983.72 585.00
Subtractions:
ACH debit (136.34)
ACH debit (28.75)
NSF check returned (4,500.00)
Interest payment (690.00)
Principal payment (2,650.00)
Service charge (63.00)
Total 39,465.37
Correct Cash Balance 39,465.37
(E) Subtractions made by the bank
books: 1,983.72
bank 1,398.72
error 585.00
Book balance is understated by $585.00
Same

LEARNING OBJECTIVES

This chapter will help you:

LO1 Know the three types of capital financing and their costs and trade-offs.

LO2 Understand the characteristics of a business that determine its ability to raise capital.

LO3 Know how to choose the right type of financing for your business.

LO4 Understand the differing needs for financial management at each stage of business life.

■ Dr. Mary Pat Moyer, pictured here, began INCELL Corporation in 1993 with her husband, Jim Janowiak. Though continually challenged by the financial needs of their company, Mary Pat and Jim are slowly but surely reaping the benefits of their substantial personal investments. Why do you think INCELL has stayed away from enlisting venture capitalists, even knowing firsthand the significant personal responsibilities this course of action entails? In their shoes, would you do the same?

CHAPTER 15

Small Business Finance: Using Equity, Debt, and Gifts

Focus on Small Business: Dr. Mary Pat Moyer and INCELL Corporation

Dr. Mary Pat Moyer ("Call me 'Mary Pat,'" she says.) knows firsthand the availability and value of nontraditional financing sources for small businesses. She has used both nontraditional and traditional means to finance the founding and growth of her successful biotech business, INCELL Corporation.

"I've used my own savings, borrowed from banks and credit card companies, and obtained grants from both the U.S. government and the state of Texas. If I had depended solely on the traditional sources of investment for small businesses—angel, seed, and venture capitalists—INCELL would not have survived its first year." "In fact," Mary Pat continued, "INCELL may be the only biotech in the world to be bootstrapped."

In 1993, after 20 years as an academic scientist, Mary Pat resigned from her tenured professorship at the University of Texas Health Science Center at San Antonio to start INCELL Corporation in partnership with her husband, Jim Janowiak. Today, INCELL is a successful small business that has 14 full-time employees.

http://www.incell.com

INCELL's success has come at a greater personal cost in both time and money than Mary Pat and Jim originally expected. As do many entrepreneurs who start firms based on prior successes as academics or executives, they initially underestimated the difficulties of managing the finances of a small business.

Mary Pat said, "After all, I reasoned, just how hard can financial management be for a Ph.D. in microbiology? Besides, I also had 'an ace up my sleeve.' Jim is a CPA with long experience in business management."

Jim agreed, "I'd worked with many businesses, both large and small. If I could do their accounting, prepare their financial statements, and provide business advice, certainly I could do these things for myself."

To their chagrin, they soon realized that financial management for an entrepreneurial business is very different from either academic microbiology or public accounting practice.

"At first, INCELL was 100 percent funded from our personal savings. From day one we bootstrapped growth by carefully using personal credit cards, accounts payable, and revenues from sales. We 'played the game' by collecting as fast as we could and paying as slowly as our personal ethics would allow. Still, we barely scraped by. Finally, about a year after INCELL was started, we received our first Small Business Innovation Research grant from the National Institute of Health. Since then, we have received over $2 million in seven additional grants. Although we've been able to keep afloat ever since, there have been those times that we've wondered whether or not we'd be able to meet the current week's payroll," Mary Pat said. "So far, with careful planning, the grace of God, and plain old good luck, we've managed."

Jim said, "Many times Mary Pat and I have worked a series of 60 hour weeks because we did not have the money to pay an employee. Still, we'd do it again. We've had to do without personally from time to time, but we've never missed a meal. Of course, when you own the business, you pay your employees first, your suppliers second, and then if there is anything left over, you might be able to pay yourself."

"Our problem right now is one of too much success, if there is such a thing!" Mary Pat said. "We have a product in human clinical trials in conjunction with Johns Hopkins, and we just signed a contract with the U.S. Air Force to begin the testing of our oral smallpox vaccine. Each of these projects will require that we raise significant additional funds. Where the business is right now, it either grows or it fails."

In an effort to meet INCELL's funding needs, for the last year Mary Pat has been making the rounds of venture capitalists. To date, she has not been successful in obtaining needed investment.

"I've been to Philadelphia, Orange County, San Francisco, even Ft. Atkinson, Wisconsin—pretty much everywhere in the U.S. where there are venture capitalists specializing in biotech and pharmaceuticals. And I've not raised a penny, at least not at a price we're willing to pay! We have given up on the venture capital route for now," she said. "While a venture capital investment seemed like an easy way to raise growth funds, the interest rates and amount of equity that were demanded were much, much too high. Instead, we are working with the Air Force, the Texas Department of Economic Development, the San Antonio Economic Development Department, and a regional commercial bank to put together a financing package. The package will include direct grants, tax abatement, tax increment financing, and commercial loans secured with buildings and equipment. The terms of the package will require that we create a specified number of new jobs, provide job training opportunities, and, of course, repay the loans with interest."

http://www.tded.state.tx.us/

http://www.sanantonio.gov/edd/

In the meanwhile, INCELL continues to increase sales of its current products and to work as both a contract research organization and as a development partner for other biotech firms.

The revenue from these activities provides funds to pay rent, payroll, and the many expenses of an operating biotech business.

"Financial management is a daily, constant, on-going process for INCELL," Jim said. "We regularly remind ourselves that every dollar must be made to work. We do not tolerate any waste, because we quite simply cannot afford to do so."

"We work hard. We have fun. We hire wonderful people," Mary Pat said. "We try to keep a spiritual center and a sense of humor—and we never, never, never give up!"

DISCUSSION QUESTIONS

1. What did Dr. Moyer mean when she said, "INCELL may be the only biotech in the world to be bootstrapped"?
2. In what ways does financial management for small start-up businesses differ from that of academic organizations and businesses?
3. What problems are created by "too much success"?
4. What did Dr. Moyer mean when she said, "We've not raised a penny, at least not at a price we're willing to pay!"?
5. How can raising money from venture capitalists be said to be expensive?

Sources of Financing for Small Businesses

LO1
Know the three types of capital financing and their costs and trade-offs.

Getting the money to start or grow a business seems like one of the greatest challenges, but in reality most people report they find the means to get their business going. There are two reasons for this. The first reason relates to ourselves. Financing is often easier than people think at first, because most of us have many assets and financial resources that we take for granted. Second, the range of financing resources available to us is so varied that few people just starting out in business know more than a fraction of the options available to them. The more you learn about your personal finances and the financing options, the greater your chances of finding the financing you need to start your business.

However, getting money to start is only the tip of the iceberg of finance for small businesses. Once you have started your business, you must continually work to keep up a constant flow of money and capital assets to meet the strategic and operating goals of your business. As Jim Janowiak of INCELL Corporation said, constant, careful management of money and other capital resources is essential for success throughout the existence of any business. A business's needs for financial management change as the business develops, as economic conditions vary, and as your needs and goals change. Although the details of financial management are unique to each business, there are patterns that can be seen as a business develops from start-up to exit. We examine these patterns, first getting money for start-up and growth and second using strategic financial management to reach your goals.

Where *does* financing come from for most small businesses? The number one source is from the owners (or potential owners) themselves. The other major sources include family and friends, credit cards, trade credit, banks, and other commercial lenders. There are also a number of other sources that exist but are used very rarely. These include angel investors, government programs, community-based financiers, stock sales, and venture capital. Table 15.1 gives you an idea about how often these different forms of financing are used by small business.

TABLE 15.1 Financing for Small Business by Phase, Type, and Source

	Sources of Capital Financing		
Phase of Business/ Financial Management Need	**Debt Financing**	**Equity Financing**	**Gift Financing**
Financing for start-ups Profits are secondary to cash flow Need cash to pay employees Need cash to pay suppliers Need cash to live on	Consumer banks Commercial banks SBA insured loans Economic development agencies Small business investment companies Incubators Accelerators Leasing companies Personal credit cards	Friends, family, and "fools" Angels Venture capital Public stock offerings	Institutional: Grants don't exist for startups Personal: Cash, picking up the tab, accelerated cash-outs, free use, free work/unpaid labor, overpayment, favored status/sweetheart deals, forgiveness, deferral, piggybacking
Financing for growth Profits consistent with risk levels Funds for investment in equipment Cash for marketing Cash for building inventory levels	Commercial banks Small Business Administration Private placement loans Economic development agencies Small business investment companies Suppliers Leasing companies Personal credit cards	Self-generated funds Venture capital Public sale of stock Mergers Acquisitions	Institutional: SBIR, STTR grants State grants Incubators, accelerators Donated capital Tax abatement Personal: Same as for start-ups
Financing for operations Profits consistent with risk Build owner wealth Cash flow "smoothing" Reinvestment for maintenance	Factor receivables Business credit cards Commercial banks Small Business Administration Private placement loans Suppliers Leasing companies	Self-generated funds Venture capital Public sale of stock	Institutional: Same as for growth Personal: Same as for start-ups
Financing for exit Investing to build equity and firm value Reinvestment to replace worn assets New technology Productivity Quality	Consumer banks Commercial banks Small Business Administration Private placement loans Economic development agencies Small Business investment companies Suppliers Leasing companies Lines of credit	Self-generated funds Venture capital Public sale of stock	Institutional: Same as for growth Personal: Same as for start-ups

Table 15.1 lists sources of financing as debt, equity, and gifts. **Debt** can take many forms. A business may borrow money directly from banks, development agencies, governments, or individuals. When you sell part of your business, the money you receive is **equity capital**. Any valuable assets or services, including money, that are donated to your business without any obligation to repay or to give any ownership interest, is a **gift**. Each of these three types of financing requires a different approach, which we cover below as we give you the details on the three different forms of financing.

debt
A legal obligation to pay money in the future.

equity capital
Money contributed to the businesses in return for part ownership of the business.

gift
Valuable assets or services donated to the business without any obligation to repay or any ownership interest.

Which of these financing sources is right for you? The answer depends largely on whether you are trying to start a new business or are trying to get financing for an existing business. Existing businesses have a track record of financial performance, which lets investors and lenders make better guesses about the firm's ability to pay back a loan or pay off an investment. This means that more forms of financing are available to existing firms than to start-ups. Even when the same form of financing is available to start-ups and existing firms, existing firms that are profitable or have made profits in the recent past are likely to get better terms for debt or equity. They may pay a lower interest rate on debt or give up a smaller part of ownership.

We start with gift capital because for most businesses the owner is one of the first sources of funds they consider. Then we consider equity capital and conclude with a look at **debt capital**. After that, we look at some of the decisions entrepreneurs make in the financing process.

debt capital
Money borrowed for the purpose of investment in a business.

Gift Financing

Gift financing has a special allure. It seems to many people like getting something for nothing. The impression might be that a government or a foundation hands out money that never has to be repaid, or a family member magnanimously offers a present at just the right time. It is unfortunate that anything that seems too good to be true, usually is. Gift capital is often anything but free. Often it costs time and money to obtain; and it often requires time and money for accounting and reporting to the granting agency, family members, and government. There are two general sources of gift financing: one is institutional, from government agencies and foundations, and the other is personal, from family or occasionally from friends.

Institutional Gifts

The most common form of institutional gift financing is in the form of reduced taxes, either through tax abatement or in the form of a credit against taxes payable. It does seem a misnomer to call reducing the amount taken from a business a gift, but as taxes are a cash cost to businesses, reducing tax burden has the same effect as receiving that same amount of cash would have.

Farmers receive gift financing from the U.S. government in the form of direct cash payments and price subsidies for not planting crops, for planting cereal grains, apples (but not peaches), cotton, tobacco, and a plethora of other crops, for raising mohair goats, and for producing lamb meat and dairy products. Payments for not growing crops are made through a program called "conservation reserve payments," in which farmers contract to not plant specified plots of erosion-prone land for a specific number of years. Direct subsidies and price supports are made through numerous programs, including payments for wetlands protection.

Tax abatements are provided by state and local governments, primarily to encourage specific activities that are expected to improve blighted areas or to provide additional employment. Most governments that impose a tax on real estate have some form of tax reduction to encourage rehabilitating old dwellings, providing housing for low-income citizens, and maintaining buildings that are deemed to be historic. Tax abatements can take many forms, depending upon the type of taxes that are imposed.

tax abatement
A legal reduction in taxes by a government.

Tax credits are provided by the U.S. and some state governments for the purpose of encouraging investment in specific types of assets, to increase economic activity in

tax credits
Direct reductions in the amount of taxes that must be paid, dependent upon meeting some legal criteria.

THE THOUGHTFUL ENTREPRENEUR

When Uncle Sam Is a Soft Touch

It is hard to even begin to grasp how many government tax abatement programs exist. They are provided to businesses both large and small.

Many small businesses have taken advantage of the U.S. government's program that encourages building low-income housing and rebuilding historic structures through reduced income taxes.

The city of Kansas City, Missouri, once forgave all property tax on Trans World Airlines' aircraft overhaul facilities.

Right now, the city of San Antonio, Texas, and Bexar County agreed to forego property taxes on a new Toyota pickup truck factory. In addition, the state of Texas, Bexar County, and San Antonio together are contributing over $23 million for the building of an 8-mile-long railroad spur from the main railroad line to the Toyota factory site.

The city of Albuquerque, New Mexico, arranged a three-way trade for city property which resulted in Eclipse Aviation (a small business of only 175 employees) receiving the gift of 150 acres of land.

Homestead, Florida, has established an enterprise zone in which there are property tax abatements, a direct refund of sales taxes, direct credits of property tax up to $50,000, as well as tax credits for job creation. Portland, Maine, offers tax increment and tax-exempt bond financing for firms that will relocate to the area.

Provo, Utah, is spending $7 million of tax money to build a new rendering[1] plant some distance from town. The city council explained this gift by pointing out that moving the plant would remove a source of unpleasant odors from the city, while keeping the taxes from the plant, which employs several hundred people.

specified disadvantaged geographical areas, increase the welfare of specific groups of citizens, or support industries that are held to be of national strategic interest. Credits provided include those for empowerment zone employment, employing (American) Indians, purchasing electric automobiles, or using ethyl alcohol for fuel. The list of available tax credits and the details of how to claim them is too voluminous to reproduce in this text. Also, the credits change with each Congress, and thus any specific information would be sorely out of date by the time this text is published.

grants
Gifts of money made to a business for a specific purpose.

Grants of money are available from the U.S. government, most state governments, and semiprivate and private economic development agencies. The purpose of the grants varies with the entity that makes the grant. U.S. grant programs for small business are primarily a response to political pressure brought upon Congress. The stated purpose of the grant programs is to encourage development of small businesses, thereby increasing the economic activity of the country. Various states also have grant programs. As with the federal program, the rationale for providing grants to small business is to increase economic activity, provide job growth, and provide increases in the overall standard of living of the citizens of the state.

Grants from governments are highly structured and require very accurate record keeping and reporting. Agencies that issue grants first publish a request for proposal (RFP) that specifies the conditions of the grant. Interested small businesses may then create a proposal, which must be submitted by the specified date and time, in the *exact* format specified. Grant proposals are then judged in a "blind" process. Winning proposals receive notification within about 30 days and funding within 6 months.

The two largest governmental grant programs that are specifically intended for small business are (1) the Small Business Innovation Research (SBIR) program and the Small Business Technology Transfer (STTR) program. These two programs require that every U.S. agency that makes research grants provide a minimum of 2 percent of its grant budget to small businesses, as defined by the SBA. Two percent may not sound like much, but in 2002, the SBIR program resulted in over $1.5 *billion* in grants made to participating small businesses. These programs are each three-phase programs. A winning proposal will initially receive about $100,000 to conduct a feasibility study, as detailed in the grant proposal. Depending upon successful completion, additional funds, which can range up into millions of dollars, are provided for stage II and stage III activities.

Grant programs vary widely among the states. As with federal programs, the agency that provides the grant will publish a request for proposal. Proposals are competitively judged, and only the best written proposals, which meet each and every requirement of the RFP ever receive funding. Accurate record keeping and timely reports are essential to maintain the right to use the grant money.

Finding SBIR Grants

SKILL MODULE 15.1

What kind of business are you interested in? Do you have any new ideas or procedures for this business that might lead to better ways of solving problems of health, national security, threats of terrorism, or any other area in which the U.S. government has an interest?

If you do, there is probably an SBIR grant for you.

Assume that you have come up with an idea that might result in stopping would-be terrorists at airports outside the United States. Your idea, if it works, will stop terrorists from getting to the United States in the first place. Do a Google search:

Follow the leads returned by Google (more than 10,000) to identify agencies and programs that will provide funds through SBIR grants for ideas that might help national security.

1. Write a report of your findings to be presented to your class.
2. Use the skill you have now developed to find an SBIR grant that would apply to a business that you are actually interested in starting.

economic development agency A government organization that works to increase economic activity in the form of job opportunities within a specific geographic area.

foundation An institution to which private wealth is contributed and from which private wealth is distributed for public purposes.

Economic Development Agency (EDA) grants are much less common than are those from general governments. Most economic development agencies prefer to provide loans rather than providing equity capital or gift capital. However, from time to time, EDAs will either provide direct grants or will assist small business owners in obtaining grants from other agencies.

Grants from foundations are rarely made to for-profit businesses. Foundations exist for the purpose of addressing some identified social need that cannot be adequately met by market forces. The Ewing Marion Kauffman Foundation supports *education* and *research* concerning entrepreneurship and small business. The Ford Foundation supports the arts, including public television programs. The Rotary Foundation supports efforts to eradicate hunger and polio worldwide. All these foundations were founded by successful entrepreneurs and business managers, but they do not specifically support the start up, expansion, or operation of for-profit enterprises. Rather, their (and those of about 30,000 other private foundations) missions clearly state that grants are made to nonprofit organizations.

However, occasionally private foundations will make grants to for-profit businesses, *if the purpose of the grant is to address some goal of the foundation.* If your business is such that it addresses a pernicious social problem, then you may be able to find private foundation grant funding for specific, limited projects.

Personal Gifts

While the type of gifts governments and foundations offer are relatively consistent, stable, and publicly known, the forms of personal gifts are as varied as human imagination

FIGURE 15.1

Forms of Personal Gifts

Cash—always useful, but also the gift most likely to have tax implications.

Picking up the tab—when someone buys something on behalf of your business and lets you benefit from it.

Accelerated cash-outs—where you might be given the funds for your business from an account your family set up for your future education or first home. Some cash-outs come when family or friends cash out their retirements or home (often via taking out a mortgage).

Free use—your family has an empty storefront, apartment, van, car, or other useful product which they let you use for free, or at a severely reduced price, for your business.

Free work—you get family or friends to help you out in the business for free, or for pizzas and drinks, or for wages significantly below minimum wage. This is sometimes called **unpaid labor.**

Overpayment—where family or friends "hire" you at higher than market rates, to help you generate cash for your business. A variant of this is **favored status** or **sweetheart deals** where family or friends give you contracts to help you fund your business, instead of giving their work to the most qualified candidate.

Forgiveness—where family or friends give up on collecting debts you owe them, so you can use the money for the business. A variant of this is **deferral,** where the repayment of debts is delayed until the business is doing well.

Piggybacking—where family or friends let you add (i.e., piggyback) your purchases with theirs in order to get lower prices.

and need can make them. Remember from Chapter 14 that not just money has value; goods and services can provide tremendous value to a start-up business. The most popular forms of gifts are shown in Figure 15.1.

Personal gift financing is tremendously popular. In the Panel Study of Income Dynamics,[2] fully one-third of the firms reported having unpaid labor contributed by family members. In business plan classes, the same one out of three ratio of personal gifts to start-ups in general is a fairly common occurrence. These gifts range dramatically in size, but the commonality of personal gifts as a major source of funding for start-ups is fairly well known.[3]

Gift giving seems so easy and straightforward that it is hard to imagine how complex it really is—for the giver and the recipient, as well as the business. Consider gifts from the standpoint of the recipient and then the giver.

You are trying to get your business off the ground, and your favorite uncle offers to provide you with start-up capital. Not just any start-up capital, not an investment, not a loan. He is going to *give* you that boost that you need to get into business. It is an entrepreneur's dream—capital without any strings.

Do you take the money? Not so fast. The simple fact is that although Freud may have believed that "sometimes a cigar is just a cigar"[4] you can bet that a gift is *always* much, much more than just a gift. Gifts are loaded with special meanings and hidden purposes. Robert Cialdini wrote that gifts "create and cement alliances, allegiances, and partnerships."[5] Are you ready to enter into an alliance or partnership with your beloved uncle?

Accepting money from family members and friends entails some real risks. That favorite uncle might really mean it when he says that he is *giving* you start-up capital. But gifts like this have a nasty way of morphing into very real expectations that you may quickly come to hate. Meanings, especially in spoken messages, are slippery little devils. Your uncle may well be saying "gift" but thinking "loan," or "investment." If you are successful, you may suddenly find that the "gift" has now transformed (at least in your uncle's mind) into something very different. So here you stand—you *accepted* a gift, but your uncle *gave* you a loan.

Lawsuits are made of just such differences of opinion.

Accepting gifts is difficult for many people. Especially when the gift is substantial. Before you accept your uncle's offer, you should examine your own feelings. Can you accept a gift? Or do you have some secret plan that you will repay the money when you become successful? If you do not like being beholding to anyone, you probably should think twice about accepting an outright gift. Taking one most likely will lead to guilty feelings and resentment.

No need to immediately refuse your uncle's offer, but you should be absolutely certain that both you and he understand just what is being given and just what is expected in return.

Now turn the example on its head. Assume now that you are the uncle who is going to give a gift of cash to your favorite niece to start her business.

Do you just write out a check and forget it? If you wish to keep your niece as a favorite, you probably shouldn't. Giving a gift is risky, just as is receiving one. Any gifts that you make had better be equitable among those who expect to receive from you. It is a simple fact that brothers, sisters, nieces, and nephews all expect to be treated fairly by their parents, grandparents, aunts, and uncles. Overtly favor one heir, and you will trigger resentment in all the others.

Giving a gift also has tax implications. Currently, any gift that exceeds $11,000 may be subject to U.S. Gift Taxes. Depending upon the size of the gift, and your own situation, current gift taxes can be as high as 47 percent of the amount given. So if you are planning to finance your niece's start-up with $500,000, you'll probably need some creative financial planning to avoid the tax implications.

You should carefully consider just why you want to make this gift. Perhaps you are one of those very rare people who are true Santa Clauses: You get real satisfaction from giving away your wealth. This is unlikely, however. Komter and Vollebergh showed that gifts given to extended kin are usually made because of feelings of obligation and rarely because of feelings of affection.[6] Probably, you are expecting to receive gratitude. If so, you'll more than likely be disappointed. Or do you think that your niece's business idea is the next Microsoft and that your support will result in untold wealth? In this case, you should not make your support a gift. Structure it as an investment in her business—make it a loan or a purchase of stock.

Given the many problems of gift giving, should you change your mind about supporting your niece's new business?

No, but you should understand exactly what you are giving, and what you expect in return. You should also be sure that your niece also understands.

For both of you to be certain that you agree, you should:

■ Even when gifts are given to help a family member or friend's business, common sense and clear communication are essential. Make sure both parties understand and assent to what exactly is being given, under which conditions, and with what kind, if any, of repayment plan.

1. **Put your agreement into writing.** As is said in Mexico, "Words walk. Paper talks." This has the same message as the saying, "Oral agreements are just as valuable as the paper they're written on!" There simply is no better way to be certain that everyone understands a transaction than to write it out, then have each party read, sign, and date the document. When disagreements arise later, the written agreement provides a permanent, immutable record of your original intentions.
2. **If it is a gift, have the agreement specifically say so.** "This is a gift, freely given between uncle (grantor) and you (recipient). No repayment is expected, and none will be accepted."
3. **If it is a loan, have the agreement specify the exact interest and payment terms.** A good idea from the point of view of the recipient is to make repayment a percentage of positive cash flows. Ideally, payments will be made either (a) until the principal amount plus accrued interest has been paid or (b) until the giver has received a specified return on the original amount. In the real world, loans between family members often go unpaid. Be clear concerning the circumstances under which the loan will be forgiven.

4. **If it is an equity investment, consider nonvoting stock.** One common problem with family and friends as equity investors is that they want to have a say in the management of your business. This may be fine if they have appropriate talents and experience. It can be a kiss of death if they just want to meddle. Nonvoting stock provides the opportunity for capital gains, but pretty much precludes interference in business operations.

Financing with Equity

Equity can come from the entrepreneur or from others. In general the entrepreneurs' own pockets are the first source of financing for most businesses, especially after they consider the risks and problems with gift capital. Because of this, understanding your own financial situation and the opportunities available to free up personal capital for use in your business become the foundation for any effort to finance using equity.

Personal Equity

How much are you worth? How is that value held? Often people underestimate their personal worth, because many parts of their wealth are seen or thought about only occasionally—such as retirement funds—or because they use it so much that they forget about it having value, like a car, home, or personal collection. But when starting a business, knowing your personal wealth is critical to your ability to fund yourself. Also if you plan to get investments or loans from other people or banks, they may ask to see your personal financial statements to understand *your* commitment to the business. Skill Module 15.2 has you determine your personal financial situation.

SKILL MODULE 15.2

Determining Personal Net Worth

Use the worksheet below to determine your personal net worth. You may either copy the form or go to the Web site for this text, **www.mhhe.com/katzesb**, and download it in Excel format. Enter into the column labeled "Cash Value" the amount of money you could get if you were to sell what you own. Enter into the next column any amount that you owe to pay off your debt on the item. Then, in the third column, enter the difference between what you could sell it for and what you owe on it (the difference could be a negative number). After you have listed all that you own and all that you owe, the difference is what you are worth financially.

Lenders and investors usually require that you furnish a personal net worth statement. You can find two different common formats for the report on the text Web site.

	Cash Value (A)	Amount Owed (B)	Net Value (A − B)
Cash			
Your personal checking account		0	
Your spouse's checking account		0	
Other checking accounts you own		0	
Money in all savings accounts		0	
Cash value of money market account		0	
Total money in other accounts		0	
TOTAL CASH			
Cash Equivalents			
Cash value of stocks owned (net of selling commissions)			
Cash value of bonds owned			
Cash value of annuity			

	Cash Value (A)	Amount Owed (B)	Net Value (A − B)
Cash value of IRAs			
Cash value of other retirement funds			
Cash value of life insurance			
TOTAL CASH EQUIVALENTS			
Personal Property			
Automobile 1			
Automobile 2			
Motorcycle			
Bicycles			
Personal watercraft			
Boat and motor			
Airplane			
Guns and rifles			
Cameras			
Sports equipment (binoculars, skis, parachutes, etc.)			
Art and collectibles			
Antiques			
Jewelry			
Shop tools			
Furniture			
TOTAL PERSONAL PROPERTY			
Real Estate			
Primary dwelling			
Second or vacation home			
Lot at the lake			
Farms, ranches, development property			
Houses, duplexes, apartment buildings that you rent to others			
Business lots and commercial buildings			
TOTAL REAL ESTATE			
Intangible Assets			
Copyrights on books, songs, videos, movies, etc., that you own			
Patents you own			
Trademarks			
URLs			
TOTAL INTANGIBLE ASSETS			
Unsecured Debt			
American Express credit card	0		
Master Card 1	0		
Master Card 2	0		
Visa card 1	0		
Visa card 2	0		
Discover card	0		
Unsecured loan from credit union	0		
Unsecured loan from bank	0		
Loan from your brother-in-law	0		
TOTALS			

outside equity
Money from selling part of your business to people who are not and will not be involved in the management of the business.

partnership
Two or more people cooperating to conduct a business enterprise.

corporation
A legal "artificial" entity that is formed by filing specific documents with a state government.

limited liability company (LLC)
A legal form of business organization that is created by filing required documentation with a state government. LLCs have a choice, under federal tax law, of being taxed as either corporations or partnerships.

limited partnership
A legal form of business organization that is created by filing required documentation with a state government; within a limited partnership, one or more partners may have no liability for the debts and actions of the partnership.

Outside Equity

Outside equity is money from selling part of your business to people who are not and will not be involved in the management of the business. People who buy ownership rights in your business are considered ***outside equity investors.***

- *Outside* because they are not part of the management of your business.
- *Equity* because they have legal ownership rights to your business.
- *Investors* because they are letting you use their money now in order to get wealth in the future.

You can sell ownership in your business only if your business is organized as one of three broad types of legal forms of business: a **partnership**, a **corporation**, or a **limited liability company**. We start the discussion of legal forms of business here, because the choice of legal form does make a difference in taxation, a critical issue in your efforts to secure financing. The other legal factors driving the choice of a form of organization are discussed later in Chapter 18 on small business law.

The decision of which type of business organization is best for you depends on a lot of factors, including tax treatment, business conduct, and legal liabilities. There are seven forms of organization commonly used by small businesses: sole proprietorship, general partnership, **limited partnership**, C-corporation, limited liability company, professional corporation, and S-corporation. You may need a different form of business organization at different times as your business grows and develops. A detailed comparison of the seven forms is given in Table 18.4 in Chapter 18, but two of the factors are introduced here because they are relevant to financing a business. (See Table 15.2.)

Businesses are either taxed as entities or the revenues and expenses of the business are "passed-through" to the owners who report them on their individual income tax forms. Limited Liability Companies (LLCs) are a relatively new form of organization whose primary advantage is that owners may easily choose whether to be taxed as an entity or have tax items pass through. Corporations, S-corporations, and partnerships have no choice of tax treatment.

In general, all the forms of business organization can be categorized along two dimensions (1) how much responsibility owners have for the organization's liabilities, and (2) how the business is taxed. In business and in law, responsibility is called *liability.* In terms of the form of the organization, the amount of responsibility (liability) the owners personally face for the debts of the business can be all or "none." If the owners have *all* of the responsibility for business debts, they are *fully liable,* and they face the potential of having to pay business debts from their own wealth. If the owners bear *none* of

TABLE 15.2 Legal Forms of Business Organization

	Taxed as an Entity	Tax Passed Through to Owners
Owners personally liable for debts and actions of the business		Sole proprietorship General partnership
Owners *not* personally liable for debts and actions of the business	C-Corporation LLC	S-corporation Professional corporation Limited partnership LLC

the responsibility for the business debts, they have *limited liability,* and may lose only what they have invested in the business, and not any other assets they own. Business organizations that provide limited liability are corporations, limited partnerships, and LLCs. However in limited partnerships, at least one partner, the *general partner,* is fully liable. In general partnerships all partners are fully liable as is the owner of a sole proprietorship, who is completely responsible for all debts of the business.

Sole proprietorships are not separate from their owners, and thus there is no specific documentation that creates their existence. The business and the owner are inseparable. Similarly, partnerships do not *have* to have a written agreement. If they don't, then they are assumed to be equally owned by the partners. However, partnerships may have a written partnership agreement covering key issues such as ownership, profit splits, buyouts, and other matters important to the partners. Thus partnerships may or may not be separate from their owners, depending upon the provisions in the written partnership agreement and the laws of the state in which they are formed. Corporations, and limited liability companies, are required by law to file specific forms with the state in which they are organized. Ownership of corporations is established by stock certificates. Ownership of partnerships is determined by partnership share agreements. Ownership of limited liability companies is shown by member share certificates.

sole proprietorship
A business owned by a single individual who is responsible for all debts and claims against the business.

Getting Equity Investment for Your Business

LO2
Understand the characteristics of a business that determine its ability to raise capital.

Small businesses get started and stay in business because their owners want to make money. Investors want to make money, too. Lenders expect a return on this money from making loans, by getting back the amount they had plus more money in the form of interest. In the same way, people invest in a business to get back the money they invest plus extra money, a gain on investment or a dividend. Governments also expect their gifts of grants and tax abatements to make a return for the people they represent. The only difference is that governments expect to be repaid in the form of the owner creating more jobs and paying more taxes. When a business succeeds and grows, it contributes to the *economic development* of an area.

Look at it from the investors' point of view. They have money to invest. They may lend it or put it to work by buying a share in someone's business. They do this to make money, so they want to invest in a business that will succeed and thereby provide them with returns. But of course, all businesses are not equal. Every year thousands of people start new restaurants. Every year, thousands go out of business. Of all the businesses that they could invest in, how do they choose the right one?

One way to decide is by analyzing the business's prospects. Investors want to know just how likely the business is to succeed and produce a gain. In other words, they want to know the business's risk. Unfortunately, they can't see risk directly, so they have to look at other things that are associated with risk. Investors know that some of their investments will fail. They just don't know exactly which ones. To protect themselves from losing everything, they diversify—invest in several businesses so that the ones that do succeed provide gains that more than offset the losses from those that don't.

Thus to get money from other people, you've got to show them that your business probably can make gains for them. Of course, you're not the only one looking for those investment dollars. You have to convince them that your business is a better place for their dollars than some other business. You do this by promising high enough gains. The minimum potential gain necessary to get someone to invest in your business depends mostly on the amount of risk they are taking by purchasing part of your business. Your investors could put their money into a bank savings account earning 2 percent, a CD earning 5 percent, or a government bond earning 3.25 percent. For these there is no risk at all.[7] Corporate bonds might offer higher rates of return, but they also offer a higher

interest
A charge for the use of money, usually figured as a percentage of the principal.

dividends
Payments of profits to the owners of corporations.

gain on investment
The percentage amount that the payout of an investment differs from original cost: calculated as (payout − investment + dividends)/investment.

risk
The level of probability that an investment will not produce expected gains.

diversify
To invest in multiple investments of differing risk profiles for the purpose of reducing overall investment risk.

risk of default—think of Enron, WorldCom, or other corporate failures. The riskier the business investment, the higher the return investors expect. Most investors, certainly those who aren't your parents, insist that they take no risk other than the potential loss of their investment. To ensure that nothing other than their investment is at risk, they will invest only if your business is organized to limit the liability of outside owners.

To estimate how much gain they might get from investing in your business, investors consider the growth potential of your business, how long it will take for them to see a return on their investment, and the options they have to receive back the original investment and their gains.

Growth potential is a primary concern for equity investors. Equity investors buy part of a "pie" of a known size. The more slices into which the pie is cut, the smaller each slice is, unless somehow the pie can be made larger. For this reason, it is much easier to get equity financing to develop a new factory to make flexible liquid crystal displays or to produce a treatment for obesity than it is to get someone to invest in a lawn care business in a city of 50,000 people. Lawn care in a small city has a limit to its growth, but there are millions and millions of computer users and overweight people who want to be slim.

The time required to receive gains can be a deal killer for potential investors. The longer they have to wait, the greater their risk that the business will fail. Also, all other things being equal, an investment that pays sooner is more profitable than one that pays later. Consider two simple situations. You are going to sell 25 percent of your business for $100,000. Your deal with the investor is that you will buy his or her share back at the end of one year for $150,000. In the second situation, you agree to buy back the investor's share for $150,000 in two years. Investors in the first case realize a 50 percent gain on investment, but investors in the second realize only 22 percent.[8] Waiting an extra year reduces the rate of gain by more than half.

Arrangements for paying gains to owners is an essential, but often ignored, facet of small business finance. Once more than one person owns equity in a small business, it *cannot* be a sole proprietorship. By law, lacking any specific legal business filings, it instantly becomes a general partnership. By making a legal filing, the business entity may become a limited partnership, a corporation, or a limited liability company. Regardless of what business form you choose, the issue of how to pay the owners is suddenly much more complex. Issues arise because of tax considerations, fairness to investors, and compensation for manager-owners. There is certainly no one right way to provide for returning gains to owners. It can take the form of salaries, stipends for serving on the board of directors, dividends, or stock repurchases. In those few cases in which a small business becomes a large business, equity investors often realize their gains by selling stock. Having a plan in place greatly aids in the process of acquiring outside equity capital.

From the point of view of an existing owner, financing with equity is (1) expensive and (2) guaranteed to create problems of control and decision making.

Equity capital is not free, as many entrepreneurs think. Suppose you sell half your business to raise capital. You have just sold half of all your future profits, half of all your future growth, half of all your future wealth. If, on the other hand, you were to borrow the money, your cost will be only the cost of acquiring the loan and making interest payments. In addition, owners of your business (even those who own only a small part) have a legal right to know how you're managing *their* business. As a matter of fact, most equity investors in small businesses insist upon having the right to inspect the accounting records *at any time they choose*. Once you accept equity investors, you will find that you'll have to keep careful records of transactions, and you'll have to make regular reports to your investors. If those investors disagree with your running of the business, they can challenge your decisions, even to the point of suing you for supposed damages, or replacing you as manager. Many, many entrepreneurs have found themselves forced out of their own businesses by minority equity investors.

So, if getting outsiders to invest in your business is so complicated, why do it? There are two primary reasons why: (1) you will reduce your own exposure to financial loss, and (2) your business will not have increased costs in the form of interest. Also, bringing outside investors into an existing business can often reenergize it by providing new ideas, procedures, and processes.

Financing with Debt: Getting a Loan for Your Business

The most common source of capital for established ongoing small businesses is borrowed funds. This is the case for several reasons, including all the reasons discussed above, and the simple fact that small businesses do not have easy access to equity financing through organized stock exchanges. Additionally, national, state, and local governments all encourage small business borrowing. This is done in three ways: (1) direct loans of cash, (2) guaranteeing loans made by commercial banks, and (3) reducing taxes by allowing interest to be deducted. However, when it comes to borrowing significant amounts of money, all firms are not created equal. Established businesses that have valuable assets that are separable from the owners are able to borrow more easily than are start-up or knowledge businesses.

So, where can a small business actually get loans to start and grow? As you might expect, your best source is the bank where you are currently doing business. After all, it is in the business of making loans. You are a customer. As such, you are a known commodity—you pay your bills, you keep your account balance positive, you don't bounce checks. Start where you're known.

But if your bank turns you down, you are not out of luck. In fact, in the Small Business Administration guaranteed loan programs, you *must* be turned down by a bank before you qualify. So, maybe your bank did you a favor. Having been turned down, you can apply for an SBA guaranteed loan. Through this avenue, you will still borrow from your own bank, but the SBA will guarantee the bank that if your business fails, the SBA will pay off your loan. Other sources for SBA guaranteed loans include community development organizations, and for small loans, *microlenders*.

A third source of SBA guaranteed loans is the numerous small business investment companies (SBIC). A directory of SBICs is maintained on the SBA Web site: http://www.sba.gov/INV/index.html. You can access the listing by clicking on the appropriate state on the map presented on the site. The directory provides not only a list of active SBICs, but also an outline of the business requirements.

You may also have access to *incubators* or accelerators in your area. These organizations exist solely for the purpose of facilitating the start up and growth of new businesses. They provide advice for finding loans, and, in some cases, have the ability to make loans to member businesses.

The main things that lenders want to see before they give businesses their money are the Four Cs of Borrowing, listed here and shown in Figure 15.2:

1. Character of the managers of the business.
2. Capacity of the business to repay both principal and interest on time.
3. Conditions of the industry and economy in which the business operates.
4. Collateral that can be used to secure the loan.

community development organization
An organization authorized by the SBA to make insured loans to small businesses that are expected to increase economic activity within a specific geographic area.

small business investment companies
Private businesses that are authorized to make SBA insured loans to start-ups and small businesses.

accelerator
An organization that supports start-up technology businesses by providing inexpensive office space, a variety of support services, and resources; most accelerators are associated with universities.

Character of the managers of the business.	**Capacity** of the business to repay both principal and interest on time.
Conditions of the industry and economy in which the business operates.	**Collateral** that can be used to secure the loan.

FIGURE 15.2

The Four Cs of Borrowing

No matter how you have organized your business, the bank is going to look at it as an extension of you. The simple fact is that you have the power to make decisions, good or bad, about all facets of operation regardless of its form, whether sole proprietorship, partnership, or corporation. Thus, although technically the loan may be made to the business entity, from the point of view of the lender, a loan is not made to a small business, a loan is made to the *owner* of a small business. The owner's character and business reputation are important considerations for lenders when they decide whether or not to let a business have money.

Owner character is judged largely by the owner's personal credit rating and by that of the business. All lenders want some assurance that a loan will be repaid as agreed. There are several private agencies called consumer **credit reporting agencies** (CRAs) which exist solely to collect, collate, and report the credit histories of individuals and businesses. Lenders pay a fee to join a credit agency, and then pay for each report received. Lenders also promise to provide information about you back to the agency.

credit reporting agency
A business that collects, collates, and reports information concerning an entity's use of debt.

There are four primary CRAs: Equifax, Experian, Innovis, and TransUnion. There are also many specialized agencies that provide special services for landlords, medical providers, and resellers of information who create customized reports from data acquired from the four primary CRAs.

The information collected and reported by the CRAs is limited to three areas:

- Identifying information.
- Credit information.
- Public record information.

Race, religious preference, medical history, personal lifestyle choices, political affiliation, criminal record, or anything not related to credit is prohibited from being reported. Of course, for a price, all this information can be obtained from sources other than credit reporting agencies.

The **Fair Credit Reporting Act** requires that all information reported by CRAs be accurate. However, the law does not require that CRAs independently confirm any information. It is incumbent upon you, the consumer, to obtain a copy of your credit report and to notify the CRA in writing of any inaccurate information. The CRA has 30 days in which to investigate. The CRA must also forward copies of all relevant information that you provide to the source of the inaccurate information. The source must then make its own investigation and report any inaccuracies to all nationwide CRAs.

Fair Credit Reporting Act
U.S. federal legislation specifying consumers' rights vis à vis credit reporting agencies.

Eventually you will get a report of the outcome of the investigation. If the information is still inaccurate, you have to send a notice of dispute to the provider. The provider does not have to change the information, but a copy of your dispute must then be included with any future credit reports.

SKILL MODULE 15.3

Obtaining Your Credit Report

Under the Fair and Accurate Credit Transactions Act consumers can request one free credit report in every 12-month period from each of the three national credit reporting agencies, Experian, Equifax, and TransUnion. You must use the toll-free telephone number, (877) 322-8228, the **annualcreditreport.com** Web site, or a special mailing address—Annual Credit Report Request Service, P.O. Box 105281, Atlanta, GA 30348-5281. You will have to supply a Social Security number and date of birth and answer a few personal questions to get instant access online. Credit agencies have up to 15 days to send out reports that are requested by phone or mail.

Use one of the methods listed here to obtain copies of your credit report. Carefully examine each report for accuracy. If you find any incorrect information, contact the CRA and have it corrected.

Commercial credit reporting agencies began in the 1830s when a silk merchant, Lewis Tappan, began to collect extensive records concerning customers of the business. Tappan eventually offered credit reports to other merchants. Through a series of mergers, Tappan's business today is known as Dun & Bradstreet (D&B).

Providers of commercial credit reports are much more entrepreneurial and less rule-bound than are CRAs. For example, Dun & Bradstreet allows businesses to self report gross sales, profits, numbers and types of customers, numbers of employees, and so on. D&B does, however, make extensive efforts to confirm the accuracy of information and also makes independent investigations of midsize to large businesses, including interviewing management.

You can create a credit file for your business with D&B by filling out an online application and paying an initial fee of $500. Once your file is established, D&B maintains it, using a sophisticated computer system to confirm accuracy.

http://smallbusiness.dnb.com/manage-business-credit/get-duns-details.asp

Although D&B is the best known provider of commercial credit reports, it is by no means the sole provider. Experian provides commercial reports as well as consumer reports. Additionally, there are numerous other commercial credit reporting agencies, including National Information Bureau, Ltd, Veritax Business Information, Inc., and Fair Isaac's® Small Business Scoring, to name a few. Finally, there are industry-specific reporting agencies; for example, Seafax provides credit reports for the seafood, poultry, meat, and associated food industries.

The capacity of the business is the most important single factor for being able to borrow significant amounts of money. Your capacity to repay loans is measured primarily by two factors: profitability and cash flows from operations. **Profitability** that has been maintained over time indicates that you are an effective manager who will produce future profits to repay the borrowed money. *Cash flows from operations* that have been constant and reliable indicate that you can reliably convert profits to cash.

profit, profitability
The amount that revenues exceed expenses.

Condition of the industry and economy includes such factors as technology, competition, and economic growth. For example, right now the telecommunications industry is undergoing huge changes. Cable providers are offering telephone service, and telephone companies are offering movies. Satellite operators are adding broadband to their television and radio services. Copper wire connectors are being replaced with fiber optic cable directly into businesses and homes. Cell phones have rendered pay phones obsolete. Now is not a good time to try to raise money for a telecommunications business.

Collateral value is simply the estimated market value of the assets of your business. Tangible, long-lived assets are the best **collateral**. Auction markets for automobiles, trucks, and commercial machinery provide both a source for estimating value and an immediate market in which they can be sold.

collateral
Something of value given or pledged as security for payment of a loan; collateral may consist of financial instruments, such as stocks, bonds, and negotiable paper, or of physical goods, such as trucks, machinery, land, or buildings.

Intangible assets, other than patents, copyrights, and trademarks, are not good collateral. For example, *goodwill,* the value of a business that exceeds the sum of the value of all individual assets, cannot be sold separately from the business. The same is true of other intangibles, such as experience, education, institutional knowledge, and customer relations. These things can be very valuable, but none can be transferred to a lender to satisfy debt.

Other factors affecting debt worthiness include why you want to borrow the money and just how much money of your own is invested in the business. Lenders eagerly loan money to purchase capital equipment. After all, if you default, they will just repossess your truck and sell it to someone else. If you are willing to pay high enough interest rates, they will even lend you money to finance marketing efforts or business growth. They will not, however, lend you money to make up for financial failure. They will not loan money to finance consumption or extravagance. In fact, it is quite difficult to even borrow working capital to finance ongoing operations of all types. Also most commercial lenders will not make a loan in an amount greater than that which, when added to existing debt, will bring the debt-to-equity ratio above 50 percent.

What Type of Financing Is Right for Your Business?

LO3
Know how to choose the right types of financing for your business.

Consider the simplest case in which a small business owner has the alternatives of using personal equity funding or borrowing funds. The business may be 100 percent capitalized by either equity or debt, or any mix of equity and debt. Equity capital costs are estimated to be 20 percent per year—the investors expect $200 in interest or dividends for every $1,000 invested in the business. Debt capital costs are estimated to be a net of 6 percent after tax, or for every $1,000 borrowed, the entrepreneur owes the bank $60 a year (plus the $1,000 will need to be paid back as agreed).

cost of capital
The percentage cost of obtaining future funds.

weighted average cost of capital (WAC)
The expected average future cost of funds.

If the owner chooses to use a capital mix of 70 percent equity and 30 percent debt, the weighted average **cost of capital** is approximately 16 percent. At a 50-50 mix of equity and capital, the **weighted average cost of capital** is 13 percent and at 30 to 70 percent equity, and debt is approximately 10 percent. The more debt that is included in the capital mix, the lower the weighted average cost will be. The lower your cost of capital, the more profits you can keep for yourself. The more money your business generates for its owners, the more the business is worth. Thus, firm value is inversely related to cost of capital at any level of operations.

In reality, you will never have such alternatives. Although you may choose to use 100 percent personal funds for equity capital, no lender will agree to loan 100 percent. In fact, most lenders, without having some sort of guarantee such as collateral or Small Business Administration insurance, will not lend an amount that exceeds the amount you have invested. Even with guarantees, as the amount of debt increases, so does the risk of default. Because of the added risk, lenders will demand higher rates of interest for those later loans. For these reasons, the cost of both equity and debt capital changes as their relative percentages of total capital change.

A more realistic case is a small business that is 100 percent funded from the owner's own personal wealth. In this case, the value of the firm can be described as the amount of profit divided by the owner's cost of capital. For now, assume that your business is producing $100,000 per year and that the cost of capital is 20 percent. The value of the business is $500,000 ($100,000 cash flow divided by 20 percent). Now suppose you have an opportunity to purchase a productive asset which will return 20 percent per year for its life, such as a computer-controlled 5-axis milling machine. The asset costs $50,000, which you decide to borrow at 8 percent interest. Firm value will increase. Profits will increase to $106,000 [$100,000 + ($50,000 × .20) − ($50,000 × .08)]. The weighted average cost of capital will be 19 percent ($500,000 at 20 percent plus the additional investment of $50,000 at 8 percent). The value of the business is now $560,600.

A few weeks later, you have an opportunity to purchase another asset which will cost $50,000 and will also produce 20 percent returns. Again, you can borrow the money, but because of the added debt and greater probability of default, the lender requires 10 percent interest. Making the same set of calculations shows that profits will now be $111,000. The weighted average cost of capital is 18 percent, and the value of the business is now $611,000.

financial leverage
A measure of the amount of debt relative to total investment.

optimum capital structure
The ratio of debt to equity that provides the maximum level of profits.

Notice that the first investment increased the value of the firm by $60,600 (12 percent), while the second investment increased the value of the firm by only $50,400 (9 percent). As debt increases as a percentage of total investment (called **financial leverage**), *the value of the firm increases at a decreasing rate.* At some debt-to-equity ratio, the firm value peaks and then begins to decrease as added debt is incurred. You may make a series of such calculations, each time increasing the interest rate to convince yourself. You will initially see firm value increase. It will eventually reach a maximum value, and then start to decrease as debt and the cost of debt increases.

Few, if any, small business owners, however, even attempt to estimate the **optimum capital structure** of their business. Making such calculations takes too much time for the value provided. If you understand the concept that having debt in your capital structure works to increase your profits and you know that interest rates do not increase smoothly as financial leverage increases, you can find that level of debt that works for you.

A similar argument holds for obtaining outside equity investors. The difficulties and costs of obtaining equity capital are so great that most owners of small businesses don't even try. A study reported in 2003[9] found that so few small businesses raised capital by selling equity to outsiders that no statistical analysis could be done. Given these facts, it is reasonable for you to approximate cost of capital by examining only a few specific debt-to-equity ratios which are reasonable for your business and which you expect to persist for significant periods of time.

The owners and managers of small businesses are quite diverse. Entrepreneurs come from all social classes. They have different levels of education ranging from no formal schooling to those with advanced degrees. People of all major religions, of every race, and from every part of the world are represented among small business owners. As you would expect, such a diverse group of people have very diverse attitudes toward work, toward investing, toward management.

Some people gleefully jump out of airplanes; others are determined to "keep one foot on the ground." Business owners similarly differ in their response to financial risk. A few seek risk, thriving on the pressure of attempting to make the big strike. Most prefer to avoid business risk to the extent possible. In academic terms, some business owners are *risk seeking,* although most small business owners are *risk averse.* The personal preferences of each owner of a small business affect choices concerning financial risk, debt, sharing of ownership, and interaction with private and governmental foundations and agencies. Because of this, the optimal capital structure for one entrepreneur may well be anathema to another. Each owner of a small business must find the levels of equity, debt, and financial risk with which he or she is comfortable.

financial risk
Uncertainty of returns; the probability of losing money.

Financial risk is the probability of financial loss. Business opportunities, projects, and assets that have a greater chance of producing a loss are considered more risky than those that have a smaller chance. In a very real sense, risk is synonymous with uncertainty. If you purchase a 30-day U.S. Treasury bond, the return is certain. On the thirtieth day the government will issue a check for the amount of the bond plus interest. Because the government has the power to create money, there is no uncertainty and thus no risk of financial loss. If, on the other hand, you use the same amount of money to invest in a business, the return is very uncertain. You might succeed greatly or the business might fail and you lose your entire investment.

Borrowing money increases financial risk. In effect, borrowing money for a business is very much like selling the business to an investor and simultaneously buying back an option to repurchase the business on specific terms of payment. If the terms of payment are not met, the lender has the right to keep the business. The lender may enforce this right through either repossession if business assets were pledged as collateral, or involuntary bankruptcy, mediated by the court system. Payments on debt must be made as agreed without regard to the cash position of the business.

Selling equity in the business provides neither the opportunity to repurchase nor the obligation to make payments to owners. If the business does not provide sufficient profits and cash flows, an equity investor must accept the situation and hope that future operations will be profitable.

So why should you borrow, if doing so increases the probability of financial loss? Borrowing money for capital investment provides two benefits: (1) Borrowing enhances the potential for higher rates of return for the owners. (2) Borrowing allows the owners to keep a greater level of control of the business. For these reasons, the majority of small business owners prefer to borrow over accepting outside equity investment.[10] The interaction of the effects of choosing between equity and debt capital results in a small business owner having to compromise among the levels of potential profits, financial risk, and control of the business. This is depicted graphically in Figure 15.3.

FIGURE 15.3

Interaction among Profitability, Control, and Risk

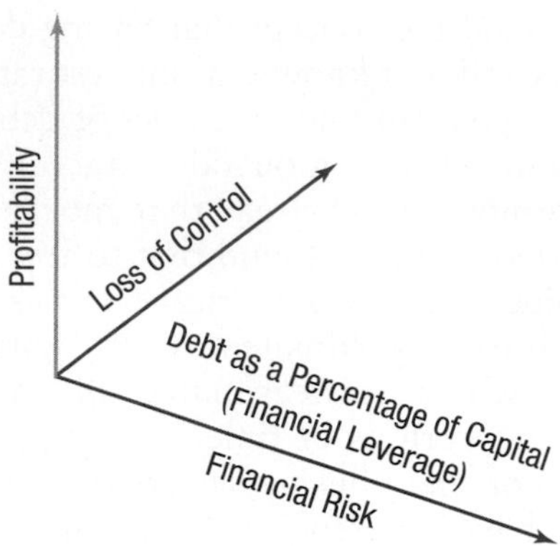

Borrowing increases potential profits by (1) lowering the weighted average cost of capital and (2) providing capital funds that allow the business to consider additional opportunities. To illustrate how this works, consider the following:

- Nucleodyne, LLC, is a biopharmaceutical start-up that owns intellectual property rights to a protein that will treat male pattern baldness. The science is sound, and the molecule grows hair on laboratory mice.
- The founders of the firm have already invested $1 million.
- To complete trials on human beings, the company must raise an additional $1 million. The owners have an agreement with a venture capital group to provide the money in return for 40 percent of the equity of the business.
- Alternatively, the money may be borrowed from a local investment bank at 10 percent annual interest.
- Based on projections of sales and expenses, the company expects to realize a profit of $300,000. Using these facts, compare the balance sheet and income statements in Figure 15.4.

return on equity
The ratio of profits to owner investment in a business.

It is immediately apparent that the business makes a greater profit if all capital is equity capital. What is not so apparent is the effect on the owners of the business. When investments are made, they are not evaluated by the number of dollars that are returned. Rather, investments are evaluated on the *percentage of return* that is realized. In this case, compare the **return on equity** (that is, the percentage of return on

FIGURE 15.4

Effect of Financing Sources on Financial Results for Nucleodyne, LLC

EFFECT OF FINANCING SOURCES UPON FINANCIAL RESULTS

100% Equity Financing		50-50 Debt-to-Equity Financing	
Balance Sheet			
Total assets	$2,000,000	Total assets	$2,000,000
Debt	0	Debt	$1,000,000
Equity	$2,000,000	Equity	$1,000,000
Total of debt and equity	$2,000,000	Total of debt and equity	$2,000,000
Income Statement			
Operating income	$300,000	Operating income	$300,000
Interest expense	0	Interest expense	100,000
Net income	$300,000	Net income	$200,000

TABLE 15.3 Owners' Return on Equity in Three Business Situations

$$\text{Owners' Return on Equity (ROE)} = \frac{\text{Net Income}}{\text{Owners' Equity Investment}}$$

Alternative 1 Use Personal Funds for Capital		Alternative 2 Issue Stock for 40% Equity		Alternative 3 Borrow Capital Funds	
Net income	$300,000	Net income	$300,000	Net income	$200,000
Original owners' equity	$2,000,000	Original owners' equity	$1,000,000	Original owners' equity	$1,000,000
New owners' equity	0	New owners' equity	$1,000,000	New owners' equity	N.A.
Original owners' ROE =	15%	Original owners' ROE =	18%	Original owners' ROE =	20%
New owners' ROE =	N.A.	New owners' ROE =	12%	New owners' ROE =	N.A.

the amount actually owned) for each the original founders of the business and new equity investors as we can see in Table 15.3.

If the *original* owners solely use their own funds, then they will realize a return of only 15 cents on each dollar invested. If they sell 40 percent of the business to outside investors, the *original* owners will realize 18 cents on the dollar (60% of $300,000 divided by $ 1,000,000). If, however, they borrow the additional funds, then they realize a 20 percent return on their investment. The total original owners' return on each dollar invested in the business is one-third greater if the needed capital is borrowed than if the business is 100 percent financed by owners' personal funds.

This analysis, of course, does beg the question, "If the owners have the additional personal funds, why not invest them into the business because the total profit realized will be greater?" There are two reasons that making the additional investment might not be the best alternative. First, obtaining equity investment from others reduces the potential loss for any single investor. Second, it is often possible to borrow at interest rates substantially lower than the opportunity cost of using the business owners' own resources. For example, you may have money invested in an IRA, 401-K, or other tax-sheltered retirement fund. Suppose your retirement is earning near the long-term market average of 10 percent. Interest rates for borrowing are currently about 8 percent. If you take money from your retirement funds, you are giving up a 10 percent tax-free gain. On the other hand, interest on money borrowed for your business is deductible for tax purposes. If you are in the 25 percent tax bracket, you will, in effect, pay interest of only 6 percent [(.08 × (1 − tax rate of .25)]. Thus, as a rule, even if you have enough money to finance your business solely with equity, you still should consider borrowing in order to get the greatest total profits.

Control issues arise under both alternatives of issuing equity to outsiders or borrowing funds. When outside investors acquire equity, they also acquire some level of influence over the operations and strategy of the firm. In the example above, Nucleodyne gave up ownership of 40 percent of the firm. The original owners retain 60 percent ownership. This provides majority voting control only so long as the original owners vote as a bloc. Should disputes arise, it is quite possible, depending upon the number of owners and their percentage of ownership, that disgruntled stockholders could form a coalition and take control of the firm from the original founders. Alternatively, disgruntled minority owners may sue majority owners. For these reasons, many owners of small businesses are loath to sell any ownership shares. They prefer to accept the added financial risk of borrowing rather than deal with stockholders.

Borrowing capital, however, is not without its own issues of control. Lenders have to trust your management to operate the business efficiently, generating sufficient cash flow to meet the repayment terms of the loan. It is common, therefore, for lenders to require borrowers to provide regular documentation of the financial condition of the business. Many banks require that a copy of each year's income tax return, income statement, and balance sheet be furnished during the term of the loan. Loan contracts may also impose restrictions on the operation of the business, such as requiring that a specific minimum net worth be maintained, a specific debt-to-equity ratio not be exceeded, no dividends be paid to stockholders, executive salaries not exceed a specified amount, no capital assets be acquired or disposed of without the concurrence of the lender, and so on. These types of restrictions, called *loan covenants,* can seriously limit management's freedom to operate the business and can make taking on shareowners seem like less of a burden. It could also make do-it-yourself funding more attractive.

Financial Management for the Life of Your Business

Financial Management for Start-Up

LO4
Understand the differing needs for financial management at each stage of business life.

financial management
A set of theories and techniques used to optimize the receipt and use of capital assets.

During the start-up phase of a small business the primary **financial management** need is to obtain sufficient funds to pay for equipment, buildings, inventory, and indeed, all the costs of starting and running a business. Generally, start-up businesses have a very limited ability to obtain funds from outside sources. Necessary funds for start-ups therefore are usually obtained through a mixture of the founders' personal resources, personal credit worthiness, and internally generated cash flows. Outsiders who provide funding during the start-up phase of a small business are often referred to as "3-F investors," that is, "friends, family, and fools." The emphasis of financial management at this stage is to obtain needed funds and to conserve scarce cash.

Figure 15.5 shows the forms of financing available to small businesses. According to the SBA, there is a pecking order of popular funding sources from most available to least.[11] Owner's capital is the most widely available source, while loans from commercial-grade lending institutions such as banks are the least available. Loan and finance companies are more likely sources of financing than banks because these lenders are "motivated" by the payoff from high-interest-rate loans. Figure 15.5

FIGURE 15.5

The Pecking Order of Funding Sources for New Firms

Source: Adapted from Charles Ou and George W. Haynes, "Uses of Equity Capital by Small Firms—Findings from the Surveys of Small Business Finances (for 1993 & 1998)". Presented at the 14th Annual Conference on Entrepreneurial Finance and Business Ventures at the De Paul University, Chicago, Illinois, on April 30–May 2, 2003, http://www.sba.gov/advo/stats/wkp03co.pdf, and from correspondence with Dr. Ou.

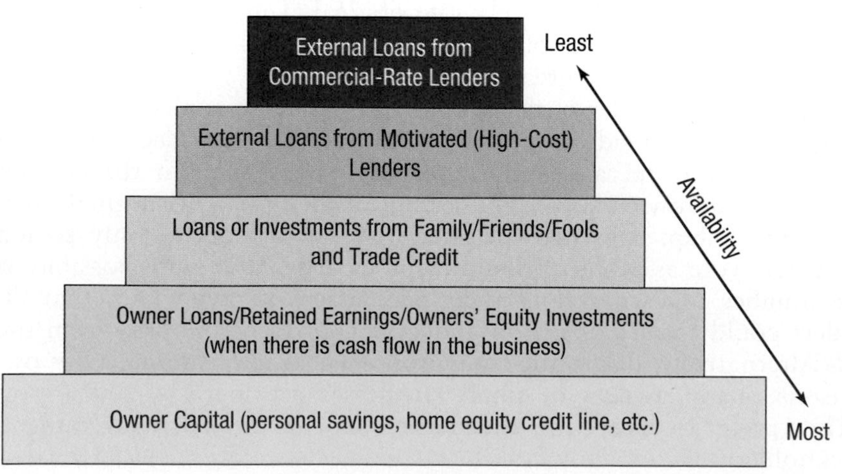

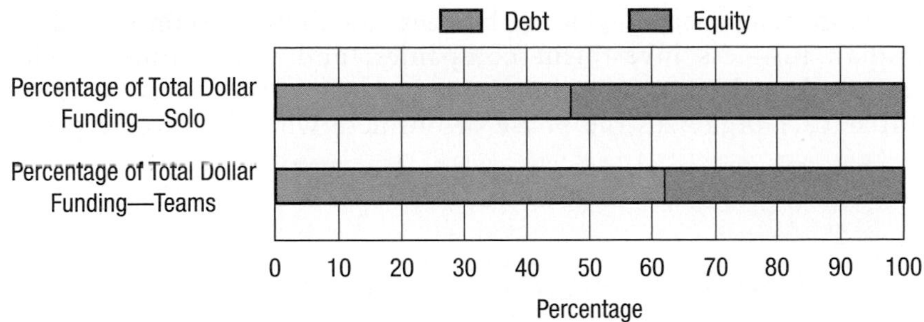

FIGURE 15.6

Use of Debt and Equity in Start-Ups From the PSED

Source: Adapted from Michael Stouder and Bruce Kirchhoff, "Funding the First Year of Business," in William B. Gartner, Kelly G. Shaver, Nancy M. Carter, and Paul D. Reynolds, (eds.), *Handbook of Entrepreneurial Dynamics: The Process of Business Creation.* (Thousand Oaks, CA: Sage, 2004), p. 368.

shows that the 3-Fs and trade credit are also fairly popular sources for funds. Once the firm gets going, a whole other source of financing becomes available as the owner uses the profits or cash generated by the business to pay for growth.

One other factor to consider in start-ups is the power of combined resources. Often solo entrepreneurs face greater pressure to use their own money in a start-up situation than do start-ups done by teams. In the Panel Study of Entrepreneurial Dynamics, teams generally reported having greater debt financing available for use at the time of start up.[12] Figure 15.6 shows from where the initial funding for team and solo start-ups comes. Solo entrepreneurs could raise only 47 percent of their start-up funds using debt, while teams could raise over 62 percent from debt sources. This means that solo entrepreneurs are more dependent on their own equity and that of the 3-F investors.

Financial Management for Growth

Many small businesses successfully start up only to find that the need for financial management is greater than ever as the business enters a phase of rapid growth. This situation is like a lame "bad news-good news" joke. The bad news is that the business has greater capital needs than ever. The good news is that more sources of money are available to meet those needs. The emphasis of financial management during periods of growth is to obtain increasing amounts of cash inflows to pay for added inventory, productive assets, and employees needed to meet growing levels of business operations.

Financial Management for Operations

Most small businesses eventually reach a size that is relatively stable: not too small to generate sufficient profits, not too large for the preferences and abilities of the owners. At this stage of the business, the emphasis of financial management is to build owner wealth, to conserve assets, to match cash inflows to outflows, and to maximize the return on capital assets by making optimal investing decisions.

Financial Management for Business Exit

Eventually, you will face the necessity of leaving the active management of your business. This may be because you want to take advantage of a different opportunity, the business needs professional management, you want to pass ownership to family members, or you want to retire. You might become ill or disabled. Regardless why, successfully leaving your business requires maximizing the value of your business for your successors. The emphasis of financial management is to create effective internal control of assets and liabilities, to develop business systems to replace your specific skills and knowledge, and to ensure that the processes of the business and personal transactions of the owners are completely separate.

There are many sources of financing for businesses. Some sources are always there, such as commercial banks and the Small Business Administration. Other sources are more temporary, including business incubators, economic development agencies, small business investment companies, and grant sources. Throughout the phases of the existence of a business, needs for and sources of investment change. Table 15.1 organizes the phase of business with the three types of capital sources.

CHAPTER SUMMARY

LO1 Know the three types of capital financing and their costs and trade-offs.

- Most people have many assets and financial resources that can be used to finance their business.
- Financing can be in the form of debt, equity, or gifts.
- An entrepreneur's own funds are the first source of financing for most small businesses.
- Forms of business organization can be categorized along two dimensions.
  - How the business is taxed.
  - How much responsibility owners have for the liabilities of the business.

LO2 Understand the characteristics of a business that determine its ability to raise capital.

- Investors put money into a business to make money for themselves.
- Lenders expect a return from making loans, by getting back the amount they loan plus more money in the form of interest.
- Equity investors expect to get back the money they invest plus extra money, a gain on investment.
- To get money from other people, owners must show them that their business probably can make gains for them.
- Financing with equity is expensive and creates problems of control and decision making.
- Other than the owner's own funds, the most common source of capital for established ongoing small businesses is borrowed funds.

LO3 Know how to choose the right type of financing for your business.

- As debt increases as a percentage of total capital, total cost of capital declines.
- Lower cost of capital results in higher firm value, all other things being held equal.
- Borrowing money increases financial risk because payments on debt must be made as agreed without regard to the cash position of the business.

LO4 Understand the differing needs for financial management at each stage of business life.

- During the start-up phase of a small business the primary financial management need is to obtain sufficient funds to pay for equipment, buildings, inventory, and indeed, all the costs of starting and running a business.
- During the growth phase, the need for financial management increases to pay for added inventory, productive assets, and employees to meet growing levels of business operations.

- During the mature phase of the business, the emphasis of financial management is to build owner wealth, to conserve assets, to match cash inflows to outflows, and to maximize the return on capital assets by making optimal investing decisions.
- Successfully leaving your business requires maximizing its value for your successors by creating effective internal controls and developing business systems to replace your specific skills and knowledge.

DISCUSSION QUESTIONS

1. Why does a business require a constant flow of money and capital assets during its existence?
2. Explain how a sole proprietorship differs from a corporation.
3. What things do you need to do to convince an investor to make you a loan or purchase equity in your business?
4. In what ways does accepting outside investment change the ways you manage your business?
5. Why do you have to give up more ownership to get outside investment if your business is risky?
6. Explain why investors prefer investments that pay back sooner to those that pay back later.
7. Name four ways that an investor can receive payment from a business. Describe the advantages and disadvantages of each.
8. Many small business owners prefer to borrow money rather than sell equity. Why is this so?
9. In what ways do the 4-Cs for borrowing differ from the requirements for being able to obtain equity capital?
10. Explain why it is easier to borrow money to buy a semi truck than to purchase rights to a business process.
11. Explain how borrowing money (1) increases firm value and (2) makes more money for a business owner.
12. Explain the differing financial management needs of a small business during the start-up, growth, mature, and exit phases.

EXPERIENTIAL EXERCISES

1. Go to the SBA directory of SBICs (http://www.sba.gov/INV/index.html). Search through the directory, specifically looking for SBICs that will invest in businesses in the industry in which you are interested. Make a chart of the minimum and maximum investments that the SBICs will make, and their requirements to invest. Present your findings to your class.
2. Contact the owner of a business you would like to own. Arrange an interview. Ask how the owner arranged for start-up financing. What sources of financing does the owner use today? Report your findings to your class.
3. Find out if your city has an office of economic development. (Almost every city with a population greater than 100,000 does.) Contact the office and inquire about the programs that it supports. Ask specifically how the office would provide support to you for start-up and operations.
4. Find out if your city or county has any tax abatement economic development zones. What must you do to be able to take advantage of the tax abatement?

5. Make an appointment with a commercial bank loan officer who handles business loans. Ask about the bank's documentation requirements. Determine what commitment, if any, the bank has for making loans to local small businesses. Present your findings to your class.
6. Do a search of *Entrepreneur, Inc.*, and *BusinessWeek Small Business* Web sites looking for information about businesses that were successful in obtaining financing. Write a report detailing how the businesses arranged financing.

Mini-Case

LIFFORCE BIOTECH, LLC

Albert Lifforce, a scientist at the University of Texas Health Science Center, has developed a molecule that stops genetically fat mice from overeating. Albert believes that the molecule will work in humans, and, as such, has enormous economic potential. Based on current National Institute of Health (NIH) statistics, more than one-third of U.S. citizens are overweight. If the drug is shown to be safe and effective, annual sales will easily exceed $1 billion. Successful biopharmaceutical companies typically produce returns on sales of 30 percent.

However, to complete the large animal studies and begin healthy normal human studies will require an investment of $20 million. It will take one year to complete the animal trials and two years to complete the two human trials. Based on other successful biotech start-ups, if the Phase 1 healthy normal studies are successful, the business will have a market value of $300 million. It will require an additional $30 million to complete Phase II trials, if Phase I trials are successful. If the drug successfully completes Phase II trials and is approved by the FDA, the business will then have a market value on the order of $1 billion.

Albert currently has savings and investments of $250,000 which he is willing to invest in the business. He also has a home in the Dominion housing development with a market value of $650,000. The house is financed with a $400,000 mortgage. Albert's wife is also an M.D. Ph.D. and has said that she is willing to return to practice and thus support the family while Albert pursues this opportunity.

Albert has been in discussion with SATAI, and TEKSA, two high-tech incubators in San Antonio, Texas. Neither of these has any money available for direct investment. However, each has worked to help Albert find angel investors.

Albert now has to choose from among three alternatives to finance his start-up.

Alternative 1: A wealthy San Antonio investor who made his fortune in the oil industry has offered to finance the start-up. He will provide $20 million. Of this, $10 million will be a loan at 15 percent. The remainder will be an equity investment. For this investment, Albert will have to give up 40 percent of his business. The investor insists that the company must complete an initial public offering (IPO) upon completion of Phase 1 trials. Both Albert and the investor will give up equity to complete the IPO. Albert will retain 30 percent, and the investor 20 percent. The 50 percent that is being sold to the public should raise approximately $150 million for the company.

Alternative 2: Albert has been assured by his colleagues at the NIH that his drug is a shoo-in for an expedited SBIR grant. The expedited path allows Albert to immediately apply for full funding. The grant would pay out $5 million. Albert would contribute $250,000 from savings, and another $120,000 by taking out a home equity loan. A local venture capitalist has pledged to invest $15 million for 30 percent of equity when the large animal trials are finished. This would be sufficient capital to then complete the Phase 1 healthy normal trials. Funding for Phase II trials would then have to be raised from other sources. One source would be to do an IPO, as in alternative 1.

Alternative 3: A group of investors from the San Francisco Bay Area has proposed the following: They will put up $40 million, which will be paid in phases—$5 million right now, $15 million when large animal trials are successfully completed, and $20 million when Phase 1 healthy normal human trials are completed. Of the $40 million, $10 million will be a loan at 12 percent interest. The remaining $30 million will be for 60 percent of equity. The venture capital group will select the chairman of the board and the chief financial officer for the business. Albert will be allowed to take a salary of $150,000 per year if he acts as the CEO and primary investigator. If the drug receives FDA approval, an IPO will be conducted. Upon completion of the IPO, Albert will retain ownership of 10 percent of equity.

Advise him which alternative to take.

LEARNING OBJECTIVES

This chapter will help you:

LO1 Understand the meaning and nature of business risk.

LO2 Recognize the specific types of risks associated with different aspects of business operations.

LO3 Manage risks to stay within your level of risk tolerance.

LO4 Learn how insurance can be used to manage business risk.

LO5 Master sharing risk with other businesses and organizations.

■ Chimney sweeping is an example of an industry that is risky to insure. Read the chapter opening scenario to learn how two chimney sweeps catalyzed change by motivating a large group of fellow workers to get involved with the insurance company. Why do you think it is so important that small business owners and workers belong to a guild or similar industry group?

Small Business Protection: Risk Management and Insurance

Focus on Small Business: The Massachusetts Chimney Sweep Guild[1]

Faced with paying twice as much for liability insurance as last year, Mike and Michelle Elliott decided to take action. Instead of simply paying the rates demanded and then griping about it, the couple prodded their industry group, the Massachusetts Chimney Sweep Guild, to use its bargaining power to get better rates for its members.

Chimney sweeps, like roofers, rough-in carpenters, and house movers, are difficult businesses to insure. Many large insurance companies do not want to deal with small businesses at all. Others will insure small businesses, but do not want to deal with businesses that involve heavy physical work, climbing ladders, and the presence of hazardous materials such as the soot and creosote that sweeps remove from flues. Such businesses have high risk of employee illnesses and injuries and high risk of damage to customers' properties—characteristics that are great disincentives for insurance companies.

The Elliotts sent a questionnaire to each of the 35 small business owners who comprised the Guild, asking for information concerning past claims, their volume of business, number of employees, and so on. Armed with the results of the survey, their own independent insurance broker, Tom Coonan, went to work to find appropriate insurance.

"Standard companies won't touch the Guild, because they have so few members. The total premium has to be over $1 million before the larger insurance companies will underwrite a group," Coonan says.

Coonan was able to find an insurance carrier that combined the desired coverages with affordable premiums. Overall, members of the Guild are highly satisfied with the insurance package. Plans are being made to obtain the group policy as an ongoing contract.

Operating a risky business such as chimney sweeping without the security of good insurance is a recipe for financial disaster. The cost of care for just one seriously injured worker or of repairing just one seriously damaged building can easily bankrupt a small business owner. On the other hand, if insurance coverage itself is excessively costly, the business cannot be profitable. By banding together, the members of the Guild were able to use their combined bargaining power to obtain appropriate coverage at affordable prices.

DISCUSSION QUESTIONS:

1. The case mentions two kinds of risks faced by chimney sweeps. Name some others.
2. What is the risk to the small business owner of operating without insurance?
3. Why do you think the data on claim experience were useful for the insurance broker in negotiating the deal?

Risk in Small Business

LO1
Understand the meaning and nature of business risk.

We have discussed two kinds of risk in the previous chapters—financial risk that comes from your capital structure and investment risk caused by accepting or providing debt, and by holding debt or equity funds. Here we discuss other kinds of risk that small business owners face.

People define risk in many different ways, depending upon their unique situations and upon their own tolerance for uncertainty. You might define risk as the likelihood of getting an A in this course. A smoke jumper might consider risk the possibility of being trapped by a rapidly advancing forest fire. A surgeon who is to perform an operation might consider risk to be the level of probability that the patient will be no better after the surgery and will sue for malpractice. The person facing major surgery might think of risk as the chance that the operation will result in death. For business owners, risk is the very real likelihood that the business may not succeed, that they may not only *not* become wealthy, but that they may well lose part or all of their investment in the firm.

We all know that people vary widely in their response to risk. Some people gleefully jump out of airplanes, while others are determined to "keep one foot on the ground." As we point out in the previous chapter, business owners similarly differ in their response to business risk. Some seek risk. Most prefer to avoid risk to the extent possible. In academic terms, some business owners are *risk seeking*, although most small business owners are *risk-averse*.

To the extent that small business owners are risk-averse, as part of every business decision, they consider what they could lose. If they can't reduce the level of risk to where they're comfortable, then they make arrangements to either insure against future losses or to spread the risk among other people or businesses.

Thinking about Risk

Generally speaking, risk is the probability that future states of being will be worse than you expect. For example, folks who build houses on or near the San Andreas fault expect those houses to survive the inevitable earthquakes. However, there is a small, but measurable, probability that an earthquake will be violent enough to destroy any building that can be built. The risk of building in an earthquake area is the *level of likelihood*, or the *probability*, that a strong earthquake will damage or destroy the house, an outcome that is definitely a worse state of being than the homeowner expects.

business risk
The level of probability that the future economic state of the business will be worse than expected.

Business risk is the probability that the future state of the business will be less successful than planned, resulting in the loss of value of business assets. No person enters a business for the purpose of losing money, but it can and does happen. The next quarter's business does not meet expectations. Investments go bad. Sales projections are not met. Products do not meet specifications. All of a sudden, investors find themselves the owners of assets that are worth much less than expected. The likelihood of this bleak outcome is the essence of business risk.

Among the most commonly identified sources of risk are:

- Financial risk that is a result of choosing among sources and types of capital investment.[2]
- Nonpayment of debts owed to the business.
- Changes in technology that render the business's product or service obsolete.
- Injury and illnesses suffered by employees as a result of their employment.
- Injury from accidents incurred by customers, vendors, and others while on business property.
- Loss or harm incurred because of the use of the business's product or service.
- Natural events, such as storms, floods, fire, and earthquakes.
- Violation of any of the multitude of laws and regulations that apply to small business.
- Theft of business property.
- Misbehavior by employees.

Risks Associated with Specific Business Operations

LO2
Recognize the specific types of risks associated with different business operations.

There are three general types of events that cause business risk. These are (1) events related to the property of the business, (2) events related to personnel, and (3) events related to customers and others.

Property of the Business

Every business owns things of value. A retail or wholesale business owns inventory. A manufacturing business owns production machinery. A consulting company owns reputation, skill, and experience. Many businesses own furniture, office equipment, vehicles, buildings, and land. Some businesses own valuable patents, copyrights, trademarks, or trade secrets.

Each and every one of these types of property involves specific forms of risk. Inventory can be stolen, spoiled, or become obsolete. Production machinery can break down. Institutional skill and experience can be diminished or lost as key employees die, retire, quit, go to work for competitors, or start their own competing businesses. Furniture, office equipment, vehicles, and buildings can be damaged or destroyed by vandalism, accidents, fire, flood, or wind. Land may become contaminated by spills of hazardous materials or rendered unsafe by cave-ins or landslides. Patents may be infringed upon. Trademarks and brand names that are not properly protected may pass into the public domain. A trade secret may be disclosed.

Events Related to Personnel

There are three main types of risk related to events involving personnel: (1) theft, (2) violation of governmental regulations, and (3) loss of key employees.

Employee Theft

employee theft
Misappropriation of business property by employees of that business.

Employee theft is a fact of life for almost all businesses. Theft by personnel may involve direct stealing of money or other assets of the business, or may be the conduct of an illegal act that is intended to provide personal benefit at a cost to the business. The most common form of employee theft is the pilfering of items of small value, such as office supplies and small hand tools, or actions such as making copies for their children to use at school or otherwise using company resources to make personal items. Thought of this way, some experts estimate that 95 percent of small businesses face at least some of this sort of loss annually.[3] Losses of these types are usually insignificant in their effect upon the financial results of your business. However, theft losses of cash and inventory can be of such magnitude that your business is significantly damaged or even fails. Large losses usually arise from embezzlement or fraud.[4]

Violation of Governmental Regulations

regulation of the workplace
Laws and governmental rules that limit the freedom of business owners to manage their businesses as they please.

Violation of government regulations has become a source of significant business risk over the last 30 years. **Regulation of the workplace** has increased, resulting in employer violations that range from having an employee one time "forget" to use required safety equipment to failing to provide required accommodations for handicapped employees and others to discrimination against a protected class (race, creed, color, national origin, age, or gender). The cost of violating any of the myriad workplace regulations can range from as little as losing a few hours of your time completing paperwork, up to huge dollar fines and judicial awards.

Violation of some of the myriad regulations is inevitable, given the complex, ambiguous, and sometimes contradictory nature of the regulations. The federal rule making agencies of which employees may run afoul are countless, including the U.S. Food and Drug Administration, the Environmental Protection Agency, the Securities Exchange Commission, the National Transportation Safety Board, the Federal Aviation Agency, the U.S. Coast Guard, the Federal Drug Agency, and the Department of the Interior, to name only a very few. In addition, most states have similar business-regulating agencies that promulgate rules which often conflict with federal standards. The Small Business Administration estimated in 2001 that small businesses had to spend roughly $1,200 per employee per year to file and keep up with all the regulatory requirements. This rate was twice what large businesses had to spend.[5]

Equal Employment Opportunity Commission (EEOC)
A commission established to enforce the provisions of the Equal Employment Opportunity Act.

Occupational Health and Safety Administration (OSHA)
A government agency created to enforce safety in the workplace.

protected classes
States of being that are expressly prohibited from suffering discrimination: race, color, religion, national origin, gender, age, or disability.

Although there are numerous government agencies that issue business regulations, what small businesses find most problematic are the rules from three agencies: the Internal Revenue Service, the **Equal Employment Opportunity Commission** (EEOC), and **Occupational Safety and Health Administration** (OSHA). The problems arise because each agency has rules that are so complex that compliance problems are almost a certainty, if enough aspects of the business are reviewed. For example, the Americans with Disabilities Act has rules that govern the furnishings, size, placement, and clear space of public toilets and those run to over four pages and include more than 10 architectural drawings to specify exact maximums and minimums to the inch. Any violation of any of the specific accessibility measurements can result in civil fines or litigation awards. We discuss the IRS and the problems of tax code compliance later in this chapter.

The risk of noncompliance with OSHA and EEOC regulations is further increased by the continual growth in the scope of government regulations. For example, the Equal Employment Opportunity Commission's rule-making authority has grown from the agency's start in 1964. At that time, EEOC established five **protected classes**: "race, color, religion, sex or national origin."[6] Since then the authority of the EEOC has grown through the passage of (1) the Age Discrimination in Employment Act of 1967 (ADEA), (2) Rehabilitation Act of 1973, (3) Americans with Disabilities Act of 1990 (ADA), and (4) the Civil Rights Act of 1991, all of which grant additional rule-making and enforcement powers. The commission has made thousands of rules that are ambiguous and, at times, contradictory.

Age Discrimination in Employment Act
An act of Congress that makes it illegal to discriminate against people who are older than 40 years of age.

Rehabilitation Act of 1973
An act of Congress that provides training for workers who are injured on the job.

Americans with Disabilities Act of 1990
An act of Congress that requires that businesses make provisions for access by disabled people.

Civil Rights Act of 1991
A series of acts by Congress that prohibit discrimination on the basis of race, color, religion, sex, or national origin.

Strategies for Dealing with Compliance

One strategy many small businesses use in coping with these rules is to stay small enough to remain below the thresholds for which these agencies' rules apply. For example, if there are no employees, there cannot be any discrimination in hiring. OSHA rules in most industries[7] do not apply to firms with fewer than 10 employees.

Some firms take the ultimate in risky strategies—indifference. Some owners figure it makes more sense not to spend time on compliance, and when they face government action, close the business. This sounds fine in theory, but government agencies can come after the owner of a business for damages and fines even after the business itself is bankrupt or closed. More often, the owner is fined and required to comply. The fines and time spent dealing with the agency are often said to cost more than complying ahead of time. You can see why indifference is the riskiest of strategies.

Another strategy is being proactive. Government agencies must post their rules and most make available summaries focused on the concerns of small business. For example:

EEOC's Small Business Page: http://www.eeoc.gov/employers/smallbusinesses.html.

EEOC's Americans with Disabilities Act Handbook: www.eeoc.gov/ada/adahandbook.html.

OSHA's Small Business Page: http://www.osha.gov/dcsp/smallbusiness/index.html.

OSHA's Small Business Handbook: http://www.osha.gov/Publications/smallbusiness/small-business.pdf.

A great listing of government small business resources can be found on the IRS's small business page, at http://www.irs.gov/businesses/small/content/0,,id=98864,00.html. Perhaps the key resource for entrepreneurs trying to be proactive is Reginfo.gov, the combined national Web site for federal, state and local regulation.

http://www.reginfo.gov

While many government agencies offer free reviews of a business for compliance, many small business owners are leery of such efforts, because they will be obligated to quickly fix any problems identified. A useful alternative is to have private contractors do assessments to check for compliance. Lawyers, especially labor lawyers, have experience in preventing EEOC compliance problems. Many consulting engineers can perform OSHA checks. In addition some of the major small business trade associations such as the NFIB and even local Chambers of Commerce offer classes on compliance for OSHA, EEOC, and other regulations.

One other strategy, which is not for the faint of heart or short of cash, is to fight for what you believe to be right. This usually entails first dealing directly with the agency's representative. Often this direct dealing is best done with an attorney present or only after being prepared by the attorney about how to handle your side of the meeting. If that meeting does not lead to a resolution, there are administrative reviews and even court actions at which the firm can stand up to the government. One famous example is that of Clint Eastwood (see Small Business Insight).

The Eastwood situation hints at one other strategy, what the original lawyer suing the hotel hoped to achieve—capitulation. In capitulation, often unscrupulous people use the threat of bringing a charge of noncompliance against a firm as a means of getting a cash settlement not to file. This type of person actively looks for minor violations of OSHA, ADA, or other laws. They then write the owner of the "offending" business, demanding a cash settlement for the alleged damage. The business owner is placed into an untenable situation: Either pay the "complainant" as demanded, or be stuck with the costs of litigation, and the risk that a jury will award even more. Many

SMALL BUSINESS INSIGHT

It's More than a Fist Full Of Dollars[8]

Clint Eastwood may not quite match your idea of a small business owner, but in fact, Mr. Eastwood owns the 32-room Mission Ranch Hotel in Carmel, California.

In early 2000, the Mission Ranch was sued for alleged violations of the Americans with Disabilities Act. Unlike many owners of small businesses, however, Mr. Eastwood is wealthy, politically savvy (he had been mayor of Carmel), and willing to bear the costs of litigation. *The Wall Street Journal* quoted him:

> These "sleazebag lawyers," the veteran actor says, his voice constricting, messed with the wrong guy when they "frivolously" sued him and hundreds of other small-business owners for failing to comply quickly enough with the Americans with Disabilities Act.

Mr. Eastwood states that he is not in any way against the ADA. Rather, he will not "roll over" for trial lawyers whom he believes are using the ADA to extort money from small businesses by filing unwarranted lawsuits. Not only is he vigorously defending the suit against the Mission Ranch, but he has joined with U.S. Representative Mark Foley of Florida in an effort to insert a requirement into the law that would provide businesses with 90 days to come into compliance before any suit could be filed. Representative Foley stated that some lawyers have exploited the ADA and targeted stretches of small businesses, such as strip malls in south Florida.

Representative Foley, who is disabled himself, claims that there is no intent to reduce the effectiveness of the ADA. Rather, he said, "I just think for the benefit of everybody, they should cut out this racket because these are morally corrupt people who are doing this."

small business owners choose to pay rather than face the risk of losing. Because these payments are never recorded in any central location, it is possible for the individuals to repeat the process.

Loss of Key Employees

key employees
Employees whose experience and skills are critical to the success of a business.

Loss of **key employees** is a particularly acute risk for small businesses. Because of the simple fact that there are only a few employees in a small business, invariably one person or a very few people are essential to the successful operation of the business. If such a key employee quits, retires, becomes disabled, or dies, the business faces a crisis. In many cases, the loss of a key employee has led to the bankruptcy and dissolution of the business.

Competition from former employees is also a constant risk. Good employees who understand the business, who successfully sell products and services, and who are skilled at the operations of the business are often tempted to become competitors. This can happen several different ways. A key employee may be "hired away" by an existing competitor who offers a higher salary and greater perks. A key employee may start her or his own business, using the knowledge and skills gained from working in your business. Customers may offer to back a key employee to establish a competing business in order to obtain lower prices and greater negotiating leverage. Vendors may offer a key employee dealerships or exclusive sales territories in a bid to increase sales of their specific products.

This risk is especially acute in knowledge and service businesses, such as accounting practices, medical practices, barber and beauty shops, and restaurants. All of these businesses have relatively low barriers to entry for qualified people. Each type of business depends upon personal relationships engendered with customers. When a key employee of a knowledge firm leaves, it is common for several customers to change to the new firm.

Events Related to Customers and Others

Although customers are, by definition, the "reason for being" of any business, they also are the source of considerable business risk. In addition to customers, you are also at risk from vendors and even trespassers on your property. This risk from customers and others primarily arises from (1) injuries suffered while upon business property and (2) injury or damage that is caused during the use of the business's products. These risks are, of course, in addition to the familiar risk of customers, who are sold products or services on credit, not paying as they have agreed.

Injuries suffered while on business property may or may not be your fault. People at times do stupid things, such as climb on shelves to get items that are "just out of reach." If the shelf collapses and dumps the customer onto the floor, you're going to pay twice: once for the broken shelf and spoiled merchandise, and once for the "pain and suffering" of the customer. A reasonable person might believe that the customer was responsible for his or her own acts and the business should not be liable. It is most unfortunate that juries are composed of "peers" and not of "reasonable persons."

Injuries on business premises may also arise from the actions of trespassers. In many cases, a business has been held responsible for harm experienced by a trespasser, as well as harm inflicted by the trespasser upon employees, customers, and vendors. An extreme example of this type of event is robbery and assault that occurs on business property. In many cases, injuries suffered by employees and customers at the hands of the criminals have been held to be the fault of the business. The rationale given has been that the business didn't provide good enough security. Again, the business pays twice: once when the robber steals money and other assets; again when the robber, employees, and customers are paid for pain and suffering caused by the robbery.

Payment for injury or damage that occurs during the use of the business's products is referred to as *product liability.* The magnitude of losses resulting from product liability claims has increased greatly in recent years with an increase in class action lawsuits. This is an issue that you must take very seriously if you are a manufacturer. Although individual customers usually get very little money from class action suits, the lawyers who pursue them often receive payments of millions of dollars, as occurred in the case of asbestos producers and tobacco companies. Certainly, the smaller your firm is, the less exposure you have to class action product liability suits. This is true for two reasons: A small business has fewer customers who can claim harm, and a small business does not have the "deep pockets" of cash and other assets that can be raided by rapacious law firms.

Individual lawsuits may also be filed when a single user claims to have been harmed by the product. Such lawsuits are actually more common than class action suits. Although the amount paid in settlement is usually a tiny fraction of that of a class action suit, a manufacturer must still take the issue very seriously. In the 1970s a rash of individual lawsuits against manufacturers of small (under 12,000 lbs. gross weight) airplanes resulted in the demise of the industry. Many small businesses that either made small airplanes or made parts and subassemblies for airplanes were forced into bankruptcy. The production of small airplanes did not resume in the United States until Congress passed a law that limited the exposure of manufacturers to product liability suits.[9]

Risk of nonpayment by customers is experienced by all businesses that offer credit. This is true whether you directly provide credit or it is provided through a third party. You have to balance two conflicting things when you decide to offer credit: (1) giving credit to customers will increase your sales, and (2) offering credit guarantees sooner or later some customer will not pay as promised. How big this risk is depends on how many customers you give credit to and how much you let any single customer charge.

Restaurants, clothing retailers, barbers, and beauticians face relatively low risks of loss from nonpayment. First, most of these businesses provide credit only by accepting credit cards, which reduces the risk of nonpayment. Second, the amount that any one customer charges is unlikely to be big enough to threaten your business if it is not paid.

If you sell large-ticket items, such as signs, house remodeling, boats, and the like, you incur large risks by offering credit to customers. Few people have credit cards that have charge limits big enough to buy such things. Therefore, you have to give credit directly to your customer. When the inevitable default occurs, the amount of the unpaid debt can be large enough to threaten the survival of a business.

Managing Risks

LO3
Manage risks to stay within your level of risk tolerance.

Although none of the risks discussed above can be completely avoided, there are strategies you can use to minimize the likelihood and magnitude of losses. The best strategy is to develop a business environment that minimizes (1) the probability of the event occurring and (2) the amount of loss that can be experienced if the event does occur. You do this by (1) making specific plans for and arrangements to deal with foreseeable events, (2) creating and enforcing an appropriate code of conduct for yourself and all employees, (3) ensuring that valuable assets are physically secure, and (4) actively working to get rid of any physical hazards in your workplace.

You should develop disaster plans for events which are unlikely, but that have a finite probability of happening. For example, those businesses that are located in the Missouri and Mississippi River flood plains near St. Louis have a very real probability of significant flooding in any year. Prudent business management for these firms includes creating a plan of action to remove valuable assets to high ground, making plans for temporary business locations, and creating provisions for subcontracting work in order to minimize the effect of business interruption from the inevitable flood. Disaster planning like this can also work to minimize the effects of fires, storms, and earthquakes upon business operations.

A written code of ethics and business conduct (like those discussed in Chapter 2) make explicit what you expect of your employees. By obtaining employee acceptance of the code, you can create an environment in which peer pressure works to discourage inappropriate behavior and works to encourage desired behavior. To be effective, it is essential that you abide by the code, leading your employees by your example of integrity and honesty.

Valuable assets of the business must be kept in secure areas. When valuable assets must be used, access to them should be carefully controlled and monitored by management. Only those employees who have a business need should be allowed access to valuable assets at any time.

Working proactively to ensure that your physical place of business is (1) free of potential hazards and (2) secure from intruders will prevent on-premises injuries and violations of EEOC or OSHA rules. It is easier and much less expensive to anticipate and prevent potential lawsuits than it is to defend yourself against them once they have been filed.

Managing Risk to Tangible Property

Managing risk to the tangible properties of your business depends upon the nature of the property. Land and buildings aren't subject to theft, but they can be damaged or destroyed by a variety of events. Equipment can be stolen, vandalized, or allowed to fall into disrepair. Small items of high value may be stolen by employees, customers, vendors, or others. The specific measures to control for each type of risk are particular to the specific asset at risk.

Managing Risk to Buildings and Land

Protection from fire for buildings may be obtained through such measures as installing smoke alarms and sprinkler systems and having a fire plug nearby. Other control measures include removing flammable ground cover such as brush, leaves, and fallen branches from proximity to all buildings.

Protection from flood can, first and foremost, be accomplished by not locating on a flood plain. Although this seems like a common sense directive, unimaginable numbers of businesses are built on flood plains, and new construction continues. In 1993, the entire flood plain of the Missouri and Mississippi Rivers in the St. Louis area, from Kansas City on the west, Hannibal, Missouri on the north, to the confluence of the Mississippi and Ohio Rivers on the south, was inundated with water up to 50 feet deep. Hundreds of businesses in the areas around St. Louis and St. Charles, Missouri, were destroyed. Despite this experience and despite a second round of severe flooding in 1994, the flood plain of the Missouri River from St. Louis upstream for over 30 miles is the site of extensive building. It is only a matter of time until the river again rises, the levees fail, and hundreds of businesses are flooded with tens of feet of muddy water.

Flooding also occurs for reasons other than streams and rivers overflowing their banks. Floods often occur from breaks in water supply pipes, from accidental activation of fire suppression sprinklers, from blockages in storm and sanitary sewers, and from run off of water that is sprayed upon burning buildings. You may protect yourself from these hazards through performing regular inspection and maintenance of the plumbing and fire suppression systems of your buildings.

Protection from storms can be accomplished by rigorously enforcing building standards concerning attachment of buildings to foundations, types and construction of roofs, and by choice of building materials and construction techniques. The specifics of storm proofing a building depends upon the geographical location of the building. Specific storm hazards, wild fire, wind, flood, or snow load are determined primarily by geography. Each geographic area has its own risk. California has frequent floods and mud slides. The mountains of the West are subject to winter snows, spring floods, and summer wild fires. The Gulf and Eastern shores south of New York are subject to frequent hurricanes. The Midwest, especially Oklahoma, Kansas, Nebraska, Iowa, Missouri, Illinois, Indiana, and Ohio, experiences thousands of tornados every year. The upper Midwest, including northern Ohio, western Pennsylvania, and western New York, is annually buried under tons of snow. Specific building techniques to withstand tornado winds are useless against five feet of snow on the roof, just as structure to withstand snow loading is useless when the entire building slides down the hillside.

Managing risks to tools, equipment, inventory, and other physical assets is largely a function of developing and enforcing appropriate business policies and procedures. Tools and equipment should be maintained on a schedule that prevents serious wear or damage. Frequent inspections should be made to ensure that any problem is detected as soon as possible, allowing repairs to be made in a systematic manner.

Physical assets that can be stolen must be kept in locked storage areas when not in use. Small items of high value should not only be kept locked away, but a procedure should be rigidly enforced that requires employees to sign for removing them from storage. A manager's signature should be required to confirm that the item has been returned to the proper storage when it's no longer needed.

Managing Risk to Intangible Property

Intellectual property rights comprise the legal rights to use unique features of products or services that provide competitive advantage. The rights to use unique features may be legally protected in several ways, including establishing precedence, keeping the process secret, filing for a copyright or trademark, or obtaining a patent. However, if the feature is successful, competitors will eventually find a way to either lessen its competitive advantage or even to render it worthless.

The problem with legal protection methods for intellectual property is that there is no governmental agency that will assist you, as the owner of a small business, in maintaining your legal rights. Copyrights, trademarks, and patents do not automatically provide any protection. Anyone may copy any of these items at any time. If, and only if the holder of the intellectual property rights promptly reacts to infringement by making written objections to any and all infractions, can the legal rights be maintained. In other words, holding legal rights to intellectual property provides the owner solely with grounds to pursue lawsuits against infringement. Immediately upon learning of any infringement, a certified letter should be sent to the suspected violator, clearly specifying the nature of the intellectual property rights held and demanding an immediate cease and desist of the infringement. If the infringement continues, a lawsuit is your only recourse. If you do nothing, you get nothing, as was the case for Harvey Ball, the inventor of the smiley face (see Small Business Insight below).

http://www.westlaw.com

http://www.wsj.com

Guarding against obsolescence is best accomplished by maintaining a diligent watch on business intelligence concerning developments within the industry. If you own a small business that depends upon valuable intellectual property, you should regularly read the journals and magazines that are unique to your industry. You also should subscribe to clipping services, such as those provided by WestLaw and Dow Jones.

Additionally, you should carefully listen to customers and vendors for information concerning developments in your industry. Although it sounds paranoid, the truth is that intellectual property is constantly under attack. Very smart people are diligently working to develop better products and processes from which they will gain wealth at your expense if you move too slowly reacting to threats to your business.

Protection from theft of business property also depends upon the type of property held. Although land is not subject to being physically stolen, you can lose your property rights through a process called *adverse possession.* Adverse possession occurs when the owner of real property does not enforce property rights and allows a nonowner to use the property as if it were his or her own. Just as land cannot be

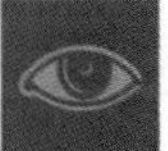

SMALL BUSINESS INSIGHT

Harvey Ball and the Smiley Face[10]

■ Does the story of Harvey Ball's design surprise you? Why do you think Harvey doesn't mind missing out on receiving royalties from use of the smiley face he invented?

You see them everywhere—yellow circles with a smiling caricature on them. The amazing thing is that as much of a cultural icon as the smiley face is, its inventor never got any money for it. Harvey Ball was a freelance designer working at State Farm Mutual Insurance in Worcester, Massachusetts, in 1963. He was asked if he could provide a design to boost morale after a merger had left some people upset. He designed the circle and smile, and he added the eyes so disgruntled employees couldn't easily turn the smile into a frown by wearing the button upside down. Ball was paid $45. He did not trademark it (which, as the designer, he could have done), nor did State Farm. State Farm gave them away—first to the employees, but then to customers who clamored for them. As the buttons spread, it got copied and copied. Franklin Loufrani of France registered the design in 1971 in over 80 countries and did receive royalties, and eventually Ball registered a version with his name on it. In the end, Loufrani made the money from the design, while Ball never got anything else for it, except a lot of satisfaction. As he said, "Never in the history of mankind or art has any single piece of art gotten such widespread favor, pleasure, enjoyment, and nothing has ever been so simply done and so easily understood in art."

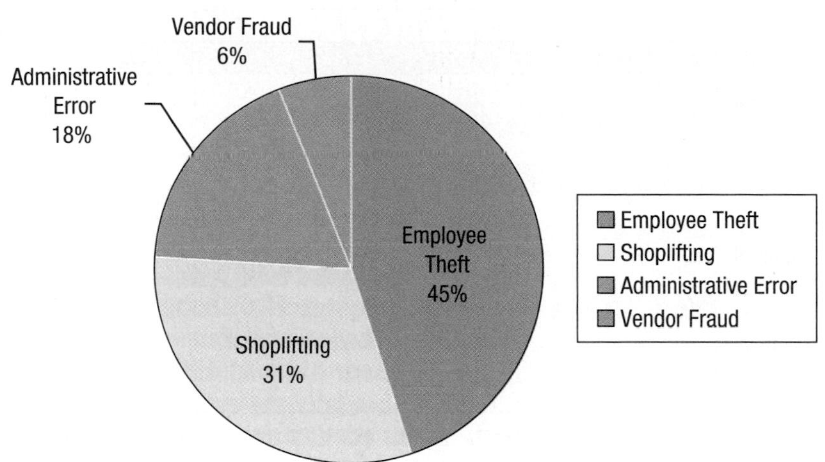

FIGURE 16.1

Sources of Theft

Source: Richard C. Hollinger and Jason S. Davis, 2001 National Retail Security Survey, University of Florida, 2002, page 4.

stolen, buildings and large equipment for which there is no ready market are similarly free from theft because of their physical nature. The property most at risk is cash and small items of high value that can be quickly and easily sold.

You need to do two things to protect yourself from theft: (1) physically protect your property, and (2) develop and enforce rules that prevent the employee responsible for the asset from being able to account for the asset. This is called **separation of duties**, and is a core management technique to safeguard money and other valuable assets of a business.[11]

separation of duties
A type of internal control that separates the physical control of an asset from the person accounting for that asset.

Although separation of duties will keep any single employee from stealing, nothing will keep two or more employees who decide to cooperate from stealing company property. Employee collusion is the source of the largest amount of employee theft.[12] When employees agree to defraud, "one lies, and the other swears to it!" This is the way that common frauds are perpetrated, such as sales of nonexistent advertising, payments to nonexistent vendors, and purchases of inventory and supplies from a vendor who will pay a kickback to the dishonest employees.

Managing Risks Resulting from Events Involving Personnel

Managing risks created by personnel starts with the hiring process, as is discussed in Chapter 19. Efforts must be made to identify people of high moral character and ethical standards. Owners of small businesses are well advised to use employment services to screen potential employees. Employment services can perform background checks, administer drug tests, and conduct psychological tests that are designed to measure an individual's level of integrity.

When potential applicants have been identified, they should be brought into the business to meet the people with whom they will be working. Current employees can participate in an informal interview with the job candidate. The purpose of these practices is to hire honest people who will become active and enthusiastic employees who consider themselves to be part of a team.

However, no hiring process is 100 percent foolproof. For that matter, no human being is 100 percent reliable. Ultimately, no one is able to withstand all temptation, regardless of ethical standards. Because all people are fallible, owners of small businesses have an obligation to employees to make theft difficult and honesty easy and rewarding. If you tempt employees with easy access to valuable property and with little likelihood of theft being detected, sooner or later most employees will succumb to temptation in ways great or small.

The Association of Certified Fraud Examiners found in a 2004 study (the Wells Report[13]) that the most costly employee frauds compared to total business assets occur in businesses with fewer than 100 employees. The median loss to these businesses was

FIGURE 16.2

Percentage of Frauds by Method of Detection

Note: Total exceeds 100 percent because of multiple responses.

Source: Association of Certified Fraud Examiners, 2004 Report to the Nation on Occupational Fraud and Abuse, 2004.

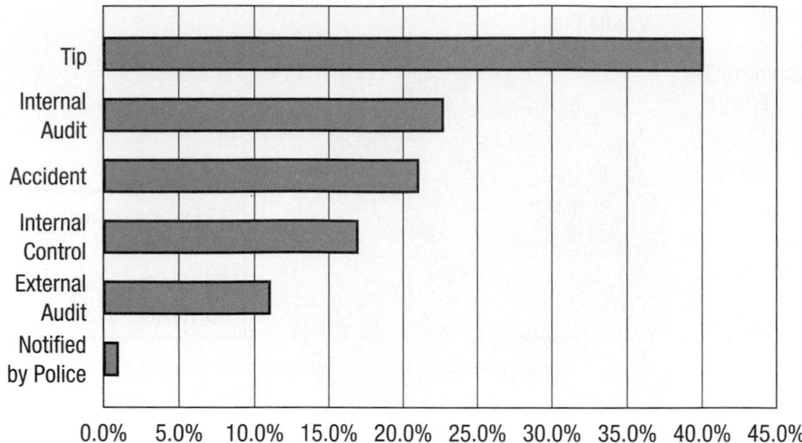

a staggering (for the owner of a small business) $98,000. This finding is interesting for two reasons: (1) The vast majority of small businesses have fewer than 100 employees, and (2) it contradicts the belief that people do not steal from people they know. The fact is that thieves come from all social classes, all levels of education, and all ethnic backgrounds. It is an unfortunate fact that the difference between many a thief and many an honest citizen is only that the citizen has not yet been caught. For these reasons, all owners and managers of small businesses must be aware of and guard against dishonesty in employees.

internal control
A set of rules and procedures that work to limit the opportunity for employee theft or malfeasance.

Internal control is the primary method of ensuring honesty in employees. Internal control is a matter of establishing policies and procedures that work to make dishonesty difficult and honesty easy. The most basic technique of internal control is to separate the duties of maintaining the security of assets from the duties of maintaining records of those assets.

While internal control will reduce the opportunity for employee fraud, it is not sufficient to disclose frauds that are currently taking place. The Wells Report found that internal controls were the fourth most likely method to discover fraud, following accidental discovery. Nearly 40 percent of all frauds that were detected were found because of a tip. About one-fourth of frauds were detected by an internal audit, and one-fifth were found by accident. Internal controls were responsible for disclosing only 18 percent of the frauds that were detected during the study period.

Separation of duties is most important for intangible assets—those things of value that have no physical "reality," such as money, accounts receivable, patents, and licensing agreements. Consider the problems of keeping money secure. Money exists primarily as an entry in the accounting records of your bank. The employee who has authority to write checks and to make deposits has free access to the things related to embezzlement. All that person needs to do is write a check made payable to a fake entity, and then cash the check and pocket the money. If one employee both writes checks and keeps accounts receivable records, theft is even easier to commit and harder to detect. The employee merely mails an invoice from a fake entity. When the fake invoice is received, the employee creates a payable account for the fake vendor. Subsequently, during the ordinary course of business, the employee writes and mails a check which will be delivered to an address held by the employee. The accounting records of the business are in perfect order. The only problem is that you are out the money that was stolen.

Such simple frauds can amount to huge amounts of money over time. The 2004 Report to the Nation on Occupational Fraud and Abuse reports on 508 cases of fraud that combined resulted in over $761 million in losses to the defrauded companies. Nearly 93 percent of the frauds detected involved misappropriation of business assets, but fewer than one-fourth of those involved assets other than cash. Fraudulent disbursements of cash comprise 74 percent of all misappropriations with an average loss to a business of $125,000.

The greatest threat of loss from employee dishonesty occurs when two or more employees *collude:* agree together to defraud your business. Employee collusion is both very common and very difficult to detect. The most common form of employee collusion is the theft of cash and inventory. Cash is most usually stolen by making false disbursements. Inventory is stolen through false employee sales.

Many small businesses allow employees to purchase inventory at cost for personal use. When two employees agree to steal, one purchases merchandise from the other. The employee who is "selling" records the sale as being less expensive items. For example, Andrew wishes to buy a complete computer from his employer's business. Brenda makes the employee sale, but records the merchandise as a hard drive. Andrew pays only the $40 cost of a hard drive, not the $400 cost of a complete computer. The owner is out the $360 difference. Of course, at some point the computer will show up as an inventory shortage. But by the time inventory is taken, there is no way to determine if the missing computer was taken by an employee or stolen by a shoplifter.

Securing valuable property is a common-sense, but often overlooked method, of keeping honest employees honest. If your business involves small items of high value, such as precision tools, jewelry, laptop computers, data projectors, computer chips, gold, platinum, and so on, those items should be kept locked in secure areas, except when being used. Employees who use such items should be required to sign for removing them from storage and obtain a manager's signature when the item is returned to storage. All items of high sensitivity, such as trade secrets, formulas, and employee and customer records, should be protected with locks, access cards, and passwords.

Risk from loss of key personnel and former employees setting up competition against your business can be managed through the contracting process. When a key employee is identified, an employment contract should be negotiated. The contract should include provisions that (1) limit the employee's freedom to go into competition, (2) contain the employee's specific promise not to disclose sensitive or secret information, and (3) offer rewards for providing adequate termination notice and a smooth transition for replacements.

Additional protection from harm resulting from loss of key employees can be obtained by cross training among employees. Although any specific employee may not be able to be directly replaced, the needed skills and talents can certainly be found within a group of employees. If employees are cross trained, the loss of one individual can be alleviated by drawing upon the diverse abilities of other employees. Finally, any truly key employee, including yourself as the owner of a small business, should be actively grooming his or her own replacement to be able to step in on an instant's notice.

Managing Risk from Violations of Tax Regulations

It is a rare business that has never run afoul of a taxing agency. Small businesses are subject to taxation from cities, counties, states, and the U.S. government. The **tax codes** of all levels of government have become ever more complex, placing more and more responsibility on businesses for calculating, collecting, and paying various taxes. Taxes imposed on small business include franchise or corporation taxes, income taxes, employee taxes, sales and use taxes, and property taxes. The regulations that relate to all these taxes are so voluminous that it is impossible for any individual to know them all. In fact, the regulations are so complex that even the enforcement personnel of various taxing agencies are often ignorant of the myriad details of the code and regulations. Perhaps then it is not surprising that the government estimates that 15 percent of taxpaying businesses are not complying with the rules.[14]

tax codes
Laws and regulations that specify the requirements of taxation.

Although there is no magic formula that will prevent financial loss that arises from being the subject of a tax audit, there are some fairly simple techniques that will work together to limit your exposure. First, you must keep complete, *accurate* accounting

SMALL BUSINESS INSIGHT

When Careful Planning and Preparation Aren't Enough

"Neither Rex nor I expected any problems when we found out that the Texas Sales Tax Commission was going to conduct an audit," said Jay Hall.

Rex said, "When the auditor came, we set up a desk for him. We kept him in coffee and gave him every record he requested. He worked for about three days checking through the last five years of our business."

"We were cool with it. After all, we have always kept our taxes squeaky clean. We knew that we had nothing to worry about."

"Little did we know," said Jay.

Rex Stone and Jay Hall are the owners and managers of Rex Stone Associates. Their business comprises planning, producing, and managing events, primarily in the San Antonio, Texas, area. They have a highly diverse client list, including businesses, unions, academic associations, and church groups. In the last few years, they have conducted training sessions, provided trail rides and chuck wagon dinners, conducted motor tours of the Hill Country, and put on numerous balls, dances, and hops for their clients.

"We were stunned when he told us that we owed the state over $125,000 in unpaid taxes, penalties, and accumulated interest. It just couldn't be so!" said Jay.

Rex continued, "When he left, we immediately called our lawyer. The issue boiled down to taxes on the services of bands and combos we had furnished for events. The auditor claimed that we had to collect sales tax on the amount that we charged our client for the music group."

"The problem was," Jay said, "we had already gotten an opinion from the Tax Commission that held that if we did not sell tickets to the event, no sales tax was due. In our business, we never sell tickets. We charge our client a fixed bid price, and only members and guests of the client group attend. Thus, no tax was due, and we had never collected for any music group."

"It took a year and cost us over $24,000 in legal fees, but finally we got a ruling that we had complied with Texas law. We did not owe the tax."

"Of course," Rex said, "we were out the twenty-four thousand. But you know, it could have been a lot worse."

records. If you use a computerized accounting system, be certain that the audit trail function is enabled. Control access to the functions of the accounting system by issuing and regularly changing passwords. File all source documents, such as purchase orders, bills of lading, requisitions, and invoices, in a systematic manner that will provide easy access if you are called upon to "prove" any transaction. Carefully document all cash transactions. Ensure that employees properly enter all cash sales into the cash register, and then reconcile the cash register tape to the cash register contents every day. Insist on receiving a *signed* receipt from vendors when you pay in cash.

The simple fact is that many, if not most, owners of small businesses "skim" in ways small and large by taking cash from their businesses before it is recorded as a revenue. Many owners also inappropriately charge personal expenses to the business as a way of extracting money without paying income taxes. Tax agents know these facts very well. As a result, when your business is audited, the agent will assume that you have understated your revenues and overstated your deductible expenses. It is your responsibility to prove that you have not.

Second, you should establish a relationship with both an accountant and a lawyer who are expert in tax issues. Although attestation by an accountant or lawyer is not evidence of lack of criminal activity (think Enron), an accountant or lawyer whose practice comprises issues of small business taxation will most likely do a much better job of representing you than you can ever do for yourself.

Third, and most important, make paying your taxes your first financial priority. The temptation to "borrow" from tax money is at times overwhelming, especially when you are being hounded by creditors for payment. Do not give in to this temptation. You can go to prison for not paying employee withholdings, for not paying sales taxes when they are due, for not paying your income taxes. If you do not pay your creditors, your credit rating will suffer. Your business may fail. But you won't go to jail for not paying your bills.

■ You won't go to jail for failure to pay your creditors, but you will spend some time behind bars if you do not pay your taxes. Keep your business in financial shape by making timely payment of taxes your first top priority.

Managing Risk from Employee Violation of Government Regulations

Reducing risk from events involving employees who violate business regulations is best accomplished through a proactive program of training and enforcing appropriate policies and procedures. The courts have consistently ruled that it is the responsibility of the employer to police employee compliance with regulations. Ignorance of either the regulations or of employee violation of regulations is not a defense against administrative action. You are financially responsible for employee violations, intentional or inadvertent. Those few cases where the employer has been held harmless all involve employers who (1) have a written policy provided to each employee, (2) have conducted training of managers and employees concerning those policies, and (3) have immediately and consistently acted upon receipt of any complaint.

Risks from violating the requirements of Equal Employment Opportunity Commission are best managed, as with risks from violations of any government regulation, by the owners being proactive:

- Know the EEOC rules that apply to your business.
- Obtain assistance from experts in EEOC regulations to assess the level of your compliance.
- Establish policies and procedures designed to prevent violations.
- Educate and train employees to know the policies and procedures and to understand the importance of following them explicitly.
- Enforce the policies and procedures by immediately dealing in a systematic manner with any employee complaint.

Knowing the EEOC rules is a daunting task for any business owner. As stated above, the rules are voluminous, ambiguous, and arcane. There are, however, many sources of information that are written to be easily understood. Most such third-party information is provided by industry associations, and thus is usually specifically written for the problems you are most likely to encounter.

Assistance can be obtained from experts in several different ways. One source that is often overlooked is the employment agency that you use to screen applicants. Employment agencies must be highly knowledgeable of the EEOC rules in order to remain in business. Often, such agencies can provide sample policy manuals and advice concerning compliance. Other sources of expert help include SCORE and the EEOC, itself.

http://www.score.org

The EEOC maintains a Web site that contains myriad resources for small business owners. The commission also publishes numerous books and pamphlets that are available from http://www.EEOC.gov.

http://www.EEOC.gov

Alleged violations of the Americans with Disabilities Act are best handled through a proactive threefold approach: (1) Determine if you are subject to any of the provisions of the ADA. (2) Obtain the services of experts on the ADA to evaluate the level of your compliance. (3) Work diligently to meet the requirements to which you are subject. Although these actions will *not* prevent you from being the target of frivolous lawsuits, you may use records of your actions as evidence of your intent to comply. This is often sufficient to persuade a mediator to pressure the complainant to either reduce the amount demanded or to withdraw the complaint entirely.

The Department of Justice maintains an ADA Technical Assistance Program which provides help directly to interested parties. By using these services, a small business owner can be assured of having current information. The Technical Assistance Program provides specific advice for your business concerning how to comply with the pertinent requirements. This program is specifically aimed at the needs of hotels, motels, restaurants, and other affected small businesses. The program provides an information hot line, printed materials, and a speakers bureau. It does not provide any inspection or affirmation services.

ADA Home Page:
http://www.usdoj.gov/crt/ada/adahom1.htm

Managing risk from violations of OSHA standards and regulations is also best accomplished through proactive efforts. As with risks from EEOC and ADA enforcement, you should first ascertain the standards to which your business is subject. The OSHA Act covers all employees except those in mining, transportation, state and local governments, and self-employment. If your business is in any other industry, you are subject to the standards of OSHA for employee health and safety. Also remember that while *you* are self-employed, anyone you hire is not. Thus, while OSHA standards and regulations do not apply to you, they do apply to your employees.

The best way to meet the basic laws of OSHA is to provide a place of employment that is free of recognized hazards and to:

1. Maintain tools and equipment in good condition.
2. Provide appropriate safety equipment and training in its proper use.
3. Provide medical examinations.

OSHA also offers free consultation services to employers who want help in identifying any deficiencies and in developing appropriate solutions. Consultations begin with a conference among the consultants and managers of the business where the scope of the consultation is set, and all parties agree on a set of working rules for the engagement. The conference is followed by an on-site inspection for hazards. The business's health program is also assessed. A final conference is held during which all findings are presented, along with suggested solutions to each identified problem. No report of any deficiency is made to OSHA for enforcement. However, if significant hazards are found, you can count on a follow-up inspection by OSHA after a reasonable time during which you must remedy the problems.

A directory of OSHA-funded consultants can be obtained by requesting OSHA Publication No. 3047, *Consultation Services for the Employer.*

You must also keep accurate records of all employee job-related illnesses and injuries. You must report within eight hours any accidents that result in a fatality or in the hospitalization of three or more employees. If your business has fewer than 10 employees or if your business is in one of the OSHA-defined "low-hazard" industries, you are exempt from the record keeping requirements of the regulations. Low-hazard industries include automobile dealers, apparel and furniture stores, eating and drinking establishments, finance, insurance, real estate, and legal, educational, personal, and business services, as well as cultural and membership organizations.

Insuring Against Risks

L04
Learn how insurance can be used to manage business risk.

Although it is impossible for the owner of a small business to avoid all business risks, it is possible, through the use of insurance, to minimize the damage that such risks can cause. However, insurance can be expensive. Because of its expense, many small business owners choose too little insurance. When the inevitable occurs, an underinsured business may well face bankruptcy and liquidation.

The key to using insurance is to obtain the "right" amount of insurance at an affordable rate. Having too little insurance leaves the business open to unsupportable losses. Carrying too much insurance wastes money.

Using Insurance to Manage Risks

Insurance is a contract between two businesses in which one, the insurance company, for a fee, agrees to indemnify the other for specific losses that are likely to occur in the future. In other words, the insurance company contracts to pay money to your business if a specific "covered" event occurs that causes your business to suffer financial loss.

insurance
A contract between two or more parties in which one party agrees, for a fee, to assume the risk of another.

Not all risks are insurable. Insurance provides a benefit by requiring a relatively small fee compared to the amount of loss that is possible. The insurance company makes a profit by collecting premiums for coverage from many businesses for the same set of risks. In effect, you and the insurance company are taking opposite gambles. You are betting that your business will be damaged or destroyed. The insurance company is betting that it won't. The insurance company wins by collecting more from all the covered companies combined than it has to pay out to those few businesses that do, indeed, suffer damage. You win (if it can be considered a "win") by having the insurance company pay when your business suffers a covered loss. Thus, the more likely an event is to occur, and the greater the potential amount that the insurance company must pay, the higher the price that you must pay for coverage. For this reason, insurance coverage is either not available or is excessively expensive for common events.

Developing a Comprehensive Insurance Program

Developing an appropriate insurance program for your business requires that you understand the risks to which your business is vulnerable. You must then know the amount of loss that your business could suffer as a result of the adverse events. Finally, you must obtain appropriate rates from reliable insurers, rates that are not too high for your business to pay but that do provide sufficient payouts if the insured event occurs.

Identifying risks is the first task to be completed before a comprehensive insurance program can be developed for your business. Risks, as discussed above, vary with the nature of your business. Risks that are common to most small businesses include fire, flood, storm, theft, business interruption, and loss of key personnel. Business-specific risks include product liability claims for manufacturers, malpractice claims for dentists and physicians, and errors and omissions claims for lawyers and accountants.

Determining which risks are to be covered is the next step. Not all identifiable risks can be or should be covered by insurance. The risk of events that are certain to occur cannot be insured at any price. Risks of events that are highly likely to occur but that have indeterminable payouts can be insured, but only at a very high price. Extremely unlikely events (being struck by a meteorite, for example) can be insured, but why would anyone do so?

Events that should be insured are those that are likely, and the economic cost of which would create a severe burden upon the finances of the business. Such events include natural disasters, liability to others, and the death or disability of key employees.

Coverages required by law exist to provide social protection from harm caused to employees, customers, and uninvolved individuals. The most common mandatory insurance coverages are liability for damages caused by vehicle accidents and illness and injury caused by employment. Most businesses are also required to pay for unemployment insurance for employees to help defray the personal cost of having one's employment terminated.

Coverages
Contractual provisions of insurance policies that specify what risks the insurance company is assuming.

Vehicle liability insurance is mandated by the legislatures of all the states and territories of the United States. Minimum amounts of coverage are specified for property damage caused by the vehicle and for injury suffered by anyone other than the driver of the vehicle.

Worker's compensation insurance is mandatory in some states. In others, it is discretionary. In all states, the worker's compensation laws provide fixed monetary

THE THOUGHTFUL ENTREPRENEUR

What Risks Can Be Insured?

Not all business risks can be covered by insurance at a reasonable cost. Insurance companies, just like you, are in business to make profits. An insurance company must charge competitive prices to be able to sell policies. At the same time, the insurance company must charge enough to be able to pay legitimate claims of its policyholders. To be able to balance these conflicting needs, an insurance company must be able to accurately predict the amount of payments that will be made to settle claims for insurable events.

The amount that an insurance company must pay out in claims is a function of (1) the frequency with which an event occurs, (2) the amount that must be paid according to the terms of the contract, and (3) the number of policies that have been issued.

- **The risk must be calculable:** An insurance company estimates the amount of potential claims payments by performing statistical analyses of the number and frequency of the occurence of the event for which the insurance is being provided. For example, the probability of an individual business being flooded can be calculated from information concerning its location relative to sources and frequencies of floods. Although a specific flood may not be predictable, the number of businesses that will encounter floods in any one year can be predicted with reasonable statistical confidence, which allows an insurance company to determine the appropriate price for a flood policy.
- **The value of any loss must be measurable in dollars:** Insurance companies contract to pay only specific amounts of money for specific types and amounts of losses. In order to determine the amount that will be paid, it must be possible for the loss to be stated in a dollar amount. Thus, an insurance company will insure you for physical damage from fire. It will not insure you for the loss of your beautiful view, should the fire burn your neighbor's property across the road.
- **The policyholder must have an insurable financial interest:** Insurance companies will not insure losses for individuals who do not suffer a financial loss from what is being insured. This requirement acts to prevent fraud by persons deliberately "creating" the event in order to profit from it. In the same vein, an insurance company will not pay more than the actual amount of the loss, regardless of the amount of the policy terms.
- **The pool of potential policyholders must be of sufficient size:** Insurance works because the insurance company diversifies its risk by insuring numerous businesses in widely separated locations. This ensures that no single disaster will result in the insurance company having to pay an excessive number of claims at any one time. Of course, this strategy occasionally fails. In the summer and fall of 2004 an unprecedented four major hurricanes hit Florida causing widespread damage. The extensive damage to a relatively large area has seriously tested the ability of several insurance companies to pay required claims and to remain in business.

awards to employees who are injured or disabled on the job. Worker's compensation is enforced through administrative procedures which preclude employees suing their employers. Federal statutes are limited to workers who are employed in some interstate commerce.

Unemployment insurance is collected by the IRS and state agencies as a percentage of tax upon payroll. The amount collected varies among industries and among businesses within an industry. Industries and businesses that have frequent seasonal layoffs pay higher amounts of unemployment premiums than do those that have stable employment.

Desired coverages beyond mandatory insurance include general liability, product liability, catastrophe, and various types of malpractice coverage. Liability insurance protects your business against claims from harm caused by inadvertent consequences of actions of the business or its employees. The list of potential causes of harm to customers, vendors, or others is nearly endless. Customers fall while on business premises. A careless worker can splatter paint on a stranger's automobile. Sparks from welding can start fires on others' property. A faulty valve can release noxious or even deadly fumes into the atmosphere. Your sewer can plug and cause flooding in your neighbor's place of business. Commercial liability insurance covers losses that are the result of such mishaps and accidents.

Product liability insurance covers losses resulting from claims made by persons who use the products of your business. The risk of customers and others being harmed by your product is largely a function of (1) the nature of your product and (2) the intended users. Those products that have historically given rise to the largest claims for injury and illness are (1) transportation equipment, such as automobiles, airplanes, and bicycles, (2) health products, such as pharmaceuticals and body implants, and (3) appliances, such as toasters, vacuum cleaners, and kitchen ranges. However, examples of huge cash settlements for product liability exist for a multitude of products that would seem to be harmless by nature. Examples of such cases include insulating foam that was discovered to emit formaldehyde, asbestos-containing products that are believed to be carcinogenic, and a multitude of toys that are alleged to cause choking and other hazards to children.

Errors and omissions insurance and malpractice insurance are examples of special types of liability insurance that cover losses from harm caused during the performance of your profession. Errors and omissions insurance covers claims made by clients of attorneys, accountants, and other consultants. Malpractice insurance covers claims made by patients of physicians, dentists, nurses, and other medical practitioners. The primary value of this type of insurance is the access to highly competent specialist lawyers that is provided by the insurance company. The insurance companies employ cadres of lawyers to represent professionals who are accused of incompetence or wrongdoing. These lawyers are usually successful in negotiating reasonable settlements with clients who have been harmed. Should a settlement be impossible, the same lawyers will vigorously defend the accused professional in the subsequent court action. Of course, in the event that the professional is held responsible for a client loss, the insurance company will pay the claim, up to the limit of the insurance contract.

You, as an individual owner or manager of a small business, can obtain a general liability insurance, which is often called an *umbrella policy,* or a *success protector policy.* General liability policies exist to pay losses that are not covered by other liability insurance. It is a sad fact of our current legal climate that actual culpability is irrelevant to many damage claims. If you are successful in your business, your success makes you a target for lawsuits because you are considered to be able to pay a judgment, either through your personal wealth or through seizure of your business property. Claims against general liability policies are usually a result of such litigation.

Insuring the Property of the Business

Commercial property insurance covers losses to the business property from causes such as fire, storm, vandalism, and theft. Other property insurance exists to pay losses resulting from floods or earthquakes. The cost of property insurance is determined largely by (1) the property's insurable value, (2) the amount of deductible loss, (3) the amount of co-insurance required, and (4) the loss limits of the policy.

All the value of a property does not have **insurable value**. For example, as a general rule, the value of land, excavation, and basement is not insurable. This is because even when a disaster occurs, the land remains. Only a very few types of disasters, such as earthquake or landslide, can change the nature and topography of land.

insurable value
The amount of an asset for which a company will write an insurance policy.

Additionally, some property has value that cannot be stated in dollar amounts. The value of the historical significance of a building often cannot be determined. For example, in Clarksville, Tennessee, the Hachland Hall Bed and Breakfast has a log cabin that was the home of President Andrew Jackson during the time that he was building

THE THOUGHTFUL ENTREPRENEUR

Heidi Klum's Unique Insurance Policy[15]

In 2004, the model Heidi Klum had her legs insured for $2 million.[16] This may seem a little strange, but it is not unprecedented. During World War II, the then-famous actress and pinup girl, Betty Grable, received widespread publicity from insuring her legs for $1 million. More recently, the soccer player, David Beckham, had his legs insured for a cool $70 million.[17]

Given that the loss of a leg is not a common occurrence, why would a model, an actor, and a sports star seek such insurance?

Given that there is not a sufficient pool of models, actors, and athletes to allow an insurance company to diversify its risk, why would an insurance company write such a policy?

In actuality, such policies are not as unusual as you might think. Insurance companies routinely write policies that place a dollar value on the loss of a person's appendages. While the occurrence of the maiming of actors is low, nationwide a significant number of people lose arms, legs, hands, feet, and eyes in a variety of accidents and illnesses. Thus, the risk of such loss is well understood by insurance companies, and the cost of paying claims for such policies can be reliably predicted. Provisions for specific dollar payments for the loss of appendages is commonly included in insurance policies that cover disability.

Despite the ordinariness of disability insurance, it is clear that the purpose of these insurance policies for Ms. Klum and Ms. Grable was the publicity value to be gained. In both cases, they and the insurance companies all received lots of press coverage from the stunts. It is interesting to note that while the amount of the insurance coverage is reported, no mention is ever made of the cost of the premium or of the term of the insurance contract.

There is a popular perception that any risk can be insured. This perception has arisen because of highly publicized events that were not actually insurance transactions but were publicity stunts. While it might be comforting to be able to insure against any loss, the fact is that businesses must constantly weight the cost of insurance coverage. In many cases, the cost of insurance coverage greatly exceeds any benefit for small business.

the famous Hermitage. Were this cabin to burn to the ground, its replacement cost for logs, timber, and finish lumber could be no more than a few tens of thousands of dollars. However, no matter how carefully rebuilt, the replacement would be a replica, not the actual cabin. As such, it might be interesting, but it would not have the special character that now makes it unique. Placing a dollar amount on the historical value of this cabin is highly problematical.

deductible
An amount of loss that will not be paid by an insurance company.

A **deductible** is an amount of loss that is specifically excluded by the insurance contract. It is common for vehicle policies to specify that in the event of loss, the insurance will pay the amount of the loss, less a deductible of $250 to $1,000. Policies on buildings and equipment usually have similar deductibles ranging from $1,000 to $10,000 or more. As a general rule, the higher the deductible, the lower the policy premium payments will be.

co-insurance
A contract stipulation that requires a policyholder to carry insurance in an amount equal to a stated minimum percentage of the market value of the property insured.

Co-insurance is a contract requirement that works to prevent property owners from deliberately underinsuring. Co-insurance requires that the owner carry insurance in an amount equal to a stated minimum percentage of the market value of the property, most usually 80 percent. If the owner allows insurance coverage to fall below this amount, then the amount that the insurance company will pay in the event of loss is reduced by an amount proportional to the amount of underinsurance.

The reason for such arcane provisions is to increase the amount of premium that the insurance company collects relative to the risk that the insurance company is taking by insuring the property. The higher the value a property has, the greater the likely payout an insurance company will have to make in the event of loss.

Consider that property losses are highly correlated with the value of the property. At one extreme, the loss can never exceed the market value of the property. At the other extreme, loss cannot be less than zero. In between the two extremes, losses are often a function of the value of the property. For example, suppose two businesses each experienced a fire that destroyed the roof of a warehouse. A 43,000-square-foot warehouse worth $3.5 million has a much more expensive roof than does a 10,000-square-foot warehouse which is worth less than $750,000. Similarly, losing your 1,600-square-foot retail space will be a much greater dollar loss if the store is located on Rodeo Drive in Beverly Hills, California, than if it is located on Main Street in Beckwourth, California.

Business interruption insurance provides funds to pay the ordinary operating expenses of your business should it be forced to close temporarily because of an insured event. Although business interruption insurance can be purchased as a stand-alone policy, it is most usually acquired as a provision of commercial property insurance.

Crime insurance offers protection against losses from crimes committed against your business. It is an unfortunate fact that the greatest number of crimes of which you are likely to be victim are committed by trusted employees.

Theft insurance is normally included in insurance on physical assets. However, the greatest threat of loss because of employee dishonesty is the misappropriation of cash, as is discussed earlier. Cash cannot be insured. An approach to obtaining insurance against employee theft of money is to require all employees with access to money or to accounting for money to be *bonded.*

Fidelity bonds, also called *dishonesty bonds,* repay employers for losses caused by dishonest or negligent employees. Fidelity bonds cover losses from employee fraud, theft, forgery, and embezzlement. Unlike **surety bonds**, fidelity bonds are purchased only for the employer's benefit.

fidelity bonds
Bonds, also called *dishonesty bonds,* that repay employers for losses caused by dishonest or negligent employees.

surety bonds
An agreement with an insurance or bonding company that will pay a specified amount in the event that the entity bonded fails to comply with specified contractual requirements.

If you have any employee who handles large amounts of cash or other valuable assets, you should consider bonding that person. Some businesses, including insurance companies, securities brokers, real estate brokers, and businesses that hold escrowed cash are required by law to carry fidelity bonds. All employees who have direct access to a company's cash, securities, and accounting records, or who handle investment or retirement funds, should be bonded. Bonds are available to cover individual specific key employees, or as blanket bonds that cover all employees.

When obtaining fidelity bonds, you should consider the following:

- The scope of coverage.
- All exclusions.
- Types of employee dishonesty not covered (e.g., salary, benefit, or computer fraud).
- Coverage for employee actions off-premises.

Credit insurance covers abnormal losses from credit customers not paying their bills. Abnormal losses are carefully defined within the insurance contract. Typical covered events include customers who cease business because of bankruptcy or business interruptions caused by fire, storm, wind, floods, and earthquakes. Less common and more expensive coverage exists that will pay for losses that arise from general economic conditions such as recession, war, or trade embargos.

Credit insurance can be obtained that covers all credit accounts or that covers only specific accounts. General credit insurance is expensive, and it is common to choose to cover only very large accounts, the loss of which would threaten survival of the business.

All credit insurance requires the merchant to provide co-insurance in the amount of 10 to 20 percent of the credit loss. The co-insurance provision works to prevent both frivolous claims and to provide a disincentive to companies to issue credit indiscriminately.

Credit insurance companies provide mandatory collection services. The insured business is required to promptly report all past due accounts. When an account is determined to be delinquent, usually after 90 days of no payment, then the account must be assigned to the insurance company which will make vigorous efforts to collect.

Credit insurance is available only for manufacturers and wholesalers. At this time no insurance company will write coverage for retailers who offer credit to customers.

Retailers who provide credit are protected in two ways. First, those few retailers who offer credit directly to customers usually have a large number of relatively small accounts receivable. This provides a greater diversification of the risk of loss than is available to wholesalers who usually have a relatively small number of large value receivables. Second, most retailers today provide credit only through credit cards, including Master Card, Visa, Discover, and American Express. Credit card companies perform credit checks before issuing cards, and thus limit the risk of nonpayment. Additionally, the credit card companies have developed rules which include checking cards for customer signatures, requiring a government-issued picture ID, and obtaining a transaction authorization prior to providing the credit sale. Retailers who follow the rules are not liable for any future nonpayment by the credit card holder.

Personnel insurance is available to protect both you and your employees from specific risks. Personnel coverages include key person insurance, life, disability, and medical coverage insurance.

THE THOUGHTFUL ENTREPRENEUR

Bring in the Clowns

Imagine a fair without a midway. Can a fair even be a fair without a carousel, a roller coaster, or a ferris wheel? Carnivals are hugely popular entertainments. Over 500 million people attend amusement parks, fairs, and carnivals in the United States each year (which is quite impressive, given that the entire population of the nation is only 300 million).

As you might expect, carnivals experience numerous accidents each year, ranging in severity from bruises and abrasions to permanent maiming and death. According to the U.S. Consumer Product Safety Commission (CPSC),[18] approximately 11,000 people are injured on amusement rides each year. Of these, about five die.

There are approximately 500 carnivals that travel the United States each year, ranging in size from 1 to over 100 portable amusement rides. The vast majority of carnivals are small family-owned businesses with second and third generation members involved in management and operation.[19]

If your carnival is large enough and you expect to have about 1 million riders in a year, then you should expect to experience approximately 20 to 25 injuries, based on CPSC statistics. If the people injured are representative of the national experience, all of them will be younger than 16. Not one will have an injury severe enough to require more than outpatient treatment. However, there is a small, but measurable risk that you will be among the unfortunate carnival operators who have patrons seriously injured to the point of maiming or death.

As the owner of a carnival, what insurance should you carry to cover the injuries of customers on your rides? Insurance to cover the potential medical expenses for twenty-some minor injuries would be prohibitively expensive. It would, on the other hand, be quite risky for your business to carry no insurance at all. A reasonable strategy is to obtain insurance that will cover only serious injury and death. Your carnival will then absorb the cost of treating minor injuries, the number of which can be reduced by a safety program that prevents customer horseplay, requires operator training, and enforces regular rigid safety inspection of the rides. Taking such measures not only reduces the probability of serious injury, but also reduces the cost of accident insurance.

Key person insurance protects you in the event that a key employee dies or is disabled and cannot work.

Life insurance is the most common kind of coverage on key persons. Usually key person insurance names you, as the owner, or your business as the beneficiary of the policy. Life insurance also is often provided to employees to provide security for their families. Life insurance provided by you, the employer, is usually term insurance. *Term insurance* is a form of insurance that does not accumulate any value over the contract term. Rather, only specific events, including disability, dismemberment, and death, are insured events. Term insurance is very inexpensive for healthy young people. The premiums increase with age, and with specified risk factors such as obesity, heart problems, and a history of driving while intoxicated.

Disability insurance is usually provided as part of life insurance, although it can be obtained as either a stand-alone policy or as part of medical coverage. You as the owner of a small business should carefully consider obtaining disability coverage not only for key persons but also for yourself. Statistics provided by the American Association of Retired Persons (AARP) show that between the ages of 22 and 65, there is a greater than 25 percent probability that you will be disabled for a period of 12 months or more.[20] Statistics provided by the Social Security Administration indicate that the greatest probability of becoming disabled for this period of time occurs between ages 50 and 65.[21] The probability of shorter periods of disability is, of course, much higher. Given the high probability of temporary disability and the devastating effects it can have upon a small business, it is becoming ever more common for disability coverage to be included in business insurance plans.

Disability insurance can take several forms. The most common disability coverage provides the insured person with funds to replace income lost because of the inability to work. While this coverage is important to the disabled person, it provides no direct benefit to your business.

Some insurance companies now offer disability coverage that provides direct benefits to small businesses and to owners of small businesses. The most common of such disability coverage is **buyout insurance** which provides funds to the business to purchase the ownership position of a disabled partner. Less common, but of similar value for small business owners, is disability coverage that will pay specific fixed costs of the business, such as rent, salaries, and utilities, in the event that the owner or other named key person becomes disabled. Even less common is disability coverage that will pay specific dollar amounts to the business to replace lost revenue caused by the disability of a key person.

buyout insurance
Insurance that provides money to owners of a business to buy the shares of any deceased owner from that owner's heirs.

Medical coverage is the most highly desired form of insurance for most employees. Medical coverage is quite expensive, and the cost has been increasing rapidly in recent years. There are many reasons, however, that you, as the owner of a small business, might wish to provide such coverage for your employees. First, receiving medical coverage is a strong retention incentive for employees. Second, if you provide medical insurance for all employees, you can obtain reduced rates and can include yourself and your family. Third, the least expensive way to obtain key person insurance is as a part of a comprehensive medical insurance plan that covers all employees.

Sharing Risk

LO5
Master sharing risk with other businesses and organizations.

One very effective method to reduce and to control business risk is to share that risk with other entities. As discussed above, one way to share risk is through insurance programs which, in effect, diversify risk across industries, businesses, and geographical areas. Additionally, risk can be directly shared without the intermediary of an insurance company, by forming joint ventures, by joining industry groups, and by obtaining government grants and guarantees.

Joint Ventures

joint venture
An agreement between two or more entities to pool resources in order to complete a project.

Joint ventures are partnerships through which two or more businesses combine to undertake a specific economic activity. Each business involved in a joint venture keeps its own identity and conducts its own business separately from that of the other partners. The businesses are partners only for the activities specified in the joint venture contract.

Joint ventures are most usually formed and taxed as partnerships. This allows for disproportionate allocation of revenues and expenses among the partner businesses. The ability to assign tax items to the partner for which they are most advantageous eases the problems of dissimilar businesses forming a partnership. A relatively large, profitable partner can be assigned the deductible costs of the joint venture, while revenues are simultaneously assigned to the smaller, less profitable (or even unprofitable) partner who will pay taxes at a lower rate.

Another advantage of joint ventures is that each partner can lose no more than its investment in the venture. The joint venture is a separate entity from any of the partners that own it. Thus, if the joint venture fails, only the resources of the joint venture are lost. The partner companies can continue in their individual businesses.

Industry Groups for Insurance Coverage

One of the primary reasons that there is at least one organized group for every conceivable industry is that joining in groups provides benefits of scale to members. The most common benefit is low-cost group insurance. The cost of insurance, as discussed above, is partly a function of the risk that the insurance provider assumes. Insurance companies diversify risk by insuring large numbers of similar businesses. It is obvious that the National Electric Sign Association can provide a much larger pool of people to be insured than can any single sign shop member. Because of the larger pool of potential insured people and because of its greater bargaining power, the NESA can obtain much lower insurance rates for its members than the members can obtain individually.

Government Funding of Risky Ventures

The final source for sharing risk is governments. Townships up to the federal government have programs to encourage economic activity. Governments do not have the profit-making requirements of businesses, but they do have the power to extract money from citizens. As a result, risk for a government is very different from risk for private business. Governments often subsidize very risky ventures that private companies would otherwise never attempt.

One example of government subsidizing risky ventures can be seen in the building of sports arenas, convention centers, and convention hotels. Cities across the nation have imposed taxes upon citizens and tourists to subsidize the building of such facilities. St. Louis has three such publicly funded arenas: one for the Cardinals baseball team, one for the Rams football team, and a half-million-square-foot convention center. Houston recently demolished an old facility and built a new one for the Houston Oilers football team. The City of San Antonio, Texas, and Bexar County recently enacted one of the nation's highest taxes on hotel rooms and rental cars to finance a new arena for the Spurs basketball team, despite having the largely unused Alamo Dome.

It is important to realize that the cities do not directly profit from these facilities. Nationwide, arenas, convention centers, and convention hotels operate at losses, which are covered by taxes imposed on nonusers of the facilities. In those rare instances in which the facilities are profitable, the profits go to private businesses which lease or operate the facilities on contract. Absent government subsidies, few, if any, of these facilities would exist.

Small businesses can obtain their share of government subsidies through direct contracting and grants. Opportunities exist for small businesses to obtain government funding for recycling of waste materials, for research and development of products for health, security, and defense, and for providing services directly to government entities.

All businesses operate in varying states of risk. The most careful planning and the best management in the world cannot remove all uncertainty from business operations. Storms, earthquakes, tsunamis, famines, recessions, and wars are facts of life with which you must sooner or later cope.

Although business risk cannot be eliminated, it can be controlled. Management techniques including security devices and internal controls can reduce the risk of misappropriation of business assets. Those risks that cannot be controlled can be insured. Insurance works to reduce the amount of loss that any individual business experiences because of natural events, dishonesty, or negligence. Because the environment in which business operates is constantly changing, you, as the owner and manager of a small business, must constantly reassess your risk controls, your exposure to disaster, and your insurance coverage.

Ben Franklin said long ago that, "A penny saved is a penny earned," and that adage is truly important for small businesses. Money saved means more flexibility and more profit. The point of spending time on risk, insurance, and protecting yourself and your business is to help you identify the ways to minimize your losses. Often thinking about the potential sources of risk and loss ahead of time makes it possible for you to take action to minimize the risk, or handle the loss should it come. The whole concept of insuring against risk works best when you can think objectively about the potential risk, loss, and cost to your firm. Only then can you be sure that you are spending your insurance dollars wisely. Despite all the talk about financial loss, it is important to note the human and emotional cost of loss. Whether through injury or criminal action, loss focuses our attention and can make us sad, angry, guilty, or a combination of the three. When it causes harm to employees or customers, it can derail a business and its owner. For all these reasons, taking the time to protect your business, its assets, and people always makes sense.

CHAPTER SUMMARY

LO1 Understand the meaning and nature of business risk.

- Business risk comes from many sources, including financial risk from capital structure, economic risks from business decisions, and the environment.
- Business risk is the probability that the future economic state of the business will be worse than is projected.

LO2 Recognize the specific types of risks associated with different aspects of business operations.

- Economic risks arise from events related to the property of the business, the personnel of the business, and the customers, vendors, and visitors to the business.
- Much of the risk related to people is created by the myriad laws, rules, and regulations of the ADA, OSHA, the EEOC, and various tax agencies.
- Businesses are usually held liable for injuries suffered on business property, regardless of the cause.

LO3 Manage risks to stay within your level of risk tolerance.

- The loss from various events can be reduced by making specific plans and arrangements to deal with them, should they occur.
- Disaster plans can reduce losses by reducing the time that business operations are interrupted when the event occurs.
- Following building codes, locating away from flood plains, and keeping property clear of flammables can reduce loss from natural events.
- The best control for risks from personnel is to hire qualified people of high integrity.

LO4 Learn how insurance can be used to manage business risk.

- Keeping the right types and levels of insurance can minimize a business's loss from adverse events.
- You should not try to insure against all risks, rather only those that have economic consequences great enough to threaten the survival of your business.
- Some insurance coverages are required by law.

LO5 Master sharing risk with other businesses and organizations.

- Risk may be reduced and insurance made affordable by joining with other similar businesses.
- The risky activity can be separated from the main part of your business through joint ventures and placing the risky activity into a separate legal entity.
- Industry groups can obtain lower insurance rates than can a single business.
- Government agencies can provide protection from risk by limiting the potential loss and by subsidizing risky ventures.

DISCUSSION QUESTIONS

1. Discuss the types of risk encountered by small businesses. Are these risks different in any way from risks facing big business?
2. What are the risks to small businesses caused by personnel issues?
3. How are the risks from personnel affected by government business regulations?
4. How does disaster planning help a small business cope with risk?
5. The text discusses methods to protect against weather. What might a business do to protect itself against earthquake?
6. Which is easier to steal, money from an employer's bank account or secret business processes? Why?
7. What types of insurance should a small business have? Give your reasons for maintaining each type of coverage.
8. Suppose you are in the business of making ladders. A customer places a board plank between two of your ladders as a scaffold. One of the ladders fails, causing your customer to fall and break a leg. Are you responsible for your customer's losses? How can you protect yourself from lawsuits in such cases?

9. You are considering offering credit to good customers to increase sales. What things should you consider to limit your risks if you do?
10. One of your partners has special skills that would be very difficult to replace. His great joy in life is single-track bicycle racing. How can you protect yourself from the probability that he will be injured and unable to work?

EXPERIENTIAL EXERCISES

1. Identify a business you would like to own. Make a list of the risks that are specific to that business. Contact an insurance broker to find out what coverages are available and what they would cost. Make a report to your class of your findings.
2. Identify a business you would like to own. Go to the OSHA Web site and find out what rules and regulations apply to this business. Create a chart of hazards of this business and the applicable OSHA rules. Make a report to your class of your findings.
3. Suppose you are going to open a consulting business. You are going to finish half of your garage to use as an office. Go to the ADA site and determine what accessibility requirements you must meet. Make a report to your class of your findings.
4. Identify a specific location (street address) where you would like to operate a business. Visit your city's planning and zoning office (or its Web site, if it has one) and determine if this site is in a flood plain. Make a copy of the city's map of flood plains. Make a report to your class of your findings.
5. Identify a business you want to own. Use the resources of your library and the Internet to identify what insurance you are legally required to carry. Contact an insurance broker to determine how and for how much you can obtain the required coverage. Make a report to your class of your findings.

Mini-Case

RISKY BUSINESS

Vicky Volare fell in love with motor scooters on her vacation trip to Aruba. "They're a blast!" Vicky said, "They are convenient, safe, inexpensive, and fun to ride." Now she is planning to buy 30 Vespa Scooters to provide scooter rental in Vail, Colorado. Vicky will need four employees, in addition to her own services. She has completed a business plan, except for determining what types and amounts of insurance coverage she should have. As soon as she completes the insurance planning, she can complete the financial section of her business plan. Vicky will invest $50,000 of her own funds and is borrowing $230,000. $180,000 of the loan will be secured with the 30 scooters. The other $50,000 is a personal note to her from her bank. She hopes to start her business within 90 days, to catch the beginning of the summer.

CASE DISCUSSION QUESTIONS

1. What financial risks is Vicky assuming?
2. What are the risks that are specific to renting motor scooters?
3. What are the risks specific to motor scooters, as physical assets?
4. What risks will Vicky face because she is hiring four people?
5. What regulatory risks will Vicky face in operating a vehicle rental service in the state of Colorado?
6. What insurance coverage will Colorado require Vicky to have?
7. What insurance must Vicky have for her employees?
8. How should Vicky structure her business to minimize the potential loss she can suffer if a customer or bystander is injured or killed by one of her scooters?

LEARNING OBJECTIVES

This chapter will help you:

LO1 Learn how to manage short-term assets.

LO2 Determine the value of the assets in your business.

LO3 Master managing fixed assets.

LO4 Understand how to analyze capital investment decisions.

LO5 Recognize the advantages of renting or leasing capital equipment.

■ Curtis Graf's company lost a significant amount in assets when a thief disguised as a worker literally walked onto a construction site and drove off in a backhoe. Managing your business's property can be a challenge. What are some of the security measures Curtis could have put into place that would have deterred this theft? What measures do you think you would need to implement for your dream business?

Assets: Inventory and Operations Management

Focus on Small Business: Curtis Graf and the Nightmare on Construction Street

It's every contractor's nightmare. You arrive on a job site at six in the morning and find that hundreds of thousands of dollars of construction equipment was stolen overnight. Work comes to a halt. Expenses escalate as workers stand around while you make a frenzied effort to buy, borrow, or rent replacement equipment.

Curtis Graf in the Dallas suburb of Mesquite, Texas, encountered something even worse. A bold thief, in broad daylight, simply walked onto one of his construction sites, started up, and drove away in a $40,000 backhoe. A worker on the site saw the whole thing, but because the thief looked and acted as if he belonged, mistook him for another worker.

"I paid $3,000 to have it burglar-proofed," Curtis said, "but they stole it anyway!"[1]

Most unfortunately, equipment theft is a nightmare that all too often comes true. Despite all efforts—those of law enforcement, the owners, and industry groups—500 pieces of heavy construction equipment are stolen in the United States *each week.* Less than 15 percent of the machines stolen are ever recovered.[2]

Curtis did not get his machine back. He faxed a report to the local police and called numerous times to see if it had been found. Curtis said that the only reply from the police was, "We will call you when we find something." He added, "That's short for, 'We don't have time to talk to you anymore.'"[3]

His insurance company was little help, as well. It not only delayed payment as long as it could, but it also canceled his policy, which resulted in his changing insurance carriers for the third time in three years. He did finally receive a payment of $24,000 nearly a year after the machine was stolen, leaving him $16,000 shy of the cost of a replacement.

DISCUSSION QUESTIONS

1. Why do you think that thieves target heavy construction machinery?
2. To what extent do you think that Curtis Graf's negative experience with insurance coverage for theft is commonly encountered by small business owners?
3. Why do you suppose that less than 15 percent of stolen heavy machines are ever recovered when the FBI reports that 62 percent of stolen automobiles are recovered?
4. Think of the business that you own or would like to own. How and to what extent would the theft of machinery or equipment be a threat to your business?

Managing Short-Term Assets

LO1
Learn how to manage short-term assets.

In many ways, you can think of your business as a collection of assets: things you own that will provide value in the future. The things that you own include the obvious, such as cash, inventory, tools, machinery, buildings, and land. Less obvious things are also owned, such as legal claims to collect money from customers in the future, patents, copyrights, trademarks, expertise, and your reputation.

Because your business *is* its assets, if you allow them to be damaged, lost, stolen, or destroyed, your wealth diminishes. At some point, if your business loses enough value, it will cease to exist. It will be bankrupt, and you will have lost your investment.

Managing your business assets to obtain their maximum value is critical to ultimate business success. Chapter 14 is dedicated to the issues of managing cash, the most liquid of all business assets. This chapter discusses managing the critical short-term assets of accounts receivable and inventory, and managing the essential long-term assets of property, plant, and equipment.

Accounts Receivable

accounts receivable
Money owed to your business by customers who purchased your product on credit.

Accounts receivable are money that is owed to your business by your customers. As is discussed in Chapter 16, relatively few small businesses today provide credit to customers. Current practice is for small businesses to provide credit only by accepting bank-issued credit cards. However, there are still some small businesses, especially those involved in wholesale distribution, that provide direct credit to customers. For these firms, managing receivables is an essential activity.

The Pros and Cons of Offering Credit to Customers

Credit is provided to customers for marketing reasons. Providing credit usually results in higher sales revenue because of increased repeat business. Providing credit also reduces the cost of selling, because it is much less expensive to obtain repeat business than it is to get new customers.

On the down side, selling your product and then allowing customers a month or two to pay has three negative effects that are often overlooked when business owners make the decision to extend credit. First, providing credit delays the receipt of cash. If your small business is like most, you exist in a state of constant cash shortages. Anything that delays receiving cash makes the problems of meeting payrolls and paying suppliers and vendors even worse. This causes the second problem: You must somehow replace the "missing" cash. Most often this means borrowing. Borrowing, of course, is expensive. You spend time to arrange a loan, and then must make regular payments of interest. Third, if you give credit to your customers, sooner or later one of them will not pay. Although you provide credit only to those customers whom you believe will pay, despite careful monitoring and despite strenuous collection efforts, eventually someone won't. The reasons why people don't pay can be almost anything, from inability to pay because they have no money to low ethics to outright fraud. Regardless of the cause, your business loses when customers don't pay.

Managing Accounts Receivable to Receive the Greatest Benefit for Your Business

As stated above, providing customer credit usually results in increased sales revenues and lowered transaction costs, which usually more than offsets the costs of interest and uncollectible accounts, resulting in greater profits. To realize this benefit, you must establish and enforce efficient and effective policies and procedures for extending credit. Your goals are to: (1) minimize the time that passes between when a credit sale is made and when the cash is received, and (2) keep the number of bad accounts as low as possible. Figure 17.1 provides a list of standards that should always be followed if you provide credit to customers.

Using Your Accounts Receivable as a Source of Financing

You can often get immediate cash from third-party finance companies if you have established and enforced policies to maintain a high quality of receivables. Having high-quality receivables lets you quickly get cash to meet unexpected needs.

You can use your receivables in two ways to quickly lay your hands on cash. First, you can pledge your receivables as collateral for a commercial loan. Depending upon

FIGURE 17.1

Policies for Managing Accounts Receivable

If you want to collect the money owed you from credit sales, you must be very careful to give credit only to those customers who are likely to pay. To make credit work for your business, you must work consistently to collect what you are owed. The following nine policies are *minimum standards* for managing customer credit:

1. Make an extensive credit check prior to authorizing credit sales to any individual customer.
2. Promptly bill each customer following each credit purchase.
3. Provide cash discounts for making timely payments.
4. Enforce significant late fees and interest on past due accounts.
5. Maintain constant "aging" of accounts to quickly identify customers who become delinquent.
6. Make consistent, vigorous efforts to collect from customers, including dunning letters and phone calls.
7. Discontinue credit sales to customers who become significantly late in paying.
8. File suits and liens against the assets of customers who default on payment.
9. Use your bank as a **lock box** for the receipt of payments.

lock box
A locked receptacle for money, the keys to which are not available to those who physically handle the receptacle; a common example of a lock box is the coin receptacle for parking meters which cannot be opened by the workers who are responsible for collecting the deposited coins.

SMALL BUSINESS INSIGHT

Put *Your* Bill on the Top of the Pile

Dwight Cooper, CEO of PPR Travel,[4] a nurse-staffing firm in Jacksonville, Florida, was in a quandary. Average time to collect payment on accounts was a crippling 60 days from the time the bill was sent. For two months, Cooper had to cover all the costs of his nurses—wages, benefits, and tax withholdings—as well as his own operating expenses. In effect, Cooper was financing the operations of his customers. On the other hand, if he pressed his clients for payment, he risked creating bad will and perhaps even losing business.

"What should I do?" he asked himself.

Owners of small businesses commonly face the same dilemma. A recent study by REL Consultancy Group of Purchase, New York, found that fully one-third of big businesses are habitually late paying vendors' bills.[5] Sooner or later, if you provide credit to customers, you too will have difficulties in collecting what is due. Customer accounts will slip ever farther into arrears. Past due accounts will accumulate: 90, days, 120 days, even 6 months in arrears. Cooper took a unique approach to his problem. He *asked* his customers why they paid late and what he could do to help them speed payment.

■ Dwight Cooper shaved 15 days off his company's average time for collection of bills receivable. Which of his steps could you see yourself imitating in your business? What ideas might you add in improving your company's collection process?

Even more unusually, he *acted* to implement the things that his customers said would help them pay more quickly. First, he established procedures to ensure that every bill was accurate. Second, he issued a single invoice to each hospital for all nurses provided, rather than sending multiple invoices, one for each nurse provided. Third, he started printing his invoices on blue paper, making them immediately recognizable. Fourth, he began sending a reminder when a customer was only one day late. To take the sting from the reminders, each is addressed by hand.

The results of Cooper's efforts is that average collection time has been reduced from 60 days to 45.[6]

the finance company, customer payments on pledged receivables may be collected either by you and forwarded to the lender, or may be made directly to the lender. Second, you can *sell* your receivables to a finance company in a process called **factoring**. A factoring company will usually pay you about 75 to 80 percent of the total amount that can be collected. The factor then collects the receivables. The difference between the gross amount of the receivables and the amount that is ultimately collected is the factor's profit margin. Skill Module 17.1 gives you a chance to work through the ways a factor might structure a deal for you.

factoring
Selling the rights to collect accounts receivable to an entity outside your business.

Pledging receivables to a commercial lender is usually less expensive than factoring. When you pledge receivables, your business is liable only for the borrowed amount and accrued interest on the loan, regardless of the amount that is subsequently collected from your customers. You have the opportunity to collect it all. On the other hand, a commercial lender will loan you only one-half of the amount that can be collected. When you factor receivables, you immediately get 75 to 80 percent of the amount due. But, you forever give up all rights to the factor's discount. Of course, for this amount, the finance company assumes your bad debt risk. If a factor does not collect enough to make a profit, it's the factor's problem, not yours.

pledging receivables
Giving a third party legal rights to debts owed your business in order to provide assurance that borrowed money will be repaid.

SKILL MODULE 17.1

Using Receivables to Raise Immediate Cash

Suppose that you need $50,000 immediately in order to purchase welded steel roof trusses for a building that you have contracted to construct. Normally, you would simply purchase the materials on account from an established supplier, but two things prevent this. First, you have reached your credit limit with your supplier, and the supplier refuses to provide more. Second, your regular supplier is operating at maximum possible output and cannot deliver the trusses within the time required by your contract.

You have found a supplier who will manufacture and deliver the trusses when you need them. However, this supplier does not offer credit. Further, the supplier demands an immediate deposit of one-half of the cost of the trusses, $25,000, with the remaining $25,000 paid on delivery. You have approached your bank, but the bank has refused you a loan because (1) you are at your borrowing limit, and (2) the business with which you have contracted is embroiled in a lawsuit with the bank, and the bank therefore will not accept the contract as collateral.

You have current receivables of $67,000. You have contacted a factor in your area that has proposed two financing deals.

1. The factor will purchase your receivables for 75 percent of their collection value. You will receive 95 percent of the cash immediately, and the factor will retain the remaining 5 percent until all the receivables are collected. If the entire $67,000 is collected, then the remaining money will be paid to you. However, the money being held will be reduced by any amount uncollected at the end of 120 days from the date of the factoring contract.
2. The factor will lend you $54,000 discounted at 12 percent interest for 90 days. You must pledge 100 percent of your receivables as collateral for the loan. The factor will collect your receivables, applying 100 percent of the amount collected against the $54,000 until it is completely repaid, dollar for dollar.

What should you do? Show calculations to support your decision.

Managing Inventory

inventory
Products that are held for sale to customers.

Inventory is a constant, everyday problem for most small businesses. It is the largest current asset that most manufacturing, wholesale, and retail firms have. Manufacturing firms, wholesalers, and retailers simply cannot operate effectively without a minimum level of inventory on hand. Even service firms such as restaurants, beauty shops, automobile garages, plumbing businesses, electrical contractors, sign companies, and so on also have to have some inventory to function efficiently. It is a rare business, indeed, that has no inventory at all.

The amount and type of inventory held for resale is important for small businesses because (1) the supply of inventory and demand of customers cannot be precisely matched at all times, and (2) holding inventory requires a nonproductive cash investment. While inventory sits on your shelves, the money required to buy it is tied up and is not making a return for you.

Determining the Appropriate Level of Inventory

The *right* amount of inventory to keep on hand and the *right* amount of inventory to order at one time is determined by (1) the cost of processing an order, (2) the cost of keeping merchandise in inventory, (3) the cost of lost sales if you run out, and (4) the time it takes to receive inventory after it's ordered. These factors vary widely with the location and type of business. Small retailers and service firms that also sell products (such as a beauty shop) and are located in urban areas usually have easy access to wholesalers and can make frequent small purchases. If the business is in a small town or if it needs hard-to-get resources, then it may have to keep a lot of merchandise on

TABLE 17.1 Inventory Costs

Costs of Carrying Inventory	Costs of Ordering Inventory
1. The opportunity cost of the funds invested in inventory	1. The transaction costs of preparing and transmitting the order
2. The cost of keeping inventory secure and in sellable condition	2. Investigating and selecting an appropriate vendor
3. Cost of warehouse or other storage facilities	3. Receiving inventory
a. Utilities	
b. Physically moving inventory into, within, and out of the storage area	
c. Security guards, fencing, access control, etc.	
4. Insurance and taxes on inventory	4. Time required to travel to suppliers to pick up inventory
5. Inventory shrinkage, i.e., loss from waste, spoilage, and theft	5. Inspecting shipments
6. The transaction costs for counting and record keeping	6. Record keeping

hand. For example, our manufacturer of fine wooden desks, from Chapter 9, may well need hardwood, such as mahogany, teak, or burled maple, which is produced in only a few places and for which there are only a few wholesalers, worldwide. The distribution system for hardwoods is such that, except in very large cities, you have to buy a lot of it at one time and then keep it in stock until it is used.

There is a way to know how much you need to order so that you have an adequate supply of inventory on hand. It is called **economic order quantity (EOQ)**, and it helps you think in terms of ordering costs and carrying costs.

economic order quantity (EOQ)
A statistical technique that determines the quantity of inventory that a business must hold to minimize total inventory cost.

The total cost of keeping inventory is the sum of the cost of buying it, the cost of keeping it on hand, and the cost of ordering more.[7] (See Table 17.1.)

If the cost of carrying inventory were the only factor in making the decision of how much inventory to obtain, it would make the most sense to purchase the smallest number of units possible at any single time. On the other hand, if ordering costs were the only consideration, you would order the largest number that you expect to sell. But if you consider both these *and* purchase price, as we do in Figure 17.2, you get the economic order quantity (EOQ)—the quantity at which the total cost of inventory is minimized.

You do not have to derive the EOQ equation to use it. You can simply substitute your business's projected annual sales demand, cost of placing one order, and cost of holding one unit in inventory to calculate your unique optimum order quantity and the number of orders that you should place each year. If you are interested, the first appendix of this chapter, entitled "Economic Order Quantity," provides a detailed explanation of how the EOC equation can be used.

Scheduling Ordering and Receipt of Inventory

Determining the right quantity to order is only part of the problem of inventory management. You also need to know *when* to place each order. The EOQ tells us only

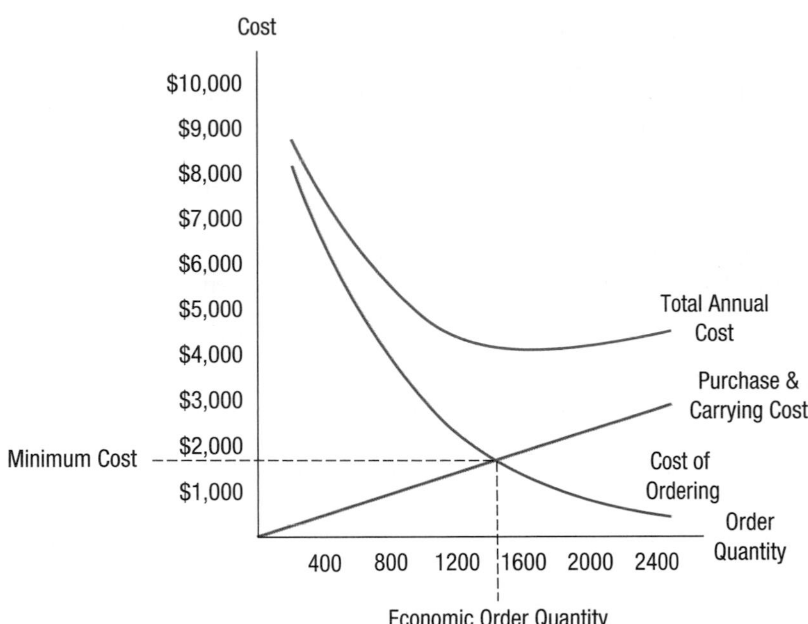

FIGURE 17.2

Economic Order Quantity Graph

how many units to order and how many orders to make. It does not tell us *when* to place each order. Deciding when to place an order is determined by (1) the rate of sales and (2) the time required to receive new stock.

The **optimum stocking level** (also called *reorder point*) is the amount of inventory that results in the minimum cost, considering (1) the cost of lost sales resulting from running out of stock, (2) the number of units sold per day, and (3) the number of days required to receive inventory.

optimum stocking level
(Also known as the *reorder point.*) The amount of inventory that results in the minimum cost, when considering the cost of lost sales resulting from running out of stock, the number of units sold per day, and the number of days required to receive inventory.

If everything worked perfectly, you would receive new inventory just as you sold the last unit from the prior order. But in business as in most things in life, things are never perfect. Delivery times vary. Sales volumes are not constant. Sometimes demand exceeds your estimate. Sometimes your estimate exceeds demand.

If you know how demand for a particular product or part changes, you can calculate the probability of being out of stock, given any initial level of inventory and time between receipts of inventory. Computing the reorder point tells you the minimum stock level at which you would place an order. Ordering at that time would ensure that you do not run out of inventory before you run out of customers, and at the same time would minimize your holding unnecessary amounts of stock.

In practice, managers of small businesses rarely attempt such statistical analyses. Rather, they use a heuristic (rule of thumb) developed from experience. Unless you are selling a product that has very high unit costs, such as automobiles, tractors, or airplanes, the effect of having too little inventory is worse than the effect of having too much. For this reason, most businesses deliberately time the placement of orders to keep some extra amount of inventory on hand as **safety stock** to provide for the possibility that sales might be greater than forecast, or that deliveries might be delayed.

safety stock
An amount of inventory carried to ensure that you will not run out of inventory because of fluctuating levels of sales.

One interesting use of optimum stocking levels comes when an entrepreneur starts to use it as a sales tool directed toward customers. If you compute customers' reorder point, you start to have an added reason to contact them and check to find out whether it is time for them to reorder your product.[8]

Just-in-Time Inventory Systems

The cost of owning and holding inventory is far greater than the cost of ordering inventory. As a result, most businesses try to acquire and keep on hand the minimum amount of inventory possible while still being able to meet customer needs. At the extreme, a few businesses hold no inventory at all. Rather, these businesses order and receive inventory only after a customer purchase has been made.

pull-through system
A term for just-in-time inventory systems in which product is ordered and placed into production only after a sale has been completed.

just-in-time inventory
The practice of purchasing and accepting delivery of inventory only after it has been sold to the final customer.

The practice of acquiring inventory only in response to a completed sale is called a **pull-through system**. Once a customer sale is made, an order is placed to either obtain or produce the product. Each stage of the production process operates in response to this order, ultimately reaching back to the acquisition of the raw materials from which the product is made.

The ultimate extension of pull-through processing is **just-in-time inventory** management. A just-in-time (JIT) inventory system attempts to reduce inventory levels to the absolute minimum by (1) accepting inventory only as it is sold, (2) assembling product in the absolute minimum time possible, and (3) shipping product to the customer immediately upon completion. In this way, the three primary inventories of manufacturing, (1) raw materials, (2) work in process, and (3) finished goods, are all kept at the minimum levels possible.

One of the best-known examples of just-in-time manufacturing is Dell Computers,[9] but small businesses use the approach too. Consider Alienware, a maker of high-end PCs for game enthusiasts started by two lifelong friends in Miami, Alex Aguila and Nelson Gonzalez. Their model is simple: "First you pay. Then we build." Having started with only $13,000, they could not afford to spend a lot on inventory. When Alienware receives a computer order from its Web site, a work order is generated that specifies each individual component to be assembled. Alienware maintains a just-in-time delivery system for needed parts, and leverages its relations with suppliers to ensure speedy delivery. With the parts together, the computer is assembled, tested, and then sent to the packing and shipping department. The use of the JIT approach originally meant that Alienware had no receivables to underwrite, no inventory to depreciate, and no bad debt.[10] Today Alienware still gets the same benefits, but it has grown to $112 million, and even has an arrangement with Best Buy.

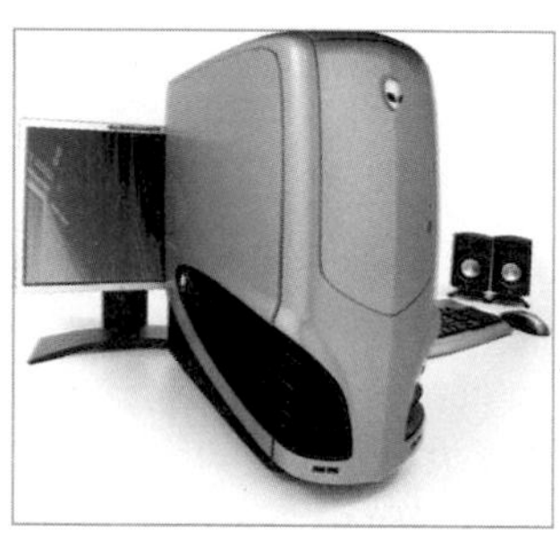

■ Alienware uses just-in-time inventory management in order to keep costs of its high-end PCs at a reasonable level

Adoption of just-in-time inventory management requires an extreme degree of cooperation with your vendors. The location, scheduling, and transportation of inventory must be as carefully choreographed as is a Broadway dance routine. A single misstep in process can result in the shut down of production and in lost sales. To ensure against this, most businesses that adopt just-in-time inventory management compromise between the theoretical "best way" and the exigencies of real-world business management and maintain some level of safety stock.

The development and growth of the eBay online auction service has provided many small businesses with the ability to practice just-in-time inventory management. Buyers on eBay know that there will be a period of a few days between winning a bid and receiving the product. Numerous eBay sellers use this time to obtain the product. Often, it is shipped directly from the wholesaler to the buyer. This practice is the ultimate just-in-time process: The eBay seller never owns or handles the products being sold. It is called **microinventory** and is a very special form of JIT found in Internet-based businesses[11] such as Alienware.

microinventory
The purchase of inventory only after a sale is made; very typical with Internet firms.

Other Approaches to Inventory Control

There are three other approaches to inventory which are very common in small businesses: (1) periodic inventory, (2) perpetual inventory, and (3) point-of-sale systems. Any one of these, applied conscientiously, can help control inventory and inventory costs.

periodic inventory
The process of physically counting business assets on a set schedule.

Periodic inventory is the process of physically counting business assets on a set schedule. The time between counts is usually one business year, although periodic inventories may be conducted twice per year, quarterly, monthly, or as often as your business needs require. Most small businesses use the periodic inventory method because it is relatively inexpensive and meets the requirements of both local and federal taxing agencies.

perpetual inventory
A system of recording the receipt and sale of each item as it occurs.

Perpetual inventory is a system of recording the receipt and sale of each item as it occurs. A perpetual inventory system maintains a constant record of the amounts and value of inventory that has been sold and the amounts and value of inventory on hand. Perpetual inventory systems provide you with instant access to accurate inventory

Stock Card					
Type of product:			Unit of measurement:		
Date	Reference	Designation	Receipts	Disbursements	Stock in hand
Total to be carried forward					

FIGURE 17.3

The Stock Card

records, thus greatly easing the problems of managing inventory levels. The main drawback to using perpetual inventory systems is the high cost in time needed for constant record keeping. (See Figure 17.3.)

Bar coding is one method used to reduce the cost of perpetual inventory systems. Bar codes are computer readable tags that are unique to each item of inventory. The most common bar codes (those that are used every time your grocery purchases are scanned at the register) are called UPCs or universal product codes.

bar coding
Obtaining a Universal Product Code number and scan-ready visual tag, and printing it on the product or its packaging. Bar codes can then be scanned and recognized by others.

UPCs are registered with and controlled by a private company, the Uniform Code Council (UCC), which is changing its name to GS1 US. Manufacturers pay an annual fee to participate in the UPC system. Each member of the system makes an application for codes for its products. In return, the UCC issues a six-digit code for each member, and an additional, unique five-digit code for each registered product. The 12-digit UPC comprises the manufacturer identification number plus the product number plus a check sum to allow for computer error checking.

http://www.uc-council.org or http://www.gs1us.org/gs1us.html

Each UPC is therefore unique to the product for which it is issued. As a member of the UCC, you have access to the database of all codes and the corresponding product information. The UCC maintains an extensive Web site that explains the system, the use of bar codes, and information necessary to join.

You may also create private bar codes of any number of digits for your internal use. Because the private codes are for your internal use, they do not have to be registered with the UCC.

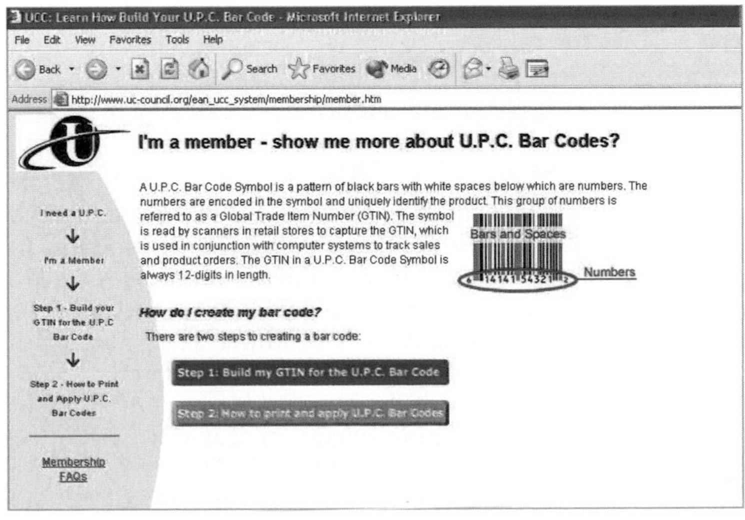

■ If it is important to you that your product be recognized universally, be sure to apply with the UCC in order to receive your product's UPC.

http://dmoz.org

To use bar codes effectively in your business, you need (1) a method to create bar codes, (2) a means to print the codes on the items that you wish to track, (3) a scanner that can read the codes, and (4) a computer software program that can interpret the codes and update a database of information associated with each code. There are hundreds, if not thousands, of businesses that provide all the elements necessary for you to use bar codes internally in your business. A search of the Internet's open directory (DMOZ) on the term "bar codes" returned 229 individual listings for firms that provide bar code software and hardware.

point-of-sale system
Hardware and software combinations that integrate inventory management directly into accounting software.

Point-of-sale (POS) systems comprise both hardware and software to integrate inventory management directly into your accounting system. You are very familiar with POS, whether or not you are aware of being so. The familiar supermarket scanner and the multibutton registers at fast food restaurants are examples of point-of-sale systems. In these systems, every sale is immediately recorded in the accounting system. Revenue is increased and inventory is decreased simultaneously.

Point-of-sale systems have recently become inexpensive enough to be used by small businesses. Today, you may acquire complete systems, including a cash drawer, credit card scanner, bar code scanner, computer, monitor, and software for less than $2,000. There are numerous providers of POS systems, including such well known companies as Intuit, Hewlet Packard, Sony, and Panasonic.

Value of Assets in Your Business

LO2
Determine the value of the assets in your business.

capital assets
Assets that are expected to provide economic benefits for periods of time greater than one year.

There are two fundamental kinds of assets in a business—inventory and operating or **capital assets**. The methods for determining the value of each are similar in many respects. Many small businesses need little in the way of capital assets. However, transportation, manufacturing, automobile repair, mining, ranching, and farming businesses all require the use of substantial capital assets in the form of land, buildings, and machinery. The value of such businesses is largely determined by the value of the physical capital assets that they own.

The value of assets in your business usually far exceeds the value that you might realize if you were to sell them. An example of such an asset is fencing for a ranch or farm. A four-strand barbed wire fence on steel posts can easily cost $4,000 per mile. However, no rancher can ever realize the value of the fence by selling it. At least half the cost of fencing is in the labor required to install it. Once installed, it would cost a similar amount to uninstall. Used barbed wire and posts will bring only a fraction of their cost new. In fact, farmers and ranchers often cannot even give away old fencing; rather, they incur significant costs to safely dispose of it.

Similar situations exist in other businesses such as manufacturing, in which equipment, especially custom-made machinery, is much more valuable as an operating asset than can ever be realized from disposal. Even restaurant equipment such as deep fryers, cooking grills, and ventilation hoods have a much greater value being used in a restaurant than they do sitting in a restaurant supply store.

Determining the Value of Your Operating Assets

The value of operating assets is a function of their utility. In other words, your assets are worth the sum of the future benefits that the assets will produce. It is this definition that is the source of the discounted cash flow methods discussed in the second appendix of this chapter. Discounted cash flow valuation methods define *utility* as being the net cash inflows that the asset will produce. The value of the asset is the sum of these cash flows discounted for time and cost of capital.

Just as estimating future cash flows is highly problematic for small businesses, predicting future utility of capital assets is so uncertain that it is largely a waste of time. Therefore, most small businesses determine the value of capital assets using some combination of the four common accounting methods of assigning asset value.

The four accounting methods to value capital assets are (1) book value, (2) disposal value, (3) replacement value, and (4) fair market value.

Book value is an accounting term that describes the difference between the original acquisition cost of capital assets and the amount of depreciation expense that has been recognized for them. Even a superficial consideration of book value discloses that it is simply an accident if book value even approximates the asset's economic value. This is true for two reasons: (1) Purchase price is not an indicator of the current value of any asset, and (2) depreciation is not, nor is it intended to be, any measure of the consumption through use of an asset's value.

Depreciation is an arbitrary, but regular and systematic, method used to take asset value as an expense for the purpose of calculating net income or loss. Depreciation is based on three assumptions: (1) that the asset has a fixed, determinable period of utility (called useful life), (2) that the asset has a fixed, determinable value that will exist when the depreciation process is complete (called *salvage value*), and (3) that the value of the asset will decline in a continuous and predictable manner over the period of utility (e.g., straight line, declining balance, etc.). In fact, none of these assumptions necessarily holds for any capital asset. Thus depreciation is arbitrary. Book value is generally considered to be not very useful for any purpose other than accounting and income taxes, each of which, through law, regulation, and practice, require its use.

disposal value
The net amount realized after subtracting the costs of getting rid of an asset from its selling price.

Disposal value is a method of estimating asset value by calculating the net amount that you would realize were you to sell the asset in an **"arm's length" transaction**. This is accomplished by subtracting from the estimated sale price the estimated costs of selling, disassembly, shipping, indeed, all costs necessary to dispose of the asset. Disposal value is the residual of many estimates. At best, you must consider the value to be a rough approximation. At worst, the value may hold no relationship to the asset's unknown, "true" economic value.

arm's length transaction
A business deal where the parties have a prior relation or affiliation, but where the business is conducted as if they were unrelated. This approach is done to help guard against potential conflicts of interest.

Replacement value can be determined with much greater confidence than can be given to either book value or disposal value. In effect, you are estimating the value of a currently owned capital asset by determining the cost that would be incurred to replace it with an identical asset. Unlike disposal value, in which you must estimate an essentially unknowable selling price for a used asset, replacement value is based on determining the price of either a new asset or a used asset for which there is an organized market. For many assets, such as machine tools and vehicles, this is done quite easily by obtaining quotes from dealers. Custom-made assets require a bit more work, but still can be accurately priced through an engineering approach.

replacement value
The cost incurred to replace one asset with an identical asset.

The primary advantage of replacement value is that you can be quite confident of its accuracy. The disadvantage is that the price of a new asset is often much greater than the price of an essentially identical asset already in your business.

Fair market value lies somewhere between disposal value and replacement value. Fair market value is an attempt to determine the price that the asset would bring, in its current location and condition, in an arm's length transaction between a willing buyer and a willing seller. In contrast to disposal value, fair market value is assigned from the point of view of the buyer, and thus includes the selling price and all costs to install, test, and prepare the asset for productive use.

fair market value
The price at which goods and services are bought and sold between willing sellers and buyers in an arm's-length transaction.

The appropriate valuation method is largely determined by the purpose for which the valuation is being made. As stated above, laws, regulations, and the requirements of **GAAP** require that book value be used for financial reporting and income tax purposes.

GAAP
Generally Accepted Accounting Principles are the standardized rules for accounting procedures set out by the Financial Account Standards Board and used in all audits and submissions of accounting reports to the government.

For any other purpose, you may use the valuation method that best meets your needs. If you are offering assets as collateral, lenders are most interested in disposal value, as that best approximates the amount that would be realized if the asset were repossessed. If you are considering an investment opportunity, disposal value provides an estimate of the timing and amounts of cash flows that can be used for net present value and internal rate of return calculations. If you are offering your business for sale, as the seller of a business you would view disposal value as a "lower limit" for the selling price because it approximates the amount that would be realized were the business to be liquidated.

On the other hand, potential buyers and investors are most interested in replacement value. Replacement value sets an "upper level" for the value of your business assets as an approximation of the cost that would be incurred to equip a start-up business.

Determining the Value of Inventory

If your business holds inventory for sale, you are faced with the problem of determining its value. The value that you assign to inventory sold and on hand affects (1) the amount of profit that you recognize and (2) the value of your business.

inventory valuation
Determination of the amount of assets held by the firm for sale or production.

physical inventory
A count of all the inventory being held for sale at a specific point in time.

Inventory valuation begins with knowing *how much* of *what* you are holding. All too often owners of small businesses purchase inventory items which are stored out of sight. These items somehow never get used or sold. Over time such "forgotten" items accumulate, tying up scarce funds. At the minimum, you should conduct a **physical inventory**—a type of periodic inventory—at least once each year, identifying and counting all items that your business owns. Items that have not been sold or used for significant periods of time should be disposed of to free their value for productive use. Slow-moving and dated inventory may be disposed of by discounting or "dumping" it to overstock resellers such as Big Lots, Dollar Stores, or junk dealers.

SMALL BUSINESS INSIGHT

James P. Smith of Signgraphics, Inc.

James P. Smith, owner of Signgraphics, Inc., of Blue Springs, Missouri, had just learned that a contract to produce signs for a chain of convenience stores had been lost to a competitor. As a result, Signgraphics was now stuck with twenty 8ft × 12ft polycarbonate plastic sign faces. The faces could not be used for any other purpose because they were vacuum molded and internally painted with the logo and name of the store chain. Each sign face, molded and painted, cost over $1,300. That meant Signgraphics had $26,000 of scrap.

Signgraphics, as would most small businesses, would be severely damaged by such a loss. Something had to be done, and done quickly.

Biting the bullet, James called the competitor who had just won the contract. The competitor quickly agreed to purchase the faces for $22,000. Although still a painful loss, $4,000 was not great enough to threaten the survival of the business. In fact, Signgraphics continued to be successful for an additional four years until the business was sold to yet another competitor in the area.

Sooner or later, you are likely to be stuck with surplus, slow-moving, or obsolete inventory. If you are like most entrepreneurs, you'll be tempted to keep the inventory, "just in case you find a use for it." Over time, such surplus inventory can build up to astonishing levels, tying up money that could and should be used in the business.

A better strategy is to constantly monitor the use of inventory and quickly dispose of any "dated" items before they become obsolete or otherwise unsellable. Such inventory items may, as in the case of Signgraphics, find a ready buyer in a competitor. If you are a wholesaler or retailer, you can offer steep discounts to existing customers. You may sell to a company that specializes in buying surplus and distressed items. Finally, you may, as a last resort, scrap such inventory, and take its acquisition cost as a business deduction against profits.

■ Signgraphics had to make a touch call on selling their extra sign faces inventory to a competitor. Having an inventory handling approach that allows for quick and easy adaptation is key to successfully managing your small business. What are some ways you think owners can build flexibility into their inventory management procedures?

Once you know what inventory you have, you can then assign it a value. One of the unpleasant surprises that many small business owners experience is the discovery that inventory is often worth far less than it cost to acquire. Inventory loses value in many ways. It can lose value because of changes in fashion or changes in technology. Some inventory items, especially food items, spoil with the passage of time. Some things get broken, dented, scratched, dirty, or otherwise shopworn. Determining the value of items being held for sale is essential to efficient inventory management.

The value of inventory items held in stock is highly problematic, especially when prices are rapidly changing. You must answer the questions, "Is inventory worth what I paid for it? Is it worth what I must pay to replace it? Or is it worth only the amount for which I can sell it?" Any of these methods, acquisition cost, replacement cost, or fair market value, respectively, can reasonably be used to determine the value of your inventory. However, your choice of valuation method affects the profit you recognize and thus the amount of taxes you must pay.

acquisition cost
The total cost of acquiring an asset, including such costs as purchase price, transportation, installation, testing, and calibrating in order to ready it for its first productive use.

If you assign a high value to inventory, you increase the amount that you deduct for cost of goods sold which results in decreased sales margin and reported profit. Less reported profit means less will be paid in income taxes. However, lowered reported profits makes your business worth less to investors, lenders, and potential buyers. On the other hand, if you assign the lowest acceptable value to inventory, you will make the results of operations of your business look better, but at the price of paying increased income taxes.

replacement cost
The total cost of replacing an asset with an essentially identical asset.

Property, Plant, and Equipment

LO3
Master managing fixed assets.

The importance of the issues of the acquisition and maintenance of real estate, buildings and machinery varies among businesses. If your business is wholesale or retail merchandising, the issues of property, plant, and equipment (PPE) are most likely of relatively minor importance to your success. If your business is manufacturing, mining, farming, ranching, or transportation, however, your greatest investments and your greatest costs are consumed by land, buildings, and machinery. Obtaining, maintaining, and efficiently using these expensive capital assets is critical to your success.

property
A general term for real estate, but it can also be applied as a legal term for anything owned or possessed.

All capital assets cause you to incur four costs over time: (1) the cost of acquiring the asset, (2) the cost of owning the asset, (3) the cost of operating the asset, and (4) the cost of disposing of the asset.

plant
A general term for the facilities of a business.

It is common for owners of small businesses to consider only the first of these costs in making an investment decision. This narrow focus on acquiring an asset is unfortunate because although you make such decisions infrequently, the ramifications of the decisions are critical to your success. Making a correct decision will increase the value of your business, and thus your wealth. Making an inappropriate decision will lead to suboptimal returns, even to your business going bankrupt. The probability of making a good capital investment decision is greatly increased when all the costs of the asset, called whole of life costs, are included in the decision process. In Skill Module 17.2 you analyze the whole of life costs for one asset.

equipment
Machinery, tools, or materials used in the performance of the work of the business.

whole of life costs
The sum of all costs of capital assets, including acquisition, ownership, operation, and disposal.

Acquisition cost of a capital asset is the sum of *everything* that you spend to acquire and prepare the asset for its first productive use. Thus, the cost of engineering to specify the details of the asset, purchase price, shipping, insurance during shipping, setup, testing, and interest on any borrowed funds are all accumulated to determine the cost of the asset.

cost of owning
Cost incurred in financing, insuring, taxing, or tracking an asset.

Costs of owning an asset include interest on funds borrowed and the opportunity costs of funds invested to acquire it. Costs of ownership also include insurance on the asset, property taxes, value of the space that the asset occupies, and the cost of record keeping and security for the asset.

cost of operating
The direct cost incurred in using an asset for the purpose for which it was intended.

Costs of operating the asset include the energy the asset consumes, maintenance, loss of economic value resulting from wear and obsolescence, and any necessary training of operators.

SKILL MODULE 17.2

Understanding Whole of Life Costs for Capital Budgeting

You are the owner of the Real Wood Furniture Company. Business has grown to the point that a bottleneck has formed at the point where the 4-ft × 12-ft lumber-core plywood sheets are cut to finish size. You have identified two automated panel saws that have identical capacity sufficient not only to eliminate the bottleneck, but also to be able to keep up with projected growth for the next 10 years.

Each machine has a useful life of 10 years. However, each will have to be rebuilt at the end of the seventh year to be able to get the final three years of use. At the end of 10 years, either machine will be technologically obsolete, and thus you will have to dispose of it at that time. Estimated cost data for each saw are shown in the chart at the left.

Real Wood Furniture Co.
Manufacturers of Fine Wood Desks
Data Concerning Automatic Panel Saw

	Kyrobi	**Delta**
Purchase price	$110,000	$80,000
Shipping	3,500	1,000
Installation	6,500	4,000
Testing	3,500	4.500
Total acquisition cost	$123,500	$89,500
Maintenance cost per year	$12,000	$14,900
Energy costs per year	8,500	13,000
Rebuilding in seventh year	25,000	35,000
Disposal cost end of tenth year	4,850	6,000

1. Examine the data in the chart. Without doing any specific mathematical analysis, state which saw you would purchase, and why you made your choice.
2. Assume that every desk to be produced for the next 10 years will be made from wood that is cut by the saw that is purchased. Sales for the year the saw is purchased are projected at $260,000 and are expected to increase by 15 percent per year for the next 10 years. Use Real Wood Furniture Co.'s cost of capital to perform a discounted cash flow analysis of purchasing each saw. Now which saw would you choose, and why?
3. **Advanced topic** Assume that Real Wood Furniture Co. is profitable and will pay 30 percent income taxes each year of the life of the saw purchased. Repeat the discounted cash flow analysis, only this time make adjustments for the effect of income taxes. Now which saw would you choose, and why?

cost of disposition
Cost incurred in the activities necessary to get rid of an asset.

Costs of disposition are composed of the value of the activities necessary to get rid of the asset. Such costs include meeting environmental regulations, disassembly, advertising, commissions, shipping, insurance, and fees. The cost of meeting environmental requirements can be huge for some assets. For example, it is nearly impossible to find affordable means to dispose of radioactive tools, anything that contains mercury or lead (e.g., computer monitors), electric motors and transformers that contain polychlorinated biphenyls (PCBs),[12] and personal computers which contain significant quantities of several poisonous heavy metals.[13]

LO4
Understand how to analyze capital investment decisions.

The Capital Budgeting Decision

capital budgeting
The process of deciding among various investment opportunities to create a specific spending plan.

Eventually small businesses get to the point where they can begin to make investment choices—do you open a new location or expand the one you have? Do you buy new machinery or invest in real estate? The process of deciding among various investment opportunities to create a specific spending plan is called capital budgeting. The goal of capital budgeting is to improve the quality of decisions about how to best use the scarce resources of the business. Capital budgeting works by determining the costs and benefits of each alternative investment, such as machinery or real estate. The question that must be answered to make a decision is, "Which of the available investment alternatives provides the greatest benefit relative to the cost of the investment?"

To do this, the alternatives are simultaneously compared by examining various financial ratios or by applying the concepts of the time value of money. The time value of money is the concept that a dollar received today is worth much more than is a dollar to be received at some time in the future. A dollar might buy you a cola today, but if it were received a year from now, it might not be enough.

The two most commonly used financial ratios for comparing investment alternatives are (1) payback period and (2) return on investment (ROI). There are also two significantly more complex approaches called *net present value (NPV)* and *internal rate of return (IRR),* which are discussed in the second appendix of this chapter. Each of these measures has both advantages and disadvantages. Not one of them is appropriate in all circumstances, although each can be useful in the capital budgeting process.

payback period
The amount of time it takes a business to earn back the funds it paid out to obtain a capital asset.

return on investment (ROI)
A capital budgeting equation used to measure the relationship between initial investment and the profits that are expected to be received from making the investment.

To illustrate each of these investment analysis tools, consider the following: The owner of a sign shop has the opportunity to contract with a rapidly growing franchise operator to install signs at all new locations. To be able to complete this contract, she will need to invest in a heavy truck and a truck-mounted crane. She has reduced the decision alternatives to two different truck-crane combinations: a Skyhook 85-foot heavy-duty crane with a service ladder mounted on a Ford diesel truck and a Sponco 87-foot medium-duty crane with a service bucket and remote controls mounted on a GMC diesel truck. The cost of the Ford-Skyhook combination, ready for use will be \$150,000. The cost of the GMC-Sponco combination will be \$185,000. Each truck and crane will have a useful life of 10 years.

Each crane has certain advantages and disadvantages. The Skyhook crane can lift 2,000 pounds to its full extension height. However, it does not have remote controls, and thus requires a crew of two people. The Sponco can lift only a 950-pound load, but its service bucket with remote controls allows it to be used by a single operator as a "cherry picker" to lift the operator into position, obviating the need (and dangers) of working from a ladder. Based on these facts, the owner has estimated future cash flows that will be provided by each alternative.

The owner has determined the following criteria to aid in making a decision:

1. The business's weighted average cost of capital is 20 percent.
2. The maximum acceptable payback period is four years.
3. Depreciation is recognized using a straight line for a useful life of 10 years.
4. Salvage value of each combination will be \$0 (zero).
5. Cash flows and profits will differ by the amount of depreciation recognized.[14] Depreciation for the Ford-Skyhook is \$15,000 a year, for the GMC-Sponco \$ 18,500 a year.

straight line for a useful life of 10 years
Depreciation is computed using a straight line method over 10 years, so an asset would lose 10% of its value each year.

Payback Period

The payback period measure is a statement of how much time must pass before your business receives back the same number of dollars in cash flow as you must pay out to obtain a capital asset. Only cash flows are considered.

Two decision rules are applied in choosing from among alternative investments:

1. Accept only those alternatives for which the time required to recoup the original investment is equal to or less than a maximum allowable time determined by management.
2. Accept the alternative with the shortest payback period among those that meet the first criterion.

Consider the following example: Using the data in Table 17.2, we can calculate that the Ford-Skyhook combination pays back in 2 years and 11 months. In the first year, \$35,000 is paid back. Another \$60,000 is received in year 2, leaving \$55,000 to be

TABLE 17.2 Data for Capital Budgeting Decisions

Estimated Cash Flows and Accounting Profits of Each Alternative				
	Ford-Skyhook		GMC-Sponco	
Years	Cash Flows	Accounting Profits	Cash Flows	Accounting Profits
0	$ (150,000)		$ (185,000)	
1	35,000	20,000	45,000	26,500
2	60,000	45,000	62,500	44,000
3	60,000	45,000	62,500	44,000
4	65,000	50,000	67,500	49,000
5	70,000	55,000	77,500	59,000
6	75,000	60,000	87,500	69,000
7	75,000	60,000	92,500	74,000
8	80,000	65,000	95,000	76,500
9	80,000	65,000	95,000	76,500
10	80,000	65,000	100,000	81,500

recovered. If we assume that the money is received evenly across the year, then it will take 55,000/60,000, or 0.917 of one year to recoup the final $55,000.

Using the same method, we find that the GMC-Sponco combination will require 3 years and 2.7 months to pay back its initial investment.

Following the decision rules, we find that both alternatives meet the minimum hurdle of paying back in four or less years. However the Ford-Skyhook alternative payback period is 3.7 months shorter, and thus we would choose this alternative.

The main advantage to using the payback period analysis is its simplicity. Second, it allows easy comparison of alternatives that are dissimilar in magnitude of cash flows and overall project life. The primary disadvantages of the payback method are that (1) it disregards the time value of money and (2) it disregards all cash flows that occur after the payback period. These disadvantages often result in managers making suboptimal investment decisions.

Rate of Return on Investment

Rate of return on investment (ROI) is a measure of the relationship between the initial investment and the profits that are expected to be received from making the investment. The calculation is straightforward:

ROI = (average annual profits)/(average investment)

As with the payback method, two decision rules are applied to choose from among alternative investments:

1. Accept only those alternatives for which the return on investment is equal to or greater than the business's weighted average cost of capital, which is the expected average future cost of funds and is discussed in Chapter 15.
2. Accept the alternative with higher ROI among those that meet the first criterion.

We can then calculate the ROI of each alternative:

	Ford-Skyhook	GMC-Sponco
(Sum of profits/length of project)	(530,000/10)	(600,000/10)
(initial investment + salvage value)/2	(150,000 + 0)/2	(185,000 + 0)/2
	= 0.707	= 0.649

Both alternatives meet the first decision rule as the ROI of each exceeds the business's weighted average cost of capital of 20%. We accept the Ford-Skyhook alternative because it has the greater ROI of the two.

Return on investment analysis has two advantages: (1) It is easy to calculate, and (2) it relies on accounting information with which business owners, lenders, and investors are comfortable. ROI's disadvantages are (1) profits are not the same as cash, and (2) the method ignores the time value of money.

Rent or Buy

LO5
Recognize the advantages of renting or leasing capital equipment.

It is often not necessary, or even advisable, to purchase capital assets. Many capital assets for which there is an active market, such as real estate, trucks, tractors, and airplanes, can easily be obtained through rental agreements.

Renting such assets provides several important advantages. First, renting requires little or no cash investment on your part. Purchasing, however, often requires that your business be able to pay cash of 20 percent or more of the purchase price in order to be able to borrow funds to finance your purchase. Second, renting usually does not require an extensive (and expensive) application process as does borrowing money. Third, renting usually protects you from unexpected costs of repairs. If you are renting a truck for your business and it breaks down, you can quickly obtain a replacement vehicle. Fourth, renting capital equipment provides an easy method to avoid ongoing costs if business conditions change. If a sudden loss of business makes the asset uneconomical, you can return it to its owner, thereby avoiding the costs of ownership, operation, and disposal.

Making the decision to rent rather than to buy an asset provides a partial answer to the problem of projecting future cash flows. You may make the same analysis that you would in order to decide to buy. However, in making this analysis, renting provides two advantages over buying: (1) The exact amount and timing of cash **outflows** is specified in the rental contract, and (2) renting provides a fall-back position should your projections prove to be incorrect. If actual cash flows fall short of your projections, you may be able to return the rented property, avoiding future rent payments. If you still wish to pursue the opportunity despite lower cash flows than expected, you can make provisions for a less expensive alternative. Should actual cash flows exceed your projections, you have the options of either purchasing the rented asset or returning the asset and purchasing a higher-capacity replacement.

outflow
Funds being paid to others by the firm.

The disadvantages to rental are, first, you do not have an ownership position. The value of a rented asset does not ever show up on your business's balance sheet. Should you need capital, rented assets cannot be used as collateral to obtain borrowed funds. Second, rental requires that you make regular, timely payments. If you own an asset, you may be able to exercise some control over cash outflows for costs of ownership and operations, such as maintenance and upgrades. These options do not exist for rented assets. Third, the number of dollars paid in rent usually exceeds the number of dollars you would spend to own the asset. The owner of the asset you are renting bears the risk of breakdowns, obsolescence, and disposal costs. Because of these risks, the owner must receive a premium over the costs that you would incur if you were to buy the asset.

Financing with Leases

A lease is simply a rental agreement that specifies a minimum period of time for which you must make rental payments. Lease periods range from as short as a few days to 99 or more years, and leases can include other sorts of provisions or specifications for how the business deal or the leased property is to be handled. Thus, as lessee, you may agree to bear the costs of maintenance, insurance, and taxes on leased assets. Alternatively, any of these costs may be born by the lessor. Leases provide a middle ground between renting and owning assets.

There are two basic types of leases, operating leases and capital leases. The two types of leases differ primarily in how the property is disposed of at the end of the lease period.

operating lease
A long-term rental in which ownership of the asset never passes to the person paying for the lease.

Operating leases are leases that are similar to renting. In an operating lease, ownership of the asset never passes to you as the lessee. At the end of the lease period, you either return the asset to its owner, or you may purchase the asset at its then current fair market value.

All other aspects of maintaining and operating the asset can be negotiated between lessor and lessee. Either party may be contractually responsible for maintenance and operating costs.

capital lease
A lease in which at the end of the lease period the asset becomes the property of the lessee, possibly with an additional payment.

Capital leases are leases that are essentially the same as buying the asset. At the end of the lease period the asset becomes property of the lessee, either without any additional payment or by the lessee paying a nominal amount. The test to determine if a lease is a capital lease, rather than an operating lease, is the existence of provisions for title of the asset to pass to the lessee at a price less than the asset's fair market value.

The benefits of leasing are numerous. First, you can usually obtain a very low down payment. Second, the process of negotiating and closing a lease is usually less complicated and expensive than making a purchase and obtaining borrowed funds. A third benefit is that it is usually much easier for you to replace leased assets than it is to replace assets you own.

Because actual ownership of the asset remains with the lessor until the provisions of the lease contract are fulfilled, the owner is not faced with the expensive and time consuming process of repossession. As owner of the asset, the lessor may simply take it back, should you default on the contract. Because of this, a lessor is less concerned with your ability to pay than is a lender and is willing to accept a lower initial investment from you in return for higher periodic lease payments. Similarly, because the lessor is in the business of acquiring and disposing of assets, the lessor assumes the responsibility of disposing of obsolete assets and providing new ones.

The primary disadvantage of leasing is that it usually costs more than would purchasing. A secondary disadvantage is that leased assets are usually subject to numerous restrictions on how they may be used, maintained, and disposed of. Restrictive lease covenants are intended to provide protection to the owner by preventing the lessee from allowing the asset to lose value through misuse, neglect, or abuse. A typical lease restriction is a prohibition on driving or flying leased transportation equipment across an international border. Were you the lessee of a business airplane, such a provision could become a serious inconvenience should you develop business that requires you to regularly travel to Monterrey, Mexico, and no airline offers such service from your home city.

Fractional Ownership and Other Forms of Joint Ventures

A less used method of reducing the costs and risks of acquiring capital assets is the process of joint venturing. A joint venture is simply a formalized partnership between two or more businesses for some specific purpose. Joint ventures are quite common among medium to large businesses and are growing among small businesses.[15]

Joint venturing makes economic sense when each party to the venture has limited use of an expensive asset or faces major investments that could be sidestepped by partnering with another firm that already has made that investment. One area in which joint ventures are relatively common among small businesses is the ownership of airplanes. Airplanes are quite expensive. Even a 30-year-old Beech King Air turbo prop airplane can easily sell for $1 million. Although old, and by some standards obsolete, a King Air can still produce more than 6 million seat miles per year: the equivalent of 1,600 transcontinental trips. Very few small businesses need even a fraction of the transportation capacity produced by such an airplane. Because of these facts, it is common for airplanes to be owned by partnership arrangements among several businesses that share the costs proportionate to their use of the plane.

Recently, some leasing companies have created an ownership structure similar to joint ventures, called *fractional ownership*. These companies offer buses, airplanes, and yachts under arrangements in which a small business may buy only that share that it can reasonably use during the course of business. In this manner, many small businesses now have access to business jets by having purchased as little as one-sixteenth of the ownership rights.

"Once bought, forgotten" might be the sort of saying that reminds all entrepreneurs about why managing assets is critical to being successful in managing a small business and its finances. Whether inventory or operating assets, most firms have substantial value tied up in the assets of the business. It is possible to make sure that these assets are being managed to be financially useful, and this chapter outlines the techniques—ranging from simple to complex—to do that. The simple techniques of inventory tracking and management can be easily grasped and implemented in a wide variety of settings. The more statistically driven approaches are increasingly workable, because they use functions built into spreadsheets or accounting programs' inventory routines. Like so much in small business, asset management works if you take the time to do it or have it done for you.

CHAPTER SUMMARY

L01 Learn how to manage short-term assets.

- Two short-term assets other than cash are critical to the success of most small businesses: accounts receivable and inventory.
- Offering credit can benefit a business in many ways, if the credit process is well thought out and carefully managed.
- High-quality receivables provide a means to quickly get cash to meet unexpected opportunities and problems.
- Inventory management is critical because for many small businesses inventory is the single greatest asset.
- Inventory requires significant cash investment that ties up capital that could be used for other business purposes.

- Careful management of inventory involves keeping the right amount of inventory available for sale and ordering the right amount of inventory at the right time to avoid both having too much on hand and running out of inventory, and thus losing sales.
- Techniques of inventory management include economic order quantity, just-in-time inventories, optimum stocking level, periodic inventory, perpetual inventory, bar coding, and point-of-sale systems.

LO2 Determine the value of assets in your business.

- Assets in use usually have a value greater than can be realized by selling them because of the value present in the assets' future use.
- Because the value of future use is very difficult to determine, accounting methods used to value capital assets are (1) book value, (2) disposal value, (3) replacement value, and (4) fair market value.
- Of these four methods, only book value and replacement value can be accurately determined.
- Each of the four accounting methods is useful in different situations:
    - Book value is used for financial reporting to outsiders.
    - Lenders prefer disposal value for the purpose of accepting collateral for a loan.
    - Disposal value is useful for estimating cash flows for discounted cash flow analysis.
    - Replacement value is useful for estimating sales prices for individual assets and for the business as a whole.

LO3 Master managing fixed assets.

- Capital assets create four costs across their useful lives: (1) the cost of acquiring the asset, (2) the cost of owning the asset, (3) the cost of operating the asset, and (4) the cost of disposing of the asset.
- Better decisions result when all the costs above, called *whole of life costs,* are considered in the investing analysis.

LO4 Understand how to analyze capital investment decisions.

- The two most commonly used financial ratios for comparing investment alternatives are (1) payback period and (2) return on investment (ROI).
- There are also two significantly more complex approaches called net present value (NPV) and internal rate of return (IRR).
- Discounted cash flow methods (NPV and IRR) are the most complete, because they include the greatest amount of data in the analysis.

LO5 Recognize the advantages of renting or leasing capital equipment.

- Renting requires little or no down payment. It therefore preserves cash.
- As a renter, you usually do not bear the costs of maintenance and repair.
- Leasing provides the same advantages as renting, but also provides assurance the asset will remain available for your exclusive use.
- Joint venturing for assets that have limited use allows you to obtain the benefits of the asset, but reduces the cost of ownership by sharing with other businesses.

DISCUSSION QUESTIONS

1. Discuss the pros and cons of providing credit to customers. If you do decide to provide credit, what policies should you establish and enforce?
2. Discuss how the use of economic order quantity (EOQ) and reorder calculations can benefit a retail business. What are the drawbacks in using these calculations?
3. Which of the asset valuation methods (book value, disposal value, replacement value, and fair market value) is the best for determining the value of your business's assets? Explain your choice, detailing how your preferred method is better than the other three.
4. How would you estimate the whole of life costs of an expensive capital asset, such as an executive airplane?
5. Discuss the advantages and disadvantages to payback and to return on investment (ROI) as analysis tools for making capital investment decisions. Which do you prefer and why?

EXPERIENTIAL EXERCISES

1. Choose a local business in the industry in which you would like to own a firm. Visit the business that you choose, and walk about to observe the amounts and types of inventory on display. Interview the owner or manager. Determine the approximate value of inventory kept on hand. Find out the average time that any single item stays in inventory before it is sold. Also find out the minimum order quantities and delivery times of inventory. Use this information to estimate the amount of working capital necessary to maintain inventory. Make a report to your class.
2. Make a search, using your library, the Internet, and your business contacts, to find factors in your area. Interview the factor and determine the terms offered. Ask what things about the receivables are considered in pricing the factor contract. Contact a commercial banker in your area and find out the bank's policy for lending against receivables. Report your findings to your class.
3. Contact a dealer who sells expensive capital assets, such as earth-moving or transportation equipment. Find out the costs of acquiring, owning, operating, and disposing of the asset. Use a spreadsheet program to estimate the amounts and timing of the whole of life costs of the asset. Estimate the cash inflows that the asset will produce. Use your estimates of costs and cash inflows to calculate the NPV, IRR, ROI, and payback of the asset. Make a presentation to your class, detailing the calculations you have made.
4. Assume that you have a plumbing business that requires the use of a backhoe. Contact equipment rental businesses in your area and find out the rental cost and terms for a suitable machine. Contact leasing companies to find out the cost of leasing a similar backhoe. Assume that, on average, you need the machine for 12 hours weekly. Which is more advantageous, renting or leasing? How would your answer change if you needed the machine an average of 20 hours per week? At what level of usage would renting and leasing not matter?
5. Assume that you own a 2005 Ford F750 Super Duty truck. The truck has been driven 32,000 miles. What is a reasonable disposal value for this truck? (Be sure to reduce your estimate of sales price by the costs of selling the asset.) What is the replacement value of this truck (in other words, how much would another F750 with 30,000 miles cost to find, buy, finance, deliver, and license?) Peruse newspaper ads, search the Internet, and talk with truck salespeople to estimate the truck's fair market value. Make a report to your class of your findings.

Mini-Case

QUALITY SIGN COMPANY

The Quality Sign Co. of Visalia, California, provides credit to customers. The firm is currently averaging receivables of $34,500. The business needs an additional truck-mounted crane to keep up with its rapidly growing business. Quality's owner, George McElroy, has worked up an estimate of the cost of a suitable crane, which is presented in the chart below. Quality's bank is willing to loan 90 percent of the purchase price of the truck, crane, and equipment. All of Quality's currently available cash is needed as working capital and is not available to invest in this project. As a result, Quality must find a way to finance the 10 percent that the bank will not loan, plus the other costs of acquisition.

Quality has contacted a factor who has offered to pay 80 percent for all accounts that are less than 60 days past due. The factor is also willing to act as a collection agency for those accounts that are 60 or more days past due for a fee of 25 percent of the amount collected. Alternatively, Quality's bank has agreed to make a 90-day loan discounted at 12 percent interest in the amount of $32,100, secured by 100 percent of outstanding receivables. The sum of $32,100, which includes accrued interest, is due on the 90th day after the loan is made. During the 90 days, all new receivables will be pledged to the bank as they are incurred. Quality will continue to collect the receivables in the normal course of business. Examine the financial information provided below and prepare a recommendation to Mr. McElroy.

Cost of Acquiring Mobile Crane	
Ford F750 Tandem truck	$ 73,000
120-ft heavy-duty crane	67,000
Hydraulic outriggers	12,500
Hydraulic pump	8,000
30-ft truck bed	5,000
Installation of bed	1,500
Delivery	1,500
Sales tax	12,338
License	1,000
Total acquisition cost	$181,838

Accounts Receivable	
Current	$34,500
>30 days	6,000
>60 days	5,000
>90 days	4,000
Deliquent	4,000
Total receivables	$53,500

Economic Order Quantity

To solve for the quantity at which total inventory costs is minimized, consider the following definitions:

EOQ = economic order quantity in units (quantity that minimizes total inventory cost)
Q = quantity in units to be ordered at one time
P = price of one unit of inventory
O = cost of placing one order
C = cost of carrying one unit in inventory for one year
D = number of units to be sold in one year (demand)
D/Q = number of order cycles per year
Q/D = length of one order cycle as a fraction of one year

The total cost of making a single order is calculated as:

$$\text{Total cost of one order} = O + P \times Q$$

The total cost of holding inventory is the cost of holding one unit in inventory times the average number of units held during one order cycle times the number of order cycles in one year. If the number of units at the beginning of an order cycle is Q, and the number at the end of the cycle is 0, and sales are made at a constant rate, then the average number of units held is (Q + 0)/2, or simply Q/2. The length of one order cycle, as a fraction of one year, lies between 1 and 1 divided by the number of units to be sold in one year.

Holding cost per order cycle = C (Q/2) (Q/D) which can be simplified to:

$$\text{Holding cost per cycle} = C\ Q2/2\ D$$

The total cost of ordering and holding inventory for one order cycle is the sum of these two equations. The total cost of inventory for one year is the cost for one cycle times the number of order cycles per year:

$$\text{Total annual cost} = [(O + P \times Q) + (C\ Q2/2\ D)] \times D/Q = (O\ (D / Q) + D\ P + C\ (Q/2)$$

The purchase price of inventory (DP) is independent of how many units are ordered at any one time and how many orders are made, and thus may be disregarded. This provides the total cost of ordering and holding inventory:

$$O\ (D/Q) + C\ (Q/2)$$

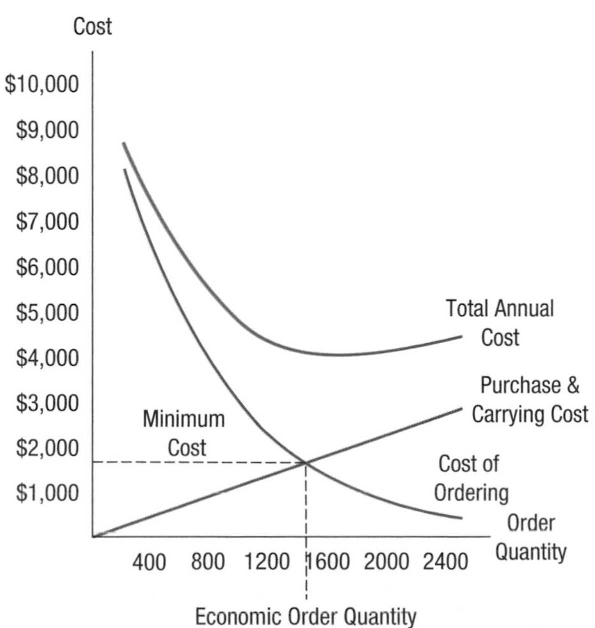

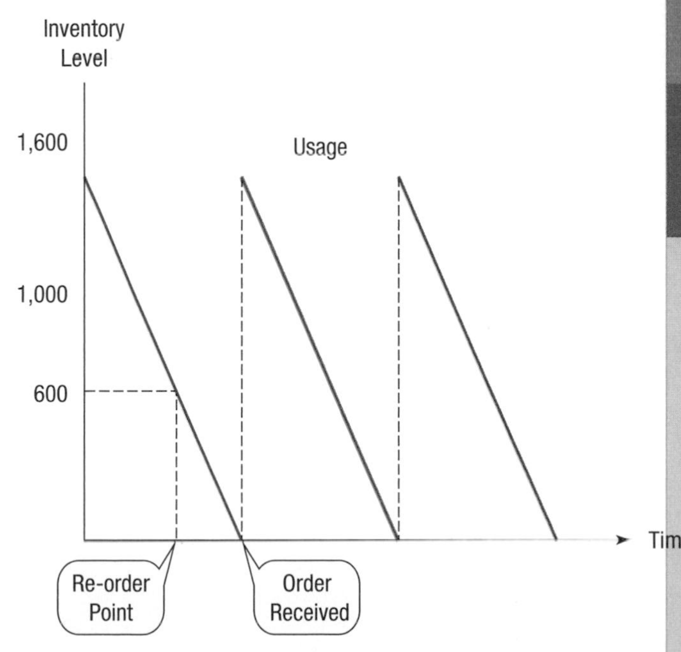

The minimum value of this equation is found by setting the first derivative equal to zero and solving for Q:

$$Q = (2OD/C).5$$

The EOQ calculation indicates how much to order at one time. It does not tell you when to order, however. To make this decision, you have to know how much time will pass between when the order is placed and when the inventory will be received. Suppose that the lead time is one month and that your business uses 600 units of inventory each month. You, therefore, must reorder when inventory levels fall to 600 units, leaving you with one month's supply on hand.

But what if your usage fluctuates, say, between 400 and 700 units of product each month? If you wait to reorder until inventory drops to 600 units and you then have a high-sales month, you could run out of inventory long before you run out of month. To protect from this, you can set a policy of maintaining a safety stock of surplus inventory over the minimum. You will reorder when inventory drops to 700 units. This will increase the cost of carrying inventory, but for almost all businesses, the cost of carrying inventory is a fraction of the cost of lost sales. Thus, for you, the cost of holding safety stock is offset by the advantages of not having a stock-out situation.

Appendix

Time Value of Money and Discounted Cash Flow Analysis

Which would you prefer? One dollar right now, or one dollar to be received one year from now?

Certainly, you'd prefer to have the dollar today. Anyone would. But consider this: Suppose you were offered the choice between one dollar now or a U.S. savings bond that will pay you $10 one year from now. Which of these would you prefer? Most people immediately see the savings bond as being more valuable.

Now ask yourself, "Why is a dollar right this minute preferable to receiving a dollar in the future, but an iron-clad guarantee of 10 dollars one year from now is preferable to one dollar now?"

Almost everyone, even young children, have an instinctual grasp of the concept that waiting for a benefit somehow lessens the immediate value of that benefit. Given the alternatives of a benefit to be received immediately and a benefit to be received later, the delayed benefit must be of significantly greater value if it is to be chosen. This simple concept is the basis of the concept of the time value of money.

Suppose you knew for a fact that to save your life, you would need to have exactly one dollar one year from today. You can make an arrangement with a bank to deposit any amount of money. The bank will pay 10 percent interest. How much must you deposit to have the one dollar when it is needed?

Let "x" represent the amount that you will deposit. Then $10\%x$ is the amount of interest that the deposit will earn in one year. The sum of the amount you deposit plus the interest earned must equal one dollar:

$$\begin{aligned} x + 10\%x &= \$1 \\ 1.1x &= \$1 \\ x &= \$1 / 1.1 \\ x &= \$.91 \end{aligned}$$

In finance terms, we would state that the *present value* of one dollar, *discounted at 10 percent for one year,* is $0.91. Alternatively, we could say that the *future value* of ninety-one cents, *compounded at 10 percent for one year,* is $1.00. The term *present value* simply refers to the amount of money that would have to be deposited now to grow into a specified amount, given an interest rate and period of time. *Future value* is the inverse: the amount that a specific amount of money would grow to be, given a specific interest rate and period of time.

With just a little bit of effort, this concept can easily be expanded to calculate the amount that you must deposit now, at any stated interest rate, to accumulate any amount desired to be received at any time in the future. For example, consider the problem of accumulating for four years:

Value at the End of Year 1	Value at the End of Year 2	Value at the End of Year 3	Value at the End of Year 4
$(1+r)X$	$(1+r)(1+r)X$	$(1+r)(1+r)(1+r)X$	$(1+r)(1+r)(1+r)(1+r)X$

Where X = amount to be deposited
r = interest rate to be earned

The property that in years 2, 3, and 4 interest is being earned on interest from the prior years is called *compounding.*

PRESENT VALUE AND FUTURE VALUE OF 1

Notice that the value at the end of each year is equal to the amount deposited multiplied by 1 plus the interest rate, raised to the power of the number of the period. This allows us to develop an equation that can be easily solved for any amount deposited, any interest rate, and any number of compounding periods:

$$FV_n = PV\,(1 + r)^n$$

Where:

FV_n = future value of the investment at the end of n years
PV = present value (the amount to be deposited)
r = annual interest rate (also called *compounding rate*)
n = number of periods that the deposit is compounded

By solving the equation for PV, we can develop a general equation that will answer the original question, "How much must you deposit now, at a stated interest rate, to accumulate a desired amount at a specified time in the future?"

$$PV = FV_n \times 1/(1 + r)^n$$

Thus, if you need one dollar four years from now, and you can earn 10 percent compounded annually, you must deposit $1/(1.1)^4$ dollars, or 1/1.4641, which equals 68.3 cents.

The calculated value of $(1 + r)^n$ is called the *future value of one,* and can be calculated for any discount rate, r, and any period of time, n. Similarly, the calculated value of $1/(1 + r)^n$ is the *present value of one.* You can easily calculate either the future value or present value of any amount by simply multiplying that amount by the appropriate future value or present value of 1. Thus, if you needed to have available $68,301.50 five years from now and you can earn an interest rate of 8 percent, you would multiply 68,301.50 times the present value of 1 for five years at 8 percent:

$$68{,}301.50 \times 1/(1.08)^5$$
$$68{,}301.50 \times 1/1.4693$$
$$68{,}301.50 \times 0.6806$$

The amount that you would have to deposit today is approximately $46,485.75.

PRESENT VALUE AND FUTURE VALUE OF AN ANNUITY

As the owner of a small business, you will often need to know information about the value of a series of equal payments over time. A series of equal payments made regularly over a set period of time is called an *annuity.*

For example, suppose you know that in three years you will have to replace an essential piece of equipment for your business. Your best estimate is that you can deposit $500 per month for three years at 8 percent interest in order to have sufficient money to make a down payment. How much would you have at the end of three years? The answer to this question can be easily, but tediously, solved by making a series of calculations. First, you must calculate the *monthly* compounding rate by dividing 8 percent by 12 months. Then, you use this monthly rate of .00666 to calculate the *future value of each payment,* then simply sum all 36 values:

$$FV = \$500 \times (1 + .00667)^{36} + \$500 \times (1 + .00667)^{35} + \$500 \times (1 + .00667)^{34} + \ldots + \$500 \times (1 + .00667)^{1}$$
$$635.119 \quad + \quad 630.912 \quad + \quad 626.734 \quad + \ldots + \quad 503.333$$

There is, however, a much less tedious, although slightly more difficult, means to calculate the future value of an annuity. The above summation equation can be solved algebraically, providing the following:

$$FV = C\left[\frac{(1 + r)^n - 1}{r}\right]$$

Where:

C = cash payment per period
r = interest rate
n = number of payments

Substituting values into this equation provides:

$$FV = 500\left[\frac{(1 + .00667)^{36} - 1}{.00667}\right] = \$20{,}403,$$

rounded to the nearest whole dollar.

The present value of a series of equal payments may be similarly solved by discounting each payment and summing all the payments. However, this summation equation has also been reduced to a formula:

$$PV = C\left[\frac{1-(1 + r)^{-n}}{r}\right]$$

Thus, by substituting in the appropriate values, you may easily calculate the present value of an installment contract, a lease, indeed, any series of equal payments.

DISCOUNTED CASH FLOW ANALYSIS

These simple concepts and calculations are the basis of all discounted cash flow analyses. Estimated current cash expenditures and net future cash inflows are discounted by some appropriate rate to derive *net present value* and *internal rate of return.*

NET PRESENT VALUE

To perform a net present value analysis, you must:

1. Estimate the *amount* and *timing* of all cash flows of the project.
2. Select an appropriate discount rate.
3. Discount to present value each cash flow using the selected discount rate and timing.
4. Sum the discounted cash flows.

As you can see from the steps above, net present value (NPV) is simply the sum of all cash flows, both negative and positive, discounted by an appropriate discount rate. The difficulty of NPV analysis lies first in accurately estimating future cash flows and second in selecting an appropriate discount rate. Performing the calculations is trivial.

Estimating future cash flows is basically a process of guessing the revenues and expenses that the project will create. Revenues and expenses are then netted for each time period, usually by month, quarter, or year. The estimating process can be as simple or as complex as you believe necessary to produce reliable numbers and dates.

Selecting an appropriate discount rate is absolutely essential to the utility of the analysis. If you select too high a discount rate, desirable projects will be rejected. Select too low a discount rate and money-losing projects will be accepted. Arguments can be made for using any of three very different discount rates: (1) cost of capital of your business, (2) the incremental cost of capital (or marginal cost of capital), and (3) a management-selected minimum acceptable rate of return.

The computation of NPV is accomplished by the following algorithm:

$$NPV = -CF_0 + \frac{CF_1}{(1 + r)^1} + \frac{CF_2}{(1 + r)^2} + \frac{CF_3}{(1 + r)^3} + \ldots + \frac{CF_n}{(1 + r)^n}$$

Where:

NPV	=	net present value of the project
CF_0	=	initial investment in the project
CF_n	=	cash flow at period n
r	=	discount rate

To illustrate the calculation of *NPV*, consider the following: You are thinking about purchasing for your restaurant a pressurized fryer that will allow you to rapidly prepare spicy deep-fried chicken wings. You believe that the demand for this product will peak within a year, then decrease to zero over three years. The total cost of the fryer, installed and ready for service, is $25,000. The cost of disposing of the fryer at the end of its useful life will be equal to its value at that time. In order to make an NPV analysis, you have determined that your weighted average cost of capital is 24 percent. You estimate that the fryer will provide the following cash flows to your business:

Cash flows	($ 25,000)	$20,000	$ 8,000	$ 4,000	$ 2,000
Time Period	Right Now (t_0)	One Year from Now (t_1)	Two Years from Now (t_2)	Three Years from Now (t_3)	Four Years from Now (t_4)

Net present value of these cash flows is calculated thusly:

Cash flows	($25,000)	+	$20,000	+	$8,000	+	$4,000	+	$2,000
Discount factor	$(1 + .24)^0$		$(1 + .24)^1$		$(1 + .24)^2$		$(1 + .24)^3$		$(1 + .24)^4$

You may easily calculate the present value of the individual cash flows by using a financial calculator, any calculator that does powers, or a computer spreadsheet such as Lotus 123, Quattro Pro, or Excel.[16] The calculated NPV is ($ 724.16). Because the NPV is less than zero (a negative number), you should reject this project because it would not provide a return as great as your business's weighted average cost of capital.

Although the decision rule for NPV indicates that the project should be rejected, remember that all the numbers on which the analysis is made are estimates. No matter how carefully you attempt to estimate future results, you can never do so with certainty. In fact, were you to purchase the fryer, you might find that the product was either much more successful or much less successful than you would ever have expected.

There are several ways to deal with this inevitable uncertainty. You can change your estimates slightly up or down, a process called *sensitivity analysis,* to determine the effects of small changes in your estimates. For example, if you were to increase your estimate of the first year cash flows by just $898, the decision would change to "accept." If you enjoy doing math, you could adjust each of your estimates for the probability of their being correct, then use the *expected* values in the analysis. You might reconsider using weighted average cost of capital for the discount rate. Perhaps you should consider using the cost at which you can borrow funds. Or you might consider using a discount rate that is the sum of the cost of borrowing and some minimum return that you are willing to accept. In fact, in this example, reducing the discount rate by less than 3/10 of one percent reverses the decision.

INTERNAL RATE OF RETURN

Another way of dealing with the uncertainty of NPV analysis is to ask the question, "If this project does not provide a return equal to the discount rate, then what rate of return does it provide?" Internal rate of return (IRR) provides the answer to this question by disclosing the actual rate of return, based on the amount and timing of the cash flow.

The internal rate of return of a project is that rate at which NPV = zero. In other words, IRR is the discount rate at which the present value of the cash inflows of the project exactly equals the present value of the cash outflows. Thus, in this example, you must solve the following equation for the value of the discount rate (IRR):

$$\frac{(\$25{,}000)}{(1 + \text{IRR})^0} + \frac{\$20{,}000}{(1 + \text{IRR})^1} + \frac{\$8{,}000}{(1 + \text{IRR})^2} + \frac{\$4{,}000}{(1 + \text{IRR})^3} + \frac{\$2{,}000}{(1 + \text{IRR})^4} = \$\,0$$

It is unfortunate that there is no way to directly solve this equation for IRR. The only way to find the value of IRR is to try different numbers in a reiterative process until you find a number that provides a solution sufficiently close to zero. Financial calculators, such as those provided by Hewlett Packard and Texas Instruments, all provide an automated means to derive the answer. Computer spreadsheet programs also provide functions to find the IRR of any series of cash flows.

If you do solve the above equation, you will find that the IRR is approximately 21.59 percent. Compare this number with your estimate of your cost of capital, 24 percent. The question you must answer is, "How confident am I that my cost of capital actually exceeds 21.6 percent?" If you are confident, reject the project. If, on the other hand, you are not so sure, perhaps you should reconsider the assumptions and estimates that you have made.

APPLYING THESE APPROACHES TO THE TRUCK AND CRANE PROBLEM

Earlier in the chapter we discuss the problem of deciding whether to buy a Ford-Skyhook or GMC-Sponco truck and crane combination. We worked through two simple methods for making a capital budgeting decision—the payback period approach and the ROI or rate of return on investment approach. We noted then that NPV and IRR approaches could also be used.

Using either NPV or IRR will avoid the shortcomings of both the payback period and the return on investment methods. Discounted cash flow methods make specific numeric adjustments to approximate the lower value of money to be received as compared to the value of money received now.

Net present value (NPV), like the payback period method, is based upon estimates of the cash flows that an investment will cause and utilizes your business's weighted average cost of capital. It is like ROI in using the weighted cost of capital, but unlike ROI because NPV uses cash flows, not profits. When Warren Buffet is deciding if he will buy a company, he uses this technique. In his case he looks at the cash flow the business generates in a year and then figures how much it would be worth—after being discounted—at some point in the future. For buying businesses, he uses a U.S. Treasury long-term bond rate[17] for the period of time that he decides is appropriate. The final result of NPV calculation is a single dollar value, which can be of any magnitude, even a negative number, although the more positive the number, the better.

For our truck and crane example, the time period is the 10 years the truck and crane would be used. We know from the owner's earlier calculations that her weighted cost of capital is 20 percent, and we saw the cash flows in Table 17.2. The computations are complex, but spreadsheets like Excel can do them quickly and easily.

As with payback and ROI, two decision rules are applied to decide among alternative investments:

- Accept only those alternatives for which the net present value is equal to or greater than zero.
- Accept the alternative with the greatest value among those that meet the first criterion.

Ford-Skyhook	GMC-Sponco
Net present value = \$108,112	Net present value = \$107,544

Both alternatives meet the first decision rule. Applying the second, you would accept the Ford-Skyhook alternative because it provides the greater positive net present value.

Internal rate of return (IRR) is a special case of net present value. IRR focuses on the return to the company, but also factors in the cost of the project. What is distinctive about the way IRR does this is that it statistically makes the net present value equal to zero, so the discount rate is thrown out as a consideration.

The decision rules for using IRR are:

1. Accept only those alternatives for which internal rate of return is equal to or greater than the business's weighted cost of capital.
2. Accept the alternative with the greatest IRR among those that meet the first criterion.

Ford-Skyhook	GMC-Sponco
Internal rate of return = 36.5197%	Internal rate of return = 33.37265%

As with net present value, both alternatives pass the first decision test. Of the two, you would choose the Ford-Skyhook alternative because it has the greater IRR.

It is important to note that NPV and IRR are considered some of the most complex of financial equations. The advantages of discounted cash flow analyses for evaluating investment alternatives are (1) all cash flows of each investment are explicitly included in the analysis, and (2) the time value of money is specifically calculated. Discounted cash flow methods do have serious drawbacks, however. First, a discounted cash flow analysis has the appearance of being extremely accurate. This appearance is highly deceiving, however. Every number in the calculation is, at best, an estimate. The weighted cost of capital, the amounts, and the timings of cash flows cannot ever be known with certainty. Second, the calculation uses a single estimate for each projected cash flow. Although cash flows that will occur soon may be reasonably accurately estimated, the longer the period of time over which projections are made, the greater the uncertainty of each estimate. Third, making good estimates of future cash flows requires considerable expertise and effort. Few owners of small businesses have either the time or the resources to do the necessary projections. All in all, discounted cash flow analyses are theoretically sound but are empirically highly problematic.

Management and Organization in the Small Business

PART

4

CHAPTER 18:

Legal Issues: Recognizing Your Small Business Needs

CHAPTER 19:

Human Resource Management: Small Business Considerations

CHAPTER 20:

Achieving Success in the Small Business

LEARNING OBJECTIVES

This chapter will help you:

LO1 Know when you need legal information and how to get it.

LO2 Understand the legal business structures that relate to small business.

LO3 Learn how to master the process of negotiating.

LO4 Recognize potential legal liabilities for your business.

LO5 Know contract terms and when a contract is needed.

LO6 Understand the basics of intellectual property.

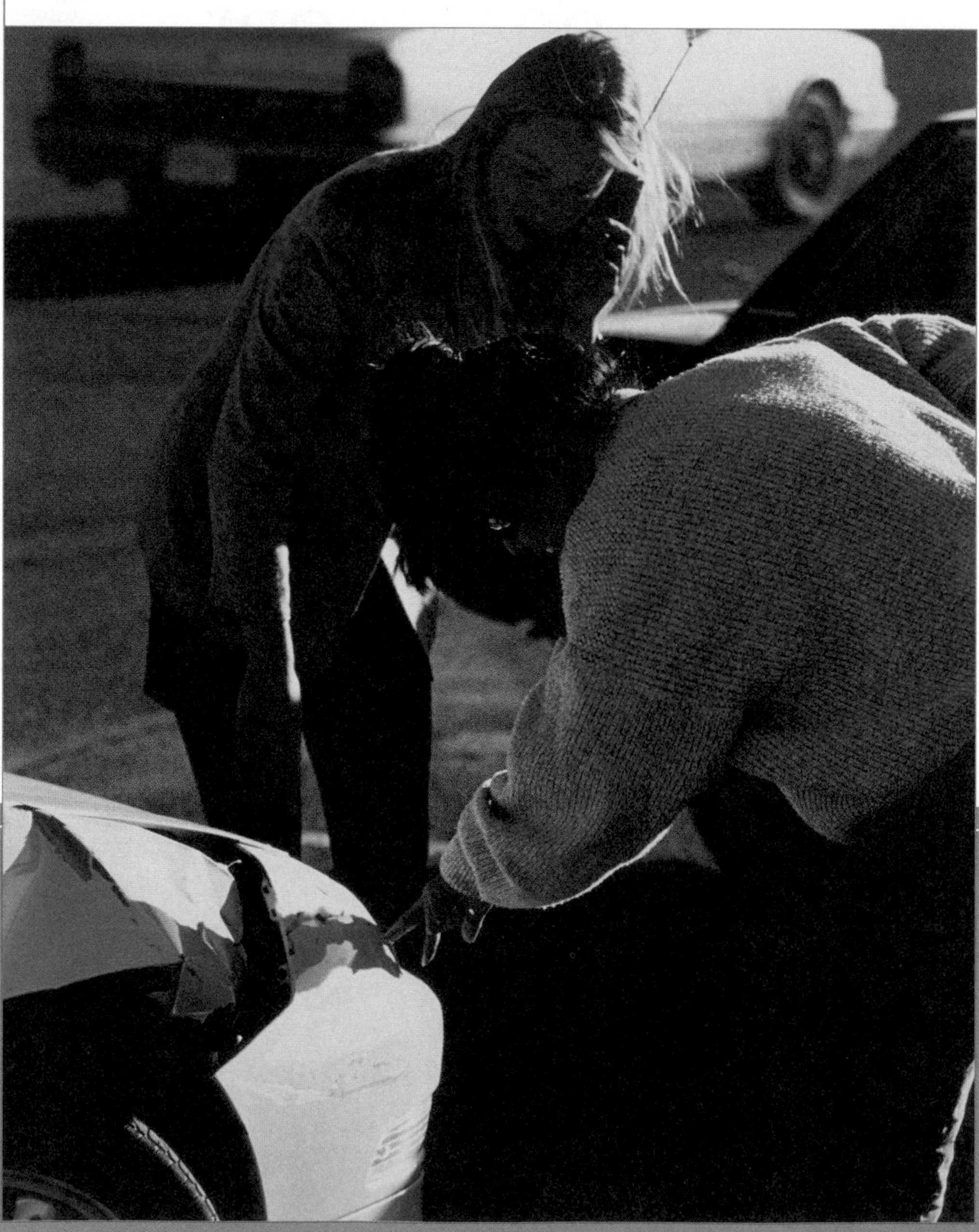

■ Preparing for possible legal interactions is a necessary step for small business owners. Utilize this chapter's tips to learn how to manage the various legal responsibilities that come with the small business territory.

Legal Issues: Recognizing Your Small Business Needs

Focus on Small Business: Kelly and Steve and To Your Door Fitness

Kelly and Steve met at the gym. Both into physical fitness, they saw a career opportunity in a personal training business for well-to-do senior citizens who wished to exercise in the privacy of their own homes. After some consideration, Kelly and Steve started To Your Door Fitness. All day long they traveled the city visiting clients' homes, sometimes alone and sometimes together, to work as personal trainers.

While delivering flyers publicizing the business, Kelly accidentally ran a red light and collided with another vehicle. As a result, several people were injured and there were extensive damages to both vehicles. Seeing the business sign on the door of the car, the injured driver wanted the information not only for Kelly, but also for Kelly's boss, figuring that each was liable for the accident. Kelly explained that she was co-owner of the business, and she gave her personal information, but the other driver insisted on Steve's contact information. Not sure what to do, Kelly gave up the information.

DISCUSSION QUESTIONS:

1. Who can be held responsible for the accident?
2. Should the business have some responsibility because Kelly was driving as part of the business?
3. Would the "form" of the business matter in determining liability?

You and the Law

L01
Know when you need legal information and how to get it.

Kelly and Steve's business faced a traffic accident, but in owning and operating a business there are always unavoidable risks. They can range from traffic accidents to products harming customers to new government regulations that change the business environment and even to deals that go bad. However, when business owners know the law, they can better protect themselves and sometimes even avoid the problems completely. This chapter will help you spot important legal issues for small businesses and provide guidance for dealing effectively with those issues.

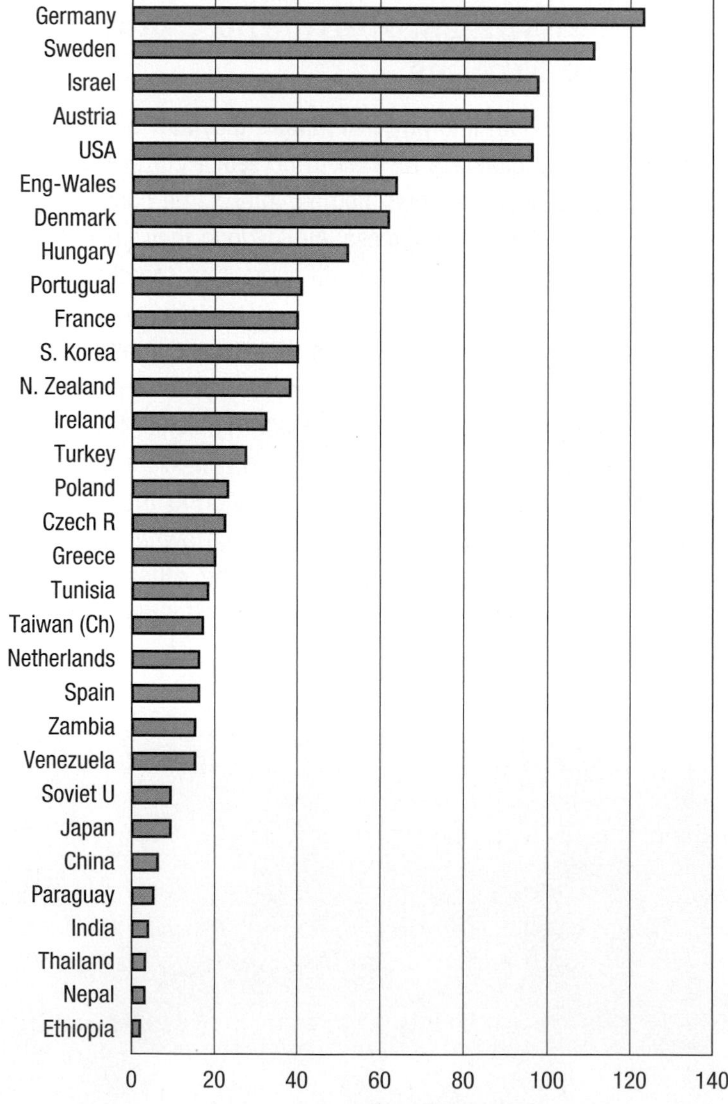

FIGURE 18.1

Estimated Litigation Rates, 1990

Source: Christian Wollschlager, "Exploring the Global Landscapes of Litigation Rates," in Jürgen Brand and Dieter Stempel (eds.), Soziologie des Rechts: Fetschrift fur Erhard Blankenburg zum 60, Geburtstag. (Baden-Baden, Germany: Nomos Berlagsgesellschaft, 1998), pp. 587–88.

The United States is one of the most *litigious* (from the word *litigate,* meaning to sue) societies in the world, along with countries such as Germany, Sweden, Israel, and Austria, as we can see in Figure 18.1.[1] On the other hand, in a 2002 National Federation of Independent Business poll of small businesses, less than 1 business in 10 had been sued in the prior five years. No matter what the perception, the law affects everything about business. Despite all the negative comments about attorneys, attorney jokes, and general resentment of the legal profession, the fact remains that if you are going to start a small business, you are going to be stuck with the legal system—virtues and faults both.

Because of that, it is important for you as a prospective small business owner to understand our legal system. Understanding the legal system will help you be less intimidated by attorneys and the law. And that knowledge can help move you from being a passive victim of the legal system, merely reacting to legal threats, to an empowered owner able to use the law to your advantage in a proactive way. Starting a business is risky enough. With the right knowledge about the law and the use of legal counsel, many of those risks can be significantly reduced or eliminated altogether.

In this chapter we start with your key legal expert—your attorney. We talk about how to select and work with an attorney. We also cover how to make some key legal decisions, such as choosing a legal form for your business, how to negotiate, liability issues, and contracts (in person and online), that come up in business. We conclude the chapter with a discussion of the latest hot topic in law—intellectual property.

You Need a Good Attorney

Setting up a business requires some familiarity with several areas of law—forms of organization, contracts, and licensing, for example. Usually with legal issues, as with health issues, it is best to confront potential problems before they have a chance to get serious. Timely decisions and action may avoid a problem altogether or may make solving the problem much easier and cheaper. Think of legal knowledge as a form of insurance. The key is finding the right lawyer.

First, look for an attorney who is experienced in forming new business entities and handling the needs of small businesses.[2] Where can you find such a person? If you do not have someone in mind, get suggestions from small business owners you know and respect. Bankers involved in commercial financing on a regular basis often know which attorneys handle small businesses well. In addition, a trade association for your industry may have suggestions.

These days, it is typical to be involved with more than one attorney. As with doctors, where you might work with one generalist and several specialists, today most businesses need to depend on one general purpose lawyer and several specialists. The law is so complex that no one can be an expert in all areas. Beware of the attorney who tells you he or she can handle all your legal needs. However, if the attorney is in a group practice, there may well be others in the firm who specialize in the other areas where you need specialized help. Ask about the legal specialties covered within the firm when you call to make an appointment. You may make several calls and visits. If one attorney does not meet your needs in terms of qualifications, work ethic, or pricing, there are many others who would like to have your business. See Figure 18.2 for legal specialties.

Again, like with physicians, once you have chosen an attorney, having an ongoing relationship helps him or her to know you and your situation when something comes up and you need legal advice on short notice.

Clients and attorneys start with a natural conflict of interest. The attorney wants to make money for the services, and you would like the services for as little cost as possible. In reality, all entrepreneurs know they will have to pay, so the key issues are how and how much you will be charged for legal services.

FIGURE 18.2

A Sampler of Legal Specialties

Source: Adapted from: http://www.multilaw.com/Template. cfm?Section=Legal_Specialties. Reprinted with permission from Multilaw-Multinational Association of Independent Law Firm.

Administrative	Estate Planning/Succession
Bankruptcy	Franchising
Biotechnology	Immigration
Business Transactions	Insurance
Competition/Antitrust	Intellectual Property
Computer and Technology	Labor/Collective Bargaining
Construction	Maritime
Contracts	Media and Entertainment
Corporate	Mergers and Acquisitions
Criminal	Real Estate
Domestic Relations/Family Law	Tax/Taxation
E-Commerce	Trade Law
Employment	Women's Rights
Environment	

Typically you and the attorney will discuss and decide on the type and rate of charges up-front, before you engage his or her professional services. The attorney-client agreement should definitely be in writing and signed by both parties.[3] Take the time to read the agreement before signing. Ask for it to be sent to you to review. If the agreement is hard to understand, think about what other work from the attorney will look like, and consider whether that attorney is right for you. There are four ways attorneys typically charge:

hourly fees
A basis for legal charges in which the rate is based on a price per hour. Often lawyers will charge for fractions of an hour.

flat fees
A method of billing for lawyers in which a fixed amount is paid for a certain task.

retainer
A fee paid by a client to an attorney to engage the attorney's services.

contingency fee
Fee paid by a client to an attorney for legal services that is dependent upon the outcome of a case.

1. **Hourly fees:** Hourly fees can vary greatly from one part of the country to another, as well as from firm to firm and even within a firm. Attorneys with more experience often charge more than new law school graduates. Prestigious law firms often charge more than smaller, less recognized firms.
2. **Flat fees:** Flat fees are a fixed amount paid for a certain task. For example, an attorney may have a flat fee for handling all the paperwork to establish a corporation.
3. **Retainers:** When using a retainer, the attorney will be paid a specified amount every month regardless of the workload for that month. Usually there is a retainer agreement which specifies what types of work that monthly fee covers and when and how much additional fees are when circumstances change.
4. **Contingency fees:** You have seen the attorney ads on television announcing, "I don't get paid unless you get paid." That ad is describing a contingency fee. Contingency fees are typical in accident (especially personal injury) situations, but are not usually used in everyday contract and business-related matters. With a contingency fee, the attorney will take a percentage of your recovery (if your side wins) as his or her fee.

Just like anything else, pricing of legal services is based on supply and demand, especially your negotiating demands. Do not be intimidated by having to negotiate price with an attorney. Regardless of what the attorney says, the attorney's fee schedule in all four types of pricing of services may be negotiable, particularly if the attorney is a more senior member of the firm with the authority to negotiate. Diplomacy is recommended in these negotiations because once the original issue of pricing is resolved, it is in your best interest for you and your attorney to have a positive working relationship.

Can I Do This for Free?

There are three elements to most aspects of business law—finding the right information, negotiating the specific outcome you want, and then taking care of the paperwork associated with it. The three elements are what you pay your lawyer to do, but when you look at paying lawyer's fees, you probably want to know if there are things you can do yourself. The good news is that you can.

These days there are many sources of reliable legal information on the Internet for small business owners who want to do the legal work themselves. Also be aware that your local library and bookstores are brimming with titles on business law and how to start your own business.

There are two basic categories of information available to small business owners: free and paid. If you are paying a nonattorney for legal services, such as using an Internet company to set up your business as a corporation, you may not be saving that much money over what an attorney would charge. Consider whether you would be better served in seeking out an attorney and getting individual, custom-tailored advice. Falling between free and paid are the do-it-yourself products. Nolo (www.Nolo.com) is one well-known company that has been established for some time and offers do-it-yourself products.

Of the free information available, some is more reliable than others. Government Web sites, such as www.business.gov (the general business site), www.reginfo.gov (the regulatory information site), www.dol.gov (for labor laws), and www.sba.gov (the Small Business Administration site), provide information to business owners that is reliable, and the government does not have the conflict of interest of wishing to make money from the business owner.[4] State government sources can be very valuable in helping you choose a business entity; check your state's secretary of state Web site. You can easily find the sites by searching Google as shown and replacing your state's name for North Carolina or you can go to www.business.gov/regions/states/ to find your state's offices, as shown in Skill Module 18.1.

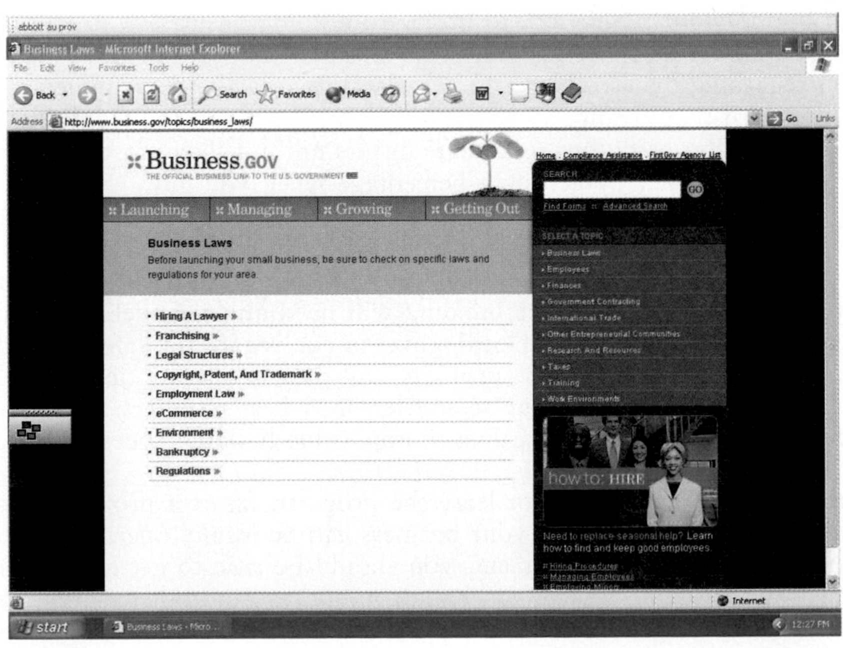

■ Visit www.business.gov to take advantage of the government's free legal resources. Looking at this and related Web sites can help you determine which legal aspects you can manage on your own and which require a paid attorney's involvement.

SKILL MODULE 18.1

Getting Started on Legal Issues Online

The Internet can be a great source of information in helping you determine which various governmental requirements apply to a business. On the state level you can go to the Web site for the state and obtain all sorts of information on starting a business in that state, required licenses, and the like.

Pretend that you wish to start business as an electrician in the state of Washington. You have questions on professional licenses required of electricians, and you are considering hiring a high school student to work part-time after school. In addition, you have concerns about safety and health rules that apply to businesses in Washington.

There is information on all these matters on state Web sites. To find it, go to **www.business.gov/regions/states** and find Washington. First click on "Starting a Business" and then check the resources under "General Information" or "Overview." You will typically find at least one guide or one-stop Web site from each state which focuses on giving you the information to start your business.

For Washington state, there is a guide to "Operating a Business In Washington State" under the "General Information" category. That guide gives you the information on where to find the answers to the questions asked above.

Now go to your state government Web page at **business.gov** and see what you can discover.

Trade associations are another source of information for business start-ups. Many trade associations compile legal information for their members, including laws particularly applicable to certain types of businesses in various jurisdictions and proposals for changing the laws that affect your industry. As you may be aware, these organizations also hire lobbyists to push the agenda of an industry or trade group within the various branches of government, both federal and state. Because of the limited resources of small businesses, membership in one of these organizations can be particularly valuable in informing the business owners and giving them more power as a group to influence legislation that affects them. In addition, through these trade associations it is possible to meet others in your industry and make noncompetitive connections that help you network and keep up with industry trends. Remember that you learned how to find your relevant trade, industry, or professional association in Skill Module 7.2 in Chapter 7.

Be wary of legal information on matters such as statutes or agency regulations offered by individuals who seek to profit from doing business with you. For instance, if you are looking for space to locate your business, be wary of what real estate agents tell you regarding the law. Never forget, these folks make their money when you buy something or if they arrange some lease agreement for you. It may not be in your best interest to buy property, but real estate agents are not likely to tell you that because they will make money by getting a percentage when you buy.

For example, in the issue of zoning, go to your local governmental unit and check on the zoning of the property before you seriously consider it.[5] Do not take the real estate agent's word on the zoning. Be sure that the business you plan may be legally operated in that location. If the building will need any remodeling to suit your purposes, be sure to contact the local government regarding safety standards, exits, entrances, and so on so that the property will pass inspection once the remodeling is done. In the contract with your remodeler, it is best to insert a provision that the remodeling has to be done according to applicable building codes before the contractor is fully paid.

In the contract to purchase or lease the property, insert a provision that the property has to be zoned such that your business can be legally operated in that location. By contacting the local government, you should be able to get guidelines on zoning, placement, and size of signage, parking, property tax, and other matters related to the

■ One key legal issue for small business owners is the matter of real estate. Before you purchase a space for any of your business's activities, make sure the site is zoned appropriately and that you can legally undertake any planned re-modeling, expansion, or re-zoning of the area.

location.[6] Also, be sure to inquire about future plans regarding street repairs, expansions, and closures in the area, which could affect your ability to do business. Do not rely on the real estate agent for any of this information.

As noted at the start of this section, there are three elements to the law—finding the right information, negotiating the specific outcome you want, and then taking care of the paperwork associated with it. Often as businesspeople become familiar with the legal specifics of their business, they take on more of the responsibilities. Most often they do the negotiating themselves (you will see how later in this chapter), and where the paperwork is standardized (as we see below with standard contracts) even handle aspects of the paperwork themselves. Even some legal research can be done, especially when the business owner is made aware of new legal concerns by the trade or professional association. But for all of these things you can eventually do for yourself, when learning the business or when facing a new or unusual situation, it makes sense to go with the pro. When in doubt, call your lawyer.

Choosing a Business Form

LO2
Understand the legal business structures that relate to small business.

Most often choosing the *form* of your business is the first legal decision you need to make. Except for sole proprietorships, business forms are types of separate, legal entities. A **legal entity** is a unit recognized as having rights and duties apart from the owners of the company. Legal entities can own property, sue, and be sued.

legal entity
A being, human or nonhuman, such as a corporation, that is recognized as having rights and duties, such as the right to own property.

The original type of legal entity recognized in England, the source of United States law, was the individual. An individual may hold property ownership and be a **plaintiff** (the party who files a lawsuit) or a **defendant** (the party who is sued) in a lawsuit. As time passed, the law recognized other legal entities that were not human beings. For example, about 1600 the corporation was recognized as a separate entity in England. In other words, a corporation itself, without its shareholders (or owners), could hold title to property and could sue or be sued in its own name, without its owners being sued.

plaintiff
Person or other entity filing a lawsuit.

defendant
Person or other entity being sued.

Today there are seven general types of business form—sole proprietorships, general partnerships, limited partnerships, C corporations (commonly known as just "Corporations"), S corporations (also known as Subchapter S corporations), professional corporations, and limited liability companies (commonly known as LLCs). Each general form has advantages and disadvantages, which are outlined in Tables 18.1, 18.2 and 18.3. For start-ups, the most popular form is the sole proprietorship, although the

FIGURE 18.3

Legal Forms of Start-Ups from the PSED

Source: Paul D. Reynolds, "Nature of Business Start-ups," in William B. Gartner, Kelly G. Shaver, Nancy M. Carter, and Paul D. Reynolds (eds.), *Handbook of Entrepreneurial Dynamics: The Process of Business Creation*, p. 250. Copyright © 2004. Reprinted by permission of Sage Publications, Inc.

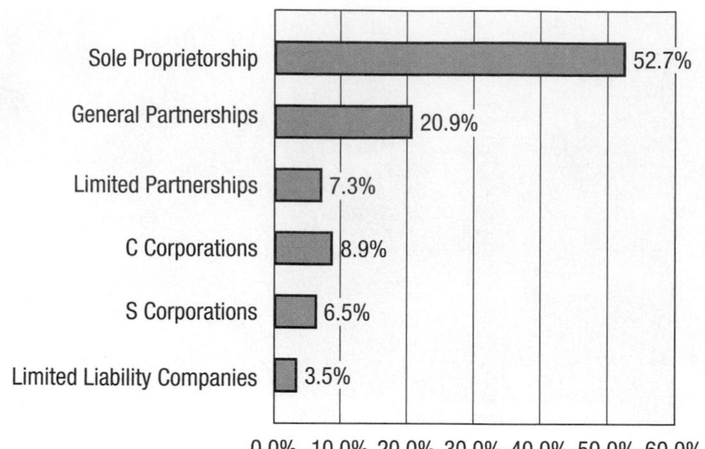

approach is not always optimal for a small start-up, as we see below. General partnerships are the second most popular, and C corporations are third. These results are shown in Figure 18.3.

These days, there is a general rule of thumb for legal form. Unless advised otherwise by your attorney, the best choice for a new small business is a limited liability company (LLC). This is because LLCs are simple to set up and relatively easy to maintain once started. They can be used for an individual or a group of partners. If you have partners, it makes sense to create an agreement specifying ownership, profit splitting, buyouts, and the like, called **articles of organization**. In addition, an LLC offers legal protection to owners for assets they personally hold outside the LLC. It also gives the owners the benefits of single taxation, if they choose to go that route. (See Table 18.1.)

articles of organization Document setting forth information about a limited liability company that is filed with the state to establish an LLC.

The major advantage of the sole proprietorship is that it is extremely easy to set up. There are no forms to file; you just start doing business. The problem is one mentioned in Chapter 15 when discussing financing. In a sole proprietorship, the owner and the firm are one and the same. If an employee has an accident while at work, the business is liable for the damages—*and the owner is personally responsible too.* This

TABLE 18.1 Advantages and Disadvantages of Corporations

Advantages	Disadvantages
Can have representative management	Impersonal
Ease of raising large amounts of capital	Owners have limited interest in firm's activities—except profits
Legal entity separate and distinct from its owners as individuals	High incorporation fees and high taxes, especially double income taxation
Relatively permanent, since life of firm not affected by loss of any shareholder	Burdensome procedures, reports, and statements required by governments
Owners' liability for the firm's debt limited to their investment in it	Powers limited to those stated in charters—may be difficult to do business in another state

Source: Adapted from Megginson/Byrd/Megginson, Small Business Management 5th edition, 2006, p. 61. Copyright © 2006 by The McGraw-Hill Companies, Inc.

TABLE 18.2 Advantages and Disadvantages of Sole Proprietorships

Advantages	Disadvantages
Secrecy	Limited capital
Unique tax advantages	Difficulty in obtaining credit
Owner doesn't have to share profits	Inadequate management and employee skills
Relative freedom of action and control	Unlimited liability for the firm's debts
Easiest and simplest form to organize, operate, and dissolve	Limited life because business and owner are legally the same

Source: Adapted from Megginson/Byrd/Megginson, Small Business Management 5th edition, 2006, p. 58. Copyright © 2006 by The McGraw-Hill Companies, Inc.

means the sole proprietor's home, stocks, savings, and even personal property could be taken to pay damages.[7] For this reason alone, having an LLC makes a lot of sense. (See Table 18.2.)

Partnerships can vary dramatically. They can be set up quickly with nothing more than with a handshake or with a formal legal agreement called **articles of partnership** (the latter is usually safer). They can be set up so all partners are equally and fully responsible for the business's obligations (called a *general partnership*) or where most partners are liable only for the amount they invested in the partnership (called a *limited partnership*—but every limited partnership has at least one general partner). The total liability issue in general partnerships is like that of sole proprietorships, so although easy to start, partnerships are something to avoid. (See Table 18.3.)

articles of partnership
Agreement between the partners of a firm on matters pertaining to the formation and operation of the partnership.

Maybe you are not sure that an LLC is right for your situation, or your lawyer has suggested another form. How do you go about thinking through the issues?

TABLE 18.3 Advantages and Disadvantages of Partnerships

Advantages	Disadvantages
Easy to form	Limited life
Division of labor and management responsibility	Unlimited liability for debts of the firm
Can use ideas and plans of more than one person	Each partner is responsible for the acts of every other partner
Specialized skills available from individual partners	An impasse may develop if the partners become incompatible
Can raise more capital since good credit may be available	Death of any one of the partners terminates the partnership
Obtains financial resources from more than one person	A partner cannot obtain bonding protection against the acts of the other partner(s)

Source: Adapted from Megginson/Byrd/Megginson, Small Business Management 5th edition, 2006, p. 59. Copyright © 2006 by The McGraw-Hill Companies, Inc.

single taxation
Earnings of the business are taxed once with the owners paying the taxes.

TABLE 18.4 Forms of Legal Organization

Factors	Sole Proprietorship	General Partnership	Limited Parnership
Personal liability of owners	Unlimited personal liability.	Unlimited personal liability of partners if partnership has insufficient assets to cover partnership liabilities.	A limited parnership has to have at least one general partner and one limited partner. The general partner has unlimited personal liability. The limited partner can lose "only" his or her investment in the business.
Taxation	**Single taxation** of income to sole proprietor.	Single taxation of income to individual partners.	Single taxation of income to individual partners.
Control or management of business	Complete control by sole proprietor.	Authority shared equally between partners unless otherwise stated in articles of partnership.	Written articles of partnership generally are required for limited partnerships. Authority of various partners is set forth in the articles.
Continuity of business	Ends at death of sole proprietor.	Whenever mix of partners is changed, that partnership is dissolved.	Whenever mix of partners is changed, that partnership is dissolved.
Raising capital	Dependent upon assets and credit of sole proprietor.	Dependent upon capital contributions of the partners, credit of the partnership, and credit of the individual partners.	Dependent upon capital contributions of the partners, credit of the partnership, and credit of the individual partners.
Complexity of setup and maintenance of business form	No government permission required, few (if any) legal costs.	May be formed by conduct of the parties, no government permission required, optional cost of articles of partnership.	Limited partnerships have to meet state statutory requirements which may vary from state to state. Filings with the state are generally required. In addition, states usually require that the business always identify itself to the public as a limited partnership.

Corporation	S Corporation	Professional Corporation	Limited Liability Company
Shareholders are not responsible for debts of the corporation. If the corporation fails, the shareholders can lose, at most, the value of their investment in the corporation.	Shareholders are not responsible for debts of the corporation. If the corporation fails, the shareholders can lose, at most, the value of their investment in the corporation.	Shareholders are not responsible for debts of the corporation. If the corporation fails, the shareholders can lose, at most, the value of their investment in the corporation.	Members (owners) are not responsible for debts of the LLC. If the LLC fails, the members can lose, at most, the value of their investment in the LLC.
Double taxation of earnings generated by the corporation. Corporation is taxed on its income at the corporate rate, and shareholders are taxed on dividends at their individual rate.	There is no taxation of the S corporation, itself. The earnings are **passed through** to the shareholders who are taxed at their individual rate on their individual tax returns.	There is no taxation of the professional corporation (PC) itself. The earnings are passed through to the shareholders who are taxed at their individual rate on their individual tax returns.	"**Check the box taxation**" An LLC can choose whether to be taxed as a corporation or as a partnership (pass through taxation).
Shareholders elect directors who set broad corporate policy. Directors appoint officers to carry out that policy, aided by employees.	Shareholders elect directors who set broad corporate policy. Directors appoint officers to carry out that policy, aided by employees.	Shareholders elect directors who set broad corporate policy. Directors appoint officers to carry out that policy, aided by employees.	Members enter into an operating agreement under which the division of management rights, e.g., committees, voting, is established.
The corporate entity can continue indefinitely if the corporation is properly formed, regardless of changes in ownership of shares.	S corporation may continue as long as the business qualifies under the Federal Tax Code and the rules and regulations of the Internal Revenue Service.	PC can continue as long as the business qualifies under state law.	Depends upon state statute creating LLCs. Some states allow perpetual existence.
Corporations may issue securities such as stocks and bonds, and/or borrow money based upon the corporation's credit.	S corporations may issue securities such as stocks and bonds, and/or borrow money based upon the corporation's credit.	PC may issue stock although ownership may be limited by state law.	In addition to the capital contributions paid in by members, the LLC can borrow money as a separate entity.
Corporations are created by the state. Incorporators must submit articles of incorporation and pay appropriate fees to the state.	S corporations are created by the state. Incorporators must submit articles of incorporation and pay appropriate fees to the state. In addition, the S corporation must elect this tax status with the Internal Revenue Service.	Professional corporations are created by the state. The incorporators must qualify under state law. An application and fees are submitted to the state.	In some states a single individual may form an LLC. In other states two or more members are required. To form the LLC, articles of organization must be filed with the state. The members also need an operating agreement. There will be minimal state filing fees.

double taxation
Earnings of the business are taxed twice with the business as well as its owners being subject to tax.

pass through (taxation)
Earnings of the business are distributed to the business owners and those owners (rather than the business) pay individual tax on the earnings.

check the box taxation
A choice LLCs can make on their tax returns to be taxed as a corporation or a partnership.

There are six major factors at play in the decision on the form of a business organization to set up:

1. Personal liability of the business owner—how much the owner can lose if there are problems arising from the business.
2. Taxation of both the entity and its owners—do owners get taxed as well as the business?
3. Complexity and organizational costs in setting up the business and maintaining that entity—how difficult and costly is it for the owner to maintain the legal form of the business?
4. Control of the business—who runs the business and how is decision making split among various people?
5. Continuity of the business—how long that particular form of business can continue and under what conditions the business could end.
6. Ability of the business to raise capital—can the business borrow money, issue stock, or issue bonds?

Table 18.4 provides a simple summary of how the forms of legal organization differ on the six issues. Note that in Chapter 15, the issues of liability and taxation are also discussed.

After going through the characteristics of these various entities, you can easily see how some of the newer and nontraditional business forms, such as S corporations and LLCs, can offer the best of both worlds, that is, limited liability of owners as well as single taxation. Of these newer forms, the easiest to form and the most user-friendly is the LLC or limited liability company. As a result, LLCs should be viewed as a default of sorts, so select an LLC unless there is a compelling reason to choose another form.

If you choose any of the forms other than the sole proprietorship, please be careful to treat your legal form of business as if it were a being separate from the owner(s). Where you keep the business separate from you personally, that business entity can have liability apart from its owners. If you fail to keep them separate, such as using personal funds for business purposes or using the business's car or equipment for personal purposes, there is a chance that a court may hold that there is no distinction between the entity and its owners in practice. If this happens, called **piercing the veil**, the court may hold that the owners have some personal liability for debts of that business entity. A good place to start in this area is to keep the finances of the business entity and those of its owners entirely separate. Company bills should never be paid from the owners' personal accounts using an owner's personal check. An asset of the business, such as a car, should not be used for personal use without accounting for that nonbusiness use.

piercing the veil
The dissolution of a corporate form, making it back into a sole proprietorship or general partnership, if the court finds that the owner carelessly mixed up personal and business assets or finances.

Another essential caution comes from recognizing that *no* form of LLC or corporation will make the owner(s) bulletproof. No matter what form of business a person owns, if he or she causes a traffic accident or accidentally hurts another person in some way (causes a tort), that person may be found "personally liable" in a lawsuit. That person may have to sell his or her car, home, or other assets (including the business) to pay the judgment. On the other hand, if the owner's employee causes the loss, as mentioned before, the business may be held liable. This is when it makes a huge difference what the structure of the business is in terms of what the owner can lose. If the business is a sole proprietorship or a partnership, the owner may lose personal assets as well as business interests. If the business is a corporation or an LLC, the owner can "only" lose what he or she has in that business.

Similarly, for a newly created LLC or C corporation going to the bank for a loan, it is unlikely that the new corporation will have the collateral base, asset base, or cash flow to convince a banker to issue a loan to the corporation. Regardless of your efforts to shield yourself from liability, the likelihood is that a bank giving a loan to your new corporation will require that you *personally* sign for the loan, in addition to the corporation's signing for it. From a banker's view, a corporation is only as strong as its balance sheet.

Everything Is Negotiable, and Negotiation Is Everything

LO3
Learn how to master the process of negotiating.

Some people argue that business is all about negotiation. While customers go into stores, find price tags, and pay the amount all the time, deals between businesses and even deals between businesses and consumers are often handled through a negotiation. Negotiations are discussions aimed at coming to an agreement about a particular outcome.

The ideal goal in a business negotiation is for each side to feel it got what it wanted. Leaving one side feeling a loss, particularly if someone thinks he or she lost and the other side won, only paves the way for future bad feelings, bad reputations, and bad negotiations. Often small businesses entering into negotiations worry that their youth, lack of experience, lack of track record, or lack of resources mean that there is no way they can win. Experience has shown that small businesses, even *new* small businesses, can do well in negotiations.

Use these four steps to structure a negotiation to achieve a winning solution for you and the other party: prepare, position, propose, and pounce.[8]

- **Prepare** what you need to achieve, what you are ready to give up, and what it takes to close rapidly once agreement is reached. Learn as much as you can about the other side, its track record, current situation, and possible needs.
- **Position** by putting your best foot forward, show confidence in yourself, your firm, and your prospects. Don't lie or mislead, but do not apologize. All businesses started small. With the right deals some small businesses grow large and bring their trading partners along with them. Talk about where you see your business in a couple of months or years. Position your firm as a good partner with which the other firm can ally.
- **Propose** solutions that provide value and balance for both you and the other party. This is often the hardest part of the negotiating process, but it is also the aspect which has received the most attention. Consider using these techniques for finding mutually winning propositions:
  - **Seek to create value:** Listen to what *drives* the other side's needs and seek alternative ways to solve the problem. For example, it says it needs money, but it may be able to work with more time, more flexibility, or a preferred treatment later. Adding new acceptable factors enlarges the negotiated pie.
  - **Seek long-term solutions:** Today you are small, but tomorrow you may be bigger, so think longer term.
  - **Seek balance:** Ideally, each side's contributions should closely balance. Where close balance is not easily achieved initially, structure contingent contracts to ensure balance later. For example, pay a small amount now to get started, but agree to pay a larger amount (e.g., a balloon payment) or a percentage of sales when sales reach a higher level.
  - **Seek mutual safety:** Where risk is faced, consider sharing risks and rewards so each party is providing some of the safety net for the other, and each shows commitment to the deal working out.
  - **Seek outcomes commensurate with investment:** Scale returns or considerations according to the size of the contribution of the party to your success. Aim to satisfy people or organizations that are major factors in your business, and realize you cannot accommodate every small contributors' every need.
- **Pounce** when agreement on any part of the negotiation appears at hand; move to close the deal on that issue. When you have an agreement, even on small issues, pounce on it as a positive outcome, an indicator of future deals to be made. Then get the deal down in writing. When stalled, ask the other party how to move forward.

One fear some people have is being dealt a dirty trick by the other side. Preparation and a long-term view help here. A dirty trick only works when the other party can be confident you will not be able to retaliate or tell others about the dirty trick, since publicizing it will ruin negotiations with others. One-time deals are more prone to dirty tricks; long-term arrangements make them harder to sustain. Also, knowing if the other party has done dirty tricks in the past can help you prepare for them. Being well networked (and letting the other party know you are) can also help since if you are tricked, you can let others know, making the chance of the other party playing dirty tricks on others much less.

What makes all negotiations work is honesty. No one expects you to give up your secrets, but to build trust, you need to offer some information that helps the other side determine where to start negotiating. The optimal strategy is called *tit-tit tat*.[9] Give up one piece of information on what you need or are willing to offer. Wait for an equal response. If you get one, your negotiation is off to a good start. If you do not get a response, offer one more piece of information. Wait for a response. If you do not get one, bring up the point that so far in the negotiation you have made all the overtures. If the other side is serious about coming to a fair deal, it needs to step up to the table and start talking seriously. If not, then it is clear it is not interested in striking a fair deal, and the negotiation must obviously be over.[10]

Along these lines, another negotiating tactic that lets you be open about your goals without giving away your secrets involves prioritizing your goals. Let us say you know three key goals you hope to achieve. Go into the negotiations asking for five or even ten goals. In the bargaining process, you can "give up" some of your demands to show the other side you are willing to compromise. As long as you gain some or all of the three key goals you wanted, you are ahead of the game by negotiating.[11]

Always keep issues of legality in the back of your mind when negotiating without a lawyer present. Let's say you negotiate a trade of services with another business—you print its ad brochure, it waterproofs your parking lot. Legal? Yes, *but* in barter arrangements, you are trading something of value. That means you need to count it when tax time rolls around. If you fail to account for it, you *have* done something illegal. Twists like that are a good reason to get lawyerly advice until you know enough to go solo.

Legal Liabilities

LO4
Recognize potential legal liabilities for your business.

agent
Person given authority to act for and represent another person or entity (the principal) within certain controls by that entity.

A huge concern for business owners is liability arising from the business. The simplest form of liability is direct liability. Simply put this means the business entity is responsible for something the entity has done. For example, when a customer goes into a fast food restaurant and places an order, the restaurant employee is there representing the restaurant. The contract formed is between the customer and the restaurant, not between the customer and the employee. The employee is an **agent** of the entity, in this case the restaurant. The employee represents the entity. Through that employee's actions, the restaurant is now bound in contract to provide certain food at a certain price. Failure of the restaurant to honor its contractual obligations will bring direct liability upon the restaurant. The liability could apply through contract or tort law, each of which is described below.

Torts: Responsibility for Your Actions and the Actions of Employees

vicarious (indirect) liability
Indirect liability or responsibility for the actions of another.

Torts here are not fancy French desserts, but are civil, not criminal, wrongs. Torts can arise when a person's legal rights are violated in ways other than from a breach of contract. For example, where a person is hurt in a car accident caused by your driver, the tort issue is that the victim's right to travel down the road was impaired by the wrongful actions of your driver. Often when this happens, the driver faces direct liability for causing the accident, but the employer can also be sued by the injured party for what is called **vicarious (indirect) liability**. Vicarious liability against a business is possible if the employee involved was an agent of the business and at the time of the accident doing work for the employer.

If your business is facing vicarious liability, there are two typical arguments you can try to deflect the liability: (1) the actor is not an employee, but an independent contractor, and (2) the actions were outside the scope of agency/employment. If you can prove that either one applies, your firm is not likely to be held for vicarious liability. The employee as an individual would face the liability alone.

■ Protect yourself and your business from unnecessary lawsuits, which can quickly cripple your best-laid plans. The very first step in doing so is to develop clear guidelines for your employees to follow in regulating their conduct on the job and give them complete training programs on how to apply the guidelines.

The Independent Contractor Argument

Sidestepping the problem of agency is one of the reasons businesses often use **independent contractors**. For example, many retail stores contract with an independent contractor to provide store security. The security officers are agents of their employer, the security company, and not of the department store. In that way, if those security officers commit a tort while detaining alleged shoplifters, such as defamation (saying something false about a person that hurts his or her reputation, such as calling the suspected shoplifter a "thief" for others to hear while detaining him or her when in fact, the person did not steal anything), false imprisonment (physically restraining a person or holding him or her against his or her will), or battery (improper touching), the department store can avoid vicarious liability because the guard is an employee of the security firm and not the store. In this instance, the security guard and the security company, but not the store, may have liability if the detention was handled improperly. Such arrangements, though sometimes more costly to the store than doing it themselves, may afford the store a measure of protection from liability.

Another approach to protection against liability is to train employees to avoid problems. Training employees on diverse issues such as safety measures, including spotting hazards at the business and how to treat customers, can drastically lower the exposure to liability for a business.

independent contractors Persons working to achieve a certain goal without being subjected to substantial controls by another.

The Scope of Authority Argument

Another important part of agency law involves the amount of authority given to each agent. Employees differ in their job descriptions and responsibilities, so it is common for them to also differ in the amount of authority they have to handle their jobs. In practice this relates to the activities an employee can do and make decisions about without checking with their boss for approval. If employees make a decision requiring more authority than they really possess, the business can argue it was not liable for the problem.

For this argument to work, the firm needs to show that it fully trains or informs the employees of the exact authority they possess—when they can decide for themselves, and when they need approval from higher-ups. It also helps to include informing employees that they may face personal liability for problems which arise from their exceeding their authority. The business also ought to take steps to convey to its customers what the authority level of an employee is. For example, calling a sales clerk a "retail manager" would give the wrong impression of how much authority the clerk possesses.

THE THOUGHTFUL ENTREPRENEUR

Dealing with Criminal Companies

Here's an example to think about. Suppose a business markets some sort of medical device used to close wounds. Assuming this device is widely sold and used, many thousands of patients may come in contact with the device. If the device is poorly designed or manufactured, one can imagine situations in which infections could result from the use of this product. Assume further that employees of the business know of the problem and do nothing to improve the product or to warn the users of this product. Perhaps the company has even been issued a warning of some sort from a governmental agency on this matter.

Even though the business entity itself cannot form criminal intent like a human being, if that entity produces or sells a product that is widely used, the potential to harm a great number of people is certainly present. The prevailing thought is that such businesses are subject to criminal prosecution in order to protect the public from harm and secondarily as a warning to others who might contemplate similar actions.

In other words, nowadays, there are cases in which the business itself (e.g., the corporation, partnership, or LLC) or management can be held *criminally* liable for damages caused by the actions of its employees. If management directs, encourages, knows of, or in some cases should have known of criminal behavior of others in the organization, the company and management may be held criminally liable. Of course, a nonhuman business form cannot be put in jail, but in such cases the business can be, and often is, fined a substantial amount of money as punishment.

There are also specific statutes which provide criminal penalties against businesses (as well as managers and under certain circumstances, owners) if those statutes are violated. Examples of these statutes are laws that protect the public health and environment, certain tax laws, and certain employment laws protecting employees from sexual discrimination and harassment.

Similarly it is important that management take appropriate steps to listen to employees. This is because one of the rules of agency law is that notice to an agent can serve as notice to the business itself. For example, if a customer comes into a retail store and announces to the employees that sleet has started falling on the steps outside, the business itself is now on notice that there is a hazard. If someone subsequently falls on that slick, frozen surface, the question may arise as to whether the business was negligent in clearing the icy area. The business will be unable to argue that it was unaware of the hazard. The court will be looking at what would be reasonable to expect of the business in terms of how quickly the area was cleaned up after any member of the business had notice of this problem. It is important to note that these issues work only where the concerns revolve around civil law. If it is a case of criminal law (see Thoughtful Entrepreneur: Dealing with Criminal Companies), another, tougher standard applies.

Litigation vs. Arbitration vs. Mediation

litigation
A formal dispute resolution method that operates using the court system, typically with a lawyer representing each party.

Problems of contract or tort law can be handled either through litigation, through arbitration, or through mediation. **Litigation** uses lawyers, and when they are unable to resolve the issue, the court system, to settle differences. The litigation approach is draining, both financially and emotionally, on both sides in a lawsuit, so before pursuing the litigation route, think through these issues to decide if litigation is right for you.

First, in litigation, the only guaranteed winners are the attorneys. That is how they make their living, and particularly in business litigation, the case is not emotionally draining for them. Second, remember that good attorneys keep their clients *out* of court by writing better contracts and negotiating on behalf of their clients. If you are going to court, it means you have failed to win at the bargaining table. Third, remember that since litigation is so expensive, large, well-funded companies have a definite advantage over small businesses. And finally, beware of any attorney who guarantees a certain outcome in a case, particularly a jury trial. Human beings are not always predictable, and it is not all that unusual for a case to be decided in an unforeseen way. Of course, litigation can have wonderful outcomes for participants, but the point is that litigation can be risky, it often is expensive, and it always is emotionally demanding for the small business owner.

Given these cautions, if litigation does not make sense, a growing alternative is called arbitration. **Arbitration** is a way of settling disputes in place of going to court. Often it involves the two sides of a case presenting their perspective, facts, and materials to a private judge. If you agree to submit your dispute to arbitration, you are giving up a legal right to sue if you do not like the result. For that reason, an agreement to arbitrate should be in writing and should be given in exchange for something (a contract) if it is to be enforceable. Many of us unwittingly sign such agreements all the time. In a standard contract, such as an agreement with a brokerage firm to open an account, a contract for wireless service, and even in employment agreements, a closer look at the written contract terms may show that the parties have agreed, as part of the contract, to settle their disputes by the use of an arbitrator rather than by litigation.

arbitration
A dispute resolution process held instead of court cases in which both sides present their case to a legal professional.

A third choice is *mediation,* in which the dispute is put to a neutral third party who is not a judge. While arbitration and court cases have decisions that are binding, mediation works only if the two sides agree to the decision and settlement. If mediation fails, arbitration and litigation are still possible. Mediations are generally much faster to complete than either arbitration or litigation, and it is the least expensive of the three approaches. Mediation can even be used with the government, based on the rules set out in the Administrative Dispute Resolution Act, which is handled by the Federal Mediation and Conciliation Service (www.fmcs.gov). Outside of government, mediators and arbitrators generally come from the same sources, such as the American Arbitration Association (www.adr.org).

A comparison of the three approaches is given in Table 18.5. Generally, the optimal situation is to include a clause in your contracts requiring binding arbitration. If

TABLE 18.5 Litigation vs. Arbitration vs. Mediation

Litigation	Arbitration	Mediation
Uses court system	Works outside of court system	Works outside of court system
Formal	Informal	Informal
Public judges	Private judges	Attorneys or mediation specialists
Multiple levels of postdecision appeal	Limited appeal possibilities	Full range of appeals
Can force other party into court	Occurs by agreement or accepting clause to arbitrate	Occurs only by mutual agreement
Binding decisions	Binding decision if agreed to beforehand	Nonbinding decision
Public	Confidential	Confidential
Most costly	Costly	Least costly
Slowest	Moderately fast	Fastest
Favors those with more money for legal help	More balanced than courts	Friendliest format for small businesses

Source: John R. McGinley, Jr., "Arbitration or Litigation? Having Trouble Choosing between the Two? Here Are Some Factors to Consider when Making Your Decision," *Entrepreneur,* April 01, 2002, http://www.Entrepreneur.com/article/0,4621,298318,00.html. Steven C. Bahls and Jane Easter Bahls, "Stuck in the Middle: You're Jammed between a Court and a Hard Place. Get Free with Third-Party Mediation," *Entrepreneur,* November 2000, http://www.Entrepreneur.com/article/0,4621,281851,00.html.

an issue arises, you can see if you can handle it yourself. If you cannot get satisfaction, think about asking for mediation, since it is the fastest and cheapest of the procedures. If mediation does not work, exercise the binding arbitration clause. If there was no clause, the route is negotiate on your own, mediate if possible, and then go to litigation.

Common Sense Ways to Avoid Torts

In addition to the obvious ways of avoiding being sued, such as making sure there are no hazards on your property, not infringing upon another's trademark, and impressing upon your employees the importance of safe driving, there is another method to avoid a lawsuit that is rarely mentioned. When it comes right down to it, transactions between businesses and customers are an interchange of communications between people.

You know from personal experience that there are various ways of dealing with conflicts besides suing, the most obvious being communication and negotiation. You might think that lawsuits come as the result of a careful decision-making process, since they are so costly and time consuming, but in reality lawsuits are often filed out of frustration or anger. It sounds simplistic, but people are less likely to sue someone they like or someone they perceive to be willing to work the problem out with them.

Take a moment to think about the actor Tom Hanks and *American Idol* judge Simon Cowell. Both are wealthy. Imagine each caused a car wreck. Which one do you think is more likely to be sued? If Hanks and Cowell are at all like their screen personalities, Hanks is much less likely to be sued. Being perceived as a likable and genuinely concerned person can sometimes save you from an angry reaction. How do you achieve this? Try to develop client loyalty and give personal service. Listen to your customers. Besides helping the bottom line of your business, developing such relationships can keep you out of court.

Contracting

LO5
Know contract terms and when a contract is needed.

The vast majority of business law in the everyday operations of a business is contract law. Contracts are essentially agreements in which the parties exchange promises. Not all contracts have to be in writing to be enforceable. For example, one neighbor wishes to buy a snow blower from the other neighbor who is relocating to Hawaii. The two discuss the purchase agreement and decide on a price of $800. Nothing is put in writing. It is a spoken promise to pay $800 in exchange for a spoken promise to give possession and title to the snow blower. If it works out as described, fine. But if there is a problem, how can it be resolved? There is likely to be a difference of opinion on what was intended. Without a written contract, there is no way to be sure what should have happened.

In business, there are several kinds of situations in which you want a lawyer to take charge in making things work, for example:

- **Standard contracts**: If you are going to use one type of contract over and over, such as a purchase order, have your attorney draft that contact so that agents of the company can just fill in the blanks as needed.
- **Specialty contracts**: Unique contract terms and/or large dollar amounts at stake usually require careful drafting and legal counsel.
- **Interstate contracts**: When doing business outside your home state, it makes sense to have your lawyer draw up the contract because state laws vary. Charging 20 percent interest on financed purchases may be all right in your state, but this rate may be illegally high in another.

- **Noncompete clauses:** In a **noncompete clause** someone promises not to open a competing business or to go to work for a competitor.[12] Such clauses are tricky because they need to be part of another agreement and cannot stand alone. They also have to be reasonable. You cannot keep people out of their line of business forever, nor can you force them to leave town to practice their business. A lawyer can tell you what is reasonable for the kind of situation you face.
- **Exculpatory clauses:** **Exculpatory clauses** say that a party to the contract will not be responsible for certain things. An example of an exculpatory agreement is the statement on the claim check for dry cleaning that says that the dry cleaner will not be responsible for any damages to clothing. This may not be true, but such statements are "cheap" to make, just the cost of the ink and paper. The only chance for having one that works is to have a lawyer draft it.
- **Hold harmless agreements:** By agreeing to a **hold harmless** clause in a contract (also called a **waiver**), one party is agreeing not to hold the other responsible for his or her actions. In other words, one party is giving up legal rights to sue or otherwise enforce his or her rights. Courts tend not to like such agreements, so again the best chance to have an agreement that holds up in court is to have a lawyer draft it. If you see such a clause in a contract, let *your* lawyer advise you what to do. A workable clause makes it possible for Ann Williams to run a children's gym (see Small Business Insight: Ann Williams and Head Over Heels).

Contracting often seems intimidating, with all the small print and often official sounding language. But the point in contracting is to make sure *your* needs and goals are covered. Three ways to help take some of the fear out of contracting includes:[13]

- Putting in a binding arbitration clause to minimize the possibility of court expenses (and because small businesses often do better before arbitrators than judges).
- When sued, call your insurance agent first. Your business liability insurance may not only cover the settlement costs, but often even your legal fees.
- Consider getting extra liability insurance if you fear you will be facing added business risks. For example, if you expand your business into a wealthy neighborhood, you might want to have an extra $1 million in insurance coverage.

■ In the photo above, a park district has attempted to warn all park users of a potential hazard while denying responsibility for any eventual damages. Do you think this sign is effective? Why or why not?

noncompete clause
Part of a contract in which a person agrees not to open a certain type business or seek employment doing certain things in a particular area for a period of time.

exculpatory clause
Part of a contract in which a party to the contract states that he or she will not be responsible for certain actions.

hold harmless
A type of waiver in which a party agrees not to hold another party responsible for certain events.

waiver
Part of a contract in which a party intentionally gives up legal rights or claims.

SMALL BUSINESS INSIGHT

Ann Williams and Head Over Heels[14]

Ann Williams and her husband Craig bought Head Over Heels, a children's gym in Birmingham, Alabama, in 2000. Ann had been a gymnast at Auburn University and had worked for another gym in town gaining experience. A key problem facing any gym—but especially one that focuses on children—is liability. Young bones and muscles are easily hurt, and while children are resilient, parents often are not.

The Williamses have liability insurance, but to keep it reasonably priced and to provide assurance to the parents (which is far more important in the long run), Ann makes sure parents know that every instructor is trained on safety issues and puts the safety of the children first. Additionally the gym has only the finest equipment. With all these in place, it is easier for Ann to get parents to sign a lawyer-drafted agreement, in which parents recognize the possibility of injury to their child and hold the business harmless for injuries.

Subcontracting

subcontract
A contract by which a new party agrees to perform a duty that one of the original parties to a contract was already legally obligated to perform.

As the term indicates, a **subcontract** may be necessary to fulfill the promises of a "larger" contract. Particularly in small businesses, many support types of tasks such as human resources and marketing are often subcontracted, thereby allowing for fewer employees and thus lower salary and benefit costs to the business. Generally speaking, the same contract principles apply to both regular and subcontracts.

Subcontracting has one unique aspect: Saying that the subcontractor did not perform does not get you off the hook. Imagine you get a contract from Ford to make rearview mirrors. You subcontract out making the glass, while you concentrate on the housing. Your subcontractor does not deliver. Who gets sued? It is you. Your firm signed the Ford contract, so you are responsible. You can sue the subcontractor, but you still have obligations to Ford, and can be sued by Ford.

Internet Issues in Contracting

Small businesses have blossomed through the Internet. They have taken their place in commerce alongside brick-and-mortar establishments. Contract law that has existed for hundreds of years is now being applied to Internet transactions. Courts are being asked to apply this old, standard, contract law to new situations arising in e-commerce as legislatures try to enact new statutes specifically addressing contract law as applied to e-commerce. In the meantime certain problems can be anticipated.

B2B
Business-to-business transactions using e-commerce.

In business to business (**B2B**), contracts are often transactions involving electronic data interchange (EDI). These systems link suppliers of raw materials and components with wholesalers and retailers, often using dedicated lines or satellites. In this way, for example, an order for new inventory may be submitted electronically. B2B systems are generally used in situations in which repeat transactions are entered into and there is generally a master contract or umbrella contract that states the terms of the transactions covered, leaving for example, quantity and prices to be determined in each transaction. These master agreements between the parties are known as *trading partner agreements*. You need to have your lawyer review these before you enter into any major EDI effort.

B2C
Business-to-consumer transactions using e-commerce.

Another type of Internet contract is the business-to-consumer (**B2C**) contract. This is commonly used by small businesses to sell over the Internet. Here are a couple of pointers for setting up the Web sites. First, if you want to ensure control over the selling process, make it very clear on the Web site that the representations of merchandise or services are not actual offers to the buyer. Direct wording to that effect is common on many Web sites. The reason for this is so that the seller is not tied into a certain price and that the buyer cannot create the contract simply by accepting in the form of placing an order. In setting up a Web site, in addition to stating that information on the Web site is merely informational and not an offer, the Web site might also contain a statement to the effect that the seller reserves the right not to sell to everyone and that the Web site seller need not accept the buyer's offer. This gives the seller some control over pricing and also in this new world of terrorism allows the seller to not sell certain merchandise if he or she considers it a risk.

Another issue with online contracting is how to handle contracts that are required to be in writing to be enforceable. For a contract written on paper to be enforceable, it must contain the "wet signature" of the party to be held to his or her contract promises. An alternative is to use technology such as encryptions, third-party certificates, or passwords to guarantee that the parties to the contract are who they say they are. The law does not yet dictate what precise technology must be used, just that there be protection from imposters purporting to be someone else. See Figure 18.4.

Although not an issue in business contracting, there is one other Internet-related issue with legal overtones—how a business handles e-mail. As business e-mail becomes more important, more problems have arisen with employee misuse of these tools. For that reason, it is very important that businesses, big and small, establish policies for employees on usage of the Internet and e-mail.

Digital Certificates (also called SSL Certificates)	Encryption Programs
Entrust: www.entrust.com	OpenSSL (a free open source program): www.openssl.org
Equifax: http://www.equifax.com/DigitalCertificates/	Comodo: www.comodogroup.com
Thwate: www.thawte.com	beTRUSTed (part of PriceWaterhouseCoopers): www.betrusted.com
Verisign: www.verisign.com	eOriginal: www.eoriginal.com
	And the digital certificate companies

FIGURE 18.4

Sources of High-Technology Alternatives to Signatures

If your employees have access to the Internet at work, make it very clear how that access can be used both in terms of amount of time spent and sites visited. Employees should be informed (ideally through a written communication such as an employee handbook or written notice) about the company's policy regarding usage of the Internet for personal business. For example, are employees allowed to access Internet sites for sports scores, sexually explicit materials, stock quotes, and online shopping while "on the clock"? If not, you need to specify this.

For e-mail, the essential message that must be conveyed (again, ideally through a written communication such as an employee handbook or written notice) to employees is that the business owns the e-mail system and has full rights to monitor that system. This even includes e-mail in outside ISPs (like a personal e-mail account) that is accessed from work. In fact, over 50 percent of U.S. companies monitor employee e-mail, and 22 percent of companies have terminated an employee for misuse.[15]

Employees should be informed of policy regarding personal use of the e-mail system at work. For example, are employees allowed to send e-mails at work informing co-workers that their children are selling cookies for scouts or candy bars for the baseball team? In addition, employees should be told explicitly what is considered inappropriate content of e-mails. Clearly, unauthorized transfer of trade secrets is a huge concern of business owners and should be prohibited as well as e-mail that contains offensive sexual, ethnic, or racial messages. Besides monitoring e-mail for misuse by employees, it can be very beneficial for a company to monitor its system as a way to ensure proper customer service. A good rule of thumb is that nothing should be sent by e-mail that you wouldn't be embarrassed to read on the front page of the newspaper. Once that send button is clicked, it may be impossible to limit access to that message.

LO6
Understand the basics of intellectual property.

intellectual property
Property coming from some sort of original thought, e.g., patents, trade secrets, trademarks, and copyrights.

intangible property
Property that has no value of its own but that represents value, such as a stock certificate.

patent
A grant by the U.S. government to an inventor for an idea that is new, useful, and nonobvious, giving the inventor the exclusive right to make, use, or sell his or her idea.

trade secret
Confidential information within a company that gives that company a competitive advantage.

copyright
Exclusive right given to the creator of a literary or artistic work to make use of that work.

trademark
Distinctive word, slogan, or image that identifies a product and its origin.

design patent
A 14-year patent for a new, original, and ornamental design for an article of manufacture.

Intellectual Property

When you worry about making copies of books or songs, you are dealing with issues of **intellectual property**. Intellectual property is a type of **intangible property** in which what is being protected is an idea or a form of expression. This includes the law of **patents**, **trade secrets**, **copyrights**, and **trademarks**. It also touches on the creation of a trade name for a business. Businesses may deal with one or more of the forms of intellectual property.

Patents and Trade Secrets

New ideas can be protected from being used by others by the owner obtaining a patent issued by the U.S. Patent Office (www.uspto.gov) or by keeping the information as a trade secret. A **design patent** (which lasts 14 years) covers the look of a product and those

utility patent
A 20-year patent covering a process, machine, article of manufacture, composition of matter, or any new or useful improvement of an existing one.

plant patent
A 20-year patent that covers new strains of living plant organisms, algae, or macro fungi.

www.uspto.gov

http://www.uspto.gov/web/offices/com/iip/index.htm

infringer
Someone who uses intellectual property without the permission of the owner.

parts that are essential or a part of the design. **Utility patents** cover processes and functions and last 20 years. There are even **plant patents** for newly created strains of living matter, which last 20 years from when the patent application is filed. A great first stop at the Patent Office Web site is the Inventor Resources page, at http://www.uspto.gov/web/offices/com/iip/index.htm. It can tell you most of what you will want to know.

Patents are essentially monopolies granted to inventors by the U.S. government giving patent owners the exclusive rights to make, use, or sell that invention for a certain period of time. Once the patent is issued, anyone can have access to the information covered by the patent, but people cannot make use of that information without the consent of the patent holder. Persons doing so are known as **infringers** and are subject to being sued by the patent holder. Because of the complexity in this area of the law (starting with the question of whether an idea *is* patentable), it is highly unlikely that an inventor could obtain a patent without the services of a patent attorney see Figure 18.5.

Whether an idea is patentable and whether it should be patented or whether an idea can or should be protected as a trade secret are questions for a patent attorney. There are certain ideas that can be patented and also would be suitable for protection as a trade secret. Once again, a patent attorney is the appropriate source to help the business owner make that determination.

Here is an important word of warning: Be extremely wary of companies stating that they will assist you in finding financial backers to develop your new idea or that they will assist you in patenting your new idea. Do not deal with these "companies." They are often out there to steal unprotected, new ideas from inventors. Before sharing information on a new idea to obtain financing or marketing assistance, that idea must first be protected as a trade secret or by a patent.

A *trade secret* is not created by the government but is information known to certain people in the company that makes that company more competitive. Trades secrets include more than patents. A trade secret can be a formula (e.g., the formula for the KFC "13 herbs and spices" chicken coating), the name of the company's top salesperson, or details of (or even acknowledgment of) the upcoming ad campaign. One rule of thumb when considering whether certain information is a trade secret is to ask whether a competitor would be willing to pay for that information. If the answer is yes, then you may have an idea that is protectable as a trade secret.

To protect a trade secret, the secret must literally be kept a secret from all except those who need to know to operate the business. The most famous example of a trade secret is the formula for Coca-Cola Classic. Had that recipe been patented back in the late 1800s, the company would have had exclusive rights to it for 17 years under the patent laws in effect at that time (today it would have had the rights for 20 years). Then, after 17 years, anyone could follow the recipe and make the beverage known to us as Coca-Cola. However, by treating the formula as a trade secret and successfully keeping the formula a secret from outsiders for all these many years, Coca-Cola still has exclusive rights to its use. There is no expiration date for trade secrets. There are five steps to protecting trade secrets:[16]

1. **Trade secrets must really be secrets:** They cannot be shared with others or be likely to be known by others.
2. **Use warning labels:** Put "confidential" on *every* page that contains trade secrets. The full legal version can go on the front page of the document, and it looks like this:

> *This item/document/material contains* CONFIDENTIAL TRADE SECRET INFORMATION *owned by [*THE LEGAL NAME OF YOUR COMPANY*] and/or its affiliated companies. This information is protected by applicable state law and may be protected by the federal Economic Espionage Act of 1996 (18 U.S.C. Sec. 1831), which provides for criminal penalties of up to 15 years in prison and/or a $5 million fine for stealing, receiving, possessing and/or duplicating any information contained herein.*

(12) **United States Design Patent** (10) **Patent No.: US D472,245 S**
Andre et al. (45) **Date of Patent: ** Mar. 25, 2003**

(54) **MEDIA PLAYER**

(75) Inventors: **Bartley K. Andre**, Menlo Park, CA (US); **Daniel J. Coster**, San Francisco, CA (US); **Daniele De Iuliis**, San Francisco, CA (US); **Richard P. Howarth**, San Francisco, CA (US); **Jonathan P. Ive**, San Francisco, CA (US); **Steve Jobs**, Palo Alto, CA (US); **Duncan Robert Kerr**, San Francisco, CA (US); **Matthew Dean Rohrbach**, San Francisco, CA (US); **Douglas B. Satzger**, San Carlos, CA (US); **Calvin Q. Seid**, Palo Alto, CA (US); **Christopher J. Stringer**, Pacifica, CA (US); **Eugene Anthony Whang**, San Francisco, CA (US)

(73) Assignee: **Apple Computer, Inc.**, Cupertino, CA (US)

(**) Term: **14 Years**

(21) Appl. No.: **29/164,950**

(22) Filed: **Aug. 2, 2002**

Related U.S. Application Data

(63) Continuation of application No. 29/153,169, filed on Oct. 22, 2001.

(51) **LOC (7) Cl.** **14-03**
(52) **U.S. Cl.** **D14/496**
(58) **Field of Search** .... D14/400, 401, D14/435, 454, 474, 446, 483, 217; D21/332, 333; 273/148 B; 463/43–47, 1; 206/308.1, 308.3, 307; 369/2, 24, 25; 370/342, 343, 344

(56) **References Cited**

U.S. PATENT DOCUMENTS

D264,969 S	*	6/1982	McGourty	D14/496
4,976,435 A	*	12/1990	Shaford et al.	345/156
5,192,082 A	*	3/1993	Inoue et al.	463/44
5,661,632 A	*	8/1997	Register	345/905
5,964,661 A	*	10/1999	Dodge	463/24
D430,169 S	*	8/2000	Scibora	D14/496
D450,713 S	*	11/2001	Masamitsu et al.	D14/496
D542,250	*	12/2001	Chan	D14/496

* cited by examiner

Primary Examiner—Prabhakar Deshmukh
(74) *Attorney, Agent, or Firm*—Beyer Weaver & Thomas, LLP

(57) **CLAIM**

We claim the ornamental design for a media player, substantially as shown and described.

DESCRIPTION

FIG. **1** is a perspective view of a media player in accordance with the present design.
FIG. **2** is a front view for the media player shown in FIG. 1.
FIG. **3** is a left side view for the media player shown in FIG. 1.
FIG. **4** is a right side view for the media player shown in FIG. 1.
FIG. **5** is a bottom view for the media player shown in FIG. 1.
FIG. **6** is a top view for the media player shown in FIG. **1**; and,
FIG. **7** is a rear view for the media player shown in FIG. 1.
The broken lines in FIGS. **1** and **2** are for illustrative purpose only and forms no part of the claimed design.

1 Claim, 5 Drawing Sheets

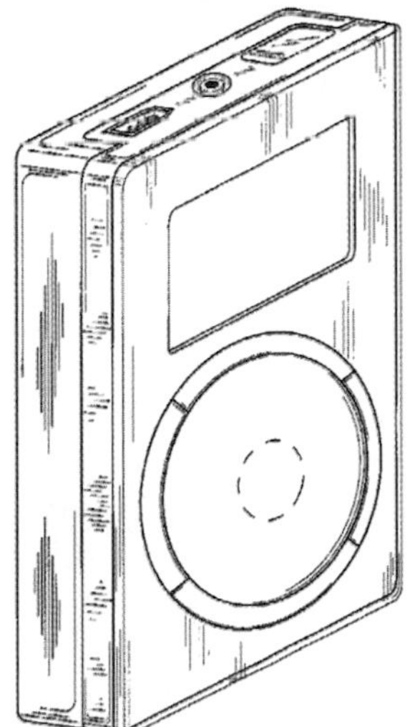

FIGURE 18.5

Section of a Patent Application

Patents protect designs, processes, or plants but are complex documents which should be handled by a patent attorney.

Source: http://patimg1.uspto.gov/.piw?Docid=D0472245&homeurl=http%3A%2F%2Fpatft.uspto.gov%2Fnetacgi%2Fnph-Parser%3FSect1%3DPTO2%2526Sect2%3DHITOFF%2526p%3D1%2526u%3D%2Fnetahtml%2Fsearch-bool.html%2526r%3D44%2526f%3DG%2526l%3D50%2526co1%3DAND%2526d%3Dptxt%2526s1%3DWKU-D%2526s2%3D'apple%252Bcomputer'.ASNM.%2526OS%3DPN%2FD%252BAND%252BAN%2F%252522apple%252Bcomputer%252522%2526RS%3DPN%2FD%252BAND%252BAN%2F%252522apple%252Bcomputer%252522&PageNum=&Rtype=&SectionNum=&idkey=E0AFABE9F82D.

3. **Restrict physical access:** Coca-Cola has a big vault. You can get by with a locked cabinet or a password protected file, but if you have a secret, it should be locked up when not in use.
4. **Confidentiality agreements:** Only people who sign one of these (have your lawyer draft it) get to handle, see, or hear the trade secret material.
5. **Keep doing Steps 1 through 4:** A trade secret is enforceable only as long as you take positive steps to protect it. If you get lazy, the secret may get out, and you have no protection.

Wrongful acquisition of a trade secret is a tort and if certain behavior, such as trespassing or bribery, is involved in getting the information, criminal violations may also have taken place. Concern over protection of trade secrets can justify use of a noncompete agreement to help protect against former employees taking that information to new employers.

Copyright

Copyright involves the expression of ideas, not (as with patents and trade secrets) the ideas themselves. For example, if a greeting card company creates a picture of a single sunflower for use on a greeting card, what can be copyrighted is that particular rendition of a single sunflower. Copyright does not mean that no one else can create a card with a single sunflower (which would use that idea). That *particular* image of a sunflower is protected, so another person or company cannot use that same image without permission. Copyrights for new works last for the creator's life plus 70 years. If it is a "work for hire" bought from the creator, the copyright lasts for 120 years after creation or 95 years after its first publication, whichever is less.

Writers, artists, and others who create unique expressions of ideas automatically copyright those expressions by creating their work. Even though it is not now required, it is a very good idea to place a notice upon your original creation such as a book, painting, sculpture, computer program, or musical score that the work is copyrighted. Placing a notice on the work is done by using the word "copyright," "copr.," or "©," the creator's name, and the year of creation. Because original works are automatically copyrighted, this notice does not create the copyright, but it puts others on notice that the materials cannot be copied without permission of the copyright holder and will prevent any infringer from successfully arguing that he or she didn't know the materials were copyrighted.

www.copyright.gov

The government does not create copyrights. However, copyrights on works can be registered with the federal government (www.copyright.gov) for more complete protection of the work(s). Registration with the government of copyrighted materials will establish a presumption as to ownership of the work. However, registration is not generally done unless wide distribution of those materials is planned.

Trademarks

One last area of intellectual property, *trademark,* can be of particular significance to small business owners. Trademarks identify certain goods. A trademark will indicate the source of particular goods, for example, a Mini Cooper automobile, and not just any automobile. A related concept using the same law is a service mark. Service marks identify services. Some words or groups of words such as Weight Watchers® can be both trademarks (applicable to foods sold under this name) and service marks (identifying services such as programs of instruction on dietary management).

Once a mark is established as identifying certain goods or services, the owner of the mark can keep others from using a similar or identical mark to identify similar or identical goods. As with other intellectual property, anyone using the mark without permission is an infringer and is subject to legal action such as Ty, Inc., learned in 2004 when it was sued by a small business (see Small Business Insight: Peaceable Planet and "Niles"). A trademark once granted lasts for 10 years and can continue to be renewed for another 10 years at a time.

SMALL BUSINESS INSIGHT

Peaceable Planet and "Niles"[17]

Peaceable Planet is a very small toy maker from Savannah, Georgia, that makes a line of plush toy dolls. In 1999 it created a camel it called "Niles," named for the Egyptian river. Niles had a name card with information on it about Egypt. Peaceable Planet trademarked the name, and it sold a few thousand in the first year. The next year, Ty, Inc., the maker of Beanie Babies bean bag dolls, introduced its camel, who also happened to be named Niles, and sold more than one million of them in the first year.

Peaceable Planet sued for trademark infringement, and lost in the U.S. district court. Peaceable Planet appealed and won. In the complex world of intellectual property protection, what this meant was that Peaceable Planet got another chance to prove in district court that Ty took advantage of the Niles name. Peaceable Planet faced another round in court, with the attendant legal fees and time spent on depositions and briefings. Like so many stories about small firms versus large in intellectual property, it may be a while for this issue to have an ending. However, in pursuing the case to the appeals court and getting a favorable ruling, the chance of getting an out-of-court settlement increases. In reality, sometimes that is what a "win" in intellectual property lawsuits looks like.

Trademark issues can come up at the very beginning when a name is being chosen for a new business. It is very important to check to see what marks are already being used to identify goods and services similar or identical to yours, *before* a mark is selected. Skill Module 18.2: Checking Out Trademarks Online can help you get a start on this.

Checking Out Trademarks Online

SKILL MODULE 18.2

Before you settle on a name for your business or product, it is very important to determine how that word or group of words is already being used in the United States to avoid trademark infringement challenges. Assume you are starting a business doing detailing work on vehicles. You are considering the name "Clean as a Whistle." In checking the name, one source of information is the U.S. Patent and Trademark Office listing of federally registered trademarks. While that list shows only federally registered marks and there may be an identical or similar name used that is not registered, this listing is a start. Go to the U.S. Patent and Trademark Web site, **www.uspto.gov,** then to "trademarks," then to "search," then to "new user form" and search for "Clean as a Whistle." According to the information in this site, is this name currently being used for a car detailing business?

All too often with small businesses, a name is chosen and used, and the business incurs all sorts of expenses in terms of labels, signs, and even advertising without considering trademark issues. Before selecting a business name, an Internet address, or the mark for products or services, an attorney should be consulted. An attorney can do a trademark search to determine what use is being made of the words or groups of words a business may want to use. Researching the desired name(s) ahead of time can avoid liability for infringement in which someone already using or having rights to that name sues the business, as well as financial costs (including loss of goodwill) in changing names. Once an attorney has established that it is unlikely that your choice of name is infringing on another's, consideration can be given to obtaining state or federal trademark registration to get additional rights for your mark.

Any size business may own valuable intellectual property such as patents, trade secrets, copyrights, and trademarks. Understanding and protecting these assets by seeking qualified, professional counsel cannot be overemphasized.

Trade Names

trade name or **assumed name** or a **doing business as (dba)**
The name under which a business is operated.

assumed name filing or a **fictitious name filing**
Filing made with a state(s) in which the business operates disclosing the trade name or assumed name of the business along with the owners of the business.

resident agent
A person who represents an out-of-state company as its agent in a state where the business is operating for purposes of contacting the out-of-state company and receiving notice of lawsuits against the out-of-state company.

A **trade name** is a name of a business used to identify itself to the public. This can also be called an **assumed name** or a **doing business as (dba)** name. If that name is something other than the name(s) of the owner(s), then the trade name must be registered in states in which the company does business. The filing is typically called an **assumed name filing** or a **fictitious name filing**. In most states, this filing is made with the Secretary of State's office. If, for example, you are sued, the first thing to do (besides contacting your attorney immediately) is to determine who, exactly, is suing you. In the case of businesses, often the name under which the business is operating is not the same as the name(s) of the owners. By contacting the Secretary of State's office, you can determine who is "behind" that name. In addition to listing the owners using that name, the filing often lists a "**resident agent**" for that entity. This is a person who represents that entity in that state and for practical purposes is the person notified in the event of a lawsuit. There may be more than one business using the same name within a state. In terms of an assumed name, this is not a problem and states allow filings from multiple entities using the same name. If however one of those businesses establishes trademark or service mark rights in that name, it may be able to prevent the later use of that mark by an entity in the same or similar business. For that reason, it is best to consider trademark implications and check with the Secretary of State for a list of all registered entity names before selecting a business name.

Whether you think we have too many laws or not enough, the stability and success of the United States' business community is based, in large part, upon our legal system. Laws guarantee rights to individuals and companies. Those rights are upheld every day in courtrooms across America. Caveat emptor (let the buyer beware) is *not* the motto in twenty-first century America. Knowing the law or even knowing when to ask for advice concerning the law gives business owners more power in pursuing their dreams. Knowledge is power. After reading this chapter, you should have a greater understanding of our legal system and particular areas of interest for business owners. This should give you more confidence in pursuing those dreams.

CHAPTER SUMMARY

LO1 Know when you need legal information and how to get it.

- Get a good attorney with experience in your areas of concern. You may need more than one attorney for various issues that arise over time.
- You can use online sources from the government or trade associations for certain legal information.

LO2 Understand the legal business structures that relate to small business.

- The most common business forms are sole proprietorships, general partnerships, limited partnerships, C corporations, S corporations, professional corporations, and limited liability companies.
- Each of various types of business entities has pros and cons in terms of personal liability of the owners, creation and maintenance of the organization, management of the organization, continuity of the organization, the raising of capital, and taxation.
- Unless there is a compelling reason to do otherwise, an LLC is probably the best choice of business entity because of its ease of formation, limited liability of owners, and flexibility in taxation.

LO3 Learn how to master the process of negotiating.

- Nearly everything in business is negotiable.
- Negotiating successfully depends on mastering the 4 Ps—prepare, position, propose, and pounce.
- The goal is to create outcomes where you and the other party win.
- Be honest in your presentation and balanced in your approach.

LO4 Recognize potential legal liabilities for your business.

- You and your business may be held responsible for the actions of agents, including employees.
- Avoid lawsuits by properly training employees, using independent contractors, or submitting disputes to arbitration.

LO5 Know contract terms and when a contract is needed.

- You are free to contract for anything that is not illegal or unethical.
- Put agreements in writing and have them reviewed by legal counsel.
- Make use of special contract terms such as noncompete clauses, exculpatory clauses, and hold harmless agreements to avoid litigation.
- The primary contractor is responsible for a subcontractor's failure.
- On the Internet make sure to specify that your site is informational and arrange for secure alternatives to "wet signatures."
- Design and implement a company e-mail policy.

LO6 Understand the basics of intellectual property.

- Intellectual property is composed of patents, trade secrets, copyrights, trademarks, and trade names.
- Ideas can be protected as patents or trade secrets.
- Expression of ideas can be protected as copyrights.
- Trademarks uniquely identify products and their origin.
- Trade names exist when a firm uses something other than the owner's name as the name of the business.
- Intellectual property is a business asset and can be extremely valuable. For that reason protection of intellectual property should be taken seriously.

DISCUSSION QUESTIONS

1. How would you go about finding a lawyer for your business?
2. Which form of business structure would be best for your new business and why?
3. In what ways could the owner of a parking lot limit his or her potential liability?
4. How could you keep your employees from going to your competitors after you have trained them?
5. How can you protect your company's trade secrets?
6. What issues should be addressed in a company policy on e-mail?

EXPERIENTIAL EXERCISES

1. Find your state's Secretary of State home page on the Internet. Find information on forming LLCs. Can the form(s) be submitted online? If not, can the form(s) be downloaded or filled in using the computer?
2. In most states you can contact the state bar, the state supreme court, or a state commission to check on whether a particular attorney has been disciplined for professional conduct violations. To find out whom to contact in your state, go to the American Bar Association Web site at **http://www.abanet.org/cpr/regulation/scpd/disciplinary.html** and check it out.
3. You may be able to represent yourself on small matters by going to small claims court. These courts of limited jurisdiction have different names in different states. Go to **http://business.gov**, click on "regions," and select the state of Indiana as an example. Select "legal assistance," and there you will find information on small claims courts in Indiana.
4. Would you like more information on LLCs? Go to **http://nolo.com**, click on "business and human resources," and then "LLC FAQs."

Mini-Case

THERESA MURRAY AND IN THE EYE OF THE BEHOLDER

Theresa Murray started a new business called In the Eye of the Beholder about two years ago. Her business is a retail store that sells art work and does framing. Theresa purchased an old house for her business. The house is in an older neighborhood in the city which is back on the "upswing" because young professionals are moving into the area. The houses in the neighborhood are all small by today's standards and have small lots. In the Eye of the Beholder is on the corner of a street that has been zoned as commercial, so Theresa's business is in full compliance with zoning regulations. The houses on that street are in the process of being or have been modified for use as businesses such as an insurance agency, a dental office, a chiropractor's office, a lawyer's office, a hair salon, and retail stores. There is on-street parking as well as three to four parking spaces in the former backyards of each house accessed by driveways running beside the houses.

The street behind In the Eye of the Beholder, however, is still zoned for single-family residences. The house directly behind Theresa's place is owned and occupied by an elderly gentleman, Elmer Ferguson.

Elmer has been nothing but trouble to Theresa from the beginning. He has complained about everything, including traffic, noise, lighting, her trash bin—you name it. Theresa has tried to be cordial to him and has met all legal requirements for parking, lighting, signage, and the like. In an attempt to keep Elmer calm, she even had a privacy fence built between the parking area behind her house and Elmer's backyard, although there was no legal requirement for the fence.

Theresa knew when she bought the house that it would need a new roof in the near future. The time has come to replace the roof and she would like to go ahead and get the job done. Theresa has a can-do attitude and is fully capable of roofing the small house herself. She worked construction during summers when she was in college and looks forward to being outside in the sunshine. Clearly, she could save money by doing the work herself. She has one lingering doubt, however. The house is close enough to the ocean that there is always a breeze, and, not infrequently, it is downright windy. Theresa is concerned that no matter how careful she is, something could blow off the roof onto Elmer's property and cause damage, or at least infuriate Elmer. In launching his tirades against her in the past, he has threatened to sue her for various aggravations, both real and imagined. Theresa has a real concern that Elmer may sue her should nails, roofing materials, or even tools blow off the roof onto his property.

CASE DISCUSSION QUESTIONS

1. If Theresa's personal negligence, not that of an employee, causes damage to Elmer's property, will it make any difference what her business structure is in terms of her personal liability and how much money she could lose, should Elmer sue her and win damages?
2. If one of Theresa's employees causes damage to Elmer's property while doing his job, would it matter what business structure Theresa has in terms of what Theresa could lose?
3. What would be the arguments, pro and con, for hiring a professional roofer to do the roof repairs on the house?

LEARNING OBJECTIVES

This chapter will help you:

LO1 Explore the decision to hire full-time or part-time help.

LO2 Understand how to recruit good employees on your budget.

LO3 Know how to match the right person to the job.

LO4 Learn about employee training methods and resources.

LO5 Gain insight in meeting employees' needs and expectations.

LO6 Learn how to develop a fair compensation and benefit plan.

LO7 Understand the complexities of managing family within your business.

■ Read this chapter's opening scenario to weigh the pros and cons of hiring employees versus hiring independent contractors to staff your business. This decision is one of many human resources considerations small business owners must take into account as their companies begin and then grow. Which hiring approach do you think would be the best fit for your business?

Human Resource Management: Small Business Considerations

Focus on Small Business: Chris Perkett and PerkettPR, Inc.[1]

As a former consultant herself, Chris Perkett had a fairly easy time deciding whether to hire independent contractors when she started her Marshfield, Massachusetts, virtual public relations agency in 1998. "I wasn't ready to hire employees because there's so much involved with doing that," says the CEO of PerkettPR Inc. "I wanted to make sure I was [building the company] right and wasn't biting off more than I could chew."

Perkett admits she initially appreciated the temporal nature as well as the flexibility of having independent contractors, but as she began to increase her client base, those very aspects began to concern her. "I needed more of a commitment from my staff," she explains. "The knowledge that they could leave at any time was always looming over my head. I needed to show my client base that I had a staff that was as committed to serving them as I was."

So at the end of last year, Perkett decided to switch to an employee-based staff, hiring many of her former consultants as full-time employees. Since then, Perkett says there's been an increase in the level of excitement in the company's projects, and her clients now feel the company is growing and stabilizing, two things that weren't happening with the contractors.

Still, employees aren't necessarily the only way to achieve a common vision and commitment for a business, according to Jennifer Johnson, principal of Johnson & Co., The Virtual Agency. With 15 contractors and only 2 employees on board, Johnson encourages dedication to her Salt Lake City public relations firm by requiring all contractors to attend regular business meetings and retreats and to meet with a senior consultant mentor. "I think it's a myth to believe that because someone is an employee, it means they're more dependable," says Johnson. "In today's fast-moving, competitive market, the best talent needs to stay motivated and driven whether they're a consultant or an employee."

According to Johnson, the ever-changing nature of today's business world has left traditional job descriptions by the wayside and forced companies to have a more flexible structure. "Consultants are used to change; they thrive on [that]," she says. "They understand they're getting paid to deliver tangible results as opposed to just punching a clock."

As for Perkett, although she's had to adjust to the variety of personalities that now exist in the core of her company, she's confident that hiring employees was the right choice for her growing business. "If you're not sure where or how you want to grow, then it's a lot to take on," she says. "But I think it helps our clients feel like we're growing, we're adding clients, and we're committed to this business."

DISCUSSION QUESTIONS

1. What are some potential advantages as well as drawbacks of having contractors in Jennifer Johnson's firm attend meetings, retreats, and be mentored by senior consultants?
2. Do you agree with Johnson's assertion that "In today's fast-moving, competitive market, the best talent needs to stay motivated and driven whether they're a consultant or an employee"? Why or why not?
3. What do you think Chris Perkett means when she mentions that "I wasn't ready to hire employees because there's so much involved with doing that"? As a small business owner, what do you think is involved in hiring that first employee to your firm?
4. How does Chris Perkett's hiring and retaining employees perspective compare or differ from Jennifer Johnson's perspective?

The Bigger Small Business: Hiring Employees

LO1
Explore the decision to hire full-time or part-time help.

Of all the decisions that differentiate the types of small businesses, no decision is as important or complex as the decision to hire an employee. Many small businesses never do. Of the more than 23 million businesses in the United States in 2002, over 17.6 million had no employees at all—only the owner. Another 5.7 million firms had one or more employees.[2] For the economy, those firms that hire employees are an important source of job generation.[3]

For the owner, adding employees is important for several reasons. Adding employees increases the amount of work that can be done—serving more customers, producing more, or staying open longer. It also increases the demands on the owner. Now sales need to be made to cover the employee's wages or salary, and, when adding employees, the owner and business become responsible for the safety and well being of the employee, as well as face legal requirements as an employer. Some owners look at the pluses and minuses and decide to stay a solo operation for as long as possible, like Chris Perkett in the early stages of her business. Others take on the opportunity and responsibility, as Chris did later. For those entrepreneurs, the next key decision is what work should be done, who the best person is to do that work, and how the firm should take care of them. Those areas are where the field of human resource management comes into small business. In this chapter we look at those three areas.

Let's start with the decision of what kind of work needs to be done. Generally we start by thinking about how much work we want to cover. As a small business owner, you can hire either part-time or full-time employees. Which one will be best for you? You need to consider the pros and cons and expand with care. Full-time employees make it possible for you to take significant time away from the business. They get to understand the business sooner, and often are willing to take on more responsibility. They provide the ability to dramatically increase your hours open, material produced, or sales. But there are many additional expenses to having a full-time employee on staff as opposed to a part-time employee. The cost of adding an employee includes compensation, training time, and employee tax and accounting costs. Presumably, such costs are outweighed by greater productivity, but you need to carefully balance the ledger. "Probably the biggest mistake I made in my early hires was hiring too early," says Louis Gudema, president of Magic Hour Communications, a marketing agency in Watertown, Massachusetts. "As a result, we were not as profitable as we might have been if I had been slower to hire."[4]

www.magic-hour.com

"While every business has its own rhythm, it's usually wise to go through the first year without hiring. Get a feel for the sales cycle and the downturns. Measure the 'just right' temperature of income and outgo. Experts suggest squirreling away at least a year's worth of expenses and overhead before hiring in order to see you through any rough patches," says Joanna Krotz, co-author of the *Microsoft Small Business Kit*.[5]

Not only are there additional expenses to consider, but also **employee fit**.[6] You can ease into an employment contract by first hiring part-time help and if he or she works well and the demand for additional help is present, you can ease into a full-time position weighing the additional expense. Before making a full-time offer, let the applicant work part time for a while so you can see how she or he fits. Likely as not, this will be a learning period for you, too. You can ease someone into the business as a part-time worker. Or, if you go ahead and hire a full-time applicant, set up a **probationary period**.[7] Usually, state law dictates how long such trials may last, so check with your state employment office. Typically, a probationary period lasts 90 days. You can find this information for your state at www.business.gov/regions/states/. A trial period can be important, and if your first choice turns memorable in all the wrong ways, chalk it up to experience and keep recruiting.[8]

employee fit
The match between the needs, expectations, and culture of the small business with the expectations and the skills of the individual employee.

probationary period
Trial period in which an employee has temporary status before a formal offer to work full time is presented.

Whether you hire a part-time or full-time employee, it is important that each type of employee values your company's mission. Don Dymer, a former Scotland Yard police inspector, started his preemployment screening business in Jacksonville Beach, Florida, in 1995. He emphasizes the need for "employees to take on the mission and values that you want the business to take on." You do that by setting an example and making sure to define those values for every new hire.[9] For some inspirational stories on how small business owners hired their first employee, see http://www.Entrepreneur.com/article/0,4621,317629,00.html.[10]

www.business.gov/regions/states/

http://www.Entrepreneur.com/article/0,4621,317629,00.html

Attracting Employees

LO2
Understand how to recruit good employees on your budget.

A lot of the time a smaller firm can actually outperform large businesses in attracting high-quality employees.[11] To attract and hire new talent into a medium to large growing organization, help wanted ads in regional newspapers or the use of an employment

■ Attracting the best talent to your company can be encouraged by the strategic use of networking. Spend time in conversation with colleagues in the field, friends, vendors, and others to learn of possible employee leads.

service have been traditional methods. For small business owners, these methods tend to be expensive and have a long turnaround time. Today there are less expensive alternatives to consider.

networking
Relatively low-cost, although time-intensive, method of recruiting that can include colleagues, business professionals (your attorney or accountant), vendors, alumni, and advisory board members.

Networking is a relatively low-cost, although time-intensive, method of recruiting. There are many benefits such as receiving a credible critique of a potential candidate's work experience and personal character. People to network with include colleagues, business professionals (your attorney or accountant), friends, vendors you have strong relationships with, alumni, and advisory board members.

Internet recruiting
Method of recruiting that allows you to search a résumé database or post a job description to the Web; a small business owner who knows exactly what he or she wants can use filters to search vast numbers of résumés with pinpoint accuracy.

Internet recruiting allows you to search a résumé database or post a job description to the Web. The main contribution of a recruiting Web site, such as Monster.com, has been to speed up hiring and vastly increase the accuracy of the job-search process. You can post a job at 2 p.m. and get your first response a minute later. An employer who knows exactly what he or she wants can use filters to search vast numbers of résumés with pinpoint accuracy.[12]

employee referral
An underused, low-cost method for finding workers that rewards your employees for recommending potential candidates that would be a great employee fit.

Employee referral is an underused, low-cost method which rewards your employees for recommending potential candidates that would be a great fit. Even for small businesses, to work successfully, referrals should be handled formally, with guidelines such as following up on all leads within 24 hours.[13]

Company Web sites can be used to post job openings. This method would be effective if your site receives a fair amount of traffic, and it would incur only a small incremental cost to your Web site budget.[14] If your business does not have a company Web site, the investment of Web site development and maintenance may be a limiting factor, but when a Web site can cost $50 a year, it is a worthwhile investment. Search Google for "cheap web hosting" and you will find plenty of services offering template-based design and hosting services.

Many universities have *career service offices* that encourage companies to post openings to their job bank to recruit at both the undergraduate and the graduate levels. This service is commonly offered at no cost to companies and allows businesses to set up an account to manage résumé selection.

Professional groups can be a resource for recruiting new talent. Many associations publish newsletters or post openings online or at their meeting locations. Try sending a one-page job description to associations to which you belong.[15]

outsourcing
Contracting with others outside your firm to do work that would otherwise be done within your firm.

Outsourcing may be the answer if your small business is not ready to hire employees, but you have a growing need to meet workload demand. Consider, as an example, outsourcing to an assistant who is an independent entrepreneur and provides

SMALL BUSINESS INSIGHT

Go Virtual

Virtual employees or assistants can change the way many small businesses are operated and managed. This field is growing tremendously and is offering employers and small business owners alike an attractive new alternative to hiring and managing employees. Virtual employees are independent contractors who provide specialized business services or support from a distance, through the Internet, telephone, fax, or another method of communication. A virtual assistant can assist a small company that needs extra people to meet seasonal demands; step in to meet the demands of business growth, locally, domestically, or globally; or provide unique skills for a special project.

In the small business, virtual employees are not hired as full-time employees. They can be business owners themselves and are hired on a contract basis. Small business owners who work with a virtual employee have the distinct advantage of not having to deal with taxes, unemployment insurance, sick leave, vacation pay, or benefits. Rather than having to provide additional office space and be responsible for the development and supervision of an employee, they can enjoy the support and assistance of a professional without the headaches of hiring and managing employees.[16]

Here are some guidelines and methods for managing and fostering productivity among virtual employees:[17]

- Hire virtual employees who have experience with being self-motivated and disciplined, including former consultants, freelancers, and salespeople who are accustomed to dealing with deadlines and working independently. As a small business owner, this is critical, given that you already have multiple deadlines and responsibilities.
- As you manage your virtual employees, make sure to spend time developing a system of task lists, schedules, and goals with varying time frames and clear deadlines. Invest in spreadsheets and project scheduling software that will help your virtual employees organize tasks. Be sure to consistently review status reports with virtual employees to ensure that tasks are completed on time and on budget.
- Maintain communication with virtual workers via voice, fax, and other electronic methods. Don't become reliant on e-mail since it is too easy to misinterpret or misunderstand the written word. Speak on the phone and schedule face-to-face meetings occasionally.
- Micromanagement is nearly impossible with a remote staff, and it will unnerve anyone who attempts it. Trust that your employees are doing the right thing until evidence proves otherwise. If you are paranoid about slacking, hire salaried, rather than hourly, workers or pay per project.

administration, creative, or technical support. The assistant works on a contractual basis online and handles such functions as keeping your schedule, customer intelligence, or database up to speed.[18] Assistants can be people from your neighborhood or city, or virtual assistants working over the Internet. The nonprofit Virtual Assistant Association can be found at www.ivaa.org, and the major Web sites for outsourcing are eLance Online and Smarterwork.[19] Advice for hiring and managing **virtual employees** can be found in the accompanying Small Business Insight: Go Virtual.

Other traditional and nontraditional hiring sources to consider include:

- Contact *local churches* and the pastors and see if they have parishioners who are looking for a new job.
- Visit local *high schools* for entry-level jobs, local community colleges for those interested in management or a technical career.
- Finally, *state unemployment offices* are a great resource, with no cost to the employer.

virtual employees
Independent contractors who provide specialized business services or support from a distance, through the Internet, telephone, fax, or another method of communication.

www.elance.com

www.smarterwork.com

THE THOUGHTFUL ENTREPRENEUR

Low-Cost and No-Cost Employees

If your budget does not allow for a paid employee, consider three alternative methods to hire an employee at no cost.[20]

1. **Barter:** Trade your products or services for those of another business, for example, a maid service trading its house-cleaning services to a designer in return for a new logo. For this method of recruiting, you must be flexible in services rendered and received. Bartered services may add great value to a particular function of your small business and can be particularly useful when money is in short supply.
2. **Internships:** Hiring students to work at no cost in exchange for work experience may be a great way to get the assistance you need. Generally, students who intern are looking to use specific skill sets or be exposed to a particular functional area of a business. If you can provide valuable work experience, offering internships may be an appealing way to attract temporary help.
3. **Volunteers:** Volunteers are a wonderful resource if your business is strapped for cash, although the search process may be time consuming. Who will work for free? Family members are always the first source, with friends a close second, although people who need relevant work experience might give a few hours to have an entry on their job applications, such as stay-at-home spouses who are looking for work experience while children are at school. Also individuals committed to your company's mission are possible candidates. If your firm is doing a promotion for a charitable organization (like operating a stand at a fair), you may be able to get customers or members of the charity to contribute their help.

Matching the Worker to the Work

LO3
Know how to match the right person to the job.

Even before your first hire, you will need to know what your basic needs are and what roles this new employee will fit into. Ultimately, you would like to "match" the job with the ideal individual who can fulfill the responsibities of the job and grow with the business. Your first step is to define and describe all the work that will be part of the new job. Then you'll need to know how to evaluate the potential employees to see how well they match your ideal set of requirements.

Writing a Job Description

job description
Defines and discusses all the essential knowledge, skills, and abilities that are needed to fill the position.

Your job description needs to define and discuss all the essential knowledge, skills, and abilities that are needed to fill the position. In addition, you will need to describe what kind of personality, experience, and education you believe a person who performs the job should have. To determine some of these attributes, sit down and do a job analysis covering the following areas:[21]

- The reason the job exists (including an explanation of job goals and how they relate to your position and other positions in the company).
- The mental or physical tasks involved (ranging from judging, planning, and managing to cleaning, lifting, and welding).
- How the job will be done (all of the methods and equipment to be used).
- The qualifications needed (what kind of training, knowledge, skills are necessary).

If some of these questions are difficult to answer, consider talking to other small business owners in your area. You may also discuss these issues with employees and supervisors at other noncompeting small businesses that offer similar positions. (See Figure 19.1.)

JOIN THE REVOLUTION: BUSINESS/ENTREPRENEURSHIP/MANAGEMENT INTERNSHIP

Company or Recruiter	Make Me Heal	**Position Level**	Entry Level
Industry	Health Care	**Position Type**	School Year Internship
Function	Corporate Business Development	**Intern Paid**	Yes
Location	Los Angeles, CA	**Intern Type**	Undergraduate

BUSINESS/ENTREPRENEURSHIP/MANAGEMENT/FINANCE INTERNSHIP

Make Me Heal Internship Associate Program

Please e-mail your resume and cover letter to: interns@makemeheal.com

We offer paid internships during the entire year (summer, fall, winter, spring) in all areas of the company, from business, marketing/press relations, to writing, journalism, and research. The nationally renowned The Princeton Review has honored our Internship Program by selecting it for inclusion in its prestigious Internship Bible, the book profiling the top U.S. internships.

Join The Revolution: The Internship Associate Program and the people who make part of this important team at Make Me Heal are an essential part of our "revolution." We are proud to have created internship positions that will not involve brainless tasks and will not only serve to try to impress or fill space on your resume. Rather, our internships are designed to actually educate, empower, challenge, inspire, and accelerate your growth before you join the workplace.

Exposure and Growth in Several Disciplines: An important element of our Philosophy is to enable our team members to acquire expertise in a number of areas of our business. If we were to align together, you would be exposed to and learn about a number of disciplines. So during the scope of the Internship, team members can be expected to delve into various facets of our business as they grow with us.

Leap from an Internship to a Full-Time Career: Due to our philosophy of cultivating long-term connections with everyone in our team, it is entirely possible that an internship may evolve into a full-time career with us if the internship experience proves to be meaningful, productive, happy, and fun for you and all of us at Make Me Heal.

We're Family: Whether one is an Internship Associate or a full-time employee with us, we care about all of our MMPeople and are dedicated to offering everyone incredibly rewarding, meaningful, and fun career opportunities. Indeed, when you become an Internship Associate with us, you also become a part of our extended family.

Selected for Inclusion in the Internship Bible: It is worthwhile to note that the nationally renowned The Princeton Review (the U.S. leader in the educational/school services industry) has selected our Internship Associate Program to be included in its prestigious Internship Bible, which is indeed the "bible" profiling the top internship opportunities in the United States.

We're looking to connect with highly entrepreneurial, ambitious individuals who thrive in an ever-changing, multibillion dollar industry where rewriting the rules is the law.

Roles involve researching, analyzing, and formulating innovative business strategies and implementing them, conceiving strategies to build our brand name to a national/international scale, creating strong operational infrastructure, assessing financial issues, among other functions. Work directly with CEO (former investment banker and Wharton Business School alum) to formulate business strategies and plans, implement new product and service lines, initiate supplier relationships with multinational cosmetics companies and leading manufacturers, devise innovative marketing and publicity initiatives, devise financial forecasts, strengthen quality of consumer experience, develop financial statements and forecasts, participate in deal-making, make presentations to institutional/high-net worth individuals and strategic business partners, and create quality controls, accounting, and legal structures for transacting with consumers.

FIGURE 19.1

Sample Job Description

Source: Copyright © 2005 Vault.com: Item posted by an employer, job/internship listing on the Vault.com Job Board.

To get started, write down the job title and whom that person will report to (define how the job relates to you or other positions in the small business). Next, develop a job statement or summary describing the position's major and minor duties. List any educational requirements, desired experience, and specialized skills or knowledge required. Include salary range and benefits (see "Compensation" later in this chapter). Finish by listing any physical or other special requirements associated with the job.

Figure 19.1 gives you an example of a job description for an internship in a growing small business. For a one-person business hiring its first employee, these guidelines may seem unnecessary. But remember, you are laying the foundation for your personnel policy, which will be essential as your small business grows. Keeping detailed records from the time you hire your first employee will make things a lot easier when you hire your tenth, twentieth, and so on.

Also, writing the job description will help you determine whether you need a part- or full-time employee, whether the person should be permanent or temporary, and whether you could use an independent contractor to fill the position.

SKILL MODULE 19.1

Crafting a Job Description

In this skill module, you have the opportunity to write job descriptions for a student and an instructor on your campus. Write a job description for the role of student, and ask one of your instructors about his or her job and write a description. In your instructor interview or when thinking about the student job, cover many of the areas and questions discussed to get a full view and perspective of the positions.

Write a half-page job description using the following how-to steps:[22]

1. **Start with a Title:** Provide a job title for the position (two–three words). Beneath the title, you want to include important information related to the job such as the status (exempt vs. nonexempt) and to whom the employee reports.
2. **Give a Job Overview (or Summary of the Job):** Be sure that this section is not more than three to four sentences long and that it explains the level and basic nature of this job position. You will be outlining details of the job in the following sections:

   Example:
   An entry-level job position providing administrative support to a technology business with three employees. Main duties include: scheduling appointments, giving information to callers, and generally relieving staff of clerical work and minor administrative and business detail.
3. **Define the Duties and Responsibilities:** Write down all the tasks that the employee will be doing in this position. (Remember that the job description is the work that you need to have done now and also the work that will need to be done.) Be flexible in writing the duties and responsibilities to accommodate growth of the position. Be clear, concise, and complete.
4. **Knowledge, Skills, and Abilities:** These are basic qualities that the employee should possess. They could include:

   Knowledge of computer software, including: PowerPoint, Excel.
   Skilled at performing multiple tasks simultaneously.
   Ability to relate to people and make them feel comfortable.
5. **Credentials and Experience:** List the level of educational and professional experience the person should have (possibly allow for additional experience to make up for the lack of an educational degree).
6. **Special Requirements:** Anything that may not have been covered up until this point should go here. For example:

Frequent travel required to other universities and conferences.
Job includes some evening and weekend hours.
Ability to lift 15 lbs or more.

Then compare the descriptions with those of other students. You might also try to find the official job description for an instructor from your school. When comparing your description with the other ones, consider the following:

1. How difficult was it to define and narrow the many responsibilities of the position?
2. Were there differences between your description and the actual description?
3. How many similarities were there between your description and the actual description?
4. If there were discrepancies, where were the "gaps" between the two?
5. As a small business owner, what can you do to ensure there is a mutual understanding between you and the employee in describing the job/position as your business grows?
6. How can you get both formal and informal feedback from employees regarding the job on a continual basis?

Evaluating Job Prospects

Once you have a job description, you can use it to help you evaluate whether an individual would be the right match for the position and your small business.[23] So what can you do to make sure you hire the right person for the job? This is probably one of the most difficult decisions you may be faced with making, especially since we are all not trained in the art and science of hiring employees. In making successful hiring

FIGURE 19.2

Typical Interview Questions that Small Business Owners Can Ask[24]

Matching the right person to the job based on personal, educational, experience, and career goals of the applicant.

Personal

1. Tell me about yourself.
2. What are your hobbies?
3. Why did you choose to interview with our organization?
4. Describe your ideal job.
5. What can you offer us?
6. What do you consider to be your greatest strengths?
7. Can you name some weaknesses?
8. Define success. Failure.
9. Have you ever had any failures? What did you learn from them?
10. Of which three accomplishments are you most proud?
11. Who are your role models? Why?
12. How does your college education or work experience relate to this job?
13. What motivates you most in a job?
14. Have you had difficulty getting along with a former professor/supervisor/co-worker and how did you handle it?
15. Have you ever spoken before a group of people? How large?
16. Why should we hire you rather than another candidate?
17. What do you know about our organization (products or services)?
18. Where do you want to be in five years? Ten years?
19. Do you plan to return to school for further education?

Education

20. Why did you choose your major?
21. Why did you choose to attend your college or university?
22. Do you think you received a good education? In what ways?
23. In which campus activities did you participate?
24. Which classes in your major did you like best? Least? Why?
25. Which elective classes did you like best? Least? Why?
26. If you were to start over, what would you change about your education?
27. Do your grades accurately reflect your ability? Why or why not?
28. Were you financially responsible for any portion of your college education?

Experience

29. What job-related skills have you developed?
30. Did you work while going to school? In what positions?
31. What did you learn from these work experiences?
32. What did you enjoy most about your last employment? Least?
33. Have you ever quit a job? Why?
34. Give an example of a situation in which you provided a solution to an employer.
35. Give an example of a time in which you worked under deadline pressure.
36. Have you ever done any volunteer work? What kind?
37. How do you think a former supervisor would describe your work?

Career Goals

38. Do you prefer to work under supervision or on your own?
39. What kind of boss do you prefer?
40. Would you be successful working with a team?
41. Do you prefer large or small organizations? Why?
42. What other types of positions are you considering?
43. How do you feel about working in a structured environment?
44. Are you able to work on several assignments at once?
45. How do you feel about working overtime?
46. How do you feel about travel?
47. How do you feel about the possibility of relocating?
48. Are you willing to work flextime?

■ Interviewing can be a nerve-wracking experience for both interviewer and candidate. As an interviewer, be prepared as fully as possible, with specific questions to ask and a clear communication of job details. See Figure 19.2 to glean sample interview questions and start you thinking of additional questions you might want to ask in your own company setting.

decisions, rely on the information developed in your job description to identify the most important knowledge areas, skills, and abilities the ideal candidate should possess. Next, create the same specific questions that you will ask of all candidates that will clearly and behaviorally demonstrate to you that they have these critical factors. Do not simply accept the candidate's word that he or she possesses a certain skill or knowledge base. Ask that person to demonstrate the skill, solve a problem, or write or create something that clearly and concretely provides you with the proof you need to make an informed decision.

Ask specific and measurable questions of the candidate. If you ask if this individual considers himself or herself a success or a failure, do not simply accept a yes or no response. Probe for specific examples of both successes and failures. The latter is especially rich in response material because you can then ask what the person could have done to turn the failure into a success. In the process, you are observing how the candidate analyzes situations, how rationally or logically the situation is presented, and whether or not, to the best of your judgment, the person is being truthful.

If at all possible, consider involving one or two other interviewers (if possible within your small business) to look at a candidate who seems promising. This helps you be sure that you understand the individual as well as possible. In that way, you can all share your insights and impressions of the candidate. Furthermore, one interviewer can add an aspect to a question that another one (or even you as the owner) may have overlooked.

Finally, make sure you know enough about a candidate before you hire that person, and never, ever hire even a moderately qualified person just because you need someone now. You want to be sure you haven't hired a problem. It can be long and painful to terminate someone and advertise, screen, interview, and hire another person. Take your time to make sure you have the person that best matches the position for your small business.

SMALL BUSINESS INSIGHT

Mavens & Moguls, a Marketing Strategy Consulting Firm[25]

I feel like my role is to connect the dots . . . I'm a conductor of a world class orchestra.

— Paige Arnof-Fenn

Paige Arnof-Fenn, founder and CEO of Mavens & Moguls, launched her company two and a half years ago. Paige had worked with companies at all stages that needed expert marketing advice, including projects for start-ups, authors, professional service firms, the Sundance Film Festival, Merrill Lynch, Sprint, and Delta Airlines. With Mavens & Moguls she has assembled a team of marketing all-stars, the best people that she has encountered in her career across all marketing disciplines. They are spread across the United States and as far away as Bangkok.

As the sole business owner of Mavens & Moguls, Paige relies on her virtual employees to knit together the network of experienced professionals who have actually "done it" for the top companies across a variety of industries. Working from their own offices, homes, or other private work spaces, they provide marketing strategy, planning, and execution. The real mavens and moguls specialize in promotion, PR, direct marketing, media, pricing strategy, positioning, customer acquisition, and new product launches. In many ways, all the areas of the marketing mix are covered that can be used to build a brand and grow a client's business.

Training Your Employees

LO4
Learn about employee training methods and resources.

Of course, it would be great if employees came to work fully prepared to meet your business needs. However, most employees (even the most ideal new hires) need training. The time and money you spend teaching employees how to do their jobs could turn out to be your small company's wisest investment.

To begin, you should first assess your small firm's training needs from the perspective of the business, the job itself (job description), and the needs of the employees. This assessment will provide answers to the following questions:

- *Where* is training needed? What key areas need the most attention?
- *What* specifically must an employee learn in order to be more productive?
- *Who* needs to be trained?

Once you have answered these questions, you can then design your training program. There are two different types of training: initial training and ongoing training. When employees first join your small business or start a new role, offering them the training they need to handle the position makes them feel valued, challenged, and rewarded.

Initial and Ongoing Training Methods

There are two broad types of training available to small businesses: on-the-job and off-the-job techniques. Individual circumstances and the where, what, and who of your training program determine which method to use.

on-the-job training
Delivered to employees while they perform their regular jobs; techniques include orientations, job instruction training, apprenticeships, internships and assistantships, job rotation, and coaching.

On-the-job training is delivered to employees while they perform their regular jobs. In this way, they do not lose time while they are learning. After a plan is developed for what should be taught, employees should be informed of the details. On-the-job techniques include orientations, job instruction training, apprenticeships, internships and assistantships, job rotation, and coaching.[26]

For on-the-job training in a small business, you need to stay abreast of all the jobs that need doing and define them so others can be trained in doing parts of the job. It is critical to design a job to make sure that nothing important is missed. To give you an idea of how to design on-the-job instruction that gives an employee a method to complete a certain task in a job, consider Skill Module 19.2: Writing Instructions and Procedures.

Writing Instructions and Procedures[27]

SKILL MODULE 19.2

- Prefix the instruction/procedure with a clear heading that summarizes the task.
- Show clearly who does what.
- Start each step or instruction with a verb that tells the reader to do something: examples: "Open the valve . . . ," "Press the emergency button . . . ," "Tell your supervisor. . ."
- Use a numbered list when the order in which tasks are to be performed is important. Use a bulleted list (like this one) when the order is not important.
- Put notes, warnings, and prerequisite conditions at the start, or *before* the list item to which they refer.
- Don't mix instructions with conceptual information. Present any necessary background information before the instructions.
- Use a level of detail that is appropriate to your employees' skill level and will ensure they will be able to know how to complete the job task.

Along with on-the-job training techniques, off-the-job methods such as lectures, special study, videos, television conferences or discussions, case studies, role-playing, simulation, programmed instruction, and laboratory training are all possible. Most of these techniques can be used by small businesses, although some may be too costly.[28] Other affordable and ongoing training methods can be less formal. In fact, training can be as simple as encouraging employees to meet regularly to discuss issues and share new ideas and perspectives. If your firm is large enough, you can also assign mentors to junior employees. Mentors give less experienced employees the opportunity to learn from seasoned veterans. Employees will be more comfortable in the face of new challenges if they know where to go for help. Mentors can inspire employees to strive for greater levels of success, help them channel their ambitions, and teach them new ways of handling ongoing problems more effectively.

Three Guidelines for Training[29]

1. **Give your employees opportunities to use their new skills:** Many small business owners complain that it is sometimes useless to train employees. Owners may argue that employees will take the knowledge and leave for a higher-paying job at another firm. While this may happen, small business owners can prevent it. Once your employees are trained, give them opportunities to use their new skills.
2. **Make training an ongoing process:** Good employees want to learn, and you should provide them with opportunities to do so. Give employees encouragement to talk to you when their learning curve goes flat and then find ways to provide them with challenges and the knowledge to meet them successfully.
3. **Think of training as an investment (as opposed to an expense):** Many small business owners hesitate to invest too much energy, time, or money in training employees. Feeling that the expense does not justify the end results, they choose instead to give new hires a crash course and then put them right to work. Results of that sink-or-swim approach include costly mistakes, unhappy workers, and low productivity.

LO5

Gain insight in meeting employees' needs and expectations.

Rewarding Employees

Congratulations! Your business is growing and you have hired your first employee(s), either full time, part time, or on a virtual basis. Most likely the hiring process was time consuming to ensure a perfect fit between your new employee and your company. So how are you going to retain your first employee and ensure you are meeting his or her needs? To retain productive employees and increase their job satisfaction, the simplest answer is to ask them what their needs are. Next, create an environment that appeals to them.

But when you do not have employees to ask, where do you start? Jill Kickul studied 23 owner promises, including everything from salary and health care to workload and opportunities for advancement, and distilled them down to five underlying factors, in order of most important to least important: autonomy and personal growth, rewards/opportunities, job security/responsibilities, benefits, and facilitating work.[30] The full list is given in Table 19.1.

Salary rewards, bonuses, and perks were not as important to employees as autonomy and personal growth; job security and responsibility were more important than benefits. But small business owners often implicitly or explicitly communicate conflicting terms when making **psychological contracts** with employees. To avoid this, denote strict limits on what you promise employees and how and when those promises will be delivered. Put what you agree to in writing to prevent problems when it comes time to evaluate whether you've delivered on the contract.

Entrepreneurs need to make job offers and manage based on an **open-book policy**. If you work this way and your company hits a downturn and promises cannot be met,

psychological contract
Refers to employees' beliefs about the promises between the employee and the firm. These beliefs are based on the perception that promises have been made (e.g., competitive wages, promotional opportunities, job training) in exchange for certain employee obligations such as giving of their energy, time, and technical skills.

open-book policy
Concept that key employees should be able to see and understand a firm's financials, that they should have a part in moving the numbers in the right direction, and that they should have a direct stake in the strategy and success of the firm.

Table 19.1 23 Rewards Offered Employees of Small Businesses

Factors	Psychological Contract Items
Autonomy and growth	Meaningful work Challenging and interesting work Participation in decision making Freedom to be creative Opportunity to develop new skills Increasing responsibilities A job that provides autonomy and control Recognition of my accomplishments Career guidance and mentoring
Benefits	Health care benefits Vacation benefits Retirement benefits Tuition reimbursement
Rewards and opportunities	Opportunities for promotion and advancement Opportunities for personal growth Pay and bonuses tied to performance Job training Continual professional training
Job security and work responsibilities	Well-defined job responsibilities A reasonable workload Job security
Work facilitation	Adequate equipment to perform job Enough resources to do the job

Source: Jill Kickul, "Promises Made, Promises Broken: An Exploration of Employee Attraction and Retention Practices in Small Business," *Journal of Small Business Management* 30, no. 4 (October 2001), pp. 320–335. Reprinted with permission.

employees are less likely to react badly since they have a better understanding of the firm's situation. Five factors are most valuable to employees:

1. **Teamwork:** Fostering a sense of teamwork allows people to interact with one another on a professional level. Sharing ideas, working toward a common goal, analyzing one another's work, and communicating cross functionally help build stronger professional bonds which increase a sense of belonging and company fit.
2. **Recognition:** Showing appreciation for a job well done or giving credit to an employee who introduced a great idea can go a long way in making your employee feel valued. Recognition can be given in person, by voice mail, through e-mail, or written in a memo or letter. You can also incorporate a reward system. Do you have star performers? Increase their motivation by recognizing their accomplishment with a certificate, plaque, or personal bonus such as a dinner or movie gift certificate. This will help them to feel valued for their hard work and dedication and encourage them to continue this behavior.[31]
3. **Training:** A common reason people leave a company is if they feel they are not developing professionally.[32] Providing learning opportunities at every level of the organization through on-the-job training or professional training will increase your employees' capabilities, allow them to expand their job responsibility, and help to

increase job satisfaction. Commitment to employees' development and growth is one way to ensure an employee is growing and will stay longer.[33]

4. **Empowerment:** Proper training and explanation of guidelines or boundaries for decision making will allow employees to use their judgment to make on-the-spot decisions for the companies' best interest. Empowerment, when embraced, will increase their personal feeling of responsibility and enhance their commitment to the company.
5. **Contribution:** Providing meaningful work for employees gives them the feeling or belief that the day's work was a valuable contribution to the company and that they made a difference.[34] Employees have to believe that the decisions they make and the work they perform have a direct impact on the product or service you provide.[35]

Although not included in the study, another key element on which the other factors depends is communication. Open communication is vital for new employees. Share your vision and the mission of the business. To be sure your employees feel valued, it is important to make time to talk about the direction of the company. Make sure *you* understand how they see what you have said and what they think you have promised.[36] To do this, you can have a casual conversation while working side by side. Or find time to schedule brief one-on-one meetings to make sure the conversation takes place and the message is understood. Employees want to know what the company is trying to do, where it is going, and what it stands for.[37] After you have communicated the goal of the position and your expectation of their performance during the hiring process, follow up with feedback on a consistent basis regarding their performance. And ask how they personally prefer to communicate and what they need in their work environment to maximize their productivity.

Increasingly, small entrepreneurial companies are implementing formal performance appraisals. Reviewing employees' performance is an ongoing process. Owners and managers need to communicate with employees and give year-round feedback to employees on the job regarding performance and company goals. Before conducting a formal review, it is important to understand that there are two parts to a review: (1) the performance review and (2) the pay review. These reviews should be held at different times of the year. The performance review typically occurs once a year to monitor your employees' job satisfaction, overall performance, and set career objectives. The goal of the performance review is to identify employee strengths, formally recognize performance, set goals to utilize the skills identified as strengths, and set direction for the upcoming year. It is also a time to identify areas of development and communicate with employees concerning how you will support them and the necessary steps they need to take to develop identified areas. It is a time to plan and set goals for the year ahead and to review work from the year past. The goal of the pay review is to reward your employees if they have performed all duties and met general requirements as discussed in initial job description conversations.

Small business owners with fewer than five employees may find formal performance reviews unnecessary or impersonal—taking away the strength of a small firm. It is a good idea to conduct written reviews to track employee performance. This gives you an out if their performance becomes unsatisfactory after coaching or retraining. To successfully conduct an employee review, you should have a clear understanding of the position.[38] Next you should create a list of questions and issues that will be discussed in preparation for creating an evaluation sheet:[39] This list can include what the current responsibilities are, how well they are performing in meeting identified responsibilities, what needs to be improved or learned to be successful in the position, and where employees are headed in their career. The evaluation sheet should include open-ended questions for the employees to fill out regarding job performance, strengths, areas of development, and what gets in the way of accomplishing the job.[40] For a sample appraisal and type of questions you may want to begin with, go to: www.bizhelp24.com.

www.bizhelp24.com

An appraisal form should be filled out and returned to you before the scheduled performance review so that you can learn the employees' goals, interests, and self-evaluation when you are crafting your comments.[41] Your comments during the review should address how the employee can grow, improve, and build on his or her current set of successes to contribute to the company, what you can do as a leader to provide resources, guidance, and opportunities, and what the individual needs to do on his or her own to continue to grow and succeed.[42]

Compensation and Benefits

L06
Learn how to develop a fair compensation and benefit plan.

One of the first steps in developing a compensation plan is to determine your organization's salary philosophy. Do you believe in raising the level of base salaries in your organization or do you appreciate the flexibility of variable pay? A small business, with variable sales and income, may be better off controlling the levels of base salaries. When times are good, the business can tie bonus dollars to goals achieved.

The next step is to find comparison factors for salary. Research the salary range for similar positions and job descriptions. Determine whether you are competitive with organizations of similar size, sales, and markets. If you can find companies in the same industry, especially in your area or region, that is another good comparison source. You can check salary surveys and want ads, and scout out competitors to see if they are underpaying or overpaying their employees. You can get a start by searching Google for "salary comparison" as shown below. Probably the best-known site for comparison information is Salary.com. You can get the same report without registering by using hotjobs.yahoo.com. Paying too much is an unnecessary drain on your resources, but paying too little will make it difficult for you to find and keep the best people.[43]

www.salary.com

Moreover, salary should be tied to a person's skills and experience. Subsequent increases need to be based on an employee's performance, value, and contribution to the small business. Use the information from the employee's performance appraisal form to help you determine the appropriate increase. You will also want to consider percentages of increase in salary in similar jobs in your local area.[44]

Bonuses and Long-Term Incentives[45]

Employee bonuses, usually paid in a single lump at the end of the year, are one way of providing performance incentives. Profit-sharing plans, stock options, or stock grants not only provide long-term incentives to employees, but they can also help retain valuable team members through your small business start-up phase. However, you also may want to consider these options once you are beyond the start-up phase and have stability in your business earnings overall.

Health Insurance[46]

Employer-sponsored health insurance is fairly standard among medium-sized companies, but not among small businesses. While an employer-sponsored plan saves employees money and gives them peace of mind in knowing that they won't be denied coverage, it is not always affordable to the small business owner. However, providing insurance to your employees sends the message that you care about their health and the health of their families. To minimize costs, consider having employees pick up part of the tab. Employees who have coverage through a spouse may want to opt out of a plan, particularly if there's a cost associated with it.

Retirement Plans[47]

401(k) plans have become popular because they are relatively easy to administer and are less expensive than traditional pension plans. Many employees like these plans

THE THOUGHTFUL ENTREPRENEUR

Labor Unions

Many employees are members of labor unions. A labor union is an organization of employees that usually work for the same employer at the same workplace. Labor unions try to get a "collective" contract for their members. The labor laws governing unions can be very complicated. If you are faced with a union organizing drive, you should contact a labor lawyer immediately to make sure that your response to the organizing drive is legal.

If your employees belong to a labor union, they probably already made a "union contract," which is also called a "collective bargaining agreement" with you. This agreement and contract covers wages, working conditions, and procedures for complaining about problems on the job.

Union contracts usually provide that employees cannot be fired, suspended, or disciplined without "good cause." This rule is usually found in a section of the contract titled "Grievance Procedure" or "Discipline." If an employee thinks you didn't have "good cause" to fire or discipline, he or she generally contacts the union. The union may decide to file a grievance for the worker against you. If the union files a grievance against you, you should see an attorney who specializes in labor law, who should help you decide how to defend against the grievance. If you have questions about labor unions, contact a business lawyer near you, or you can start some of the research yourself by contacting the U.S. Department of Labor, **http://www.dol.gov/compliance/**. Its main goal is to help employers and employees comply with Department of Labor laws and regulations as well as to give you additional information related to your state's laws and compliance issues specific to managing and operating your small business.

because they maintain some control over the amount of their contribution and how the money is invested. Most small companies try to put some kind of savings or 401(k) plan in place, even if they don't contribute money to them. Other incentives that you may want to consider include time off and flexible schedules such as holidays, vacations, sick days, and personal days. An employer unable to offer competitive salaries may close part of the gap by offering more time off or flexible work hours. Some employers make no distinction between sick, vacation, and personal days and allow employees a set number of days off each year to be used at their discretion. This prevents employees from abusing sick days and keeps employees from feeling that they need to lie when a child is ill or a personal emergency arises.

Human Resource Issues in the Family Business

LO7
Understand the complexities of managing family within your business.

Small business management problems in a family-owned business are somewhat different from the same problems in a nonfamily business. When close relatives work together, emotions often interfere with business decisions. In some family companies, control of daily operations is a problem. In others, a high turnover rate among nonfamily members is a problem. In still other companies, growth is a problem because some of the relatives are unwilling to plow profits back into the business.[48] When you put up your own money and operate your own small business, you prize your independence. "It's my business," you tell yourself in good times and in bad times. However, "It's our business," in a family company. Conflicts sometimes abound because relatives look upon the business from different viewpoints. Those relatives who are silent partners, stockholders, and directors see only dollar signs when judging capital expenditures, growth, and other matters. Relatives who are engaged in daily operations judge matters from the viewpoint of the production, sales, and personnel necessary to make the company successful. Obviously, these two viewpoints may conflict in many instances.

This natural conflict can be aggravated by family members who have no talent for money or business. Sometimes they are the weak offspring of the founders or the small business owner—sons and daughters who lack business acumen—and sometimes they are in-laws who must be taken care of regardless of their ability or the company's needs. Basically, the management problems that face the manager of a family-owned business are the same as those that confront the owner-manager of any small company. But the job of the "family manager" is complicated because of the relatives who must be reconciled to the facts of the marketplace, the factory, and the house.

■ Family members who work together in a shared small business can encounter serious conflict when emotional ties escalate everyday problems into crises. What are some suggestions you have for problem-solving methods within a family business?

When the Sparks Fly between Family Members[49]

Different opinions do not always produce discord, but sometimes they cause sparks to fly, especially in a family-operated firm. Emotion is an added dimension as brothers and sisters, uncles and aunts, nephews and nieces, and fathers and children work together in such a small business. For the individual who must head such a company, the important thing is to recognize this dimension of emotions and to make objective decisions that are difficult to come by in such situations. When members of a family are active in the small business, it is hard to make objective decisions about the knowledge, skills, and abilities of one another. For instance, one says about another relative, "He was lazy when we were kids, and he's still lazy." Or a disgruntled wife says about an aunt, "What does she know about the business? She's only here because of her father's money."

If such emotional outbursts affected only the family, the manager might "knock a few heads together" and move along. However, often it is not that easy. The bad feelings and quarrels of relatives have a way of spreading out to include the nonfamily employees. Then the owner's problem is to keep the bickering from interfering with the real work. You cannot afford to let the company become divided into warring camps. You have to convince nonfamily employees that their interests are best served by a profitable organization rather than by allegiance to particular members of the family. Another aspect of the emotional atmosphere is that often nonfamily employees tend to base their decisions on the family's tensions. They know how their bosses react and are influenced by this knowledge.

Is the Small Business Owner Really in Control?[50]

The president of a small business is not always necessarily the person in charge. In many family-owned firms, the elder statesperson of the family becomes president or chairperson of the board of directors. But day-to-day management is in the hands of other members of the family. In some cases, even the best hands are tied as the family member tries to manage the business. As an example, the ceiling on the amount of money that can be spent without permission from the rest of the family may be too low for the situation confronting the company. Having to clear operating expenditures may mean missing opportunities for increased profits, such as taking advantage of a good price on raw materials or sales inventory.

In other cases, an employee/manager may be in a bind because of emotional involvement. For example, you may feel that you have to clear routine matters with top family members because "Uncle Joe never lets you forget your mistakes." Personalities and emotional reactions create bottlenecks that work against an efficient operation. In some family-owned companies, the day-to-day manager may be a bottleneck. You may be a bottleneck because you do not have the ability to delegate work and authority. You may be the manager because of age or the amount of capital you have in the business without regard to your qualifications. In other instances, you may hold up progress because you do not listen to others in the company.

One way to obtain objective control in a family-owned business is to hire an outsider to manage the day-to-day operations, when the company can afford it. Any manager may become as biased as any family member. With a hired manager, the family members will have their hands full in setting policies and in planning for growth. An efficient hired manager will see to it that all employees—family and nonfamily alike—know to whom to report at all times. Such definite lines of authority are even more important when a member of the family manages operations with other relatives filling various jobs. The responsibilities of family members should be spelled out. Family employees should discipline themselves to work within the bounds of these lines of authority. Even then, it is wise to have a nonfamily employee high in the organization so that he or she can be involved in operations and help smooth out any emotional decisions which family members may make.[51]

The manager's authority to suspend or discharge flagrant violators of company rules should also be spelled out. Management control is weakened if special allowances are made for family employees. An important question connected with authority is: Who takes over when something happens to the family member who heads the business? A position may be up for grabs if the family hasn't provided for an orderly succession. This need is especially critical when the top family member is approaching retirement age or is in poor health.

What to Do When the Brother-in-Law Needs a Job[52]

One of the most common problems in a family business is the hiring of relatives who do not have talent. But what are you to do when your brother or another close relative says, "Tom needs a job badly"? The emotional aspect of such family relationships is hard to fight. It will be hard to fire Tom if he turns out to cost you more money than his presence is worth. The main thing is to recognize the talent or lack of it. Suppose your brother-in-law, for example, has little or no ability as far as your company is concerned. Perhaps you can put him in a job where in spite of his weaknesses he can make a contribution and not disturb your employees.

The major concern is not necessarily the relative but how he or she affects other employees. In some cases, a relative can demoralize the small business by his or her dealing with other employees. For example, he or she may loaf on the job, avoid unpleasant tasks, take special privileges, and make snide remarks about you and other relatives. If you are stuck with such a relative, try putting him or her in a job where he or she will have minimum contact with other employees, out of the mainstream of decision making. For instance sister-in-law Sue might be placed in a sales office in another city some distance from the company's headquarters where she will be under the supervision of a top producer. Another alternative is to change her attitude by formal or informal education. The key is to see that the nontalented relative does not affect the relationship that you, the owner, have with other members of your staff. Other employees will respect you for keeping relatives in line.

Is Nonfamily Turnover High?

Some family-owned businesses are plagued with a high turnover among their nonfamily executives. In other cases, top-notch employees leave because promotions are closed to them because they see your relatives being promoted instead. An exit interview is a useful device for getting at the root of this type of turnover. A key employee who has decided to leave may be eager to tell you the true story—or at least enough of the facts to help you develop a course of action. When a small business owner has the facts, he or she may have to confront the trouble-causing relative with an unpleasant story. Rare is the owner-manager who can fire a troublesome and close relative and make it stick. One way to remove such a thorn from the side of key employees is to help the relative start a business in a noncompeting line—provided he or she has the management ability that is necessary for success. Another way is to "exile" him or her to a branch office or find a job with another business.

How Is the Pie Divided?[53]

Paying family members and dividing profits among them can also be a difficult affair. Many persons feel that they are underpaid, but what about relatives who comment as follows:

- "Uncle Jack sits around and gets more than I do."
- "Aunt Sue goes to Europe on the returns of money her husband put into the business before he died 10 years ago."
- "Your brother goofs off and rakes in more than you do."

How do you resolve such complaints? You won't be able to entirely. If the business is a small corporation, certain equalizing factors can be accomplished by stock dividends. By recapitalizing the company, some stockholders can take preferred stock with

SMALL BUSINESS INSIGHT

Hiring and Managing Family

So you want to employ family members to help run your business. There are many benefits to working with family members including lower cost of governance, the commitment a family member brings, and seeing relatives grow professionally. Because you are intimate with the family member's values and work ethic, you may feel inclined to skip the job interview and bring him or her onboard. In a job interview a prospective candidate will learn of the job description and what the performance expectations are. Or you may be in desperate need of help and instead of interviewing and reviewing a job description or performance expectation you put someone to work right away. He or she might be your first employee, and it is possible that you don't have a job description or haven't thought through your expectations. This is a good time to determine what you are looking for in terms of assistance and what you expect from the employee. This will become your guideline. For a successful employer-employee relationship it is essential to set guidelines on the job description, expectations, and contingency plans before an issue arises. This way you are limiting the potential for a family feud or nonfamily member to feel undervalued. If you plan carefully enough, a family business can be rewarding as well as profitable.[54]

"While it is satisfying to build a business with the people you love and will allow you to spend more time with them, unfortunately, that's not enough of a foundation on which to build a solid business."[55] Formal guidelines which outline job description and performance expectations should be established even for small family-run businesses. In most cases family members will not go through a formal hiring process and therefore have not learned what is expected. It is best to have a conversation early to review guidelines so that the new employee can learn what is expected in terms of work performance. "Families don't need written guidelines to operate, but family businesses do," says Dr. David Gage, clinical psychologist and founder of Business Mediation Associates in Washington, D.C. "It isn't viable for a firm of, say, 10 people to have a human resources department, but it should have formal personnel policies."[56]

dividends. Salaries are best handled by being competitive with those in the area. Find out what local salary ranges are for various management jobs and use these ranges as a guide for paying both family and nonfamily personnel. When you tie pay to the type of work that the individual does, you can show disgruntled relatives the value that the industry puts on their jobs. Fringe benefits can also be useful in dividing profits equitably among family members. Benefits, such as deferred profit-sharing plans, pension plans, insurance programs, and stock purchase programs, offer excellent ways to placate disgruntled members of the family and at the same time help them to build their personal assets.

Fair Personnel Policies across Family and Nonfamily Members

As family members are integrated within the small business, you should be careful in making sure that your hiring standards are consistent across employees and that there are clear boundaries for each position. Your policies should be communicated to all. Here are a few guidelines to consider when developing policies across family and nonfamily members:

- **Hiring standards:** You should employ the same hiring standards with family members as you do with nonfamily members—to hire the best possible candidate for the position. You will want to determine if family members are qualified for the position and if they have the desire to contribute. Before bringing on family members, you should "articulate your company's philosophy and practices to them to head off inappropriate or unrealistic expectations."[57]
- **Boundaries for each role:** The important thing is that each role be well defined and that employees and managers respect one another's boundaries. For instance, an employee-daughter should not be asking a CEO-dad to "take care of" this or that because she has a softball game that afternoon, and vice versa. Essentially, family members must be prepared to behave in their role exactly as they would in a traditional office setting.[58] If problems arise, as with any employee, it is best to have a conversation with the employee to address the issue. If not addressed, the employee will be unaware of his or her inappropriate behavior and be likely to repeat it.
- **Clearly defined job description:** Ira Bryck, director of the University of Massachusetts Family Business Center in Amherst, Massachusetts, says, "People [involved in family businesses] need to do what they're especially good at. They need to know what their job is and what their job isn't. By defining everyone's job titles, compensation and responsibilities upfront, you can prevent any kind of future drama."[59] To do this have a conversation with the family member about what the job entails, what the pay will be, and what he or she will be responsible for before he or she starts on the job. Mapping out clear responsibilities "works well for a relative who's an ideal fit for a job as s/he knows full well what his/her job entails, and that can bolster performance."[60] It also is helpful to have the job description documented in case responsibilities are left unmet. It gives you a concrete document to refer to if job performance is not met.
- **Performance expectations:** "Make sure that you establish clearly what you expect of any employee family member"[61] and what happens when expectations are not met before a performance issue arises. As mentioned above, nonfamily new hires learn of performance expectations during the hiring process. If your family member did not go through the formal hiring process, he or she may not have complete information about performance expectations which is critical to employee success. You can have a conversation to explain performance expectations, employee responsibility, and cultural norms of the work environment. "Sometimes people think just because they're family, they can take advantage of the rules," says Leon Eastmond, president of A. L. Eastmond & Sons Inc.,

a second-generation, family-run boiler/tank manufacturing and repair company in New York City. "But I won't tolerate such foolishness. Business is business, and I tell them that I don't dictate the terms of their behavior; the business does. If they don't act properly on the job, they'll be on a slippery banana with this company—even if they're members of the family."[62]

- **Personnel policies apply to everyone:** Just as a certain standard of workplace behavior is expected of all employees, benefits afforded family members should be applicable to nonfamily employees as well. According to DeWitt, who runs a decidedly family-friendly firm, "We set up a flexible-schedule work arrangement initially because Lisa was pregnant. But it's not just for our benefit. Everyone here can flex their work time and place, as long as the results meet the company's high expectations. That's company policy."
- **Procedure to express objections:** In small family businesses, whom to complain to can become a real issue. Under normal circumstances, if an employee has a gripe, he or she brings it to an immediate supervisor rather than the head of the company. That procedure often becomes blurred when it's a family business and the griper is the son or daughter of the owner—even if the parent isn't the child's immediate supervisor.[63] Depending on the organizational environment, there are different preferred channels of communication. Small business owners may have an open-door policy in which any employee is welcome to address business issues. Some organizations are hierarchical, and employees are expected to address the next level in the chain of command such as their supervisor or manager. Other organizations are flat and do not have many management levels. In these organizations there is more flexibility as to whom to address when you have an issue. What is important is communicating through the company's preferred channel of communication and holding all employees, family employees and nonfamily employees, accountable for following the same guidelines.
- **Procedures to let a family member go:** It is often a lot harder to let a family employee go than a nonfamily employee because of the potential for a family crisis and the awkwardness it may bring at Thanksgiving time when the family gets together.[64] "It's almost impossible to 'effectively' fire a family member, because of family issues," says Quentin Fleming, author of the book *Keep the Family Baggage out of the Family Business*. "It's a family incident. The person who's fired will turn to other family members. The owner who fires another family member will be contacted by family members who are going to condemn him for disloyalty." That sort of stress makes it essential to approach the decision purely within a business framework. Emphasize performance and suitability to a position. If someone simply isn't up to the job, it's important that change occur, no matter if the employee is a relative or not. "Owners need to give themselves permission to operate the business like a business," Fleming says. "When faced with a decision, they should ask themselves what good business practice dictates. Then they should do it. The business can't allow the fact that someone happens to be a family member to interfere with what the situation demands."[65]

The idea of small businesses hiring employees has grown in importance. It turns out that while the Fortune 500 companies have laid off millions of workers over the past 20 years, most new jobs came from small businesses.[66] While some complained initially that small business jobs are somehow inferior to those of big business,[67] these days it is small business that often leads the way in employee satisfaction and innovative practices.[68] What has happened over the past 20 years is that small business owners have realized how important it is to hire, train, and reward people in the best way they can. Small businesses do not always pay the highest wages (although some do), but often they can get fierce loyalty from their employees because they treat people right.[69] That comes from doing the right things, the right way.

CHAPTER SUMMARY

LO1 Explore the decision to hire full-time or part-time help.

- There are many additional expenses to having a full-time employee as opposed to a part-time employee. You need to consider the pros and cons and expand cautiously.
- The cost of adding an employee includes compensation, training time, employee taxes, and accounting costs.
- Whether you hire a part-time or full-time employee, it is important that the employee values your company's mission.

LO2 Understand how to recruit good employees on your budget.

- For the small business owner, there are inexpensive, alternative methods to consider in attracting and recruiting key employees.
- Networking, Internet recruiting, employee referrals, and company Web sites are several ways to look for talent for your small business. Also consider bartering and internships for part-time employees.
- Hire virtual employees that have experience with being self-motivated and disciplined, including former consultants and freelancers who are accustomed to dealing with deadlines and working independently.
- As you manage your virtual employees, make sure to spend time developing a system of task lists, schedules, and goals with varying time frames and clear deadlines.

LO3 Know how to match the right person to the job.

- The first step in hiring is writing a job description that discusses and reveals all the essential knowledge, skills, and abilities that are needed to fill the position.
- Use the job description to help you evaluate whether an individual would be the right match for the position and your small business.
- Use the information developed in the job description to identify the most important knowledge areas, skills, and abilities the ideal candidate should possess. Next, create specific questions that you will ask of all candidates that will clearly and behaviorally demonstrate to you that they have these critical factors.

LO4 Learn about employee training methods and resources.

- To begin, you should first assess your small firm's training needs from the perspective of the business, the job itself (job description), and the needs of the employees.
- There are two different types of training: initial training and ongoing training.
- There are two broad types of training available to small businesses: on-the-job and off-the-job techniques. Individual circumstances and the where, what, and who of your training program determine which method to use.

LO5 **Gain insight in meeting employees' needs and expectations.**

- Factors conducive to a positive and rewarding work environment include communication, teamwork, recognition, training, empowerment, and contribution.
- Increasingly, small entrepreneurial companies are implementing formal performance appraisals. Reviewing employees' performance is an ongoing process.
- The performance appraisal sheet should include open-ended questions for the employee to fill out regarding job performance, strengths, areas of development, and what gets in the way of accomplishing the job.

LO6 **Learn how to develop a fair compensation and benefit plan.**

- One of the first steps in developing a compensation plan is to determine your organization's salary philosophy. The next step is to find comparison factors for salary. Subsequent increases need to be based on employee performance, value, and contribution to the small business.
- Employee bonuses, usually paid in a single lump at the end of the year, are one way of providing performance incentives (consider also profit-sharing plans, stock options, or stock grants early or later on).
- While an employer-sponsored medical insurance plan saves employees money and gives them peace of mind in knowing that they won't be denied coverage, it's not always affordable to the small business owner.

LO7 **Understand the complexities of managing family within your business.**

- Small business management problems in a family-owned business are somewhat different from the problems in a nonfamily business.
- One way to obtain objective control in a family-owned business is to hire an outsider to manage the day-to-day operations, when the company can afford it.
- Some family-owned businesses are plagued with high turnover among their nonfamily executives. In other cases, key employees leave because promotions are closed to them because they see relatives being promoted instead.
- As family members are integrated within the small business, you should be careful in making sure that hiring standards are consistent across employees and that there are clear boundaries for each position. Policies should be communicated to all employees.

DISCUSSION QUESTIONS

1. As a small business owner, you will most likely have the opportunity to hire either part-time or full-time employees. What do you need to consider in determining which one will be best for you and when to hire the first or another employee for your business?
2. Whether you hire a part-time or full-time employee, in what ways can you ensure that each type of employee knows and values your company's mission?
3. While a smaller firm can actually outperform large businesses in attracting high-quality employees, how can you communicate to the job market the multiple benefits of working within your firm? How can you get the word out about these advantages in a cost-effective manner?

4. What are the multiple benefits of hiring virtual employees for your small business? What are some of the ways to manage and foster productivity among your virtual employees? Are there any drawbacks to these methods?

5. What recommendations or suggestions would you give Paige Arnof-Fenn, founder and CEO of Mavens & Moguls, on how to manage and "orchestrate" her multiple virtual employees?

6. What are some of the different ways small business owners can write a job description for the first time? How can they ensure that they cover all the essential knowledge, skills, and abilities that are needed for the position? Why is this important?

7. As a new small business owner, what can you do to make sure you hire the right person for the job? This is probably one of the most difficult decisions you may be faced with making, especially since we all are not trained in the art and science of hiring employees.

8. What specific training guidelines would you incorporate into your business? What inexpensive techniques (on-the-job training) can you use after you make the first hire? Did the owner of the business where you are employed use any of these techniques with you? If so, how beneficial were they to your own development and learning?

9. What are creative ways that you can retain your first employee and ensure you are meeting his or her needs? Consider how you can meet or exceed the employee's "psychological contract."

10. Consider your previous employment position; did the firm have an open-book philosophy? How much information was shared regarding the strategy and financials of the business? What are the advantages and disadvantages of sharing too much or too little information with employees, particularly from a small business owner perspective?

11. Managing health care costs is one of the biggest concerns for small business owners; what are some creative ways that they can minimize some of these costs? In your own community, how have owners confronted these concerns and costs? Be specific with types and the size of the small firms you believe are being innovative in how they manage health care costs.

12. As mentioned by Dr. David Gage, clinical psychologist, "Families don't need written guidelines to operate, but family businesses do." What are some initial guidelines that should be defined in the family business?

13. As mentioned, one of the most common problems in a family business is the hiring of relatives who do not have talent to fulfill the necessary job responsibilities. What can you do if you are "stuck" with an unproductive family member to ensure that he or she does not disturb the work and interfere with the operations of the business?

EXPERIENTIAL EXERCISES

1. At ReCellular, Inc., a cellular phone remanufacturing company in Ann Arbor, Michigan, the small business owner put together a list of interview questions that immediately improved the hiring process. The owner first defined the qualities, characteristics, and basic aptitude he wanted to find in a potential remanufacturing employee. The owner wanted to find people who shared these characteristics:

   - Excellent attendance and dependability
   - Flexibility
   - Integrity and honesty
   - Motivated and dedicated

- Detail-orientated
- Team-orientated
- Strong work ethic
- Positive, polite, and approachable
- Continuous improvement oriented
- Good communication skills
- Actual hands-on demonstration of capability to sort phones and identify cosmetic problems with phones

The owner then worked with several online resources to structure questions that would indicate whether candidates had these characteristics. No list of questions is totally comprehensive; however, these questions are helping the interviewers find better candidates:

- What made you decide to apply at ReCellular?
- Tell me about yourself and your last/current job/class.
- When we call your previous employer for references, what are they likely to tell us in regard to your dependability/attendance?
- Tell me about a time when you demonstrated your trustworthiness or integrity in school or at work.

This is, of course, a start—you job is to think of other questions that the small business owner may want to ask a potential employee (either for a full-time, part-time, or virtual assistant position).

2. You have just been asked by a small business owner to uncover U.S. and state laws that are relevant to managing people (in the future, when the small business owner is interested in hiring). Go to Businesslaw.gov and obtain three to four critical areas of information about specific laws within your state regarding: hiring issues, wage laws, taxes, health and safety, and termination.

3. Small business owner Jeff Birdsell opened Shauncey's Gourmet Ice Cream, Inc., in Battlefield Shopping Center in Springfield, Missouri, during April 2000 (for the business plan, go to: **http://www.mgt.smsu.edu/shaunceys/index.htm**). Like any small business owner, Jeff Birdsell realized that starting this venture would entail a tremendous commitment of time and energy. He had expected to work 60–80 hours a week indefinitely, and finds he works at least that. He estimates that he and his parents frequently tally up to 250 hours per week in the organization. Employee turnover at Shauncey's runs at 100 percent per year. What creative and innovative hiring and retention recommendations would you give Jeff as he manages both his family and part-time workers (especially with 100 percent employee turnover)?

Mini-Case

ALASKA WILDLAND ADVENTURES[70]

Between August 10 and 11, 2003, a 500-acre fire raged across Alaska's Kenai Peninsula. Caught in the path of this blaze was a small lodge owned by Alaska Wildland Adventures, a Girdwood, Alaska-based ecotourism company. The facility was situated in a remote area inaccessible by car, and owner Kirk Hoessle feared firefighters would not reach it in time. What's more, it was the height of the company's peak season and the majority of his staff was occupied with running tours in other parts of the state, leaving him short on help. Hoessle assembled as many of his people as he could, but with the fire fast encroaching on the lodge, the situation was growing dire. It was at this point that help came from a most unexpected source: his former employees.

Dennis Weber, a former camp manager and owner of his own construction business, received word of Hoessle's emergency around midnight on August 10. He immediately packed up some equipment and made the three and a half hour trek from his home, about a mile north of Anchorage, to the Kenai Peninsula. He arrived in the early morning hours and joined a group of 15 people, about half of whom were former employees, in fighting the blaze. The group cleared trees and brush from the lodge's perimeter. "The firefighters didn't arrive until around evening," says Weber. "By that time we had the fire ring cut." With the help of Weber and other former employees as well as some assistance from Mother Nature—the winds shifted, diverting the fire—the lodge was spared.

The incident was a testament to the goodwill Hoessle has garnered over the years with his employees. "It was truly a beautiful thing," he says. "We would've struggled to keep the business intact had the fire gone through."

Hoessle attributes the loyalty of his former and current employees to creating a work environment grounded in trust and open communications. "I don't like to make decisions in a vacuum," he says. The majority of the company's workers are seasonal tour guides, and every year they are given an employee survey. Hoessle addresses his seasonal people's concerns and communicates all improvements at the beginning of each season. Hoessle also delegates a lot of decision making to employee committees. At times, these committees serve a strictly advisory function. On other issues, such as the company's holiday schedule, the employees are empowered to make the final decision. In order to avoid giving his people false expectations, Hoessle tells employees when their deliberations will be taken on a strictly advisory basis.

Not only does the company engage employees in the decision making process, but it practices open-book management. Alaska Wildland Adventures has a revenue sharing plan, and Hoessle believes that sharing the company's financial information helps to instill trust in the program. What's more, practicing open-book management has helped engage the employees. "Knowing the financials helps me understand the big picture," says sales manager Alicia Foster. "I know what we can afford and can make decisions from the perspective of my job."

Foster says that creating a good workplace has benefited the organization in a number of ways. For example, the company is involved in ecotourism, which entails providing an educational experience that does not disturb wildlife and other natural resources. It is a complex operation that requires heavy training for new guides. The company, however, has been able to keep its training expenditures at a reasonable level because many of its seasonal employees return year after year.

Sales representative Glenda Denny first heard of the company when she worked at a nearby hotel. There she had the opportunity to come in contact with its guides, and she says meeting them convinced her to join the company. "They were all so knowledgeable, and you could tell that they loved their jobs," she says. This stable and knowledgeable staff has helped to create a loyal clientele, as evidenced by the fact that about 40 percent of the company's business comes from referrals. What's more, it has fishing guests who have been returning for 15 years.

Most importantly, Alaska Wildland Adventures' inclusiveness and open-book management style has helped the company survive during tough economic times. The August 2003 fire wasn't the first time the company's viability was threatened. The travel industry has struggled since the terrorist attacks of September 11, 2001. And unlike its competitors who offer a more diversified catalog of vacation spots, Alaska Wildland Adventures is home grown and solely dependent on travel to the state.

The downturn in business has forced the company to make some difficult choices over the last couple of years. Faced with dwindling revenues, the organization needed to cut costs. Ultimately, Hoessle decided to reduce work schedules rather than lay people off. Everyone would take off 30 days without pay. Hoessle sought the insight of employees on how they would like to handle their schedules. Some chose to take their time off all at once; others chose to work four-day weeks. Hoessle extended loans to people who were struggling to get by on the new schedules.

Understanding the sacrifices his employees made, Hoessle found inexpensive ways to reward them. For example, the company has tried to give employees greater flexibility in their scheduling. Marketing coordinator Heather Dudick is a mother and she says that working a reduced, flexible schedule has made it easier to care for and spend quality time with her eight-year-old child. The company operates several lodges and encourages employees to make use of them during the off-season. The organization also owns a transferable ski pass, which staff members can use on their down time.

It appears that Alaska Wildland Adventures has weathered the worst of the downturn. According to a recent Associated Press article, January and February were the strongest months in the adventure travel industry since 1999. Hoessle says that the company appears poised for a good year when Alaska's travel season starts in May. And the importance of his employees' loyalty, both past and current, in surviving the tough times is not lost on him. "People work here because they are attracted to our mission and environmental beliefs," he says. "They stay because they are treated well."

CASE DISCUSSION QUESTIONS

1. How would you characterize Hoessle's open-book management style?
2. How do you think this style motivates and retains key staff and employees?
3. In what ways has Hoessle been able to reward employees despite slower growth and having to cut costs throughout the small business?
4. What additional recommendations would you make to Hoessle if he needed to bring in new employees, especially as the adventure travel industry begins to heat up?

LEARNING OBJECTIVES

This chapter will help you:

LO1 Know how to recognize the stages of the small business life cycle.

LO2 Understand the four types of firm-level growth strategies.

LO3 Understand the options for harvesting or closing the small business.

LO4 Know the firm-level critical success factors for small business.

LO5 Understand what success means with the quadruple bottom line.

■ From tires to wholesale foods to sporting goods, Shoppers' Service evolved spinoffs, grew larger and smaller, and changed hands over the 42 years of its existence. By remaining flexible, creative, and committed, the owners enjoyed these changes—and made good profits, as well. How are you encouraged about small business ownership as a result of reading this story?

CHAPTER 20

Achieving Success in the Small Business

Focus on Small Business: The Many Lives of Shoppers' Service Store

From 1962 to 2004, Shoppers' Service was an entrepreneurial company serving a variety of customer needs. Originally founded as a discount department store—sort of a mini-Wal-Mart—in Memphis in 1962, its original owners, three European immigrants to Memphis—Morris, Sol, and Karl—combined their money, skills, and energy to start the business. Each had prior experience in small business ownership, and with their combined savings, contacts, and experience, Shoppers' grew to encompass the mini-discount store, a second store branch in the suburbs, a sporting goods wholesaling warehouse, a food wholesaling company, a tire store, and three pharmacies.

Along the way, the partners decided to go their separate ways. First Karl asked to leave, and he was given the pharmacies and tire store as his share of the assets. A few years later Sol left, taking with him the suburban branch discount store. Working solo, Morris sold off the warehouse and the original store, keeping the food wholesaling company going as his major source of income.

At each change in the business, the partners obtained expert assistance, working with attorneys, accountants, and industry consultants to make sure the valuations of the businesses were fairly determined. They also worked with the experts to minimize tax burdens on each of the soon-to-be separated firms and owners.

When Shoppers' closed with the death of Morris in 2004, the business had gone through three owners, five changes of its legal structure, over one dozen additions and deletions of subsidiary business entities, and forty-two years of profitable operations. Along the way it supported more than a dozen members of the three owners' families, and, at its peak, nearly twenty other employees. For all of that, the story of Shoppers' Service is like millions of other small businesses that start, grow, survive, and eventually succeed.

DISCUSSION QUESTIONS

1. How would you describe the stages in the life of Shoppers' Service Store?
2. How did Shoppers' Service make use of outside help?
3. How do you imagine long-term customers would describe Shoppers' Service over the years?
4. How successful would you say Shoppers' Service was as a business?

Small Business Life Cycle

LO1
Know how to recognize the stages of the small business life cycle.

business life cycle
The sequence or pattern of developmental stages any business goes through during its life span.

Like every person, every small business is unique. But just as we all go through childhood and adolescence on the way to adulthood, as we saw with Shoppers' Service, so do small businesses. There is a lot of predictability in this growth process, and knowing the developmental stages of the **business life cycle** can help you better understand your business and your career as a small business owner. The small business life cycle is shown in Figure 20.1.

Several models exist for the life cycle of the small business firm.[1] Each divides the stages a bit differently. But all models have the same general ideas: (1) there are multiple stages, (2) the key issues, actions, and lessons at each stage are different from the other stages, and (3) the level of risk the business faces changes from stage to stage.

For most small businesses, though, the usual sequence of stages is emergence, existence, survival, success, and resource maturity. Let's look at each of these stages to see what they involve for the small business and the key issue you can expect to face in each. These stages and business growth patterns are shown in Figure 20.1.

Emergence

Morris, Sol, and Karl were friends before they opened the business, and over several years they talked about a variety of business prospects before finally settling on Shoppers' Service. They were engaged in the stage called *emergence,* in which a person

FIGURE 20.1

The Small Firm Life Cycle

Sources: Adapted from Churchill and Lewis (1983), Baumol (1968), Chandler and Hanks (1994), and Katz and Gartner (1988).

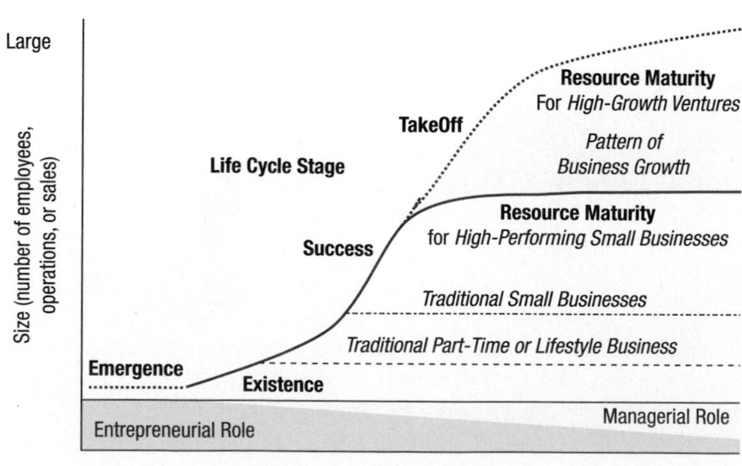

thinks about and takes actions toward starting a firm. Typically a lot more people think about starting a firm than actually take steps to do so. In 2002, 50 percent of the general population expressed an interest in owning their own firm, and among young adults, the rate was an even higher 80 percent. But in 2002, only 7 percent of the population was actually taking steps to start a firm.[2]

Getting from entrepreneurial thinking to entrepreneurial action is the challenge of the emergence stage.[3] Two techniques discussed earlier in the book can help you move from thought to action. One is using the BRIE behaviors from the Chapter 1 checklist to start on the road to creating a firm. The other is to get into business part time (as discussed in Chapter 5) as a way to lay a foundation for future entrepreneurial action.

Existence

When Shoppers' Service opened in 1962, the three partners had a lot of ideas, a fair amount of merchandise, an absolutely certain set of overhead costs, and no guarantee of sales. Sales did come, but it was a rocky first couple of years. This is typical of the *existence* stage, which is defined by having the business in operation, but not yet stable in terms of markets, operations, or finances. In 2002, about 4.5 percent of Americans were involved with businesses in their existence stage.[4] Survival is the second riskiest period after emergence. The reason risk is so high is that many business owners lack the key information or experiences they need in marketing, production, and management.[5] The problems of mastering these three areas form what are called the **liabilities of newness** for small businesses in their survival stage.

liability of newness
The set of risks faced by firms early in their life cycles that comes from a lack of knowledge by the owners about the business they are in and by customers about the new business.

The solutions for liabilities of newness come from getting expertise as quickly as possible. For most owners of firms, personally getting more experience is risky because it takes too long. The safer way is to obtain help from others. As noted in Chapter 2, developing an extensive social network is essential for the success of any firm. Whether you use family, friends, industry contacts, or free or paid advisers, getting help helps you survive.

Success

Woody Allen once said that "Eighty percent of success is showing up,"[6] and it seems to be particularly true for small businesses transitioning from survival to success. The success stage occurs once the firm is established in its market. For Shoppers' Service, success came in the 1970s, when it was well known in the local market and started to have the profits for expansion. Success stage firms show consistently growing financial performance, usually with slowly rising sales.

Firms at this stage develop the information, skills, and most importantly the routines to grow the business's profits. Those profits aren't always taken in the form of money. Time off from work, a slower pace at work, or hiring additional personnel to take on more of the tasks of the owner are all ways that these profits can be used to make the owner's life easier. Used that way, the extra profits are called **slack resources** by economists, because they can be rechanneled into the business if needed. For most owners, though, these profits are called *flexibility.* All new businesses—from small businesses to high-growth firms—go through this stage. For most small business owners, this is a stage that lasts a long time. For the owners of high-growth businesses, this is only a chance to catch their breath and lay the groundwork for the period of takeoff.

slack resources
Profits that are available to be used to satisfy the preferences of the owner in how the business is run.

Resource Maturity

For most small businesses, resource maturity will follow the success stage. This stage is characterized by a stable level of sales and profits over several years. At this stage, the functional areas, the market, and the products or services are all being dealt with consistently and efficiently. The challenge of maturity is to avoid complacency. Shoppers'

Service was able to sidestep that problem because of its changes in what would have been the maturity years, as the partners broke up and took pieces of the business with them, requiring adaptation. After years of consistency, customers and businesses can begin to take each other for granted. For your business, that can be deadly, because a competitor can come to your customer, show personal interest and competitive products or services or prices, and take your customer away. Since the rule of thumb is that getting a new customer costs five times as much as keeping an existing customer,[7] every lost customer is important. How do you avoid customer complacency?

Supersalesman Zig Ziglar says he learned from Australian psychologist Joseph Braysich the four key components for staving off customer complacency—recency, frequency, potency, and recommendation:[8]

- **Recency:** Be among the people your customers have seen in the past few days. Do this through magnetic business cards on their file cabinet, a phone call or e-mail to make sure they have everything they need, or a thank-you note saying that you appreciate their business.
- **Frequency:** You never know when your competitors will show up, so to make recency work, you have to stay in touch with customers on a frequent basis. This might be on a quarterly or monthly basis in cases where customers buy only a few times a year, but contacts can even be on a daily basis if that is how often customers buy from you. All forms of contact count here—visits, phone calls, e-mails, newsletters, business letters, and so on.
- **Potency:** Did you ever see a funny TV advertisement but a few days later could only recall the joke, but not the company being advertised? The problem was the potent part of the ad—the joke—was not related to the important part of the message—the business. When you contact customers, your message has to remind them that your firm values their business. A potent message is one that is remembered, and remembered for the right reasons.
- **Recommendation:** We all seek recommendations. It is a powerful way to get help and advice. Your customers hopefully see you and your firm as experts in certain areas of business. After all, you've been in business for years at this point. Making clear recommendations that can help your customers provides a memorable way to show that you think about, understand, and care about your customers and their business.

Takeoff

Although rare among small businesses, one possible complication is when the survival stage leads into takeoff rather than resource maturity. Takeoff happens if a business embarks on a period of exceptional growth. For small businesses, it might come from landing an unexpectedly gigantic contract, expanding into multiple locations, or just being in the right place at the right time, as was the case for Sun-Hill Industries when it created the Stuff-a-Pumpkin.

The challenge Sun-Hill and other firms face in the possible takeoff stage is to understand the nature and demands of growth and get some control over it. Managing takeoff involves working extensively with potential sources of funding and

SMALL BUSINESS INSIGHT

Success = Opportunity + Danger

Stuff-a-Pumpkins are the pumpkin-colored leaf bags you see on lawns around Halloween. You know the ones—they have a jack-o-lantern's face on them. They were the brainchild of Anita Dembiczak and Ben Zinbarg. Zinbarg's company, Sun-Hill Industries, had been operating consistently for 17 years in Stamford, Connecticut. When he came up with the idea, he spent his own money to get the first run of bags made. They sold out instantly at the discount stores where he tried them out. The stores clamored for more and demanded immediate delivery! But Dembiczak's, Zinbarg's and Sun-Hill's finances were tapped out, and the discount stores were months away from paying for the bags they'd sold. Zinbarg went to his business banker, who refused to extend credit, even though Ben had contracts from big retailers. Twenty-three other banks also turned Ben down. He got the money needed to get out the next order by investing all his remaining personal money, securing a loan from a friend, and convincing suppliers and employees to delay receiving money owed them. He got the bags made and out to the retailers. But competitors meanwhile started to copy his bag, so he took the remaining money and started legal proceedings against these concept pirates.[9] Eventually he succeeded in getting the pirates on the run, but Zinbarg probably came to a new understanding of why the Chinese term for crisis consists of the symbols for opportunity and danger.[10]

other key resources, as well as working with markets outside and employees within the firm. It also often entails relearning the processes that led to this level of success, as a growth-oriented firm often needs to do things differently from one content with maintaining a stable state. One example of this is outsourcing or subcontracting for the growth-oriented firm to let the firm stay focused on its own key competencies. A growing nursery might subcontract out its bookkeeping and human resources functions so the managers at the nursery can focus on increasing sales and managing the expansion.

It is important to remember that most small businesses never go through the takeoff stage, and for those that do, the takeoff path often moves them into the high-growth firm model (discussed next) and away from small business. For firms that don't reach a possible takeoff stage situation, the jump is from the success stage to the maturity stage.

The lesson of the life cycle model of business is that much of your firm's development as a business is predictable within some broad terms. Knowing the stages of the life cycle and where your firm is among those stages can serve as a powerful reminder of the kinds of issues for which you need to watch. Knowing the different possible life cycle paths for the resource maturity stage makes it possible to clearly choose when to grow, and what to expect if a higher-growth approach is in the cards for your firm.

Growth Strategies

LO2
Understand the four types of firm-level growth strategies.

As entrepreneurs come to develop an understanding of their firm, from the planning process or from getting into the business itself, they usually find that they have the chance to decide the overall growth strategy for their firm. The *overall growth strategy* describes the kind of business the owner (or owners) would like to have, from the perspective of how fast and to what level they would like the firm to grow. There are four generic growth strategies that account for nearly all businesses. They are:

high-growth venture
A firm started with the intent of eventually going public, following the pattern of growth and operations of a big business.

high-performing small business
A firm intended to provide the owner with a high income through sales or profits superior to those of the traditional small business.

traditional small business
A firm intended to provide a living income to the owner, and operating in a manner and on a schedule consistent with other firms in the industry and market.

lifestyle or part-time firm
A small business primarily intended to provide partial or subsistence financial support for the existing lifestyle of the owner, most often through operations that fit the owner's schedule and way of working.

- **High-growth ventures**: These aim to achieve growth rates of 25 percent or more a year, with sales of more than $1 million. These businesses typically go through all the stages, beginning with takeoff and going through resource maturity. These firms aim to become big businesses and pursue high levels of professionalization and external funding. Such firms represent about 5 percent of all businesses.
- **High-performing small businesses**: These tend to level off after the success stage, with sales of between $100,000 and $1,000,000, depending on the industry. These firms grow at rates more like 5 to 15 percent a year, adding employees, and often growing through multiple locations and higher levels of professionalization, in order to maximize their profitability over a long term, while reaching a plateau that lets them remain manageably small. Many of the millionaires Stanley and Danko described in *The Millionaire Next Door* had businesses in this range. About 20 percent of businesses fall into this category, including Shoppers' Service.
- **Traditional small businesses**: These are the smallest full-time businesses, with schedules defined by customer, not owner, needs. Most often, these are one-site businesses with sales of between $25,000 and $100,000. Growth levels off after operations settle into a consistent, money-making pattern, generating enough income to provide a living for the owner and family. Around 22 percent of small businesses fall into this category.
- **Lifestyle or part-time firms**: These typically have sales of $25,000 a year or less, which provides enough profit or salary to supplement an income but usually not enough on which to live. These businesses start and stay very small, often operating seasonally or when the owner wants to work in the business. Growth in these firms tends to quickly level off after the owners operate long enough to learn the basics of making money in their industry and setting. About 53 percent of all small businesses fall into this category. (See Figure 20.2.)

FIGURE 20.2

Types of Firms

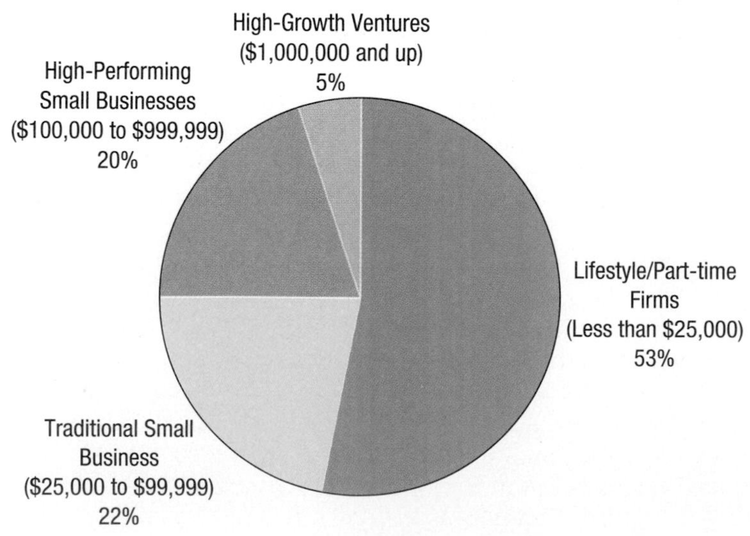

Closing the Small Business

LO3
Understand the options for harvesting or closing the small business.

As we note in Chapter 1, about 1 million businesses start each year, or about 1 million firms move into the existence stage of the life cycle each year. This sounds like a lot of activity, and it is important for our economy, but the really high levels of activity happen farther along in the life cycle. Every year, nearly 4 million firms go through changes in ownership or existence.

The ideal goal for most entrepreneurs is to be able to **harvest** from the firm some of the value of the hard work they put into it over the years. For the owners, a central goal of a harvest is to get the maximum value they can for their business.[11] Often the harvest will represent their last major return from the firm and a key pool of money for retirement or further businesses.

harvest
Recovery of value through a sale of a firm or its assets.

Some of the ways harvests take place are so well known they have become part of our everyday language. For example an **initial public offering** or IPO is where a business sells its stock to the public on a major stock exchange. Google's IPO in 2004 was a famous example, but there were only 71 IPOs in 2004, out of 4 million firm transitions.

initial public offering (IPO)
Transfer method describing the first-time public sale of a stock listed on a public stock exchange.

Other techniques are similar and nearly equally rare. *Mergers and acquisitions* are where one firm combines (i.e., merges) or absorbs (acquires) another through a purchase. In 2003, there were only 4,934 mergers and acquisitions in the United States,[12] with most of these involving multibillion dollar companies like NBC and Vivendi. A similar approach is called **consolidation** and involves a company buying up many smaller competitors to form a giant firm, such as the case of how Blockbuster Video was originally created, but consolidations accounted for only a few thousand purchases all year. An **employee stock ownership plan** (ESOP) is a special tax-protected way to sell a firm to its employees, but these are very rare, accounting for around 11,000 businesses in the United States[13] altogether, and fewer than 100 are done in any year.[14]

consolidation
A transfer method in which a small business is bought by a larger firm for the purpose of quickly growing the larger firm.

employee stock ownership plan
A formalized legal method to transfer some or all of the ownership of a business to its employees.

So what does happen to the other 4 million businesses? There are two general possibilities that happen to most small businesses. About half of the changes are **transfers**, which involve moving ownership from one legal entity, person, or group to another. Examples of transfers include selling a business in whole or in part, or arranging a succession of the business between family members, or giving the firm as a gift to someone who will keep the business a going concern. The other half are **terminations**, which refer to the methods for closing down a business, and include three major methods—walkaways, workouts, and bankruptcies.

transfer
An endgame strategy in which ownership is moved from one person or group to another.

termination
An endgame strategy in which the owner closes down a business.

As mentioned above, the goal of the owners is ideally to obtain value from the firm when they transfer or terminate it, but that goal sits at the top of a hierarchy of business outcomes that are a part of the way every owner thinks about their firm. The hierarchy is shown in Figure 20.3. The top of the hierarchy describes situations in which the owner leaves the firm with substantial funding, while the other extreme has situations of bankruptcy. Obviously owners would prefer to end up as high on the hierarchy as possible, and transfers are the technique that yield those results.

Transfers

In 2003, around 860,000 firms were transferred within the family, a process called *family business succession*. That year nearly 1 million *business sales* took place, where the business was transferred to people other than family. Successions and business sales generally occur only among the largest small businesses, such as high-performing small businesses and high-growth ventures, because only these firms generate the kinds of cash flows and profits that make paying the former owner possible.

Regardless of the method used for transferring or harvesting, the key issue remains the same—doing it right. All transfers are legally, financially, and operationally complex.

FIGURE 20.3

The Hierarchy of Business Outcomes

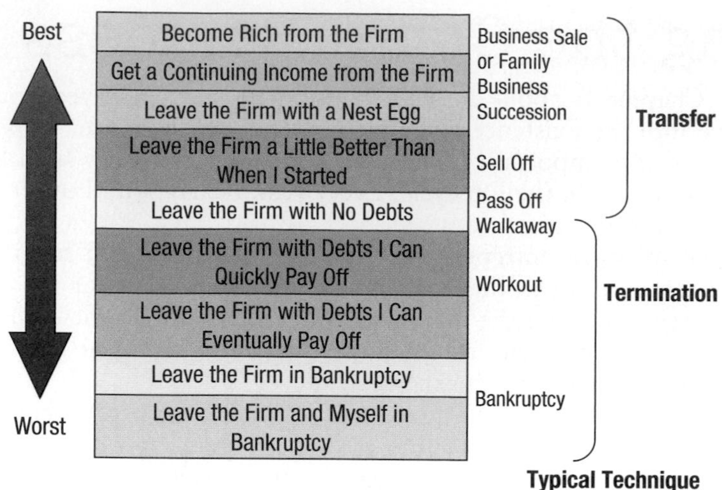

For example, one key goal is minimizing the tax effects of the transfer.[15] Between federal and state taxes on transfers, portions of larger estates and capital gains, a business can lose as much as half of its value to the government. The specifics of structuring transfers are highly technical. For example, the federal laws governing estate taxes on business transfers are changing on a yearly basis until 2011.[16] Meanwhile many states are decoupling their own estate tax laws from the federal approach.[17] In such a situation the best advice is to enlist the aid of lawyers and accountants with expertise in business buying and selling, and leave time to let the transfers take place in ways that minimize the tax burden on everyone.

For most part-time businesses and traditional small businesses, the firm cannot easily be sold because it does not generate enough profits to pay a current owner and a former owner. In such cases, the original owner must decide if it makes sense to close the business down and lose all invested value, or transfer the business in a way that lets some of the value be realized.

Several approaches are available. For small firms these include approaches such as a *pass off,* which happens when the owner realizes there is little chance of being able to sell the firm, but in the interest of keeping the firm going, or providing employees with a source of income, the owner gives the firm to someone as a gift, without compensation.[18] In a 1998 survey of family business transfers, around 38 percent of firms used gifts as a major way to transfer firms.[19] For pass offs, legal and accounting advice is necessary to make sure that the owner leaves all financial and tax obligations with the firm, permitting a clean exit.

Another typical form is the *sell off.* In this approach the assets of a firm—perhaps including the customer list, real estate, and even the inventory—are sold to another business, with the proceeds used to pay off the firm's remaining debts, and perhaps leaving the owner some small profit. Often the purchasing firm absorbs the assets, so the customers or real estate appear to move to another business. Transfers are estimated in the tens of thousands annually, but reliable statistics are hard to come by. The key to a successful sell off is finding customers for the assets and determining a price for the different assets. For assets that lead to revenue, such as customer lists or working real estate, it is typically possible to get an amount ranging from one-half year to two years profits from the asset, with more possible for negotiators with information on comparable deals.

Terminations

There are nearly as many terminations as transfers—around 1.8 million a year. Terminations are more likely for young firms, those four years old and less.[20] As noted above, there are three types of terminations—walkaways, workouts, and bankruptcies. In a walkaway the entrepreneur ends the business with its obligations met. In a workout the firm's legal or financial obligations are not fully met at closing,[21] while **bankruptcy** refers to a legal method for closing a business and paying off creditors in extreme situations, and is quite rare with only 150,000 a year.

■ Bankruptcy is the most extreme business closing situation, which occurs when the business has such high debt that it cannot reasonably expect to earn back the funds required by its creditors. A lawyer's involvement can help owners protect as much of their personal assets as possible throughout the process and eventually recover their financial standing.

Walkaways

A **walkaway** describes the single most typical way businesses close down. Walkaways are businesses that close down with all debts paid. The entrepreneur might consider the business successful or unsuccessful at closing. About one-third of closing firms, around 600,000 a year, are considered by their owners to be successful, with the business ending voluntarily, often due to illness, old age, family moves, and choosing new opportunities.[22]

A successful walkaway depends on the owner having completed meeting all the firm's financial and organizational obligations. The goal in closing a business is "doing it right"—being able to walk away from the business with a sense of satisfaction.[23] The factors that lead to this include:

- All bills are paid off (or scheduled).
- All taxes are paid up, and the various levels of government are informed of the closure.
- Contracts, leases, and the like are fulfilled or formally terminated.
- Employees are let go as they find other jobs.
- Assets or inventory are depleted.
- No lawsuits consuming money and time.
- Customers placed so they get needed goods or services.
- If needed, insurance is continued to cover unexpected claims after the firm closes.

bankruptcy
An extreme form of business termination which uses a legal method for closing a business and paying off creditors when debts are substantially greater than assets.

walkaways
Business terminations in which the entrepreneur ends the business with its obligations met.

workout
A form of business termination in which the firm's legal or financial obligations are not fully met at closing.

Workouts and Bankruptcy

In a **workout**, the entrepreneur feels that the business was less than successful, usually because of the result of poor use of the firm's human or financial assets, with an unsatisfying business experience (e.g., not enough leisure time, not enough time for family needs, too much conflict, not good at selling, etc.) the second most likely reason.[24] In a workout the entrepreneur arranges to pay off all debts, often doing this after the business is officially closed. This approach accounts for about one-half of all business closings, or roughly 1 million closings.

In preparing the workout, the owner personally makes arrangements to pay off creditors. Often this involves asking for extended terms and smaller payments. The money for these payments might come from the sale or refinancing of a home, through selling business and personal assets, cashing out pensions or stocks, money from personal bank loans, or credit card advances. Most often, the funds come from a mixture of these efforts as well as from paychecks as the former owner becomes an employee for someone else.

In walkaways and workouts, a key goal for entrepreneurs is to maintain their goodwill and reputation in the business community, often as a means of maintaining trust for future entrepreneurial efforts. All small businesses face tough times, and entrepreneurs are often willing to extend terms to a former entrepreneur (and customer) who has fallen on hard times. As long as they feel confident they will get their money from the former owner and their own cash situation is not life-or-death tight, they are likely to accept extended terms.

When facing severe difficulties in arranging a payback, one worthwhile strategy is to enlist the aid of a consumer credit bureau. These agencies provide low-cost debt reduction advice and have experience in negotiating repayment schedules and making credit bureaus aware of debt remediation efforts. A good source for finding these bureaus in your area is to use the Web site of the National Foundation for Credit Counseling (http://www.nfcc.org/), which is the professional association for nonprofit credit counseling agencies. Your local Small Business Development Center can also refer you to local credit counseling agencies with small business experience.

In the more extreme cases of closing, entrepreneurs are so far in debt at the business's end that they have little or no chance to earn the money to pay back all the major debts. In such cases owners and firms need to declare bankruptcy. Because bankruptcy is a formal legal situation and one handled in the courts, it is important to involve a lawyer early in the process. The lawyer will not only help you work out the legal papers but will advise you on restructuring your debt and taking other actions to protect as much of your personal assets as possible.

For entrepreneurs, the message of harvesting is an upbeat one. Of the 4 million firms that will change hands or close down this year, almost half will make the entrepreneurs richer, through sale and succession. Another quarter will have benefited from their businesses, and walk away ready to start their next firm. And start them they do. There is a special term for those owners who start multiple businesses in their careers—**serial entrepreneurs**. What do these entrepreneurs know? For those who are determined not only to survive but also to truly do well, the key is recognizing and building a firm along the lines of the critical success factors for small business.

serial entrepreneurs
People who open multiple businesses throughout their career.

The Not-So-Secret Secrets of Success

LO4
Know the firm-level critical success factors for small business.

Ask entrepreneurs what they hope to achieve and the universal answer is "success." But what is the measure of success for a business firm? One of the most famous models for success was offered by Daniel Katz and Robert Kahn. They suggest that the measure of success for any organization in the short term is profit, and in the long term is survival. In practice however, new businesses often face challenges in the reverse. In the short term their greatest need is to survive, even if there is no profit. For example, the typical mail order business will not show a profit for three to five years, according to John Schulte, chairman of the National Mail Order Association (NMOA).[25] The key for new firms is to do those things that will help them survive so that they get to the longer term, when to prove their legitimacy as a business, they need to show a profit.

Over the years the experience of small business consultants, experts, and researchers has converged on a set of critical success factors for small business.[26] Critical success factors (CSF) are processes, benchmarks, or components of the business that are essential for the business to be profitable and competitive in its market. They are by definition best practices for a given industry.

CSFs are important because they come from sources external to entrepreneurs, who are prone to biases in assessing the causes of success and failure in their businesses.[27] CSFs fall into two broad types—outside help and entrepreneurial experience. The CSFs below will seem familiar to you because they have been some of the major pieces of advice we have offered throughout the book. As we conclude our thinking about small

- Contact your local SBDC or SCORE or economic development office.
- Join the trade or professional association for your industry and get help or referrals from it.
- Ask successful entrepreneurs for advice and referrals.
- Talk to a lawyer or accountant or other for-profit expert.

FIGURE 20.4

How to Get Help

business, it makes a lot of sense to bring together some of the most important CSFs that are under the control of the entrepreneur and give the firm the greatest possible chance of success.

To put it simply, help helps. People who get help from experts are far more likely to survive and achieve profitability than those who do not. Consider this. While the SBA has reported that 50 percent of firms fail in four years, 81.5 percent of clients of Small Business Development Centers are still going strong five years after starting.[28] As noted in the first chapter, 87 percent of incubator based start-ups are still going after five years.[29] Time and time again similarly positive results are reported for students taking entrepreneurship and small business courses,[30] proving that small business education works.

Entrepreneurial Experience

The more you know, the better the chances for your firm to succeed. This can come from formal education past high school[31] (like this course) or from working in the industry or market. Anything that gives you the kinds of entrepreneurial or managerial competencies[32] (discussed in Chapter 3) or social[33] or networking[34] skills (discussed in Chapter 2) needed to start and run a business is useful.

But there is also a collection of other CSFs that have been repeatedly shown to be important. These CSFs help identify those businesses more likely to survive. These include:

- **Being incorporated:** Because incorporation usually involves a lawyer, who is likely to give small business owners advice and help them avoid some of the major pitfalls of a new firm.[35]
- **Employees:** Because employees are a way to get more done, to appeal to a larger market, a great source of expertise and feedback, as well as a larger responsibility, which usually means the owner has to make more sales to pay wages.[36]
- **Extreme start-up capital:** Businesses starting with no start-up capital and those starting with more than $50,000 are among those most likely to survive long term.[37] For those with the higher amounts, getting those funds implies prior hard work, and funds that size indicate a major investment, one an owner is more likely to work hard to protect. On the other hand, bootstrap entrepreneurs, who start with nothing, are likely to keep overhead low, live on a shoestring, and build their business over the long term, or change tracks quickly when new opportunities arise. The folks in the middle are those most likely to be undercapitalized for their industry and start-up situation.
- **Protectable intellectual property:** Such as patents or trademarks show preparation for the business, a potential asset, and implied expert assistance.[38]

- **Brand name affiliations or partners:** Having a major brand name shows that you have been checked out and found to be acceptable. It also increases the chances of favorable customer response.[39]
- **Optimal strategies:** Picking to start a business in a growing industry offers above average prospects of business growth.[40] Pursuing an imitator strategy shows a lower risk and greater learning from the mistakes of pioneers.[41]
- **Presales:** Perhaps the strongest benchmark is to have proven your idea through sales—in a pilot test, or through contracts, orders, or letters of intent from customers.[42]

Few businesses achieve all CSFs, but they provide a checklist for running your business in a way that increases its chances for survival. In addition, many of these CSFs are visible to customers, suppliers, and financiers, and convey the idea that you are running your business in a manner likely to lead to continued success.

Measuring Success with Four Bottom Lines

LO5
Understand what success means with the quadruple bottom line.

Originally, the *bottom line* referred to the profitability of a business, figured from the financial statements. For more than a hundred years in the thinking of economists, financiers, and accountants, it had been the ultimate and sovereign criterion of business success.

Today entrepreneurs and consultants realize that success can no longer be measured solely in terms of profits.[43] Financial success in business with a miserable family life or profits at the expense of public approval represent forms of "success" that leave a lot to be desired. There are four domains in which balanced entrepreneurs need to achieve success to be truly happy: the firm, the community, the family, and their own life.

But the bottom line concept, with its implication of some sort of adding up of pluses and minuses, still makes a lot of sense as a way for entrepreneurs to think about their business and life. In this section we talk about the four bottom lines of business—the firm, the community, the family, and the entrepreneur.

The Firm

Once started, it often seems that a firm takes on a life of its own. That is not surprising. Social systems researchers tell us that firms, as well as other types of groups, are living systems. Just as we think of a nation or culture as a living, growing entity, businesses are too.[44] As noted earlier, Daniel Katz and Robert Kahn suggest that the short-term measure of success for any organization is profit with survival the long-term measure, but in reality these are probably reversed for small businesses just starting out because new firms need to survive long enough to generate a profit. In effect, in order to succeed, you need to survive.

Entrepreneurs have the opportunity to define the level of profit that they seek. There are generally three levels: **supplemental profits** are intended as a secondary income for the entrepreneur, who has another job which provides his or her main income; **substitution profits** are intended to equal and replace the salary or wages the entrepreneur could draw working for someone else; **success profits** represent income levels higher than the person could make working for others.

supplemental profits
Returns above costs intended as a secondary income for entrepreneurs (where self-employment is secondary to their main job).

substitution profits
Returns intended to equal and replace the salary or wages the entrepreneur could draw working for someone else.

success profits
Returns at levels higher than the entrepreneur could make working for others.

The other measures of firm success can come from leadership of the industry. This can come through inventions and patents the business holds, which show its thought leadership, or from positions in professional and trade associations or in the marketplace, which make the firm distinctive in the eyes of customers and competitors.

For small businesses with employees, employee satisfaction and well being become a big part of the measure of success. Typically owners and employees in small businesses become a business family, with the owner taking on the parental role and responsibility. Making sure that the employees are taken care of becomes a key measure of success. In the opening vignette, at Shoppers' Service one of the key goals in closing down the firm was to first find a job for the one remaining employee.

Community

In the end, every small business is a part of its larger community, and one of the ways success gets measured is how the business relates to its community. Simply put, is the community better off for having the business present? In businesses operating for the long term, managing this bottom line is important to some extent. Few businesses operate to maximize the social bottom line over the profit one, but taking steps to be seen as a net benefit to the community is an expenditure worth making in the long run.

In small business, doing good takes many forms. In Chapter 2, we talk about five areas in which firms want to do good:

- Community impact, such as providing jobs to employees, business for other firms, and goods and services to customers.
- Building trust, such as through dependability and "doing the right thing."
- Promoting a positive culture, such as through promoting hard work, fair treatment, and developing the industry, market, and community.
- Enhancing flexibility by increasing the firm's and community's ability to respond to changes in the marketplace, economy, and environment.
- Fostering innovation, which is the basis for increasing profits, services, or goods offered, and competitive ability.

But many small business owners, like Michael McMyne (Small Business Insight: The Giving Back Foundation) find themselves taking a more active role in the community, through charitable works, sponsoring others as they do good, and taking steps to ensure that the community remains a good place to be. This can range from picking up trash around the business to promoting professional standards and self-monitoring in the trade or industry association to taking a stand on issues important to the community.

Family

Time and time again, family has been shown to be the area that entrepreneurs worry about the most.[45] Running a business is time consuming, and often the demands of customers mean that the entrepreneur cannot control the schedule. Often that time comes out of family time. Making sure that you spend the time with your family and tackle the issues of communication and commitment that often underlie family problems is the key to success in this factor.

It is not easy. Reflecting on her years as founder and president of Tocquigny Advertising, Interactive and Marketing, in Austin, Texas, Yvonne Tocquigny observes, "I sometimes had a difficult time adjusting to the slower, gentler pace of home and was impatient and less nurturing than I should have been."[46]

Often the key is to leave personal time to make the transition from work to family—clearing your work list and your mind. It also helps to declare certain times as ones when you are unavailable, either letting others fill in, or letting voice mail take the messages.

Another key factor is keeping a portion of family time free of business issues, especially when other family members are involved in the business. Family time needs to be focused on the family, not the family business.[47]

Note that some entrepreneurs work best when combining family and work, while others work best when each is separate.[48] While you might quickly recognize which type you are, the measure of success is not based on your preference, but on that of your family. If your family complains that you do not seem to "be all here," then you are integrating too much and need to segregate business and family life more.

SMALL BUSINESS INSIGHT

Michael McMyne and the Giving Back Foundation

Michael McMyne has made a business of giving back to the community. Stricken with chronic obstructive pulmonary disorder in his teens, a life-saving procedure at Denver's National Jewish Hospital gave him back his health and life. Shortly after this, Michael was asked to talk to a student group about overcoming adversity. The response was so positive that Michael started McMyne & Associates, a motivational speaking company. With a professor he knew, he co-authored *Real Life University,* expanding his services to help promote college students completing their education. Michael was doing well.

But Michael had made a promise to give back if he were cured. He had done what he could as he built his business, such as a fund raiser for a local police officer injured in the line of duty. However, now that Michael was truly successful, he had better means to give back. His idea was to create the Giving Back Foundation to help other terminally ill and underprivileged children nationwide. Today the mission of the Foundation has expanded to include helping students finish college. Michael shows how giving back helps the community and the business, "The Giving Back Foundation has created a lot of good in the community, but it has also let people know who I am as a person and that I am a man who stands behind his word."

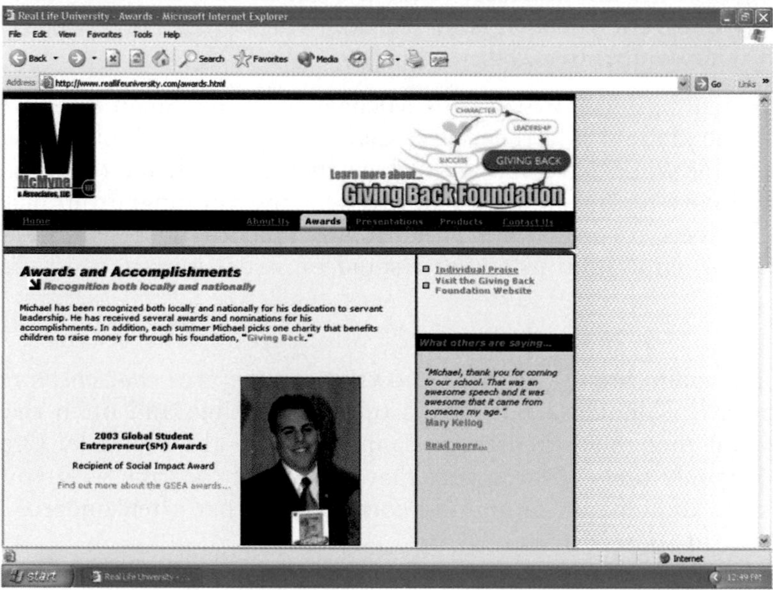

■ Michael McMyne's Giving Back Foundation is what some would call the best outcome for a business—success to an extent that the owner is able to give extensively to others in need. Even without as much capital as Michael's business has accumulated, what are some of the ways you and your business can help grow your community with the skills and assets that are uniquely yours?

Yourself

So far, the domains discussed—the firm, the community, and the family—are external environments for the entrepreneur. You and your personal goals and desires count, too. They deserve the same chance for success that you strive for in the other settings. Part of what makes owning a small business rewarding to the entrepreneur is the possibility of personal returns—the fourth bottom line. Returns to the entrepreneur reflect the kinds of outcomes that the individual values. In Chapter 1, you learned about the rewards mentioned by most entrepreneurs—flexibility, income, and growth—as well as a collection of rewards that crop up occasionally, things like admiration, recognition, wealth, product creation, power, and family.[49]

The returns to the entrepreneur can include these and much more. Consider fun as an outcome. Sergey Brin and Larry Page of Google actually delayed growing their business to the IPO stage because they were afraid of having less fun when they became a public company.[50]

In the end, entrepreneurs go into business with a variety of expectations, dreams, and goals. A large reason for much of what we do—schooling, marrying, raising children, helping the community, and perhaps most of all, working—is to help us achieve those dreams. Entrepreneurship is one area in which, because you create the business and its goals, you have your best chance of capturing or creating your dream. Because of that, to be a successful entrepreneur, you need to be able to achieve those things in your life that are important to you.

Often the biggest risk to achieving that dream is getting caught up in the thousands of immediate demands on your time, attention, and life. Keeping track of your personal bottom line requires two key actions from yourself—keeping the dream alive and occasionally assessing yourself from the perspective of your dream.

Keeping the dream alive starts with giving a name to your dream and putting that name somewhere where you can remind yourself about your own personal ultimate goal. The other part is to schedule a meeting with yourself every once in a while—perhaps quarterly for a start—to assess how you are doing in achieving your dream and what you should do to help yourself.

Simply put, when you talk with entrepreneurs who consider themselves completely successful, you will find that they talk about what they were able to accomplish in their business, their community, their family, and their personal life. Knowing the four areas where success is critical, you can begin to think about how well you are achieving in each and begin the process for working up a plan to maximize your achievement of all forms of success. The procedure for doing this is discussed in Skill Module 20.1.

Assessing the Four Bottom Lines

SKILL MODULE 20.1

As discussed in this chapter, the four bottom lines of business refer to yourself, your family, your firm, and your society or community. In planning a business or evaluating it every once in a while (say once or twice a year), it makes sense to think about how well you and your business are doing at meeting the four bottom lines. Here is how to do it:

1. For yourself, pick the two or three personal goals you have for the business. Ask yourself what it is that you want to achieve through running your business or what you would miss the most if it were gone. List these.
2. For your family, ask what family members want from you personally (time with you, money to support their efforts and needs, etc.). List these.
3. For your firm, there are always three items of critical importance—profits, how well the firm does its job (making or selling products or services—this is based on customer and industry information), and how satisfied are the people involved in the business (owners and employees).
4. For your community, there are also clear indicators of outcome—economic contributions (profits, salaries, taxes), quality of life contributions (lack of pollution, providing needed products or services, supporting civic betterment), and industrial contributions (supporting the industry, operating responsibly, developing the industry through innovation and improvement).

In the example matrix below, you can see that to evaluate these goals you need two pieces of information for each. The first is some sort of metric—a way to measure the degree of achievement. Despite the name, metrics do not have to be "hard" measures like dollars or customers. Opinions are acceptable, and behaviors are even better. With a metric in hand, you are ready to get the second piece of information, the achievement level. This is how you have scored on the metric. To really understand how well your firm is doing on all four bottom lines, you will want to ask others for their assessment on relevant goals. In the end, the evaluation of your business is your opinion, but checking your perceptions against those of knowledgeable others can help you identify areas for improvement and reinforce your recognition of areas of achievement.

Table 20.1 The Four Bottom Lines

Area	Goal	Metric	Achievement Level
Yourself	Feel in control of my life	Personal opinion	Achieved
Family	Have time for spouse and children	Their opinions	Spouse—Not Achieved Kid (Ann)—Achieved Kid (Roger)—Not Achieved
Firm	Profits or take outs	Practical income of $75,000 in cash or services a year	$71,000
	Satisfied employee	Her opinion	"Generally yes"
Community	Support local charities	5% of sales minimum	4.88%

Conclusion

The quadruple bottom line does a wonderful job of showing how starting and running your own small business can reward not only you, but your family, your firm, and your community. It is a means to gain control over the working portion of your life, and perhaps even all of it. It offers communities services and goods, employment, and innovations that make all our lives better. Doing a small business well is not easy. Even knowing the critical success factors for small firms does not mean that you can develop or achieve them. That means that in every small business effort there is always an element of risk.

But millions look at the prospects and decide to take those risks—nearly 40 million people in 2003, with 27 million already self-employed and another 13 million who have been, or are planning to be again. Why do so many do this? The answer is simple—because they want to and they can! Today, with the ready availability of help and the many ways to get into small business with less financial and personal risk than ever before, the chances for success in small business have never been higher.

And the returns from small business have never been greater. The opportunity to work your own way, with flexibility and support, increases as more different types of people, technologies, and businesses remake entrepreneurship for the twenty-first century. The chance for people to learn the right way to run businesses, whether part time or full time, local or global, has never been greater. Classes like the one you've taken and resources like the ones in this book are just the start. Having the right help can help, and now you know the kind of help available to you. You can do this. The time to do it is right now.

CHAPTER SUMMARY

LO1 Know how to recognize the stages of the small business life cycle.

- Every firm goes through a similar sequence of developmental stages.
- Emergence comes before the firm starts, followed by existence.
- Survival happens to most firms, as does resource maturity.
- Some firms experience the takeoff stage, but most do not.
- Each stage poses a distinct challenge to the small business and owner.

LO2 Understand the four types of firm-level growth strategies.

- Every owner has a chance to decide on his or her firm's approach to growth.
- Lifestyle/part-time firms start and remain small and centered on the owner's needs.
- Traditional small businesses are more customer-driven, but remain small and simple, providing an income for the owner.
- High-profit businesses add employees and locations in order to provide a substantial income to the owner.
- High-potential ventures attempt to grow enough to become a big business.

LO3 Understand the options for harvesting or closing the small business.

- Harvests reflect an owner's efforts to take value out of a firm.
- Firms get transferred through sales or family succession.
- Terminations can be walkaways, workouts, or bankruptcies.
- The terminations that have legal repercussions, like bankruptcies, and almost any sort of transfers are complex enough that expert assistance is necessary.
- IPOs, ESOPs, mergers and acquisitions, and other specialized transfer techniques exist but are rarely used.

LO4 Know the firm-level critical success factors for small business.

- Critical success factors are processes, benchmarks, or components of the business that are essential for the business to be profitable and competitive in its market.
- CSFs fall into two broad types—outside help and entrepreneurial experience.
- Specific experience factors that lead to success include being incorporated, having employees, having large or no start-up capital, protectable intellectual property, brand name affiliations, an optimal strategy, and preopening sales.

LO5 Understand what success means with the quadruple bottom line.

- Today entrepreneurs and consultants realize that success can no longer be measured solely in terms of profits.
- There are four domains in which balanced entrepreneurs need to achieve success to be truly happy: the firm, the community, the family, and their own life.
- Auditing the four bottom lines requires specifying the goal, the metric, and the achievement level.

DISCUSSION QUESTIONS

1. What is the difference between a lifestyle business and a traditional small business?
2. What are some of the differences between a lifestyle business and a high-performing small business?
3. What are the stages of the small business life cycle? What stage do high-growth ventures go through that other forms of small business do not?
4. What is the difference between a transfer and a termination?
5. From the entrepreneur's perspective, what is the major reason for preferring a transfer of the business to a termination?
6. What are the key business characteristics needed for a successful walkaway?
7. Give and compare three critical success factors for small businesses.
8. What are the four bottom lines of small business?
9. Why are separate bottom lines broken out for the family and the firm, rather than just including it in the "yourself" category?
10. In assessing the four bottom lines, what is the difference between the goal and its metric? Why is each needed?

EXPERIENTIAL EXERCISES

1. Look up businesses for sale in an industry of your choice (or the industry assigned you by your professor), at a site such as **www.bizbuysell.com**. What kind of information does the Web site provide you? List three additional pieces of information you would most want to get. Can you think of other online or print resources you could use to find this information, such as online business databases your library has? Try and find at least one of these key pieces of information using these other resources.
2. Make your list of your personal goals for the "yourself" assessment in the quadruple bottom line exercise. Compare this list to the major reasons people give for going into business (covered in Chapter 1). Which of your goals overlap the popular reasons and which are unique to yourself?
3. One of the most common ways to evaluate firm success is by profitability. Use a financial database such as the Risk Management Association's Annual Statement Studies to find out target profitability levels for your business.

Mini-Case

JOSEPH SHAUGHNESSY, BSI CONSTRUCTORS, ST. LOUIS

To his family and friends, Joseph "Joe" Shaughnessy became a local TV star at age 68, appearing on screen with a new Fox TV sportscaster as honorary co-chair of the 2004 United Negro College Fund's Annual St. Louis Walkathon. How many construction company executives would be so well known that they would be used as a local charitable pitchman? Not many, and that speaks volumes about Joe Shaughnessy's career.

Joe's firm, BSI Constructors, shows the unexpected paths one entrepreneur's life can take. After graduating in Civil Engineering from Saint Louis University, Joe and friend Lorry Bannes went to work for St. Louis's Gamble Construction Company, where over 10 years they rose to executive positions. Wanting to get out on their own, they formed Bannes-Shaughnessy Incorporated in 1972 with carpenter and field supervisor Ed Clinard as the third owner, and a grand total of $27,500 in capital between them. Despite their prior experience, it took five years before they received their first million dollar contract. But once that milestone was passed, their firm grew. Clinard retired in 1980 and Bannes in 1988, so by 1989 Joe was the sole owner of the firm, now called BSI Constructors, Inc.

Throughout its life the firm was innovative, pioneering building the region's first earthquake proof building at the Missouri Botanical Garden. The company also had a reputation for high-quality building. Churches, hospitals, universities, and companies looking to build for the long term turned to Joe Shaughnessy's firm.

The firm was also compassionate. In 1975, it won the first national Build America award given by the Associated General Contractors of America for promoting minority subcontractor participation in the building industry. In 1989, Joe's firm would renovate a statue commemorating the first Jewish settlers in the New World on a no fee basis. In 1999, Joe (a devout Catholic) would give up weeks of his time and use of company facilities to organize the transportation for the St. Louis visit of Pope John Paul II.

Even when Joe solely owned BSI, he knew it was important to transition the ownership. He hoped to involve his children in the company and eventually pass it on to them. It was a close-knit family, and the company was like the eighth child for all seven. Many of the children worked in the company doing summer jobs, and helped on projects when needed. Eldest son Paul worked his way up through the ranks of the firm after working in mortgage banking for five years. Son Jim, who originally intended to pursue medicine, came back to the company after being successfully cured of leukemia and realizing he wanted to be productive immediately after graduating from Saint Louis University's Business School. Youngest son Dan, a Washington University Architecture School graduate, went into the business after six years with an international architecture firm. To set things straight, Joe started his transition process by writing a letter to all seven children explaining his view about the company and its need for clear management and control. Paul, with the most experience, would become president, with Jim and Dan continuing to work as executives of the company and being involved in business development and all company operations.

Today, Joe is the chairman of the board of BSI, and Paul is the president. The firm's revenues have reached $200 million a year and it continues to get many of the premier building contracts in the St. Louis region. Joe's involvement in civic activities makes him one of the best known entrepreneurs in St. Louis, and winner of the area's Ernst & Young Constructor Entrepreneur of the Year award in 1998.

CASE DISCUSSION QUESTIONS

1. How did Joe Shaughnessy seem to do in achieving the four bottom lines?
2. Did Joe balance with the four bottom lines at the same time, or did some come before others?
3. How did Joe use the business to promote beliefs he felt were important?
4. Some folks would say the solution to balancing the four bottom lines is to never sleep. How do you think Joe Shaughnessy would respond? Do you agree with that approach for yourself?

Appendix A

Consulting to Small Business—SBI and Beyond

In some small business management and entrepreneurship courses, students have an opportunity to work either individually or in teams on consulting projects. These projects are called "live" cases, because they involve working closely with real businesses usually located near their campus community. Throughout the project, students interact with the owner, manager, or employees of the business. These consulting projects are "fieldwork," so named because students work directly with companies in the field of business. This appendix will provide you with some key guidelines and information about how to carry out effective fieldwork.

Fostering Entrepreneurial Education Together

HOW DOES FIELDWORK DIFFER FROM TEXTBOOK CASES?

Fieldwork and the analysis of text or written cases are both valuable components of your study of small business. We use the phrase "textbook cases" to refer to all types of cases in which the information and material are available for you to read and analyze, whether the case is found in a textbook, workbook, journal or magazine, or online. There are many differences between fieldwork and written cases.

In textbook cases, all the pertinent information is available to you, including the history of the firm and its founders, financial records, and a description of the major problems or opportunities relevant to the business. When you conduct fieldwork in conjunction with a real business, you become the detective, seeking out information you feel you need, and doing an analysis of data you collect. In this way, fieldwork often reveals the nature of what it is like to work in or with small businesses. Fieldwork gives you a dose of reality, and when you combine this experience with the material you learn in the classroom, you will find that you are well prepared to make a difference in the world of small business management.

Consider the words of a management student, describing the experience:

"The fact that these were real businesses with real problems made it different than the cases we were used to doing in other management courses from a reading. We felt that we had some real impact on the business if we would offer help, instead of just commenting on the problems of the written cases without knowing what impact it might have on the business."[1]

Fieldwork sharpens your managerial skills as you:

- Identify a problem faced by a business, or help a business discover new opportunities.
- Consider what in fact needs to be done. This involves exploring the perspectives of key players in the business (e.g., the founder, a key officer or manager, an employee, a customer) to view the business through their eyes.

- Determine what information you need to solve the problem or capture the opportunity, and decide how to interpret the information you collect.
- Prepare and present the findings of your consultation to the client business, and help develop a plan for implementation of your recommendations.

SUPPORT FOR CONSULTING PROJECTS

Often, live cases are organized through a unit or faculty of your school. Some of these units may be based on the Small Business Institute® (SBI),[2] which originated the live case consulting project in the 1970s to improve the economic health of client businesses.[3] In schools without an SBI program other institutions and centers that organize and support live cases include Entrepreneurship Centers, Small Business Development Centers, legal clinics for law-related issues, technology assistance centers, or the Service Corps of Retired Executives (SCORE, affiliated with the Small Business Administration). In other schools it is the professors who provide the support on their own.

PREPARING FOR THE CONSULTING PROJECT

The live case is usually done following a series of steps or stages. These stages help students know what to expect and what needs to be done. The five stages of the live case typically are: assessment, meeting with the client, working on the project, preparing the final report, and completing the consulting project. Each of these stages is detailed below. One person who will pop up repeatedly in the discussion will be your *team adviser,* who might be a professor, a staff member of one of the entrepreneurship support units, or even an entrepreneur, consultant or alum who has volunteered to help work with you on the live case.

STAGE 1: ASSESSMENT

During the assessment phase, the student consultant or consulting team will gather information about the client firm, the general and industry environment of the client firm, and the nature of the project itself. The team will meet with the client and identify the client's needs and the scope of the proposed project. The outcome is a determination of the project "deliverables"—the results that you will present to the client. Before you meet with your client, determine as much as you can about your client.

- **Why does the client need assistance?** Obtain any information you can about the client's company, its history and its performance. Often, your team adviser will have preliminary information on the client, including a business plan, market research, brochures, and financials. Just as a physician reviews a patient's medical records and symptoms before entering the examination room, so should you examine what is known about your client's business and need for assistance.
- **Conduct research on the external environment of the client's business.** Do not neglect this research, even if you have a fairly narrowly defined project. Without knowledge of the client's general business environment, you may make recommendations that are neither practical nor useful. The key areas you need to know about are (1) whether the industry sees itself as growing, stable, or declining, (2) whether the industry or firms in it are facing legal or political issues, such as legal liability for pizza delivery firms or offshore outsourcing for computer programming firms, (3) social issues such as changes in society that can affect a firm, like the aging of America, and (4) technological issues, such as how the Internet has replaced the garage sale with eBay. Knowing how each of these could influence the client firm will go a long way to helping you make suggestions that are grounded in reality and more likely to be used.
- **Define and examine the industry in which the client firm operates.** Begin by asking, "What business is the client *really* in?" Define the business not only as the product or service offered by the client, but by the *experience* the business provides to its customers. For example, some fancy restaurants are as much in the entertainment business as in the food business.

An industry is a group of firms that produces products or services that are similar in nature and are intended to satisfy a common defined demand. As part of your consulting project, you will want to analyze those factors that influence the specific product and market of the client firm. Depending on the nature of the business, you will conduct a competitive analysis that can span from local (neighborhood) firms to international, if the business exports or has an online presence. Where possible, doing a preliminary analysis before your first meeting using resources at your school library is a great way to show clients that you are trying to understand their business and that you have access to information that can help them. Having a working knowledge of the client or the industry raises your self-confidence and provides a basis for meaningful discussions with the client.

STAGE 2: MEETING WITH THE CLIENT

Once the student consultant or consulting team has gathered information from secondary sources about the client firm and completed a preliminary analysis, it is time to meet the client face to face and begin the fieldwork consultation process. This is an exciting time, since you are looking forward to meeting the client and learning first hand about the client's needs and concerns. The client is anxious to have the team begin work to address the client's needs and concerns.

Usually the first meeting with your client takes place at your college or university, or at the client's business. Presumably, your team adviser has already met with the client and gave the client a realistic preview of the fieldwork project. You should talk to the team adviser about that meeting, and get copies of any documents the adviser gave the client. Included in the team adviser's preview is typically a description of the fieldwork project and process, expectations regarding the client's support of the team, information on the expected time frame and project management, and procedural matters pertaining to project administration.

Dress professionally because the image you project will set the tone for the project. If you are working in a consulting team, it is advised that you elect a team leader who will establish contact with the client and communicate with your team. This role can rotate during the project, but it is important that the team leader be reliable in carrying out duties, especially for meetings with the client.

At this first meeting, you will learn what your client expects from the team and the project.

Below are some questions you will want to ask at this meeting. These are phrased as if you are talking directly to your client:

- What specifically would you like me (or the team) to do?
- On what issues or for what problems do you need assistance?
- What questions would you like me (us) to answer?
- How do you envision the nature and scope of the project?
- What do you believe you already know in relation to this problem/opportunity?

Establish the Purpose and Deliverables of the Consulting Project

After you meet with the client, your next task is to identify the exact purpose of the consulting project. Consider what information the client is searching for and what outcome the client wants, such as information, advice, or support. Almost always you end up needing to narrow the client's needs into the time frame allowed for your project. While consulting projects can continue over the course of a few academic terms and across students or teams, most often the goal is to handle the project in one academic term, with one team.

Your project may have several steps with a logical progression to them (e.g., performing a competitive analysis before recommending a marketing plan). To manage your time, you will need to prioritize tasks. How do the clients' needs match the time available and your individual skills (or the skills of your teammates)? Consulting projects can fail because too much is promised, not enough resources are available, or poor advice is given under a time crunch. The statement of project purpose contains three parts:

- Objective: What you intend to do and why (should contain the problem or opportunity you will research).
- Methodology: How you intend to do it? (activities and procedures you will perform: e.g., library/Web research, collection and analysis of data, development of materials such as brochures).
- Deliverables: What your deliverables to the client will be (e.g., market research, financial reports, etc.).

A sample agreement is included at the end of this appendix. It presents the points above as a series of bullet points, but it is also possible to give the information in narrative form. Below are sample narrative statements of project objective, methodology, and deliverables:

> "The purpose of this project is to provide Ms. Susan Jones, the owner of the XYZ Company, with information that will enable her to determine how to most effectively make potential customers aware of the company's services. To do so, it will be necessary to determine the characteristics of the firm's potential customers—particularly with respect to their buying habits—and to review the potential media available for communicating information about the company. This information will enable Ms. Jones to develop a cost-effective advertising program that will secure additional customers for the company and increase the firm's revenues and profitability."
>
> "To provide Ms. Jones with the requested information, the team intends to conduct a survey of potential customers to obtain information on customer needs, perceptions of Ms. Jones's services, and the types of information media used by potential customers. In addition, the team will investigate alternative advertising and communications media for possible use by Ms. Jones. This will include information on the costs of various types of media, the effectiveness of each type, and the potential impact of each on Ms. Jones's business."
>
> "At the conclusion of the project, the team will present Ms. Jones with the results of a survey of potential customers, in graphic and table form, that will explain the customers' needs, perceptions of the service, and buying decision process, including sources of information. In addition, the team will provide Ms. Jones with a description of the alternative forms of advertising available within the XYZ Company's market area, including the costs of each, number of exposures, and potential reach to the target customers. The team will perform a financial analysis of the various alternative forms of communication and provide recommendations for the media to be used based on cost-effectiveness of each type. Finally, the team will furnish Ms. Jones with a media plan, including advertising copy, artwork, and sample ads; dates and times for ad placement; and procedures for placing the ads with each media source."[4]

The statement should be signed by your team and the client. It provides a basis for agreement and a definition as to what constitutes successful completion of the fieldwork. It also protects you and the client's interests. The client can evaluate the project according to the statement, and the student can avoid having additional work requested by the client later in the project. It is also recommended that you include in your statement the approximate number of hours per week you will commit to the project, any limits imposed by funding or other resources, how often you will be in touch with the client, and a list of budget items needed to carry out the project.

Another aspect of many projects that can be new to students is the need for confidentiality. This can come from several sources. The business may be sharing proprietary information (such as trade secrets, see Chapter 18 for more on this) with the team, information that it does not want others, especially competitors, to know. Can you imagine talking about a project in class, and it turns out another student in the class works part time at a competing business? It happens, and the results of disclosure can be catastrophic for your client! Another reason to keep confidentiality is that sometimes student projects look at problems the business faces, and few businesses want their problems to be publicly known. Letting the word get out can ruin investors, bankers, or other creditors' confidence in the firm. As a result, SBI and many schools have confidentiality agreements that the student team members sign and provide the client to ensure both sides that what is said in the project *stays* in the project. A sample confidentiality and nondisclosure agreement is also included at the end of this appendix.

STAGE 3: WORKING ON THE PROJECT

Setting Objectives and Responsibilities

Once you begin carrying out the consulting project, it helps to develop a set of objectives that specifies a time frame and the delegation of responsibility. If you are working with a team, you can make assignments based on each student's area of expertise. Marketing majors tend to be assigned marketing surveys, accounting majors tend to be assigned financial analyses, and so on. However, don't be hesitant to work on a part of the project that doesn't align with your major. You can apply some creative thinking to areas outside your domain and expand your skills by applying your business knowledge in this way. Be sure your consulting objectives meet the following criteria:

- They are as specific as possible. A general objective, such as "conduct a market survey" is not specific. "Perform a survey of at least 50 potential customers in the defined market area via telephone to determine if these individuals are aware of the company, the types of information used by customers in making a purchasing decision, and the characteristics customers look for in deciding on a particular firm's products or service,"[5] is a much more detailed and clear objective.
- If you are working in a student team, make sure every member is involved in setting and sharing the objectives. Responsibility and accountability ensure project success.
- Project objectives should have a time frame, and be realistic and attainable. Without these, motivation will drop, and the project will veer off course.
- Develop a project management chart (an action plan), with all steps, time frame, and person responsible listed. Some examples of steps needed to complete a market survey could include: define the market area, develop the initial design of the survey; send the team adviser and the client a copy of the survey for feedback, revise survey, select the survey sample, pilot the survey on a subsample of respondents, revise and edit survey based on pilot test, administer the survey.

As you continue work on the project, remember to communicate with the client regularly, including informing the client about project issues or problems as they occur. Your client may be able to help you with additional resources and information if you interact frequently and honestly throughout the project. Adhere to your action plan and manage your deadlines. If you anticipate problems with the project or if you encounter problems with team members or the client, see your team adviser or professor immediately.

Gathering Appropriate, High-Quality Information

A typical project involves gathering both primary (original research collected by you) and secondary (published data collected by others) sources of information. Hopefully your preliminary analysis (mentioned above) will help you narrow your later searches to only the exact data you need. Depending on the data needed, you may need to use creative thinking techniques to find data. For example, a banker or investment analyst who specializes in a particular industry or an officer of the trade or professional association for your client's industry might be able to give you very specific information about survival rates, causes of problems, or companies that have beaten the odds. Also think about others at your school whom you might ask for information, including librarians and small business reference specialists.

It often makes sense to start with online and library print sources such as Hoover's or Standard & Poor's Industry Reports. Many college/university libraries have access to online searchable databases such as McGraw Hill's Standard & Poor's database or Gales's Business & Company Resource Center, and you can always find government census data (www.census.gov), and trade association Web sites (the Strategy chapter has a skill module on finding trade or industry associations). Primary data that you collect on your own can include surveys and interviews to measure attitudes or opinions about your client's product or service.

Guidelines for good survey design (which is also covered earlier in the marketing chapters) include the use of open-ended as well as closed-ended questions. An example of an open-ended question is, "What do you like best about this product?" This permits the people completing your survey to tell you as much as they want to about the issue. You can also include some structured questions, such as, "How would you classify the 'sweetness' of this pastry?" following with a scale of responses that range from "very sweet" to "not at all sweet." Open-ended questions give you information that you couldn't possibly otherwise obtain, since you may not have thought to ask all the right questions. Surveys often are anonymous and confidential, so that the information you collect is more likely to be accurate and honest. If you are conducting a survey, you can choose to do it in person, by telephone, or online. We do not recommend mailed surveys because they take too long to collect. Try to obtain a minimum 10–30 percent response rate, so that your findings are generalizable to a larger population.

Interviews give you rich, highly detailed information, but they are much more time consuming than distributing surveys. Therefore, it is not realistic to expect to collect information from as many people by interviewing them as you could by surveying them. But, there are advantages for choosing the interview method. If interviews are conducted in person, you have the opportunity to observe the facial and body gestures of the subjects, which can often communicate much more to you than their words. Even on the phone, you are able to pursue and probe topics "off the main point" that might turn out to be very interesting and relevant. Ask permission to tape-record the interview so that you don't have to rely on memory or notes.

Finally, consider using nonreactive methods, so-called because people are unaware that they are being "measured." For example, observe the number of customers that enter a store, which displays they visit, and their reactions to these displays. These nonreactive methods can yield very important information since your measures are not biased by people's tendency to sometimes tell you what you expect to hear. When you interpret your data, take care not to make unwarranted projections or conclusions based on data analysis. One way to avoid this is to be sure you can support each and every conclusion or recommendation you make. Cite the numbers, statistics, and actual responses (anonymously, of course) that led you to the conclusion.

Wherever you gather your data, make sure you have permission to do so. Malls for example are popular places to find potential customers, but doing a survey in a mall without permission may get you charged in some places with trespassing. Usually explaining you are students from a local college who are working on a project is enough to get permission to observe or survey, but always make sure first.

STAGE 4: PREPARING THE FINAL REPORT

The consulting report you present to your client should meet the following criteria:

- The report addresses the client's needs that were assessed at the start of the fieldwork and mutually agreed upon between the student(s) and the client. Clearly demonstrate how your work has (or will) make a difference in the client's business (e.g., profitability, increased market awareness, ROI, reducing costs, etc.).
- The report is well-documented, written logically and cohesively, and uses language understood by the client for whose benefit it is written. It should look professional and be free of grammatical errors.
- Recommendations include options and alternative courses of actions that can be taken. A set of action steps is given, with time frame, personnel and other resources required, and agreed upon between the student(s) and the client. Any knowledge or instructions that the client needs to carry out your recommendations are provided or a referral is given.
- Supporting evidence from external sources is included, with references to all works cited.

What should be included in the final consulting report?

1. Letter of transmittal thanking the client for working with the student team.
2. Cover page, including the client and business name, and the student(s)' names.
3. Executive summary, containing the key ideas of the report. It should contain a brief statement of the project purpose, a summary of the methodology employed, summaries of the key findings and results from the team's research, and the key recommendations the team wishes to offer to the client. The summary should be no more than three pages long.
4. Table of contents.
5. Statement of the project purpose (you can put the signed statement here). This defines the business problem.
6. Brief history and background of the client organization.
7. Detailed description of the methodology employed by the team and the analyses conducted.

8. Findings and results: presentation of data; the facts you discovered through research and conducted at the client's request.
9. Discussion of the team's findings: draw on information from various parts of the project and present new conclusions that are meaningful to the client. This section should list the alternative courses of action for the client.
10. Recommendations: a detailed description of the proposed course of action and the specific methods the client should use to implement the recommendations.
11. Bibliography: Provide complete citations of all sources of information you used in the project.
12. Appendixes: Exhibits, figures, tables, and other supporting documents that illustrate key points from the report.
13. A client letter acknowledging receipt and presentation of the report.

Your final consulting report and presentation to the client are the "deliverables," and they reflect the major focus of your efforts during the project. Your report and its recommendations essentially answer these questions for your client: What did you (or the student team) learn as a result of the research? What new information can you provide the client that will help the client increase his or her firm's performance? What do you suggest the client might do to improve operations? Before you present your findings to your client, you might even ask, "What do I think I found out in this research?" That can be a springboard for discussion and help you avoid a reaction of, "I already knew that."

STAGE 5: COMPLETING THE CONSULTING PROJECT

The Client's Evaluation of the Fieldwork

Although the primary consulting activities have been completed after you submit your final report and present your findings to your client, the consulting process has not yet concluded. There is usually a formal mechanism that allows the client to evaluate the project and the performance of the student consultant(s). This can consist of a rating sheet, a narrative summary describing strengths and weaknesses of the project, oral discussion with the student consultant(s) or the team adviser, or some combination of these evaluation methods. You will receive feedback on your performance from the client's perspective, helping you determine how well you met the client's needs. The client evaluation is an important part of the fieldwork process. Most students have little or no consulting experience with firms in the community when they undertake a consulting project, so this feedback gives you insights that can help you develop your professional skills within the learning environment of the college/university.

Ongoing Communication with the Client

Some of the recommendations from student consultants take months to put into practice, and it may be helpful to the client to talk to or e-mail you occasionally to get additional insights, opinions, or assistance, or just to ask questions. It is not always possible to consider every possible circumstance that will arise in the course of implementing a consultant's recommendations. Therefore, if the client can maintain some contact with the students, further help can be given and the likelihood that the client will be able to successfully implement the team's recommendations improves significantly. When providing counsel or advice on matters that impact people's businesses and ultimately their lives, there is a greater responsibility to ensure that the client receives the best possible consultation and makes the right decisions.[6]

The world of small business consulting is complex, and many issues and problems must be resolved and actions taken to make it a positive experience and a high-quality result for the students and the clients. Student consulting teams need to understand the fieldwork process and must be actively involved in the management of the process to satisfy the client. A well-managed process is crucial to the overall success of the project. There are numerous examples of a well-managed team working with an "average" client and doing outstanding work. At the same time, we have seen many instances of potentially "good" cases and clients ruined by a team that does not control the fieldwork process. A commitment to understanding the nature of the client's needs, developing and executing a plan of action, and providing high-quality results is essential to maximize the benefit of the consulting experience.[7]

ETHICS AND THE SMALL BUSINESS CONSULTING PROJECT

As a student consultant to small businesses in your community, you must uphold the highest level of ethical standards as a representative of your university or college and as a citizen of your community. SBI has drafted a set of ethical guidelines. Accordingly, student consultants *should not:*

- Hold a vested interest in companies that maintain business relationships with client firms.
- Accept personal gifts or gratuities from clients.
- Accept employment or remuneration from a client firm while still engaged in consulting.
- Consult personally to a client firm that is owned or managed by an immediate family member.
- Share current client data with others outside the student team, case supervisor, faculty advisers, and SBI class members without a signed client waiver of confidentiality.
- Practice discriminatory case selection procedures against any potential client.[8]

CONCLUSION: THE ROLE OF SMALL BUSINESS CONSULTING IN YOUR EDUCATION

No other situation gives you quite the same opportunity to integrate your education with practical experience in the community of small business. In a live case you are able to use your business skills to conduct an assessment of an existing company, not an artificial case study. You have the chance to immerse yourself in the business for an extended period of time with the perspective of an objective outsider (rather than an employee), pursue alternative solutions (calling for your creativity as well as your business ingenuity), and present the findings to your client in the hope of having real impact on the lives of others.

Baylor University has a program entitled, Business Excellence Scholarship Team (BEST). According to Kendall Artz, chairman of the Department of Management & Entrepreneurship at Baylor Business School:

"Consulting projects are a unique opportunity for students to take their theoretical training and apply it to real-world problems. It is really invaluable to enable them to see that just because we talk about things in the classroom, they are not always applicable to the situation you may find yourselves in."[9]

Some universities and colleges sponsor contests showcasing the best student consulting projects. SBI sponsors a case of the year competition as well. In one example, at the University of North Texas, teams of students engage in competition to provide the best quality business case project on real firms. The contest helps students develop and communicate their ideas clearly, and presentation skills are much in demand by employers. Cheryl Taylor Pruden, of Irving, Texas, who graduated with a degree in human resource management, felt that the experience was very worthwhile. She noted:

"It was hard, fast-paced and made you think. The competition offers many practical applications that greatly enhance students' ability to work in a team environment, negotiate and compromise, communicate effectively, and speak confidently in public."[10] Similarly, Robert Skains, a nontraditional student in his 30s and a senior at the University of North Texas, said the experience was worthwhile because it "brought together a variety of subjects like accounting, finance, marketing, management, and information systems . . . These projects let you see the whole picture of strategic planning and implementation of solutions for companies."[11]

For more information on student consulting projects, see the SBI Web site, available at http://smallbusinessinstitute.org, that contains guidelines, tips, and other resources for students and case supervisors. There is also a book devoted to the live case by Lisa Gundry and Aaron Buchko, called *Field Casework: Methods for Consulting to Small and Start-up Businesses* (Sage Publications, 1996).

SAMPLE

Consulting Agreement

Client: (Name of Client)

Project (Title of Project)
Student Consultants:
(Names of Students)

Re: Consulting Contract

Objective

The primary objective of this project is to develop a comprehensive business plan for (Client Name). The business plan will have emphasis placed on the business and industry rather than on detailed financial projections. Through comprehensive research, the Student Consulting Team (SC Team) will also achieve the following objectives:

- Define the mission and goals of your business.
- Identify your customers and potential customers.
- Identify your strengths, weaknesses, opportunities, and threats.
- Determine your competitive advantages and disadvantages.

Methodology

The Student Consulting Team will conduct research in the areas of industry, product analysis, market research, marketing, operations (organization of management team, staffing), and financing.

Business plan research will concentrate on the following areas:

1. People: This section will include a brief biography (including résumé) of each of the members of the entrepreneurial team.
2. Opportunity: A synopsis of the business, industry analysis, opportunities within the industry, and how the business may plan to take advantage of these opportunities.
3. Context: The group will research the market as a whole including macroeconomic issues as well as industry regulations.
4. Risk/Reward: Although little emphasis will be placed on this section, the group will do a brief analysis.

Deliverables

The SC Team will provide (Client Name) with the following:

1. A comprehensive business plan that allows the business to become more focused in determining the future direction and strategy of (Client Name).
2. A final report and presentation that includes the following research objectives:
   - Summary of the people involved in the (Client Name) entrepreneurial team.
   - The business opportunity—a description of the business.
   - Context analysis of the external environment, industry, and opportunities within the industry relating to (Client Name).

- Research of the market and its regulations.
- Risk/Reward: brief and limited financial projections of the business.
- Conclusions and recommendations.

Estimated Timetable

Stage	**Timeline**
Contract Approval	Wednesday January 19
Context Analysis	Thursday, Jan. 20–Thursday, Feb. 3
Opportunity Analysis	Thursday, Feb. 3 – Thursday, Feb. 17
People and Risk/Reward	Thursday, Feb. 17 – Tuesday, Feb. 29
Wrap-up	Tuesday, Feb. 29 – Tuesday, March 7

SAMPLE

Confidentiality and Nondisclosure Agreement

WHEREAS, (Client), owner, (Name of Client's Business) agrees to furnish (Student Consultants' Names), hereby known as the Student Consulting Team (SC Team), certain confidential information relating to ideas, inventions, or products for the purposes of determining an interest in developing, manufacturing, selling, and/or joint venturing.

WHEREAS, (SC Team) agrees to review, examine, inspect, or obtain such confidential information only for the purposes described above, and to otherwise hold such information confidential pursuant to the terms of this Agreement.

BE IT KNOWN, that (Client Name) has or shall furnish to the SC Team certain confidential information and may further allow the SC Team the right to discuss or interview representatives of (Client Name) on the following conditions:

1. SC Team agrees to hold confidential or proprietary information or trade secrets ("confidential information") in trust and confidence and agrees that it shall be used only for the contemplated purposes, shall not be used for any other purpose, or disclosed to any third party.
2. No copies will be made or retained of any written information or prototypes supplied without the permission of (Client Name).
3. At the conclusion of any discussions, or upon demand by (Client Name), all confidential information, including prototypes, written notes, photographs, sketches, models, memoranda, or notes taken shall be returned to (Client Name).
4. Confidential information shall not be disclosed to any employee, consultant, or third party unless they agree to execute and be bound by the terms of this Agreement, and have been approved by (Client Name).

I have read the terms and conditions of this consulting contract and confidentiality agreement. I agree and approve of the above details and conditions herein. I hereby authorize (Client Name)'s SC Team to commence work on this project/projects as of the undersigned date.

Client

Signature: ________________ Date: __________

Print name: ________________

Student

Consultants' Date: __________

Signatures: ________________

SIFE[1]

WHAT IS SIFE?

Founded in 1975, Students in Free Enterprise (SIFE) has grown to become one of the largest collegiate organizations in the world. SIFE teams are active on more than 1,500 college and university campuses in 41 countries around the world. In the United States, approximately 900 schools are enrolled in SIFE. (Find out more at www.sife.org)

Working together as a team and through the mentoring of a faculty adviser(s), SIFE students apply their classroom experiences to develop and implement educational outreach programs that teach individuals in their communities the principles of market economics, entrepreneurship, personal financial success, and business ethics.

The challenge to SIFE teams is not simply to inform, but also to empower—to help their targeted audiences reach their full potential through a better understanding of the principles of free enterprise. Individually, SIFE teams are improving the quality of life and standard of living for members of their communities. Collectively, the focused effort of hundreds of SIFE teams and the thousands of faculty, students, and supporting community leaders driving these teams has created a positive and sweeping force for change that affects the lives of millions and is literally changing the world.

> SIFE's mission is: "To provide college and university students the best opportunity to make a difference and to develop leadership, teamwork and communication skills through learning, practicing and teaching the principles of free enterprise."

Check out SIFE at www.sife.org

THE SIFE PROCESS

The development of a SIFE team is a simple, five-part process;

1. Identification of a faculty adviser.
2. Recruiting SIFE team members.
3. Developing a business advisory board.
4. Funding.
5. Selecting projects.

The Faculty Adviser

The faculty adviser is referred to as a Sam Walton Fellow (or SWF), thanks to the pioneering efforts of Wal-Mart founder Sam Walton and the contributions made to SIFE by the Wal-Mart organization. More than one Sam Walton Fellow can be associated with the team. The Sam Walton Fellow serves as the liaison between the team, community, school, and SIFE headquarters. The amount of time required of the Sam Walton Fellow will vary based on the complexity of projects, number of students on the SIFE team, support and release time offered by the college or university, and the individual dedication of the Sam Walton Fellow. SIFE does offer a stipend for the Sam Walton Fellow(s), which helps to offset the time spent on SIFE activities.

Developing the SIFE Team

The typical SIFE team has 20 members. These team members are generally business majors; however, SIFE teams are encouraged (one of the judging criteria discussed later) to get members from outside the business major. Time commitments vary among each team, with the typical team member contributing from 25 to over 100 hours per year on SIFE-related projects. As an incentive for SIFE team members who contribute a minimum of 100 hours individually, SIFE offers a Service Leadership certificate.

Recruitment starts at the beginning of the school year typically with a kickoff barbeque or other gathering. New members can come to the team in various ways. The main way is as a result of current SIFE members bringing them to a meeting. A second way is the success of the team, which ignites interest of potential members to seek out SIFE. A third way is during club fairs that are usually held on campus at the start of the year. During the club fair the different clubs and organizations set up booths that explain what the club is about, and students are encouraged to sign up. This works especially well to get nonbusiness majors to sign up for the team.

The goal of the SWF is the perpetuation of the team. The members must be kept involved and feel that they have made a contribution not only to the team, but also to the community. Team member involvement in SIFE projects is a concern. Too much involvement has the potential of burning out the members, yet little or no involvement makes it easy for the student to justify quitting. As noted earlier, members in successful teams report involvement ranging from 25 to 100 hours. Typically students involved in multiple activities (work, religious, and other extracurricular activities) may tend toward the lower end of the range, while students for whom SIFE is their primary focus tend toward the high end. Obviously SIFE officers are also likely to put in more than the average number of hours, too.

The organizational structure can vary depending on the team. Some teams have a very formal organization with a president and other officers, while others have project leaders with the overall decisions made on a group basis. The actual organization of the team depends on the Sam Walton Fellow and the team dynamics.

Organization of a Business Advisory Board

The business advisory board is made up of community members. Generally the SWF recruits the board, often with help and suggestions from administrators, faculty, and former and current SIFE students. The businesses advisory board, or BAB, is a tremendous asset to the team and can provide mentorship, project ideas, and funding. Some large corporations, such as 7-Eleven, Aflac, AIG, Birds Eye Foods, Campbell's Soup, Colgate-Palmolive, Korn/Ferry, KPMG, Quaker-Foods, Sunbeam, and Walgreens have their CEOs serving on the board of SIFE and encourage their employees to participate in SIFE projects. The size of the BAB can vary but is typically from five to fifteen members. Most teams work on a regular basis with the advisory board. During the meetings the BAB will offer project ideas and will provide assistance to help the projects reach completion.

Funding a Team and Projects

Funding is an integral part of any organization, and SIFE is no exception. Projects often depend on getting the right amount of funding at the right time to make the project possible within an academic year. Teams use a variety of funding sources including membership fees or dues (try the Google search to get an idea about the range in dues), fund raising activities, special events, raffles, and other sources. Some teams have corporate sponsors that contribute funds or provide services such as printing or video equipment. It should be noted that, while a large fund source is good to have, it is not necessary. True entrepreneurs will find a way to get the funds they need. Remember the lessons of the book on bootstrapping. Also note that teaching-based projects can often get by on limited funds or facilities and services freely available on a college campus.

Selecting Projects

The individual SIFE teams develop educational outreach projects designed to teach the four fundamental principles of SIFE:

- Knowing how free markets work in the global economy.
- Knowing how entrepreneurs succeed by identifying a market need and then profitably producing and marketing a product or service to fill that need.
- Knowing the personal entrepreneurial, communications, technology, and financial management skills needed to successfully compete.
- Practicing business in an ethical and socially responsible manner that supports the principles of a market economy.

The team members, BAB, and the Sam Walton Fellow individually and together work on ideas for potential projects. Often there are many more opportunities than time or people. Historically the projects seen as most rewarding by SIFE team members and communities are those which maximize three factors: (1) it meets the needs of the community, (2) it focuses on the four main principles of SIFE, and (3) it helps the residents in the community learn about free enterprise in fun and interesting ways.

After identifying the various needs, projects are developed that correspond with the four fundamental principles of SIFE, described above. While not every project will have all principles incorporated within it, the teams are encouraged to develop an overall program that covers these principles.

DEVELOPING AND COMPLETING A PROJECT

Given the objectives of SIFE, it should not be suprising to learn that SIFE projects build on the very skills you learn in your small business classes. SIFE teams explore opportunities and when they find promising ones, the teams do quick feasibility analyses (often by talking the ideas out with the SWF and BAB members) to pick the most promising ideas to pursue.

Because SIFE teams need to get their projects done during the school year and most SIFE students are juggling hectic class, work, and personal schedules, planning becomes essential. The planning takes two forms: business planning to describe the project and determine the best way to do it, and time planning to make sure the SIFE team members can put in the time and work necessary to get the project done. While the planning is often a part of the SIFE project process, most groups do not create formal written plans like those discussed in the book. While the planning process is essential, the written plan often is not.

What does a SIFE project look like in real life? A good example comes from the SIFE team at Chadron State College in Chadron, Nebraska. This team developed a project based on the needs of its community. Chadron is a rural community located in the northwest corner of Nebraska, with a county population of fewer than 10,000. Chadron State College has fewer than 3,000 students and a service area of 34,000 square miles. Within this service area are five of the nation's poorest counties.

With the help of the advisory board, the 15-member SIFE team from Chadron State developed a project designed to meet the needs of the community, focus on the four main principles of SIFE, and taught residents in the community about free enterprise in fun and interesting ways.

The project was called "Raising Dough." The Chadron State team helped 50 middle school students raise funds to travel to Washington, DC. The team developed a project to help these students sell premade pizzas for Super Bowl Sunday. The twist, developed by the SIFE team, was to have the students make the pizzas they sold.

How Did This Project Begin? Why Pizzas? Why SIFE?

Every two years students from Chadron middle schools travel to Washington, DC, to learn more about our nation's capital. While this is a part of the school curriculum, the school does not fund the trips, and each student is required to raise $1,500 to pay for travel, rooms, and meals. One of the parents of the students was also a BAB member, and she believed the entrepreneurial activities of the Chadron State SIFE team might be just what the middle school students needed to help raise funds. The team met with the parents to brainstorm. Ideas from a bake sale to a car wash were discussed.

Using techniques much like the feasibility analyses described in Chapter 4, the SIFE team analyzed the needs of the students and the problems that exist to raise a large amount of money in a small town. Team members also realized that these students were too young to get a job, yet these students had a tremendous amount of energy. After several meetings and discussion sessions, the SIFE team determined that if the fundraising was carried out over too long a period of time, some of the students might lose interest and give up before reaching their financial goal. They also determined that a bake sale could generate some money, but the real source of sales were in most cases the parents baking the items for the students to sell (not really fund raising but a transfer of funds). The dilemma facing the SIFE team was to develop a "big" project capable of making a large amount of cash in a short time with little or no help from parents.

Since pizza is a popular food choice for many families, the SIFE team proposed that the students sell pizzas for a price of $10.00 each. Super Bowl Sunday provided a target date and theme, but what about the costs? The team asked the local pizza restaurant if it would make an uncooked pizza (frozen or fresh) and sell it at a wholesale price to the students allowing them to resell the pizza for a profit. The "best" wholesale price offered to SIFE was $6.95 per large pizza, which gave a profit of $3.05 each.

The SIFE team members believed they could do better and performed an industry analysis (like those described in Chapter 7) to research the wholesale market and to find out what the ingredients would cost to make a pizza. They found that they could purchase the ingredients to make a pizza cheaper than purchasing the wholesale pizza. The saving came in the overhead and labor costs.

Based on its industry analysis, the SIFE team did the initial planning and determined the quantities of ingredients needed to make each sixteen-inch pepperoni, beef, and cheese pizza. With this information the team determined the average cost for each pizza to be $3.64. After meeting with the students, a selling price of $10.00 for each pizza was determined to still be viable, but with the new make-it-yourself model the average profit potential was estimated to be $6.36, which was more than double the profit from purchasing the premade pizzas from the restaurant.

The catch would be that the middle school students, not the parents, had to donate one Saturday morning to make the pizzas. The students thought this was a great idea. They argued that any time you can give 50 middle schools students the opportunity to get together in a group, it is a "good thing."

The second step was for the SIFE team to teach the students how to sell. Most of the students had never had a job, and this was their first real selling experience. The SIFE team emphasized that the major selling feature was the quality of the pizza and how the purchase was not just a donation. Customers actually received a quality, freshly made product for a very reasonable price. Based on the SIFE team's initial market analysis (see Chapter 12 on marketing plans) projections, it set a goal for each student of selling 10 pizzas. While some would sell more and others might not sell ten, the benchmark was 500 pizzas. Based on the financial analyses, selling 500 pizzas would provide a total estimated profit of $3,180. This was a lot better than a car wash.

Following a discussion and demonstration on selling to the students, the SIFE team introduced the theme of a fresh pizza to be delivered for Super Bowl Sunday. These young middle school entrepreneurs developed some great selling ideas on their own. One student brought a tape measure to show prospective customers just how big a 16-inch pizza really was. While another used a cardboard pizza circle with a picture of a pepperoni pizza on it to demonstrate what a customer would receive. With the kind of ideas and energy these motivated and trained middle school students had, they beat the target, preselling 673 for Super Bowl Sunday. The top salesperson sold 55 pizzas.

But the job was only partially done. The next step was the manufacturing process. Three production lines were set up in the local fellowship hall. The layout was done to provide one line each for pepperoni, beef, and cheese pizza. Before the students were able to start making pizzas, they were given health and safety instructions, again by the SIFE team with some local help. This turned out to be a big surprise to the young girls who came to the pizza-making session all dressed up with their hair done and makeup on. They were instructed to put on hairnets, aprons, and sanitized gloves. The SIFE team served as quality control, making sure the pizzas were made properly and waste was kept to a minimum. With the guidance of the SIFE team the students made 673 pizzas in just over two hours. That's a pizza every 12 seconds.

What Did the Students Learn?

These students learned how assembly lines work, quality control, and how to organize, market, and get a product ready. They also learned proper health practices, how to get along in a group, and how to take orders and directions from others.

What Did the SIFE Team Learn?

The SIFE team learned some unexpected lessons, such as the limited attention span of middle schoolers. The team was also surprised at just how much time it took to organize and plan a project and see it to its completion. For the first time, team members could see how they were able to apply what they learned in class to a real life situation.

This is an example of a "win-win" situation in which a small SIFE team was able to empower others to complete a task. The project was fun and rewarding. The budgeted cost estimates made (just like those described in Chapter 13) were very close to the actual expenses. After allowing for waste, there were enough pizza ingredients left over to give a large pizza to each of the ten SIFE members and to give a pizza to each of the top five sales leaders among the middle schoolers. The profit for the group was just over $4,280. This was the largest fund raiser for the group and helped several of the students reach their financial goal.

In practice, a SIFE team may often do more than one project during the year, so when it presents to its school or at the SIFE competitions, it often consolidates several projects into one presentation. Those competitions are described below.[2]

THE SIFE COMPETITION PROCESS

The individual projects are important to the community and school. They provide team members an opportunity to give back to the community, apply what they have learned, and help prepare them for the real world of work. In addition to completing projects and helping the local community, SIFE offers several regional competitions. The SIFE overall competition provides SIFE teams with the opportunity to compete against each other and ultimately determine which team had the most impact on improving the quality of life and standard of living for members of its community. The competitive format consists of a four-page written annual report and a 24-minute live, audiovisual presentation, which the teams present to a panel of entrepreneurs and executives serving as judges. The judging is based on the set of judging criteria given in Figure B-1.

Winners at the regional competitions travel to Kansas City, MO, to compete in the national expo. This annual gathering is tremendously exciting and extremely competitive. Not only is

How creative, innovative, and effective were the students in teaching:

Point Value	
1. How free markets work in the global economy.	20
2. How entrepreneurs succeed by identifying a market need and then profitably producing and marketing a product or service to fill that need.	20
3. The personal entrepreneurial, communications, technology, and financial management skills needed to successfully compete.	20
4. Practicing business in an ethical and socially responsible manner that supports the principles of a market economy.	20
In their educational programs, how effective were the students at:	
5. Measuring the results of their projects.	5
6. Utilizing mass media and the Internet.	5
7. Involving nonbusiness majors and utilizing a business advisory board.	5
8. Communicating their program through their written report and oral presentation.	5
Total	**100**

FIGURE B-1

The SIFE Competition Judging Criteria

Source: http://www.sife.org/united_states/competition/judges_judging_criteria.asp?ID=US&ID2=Expo.

there money on the line for final placement, but it also gives the students an opportunity to be seen by company executives. This can be critically important for many SIFE teams. For a small college, the national expo is a key opportunity. At a small school or one in an out-of-the-way location, there are not always other opportunities to meet one-on-one with this caliber of employer or company.

During the competitions, several major businesses with ties to SIFE participate in a career fair. During these fairs, students have the opportunity to meet with top CEOs of major firms, and many SIFE students are offered jobs or internships from such meetings. At the national expo four of the students from Chadron State were offered jobs, and another three were offered paid internships. Because the judges at the national exposition are themselves business people, it is not unheard of for students to be offered jobs or internships.

The Presentation

The formal presentation is the highlight of the year for the SIFE teams. The presentations are typically given in a conference room at one of several regional competition sites around the United States. The winners of the various regional competitions are eligible to compete at the national expo. At the national expo, the regional champion teams are divided into 20 leagues of six to eight teams. All teams currently present at the Kansas City Convention Center, in Kansas City, Missouri. Each competing team will have a 37-minute time block for its verbal/audiovisual presentation. After the Sam Walton Fellow and team are formally introduced, the time will be precisely divided as follows:

1. Immediately after the introduction, the team will have 7 minutes to distribute written annual reports for the judges to review prior to their presentation, and to set up the presentation equipment (boot computers, check lighting and sound, etc.)
2. The team will have 24 minutes to give the formal verbal/audiovisual presentation.
3. There will be a mandatory 5-minute question and answer session for the judges.
4. The team will have 1 minute to return the presentation area to the original setup and exit the room.

Typically four to seven team members give the presentation to a group of judges. The judges are selected from SIFE board members and area business executives.

Preparing Your Presentation

With only 24 minutes to present the year in review, the presentation must be creative, informative and exciting. SIFE teams are encouraged to focus on the four fundamentals of SIFE as a center to their presentation. The individual projects are presented based on the major judging criteria that the project achieved. This makes the judging easier for the judges. The annual report (see page A-18 for an example), which is limited to four printed pages, should follow the presentation and be simple and easy to read. (Remember that based on the very strict time schedule the judges have only seven minutes to preview the report before the presentation starts.)

The video or media presentation is often an integral part of the presentation. The media presentation should supplement the oral presentation and not overpower it. Slides or video of the SIFE team and the target group of the particular project are usually shown while each presenter speaks.

The typical presentation is usually divided into segments. Each represents a project or group of projects. Some presentations also have an introduction about the presenters' school and a conclusion or summary of the projects. Since the judges know the basics about SIFE, it is important to refresh their memory and tell a story of how the SIFE team had an impact on the community and the college.

Incorporating a Project in the Presentation

The pizza project was fun with the main focus in judging criteria 2 and 3.

2. How entrepreneurs succeed by identifying a market need and then profitably producing and marketing a product or service to fill that need.
3. The personal entrepreneurial, communications, technology, and financial management skills needed to successfully compete.

This project was considered important and was given approximately 3.5 minutes of the 24-minute presentations. Four team members presented this project, which was called "Raising

Dough." The first presenter gave an overview of the judging criteria the project focused on. This alerted the judges to what was to come in this section of the presentation. The next part showed the initial meeting with the parents and students and estimating of the ingredients. The video component, which was playing on the screen, showed the SIFE team measuring and estimating ingredients. Following the estimating segment, the students were shown selling and making pizzas in three assembly lines, while the presenter explained the manufacturing process. The third segment explained the problems that came up during the process. The video segment showed the young girls getting ready for the work with their hairnets; it also showed students tossing dough in the air and the mess that was made by the young entrepreneurs. The last segment gave the results of the pizza sale, reinforced the judging criteria, and gave the impact of the project on the community and target group.

WHY SIFE?

As mentioned before, the majority of the students attending Chadron State College graduated from rural high schools of fewer than 100 students each. Most of these students were very active in their hometowns. The projects that a SIFE team does provide the students with the opportunity to give back to the community what they have learned in college and get involved. SIFE students also have the opportunity to meet business leaders in the community and work with youngsters. SIFE helps to get students involved and form relationships, and it helps to bridge the gap between home, school, and work.

At the national expo the SIFE students have the opportunity to meet with senior executives from major firms. They find out what businesses are looking for in new employees and have the opportunity to be interviewed for jobs and internships.

For an instructor and Sam Walton Fellow, SIFE provides an opportunity for student learning that is otherwise very hard to provide. Because of the design of the competition, even a small SIFE team (or a team from a small school) has the opportunity to successfully compete on a level playing field with colleges and universities and teams that are much larger. Regardless of the size of the team or the school, this experience helps the SIFE students realize that through their formal education and the SIFE experience, they have the skills to get a job in a competitive market environment, or even start a business on their own.

What do student organizations such as SIFE cost the school? In most cases nothing or very little. The school pays for transportation to the competitions. SIFE reimburses members for a portion of their rooms and meals and provides a small stipend for the sponsor. SIFE provides numerous opportunities for a school to earn funds through special competitions. These funds are provided through individual corporate sponsors of SIFE.

SIFE INTERNET RESOURCES

www.sife.org

School sites include:

- http://www.nsula.edu/sife/
- http://data.gc.peachnet.edu/www/clubs/sife/sifeweb/default.htm
- http://www.methodist.edu/SIFE/index.htm
- http://www.jbu.edu/campus life/clubs/SIFE/index.htm

To find academic presentations on SIFE and its impact on education, use the Google search of the resources at the Small Business Advancement Electronic Resource:

Chadron State College	Sixth Annual Report	2004 - 2005

Inside This Issue

Team Statistics

Total Team Members
15
Areas of Academic Study
8
Team G.P.A.
3.33
Total Projects
30
Total Hours
2,720
Gross Media Impressions
3,618,000

About Chadron State

Chadron State College, the "Best Kept Secret in Western Nebraska," is located in the Pine Ridge area of Nebraska. Historic Chadron, Nebraska is a city of 5,500 and is a regional trade center serving residents in western Nebraska, South Dakota and Wyoming. Chadron State College was founded in 1911 and is the only accredited four-year institution in western Nebraska. Chadron State has a service area of 34,000 square miles—an area greater than the states of Connecticut, Rhode Island and New Jersey combined. Chadron State enrolls approximately 2,700 students of which 70% graduated from high schools of less than 100 students.

Mission Statement

Chadron State College Students In Free Enterprise Team supports the national leadership, teaching, and community service philosophies of SIFE. Our projects teach the effectiveness of a market economy which is based on good business practices, ethics, honesty, and integrity throughout Nebraska and the World.

Chadron Apprentice

The Chadron version of the popular ***Apprentice*** television series was started this year by our SIFE team. With the help of our Advisory Board, we applied what we have learned in class to real life business situations where your decisions can mean profit or loss. This program taught us how a business operates as well as teamwork and communication skills. Following the ***Chadron Apprentice,*** we are using the techniques we learned to conduct a survey for a new business and we have started a training center to help others sell products using the Internet.

SAMPLE

First page of Chadron State SIFE annual report.

For complete report see www.mhhe.com/katzesb.

A Marketing Plan

"Asian Eden," A Boba/Snack Bar In Folsom, California[1]

TABLE OF CONTENTS

EXECUTIVE SUMMARY

The Boba/Snack Bar will be named Asian Eden. It is a new business that will be opened in December 2005. Asian Eden will mainly serve tea, juices, smoothies, other beverages, and some Asian style snacks. The potential customers of Asian Eden may include local residents, residents from the cities neighboring Folsom, local students, and business people. Asian Eden will be located in the city of Folsom, California. In order to build a large base of customers, the proposed location of Asian Eden will be inside the Kohl's Shopping Center. Asian Eden's exotic appearance will impress the customers in the first place. Asian Eden's artistic interior design will provide customers with a fully relaxing and enjoyable dining environment. Asian Eden is not only a snack bar, but it is more like an Asian style Starbucks for people to hang out with friends, to sit down to read books or newspapers, to relax after a long work day, to escape from the routine of a daily life, or to explore some Asian culture and arts while sipping a cup of well-prepared tea and listening to some exotic music from Asia.

The Folsom area has been booming rapidly during the past several years, and it is still fast-growing; the food-service industry in that area is competitive but it is not saturated. For Asian style restaurants or bars, the competition is low; currently there are not many Asian style restaurants in Folsom, and there is no bar or snack bar in Asian style like Asian Eden in that area. Asian Eden will be able to compete successfully and differentiate itself by serving authentic Asian style snacks and well-prepared drinks, offering high-quality customer service and high-quality products and providing customers with a unique social environment filled with exotic Asian culture.

Based on the financial analysis, the total start-up capital will be $150,000, financed by small business loans from banks and my personal savings. The initial start-up expenses will be $50,000. The first year's projected sales will be at least $250,000.

Asian Eden is expected to reach the breakeven point in the first business year. Asian Eden will be a sole proprietorship business that will be owned by Yong Xu, the author of this business plan.

MISSION

Asian Eden will provide customers with a fully relaxing and enjoyable environment for people to hang out with friends, to sit down to read books or newspapers, to relax after a long work day, to escape from the routine of daily life, or to explore some Asian culture and arts while sipping a cup of well-prepared tea, tasting some authentic Asian snacks, and listening to some exotic music from Asia. Asian Eden will provide customers not only a nice dining place but also a social center to experience exotic Asian culture.

Asian Eden will be a sole proprietorship business that will be owned by Yong Xu, the author of this marketing plan.

SWOT ANALYSIS

Strengths

- The owner is Chinese and can provide an authentic Asian experience for her customers. She has also lived for a number of years in California and understands when the Asian experience needs to be adapted for local tastes.
- Asian Eden will provide customers with authentic Asian style snacks and drinks. Real Asian taste, real Asian style! Based on the results of interviews, more than 85 percent of the interviewees prefer to go to an Asian restaurant that serves authentic Asian food instead of American-Asian food.
- Asian Eden is not just a snack bar. Asian Eden's artistic design will give customers an experience of the exotic Asian culture, providing customers with a very comfortable, relaxing, and unique social environment.
- Asian Eden provides customers with high-quality customer service and high-quality products.
- A snack/bar restaurant opened by a friend of the owner in another northern California town with similar demographics has done very well. The friend has also provided much of her insight and experiences into developing this plan and will continue to offer additional support.
- The owner has extensive business experience both in the United States and China and possesses an MBA.

Weaknesses

- Asian Eden is a new business—not a franchise—and lacks brand recognition.
- Asian Eden's authentic Asian style snacks and drinks may be unfamiliar to many of the Folsom community.
- Since the majority population in Folsom is white, non-Hispanic people, Asian Eden's strong Asian culture may not be as acceptable as it would be in an area with a larger Asian concentration.

Opportunities

- Fast-growing industries and significant increasing population provide tremendous opportunities to Asian Eden to expand its business areas.
- No similar concept restaurants exist in the Folsom area.
- Folsom is conveniently located on the northern border of Folsom Lake, which attracts more than 4 million visitors a year. The recreation area attracts year round visitors. The target location of Asian Eden is along the main road to the area.
- On December 14, 1999, Folsom's City Council voted to enter a sister-city relationship with Jiaohe City, Jilin Province, China. The city of Folsom and its citizens are eager to learn more about Asian culture and products. Asian Eden brings a wind of Asia to this booming area, more culture, more color, and more excitement!

Threats

- The barriers to entry in this sort of industry are relatively low.
- The environment of this industry is becoming more and more competitive.

COMPETITIVE ANALYSIS

Asian Eden is an Asian style snack bar; it is neither a formal restaurant nor a fast food restaurant. Therefore the Asian/Chinese restaurants in Folsom are not Asian Eden's direct competitors. More likely Asian Eden will compete with local coffee stores or bars.

Asian Eden's possible direct competitors are: Starbucks Coffee, Courtyard Café, Bella Bru, Java Station, Jitters Coffee & Espresso, Coffee Republic, Mob Coffee, City Slickers Sports Bar & Grill, Powerhouse Pub, Carmelitas Folsom Mexican Bar, and TDS Sports Bar-B-Q. The major direct competitors are Starbucks, Coffee Republic, Bella Bru, and Powerhouse Pub.

Starbucks Coffee Store

Starbucks is well known nationwide, even worldwide, with very high customer loyalty, high product quality, and high service quality. It is always a popular place for people to hang out with friends. It is popular to people of all ages. Within four miles of Asian Eden's future location, there are four Starbucks Coffee stores. The table on the next page shows their addresses. Those Starbucks are Asian Eden's strongest competitors.

Powerhouse Pub

Powerhouse Pub was one of the winners of the "Best of Folsom" in 2003 and 2004, and there is

Comparison	Asian Eden	Starbucks Coffee	Coffee Republic	Bella Bru	Powerhouse Pub
Customer Loyalty	9	10	8	8	10
Service Quality	9	9	8	8	9
Service Variety	8	5	4	4	8
Food Quality	10	9	7	7	9
Food Variety	6	6	5	5	8
Environment Comfortable Level	10	7	5	5	10
Culture Gap	9	0	0	0	0

3.6 miles	2.2 miles
Starbucks Coffee 2791 E Bidwell St Folsom, CA 95630-6407	Starbucks Coffee 1860 Prairie City Rd Folsom, CA 95630-9580
2.0 miles	**2.0 miles**
Starbucks Coffee 195 Blue Ravine Rd Folsom, CA 95630-4722	Starbucks Coffee 195 Blue Ravine Road Folsom, CA 95630-4722

no doubt about its local popularity. Powerhouse Pub is rated a popular place to meet up with friends. With its live music bands, it became a popular nightspot in the Folsom area.

Coffee Republic and Bella Bru

Coffee Republic and Bella Bru are also popular coffee stores ranked by local customers. Bella Bru was even ranked as the best local coffee shop in Folsom in 2003.

The following table and chart show the results of the comparison between Asian Eden and its major direct competitors from the marketing point of view. The scale of the measurement ranged from

Comparison between Asian Eden and Its Major Competitors

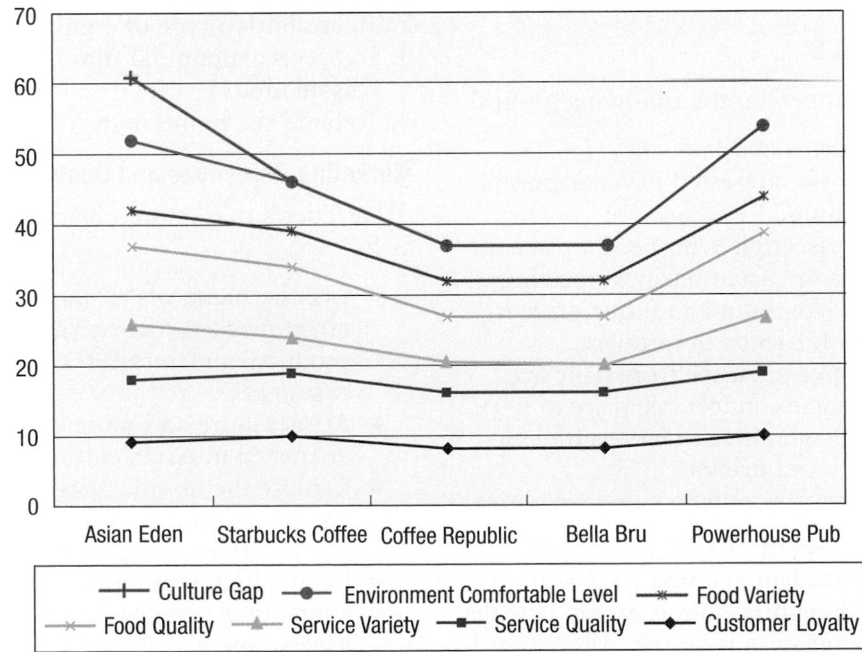

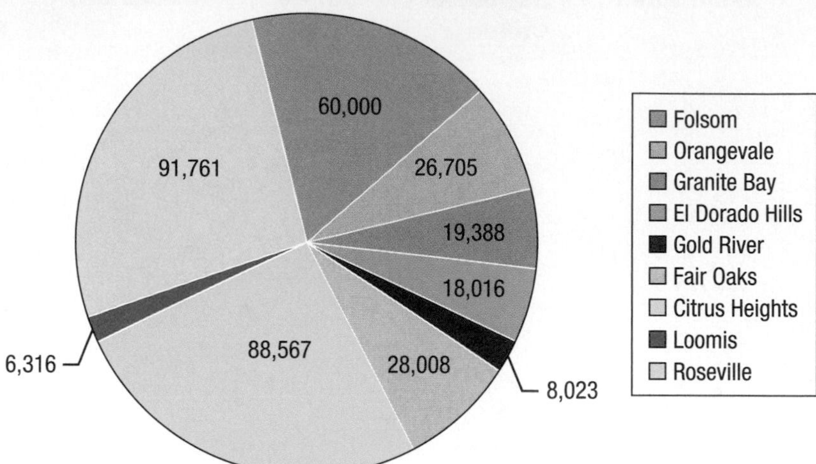

one to ten (ten = very good) and is based on the researcher's opinion, critic's reviews, and consumer opinions.

TARGET MARKET

Asian Eden's target market includes everyone in the city of Folsom and everyone in the nearest cities to Folsom, as well as visitors to the Folsom Lake Recreation Area. The current population of Folsom is about 60,000. The total population of the nearest cities to Folsom is about 286,784 (www.censuscd.com, 2000). The population of each city is shown in this chart.

CUSTOMER PROFILE

Asian Eden will appeal to the following groups:

- College students and faculty.
- People who are interested in Asian cuisine or Asian culture.
- Local businesspeople who need a place for lunch breaks or casual business meetings.
- People who like to find a unique place to hang out with friends or families.
- People who like to escape from daily lives and to find some comfortable place to relax.
- Asian people who love to have authentic Asian snacks and drinks.
- Visitors to this area or who pass by this area.

According to the record of U.S. Census 2000, in Folsom City, the median age was 35.9 years old. Therefore, even though Folsom is an old city, the majority of its population is young. Also, according to the record of U.S. Census, the majority population of Folsom is white, non-Hispanic people (www.censuscd.com, 2000). Overall, Asian Eden's target market will initially focus on young, white non-Hispanic people and all Asian people at every age. The potential customer base for Asian Eden is very large. The customers in the target market are less price-sensitive. (More demographic information is available in Appendix C-1).

OBJECTIVES

The overall objectives of Asian Eden are:

1. To achieve breakeven by the end of the first year.
2. To establish a core of regular customers.
3. To become a popular dining place in the Folsom area.
4. To build the brand name of Asian Eden.

Marketing Objectives and Goals

Asian Eden's marketing objectives and goals are as follows:

- Get the name of "Asian Eden" out in the target market; increase the awareness of its products and services among its potential customers.
- Attract more and more customers who are interested in Asian culture and food.
- Explore the unique image of Asian Eden among customers, differentiating Asian Eden from its competitors.
- Build a high reputation of Asian Eden's authentic Asian snacks and drinks among its customers.

■ The success of Starbucks in Beijing motivated the owner of Asian Eden to attempt something similar—attract customers by building a store with a different culture in its atmosphere and products than the surrounding area. Asian Eden hopes to attract people with the careful use of details, such as Asian food products and décor.

MARKETING STRATEGIES AND PLANS

The focus of the marketing strategy is to increase the awareness of its unique services and products among the potential customers and to differentiate itself from its competitors.

Product Strategy

Store Design

Asian Eden will impress and attract customers with its exotic appearance and artistic interior design. This is an idea from Starbucks Coffee business in China.

To most Chinese people, Starbucks coffee represents the culture from western countries. Seeing a Starbucks Coffee Store open inside the Forbidden City Palace in Beijing not only made Chinese people feel disbelief, but also make visitors from western counties feel shock. Starbucks' stories of success showed that culture difference could be part of attracting customers instead of a threat to the business.

Using this idea, the owner will design Asian Eden as a mini Forbidden City Palace. The appearance of Asian Eden will be similar to the Starbucks in Forbidden City in China.

The interior design will be in the same style with a gallery showing pictures of the Forbidden City in China. Other pictures of Asian arts, especially arts from China, will also be used for interior decorations.

Service

Asian Eden is designed to be a sit-down dining place. However, customers can choose to dine in-store or to order over the phone for pick up. Fax or Internet orders may be accepted in the future based on the market demand.

High-quality customer service will be provided to make sure all customers feel comfortable. Knowledgeable waitresses will be ready to assist customers to place an order and answer any questions.

In the future, free delivery service may be provided for local companies if the market demands.

Menu Design

The chef special and daily special will be seen on the red lanterns hanging next to the store entrance. The regular menu will be designed and printed nicely showing all the names, pictures, brief descriptions, and prices of the snacks and drinks selling in-store. All the snacks and drinks will be made fresh to ensure high quality and good taste. The regular menu will also show Asian Eden's business hours, address, fax and phone numbers, and a calendar of Chinese holidays. (Please see a menu list in Appendix C-2.)

Promotional Strategy

Advertising

Advertising of the grand opening will be placed on http://www.myfolsom.com. This is a popular local Web site showing Folsom's local news, providing resident guide and visitor guide and averages 90,000 page views per month. The cost of advertisement is affordable. A super size advertisement (746 × 60 pixels) costs only $125 per month; it is perfect for the first business month of the grand opening. An economical advertisement (100 × 60 pixels) costs only $350 per year; it is good for doing an on-going advertisement for Asian Eden's first business year (http://www.myfolsom.com/advertising.shtml).

Sales Promotion

The result of a survey showed that customers tend to buy products that they have sampled or they are familiar with. Some interviewees said they do not buy Asian drinks because they are not sure what those drinks would taste like. In order to promote Asian Eden's food products, free samples of drinks and snacks will be offered to customers especially during the time of the grand opening.

Customers can get a 15 percent discount coupon that is good for the next time for a purchase over $20.00.

Special Events

During Chinese holidays, Asian Eden will have some small gifts for customers. For example, during Chinese Moon holiday, customers can get free moon cakes for desserts. For Chinese New Year holiday, live Chinese lion dancing along with traditional Chinese music show may be seen in front of the store; customers can also get free red fortune cookies and lucky candies wrapped with golden papers.

Public Relations

Asian Eden will consider itself not only a new style of business but also an advocate of the diversity of community and an educator of Asian/Chinese culture. In addition to having in-store celebrations for Chinese holidays, Asian Eden will support the local Asian-American community by holding or sponsoring some events of Asian culture. For example, June 1 is Children's day in China. Asian Eden will hold a Chinese-speaking contest to encourage Chinese-American children to learn Chinese.

Asian Eden will work with the Chamber of Commerce to discover and develop any possible business opportunity with China. Overall, Asian Eden will devote itself to make Folsom an even better city in which to live.

Location Strategy

Store Location

Asian Eden will be located inside the Kohl's Shopping Center that is across the street from the

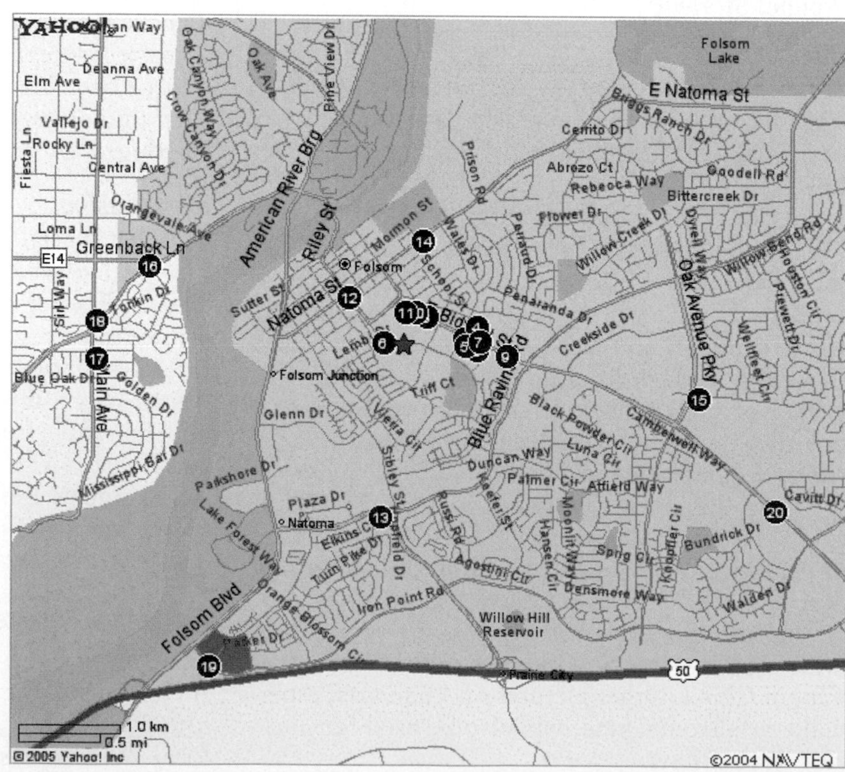

■ The map shown here depicts Asian Eden's proposed location, marked with a star, as well as the locations of other nearby businesses that will help supply a strong customer base.

Wal-Mart Shopping Center. This location is also close to the Century Folsom 14 movie theater and surrounded by grocery stores and supermarkets. Asian Eden will be strategically positioned in this location in order to build a large base of customers.

The grocery stores and supermarkets marked on the map on the previous page are listed as the following (http://www.folsomliving.com/modules/guide/shop.php):

Map#	Business/Landmark Info	Distance
1	**Malabar Indian Store** 705 E Bidwell St # 12 Folsom, CA **Phone:** (916) 984-4845	**0.4 miles**
2	**Raley's Supermarket & Drug Ctr** 715 E Bidwell St Folsom, CA **Phone:** (916) 983-6574	**0.4 miles**
3	**Yogurt Delite** 711 E Bidwell St # 10 Folsom, CA **Phone:** (916) 983-1943	**0.4 miles**
4	**Raley's Supermarket** 715 E Bidwell St Folsom, CA **Phone:** (916) 983-7267	**0.4 miles**
5	**Tower Mart** 700 E Bidwell St Folsom, CA **Phone:** (916) 983-4922	**0.4 miles**
6	**Food Source** 1006 Riley St Folsom, CA **Phone:** (916) 983-1065	**0.4 miles**
7	**Trader Joe's Co** 810 E Bidwell St Folsom, CA **Phone:** (916) 817-4193	**0.4 miles**
8	**Folsom Food Mart** 500 E Bidwell St Folsom, CA **Phone:** (916) 983-3532	**0.4 miles**
9	**Albertsons** 1003 E Bidwell St Folsom, CA **Phone:** (916) 983-0186	**0.5 miles**
10	**India Bazar** 422 E Bidwell St Folsom, CA **Phone:** (916) 983-5599	**0.5 miles**

(Continued)

11	**Palika Bazar** 333 E Bidwell St Folsom, CA **Phone:** (916) 984-4460	**0.5 miles**
12	**Circle K** 703 Natoma St Folsom, CA **Phone:** (916) 985-7816	**0.7 miles**
13	**India Market** 241 Blue Ravine Rd Folsom, CA **Phone:** (916) 608-9930	**0.7 miles**
14	**Circle K** 95 Natoma St Folsom, CA **Phone:** (916) 985-2857	**0.9 miles**
15	**Lexington Food Store** 316 S Lexington Dr Folsom, CA **Phone:** (916) 984-7565	**1.6 miles**
16	**Ralph's** 9522 Greenback Ln Folsom, CA **Phone:** (916) 989-1160	**1.8 miles**
17	**American Food Stores** 5682 Main Ave Orangevale, CA **Phone:** (916) 989-4049	**2.0 miles**
18	**Save Mart Liquor** 5920 Main Ave Orangevale, CA **Phone:** (916) 988-5104	**2.0 miles**
19	**Tosco Corp** 191 Iron Point Rd Folsom, CA **Phone:** (916) 608-9118	**2.1 miles**
20	**Bel Air Supermarket** 2760 E Bidwell St Folsom, CA **Phone:** (916) 983-8844	**2.2 miles**

Price Strategy

Menu items will be priced comparable to competitive products in and around the area. (Please see menu in Appendix C-2.)

FINANCIAL PLAN

In this business plan, the financial analysis will be limited to the breakeven analysis. The goal is for this small shop to reach breakeven within a year. Please note: where actual cost figures were unavailable, estimates were used based on a similar shop in Pleasant Hill, California, adjusted for inflation. This shop opened four years ago in another northern California town with similar demographics, population size, and competitive situation as Folsom.

The assumptions for this breakeven analysis are as follows:

- The costs of goods sold will remain stable.
- There will be no dramatic changes of demographic data in the city of Folsom and its neighbor cities during this time period.
- No new government regulations will be introduced and will affect Asian Eden's business in a negative way.
- The average selling price for snacks is $5.30 per unit. As for the drinks, the average selling price is $3.00 per unit. Therefore the estimated average selling price for snacks and drinks is $4.15 per unit. The average price per unit is estimated according to the average price per unit in the Boba/Snack bar in Pleasant Hill, California.
- The first year's projected sales will be at least $250,000. Again, this number is based on the experience of a Boba/Snack bar in Pleasant Hill, California, a city with a similar demographic makeup and size as Folsom. Folsom actually has a slightly higher percentage of Asian people, making the estimated sales number likely to be higher in Folsom. Therefore, the projected sales will be $20,833 per month.
- The estimated fixed cost for the first year will be $17,991 per month based on the Pleasant Hill store's experience.
- Rent expenses for the selected location will be $2,400 per month.
- Utility costs will be $400 per month.
- Insurance will be $2,400 per year, $200 per month.
- Sales and marketing costs for the first year will be $1,200 per month. It will include the costs of holding special events, advertising, etc.
- Premises remodeling will cost about $100,000, which will be about $8,333 per month.
- Legal expenses for obtaining business licenses and permits will be $1,500 during the first year; it will be $125 per month.
- Inventory purchase including materials and others will cost $24,000 per year; it will cost $2,000 per month.
- Equipment costs will be $40,000 for the first year, which will be $3,333 per month.
- Therefore, for the first business year, the estimated fixed cost will be about $17,991 per month.
- The average variable cost is assumed to be $2.50 per unit.

Breakeven Result

Based on the above assumptions, the breakeven point for Asian Eden is at 10,904 selling units per month.

Contingency Plan

The success of Asian Eden depends on several key factors working as described above. Recognizing that there are always problems in new start-up businesses, the most likely problems have been identified, and contingency plans developed to handle them. The owner and staff will be on the lookout for these situations, so immediate action can be taken.

Problem: *Lower customer numbers than planned (but customers like food)*

- Try alternative promotions: deliver samples and lunch menus to local businesses/industries; try a customer loyalty program; distribute additional flyers/handbills with a "free drink with meal purchase" promotion.
- Add new menu items to attract more customers.
- Try to link with local businesses; example: customers can bring a receipt from the dry cleaner next door and get 10 percent off a drink.

Problem: *Perceived as "too Asian;" tastes are too unfamiliar to the locals.*

- Add non-Asian items to appeal to those tastes.
- "Americanize" slightly some of the recipes.

Problem: *A new Asian restaurant tries to duplicate our menu or existing restaurants try to expand into a similar menu.*

- Emphasize our unique attributes in all ads and other messages.
- Develop a customer loyalty program.
- Develop "next generation" menu items to stay ahead of competition.
- Compete back, adding popular items from competing restautants.

Problem: *Food or other costs rise more than anticipated.*

- Wherever possible, minimize these effects with long-term contracts.
- Constantly be on the lookout for alternative suppliers.
- Try to create a close relationship with suppliers so that you can receive advanced notice whenever possible: With advanced notice, it may be possible to make a couple of small incremental price increases or small adjustments in serving sizes without customer complaints.

Problem: *Road construction or other unanticipated project makes access to restaurant difficult.*

- Offer and promote delivery

Schedule

The implementation of the Asian Eden plan would follow the schedule identified below, with the intent to open around Chinese New Year, when interest in Chinese traditions, customs, and foods are at their peak.

September

- Incorporate, Set Up Bank Accounts
- Investigate Equipment Options
- Investigate Suppliers
- Procure Lease
- Secure Utilities

October

- Begin Remodeling
- Order Equipment
- Develop Menus
- Develop Newspaper and Web Ads
- Develop Mailers
- Design Web Site

November

- Continue Remodeling

December

- Install Equipment
- Order Nonperishable Supplies/Furnishings
- Finishing Touches on Remodeling
- Print Menus, Mailers, Handbills

Late December/Early January

- Order Perishables
- Final Inspections
- Run Ads
- Contact Newspaper for PR
- Open Web Site
- Send Out Mailers/Place Handbills on Cars

Late January to Mid-February

- Open for Business by Chinese New Year

APPENDIX C-1: CITY OF FOLSOM CENSUS DATA

Folsom City, California Statistics and Demographics

(U.S. Census 2000)

	Number	Percent
Folsom Population:	**51,884**	**100.00%**
Sex and Age		
Male	28,658	55.23%
Female	23,226	44.77%
Under 5 years	3,591	6.92%
5 to 9 years	3,647	7.03%
10 to 14 years	3,457	6.66%
15 to 19 years	2,809	5.41%

20 to 24 years	2,476	4.77%
25 to 34 years	8,935	17.22%
35 to 44 years	11,306	21.79%
45 to 54 years	7,566	14.58%
55 to 59 years	2,036	3.92%
60 to 64 years	1,492	2.88%
65 to 74 years	2,276	4.39%
75 to 84 years	1,735	3.34%
85 years and over	558	1.08%
Median age (years)	35.9	
Race		
One race	50,103	96.57%
White	40,415	77.89%
Black or African American	3,109	5.99%
American Indian and Alaska Native	302	0.58%
Asian	3,731	7.19%
Asian Indian	1,153	2.22%
Chinese	730	1.41%
Filipino	710	1.37%
Japanese	297	0.57%
Korean	281	0.54%
Vietnamese	278	0.54%
Other Asian	282	0.54%
Native Hawaiian and Other Pacific Islander	100	0.19%
Native Hawaiian	30	0.06%
Guamanian or Chamorro	22	0.04%
Samoan	5	0.01%
Other Pacific Islander	43	0.08%
Some other race	2,446	4.71%
Two or more races	1,781	3.43%
Households by Type		
Total households	17,196	100.0 %
Family households (families)	12,527	72.85%
With own children under 18 years	6,727	39.12%
Married-couple family	10,609	61.69%
With own children under 18 years	5,508	32.03%
Female householder, no husband present	1,379	8.02%
With own children under 18 years	874	5.08%
Nonfamily households	4,669	27.15%
Householder living alone	3,754	21.83%
Householder 65 years and over	1,225	7.12%

(Continued)

Households with individuals under 18 years	7,019	40.82%
Households with individuals 65 years and over	3,186	18.53%
Average household size	2.61	
Average family size	3.08	
Housing Tenure		
Occupied housing units	17,196	100.00%
Owner-occupied housing units	13,124	76.32%
Renter-occupied housing units	4,072	23.68%
Average household size of owner-occupied units	2.75	
Average household size of renter-occupied units	2.18	

APPENDIX C-2: A PARTIAL LIST OF ASIAN EDEN'S PRODUCTS

Special Milk Tea (Hot/Iced)	
House Blended Milk Tea (Green/Black Tea)	$3.00
Pearl Milk Tea (Boba Tea)	$3.00
Wheat Green Milk Tea (Green/Black Tea)	$3.00
Thai Iced Milk Tea	$3.00
Coffee Milk Tea	$3.00
Almond Milk Tea	$3.00

Flavored Iced Tea	
Plum Green Tea	$3.00
Passionfruit Kumquat Green Tea	$3.00
Lemon Iced Tea With Honey	$3.00
Iced Osmanthus OoLong Tea	$3.00
Rose Tea	$3.00
Peach Iced Tea	$3.00
House Blended Iced Tea	$3.00
Strawberry Iced Tea	$3.00
Apple Iced Tea	$3.00
Honey Iced Tea	$3.00

Tea Snack	
Meat Ball With Rice Noodle	$5.50
Salt + Pepper Chicken Nugget With Rice	$5.50
Tea Marinated Eggs	$3.50
Baked Squid	$3.50
Deep Fried Tofu	$3.50
BBQ Fish Cake	$3.50
Fried Wonton	$4.00
Egg Rolls/Beef Rolls	$4.00
Three Flavored Chicken with Rice	$5.50
Pork Chop with Rice	$5.50
Sausage with Rice	$5.50
Beef Stew with Rice	$5.50
Sweet Crepe	$4.00
Fish Ball Soup	$3.50
Won Ton Soup	$3.50

Short Business Plan

Emergency Bridal LLC

Emergency Bridal LLC is an example of a full business plan that presents all the necessary elements to get the job done in a shorter than usual format. This plan builds on established business ideas and markets to offer an innovative service, but is able to get the point across quickly. The plan follows the format for a full plan quite closely. The only major omissions are the assumptions for the financials and the critical risks.

Because the plan was going to be funded from a personal loan to Rachel (not a business one), there was no one who needed to see the plan except Rachel, and she knew what her assumptions were. During her presentation, the majority of the judge's questions were on the assumptions underlying the numbers, so it proves the point that including an assumptions section in your business plan can make life a lot easier all around. The lack of critical risks also reflected this approach. Rachel's point was she could easily pay off the $10,000 loan from nearly any job she could get, so the downside risk was negligible. If she encountered an unexpected risk that she could not handle, she would perform a walkaway and pay off her loan from another job. To find out what happened to Rachel and the plan, look at the postscript at the end of the plan.

Emergency Bridal LLC

Emergency Bridal LLC

1.0 Executive Summary

Introduction There is an untapped part of the wedding market for brides in the middle planning stage[1] who would benefit from extra help planning their event, selecting reliable and reasonably priced vendors, and additional wedding day assistance. We are proposing the creation of a company that will be modeled after traditional wedding/event planning companies, but with a twist. Rather than marketing directly to the bride like other wedding consultants, we will market to venues first and then to the bride, in order to target those in the middle planning stage. Emergency Bridal LLC is being established as a third-party contracting service to team up with venues, so they can pass along our services in order to help their clients complete the planning process successfully while remaining on budget.

The Services We will specialize in wedding planning services and concentrate on stationery, favors, decorations, music, and flowers. In addition to planning, we will help clients keep track of budgets and bills. We will also help our clients with last minute details and overseeing the actual event.

The Market Emergency Bridal has two market segments that will be targeted; event venues and engaged couples. Our target venue is located in Des Moines City or Des Moines County and has two or more ballrooms/event rooms and holds one–two events per week in off-peak season and three–four in peak season.[2] Our target clients are Des Moines County residents between the ages of 22 and 35, who are engaged, and are budgeting $18,000 to $25,000 on their wedding. Our clients are individuals who want a well-run event that is creative and personalized within their budget.

Management Emergency Bridal will be owned and solely operated by Rachel Evans.

Financial Considerations Emergency Bridal's initial start-up expenses are estimated at $4,405, with an additional $5,600 to finance receivables. Start-up cost will be covered by a $10,000 loan. The loan is due in five years with a 6.99 percent fixed interest rate. Rachel Evans will personally secure the loan.

In the first year Emergency Bridal will be making a profit of $4,783 after taxes. In the following years, Emergency Bridal will continue to grow and earn more business while increasing profits. It is projected that in the fifth year of business Emergency Bridal will have a profit of $67,015 after taxes.

1.1 OBJECTIVES Our objective is to develop relationships with local venues and offer our services to their clients. By teaming up with venues, we would be able to target a niche market of brides who originally passed up the idea of wedding planners, but after starting the planning process have decided that they would benefit from professional services. In addition to pairing up with venues, we will also work to develop relationships with vendors that we can repeatedly rely on for quality and reasonable prices. Emergency Bridal LLC is entering a market that is currently populated by 11 Des Moines area wedding planning professionals, which are small businesses that typically employ only one to two people. These planners are traditional planners in the sense that they target brides before planning begins; however, Emergency Bridal intends to target the brides who are in the midst of planning and need help in the continuation of the planning process.

1.2 MISSION Emergency Bridal's mission is to be the sole service provider of wedding planning services for major reception venues in Des Moines. We help brides orchestrate their wedding day, while ensuring the hiring of quality vendors and maintaining the established budget. As professionals we will use our network of vendor relationships and use our expertise to aid brides in planning memorable events and help ease their stress. Our experience and knowledge in the industry will ensure reliable services, organization, and event excellence.

1.3 KEYS TO SUCCESS With our strategy in selling to the venue first and then to the bride, our keys to success can be segmented into two stages.

Our first market is the venue. In selling our services to the venue, we are dedicated to:

- Reliable, professional, and quality work.
- Promoting the venue and helping to further satisfy its clients.

- Working with management to motivate the sales staff through incentive programs.

Next, in order to serve the bride and groom, we believe in listening to the customers' needs and wedding dreams, while providing the reliable quality service they deserve which includes but is not limited to:

- A detailed list of wedding objectives and services designed to fit the needs of the client.
- Dedication to established budget.
- Creativity and personalized events.
- Organization and seamless execution of events.

We are dedicated to offering a variety of event services and will strive to satisfy customer demands and continue working relationships with venues and vendors.

2.0 Company Summary

Emergency Bridal LLC is a start-up company that will provide third-party wedding planning services to catering venues, which they will then make available to their clients. We will work with their clients and help them with the various other details that go into planning their event. We will focus on stationery/invitations, favors, decorations, transportation, music, and photography. However, we will work with the clients to ensure that their wedding dreams come true, and do so within their budget. Our main objective is to help the client with vendor decisions and help eliminate the time and guess work that comes along with major wedding decisions. We will use our knowledge in the industry and relationships with local vendors to find what the clients are looking for at the most reasonable price. In developing relationships with local vendors through networks and repeat business, we will be able to provide our clients with a list of reliable vendors whom we are familiar with.[3] We will also take care of the stress of scheduling, contracts, and follow-up calls. It is our mission to design our services around what clients want and help plan and execute their wedding, while letting them enjoy their special day with confidence and assurance.

2.1 COMPANY OWNERSHIP This business will form as a limited liability company with complete ownership by its founder and president Rachel Evans.

2.2 START-UP SUMMARY Emergency Bridal LLC's original start-up costs will amount to $4,422 of which $1,622 will be office equipment including a computer and software; $557.00 will be used for office supplies[4] and furniture, and $1,500 will be dedicated to legal fees. The remaining balance will be used for other miscellaneous supplies, stationery, furniture, and other start-up fees. In addition, Emergency Bridal LLC projects the need for an additional financial commitment of $5,578 to finance receivables and other start-up expenses for the first 12 months of operations.

Funding of this initial $10,000 will be provided by a business loan. The owner Rachel Evans will personally secure the loan.

For spreadsheet, see Appendix 8-a.

2.3 COMPANY LOCATIONS AND FACILITIES Initially this will be a home-based business that will be stationed at 3701 Parkway Avenue, which is two miles from downtown and one mile from Highway 8 and 235 entrance ramps. We see no need to purchase office space since much of our time will be spent meeting with clients on site and traveling to build relationships with venues and vendors. However, we are willing to look into an incubator or office space once we have established ourselves in the industry.

3.0 Services

Emergency Bridal provides services to two target segments, one being venues looking to enhance their clients' experience and to the brides themselves. Emergency Bridal will offer our wedding planning services in a contractual relationship with catering venues to serve their clients. We will work to serve their clients and therefore serve the venue. By satisfying and further helping their clients, we can help the venue promote its image and increase the overall satisfaction of its clients. The idea that a venue can provide clients with additional wedding planning help on other aspects of its event can be used as a selling device for venues when booking events. By teaming up with venues, we can offer their clients a service and help to ensure the overall success of the events at their venue.

Emergency Bridal will specialize in helping clients complete the aspects of their wedding. We will offer middle-planning stage brides, who are in need of a little extra expertise and organization, help with stationery/invitations, favors, decorations, transportation, music, and photography, but we are not limited to those services. We will take care of the stress of scheduling, vendor agreements, confirmation calls, and guest list finalization and R.S.V.P.s. In addition, if desired, we will have a bill pay option where we will organize expenses, make sure payments are on time, and keep track of the budget and expenditures.[5] We will offer various service packages that cater to the clients' needs and wishes that will vary from day of services to complete wedding orchestration. The goal of our services is to allow brides to enjoy their special day and help them avoid getting bogged down by all of the details and technicalities that go into making their event successful.

3.1 COMPETITIVE COMPARISON Emergency Bridal LLC is entering a market that is nationally populated with small businesses that have one to two employees. The local Des Moines market is similar to national norms and of the 11 wedding consultants,[6] most work by themselves. However, there are two bigger names in the Des Moines area: Katie Fisher of The Bridal Group and Jenny Little of Wedding Dreams. Both are synonymous with Des Moines upscale events. Other competitors are smaller, single-person businesses that operate from suburban Des Moines. Research shows that the Des Moines area wedding consultants follow a traditional format as wedding consultants and mainly concentrate on the entire event from start to finish. What makes Emergency Bridal different from the competition is that we are making our connection with brides at a different stage in the planning process. While our competition is marketing to them right after their engagement, we are zoning in on brides who have already begun the planning process and could use extra help on the more tedious tasks. With that said, the areas in which we would specialize are stationery, favors, decorations, transportation, music, and flowers, which account for only 50 percent of the total average wedding budget.[7] Even though we would follow the traditional pricing structure of charging 10 percent of the total services used, with additional hourly rates, our profits will be significantly less, since they are based on a smaller percentage of the total wedding. Therefore competing with us on a direct level would not be lucrative for existing wedding planners who customarily plan and are compensated for all aspects of weddings. Our strategy is to work with the brides who the traditional wedding planners have missed out on. Even if other wedding planners caught on to our tactics and ideas, we would retain our competitive advantage with venue/vendor contracts, our established working relationships and reputation.

3.2 TECHNOLOGY As mentioned in our start-up summary, we are planning on purchasing The Wedding Workshop software (MicroPrecision, $29.95) in addition to the standard Microsoft Office and QuickBooks. The Wedding workshop software will help us manage guest lists, track expenses, and set up budgets for our clients.

We are also planning on having a Web site designed that will provide general information about our services and contact information. Ideally this Web site will be used as a tool for advertising and reaching potential clients and can be linked with Des Moines and national wedding reference sites, such as www.theweddingchannel.com and www.theknot.com.

3.3 PRICING AND PAYMENT Traditionally a bride books the reception location six to nine months before the wedding date. It is after she books the reception, about six months before the wedding date, that the bride would be contacted by Emergency Bridal. At the first consultation with the bride there will be an information session describing what Emergency Bridal has to offer. If the bride is satisfied and wants to use Emergency Bridal as her event planner, she will sign a contract and pay 20 percent of the package up front. This original deposit will be nonrefundable. Depending on the time frame, the remaining amount will be split in even monthly payments. The bill for our services will be 10 percent of the Emergency Bridal budget if contracted six months or longer before the event and 12 percent if contracted within six months of the wedding date. In addition, for each event there will be an additional $20 an hour fee.[8] For example, if the package purchased six months before the wedding was $10,000.00[9] and the bride pays 20 percent or $2,000.00 up front, the remaining 80 percent or $8,000.00 will be split up into $1,600.00 payments due each month for the next five months, and the billable hours will be totaled before each payment is due and added to that payment. The fees paid to Emergency Bridal will be used to pay contracts, sales commission to our contracted venue, and Ms. Evans's salary.

In 2006, after our first year, when Emergency Bridal has grown more stable, an R.S.V.P. package, a Week Of package, and a Day Of package will all be offered to the bride. The R.S.V.P. package includes Emergency Bridal contacting people on the bride's guest list who have not returned their R.S.V.P. This will be billed on a per call basis plus an additional package fee of $200. If there are 200 guests or less, the price will be $0.90 per call, and if the wedding has over 200 guests, the price per call will be $0.80. The Week Of package, which includes calling vendors and verifying times and locations, will cost the bride $500.00 for a wedding with 150 guests or less, $700.00 for a wedding with 150 to 300 guests, and a wedding with more than 300 guests will be given a personalized quote. The Day Of package includes getting people where they need to be, when they need to be there, and will include the services of Ms. Evans and another onsite assistant. This package costs $600.00 for 10 hours of service, and each additional hour will cost $70.00.[10] All packages are to be paid in full the day of the wedding. All payments will be in the form of cash, check, or money order.

4.0 Market Analysis Summary

Wedding planning/consulting is one of the more difficult industries to obtain exact estimates and sales projections on. It is classified by the S.I.C. /N.A.I.C.S. codes as 7299/812990 which are miscellaneous personal services not elsewhere classified, which places them in a category with 84,994 other services[11] which employ an estimated 290,937 individuals. This category includes everything varying from physical fitness facilities and dating services to scalp treating services and valet parking establishments. Market analysis by specialty, code 7299-0504, states that there are 2,140 wedding consultant services in the United States, 11 of which are in the Des Moines area.[12]

The search for information is even more difficult because over 90 percent of all consultants are self-employed and typically work from the home[13] and therefore have privately held companies. However, it has been quoted that the wedding market is a $35–$38 billion per year industry. Gerard Monaghan of the

Association of Bridal Consultants stated "the entire wedding industry—encompassing everything a bride and groom do six months before the ceremony to six months after—is pushing $100 billion dollars a year."[14] Monaghan also noted that the industry itself has only developed in the past 25 years. It is difficult to estimate this young industry's growth potential and future profit, because the large majority of companies are privately held. However, Gerard Monaghan, president of the Association of Bridal Consultants, and Ann Nola, president of the Association of Certified Professional Wedding Consultants, predict the industry is growing and that the demand is increasing. In her article "Alter-Bound, Wallets Open" Karen Benezra predicts "engagements will be up 14% in the next four years and 30% in the next 15 years."[15] An article by Raye Robertson also deals with the increase in recent engagements and states that the increase is due to the increased marriage of Generation Xers, 25–34-years-old, who have taken their time to marry, and the trend of Generation Yers, 18–24 years old, to get married at an earlier age than the previous generation.[16] With the Generation Xers getting married later, a majority are busy professionals as confirmed by *Entrepreneur* magazine's *How to be a Wedding Planner* booklet. It stated that 83 percent of brides and 89 percent of grooms are employed full time. These working individuals are benefiting from the use of wedding planners and therefore contributing to industry growth.

In addition to an increase in engagements, there has been a constant rise in the amount couples spend on their big day. A recent survey by the WeddingChannel.com stated that the average bride and groom are spending $27,600 on their wedding, and 85 percent of the couples surveyed said they would spend the "same amount of money" if they had the chance to plan their weddings again. With couples spending upwards of $27,000 on the big day and increases in engagements by all age groups, the possibility of niche services is increasing.

4.1 MARKET SEGMENTATION According to the Annual Statement Studies: 2002–2003 there were 2.327 million marriages in the United States in 2001. Of those, 42,000 were in Iowa, and an estimated 7,560 were Des Moines County Residents.[17] According to 2002 census data, there were 162,883 Des Moines County residents in the age group 22–34. In the "Wedding Statistics" prepared by the Association of Bridal Consultants, the average age of couples ranged from 24 for brides and 26 for grooms. With that being said, in Des Moines County there are a large number of prospective couples, therefore prospective clients. With the large number of engaged couples in the area, this will lead to a large number of receptions, and statistics from the Association of Bridal Consultants show that 98 percent of couples will have a reception. One-third of all brides say that their number one choice for a reception site is a catering hall, the exact type of venue we are looking to contract with. Another 35 percent say that their first choices would be a country club or hotel, also one of our major targets.[18]

4.2 TARGET MARKET SEGMENT STRATEGY The target market of Emergency Bridal is different from typical wedding consultants. Our first market is finding and creating relationships with reception venues. We will contract our services to the venues, and they will then offer our services to their clients. Our ideal venue to build a contractual relationship with has at least two rooms and does an average of three weddings a week. After contacting various Des Moines area venues, we discovered that a majority of venues will only offer catering, rentals, and possible references. This shortcoming of venue services allows for a market niche. Emergency Bridal will highlight this inadequacy to venues and show them that our services will pick up where theirs leave off. By contracting our services to their clients, we can increase the success of their events, reduce the stress of their clients, and help promote their image as a full-service venue. In addition to helping with their image and event success, Emergency Bridal will give venues a commission on our profits of 1.5 percent. Once we have contractual agreements with venues, our next objective is to sell our services to their clients.

What is special about Emergency Bridal is that our major target market is a bride who does not think she needs a wedding planner. Our services are designed to help the bride who wants to do it on her own, but after the struggle to select a date and a venue is ready for some extra help. The list of things to do when planning a wedding is often endless and it often only takes a bride a month of planning before she is frustrated, overwhelmed, and exhausted. As a little girl when you dream of your wedding, you do not think about contracts, stationery, and playing phone tag with vendors. Our bride is someone with a moderately average budget from $18,000 to $25,000 who wants an upscale well-run event within her budget and does not have the time to compare vendors and orchestrate all the details of her wedding the way she would like. By teaming up with venues, we will have access to all of their brides who have booked events and we can target brides in the middle planning stage. Once brides have booked their event, we will contact them and offer our services for the coordination of the rest of their event.

4.3 MARKET NEEDS Our bride is someone who is just establishing her career or is already established and is too busy to deal with the stresses and time-consuming organization it takes to plan a wedding, but thinks that she can do it on her own. The market needs for our services are rooted in the conflict between time and desired perfection. Our bride is an individual who began the planning process on her own, but after realizing the magnitude of the planning process is willing to ask for professional help. Our customer seeks our professional services to ensure that all aspects of the wedding meet her expectations and run seamlessly, the way they would have if she had done it on her own. It is our desire to help brides who have already begun the planning process and need help completing their event and would rather spend time enjoying their engagement than being stressed out about the details.

5.0 Strategy and Implementation Summary

As noted earlier, the average wedding costs $27,000 and the U.S. weddings industry amasses $38 billion to $42 billion in sales annually.[19] Typically wedding planners can be found and contacted through Web sites and are contacted soon after the engagement, before the planning process begins. A bride without a wedding planner typically plans everything on her own, in addition to her already busy schedule. While the excitement of her engagement may give her the adrenaline she needs to push through the first months of planning, it doesn't take long for her to get stressed out and discouraged. At this point in time there are few wedding planners who are willing to come in and plan an event from the middle of the planning stage.

Emergency Bridal will step in when the bride needs a planner the most, after the frustration sets in. Shortly after booking the venue is typically when the bride will experience major stresses from calling vendors, choosing the best ones, and trying to stay on budget. By being the sole planner contracted to a venue, the services Emergency Bridal offers will be made available to a bride[20] once she has booked her reception location.

From there Emergency Bridal will pick up where the bride left off. From playing phone tag with vendors to confirming R.S.V.P.s, Emergency Bridal can make the special event come off without a hitch, all the while staying on budget. The benefits offered by Emergency Bridal will be unbeatable service, incredible shopping ease, and quality assurance that everything will be completed as requested. No more will this stressed out bride have to worry about her special day.

Initially the bride may have wanted to stay away from hiring a wedding planner because of the typically high costs, but at Emergency Bridal we provide all the benefits of a wedding planner, while working with vendors to make relationships and provide discounts to pass on to the bride. So that even with the added expense of the wedding planner, her budget can still be maintained.

In addition to venue contracts and relationships, Emergency Bridal will have a Web site. The Web site will provide a list of our services and contact information. This Web site can be used as a tool for advertising and reaching potential clients, and can be linked with Des Moines and national wedding reference sites.

5.1 COMPETITIVE EDGE By being the sole planning service to a venue, Emergency Bridal has a contracted relationship along with business and personal networks with vendors. A competitor cannot break this relationship due to the contractual agreement. Our contract with venues will outline our agreement and state that they (the venue) will hire us (Emergency Bridal LLC) as their sole wedding planners and will offer our services to their clients who have booked events. In return we will compensate the venue with 1.5 percent of our profit from each event and offer incentive programs for their sales staff. Under the contract the venue will not be able to hire anyone who provides services similar to ours, contractor or employee. Emergency Bridal will however be permitted to plan events for other venues and for individuals who have contacted them on their own (i.e., through the Web site or word of mouth). The contracts will have time constraints, but we are confident in the reputation, experience, and relationships built by Ms. Evans before the establishment of Emergency Bridal and that the success of Emergency Bridal will sustain our competitive edge.

5.2 SALES STRATEGY As noted in the Target Market Segmentation Strategy, Emergency Bridal has two target markets: first the venue and then the client. In order to sell our services to the venues, we will promote the influence Emergency Bridal can have on the overall success of the event and the positive experience of the bride, which will have a positive impact on the venue reputation. We will also give vendors 1.5 percent of all of the profits that we earn from their contacts, which will be documented in our contract.[21] In addition Emergency Bridal will offer incentives to salespeople at the venue for giving our promotional items and references to brides booking with them and larger rewards when a client signs a contract. For example, there would be a points system. For each referral, they would receive one point and for each client who uses our services, they would receive five points. After a specified number of points are accumulated, we would reward them with gift certificates.[22] This system is designed to increase the willingness of the salespeople to sell our services to their customers. Incentives for salespeople would also be a benefit to the company because it would motivate their employees for rewards.

To sell our services to brides, we would promote our professional experience and the fact that using our services would alleviate planning frustrations. In addition to the stress relief benefit, using our services would also ensure that only quality reliable vendors are used and that they get the most for the money that they spend. Our experience and networks would also influence the prices they are charged and ideally our repeat use of vendors would lead to discounts or commissions which would then be passed along to our clients or kept as profit.[23]

Another possibility for Emergency Bridal to explore is referrals from local traditional wedding coordinators. Typically wedding coordinators will not complete wedding plans that have already begun; especially the time period we are targeting, which is halfway through the planning stage. Therefore, if there is a bride in a panic who needs extra help and contacts another local wedding coordinator who cannot or will not take on her event, they could refer her to Emergency Bridal. Our specialties in wedding completion and Week Of and Day Of services would be ideal for most brides in this situation.

6.0 Management Summary

Our owner and president, Rachel Evans, will do all of the wedding consulting and event planning. In addition, she will work with venues and vendors to establish relationships and promote her company. She is originally from Cleveland, Ohio, and has been in Des Moines since 2001. Ms. Evans will be graduating in December of 2004 from Des Moines University with a degree in entrepreneurship. She has worked in various aspects of the wedding industry for several years and has had experience selling bridal gowns and bridesmaid attire at the Jessica McClintock Boutique in Cleveland, inventorying and preparing linens for rental for Cleveland Party Rental, and banquet serving and working as a party manager at Windows On/Off Washington. Currently she has an internship in the sales department at the Norman K. Probstien Golf Course and Catering Center. In addition to her work experience, she has developed her time management skills through the Service Leadership Program, University Ambassadors, and held various leadership positions in Delta Gamma, all while achieving academic honors of Alpha Sigma Nu, Order of Omega, Beta Gamma Sigma, Golden Key, and Dean's list. Ms. Evans has done extensive research about wedding planning and is currently researching membership in the Association of Bridal Consultants, Association of Certified Professional Wedding Consultants, and International Special Events Society. She is very interested in combining her business skills with her creativity, planning abilities, and love of weddings to make her dreams of owning her own event planning business become a reality.

6.1 PERSONNEL PLAN Initially, Emergency Bridal LLC's event planning personnel will include only the owner. Rachel Evans will work full time. In the first three months most of her time will be spent building relationships with venues and organizing contracting agreements. After the business has established these relationships, much of her time will be spent planning weddings, while still continuing to network. She expects to work alone in the beginning, and as noted accept no salary for the first year and then will start receiving a salary of $10,525 and have a significant pay increase each year after due to increase in sales. She will be paid on a commission basis and receive 4 percent of each wedding's total package price.

With growth she intends to hire two part-time employees to help with R.S.V.P., day of and week of event services. The hire would ideally be a junior or senior in college or a college graduate with a background in marketing or communications and events services. For typical events there would be one part-time worker present, unless otherwise requested by the client, and that worker would be compensated $18 an hour.

Personnel Plan	2005	2006	2007	2008	2009
Rachel Evans	$10,525	$21,144	$26,343	$26,879	$26,958
Part-time employee(s) (20 hrs/week total)		18,720	19,420	19,820	20,740
Total people	1	2	2	2	2
Total payroll		$39,864	$45,763	$46,699	$47,698

1.0 Financial Plan

7.1 Pro forma Income Statement Year 1

Emergency Bridal, LLC
Pro forma Income Statement by Month
for the Year Ended December 31, 2005

	Jan	Feb	Mar	Apr	May	Jun	Jul	Aug	Sep	Oct	Nov	Dec	Total
Gross Sales	$35,550	$9,850	$8,100	$20,450	$32,300	$10,600	$9,850	$9,850	$8,100	$9,850	$10,600	$32,300	$197,400
Cost of Goods Sold	31,284	8,668	7,128	18,405	29,070	9,328	8,668	8,668	7,128	8,668	9,328	29,070	175,413
Vendor Commission (1.5%)	469	130	107	276	436	140	130	130	107	130	140	436	2,631
Gross Margin	**3,797**	**1,052**	**865**	**1,769**	**2,794**	**1,132**	**1,052**	**1,052**	**865**	**1,052**	**1,132**	**2,794**	**19,356**
Operating Expenses													
Travel	124	34	28	72	113	37	34	34	28	34	37	113	688
Telephone	142	39	32	82	129	42	39	39	32	39	42	129	786
Internet	20	20	20	20	20	20	20	20	20	20	20	20	240
Web Site	250	100	100	100	100	100	100	100	100	100	100	100	1,350
Insurance	10	10	10	10	10	10	10	10	10	10	10	10	120
Legal	1,500	150	150	150	150	150	150	150	150	150	150	150	3,150
Accounting			250	100									350
Licenses	150												150
Office Supply	457	50	50	50	50	50	50	50	50	50	50	50	1,007
Postage	37	37	37	37	37	37	37	37	37	37	37	37	444
Equipment	1,722												1,722
Miscellaneous	210												210
Total Operating Expenses	**4,622**	**440**	**677**	**621**	**609**	**446**	**440**	**440**	**427**	**440**	**446**	**609**	**10,217**
Selling & Administrative													
Advertising	300	100	100	100	100	100	100	100	100	100	100	100	1,400
Owner's Draw	1,877	520	428	1,104	1,744	560	520	520	428	520	560	1,744	10,525
Payroll Taxes*	260	73	60	153	242	78	73	73	60	73	78	242	1,465
Other													
Interest		58	57	57	56	55	54	53	52	52	51	50	595
Total Expenses	**7,059**	**1,191**	**1,322**	**2,035**	**2,751**	**1,239**	**1,187**	**1,186**	**1,067**	**1,185**	**1,235**	**2,745**	**24,202**
Total Operating Income	(3,262)	(139)	(457)	(266)	43	(107)	(135)	(134)	(202)	(133)	(103)	49	(4,846)
Other Income	100	146	147	149	148	148	167	179	192	206	216	221	2,021
Net Income (Loss) Before Taxes	(3,162)	7	(310)	(117)	191	41	32	45	(10)	73	113	270	(2,825)
Income Taxes (10%)	(317)	1	(31)	(12)	20	5	4	5	(1)	8	12	27	(279)
Net Income (Loss) After Taxes	**(3,479)**	**6**	**(341)**	**(129)**	**171**	**36**	**28**	**40**	**(11)**	**65**	**101**	**243**	**(3,104)**

*6.2% FICA on employee wages to $90,000 12.4% on self-employment to $90,000 1.45% medicare on wages 2.9% medicare on net earnings (self-employed)
6.2% FUTA on wages to $7,000

7.2 Pro forma Income Statement Year 2

Emergency Bridal, LLC
Pro forma Income Statement by Quarter
for the Year Ended December 31, 2006

	Quarter 1	Quarter 2	Quarter 3	Quarter 4	Total
Gross Sales	$108,702	$135,455	$81,909	$122,052	$448,118
Cost of Goods Sold	85,236	107,419	63,896	95,841	352,392
Vendor Commission (1.5%)	1,279	1,611	958	1,438	5,286
Gross Margin	**23,466**	**28,036**	**18,013**	**26,211**	**95,726**
Operating Expenses					
Travel	380	474	287	427	1,568
Telephone	435	542	328	488	1,792
Internet	60	60	60	60	240
Web Site	300	300	300	300	1,200
Insurance	31	31	31	31	125
Legal	450	450	450	450	1,800
Accounting	250	100			350
Licenses	75	75	75	75	300
Office & Supply	150	150	150	150	600
Postage	111	111	111	111	444
Payroll Expense	2,740	2,880	2,200	2,880	10,700
Miscellaneous					
Total Operating Expenses	**4,982**	**5,173**	**3,992**	**4,972**	**19,119**
Selling & Administrative					
Advertising	300	300	300	300	1,200
Owner's Draw	5,114	6,445	3,834	5,751	21,144
Payroll Taxes*	1,014	1,198	780	1,112	4,104
Interest	144	137	129	120	530
Other	215	205	234	299	953
Total Expenses	**11,769**	**13,458**	**9,269**	**12,554**	**47,050**
Total Operating Income	11,697	14,578	8,744	13,657	48,676
Other Income	215	205	234	299	953
Net Income (Loss) Before Taxes	11,912	14,783	8,978	13,956	49,629
Income Taxes (10%)	1,192	1,479	898	1,396	4,965
Less Tax Credit previous year	(279)				
Net Income (Loss) After Taxes	**10,441**	**13,304**	**8,080**	**12,560**	**44,385**

*6.2% FICA on employee wages to $90,000
12.4% on self-employment to $90,000
1.45% medicare on wages
2.9% medicare on net earnings (self-employed)
6.2% FUTA on wages to $7,000

7.3 Pro forma Income Statement Years 3 through 5

Emergency Bridal, LLC
Pro forma Income Statement by Year
for the Years Ended December 31, 2007, 2008, 2009

	2009	2008	2007
Gross Sales	$697,730	$684,730	$674,110
Cost of Goods Sold	539,158	537,583	526,853
Vendor Commission (1.5%)	8,087	8,064	7,903
Gross Margin	**150,485**	**139,083**	**139,354**
Operating Expenses			
Travel	2,442	2,397	2,359
Telephone	2,791	2,739	2,696
Internet	240	240	240
Web Site	1,200	1,200	1,200
Insurance	125	125	125
Legal	1,000	1,000	1,000
Accounting	350	350	350
Licenses	300	300	300
Office & Supply	600	600	600
Postage	456	456	456
Payroll Expense	20,740	19,820	19,420
Miscellaneous			
Total Operating Expenses	**30,244**	**29,227**	**28,746**
Selling & Administrative			
Advertising	1,200	1,200	1,200
Owner's Draw	26,958	26,879	26,343
Payroll Taxes*	6,215	6,078	5,956
Interest	71	178	397
Other			
Total Expenses	**64,688**	**63,562**	**62,642**
Total Operating Income	85,797	75,521	76,712
Other Income	812	535	317
Net Income (Loss) Before Taxes	86,609	76,056	77,029
Income Taxes (15%)	12,992	11,409	11,555
Less Tax Credit previous year			
Net Income (Loss) After Taxes	**73,617**	**64,647**	**65,474**

*6.2% FICA on employee wages to $90,000
12.4% on self-employment to $90,000
1.45% medicare on wages
2.9% medicare on net earnings (self-employed)
6.2% FUTA on wages to $7,000

7.4 Pro forma Cash Flows Years 1 through 5

Emergency Bridal, LLC
Pro forma Cash Flow by Year
for the Years Ended December 31

	2009	2008	2007	2006	2005
Net Income	73,617	64,647	65,474	44,385	(3,104)
Less increase in receivables	(1,896)	-0-	(32,504)	(53,106)	(47,208)
Plus increase in payables	55,216	54,048	76,235	73,107	52,279
Cash Flow from Operations	126,937	118,695	109,205	64,386	1,967
Cash Flow from Investing	-0-	-0-	-0-	-0-	-0-
Long Term Borrowing	-0-	-0-	-0-	-0-	10,000
Repayment of Long Term Debt	(2,275)	(2,122)	(1,979)	(1,846)	(1,582)
Cash Flow from Financing	(2,275)	(2,122)	(1,979)	(1,846)	8,418
Beginning Cash Balance	296,725	180,151	72,925	10,385	-0-
Ending Cash Balance	421,386	296,725	180,151	72,925	10,385

7.5 Pro forma Balance Sheet Years 1 through 5

Emergency Bridal, LLC
Pro forma Balance Sheet by Year
As of December 31

	2009	2008	2007	2006	2005
Current Assets					
Cash	421,386	296,725	180,151	72,925	10,385
Accounts Receivable	134,714	132,818	132,818	100,314	47,208
Long Term Assets*	-0-	-0-	-0-	-0-	-0-
Total Assets	556,100	429,543	312,969	173,239	57,593
Current Liabilities					
Accounts Payable	310,885	255,669	201,621	125,386	52,279
Long Term Liabilities					
Long Term Note	197	2,472	4,593	6,572	8,418
Owner's Equity					
Beginning Retained Earnings	171,402	106,755	41,281	(3,104)	-0-
Plus Net Income	73,617	64,647	65,474	44,385	(3,104)
Less Dividends	-0-	-0-	-0-	-0-	-0-
Ending Retained Earnings	245,019	171,402	106,755	41,281	(3,104)
Liabilities plus Owner's Equity	556,100	429,543	312,969	173,239	57,593

note: equipment and furniture is expensed in first year

7.6 Sales, Receivables, and Payables Projections

2005	Jan	Feb	Mar	Apr	May	Jun	Jul	Aug	Sep	Oct	Nov	Dec	Total
Number of Weddings	3	1	1	2	3	1	1	1	1	1	1	3	19
Package price	13,100	9,850	8,100	10,600	11,850	10,600	9,850	9,850	8,100	9,850	10,600	11,850	
	11,850			9,850	10,600							10,600	
	10,600				9,850							9,850	
Gross Sales	35,550	9,850	8,100	20,450	32,300	10,600	9,850	9,850	8,100	9,850	10,600	32,300	197,400
Cash Sales	7,110	1,970	1,620	4,090	6,460	2,120	1,970	1,970	1,620	1,970	2,120	6,460	39,480
Credit Sales	28,440	7,880	6,480	16,360	25,840	8,480	7,880	7,880	6,480	7,880	8,480	25,840	157,920
Collections			5,688	5,688	5,688	5,688	1,696	1,696	1,696	1,696	1,696	1,696	
			1,576	1,576	1,576	1,576	1,576	1,576	1,576	1,576	1,576	1,576	
				1,296	1,296	1,296	1,296	1,296	1,576	1,576	1,576	1,576	
					3,272	3,272	3,272	3,272	3,272	1,296	1,296	1,296	
						5,168	5,168	5,168	5,168	5,168	1,576	1,576	
Total Collections	0	0	7,264	8,560	11,832	17,000	13,008	13,008	13,288	11,312	7,720	7,720	110,712
Total Accounts Receivable	28,440	36,320	35,536	43,336	57,344	48,824	43,696	38,568	31,760	28,328	29,088	47,208	47,208
Purchases	31,284	8,668	7,128	18,405	29,070	9,328	8,668	8,668	7,128	8,668	9,328	29,070	175,413
Payments	4,693	4,693	4,693	4,693	4,693	4,693	1,300	1,300	1,300	1,300	1,300	1,300	
		1,300	1,300	1,300	1,300	1,300	1,300	1,300	1,300	1,300	1,300	1,300	
			1,069	1,069	1,069	1,069	1,069	1,069	1,069	1,069	1,069	1,069	
				2,761	2,761	2,761	2,761	2,761	2,761	1,300	1,300	1,300	
					4,361	4,361	4,361	4,361	4,361	4,361	1,399	1,399	
						1,399	1,399	1,399	1,399	1,399	1,399	4,361	
Total Payments	4,693	5,993	7,062	9,823	14,183	15,582	12,190	12,190	12,190	10,730	7,768	10,730	123,134
Total Accounts Payable	26,591	29,266	29,332	37,914	52,801	46,547	43,025	39,503	34,441	32,379	33,939	52,279	52,279

Income from RSVP Services

				2006				2007	2008	2009
				Qtr1	Qtr2	Qtr3	Qtr4	Year3	Year4	Year5
RSVP	Fee	200	RSVP	4,322	5,375	3,449	4,882	24,410	25,080	26,580
200 guests	per call	0.90	Week Of	5,000	5,500	4,400	4,600	32,000	33,100	35,600
200+ guests	per call	0.80	Day Of	4,230	4,480	2,610	5,570	30,800	27,800	35,200

2006	Jan	Feb	Mar	Apr	May	Jun	Jul	Aug	Sep	Oct	Nov	Dec	Total
Number of Weddings	4	2	3	4	4	3	2	2	3	2	3	5	37
Package prices	13,100	11,850	10,600	13,100	11,850	10,600	10,600	11,850	13,100	13,100	11,850	10,600	
	9,850	8,100	13,100	9,850	8,100	13,100	9,850	8,100	9,850	9,850	8,100	13,100	
	10,600		9,850	11,850	10,600	9,850			8,100		11,850	10,600	
	8,100			8,100	13,100							9,850	
												8,100	
Gross Sales	41,650	19,950	33,550	42,900	43,650	33,550	20,450	19,950	31,050	22,950	31,800	52,250	393,700
Cash Sales	8,330	3,990	6,710	8,580	8,730	6,710	4,090	3,990	6,210	4,590	6,360	10,450	78,740
Credit Sales	33,320	15,960	26,840	34,320	34,920	26,840	16,360	15,960	24,840	18,360	25,440	41,800	314,960
Collections	1,696	1,696	1,696	1,696	6,864	6,864	6,864	6,864	6,864	4,968	4,968	4,968	
	5,168	5,168	5,168	5,168	5,168	6,984	6,984	6,984	6,984	6,984	3,672	3,672	
	1,576	6,664	6,664	6,664	6,664	6,664	5,368	5,368	5,368	5,368	5,368	5,088	
	1,296	1,296	3,192	3,192	3,192	3,192	3,192	3,272	3,272	3,272	3,272	3,272	
	1,576	1,576	1,576	5,368	5,368	5,368	5,368	5,368	3,192	3,192	3,192	3,192	
Total Collections	11,312	16,400	18,296	22,088	27,256	29,072	27,776	27,356	25,680	23,784	20,472	20,192	270,184
Total Accounts Receivable	77,546	77,106	85,650	97,882	105,546	103,314	91,898	80,002	79,162	73,738	78,706	100,314	100,314
Purchases	37,485	17,556	30,195	38,610	39,285	29,524	17,996	17,955	27,945	20,196	28,620	47,025	352,392
Payments	5,623	5,623	5,623	5,623	5,623	5,623	2,699	2,699	2,699	2,699	2,699	2,699	
	1,300	2,633	2,633	2,633	2,633	2,633	2,633	2,693	2,693	2,693	2,693	2,693	
	1,069	1,069	4,529	4,529	4,529	4,529	4,529	4,529	4,192	4,192	4,192	4,192	
	1,300	1,300	1,300	5,792	5,792	5,792	5,792	5,792	5,792	3,029	3,029	3,029	
	1,399	1,399	1,399	1,399	5,893	5,893	5,893	5,893	5,893	5,893	4,293	4,293	
	4,361	4,361	4,361	4,361	4,361	4,429	4,429	4,429	4,429	4,429	4,429	7,054	
Total Payments	15,052	16,385	19,845	24,337	28,830	28,898	25,975	26,035	25,697	22,935	21,335	23,961	279,285
Total Accounts Payable	74,712	75,883	86,233	100,506	110,961	111,587	103,608	95,528	97,776	95,037	102,322	125,386	125,386

2007	Jan	Feb	Mar	Apr	May	Jun	Jul	Aug	Sep	Oct	Nov	Dec	Total
Number of Weddings	7	4	3	7	7	3	3	3	4	3	3	7	54
Package Prices	13,100	13,100	11,850	13,100	13,100	13,100	13,100	11,850	11,850	11,850	11,850	13,100	
	11,850	11,850	10,600	11,850	11,850	11,850	11,850	10,600	10,600	10,600	10,600	11,850	
	10,600	10600	9,850	10,600	10,600	10,600	10600	9850	9,850	9850	9,850	10,600	
	9,850	9850		9,850	9,850				8100			9,850	
	8,100			8100	8100							8,100	
	11,850			11,850	11,850							11,850	
	9,850			9,850	9,850							9,850	
Gross Sales	75,200	45,400	32,300	75,200	75,200	35,550	35,550	32,300	40,400	32,300	32,300	75,200	586,900
Cash Sales	15,040	9,080	6,460	15,040	15,040	7,110	7,110	6,460	8,080	6,460	6,460	15,040	117,380
Credit Sales	60,160	36,320	25,840	60,160	60,160	28,440	28,440	25,840	32,320	25,840	25,840	60,160	469,520
Collections	4,968	4,968	7,264	7,264	7,264	7,264	7,264	5,688	5,688	5,688	5,688	5,688	
	3,672	3,672	3,672	5,168	5,168	5,168	5,168	5,168	5,168	5,168	5,168	5,168	
	5,088	5,088	5,088	5,088	12,032	12,032	12,032	12,032	12,032	6,464	6,464	6,464	
	8,360	8,360	8,360	8,360	8,360	12,032	12,032	12,032	12,032	12,032	5,168	5,168	
	3,192	12,032	12,032	12,032	12,032	12,032	5,688	5,688	5,688	5,688	5,688	5,168	
Total Collections	25,280	34,120	36,416	37,912	44,856	48,528	42,184	40,608	40,608	35,040	28,176	27,656	441,384
Total Accounts Receivable	135,194	102,514	89,738	122,562	115,618	80,226	86,570	85,546	92,026	91,114	97,978	132,818	132,818
Purchases	67,680	40,860	29,070	67,680	67,680	31,284	31,995	29,070	36,360	29,070	28,424	67,680	526,853
Payments	10,152	10,152	10,152	10,152	10,152	10,152	4,799	4,799	4,799	4,799	4,799	4,799	
	2,693	6,129	6,129	6,129	6,129	6,129	6,129	4,361	4,361	4,361	4,361	4,361	
	4,192	4,192	4,361	4,361	4,361	4,361	4,361	4,361	5,454	5,454	5,454	5,454	
	3,029	3,029	3,029	10,152	10,152	10,152	10,152	10,152	10,152	4,361	4,361	4,361	
	4,293	4,293	4,293	4,293	10,152	10,152	10,152	10,152	10,152	10,152	4,264	4,264	
	7,054	7,054	7,054	7,054	7,054	4,693	4,693	4,693	4,693	4,693	4,693	10,152	
Total Payments	31,413	34,849	35,018	42,141	48,000	45,639	40,286	38,518	39,611	33,820	27,932	33,391	450,618
Total Accounts Payable	161,653	167,664	161,716	187,255	206,935	192,580	184,289	174,841	171,590	166,840	167,332	201,621	201,621

2008	Jan	Feb	Mar	Apr	May	Jun	Jul	Aug	Sep	Oct	Nov	Dec	Total
Number of Weddings	7	5	3	7	7	3	3	3	4	3	3	7	55
Package prices	13,100	13,100	11,850	13,100	13,100	13,100	13,100	11,850	11,850	11,850	11,850	13,100	
	11,850	11,850	10,600	11,850	11,850	11,850	11,850	10,600	10,600	10,600	10,600	11,850	
	10,600	10600	9,850	10,600	10,600	10,600	10600	9850	9,850	9850	9,850	10,600	
	9,850	9850		9,850	9,850				8100			9,850	
	8,100	11850		8100	8100							8,100	
	11,850			11,850	11,850							11,850	
	9,850			9,850	9,850							9,850	
Gross sales	75,200	57,250	32,300	75,200	75,200	35,550	35,550	32,300	40,400	32,300	32,300	75,200	598,750
Cash Sales	15,040	11,450	6,460	15,040	15,040	7,110	7,110	6,460	8,080	6,460	6,460	15,040	119,750
Credit Sales	60,160	45,800	25,840	60,160	60,160	28,440	28,440	25,840	32,320	25,840	25,840	60,160	479,000
Collections	12,032	12,032	12,032	12,032	12,032	12,032	12,032	12,032	12,032	12,032	5,168	5,168	
	5,168	12,032	12,032	12,032	12,032	12,032	5,688	5,688	5,688	5,688	5,688	5,168	
	6,464	6,464	9,160	9,160	9,160	9,160	9,160	5,688	5,688	5,688	5,688	5,688	
	5,168	5,168	5,168	5,168	5,168	5,168	5,168	5,168	5,168	5,168	5,168	5,168	
	5,168	5,168	5,168	5,168	12,032	12,032	12,032	12,032	12,032	6,464	6,464	6,464	
Total Collections	34,000	40,864	43,560	43,560	50,424	50,424	44,080	40,608	40,608	35,040	28,176	27,656	479,000
Total Accounts Receivable	158,978	163,914	146,194	162,794	172,530	150,546	134,906	120,138	111,850	102,650	100,314	132,818	132,818
Purchases	67,680	51,525	28,424	67,680	67,680	31,995	31,995	28,424	36,360	29,070	29,070	67,680	537,583
Payments	10,152	10,152	10,152	10,152	10,152	10,152	4,799	4,799	4,799	4,799	4,799	4,799	
	4,361	7,729	7,729	7,729	7,729	7,729	7,729	4,264	4,264	4,264	4,264	4,264	
	5,454	5,454	4,264	4,264	4,264	4,264	4,264	4,264	5,454	5,454	5,454	5,454	
	4,361	4,361	4,361	10,152	10,152	10,152	10,152	10,152	10,152	4,361	4,361	4,361	
	4,264	4,264	4,264	4,264	10,152	10,152	10,152	10,152	10,152	10,152	4,361	4,361	
	10,152	10,152	10,152	10,152	10,152	4,799	4,799	4,799	4,799	4,799	4,799	10,152	
Total Payments	38,743	42,111	40,920	46,712	52,600	47,248	41,895	38,430	39,620	33,829	28,037	33,390	483,535
Total Accounts Payable	230,558	239,972	227,476	248,444	263,524	248,271	238,371	228,365	225,105	220,346	221,379	255,669	255,669

2009	Jan	Feb	Mar	Apr	May	Jun	Jul	Aug	Sep	Oct	Nov	Dec	Total
Number of Weddings	7	5	3	7	7	3	3	3	4	3	3	7	55
Package Prices	13,100	13,100	11,850	13,100	13,100	13,100	13,100	11,850	11,850	11,850	11,850	13,100	
	11,850	11850	10,600	11,850	11,850	1,850	11850	10600	10,600	10600	10,600	11,850	
	10,600	10600	9850	10,600	10,600	10600	10600	9850	9850	9850	9850	10,600	
	9,850	9850		9850	9850			11850	8100			9,850	
	8,100	11,850		8,100	7,850							8,100	
	11,850			11,850	11,850							11,850	
	9,850			9,850	9,850							9,850	
Gross Sales	75,200	57,250	32,300	75,200	74,950	25,550	35,550	44,150	40,400	32,300	32,300	75,200	600,350
Cash Sales	15,040	11,450	6,460	15,040	14,990	5,110	7,110	8,830	8,080	6,460	6,460	15,040	120,070
Credit Sales	60,160	45,800	25,840	60,160	59,960	20,440	28,440	35,320	32,320	25,840	25,840	60,160	480,280
Collections	5,168	5,168	5,168	5,168	5,168	5,168	5,168	5,168	7,064	7,064	7,064	7,064	
	5,168	5,168	5,168	5,168	12,032	12,032	12,032	12,032	12,032	6,464	6,464	6,464	
	12,032	12,032	12,032	12,032	12,032	11,992	11,992	11,992	11,992	11,992	5,168	5,168	
	5,168	12,032	12,032	12,032	12,032	12,032	4,088	4,088	4,088	4,088	4,088	5,168	
	6,464	6,464	9,160	9,160	9,160	9,160	9,160	5,688	5,688	5,688	5,688	5,688	
Total Collections	34,000	40,864	43,560	43,560	50,424	50,384	42,440	38,968	40,864	35,296	28,472	29,552	478,384
Total Accounts Receivable	158,978	163,914	146,194	162,794	172,330	142,386	128,386	124,738	116,194	106,738	104,106	134,714	134,714
Purchases	67,680	51,525	29,070	67,680	67,455	22,484	31,995	39,735	36,360	29,070	28,424	67,680	539,158
Payments	10,152	10,152	10,152	10,152	10,152	10,152	4,799	4,799	4,799	4,799	4,799	4,799	
	4,264	7,729	7,729	7,729	7,729	7,729	7,729	5,960	5,960	5,960	5,960	5,960	
	5,454	5,454	4,361	4,361	4,361	4,361	4,361	4,361	5,454	5,454	5,454	5,454	
	4,361	4,361	4,361	10,152	10,152	10,152	10,152	10,152	10,152	4,361	4,361	4,361	
	4,361	4,361	4,361	4,361	10,118	10,118	10,118	10,118	10,118	10,118	4,264	4,264	
	10,152	10,152	10,152	10,152	10,152	3,373	3,373	3,373	3,373	3,373	3,373	10,152	
Total Payments	38,744	42,209	41,116	46,907	52,664	45,885	40,532	38,763	39,856	34,065	28,211	34,990	483,942
Total Accounts Payable	284,605	293,921	281,875	302,648	317,439	294,038	285,501	286,473	282,977	277,982	278,195	310,885	310,885

8.0 Appendix

8-A START-UP SUMMARY TABLE

START-UP SUMMARY

Office Equipment		
Computer	$1,172.00	
Software		
Quick Books	$200.00	
Wedding Software	$30.00	
Zip Drive	$150.00	
Phone	$70.00	
Subtotal		$1,622.00
Office Furniture		
File Cabinet	$100.00	
Subtotal		$100.00
Office Supplies		
Stationery	$200.00	
Misc. Supplies	$50.00	
Copy Paper	$25.00	
Ink Cartridge	$50.00	
Zip Disks	$25.00	
3.5 Floppy	$7.00	
Binders	$100.00	
Subtotal		$457.00
Total		$2,179.00
Start-Up Expenses		
Equip., Supp., Furn.		$2,179.00
Business License		$150.00
Phone Line Install (2)		$92.00
Voice Mail		$11.00
Promotion		$250.00
Legal		$1,500.00
Insurance		$10.00
Online Service		$20.00
Subtotal		$4,212.00
Misc. Expenses (5%)		$210.00
Total Start-Up Expense		**$4,422.00**
Funding		
Bank Loan		$10,000.00
Investment Needed		$4,422.00
Total Reserve		$5,578.00

8-B SAMPLE AVERAGE WEDDING BUDGET

ITEM		$ Amount	% of Total
Apparel	Bridal Gown	800	
	Headpiece, Veil	175	
	Alterations, Accessories	315	
	Groom's Tux Rental	100	
	Apparel Sub-Total	**1390**	**7%**
Rings	Engagement Ring	3000	
	Wedding Rings	1000	
	Rings Subtotal	**4000**	**20%**
Music	Ceremony Music	150	
	DJ at Reception	400	
	Music Subtotal	**650**	**3%**
Miscellaneous	Marriage License	30	
	Attendants Gifts	320	
	Other Stuff	450	
	Misc. Subtotal	**800**	**4%**
Ceremony Site and Officiate		200	1%
Flowers		900	5%
Cake		525	3%
Reception/Catering		8,400	42%
Photography		1,500	8%
Videography		1,000	5%
Invitations		390	2%
Limo/Transportation		190	1%
TOTAL		**$19,945**	**100%**

Postscript

Rachel answered the judges' questions on assumptions without missing a beat. In the process of researching for her plan, her grasp of the industry and potential was noted by one of the planners she interviewed. Rachel ended up taking a job with one of the premier wedding planners in her home town. The plan is still there and ready should she need it, and if she does, her own experience and contacts in the industry and community will strengthen her situation.

Full Business Plan

Blue Water Boatworks, Inc.

Blue Water Boatworks is a well done plan, which falls between the full business plan and the operational plan. While the plan generally follows the outline from Chapter 8, Table 8.3, it shows how plans are adjusted based on the thinking of the entrepreneur and the purpose the plan serves. In putting this plan together, JP wanted to demonstrate to potential customers and bankers (the plan was going to be funded from his own capital and a line of credit from a bank) that he had thought through the business. For that reason he included a section on the "operational plan." This gave a general overview of operations, but fell short of the level of detail you would see in a true operational plan, which would be used as an internal "how-to" book for the business.

Note also that JP did a *very* detailed section on critical risks. This was done to assure the banker that JP did recognize the problems of a start-up and had taken steps to anticipate the problems and solve them if they appeared. JP did this plan as he was just finishing his undergraduate degree in entrepreneurship at Saint Louis University, and he realized that his youth and lack of experience in owning and running a business (or paying back a loan) were going to be major factors for the banker. It is also important to note what is *not* present, namely the balance sheet in the financials. From the standpoint of the banker, since the loan would have to be paid back from cash flow, the balance sheet was seen as JP's concern, not the bank's. Leaving off a balance sheet is not recommended as a "best practice," but in this case it did not cause a problem. You can find out how JP and BWB did in the postscript at the end of the plan.

Blue Water Boatworks, Inc.
St. Louis, Missouri
J. P. Keating—President & CEO

Table of Contents

I. EXECUTIVE SUMMARY

Blue Water Boatworks Inc. is a watercraft detailing and cleaning service in the St. Louis area catering strictly to watercraft dealers and marinas. Blue Water Boatworks (BWB) will specialize in servicing recreational fiberglass and aluminum watercraft; bass boats, cruisers, yachts, etc., for the purposes of resale. Monthly cleaning services will be offered to marinas as well. Operations are scheduled to begin in January 2004.

BWB offers on-site only detailing and cleaning and will go to the customer. By conducting business this way, BWB expects to reduce its own liability and keep costs low for the customer. BWB will seek to enter into contracts with marinas and boat dealerships in the St. Louis area to service their sales inventory or customers' boats.

Based upon the financial projections, it is estimated that $175,000 is required to begin operations successfully. $145,000 is needed from bank loans and $30,000 will be invested by the principal owner. The estimated interest rate on the $145,000 loan is projected to be about 8 percent. The funds will be used for start-up and three month's operating expenses.

MARKET POTENTIAL There are over 20 boat dealerships in the St. Louis area as well as over a dozen marinas. However, BWB will focus on just a handful of dealers and marinas in the first few years. BWB plans to contract with two large dealerships and one marina during the first year of operation. An increase of one to two additional dealers and one marina per year is the projected growth rate of the company after the first year. Service for a total of four dealers and two marinas is projected in years 3 and 4.

DISTINCTIVE COMPETENCE BWB will provide a much needed and reliable service to the watercraft dealer and marina owner. BWB can offer the boat dealer a cost savings in personnel (wages, insurance, benefits), materials, facilities and any other costs associated with having a cleaning shop or department. BWB can be contracted on an as-needed basis if services are needed for only a few boats or services can be contracted for dozens of boats. BWB is flexible and will be able to accommodate the needs of large and small dealers and marinas.

There is no operation comparable to Blue Water Boatworks in the area. There are detailing and clean-up shops in most dealerships and a few marinas, as well as one or two small mobile detailing operations in the area. However, dealers and marinas can have difficulties with employees or can incur excess costs related to personnel. The other small operations in the area deal specifically with retail customers—individual boat owners. BWB will deal strictly on a commercial basis, working mainly as a wholesale service provider.

FINANCIAL SUMMARY Based on detailed financial projections, Blue Water Boatworks will require debt financing and is expected to repay the loan in four years. The first operating profit is projected to occur in the third month of operations. Future growth is expected to be funded through generated earnings.

II. Company Description

The goal of BWB is to offer clients a valuable service at a reasonable cost while helping them become more profitable. Professionally detailed boats can return higher profits for the dealer; increased returns could range from 1 percent to over 100 percent depending on the original condition of the boat. It is also known that clients want their merchandise ready to sell as soon as possible so quick turnaround is a necessity. BWB can offer the dealer several options. For example, if the dealer is large enough and has a high turnover rate of inventory, BWB can assign a crew to its location on a somewhat permanent basis to handle the backlog of work. Dealers which also have repair shops or storage facilities could offer cleaning and detailing services to their customers as an additional service. A quick profit can be made by marking up BWB's service.

BWB can offer marinas cleaning services for their customers. Monthly cleaning services can be offered by BWB which in turn could be sold by the marina for a profit. No personnel and scheduling issues for the marina owner, just pure profit every month.

BWB will strive to offer its customer the highest quality service with the greatest amount of professionalism. Attention to detail and the needs of the customer will always come first.

III. Description of Services

BWB is an entirely mobile operation able to provide services to dealers and marinas in the St. Louis metropolitan area. There are three types of services we provide:

- Detailing
- Marina service
- General cleaning

Detailing is the most expensive service we offer because it requires the most time and materials to provide. Everything on the boat is meticulously cleaned and polished to ready it for resale by the dealer. Boat dealers need to present their inventory in flawless condition to make higher profits on the sale. Detailing will normally include:

- Hull cleaning
- Interior cleaning and detailing
- Hull waxing and sealing
- Carpet and upholstery cleaning
- Chrome and stainless polishing
- Plastic and glass maintenance
- Sealing
- Bilge cleaning
- Canvas and vinyl cleaning
- Cleaning and treatment of fenders
- Sealing
- Engine cleaning

The price for this type of service would be broken down as follows:

> Open bow boats from 15′–26′ will cost $350.
>
> Cabin boats with lengths up to 25′ will be $450.
>
> Anything over that length would have to be inspected by BWB management to determine a price. These prices were formulated barring any extenuating circumstances which could include severe oxidation, severe stains, etc.

A general cleaning can also be used by dealers to maintain their inventory. This type of service would consist of a rinsing, drying, and wiping down boats which may have collected dust or light dirt from sitting on the dealer's lot for a few weeks. This service is not as expensive as a detail because a lesser amount of materials and labor are used. The price for this type of service would be approximately $80 per boat. A modified general cleaning service may also be offered. This would be offered to dealers who own storage facilities or repair shops. Dealers could offer this service to customers who wanted to get their boat cleaned after a repair or before the boat was winterized. Some other services could be added to the general cleaning like waxing the hull, cleaning and sealing vinyl or canvas, cleaning fenders, etc. The pricing for this service would have to be determined by the job.

A marina service consists of a monthly maintenance contract with a marina. This type of service is similar to a general cleaning service except that it is done for an entire marina. The marina owner would charge the boat owner a specific price for this service, and BWB will provide the service. The marina owner is able to charge whatever he or she wants over the wholesale price and realize another revenue source. A crew would most likely be permanently assigned to the marina to handle this service because a job of this nature can take up to a month to complete. The services included are:

- Hull cleaning to waterline
- Plastic and glass maintenance
- Wipe down of all hardware

This type of service will be charged by the foot. The wholesale price will be $2.75 per foot.

All of the prices listed are tentative and can be negotiated. For example, volume discounts can be offered for dealer services. Prices may also increase due to rising materials costs.

It is projected that that 60 percent of BWB business will be detailing, 35 percent will be marina servicing, and 5 percent will be general cleaning services.

All of the cleaning products used by BWB (boat washes, polishes, waxes, sealers, plastic cleaners, etc.) are premium brand, environmentally friendly and are specifically formulated for a marine environment.

IV. Marketing Plan

BWB will be a strictly commercial operation, marketing only to boat dealers and marinas. There are over a dozen marinas and over twenty boat dealers in the St. Louis metropolitan area. However, only a few dealers and a few marinas will be targeted during start-up. The main target market is boat dealers, with marinas being second. Dealers are in need of this service because their boats need to be in exceptional condition in order to increase sales and achieve acceptable profits. Having in-house cleaning crews and clean up shops can be expensive for a dealer to operate. BWB provides value for the dealers by alleviating their employment burden and the costs associated with maintaining an in-house cleaning facility. BWB can provide boat detailing services on an on-call basis or on a longer-term contractual basis. For example, smaller dealers may only require BWB on-call services for a few boats a week. Larger dealers who need detailing services on a dozen or more boats a week may need a dedicated crew for an extended period of time. BWB will have 15 employees to serve clients, so someone will always be able to support a dealership.

Marinas will also be able to benefit from the services of BWB. BWB will offer cleaning services which marinas can resell to their customers. Basic cleaning services, which include exterior washing and cleaning and drying, will be the standard offering. This type of service allows boat owners to enjoy their boats on the weekends and not spend hours cleaning them every time they come out to use them. We can offer this service at a wholesale price to marina owners which they can mark up as high as they like and then sell for retail. They too will benefit from the convenience of not employing an in-house cleaning crew.

There is no other way to market this service except through the use of personal sales calls. Dealers need their inventory processed and ready to go as soon as possible so they can resell and make a profit. BWB will have to prove to them that our service is exceptional and can provide them with what they need.

A Web site may also be established in Year 2 for scheduling and customer relationship management purposes.

The owner of a local St. Louis dealership has expressed a great interest in this venture. He has agreed to aid in the acquisition of other clients (mainly other St. Louis dealers he is friendly with as well as some marina owners) if the services of BWB prove to be valuable to his business. A local Marina owner has also expressed an interest in using BWB as well as agreeing to assist in organizing additional clients. Both will be key to the success of this venture. Even though these individuals can assist in opening the door for new business, it will still be necessary to make personal visits and sales calls to dealers and marinas to sell the services and inform them of the benefits of working with BWB. If the dealer or marina can benefit from our services, we would then discuss any special needs they may have such as volume discount possibilities, or reliability. The best way to market our services will be to give a free detail to the dealer to show the quality of work that can be done by BWB. The dealers must feel that they are benefiting from using our service as opposed to having an on-site shop. If the dealer is satisfied and still interested in our services, pricing and terms for contracts would then be discussed.

The aforementioned dealership and marina will be launch customers in this venture; promoting our business by word of mouth. Since they have commanding positions in the boating industry in St. Louis, their opinions are very valuable.

BWB will focus on quality, dependability and personal service. The owner/manager of the company will visit the job sites on a daily basis and communicate with customers. Any problems or questions that customers may have will be handled by the owner personally.

Due to the seasonality of the boating industry in St. Louis, it is inevitable that business will see a drop in the month of September and will not recover until March. BWB will not head south. The customers in St. Louis will still need our services. Marinas will still be serviced, and dealers will still need some detailing work done on their inventory. Dealers will also need our services when they present their inventory at boat shows in the fall and winter.

V. Operational Plan

BWB will be open for customer appointments Monday through Friday from 8:00 A.M.–5:00 P.M. However, there may be some instances where hours may vary; such as if there is work to be done for a boat show or similar event. BWB will be closed for most major holidays.

Depending on the needs of the customer, appointments may not be feasible. For example, if a dealer has a steady flow of boats coming through the dealership, it may be possible to permanently assign a crew to that location. The same would work for marinas. Since there is going to be a large number of boats to be cleaned in no particular order, it would be more feasible to just assign a crew to the marina. However, small dealers will more likely call on an as needed basis. In this instance BWB would have to react rather than "ride a circuit."

BWB will have six full-time cleaners which will be split into three crews. Two part-time employees will be hired to assist the full-time crews. If BWB works with two large dealerships, one crew will be assigned to each dealership. The third crew will be assigned to the marina. One part-time worker will be sent to the marina, and the other part-time worker will be sent to the dealership with the largest amount of work to be done. The marina crew can also act as a support crew for the other two crews in the case of excessive work orders at a dealership. Finally, the owner/manager of BWB will be traveling between dealerships and the marinas to supervise the three crews, communicate with dealers and marina owners, and handle any job estimates or special requests from clients. The owner will manage the daily operation of the company, be the main salesperson, and will also service all accounts. As business increases, it may be necessary to hire additional staff to service accounts.

Each day crew members will be given assignments and sent to the respective job site. Crews will always be in communication with the main office and manager through cellular phones. Once the crew reaches the job site, contact will be made with a representative of the dealership or marina to determine what special needs he or she may have. If there are any problems or questions, the crew will call the office or the manager directly and resolve the problem. Once the situation is assessed, the crew will go to work. After the service is completed, billing statements will be mailed to the dealer or marina manager.

The approximate time to properly detail and clean a boat will vary. It could take from two hours to two days depending on the size and condition of the boat. A fair estimate can be three to four hours for most boats. Marina servicing can take weeks because of the number of boats at a single location. However, the time to rinse and dry a boat at a marina may take only one half of an hour with three people working on it at once. A marina with 150 boats will take approximately 9–10 days to complete. The marina crews could then assist the other two dealership crews.

BWB employees will not be permitted to operate or transport any of the watercraft which they will be servicing due to insurance reasons. For example, they will not be permitted to move the boat to a better location for servicing or operate a boat lift on which the boat is moored. The dealer or marina owners will have to do this themselves. BWB will not be responsible for hauling the boat out of the water for a complete detail job and will also not be responsible for cleaning any part of the dock surrounding the watercraft if moored at a marina; unless of course there was a mess left by the crew. In the case of inclement weather such as snow, rain, or below freezing temperatures, services may have to be postponed until a later date at marinas. However, dealers will have less of a problem with this. BWB will be able to detail boats under 35 feet in length in almost any weather because a portable, heated, inflatable tent will be used. This tent can be completely set up and taken down in under 10 minutes. Dealers just have to pull the boat in the tent and pull it out when the service is completed.

BWB is dedicated to the preservation of the marine environment and will only use environmentally friendly products such as citrus based cleansers and detergents. Workers will also obey all laws and regulations set forth by the state regarding the preservation of the environment. For example, there will be no illegal dumping of any harsh cleaning agent such as bleach or acid into the water. Employees working at marinas will be monitored by the manager or assistant manager of BWB as well as the owner of the marina. Any employee found breaking these laws will be terminated. Our employees will also be required to obey all safety precautions necessary when working with special cleaning agents and around a marine environment. There are a few safety precautions regulated by OSHA and the Longshoreman's Act. For example, there will be no smoking near the watercraft, and everyone will wear a personal flotation device when working on a dock or on a boat. BWB will supply employees with all necessary sun screens and uniforms.

A uniform supply company such as Aramark or Cintas will be used to provide uniforms for the workers. Uniforms will consist of a blue long- or short-sleeved shirt, and navy blue pants or shorts. Insulated coats will also be supplied in the fall and winter. There will be no markings referring to BWB on the uniforms. The only markings will be the workers' name tapes. All of the vehicles operated by BWB will also be free of any distinguishing markings; just plain white minivans. The reason for the generic uniforms is to create a low profile; making the appearance that our workers may actually be the dealer's or marina's workers. Thus the customers have no idea that the people cleaning their boats are actually outside contractors. Cleaning supplies will need to be ordered in large quantities, so orders will be placed with the manufacturers or wholesalers of these products. Office supplies, equipment, and vehicles will be purchased from local dealers. Orders for cleaning supplies will be placed during the third week of every month.

Fees are determined on the attached rate sheet. Payment can be made by cash, check, or money order. Customers can be billed later for service or will be able to pay at the time of service. If customers are billed, then payment will be due 14 days after services are rendered.

VI. Management and Organization

BWB will be set up as a close corporation under Missouri State law and a subchapter S corporation under U.S. federal law. The close corporation does not require a board of directors, bylaws, annual stockholder meetings, or more than one stockholder. However, the close corporation does provide the same type of protection to the small business owner as a general business corporation does for large corporations.

The subchapter S corporation will be chosen strictly for tax purposes. The subchapter S corporation will eliminate the corporate tax to which subchapter C corporations are subject.

BWB will have a total of 9 employees in the first year with an increase to 15 in year two. The owner will be the president/CEO/manager of the entire operation. His résumé as well as those of potential employees can be furnished upon request.

All of the potential employees being considered have all had multiple years of experience in detailing. The experienced boat detailers will train the other employees on detailing boats. One of the boat detailers will be hired as the assistant manager and will be responsible for directing the training of other employees. This employee will require some management experience in the past. The part-time workers will be high school or college students and will be hired between the months of March and September; however, part-time workers may be retained for the entire year if necessary.

The six full time employees will be split into three crews. The part-time workers will be assigned to the crews which have the largest workload during the day. The owner anticipates a yearly salary of $45,000 and an anticipated 5 percent per year increase thereafter. The assistant manager will receive a salary of $27,000 per year with an anticipated 3 to 4 percent increase thereafter. All other full-time employees will make $11.00 per hour, and part-time employees will receive $8.00 per hour initially and an anticipated annual increase of 3 percent per year thereafter. A bonus plan may also be established. All full-time employees will receive medical benefits. An answering service will be used to handle any incoming calls. The manager or the assistant manager will then handle all of the calls taken by the answering service.

VII. Exit Strategy

There has been no specific exit strategy planned. This venture is being planned as a long-term, possibly family business with plans for growth and expansion. However, there has been no succession strategy planned because the owner is neither married nor has any children. It will be determined at a later date who will take control of the business in the event that the owner dies or is incapacitated. It has been discussed that if there are any shareholders in the company that they will share control with the assistant manager. However, no definitive plans have been made concerning this issue.

VIII. Critical Risks

There are several details of this business plan which may cause concern. These issues are discussed in the following paragraphs. The following points will be evaluated: financing, seasonality of the business and the economy, competition, and employee issues.

BWB will be a customer-financed venture. Meaning, without certain launch customers signed on prior to start-up, there will be no start-up. The dealership and marina mentioned in the marketing plan have offered to assist in compiling a consortium of boat dealers and marinas in the St. Louis area to secure an adequate amount of business for BWB. Assistance and experience in the industry will be an invaluable asset to the start-up and future of BWB. The dealership owner has also offered to assist in securing a business loan for this venture and has agreed to enter into a long-term contract with BWB to service the inventory if BWB does launch.

Another important factor to consider in the financing of this venture is cash flow. If cash flow problems arise in the future, it may be necessary to take several different courses of action. If BWB is not able to raise extra financing itself, it may be necessary to enter into prepayment contracts (discounted services based on an estimated number of cleanings) with dealers and marina owners, enter into joint ventures with customers, or even sell parts of the company. These issues will be addressed as they arise.

Seasonality will be a major issue for BWB. It is obvious that business will drop severely in the month of October and will not recover until March. However, as stated earlier, BWB will not head to other areas of the country in the winter months. Our services will still be needed in St. Louis. Revenues will not be strong in these months, but dealers and marinas will still need our services. Another issue which also deals with seasonally is inclement weather and flooding. Flooding in the area would hurt marina servicing in the short term. However, after the floods are over, there may be a boom in the marina servicing business as well as some dealer servicing. Opportunities may also arise where a considerable amount of retail business could be done after a flood. If this would occur and it was a feasible plan, BWB could temporarily operate as a retail watercraft cleaning and detailing business; servicing private individuals' boats as well as servicing wholesale customers. (There have been no and there will be no estimates factored in this plan concerning retail business.)

The boating industry is a luxury industry. If the economy is waning, luxury industries will see declines in business. This will severely harm the dealer servicing part of BWB. However, there is an upside. People will have to keep their boats in good condition in order for them to hold their value or if they wish to sell them. Therefore, BWB may have to focus on some retail servicing again. If retail servicing becomes a necessity in the future, it would be done through the dealer or marina. As explained earlier in this plan, the dealer or marina would be the main contact for any retail servicing. BWB would be the subcontractor.

The next issue to address is that of competition. This business is incredibly easy to copy. Labor does not have to be very skilled, the equipment used is readily available, this operation does not require an inordinate amount of start-up capital, and quality and service is easily copied as well. The way BWB is set up makes it somewhat obscure to potential competition. First, there will be very little advertisement; direct calls to marina owners and boat dealerships only. There will be no markings on any of the uniforms or equipment stating what the company does. BWB will be somewhat "invisible" to potential competition for a period of time.

Entering into exclusive contracts with marinas and boat dealers will also help protect BWB from competition for a short time. However, when competitors begin to offer the same service for the same price with the same quality and service, sustaining business will become much more difficult. If BWB is the first to do this and can secure the necessary clients, the competition will have a difficult time breaking into the market. The key to staying ahead will be to constantly improve and innovate the way boats are cleaned and serviced.

Competition from exiting employees can also be somewhat protected against. Having all employees sign noncompete contracts will offer some protection to BWB. However, we feel that if the employees are paid fairly, given their benefits for free, and are made happy, this type of competition will be minimal. Employee issues can include human resource issues, employee mistakes, accidents, behavior, and performance.

The type of work that BWB does can at times be grueling, dirty, and tough. This would normally hurt the human resource plan because of high employee turnover. However, by paying the full-time workers approximately $22,000 per year with a possible bonus at year end and annual increases, benefits, and paid vacation time, BWB will be able to keep most employees for a long period of time.

Employee mistakes and accidents could also cause problems for the business. For example, accidents with the vehicles, customers' boats, equipment, accidents which would cause personal injury to the employee (such as falls), and property damage could severely hinder business operations, strain cash flow, decrease productivity, and hurt quality. Therefore, a considerable amount of insurance has been taken out on this venture, expenses for safety equipment were factored into the monthly equipment costs, and minor damage costs were factored into monthly miscellaneous costs. Some examples of employee mistakes could include damage to the exterior or interior of the boat; using the wrong types of solvents, cleaners, etc.; damaging glass, plastic, or chrome; etc. These costs would be paid out of miscellaneous expenses or if the damage is too severe, from an insurance claim.

Employee behavior and performance are also important factors to the success of this venture. If employees do not perform properly, then, as stated earlier, quality, productivity, and cash flow will suffer, therefore losing business. Employees will be expected to act accordingly when servicing clients' boats; if not, they will be reprimanded and, if necessary, terminated. Specific policies have not yet been finalized and are not included in this plan. However, BWB will adhere to all laws pertaining to employee issues. The merchandise BWB will be working on can cost from a few thousand to over one million dollars, a significantly valuable commodity for the client. There will be an acting supervisor at each job when the manager/owner is not present. The supervisors have not yet been determined but will be chosen later based on performance and experience.

Due to the fact that BWB will have a small number of clients, supervision of the crews will be manageable. The marinas and dealerships targeted are located relatively close to one another, which equates to relatively easy access to all of the crews for the owner/manager. If problems arise, it may be necessary for the assistant manager to handle some of the duties of the manager.

These are only a few foreseen problems; more may possibly arise. However, it is difficult to determine what problem will occur when. The above solutions are only options which may be exercised in the event of a future problem.

IX. Financial Plan

The following statements have been reviewed by an independent CPA. They provide financial information for years 1 through 4 for BWB.

SALES It has been estimated that the average price for a marina service is $70 per boat. A marina of 150 boats would yield revenues of $10,500 per month. Detailing services were calculated at 80 percent open bow ($350 per) and 20 percent cabin boats under 26 feet in length ($450 per). There were no boats over 26 feet taken into account for this model because pricing would depend on the type of boat and the condition. No price increases will take effect until after year 4.

COLLECTIONS Payments for services will be paid within 14 days after services rendered unless otherwise determined beforehand between BWB and the customer. Any additional fees incurred for services rendered will also be paid immediately upon completion of services unless otherwise discussed.

DISBURSEMENTS Accounts payable will be paid the first week of the following month. All orders for supplies will be done the third week of every month. Wages will be paid every two weeks.

EXPENSES Expenses for the first year will include telephone, mobile telephone, rent, utilities, fuel, advertising, supplies, benefits, and accounting and legal fees. Insurance costs will be $25,000 per year for the first year with rates increasing as more employees and vehicles are added. (Insurance quotes were provided by an independent insurance agency.) Salary expense is $3,750 per month for the first year with an increase of 5 percent thereafter. The full-time employees will receive $11/hr. and the part-time employees will receive a wage of $8.00/hr. for the first year and an increase of 3 percent thereafter. The assistant manager will receive a monthly salary of $2,250 with an increase of 3 percent per year thereafter. Vehicle and equipment expenses will be incurred in the first month of operations. Three used GMC Safari mini vans will be purchased for $11,000 each. These will be used as the servicing vehicles. One used GMC truck will be purchased for $9,000. This vehicle will be used by the manager/owner to travel between sites to supervise operations and communicate with customers. The truck can also be used as a service vehicle if a van is temporarily out of service. All of these vehicles will be purchased with less than 40,000 miles on each on them. An extended warranty can be purchased for $720 per vehicle which extends the service warranty to 100,000 miles. Vehicles will not be leased because of the restrictive mileage requirements. Vehicles will not be purchased new because of the limited amount of capital available and the fact that the value of new vehicles drops approximately 20 percent after the purchase. If used vehicles are purchased, it is possible to recover nearly all the investment if the business needs to liquidate. (This information was supplied by a local GMC dealership.) A down payment of $10,000 for the four vehicles is needed. The vehicles will be financed for 8 percent through GMAC. Two more vans will be purchased in year 2. All equipment (power washers, generators, buffers, brushes, sponges, etc.) will be purchased new for $12,000. All equipment will be purchased in sets of four; one set for every van as well as a spare set if any equipment breaks. A list of all equipment needed is listed in the attachments section. Each inflatable tent will cost $10,000. Two tents will be purchased in the first year. All office equipment, such as desks, a computer, equipment lockers, etc., has already been obtained and is not reflected in the financial statements. Also there were no volume discounts taken into consideration for this model.

The loan is scheduled to be retired by late 2007. A monthly loan expense of $3,539 was calculated on an 8 percent interest rate for $145,000.

An estimated breakeven point is at about 75 boats per month (80% @ $300 and 20% @ $400) plus a marina service of over 150 boats; totaling 225 per month. However, variable costs such as fuel and supplies expense will change the breakeven point.

The financial statements for year one are based on sales for two large dealerships, one small dealership, and one marina of 150 boats. Year 2 will show an increase of one large dealership and one marina of 150 boats. (A large dealership is a dealership with sales of over $2.5 million.) There has been an estimated increase of $50 per boat in year 3 based on rising supply and labor costs in year 3. There will be a total of four dealers and two marinas that will be serviced. There will be no more clients added until after year 4.

X. Financial Projection

Projected Start-Up Costs for Blue Water Boatworks

Down Payment for Four Vehicles	$10,000
Equipment for Three Vehicles plus Spare	$12,000
Two Inflatable Tents	$20,000
Legal Fees (Set-Up, Incorporation, and Contracts)	$1,000
Three Months Operating Expenses	$109,090
Reserve for Taxes and Misc.	$20,000
Expenses TOTAL	$172.090
Extra Cash	$2,910

RATE SHEET:

Marina service is $70 per boat (minimum 25 boats)

General cleaning—$80

Open bow to 25'—$350 per boat

Cabin Boats under 26 ft. in length—$450 per.

Cabin Boats over 26 ft. in length—inspection required

Postscript

JP presented his plan to the owner of a local boat dealership, who was so impressed that he took JP to his competitors to create a consortium to employ JP, and then to his own banker. The boat dealer informed the banker that JP would get the exclusive contract for boat detailing from several local dealerships, *if* the banker approved the loan. On the strength of the dealer's recommendation (and the consortium's willingness to sign long-term contracts), JP's professionalism, *and* the plan, the banker approved the loan.

BWB did not start, however. The one critical risk JP did not anticipate was that he would find the woman of his dreams, propose, and have her accept. After she accepted and discovered she would be losing her new husband to a multiyear effort to get Blue Water Boatworks going as a profitable business, she gave JP an ultimatum—her or the business. He had a good idea in BWB and a good head on his shoulders, and he understood the four bottom lines. He chose marriage, but used his knowledge as an auditor at Boeing to work with teams involved in developing new technologies and products. To them, JP is the rare finance person who "gets" corporate entrepreneurship and innovation.

ANALYSIS FOR YEAR 1 ONLY

Projected Cash Flow Statement for Blue Water Boatworks Year 1

Month	Start-Up Costs	Jan-04	Feb-04	Mar-04	Apr-04	May-04
Beginning Cash Balance			148,750.07	154,993.47	168,401.51	187,195.68
Total Sales		$ 18,500.00	$ 27,750.00	$ 44,400.00	$ 55,500.00	$ 44,400.00
		50	75	120	150	120
Marina Servicing (150 Boats estimated @ $70 per)		$ 10,500.00	$ 10,500.00	$ 10,500.00	$ 10,500.00	$ 10,500.00
Net Sales:		$ 29,000.00	$ 38,250.00	$ 54,900.00	$ 66,000.00	$ 54,900.00
Loan:		**145,000.00**				
Owner's Equity		**$30,000**				
Total Cash Available:		204,000.00	187,000.07	209,893.47	234,401.51	242,095.68
Disbursements:						
Operating Expenses:						
Telephone		50.00	60.00	100.00	100.00	100.00
Cellular & Paging		150.00	150.00	300.00	300.00	300.00
Rent		1,000.00	1,000.00	1,000.00	1,000.00	1,000.00
Utilities		200.00	200.00	200.00	200.00	200.00
Fuel		500.00	500.00	800.00	800.00	800.00
Advertising		200.00	200.00	200.00	200.00	200.00
Accounting Fees		500.00			500.00	
Legal Fees		1,000.00	200.00	200.00	200.00	200.00
Insurance		6,250.00			6,250.00	
Wages		12,750.00	12,750.00	12,750.00	12,750.00	12,750.00
Owner's Salary		3,750.00	3,750.00	3,750.00	3,750.00	3,750.00
Payroll Taxes				4,300.00		
Benefits		3,000.00	3,000.00	3,000.00	3,000.00	3,000.00
Miscellaneous (answering service, repairs, uniforms, etc.)		2,000.00	2,000.00	2,000.00	2,000.00	2,000.00
Supplies		1,000.00	1,000.00	2,000.00	2,500.00	2,500.00
Equipment		12,000.00	200.00	200.00	200.00	200.00
Loan Payments 8%		**3,539.00**	**3,539.00**	**3,539.00**	**3,539.00**	**3,539.00**
Expense for Tents		20,000.00				
Bad Debt Expense (1%)		290.00	382.50	549.00	660.00	549.00
Total Disbursements		68,179.00	28,931.50	34,888.00	37,949.00	31,088.00
Total Cash Flow		(39,179.00)	9,318.50	20,012.00	28,051.00	23,812.00
Tax Reserve		(12,929.07)	3,075.11	6,603.96	9,256.83	7,857.96
Net Cash Flow		(26,249.93)	6,243.40	13,408.04	18,794.17	15,954.04
Ending Cash Balance		***148,750.07***	***154,993.47***	***168,401.51***	***187,195.68***	***203,149.72***
350 80%						
450 20%						
80						
$2.75/ft						
	($3,539.87)					
60% Detail						
35% Marina						
5% GC						

Jun-04	Jul-04	Aug-04	Sep-04	Oct-04	Nov-04	Dec-04	Totals
203,149.72	223,585.39	235,351.93	251,305.97	259,470.59	255,397.66	250,603.81	
$ 55,500.00	$ 44,400.00	$ 44,400.00	$ 37,000.00	$ 18,500.00	$ 11,100.00	$ 11,100.00	$ 412,550.00
150	120	120	100	50	30	30	
$ 10,500.00	$ 10,500.00	$ 10,500.00	$ 10,500.00	$ 10,500.00	$ 10,500.00	$ 10,500.00	$ 126,000.00
$ 66,000.00	$ 54,900.00	$ 54,900.00	$ 47,500.00	$ 29,000.00	$ 21,600.00	$ 21,600.00	$ 538,550.00
							145,000.00
269,149.72	278,485.39	290,251.93	298,805.97	288,470.59	276,997.66	272,203.81	
100.00	100.00	100.00	100.00	50.00	50.00	50.00	960.00
300.00	300.00	300.00	300.00	150.00	150.00	150.00	2,850.00
1,000.00	1,000.00	1,000.00	1,000.00	1,000.00	1,000.00	1,000.00	12,000.00
200.00	200.00	200.00	200.00	200.00	200.00	200.00	2,400.00
800.00	800.00	800.00	800.00	500.00	500.00	500.00	8,100.00
200.00	200.00	200.00	200.00	200.00	200.00	200.00	2,400.00
						500	1,500.00
200.00	200.00	200.00	200.00	200.00	200.00	200.00	3,200.00
	6,250.00			6250.00			25,000.00
12,750.00	12,750.00	12,750.00	12,750.00	12,750.00	12,750.00	12,750.00	153,000.00
3,750.00	3,750.00	3,750.00	3,750.00	3,750.00	3,750.00	3,750.00	45,000.00
4,300.00			4300.00			4300.00	17,200.00
3,000.00	3,000.00	3,000.00	3,000.00	3,000.00	3,000.00	3,000.00	36,000.00
2,000.00	2,000.00	2,000.00	2,000.00	2,000.00	2,000.00	2,000.00	24,000.00
2,500.00	2,500.00	2,500.00	2,500.00	1,000.00	1,000.00	1,000.00	22,000.00
200.00	200.00	200.00	200.00	200.00	200.00	200.00	14,200.00
3,539.00	**3,539.00**	**3,539.00**	**3,539.00**	**3,539.00**	**3,539.00**	**3,539.00**	42,468.00
660.00	549.00	549.00	475.00	290.00	216.00	216.00	5,385.50
35,499.00	37,338.00	31,088.00	35,314.00	35,079.00	28,755.00	33,555.00	437,663.50
30,501.00	17,562.00	23,812.00	12,186.00	(6,079.00)	(7,155.00)	(11,955.00)	100,886.50
10,065.33	5,795.46	7,857.96	4,021.38	(2,006.07)	(2,361.15)	(3,945.15)	33,292.55
20,435.67	11,766.54	15,954.04	8,164.62	(4,072.93)	(4,793.85)	(8,009.85)	67,593.96
223,585.39	***235,351.93***	***251,305.97***	***259,470.59***	***255,397.66***	***250,603.81***	***242,593.96***	

ANALYSIS FOR YEAR 1 ONLY

Income Statement for Blue Water Boatworks Year 1

	Jan-04	Feb-04	Mar-04	Apr-04	May-04
Net Sales	29000	38250	54900	66000	54900
Materials	2000	2000	2000	2000	2000
Gross Profit	**27000**	**36250**	**52900**	**64000**	**52900**
Expenses					
Payroll Expense	12750	12750	12750	12750	12750
Salary Expense	3750	3750	3750	3750	3750
Rent/Utilities/Telephone/Cellular	2400	2400	2400	2400	2400
Ins., Legal and Acct	7750	200	200	6950	200
Benefits/	3000	3000	3000	3000	3000
Office & Supplies	500	500	500	500	500
Equipment Expense	32000	200	200	200	200
Maintenance/Misc	2000	2000	2000	2000	2000
Auto Expense, Fuel	10500	1610	1610	1610	1610
Depreciation	930	930	930	930	930
Interest Expense	**967**	950	932	915	897
TOTAL	**76547**	**28290**	**28272**	**35005**	**28237**
PROFIT/LOSS	−49547	7960	24628	28995	24663
Income Taxes (33%)	−16350	2627	8127	9568	8139
NET PROFIT	**−33196**	**5334**	**16501**	**19427**	**16524**

Jun-04	Jul-04	Aug-04	Sep-04	Oct-04	Nov-04	Dec-04
66000	54900	54900	47500	29000	21600	21600
2000	2000	2000	2000	2000	2000	2000
64000	**52900**	**52900**	**45500**	**27000**	**19600**	**19600**
12750	12750	12750	12750	12750	12750	12750
3750	3750	3750	3750	3750	3750	3750
2400	2400	2400	2400	2400	2400	2400
200	6450	200	200	6450	200	700
3000	3000	3000	3000	3000	3000	3000
500	500	500	500	500	500	500
200	200	200	200	200	200	200
2000	2000	2000	2000	2000	2000	2000
1610	1610	1610	1610	1610	1610	1610
930	930	930	930	930	930	930
862	844	826	808	790	772	753
28202	**34434**	**28166**	**28148**	**34380**	**28112**	**28593**
35798	18466	24734	17352	−7380	−8512	−8993
11813	6094	8162	5726	−2435	−2809	−2968
23985	**12372**	**16572**	**11626**	**−4945**	**−5703**	**−6025**
		69375.15	189393.59	238556.18	238401.41	

ANALYSIS FOR YEAR 2 ONLY

Projected Cash Flow Statement for Blue Water Boatworks Year 2

Month	Jan-05	Feb-05	Mar-05	Apr-05	May-05
Beginning Cash Balance	242,593.96	232,752.46	253,776.46	279,353.96	334,462.96
Total Sales	$ 27,750.00	$ 40,700.00	$ 64,750.00	$ 77,700.00	$ 64,750.00
	75	110	175	210	175
Marina Servicing (300 Boats estimated @ $70 per)	$ 21,000.00	$ 21,000.00	$ 21,000.00	$ 21,000.00	$ 21,000.00
Net Sales:	$ 48,750.00	$ 61,700.00	$ 85,750.00	$ 98,700.00	$ 85,750.00
Loan:					
Total Cash Available:	291,343.96	294,452.46	339,526.46	378,053.96	420,212.96
Disbursements:					
Operating Expenses:					
Telephone	75.00	80.00	125.00	125.00	125.00
Cellular & Paging	200.00	400.00	600.00	600.00	600.00
Rent	1,000.00	1,000.00	1,000.00	1,000.00	1,000.00
Utilities	300.00	300.00	300.00	300.00	300.00
Fuel	500.00	500.00	800.00	800.00	800.00
Advertising	300.00	300.00	300.00	300.00	300.00
Accounting Fees	750.00				
Legal Fees	1,000.00	300.00	300.00	300.00	300.00
Insurance			10,000.00		
Wages	21,500.00	21,500.00	21,500.00	21,500.00	21,500.00
Owner's Salary	3,940.00	3,940.00	3,940.00	3,940.00	3,940.00
Payroll Taxes			6,711.00		
Benefits	3,500.00	3,500.00	3,500.00	3,500.00	3,500.00
Miscellaneous (answering service, repairs, uniforms, etc.)	3,000.00	3,000.00	3,000.00	3,000.00	3,000.00
Supplies (80% Cleaning Supplies, 20% Office Supplies)	1,500.00	1,500.00	3,500.00	3,500.00	3,500.00
Equipment	7,000.00	200.00	200.00	200.00	200.00
Loan Payments	3,539.00	**3,539.00**	**3,539.00**	**3,539.00**	**3,539.00**
Expense for Tents	10,000.00				
Bad Debt Expense (1%)	487.50	617.00	857.50	987.00	857.50
Total Disbursements	58,591.50	40,676.00	60,172.50	43,591.00	43,461.50
Total Cash Flow	(9,841.50)	21,024.00	25,577.50	55,109.00	42,288.50
Tax Reserve	(3,247.70)	6,937.92	8,440.58	18,185.97	13,955.21
Net Cash Flow	(6,593.81)	14,086.08	17,136.93	36,923.03	28,333.30
Ending Cash Balance	***232,752.46***	***253,776.46***	***279,353.96***	***334,462.96***	***376,751.46***

Jun-05	Jul-05	Aug-05	Sep-05	Oct-05	Nov-05	Dec-05	Totals
376,751.46	415,149.46	456,687.96	498,976.46	515,396.46	523,304.96	520,724.46	
$ 77,700.00	$ 64,750.00	$ 64,750.00	$ 55,500.00	$ 27,750.00	$ 16,650.00	$ 16,650.00	$ 599,400.00
210	175	175	150	75	45	45	
$ 21,000.00	$ 21,000.00	$ 21,000.00	$ 21,000.00	$ 21,000.00	$ 21,000.00	$ 21,000.00	$ 252,000.00
$ 98,700.00	$ 85,750.00	$ 85,750.00	$ 76,500.00	$ 48,750.00	$ 37,650.00	$ 37,650.00	$ 851,400.00
475,451.46	500,899.46	542,437.96	575,476.46	564,146.46	560,954.96	558,374.46	
125.00	125.00	125.00	125.00	75.00	75.00	75.00	1,255.00
600.00	600.00	600.00	600.00	200.00	200.00	200.00	5,400.00
1,000.00	1,000.00	1,000.00	1,000.00	1,000.00	1,000.00	1,000.00	12,000.00
300.00	300.00	300.00	300.00	300.00	300.00	300.00	3,600.00
800.00	800.00	800.00	800.00	500.00	500.00	500.00	8,100.00
300.00	300.00	300.00	300.00	300.00	300.00	300.00	3,600.00
	750.00					750	2,250.00
300.00	300.00	300.00	300.00	300.00	300.00	300.00	4,300.00
10,000.00			10,000.00			10,000.00	40,000.00
21,500.00	21,500.00	21,500.00	21,500.00	21,500.00	21,500.00	21,500.00	258,000.00
3,940.00	3,940.00	3,940.00	3,940.00	3,940.00	3,940.00	3,940.00	47,280.00
6,711.00			6711.00			6711.00	26,844.00
3,500.00	3,500.00	3,500.00	3,500.00	3,500.00	3,500.00	3,500.00	42,000.00
3,000.00	3,000.00	3,000.00	3,000.00	3,000.00	3,000.00	3,000.00	36,000.00
3,500.00	3,500.00	3,500.00	3,500.00	2,000.00	1,500.00	1,500.00	32,500.00
200.00	200.00	200.00	200.00	200.00	200.00	200.00	9,200.00
3,539.00	**3,539.00**	**3,539.00**	**3,539.00**	**3,539.00**	**3,539.00**	**3,539.00**	
987.00	857.50	857.50	765.00	487.50	376.50	376.50	8,514.00
60,302.00	44,211.50	43,461.50	60,080.00	40,841.50	40,230.50	57,691.50	593,311.00
38,398.00	41,538.50	42,288.50	16,420.00	7,908.50	(2,580.50)	(20,041.50)	258,089.00
12,671.34	13,707.71	13,955.21	5,418.60	2,609.81	(851.57)	(6,613.70)	85,169.37
25,726.66	27,830.80	28,333.30	11,001.40	5,298.70	(1,728.94)	(13,427.81)	172,919.63
415,149.46	***456,687.96***	***498,976.46***	***515,396.46***	***523,304.96***	***520,724.46***	***500,682.96***	

ANALYSIS FOR YEAR 2 ONLY

Income Statement for Blue Water Boatworks Year 2

	Jan-05	Feb-05	Mar-05	Apr-05	May-05
Net Sales	48750	61700	85750	98700	85750
Materials	3000	3000	3000	3000	3000
Gross Profit	**45750**	**58700**	**82750**	**95700**	**82750**
Expenses					
Payroll Expense	21500	21500	21500	21500	21500
Salary Expense	3940	3940	3940	3940	3940
Rent/Utilities/Telephone/Cellular	2725	2725	2725	2725	2725
Ins., Legal and Acct	1750	300	10300	300	300
Benefits/	3500	3500	3500	3500	3500
Office & Supplies	500	500	500	500	500
Equipment Expense	7000	200	200	200	200
Maintenance/Misc	3000	3000	3000	3000	3000
Auto Expense, Fuel	2800	2550	2550	2550	2550
Depreciation	1382	1382	1382	1382	1382
Interest Expense	735	716	697	678	659
TOTAL	**48832**	**40313**	**50294**	**40275**	**40256**
PROFIT/LOSS	−3082	18387	32456	55425	42494
Income Taxes (33%)	−1017	6068	10710	18290	14023
NET PROFIT	**−2065**	**12319**	**21746**	**37135**	**28471**

Jun-05	Jul-05	Aug-05	Sep-05	Oct-05	Nov-05	Dec-05
98700	85750	85750	76500	48750	37650	37650
3000	3000	3000	3000	3000	3000	3000
95700	**82750**	**82750**	**73500**	**45750**	**34650**	**34650**
21500	21500	21500	21500	21500	21500	21500
3940	3940	3940	3940	3940	3940	3940
2725	2725	2725	2725	2725	2725	2725
10300	1050	300	10300	300	300	10300
3500	3500	3500	3500	3500	3500	3500
500	500	500	500	500	500	500
200	200	200	200	200	200	200
3000	3000	3000	3000	3000	3000	3000
2550	2550	2550	2550	2550	2550	2550
1382	1382	1382	1382	1382	1382	1382
640	620	601	581	562	542	522
50237	**40967**	**40198**	**50178**	**40159**	**40139**	**50119**
45463	41783	42552	23322	5591	−5489	−15469
15003	13788	14042	7696	1845	−1811	−5105
30460	**27994**	**28510**	**15625**	**3746**	**−3877**	**−10364**

ANALYSIS FOR YEAR 3 ONLY

Projected Cash Flow Statement for Blue Water Boatworks Year 3

Month	Jan-06	Feb-06	Mar-06	Apr-06	May-06
Beginning Cash Balance	500,682.96	497,958.96	511,559.96	532,071.96	573,530.96
Total Sales	$ 31,500.00	$ 46,200.00	$ 73,500.00	$ 88,200.00	$ 73,500.00
	75	110	175	210	175
Marina Servicing (300 Boats estimated @ $70 per)	$ 21,000.00	$ 21,000.00	$ 21,000.00	$ 21,000.00	$ 21,000.00
Net Sales:	$ 52,500.00	$ 67,200.00	$ 94,500.00	$ 109,200.00	$ 94,500.00
Loan:					
Total Cash Available:	553,182.96	565,158.96	606,059.96	641,271.96	668,030.96
Disbursements:					
Operating Expenses:					
Telephone	125.00	125.00	125.00	125.00	125.00
Cellular & Paging	600.00	600.00	600.00	600.00	600.00
Rent	1,500.00	1,500.00	1,500.00	1,500.00	1,500.00
Utilities	500.00	500.00	500.00	500.00	500.00
Fuel	900.00	900.00	900.00	900.00	900.00
Advertising	300.00	300.00	300.00	300.00	300.00
Accounting Fees	750.00				
Legal Fees	1,000.00	300.00	300.00	300.00	300.00
Insurance			10,000.00		
Wages	22,145.00	22,145.00	22,145.00	22,145.00	22,145.00
Owner's Salary	4,140.00	4,140.00	4,140.00	4,140.00	4,140.00
Payroll Taxes			6,711.00		
Benefits	3,500.00	3,500.00	3,500.00	3,500.00	3,500.00
Miscellaneous (answering service, repairs, uniforms, etc.)	3,000.00	3,000.00	3,000.00	3,000.00	3,000.00
Supplies (80% Cleaning Supplies, 20% Office Supplies)	4,000.00	4,000.00	4,000.00	4,000.00	4,000.00
Equipment	7,000.00	200.00	200.00	200.00	200.00
Vehicle Expense	1,700.00	1,700.00	1,700.00	1,700.00	1,700.00
Loan Payment	**3,539.00**	**3,539.00**	**3,539.00**	**3,539.00**	**3,539.00**
Expense for Tents					
Bad Debt Expense (1%)	525.00	672.00	945.00	1,092.00	945.00
Tax Reserve		6,478.00	9,883.00	20,200.00	15,378.00
Total Disbursements	55,224.00	53,599.00	73,988.00	67,741.00	62,772.00
Net Cash Flow	(2,724.00)	13,601.00	20,512.00	41,459.00	31,728.00
Ending Cash Balance	***497,958.96***	***511,559.96***	***532,071.96***	***573,530.96***	***605,258.96***

Jun-06	Jul-06	Aug-06	Sep-06	Oct-06	Nov-06	Dec-06	Totals
605,258.96	635,521.96	666,727.96	698,436.96	711,984.96	715,834.96	708,886.96	
$ 88,200.00	$ 73,500.00	$ 73,500.00	$ 63,000.00	$ 31,500.00	$ 18,900.00	$ 18,900.00	$ 680,400.00
210	175	175	150	75	45	45	
$ 21,000.00	$ 21,000.00	$ 21,000.00	$ 21,000.00	$ 21,000.00	$ 21,000.00	$ 21,000.00	$ 252,000.00
$ 109,200.00	$ 94,500.00	$ 94,500.00	$ 84,000.00	$ 52,500.00	$ 39,900.00	$ 39,900.00	$ 932,400.00
714,458.96	730,021.96	761,227.96	782,436.96	764,484.96	755,734.96	748,786.96	
125.00	125.00	125.00	125.00	125.00	125.00	125.00	1,500.00
600.00	600.00	600.00	600.00	600.00	600.00	600.00	7,200.00
1,500.00	1,500.00	1,500.00	1,500.00	1,500.00	1,500.00	1,500.00	18,000.00
500.00	500.00	500.00	500.00	500.00	500.00	500.00	6,000.00
900.00	900.00	900.00	900.00	900.00	900.00	900.00	10,800.00
300.00	300.00	300.00	300.00	300.00	300.00	300.00	3,600.00
	750.00					750	2,250.00
300.00	300.00	300.00	300.00	300.00	300.00	300.00	4,300.00
10,000.00			10,000.00			10,000.00	40,000.00
22,145.00	22,145.00	22,145.00	22,145.00	22,145.00	22,145.00	22,145.00	265,740.00
4,140.00	4,140.00	4,140.00	4,140.00	4,140.00	4,140.00	4,140.00	49,680.00
6,711.00			6711.00		6,711.00	26,844.00	
3,500.00	3,500.00	3,500.00	3,500.00	3,500.00	3,500.00	3,500.00	42,000.00
3,000.00	3,000.00	3,000.00	3,000.00	3,000.00	3,000.00	3,000.00	36,000.00
4,000.00	4,000.00	4,000.00	4,000.00	4,000.00	4,000.00	4,000.00	48,000.00
200.00	200.00	200.00	200.00	200.00	200.00	200.00	9,200.00
1,700.00	1,700.00	1,700.00	1,700.00	1,700.00	1,700.00	1,700.00	20,400.00
3,539.00	**3,539.00**	**3,539.00**	**3,539.00**	**3,539.00**	**3,539.00**	**3,539.00**	42,468.00
1,092.00	945.00	945.00	840.00	525.00	399.00	399.00	9,324.00
14,685.00	15,150.00	15397	6452	1676			
78,937.00	63,294.00	62,791.00	70,452.00	48,650.00	46,848.00	64,309.00	748,605.00
30,263.00	31,206.00	31,709.00	13,548.00	3,850.00	(6,948.00)	(24,409.00)	183,795.00
635,521.96	***666,727.96***	***698,436.96***	***711,984.96***	***715,834.96***	***708,886.96***	***684,477.96***	

ANALYSIS FOR YEAR 3 ONLY

Income Statement for Blue Water Boatworks Year 3

	Jan-06	Feb-06	Mar-06	Apr-06	May-06
Net Sales	52500	67200	94500	109200	94500
Materials	3500	3500	3500	3500	3500
Gross Profit	**49000**	**63700**	**91000**	**105700**	**91000**
Expenses					
Payroll Expense	22145	22145	22145	22145	22145
Salary Expense	4140	4140	4140	4140	4140
Rent/Utilities/Telephone/Cellular	2725	2725	2725	2725	2725
Ins., Legal and Acct	1750	300	10300	300	300
Benefits/	3500	3500	3500	3500	3500
Office & Supplies	500	500	500	500	500
Equipment Expense	7000	200	200	200	200
Maintenance/Misc	3000	3000	3000	3000	3000
Auto Expense, Fuel	2600	2600	2600	2600	2600
Depreciation	1382	1382	1382	1382	1382
Interest Expense	502	481	461	441	420
TOTAL	**49244**	**40973**	**50953**	**40933**	**40912**
PROFIT/LOSS	−244	22727	40047	64768	50088
Income Taxes (33%)	−80	7500	13216	21373	16529
NET PROFIT	**−163**	**15227**	**26831**	**43394**	**33559**

Jun-06	Jul-06	Aug-06	Sep-06	Oct-06	Nov-06	Dec-06
109200	95400	95400	84000	52500	39900	39900
3500	3500	3500	3500	3500	3500	3500
105700	**91900**	**91900**	**80500**	**49000**	**36400**	**36400**
22145	22145	22145	22145	22145	22145	22145
4140	4140	4140	4140	4140	4140	4140
2725	2725	2725	2725	2725	2725	2725
10300	1050	300	10300	300	300	10300
3500	3500	3500	3500	3500	3500	3500
500	500	500	500	500	500	500
200	200	200	200	200	200	200
3000	3000	3000	3000	3000	3000	3000
2600	2600	2600	2600	2600	2600	2600
1382	1382	1382	1382	1382	1382	1382
399	378	357	336	314	293	271
50891	**41620**	**40849**	**50828**	**40806**	**40785**	**50763**
54809	50280	51051	29672	8194	−4385	−14363
18087	16592	16847	9792	2704	−1447	−4740
36722	**33688**	**34204**	**19880**	**5490**	**−2938**	**−9623**

ANALYSIS FOR YEAR 4 ONLY

Projected Cash Flow Statement for Blue Water Boatworks Year 4

Month	Jan-07	Feb-07	Mar-07	Apr-07	May-07
Beginning Cash Balance	684,477.96	686,937.96	700,119.96	718,584.96	759,625.96
Total Sales	$ 31,500.00	$ 46,200.00	$ 73,500.00	$ 88,200.00	$ 73,500.00
	75	110	175	210	175
Marina Servicing (300 Boats estimated @ $70 per)	$ 21,000.00	$ 21,000.00	$ 21,000.00	$ 21,000.00	$ 21,000.00
Net Sales:	$ 52,500.00	$ 67,200.00	$ 94,500.00	$ 109,200.00	$ 94,500.00
Loan:					
Total Cash Available:	736,977.96	754,137.96	794,619.96	827,784.96	854,125.96
Disbursements:					
Operating Expenses:					
Telephone	125.00	125.00	125.00	125.00	125.00
Cellular & Paging	700.00	700.00	700.00	700.00	700.00
Rent	1,500.00	1,500.00	1,500.00	1,500.00	1,500.00
Utilities	500.00	500.00	500.00	500.00	500.00
Fuel	1,000.00	1,000.00	1,000.00	1,000.00	1,000.00
Advertising	300.00	300.00	300.00	300.00	300.00
Accounting Fees	750.00				
Legal Fees	1,000.00	300.00	300.00	300.00	300.00
Insurance			12,000.00		
Wages	22,809.00	22,809.00	22,809.00	22,809.00	22,809.00
Owner's Salary	4,340.00	4,340.00	4,340.00	4,340.00	4,340.00
Payroll Taxes			7,142.00		
Benefits	3,500.00	3,500.00	3,500.00	3,500.00	3,500.00
Miscellaneous (answering service, repairs, uniforms, etc.)	3,000.00	3,000.00	3,000.00	3,000.00	3,000.00
Supplies (80% Cleaning Supplies, 20% Office Supplies)	4,500.00	4,500.00	4,500.00	4,500.00	4,500.00
Equipment	300.00	300.00	300.00	300.00	300.00
Vehicle Expense	610.00	610.00	610.00	610.00	610.00
Loan Payment	**3,539.00**	**3,539.00**	**3,539.00**	**3,539.00**	**3,539.00**
Expense for Tents					
Bad Debt Expense (1%)	525.00	672.00	945.00	1,092.00	945.00
Tax Reserve	1,042.00	6,323.00	8,925.00	20,044.00	15,242.00
Total Disbursements	50,040.00	54,018.00	76,035.00	68,159.00	63,210.00
Net Cash Flow	2,460.00	13,182.00	18,465.00	41,041.00	31,290.00
Ending Cash Balance	***686,937.96***	***700,119.96***	***718,584.96***	***759,625.96***	***790,915.96***

Jun-07	Jul-07	Aug-07	Sep-07	Oct-07	Nov-07	Dec-07	Totals
790,915.96	819,131.96	849,919.96	881,209.96	892,710.96	896,142.96	888,620.96	
$ 88,200.00	$ 73,500.00	$ 73,500.00	$ 63,000.00	$ 31,500.00	$ 18,900.00	$ 18,900.00	$ 680,400.00
210	175	175	150	75	45	45	
$ 21,000.00	$ 21,000.00	$ 21,000.00	$ 21,000.00	$ 21,000.00	$ 21,000.00	$ 21,000.00	$ 252,000.00
$109,200.00	$ 94,500.00	$ 94,500.00	$ 84,000.00	$ 52,500.00	$ 39,900.00	$ 39,900.00	$ 932,400.00
900,115.96	913,631.96	944,419.96	965,209.96	945,210.96	936,042.96	928,520.96	
125.00	125.00	125.00	125.00	125.00	125.00	125.00	1,500.00
700.00	700.00	700.00	700.00	700.00	700.00	700.00	8,400.00
1,500.00	1,500.00	1,500.00	1,500.00	1,500.00	1,500.00	1,500.00	18,000.00
500.00	500.00	500.00	500.00	500.00	500.00	500.00	6,000.00
1,000.00	1,000.00	1,000.00	1,000.00	1,000.00	1,000.00	1,000.00	12,000.00
300.00	300.00	300.00	300.00	300.00	300.00	300.00	3,600.00
	750.00					750	2,250.00
300.00	300.00	300.00	300.00	300.00	300.00	300.00	4,300.00
12,000.00			12000.00			12000.00	48,000.00
22,809.00	22,809.00	22,809.00	22,809.00	22,809.00	22,809.00	22,809.00	273,708.00
4,340.00	4,340.00	4,340.00	4,340.00	4,340.00	4,340.00	4,340.00	52,080.00
7,142.00			7142.00			7142.00	28,568.00
3,500.00	3,500.00	3,500.00	3,500.00	3,500.00	3,500.00	3,500.00	42,000.00
3,000.00	3,000.00	3,000.00	3,000.00	3,000.00	3,000.00	3,000.00	36,000.00
4,500.00	4,500.00	4,500.00	4,500.00	4,500.00	4,500.00	4,500.00	54,000.00
300.00	300.00	300.00	300.00	300.00	300.00	300.00	3,600.00
610.00	610.00	610.00	610.00	610.00	610.00	610.00	7,320.00
3,539.00	**3,539.00**	**3,539.00**	**3,539.00**	**3,539.00**	**3,539.00**	**3,539.00**	42,468.00
1,092.00	945.00	945.00	840.00	525.00	399.00	399.00	9,324.00
13,727.00	14,994.00	15242	5494	1520			
80,984.00	63,712.00	63,210.00	72,499.00	49,068.00	47,422.00	67,314.00	755,671.00
28,216.00	30,788.00	31,290.00	11,501.00	3,432.00	(7,522.00)	(27,414.00)	$ 176,729.00
819,131.96	***849,919.96***	***881,209.96***	***892,710.96***	***896,142.96***	***888,620.96***	***861,206.96***	

ANALYSIS FOR YEAR 4 ONLY

Income Statement for Blue Water Boatworks Year 4

	Jan-07	Feb-07	Mar-07	Apr-07	May-07
Net Sales	52500	67200	94500	109200	94500
Materials	4000	4000	4000	4000	4000
Gross Profit	**48500**	**63200**	**90500**	**105200**	**90500**
Expenses					
Payroll Expense	22809	22809	22809	22809	22809
Salary Expense	4340	4340	4340	4340	4340
Rent/Utilities/Telephone/Cellular	2825	2825	2825	2825	2825
Ins., Legal and Acct	1750	300	12300	300	300
Benefits/	3500	3500	3500	3500	3500
Office & Supplies	500	500	500	500	500
Equipment Expense	300	300	300	300	300
Maintenance/Misc	3000	3000	3000	3000	3000
Auto Expense, Fuel	1610	1610	1610	1610	1610
Depreciation	1382	1382	1382	1382	1382
Interest Expense	249.5	227.56	205.48	183.25	160.88
TOTAL	**42265.5**	**40793.56**	**52771.48**	**40749.25**	**40726.88**
PROFIT/LOSS	6235	22406	37729	64451	49773
Income Taxes (33%)	2057	7394	12450	21269	16425
NET PROFIT	**4177**	**15012**	**25278**	**43182**	**33348**

Jun-07	Jul-07	Aug-07	Sep-07	Oct-07	Nov-07	Dec-07
109200	95400	95400	84000	52500	39900	39900
4000	4000	4000	4000	4000	4000	4000
105200	**91400**	**91400**	**80000**	**48500**	**35900**	**35900**
22809	22809	22809	22809	22809	22809	22809
4340	4340	4340	4340	4340	4340	4340
2825	2825	2825	2825	2825	2825	2825
12300	1050	300	12300	300	300	13050
3500	3500	3500	3500	3500	3500	3500
500	500	500	500	500	500	500
300	300	300	300	300	300	300
3000	3000	3000	3000	3000	3000	3000
1610	1610	1610	1610	1610	1610	1610
1382	1382	1382	1382	1382	1382	1382
138.35	115.67	92.84	69.86	46.73	23.44	0
52704.35	**41431.67**	**40658.84**	**52635.86**	**40612.73**	**40589.44**	**53316**
52496	49968	50741	27364	7887	−4689	−17416
17324	16490	16745	9030	2603	−1548	−5747
35172	**33479**	**33997**	**18334**	**5284**	**−3142**	**−11669**

Case 1

BROTHERS GOING SEPARATE WAYS OR NOT?

Derrick and Kevin Petersen, twin brothers from a small town outside of Chicago, will soon graduate from a local business school. The boys have remained inseparable throughout their lives, including sports, hobbies, friends, and work. Decision time is now facing the young men in terms of career choices and tracks. While the brothers have always shared an interest in becoming business owners, their individual goals and newly acquired management training and vision may very well have them going separate ways after all these years.

The Petersen family owns and operates a very successful auto repair and towing business. Each of the five children in the family has worked for their parents throughout high school and during summers throughout college. The boys' parents took over the one-man business nearly 30 years ago. Since that time, they have purchased and now maintain a fleet of seven tow trucks and have expanded the garage to include four bays that provide a wide range of auto and truck repair services. The business generates about $4,000,000 in sales, a higher than industry average profit margin, and has provided the once poor family with a very good life.

The elder Petersens are approaching retirement and would love to see one of their kids continue the tradition. Kevin and his three other siblings have come and gone and made it very clear that they want no part of the business. Derrick remains as the lone ranger and is seriously considering the opportunity.

The elder Petersens are well known and respected for their quality work and service and for their active role in the community. They are set in their ways and have a hard time dealing with new ideas and with letting go. Derrick has many new ideas as to how he would grow the next generation of the business.

There is unused space above the garage that Derrick has talked about turning into a custom auto parts showroom. There is unused space on the property that Derrick would like to convert into self-service gas pumps and an automated car wash. Derrick has also commented on the great success that area competitors enjoy through the addition of a convenience store.

This has all resulted in a family-business conflict of sorts, as the parents want to work something out and get out, but continue to resist the changes that Derrick has offered. Derrick appreciates the knowledge, experience, and success that his parents have, but wants to be his own man and build his own empire if he is to stay on and make this his career. Derrick wants to take on his own new challenges and achieve his own personal rewards. A close friend of the family has recommended bringing in an objective outside consultant and attorney to work up a formal contract that everyone can live with.

Derrick's parents want the business to provide them with retirement income and would like the option of staying on as seasonal employees, as they plan to winter in the south and come home for the summer.

Derrick has many questions that need answering. He is unsure about the best legal form for the business to have. He is not sure how to best deal with his parents. He is not sure about the particulars for the best financial package, one that will reward his parents accordingly, and at the same time provide him with the best opportunity for continued success.

Brother Kevin has a very different mindset. He wants to start up and own several businesses, but he does not want to be tied down or committed to any single one. He has $200,000 of seed money available to him through the family. He has taken the time to build a relationship with three of the bankers that the family has worked with for many years. He participated in an internship through the SBA while in school in order to familiarize himself with the programs and opportunities that that organization has to offer. He also spent a semester in London in order to learn more about the way business is conducted in Europe.

Kevin is interested in franchising. He envisions himself starting and perfecting a number of service businesses that he can eventually take national and international. He is interested in going public in order to raise large sums of capital and to expedite his expansion plans. Kevin is interested in e-commerce. He views that industry as being in the early growth stages of the product life cycle and feels that the time is right to enter that industry. There appears to be many opportunities to buy low and sell high to worldwide markets. Kevin is interested in real estate development. The family lives in the urban/suburban area of Chicago, which is the site of very active construction of new homes, condo units, and commercial developments. Kevin knows that there are many other such venues around the country and world with plenty of room for new developers.

Kevin is also interested in other parts of the world. He wants to live and work in China and South America and possibly eastern Europe. While he greatly enjoyed the people, activities, and surroundings of his childhood, he really does not want to go home. At the same time, graduation is just three months away, and Kevin does not have a job.

Derrick is encouraging Kevin to come home for a year and help him take over and grow the family business. Derrick feels that this will be an exciting and fun challenge and that it will give his brother time to put together a more specific plan for his own endeavors. That choice also comes with an immediate source of income and a free place to live.

QUESTIONS

1. Profile the brothers. Are they typical "small business" people or "entrepreneurs" or both? Is there really a difference?
2. Advise the brothers. Develop a strategic and tactical plan that best fits their goals and aspirations and that has the highest likelihood for success.
3. How would each brother make a contribution to the family, community, and economy if their efforts were successful?

Case 2

G & R GARDEN CENTER: LAWN CARE SERVICES DIVISION

Rick and Gloria Ash started a new business in 1986 on the outskirts of Columbus, Ohio. Their original retail store with greenhouse attachment featured fresh-cut flowers, annuals, vegetables, and perennials. The building is on the grounds of Gloria's family farm, which enables the Ashes to grow some of their retail products from scratch. Gloria's parents gave the couple several acres of commercially zoned land as a wedding gift in 1982. The building and greenhouse construction were completed by Rick with a little help from his brothers. This combination of land acquisition and building construction resulted in a very low overhead situation that contributed to their start-up success.

An addition to the building was completed in 1991 and included several new and related product lines such as garden tools, soil and mulch products, gifts, seeds, and related accessories.

Gloria earned a horticulture degree at the local community college prior to the establishment of the business, and in 1997 she was able to fulfill a lifelong dream of starting a landscape design and installation service that became the company's next and newest product line. Gloria set up a small studio and office in the couple's nearby home and was able to acquire some new clients. Her timing was good, as the Columbus area experienced a housing boom during that period. New houses and new developments sprang up in every direction from the city. Their garden center was able to supply the plant materials that each new job required. Soon after, the Ashes expanded their product lines to include a new and wider variety of trees, shrubs, landscape terraces, patios, and walkways as a means to generate new sales and to complement Gloria's new service line.

The original start-up business and each expansion project (building addition, new products, design and installation service) have more than covered their costs but have only generated fair to moderate profit margins according to the Ashes. They attribute this mostly to the presence of their competition, which always seems to be growing. As a result, they have been reluctant to raise prices even though some product costs have risen.

One year later, the Ashes completed the final phase of their original long-range business plan with the addition of another new service—Big Rick, The Lawn & Garden Doctor. This new product line was added because of its very high profit projections coupled with the fact that the Ashes would (temporarily at least) have a monopoly on this market, as none of their competitors currently offer the service.

This new division specializes in the treatment and eradication of lawn and garden pests. There are many insects and diseases that affect plant life, some of which are fatal. In spite of the fact that the Ashes and other local garden centers offer high-quality plants to consumers, Mother Nature has a way of wreaking havoc on lawns, gardens, shrubs, and trees over time.

The start up of this division required a tremendous amount of time, effort, and expense as a result of the environmental and safety-related hazards of some of the products such as insecticides and fungicides.

The Ashes were required to train and license two of their employees as certified applications technicians. A custom built, high-security storage facility was required and built to house all hazardous materials. The building was secured with a locked, barbed-wire fence, an alarm system, and a hazardous material runoff-proof partition. A special liability insurance policy was purchased as well.

As expected, the new division turned out to be very profitable. Demand was strong, and the technicians' work was professional and effective. In fact, at the end of its first full year of existence, Big Rick, The Lawn & Garden Doctor turned a profit that almost matched that of all other divisions combined. At the company's monthly staff meeting, it therefore came as quite a surprise to everyone when Rick announced that he was seriously considering dropping the division entirely.

Rick Ash is a local native of the area. He has very strong family and community values and has always felt responsible for the welfare and happiness of his friends, neighbors, and especially his customers. He was always nervous and apprehensive that something bad would happen as a result of the pesticide or fungicide applications.

And then it happened. A customer's dog died as a result of eating some grass from a recently treated lawn. Big Rick's technician had taken every precaution. The area was properly treated, marked, and roped off, and the customer was instructed as to the after-care safety precautions which included a well-written handout and a signed liability waiver form. While the company was clearly not negligent, Rick was clearly upset.

Two months later, a lawsuit was filed against the company, claiming that the water runoff from the property of one of their customers had tainted a neighbor's well. The Ashes were forced to hire an attorney, and following a full and costly investigation were found to be not guilty of that charge. In fact, the case never even made it to court.

Gloria feels that Rick is overreacting. She points out that the company is in full compliance with every regulation and that Rick has gone out of his way to ensure the safety of all. Gloria also noted that no business can control the behavior or responsibility of its customers or of the population in general and that incidents beyond their control will naturally and always occur. In addition, the high profitability of the division will allow the Ashes to embark upon an aggressive advertising campaign aimed at improving the sales and profits of their other divisions.

Rick is losing sleep over all of this and is not sure what to do. He is worried about the image and reputation of his family and their business. He feels that the conditions surrounding the lawn and garden doctor business are in conflict with his values and conscience.

QUESTIONS

1. Present an argument in favor of retaining the new division that considers and incorporates the ethical and moral conflicts that Mr. Ash is experiencing.
2. Present an argument in favor of eliminating the new division, and make recommendations to improve overall company profits through means that will be socially and morally acceptable to Mr. Ash.
3. Aside from compliance with the law, just how much additional responsibility does a business owner have to his or her customer base, employees, suppliers, and the community at large? How do you feel about the old saying, "buyer beware"?

Case 3

REAL ESTATE MILLIONAIRES OF MEMPHIS

The one sure way to make money in Memphis, Tennessee, has always been through real estate, but the kinds of people who became millionaires this way defied a single, simple description. Consider five people who became millionaires within a few years of each other. All were in their early 30s when they struck it rich, but otherwise, they were a very varied group.

For example, Abe was the local "do it right" guy. He went to college, got his start in real estate working for a successful firm (he was one of the few African Americans in the local industry who specialized in commercial real estate), and built a nest egg. He left the firm after about five years to start his own, and he kept up his conscientious ways. He made a profit in his first year of operations through frugality and careful money management. He studied the market, the competition, and how and where the city was growing. He negotiated tirelessly but fairly to get the best price on land, and he developed it for the commercial market because that is where the money was.

Cal was the promoter. He was college-educated but seemed to have majored in partying. He was always talking up one big deal or another, developing major projects for tourists. More than anyone else in town, he sold visions of a future Memphis. He built his deals from the downtown out, looking for opportunities near the Mississippi River, which he saw as Memphis's key tourist attraction. He was always putting together consortia, but often forgot or failed to cover key details. His relationships with people were emotional roller coaster rides, and he likewise led a life of financial feast or famine, depending on where he and his latest project was. Just after his 30th birthday, one of his projects "came in," and he became a millionaire.

Lee went to college in engineering and joined her father's construction company right after graduation. She knew business as well as engineering and made the family firm a major force in home construction. She had a keen eye for where new subdivisions should go and was able to get the best work out of local architects and subcontractors. She was considered not only sharp, but kind to people and careful about the details of her homes and her firm. She prospered because her subdivisions were the best in town.

Dave ran a grocery on the outskirts of Memphis and said he "dabbled" in real estate. Self-educated, he largely limited his real estate dealings to when one came across the butcher shop refrigerated case in his grocery. All the locals knew him, and he knew every piece of property and its history from experience and listening to his customers. When someone needed to move or sell a deceased parent's farm, Dave was there with his checkbook, financed through the grocery. He did not prospect, and he resold land rather than developing it.

Frank also lived on the outskirts of town. Never graduating from high school, he apprenticed himself to a gas station owner as a teen. When the company needed to open a gas station just outside of Memphis, Frank agreed to do it, and the company financed his purchase of the gas station. At his gas station, Frank mostly sat outside in a rocking chair by the gas pump. He became a millionaire when gravel was discovered on his land and was mined by local gravel and building companies. Armed with serious money, Frank always said he was looking for his next deal, but he never found one.

QUESTIONS

1. In terms of the five types of entrepreneurial personalities mentioned in the chapter, do any of them fit the description of the Memphis real estate tycoons?
2. What role in their development as entrepreneurs would you think special conditions had—for example, Abe being African American, Lee being a female in a male-dominated industry or working within a family business, or Frank or Dave going into serious business without a college education?
3. What kinds of competencies do you see these real estate entrepreneurs bringing to their business?
4. Are there any conclusions you can draw about there being an entrepreneurial personality type for the real estate business? What does it say about the kind of entrepreneur *you* can become with the personality you have?

BIG BUSINESS IN A SMALL RURAL CITY

Bud Collier grew up "smack in the middle of a 100 mile-long hay field," as he puts it, near central Kansas. That part of the country features a lot of land, a lot of cattle, very large farms, agricultural processing centers, and relatively few people. The region has a number of very small farm towns, with populations of less than 1,000 located as much as 30 to 50 miles apart, and a much smaller number of small cities, with populations of 10,000 to 30,000 widely scattered throughout the state. There is an ongoing effort by state and federal agencies to support the development of commerce in those regions. Outside of farming and the few small retail shops that serve those small towns, there is not much happening in the way of new employment opportunities. The farm base continues to shrink, and natives of the area continue to move to other parts of the country after high school, college, or a hitch in the military.

Bud's small family farm is located near one of those small cities. He has earned a degree in marketing and graphic arts and now faces a dilemma and turning point in his life. He very much wants to go home and settle down in the community that he loves, wants to start a career related to his newly acquired skills and knowledge, but has no idea as to what or if that area has to offer him.

He developed a great interest in market research and data analysis while in school. Bud has studied national and international trends in business in an attempt to discover where the opportunities and connections lie between future product and service demand, his graphic arts and marketing skills, and his desired home base. He is trying hard to be creative and innovative and to "think outside the box" as he was often encouraged to do while in school. Bud is also trying to "make the data work for you" as his statistics professor often spoke about.

He has thought about and studied the data regarding food production and world hunger. His area of the country is capable of producing additional and abundant quantities of much needed agricultural products. The only thing standing in the way seems to be governments and politics. His area of the country is a national hub for the transportation and distribution of products from coast to coast and includes a number of major interstate highways. Bud has learned that health care and wellness and its many related industries are projected to become the number one source of jobs and opportunities to the new generation of college graduates. That industry offers options ranging from traditional forms of health care, to fitness, recreation and leisure, diet and nutrition, and nontraditional programs and practices. From a global perspective, Bud knows that China and the Pacific Rim and all of the so-called "Latino Nations" represent two gigantic and growing markets for virtually all consumer goods and services. His mind continues to race with thoughts and ideas as to how to connect these opportunities with his desired home base.

Bud also gained skills in the process and art of new product development while in school. He was often assigned to work with small groups of classmates to brainstorm ideas, to shrink the list to the best and most feasible, to conduct research and analysis, and to finally develop prototypes and test marketing strategies. Bud is now ready to do this for real; he also wants to incorporate his graphic arts skills into the mix. Bud has become very proficient in desktop publishing, computer animation, and video production. He is familiar with and proficient in current multimedia marketing software.

Soon after his return home, Bud learned that an old friend of the family was about to retire and sell his printing and stationery business. That business is located in the downtown of a nearby small city, population 26,000, near Bud's home and has provided a nice income and lifestyle for the proprietor. The shop sells greeting cards, office supplies, and other complementary paper products and includes a small warehouse and processing center where the owner is able to produce custom business cards, office stationery, and a limited line of brochures and flyers. Most of the equipment is old and labor-intensive with limited capabilities.

QUESTIONS

1. Use your imagination and creativity along with the information provided to identify a short list of the best opportunities for Bud to consider.
2. Should Bud consider purchasing the printing and stationery business, and if so, what do you see as his goal for the business, especially how could he expand production and sales given the limited opportunities that the location offers?
3. Business ideas are easy to come by. The more difficult task is determining the feasibility of business success. How will you go about doing that? What kind of information does Bud need in order to make an informed decision? What types and sources of data are available to assist you in determining your best opportunities?

THE AMBITIOUS COLLEGE KID WHO JUST CAN'T WAIT

Lyle Wong has been carrying a briefcase everywhere he goes since the age of 12 and has always been glad to let anyone and everyone know that he is an up and coming entrepreneur. At the age of 14, Lyle started and ran a flea market on weekends on a field next to his house. He rented space to vendors and sold his own merchandise on consignment for a commission. He then started and ran his own landscaping company during the following three summers. This required Lyle to first persuade his older brother to use his truck and become an employee, as Lyle was not yet old enough to drive. He then started and ran a DJ business during his last two years of high school. By the time Lyle graduated from high school, he had more than $75,000 in savings and mutual fund investments.

His parents had all they could do to keep him in high school. Although he earned straight A's, Lyle considered high school to be a waste of time and nothing but an obstacle to earning his first million. He was offered a full scholarship at a Michigan college. Thanks to some friendly and persistent convincing from his parents and from his already established business associates, Lyle agreed to give college a try as long as he could continue to conduct business.

Lyle is now a 19-year-old sophomore, majoring in computer science, with minors in business and international marketing, and lives in a dorm. He started a T-shirt business during his freshman year, which he says pacifies him for now, earns him spending money, and allows him to continue investing in his retirement portfolio.

He is ready to take it to the next level. Lyle has set a goal of accumulating $1,000,000 by the time he graduates from college. He is willing to do this "part time" since he is in school. Lyle has discovered that college takes up much less time than high school. He figures that he needs only about 30 hours a week to attend class, study, complete all assignments, and continue to earn straight A's. He has decided to dedicate an additional 40 or 50 hours per week, his version of part time, to the next venture in order to earn him his first million.

Lyle is still undecided as to which direction to go with his next venture. He is thinking about setting up and running an entire operation from his dorm room. He views this as a location with free overhead. As a full-time student, Lyle also has access to many other on-campus resources. Those resources include an abundance of cheap help if needed, access to all computer technology, access to most on-campus buildings and facilities, free public transportation, and access to the student newspaper and radio station.

Lyle is thinking a lot about e-commerce. He knows that this gives him access to a worldwide customer base. Unlike his previous ventures, which were all very small and localized, Lyle is excited about the prospect of selling merchandise on a global basis. He has always liked the concept and role of the middleman, and is searching for product lines that he can buy low and sell high in volume. Lyle knows that the necessary infrastructure is already well established. There are an abundance of manufacturers, shippers, and consumers throughout the world. Lyle figures it is just a matter of putting together the right mix of those entities with him properly placed to reap the benefits.

Lyle's current and past ventures have given him a lot of good experience in key areas of business. Those include customer and employee relations, handling merchandise, and managing cash and the many details and tasks that arise from the normal day-to-day operations of most any business. He is now very computer literate, and in spite of his passion and drive for business success, Lyle has lots of friends, good social skills, and enjoys and participates in many hobbies, social events, and extracurricular activities.

QUESTIONS

1. Do you believe that Lyle can achieve his goal of earning $1,000,000 by graduation? Why or why not?
2. Help your colleague. You are familiar with the resources available to students on a typical college campus. Consider those resources and Lyle's goals, and develop a short list of the

best products or services to consider. Include an outline and action plan to make it all happen.

3. Trying to start up a part-time business while being a full-time student in college could pose some problems for Lyle. What are the ones you think are most likely? How could he minimize their impact?
4. Do you see yourself taking a route similar to Lyle's? Could you do it? Will you do it?

THE GRANDE GENERAL STORE, EST. 1948—IT'S TIME TO SELL

Three generations of Grandes have dedicated their lives and careers to a small general store located on the outskirts of Denver, Colorado. Rocky and Anita Grande, the current owner-operators, have decided to sell the family business. They have declared themselves "tired, burned out, and ready to get out." Their two adult children have no interest in the business, and Rocky and Anita want to spend more time with their three young grandchildren.

They need help with setting a fair price for the business, with finding a qualified buyer, and with preparing a formal prospectus for use by investors, bankers, and others. The Grandes want the highest price possible and at the same time sincerely wish to see the business survive and prosper. It has been in the family for a long time, is a well-established part of the community, and has a dedicated workforce. Most of the employees have been with the company for more than 10 years. The Grandes will allow a buyer to continue to use the family/business name if desired.

What began as an old-fashioned general store (1940s–1960s) carrying everything from food and clothing, to tools, farm supplies, penny candy, and train tickets evolved into a traditional hardware store (1970s – present). The current 4,200 square feet of floor space is divided into four major departments: lawn and garden, paints, electrical and plumbing, and general hardware.

Sales and profits are divided equally between consumers and contractors. The store is located adjacent to a railroad siding with a storage building that allows for large shipments of merchandise to be received, stored, and sold. Building materials of all types (lumber, roofing, siding, Sheetrock, and so on) are picked up and delivered to local construction sites, which represent the mainstay of the contractor business.

The Grande family is well respected by all. Their honesty, loyalty, hard work, and community involvement have come back to bless them on many occasions. During tough economic times, suppliers often extend credit terms far beyond the norm. Customers and contractors are fiercely loyal to the Grande's business even with the presence of modern-day giant warehouse outlets that offer a wider variety of the same products for less money.

While the main buildings date back to 1948, the Grandes have upgraded their fleet of delivery trucks and forklifts. The inside of the store is a mix of the old and the new. State-of-the-art computers, paint processing equipment, and landscape machinery rentals are scattered around the old wooden building that still sports some original display fixtures and the wormy chestnut paneling that Rocky's grandfather Jeb installed during construction of the original building.

The principals have compiled the following summary financials for the past five years of operation:

Income (Profit and Loss) Statement Summary: 1998–2002 (in 000s)

	1998	1999	2000	2001	2002
Sales	$1,100	$1,215	$1,500	$1,800	2,200
CGS-Cost of Goods Sold	550	600	732	822	995
GM-Gross Margin	$ 550	615	768	978	1,205
Operating Expenses:	500	520	600	720	795
• Payroll					
• Mortgage/Debt					
• Insurance					
• Utilities					
• Supplies					
• Transportation					
• Depreciation					
Net Income Before Taxes	$ 50	$ 95	$ 168	$ 258	$ 410
Taxes	15	29	50	77	123
Net Income	$ 35	$ 66	$ 118	$ 181	$ 287

Net Cash Flow from Operations: 1998–2002 (in 000s)

	1998	1999	2000	2001	2002
Cash In	$1,014	$1,098	$1,360	$1,617	$1,996
Cash Out	945	1,014	1,250	1,430	1,760
Net Cash Flow from Operations	$ 69	$ 84	$ 110	$ 187	$ 236

Balance Sheet Summary: January 1, 1998–2002 (in 000s)

	1998	1999	2000	2001	2002
Cash	$ 12	$ 19	$ 22	$ 23	$ 21
Inventory	41	47	59	65	80
Accounts Receivables	80	102	124	148	187
Land	$ 35	$ 35	$ 35	$ 35	$ 35
Buildings	612	567	505	459	414
Equipment	84	190	171	241	214
Accounts Payables	$ 36	$ 46	$ 51	$ 61	$ 71
Notes Payables	21	6	7	9	6
Long-Term Debt	$ 121	$ 225	$ 211	$ 278	$ 261
Owner's Equity/ Net Worth	$ 686	$ 683	$ 647	$ 623	$ 613

Suburban Denver is considered a moderate- to high-growth region of the state and is projected to stay that way for years to come. New housing, new neighborhoods, new schools, new malls, and the like are under construction and in the planning stages throughout the area.

The Grande business sits on seven acres of land and includes room for growth, in terms of new buildings, increased parking, and other business options. The business was recently appraised by certified professionals. The assessed values are as follows:

- Land $110,000
- Buildings 515,000
- Equipment 155,000
- Inventory 70,000
- Total Current
- Assessed Value $850,000

The Grandes have compiled all their data into a prospectus and are about to formally put the business on the market. They have yet to settle on an asking price.

Two local area banks have indicated a willingness to offer a 15-year note to a qualified buyer for a maximum of $624,000 (which represents 80 percent of the assessed value of the land, buildings and equipment).

QUESTIONS

1. Use your entrepreneurial skills to evaluate this investment opportunity. Is this a business worth buying? If so, why? How much would you be willing to invest? Why?
2. Given the economic outlook in the Denver area, the land and physical plant, and the competition, what short- and long-term operational and growth strategies would you consider?

THE COMPUTER GURU: A ONE-MAN SHOW OR AN EMPIRE?

Juan De Jesus, of San Antonio, Texas, earned a computer science degree from The University of Texas in 1994. Upon graduation, Juan was hired as a sales and service technician for one of the large national computer corporations. That job provided him with a tremendous amount of experience in the small business sales and service sector. Four years later, he left the company, deciding to go it alone as an independent computer consultant.

Juan set up an office and computer-testing lab in his home and worked hard to grow the business. He was able to take advantage of some of the relationships and contacts that he established during his tenure at his last job that resulted in several immediate clients. His wife Conchita helps with some of the office work on a part-time basis.

The business grew rapidly thanks to Juan's excellent work and reputation. He has the ability to install hardware and software systems, including industry-specific software, is very effective at training, can fix almost any computer, and is readily available by phone to answer questions and solve problems that occur after the installation and training.

Four years into the business, Juan finds himself charging $100 per hour and earning nearly $150,000 per year for his services. He is good at what he does, and people want him—his phone is ringing off the hook. He also feels that it is time to take a step back to reevaluate his current position, his business options, and his personal goals.

Juan recalled the internship program that is offered at his alma mater and arranged to have three current business students conduct a feasibility study on his behalf. The project began with an interview at his home office. The highlights and key points of that interview follow.

Juan reported that he is making a good living, currently billing about 1,500 hours per year at $100 per hour. He actually works about 60 hours per week, however, with the addition of travel time, seemingly endless phone calls, searching for and ordering parts, office paperwork, and attending classes and seminars to remain current with new technology. Conchita works about 20 hours per week in the office. She indicated this to be her limit, as she has another part-time job and is expecting the couple's first child in a few months. She plans to give up the second job and to continue working with Juan at their home office.

Juan is concerned about the fact that his entire business is just Juan. He gets paid only when he works. He sells no actual products, just services. If he is sick or if he takes a vacation, he earns nothing. He wondered out loud whether he had already reached his maximum potential. He is worried about the fact that there are no growth opportunities under his current setup. He is not sure whether he should just keep doing what he is doing or whether he should change.

The conversation then turned to "the building of an empire" as Juan put it. He wants the student team to take a close look at some other business options that include:

- Hire an additional computer technician or two and grow the existing business.
- Open a retail computer store as a complement to his current services. If he were to establish a retail store, should he rent, lease, or buy the building?
- Hire an outside salesperson or two to generate new business either as part of the retail store or as an extension of his current business.
- Establish a Web site rather than a retail store as a complement to his current services.
- Consider new and related ideas generated by the student team.
- Do nothing.

Juan indicated to the students that he likes the idea of building an empire, but that he feels as if he is wading into new waters that he is unfamiliar with. For example, if he were to open a retail store, could he possibly compete with the Circuit Citys and Best Buys of the world? He wants his success story to continue and wants to make more money while working fewer hours. He also wants to earn money when he is not working.

Juan is not sure about the best product mix and about the pricing of those products. He is very concerned about the very rapid product life cycle that is inherent to the computer industry and is afraid of getting stuck with suddenly obsolete products. Juan is also accustomed to getting paid very quickly for his services and has not had to deal with credit and cash flow issues.

QUESTIONS

1. Form small groups and brainstorm and develop a strategic plan for Juan. Compare and contrast each group's plan and gain consensus as to the best.
2. Using that best plan, return to your original group and develop a tactical plan for Juan.
3. Having now developed a tactical plan, what are the major challenges facing Juan if he were to go forward with your plan? Include a SWOT analysis as part of your assessment.

THE OLD TIMER'S WOODSTOVE SHOP

Matty Gee took a job in computer sales upon graduation from his local community college business program. About three years later, Matty became a downsizing victim of the high-tech crash of the mid-to-late nineties. Always the optimist, Matty declared that it was his fate and his time to turn a negative into a positive and fulfill a lifelong dream of owning a business.

Matty returned to his suburban Minneapolis roots and spent several months studying the local markets. As a business student and sales associate, Matty was always fascinated by and attracted to the niche market concept. With that in mind, he rented a small downtown retail space and opened the Old Timer's Woodstove Shop.

Minnesota is home to long and cold winters, and with fluctuating costs and uncertain supply cycles of oil and natural gas, many locals turn to wood and sometimes coal as alternative sources of heat. Matty determined that there are two distinct niche markets for woodstoves and related accessories and products. There are the rational buyers who burn wood as a primary heat source and the emotional buyers who burn wood for its aesthetic, romantic, and cozy appeal. Matty's research also revealed that the availability of fuel wood is plentiful and reliable and that depending on a given year's oil and gas prices, wood is sometimes more economical as well.

The Old Timer's Woodstove Shop is a 40 foot × 60 foot retail store on the main street of the downtown. Some of its neighbors include the local barbershop, convenience store, photography studio, grocery store, clothing boutique, and bakery. Matty loves being a part of the downtown mom and pop business community. Most of the neighbor stores have been in existence for many years and have provided a respectable income and lifestyle for the proprietors and employees.

Matty filled every possible square foot of his small shop with a variety of woodstoves, coal stoves, fireplace inserts, and accessories such as pokers and brushes, ash buckets, wood carriers and storage containers, axes, and splitting mauls. Matty also offered a delivery and installation service.

For the next three to four years, the store provided Matty with an adequate living. He earned between $65,000 to $80,000 per year after taxes. Matty also worked many hours. The store was open six days and sixty hours per week, most of which were worked by Matty. That did not include the deliveries and installations and assorted paperwork requirements that generally took place after hours.

Matty feels that he has reached a turning point in his business career. For the first time ever, he feels stagnant and trapped. It is plain for him to see that his small retail space is not capable of generating any appreciable increase in sales or profits. Matty wants more. He has established a very good reputation for product quality and service and is well respected as a member of the business community. Matty contributes to a variety of local events and coaches a little league team each spring.

Matty went back to the market research drawing board, including a close analysis of his customer database files, and concluded that it is time to take his business to the next level. Matty notes that the vast majority of his customers are middle- to upper-middle-class working professionals with nice suburban/rural homes. His strategy is to find a new and more spacious location and to offer an expanded product mix that will complement and grow his business.

Following a meeting with his wife and his banker, Matty contacted a local real estate agent, who after a time found a much larger building just outside of town. The 15,000 square-foot space is a stand-alone building (abandoned restaurant) located on one of the main roads leaving town. The road and building are adjacent to an excellent flow of traffic (30,000 cars per day) and offers much better visibility than the downtown location.

From a financial perspective, the breakeven sales point of the new building ($600,000) is more than the current location has ever generated ($480,000). From a product perspective, Matty can more than triple the volume of wood and coal stove inventory on his new showroom floor and still use up about only one-third of that available space. Matty needs a new and expanded product line. Matty also needs to greatly increase sales just to match his historical earnings.

Matty is not quite sure which way to go. He has thought about adding a line of outdoor furniture. He has also considered everything from hot tubs to gas grills to plumbing and air-conditioning. His other considerations include the outdoor enthusiast market (hiking, boating) and the environmentally friendly market (all natural products). Matty has also thought about seasonal product lines. The bulk of wood and coal stove sales takes place between August and December. Sales at the current location slow down dramatically during the dead of winter and are almost nonexistent during the spring and early summer. Matty believes that some combination of the above-mentioned product lines along with possible others will complement both his current product lines and customer base.

Matty's market radius includes the normal mix of competition that is found in many regions around the country. There are a small number of the large superstores, home care centers, and national chain mall stores. There are a larger number of smaller independently owned stores such as furniture, hardware, pools and spas, and sporting goods.

The consumer markets are also quite similar to many suburban/rural regions of the country. The majority of consumers are middle- to upper-middle-class working professionals. Most households include two-income families with kids. There are a smaller number of senior citizen and young singles households. The major employers are service businesses, schools and government agencies, retail establishments, and a small number of manufacturers.

Matty is also concerned about the image that he has created. While his reputation for quality products and service is excellent, he is known as a woodstove specialist and retailer as the store name implies. He is not sure if he should change or add to the name of the business. He is not sure if people will take him seriously if he suddenly begins to sell furniture or hot tubs or air-conditioning. His good name and reputation has suddenly become a double-edged sword. His current store will close its doors for good on April 30. The grand opening of the new store is scheduled for August 1.

QUESTIONS

1. Help Matty by composing an outline for a new business plan.
2. What unique challenges face Matty as compared to someone preparing a traditional business plan for an all new venture?

Case 9

THE HOUSE OF WINE—GRAND OPENING

CASE PERSPECTIVE

Fred and Larry Butts are excited and a bit nervous about their new wine and specialty store that is scheduled to celebrate its grand opening in about four months. Fred and Larry have spent the past year choosing a location for their new venture and completing a market research and business plan.

The couple purchased a lakeside parcel of property in the heart of the lakes region of upstate New York. Their newly built structure includes a 7,200-square-foot retail showroom (72 × 100) with a below-ground wine and inventory storage area of the same dimensions. The retail showroom is very elegant, featuring wood floors, a large number of beautiful windows, many of which overlook a scenic lake vista, bright stucco walls adorned with works of art and a high-end surround-sound system. The building is located on a busy road, and the parcel includes plenty of room for parking and possible building expansion.

Fred and Larry's market research indicates that the area is evenly divided between an upper-middle-class population of second home seasonal and year-round retirees, a white-collar population of insurance and banking people, and a blue-collar population of factory workers. The total population of the multitown region nearly doubles between Memorial Day and Labor Day each year (from 50,000 to 100,000+), as there are a large number of summer cottages and campgrounds that surround the many small lakes within their market radius. The region also enjoys a "leaf-peeping" tourist season in the fall and a pass-through and nearby ski market during the winter months.

Tourism is the area's major industry, followed closely by the manufacturing sector. There are no major cities nearby. The area consists of several small towns surrounded by beautiful hardwood forests, fresh water lakes and ponds, and several nearby small mountain ranges.

Fred and Larry's market research also revealed that there is currently very little direct competition in the area and that the fine wine and related products markets are growing steadily. Wine is currently available only in local convenience stores and supermarkets. Those establishments typically carry the lower-priced, lower-end, faster-moving selections. Fred and Larry are very optimistic about their chances for success, but are still faced with several important decisions to make prior to their grand opening.

Highlights of the financial section of Fred and Larry's business plan include the following:

- A budget of $150,000 for store fixtures, furniture, and other equipment.
- A budget of $250,000 for merchandise inventory.
- A beginning working capital balance of $100,000 (they expect this and their initial sales to support the net cash flow from operations for a period of six months, at which time the business is projected to support itself).
- A breakeven sales volume of $650,000.
- All sales are for cash or credit.
- About half of their wine inventory must be paid for up front; the other half is purchased under 2/10/ net/30 terms.
- All complementary products (described below) are purchased under 2/10 net/30 and/or 2/10 net/45 terms.

Fred and Larry's major remaining unfinished business and related decisions revolve around their specific product mix, the specific layout of the store and warehouse, and their short-, medium-, and long-range marketing and promotion plan. Each is described below in more detail.

PRODUCT MIX

While wine is obviously Fred and Larry's major product line, there are a very wide range of products and prices to choose from. A single bottle of wine can sell from as little as $5 to as much as $10,000 or more. Wines are generally grouped into categories that sell from $5 to $8, $9 to $17, $18 to $30, $35 to $75, and $100+. There are red wines and white wines, small- to standard- to large-sized bottles, champagnes, after-dinner wines, and dessert wines. Wines can be sold by the case, as part of a gift set, on site and through the mail. The major producers of wine are found in France, Italy, Germany, South America, Australia, and California.

Fred and Larry need to select the "right" mix of complementary products. They already find themselves with vendors offering more products than they can possibly handle. Those products include but are not limited to assorted glassware; wine racks and storage units; corkscrews; cookbooks; party platters; serving utensils; coasters; dry, fresh, and frozen food products; tablecloths and napkins; newspapers and magazines; and so on.

Their goal is to operate an upscale, classy establishment and to make as much money as possible. They must pay attention to cash flow and store image. The cheaper wines move fast but generate a smaller profit per unit and portray a "lower-class image." The more expensive wines move more slowly, generate a much larger per unit profit, and portray an image of "upper-class elegance." They must also consider services as well as products. Those include but are not limited to delivery, catering, wine-tasting parties, wine classes, and so on.

STORE LAYOUT

With building construction nearly complete, Fred and Larry keep staring at their (now empty) 72 by 100 feet of retail/showroom space that they must soon fill with equipment, fixtures, products, and other accessories. The lower level must soon be filled with storage equipment, inventory, supplies, and other operational necessities. How should each level be laid out? What kind of display cases should they buy? How should they incorporate light, music, and other presentation aspects into their business? Where should the cash register be? What about an office? How should inventory be received, stored, and handled?

They must design their layout in a way that will maximize sales and profits; maximize their customer's buying experience; maximize the use of wall, floor, ceiling, and window space; minimize shoplifting; maximize safety; and minimize liability.

Outdoor presentation and layout decisions must be made as well. Those include but are not limited to road and building signage, lighting, parking lot design, trash and snow removal, landscaping, traffic flow, and safety.

SHORT-, MEDIUM-, AND LONG-RANGE MARKETING AND PROMOTION PLAN

Fred and Larry envision a three-phase marketing and promotion plan. In the short term (first six months), they want to maximize exposure by having as many people learn about and visit the store as possible. They want people to show up and have an experience that makes them want to come back soon and often. They want to generate enough sales to establish and sustain a positive cash flow within six months of their grand opening.

Their medium-range (six months to one year) goals call for the establishment of a never-ending positive cash flow from operations, a year-round local clientele to support that cash flow, and the beginning of a long era of word-of-mouth referrals.

Their long-range goals are focused on sales and profit stability and flexibility. Fred and Larry's first, second, and third year sales projections are $1,000,000, $1,500,000 and $2,000,000, respectively. At that point, their goal is to achieve an annual increase in sales of 5–10 percent. By the end of their fifth year, they want to be in the position of being able to sell the business for a substantial profit ($1,000,000 or more) or continue to run and grow the business if they are having fun.

QUESTIONS

1. Fred and Larry raised several issues regarding the product mix for their business. What product strategy do you think makes the most sense for The House of Wine? Why?
2. Given the market and product line options for this new business, what kind of pricing strategy do you think makes the most sense for the business?
3. Prepare a time line of strategies and actions that will help the principals achieve their short-, medium-, and long-term goals.

SAUNDERS AND COMPANY, INC.: AN INTERNATIONAL ENTREPRENEURIAL ENTERPRISE

George L. Saunders and his son Lorin operate Saunders and Company. This small entrepreneurial enterprise is actively involved in international business. It has fabric suppliers in Europe, Thailand, and the United States. Most of its tailors are in Thailand. It sells custom-made design jewelry, exquisite diamonds and pearls from China, Greece, and other countries. The company is on the verge of substantial growth if it can surmount four challenges in the near future. To realize substantial future growth, the company must build a broader customer base, build a sales force, find additional suppliers of raw materials, and establish a brand identity for the custom suits it now sells.

PRODUCTS

Saunders and Company offers a full line of custom-made men's and women's suits and accessories, including shirts/blouses, blazers/jackets, overcoats, tuxedos, furs, leather goods, and jewelry. It also makes women's after-five dresses, wedding dresses, and evening wear. The primary product line and major revenue source is custom-tailored suits. The suits are available in a wide array of styles and fabrics and are tailored to specific measurements for each customer. Saunders and Company prides itself on being able to match any style the customer wants and do so in a range of fabric choices. The primary cost determinant is the fabric choice. Contract tailors in Thailand and the United States assemble the suits. The fabrics offered are from Europe, Thailand, and North America. The styles available are virtually unlimited. While it has a wide selection of styles available from design catalogs from Europe and the United States, it is able to work from any picture the customer may supply as well. The price of a suit is primarily a factor of the fabric chosen and, in most cases, there are no charges for suit features and styles. The company makes suits in prices ranging from less than $500 to well over $1,000, and it recently established the George Saunders' Collection line, which starts at $1,500.

To complement the suits, Saunders will also supply shirts, blouses, overcoats, and other accessories that are custom-made. The lines of accessories available include shoes, belts, jewelry, and leather or fur coats. A manufacturer in New York supplies the furs and leather coats. The firm also offers a line of jewelry it sells for the manufacturers. The jewelry includes a line of custom-made pearls from China, as well as custom-made diamond and gold pieces from Greece and other countries. The leather goods are available in exotic skins such as alligator and snake, which it receives from a supplier in Florida.

THE MANUFACTURING PROCESS

As noted, tailors in Thailand and the United States make the suits. The tailors work from measurements taken by George or Lorin Saunders using techniques and measuring standards identified by the Thailand tailors. The customer chooses fabric for each suit from samples the company maintains. The customer is measured at his or her home, office, or at one of the many shows Saunders and Company holds in upscale hotels. The customer chooses the style from one of the design catalogs available from Saunders, or from any picture she/he provides. The company currently has over 100 tailors in Thailand and six in the United States. The number of suppliers the company has been able to contract with limits the availability of fabrics. It currently has over 2,000 fabrics that customers can select from, with turnover of fabrics twice a year. It is able to supply fabrics identical to many of the top European brands.

CUSTOMERS

Current customers include doctors, college coaches, professors, entertainers, business executives, clergy, professional athletes, and Hollywood personalities. The primary source of new customers is word-of-mouth. Since the company promises confidentiality to its customers, Saunders and Company is able to attract clients who want to be able to purchase suits and accessories away from public attention. However, that guarantee of confidentiality also means the company cannot advertise its success. Without advertising it has developed a customer base of hundreds.

A potential new source of customers was recently identified. Saunders and Company is in the process of preparing to bid on a contract to supply suits and accessories to a church. That contract will mean supplying over 200 suits per year as well as shirts and ties. The contract is valued at more than $100,000, a substantial annual revenue increase for this company. The company sees similar opportunities as an excellent avenue for growth.

FUTURE DIRECTIONS

One of the primary challenges Saunders and Company faces is building its customer base. While it currently has hundreds of private customers, it thinks it can expand that number substantially with an active sales force. Since George Saunders is still employed full time at InspireWorks, the only full-time sales person currently is his son Lorin. The vision they have at this time would allow new salespeople to immediately begin earning commission by assigning current clientele to each salesperson. The sales force will operate essentially as independent agents. The primary advantage offered by having an active sales force, besides the obvious effect of building the customer base, is the freedom that George and Lorin would gain to focus on growing the business.

One clear avenue for growing the company is in the contract arena. The potential for growth in this area is substantial. Contract sales would include customers such as churches, choirs, orchestras, teams, and any group that is looking for a uniform look. One such prospect is supplying suits to clergy, such as priests.

The company is always looking to expand its fabric offerings. The primary source of profits is the markup of fabrics. Clearly the more fabric offerings it has, the more it will be able to attract customers. Saunders and Company already supplies fabric from some of the premier names in men's and women's suits, but expanding that capability will directly contribute to attracting more lucrative customers. With an extensive fabric selection and a larger customer base, Saunders and Company anticipates transitioning to its own manufacturing operation and the development of a brand identity.

QUESTIONS

1. Since Saunders and Company's primary means of promotion is word-of-mouth, how can they make that approach more effective?
2. Given Saunders and Company promises confidentiality to their customers, what other means of promotion might they employ?
3. What kinds of problems do you see cropping up for managing and getting the most from an outside sales force, if George and Lorin decide to go this route? What can be done to minimize the problems?
4. Other than the offering of more profitable fabrics, what other things might George and Lorin do to increase profitability?

The case was written by Robert E. Ledman, Morehouse College, Rledman@morehouse.edu and submitted to Babson University HBCU Case Consortium. The information provided in this case is derived from an interview with Lorin Saunders, a principal of the company.

S & Z EAST COAST IMPORTERS

OVERVIEW

Herbie Shapiro has worked as a retail footwear salesman in the New York City area for nearly 20 years. The New York City native has always worked for someone else but knows the business and its people very well. Herbie has always felt that the supply side of the retail footwear business is poorly organized, and that few if any distributors provide good service to the hundreds of retail outlets in the metropolitan area.

Mei Zhao, a native of China, is a long-time acquaintance of Herbie, and a manufacturer's rep for several of the Pacific Rim footwear manufacturers. Mei functions primarily as a foreign agent and freight forwarder for the Asian manufacturers, overseeing the unloading and trucking of container ship cargo.

Mei shares many of the same views as Herbie when it comes to the distribution and supply side of the retail footwear business. Both men are at the midpoint of their careers, have built a solid business and personal relationship with each other, and following several meetings, have decided to form a partnership. S & Z East Coast Importers has the opportunity to lease a 60,000-square-foot warehouse with a buy option in northern New Jersey for purposes of establishing a distribution center for the metropolitan area retail footwear business.

Mei already has many good links and relationships with the major suppliers and shippers of retail footwear. The partners plan to import a wide range of products including casual shoes, athletic footwear, fashion and outdoor boots, slippers, socks, laces, pads and inserts. Mei has access to all the major national brands as well as the bargain priced no-name lines.

In addition to his long association and membership in local and national footwear organizations, Herbie knows many store owners and employees within the New York-New Jersey metro area. Herbie is well liked and well respected. The partners believe that their strong combination of supply side and retail experience will provide them with access to many good markets.

As is the case in many industries, there are a very small number of large suppliers of manufactured products coupled with a very large number of small retail stores. One of the major keys to success therefore is the existence of an efficient, well-organized system of distribution. Herbie and Mei are focusing their efforts on doing a better job than the competition and on filling that niche in the footwear market.

LOGISTICAL ISSUES AND CHALLENGES

Most of the aforementioned footwear products arrive at the West Coast on giant container ships. After clearing customs, the containers are off-loaded onto tractors for local (western) delivery and onto railcars for Midwestern and East Coast distribution. Herbie and Mei plan to set up their building as a warehouse and distribution center.

Warehouse and distribution centers must purchase virtually all their products in large quantities. Herbie and Mei will be faced with buying stock shipments ranging from no less than 1,000 to as many as 50,000 to 100,000 units of laces, shoes, socks, running shoes, and so on.

Retailers on the other hand typically must purchase very small quantities of mixed loads of products, primarily because of a lack of retail and storage space. Herbie and Mei will be faced with orders that call for 50–150 pairs of laces, shoes, socks, running shoes, and so on.

Warehouse and distribution centers must therefore be set up to receive, unload, and store large shipments of product (railroad cars/tractor trailers), to "break bulk" (unpack, count, inventory, and repack) and to load and deliver small mixed loads to retail establishments. Many metro area retailers are located on cramped and busy streets with limited access.

The financial side of Herbie and Mei's business looks very promising. Thanks to Mei's connections with suppliers and Herbie's connections with the New York-New Jersey metro market, the partners anticipate an average markup of 30–40% for their products. That is about twice as much as Mei earns as a manufacturer's rep.

In order for their business to succeed, several variables and logistics must fall into place and be properly managed. Their warehouse and distribution process, quality of service, and financial management must operate at maximum efficiency. In addition to in-house efficiency and cost control, the company must also buy and sell enough volume of product to cover all costs and generate profits.

Retail customers are looking for timely and frequent deliveries of small quantities of very specific products. Some of those customers may need merchandising help as well. If their products are not selling, the distribution centers and manufacturers will soon be backed up with product as well. Retail sales are the key to avoiding a "bottleneck" in the process and flow of manufacturing and distribution.

The financial side of this business requires close and careful management of receivables and payables. Many manufacturers expect and receive payment for their products in about 10 days. This is essential to the sustained cash flow of their operations (primarily for payroll and raw materials purchases). Some manufacturers are in a position to offer credit terms of up to 30 days. Retailers on the other hand often require accounts payable terms ranging from 30 to 60 days. This is essential to the sustained cash flow of their operations, as customer sales are the primary source of funds.

So while the prospect of a 30–40% markup is clearly attractive, there is a cash flow situation and challenge that must be met.

Herbie and Mei are unsure about the best way to facilitate and manage trucking and insurance. They have the option of buying or leasing their own trucks on both the supply and delivery side and also have the option of using independent trucking companies. They could select some combination of those two options. In addition, merchandise must be insured, but who exactly is responsible for that coverage and when does that "ownership" change hands?

The partners project monthly warehouse operating expenses of $55,000 (building, payroll, administration, and salaries). This does not include merchandise, trucking, or insurance. The partners have conservatively projected first year sales to be $3 million.

Their warehouse inventory capabilities are in excess of $30 million. Herbie and Mei realize that it will take some time to approach that level from both a sales and cash flow perspective. Their facility and market base clearly present the potential to achieve sales of $40 million or more. Cash flow is the current obstacle. They have just over $4 million in cash and working capital (line of credit) for their start-up and believe that that will accommodate first year sales of $3 million given their logistics of inventory purchase, sales, and cash flow.

From a distance, the prospect of success is promising. The partners have the opportunity to buy low and sell high in large volume. There is a market niche to fill. The partners have the experience and the connections on both the supply and sales sides of the business.

QUESTIONS

1. What model for distribution does S & Z plan to pursue? What does its distribution channel chain look like?
2. Does its site selection make sense for the kind of business S & Z plans to pursue?
3. How should Herbie and Mei go about figuring the right mix of using their own trucks and using independent trucking companies?
4. How can the principals use technology to achieve success in their new venture? Be sure to address each of the major categories presented, i.e., purchasing, transportation, operations, distribution, and financial management.
5. Select a specific business or industry that you may become a part of; how would you incorporate the technological aspects described in the text into your day-to-day operations?

THE WALLINGFORD BOWLING CENTER

A group of 12 lifelong friends put together $2 million of their own funds and built a $13 million, 48-lane bowling alley near Norfolk, Virginia. Two of the investors became employees of the corporation. Ned Flanders works full time as general manager, and James Ahmad, a licensed CPA, serves as controller.

The beautiful, modern-day facility features a multilevel spacious interior with three rows of 16 lanes on two separate levels of the building, a full-service bar, a small restaurant, a game room (pool, video games, pinball), and two locker rooms. The facility sits on a spacious lot with plenty of parking and room to grow.

The bowling center is located in the small blue-collar town of Wallingford. There is no direct competition within the town. The surrounding communities include a wide-ranging mix of ethnic groups, professionals, middle- to upper-middle-class private homes, and several apartment and condominium complexes ranging from singles to young married couples to senior citizen retirement units. Nearly 200,000 people live within 15 miles of Wallingford.

The bowling center is open 24 hours per day and has a staff of 27 part- and full-time employees. After four years of operation, the partners find themselves frustrated with the low-profit performance of the business. While sales are covering expenses, the partners are not happy with the end-of-year profit sharing pool. The most recent income statement follows:

Wallingford Bowling Center
Income Statement—2004

Sales		$ 3, 844,000
Cost of Goods Sold		1, 315,000
Gross Margin		$ 2, 529,000
Operating expenses:		$ 2, 381,000
Mortgage	$ 960,000	
Depreciation	195,000	
Utilities	138,000	
Maintenance	125,000	
Payroll	700,000	
Supplies	127,000	
Insurance	136,000	
Taxable income		148,000
Taxes		54,000
Net income		$ 94,000

The bowling center operates at 100 percent capacity on Sunday through Thursday nights from 6:00 P.M. until midnight. Two sets of men's leagues come and go on each of those nights, occupying each lane with mostly five-person teams. Bowlers from each league consistently spend money at both the bar and restaurant. In fact, the men's leagues combine to generate about 60 percent of total current sales.

The bowling center operates at about 50 percent capacity on Friday and Saturday nights and on Saturday morning. The Friday and Saturday "open bowling" nights include mostly teenagers, young couples, and league members who come to practice in groups of two or three. The Saturday morning group is a kid's league, ages 10 through 14.

There are four women's leagues that bowl on Monday and Wednesday afternoon.

Business is extremely slow at the bowling center on Monday through Friday and Sunday mornings, and on the afternoons of Tuesday, Thursday, Friday, Saturday, and Sunday. It is not uncommon to have just three or four lanes in operation during those time periods.

The owners have taken a close look at the cost side of their business as a way to improve profitability. They concluded that while the total operating expense of $2,381,000 might appear to be high, there was in fact little room for expense cutting.

At a recent meeting of the partners, James Ahmad reported on the results of his three-month long investigation into the operating cost side of other bowling alleys and discovered that The Wallingford Bowling Center was very much in keeping with their industry. James went on to report that bowling alleys were considered to be "heavy to fixed cost operations" and that the key to success and profitability lies in maximizing capacity and sales dollars.

QUESTIONS

1. Develop a complete short marketing plan for this company. The goal of the plan is to increase capacity to as close to 100 percent as possible.
2. Given the particulars of this case, develop a list of the five best target market groups and the distinct features of the "4Ps" for each of those groups.

PARKER MOUNTAIN PRODUCTS, INC.

COMPANY HISTORY

The New England region of the United States includes a beautiful coastal stretch that extends from Maine to Rhode Island, through the states of New Hampshire, Massachusetts, and Connecticut. The area is famous for its summer tourism, which includes beaches, quaint villages and towns, restaurants, shops, historic sites and landmarks, and lobsters. Tens of thousands of people from around the world vacation in the area each year, especially during the summer season, which extends from Memorial Day to Labor Day.

Shortly after World War II, Ernest Parker returned to his hometown of Rochester, New Hampshire, and built a small factory that produces low-end glass and ceramic regional souvenirs. These products include wine glasses, general glassware, ceramic cups and bowls, and small platters. Each of these is decorated with a variety of painted images and words related to the specific coastal tourist towns and markets, that is, pictures of lobsters, seagulls, ocean waves, famous towns, and famous sites.

Ernest has provided steady employment for 35 production and support staff. The business has grown at a rate of about 5 percent per year (in sales). The most recent profit and loss statement is shown:

Parker Mountain Products, Inc.
Profit and Loss Statement—2001

Sales	$ 2,000,000
Cost of sales*	990,000
Gross profit	$ 1,010,000
Expenses	930,000
Net income	$ 80,000

* Includes direct materials only.

The entire production is sold through a small number of manufacturer's reps, wholesalers, and brokers. While the opportunity was always there to sell direct, Ernest chose to focus all his efforts on the production side of the business, allowing others to market, sell, and distribute the products to retail shops, hotels, and other vendors. The industry average or norm for profits is between 5 and 7 percent (net income to sales).

CURRENT SITUATION

Having now reached the age of 75, Ernest has decided to retire and turn the business over to his grandsons Chris and Ben, two young and ambitious entrepreneurs who recently graduated with honors from the renowned Applied Business Management program at the University of New Hampshire's Thompson School.

Chris and Ben are anxious to improve efficiency on the production side and to develop a variety of direct niche markets to complement their wholesale distribution on the marketing and sales side. The opportunity to add, drop, or shift the product mix, and to increase production and sales exists. In order to properly analyze and act on this, they have asked their bookkeeper to provide more specific production and cost data.

This information is presented below:

Product Line	No. of Units Produced	Selling Price per Unit	CGS per Unit	Total Variable Costs per Year
Platter	300,000	$2.00	$ .60	$240,000
Cups	200,000	2.50	1.50	160,000
Bowls	100,000	2.00	.20	80,000
General glassware	100,000	1.00	.70	80,000
Wine glasses	300,000	2.00	1.40	240,000

The total variable costs of $800,000 are assigned or charged to each product line based on the number of units produced. Total fixed costs for the factory are $80,000; selling and administrative costs for the total company are $50,000.

Chris and Ben have determined that the factory is now at 85 percent of capacity. They are certain that production can be increased without incurring any extra expense beyond direct materials.

They also know that the selling price could be increased by 15 percent as a result of a direct sales program. Their only uncertainty or fear is in disrupting the long-standing relationships that exist with the various manufacturers' reps, wholesalers, and brokers who have been able to sell all of the company's production for many years. They are afraid of "biting the hand that feeds them" by selling to an end user who currently buys from one of their own distributors.

QUESTIONS

1. As a first step, conduct a financial analysis of current operations by reformatting the income statement to include individual product lines as well as the total company. Analyze those data.
2. Use the information provided along with any assumptions you wish to make and construct a balance sheet and cash flow statement. Analyze those data.
3. What specific goals and standards of performance would you recommend for the new managers? What control process or audit system would you include for follow-up purposes?

NATE MOWER & SON, RESIDENTIAL PLUMBER(S)

Nate Mower has worked as a plumber in the Minneapolis area for 20 years. Nate has operated his business as a one-man show and has also had as many as six employees working on two or three jobs at a time.

During the winter months, Nate traditionally works alone, servicing local residents with routine plumbing repairs, furnace maintenance, and frozen pipes. During the summer months, Nate takes on a few new home construction plumbing and heating installations that call for the help of additional workers.

Nate has an excellent reputation for honesty and high-quality work. He has never had to advertise, as the work requests seem to be endlessly lined up and waiting. Nate works long hours, yet has managed to earn only a modest living for his wife Jessie and son Brett. In fact, Jessie has been heard to comment out loud to friends and family that Nate is "always busy and always broke." Several years back, Jessie had to take on a part-time cashier position at the local supermarket "just to put groceries on the table." The Mowers inherited Nate's grandparent's old farmhouse and have no mortgage. Nate drives around in his grandfather's old panel truck that he converted into the company work vehicle.

Nate is from the old school. He is a down-to-earth, hard-working country boy who loves to hunt and fish in his spare time. As Nate puts it, "I love my job and don't want to charge people too much for my work." Nate charges $25 per hour for his time (while onsite only) and provides all parts at cost. Nate believes that "it would be stealing" to markup the price of parts that he buys from a nearby wholesale distribution center. Nate mails out bills when he gets around to it, usually late at night if he's not too tired.

Brett Mower has learned a lot about the trade from his father. He often went along with Nate on jobs when he was young, and worked for his father throughout high school, mostly during the summers. Brett has returned home from a tour of duty in the military and is thinking about becoming a partner in the family business. He has several serious concerns, however, and is not sure which way to turn.

Although Brett would never say so out loud, he acknowledges that his father does seem to be always busy and always broke. He wonders why his mother is forced to work to put groceries on the table and help pay the bills. The family has no mortgage and no car payments. His folks have never taken a vacation, rarely go out, and still don't own a personal computer.

Brett recalls many incidents of receiving angry letters from creditors and parts suppliers over past-due bills. There have also been a few bounced and delayed paychecks over the years. Nate is currently on "c.o.d. - only" status with his suppliers who also expect some payment toward outstanding payables.

Brett wonders whether the business could ever support two families. He is planning on marrying his childhood sweetheart within the next year and has dreams of a house, family, and career of his own.

And yet, business is booming. The phone never stops ringing, especially during the long winter months, and Nate has barely scratched the surface of the new home installation market. The Minneapolis area is booming with new home construction. There have been reports in the local papers that several jobs have been delayed because of a shortage of contractors, including plumbing and heating. The short- and long-term market outlook is excellent.

Brett has been anguishing over his next move. Nate is thrilled at the prospect of forming a partnership with his son. Brett wants to start a new life and career in his hometown but has serious concerns about the condition and future of his father's business. Jessie suggested that perhaps someone in the know should take a look at their books and point them in the right direction.

Nate's most recent IRS returns reveal the following:

Schedule C—Profit and Loss Statement—2004
Nathan Mower, Residential Plumber

Sales		$221,250
CGS		135,000
GM		$ 86,250
Expenses:		$ 49,500
Outside		
labor	$39,500	
Truck	2,000	
Supplies	4,000	
Insurance	4,000	
Taxable income		$ 36,750

Balance Sheet Accounts—12/31/2004
Nathan Mower, Residential Plumber

Cash	$ 600	Accounts payable	$ 98,000
Accounts receivable	97,500	Notes payable	14,000
Inventory	143,400		
Land	0	Long-term debt	0
Buildings	0		
Equipment	36,000	Net worth	$165,500
	$277,500		$277,500

QUESTIONS

1. Using the above statements, provide specific recommendations that will alleviate Nate's cash flow problems.
2. Given the history of the company, is it possible for Brett to come onboard, earn a living, and successfully grow the company? If so, how?

THE LANDLORDS: INVESTMENTS IN COMMERCIAL REAL ESTATE

Greg, Chris, and Nancy are midcareer high school teachers in the Pittsburgh area. They love their jobs, are very dedicated, and plan to stay on until they are eligible for retirement in about 15 or 20 years. The three teachers and friends have met on several occasions to brainstorm ideas for an outside business partnership. With kids about to enter college and a somewhat pessimistic outlook toward their retirement pensions, the three want to make some extra money.

Their financial goals are to supplement their annual incomes by $10,000 to $15,000 each for college tuition purposes and to build an equity base of about $300,000 each for retirement.

Following several meetings, some consultation with friends and advisers, and some local market research, they have settled on the business of commercial real estate investment, more specifically, multiunit rental properties.

The Pittsburgh and surrounding communities are currently experiencing and are projected to sustain above-average growth in both jobs and housing. In fact, there is a current shortage of both rental units and single-family housing in the area. As a result, rents have increased steadily during the past three to five years and currently average:

1-bedroom apartment	$750–$900	per month
2-bedroom apartment	$1,000–$1,200	per month
3-bedroom apartment	$1,200–$1,400	per month
4-bedroom apartment	$1,400–$1,800	per month

Tenants are responsible for heat, hot water, and electricity. Landlords provide parking and maintenance.

Interest rates are very low at this time and are therefore very attractive for borrowing and investing purposes. Greg has learned that local banks will finance commercial properties for up to 25 years at 6 percent interest. In addition, those banks will provide loans for up to 85 percent of assessed property values.

Multi-unit apartment buildings in the area range from $300,000 to $600,000 depending on size, condition, and neighborhood location. Most buildings include three to six separate units ranging from one to four bedrooms in size.

Greg, Chris, and Nancy want to locate and purchase enough buildings to meet their financial goals. Each building must therefore generate enough rental income to offset all costs and generate an after-tax profit. The buildings must also be carefully selected with regard to their expected growth in appreciation.

In addition to building and outside maintenance, the landlords are responsible for mortgage payments, city water and sewer bills, insurance, and local taxes. The IRS requires that depreciation be spread over a 28-year period.

The landlords each have $30,000 to invest for down payments on properties. One of their advisers urged them to set aside a portion of that amount for working capital depending on their cash flow outlook.

QUESTIONS

1. Greg, Chris, and Nancy could do their real estate rental business strictly self-financed or with bank loans. Which do you recommend and why? What are the monthly financial obligations under each approach?
2. Given their starting funds and loan opportunities, how large a real estate deal can they handle their first time out if they go the bank loan route?

3. One adviser mentioned putting aside a portion of their money for working capital. How much would you recommend they put aside? On what do you base your suggestion?
4. What are the typical cash flow problems that people in real estate rentals face? How can Greg, Chris, and Nancy prepare themselves to meet these?
5. Many real estate investments or projects are of a much greater magnitude than those in this case. How would you go about organizing and financing a project that required an investment of say $300 to $350 million dollars?

Case 16

RICHARD HARRIS AND HARRIS HOMES LLC

Many people who thought the devastation from 2005's Hurricane Katrina would be a golden opportunity for the Gulf Coast construction industry were sadly mistaken. Consider the situation of Richard Harris.

Harris had owned Harris Homes LLC about ten years when Katrina hit Ocean Springs, Mississippi. By 2004, his sales had grown to $3.5 million and his 2005 sales were on track for $5 million when the storm hit. Before the storm, he had $3 million in projects and $300,000 worth of vacant property. Before the storm, he was building 24 houses, and 12 of them were already under contract. When Katrina hit, those homes sustained damage, and even with insurance, Harris' out-of-pocket expenses to cover his deductible were around $100,000. The bad news was that paying those deductible expenses would eat up all of his working capital.

That money problem fed into another problem – people. Harris was employing 60 to 80 subcontracted workers, but now he couldn't make competitive offers to get the workers back. FEMA (the Federal Emergency Management Agency) was spending money for their Blue Roof emergency repair program, out-of-state contractors with fat bank accounts were hiring local workers at premium rates to help them start repairing and rebuilding, and the area's worker base was still depleted because of the people who evacuated the area and had not yet returned. Just as workers were scarce and going for premium prices, so were lumber and all building materials, as an entire region tried to rebuild at the same time.

Those 12 homes under contract were sold at pre-Katrina prices, in effect "locking-in" low prices the region will not see for months, perhaps years to come. Harris was obligated to finish those homes. However, the cabinetmaker, plumber and electrician he had favored all had businesses underwater after Katrina, and may be out of business.

It is now about three weeks after Katrina (and the glancing blow from Hurricane Rita) hit. Looking at his immediate future, Harris knows he needs to get to work on the other nearly finished homes, which would get some new cash flowing into his business. He has applied for SBA disaster relief, but has been told it would be 90 days before any money became available—if he qualifies. He needs to move to get some of the potentially lucrative government contracts for rebuilding that are being offered. But even here, it is hard to know how to bid when prices are so unpredictable. For example, the cost of dumping debris from cleared land jumped from $1 a cubic yard to $4 after Katrina.

Harris had done several things right. He had insurance. He kept a set of records where they would be safe, making it easier to apply for government relief and insurance after the storm. He even had kept ready cash for expenses. Despite all of that, Katrina hit, and Richard Harris is looking at the possible loss of his business, right at the moment when the construction industry in his area appears about to enter a golden age of rebuilding.

QUESTIONS

1. What do you think are the two greatest risks facing Richard Harris's business? Why?
2. What actions can Richard take now to manage the risks you mentioned above?
3. From this experience, what recommendations would you make to Richard Harris to do an even better job of preparing for future hurricanes?

Source: Jackie Larson, "Gulf Coast Entrepreneurs Face Reality" *Entrepreneur.com,* September 22, 2005 http://www.entrepreneur.com/article/0,4621,323569,00.html.

Case 17

THE HOUSE OF WINE (REVISITED)

Please refer back to Case 9. The focus now shifts to inventory management. The proprietors have a somewhat limited start-up budget for inventory and working capital. It is very important for them to buy the right quantity of the right products (part of asset management).

Inventory may be purchased with cash, through short-term loans from a bank (notes payable/line of credit), or through a credit arrangement with suppliers (accounts payable). There are also a variety of shipping and receiving programs and systems available.

QUESTIONS

1. Use the information from this case, Case 9, and your classroom discussions to create a detailed inventory management program for the proprietors.
2. How would you recommend they pay for the inventory?
3. What milestones in the House of Wine's operations do you think should occur in order to signal when a different approach to inventory might make sense?
4. When thinking about the House of Wine's inventory, will it make any difference that some inventory is time-limited (i.e., can spoil), other parts of it are seasonal, and some can be sold or held for long periods of time? If it is an issue, how do you propose to handle it?
5. Will the House of Wine face much in the way of accounts receivable problems? Why or why not?

Case 18

ELI ASSOCIATES: PROFESSIONAL WRITERS, SPEAKERS, CONSULTANTS

A small group of successful executives from different but related industries have decided to say good-bye to their 80-hour workweeks and constant travel, and start a new career. The executives, now in their late forties to early fifties, have worked together for many years in varying capacities and have established a name for themselves in their respective industries. Their extracurricular activities outside their former jobs have allowed them to already establish some markets for their new products and services even though the business has not yet begun formal operations.

D. Eli, the firm's president, spent many years in the shipping industry, working in both the container ship and rail areas of the international product distribution system. Eli has extensive experience in the Pacific Rim markets and in the West Coast rail network. Eli is fluent in Chinese.

Dave Howell spent more than 20 years as a production and general manager in the lumber industry. Dave has managed manufacturing facilities all over the continental United States and eventually moved up to the general manager role, where he was responsible for the overall operation of several large plants.

Fred Malone just sold his building products distribution yard. Fred started from scratch and over a 25 year period built a wholesale distribution operation that features a 60,000-square-foot warehouse with a high-tech shipping and receiving and order processing system. Fred has contributed to the wealth of many small manufacturers, shippers, and retailers thanks to his astute marketing and organizational skills.

Pam Waller spent many years in the banking business, moving all the way up the ranks from teller to loan officer to vice president of finance. Pam is responsible for facilitating many new and growth business ventures. She built a reputation as being able to bring the right people together on big projects and in knowing how to negotiate deals so that everyone involved could realize his or her own success story.

The new partners have crossed paths many times over the years and have become good friends. In addition to formal business transactions, the partners have been active in many industry and trade associations and are often asked to speak and write articles on behalf of those groups. Each also serves as a member of the board of directors of a number of organizations, both in the business and philanthropic arenas. They have also had a little taste of consulting, as their experience and connections have resulted in a number of those opportunities.

The new partners have a home base in the Portland, Oregon, area and have located a parcel of land to purchase just outside of the city. They plan to construct a professional office complex; the new firm will occupy about 50 percent of that building, and they plan to rent or lease the additional space to "just the right neighbors," as Eli puts it.

The new partners are very confident that sales will flow in the door almost immediately, given their history and current activities. They are however wading into unfamiliar waters and have many questions regarding liability, intellectual property, contracts, errors and omissions, and insurance coverage, staffing, subcontracting, and so on.

They now find themselves in the business of selling advice and recommendations on the consulting side, in developing intellectual property on the writing side, and in becoming spokespeople and speech-givers on behalf of other companies and organizations. They are suddenly worried about conflict of interest situations that may arise. They wonder what might happen if someone takes their advice and then fails? This has led them to discuss the possibility of formulating some sort of mission statement or corporate policy/philosophy and developing some package of disclaimers and contractual agreements for clients to sign. They are also concerned about protecting the individual wealth and assets that they have earned throughout their careers. They wish to somehow separate and protect that wealth from this new venture.

QUESTIONS

1. Given the information provided, create a list of potential problems and challenges that the group may face on the legal and liability side of their new venture.
2. Advise the advisers. What should they do?
3. Although this case focuses primarily on legal issues, the partners have many marketing options to consider. Advise the advisers. Create a list of best prospects for each of the principals and for the firm as a whole.

WAYNE MANOR COMIX

Jared Wayne began buying, selling, and trading comic books in grade school. By the time he graduated from college, his collection filled his apartment and his parent's basement. He lived near Flagstaff, Arizona, and was well known in the community, having sold at nearly every comic book and science fiction convention in that university town. It was only natural for him to open a shop.

Jared opened a small shop in an old strip mall near the Northern Arizona University campus and a local high school. He called it Wayne Manor Comix. As a one-person operation, Jared stayed open only afternoons and weekends. He occasionally had a friend or one of his parents stay at the shop on convention weekends, while Jared ran his booth at the convention. Since this was maybe four to six weekends a year, he figured that his employing others required no paperwork.

It was at one of those conventions that Jared met Xandra Kent. It was love at first sight, and they were married six months later. Xandra worked at a dress shop during the week, and in the comic shop on weekends when Jared did his convention runs, so life—and Jared's paperwork—remained simple. Then Xandra announced she was pregnant. She had the baby, and they named him Bruce (what else would two comic loving parents call a kid named Wayne?).

Jared loves being around Bruce, and Xandra has suggested that Jared hire someone to work at the shop. That way, Jared would have time on weekends with the family. Jared likes the idea, and has several customers he trusts and who know comic books really well. He could hire one of them. The shop is making enough money that Jared thinks he can afford a part-time employee, but he does not know how to determine what a fair hourly wage would be or what would be the best way to train the new employee. He is also worried that there may be government requirements for a permanent part-time employee that might trip him up.

QUESTIONS

1. What kinds of things would a regular customer need to learn in order to be successful as an employee? What would that suggest as skills Jared might want to make sure he finds in a successful candidate for the job?
2. How could Jared find out the going local hourly wage for a part-time employee in a small shop? In addition to a wage, are there any other ways Jared could "pay" an employee without using cash?
3. Are there government regulations that apply when you add a permanent part-time employee? Where could Jared get help about that?
4. If Jared can get satisfactory answers for all his questions and can hire someone, how would you recommend for Jared to supervise the employee, especially when he plans to spend most of his weekend with his family?

Case 20

THE DAUGHTER OF THE IMMIGRANT

This is the story of a journey through poverty, a large and loving family, and a quest for wealth and social good. This is the story of a twenty-first century woman with a wide-reaching agenda that would touch many lives. This is the story of Eva Sanchez, the youngest of eight children, born in Mexico, born in poverty. There was never any money, but there was always lots of love and culture and religion—plenty of sources of hope and inspiration.

Soon after Eva's father died, the family moved to Los Angeles to start a new life. Her mother and most of her siblings were forced to find work, but Eva was pushed to stay in school. She was always the brightest, and she always had big goals and plans that went far beyond her immediate family.

Eva is determined to achieve great wealth. Eva is also determined to break the cycle of poverty and hopelessness and to help and inspire members of her Mexican/Latino cultures to "get educated and get out," as she puts it, and to live and be a part of the American dream. Eva was the first in her family to attend college, and through hard work, straight A's, and much determination, is about to graduate with a degree in business. Eva still has no money and now has nearly $60,000 in outstanding school loans. She is very happy and very excited to begin to fulfill her dreams.

Eva has many goals. She already sees her life as a blended mission of family, career, and community service. She does not believe in the separation or distinction of work and play or work and family that others do. At the moment, however, Eva has no specific agenda and no money. Her major goals are:

- A successful career in real estate and business consulting. Eva believes in capitalism, is proud to be an American, and intends to become a millionaire. She plans to achieve this through her real estate work and through "outside projects," as she puts it. Eva is thinking about real estate investment, in particular, the purchase and development of multi-unit apartment buildings.
- A program to improve the lives of women and minorities and the Latino culture in particular. Eva believes that education and motivation are the foundations of success. As a woman and a minority and a poor person, she believes that she can use her education and motivation to inspire others to do the same. Eva would like to have a hand in helping others achieve a successful career in family, business, and community service.
- A strategy of high growth and high performance. Eva plans to earn a good living through traditional real estate sales and to achieve wealth and high earnings through real estate development.
- A productive and satisfying balance of wealth, family and social values, community, and lifestyle. Eva also wants to have at least five kids.

One would describe Eva's characteristics as very hard working and ambitious, very conservative, very religious and traditional, and very bright. One would describe Eva's competencies as having good common sense, a good education and basic training in business, and being very personable.

While this is not the end of Eva's story, it is the end for you for now. Most of you are reaching the point where it is time to formulate your own mission of family, career, lifestyle, and community service. You can help yourself by first helping Eva through your responses to the following:

QUESTIONS

1. How does Eva's life and expectations fit with the four bottom lines mentioned in Chapter 20?
2. Does Eva have the characteristics and competencies to pull this off? Are her plans realistic? Why or why not?
3. Given her current status of no job, no money, and a large debt to pay off, how specifically would you advise Eva to proceed? Be sure to include both a short- and long-range plan, as her goals are not likely to become realities all at once.
4. Now think about yourself and list and briefly describe your own goals in each of the categories discussed. Writing them down is the first step to making them happen.

Glossary

A

Accelerator An organization that supports start-up technology businesses by providing inexpensive office space, a variety of support services, and resources; most accelerators are associated with universities.

Access The opportunity to find and obtain opportunities offered to others.

Accounting equation The statement that assets equal liabilities plus owners' equity (assets = liabilities + owners' equity).

Accounts receivable Money owed to your business by customers who purchased your product on credit.

Acquisition cost The total cost of acquiring an asset, including such costs as purchase price, transportation, installation, testing, and calibrating in order to ready it for its first productive use.

Advertising Advertising is often used to support the corporate identity and value propositions that are established through public relations efforts. Part of conveying your message to your customers, advertising outlets include newspapers, magazines, billboards, television, and Internet banner ads, to name a few.

Age Discrimination in Employment Act An act of Congress that makes it illegal to discriminate against people who are older than 40 years of age.

Agent Person given authority to act for and represent another person or entity (the principal) within certain controls by that entity. (Ch. 18)

Agent A middleman business which represents a manufacturer's product or service to other business-to-business middleman firms. (Ch. 11)

Aggrandizing Attempting to make your business or yourself seem more accomplished or grander than reality.

Americans with Disabilities Act of 1990 An act of Congress that requires that businesses make provisions for access by disabled people.

Arbitration A dispute resolution process held instead of court cases in which both sides present their case to a legal professional.

Arm's length transaction A business deal where the parties have a prior relation or affiliation, but where the business is conducted as if they were unrelated. This approach is done to help guard against potential conflicts of interest.

Articles of organization Document setting forth information about a limited liability company that is filed with the state to establish an LLC.

Articles of partnership Agreement between the partners of a firm on matters pertaining to the formation and operation of the partnership.

Articulate The concept that information flows from the income statement through the statements of retained earnings and owners' equity to the balance sheet.

Asset Something the business owns that is expected to have economic value in the future.

Assumed name filing or a fictitious name filing Filing made with a state(s) in which the business operates disclosing the trade name or assumed name of the business along with the owners of the business.

Auction A business setting in which products consigned from multiple sellers are available for bidding by customers.

Augmented product Core product plus features that tend to differentiate it from the competition.

B

B2B Business-to-business transactions using e-commerce.

B2C Business-to-consumer transactions using e-commerce.

Balance sheet A statement of what a business owns (assets), what it owes to others (liabilities), and how much value the owners have invested in it (equity).

Baldridge Award The Malcolm Baldridge National Quality Award is given by the US Government to businesses and nonprofit organizations that have been judged outstanding in seven measures of quality leadership; strategic planning; customer and market focus; measurement, analysis, and knowledge management; human resource focus; process management; and results (see http://www.quality.nist.gov).

Bank available balance The sum of money that has actually been received and paid out of a depositor's account.

Bank ledger balance The sum of deposits and withdrawals recorded in a bank's accounting records.

Bankrupt The financial state of having more debt than assets, such that net worth is negative.

Bankruptcy An extreme form of business termination which uses a legal method for closing a business and paying off creditors when debts are substantially greater than assets.

Bar coding Obtaining a Universal Product Code number and scan-ready visual tag, and printing it on the product or its packaging. Bar codes can then be scanned and recognized by others.

Barter The practice of trading goods and services without the use of money.

Bearer Any person or business entity who possesses a security.

Benefits Characteristics of a product or service that the target customer would consider worthwhile.

Billboard principle Is an ethical model that asks whether someone would be comfortable having his or her decision and name advertised on a billboard for the public to see.

Book value The difference between original acquisition cost and the amount of accumulated depreciation.

Bootstrapping Using low-cost or free techniques to minimize your cost of doing business.

Born international A new firm that opens a Web site immediately, thus being exposed to customers from around the world.

Bot A Web-based program that uses artificial intelligence techniques to automate tasks such as searches.

Brainstorming A group discussion in which criticism is suspended in order to generate the maximum number of ideas.

Breakeven The point at which total costs equal total sales.

Brochure A sales document, typically consisting of multiple panels (when folded) or multiple pages, describing your business or specific products or services.

Budget A financial plan for the future, based on a single level of operations; a quantitative expression of the use of resources necessary to achieve a business's strategic goals.

Bundling Combining two or more products in one unit and pricing it less than if the units were sold separately.

Business cards A 2- × $3\frac{1}{2}$-inch cardboard card with your personal and company contact information; the key way of leaving information about yourself.

Business entity concept The concept that a business has an existence separate from that of its owners.

Business format franchising An agreement that provides a complete business format, including trade name, operational procedures, marketing, and products or services to sell.

Business life cycle The sequence or pattern of developmental stages any business goes through during its life span.

Business plan A document designed to detail the *major* characteristics of a firm—its product or service, its industry, its market, its manner of operating (production, marketing, management), and its financial outcomes with an emphasis on the firm's *present* and *future.*

Business risk The level of probability that the future economic state of the business will be worse than expected.

Business stationery A standard $8\frac{1}{2}$- × 11-inch page of blank paper typically imprinted with your company's name and contact information.

Buyers People who purchase an existing business.

Buy-in The purchase of substantially less than 100 percent of a business.

Buyout insurance Insurance that provides money to owners of a business to buy the shares of any deceased owner from that owner's heirs.

Buyout The purchase of substantially all of an existing business.

C

Cannibalizing Taking business away from your employer.

Capital assets Assets that are expected to provide economic benefits for periods of time greater than one year.

Capital budgeting The process of deciding among various investment opportunities to create a specific spending plan.

Capital lease A lease in which at the end of the lease period the asset becomes the property of the lessee, possibly with an additional payment.

Captive pricing Setting the price for an item relatively low and then charging much higher prices for the expendables it uses.

Career A lifelong series of jobs or occupations.

Cash budget A cash budget identifies when, how, and why cash is expected to come into the business, and when, how, and why it is expected to leave.

Cash equivalents Assets that may be quickly converted to cash.

Cash flow statement A statement of the sources and uses of cash in a business for a specific period of time.

Cash flow The actual receipt and disbursement of money by a business.

Cash receipts budget A schedule of the amounts and timings of the receipt of cash into a business.

Cash Money that is immediately available to be spent.

Cash-to-cash cycle The time that is required for a business to acquire resources, convert them into product, sell the product, and receive cash from the sale.

Categorical questions Questions that are answered by selecting the proper category; for example, "What is your ethnicity? White, African American, Hispanic, Asian, American Indian, Other."

Caveat emptor Latin: let the buyer beware.

Certification An examination based acknowledgement that the firm is owned and operated as specified.

Charge back A reduction in the bank account of a merchant by a credit card company.

Check kiting The practice of writing checks when there is not enough money on deposit to cover them.

Check the box taxation A choice LLCs can make on their tax returns to be taxed as a corporation or a partnership.

Civil Rights Act of 1991 A series of acts by Congress that prohibit discrimination on the basis of race, color, religion, sex, or national origin.

Clearing house An entity that processes checks and electronic fund transfers for banks and other financial organizations.

Cognitive dissonance Doubt that occurs after a purchase has been made. An inconsistency between experience and belief.

Co-insurance A contract stipulation that requires a policyholder to carry insurance in an amount equal to a stated minimum percentage of the market value of the property insured.

Collateral Something of value given or pledged as security for payment of a loan; collateral may consist of financial instruments, such as stocks, bonds, and negotiable paper, or of physical goods, such as trucks, machinery, land, or buildings.

Combinational competencies Organizational capabilities that come from combining tangible and intangible resources in ways superior to the competition.

Commercial paper Notes issued by credit-worthy corporations.

Community development organization An organization authorized by the SBA to make insured loans to small businesses that are expected to increase economic activity within a specific geographic area.

Company book balance The sum of cash inflows and cash outflows recorded in the firm's accounting records.

Competencies Forms of business-related expertise.

Competitive advantage The particular way a firm implements customer benefits that keeps the firm ahead of other firms in the industry or market.

Comprehensive budget Comprehensive budgets, also often referred to as *master budgets,* are sets of budgets that detail all projected receipts and spending for the budget period.

Concentrated strategy A marketing strategy in which a marketer selects one specific group of consumers and designs a marketing mix specifically for that group.

Conflict of interest A situation in which a person faces two or more competing standards or goals.

Consignment The practice of accepting goods for resale, without taking ownership of them and without being responsible to pay prior to their being sold.

Consignment shops Retail stores in which customers can come and buy products placed in the shops by a wide variety of sellers.

Consistency Maintaining of the same behavior, attitude, or value over long periods of time.

Consolidation A transfer method in which a small business is bought by a larger firm for the purpose of quickly growing the larger firm.

Consumer A private individual or household who is the end-user of (the entity that "consumes") a product or service.

Contingency fee Fee paid by a client to an attorney for legal services that is dependent upon the outcome of a case.

Contract manufacturing An existing firm with the correct manufacturing capabilities makes your product for you.

Copyright Exclusive right given to the creator of a literary or artistic work to make use of that work.

Core competency The main work of a firm in a particular line of business.

Core product The very basic description of what a product is—a bar of soap, a house-cleaning service.

Corporation A legal "artificial" entity that is formed by filing specific documents with a state government.

Cost of capital The percentage cost of obtaining future funds.

Cost of disposition Cost incurred in the activities necessary to get rid of an asset.

Cost of goods sold budget A schedule of the expected amounts of direct materials, direct labor, and manufacturing overhead that is included in products sold during the accounting period.

Cost of operating The direct cost incurred in using an asset for the purpose for which it was intended.

Cost of owning Cost incurred in financing, insuring, taxing, or tracking an asset.

Cost strategy A generic strategy aimed at mass markets in which a firm offers a combination of cost benefits that appeals to the customer.

Cost The value given up to obtain something that you want.

Cover letter A one-page document on business stationery (also called *letterhead*) that introduces the business plan and the business owner to the recipient and indicates why the recipient is being asked to read the plan.

Coverages Contractual provisions of insurance policies that specify what risks the insurance company is assuming.

Creative destruction The way that newly created goods, services, or firms can hurt existing goods, services, or firms.

Creativity A process producing an idea or opportunity that is novel and useful, frequently derived from making connections among distinct ideas or opportunities.

Credit reporting agency A business that collects, collates, and reports information concerning an entity's use of debt.

Cultural resonance A concept in public interest which alludes to events with a broad appeal within the market or population.

Culture A set of shared norms, values, and orientations of a group of individuals, prescribing how people should think and behave in the organization.

Currency A concept in public importance which alludes to the degree to which the issue is immediate in its impact. (Ch. 10)

Currency The bills and coins printed by governments to represent money. (Ch. 14)

Current ratio The value of current assets divided by current liabilities.

Customer segment A group or subgroup of potential purchasers that can be approached in a coherent manner.

Debt capital Money borrowed for the purposes of investment in a business.

Debt A legal obligation to pay money in the future.

Decline stage A life cycle stage in which sales and profits of the firm begin a falling trend.

Deductible An amount of loss that will not be paid by an insurance company.

Defendant Person or other entity being sued.

Degree of similarity The extent to which a product or service is like another.

Delegation The assignment of work to others over whom you have power.

Demand deposits Money held in checking and savings accounts.

Deposits and progress payments Cash payments received before product is completed or delivered.

Depreciation Regular and systematic reduction in income that transfers asset value to expense over time.

Design patent A 14-year patent for a new, original, and ornamental design for an article of manufacture.

Determination competencies Skills identified with the energy and focus needed to bring a business into existence.

Dichotomous questions Questions that have only two possible choices; for example, "Have you shopped here before?"

Differential advantage The characteristic that separates one company from another in product, price, promotion, and/or distribution.

Differentiated strategy A marketing strategy in which a marketer selects two or more distinct groups of consumers and designs specific marketing mixes to meet their needs.

Differentiation strategy A type of generic strategy aimed at clarifying how one product is unlike another in a mass market.

Difficult to imitate A resource characteristic which enhances value through offering uniqueness to the buyer.

Direct competition Other companies that make a similar product or provide a similar service; for example, direct competition for Coca-Cola includes all other soft drink providers.

Direct exporting Exporting using no middlemen.

Direct mail A method of selling in which catalogs, brochures, letters, videos, and other pieces of marketing materials are mailed directly to customers from which they can mail, call, or e-mail an order. Direct faxing and direct e-mailing are more modern forms of direct mail.

Direct response advertising Placing an advertisement in a magazine or newspaper, on television or radio, or in any other media. The ad contains an order blank with a phone number and e-mail or regular mail address with the intent of having the customer place an immediate order.

Direct sales Methods of going directly to your customer in order to sell your product. Vending machines, door-to-door salespeople, leasing space at a craft fair, farmers' markets, party sales, and most industrial sales are methods of direct selling.

Discounted cash flows Cash flows that have been reduced in value because they are to be received in the future.

Discounts for prompt payment A reduction in sales price provided to credit customers for paying outstanding amounts in a timely manner.

Disposal value The net amount realized after subtracting the costs of getting rid of an asset from its selling price.

Distributive view An ethical overview which involves thinking of problem solving as a win-lose issue. (Compare to the integrative view.)

Diversify To invest in multiple investments of differing risk profiles for the purpose of reducing overall investment risk.

Dividends Payments of profits to the owners of corporations.

Documentary draft A draft which can be exercised only when presented with specified shipping documents.

Double taxation Earnings of the business are taxed twice with the business as well as its owners being subject to tax.

Due diligence The process of investigating a business to determine its value.

E

Early adopters A customer adoption segment that purchases after pioneers.

Early majority Customer adoption segment that purchases after early adopters, and whose demand creates a mass market.

Earnings multiple The ratio of the value of a firm to its annual earnings.

Economic development agency A government organization that works to increase economic activity in the form of job opportunities within a specific geographic area.

Economic order quantity (EOQ) A statistical technique that determines the quantity of inventory that a business must hold to minimize total inventory cost.

Elastic product Product for which there are any number of substitutes and for which a change in price makes a difference in quantity purchased.

Electronic malls A group of companies, usually with a common target market, selling via the Internet through a specific site.

Elevator pitch A 30-second (100 words or less) action-oriented description of a business designed to sell the idea of the business to another.

Employee fit The match between the needs, expectations, and culture of the small business with the expectations and the skills of the individual employee.

Employee referral An underused, low-cost method for finding workers that rewards your employees for recommending potential candidates that would be a great employee fit.

Employee stock ownership plan A formalized legal method to transfer some or all of the ownership of a business to its employees.

Employee theft Misappropriation of business property by employees of that business.

Entrepreneur A person who owns or starts an organization, such as a business.

Entrepreneurial alertness A special set of observational and thinking skills that help entrepreneurs identify good opportunities; the ability to notice things that have been overlooked, without actually launching a formal search for opportunities, and the motivation to look for opportunities.

Entry wedge An opportunity that makes it possible for a new business to gain a foothold in a market.

Equal Employment Opportunity Commission (EEOC) A commission established to enforce the provisions of the Equal Employment Opportunity Act.

Equipment Machinery, tools, or materials used in the performance of the work of the business.

Equity capital Money contributed to the businesses in return for part ownership of the business.

Equity Ownership of a portion of a business.

ESOP (Employee stock option plan) A method for employees to purchase the business for which they work.

e-tailer An electronic retailer; a store that exists only on the Internet.

Ethical dilemma A situation that occurs when a person's values are in conflict, making it unclear whether a decision is the right thing to do.

Ethics A system of values that people consider in determining whether actions are right or wrong.

Ethics planning A process used to better consider issues of right and wrong.

Ethnographic research Data gathered by simple observation—seeing what consumers do, rather than asking them.

Exculpatory clause Part of a contract in which a party to the contract states that he or she will not be responsible for certain actions.

Executive summary A one to two-page (250–500 word) overview of the business, its business model, market, expectations, and immediate goals. It is typically put at the start of a business plan and is the most popular summary form for a business plan.

Expense A decrease in owners' equity caused by consuming your product or service.

Expert business professionalization A situation that occurs when all the major functions of a firm are conducted according to the standard business practices of its industry.

External legitimacy The extent to which a small business is taken for granted, accepted, or treated as viable by organizations or people outside the small business or the owner's family.

External reference price An estimation of what a price should be based on information external to a consumer, such as advice, advertisements, or comparison shopping.

F

Factoring receivables Borrowing money secured by a firm's accounts receivable.

Factoring Selling the rights to collect accounts receivable to an entity outside your business.

Fair Credit Reporting Act U.S. federal legislation specifying consumer's rights vis à vis credit reporting agencies.

Fair market value The price at which goods and services are bought and sold between willing sellers and buyers in an arms-length transaction.

Family business A firm in which one family owns a majority stake and is involved in the daily management of the business.

Famous faces A concept in public recognition which alludes to connections of your event or firm to individuals the general public would recognize.

Favorable/unfavorable variance A label applied to variances to indicate their effect upon the income statement; favorable variances would result in profits being greater than budgeted, all other things being equal. Unfavorable variances would result in profits being less than budgeted, all other things being equal.

Feasibility The extent to which an idea is viable and realistic and the extent to which you are aware of internal (to your business) and external (industry, market, and regulatory environment) forces that could affect your business.

Fidelity bonds Bonds, also called *dishonesty bonds,* that repay employers for losses caused by dishonest or negligent employees.

Financial accounting A formal, rule-based set of accounting principles and procedures intended for use by outside owners, investors, banks, and regulators.

Financial flexibility A business's ability to manage cash flows in such a manner that the company can respond appropriately to unexpected opportunities and needs.

Financial leverage A measure of the amount of debt relative to total investment.

Financial management A set of theories and techniques used to optimize the receipt and use of capital assets.

Financial risk Uncertainty of returns; the probability of losing money.

Financial statements Formal summaries of the content of an accounting system's records of transactions.

Financial strength The ability of a business to survive adverse financial events.

Financing activities Activities through which cash is obtained from and paid to lenders, owners, and investors.

First principles Basic ideas about what constitutes right behavior.

Fixed costs Those costs that remain constant regardless of the quantity, for example, rent.

Flat fees A method of billing for lawyers in which a fixed amount is paid for a certain task.

Flexibility rewards The ability of business owners to structure life in the way that suits their needs best.

Flexibility The freedom of not having lots of rules, policies, and procedures.

Float Delays in the movement of money among depositors and banks.

Flyers A sales document to be posted or handed out, typically printed on a $8^1/_2$- $\times$11-inch sheet of colored paper (or printed in color on white stock to increase visibility).

Focus group A form of data gathering from a small group led by a moderator.

Focus strategy A generic strategy that targets a portion of the market, called a *segment* or *niche.*

Foundation An institution to which private wealth is contributed and from which private wealth is distributed for public purposes.

Founders People who create or start new businesses.

Franchise A prepackaged business bought, rented, or leased from a company called a *franchisor.*

Freight forwarders Firms specializing in arranging international shipments—packaging, transportation, and paperwork.

Fulfillment center A company that will warehouse your products and fill your customers' orders for you.

Full (or classic) business plan Contains a maximum of 25 single-spaced pages of text and 15 pages of financials and appendixes.

Full-time self-employment Working for yourself for more than 35 hours a week.

G

GAAP Generally Accepted Accounting Principles are the standardized rules for accounting procedures set out by the Financial Account Standards Board and used in all audits and submissions of accounting reports to the government.

Gain on investment The percentage amount that the payout of an investment differs from original cost: calculated as (payout − investment + dividends)/investment.

Gaming the payment process Using methods to appear to be paying bills on time, when in fact payment is being delayed or avoided.

Generic strategies Three widely applicable classic strategies for businesses of all types—differentiation, cost, and focus.

Gift Valuable assets or services donated to the business without any obligation to repay or give up any ownership interest.

Going concern The accounting concept that a business is expected to continue in existence for the foreseeable future.

Golden Rule An ethical model which suggests you treat others in the manner you wish to be treated.

Good story A concept in public interest which alludes to an incident with good triumphing.

Grants Gifts of money made to a business for a specific purpose.

Gross profit Funds left over after deducting the cost of goods sold.

Growth rewards What people get from facing and beating challenges.

Growth stage An industry life cycle stage in which customer purchases increase at a dramatic rate.

Growth trap A financial crisis that is caused by a business growing faster than it can be financed.

Guerilla marketing The use of creative and relatively inexpensive ways to reach your customer. Examples include door-knob hangers, flyers under windshield wipers, T-shirts, balloons, and messages written on sidewalks.

H

Harvest Recovery of value through a sale of a firm or its assets.

Heir A person who becomes an owner through inheriting or being given a stake in a family business.

Heterogeneity A quality of a service in which each time it is provided it will be slightly different from the previous time.

Heuristic A common-sense rule, a rule-of-thumb.

High-growth venture A firm started with the intent of eventually going public, following the pattern of growth and operations of a big business.

Highly fragmented industries Collections of similar businesses in which virtually all firms have small market shares.

High-performing small business A firm intended to provide the owner with a high income through sales or profits superior to those of the traditional small business.

Hold harmless A type of waiver in which a party agrees not to hold another party responsible for certain events.

Home-based business A business that is operated from the owner's home.

Hourly fees A basis for legal charges in which the rate is based on a price per hour. Often lawyers will charge for fractions of an hour.

Human interest A concept in public interest which alludes to a character to whom the public can relate.

I

Imitative strategy An overall strategic approach in which the entrepreneur does more or less what others are already doing.

Imitative Characterized by being like or copying something that already exists.

Income rewards The money made by owning one's own business.

Income statement A statement that lists revenues and expenses and shows the amount of profit a business makes for a specified period of time.

Incremental innovation An overall strategic approach in which a firm patterns itself on other firms, with the exception of one or two key areas.

Incremental strategy Taking an idea and offering a way to do something slightly better than it is done presently.

Incubator A facility which offers subsidized space and business advice to companies in their earliest stages of operation.

Independent contractors Persons working to achieve a certain goal without being subjected to substantial controls by another.

Independent small business A business owned by an individual or small group.

Indirect competition Companies that provide alternatives that are dissimilar to your product/service that consumers might choose to meet a similar need; for example, indirect competition for Coca-Cola includes any other company providing items to quench thirst.

Indirect exporting Exporting using middlemen such as agents, export management companies, or export trading companies.

Industry The general name for the line of product or service being sold, or the firms in that line of business.

Industry analysis (IA) A research process that provides the entrepreneur with key information about the industry, such as its current situation and trends.

Industry-life cycle The stages an industry goes through from its birth to its ending. There are five stages: introduction, growth, maturity, decline, and death.

Industry specific knowledge Activities, knowledge, and skills specific to businesses in a particular industry.

Inelastic product Product for which there are few substitutes and for which a change in price makes very little difference in quantity purchased.

Informational plans Give potential customers or suppliers information about the company and its product or service.

Infringer Someone who uses intellectual property without the permission of the owner.

Initial public offering (IPO) Transfer method describing the first-time public sale of a stock listed on a public stock exchange.

Innovation Implementation of a creative idea or opportunity leading to profitable and effective outcomes.

Innovative strategy An overall strategic approach in which a firm seeks to do something that is very different from what others in the industry are doing.

Inseparability A quality of a service in which the service being done cannot be disconnected from the provider of the service.

Insurable value The amount of an asset for which a company will write an insurance policy.

Insurance A contract between two or more parties in which one party agrees, for a fee, to assume the risk of another.

Intangible assets Things of value that have no physical existence, for example, patents and trade secrets.

Intangible property Property that has no value of its own but that represents value, such as a stock certificate.

Intangible resources Capabilities, organizational processes, information, or knowledge of a firm that are not clearly evident.

Integrative view An ethical overview which involves considering what is best for everyone involved in a situation. (Compare to the distributive view.)

Intellectual property Property coming from some sort of original thought, e.g., patents, trade secrets, trademarks, and copyrights.

Interest A charge for the use of money, usually figured as a percentage of the principal.

Internal control A set of rules and procedures that work to limit the opportunity for employee theft or malfeasance.

Internal reference price A consumer's mental image of what a product's price should be.

Internal understanding The extent to which employees, investors, and family members involved in the business know the business's purposes and operations.

Internet recruiting Method of recruiting that allows you to search a résumé database or post a job description to the Web; a small business owner who knows exactly what he or she wants can use filters to search vast numbers of résumés with pinpoint accuracy.

Introduction stage The life cycle stage in which the product or service is being invented and initially developed.

Invention plan A business plan that provides information to potential licensees. Invention plans focus on the details of an invention, including intellectual property rights.

Inventory valuation Determination of the amount of assets held by the firm for sale or production.

Inventory Products that are held for sale to customers.

Investing activities The purchase and sale of land, buildings, equipment, and securities.

ISO Stands for the International Standards Organization, and refers to certification for having met a standard of quality that is consistently evaluated around the world (see http://www.iso.org).

Issue recognition A concept in public recognition which alludes to the extent to which the public is familiar with the issue or problem at hand.

J

Job description Defines and discusses all the essential knowledge, skills, and abilities that are needed to fill a position.

Joint venture An agreement between two or more entities to pool resources in order to complete a project.

Just-in-time inventory The practice of purchasing and accepting delivery of inventory only after it has been sold to the final customer.

K

Key business functions Activities common to all businesses such as sales, operations (also called *production*), accounting, finance, and human resources.

Key employee/partner plans Provides information on the company, product/service, market, and critical risks to prospective business or marketing partners or to prospective key employees.

Key employees Employees whose experience and skills are critical to the success of a business.

Keyword and description tags Terms included in the hidden portion of a Web page (called the document head) which are used by search engines such as Yahoo! and Google to describe your Web site and evaluate its focus and category placement.

Keyword optimization The selection of words that describe a Web site ad that results in the site being displayed toward the beginning of a search engine's (e.g., Google, Yahoo!, etc.) listing for that term.

L

Laggard A customer adoption segment that holds off buying new products or services until either they are forced to or prices reach rock-bottom.

Late career entrepreneurs (also known as *second career entrepreneurs*) People who begin their businesses after having retired or resigned from work in corporations at age 50 or later.

Late majority A customer adoption segment describing people who wait until the technology has stabilized and the costs have begun to drop.

Legal entity A being, human or nonhuman, such as a corporation, that is recognized as having rights and duties, such as the right to own property.

Legitimacy The belief that a firm is worthy of consideration or doing business with because of the impressions or opinions of customers, suppliers, investors, or competitors.

Letter of credit A document issued by a bank that guarantees a buyer's payment for a specified period of time upon compliance with specified terms.

Liabilities Legal obligations to give up things of value in the future.

Liability of newness The set of risks faced by firms early in their life cycles that comes from a lack of knowledge by the owners about the business they are in and by customers about the new business.

Licensing Documented permission from the government to run your business.

Lifestyle or part-time firm A small business primarily intended to provide partial or subsistence financial support for the existing lifestyle of the owner, most often through operations that fit the owner's schedule and way of working.

Limited liability company (LLC) A legal form of business organization that is created by filing required documentation with a state government. LLCs have a choice, under federal tax law, of being taxed as either corporations or partnerships.

Limited partnership A legal form of business organization that is created by filing required documentation with a state government; within a limited partnership, one or more partners may have no liability for the debts and actions of the partnership.

Liquidity A measure of how quickly a company can raise money through internal sources by converting assets to cash.

Litigation A formal dispute resolution method that operates using the court system, typically with a lawyer representing each party.

Lock box A locked receptacle for money, the keys to which are not available to those who physically handle the receptacle; a common example of a lock box is the coin receptacle for parking meters which cannot be opened by the workers who are responsible for collecting the deposited coins.

M

Managerial accounting Accounting methods that are specifically intended to be used by managers for planning, directing, and controlling a business.

Manufacturer The entity which produces a product or service to be sold.

Market research Research conducted to uncover market and customer needs and opportunities; it exists at two levels, primary and secondary.

Market segmentation The process of dividing the market into groups that have somewhat homogeneous needs for a product or service.

Market The business term for the population of customers for your product or service.

Marketable securities Stocks and bonds that are traded on an open market.

Marketing plan A systematic written plan of all phases of marketing for a business, including information on the product, price, distribution, and promotion strategy, as well as a clear identification of the target market and competition.

Marketing research Systematic collection and interpretation of data to support future marketing decisions.

Mass market A customer group that involves large portions of the population.

Mat release A news release that is typeset and thus may be photographically reproduced for inclusion in a newspaper.

Maturity stage The third life cycle stage, marked by a stabilization of demand, with firms in the industry moving to stabilize or improve profits through cost strategies.

Me-too products Products essentially similar to something already on the market.

Microinventory The purchase of inventory only after a sale is made; very typical with Internet firms.

Middleman Any firm that assists in getting your product to your end customer—distributors, retailers, and so forth.

Minimalized business professionalization A situation that occurs when the entrepreneur does nearly everything in the simplest way possible.

Mission statement A paragraph that describes the firm's goals and competitive advantages.

Modeling When small business owners act in ways they want their employees to act.

Money An accepted medium of exchange.

Moonlighting Working on your own part time after your regular job.

Multichannel marketing The use of several different channels to reach your customers, for example, a Web site, direct mail, and traditional retailing.

Multiple or bonus pack Combining more than one unit of the same product and pricing it lower than if each unit were sold separately.

Mutuality The action of each person helping another.

N

Net profit The amount of money left after operating expenses are deducted from the business.

Net realizable value The amount for which an asset will sell, less the costs of selling.

Network marketing An approach to selling in which the salesperson recruits customers to become distributors of the product or service to others.

Networking Interacting with others in order to build relationships useful to a business.

New entrant business A firm whose product or service is established elsewhere and is new to this market.

Newsworthy events To garner serious attention from the media and the public, a news story needs to deliver certain essentials that will hold their attention and keep your news in their thoughts. It should have public recognition, importance, and interest.

Niche market A narrowly defined segment of the population that is likely to share interests or concerns.

Noncash incentives Rewards that do not require payment of cash, such as stock options, compensating time off, or added vacation days.

Noncompete clause Part of a contract in which a person agrees not to open a certain type business or seek employment doing certain things in a particular area for a period of time.

Noncore projects Revenue-producing tasks and activities related to, but not part of, the primary strategy of a business.

Nonsufficient funds A situation that occurs when a check is returned to a depositor because the writer of the check did not have a bank available balance equal to or greater than the amount of the check.

Novelty Characterized by being different or new.

O

Obligations The social force which impels people who make decisions or have responsibilities to act ethically because the actions they take could affect many other people.

Occupational Health and Safety Administration (OSHA) A government agency created to enforce safety in the workplace.

Occupational structure The sequence or organization of jobs and careers in the economy.

Odd-even pricing Setting a price that ends in the number 5, 7, or 9.

Off-peak pricing Charging lower prices at certain times to encourage customers to come during slack periods.

On-the-job training Delivered to employees while they perform their regular jobs; techniques include orientations, job instruction training, apprenticeships, internships and assistantships, job rotation, and coaching.

Open-book policy Concept that key employees should be able to see and understand a firm's financials, that they should have a part in moving the numbers in the right direction, and that they should have a direct stake in the strategy and success of the firm.

Open-ended questions Questions that allow respondents to express themselves as they choose; for example, "What do you like about this book?"

Operating activities Activities involved in producing and selling goods and services.

Operating cycle See cash to cash cycle.

Operating lease A long-term rental in which ownership of the asset never passes to the person paying for the lease.

Operational plan Business plans designed to be used internally for management purposes.

Opportunity competencies Skills necessary to identify and exploit elements of the business environment that can lead to a profitable and sustainable business.

Opportunity cost The value of an economic activity or event that is foregone in order to be able to undertake a different, specific activity or event.

Opportunity recognition Searching and capturing new ideas that lead to business opportunities. This process often involves creative thinking that leads to discovery of new and useful ideas.

Optimum capital structure The ratio of debt to equity that provides the maximum level of profits.

Optimum stocking level The amount of inventory that results in the minimum cost, when considering the cost of lost sales resulting from running out of stock, the number of units sold per day, and the number of days required to receive inventory.

Organizational capabilities The abilities, skills, and competencies used by the firm to make profits from tangible and intangible resources.

Organizational culture A set of shared beliefs, basic assumptions, or common, accepted ways of dealing with problems and challenges within a company that demonstrate how things get done.

Outflow Funds being paid to others by the firm.

Outside equity Money from selling part of your business to people who are not and will not be involved in the management of the business.

Outsourcing Contracting with people or companies outside your business to do work for your business.

Overdraft A negative balance in a depositor's bank account.

Owner-manager The individual who owns and runs a business.

Owners' equity The difference between assets and liabilities of a business.

P

Parallel competition An imitative business that competes locally with others in the same industry.

Partitioned pricing Setting the price for a base item and then charging extra for each additional component.

Partnership Two or more people cooperating to conduct a business enterprise.

Part-time self-employment Working for yourself for 35 or fewer hours a week.

Pass through (taxation) Earnings of the business are distributed to the business owners and those owners (rather than the business) pay individual tax on the earnings.

Patent A grant by the U.S. government to an inventor for an idea that is new, useful, and nonobvious, giving the inventor the exclusive right to make, use, or sell his or her idea.

Payables Amounts owed to vendors for merchandise or services purchased on credit (see receivables).

Payback period The amount of time it takes a business to earn back the funds it paid out to obtain a capital asset.

Periodic inventory The process of physically counting business assets on a set schedule.

Periodic or random discounting Sales conducted at either predictable or nonpredictable intervals.

Perishability A service exhibits perishability in that if it is not used when offered, it cannot be saved for later use.

Perpetual inventory A system of recording the receipt and sale of each item as it occurs.

Personal accountability A process in which people take responsibility for decisions they make and the consequences of these decisions.

Personal ethics Beliefs about what is right and wrong which guide decisions in everyday life.

Personal values Attitudes regarding what a person believes is important in life and the best way to live one's life.

Physical inventory A count of all the inventory being held for sale at a specific point in time.

Piercing the veil The dissolution of a corporate form, making it back into a sole proprietorship or general partnership, if the court finds that the owner carelessly mixed up personal and business assets or finances.

Pioneering business A firm whose product or service is new to the industry or is itself creating a new industry.

Pioneers A customer adoption segment characterized by customers most willing to be the first to try or have something new.

Plaintiff Person or other entity filing a law suit.

Plant patent A 20-year patent that covers new strains of living plant organisms, algae, or macro fungi.

Plant A general term for the facilities of a business.

Pledging receivables Giving a third party legal rights to debts owed your business in order to provide assurance that borrowed money will be repaid.

Point of indifference The price at which a buyer is indifferent about buying or not buying the business.

Point-of-sale system Hardware and software combinations that integrate inventory management directly into accounting software.

Poisoning the well Creating a negative impression among your employers' customers.

Power A concept in public importance which alludes to potential shifts in control or influence.

Preselling Involves introducing your product to potential customers and taking orders for later delivery.

Press kits Another vehicle to use for promotional purposes, press kits should include product or service brochures, press releases with the latest news about your company (new product, media mentions, etc.), biographies on you and key employees, and photos or digital images of products or services, if appropriate.

Press release A written announcement intended to draw news media attention to a specific event.

Prestige or premium pricing Setting a price above that of the competition so as to indicate a higher quality or that a product is a status symbol.

Price lining The practice of setting (usually) three price points: good quality, better quality, best quality.

Primary data Information collected to solve a problem at hand or answer current questions.

Primary research Research conducted by the small business owner that is customized to answer specific questions regarding the marketplace and assess customer needs and demands.

Probationary period Trial period in which an employee has temporary status before a formal offer to work full time is presented.

Process of personal selling The process of selling your products and service; includes prospect and evaluate, prepare, present, and the close.

Product distribution franchising An agreement that provides specific brand name products which are resold by the franchisee in a specified territory.

Professionalization The extent to which a firm meets or exceeds the standard business practices for its industry.

Profit before taxes The amount of profit earned by a business before calculating the amount of income tax owed.

Profit, profitability The amount that revenues exceed expenses.

Pro forma Latin for "in the form of" when used to describe financial statements, indicates estimated or hypothetical information.

Proof-of-concept Web site An Internet-based type of business plan providing information or demonstration of a product or service designed to solicit information on customer interest.

Property A general term for real estate, but it can also be applied as a legal term for anything owned or possessed.

Proprietary technology A product or service or an aspect of one that is kept as a trade secret or is protected legally using patent, copyright, trademark, or service mark.

Protected classes States of being that are expressly prohibited from suffering discrimination: race, color, religion, sex, national origin, gender, age, or disability.

Proximity A concept in public recognition which alludes to the impact level of the issue being discussed.

Psychological contract Refers to employees' beliefs about the promises between the employee and the firm. These beliefs are based on the perception that promises have been made (e.g., competitive wages, promotional opportunities, job training) in exchange for certain employee obligations such as giving of their energy, time, and technical skills.

Public importance (1)Things that are considered important to large numbers of otherwise unrelated people (2) things that are of civic importance, as opposed to private or corporate entities.

Public interest (1)Things that are generally considered to be beneficial to large numbers of people (2) civic causes and benefits, as opposed to private and corporate benefits.

Public recognition Being recognized or acknowledged by large numbers of people, similar to "fame."

Public relations Activities used to establish and promote a favorable opinion by the public.

Pull-through system A term for just-in-time inventory systems in which product is ordered and placed into production only after a sale has been completed.

Pure innovation The process of creating new products or services, which results in a previously unseen product or service.

Q

Qualitative research Techniques for gathering information that rely on opinions expressed without a numerical basis ("real good" instead of "4 on a 5-point scale"). Popular techniques for qualitative research include interviews, small groups discussions, and observation.

Quantitative research Techniques that depend on categorizing responses into numbers, enabling statistical analysis of opinions. Examples include surveys and focus groups.

R

Radical innovation strategy Rejecting existing ideas, and presenting a way to do things differently.

Rare resource An asset, capability, organizational process, information, or knowledge that is not generally available to competitors.

Receivables Amounts that are owed to a business for merchandise that was sold on credit (see payables).

Reconciling An accounting process that identifies the causes of all differences between book and bank balances.

Referral discount A discount given to a customer who refers a friend to the business.

Registration Information provided to the government concerning the existence of, name of, nature of, and contact information for your business.

Regulation of the workplace Laws and governmental rules that limit the freedom of business owners to manage their businesses as they please.

Rehabilitation Act of 1973 An act of Congress that provides training for workers who are injured on the job.

Replacement cost The total cost of replacing an asset with an essentially identical asset.

Replacement value The cost incurred to replace one asset with an identical asset.

Research and development (often abbreviated R&D) The part of a business (and a business plan) that is focused on creating new products or services and preparing new technologies, ideas, products, or services for the firm's market.

Resident agent A person who represents an out-of-state company as its agent in a state where the business is operating for purposes of contacting the out-of-state company and receiving notice of lawsuits against the out-of-state company.

Resource competencies The ability or skill of the entrepreneur at finding expendable components necessary to the operation of the business such as time, information, location, financing, raw materials, and expertise.

Resource Any asset, capability, organizational process, information, or knowledge that contributes to the firm's performance.

Retailer A middleman business which sells to consumers or end-users of a product (typically in single or small quantities).

Retained earnings The sum of all profits and losses, less all dividends paid since the beginning of the business.

Retainer A fee paid by a client to an attorney to engage the attorney's services.

Retrenchment An organizational life cycle stage in which established firms must find new approaches to improve the business and its chances for survival.

Return on equity The ratio of profits to owner investment in a business.

Return on investment (ROI) A capital budgeting equation used to measure the relationship between initial investment and the profits that are expected to be received from making the investment.

Return pricing A price that is set so as to achieve a certain profit level.

Revolving credit A credit agreement that allows the borrower to pay all or part of the balance at any time; as the loan balance is paid off, it becomes available to be borrowed again.

Risk The level of probability that an investment will not produce expected gains.

Risks The parts of a business or business plan that expose the firm to any kind of loss—profits, sales, reputation, assets, customers, and so on.

Role conflict The kind of problem that arises when people have multiple responsibilities, such as parent and boss, and the different responsibilities make different demands on them.

Safety stock An amount of inventory carried to ensure that you will not run out of inventory because of fluctuating levels of sales.

Scalar questions Questions that are answered by some sort of scale; for example, "On a scale of 1 to 5, how do you like this book?"

Scale A characteristic of a market that describes the size of the market—a mass market or a niche market.

SCAMPER A creativity tool that provides cues to trigger breakthrough thinking. The letters stand for substitute, combine, adapt, modify, put to other uses, eliminate, and rearrange.

Scope A characteristic of a market that defines the geographic range covered by the market from local to global.

Screening plan Also called a *mini-plan*, gives the basic overview of the firm and a detailed look at the financials.

Search engine optimization A general approach to Web site design intended to result in the site being displayed toward the beginning of a search engine's (e.g., Google, Yahoo!, etc.) listing for that term.

Secondary data Information already collected for some other purpose than the current problem or questions.

Secondary research Research conducted by a third party that can be used to substantiate and generalize characteristics of the small business owner's target market.

Self-employed Working for yourself.

Separation of duties A type of internal control that separates the physical control of an asset from the person accounting for that asset.

Serial entrepreneurs People who open multiple businesses throughout their career.

Set-asides Government contracting funds which are earmarked for particular kinds of firms, such as small businesses, minority-owned firms, women-owned firms, and the like.

Sheltered workshop A nonprofit organization or institution that provides business services by using handicapped or rehabilitated workers.

Short-term debt Any debt that must be paid in less than one year from the date of the financial statement on which it is reported.

Single taxation Earnings of the business are taxed once with the owners paying the taxes.

Skimming Setting a price at the highest level the market will bear, usually because there is no competition at the time.

Slack resources Profits that are available to be used to satisfy the preferences of the owner in how the business is run.

Small and medium enterprise The international term for small businesses.

Small business Involves 1–50 people and has its owner managing the business on a day-to-day basis.

Small Business Administration A part of the United States government which provides support and advocacy for small businesses.

Small Business Development Center Offices co-sponsored by states and the Federal government that offer free or low-cost help to existing and potential small businesses.

Small business investment companies Private businesses that are authorized to make SBA insured loans to start-ups and small businesses.

Social capital Characteristics of a business, like trust, consistency, and networks, that represent potential social obligations which are an asset of the firm or entrepreneur.

Social network The entrepreneur's set of relationships and contacts with individuals and institutions.

Sole proprietorship A business owned by a single individual who is responsible for all debts and claims against the business.

Specialized business professionalization A situation that occurs when businesses have founders or owners who are passionate about one or two of the key business functions, such as sales, operations, accounting, finance, or human resources.

Spin-off A business that is created by separating part of an operating business into a separate entity.

Sponsored link A form of paid advertising that gets your company's Web site at the top of a search list.

Standard business practice A business action that has been widely adopted within an industry or occupation.

Start-up A new business that is started from scratch.

Straight line for a useful life of 10 years Depreciation is computed using a straight line method over 10 years, so an asset would lose 10% of its value each year.

Strategic direction The conceptualization of how a business might best move in response to the findings of a SWOT analysis—Flaunt, Fix, Fight or Flee.

Subcontract A contract by which a new party agrees to perform a duty that one of the original parties to a contract was already legally obligated to perform.

Substitution profits Returns intended to equal and replace the salary or wages the entrepreneur could draw working for someone else.

Success profits Returns at levels higher than the entrepreneur could make working for others.

Succession The process of intergenerational transfer of a business.

Succinct message Your key point in as few and as memorable words as possible.

Supplemental profits Returns above costs intended as a secondary income for entrepreneurs (where self-employment is secondary to their main job).

Surety bonds An agreement with an insurance or bonding company that will pay a specified amount in the event that the entity bonded fails to comply with specified contractual requirements.

Survey A data-collection method using a questionnaire—in person, on phone, on paper, or on the Internet.

Synergy A combination in which the whole is greater than the sum of its component parts.

T

Tagline (also known as a slogan) Memorable catchphrase that captures the key idea of a business, its service, product, or customer.

Takeover Seizing of control of a business by purchasing its stock to be able to select the board of directors.

Tangibility An item's capability of being seen, touched, tasted, or felt.

Tangible resources Assets of a firm that can be easily and concretely identified.

Target market The group of people on which a marketer focuses promotion and sales efforts.

Tax abatement A legal reduction in taxes by a government.

Tax accounting An accounting approach based on specific accounting requirements set by governmental taxing agencies.

Tax codes Laws and regulations that specify the requirements of taxation.

Tax credits Direct reductions in the amount of taxes that must be paid, dependent upon meeting some legal criteria.

Telemarketing Contact via telephone for the express purpose of selling a product or service. Telemarketing can either be inbound (customer calls company) or outbound (company calls customer).

Termination An endgame strategy in which the owner closes down a business.

Test marketing Selling your product or service in a limited area, for a limited time.

Timing purchases A method of controlling the timing of cash outflows that is invisible to suppliers and vendors.

Total product The entire bundle of products, services, and meanings of your offering; includes extras like service, warranty, or delivery, as well as what the product means to the customer.

Trade association (also known as professional association) A group of people in the same industry who band together to gather and share information and present and represent the industry to the public and government.

Trade discounts Percentage discounts from gross invoice amounts provided to encourage prompt payment.

Trade magazines The magazines that target specific industries and professions.

Trade name franchising An agreement that provides to the franchisee only the rights to use the franchisor's trade name and/or trademarks.

Trade name or assumed name or a doing business as (dba) The name under which a business is operated.

Trade secret Confidential information within a company that gives that company a competitive advantage.

Trademark Distinctive word, slogan, or image that identifies a product and its origin.

Traditional small business A firm intended to provide a living income to the owner, and operating in a manner and on a schedule consistent with other firms in the industry and market.

Traffic generators Other businesses that bring customers (generate traffic) to the area.

Transfer An endgame strategy in which ownership is moved from one person or group to another.

Transformational competencies The abilities of a firm to make its product or service in a way that enhances value or efficiency compared to other firms.

Trendiness A concept in public recognition which alludes to the fit of the topic to current fashion or public interest.

Trust A feeling of fairness in all business transactions in which the firm engages, such as financial transactions, employee matters, regulatory compliance, and complaint resolution.

U

Undercapitalization Not having enough money available to the business to cover shortfalls in sales or profits.

Undifferentiated strategy A marketing strategy that uses no segmentation; assumes that all consumers have virtually identical needs and can be reached by the same marketing mix.

Universalism An ethical model that suggests that there is a code of right and wrong that everyone can see and follow.

Utilitarianism An ethical model that supports seeking the greatest good for the greatest number of people.

Utility patent A 20-year patent covering a process, machine, article of manufacture, composition of matter, or any new or useful improvement of an existing one.

V

Valuable resource An asset, capability, organizational process, information, or knowledge that lets a firm take advantage of opportunities or lock out competitors.

Value chain A collection of processes and activities a small business conducts to design, produce, market, deliver, and support its product or service.

Value proposition Small business owners' unique selling points that will be used to differentiate their products and/or services from those of the competition.

Variable costs Those costs that change with each unit produced, for example, raw materials.

Variance analysis The process of determining the effect of price and quantity changes on revenues and expenses.

Variance The difference between an actual and budgeted revenue or cost.

Viability The preliminary assessment of the potential for a business to be created or, once created, to survive.

Vicarious (indirect) liability Indirect liability or responsibility for the actions of another.

Virtual employees Independent contractors who provide specialized business services or support from a distance, through the Internet, telephone, fax, or another method of communication.

Visibility Demonstration of a behavior, attitude, or value in ways that are evident to others.

Vision statement A very simple 5-10 word sentence or tagline that expresses the fundamental idea or goal of the firm.

Visuals A concept in public interest which alludes to the graphic interest held by an event.

Volatility The frequency of business starts and stops.

W

Waiver Part of a contract in which a party intentionally gives up legal rights or claims.

Walkaways Business terminations in which the entrepreneur ends the business with its obligations met.

Weighted average cost of capital (WAC) The expected average future cost of funds.

Whole of life costs The sum of all costs of capital assets, including acquisition, ownership, operation, and disposal.

Wholesaler A middleman business which buys (typically in large quantities) and sells (typically in smaller quantities) to businesses rather than consumers.

Word-of-mouth A means of spreading information about your business through the comments friends and customers make to other potential customers.

Workout A form of business termination in which the firm's legal or financial obligations are not fully met at closing.

Z

Zoning Government specifications for acceptable use of land and buildings in particular areas.

End Notes

Chapter 1

1. David Astor, "Boom in 'Boondocks' Client Papers as Comic Strip Sets Start-Up Record" *Editor & Publisher,* 132, no. 16 (April 17, 1999), p. 53. David Astor, "'Boondocks' Artist Still Living on the Edge of Controversy," *Editor & Publisher* 132, no. 41 (October 9, 1999), p. 47. David Astor, "High-Profile Year for 'Boondocks,'" *Editor & Publisher* 132, no. 33 (August 14, 1999), p. 29. F. Romall Smalls, "Blowin' Up in 'The Boondocks'", *Black Enterprise* 30, no. 12 (July 2000), p. 64. John Simpkins, "The Equal-Opportunity Offender (Cartoonist Aaron McGruder's 'Boondocks')," *The New York Times Magazine,* June 24, 2001, p. 42. Aaron McGruder's Web site can be found at http://www.boondocks.net. Jennifer A. Carbin, "Boondocks Speaks: An Interview with Aaron McGruder," *City Paper (Philadelphia),* November 5, 2001, http://www.alternet.org/story/ 11859. United Press Syndicate Web site, "Aaron McGruder," http://www.amuniversal.com/ups/features/ boondocks/bio.htm.

2. The GEM study for 2002 reported that 50 percent of adults surveyed had thought about starting a business. Only 7 percent had taken any actions toward starting one, and 4.5 percent of the population actually started a business. Heidi M. Neck, Andrew L. Zacharakis, William D. Bygrave, and Paul D. Reynolds, *Global Entrepreneurship Monitor: National Entrepreneurship Assessment—United States of America, 2002 Executive Report.* (Wellesley, MA: Babson College, 2003) http://www.gemconsortium.org/document.asp?id=287.

3. Estimates peg new starts at around 4 percent of all businesses, which given 23.7 million firms, would place the estimate at 948,000. The SBA, counting only new firms with employees, reported 572,900 opening in 2003. This does not count partial-year businesses or sellers on the Internet based in the United States, so 1 million is a conservative estimate. Heidi M. Neck, Andrew L. Zacharakis, William D. Bygrave, and Paul D. Reynolds, *Global Entrepreneurship Monitor: National Entrepreneurship Assessment—United States of America, 2002 Executive Report* (Wellesley, MA: Babson College, 2003) http://www.gemconsortium.org/download/ 1061664039492/GEM%20US%202002.pdf. *Small Business by the Numbers* (Washington DC: Small Business Administration, 2004) http://www.sba.gov/advo/stats/sbfaq.pdf.

4. This is the latest version of the idea called "fear of failure" by researchers in achievement motivation in the 1960s and 1970s. For fear of failure, see Ray Smilor, *Love and Fear: The Great Motivators of Entrepreneurial Achievement* EntreWorld, n.d., http://www.entreworld.com/content/topAdvise.com? ColumnID=192, July 9, 2005, or Emmeline G. de Pillis, "What's Achievement Got to Do With It? The Role of National Culture in the Relationship Between Entrepreneurship and Achievement Motivation," *Frontiers of Entrepreneurship Research* (Wellesley, MA: Babson College, 1998). http://www.babson.edu/entrep/fer/papers98/IV/IV_A/IV_A_text.htm. For the latest version, see Jeffrey Pfeffer and Robert I. Sutton, *The Knowing-Doing Gap: How Smart Companies Turn Knowledge into Action,* (Cambridge, MA: Harvard Business School Press, 1999), or see Alan M. Webber, "Why Can't We Get Anything Done?" *Fast Company,* June 2000, http://www.fastcompany.com/magazine/35/pfeffer.html.

5. U.S. Small Business Administration, Office of Advocacy, *Small Business by the Numbers* (Washington DC: Small Business Administration, 2004), http://www. sba.gov/advo/stats/ sbfaq.pdf. These numbers are for firms with employees. The SBA believes that the survival rate is lower for businesses without employees. They typically use a 50 percent survival rate for four years, based on Brian Headd, "Redefining Business Success: Distinguishing between Closure and Failure," *Small Business Economics.* 21, no. 1 (August 2003), pp. 51–61.

6. James J. Chrisman, "The Influence of Outsider-Generated Knowledge Resources on Venture Creation," *Journal of Small Business Management* 37, no. 4 (October 1999), pp. 42–58. James J. Chrisman and W. Edward McMullan, "A Preliminary Assessment of Outsider Assistance as a Knowledge Resource: The Longer-Term Impact of New Venture Counseling," *Entrepreneurship: Theory & Practice* 24, no. 3 (Spring 2000), pp. 37–53. James J. Chrisman and W. Edward McMullan, "Outsider Assistance as a Knowledge Resource for New Venture Survival," *Journal of Small Business Management* 42, no. 3 (July 2004), pp. 229–244.

7. Devron A. Veasley, "Incubators Build Economies, Benefit Communities, In Depth: Small Business Resource Guide—Business Incubation," *Birmingham Business Journal*, 2003, http://birmingham.bizjournals.com/birmingham/stories/2003/08/11/focus6.html.

8. Alberta Charney and Gary Libecap, *Impact of Entrepreneurship Education* (Kansas City, MO: Kauffman Center for Entrepreneurial Leadership, 2000). Nancy B. Upton, Donald L. Sexton, and Carlos Moore, "Have We Made a Difference? An Examination of Career Activity of Entrepreneurship Majors since 1981" (abstract), *Frontiers of Entrepreneurship Research* (Wellesley, MA: Babson College, 1995), pp. 727–728. Zenas Block and Stephen A. Stumpf, "Entrepreneurship Education Research: Experience and Challenge." In Donald L. Sexton and John D. Kasarda (eds.), *The State of the Art of Entrepreneurship* (Boston, MA: PWS-Kent Publishing, 1992). Bryan W. Clark, Charles H. Davis, and Verne C. Harnish, "Do Courses in Entrepreneurship Aid in New Venture Creation?" *Journal of Small Business Management* Vol 22, no. 2 (April 1984), pp. 26–31. Calvin A. Kent, "Entrepreneurship Education at the Collegiate Level: A Synopsis and Evaluation," In Calvin A. Kent (ed.) *Entrepreneurship Education* (New York: Quorum Books, 1990), pp. 111–122. Lawrence A. Klatt, "A Study of Small Business/Entrepreneurial Education in Colleges and Universities," *The Journal of Private Enterprise* 4 (Fall 1988), pp. 103–108. Peter Robinson and Max Hayes, "Entrepreneurship Education in America's Major Universities," *Entrepreneurship: Theory & Practice* 15, no. 3 (Spring 1991), pp. 41–52. Donald L. Sexton. and Nancy B. Upton, "Evaluation of an Innovative Approach to Teaching Entrepreneurship," *Journal of Small Business Management* 25, no. 1 (January, 1987) pp. 35–43. Van G. H. Clouse, "A Controlled Experiment Relating Entrepreneurial Education to Students' Start-up Decisions," *Journal of Small Business Management.* 28, no. 2 (April 1990), pp. 45–53.

9. Ulla Hytti and Paula Kuopusjärvi, "Evaluating and Measuring Entrepreneurship and Enterprise Education," *Methods, Tools and Practices* (Turun Yliopisto, Finland: Turku School of Economics and Business Administration, 2004). http://webct.tukkk.fi/entreva/entredu/tiedostot/report_web.pdf. Lars Kolvereid and Øystein Moen, "Entrepreneurship among Business Graduates: Does a Major in Entrepreneurship Make a Difference?" *Journal of European Industrial Training* 21. no. 4, (1997), pp. 154–160. W. Edward McMullan and L. Murray Gillin, "Entrepreneurship Education: Developing Technological Start-up Entrepreneurs, A Case Study of a Graduate Entrepreneurship Programme at Swinburne University," *Technovation* 18, no. 4 (April 1998), pp. 275–286. Teresa V. Menzies and J. C. Paradi, "Encouraging Technology-Based Ventures: Entrepreneurship Education and Engineering Graduates," *New England Journal of Entrepreneurship* 5, no. 2 (Fall 2002), pp. 57–64. Teresa V. Menzies and J. C. Paradi, "Entrepreneurship Education and Engineering Students: Career Path and Business Performance," *International Journal of Entrepreneurship and Innovation* 4, no. 2 (May 2003), pp. 85–96. Thomas N. Garavan and Barra O'Cinneide, "Entrepreneurship Education and Training Programmes," *Journal of European Industrial Training* 18, no. 8/9 (1994), pp. 3–13. Thomas N. Garavan and Barra O'Cinneide, "Entrepreneurship Education and Training Programmes," *Journal of European Industrial Training.* 18, no. 11 (1994), pp. 13–22.

10. U.S. Small Business Administration, Office of Advocacy, *Small Business by the Numbers.* (Washington DC: Small Business Administration, 2004), http://www.sba. gov/advo/stats/sbfaq.pdf.

11. For details on the SBA size standards, look at the Office of Size Standards Web site at the U.S. Small Business Administration—http://www.sba.gov/size/.

12. Even among small business owners, calling someone an entrepreneur can be problematic. About one owner in eight was offended by the term in a 2001 poll, although "small business owner" was almost universally accepted. *NFIB—National Small Business Poll—Success, Satisfaction and Growth* (Washington, DC: NFIB Research Foundation, 2001).

13. This fight among professors seems to have settled down to three competing camps—wealth creation, opportunity recognition, and firm creation. Wealth creation proponents usually define entrepreneurship as efforts to create wealth, especially through high-growth new ventures. Major centers for this approach are Harvard University and Babson College. The opportunity recognition approach is centered at University of Chicago and University of Virginia. This approach sees entrepreneurship occurring when an individual finds and exploits some technological, economic, or market mismatch. The firm creation approach says that starting a business is where entrepreneurship occurs, and it is the favored model at Clemson University and Saint Louis University.

14. M. Dell and C. Freedman, *Direct from Dell: Strategies That Revolutionized an Industry* (New York: Harper Business, 2000), http://www.amazon.com/exec/obidos/tg/detail//0756718775/102-2417352-1853726?v=glance&vi=excerpt.

15. Robert X. Cringley, *Accidental Empires: How the Boys of Silicon Valley Make Their Millions, Battle Foreign Competition, and Still Can't Get a Date* (New York: HarperInformation, 2000).

16. There were 335,000 high growth ventures according to a 2002 report on business growth issues by Cognetics (now Arc Analytics) of Waltham, MA. The 22.9 million estimate came from the U.S. Small Business Administration for 2002. The 2003 version of that number was reported earlier in the chapter as 23.7 million firms. The SBA report is available at http://www.sba.gov/advo/stats/sbfaq.pdf.

17. Jerome A. Katz, "A Psychosocial Cognitive Model of Employment Status Choice," *Entrepreneurship: Theory & Practice* 17, no. 1 (Fall 1992), pp. 29–37.

18. Sources include: John Case, "Why 20 Million of You Can't Be Wrong: A Long-Time *Inc.* Contributor Surveys the Current Entrepreneurial Scene and Reports His Findings. How do things look? Well, one answer might be "Never better, thanks!" *Inc. Magazine,* April 2004, p. 100. URL: http://www.inc.com/magazine/20040401/20million_2.html. John Case, "Start-Up Nation: Who's Looking at Start-Ups? The Birthing of Companies Is the Process by Which an Economy Reinvents and Re-Creates Itself," *Inc. Magazine,* May 2001. URL:http://www.inc.com/magazine/20010515/ 22623.html. Janean Chun, "More Power to You: A New Empowerment Contracting Program Offers Small Business a Huge Advantage," *Entrepreneur,* March 1997. URL:http://www.entrepreneur.com/Magazines/Copy of MA SegArticle/0,4453,226989—2-,00.html. Janean Chun, "Ground Zero: An Ambitious New Study Aims to Uncover What Really Happens in the Start-Up Stage," *Entrepreneur,* December 1996. URL: http://www.entrepreneur.com/mag/article/0,1539, 226706,00.html.

19. Including one of the Entrepreneurial Small Business authors. Both authors developed the financial sophistication questions for the PSED. In addition, the design for identifying existing firms came from work done by Jerome Katz and William Gartner. Jerome A. Katz and William B. Gartner, "Properties of Emerging Organizations," *Academy of Management Review, 13*(3), (July 1988) 429–441.

20. Many of the PSED analyses done for *Entrepreneurial Small Business* were done by Dr. Jennifer Shaver. For background on the PSED, see Paul D. Reynolds, "National Panel Study of U.S. Business Startups: Background and Methodology." In Jerome A. Katz (ed.), *Advances in Entrepreneurship, Firm Emergence and Growth* Volume 4: *Databases for the Study of Entrepreneurship* (Greenwich, CT: JAI Press, 2000), or William B. Gartner, Kelly G. Shaver, Nancy M. Carter, and Paul D. Reynolds (eds.), *Handbook of Entrepreneurial Dynamics: The Process of Business Creation* (Thousand Oaks, CA: Sage, 2004).

21. Marc Fleury, "Doing It Wrong, Getting It Right," Entrepreneur's Byline, *BusinessweekOnline.* September 3, 2003, http://www.businessweek.com/smallbiz/content/sep2003/ sb2003093 8638.htm.

22. The "universally mentioned" rewards were those mentioned by 75 percent or more of potential or new small business owners—a much higher rate than working people in general mention. The "occasionally mentioned" rewards were those mentioned by less than 50 percent of potential or new small business owners, but were still mentioned more often than by working people. The "rarely mentioned" rewards were those in which entrepreneurs mention a reward significantly less often than working people do in general. The sample was 871 potential and new entrepreneurs, compared to a control group of 431 individuals. For details on the measures see Nancy M. Carter, William B. Gartner, and Kelly G. Shaver, "Career reasons." In William B. Gartner, Kelly G. Shaver, Nancy M. Carter, and Paul D. Reynolds (eds.), *Handbook of Entrepreneurial Dynamics: The Process of Business Creation* (Thousand Oaks, CA: Sage, 2004), pp. 142–152. The PSED analyses reported here were custom analyses performed by Dr. Jennifer Shaver.

23. Thomas. J. Stanley, *The Millionaire Mind* (Kansas City, MO: Andrews McNeel, 2001). Thomas J. Stanley and William D. Danko, *The Millionaire Next Door* (New York: Pocket Books, 1996).

24. Devlin Smith , "Women of Substance—Experience: A Secret to Success," *Entrepreneur,* November 2003,http://www.entrepreneur.com/Magazines/Copy of MA SegArticle/ 0,4453,311442—2-,00.html.

25. The GEM study for the United States in 2002 reported that 50 percent of respondents were thinking about starting a business. About 7 percent had taken some sort of action to start a business, and 4 percent had actually started a firm. Heidi M. Neck, Andrew L. Zacharakis, William D. Bygrave, and Paul D. Reynolds, *Global Entrepreneurship Monitor: National Entrepreneurship Assessment—United States of America 2002 Executive Report* (Wellesley, MA: Babson College, 2003), http://www.gemconsortium.org/download/1061664039492/GEM%20US%202002.pdf.

26. NFIB, *Small Business Problems and Priorities,* (Washington DC: NFIB Research Foundation, 2000), http://www.nfib.com/object/IO_16191.html.

27. Heidi M. Neck, Andrew L. Zacharakis, William D. Bygrave, and Paul D. Reynolds *Global Entrepreneurship Monitor: National Entrepreneurship Assessment—United States of America, 2002 Executive Report* (Wellesley, MA: Babson College, 2003), http://www.gemconsortium.org/download/1061664 039492/GEM%20US%202002.pdf.

28. "Small Business Economic Indicators for 2002" (2003), Office of Advocacy, U.S. Small Business Administration (SBA), Table 11, Nonfarm Private Employment by Industry, 2000–2001.

29. Fast Pass: Passport Express Services Inc. offers an automated way for travelers to obtain or renew passports in as few as 24 hours. Pamela Rohland, *Entrepreneur's Start-Ups,* January 2001. http://www.entrepreneur.com/mag/article/0,1539,284528,00.html. See also Julie Bawden Davis, "50 Low-Cost Businesses: Part I—Start Your Business on a Shoestring for Less Than $12,000!" *Business Start-Ups,* November 1997. http://www.entrepreneur.com/mag/article/0,1539,227766,00.html. Marcie Geffner, "Shoestring Startups: 24 Businesses You Can Start for $3,000 or Less," *Business Start-Ups,* April 1998. http://www.entrepreneur.com/Your_Business/YB_SegArticle/ 0,4621,276405—,00.html.

30. T. J. Stanley, and W. D. Danko, *The Millionaire Next Door.* (New York: Pocket Books, 1996).

31. The 50 percent survival rate is the rate reported in SBA Office of Advocacy, *Small Business by the Numbers* (Washington, D.C: Small Business Administration, 2004), http://www.sba.gov/advo/stats/sbfaq.pdf. This comes from original work done by the SBA and is reported in B. D. Phillips and B. A. Kirchoff, "Formation, Growth Survival: Small Firm Dynamics in the U.S. Economy," *Small Business Economics* 1 (1989), pp. 65–74 and B. D. Phillips, "Using Census Bureau Data by Firm Size, 1988–1996," in Jerome A. Katz (ed.), *Advances in Entrepreneurship, Firm Emergence and Growth Volume 4: Databases for the Study of Entrepreneurship,* (Greenwich, CT: JAI Press, 2000). These figures supersede a study done by the census bureau for the SBA and reported in SBA Office of Advocacy, "Small Business Answer Card 1998, Table: Survival Rates of All Firms Existing in 1992 by 1996," 1998. http://www.sba.gov/advo/stats/answer.pdf. The four-year survival figure for all firms was 75.5 percent. For firms with no employees (owner-only firms) 72.4 percent survived. For firms with employees, the survival rate was 90.5 percent. There are still many places where the myth gets repeated. Devron A. Veasley, "In Depth: Small Business Resource Guide—Business Incubation. Incubators Build Economies, Benefit Communities," *Birmingham Business Journal,* August 11, 2003. http://birmingham.bizjournals.com/birmingham/stories/2003/08/11/focus6.html. Robert A. Gardner, CPP, "Loss Prevention Management," 1995. ADT company Web site. http://www.adt.com/divisions/small_business/loss_prevention_center/news/loss_prevention_management.cfm. Tracey Drury, "For Entrepreneurs, It's All about Good Planning," *Buffalo Business First,* June 30, 2003, http:// www.bizjournals.com/buffalo/stories/ 2003/06/30/story8.html. Even the SBA is not immune to this statistical error. Although its own research shows that 50 percent of firms survive five years (see SBA Office of Advocacy, *Small Business by the Numbers.* (Washington D.C: Small Business Administration, 2004, http://www.sba.gov/advo/stats/sbfaq.pdf), there are still places on the SBA Web site where the five-year failure rate is pegged at 95 percent. See "Are You Ready?" in the "Startup Basics" section at http://www.sba.gov/starting_business/ startup/areyouready.html.

32. Devron A. Veasley, "In Depth: Small Business Resource Guide—Business Incubation. Incubators Build Economies, Benefit Communities," *Birmingham Business Journal,* August 11, 2003. http://birmingham.bizjournals.com/birmingham/stories/2003/08/11/focus6.html.

33. For example, see Oregon SBDC Network, "ASBDC Accreditation Self-Study," Oregon SBDC Network, Eugene, Oregon, November 2002. http://www.bizcenter.org/networkselfstudy/2002OregonSelf-Study.pdf. James J. Chrisman, "The Influence of Outsider-Generated Knowledge Resources on Venture Creation," *Journal of Small Business Management* 37, no. 4 (October 1999), pp. 42–58. James J. Chrisman, and W. Edward McMullan, "A Preliminary Assessment of Outsider Assistance as a Knowledge Resource: The Longer-Term Impact of New Venture Counseling," *Entrepreneurship: Theory & Practice* 24, no. 3 (Spring 1999), pp. 37–53. James J. Chrisman and W. Edward McMullan, "Outsider Assistance as a Knowledge Resource for New Venture Survival," *Journal of Small Business Management* 42, no. 3 (July 2004), pp. 229–244.

34. Alberta Charney and Gary Libecap, *Impact of Entrepreneurship Education* (Kansas City, MO: Kauffman Center for Entrepreneurial Leadership, 2000). Lars Kolvereid and Øystein Moen, "Entrepreneurship among Business Graduates: Does a Major in Entrepreneurship Make a Difference?" *Journal of European Industrial Training* 21, no. 4 (1997), pp. 154–160. W. Edward McMullan and L. Murray Gillin, "Entrepreneurship Education: Developing Technological Start-up Entrepreneurs. A Case Study of a Graduate Entrepreneurship Programme at Swinburne University," *Technovation* 18, no. 4 (April 1998), pp. 275–286. Teresa V. Menzies and J. C. Paradi, "Encouraging Technology-Based Ventures: Entrepreneurship Education and Engineering Graduates," *New England Journal of Entrepreneurship* 5, no. 2 (Fall 2002), pp. 57–64. Teresa V. Menzies and J. C. Paradi, "Entrepreneurship Education and Engineering Students: Career Path and Business Performance," *International Journal of Entrepreneurship and Innovation* 6, no. 2 (May 2003), pp. 85–96. Nancy B. Upton, Donald L. Sexton, and Carlos Moore, "Have We Made a Difference? An Examination of Career Activity of Entrepreneurship Majors since 1981" (abstract), *Frontiers of Entrepreneurship Research 1995* (Wellesley, MA: Babson College, 1995), pp. 727–728.

35. Jerome Katz and William B. Gartner, "Properties of Emerging Organizations," *Academy of Management Review* 13, no. 3 (July 1988), pp. 429–441. Jerome A. Katz and Scott Safranski, "Standardization in the Midst of Innovation: Structural Implications of the Internet for SMEs," *Futures: the Journal of Policy, Planning and Future Studies* 35, no. 4 (May

2003), pp. 323–340. Sumit K. Kundu and Jerome A. Katz, "Born-International SMEs: Bi-Level Impacts of Resources and Intentions," *Small Business Economics* 20, no. 1 (February 2003), pp. 25–47. Jerome A. Katz and Susan Peters, "Understanding the Entrepreneur in the Growth Process of SMEs," *The International Journal of Entrepreneurship and Innovation Management* 1, no. 3/4(2001), pp. 366–380. Nancy M. Carter, William B. Gartner, and Paul D. Reynolds, "Exploring Start-Up Sequences," *Journal of Business Venturing* 11, no. 3 (May 1996), pp. 151–166.

36. The theory was developed in the article: Jerome Katz and William B. Gartner, "Properties of Emerging Organizations," *Academy of Management Review* 13, no. 3 (July 1988), pp. 429–441. And extended in J. A. Katz and S. Peters, "Understanding the Entrepreneur in the Growth Process of SMEs," *The International Journal of Entrepreneurship and Innovation Management* 1, no. 3/4 (2001), pp. 366–380. Empirical work in the PSED study was reported in Nancy M. Carter, William B. Gartner, and Paul D. Reynolds, "Exploring Start-Up Sequences," *Journal of Business Venturing* 11, no. 3 (May 1996), pp. 151–166. An independent confirmation was reported in Sumit K. Kundu and Jerome A. Katz, "Born-International SMEs: Bi-Level Impacts of Resources and Intentions," *Small Business Economics* 20, no. 1 (February 2003), pp. 25–47. A shortened form of the scale they developed for the PSED remains in use in the Global Entrepreneurship Monitor.

37. Nancy M. Carter, William B. Gartner, and Paul D. Reynolds, "Exploring Start-Up Sequences," *Journal of Business Venturing* 11, no. 3 (May 1996), pp. 151–166.

38. Nancy M. Carter, William B. Gartner, and Paul D. Reynolds, "Exploring Start-Up Sequences," *Journal of Business Venturing* 11, no. 3 (May 1996), pp. 151–166 and Monica Diochon, Yvon Gasse, Teresa Menzies and Denis Garand, "From Conception to Inception: Initial Findings from the Canadian Study on Entrepreneurial Emergence (2001). ASAC 2001 Annual Meeting. www.sauder.ubc.ca/research/research_centres/cra/arena5/papers/ASAC2001Revised%20Submission.pdf.

39. This is the latest version of the idea called *fear of failure* by researchers into achievement motivation in the 1960s and 1970s. For fear of failure, see Ray Smilor, *Love and Fear: The Great Motivators of Entrepreneurial Achievement*, or Emmeline G. de Pillis, *What's Achievement Got to Do With It? The Role of National Culture in the Relationship between Entrepreneurship and Achievement Motivation.* (1998). http://www.babson.edu/entrep/fer/papers98/IV/IV_A/IV_A_text.htm. For the latest version, see Jeffrey Pfeffer and Robert I. Sutton, *The Knowing Doing Gap: How Smart Companies Turn Knowledge into Action* (Cambridge, MA: Harvard Business School Press, 1999), or see Alan M. Webber, "Why Can't We Get Anything Done? *Fast Company*, June 2000, Issue 35. http://www.fastcompany.com/magazine/35/pfeffer.html

40. The numbers are for 1999–2000, the latest year that data were available. SBA Office of Advocacy, *Small Business by the Numbers* (Washington DC: Small Business Administration, 2003), http://www.sba.gov/advo/stats/sbfaq.pdf.

41. SBA Office of Advocacy, *Small Business by the Numbers.* http://www.sba.gov/advo/stats/sbfaq.pdf and Z. J. Acs and C. Armington, "Endogenous Growth and Entrepreneurial Activity in Cities," Center for Economic Studies, U.S. Bureau of the Census, Working Paper #CES-WP-03-2, January 2003.

42. The last actual count was in 2000: small business—57.1 million, large business—56.9 million. SBA Office of Advocacy, *Small Business by the Numbers.* http://www.sba.gov/advo/stats/sbfaq.pdf

43. Jerome A. Katz, "Modelling Entrepreneurial Career Progressions: Concepts and Considerations," *Entrepreneurship: Theory & Practice* 19, no. 2 (Winter 1994), pp. 23–40.

44. Jerome A. Katz, "A Psychosocial Cognitive Model of Employment Status Choice," *Entrepreneurship: Theory & Practice* 17, no. 1 (Fall 1992), pp. 29–37.

45. Joseph A. Schumpeter, *The Theory of Economic Development* (New York: Oxford, 1961) (1934).

46. Robert X. Cringley, *Accidental Empires: How the Boys of Silicon Valley Make Their Millions, Battle Foreign Competition, and Still Can't Get a Date,* (New York: HarperInformation, 1996).

47. Scott A. Shane, "Is the Independent Entrepreneur a Valuable Organizational Form?" *RISEbusiness,* http://www.riseb.org/shane.html.

48. SBA Office of Advocacy, *Small Business by the Numbers.* http://www.sba.gov/advo/stats/sbfaq.pdf.

49. U.S. Small Business Administration, *The State of Small Business: A Report of the President, 1994 (*Washington, DC: U.S. Government Printing Office, 1995), p. 114.

50. History of Snowboarding Web site, http:// www.sbhistory.de/.

51. "Behind the Earmuff," *Kids World.* http://www.kidzworld.com/site/p880.htm. Mary Bellis, "Chester Greenwood, Earmuffs," *Inventors,* About.com, http://inventors.about.com/library/inventors/blgreenwood.htm. "Fascinating Facts about the Invention of Earmuffs by Chester Greenwood in 1873" *The Great Idea Finder,* URL: http://www.ideafinder.com/history/inventions/story091.htm.

52. Krisztina Holly, "Visual Voice(TM) Telephony Software," *Thinkquest.*http://library.thinkquest.org/26451/contents/inventors/krisztinaholly.htm?tqskip1=1; Mary Bellis, About.com, Inventors "Krisztina Holly," http://inventors.about.com/library/inventors/blholly.htm.

53. Don Debelak, "A Novel Dilemma: To Reach Potential Customers with an Avant-Garde Product, You'll Need to Have a Few Tricks Up Your Sleeve," *Entrepreneur,* June 2003. http://www.entrepreneur.com/Magazines/Copy_of_MA_SegArticle/0,4453, 308735—1-,00.html. And Drinksafe Technologies Web site, http://www.drinksafetech. com.

54. "Our Founders: Ed Lowe and Darlene Lowe," URL: http://edwardlowe.org/index.peer?page=FDNfounders, July 9, 2005. Jenny Kee, "Author Mark Baven on Being Extreme: Do You Have What It Takes to Be an Extreme Entrepreneur? Let Mark Baven Show You the Ropes of Rule-Breaking, Risk-Taking Entrepreneurship," *Entrepreneur,* June 18, 2001, http://www.entrepreneur.com/article/ 0,4621,290325,00.html.

55. Small Business Administration, "The New American Revolution: The Role and Impact of Small Firms" (Washington, DC: U.S. Small Business Administration, Office of Economic Research, 1998).

56. Small Business Administration, *Rural and Urban Areas by Firm Size, 1990–1995* (Washington, DC: Office of Advocacy, 1999), http://www.sbaonline.sba.gov/advo/stats/urb_rur.pdf.

57. Economic development experts call these *central place theorems,* with the efforts to figure out how many stores a population can support called *demand-threshold studies.* Examples tend to be fairly localized and include. Thomas R. Harris. and J. Scott Shonkwiler, "Interdependence of Retail Businesses," *Growth and Change* 28 no. 4 (Fall 1997), pp. 520–533. J. Scott Shonkwiler and Thomas R. Harris, "Rural Retail Thresholds and Interdependencies," *Journal of Regional Studies* 36 (1996), pp. 617–630. H. Gale, Jr., "Retail Sales Pull Factors in U.S. Counties," *The Review of Regional Studies* 26 (1996), pp. 177–196. David Darling and Stephen Tubene, "Determining the Population Thresholds of Minor Trade Centers: A Benchmark Study of Non-Metropolitan Cities in Kansas," *Review of Agricultural Economics* 18 no. 1, (January 1996), pp. 95–102. G. Ebai and T. Harris, "Factors Influencing Trade Area Activity in the Great Basin Area," *The Review of Regional Studies* 27 (1997), pp. 251–276.

58. The idea that living spaces are important to creativity (such as the kind we find in entrepreneurial and high growth ventures) comes from Richard Florida, *The Rise of the Creative Class: And How It's Transforming Work, Leisure, Community and Everyday Life* (New York: Basic Books, 2004).

59. Robert Berner, "P&G: New and Improved: How A.G. Lafley Is Revolutionizing a Bastion of Corporate Conservatism," *BusinessWeek,* July 7, 2003. http://www.businessweek.com/magazine/content/03_27/b3840001_mz001.htm. You can find information about Trillium Health Care Products at http://www.brockville. com/newsdetails.cfm?IDln=17201.htm or at their corporate website www.trilliumhealth care.com.

60. John E. Harmon, "On the Wings of a Buffalo or 'Mother Teressa's Wings'" *Atlas of Popular Culture in the Northeastern United States.* (Undated). http://www.geography.ccsu.edu/harmonj/atlas/buffwing.htm; Anchor Bar Web site, http://www.buffalowings.com/. Calvin Trillin, "An Attempt to Complile a Short History of the Buffalo Chicken Wing," *The New Yorker,* August 25, 1980, pp. 82–87 (Also reproduced in his book, *The Tummy Trilogy*) J. Ferrary, "Mother Teressa's Wings," *Travel-Holiday* 175, no. 5 (June 1992), p. 31.

61. John M. Mcguire, "Our Town 2000, They've Got the World on a Shelf," *St. Louis Post-Dispatch,* August 28, 2000, p. E1 (Everyday). Repps Hudson, "Small-Firm Owners Strive to Meet Their High Expectations," *St. Louis Post-Dispatch,* May 13, 2002, p. P. 22 (Business Plus). Janet Mcnichols, "Kirkwood City Council Honors Three Residents," *St. Louis Post-Dispatch,* January 1, 2001, p. P. 3 (West Post). John M. Mcguire, "Our Town 2000—Thai Dynamo Is a Reminder of How a Grocer Looks, Acts," *St. Louis Post-Dispatch,* August 28, 2000, p. E1 (Everyday). Dan Mihalopoulos, "Immigrant's Motto: "You Work Hard, You Can Make It," *St. Louis Post-Dispatch*, May 9, 1999, p. B 1 (Imagine St. Louis). Joan Little, "New Food Store Will Offer Exotic and Ethnic Variety: Opening of Global Food Market Set for March '99," *St. Louis Post-Dispatch*, November 26, 1998 p. P. 6 (West Post).

Chapter 2

1. This example came from an interview conducted by Prof. Kathy Lund-Dean of Idaho State University-Pocatello, in May 2004. At the request of the entrepreneur, his name, his town, and his business' name are disguised.

2. Johan Graafland, Bert van de Ven, and Nelleke Stoffele, "Strategies and Instruments for Organising CSR by Small and Large Businesses in the Netherlands," *Journal of Business Ethics* 47, no. 1 (September 2003), pp. 45–60. Barko Bucar and Robert D. Hisrich, "Ethics of Business Managers vs. Entrepreneurs'," *Journal of Developmental Entrepreneurship* 6, no. 1 (April 2001), pp. 59–82.
3. Scott J. Vitell, Erin B. Dickerson, and Troy A. Festervand, "Ethical Problems, Conflicts and Beliefs of Small Business Professionals," *Journal of Business Ethics* 28, no. 1(November 2000), pp. 15–24. Ruth Clark and John Aram, "Universal Values, Behavioral Ethics and Entrepreneurship," *Journal of Business Ethics* 16, no. 5 (April 1997), pp. 561–572.
4. R. Kogan, "What do people pay in taxes?", published on the website of the Center on Budget and Policy Priorities, http://www.cbpp.org/whatdo.htm.
5. This example came from an interview conducted by Prof. Kathy Lund-Dean of Idaho State University-Pocatello, in May 2004. At the request of the entrepreneur, his name, his town, and his business' name are disguised.
6. Lisa Miller, "Ethics: It Isn't Just the Big Guys," *BusinessWeek online*, July 25, 2003, http://www.businessweek.com/smallbiz/ content/10/2003/sb20030725_3531.htm.
7. Pat Auger, Paul Burke, Timothy M. Devinney, and Jordan J. Louviere, "What Will Consumers Pay for Social Product Features?" *Journal of Business Ethics* 42, no. 3 (February 2003), pp. 281–304.
8. Richard P. Green, Pamela M. Williams, and Jerome A. Katz, "Trust as a Defining Characteristic of Entrepreneurs," Proceedings of the 1998 Conference of the U.S. Association for Small Business and Entrepreneurship, 1998, pp. 82–192. Jerome A. Katz and Pamela M. Williams, "Gender, Self-Employment and Weak-Tie Networking through Formal Organizations: A Secondary Analysis Approach," *Entrepreneurship and Regional Development* 9 no. 3 (July–September 1997), pp. 183–197.
9. David Newton, *Entrepreneurial ethics: Values and decision-making in successful new ventures,* 1997. Dubuque Id: Kendall/Hunt, pp. 85–86.
10. The speaker here is John Bauer, whose story is given in "Small Business Insight. How trust pays off."
11. Amar Bhide. and Howard Stevenson, "Why Be Honest When Honesty Doesn't Pay: Business Men and Women Keep Their Word Because They Want To, Not Because Honesty Pays" *Harvard Business Review* 68, no. 5 (September/October 1990), pp. 121–130.
12. See note 5.
13. Peter Economy (2001). "Let's Get Ethical." From the online newsletter, 1099, Accessed 10/31/04.
14. Definition is a paraphrase from Steve Robbins, *Essentials of Organizational Behavior,* 7th ed. (Upper Saddle River, New Jersey: Prentice-Hall, 2003) p. 231, and Edgar Schein, "The Role of the Founder in Creating Organizational Culture," *Organizational Dynamics*, Summer 1983, p. 14.
15. M. H. Morris, M. Schindehutte, J. Walton, and J. Allen, "The Ethical Context of Entrepreneurship: Proposing and Testing a Developmental Framework," *Journal of Business Ethics* 40, no. 4 (November 2002), pp. 331–361.
16. Ethics Resource Center, National Business Ethics Survey, 2003, http://www.ethics.org/ nbes2003/2003nbes_summary.html.
17. Brenda E. Joyner, Dinah Payne, and Cecily A. Raiborn, "Building Values, Business Ethics and Corporate Social Responsibility into the Developing Organization." *Journal of Developmental Entrepreneurship* 7, no. 1 (April 2002), pp. 113–131. E. H. Schein, "The Role of the Founder in Creating Organizational Culture," *Organizational Dynamics* 12 no. 1 (Summer 1983), pp. 13–28.
18. Edgar H. Schein, "The Role of the Founder in Creating Organizational Culture," *Organizational Dynamics*" 12 no. 1 (Summer 1983), pp. 13–28.
19. Charles Brown, James Hamilton, and James Medoff, *Employers Large and Small* (Cambridge, MA: Harvard University Press, 1990).
20. Stuart Dawson, John Breen, and Lata Satyen, "The Ethical Outlook of Micro Business Operators," *Journal of Small Business Management* 40, no. 4 (October 2002), pp. 302–313. LaRue Tone Hosmer, *Moral Leadership in Business* (New York: McGraw-Hill Irwin, 1994), p. 35.
21. Graham L. Staines, "Spillover versus Compensation: A Review of the Literature on the Relationship between Work and Nonwork," *Human Relations* 33, no, 2 (1980), pp. 111–129.
22. Scott J. Vitell, Erin B. Dickerson, and Troy A. Festervand, "Ethical Problems, Conflicts and Beliefs of Small Business Professionals," *Journal of Business Ethics* 28, no. 1. (November 2000), pp. 15–24.
23. Robert C, Solomon, *A Better Way to Think About Business* (New York: Oxford University Press, 1999).
24. Hai Y. Teoh and Siang L. Foo, "Moderating Effects of Tolerance of Ambiguity and Risk Taking Propensity on the Role Conflict-Perceived Performance Relationship: Evidence from Singaporean Entrepreneurs," *Journal of Business Venturing* 12, no. l (January 1997), pp. 67–81.
25. Howard E. Aldrich and Ellen R. Auster, "Even Dwarfs Started Small: Liabilities of Age and Size and Their Strategic Implications," *Research in Organizational Behavior* 8, no. 2 (1986), pp. 165–198.
26. Lisa Miller, "Ethics: It Isn't Just the Big Guys," *BusinessWeek online*, July 25, 2003, http://www.businessweek.com/smallbiz/ content/10/2003/sb20030725_3531.htm.
27. M. H. Morris, M. Schindehutte, J. Walton, and J. Allen, "The Ethical Context of Entrepreneurship: Proposing and Testing a Developmental Framework," *Journal of Business Ethics* 40, no. 4 (November 2002), pp. 331–361. Hai Y. Teoh, and Siang L. Foo, "Moderating Effects of Tolerance of Ambiguity and Risk Taking Propensity on the Role Conflict-Perceived Performance Relationship: Evidence from Singaporean Entrepreneurs," *Journal of Business Venturing* 12, no. l (January 1997), pp. 67–81.
28. Amy Tsao, "A Primer on Drug 'Reimporting,'" *BusinessWeek* online, April 21, 2004. http://businessweek.com/bwdaily/dnflash/apr2004/nf20040421_1767_db_080.htm.
29. For more about Rx Depot see Associated Press, "Judge Hears Testimony in Canada Drug Case." *St Louis Post-Dispatch,* October 10, 2003, p C2. Also see Theresa Agovino, "Entrepreneur Fills an Order for Trouble," *St. Louis Post-Dispatch*, October 8, 2003, p. E1.
30. For information on online pharmacies and some of the issues lawmakers are wrestling with, see Amy Tsao, "An Iffy Prognosis for Online Pharmacies," *BusinessWeek* online, November 25, 2003. http://www.businessweek.com/technology/content/nov2003/tc20031125_2272_tc136.htm.
31. This example came from an interview conducted by Prof. Kathy Lund-Dean of Idaho State University-Pocatello, in May 2004. At the request of the entrepreneur, his name, his town, and his business' name are disguised.
32. LaRue Tone Hosmer, *Moral Leadership in Business* (New York: McGraw-Hill Irwin, 1994), p. 35. http://www.nvca.org/med_industry_71603.html accessed and printed 9/26/03 E. H. Waterman. Statement of Elizabeth H. Waterman, Vice Chair, Medical Group, National Venture Capital Association, Managing Director, Warborg Pincus LLC, Before the Antitrust, Business Rights and Competition Subcommittee of the U.S. Senate Judiciary Committee, July 16, 2003, NUCA website.
33. Available at Walmart.com. Sales figure quoted YTD as of October 2003 per balance sheet.
34. From Stephen P. Robbins, *Essentials of Organizational Behavior,* 7th ed. (Upper Saddle River, NJ: Prentice-Hall, 2003), pp. 171–173.
35. Ibid.
36. Darren Dahl, "Do the Right Thing—or Else," *Inc*, November 2004, p. 48. Available at http://pf.inc.com/magazine/20041101/law.html.
37. Ibid.
38. Patricia Carr, "Revisiting the Protestant Ethic and the Spirit of Capitalism: Understanding the Relationship between Ethics and Enterprise," *Journal of Business Ethics* 47, no. 1 (September 2003), pp. 7–16. Jeffrey R. Cornwall and Michael J. Naughton, "Who Is the Good Entrepreneur? An Exploration within the Catholic Social Tradition," *Journal of Business Ethics* 44, no. 1 (April 2003), pp. 61–75.
39. A. Bhide and H. Stevenson, "Why be Honest When Honesty Doesn't Pay," *Harvard Business Review* 68, no. 5 (September/October 1990), pp. 121–130. Stuart Dawson, John Breen, and Lata Satyen. "The Ethical Outlook of Micro Business Operators," *Journal of Small Business Management* 40, no. 4 (October 2002), pp. 302–313.
40. Robert D. Putnam, *Making Democracy Work: Civic Traditions in Modern Italy* (Princeton, NJ: Princeton University Press, 1993), p. 167. Laura J. Spence and Rene Schmidpeter, "SMEs, Social Capital and the Common Good," *Journal of Business Ethics* 45, no. 1 (June 2003), pp. 93–108.
41. Robert A. Baron and Gideon D. Markman, "Beyond Social Capital: The Role of Entrepreneurs' Social Competence in Their Financial Success," *Journal of Business Venturing* 18, no. 1 (January 2003) pp. 41–60. Julie Hite and William Hesterley, "The Evolution of Firm Networks: From Emergence to Early Growth of the Firm," *Strategic Management Journal*, 22, no. 3 (March 2001), pp. 275–286. Helena Yli-Renko, Erkko Autio, and Harry J. Sapienza, "Social Capital, Knowledge Acquisitions, and Knowledge Exploitation in Young Technology-Based Firms," *Strategic Management Journal* 22, no. 6/7 (June–July 2001), pp. 587–613. S. Venkatraman, A. Van de Ven, J. Buckeye, and R. Hudson, "Starting Up in a Turbulent Environment: A Process Model of Failure among Firms with High Customer Dependence," *Journal of Business Venturing* 5, no. 5 (September 1990), pp. 277–295.
42. This is the concept of cognitive legitimacy as discussed in: Freeman, John; Carroll, Glenn R.; and Hannan, Michael T. (1983). The liability of newness: Age dependence in organizational death rates. *American Sociological Review. 48*(5), Oct, 692–710. Hannan, Michael T. and Freeman, John (1984). Structural inertia and organizational change. *American Sociological Review, 49*(2), April, pp. 149–164. Aldrich, Howard E. & Fiol, C. Marlene (1994). Fools rush in? The institutional context of industry

creation. *Academy of Management Review*, *19*(4), October, pp. 645–670.
43. Dean Shepherd and Andrew Zacharakis, "A New-Venture's Cognitive Legitimacy: An Assessment by Customers," Journal of Small Business Management 41, no. 2 (April 2003), pp. 148–167.
44. By the way, the fact that outsiders see entrepreneurs as a key source of legitimacy, while the entrepreneurs look outside themselves to their product as the legitimacy source, is a wonderful example of the classic psychological idea of causal attribution. People tend to see causes as being outside themselves, while outsiders are more likely to attribute cause to a person. For more on this in general, see Richard Nisbet, and Lee Ross, *Human Inference: Strategies and Shortcomings of Social Judgement* (Englewood Cliffs, NJ: Prentice Hall,1980). For an example in entrepreneurship, see Kelly G. Shaver, William B. Gartner, Elizabeth Crosby, Karolina Bakalarova, and Elizabeth J. Gatewood, "Attributions about Entrepreneurship: A Framework and Process for Analyzing Reasons for Starting a Business," *Entrepreneurship: Theory and Practice* 26, no. 2 (Winter 2001), pp. 5–32.
45. Kim T. Gordon, "Cross-Training: Join the Multichannel Marketing Revolution, and Get Ready to Pump Up Your Sales," *Entrepreneur,* July 2003. http://www.Entrepreneur.com/ article/0,4621,309488,00.html.
46. Anat BarNir and Ken A. Smith, "Interfirm Alliances in the Small Business: The Role of Social Networks," *Journal of Small Business Management* 40, no. 3 (July 2002), pp. 219–232. T. A. Ostgaard and S. Birley "Personal Networks and Firm Competitive Strategy—A Strategic or Coincidental Match?" *Journal of Business Venturing* 9, no. 4 (July 1994), pp. 281–305. Herminia Ibarra, "Personal Networks of Women and Minorities in Management: A Conceptual Framework," *Academy of Management Review* 18, no. 1 (January 1993), pp. 56–87. Sue Birley,. "The Role of Networks in the Entrepreneurial Process," *Journal of Business Venturing* 1, no. 1 (Winter 1985), pp. 107–117.
47. Heidi M. Neck, G. Dale Meyer, Boyd Cohen, and Andrew C. Corbett, "An Entrepreneurial System View of New Venture Creation," *Journal of Small Business Management* 42, no. 2 (April 2004), pp. 190–209. Danny Mackinnon, Keith Chapman, and Andrew Cumbers, "Networking, Trust and Embeddedness amongst SMEs in the Aberdeen Oil Complex," *Entrepreneurship and Regional Development* 16, no. 2 (March 2004), pp. 87–106. Robert A. Baron and Gideon D. Markman, "Beyond Social Capital: The Role of Entrepreneurs' Social Competence in Their Financial Success," *Journal of Business Venturing* 18, no. 1 (January 2003), pp. 41–60. Sarah D. Dodd, "Social Network Membership and Activity Rates: Some Comparative Data," *International Small Business Journal* 15, no. 4 (July/September 1997), pp. 80–87. Eric L. Hansen, "Entrepreneurial Networks and New Organization Growth," *Entrepreneurship Theory and Practice* 19, no. 4 (Summer 1995), pp. 7–20. Tone A. Ostgaard and Sue Birley, "Personal Networks and Firm Competitive Strategy—A Strategic or Coincidental Match?" *Journal of Business Venturing* 9, no. 4 (July 1994), pp. 281–306. Howard E. Aldrich and Carlos Zimmer, "Entrepreneurship through Social Networks." In Donald L. Sexton and Ray W. Smilor (eds.), *The Art and Science of Entrepreneurship* (Cambridge, MA: Ballinger, 1986), pp. 3–24. Sue Birley,. "The Role of Networks in the Entrepreneurial Process," *Journal of Business Venturing* 1, no. 1 (Winter 1985), pp. 107–117.
48. David A. Whetten and Alison Mackey. "A Social Actor Conception of Organizational Identity and Its Implications for the Study of Organizational Reputation," *Business & Society* 41, no. 4 (December 2002), pp. 393–414. Concept taken from p. 394.
49. Howard E. Aldrich and Nancy M. Carter, (2004). Social Networks. In William B. Gartner, Kelly G. Shaver, Nancy M. Carter, and Paul D. Reynolds, (Eds.)(2004). *Handbook of Entrepreneurial Dynamics: the process of business creation.* Thousand Oaks, CA: Sage.
50. Paula Caproni, *The Practical Coach: Management Skills for Everyday Life* (Upper Saddle River NJ Prentice Hall, 2000). Other articles that use similar approaches and show positive effects include: Jeff Gold, Dave Devins, and Alistair Johnson, "What Is the Value of Mentoring in a Small Business? Using Narrative Evaluation to Find Out," *British Journal of Guidance & Counselling* 31, no. 1 (February 2003), pp. 51–62. Tony Kent, Charles Dennis, and Sue Tanton, "An Evaluation of Mentoring for SME Retailers," *International Journal of Retail & Distribution Management*. 31, no. 8/9 (2003), pp. 440–465. R. Sullivan, "Entrepreneurial Learning and Mentoring," *International Journal of Entrepreneurial Behaviour & Research* 6, no. 3 (2000), pp. 160–175.
51. Ivan Misner, "Start by Learning How to Tailor Your Networking Approach for Different Occasions," *Entrepreneur—Sales & Marketing* March 22, 2004, http://www.entrepreneur.com/article/0,4621,314878,00.html. Kim T. Gordon, "Attracting Customers: Use Your Business's Assets to Bring in More Clients, *Entrepreneur,* August 07, 2000, http://www.entrepreneur.com/article/0,4621,278263,00.html. Dorothy P. Moore, *Careerpreneurs-Lessons from Leading Women Entrepreneurs on Building a Career Without Boundaries* (Palo Alto, CA: Davies-Black Publishing, 2001). Cynthia E. Griffin, "Gender Blender: Boys Don't Have Cooties, So Don't Be Afraid to Mingle at Mixed-Gender Functions, *Entrepreneur* (October 2001), http://www.entrepreneur.com/article/0,4621,292826,00.html. Erin Chambers, "A Warm Reception for Female Execs," *BusinessWeek Online*, December 9, 2004. http:// www.businessweek.com/smallbiz/content/dec2004/sb2004129_3272_sb013.htm. Sherry Alpert, "Making a Network Connection," *BusinessWeek Online,* September 18, 2003, http://www.businessweek.com/smallbiz/content/sep2003/sb20030918_4557.htm.
52. Amanda C. Kooser, "Crowd Control: Having Trouble Finding the Ideal System for Managing Your Customer Relationships? We've Got Advice to Get You Moving in the Right Direction," *Entrepreneur*, August 2003, http://www.Entrepreneur.com/article/0,4621,309894,00.html. Kimberly L. McCall, "Contact Solution: Face It, Post-its and Spiral Notebooks Won't Cut It When It Comes to Contact Management. Go High-Tech and Save Yourself the Headache," *Entrepreneur,* June 2002. http://www.entrepreneur.com/mag/article/0,1539,299744,00.html. Kim T. Gordon. "Managing Your Contacts: Our Homebased Expert Tells You Why You Can't Live without a Good Contact Management Program," *HomeOfficeMag.com,* December 2000, http://www.Entrepreneur.com/article/0,4621,284147,00.html.
53. Ian I. Mitroff and Murat C. Alpaslan, "Preparing for Evil," *Harvard Business Review,* 81, no. 4 (April 2003), pp. 109. Ian I. Mitroff, *Crisis Leadership: Preparing for the Unthinkable* (New York: Wiley, 2003). D. Creelman, Interview: Ian Mitroff on crisis leadership, 2004, *HR.com,* http://hradmin1.hr.com/HRcom/index.cfm/WeeklyMag/9A954EE7-B500-4AC4-A13DF077B83214E2?ost=wmFeature
54. Norman R. Augustine, "Managing the Crisis You Tried to Prevent," *Harvard Business Review,* 73, no. 6 (November/December 1995), pp. 147–158.
55. Dan Millar, "ICM Crisis Report: News Coverage of Business Crises during 2002" 12 no. 1 (May 2003) The Institute for Crisis Management http://www.crisisexperts.com/02creport.htm. Theresa Forsman, "Contemplating the Unthinkable: An Entrepreneur Who Lacks a Plan for Coping with Catastrophe Is a Victim in the Making, Says Crisis-Management Expert Debra Traverso," *BusinessWeek*, October 2, 2001, http://www.businessweek.com/smallbiz/content/oct2001/sb20011003_514.htm. Michael Seid and Kay Marie Ainsley, "Managing Your Reputation: Follow These Tips to Save Your Brand during a Crisis," *Entrepreneur,* October 22, 2001, http://www.entrepreneur.com/article/0,4621, 294000,00.html. Christopher D. Lancette, "Critical Thinking: A Crisis Has Hit. Now What?" *Entrepreneur,* June 1999, http://www.entrepreneur.com/mag/article/0,1539,230335, 00.html.
56. Daniel Tynan, "In Case of Emergency: A Smoke Alarm or a Life Preserver May Save Your Life, But They Won't Save Your Business. You Need a Real Disaster Plan Now. Your Business's Survival Depends on It, *Entrepreneur,* April 2003, http://www.Entrepreneur. com/article/0,4621,307161,00.html. Institute for Crisis Management," Crisis Management and Crisis Communications (Louisville, KY: The Institute for Crisis Management, 2000). http://www.crisisexperts.com/management.htm. Michael Seid and Kay Marie Ainsley, "Managing Your Reputation: Follow These Tips to Save Your Brand during a Crisis," *Entrepreneur*, October 22, 2001, http://www. entrepreneur.com/article/0,4621,294000,00.htm. Christopher D. Lancette, "Critical Thinking: A Crisis Has Hit. Now What?" *Entrepreneur* June 1999, http://www.entrepreneur.com/mag/article/0,1539,230335,00.html.
57. This mini-case is adapted from J. Kilpatrick, G. Gantt and G. Johnson, "The Gift," *Annual Advances 1990*, 1990. New York: McGraw Hill, pp. 300–301.

Chapter 3

1. Information about Laura Tidwell can be found at "*GirlGeek of the Week*," January 2001, http://www.girlgeeks.org/innergeek/ gkwk/gkwk_tidwell.shtml, (July 9, 2005). Kathleen Williams, "Enginehouse Media's CEO Honored by Business Community." *PRWeb,* December 15, 2000 http://www.prweb.com/releases/2000/12/prweb21075.htm. (July 9, 2005). [no author], "Laura Tidwell: An Internet Entrepreneur's Tips for Success." Women of.com. [No date]. http://www.womenof.com/Articles/cb121800.asp. (July 9, 2005).
2. There are some wonderful explorations on the history of the term *entrepreneur*. See R. F. Herbert and A. N. Link, *The Entrepreneur* (New York: Praeger, 1982). Here is the simple version. Trade, barter, and the family farm have existed since the earliest days of recorded history. Entrepreneurs—as people willing to take risks to pursue opportunities in order to gain wealth—have also been around a long time. Explorers like Marco Polo, ship captains, and the like were running businesses focused on the opportunity of attaining great wealth. The French economist Richard

Cantillon was both an entrepreneur in his own right and the man who focused and popularized the term *entrepreneur* in its classic sense during the 1750s. Economists and early entrepreneurship researchers used the term in Cantillon's classic sense, with perhaps the last major study using the model being the Collins and Moore studies out of MSU in the early 1960s [Orvis F. Collins, David G. Moore, and Darab B. Umwalla, *The Enterprising Man* (East Lansing, MI: Michigan State University Bureau of Business and Economic Research, 1964); and Orvis F. Collins and David G. Moore, *The Organization Makers: A Behavioral Study of Independent Entrepreneurs* (New York: Appleton-Century-Crofts 1970)] although organizational researchers of a psychoanalytic persuasion continued with such models even later. Abraham Zaleznik and Manfred F. R. Kets deVries, *Power and the Corporate Mind* (Boston: Houghton Mifflin, 1975); M. F. R. Kets de Vries, "The Entrepreneurial Personality: A Person at the Crossroads," *The Journal of Management Studies* 14, no. 1 (1977), February pp. 34–75; Elliot Jaques, *A General Theory of Bureaucracy* (New York: Halsted, 1976); M. F. R. Kets de Vries and Danny Miller, *The Neurotic Organization* (San Francisco: Jossey-Bass Publishers, 1984); Danny Miller and Jean Marie Toulouse, "Chief Executive Personality and Corporate Strategy and Structure in Small Firms," *Management Science* 32, no. 11 (November 1986), pp. 1389–1409.

3. Small Business Administration, "SBA Quarterly Indicators: Second Quarter 2005—The Economy and Small Business" (Washington DC: US Small Business Administration, Office of Advocacy, August 24, 2005), http//www.sba.gov/advo/research/sbqei0501.pdf.

4. The inclusion of new types of entrepreneurial personalities really started with Norman Smith's reanalysis of the Collins and Moore study. Norman R. Smith, *The Entrepreneur and His Firm* (E. Lansing, MI: Michigan State University Bureau of Business and Economic Research, 1967). Smith identified types he called the *opportunistic entrepreneur* (our modern classic entrepreneur), the *craftsman entrepreneur* (our small business owner), and a third possible group who consisted of technology-related entrepreneurs (what we call here the *idea generators*). Smith started a long productive collaboration with John Miner, and together over the next 40 years they and their colleagues published dozens of papers on the different entrepreneurial personality types, culminating in John B. Miner's *The Four Routes to Entrepreneurial Success* (San Francisco: Berrett-Koehler, 1996). Despite the title, Miner's book actually has six routes, with type combinations and what he calls a "sales or professional practice" which is the modern version of the small business owner or craftsman entrepreneur. But however researchers come to it, the idea of many personality types among the population of entrepreneurs remains the predominant model in consulting and research. See W. H. Stewart, Jr., Jo Ann C. Carland, and J. W. Carland, "Empirically Defining the Entrepreneur," *Journal of Business and Entrepreneurship* 8, no. 1 (1996), pp. 1–18. Smith's small business owner appeared in several other places. Sociologists had long studied small business owners, describing them as socially marginal individuals, but in general following the personality model given here. Charles M. Bonjean, "Mass, Class, and the Industrial Community: A Comparative Analysis of Managers, Businessmen, and Workers," *American Journal of Sociology*, 72, no. 2 (September 1966), pp. 149–162. Joel I. Nelson, "Participation and Integration: The Case of the Small Businessman," *American Sociological Review* 33, no. 3 (June 1968), pp. 427–438. Edna Bonacich and John Modell, *The Economic Basis of Ethnic Solidarity: Small Business in the Japanese-American Community* (Berkeley, CA: University of California Press, 1980). Psychologist Al Shapero popularized this model in an article in Psychology Today. Albert Shapero, "The Displaced, Uncomfortable Entrepreneur," *Psychology Today*, November 1975, pp. 83–88. Edgar Schein reported a group of MIT alums who were self-employed and carrying a career anchor he called *autonomy*, which was very similar. Edgar H. Schein, *Career Dynamics: Matching Individual and Organizational Needs* (Reading, MA: Addison-Wesley, 1978). Carland, Hoy, Boulton, and Carland established what has become the standard model for small business owners, and their differentiation from the contemporary classic entrepreneur. J. W. Carland, F. Hoy, W. Boulton, and J. A. C. Carland, "Differentiating Entrepreneurs from Small Business Owners: A Conceptualization," *Academy of Management Review* 9, no. 2 (April 1984), pp. 354–359. Today the small business owner profile is considered a distinct subgroup in the population of entrepreneurs and remains a lively topic of study. See for example T. M. Stearns and G. E. Hills, "Entrepreneurship and New Firm Development: A Definitional Introduction," *Journal of Business Research* 36, no. 1 (May 1996), pp. 1–4.

5. This model comes from Miner's "expert idea generator" as well as the entrepreneurial or creativity career anchor described by Edgar Schein, and the high-technology entrepreneur described by Ed Roberts of MIT. E. B. Roberts, *Entrepreneurs in High Technology* (New York: Oxford University Press, 1991).

6. This type is based on several sources also. Foremost is Miner's "Real Manager Entrepreneur," but even the psychoanalysts have mentioned this type, in Michael Maccoby, *The Gamesman* (New York: Simon & Schuster, 1976), as well as the power-oriented entrepreneurs in Wainer and Rubin's study of entrepreneurs. Herbert A. Wainer and Irving M. Rubin, "Motivation of Research and Development Entrepreneurs: Determinants of Company Success," *Journal of Applied Psychology* 53, no. 3 (June 1969), pp. 178–184. Ed Roberts also talks about entrepreneurs who come in to manage high-technology companies and contribute managerial, as opposed to technological, skills.

7. Burt Helm, "Big Business Tactics for Small Outfits," *BusinessWeek* online, January 6, 2005, http://www.businessweek.com/smallbiz/content/jan2005/sb2005016_0877_sb013.htm.

8. H. Chang, "Atiba is the Success of a Self-Taught Man," *The Tennessean*, September 10, 2003; "Enterprise Executive Profile: J. J. Rosen, Chief Executive Officer," *Nashville Business Journal*, March 2, 2001, http://nashville.bizjournals.com/nashville/stories/2001/03/05/smallb1.html.

9. Although Miner talks about the "supersalesperson" as an entrepreneurial type, it has been around by other names for a long time. Although Miner thinks in terms of growth-oriented firms, many part-time entrepreneurs are oriented toward the sales aspect of business, sometimes to the exclusion of good business sense. For example, the type had appeared earlier as the socially oriented entrepreneur in Wainer and Rubin's study of entrepreneurs, Herbert A. Wainer and Irving M. Rubin, "Motivation of Research and Development Entrepreneurs: Determinants of Company Success," *Journal of Applied Psychology* 53, no. 3 (June 1969), pp. 178–184. Furthermore, in talking about entrepreneurial efforts in low-income groups, the socially driven entrepreneur type pops up, see S. Balkin, *Self-Employment for Low Income People* (New York: Praeger-Greenwood, 1989); and Eugene Gomolka, "Characteristics of Minority Entrepreneurs and Small Business Enterprises," *American Journal of Small Business* 2, no. 1 (July 1977), pp. 12–21. Among marketing based entrepreneurship researchers, the type has long been known. See Morgan P. Miles and D. R. Arnold, "The Relationship between Marketing Orientation and Entrepreneurial Orientation," *Entrepreneurship: Theory & Practice* 15, no. 4 (Summer 1991), pp. 49–65.

10. The modernization of the classic entrepreneur really began with the works of David McClelland in his books *The Achieving Society* (Princeton, NJ: Van Nostrand, 1961) and with David Winter, *Motivating Economic Achievement* (New York: Free Press, 1969). Central to this was the concept of moderate or managed risk taking, a concept proven in the early works of R. H. Brockhaus, "Risk-Taking Propensity of Entrepreneurs," *Academy of Management Journal* 23, no. 3 (September 1980), pp. 509–520. Economists revisited their definition of *entrepreneur*, adopting the modern version in the 1980s. See Mark Casson, *The Entrepreneur: An Economic Theory* Second Edition (Cheltenham, UK: Edward Elgar Publishers, 2003). Today this modern version is called the *proactive entrepreneur* [see Jill Kickul and Lisa K. Gundry, "Prospecting for Strategic Advantage: The Proactive Entrepreneurial Personality and Small Firm Innovation," *Journal of Small Business Management* 40, no. 2 (April 2002), pp. 85–97] or the *high-growth entrepreneur* [see M. Y. Bhave, "A Process Model of Entrepreneurial Venture Creation," *Journal of Business Venturing* 9, no. 3 (May 1994), pp. 223–242].

11. There are two major models of entrepreneurial competency—Mitchell *et al.* and Chandler/Hanks models. The Mitchell *et al* model has been validated cross culturally, with very strong results, while the Chandler/Hanks model has seen wider use in U.S. studies. Although each model labels the competencies differently, the content of the competencies is very similar. The model presented here builds from the Mitchell et al. and Chandler/Hanks models, mapping their specific competencies to the BRIE model of Katz and Gartner introduced in Chapter 1. The key article on competencies is Ronald K. Mitchell, J. Brock Smith, Eric A. Morse, Kristie W. Seawright, Ana Maria Peredo, and Brian McKenzie, "Are Entrepreneurial Cognitions Universal? Assessing Entrepreneurial Cognitions across Cultures," *Entrepreneurship: Theory & Practice* 26, no. 4 (Summer 2002), pp. 9–32. Note that what are called *competencies* in this text are called *scripts* in the Mitchell works. The scripts are observed through their related cognitions. Gaylen N. Chandler and Steven H. Hanks, "Founder Competence, the Environment, and Venture Performance," *Entrepreneurship: Theory & Practice* 18, no. 3 (Spring 1994), pp. 77–89.

12. This skill is called *business ability competency* by Mitchell *et al.* and *managerial competency* by Chandler and Hanks.

13. This is called *organizational resources and capabilities* by Chandler and Hanks, while in the Mitchell *et al.* model resources are a part of arrangement competencies. The social competencies that make these easier or harder for the entrepreneur come from R. A. Baron and G. D. Markman, "Beyond Social Capital: The Role of Entrepreneurs' Social Competence in Their Financial Success," *Journal of Business Venturing* 18, no. 1 (January 2003), pp. 41–60.

14. In the Mitchell *et al.* model these are called *willingness competencies*, while in the Chandler/Hanks approach they make up a part of the entrepreneurial competence factor.

15. In the Chandler/Hanks model, this is called the *quality of the opportunity,* while opportunity factors make up much of the arrangements competency cluster.

16. See R. Mitchell and S. Chesteen, "Enhancing Entrepreneurial Expertise: Experiential Pedagogy and the Entrepreneurial Expert Script," *Simulation & Gaming* 26, no. 3 (September 1995), pp. 288–306.

17. While this exact model is new to this text, three part approaches to firms have been around more than 45 years. The two works that are the major contributors to the approach are Norman Smith's "Artisan, Technological and Opportunistic Firms" from his 1967 report, *The Entrepreneur and His Firm* (East Lansing, MI: Michigan State University Bureau of Business and Economic Research), Ron Mitchell and Susan Chesteen's 1995 article, "Enhancing Entrepreneurial Expertise: Experiential Pedagogy and the Entrepreneurial Expert Script. (*Simulation & Gaming* 26, no. 3 September, pp. 288–306), which talked about novice, enhanced, and expert types in organizing a business.

18. You can learn more about ISO9000 certification from the International Organization for Standardization's web site at www.iso.org.

19. S. S. Smith, "Five Minutes with Author Jim Collins: What Does It Take to Be Great, Not Just Good? This Built to Last Author Reveals What It Takes to Reach the Top—and Stay There," *Entrepreneur,* October 1, 2001 http://www.Entrepreneur.com/article/0,4621,293352,00.html. For the Baldridge Award, see Malcolm Baldridge National Quality Award 1992 Winner—Granite Rock Company, http://www.quality.nist.gov/Granite_Rock_Co.htm.

20. In organizational theory, this favored business function is called a leading subsystem. D. Katz and R. L. Kahn, *The Social Psychology of Organizations,* 2nd ed. (New York: Wiley, 1978).

21. J. Plazonja and A. Zildjian, *Avedis Zildjian—The Father of Cymbals* (2003), http://www.zildjian.com/adaa/adaa_2003_legacy_6.asp. (Accessed July 9, 2005).

22. [No Author] Historical Timeline. Zildjian Company Website. http://www.zildjian.com/EN-US/about/timeline.ad2. (July 10, 2005).

23. C. L. Shartle, *Occupational Information,* 3rd Edition. (Englewood Cliffs, NJ: Prentice Hall, 1959) p. 23.

24. This approach builds on the career theory of Edgar Schein, from his work *Career Dynamics* (Reading, MA: Addison-Wesley, 1978). The original adaptation of Schein comes from Jerome A. Katz, "Modeling Entrepreneurial Career Progressions: Concepts and Considerations," *Entrepreneurship: Theory & Practice* 19, no. 2 (Winter 1994), pp. 23–40, with the entrepreneur's version presented here coming from Jerome A. Katz, "What Track Are You On?" *Inc,* October 1, 1995. http://www.inc.com/magazine/19951001/ 2430.html.

25. William Gartner [W. B. Gartner, "A Conceptual Framework for Describing the Phenomenon of New Venture Creation," *Academy of Management Review* 10, no. 4 (October 1985), pp. 696–706.] defined the entrepreneurial event as the interaction of the entrepreneur, the business itself, the process by which it is started, and the context or environment in which all this happens. Other works that have built on the Gartner idea include: L. Herron and H. J. Sapienza, "The Entrepreneur and the Initiation of New Venture Launch Activities," *Entrepreneurship: Theory & Practice* 17, no. 1 (Fall 1992), pp. 49–55; Douglas W. Naffziger, Jeffrey S. Hornsby, and Donald F. Kuratko, "A Proposed Research Model of Entrepreneurial Motivation." *Entrepreneurship: Theory & Practice* 18, no. 3 (Spring 1994), pp. 29–42; Carolyn Y. Woo, U. Daellenbach, and C. Nicholls-Nixon, "Theory Building in the Presence of 'Randomness': The Case of Venture Creation and Performance," *Journal of Management Studies* 31, no. 4 (July 1994), pp. 507–524; Richard C. Becherer and John G. Maurer, "The Proactive Personality Disposition and Entrepreneurial Behavior among Small Company Presidents," *Journal of Small Business Management* 37, no. 1 (January 1999), pp. 28–36. The term *entrepreneurial settings* follows the idea of environment in these studies. However, neither Gartner nor the subsequent researchers specified the exact nature of different types of settings. The settings described here are chosen because of their frequency.

26. Joseph Weber and Louis Lavelle, "Family, Inc." *BusinessWeek* online, (November 10, 2003), http://www.businessweek.com:/print/magazine/content/03_45/b3857002.htm?mz.

27. R. Kurtz, "When Business Is in the Blood", *BusinessWeek* online, January 25, 2005, http://yahoo.businessweek.com/smallbiz/content/jan2005/sb20050125_3409.htm. D. Miller and I. Le Breton-Miller, *Managing for the Long Run: Lessons in Competitive Advantage from Great Family Businesses* (Boston: Harvard Business School Press, 2005).

28. Joseph Astrachan and Melissa C. Shanker, "Family Businesses' Contribution to the U.S. Economy: A Closer Look," *Family Business Review* 16, no. 3 (September 2003), pp. 211–219.

29. Joseph Weber and Louis Lavelle, "Family, Inc." *BusinessWeek* online, November 10, 2003, http://www.businessweek.com:/print/magazine/content/03_45/b3857002.htm?mz.

30. A. P. Sherman, "Connect the Daughters: Sons Aren't the Only Offspring Taking Over Family Businesses," *Entrepreneur* 30, no. 2 (December 2002), p. 36.

31. W. Gibb Dyer and Wendy Handler, "Entrepreneurship and Family Business: Exploring the Connections," *Entrepreneurship: Theory & Practice* 18, no. 1 (Fall 1994), pp. 71–83.

32. W. Gibb Dyer and Wendy Handler, "Entrepreneurship and Family Business: Exploring the Connections," *Entrepreneurship: Theory & Practice* 18, no. 1 (Fall 1994), pp. 71–83. Frank Hoy and Trudy Verser, "Emerging Business, Emerging Field: Entrepreneurship and the Family Firm," *Entrepreneurship: Theory & Practice* 18, no. 1 (Fall 1994), pp. 9–23.

33. David N. Laband and Bernard F. Lentz, "Like Father Like Son: Towards an Economic Theory of Occupational Following," *Southern Economic Journal* 50, no. 2 (October 1983), pp. 474–493. Bernard F. Lentz and David N. Laband, "Entrepreneurial Success and Occupational Inheritance among Proprietors," *Canadian Journal of Economics* 23, no. 3 (August 1990), pp. 563–579. Robert F. Scherer, James D. Bordzinski, and Frank A. Weibe, "Assessing Perception of Career Role-Model Performance: The Self-Employed Parent," *Perceptual and Motor Skills* 72, no. 2 (1991), pp. 555–560. Robert F. Scherer, James D. Brodzinski, and Frank A. Wiebe, "Entrepreneurship Career Selection And Gender: A Socialization Approach," *Journal of Small Business Management* 28, no. 2 (April 1990), pp. 37–44.

34. John L. Ward, *Perpetuating the Family Business: 50 Lessons Learned from Long Lasting, Successful Families in Business* (New York: Palgrave Macmillan, 2004).

35. Charles R. Stoner, Richard I. Hartman, and Raj Arora, "Work-Home Role Conflict in Female Owners of Small Business: An Exploration Study," *Journal of Small Business Management* 28, no. 1 (January 1990), pp. 30–38.

36. E. H. Updike, "How to Avoid a Dysfunctional Family Business," *BusinessWeek,* March 2, 1998, p. 3. K. E. Gersick, J. A. Davis, M. McCollom Hampton, and I. Lansberg, *Generation to Generation: Life Cycles of the Family Business* (Boston: Harvard Business School Press, 1997).

37. Nancy J. Miller, Mary Winter, Margaret A. Fitzgerald, and Jennifo Paul, "Family Microenterprises: Strategies for Coping with Overlapping Family and Business Demands," *Journal of Developmental Entrepreneurship* 5, no. 2 (August 2000) pp. 87–114. Frank Hoy and Trody Verser, "Emerging Business, Emerging Field: Entrepreneurship and the Family Firm," *Entrepreneurship: Theory & Practice* 18, no. 1 (Fall 1994), pp. 9–23. Eric G. Flamholtz, *How to Make the Transition from an Entrepreneurship to a Professionally Managed Firm* (San Francisco: Jossey-Bass, 1986).

38. Joseph Astrachan and Melissa C. Shanker, "Family Businesses' Contribution to the U.S. Economy: A Closer Look," *Family Business Review* 16, no. 3 (September 2003), pp. 211–219. Arthur Andersen Center for Family Business, *American Family Business Survey* (St. Charles, IL: Arthur Andersen Center for Family Business 1995). John Ward, *Keeping the Family Business Healthy: How to Plan for Continuing Growth, Profitability and Family Leadership* (San Francisco: Jossey-Bass, 1987). Ward suggested that around 88 percent of family firms fail by the third generation, with family infighting, rather than a lack of succession planning, taking a toll in later generations. Ward's sample was relatively small. A very large, multigenerational study of family firms in France suggested a much higher survival rate [see Dean Savage, *Founders, Heirs and Managers: French Industrial Leadership in Transition* (Beverly Hills: Sage, 1979)].

39. W. Gibb Dyer, Jr., *The Entrepreneurial Experience: Confronting Career Dilemmas of the Start-Up Executive* (San Francisco: Jossey-Bass, 1992), p. 184.

40. David Whitford, "Century-Old Companies Built to Last," *Fortune Small Business* 12, no. 5 (2002), pp. 28–34.

41. Ernesto J. Poza, *Family Business* (Mason, OH: South-Western, 2004), pp. 28–9, 33.

42. Ibid., p. 33.

43. John Ward, *Keeping the Family Business Healthy: How to Plan for Continuing Growth, Profitability and Family Leadership* (San Francisco: Jossey-Bass, 1987). Ward suggested that around 88 percent of family firms fail by the third generation, with family infighting, rather than a lack of succession planning, taking a toll in later generations. Ward's sample was relatively small. A very large, multigenerational study of family firms in France suggested a much higher survival rate [see Dean Savage, *Founders, Heirs and Managers: French Industrial Leadership in Transition* (Beverly Hills: Sage, 1979)].

44. William G. Shuster, "Family Business in Crisis: Letting Go," *Jewelers Circular Keystone,* (March 2003) p. 84.

45. Eric G. Flamholtz and Yvonne Randle, *Growing Pains: Transitioning*

from an Entrepreneurship to a Professionally Managed Firm (San Francisco: Jossey-Bass, 2000), pp. 64–5.

46. W. Gibb Dyer, Jr., *The Entrepreneurial Experience: Confronting Career Dilemmas of the Start-Up Executive* (San Francisco: Jossey-Bass, 1992), p. 184.

47. Joseph Weber and Louis Lavelle, "Family, Inc." *BusinessWeek* online, November 10, 2003, http://www.businessweek.com:/print/magazine/content/03_45/b3857002.htm?mz.

48. W. Gibb Dyer, Jr., *The Entrepreneurial Experience: Confronting Career Dilemmas of the Start-Up Executive* (San Francisco: Jossey-Bass, 1992), p. 184.

49. Barnet Helzberg, Jr., "Sage Counsel for All Seasons," *BusinessWeek* online, August 13, 2003, http://www.businessweek.com:/print/smallbiz/content/aug2003/sb20030813_2077_htm?sb.

50. Ernesto J. Poza, *Family Business* (Mason, OH: South-Western, 2004), pp. 28–9, 33.

51. Ibid.

52. D. Bork, D. T. Jaffee, S. H. Lane, L. Dashew, and Q. G. Heisler, *Working with Family Businesses: A Guide for Professionals* (San Francisco: Jossey-Bass, 1996). N. C. Churchill and K. J. Hatten, "Non-Market Based Transfers of Wealth and Power: A Research Framework for Family Businesses," *American Journal of Small Business* 11, no. 3 (Spring 1987), pp. 51. E. G. Flamholtz, *How to Make the Transition from an Entrepreneurship to a Professionally Managed Firm* (San Francisco: Jossey-Bass, 1986). R. Beckhard and W. G. Dyer, "Managing Continuity in the Family-Owned Business," *Organizational Dynamics* 12, no. 1 (Summer 1983), pp. 5–12.

53. S. Foley and G. N. Powell, "Reconceptualizing Work-Family Conflict for Business/ Marriage Partners: A Theoretical Model", *Journal of Small Business Management* 35, no. 4 (October 1997), pp. 36–47.

54. Linda Moraski, "When a Partnership Turns Toxic," *BusinessWeek* online, December 17, 2003, http://www.businessweek.com:/print/ smallbiz/content/dec2003/sb20031217_7845.htm?sb.

55. Robert D. Hisrich, *Small Business Solutions: How to Fix & Prevent the 13 Biggest Problems That Derail Business* (New York: McGraw-Hill, 2004), pp. 70–71. J. A. Cox, K. K. Moore, and P. M. Van Auken, "Working Couples in Small Business," *Journal of Small Business Management* 22, no. 4 (October 1984), pp. 24–30.

56. Howard E. Aldrich, Nancy M. Carter, and Martin Ruef. "Teams." In William B. Gartner, Kelly G. Shaver, Nancy M. Carter, and Paul D. Reynolds, (Eds.). *Handbook of Entrepreneurial Dynamics: the Process of Business Creation*. Thousand Oaks, CA: Sage, 2004, Table 27.1, page 307.

57. In Chapter 1, endnote 3, we explored the number of new firms annually. Applying the PSED findings from footnote 56 above, we have about 600,000 new firms started by teams.

58. The term "equity" comes from J. Stacy Adams motivational model called Equity Theory, which is often discussed in Introduction to Psychology courses. Two examples of applying it in partner situations include: Brian Tracy, "Is a Business Partnership Right for You?" *Entrepreneur,* February 21, 2005, http://www.Entrepreneur.com/article/0,4621,320162,00.html and John A. Gromala and David F. Gage, "Mediating Personality Differences Behind Internal Business Disputes," *The CPA Journal, 72,* no. 3, (March 2002), pp. 68-69.

59. Paige Arnof-Fenn, "The Partner Track: How To Decide if You Should Fly Solo Or Not: The Second In A Two-Part Series On Business Partnerships," *Entrepreneur,* July 14, 2005, http://www.Entrepreneur.com/article/0,4621,322335,00.html.

60. Robert D. Hisrich. *Small Business Solutions: How to Fix & Prevent the 13 Biggest Problems That Derail Business*, New York: McGraw-Hill, 2004, pp. 70–1. Joe A. Cox; Kris K. Moore; Philip M. Van Auken. "Working Couples In Small Business." *Journal of Small Business Management,* 22, no. 4, (October 1984), pp. 24–30.

61. Center for Women's Business Research, *Completing the Picture: Equally-Owned Firms in 2002* (Washington DC: Center for Women's Business Research, 2003), URL: http:www. womensbusinessresearch.com/completingthepicture.htm. (July 10, 2005)

62. Center for Women's Business Research, *Privately-Held, 50% or More Women-Owned Businesses in the United States, 2004: A Fact Sheet* (Washington, DC: Center for Women's Business Research, 2004), http://www.womensbusinessresearch.org/pressreleases/nationalstatetrends/total.htm.

63. Ibid.

64. Center for Women's Business Research, *Seizing the Opportunities: A Report on the Forces Propelling the Growth of Women-Owned Enterprises* (Washington, DC: Center for Women's Business Research, 2003), http:// www.womensbusinessresearch.org/pressreleases/6-24-2003/6-24-2003.htm.

65. U.S. Small Business Administration Office of Advocacy *The Small Business Economy,* (Washington DC: Government Printing Office, 2004), http://www.sba.gov/advo/stats/sb_econ2004.pdf. (July 10, 2005) U.S. Small Business Administration Office of Advocacy, Minorities in Business, 2001, Washington DC: US Small Business Administration Office of Advocacy http://www.sba.gov/advo/stats/min01.pdf. (July 10, 2005).

66. U.S. Small Business Administration Office of Advocacy, *The Small Business Economy* (Washington DC: Government Printing Office, 2004), http://www.sba.gov/advo/stats/sb_econ2004.pdf. (July 10, 2005) U.S. Small Business Administration Office of Advocacy, Minorities in Business, 2001, http://www.sba.gov/advo/stats/min01. pdf.

67. U.S. Small Business Administration Office of Advocacy, *Minorities in Business,* 2001. http://www.sba.gov/advo/stats/min01.pdf.

68. Alicia M. Robb, "Entrepreneurial Performance by Women and Minorities: The Case of New Firms," *Journal of Developmental Entrepreneurship* 7, no. 4 (December 2002), pp. 383–397.

69. Karen E. Klein, "Women, the Loan Strangers," *BusinessWeek* online, May 28, 2004, http://www.businessweek.com/smallbiz/content/may2004/sb20040528_5382_sb010. htm. A. M. Robb, "Entrepreneurial Performance by Women and Minorities: The Case of New Firms," *Journal of Developmental Entrepreneurship* 7, no. 4 (December 2002), pp. 383–397.

70. Center for Women's Business Research, *Access to Markets: Perspectives from Large Corporations and Women's Business Enterprises* (Washington, DC: Center for Women's Business Research, 2003), http://www.womensbusinessresearch.org/pressreleases/2-4-2003/2-4-2003.htm.

71. K. S. Cavalluzzo and L. C. Cavalluzzo, "Market Structure and Discrimination: The Case of Small Business," *Journal of Money, Credit and Banking* 30, no. 4 (November 1998), pp. 771–792.

72. National Women's Business Council, *Federal Contracting with Women-Owned Businesses, FY1997 to FY2002* (Washington DC: National Women's Business Council, 2004), http://www.womenbiz.gov/Issue_briefFederal%20Contracts.pdf.

73. National Minority Supply and Diversity Council, MBE—Certification NMSDC website (2005), http://www.nmsdc.org/MBEs/tool_kit_certification.html. (July 10, 2005).

74. American Express Company, "Should You Consider Government Contracting?" Entrepreneur.com website. (2002), http://www. entrepreneur.com/amex/article/0,5742,307414,00.html (July 10, 2005). J. B. Howroyd, "Minority Loan and Grant Programs: The Right Program Can Ease the Transition from Pre-Funding Planner to Full-Fledged Entrepreneur," *Entrepreneur Biz Startups,* May 20, 2002, http://www.entrepreneur.com/article/0,4621,299866,00.html.

75. Stephen Roper, "Entrepreneurial Characteristics, Strategic Choice and Small Business Performance," *Small Business Economics* 11, no. 1 (1998), pp. 11–24. Gangaram Singh and Alex DeNoble, "Early Retirees as the Next Generation of Entrepreneurs," *Entrepreneurship: Theory & Practice* 27, no. 3 (Spring 2003), pp. 207–226.

76. Joshua Kurlantzick, "About Face: The Face of Entrepreneurship Has Evolved Over the Years, and Today, It's Dramatically Different. But What Will the Entrepreneur of the Future Look Like?" *Entrepreneur,* January 2004, URL: http://www.Entrepreneur.com/article/0,4621,312260,00.html. David A. Baucus and Sherrie E. Human, "Second Career Entrepreneurs: A Multiple Case Study Analysis of Entrepreneurial Processes and Antecedent Variables," *Entrepreneurship: Theory & Practice* 18, no. 2 (Winter 1994), pp. 41–71. Wallace N. Davidson, Dan L. Worrell, and J. Fox, Jercary B. "Early Retirement Programs and Firm Performance," *Academy of Management Journal* 39, no. 4 (August 1996), pp. 970–984.

77. Gangaram Singh and Anil Verma. "Is There Life after Career Employment? Labour Market Experience of Early Retires." In Victor W. Marshall, Walter R. Heinz, Helga Krueger, and Anil Verma (eds.), *Restructuring Work and the Life Course* (Toronto: University of Toronto Press, 2001).

78. Gangaram Singh and Alex DeNoble, "Early Retirees as the Next Generation of Entrepreneurs," *Entrepreneurship: Theory & Practice* 27, no. 3 (Spring 2003), pp. 207–226.

79. Andrea C. Poe, "Start a Business . . . Even After 50: Neither Shy nor Retiring, People over 50 Are Proving There's Life—and Profits—after Retirement as They Launch Second Careers as Entrepreneurs," *Entrepreneur* online—Entrepreneur Extra, August 19, 2003, http://www.Entrepreneur.com/article/0,4621,310607,00.html. G. Singh and A. DeNoble, "Early Retirees as the Next Generation of Entrepreneurs," *Entrepreneurship: Theory & Practice* 27, no. 3 (Spring 2003), pp. 207–226.

80. Nichole L. Torres, "Late Bloomer: If You're Just Now Realizing You're an Entrepreneur at Heart, Not to Worry. Here's Why Starting a Business after 40 Could Be the Best Thing that Ever Happened to You," *Entrepreneur's Be Your Own Boss,* October 2003, http://www.Entrepreneur.com/article/ 0,4621,311174,00.html.

81. Andrea C. Poe, "Start a Business . . . Even After 50: Neither Shy nor Retiring, People over 50 Are Proving There's Life—and Profits—after

Retirement as They Launch Second Careers as Entrepreneurs," *Entrepreneur* online—Entrepreneur Extra, August 19, 2003, http://www.Entrepreneur.com/article/0,4621,310607,00.html.

Chapter 4

1. This case is based on J. Samuelson, "Aaaaa-choo!" *Forbes, 157* no. 5, (March 11, 1996, pp. 82–86); R. Lieber, *Upstart Start-Ups* (New York: Broadway Books, 1998); and information from the corporate website of Magnetic Poetry, www.magneticpoetry.com.
2. R. Lieber, *Upstart Start-ups* (New York: Broadway Book, 1998).
3. "Poetry Makes a Fashion Statement," press release, July 10, 2001, www.magneticpoetry.com.
4. C. M. Gaglio, "Opportunity Identification: Review, Critique and Suggested Research Directions," in J. A. Katz (ed.), *Advances in Entrepreneurship, Firm Emergence and Growth,* vol. 3 (Greenwich, CT: JAI Press, 1997), pp. 139–202. S. Venkataraman, "The Distinctive Domain of Entrepreneurship Research," in J. A. Katz (ed.), *Advances in Entrepreneurship, Firm Emergence and Growth,* vol. 3 (Greenwich, CT: JAI Press, 1997), pp. 119–138. I. Kirzner, *Perception, Opportunity, and Profit* (Chicago: University of Chicago Press, 1979). H. H. Stevenson and J. C. Jarillo, "A Paradigm of Entrepreneurship: Entrepreneurial Management," *Strategic Management Journal* 11, Summer 1990, pp. 17–27.
5. I. Kirzner, *Competition and Entrepreneurship* (Chicago: University of Chicago Press, 1973). I. Kirzner, *Perception, Opportunity, and Profit* (Chicago: University of Chicago Press, 1979). I. Kirzner, *Discovery and the Capitalist Process* (Chicago: University of Chicago Press, 1985).
6. C. M. Gaglio and J. A. Katz, "The Psychological Basis of Opportunity Identification: Entrepreneurial Alertness," *Small Business Economics* 16, no. 2, 2001, pp. 95–111.
7. G. E. Hills and R. P. Singh, "Opportunity Recognition." In *Handbook of Entrepreneurial Dynamics: the process of business creation,* ed. W. B. Gartner, K. G. Shaver, N. M. Carter, and P. D. Reynolds. Thousand Oaks, CA: Sage, 2004, Table 24.1, page 266.
8. Dame Anita Roddick, "Our history and values: a message from Dame Anita Roddick, The Body Shop founder" *The Body Shop* (corporate website), 2004, http://www.thebodyshop.com/bodyshop/company/index.jsp, accessed July 17, 2005.
9. Geoff Williams, "Innovative Model: Joey Reiman has thought up stuff you've only dreamed about and now he's going to share his secrets of innovation with you," *Entrepreneur,* September 2002, http://entrepreneur.com/article/0.4621.302457-1.00.html, accessed July 17, 2005.
10. R. Lieber, *Upstart Start-ups* (New York: Broadway Books, 1998).
11. URL for this article http://www.entrepreneur.com/article/0,4621,307944,00.html
12. Information comes from the corporate website of The Fat Hat Company, www.fathat.com.
13. G. E. Hills and R. P. Singh, "Opportunity Recognition." In *Handbook of Entrepreneurial Dynamics: the process of business creation,* ed. W. B. Gartner, K. G. Shaver, N. M. Carter, and P. D. Reynolds. Thousand Oaks, CA: Sage, 2004, Table 24.4, page 268.
14. The information for this case came from Chiquita Miller-Nolan, "Determined to be 'a cut above the rest'," In Michael McMyne and Nicole Amare, *Beyond the Lemonade Stand 14 Undergraduate Students Tell Their Stories of Ethics in Business.* St. Louis: Premium Press America, 2004, and from a personal interview of Chiquita Miller-Nolan by Lisa Gundry, October 26, 2003.
15. T. W. Knox, "Evaluating Your E-Business Idea," *Entrepreneur* 2003, http://www.entrepreneur.com/article/0,4621,308896,00.html.
16. R. Maclean, "Where really bad ideas come from," *INC* (October 1998), 20 no. 15 http://www.inc.com/magazine/19981015/1114.html.
17. M. Michalko, *Thinkertoys* (Berkeley, CA: Ten Speed Press, 1991).
18. L. K. Gundry and M. LaMantia, *Breakthrough Teams for Breakneck Times: Unlocking the Genius of Creative Collaboration* (New York: Dearborn Books, 2001).
19. Ibid.
20. G. Wallas, *The Art of Thought* (New York: Franklin Watts, 1926).
21. S. G. Isaksen, K. B. Dorval, and D. J. Treffinger, *Creative Approaches to Problem Solving* (New York: Kendall-Hunt Publishing Co., 2000).
22. C. W. Prather and L. K. Gundry, *Blueprints for Innovation* (New York: American Management Association, 1995).
23. Dean A. Shepherd and Mark Shanley, *New Venture Strategy* (Thousand Oaks, CA: Sage Publications, 1998).
24. Connie M. Gaglio and Jerome A. Katz, "The Psychological Basis of Opportunity Identification: Entrepreneurial Alertness," *Small Business Economics* (2001), 16 no. 2 pp. 95–111.
25. These results come from a custom analysis of the Panel Study of Entrepreneurial Dynamics (PSED) done by Dr. Jennifer L. D. Shaver. Additional information on the PSED can be found in *Handbook of Entrepreneurial Dynamics: the process of business creation,* ed. W. B. Gartner, K. G. Shaver, N. M. Carter, and P. D. Reynolds. Thousand Oaks, CA: Sage, 2004.
26. This outline is adapted from, Ewing Marion Kauffman Foundation, *The Business Mentor CD-ROM,* Kansas City, MO: Ewing Marion Kauffman Foundation, 2001.
27. A. Daniels, "Generating Great Ideas from Employees," *Entrepreneur* (September 18, 2000), http://www.entrepreneur.com/article/0,4621,279678.00.html.
28. The example of AltiTunes came from R. Lieber, *Upstart Start-ups* (New York: Broadway Books, 1998), and from the corporate website of AltiTunes, www.altitunes.com.

Chapter 4 Appendix

1. This feasibility study was developed by Laurel Ofstein, a student at DePaul University in May 2005, under the direction of Professor Lisa Gundry of DePaul University.
2. http://www.newmansownorganics.com/pet/home/index.php.
3. http://www.naturapet.com.
4. http://www.onlynaturalpet.com.
5. http://www.omhpet.com.
6. http://www.threedog.com.
7. http://www.flintriver.com.
8. http://www.howlinghound.com.
9. http://www.happydogtoys.com.
10. http://www.kongcompany.com.
11. http://www.fatcats.com.
12. http://www.woofonline.com.
13. http://www.dogztogz.com.
14. http://www.ruffruffandmeow.com.
15. http://www.sba.gov/starting/regulations.html.
16. http://www.illinoisbiz.biz/bus/step_by_step.html.
17. Mike Troy, "Knows No Bounds for Love of Fido," *DSN Retailing Today* 41, no. 23(December 16, 2002), pp. 40–41.
18. Rebecca Gardyn, "Animal Magnetism," *American Demographics* 24, no. 5 (May 2002), pp. 30–37.
19. April Y. Pennington, "Hot Stuff: Want to Know What's Hot for 2004? We've Got the Businesses, Markets and Trends You Shouldn't Miss Out On," *Entrepreneur* (December 2003), http://www.entrepreneur.com/article/ 0,4621,311833,00.html. Steve Cooper, "Fever Pitch," *Entrepreneur* (December 2004), http://www.entrepreneur.com/article/ 0,4621,318038,00.html.
20. Alicia Suman, "Pet Owners," *Target Marketing* 26, no. 8 (August 2003), pp. 61–62.
21. Steve Cooper, "Fever Pitch."
22. "Organic Pet Food Gets Paws Up: Niche Grows Fast, Despite High Prices," *USA Today* (July 14, 2004), http://www.usatoday.com/money/industries/food/2004-07-13-organicx. htm.
23. American Pet Products Manufacturers Association, Inc., "Fact Sheet: Industry Statistics & Trends." *American Pet Products Manufacturers Association, Inc.* (corporate website), http://site05.fuzweb2.fuzint.com/press_industrytrends. asp.
24. Alicia Suman, "Pet Owners" (citing Mediamark Research).
25. Suman, Alicia. "Pet Owners" (citing U.S. Census Bureau).
26. Alicia Suman, "Pet Owners" (citing Mediamark Research and Third Wave Research Group analysis of BLS 1999 Consumer Expenditure Survey data).
27. http://site05.fuzweb2.fuzint.com/press_industrytrends.asp.
28. April Y. Pennington, "Hot Stuff."
29. June Campbell, "Mark Your Territory in the Pet Industry," *Entrepreneurnewz* (September 8, 2003), (http://www.entrepreneurnewz.com/entrepreneurnewz-19-20030908Mark YourTerritoryinthePetIndustry.html).
30. http://www.bccresearch.com/food.
31. Rebecca Gardyn, "Animal Magnetism" (citing pet industry analyst Julia Dvorko of Business Communications Co.).
32. http://site05.fuzweb2.fuzint.com/press_industrytrends.asp.
33. Ibid.
34. Joseph Tarnowski, "Pet Project: Giant Eagle Mixes Creative Merchandising, Special Events, and Just Plain Love to Create a Pet Program that Caters to Owners as Much as Animals," *Progressive Grocer* 83, no. 13 (September 15, 2004), p. 68.
35. http://www.petco.com.
36. http://www.petsmart.com.
37. http://www.omahasteaks.com.
38. http://www.oldnavy.com ; http://www.harley davidson.com.
39. http://www.samandwillys.com.

40. http://egov.cityofchicago.org/webportal/ COCWebPortal/COC EDITORIAL/RetailChicago 2004 North 2.pdf.
41. http://egov.cityofchicago.org/webportal/COCWebPortal/COC EDITORIAL/RetailChicago 2004 North 2.pdf.
42. http://factfinder.census.gov/servlet/QT Table? bm=y&-geo id=86000US60657&-qr name=DEC 2000 SF3 U DP3&-ds name=DEC 2000 SF3 U&- lang=en&-redoLog=false&- sse=on.
43. http://www.salary.com.

Chapter 5

1. Dan Murza, "Tranforming work into fun and your fun into money!" In Michael McMyne and Nicole Amare, *Student Entrepreneurs: 14 Undergraduate All-Stars Tell Their Stories*. St. Louis: Premium Press America, 2003.
2. PSED, question 331a asks people starting a business if they work for someone else more or less than 35 hours a week. 74.4 percent reported working for others full time, i.e., more than 35 hours a week.
3. Sources include: Joseph J. Fucini and Suzy Fucini, *Entrepreneurs: The Men and Women behind Famous Brand Names and How They Made It* (Boston: G. K. Hall, 1985). Brendan Howard, "Making Time: Not Ready for the Burden of a Full-Time Business? How Do Your Evenings and Weekends Look?" *Entrepreneur,* June 2000, http://www.Entrepreneur.com/article/0,4621,275163,00.html. Adam Cohen, *The Perfect Store: Inside eBay* (Boston: Back Bay Books, 2003), http://www.businessknowhow.com/manage/perfectstore2.htm.
4. Small Business Administration. *Small business by the Numbers*. (Washington, DC: Small Business Administration Office of Advocacy, June, 2004). URL: http://www.sba.gov/advo/stats/sbfaq.html. Accessed July 17, 2005.
5. J. A. Katz and W. B. Gartner. "Properties of emerging organizations." *Academy of Management Review, 13,* no. 3, July, 1988, pp. 429–441.
6. J. A. Katz, S. R. Safranski and O. Khan, "Virtual Instant Global Entrepreneurship: Cybermediation for Born International Service Firms." *Journal of International Entrepreneurship, 1,* no. 1, March 2003, pp. 43–57.
7. David Gumpert in *Burn Your Business Plan* [Needham, M A: Lauson Publishing, 2002,] suggests 100 hours, but the range is given as rules of thumb in government (http://bellzinc.sympatico.ca/en/content/503613?skin=sli) and commercial (e.g. http://www.capital-connection. com/bpconsulting.html) sites.
8. Chris Penttila, "Retailiatory Strike: Don't Let the Big Boxes Win without a Fight. There's Plenty of Room for Start-ups to Make Their Mark in Retail," *Entrepreneur,* December 2002, http://www.Entrepreneur.com/article/0,4621,304515,00.html.
9. Jan Kingaard, "How to Select a Shopping Center Location: Your Plan for Retail Success Requires a Shopping Center or Mall Location," *Entrepreneur* online, Management Section. February 10, 2005, http://www.entrepreneur.com/article/0,4621,319969,00.html.
10. Jan Kingaard, "How to Select a Shopping Center Location: Your Plan for Retail Success Requires a Shopping Center or Mall Location," *Entrepreneur* online, Management Section. February 10, 2005, http://www.entrepreneur.com/article/0,4621,319969,00.html.
11. Paul Edwards and Sarah Edwards, "Treasure Hunt: Hit the Mark When You're Hunting for Products to Sell," *Entrepreneur,* December 2003, http://www.entrepreneur.com/article/0,4621,312023,00.html.
12. Devlin Smith, "Parties Victorian: Build a Business around Tea Time . . . and Victorian Times," *HomeOfficeMag.com*, July 2001, http://www.entrepreneur.com/article/ 0,4621,290629,00.html.
13. Michael L. Sheffield, "Closing the sale as a Network Marketer: How to Get a Commitment Out of Prospective Customers," *Entrepreneur* online, April 21, 2003, http://www.Entrepreneur.com/article/0,4621,308127,00.html.
14. Multilevel marketing resources are also available at *Entrepreneur* magazine, http://www. entrepreneur.com/search/dir/0,4733,651,00.html.
15. Sean M. Lyden, "Make Newspaper Ads Work for You," *Entrepreneur,* May 27, 2002, http://www.Entrepreneur.com/article/0,4621,300275,00.html. Reprinted with permission of Entrepreneur.com.
16. J. A. Katz, "Virtual Instant Global Entrepreneurship: Agendas for Research and Policy," Keynote presentation, Third Biennial McGill Conference on International Entrepreneurship, Montreal, Canada, September 14, 2002, J. A. Katz, "Trajectories and Simultaneities—The Impact of Electronic Networks on Facilitating and Professionalizing Part-Time Entrepreneurship," Presented at the Symposium "Building a Career—An Interactive Network Of Relationships," Academy of Management National Meeting. Denver, CO, August 13, 2002.
17. See note 2.
18. Mark Henricks, "Just To-Do It: Having Trouble Getting Organized?" *Entrepreneur,* August 2004, http://www.entrepreneur.com/article/0,4621,316414,00.html.
19. Nichole L. Torres, "Juggling Multiple Tasks: How to Find the Time to Do All You Need to Do–and Then Some," *Entrepreneur*, July 6, 2004, http://www.entrepreneur.com/article/0,4621,316299,00.html.
20. Another useful site is maintained by the U.S. Small Business Administration at http://www.sba.gov/hotlist/license.html.
21. American Express - The Open Network. "Learning to Delegate." *Entrepreneur,* December 09, 2002. http://www.Entrepreneur.com/article/0,4621,305082,00.html, Accessed July 19, 2005. "Delegation and Organizational Structure in Small Businesses: Influence of Managers Attachment Patterns," M. A. Johnston, *Group & Organization Management* 25, no. 1 (March 1, 2000) pp. 4–22. Robert McGarvey, "To the Rescue: Always Stepping in to Save the Day?" *Entrepreneur,* March 2000, http://www.Entrepreneur.com/article/0,4621,229979,00.html. Alexander Ardichvili, Brian Harmon, Richard N. Cardozo, Paul D. Reynolds, and Mary L. Williams, "The New Venture Growth: Functional Differentiation and the Need for Human Resource Development Interventions," *Human Resource Development Quarterly* 9 no. 1 (Spring 1998) pp. 55–70. Robert McGarvey, "Ready, Set, Delegate! Handing Out Tasks Is the Key to Growing Your Business" *Entrepreneur,* – July 1998, http://www.Entrepreneur.com/article/0,4621,228958,00.html. Glenn H. Matthews, "Run Your Business or Build an Organization?" *Harvard Business Review* 62 no. 2 (March/April 1984), pp. 34–39.
22. Dun & Bradstreet, D&B 21st Annual Small Business Survey Summary Report/Full Report, 2002, http://sbs.dnb.com/survey/ 2002survey.pdf. The sample was 543 firms with 1–25 employees, although only about half that number reported on the Web site and computer functions.
23. R. N. Lussier, "A Nonfinancial Business Success versus Failure Prediction Model for Young Firms," *Journal of Small Business Management* 33 no. 1 (January 1995), pp. 8–20. R. N. Lussier, and S. Pfeifer. "A Crossnational Prediction Model for Business Success," *Journal of Small Business Management* 39 no. 3 (July 2001), pp. 228–239.
24. Teresa A. Sullivan, Elizabeth Warren, and Jay Westbrook, *Financial Difficulties of Small Businesses and Reasons for Their Failure* (Washington, DC: U.S. Small Business Administration, Office of Advocacy, 1998), http://www.sba.gov/advo/research/rs188tot.pdf.
25. Lynn Neeley, "Bootstrap Finance," Coleman Foundation White Paper, 2002, http://www.colemanchairs.org/files/documents/4/Neeley.pdf. Verne Harnish, "Finding Money You Didn't Know You Had," *Fortune Small Business* 12 no. 5 (June 2002), pp. 67–68. Mary Kay Sullivan, "Small Business Familiarity with Sources of Financing: Impact of Location and Size". U.S. Association for Small Business and Entrepreneurship, annual meeting, 2000, www.usasbe.org/knowledge/proceedings/2000/sullivan.pdf. Bob Weinstein, "Walk This Way: Lessons in the Fine Art of Bootstrapping," *Entrepreneur*, October 1998, http://www.Entrepreneur.com/article/ 0,4621,229429,00.html. Howard E. Van Auken and Lynn Neeley, "Evidence of bootstrap Financing among Small Start-Up Firms," *Journal of Entrepreneurial and Small Business Finance* 5 no. 3 (1996), pp. 235–249.
26. Chris Penttila, "Close the Loop: If You're Outsourcing Projects Right and Left, Make Sure the Information You Need Is Rolling Back to You," *Entrepreneur*, October 2003, http://www.entrepreneur.com/Your Business/YB SegArticle/0,4621,311034,00.html. P. Jacobs. "So You Want to Be a Mountain Climber — Changing Careers One New Experience at a Time," *Global Career Coaching* (corporate website), http://www.gccoach.com/documents/SoYouWanttoBeAMountain ClimberOct03 000.pdf, accessed July 17, 2005; Additional information was also obtained from the Gourmet Gatherings corporate website. www.gourmetgatherings.com.
27. Michael McMyne and Nicole Amare, *Student Entrepreneurs: 14 Undergraduate All-Stars Tell Their Stories* (St. Louis, MO: Premium Press America, 2003), pp. 42–50.
28. J. Finegan, "Bootstrapping: Great Companies Started with Less than a Thousand Dollars: CEOs from 11 different companies share tips and suggestions on how to fund a start-up with under $1,000." *Inc.,* August 1995. http://www.inc.com/magazine/19950801/2363.html, accessed July 17, 2005. Jerry Useem, "Should You Lie? Permissible or Not, Lying Has a Hallowed Place in the World of Business," *Fortune Small Business,* October 14, 1999, http://www. fortune.com/fortune/smallbusiness/managing/ articles/0,15114,360720,00.html. MSGI Security Solutions Inc., "Board of Directors," *MSGI Security Solutions, Inc.* (corporate website). http://www.mediaservices.com/about/board.cfm, accessed July 17, 2005.
29. Carla Goodman, "The Big Time: You've Tested the Part-Time Waters; Now Take the Full-Time Plunge," *Business Start-Ups,* August 1998, http://www.entrepreneur .com/article/ 0, 4621,229016,00.html.
30. K. Petrova, "Part-Time Entrepreneurship and Wealth Effects: New Evidence from the Panel Study of Entrepreneurial Dynamics," Working Paper, Boston College Department of Economics, September 2004, http://www2.bc.edu/~petrovak/html/research/jmp.pdf, accessed July 17, 2005.

Chapter 6

1. Amanda Bower, *Time* 162, no. 9 (September 1, 2003), p. TB10.
2. Small business investment companies (SBICs) are private lending institutions that are licensed by the U.S. government's Small Business Administration (SBA).
3. Lyrics and tune by Paul Simon.
4. B. Headd, "Redefining Business Success: Distinguishing between Closure and Failure," *Small Business Economics* 21 no. 1 (August 2003), pp. 51–61.
5. D. A. Veasley, "Incubators Build Economies, Benefit communities," Birmingham Business Journal, August 15, 2003, July 2005. http://birmingham.bizjournals.com/birmingham/stories/2003/ 08/11/focus6.html.
6. For example, see Oregon SBDC Network, *ASBDC Accreditation Self-Study* (Eugene, OR: Oregon, SBDC Network, November 2002). http://www.bizcenter.org/networkselfstudy/ 2002OregonSelf-Study.pdf; p. 25. J. J. Chrisman, "The Influence of Outsider-Generated Knowledge Resources on Venture Creation," *Journal of Small Business Management* 37, no. 4 (1999), pp. 42–58. J. J. Chrisman and W. E. McMullan, "A Preliminary Assessment of Outsider Assistance as a Knowledge Resource: The Longer-Term Impact of New Venture Counseling," *Entrepreneurship Theory and Practice* 24 no. 3 (2000), pp. 37–53. James J. Chrisman and W. Ed McMullan, "Outsider Assistance as a Knowledge Resource for New Venture Survival," *Journal of Small Business Management* 42, no. 3 (2004), pp. 229–244. A. Charney and G. Libecap, *Impact of Entrepreneurship Education* (Kansas City, MO: Kauffman Center for Entrepreneurial Leadership, 2000). L. Kolvereid and O. Moen, "Entrepreneurship among Business Graduates: Does a Major in Entrepreneurship Make a Difference?" *Journal of European Industrial Training* 21 no. 4 (1997), pp. 154–160. W. E. McMullan and L. M. Gillin, "Entrepreneurship Education: Developing Technological Start-up Entrepreneurs. A Case Study of a Graduate Entrepreneurship Programme at Swinburne University," *Technovation* 18 no. 4, (1998), pp. 275–286. T. V. Menzies, and J. C. Paradi, "Encouraging Technology-Based Ventures: Entrepreneurship Education and Engineering Graduates," *New England Journal of Entrepreneurship* 5, no. 2 (2002), pp. 57–64. T. V. Menzies and J. C. Paradi, "Entrepreneurship Education and Engineering Students: Career path and Business Performance," *International Journal of Entrepreneurship and Innovation* 6, no. 2 (2003), pp. 85–96. N. B. Upton, D. L. Sexton, and C. Moore, "Have We Made a Difference? An Examination of Career Activity of Entrepreneurship Majors since 1981" (abstract), *Frontiers of Entrepreneurship Research,* 1995 edition, pp. 727 728.
7. Brian Headd, "Redefining Business Success: Distinguishing between Closure and Failure," *Small Business Economics* 21, no. 1 (2003) pp. 51–61.
8. These statistics come from the Panel Study of Entrepreneurial Dynamics. William B. Gartner, Kelly G. Shaver, Nancy M. Carter, and Paul D. Reynolds (eds.). *Handbook of Entrepreneurial Dynamics: The Process of Business Creation* (Thousand Oaks, CA: Sage, 2004).
9. U.S. Small Business Administration, *The Small Business Economy* (Washington: DC: U.S. Small Business Administration, Office of Advocacy, 2004).
10. Jim Collins, *Good to Great.* New York: HarperCollins Publishing Company, 2001, p. 63.
11. R. Green, and J. J. Carroll, *Investigating Entrepreneurial Opportunities* (Thousand Oaks, CA: Sage 2000).
12. Professional Association of Innkeepers International (PAII), *Eighth Biennial Industry Study of Bed-and-Breakfast & Country Inns* (Santa Barbara, CA, 2003).
13. L. Marx and G. Shaler, "Bargaining Power in Sequential Contracting," Duke/UNC Micro-Theory Working Paper 3, 2002.
14. Financial Accounting Standards Board, "Statement of Financial Accounting Standards No. 142," *Goodwill and Other Intangible Assets* (2001).
15. McDonald's Corporation, *Annual Report.* 2002, p. 10.
16. Sarah E. Lockyer, "One Year Later: Ground Round Sizzles under Franchisee Co-op," *Nation's Restaurant News,* February 28, 2005. Carlye Adler, "The Ground Round Rebound: Stunned by a Sudden Bankruptcy, Stubborn Franchisees Step in to Buy Their Parent Company," *Fortune Small Business Magazine,* February 2005. Michael Peña, "Richmond's Job Center Gets Downsized," *East Bay Business Times,* April 2004.
17. Sandra King, Organizational Performance and Conceptual Capability: The Relationship between Organizational Performance and Successors' Capability in a Family-Owned Firm, "*Family Business Review* 16, no. 3 (September 2003) pp. 173–182. Patricia Schiff Estess," Class Acts: Family Business Forums Are a One-Stop Education Resource, *Entrepreneur* December 1996, http://www. Entrepreneur.com/article/0,4621,226658,00.html. A. Ibrahim and W. Ellis, *Family Business Management: Concepts and Practices* (Dubuque, IA: Kendall/Hunt Publishing, 1994).
18. Rod P. Burkert, "A Good Deal Depends on Preparation," *Journal of Accountancy,* 196, no. 5 (November 2003), pp. 47–52.
19. Stephen Weinstein, "Add a New Owner to Your Firm," *Journal of Accountancy* 196, no. 2 (August 2003), pp. 43–48.
20. The ideas here are derived from Chris Kelleher, "Preventing Feuds in the Family Business: Handling Delicate Topics—Like Succession Planning—with Care Is Key to Keeping the Peace in Any Family Business," *Entrepreneur,* June 14, 2004, http://www.Entrepreneur.com/article/0,4621,315884,00.html. Nichole L. Torres, "Family Affair When Business and Family Mix, the Key to Success is Communication," *Entrepreneur's Be Your Own Boss,* - September 2004, http://www.Entrepreneur.com/article/0,4621,316835,00.html. Patricia Schiff Estess, "Class Acts: Family Business Forums Are a One-Stop Education Resource," *Entrepreneur* - December 1996, http://www.Entrepreneur.com/article/0, 4621,226658,00.html.
21. Dominique Besson and Slimane Haddadj, "Dysfunctions in Owner-Manager Succession Process in Family Firms and How a SEAM Intervener-Researcher Can Address Them," *Journal of Organizational Change Management* 16, no. 1 (2003), pp. 83–89.
22. Isabelle Le Breton-Miller, Danny Miller, and Lloyd P. Steier, "Toward an Integrative Model of Effective FOB Succession," *Entrepreneurship: Theory & Practice* 28, no. 4 (Summer 2004), pp. 305–328. William S. White, Timothy D. Krinke, and David L. Geller, "Family Business Succession Planning: Devising an Overall Strategy," *Journal of Financial Service Professionals* 58, no. 3 (May 2004), pp. 67–86.
23. Scott Bernard Nelson, "Leave It to Them: Make Sure Your Family Gets What It Needs by Including a Disclaimer Provision in Your Estate Plan," *Entrepreneur,* August 2004, http://www.Entrepreneur.com/article/0,4621,316380,00.html. Paul DeCeglie, "State of the Estate: What Is Estate Planning and Why Should You Be Doing It Now?" Entrepreneur's Start-Ups, - January 2001, http://www.entrepreneur.com/article/0,4621,284549,00.html.

Chapter 7

1. This case is based on Nick Tostenrude, "Turning 25¢ into $1: The Unique Advantages and Disadvantages of Being Young Entrepreneurs," in Michael McMyne and Nicole Amare, *Student Entrepreneurs: 14 Undergraduate All-Stars Tell Their Stories.* (Nashville: Premium Press, 2003).
2. SIC codes are slowly being replaced by the North American Industry Classification System (NAICS). NAICS uses a six-digit code and offers original categories reflecting newer industries, such as those related to the Internet. For NAICS information, check out the NAICS page at the Census Bureau, http://www.census. gov/epcd/naics02/.
3. Thomas J. Stanley and William D. Danko, The Millionaire Next Door. (New York: Pocket Books, 1996).
4. SIC codes are slowly being replaced by the North American Industry Classification System (NAICS). NAICS uses a six-digit code and offers original categories reflecting newer industries, such as those related to the Internet. For NAICS information, check out the NAICS page at the Census Bureau, http://www.census. gov/epcd/naics02/.
5. Nichole L. Torres, "Designing Women—A "by Women, for Women, about Women" Attitude Is Making this Greeting Card Company a Success," *Entrepreneur,* July 2001, http:// www.entrepreneur.com/mag/article/0,1539, 290274, 00. html.
6. This is question Q291 in the PSED, "Within the first three to four years, what percentage of your customers do you expect to be . . . located within x miles?" Because the numbers are averages of percentages reported, they don't necessarily add up to 100 percent.
7. PSED Q327, "If someone asked you which kind of person you are, would you say that you preferred doing things better or doing things differently?" Of respondents, 63.3 percent said doing things better, while 32.4 percent said doing things differently.
8. The ideas in this section build on three works. Michael Porter talked about the topic in general in his 1980 masterpiece *Competitive Strategy* (Free Press). Karl Vesper really gave the first detailed workup of imitation-innovation strategies in his 1990 book *New Venture Strategy* (Prentice Hall). The most advanced thinking on the topic can be found in Dean Shepherd and Mark Shanley's 1998 book *New Venture Strategy* (Sage).
9. Sheila Himmel, "Feeling Welcome at Satay House," *The Mercury News,* May 3, 2002, http://www.bayarea.com/mld/mercurynews/entertainment/ eye/3189323.htm.
10. This convention follows Michael Porter (1980), p. 192.
11. Adapted from the drivers of value and costs, Walker, pp. 27–34 and Porter, 1980.
12. Karl Vesper, *New Venture Strategy* (Prentice-Hall, 1990).
13. Tax Resources, Inc. http://www.taxaudit.com.
14. "Initiative for a Competitive Inner City," Inner city 100 Winners 2003 SLR contracting. http://www.icic.org/vsh/oin/smRenderfs.php?phpsessid

=b5238b7a7e0007c805caf97833ab6fda&cerror Fred O. Williams, Inner-City Success Story, *Buffalo News*, April 26, 2003, http://www.buffaloniagara.org/news.asp?ID=25&ARCHIVED=1.

15. The latest news can be found at the SBA's Regulatory Flexibility Act Enforcement Page, http://www.sba.gov/advo/ laws/law_lib.html.

16. This list adapts and labels Shepherd and Shanley (p. 59) with two exceptions. One of their categories, "Products with special features appealing to specific niches" is treated here as a variant of customization. Instead, the comprehensiveness supra-strategy is provided.

17. Gary Nabham, "Food for Thought: Eating In—the Benefits of Locally Grown Food," *Sierra Magazine*. November/ December 2002, http://www.sierraclub.org/sierra/200211/ food.asp.

18. James Carpenter, "Little Guy' Is No. 1 Volume Car dealer," *The Salt Lake Tribune and Deseret Morning News*. http://www.utahbusinessandindustry.com/2003article/menlove2.asp

19. Adapted from "The Vermont Teddy Bear Company Story," http://store.yahoo.com/vtbear/ourstory.html; Elizabeth J. Goodgold, "Bear Market: How One Company Repositioned Itself for a Plush Success Story," *Entrepreneur*, September 2002, http://www.Entrepreneur.com/article/0,4621,302227,00.html; Joyce P. Vincelette, Ellie A. Fogarty, Thomas M. Patrick, and Thomas L. Wheelen, "The Vermont Teddy Bear Co., Inc.: Challenges Facing a New CEO," 1998, https://www.bus.iastate. edu/jdhunger/ 581AFall03/VermontTeddyBear.doc.

20. This section draws heavily on the original and interpreted works of Jay Barney. These include Jay Barney, *Gaining and Sustaining Competitive Advatage (2nd ed.)*. (Upper Saddle River, NJ: Prentice Hall, 2002); Sharon Alvarez and Jay Barney, "Entrepreneurial Capabilities: A Resource-Based View," in G. Dale Meyer and Kurt A. Heppard, *Entrepreneurship as Strategy* (Thousand Oaks, CA: Sage, 2000); Gregory G. Dess and G. T. Lumpkin, *Strategic Management* (Boston: McGraw-Hill, 2003); and Gordon Walker, *Modern Competitive Strategy* (Boston: McGraw-Hill, 2004).

21. Elizabeth J. Goodgold, "Bear Market: How One Company Repositioned Itself for a Plush Success Story," *Entrepreneur,* September 2002, http://www.Entrepreneur.com/ article/0, 4621,302227,00.html.

22. Mark Henricks, "A Mixed Blessing: That Unexpected Windfall May Feel Like Winning the Lottery, but If You Aren't Careful, It Could Wreak Havoc on Your Business," *Entrepreneur,* July 2003, http://www.Entrepreneur.com/article/0,4621,309368,00.html.

23. Barney, J. B., "Firm Resources And Sustained Competitive Advantage," *Journal of Management,* 7 no. 1 (Mar. 1991). pp. 99–121.

24. Lumpkin, G. T. and G. G. Dess, "Linking Two Dimensions Of Entrepreneurial Orientation To Firm Performance: The Moderating Role Of Environment And Industry Life Cycel." *Journal of Business Venturing,* no. 16, (Sep. 2001); pp. 176–182. Romanelli, E. "Environments And Strategies Of Organizations Start-Up: Effects On Early Survival," Administrative Science Quarterly; 34 no. 3, (Sep. 1989); pp. 369–387. Shepherd, D. A. and Shanley, M. New venture strategy: timing, environmental uncertainty and performance. (Thousand Oaks: Sage, 1998), pp. 63.

Chapter 8

1. Lisa K. Gundry and Aaron A. Buchko, *Field Casework: Methods for Consulting to Small and Startup Businesses* (Thousand Oaks, CA: Sage Publications, 1996). B. Honig, "Who Gets the Goodies? An Examination of Microenterprise Credit in Jamaica," *Entrepreneurship and Regional Development,* 10 (1998), pp. 313–334.

2. The ideas in this table come from David Gumpert, *How to Really Create a Successful Business Plan: Step-by-Step Guide* (4th ed.) (Needham, MA: Lauson Publishing, 2003), chap. 10. D. A. Shepherd, and A. L. Zacharakis, "A New Venture's Cognitive Legitimacy: An Assessment by Customers," *Journal of Small Business Management* 41, no. 2 (April 2003), pp. 148–167. D. A. Shepherd and A. L. Zacharakis, "Venture Capitalists' Expertise: A Call for Research into Decision Aids and Cognitive Feedback," *Journal of Business Venturing* 17, no. 1 (Jan 2002), pp. 1–20. Dean Shepherd and Evan Douglas *Attracting Equity Investors* (Sage, 1999). J. Hall and C. W. Hofer, "Venture Capitalists' Decision Criteria in New Venture Evaluation," *Journal of Business Venturing*, 8, no. 1 (January 1993), pp. 25–42. Robert Ronstadt, *Entrepreneurial Finance*. (Lord Publishing, 1988), chap. 10.

3. John L. Nesheim, *High Tech Start-up* (revised and updated ed.) (New York: Free Press, 2000).

4. Twenty-eight percent of owners wrote a formal plan while 26 percent had an informal or partial plan. Sarah Bartlett, "Seat of the Pants," *Inc.*, October 2002, http://www.inc. com/magazine/20021015/24772.html.

5. F. Delmar and S. Shane, "Does Business Planning Facilitate the Development of New Ventures?" *Strategic Management Journal* 24, no. 12: (December 2003) p. 1165. "Strategic and Business Planning Practices of Fast Growth Family Firms," Nancy Upton, Elisabeth J. Teal, Joe T. Felan, *Journal of Small Business Management* 39, no. 1 (January 2001), pp. 60–72. Brian Gibson Gavin Cassar, "Planning Behavior Variables in Small Firms," *Journal of Small Business Management* 40, no. 3 (July 2002) p.171 (16 pgs).

6. F. Delmar, and S. Shane, "Does Business Planning Facilitate the Development of New Ventures?" *Strategic Management Journal* 24, no. 12 (December 2003), p. 1165. B. Honig, and T. Karlsson (forthcoming), "Institutional Forces and the Written Business Plan," *Journal of Management*. B. J. Orser, S. Hogarth-Scott, and A. L. Riding "Performance, Firm Size, and Management Problem Solving," *Journal of Small Business Management* 38, no. 4 (October 2000) pp. 42–58. Stephen C. Perry, "The Relationship between Written Business Plans and the Failure of Small Businesses in the U.S," *Journal of Small Business Management* 39, no. 3 (July 2001), pp. 201–209.

7. B. Honig and T. Karlsson (forthcoming), "Institutional Forces and the Written Business Plan," *Journal of Management.*

8. John L. Nesheim, *High Tech Start-up* (rev. and updated ed.) (New York: Free Press, 2000).

9. Question 114 in the PSED: What is the current form of your business plan. unwritten or in your head, informally written, formally prepared, or something else?

10. Sources include: Cliff Ennico, "The 30-Second Business Plan: Want to Impress a Potential Investor Quickly? Here's Exactly What to Say," *Entrepreneur*. January 20, 2003, http://www.entrepreneur.com/Your Business/YB_SegArticle/0,4621,306110,00.html. Ben Casnocha, "Perfecting the Elevator Pitch: Learn to Rattle Off a Spiel Quickly about Your Company, and Soon You'll Have More Contacts Than You'll Know What to Do With," *TeenStartUps.com*, February 2003, http:// www.entrepreneur.com/mag/article/ 0,1539,306421,00.html. Stan Mandel, "The Elevator Pitch: Engage People, Move to Action . . . in 2 Minutes," Wake Forest University, 2003.

11. A. L. Zacharakis, "Writing a Business Plan," in W. Bygrave and A. Zacharakis (eds.), *The Portable MBA in Entrepreneurship*, 3rd ed. (New York: Wiley, 2003).

12. Dess G. Gregory and G. T. Lumpkin, *Strategic Management: Creating Competitive Advantage* (Boston: McGraw Hill-Irwin, 2003), pp. 27–29. Gordon Walker, *Modern Competitive Strategy* (Burr Ridge, IL: McGraw-Hill/Irwin, 2003), pp. 263–264.

13. Gregory G. Dess, and G. T. Lumpkin, *Strategic Management: Creating Competitive Advantage* (Boston: McGraw-Hill Irwin, 2003), p. 27.

14. Robert X. Cringley, *Accidental Empires* (New York: HarperBusiness, 1996).

15. Mark Henricks, "Words to Live By," *Entrepreneur,* September 1998, http://www. Entrepreneur.com/article/0,4621,229232,00.html.

16. Excalibur Seasoning, Mission Statement (Pekin, IL: Excalibur Seasoning), http://www. excaliburseasoning.com/About.htm.

17. Gregory G. Dess, and G. T. Lumpkin, *Strategic Management: Creating Competitive Advantage* (Boston: McGraw-Hill-Irwin, 2003), pp. 28–29. Gordon Walker, *Modern Competitive Strategy* (Burr Ridge, IL: McGraw-Hill/Irwin, 2004) pp. 263–264.

18. Fantastic Gift Baskets, Inc., "Why We're Different." Raleigh, NC, http://www.fantasticbaskets.com/Different.html.

19. There is no standard time for elevator pitches. For example, the Wake Forest Elevator Pitch Competition allows two minutes for the pitch, but that is one of the longest times. For the MIT Enterprise Forums, the pitch is limited to one minute. Outside of these formal settings, communications experts tell us that listeners lose interest after 30 seconds. That in large part explains why 30 seconds is the length of the typical television commercial.

20. These come from AdSlogans.com, http://www.adslogans.com/samples/index.html.

21. These numbers are fairly standard in a number of settings. For example, Linda Pinson and Jerry Jinnett gave these numbers in their SBA how-to guide, "How To Write A Business Plan" (Managing and Planning Series, MP-32, 1993, http://www.sba.gov/library/pubs/mp-32.txt or www.sba.gov/library/pubs/mp-32.pdf, and the same numbers are consistently used in the major business plan competitions.

22. This outline for the full business plan was developed specifically for small businesses, but its roots are in a number of works on business planning. These include Jeffry Timmons and Stephen Spinelli, *New Venture Creation: Entrepreneurship for the 21st Century* (McGraw-Hill/Irwin, 2003); David Gumpert *How to Really Create a Successful Business Plan: Step-By-Step Guide* (4th ed.) (Lauson Publishing, 2003); Edward G. Rogoff, *Bankable Business Plans* (Thompson/Texere, 2004); Kauffman Foundation, *New Business Mentor* (Kauffman Foundation, 2002); and J. D. Ryan and Gail Hyduke, *Small Business: An Entrepreneur's Plan* (Southwestern, 2003).

23. Edward G. Rogoff, *Bankable Business Plans* (Thompson/Texere,

2004). David Gumpert, *How to Really Create a Successful Business Plan: Step-By-Step Guide*, 4th ed., (Lauson Publishing, 2003). David Gumpert, *Burn Your Business Plan* (Lauson Publishing, 2002).
24. Dean Shepherd and Mark Shanley. *New Venture Strategy* (Sage, 1998).
25. There is a tremendous range of models for different types of plans. Examples include: Edward G. Rogoff, *Bankable Business Plans* (Thompson/Texere, 2004); A. L. Zacharakis, "Writing a Business Plan," in W. Bygrave and A. Zacharakis (eds.) *The Portable MBA in Entrepreneurship*, 3rd ed. (New York: Wiley, 2003); David Gumpert, *How to Really Create a Successful Business Plan: Step-By-Step Guide,* 4th ed. (Lauson Publishing, 2003); Jill E. Kapron, *BizPlan Builder* (JIAN/Southwestern, 1999); the ICVE model developed through R. K. Mitchell, J. B. Smith, K. W. Seawright, and E. A. Morse, "Cross-Cultural Cognitions and the Venture Creation Decision, "*Academy of Management Journal*, 43 no. 5 (October 2000) pp. 974–993; and Dean Shepherd and Evan Douglas *Attracting equity investors* (Sage, 1999).
26. Michael McMyne and Nicole Amare, *Student Entrepreneurs: 14 Undergraduate All Stars Tell Their Stories* (St. Louis: St. Louis University/Premium Press, 2003).
27. The six-fold model here is inspired by three sources on the critical analysis of business plans: Robert C. Ronstadt, *Entrepreneurial Finance: Taking Control of Your Financial Decision Making* (Lord Publishing, 1988); David Gumpert, *Burn your Business Plan* (Lauson Publishing, 2002); and most of all Dean Shepherd and Evan Douglas, *Attracting Equity Investors* (Sage, 1999).
28. R. K. Mitchell, J. B. Smith, K. W. Seawright, and E. A. Morse, "Cross-Cultural Cognitions and the Venture Creation Decision," *Academy of Management Journal* 43, no. 5 (October 2000), pp. 974–993. G. N. Chandler and S. H. Hanks, "Founder Competence, the Environment, and Venture Performance, "*Entrepreneurship Theory and Practice* 19 (1999), pp. 77–89. G. N. Chandler, and E. Jansen, "The Founder's Self-Assessed Competence and Venture Performance," *Journal of Business Venturing* 7 (1992), pp. 223–236.
29. Margaret Fletcher and Simon Harris, "Seven Aspects of Strategy Formation," *International Small Business Journal* 20, no. 3 (August 2002), p. 297 (16 pgs).
30. C. L. Nicholls-Nixon, A. C. Cooper, and C. Y. Woo, "Strategic Experimentation: Understanding Change and Performance in New Ventures," *Journal of Business Venturing* 15, no. 5-6 (September-November 2000), pp. 493–521.
31. Adapted from "Michael Cain," in Michael McMyne, and Nicole Amare, *Student Entrepreneurs: 14 Undergraduate All Stars Tell Their Stories* (St. Louis: St. Louis University/Premium Press, 2003) pp. 59–67.
32. http://www.slu.edu/services/cc/jobsearch/chronologicalresume.pdf. Used with permission.

Chapter 9

1. http://www.beyondfleece.com/about_us/bio/
2. Susan Fournier, "Consumers and Their Brands: Developing Relationship Theory in Consumer Research," *Journal of Consumer Research,* March 1998, pp. 343–373.
3. Chiranjeev Kohli and Douglas W. LaBahn, "Creating Effective Brand Names: A Study of the Naming Process," *Journal of Advertising Research,* January/February 1997, pp. 67–75. See also Leonard L. Berry, Edwin F. Lefkowith and Terry Clark, "In Services, What's in a Name?" *Harvard Business Review,* September/October 1998, pp. 28–30.
4. Tomima Edmark, "On Your Mark . . .," *Entrepreneur,* April 1999, http://www.entrepreneur.com/article/0,4621,230153,00.html.
5. Robert G. Cooper and Elko J. Kleinschmidt, "Benchmarking the Firm's Critical Success Factors in New Business Development," *The Journal of Product Innovation Management* 12, (1995) pp. 374–391.
6. Albert H. Rubenstein, "At the Front End of the R&D/innovation Process: Idea Development and Entrepreneurship," *International Journal of Technology* 9, nos. 5, 6, 7 (1994) pp. 652–678.
7. Don Debelak, "Inspired Minds Want to Know," Entrepreneur, January 1999, http://www.entrepreneur.com/article/0,4621,229775,00.html.
8. Don Debelak, "Where's the Big Idea?" *Entrepreneur,* March 1998, http://www.entrepreneur.com/article/0,4621,228229,00.html.
9. Don Debelak, "Testing the Waters," *Entrepreneur,* February 1998, http://www.entrepreneur.com/article/0,4621,228009,00.html.
10. "McDonald's Tests Self-Service Kiosks," *Los Angeles Times,* July 6, 2004, p. C5.
11. www.kyptonitelock.com and http://www.kryptonitelock.com/inetisscripts/abtinetis.exe/templateform@psublic?tn=aboout_media.
12. Greg A. Stevens and James Burley, "Piloting the Rocket of Radical Innovation," *Research Technology Management* 46, no. 2 (Mar/Apr 2003), pp. 16–26. See also Greg A. Stevens and James Burley, "3000 Raw Ideas, 1 Commercial Success!" *Research Technology Management* 40, no. 3, (May/June 1997), pp. 16–27.
13. Phillip Kotler and Gary Armstrong, *Principles of Marketing,* 9th ed., (New York: Prentice Hall 2000).
14. Don Debelak, "I Needed That," *Entrepreneur,* May 2002, http://www.entrepreneur.com/article/0,4621,299050,00.html.
15. Laura Tiffany, "Got A Lemon?" *Entrepreneur,* May 1999, http://www.entrepreneur.com/article/0,4621,230210,00.html.
16. Tim W. Know, "Evaluating Your e-Business Idea," *Entrepreneur,* May 26, 2003, http://www.entrepreneur.com/article/0,4621,308896,00.html.
17. Robert McMath and Thom Forbes, "Look Before You Leap," *Entrepreneur,* April 1998, http://www.entrepreneur.com/article/0,4621,228323,00.html.
18. Teresa McUsic, "Differentiate Those Differences to Stay Competitive," *St. Louis Post Dispatch,* April 17, 2000, p. BP17.
19. Kim T. Gordon, "Pros and Cons of Expanding Your Product Line," *Entrepreneur,* June 7, 2004, http://www.Entrepreneur.com/article/0,4621,315840,00.html.
20. Rosabeth Moss Kantor, "The 15-Minute Competitive Advantage" *Business 2.0,* February 2002, p. 87.
21. *Op. cit.,* McMath and Forbes.
22. Arundhati Parmar, "Where Are They Now?" *Marketing News,* April 14, 2003, pp. 1, 13, 14.
23. Adam Barak and Geoffrey Wilson, "Pricing Policies to Handle Patent Loss or Expiry," *International Journal of Medical Marketing* 3, no. 3 June 2003, p. 245.
24. *Ibid.*
25. Jay B. Lipe, "How to Set (and Get) the Right Prices," 2004, http://marketing.about.com/cs/advertising/a/pricingstrtgy_p.htm.
26. "Gross Profit Margin and Markup," *Entrepreneur,* August 23, 2000, http://www.entrepreneur.com/article/0,4621,265229,00.html.
27. Ian Benoliel, "Calculating Your Breakeven Point," *Entrepreneur,* March 25, 2002, http://www.entrepreneur.com/article/0,4621,298145,00. html.
28. European Telework Online, April 3, 2000, http://www.eto.org.uk/faq.faqprice.htm.
29. Kim T. Gordon, "How To Price Your Product," *Entrepreneur,* March 5, 2001, http://www.entrepreneur.com/article/0,4621,287402,00.html.
30. Roberta Maynard, "Take the Guesswork out of Pricing," *Nation's Business,* December 1997, pp. 27–30.
31. Bob Weinstein, "What Price Success," *Entrepreneur,* March 1999, http://www.entrepreneur.com/article/0,4621,229999,00.html.
32. Jacquelyn Lynn, "The Middle of the Road," *Business Start Ups,* December 1996, p. 33.
33. Julie Monahan, "Name Your Price," *Entrepreneur,* December 1999, http://www.entrepreneur.com/article/0,4621,231863,00.html.
34. Robert McGarvey and Babs S. Harrison, "Name Your Price," *Entrepreneur,* July 2000, http://www.entrepreneur.com/article/0,4621,276150,00.html; Beverly Williams, "The Price is Right," *Entrepreneur,* October 3, 2000, http://www.entrepreneur.com/article/0,4621,280990,00.html; Ian Benoliel, "Pricing Your Product," *Entrepreneur,* July 22, 2002, http://www.entrepreneur.com/article/0,4621,301698,00.html; Rosalind Resnick, "Setting the Right Price," *Entrepreneur,* November 10, 2003, http://www.entrepreneur.com/article/0,4621,311820,00.html; Tim W. Knox, "Secrets to Setting Your Price," *Entrepreneur,* April 2, 2004, http://www.entrepreneur.com/article/0,4621,314970,00.html; *Op. cit.,* Lipe; Small Business Administration, "Pricing Your Product."
35. *Op. cit.,* European Telework Online.
36. *Op. cit.,* European Telework Online.
37. Darrell Zahorsky, "Super Charge Your Business With Profit Pricing Strategies," 2004, http://sbinformation.about.com/cs/marketresearch/a/pricing_p.htm.
38. "Inventing Success," *Business 2.0,* April 2003, p. 105.
39. Marty Nemko, "Perfecting Your Pricing Strategies," *Entrepreneur,* March 2000, http://www.entrepreneur.com/article/0,4621,267541,00.html.
40. Michel A. Habib and Alexander P. Ljungqvist, "Underpricing and Entrepreneurial Wealth Losses in IPOs: Theory and Evidence," *The Review of Financial Studies* 14, no. 2 (Summer 2001), pp. 433–458.
41. Cliff Ennico, "Set the Right Price for Your Product or Service," *Entrepreneur,* June 1, 2003, http://www.entrepreneur.com/article/0,4621,309134,00.html.
42. J. R. Baum, E. A. Locke, and K. G. Smith, "A Multidimensional Model of Venture Growth," *Academy of Management Journal* 44, no. 2, (2001), pp. 292–303; see also, Elisabeth J. Teal, Nancy Upton, and Samuel L. Seaman, "A Comparative Analysis of Strategic Marketing Practices of High-Growth U.S. Family and Non-family Firms," *Journal of Developmental Entrepreneurship* 8, no. 2 (August 2003), p. 177.
43. Timothy Matanovich, Gary L. Lillien, and Arvind Rangaswamy, "Engineering the Price-Value Relationship," *Marketing Management,* Spring 1999, pp. 48–53.

44. *Op. cit.,* Monahan.
45. *Op. cit.,* Ennico; and Knox.
46. *Op. cit.,* Gordon; Weinstein; Monahan.
47. Don Debelak, "Look What I Found!" *Entrepreneur,* July 2002, http://www.entrepreneur.com/article/ 0,4621,300831,00.html.
48. K. Carroll and D. Coates, "Teaching Price Discrimination: Some Clarifications," *Southern Economic Journal* 66 (1999), pp. 466–480.
49. Mark Hendricks, "The Art of (Price) War," *Entrepreneur,* April 2002, http://www.entrepreneur.com/article/ 0,4621,297992,00.html.
50. *Op. cit.,* Small Business Administration.
51. Eric Anderson and Duncan Simester, "Mind Your Pricing Cues," *Harvard Business Review* 81, no. 9 (September 2003), p. 96.
52. Joel Dean, "Pricing Policies for New Products," *Harvard Business Review* (November/December 1976), p. 141–153.
53. Jean-Noel Kapferer, "Managing Luxury Brands," *Journal of Brand Management,* July 1999, pp. 251–260.
54. *Op. cit.,* Weinstein.
55. http://www.makersmarkcollector.com/home.shtml.
56. Robert M. Schindler and Thomas Kilbarian, "Increased Consumer Sales Response Through Use of 99-Ending Prices," *Journal of Retailing,* Summer 1996, pp. 187–199. See also Robert M. Schindler, "Patterns of Rightmost Digits Used in Advertising Prices: Implications for Nine-Ending Effects," *Journal of Consumer Research,* September 1997, pp. 192–201.
57. "When the Price is Right," *Entrepreneur,* http://www.entrepreneur.com/article/0,4621,302807,00.html.
58. Barbara Kiviat, "Sneaky Pricing," *Time Magazine,* September 19, 2003.
59. Priya Raghubir and Kim Corfman, "When Do Price Promotions Affect Pretrial Brand Evaluations?" *Journal of Marketing Research* 36 (1999), pp. 211–222.
60. *Op. cit.,* Kiviat.
61. Thea Singer, "Upstarts: Children's Hair Salons," *Inc.,* July 2001, http://pf.inc.com/magazine/20010701/22874.html.
62. Corliss L. Green, "Media Exposure's Impact on Perceived Availability and Redemption of Coupons by Ethnic Customers," *Journal of Advertising Research,* 25 no. 2 (March-April 1995) pp. 55–64.
63. Kapil Bawa and Srini S. Srinivasan, "Coupon Attractiveness and Coupon Proneness: A Framework for Modeling Coupon Redemption," *Journal of Marketing Research* 14 no. 4 (November 1997), pp. 517–525.
64. Peter Tat, William A. Cunningham III, and Emin Babakus, "Consumer Perceptions of Rebates," *Journal of Advertising Research* 28, no. 40 (August/September 1994), pp. 45–50.
65. John Burtzloff, "Keep Customers Coming Back For More," *Entrepreneur,* June 10, 2002, http://www.entrepreneur.com/article/0,4621,300846,00.html;
66. *Op. cit.,* Ennico; also Tony Parinello, "Should You Offer Extra Services or Lower Prices?" *Entrepreneur,* July 1, 2002, http://www.entrepreneur.com/article/0,4621,301285,00.html.
67. See G. Bruce Friesen, "Dynamic Pricing: Teaching Your Clients to Dance," *Consulting to Management* 14, no. 1 (March 2003), pp. 33–38. Also Ellen Garbarino and Olivia F. Lee, "Dynamic Pricing in Internet Retail: Effects on Consumer Trust," *Psychology & Marketing* 20, no. 6 (June 2003), pp. 495–513.
68. Ellen Rohr, "Keep Your Business From Closing," *Entrepreneur,* July 3, 2000, http://www.entrepreneur.com/article/ 0,4621,277102,00.html.
69. Gwen Moran, "Flash!" *Entrepreneur,* June 2000, http://www.entrepreneur.com/article/0,4621,274950,00.html.
70. Personal interviews with Dongzhou Gongbu and from a business plan for the Aba Sichuan Dairy Company written by Dr. Susan D. Peters, July, 2002.

Chapter 10

1. This vignette was developed using material taken from an interview with Addie Swartz, conducted by Jill Kickul in April 2004, as well as excerpted from the Beacon Street Girls press release "Introducing The Beacon Street Girls, Entrepreneur/Mother of Two Creates Fun, Values-oriented Books and Accessories for Girls who are "Between Toys and Boys" written by Ellen Miller and Alan Ryan.
2. R. Cooper, "Marketing From the Inside Out: Analyzing Your Market," *Entrepreneur,* May, 28. 2002. http://www.entrepreneur.com/article/0,4621,300281,00.htm.
3. See for example William O. Bearden, Thomas N. Ingram and Raymond W. LaForge (2004). *Marketing: Principles & Perspectives (4th Edition).* Boston: McGraw Hill, pp. 147–176.
4. Laura Clampitt Douglas (December 18, 2000) "Sizing Up Your Market" http:// entrepreneur.com/article/0,4621,284832,0.html
5. Michael Warshaw, *Inc.,* November 2001.
6. Excerpted from Lydia Ramsey, "Overcoming Stumbling Blocks to Spread Word of Your Business," from *Five Stumbling Blocks To Successful Networking And How To Overcome Them,"* allbusiness.com, URL: http://www.allbusiness.com/business_advice/articles/4041.html.
7. "301 Great Ideas for Selling Smarter," *Inc.,* January 1998.
8. "301 Do-It-Yourself Marketing Ideas," *Inc.,* January 2000.
9. From Chapter 20 Personal Selling and Sales Management site and info from entrepreneur.com
10. *From Cord Cooper, "The Art of Closing a Deal." Investor's Business Daily, March 5, 2003. Copyright © 2003 Investor's Business Daily, Inc. You may not copy, modify, redistribute, or display these materials without the written consent of Investor's Business Daily. Investor's Business Daily and its licensors expressly disclaim any express or implied warranties or representations regarding the accuracy, completeness, timeliness, or reliability of information, facts, view, opinions or recommendations contained in this publication.*
11. For more information on the steps of personal selling, visit www.udel.edu/alex/chapt20.html and Sales & Marketing Top Secrets at www.entrepreneur.com.
12. Excerpted from Randall Hansen, "A Barebones Guide to Writing Successful Press Releases," 2005, Deland FL: Stetson University Marketing Department. http://www.stetson.edu/~Rhansen/prhowto.html. Used with permission.
13. Ibid.
14. Charlotte Ryan, *Prime Time Activism* (Boston: South End Press, 1991) p. 35.
15. Excerpted from Kirk Hallahan, "A publicity primer" in Hallahan Course Resources (website), 1996, Fort Collins CO: Colorado State University. URL: http://lamar.colostate.edu/Hallahan/hpubty.htm. Used with permission.
16. http://lamar.colostate.edu/~hallahan/hpubty.htm.
17. Excerpted from Kirk Hallahan, "Ideas to Generate News for Your Organization: Thirty-two ways to create news for your organization," in Hallahan Course Resources (website), 1996, Fort Collins CO: Colorado State University URL: http://lamar.colostate.edu/~hallahan/hpubty.htm. Used with permission.
18. Excerpt from "Fashion Statement," by Naomi Aoki, *Boston Globe,* May 13, 2004. Copyright © 2004 by Globe Newspaper Co. Reproduced with permission of Globe Newspaper Co. via Copyright Clearance Center.

Chapter 11

1. Don Debelak, "Rookie Rules," *Entrepreneur,* September 1999, http://www.entrepreneur.com/article/0,4621,230661,00.html.
2. Gary L. Frazier, "Organizing and Managing Channels of Distribution," *Journal of the Academy of Marketing Science* 27, no. 2 (1999), pp. 226–240.
3. E. Rosen, *The Anatomy of Buzz: How to Create Word of Mouth Marketing* (New York: Doubleday, 2000).
4. David Stokes, "Entrepreneurial Marketing: A Conceptualisation from Qualitative Research," *Qualitative Market Research* 3, no. 1 (2000), pp. 47–54.
5. Lissan Levin and Jacob Zhavi, "The Economics of Selection of Mail Orders," *Journal of Interactive Marketing* 15, no. 3 (2001), pp. 53–71; Fűsan F. Gőnűl and Byung-Do Kim, "Mailing Smarter to Catalog Customers," *Journal of Interactive Marketing* 14, no. 2 (2000), pp. 2–16.
6. Kristin Zhivago "You and CAN-SPAM" January 23, 2004 http://www.marketing-technology.com/MT/canspam.cfm.
7. 2003 figures from the Outdoor Advertising Association of America, Inc. Web site (www.oaaa.org/outdoor/facts/cpmcomparison.asp).
8. Don Debelak, "Lights, Camera, Action," *Entrepreneur,* April 2003, http://www.entrepreneur.com/article/0,4621,307359,00.html.
9. Michael H. Morris, Minet Schindehutte, and Raymond W. LaForge, "Entrepreneurial Marketing: A Construct for Integrating Emerging Entrepreneurship and Marketing Perspectives," *Journal of Marketing Theory and Practice,* 10, no. 4 (2002), pp. 1–19; K. J. Clancy and P. C. Krieg, *Counterintuitive Marketing: Achieve Great Results Using Uncommon Sense* (New York: Free Press, 2000).
10. Personal story, used with permission.
11. Michael McMyne, *Student Entrepreneurs* (St. Louis: Premium Press America, 2003).
12. Kim T. Gordon, "Cross-Training," *Entrepreneur,* July 2003, http://www.entrepreneur.com/article/0,4621,309488,00.html.
13. For more information regarding the impact of the Internet on small and medium businesses see Judith Jeffcote, Caroline Chappel, and Sylvia Feindt, "Best Practice in SME Adoption of e-Commerce," *Benchmarking,* 9, no. 2 (2002) pp. 122–132; S. McCue, "Small Firms and the Internet: Force or Farce?" *International Business Trade Forum,* 1999; Geneva; B. Kleindl, "Competitive Dynamics and New Business Models for SMEs in the Virtual Marketplace," *Journal of Developmental Entrepreneurship* 5, no. 1 (2000), pp. 73–85; C. Chappel and S. Feindt, "Analysis of E-Commerce Practice in SMEs," 1999 http://kite/tsa/de; P. Haynes, R. Becherer, and M. L. Helms, "Small and Mid-Sized Businesses and Internet Use: Unrealized Potential?" *Internet Research: Electronic Networking Applications and Policy"* 8, no. 3 (1990); Dick Anderson, "Marketplace: Creating and Nurturing a Premier E-business," *Journal of Interactive Marketing* 14, no. 3 (2000), pp. 67–78.

14. Conversation with David W. Peters, vice president of Letrah, used with permission. June 20, 2005.
15. Don Debelak, "Working the Web," *Entrepreneur,* 1998, http://www.entrepreneur.com/article/0,4621,229049,00.html.
16. Gerry Grant, "Search Optimization Campaigns Build Brand," *Marketing News,* September 29, 2003.
17. Yong Seck Sohn, Hangun Houn, and Dae Ryon Chang, "A Model of Consumer Information Search and Online Network Externality," *Journal of Interactive Marketing* 16, no. 4 (2002), pp. 2–14.
18. Nancy Einhart, "How to Get Them Buzzing to Your Site," *Business 2.0,* October 2003.
19. Philippa Gamse, "Are Search Engines Worth It Any More?" (2003), http://www.jbsba.com/cgi-bin/articlesbybtsub.cgi?art=441.
20. Philippa Gamse, "Unlocking the Keys to Your Web Site Traffic," (2003), http://www.jbsba.com/cgi-bin/articlesbybtsub.cgi?art=296.
21. Shannon Kinnard, "Get Malled," *Entrepreneur,* April 1999, http://www.entrepreneur.com/article/0,4621,265451,00.html.
22. Stephen P. Bradley and Kelly A Porter, "eBay, Inc.," *Journal of Interactive Marketing* 14, no. 4 (2000), pp. 73–97.
23. Cliff Ennico, "Selling Your Specialty Merchandise Online," *Entrepreneur,* 2003, http://www.entrepreneur.com/article/0,4621,311666,00.html.
24. Jacquelyn Lynn, "Let the Bidding Begin," *Entrepreneur,* 2003, http://www.entrepreneur.com/article/0,4621,310583,00.html.
25. Tim W. Knox, "The Secret to eBay Success," *Entrepreneur,* 2003, http://www.entrepreneur.com/article/0,4621,312476,00.html.
26. Compiled from information from Tim W. Knox, "The Secret to eBay Success," *Entrepreneur,* 2003, http://www.entrepreneur.com/article/0,4621,312476,00.html; Marsha Collier, "Ten (or So) Golden Rules for eBay Buyers and Sellers,"*Entrepreneur,* 2002, http://www.entrepreneur.com/article/ 0,4621,305285,00.html.
27. Op cit., Jacquelyn Lynn.
28. Michael Krauss, "EBay 'Bids' on Small-biz Firms to Sustain Growth," *Marketing News,* (December 8, 2003).
29. Sandy D. Jap, "An Exploratory Study of the Introduction of Online Reverse Auctions," *Journal of Marketing* 67 (July 2003) pp. 96–107.
30. Melissa Campanelli, "Help Wanted," *Entrepreneur,* 2003, http://www.entrepreneur.com/article/0,4621,310424,00.html.
31. Melissa Campanelli, "Fulfilling Orders," *Entrepreneur,* 2000, http://www.entrepreneur.com/article/0,4621,274296,00.html.
32. Art Avery, "Order Fulfillment for Your Small E-business: Should You Beg, Borrow or Buy?" (2000), http://wwwetailersdigest.com/resources/Specials/BegBorrow.htm.
33. Melissa Campanelli, "Delivering the Goods," *Entrepreneur,* 1999, http://www.entrepreneur.com/article/0,4621,229968,00.html.
34. George Matyjewicz, 'Doc' Don Avery, Kris Campbell, and Dave Campbell, "Online Logistics and Order Fulfillment Solutions for E-Tailers" (1999). http://wwwetailersdigest.com/resources/Specials/Logistics.htm.
35. Andy Gibbs, "How to Sell Your Product," *Entrepreneur,* 2000, http://www.entrepreneur.com/article/0,4621,279119,00.html.
36. Paul Edwards and Sarah Edwards, "It's in the Mail," *Entrepreneur,* 2003, http://www.entrepreneur.com/article/0,4621,307366,00.html.
37. For academic studies on e-tailers, see Heiko de B. Wijnolds and Michael W. Little, "Regulatory Issues for Global E-Tailers: Marketing Implications," *Academy of Marketing Science Review,* 2001, pp. 1–17; Gary J. Stockport, George Kunnarth, and Rashida Sedik, "Boo.com, the Path to Failure," *Journal of Interactive Marketing* 15, no. 4 (2001), pp. 56–70.
38. Don Debelak, "Who Needs 'Em?" *Entrepreneur,* 2000, http://www.entrepreneur.com/article/0,4621,276496,00.html.
39. Laura Tiffany, "Import/Export," *Entrepreneur,* 2001, http://www.entrepreneur.com/article/0,4621,290657,00.html.
40. Oystein Moen, "The Relationship Between Firm Size, Competitive Advantages and Export Performance Revisited," *International Small Business Journal* 18, no. 1 (1999), pp. 53–72.
41. *Ibid.*
42. Benjamin M. Oviatt and Patricia Phillips McDougall, "Towards a Theory of International New Ventures," *Journal of International Business Studies* 25, no.1 (1994), pp. 45–65; S. K. Kundu and J. A. Katz, "Born-International SMEs: Bi-level Impacts of Resources and Intentions," *Small Business Economics* 20, no. 1 (2003), pp. 25–47.
43. For more about SMEs and exporting, see Pierre-Andre Julien and Charles Ramagalahy, "Competitive Strategy and Performance of Exporting SMEs: An Empirical Investigation of the Impact of Their Export Information Search and Competency," *Entrepreneurship Theory and Practice* 27, no. 3 (2003), pp. 227–246; Neil A. Morgan, Anna Kaleka, and Constantine S. Katsikeas, "Antecedents of Export Venture Performance: A Theoretical Model and Empirical Assessment," *Journal of Marketing* 68 (January 2004), pp. 90–108.
44. Carla Goodman, "Going Global," *Entrepreneur,* 1996, http://www.entrepreneur.com/article/0,4621,226568,00.html.
45. Jerome A. Katz, Scott R. Safranski, and Omar Khan, "Virtual Instant Global Entrepreneurship: Cybermediation for Born International Service Firms," *Journal of International Entrepreneurship* 1 (2003), pp. 43–57.
46. S. K. Kundu and J. A. Katz, "Born-International SMEs: Bi-level Impacts of Resources and Intentions," *Small Business Economics* 20, no. 1 (2003), pp. 25–47.
47. "How to Take Your Country Global" *Entrepreneur,* 2003, http://www.entrepreneur.com/article/0,4621,312297,00.html.
48. *Op cit.,* George Matyjewicz, et al.
49. *Op cit.,* Laura Tiffany.
50. *Op cit.,* Carla Goodman.
51. Beverley Williams, "Zoning Information and Resources," http://www.jbsja.com/content/suites/hb_teleworking/zoning.shtml.
52. Virginia Baldwin Gilbert, "Startups Are Poised to Fly Away from Incubator Nest." *St. Louis Post-Dispatch,* February 2, 2002, www.niduscenter.com/m_arts_html/post_02-25-02a.html.
53. Michael H. Seid and Kay Marie Ainsley, "What Makes a Location Great?" *Entrepreneur,* March 2001, http://www.entrepreneur.com/article/0,4621,287982,00.html.
54. Julie Bennett, "Location Is Everything to Franchise Hopefuls," http://startupjournal.com/columnist/franchiseinsight/20020814-bennett.html
55. Michael H. Seid and Kay Marie Ainsley, "Finding a Great Location," *Entrepreneur,* April 2001, http://www.entrepreneur.com/article/0,4621,288851,00.html.
56. *Op cit,* Julie Bennett.
57. Rieva Lesonsky, "Cart Blanche," *Entrepreneur,* 2003, http://www.entrepreneur.com/article/0,4621,265101,00.html.
58. Michael H. Seid and Kay Marie Ainsley, "Finding a Great Location," *Entrepreneur,* April 2001, http://www.entrepreneur.com/article/ 0,4621,288851,00.html.
59. Peter Carbonara and Maggie Overfelt, "The Dot-Com Factories," *Fortune,* 2000, http://www.fortune.com/fortune/print/0,15935,360353,00.html.
60. Michael H. Seid and Kay Marie Ainsley, "Finding a Great Location," *Entrepreneur,* April 2001, http://www.entrepreneur.com/article/0,4621,288851,00.html.
61. Michael H. Seid and Kay Marie Ainsley, "What Makes a Location Great?" *Entrepreneur,* March 2001, http://www.entrepreneur.com/article/0,4621,287982,00.html.
62. The material in this section is based on the following articles: Broderick Perkins, "Create the Ideal Space For Business at Home," 2001, http://www.startupjournal.com/howto/workhome/20011012-perkins.html; Meredith Gould, "Space Quest," *Entrepreneur,* 2000, http://www.Entrepreneur.com/article/0,4621,280012,00.html; Broderick Perkins, "Realize the Dream of a Home-Based Business," 2001, http://www.startupjournal. com/howto/workhome/20011026-perkins.html; Cliff Ennico, "The Reality of Working from Home," *Entrepreneur,* 2002, http://entrepreneur. com/article/0,4621,301177,0.html; Paul Edwards and Sarah Edwards, "Handling Houseguests in Your Home Office," *Entrepreneur,* August 2003, http://entrepreneur.com/article/0,4621,310492,00.html; *Owen Thomas* "You, Incorporated," *Business 2.0,* December 2002/January 2003.
63. Meredith Gould, "Space Quest," *Entrepreneur,* October 2000, http://www. Entrepreneur.com/article/0,4621,280012,00.html. Reprinted with permission of Entrepreneur.com.
64. Personal story, used with permission.
65. Azreila Jaffe, "When Is It Time to Move the Office Out of the Home?" http://www.jbsa.com/content/suites/hb_teleworking/time_to_move.shtml.
66. Julie Baker, A. Parasuraman, Dhruv Grewal, and Glenn B. Voss, "The Influence of Multiple Store Environment Cues of Perceived Merchandise Value and Patronage Intentions," *Journal of Marketing* 66 (April 2002), pp. 120–140.
67. "Release Me?" *Entrepreneur,* 1998, http://www.entrepreneur.com/article/0,4621,266181,00.html.
68. Information from this case comes from Chris Taylor, "E-Commerce," *Fortune,* 2004, http://www.fortune.com/fortune/print/ 0,15935,575869,00.html, and Lisa Baertlein, eBay Gets Boost as Middlemen Make Comeback, *Los Angeles Times,* (January 20, 2004).

Chapter 12

1. Personal and Internet interviews with Mingkit "Jerry" Lai conducted spring 2004 by Professor Susan Peters.
2. See Tim Mazzavol, "Do Formal Business Plans Really Matter?—A Survey of Small Business Owners in Australia," paper presented at the International Council for Small Business Conference, 2000. Available online at www.scbaer.acu.edu. See also R. Brooksbank, "The Basic Marketing Planning Process: A Practical Framework for the Smaller Business," *Marketing Intelligence and Planning,* 14 no.1 (1996); G. Lancaster, and I. Waddelow, "An Empirical Investigation into the Process of Strategic Marketing Planning in SMEs: Its Attendant Problems and Proposals Towards a New Practical Paradigm," *Journal of Marketing Management* 14 (1998), pp. 853–878.

3. An Dugan, "The Value of Research," *Entrepreneur,* October 22, 2001, http://entrepreneur.com/article/0,4621,293951,00.html.
4. Karen E. Spaeder, " Define Your Target Audience to Grow Sales," - *Entrepreneur,* June 1, 2003, http://entrepreneur.com/article/0,4621,309165,00.html.
5. Don Debelek, "Want Some of This?" *Entrepreneur,* June 2002, http://entrepreneur.com/article/0,4621,299768,00.html.
6. "Seems the Only Problem With New Products Is That They're New," *Brandweek,* August 22, 1994, pp. 36–40.
7. See, for example, G. Dean Kortge and Patrick A. Okonkwo, "Simultaneous New Product Development: Reducing the New Product Failure Rate," *Industrial Marketing Management,* 18, no. 4 (1989), pp. 301–306; Sharad Sarin and Gour M. Kapur, "Lessons From New Product Failure: Five Case Studies," *Industrial Marketing Management* 19, no. 4 (1990), pp. 301–314; Peter L. Link, "Keys to New Product Success and Failure," *Industrial Marketing Management* 16, no. 2 (1987), pp. 109–118.
8. Gwen Moran, "3 Hours to a Great Marketing Plan," *Entrepreneur,* March 26, 2001, http://entrepreneur.com/article/0,4621,297622,00.html.
9. Laura Tiffany, "Researching Your Market," *Entrepreneur,* August 7, 2001, http://www.entrepreneur.com/article/0,4621,391713,00.html.
10. S. Hogarth-Scott, K. Watson, and N. Wilson, "Do Small Businesses Have to Practice Marketing to Survive and Grow?" *Marketing Intelligence and Planning* 14, no.1 (1996).
11. Data for this table were extracted from www.Websurveyor.com.
12. See Gerald Zaltman, "Rethinking Market Research: Putting People Back In" *Journal of Marketing* Research, November 1997, pp. 424–437; Stephen Groves, and Raymond P. Fisk "Observational Data Collection methods for Services Marketing: An Overview," *Journal of the Academy of Marketing Science,* Summer 1992, pp. 216–224; Rebecca Piirto, "Socks, Ties, Videotapes," *American Demographics,* September 1991.
13. Stever Robbins, "Down and Dirty Market Research," *Entrepreneur,* August 12, 2002, http://entrepreneur.com/article/0,4621,302407,00.html.
14. Judith Langer, "15 Myths of Qualitative Research: It's Conventional, But Is It Wisdom?" *Marketing News,* March 1, 1999, pp. 13–14.
15. See Janet Ilieva, Steve Baron, and Nigel M. Healey, "Online Surveys in Marketing Research: Pros and Cons," *International Journal of Marketing Research* 44, no. 3 (2002), pp. 361–376; Michael P. Cronin, "On-the-Cheap Market Research," *Inc.* June 1992, p. 108; Robert Hayes, "Internet-based Surveys Provide Fast Results," *Marketing News* April 13, 1998, p. 13; Phil Levine, Bill Ahlauser, Dale Kulp, and Rick Hunter, "Internet Interviewing," *Marketing Research,* Summer 1999, pp. 33–36.
16. Paul E. Green, Yoram Wind, Abba M. Krieger, and Paul Saatsoglou, "Applying Qualitative Data," *Marketing Research,* Spring 2000, pp. 17–25.
17. Don Debelek, "Want Some of This?" *Entrepreneur,* June 2002, http://entrepreneur.com/article/0,4621,299768,00.html.
18. Phaedra Hise, "Grandma Got Run Over by Bad Research," *Inc.,* January 1998, http://pf.inc.com/magazine/19980101/851.html.
19. See, for example, David M. Georgoff, and Robert G. Murdock, "Manager's Guide to Forecasting," *Harvard Business Review,* January–February 1986, pp. 110–120; Angelo Guadagno, "Mastering the 'Magic' of Sales Forecasting," *American Salesman* November 1, 1995; Carlo D. Smith, "An Integrated Model of Factors Affecting Sales Forecasting Management," *Academy of Marketing Science* 90 1999; Donald McBane, "Benchmarking Sales Forecasting Performance Measures," *Journal of Personal Selling and Sales Management,* 2001.
20. Stever Robbins, "Down and Dirty Market Research," *Entrepreneur,* August 12, 2002, http://entrepreneur.com/article/0,4621,302407,00.html.
21. Steven K. Baker, "Forecasting Your Sales Revenue," *Entrepreneur,* May 7, 2001, http://www.entrepreneur.com/article/0,4621,389242,00.html.
22. David Carson and Audrey Gilmore, "Marketing at the interface: Not 'What' But 'How,'" *Journal of Marketing Theory and Practice* 8, no. 2 (Spring 2000), pp. 1–8.
23. Kenneth J. Cook, "Why You Are in Trouble if You Think Marketing Is Just Sales," *Small Business Forum* 14, no. 3 (winter 1996–1997), pp. 43–49.
24. Rebecca Cooper, "Marketing From the Inside Out: A Coach's Perspective," *Entrepreneur,* May 20, 2002, http://entrepreneur.com/article/0,4621,299859,00.html.
25. Doran, G. David, "Upper Crust," *Entrepreneur,* June 1999, http://www.entrepreneur.com/article/0,4621,230374,00.html; Ruth's Chris Steak House Web site www.ruthchris.com.
26. Ellen Rohr, "Price Wars," *Entrepreneur,* April 20, 2000, http://entrepreneur.com/article/0,4621,297622,00.html.
27. Personal and Internet interviews with Mingkit "Jerry" Lai conducted spring 2004 by Professor Susan Peters.
28. Laura Tiffany, "The Ingredients of a Marketing Plan," *Entrepreneur,* August 7, 2001, http://www.entrepreneur.com/article/0,4621,291716,00.html.
29. *Op cit.,* Cook.
30. Sumit K. Kundu and Jerome A. Katz, "Born-International SMEs: Bi-level Impacts of Resources and Intentions," *Small Business Economics,* 20, no. 1 (2003), pp. 25–47.
31. http://www.backbonemedia.net/clientBite.html.
32. Laura Clampitt Douglas, "Sizing Up Your Market," *Entrepreneur,* December 18, 2000, http://entrepreneur.com/article/0,4621,284832,00.html; and "Landing Customers," *Entrepreneur,* March 2, 2002, http://entrepreneur.com/article/0,4621,297622,00.html.
33. Karen E. Spaeder, "Who Is Your Market—and What Do They Want?" *Entrepreneur,* March 18, 2002, http://entrepreneur.com/article/0,4621,298041,00.html.
34. Cliff Ennico, "Expanding Your Target Market," *Entrepreneur,* October 28, 2002, http://www.entrepreneur.com/article/0,4621,304103,00.html.
35. Based on www.entrepreneur.com/Home/HM Static/1,4472,formnet analysis,00.html.
36. Kathy Ellis, "Today's Marketing Plan," *The American Salesman* 49, no. 3 (March 2004.), pp. 21–25.
37. Kim T. Gordon, "The Structure of a Marketing Plan," *Entrepreneur,* November 2000, http://www.entrepreneur.com/article/0,4621,283011,00.html.
38. Donald Lehmann and Russell Winer, *Analysis for market planning, 6th ed.,* (Burr Ridge, IL: McGraw-Hill, 2005); also, see virtually any marketing textbook for similar layouts.
39. Laura Tiffany, "How to Create a Marketing Plan," *Entrepreneur,* August 7, 2001, http://www.entrepreneur.com/article/0,4621,291706,00. html.
40. Larry Chiagouris and Brant Wansley "Start-Up Marketing," *Marketing Management* 12, no. 5 (September/October 2003), P. 39.
41. *Op cit.,* Lehman and Winer.
42. *Op cit.,* Gwen Moran.
43. *Ibid.*
44. Mark Henricks, "Change of Face," *Entrepreneur,* April 2000, http://www.entrepreneur.com/article/0,4621,269292,00.html.
45. This marketing plan was written by Shannon Shehee of California State Polytechnic University—Pomona, under the direction of Prof. Susan Peters.

Chapter 13

1. R. P. Green. Interview with Tracy Butler. August 2, 2005. 4:25PM CDT; Dalin, S., "Brothers' IT firm was going nowhere until outside analyst set it straight." *St. Louis Post-Dispatch,* http://www.stltoday.com/stltoday/business/stories.nsf/smallbusiness/story/E689F0D55F363DAD8625701900823288?OpenDocument (June 07, 2005); Sorrell, M., "Butler's Acropolis a rising star in computer industry." *St. Louis Biz Journal,* July 18, 2003, http://stlouis.bizjournals.com/stlouis/stories/2003/07/21/focus18.html.
2. This is a loose interpretation of the bases for accounting. The definitive explanation is found in the FASB's Statements of Financial Accounting Concepts, numbers 1 through 7. Available in pdf format at http://www.fasb.org/st/#cons.
3. A complete description of the quality of financial accounting information is presented in Concepts Statement No. 2, "Qualitative Characteristics of Accounting Information." Available in pdf format at http://www.fasb.org/st/#cons.
4. It is common for these statements to be presented as only three separate documents by combining the statements of retained earnings and owners' equity into the equity section of the balance sheet. Regardless of whether they are combined or presented as separate statements, they contain the same information and follow the same general format.
5. An economist defines *income* as a change in wealth. This implies, for example, that if a business purchased a plot of land some time ago for $100,000, and today, because of the development of adjacent property, several potential buyers each offered to pay $200,000 to purchase the land, then the business has income equal to the $100,000 increase in the value of the real estate. Accounting does not, however, recognize as income the increase in wealth caused by the increase in value of the land. If, and only if, the land is sold to an outside party will the increase in value be recognized as income in the accounting statements. For accounting purposes, income, gains, expenses, and losses are recognized only when a transaction takes place between nonrelated entities.
6. An economist would say that it is converted without facing any discount from the true economic value of the asset.
7. C. Koornhof, "Accounting Information on Flexibility," dissertation. University of Pretoria, 1997.
8. Technically, owners are insiders. However, absentee owners often have little, if any, access to the financial records of small businesses. Thus they are listed as outside investors for the purposes of using financial accounting statements for disclosure.
9. S. Holmes, and D. Nicholls, "An Analysis of the Use of Accounting Information by Australian Small Business," *Journal of Small Business Management,* April 1988, pp. 57–68.

10. In fact some definitions of entrepreneurship hinge on creating wealth, such as those found in the 2001 *Strategic Management Journal* special issue, *Strategic Entrepreneurship: Entrepreneurial Strategies for Wealth Creation.*
11. R. C. Cressy, "Small Business Failure: Failure to Fund or Failure to Learn?" in Z. Acs, B. Karlsson, and C. Karlsson (eds.), *Entrepreneurship, Small and Medium Sized Enterprises and the Macro Economy,* (Cambridge: Cambridge University Press, 1999), pp. 161–185.
12. C. Bianchi, "Commercial and Financial Policies in Family Firms: The Small Business Growth Management Flight Simulator" *Simulation & Gaming* 31, no. 2 (2000), pp. 197–230.
13. M. J. Peel, and J. Bridge, "Planning Business Objectives and Capital Budgeting in Japanese, German and Domestic SMEs: Some Evidence from the UK Manufacturing Sector," *Journal of Small Business and Enterprise Development* 6, no. 4 (2000), pp. 350–365.
14. Dorothy A. Davis. "Internal Controls for the Small Owner-Operated Business," Small Business Institute Directors Association National Meeting, http://www.Sbaer.Uca.Edu/Research/Sbida/1991/Pdf/03.Pdf.
15. R. N. Lussier and S. Pfeifer, "A Cross-National Prediction Model for Business Success," *Journal of Small Business Management* 39, no. 3 (2001), pp. 228–239.
16. M. J. Peel, "Timeliness of Private Company Accounts and Predicting Corporate Failure," *The Investment Analyst: The Journal of the Society of Investment Analysts,* no. 83. pp. 23–27.
17. This definition is deliberately simple. The analysis as presented overstates both the price variance and the efficiency variance by ignoring the common variance. In practice this analysis is sufficient for all but the most sophisticated cost analysis systems.
18. H. A. Simon, "Rational Decision Making in Business Organizations," in L. Green and J. H. Kagel (eds.), *Advances in Behavioral Economics,* vol. 1 (Norwood, NJ: Ablex, 1987), pp. 18–47.
19. In practice, an outsourcing decision should not be made based solely on a financial analysis. Multiple factors, especially the effect upon the strategy of the business should be considered. See J. Bowles, "Outsourcing for Competitive Advantage," Forbes, June 7, 2004, p. 101.

Chapter 14

1. This follows some popular advice on managing cash flow using credit, see Doug Hood, "Can't Go With the Flow? Simple Solutions for Winning the Cash-Flow Battle," *Entrepreneur* August 2001, http://www.entrepreneur.com/article/0,4621,291139,00.html.
2. Michael Selz, "Seasonal Business Struggles To Refinance Its Debt," *Wall Street Journal Startup Journal,* http://www.startupjournal.comfinancing/credit/200002290929-selz.html. Dwight B. Crane, and Penny Joseph, "Be Our Guest, Inc"., (Boston: Harvard Business School Publishing, 1999), Be Our Guest Web site http://www.beourguestpartyrental.com.
3. NFIB Educational Foundation, National Small Business Poll: The Cash Flow Problem, Washington, DC, 2001.
4. NFIB Education Foundation, "Business Starts and Stops," (Washington, DC: NFIB Education Foundation, 1999).
5. Evan Smith, "John Mackey," *Texas Monthly* 33, no. 3 (2005), pp 122–132.
6. Federal Reserve Bank of Dallas, Money, Banking and Monetary Policy, 1995 p. 1.
7. See David E. W. Laidler and George W. Stadler, "Monetary Explanations of the Weimar Republic's Hyperinflation: Some Neglected Contributions in Contemporary German Literature," *Journal of Money, Credit and Banking* 30, no. 4 (1998), pp. 816–831, http://ideas.repec.org/a/mcb/jmoncb/v30y1998i4p816-31.html; or look at the Labor Law Talk page at http://encyclopedia.laborlawtalk.com/Weimar_Republic.
8. In case the term is new to you, it comes from Joseph Heller's 1961 classic book (and 1970 movie) of the same name. It means that the situation is hopeless no matter what you do.
9. If you're interested, look at the 1998 Survey of Small Business Finance, which is conducted every five years. See "Financing Patterns of Small Firms: Findings from the 1998 Survey of Small Business Finance," done by the Federal Reserve and stored by the SBA at: http://www.sba.gov/advo/stats/ssbf_98.pdf. A particularly interesting look at financing (especially self-financing) comes from Charles Ou and George W. Haynes, "Uses of Equity Capital by Small Firms—Findings from the Surveys of Small Business Finances (for 1993 & 1998)," Paper presented at the Academy of Entrepreneurial Finance 14th International Conference, April 30–May 2, 2003, Chicago, Illinois.
10. http://www.startupjournal.com/financing/credit/20011005-clark.html; http://www.babyeinstein.com/B2C/about_founder_F32.shtml; http://www. usatoday.com/life/2002/2002-06-25-baby-genius.htm.
11. Paul Deceglie, "Fun With Funding: If You Left Your Creativity Somewhere with Your Coloring Books, You're Not Ready to Find Financing in the Post-Dotcom Era." *Entrepreneur,* BizOpp Zone, September 14, 2001, http://www.Entrepreneur.com/article/0,4621,292986,00.html. John F Dalrymple, *International Business Profile Benchmarking for the SME Sector-Does it Work?* (RMIT University, Centre for Quality Management Research, 2001), http://www.cmqr.rmit.edu.au/publications/jdimprov. pdf. S. Mian and C. Smith, "Accounts Receivable Management Policy: Theory and Evidence," *Journal of Finance* 47 (1992), pp. 169–200.
12. Jonathan A. Scott and Morris G. Danielson, "Bank Loan Availability and Trade Credit Demand," *The Financial Review* 39 (2004), pp. 579–600, http://www.blackwell-synergy.com/links/doi/10.1111/j.07328516.2004.00089.x/pdf. A. N. Berger and G. F. Udell, "Small Business Credit Availability and Relationship Lending: The Importance of Bank Organizational Structure," *Economic Journal* 112 (2002), pp. 32–53.
13. Judy Gedge, "Does Your Collections System Need a Checkup?" *Entrepreneur,* March 29, 2004, http://www.Entrepreneur.com/article/0,4621,314904,00.html. Paul DeCeglie, "Gimme My Money: Steps You Can Take to Collect on Past Due Accounts Receivable," *Business Start-Ups,* August 2000, http://www.entrepreneur.com/mag/article/0,1539,277364,00.html. W. Lim and M. Rashid, "An Operational Theory Integrating Cash Discount and Product Pricing Policies," *Journal of American Academy of Business* 2(2002), pp. 282–288. W. Beranek, "Behavioral Relations, Operating Factors and the Optimal Cash Discount," The 7th International Symposium on Cash, Treasury and Working Capital Management, Chicago, October 1991.
14. See G. Udell, *Asset-Based Finance* (New York: The Commercial Finance Association, 2004); A. N. Berger and G. F. Udell, "Small Business and Debt Finance," in Zoltan J. Acs and David B. Audretsch (eds.), *Handbook of Entrepreneurship* (Norwell, MA: Kluwer Academic Publishing, 2003); M. R. Bakker, L. Klapper, and G. F. Udell, "The Role of Factoring in Commercial Finance: The Case of Eastern Europe," Working Paper, 2004.
15. See Mie-Yun Lee, "Factor Your Receivables for More Cash: Need a Quick Cash Infusion? A Factoring Service Can Help You Out," *Entrepreneur,* June 03, 2002, http://www.entrepreneur.com/article/0,4621,300447,00.html. Jan Norman, "How to Factor: Get Money to Grow!" *Business Start-Ups,* November 1998, http://www.entrepreneur.com/article/ 0,4621,229452,00.html.
16. One other approach is called *activity-based costing* (or ABC), which looks at which services, products, or internal operations add to your profits or add to your costs. It is used most often for companies with several different types of products, services, or markets and can help you pare down to those things that can truly make a positive difference in your bottom line. For an introduction, see Mark Henricks, "Beneath The Surface: Suspicious Not All Areas of Your Company Are Bringing in a Profit? Break It Down with Activity-Based Costing," *Entrepreneur,* October 1999, http://www.Entrepreneur.com/article/0,4621,230997,00.html.
17. For some other ideas, look at Jan Norman, "How to Manage Your Cash Flow: You're Making Sales, But Are You Making Money?" *Business Start-Ups,* June 1998, http://www.Entrepreneur.com/article/0,4621,228680,00. html.
18. Nancy R. Lockwood, "Work-Life Balance: Challenges and Solutions," Society for Human Resource Management, *2003 SHRM Research Quarterly,* 2003, http://www.ispi.org/pdf/suggestedReading/11_Lockwood_WorkLifeBalance.pdf. Aubrey C. Daniels, "Choosing an Employee Incentive Program: With So Many Choices Out There, How Do You Pick the Best One for Your Business?" *Entrepreneur,* September 02, 2002, http://www.entrepreneur.com/article/0,4621,302766,00.html. G. A. Marken, "Ten Low-Cost Steps to Keep Employees from Job Hunting," *Water Quality Products* 7, no. 4 (April 2002) http://www.wwdmag.com/wwd/index.cfm/powergrid/rfah=%7Ccfap=/CFID/2522697/CFTKEN/34858572/fuseaction/showArticle/articleID/3032. Marvin Collins, *The Human Use of Human Resources* (New York: McGraw Hill, 1981).
19. Mark Henricks, "Trading Up: No Cash? No Problem," *Entrepreneur's Be Your Own Boss,* February 2005, http://www.entrepreneur.com/article/0,4621,319918,00.html. Kirk Whisler and Nichole Torres, "Barter to the Cause: Does Cutting Costs Sound Like a Good Start-Up Idea?" *Entrepreneur,* October 2002, http://www.entrepreneur.com/article/0,4621,303206,00.html. Kurt J. Samson, "Better Business? Think Barter Business Why Trading for Products and Services Makes Great Financial Sense *Home Office,*" August 1999, http://www.entrepreneur.com/mag/article/0,1539,270309,00.html.
20. See C. O'Gorman. "The Sustainability of Growth in Small- and Medium-Sized Enterprises," *International Journal of Entrepreneurial Behaviour and Research* 7, no. 2, (February 2001), pp. 60–75. Kevin Mole, "Business Advice to Fast Growth Small Firms," Telford : University of Wolverhampton, 1999, http://mubs.mdx.ac.uk/research/Discussion_Papers/Business_and_Management/dpapmsno_4.pdf.

Chapter 15

1. Rendering is the process of converting dead animals into usable fats and protein.
2. J. A. Katz, "Modelling Entrepreneurial Career Progressions: Concepts and Considerations," *Entrepreneurship: Theory and Practice,* 19 no. 2

(Winter 1994), pp. 23–40. J. A. Katz, "A Psychosocial Cognitive Model of Employment Status Choice," *Entrepreneurship: Theory and Practice* 17, no. 1 (1992), pp. 29–37. J. A. Katz, "Secondary Analysis in Entrepreneurship: An Introduction to Data Bases and Data Management," *Journal of Small Business Management* 30, no. 20 (1992), pp. 74–86.
3. Crystal Detamore-Rodman, "The Search Is On: Entrepreneurs and Experts All Agree: If You're Willing to Hunt Around, You Can Score Financing to Get Your Homebased Business Off the Ground," *Entrepreneur's Be Your Own Boss,* June 2003, http://www.entrepreneur.com/article/0,4621,308997,00.html. Cliff Ennico, "Accepting Money from Friends & Family: 4 Ways to Get Your Cash without Wreaking Havoc on Your Personal Relationships," *Entrepreneur.com—Money & Finance,* May 06, 2002, http://www.entrepreneur.com/article/0,4621,299420,00.html. Stever Robbins, "Asking Friends and Family for Financing: Heed our Warnings before You Play This Dangerous Game," *Entrepreneur,* October 01, 2001, http://www.entrepreneur.com/article/0,4621,293174,00.html.
4. Actually, Freud most likely never made this statement; however, it has entered popular folklore and is usually attributed to him.
5. R. Cialdini, *Influence: The Psychology of Persuasion* (New York: William Morrow and Company, 1993).
6. A. Komter and W. Vollebergh, "Gift-Giving and the Emotional Significance of Family and Friends," *Journal of Marriage and the Family* 59, no. 3 (August 1997), pp. 747–757.
7. Certainly, these investment vehicles are not truly risk-free. At the minimum, they have term risk. A full discussion of the elements of investment is far beyond the scope of this text.
8. The actual annual effective interest rate is 22.47 percent.

$$r = \left[\frac{fv}{c}\right]^{\frac{1}{n}} - 1 \quad r=(150{,}000/100{,}000)^{1/2}-1 \quad r=0.224745$$

10. Ou, C. and G. W. Haynes, "Uses of Equity Capital by Small Firms—Findings from the Surveys of Small Business Finances (for 1993 & 1998)," presented at the 14th Annual Conference on Entrepreneurial Finance and Business Ventures at the De Paul University Chicago, Illinois, on April 30–May 2, 2003, http://www.sba.gov/advo/stats/wkp03co.pdf.
11. R. Pettit, and R. Singer. "Small Business Finance: A Research Agenda," *Financial Management,* Autumn 1985, pp. 47–60.
12. Op cit., Ou and Haynes.
13. Michael Stouder and Bruce Kirchhoff, "Funding the First Year of Business," in William B. Gartner, Kelly G. Shaver, Nancy M. Carter, and Paul D. Reynolds, (eds.), *Handbook of Entrepreneurial Dynamics: The Process of Business Creation* (Thousand Oaks, CA: Sage, 2004).

Chapter 16

1. K. Kline, "No More Brush-Offs for This Crew," *BusinessWeek,* October 29, 2003.
2. Financial risk is discussed in detail in Chapter 15, "Finance for Small Business."
3. Doris A. Christopher, "Small Business Pilfering: The "trusted" Employee(s)," *Business Ethics: A European Review* 12, no 3 (2003), pp. 284–297. Note that there is a lot of disagreement on how much theft there is. In an SBA-sponsored survey, only 2 percent of small businesses reported employee theft in the prior year, but it is better to be safe than sorry. The SBA study was Bonnie Fisher, "Small Businesses, Big Burdens: The Nature and Incidence of Crime Within and Against Small Business and Its Customers and Employees, Their Causes, Their Effects, and Their Prevention," Washington: U.S. Small Business Administration, Office of Advocacy Research Report no 176. March 1997, http://www.sba.gov/advo/research/rs176.pdf.
4. *Op cit.,* Christopher. Anita Dennis, "The Downside of Good Times," *Journal of Accountancy* 190, no. 5 (2002), pp. 53–55. Neil H. Snyder, O. Whitfield Broome, Karen Zimmerman "Using Internal Controls to Reduce Employee Theft in Small Businesses," *Journal of Small Business Management* 27, no. 3 (July 1989), pp. 48–55.
5. Thomas M. Sullivan, "Closing the Tax Gap and the Impact on Small Business," Testimony of the Chief Counsel for Advocacy to the U.S. House of Representatives, Committee on Small Business, April 27, 2005, http://www.sba.gov/advo/laws/test05_0427.html. W. M. Crain, and T. D. Hopkins, "The Impact of Regulatory Costs on Small Firms," U.S. Small Business Administration, Office of Advocacy (SBAHQ-00-R-0027), October 2001, http://www.sba.gov/advo/research/rs207tot.pdf.
6. 42 USC Pub. L. 88-352, Title VII, Sec. 701 (b).
7. Except industries in SIC codes 55–69, 71–74, and 81–89.
8. M. Johnson, *Make Them Go Away: Clint Eastwood, Christopher Reeve and the Case Against Disability Rights* Louisville, KY: (Advocado Press, 2003). K. Wexler, "Big Winners in Disabled Crusade? Lawyers." *St. Petersburg Times.* March 24, 2002. *Newsweek,* U.S. Edition: *Perspectives.* May 29, 2000. J. Vandehei, "Clint Eastwood Saddles Up For Disability-Act Showdown," *The Wall Street Journal.* May 9, 2000. B. Van Voris, "South Florida's ADA Industry," *National Law Journal,* July 9, 2000.
9. General Aviation Revitalization Act (GARA), 1994.
10. Gene Gable (ed.), "Heavy Metal Madness: Put on a Happy Face!" *Creativepro.com,* April 22, 2004, http://www.creativepro.com/story/feature/21223.html. See also Yahoo's answer at http://ask.yahoo.com/ask/20011213.html, and the international angle on the "smiley face" story at http://www.goodbyemag.com/apr01/ball.html.
11. Separation of duties is discussed more fully in Chapter 17, "Assets: Inventory and Operations Management."
12. R. Hollinger, 2001 "National Retail Security Survey Final Report," University of Florida, 2001.
13. J. Wells, "2004 Report to the Nation on Occupational Fraud and Abuse," Association of Certified Fraud Examiners. Austin, TX, 2004, http://www.cfenet.com.
14. Thomas M. Sullivan, "Closing the Tax Gap and the Impact on Small Business," Testimony of the Chief Counsel for Advocacy to the U.S. House of Representatives, Committee on Small Business, April 27, 2005, http://www.sba.gov/advo/laws/test05_0427.html.
15. Leo Standora, "Heidi Has a Leg Up—$2m Insurance!" *New York Daily News,* September 7, 2004, p. 3.
16. Ibid.
17. Ibid.
18. U.S. Consumer Product Safety Commission, "Amusement Ride-Related Injuries and Deaths in the United States:" 1987–2000, Bethesda, MD, 2001.
19. The Outdoor Amusement Association Web Site, November 27, 2004, http://www.oaba.org/facts2.htm/.
20. M. Holmer, "The Value of Social Security Disability Insurance," Public Policy Institute of AARP. Washington, DC, 2001.
21. T. Zayatz, "Social Security Disability Insurance Program Worker Experience: Actuarial Study No. 114," Social Security Administration, Washington, DC, 1999.

Chapter 17

1. B. Cummings, "They Even Stole a Backhoe in Broad Daylight," *The New York Times,* January 6, 2005.
2. C. D. Bader, "Construction Equipment Theft: A Billion-Dollar Problem," *Grading & Excavation Contractor,* November/December 2004.
3. *Op. cit.,* Cummings.
4. http://www.pprhealthcare.com/index.shtml.
5. REL's Annual Working Capital surveys, 2004, http://www.relconsult.com/website/website.nsf/Articles/.
6. Ellyn Spragins, "Get Paid First!" *Fortune Small Business* 15, no. 1 (February 2005), p. 85.
7. Rieva Lesonsky, "Inventory Control: When It Comes to Inventory, the Key Is Striking a Balance between Too Little and Too Much," *Entrepreneur,* 1998, http://www.entrepreneur.com/article/0,4621,265105,00.html.
8. Gwen Moran, "Cover Your Bases: If You Thought Database Marketing Was Just Wasting Your Time with Fliers and Mailing Lists, Take Another Look—at the Net," *Entrepreneur,* February 2000, http://www.Entrepreneur.com/article/0,4621,232630,00.html.
9. "Dell Does What Others Have Given Up," *Forbes World Media Digest,* 2005, http://Forbes.com/technology.
10. Mike Hogan, "The Outer Limits: With Larger PC-Makers Struggling, Why Is Alienware Doing So Well?" *Entrepreneur,* March 2005, http://www.Entrepreneur.com/article/0,4621,320044,00.html. "Cutting the Edge Hardware," interview with Alex Aguila, http://www.ownt.com/hardware/interviews/2003/alienware/alienware.shtm. Ed Duggan, "Alienware, a Miami Computer Maker, Could Top Sales of $50 million," *South Florida Business Journal,* August 16, 2002, http://www.bizjournals.com/ southflorida/stories/2002/08/19/smallb1.html?t=printable.
11. Jerome A. Katz, Scott R. Safranski, and Omar Khan, "Virtual Instant Global Entrepreneurship: Cybermediation for Born International Service Firms," *Journal of International Entrepreneurship* Volume 1, Issue 1 (March 2003), pp. 43–57.
12. Stephen Barlas, "Industrial Cleanser: The EPA Is Targeting Small Business for Pollution Cleanup," *Entrepreneur,* January 2000, http://www.Entrepreneur.com/article/0,4621,232505,00.html.
13. Amanda C. Kooser, "Who's Paying for Computer Recycling: The Newest Standard for Modems," *Entrepreneur,* August 2, 2002, http://www.Entrepreneur.com/article/0,4621,301626,00.html.
14. Because depreciation is a noncash expense, it causes net operating profit to be an amount less than net cash inflows, all other things being equal. (Refer to Chapter 13 "Accounting for Small Business" for a more complete discussion of depreciation.)
15. David A. Kirby and Stefan Kaiser, "Joint Ventures as an Internationalisation Strategy for SMEs," *Small Business Economics* 21, no. 3 (Spring 2003), pp. 229–242. Marc. J. Dollinger, Peggy. A. Golden, and Todd Saxton,

"The Effect of Reputation on the Decision to Joint Venture," *Strategic Management Journal* 18, no. 2 (1997), pp. 127–140.
16. There is a caveat if you use Excel, however. The builtin net present value function of Excel does not provide for time period 0. Therefore, you must calculate the present value of the cash flows of periods 1, 2, 3, . . . , *n* and then add the initial negative investment cash flow to the number provided by the Excel function.
17. Stever Robbins, "How Much Is This Business Worth? If You're Interested in Purchasing an Existing Business, Here Are a Few Ways to Gauge Its value," *Entrepreneur,* January 12, 2004, http://www.Entrepreneur.com/article/0,4621,312644,00.html.

Chapter 18

1. Robert A. Kagan, "On Surveying the Whole Legal Forest," *Law and Social Inquiry,* vol. 28, 2003, pp. 833–872, http://www.journals.uchicago.edu/cgi-bin/resolve?id=doi:10.1086/380082&erFrom=4450405588134652 20Guest. Christian Wollschlager, "Exploring the Global Landscapes of Litigation Rates," in Jürgen Brand and Dieter Stempel (eds), Soziologie des Rechts: Fetschrift fur Erhard Blankenburg zum 60, Geburtstag. (Baden-Baden, Germany: Nomos Berlagsgesellschaft, 1998), pp. 587–88.
2. Pamela Rohland, "Follow Suit: What to Do when You Get Sued," *Entrepreneur—Business Start-Ups,* April 2000, http://www.Entrepreneur.com/ article/0,4621,269539,00.html.
3. Cliff Ennico, "How to Hire an Attorney: Hiring a Good Lawyer Is Crucial to Any Successful Business," *Entrepreneur,* January 20, 2003, http://www.Entrepreneur.com/article/0,4621,305623,00.html.
4. Other than taxes, but for most governments, your success in profit-making becomes in part their success in profit-taxing.
5. Karen E. Spaeder, "Is Your Home Zoned for Business? How to Research, Comply with and Change Local Zoning Laws in Your Homebased Business's Favor," *Entrepreneur Home Office,* January 26, 2004, http://www.Entrepreneur.com/article/0,4621,313950,00.html.
6. Christopher L. Hansen, "Special Report: Homebased Zoning: What Issues Are at Stake for Homebased Businesses Fighting Zoning Ordinances?" *Entrepreneur—Home Office,* January 1, 2001, http://www.entrepreneur.com/article/0,4621,285818,00.html. Laura Tiffany, "Zoning: Home Is Where the Business Is, and It's Also Where a Lot of Regulations Are," *Entrepreneur—Home Office,* March 21, 2001, http://www.Entrepreneur.com/ article/0,4621,287928,00.html.
7. "The Basics of Sole Proprietorships: Chances Are, You're Already Running a Sole Proprietorship," *Entrepreneur,* May 12, 2005, http://www.Entrepreneur.com/article/0,4621,321392,00.html.
8. These tips are adapted from Asheesh Advani, "Negotiation Tips for Startups: Follow These Suggestions for Negotiating with Employees, Investors and Suppliers When Your Business Has No Revenue," *Entrepreneur,* April 4, 2005, http://www.Entrepreneur.com/article/0,4621,320642,00.html. Max H. Bazerman, "Creating Value, Weighing Values." *Negotiation,* April 2005, pp. 3–5. Tony Parinello, "Dealmaking Basics: Tips for Negotiating Your Way to a Smooth Sale," *Entrepreneur,* May 12, 2003, http://www.Entrepreneur.com/article/0,4621,308526,00.html. Sean Silverthorne, "Five Questions for Max Bazerman," *HBS Working Knowledge,* September 4, 2001, http://hbswk.hbs.edu/item.jhtml?id=2472&t=negotiation&noseek=one. Max H. Bazerman, and James J. Gillespie, "Betting on the Future: The Virtues of Contingent Contracts," *Harvard Business Review* 77, no. 5 (September/October 1999), pp. 155–160.
9. This is a variation of the idea of "tit for tat," where two parties immediately achieve balance.
10. Robert Axelrod, *The Evolution of Cooperation* (New York: Basic Books, 1984). See also the Evolution of Cooperation Web site at http://pscs.physics.lsa.umich.edu/Software/CC/ECHome.html. For a business-oriented approach, consider looking at John Stewart, *Evolution's Arrow: The Direction of Evolution and the Future of Humanity* (Steamboat Springs, CO: Chapman Press, 2000). The entire text is available for a free download at http://users.tpg.com.au/users/jes999/index.htm.
11. The key books on negotiating come from the Program on Negotiating at Harvard Law School (http://www.pon.harvard.edu/main/home/index.php3). They are R. Fisher, W. Ury, and B. Patton, *Getting to Yes: Negotiating without Giving In* (New York: Penguin Books, 1991), and W. Ury, *Getting Past No: Negotiating Your Way from Confrontation to Cooperation* (New York: Bantam Books, 1993). Another book you might find useful for working with very problematic types is R. M. Bramson, *Coping with Difficult People* (New York: Dell, 1981).
12. Steven C. Bahls and Jane Easter Bahls, "RA-A-A-ID! Creepy Competitors Raiding Your Work Force? The Law Can Be the Perfect Bug Spray," *Entrepreneur,* September 2000, http://www.Entrepreneur.com/article/0,4621,278653,00.html.
13. Chris Kelleher, "5 Litigation Secrets: These Tips May Keep Your Business Out of Court—or Possibly Help You Win If You Get There," *Entrepreneur,* July 12, 2004, http://www.entrepreneur.com/article/0,4621,316368,00.html.
14. David Rountree, "Head Over Heels: Former Auburn Gymnast and Husband Turn Her Talent into Success," *Birmingham Business Journal,* June 6, 2005, http://birmingham.bizjournals.com/birmingham/stories/2005/06/06/smallb1.html.
15. W. Michael Hoffman, Laura P. Hartman, and Mark Rowe, "You've Got Mail . . . and the Boss Knows: A Survey by the Center for Business Ethics of Companies' Email and Internet Monitoring," *Business and Society Review* 108, no. 3 (2003), pp. 285–307. American Marketing Association with the ePolicy Institute and Clearswift. 2003 E-Mail Rules, Policies and Practices Survey. (New York: American Marketing Association, 2003). http://www.amanet.org/research/pdfs/Email Policies Practices.pdf. Robert McGarvey, "Watch and Learn . . . or Watch and Feel Like a Slimy Interloper," *Entrepreneur,* December 2000, http://www.Entrepreneur.com/article/0,4621,283614,00.html.
16. Chris Kelleher, "How to Protect Your Business's Trade Secrets: These Five Rules Will Help Safeguard Some of Your Company's Most Important Assets," *Entrepreneur,* May 1, 2005, http://www.entrepreneur.com/article/0,4621,321263,00.html.
17. Jane Easter Bahls, "The Name Game: You Can Shield Your Trade Name from Being Ripped Off by a Larger Company—If It's Distinctive Enough," *Entrepreneur,* January 2005, http://www.Entrepreneur.com/article/0,4621,318885,00.html. "The Source of the Nile(s):Trademark Law's Personal Name rule Shows Flexibility," *Ideas on Intellectual Property Law* (Manchester, NH: McLane Intellectual Property Practice Group, October/November 2004), pp. 2–3. Eugene R. Quinn, Jr., *Beanie Babies Trademark Infringement?* (Albany NY: Hiscock & Barclay, LLP, 2004), http://www.hiscockbarclay.com/pdf/IPnewsletter hb 0504.pdf.

Chapter 19

1. Talicia A. Flint, "Employees vs. Contractors Who are the Best Players for your Team?" *HomeOfficeMag.com,* May 2001, http://www.entrepreneur.com/mag/article/0,1539,289098,00.html.
2. U.S. Small Business Administration, "Private Firms, Establishments, Employment, Annual Payroll and Receipts by Firm Size, 1988–2002," http://www.sba.gov/advo/stats/us tot.pdf.
3. B. A. Kirchhoff, *Entrepreneurship and Dynamic Capitalism* (Westport, CT: Quorum Books, 1994). B. Phillips, and B. A. Kirchhoff, "Formation, Growth and Survival Small Firm Dynamics in the U.S. Economy," *Small Business Economics* 1 (1989), pp. 65–74. D. Birch, *Job Creation in America* (New York: Free Press, 1987).
4. Joanna L. Krotz, "5 Tips For Hiring Your First Employee," *Microsoft Small Business Center* (2005). http://www.microsoft.com/smallbusiness/ issues/management/recruiting Staffing/5 tips for hiring your first employee.mspx
5. *Op cit.,* Krotz, "5 Tips For Hiring Your First Employee."
6. Gideon D. Markman and Robert A. Baron, "Individual Differences and the Pursuit of New Ventures: A Model of Person-Entrepreneurship Fit," in Jerome A. Katz and Theresa M. Welbourne (eds), *Advances in Entrepreneurship, Firm Emergence and Growth,* vol. 5 (Oxford: JAI/Elsevier, 2002), pp. 23–54.
7. Allbusiness.com, "Is Employee Probation a Good Idea?". *Allbusiness.com* (2005). http://www.allbusiness.com/articles/EmploymentHR/749-33-1817. html
8. *Op cit.,* Krotz. "5 Tips for Hiring Your First Employee."
9. Joanna L. Krotz, "Are You A Control Freak? 5 Ways to Stop," *Microsoft Small Business Center* (2005). http://www.microsoft.com/smallbusiness/issues/management/leadership training/are you a control freak 5 ways to stop.mspx.
10. "Young Millionaires on . . . Hiring, The Only Thing More Frightening Than Starting Your Own Business May Be Hiring Your First Employee," *Entrepreneur,* October 22, 2004, http://www.Entrepreneur.com/article/0,4621,317629,00.html.
11. Ian O. Williamson, Daniel M. Cable, and Howard E. Aldrich, "Smaller But Not Necessarily Weaker: How Small Businesses Can Overcome Barriers to Recruitment. Managing People in Entrepreneurial Organizations," *Advances in the Study of Entrepreneurship Firm Emergence and Growth,* vol. 5 (Greenwich, CT: JAI Press, 2002), pp. 83–106.
12. Jeff Taylor, "A Monster Success," *The Economist* 307, no. 8368 (March 27, 2004), p. 66.
13. Chris Penttila, "How Embarrassing! Highly Publicized Dry Spells Are Poor Recruiting Tools," *Entrepreneur,* August 2002, pp. 66.
14. Dale Duncan and Peter Hausdorf, "Firm Size and Internet Recruiting in Canada," *Journal of Small Business Management* 42, no. 3, (July 2004) p. 325.
15. Businesstown.com, "Hiring Top Performers." *Businesstown.com* (undated). http://www.businesstown.com/hiring/hiring-top.asp, adapted from Bob Adams and Peter Veruki, *Adams Streetwise Hiring Top Performers: 600 Ready-To-Ask Interview Questions and Everything Else You Need to Hire Right* (Cincinnati: Adams Media Corporation, 1997).

16. Gisda M. Pedroza, "Hiring Telecommuters, Before You Set Up Employees in Their Own Home Offices, Make Sure You Can Handle the Costs," *Entrepreneur,* January 2002, http://www.Entrepreneur.com/article/0,4621,295960,00.html.
17. Jerome A. Katz, Scott R. Safranski, and Omar Khan, "Virtual Instant Global Entrepreneurship: Cybermediation for Born International Service Firms," *Journal of International Entrepreneurship* 1 (2003), pp. 43–57. Robyn Greenspan, "Managing Virtual Employees," *ecommerce-guide.com,* February 28, 2002, //e-commerceguide.com/news/news/article.php/983281.
18. Joanna L. Krotz, "Tips for outsourcing your small-business needs," *Microsoft Small Business Center* (2005). http://www.microsoft.com/smallbusiness/resources/management/recruiting_staffing/tips_for_outsourcing_your_small_business_needs.mspx
19. *Op cit.,* Katz, Safranski, and Khan.
20. The ideas in the following section are from No-Cost Staffing Options on www.toolkit.cch.com.
21. Entrepreneur.com, "How to Write a Job Analysis and Description," *Entrepreneur.com,* October 23, 2002, http://www.entrepreneur.com/article/0,4621,304062,00.html.
22. Chris Kelleher, "Writing Great Job Descriptions," *Entrepreneur,* May 10, 2004, http://www.entrepreneur.com/article/0,4621,315429,00.html.
23. Gideon D. Markman and Robert A. Baron, "Individual Differences and the Pursuit of New Ventures: A Model of Person-Entrepreneurship Fit," in Jerome A. Katz and Theresa M. Welbourne (eds), *Advances in Entrepreneurship, Firm Emergence and Growth,* vol. 5 (Oxford: JAI/Elsevier, 2002), pp. 23–54.
24. This list can be found in several places on the Internet, although the original source is not evident. For example, see "Questions Asked by Employers", University of Buffalo Career Services website, http://www.student-affairs.buffalo.edu/career/empask.shtml; University of Arizona C.A.T.S. Program website, http://www.u.arizona.edu/~cats/quesbyemp.html, or Central Georgia Technical College Career Services website, http://cgtcollege.org/studserv/career_services/resources/interview2.html.
25. Adapted from the Mavens and Mogul website, http://www.mavensandmoguls.com/ and from Inc Magazine, "Entrepreneur of the Year: The Accidental Entrepreneur—Paige Arnof-Fenn," http://www.inc.com/entrepreneur/profile/index.php?arnof-fenn52.
26. The ideas here are excerpted and adapted from Gary Roberts, Gary Seldon and Carlotta Roberts, "Human Resources Management" Emerging Business Series, Monograph EB-4. (Washington DC: U.S. Small Business Administration, undated), http://www.sba.gov/library/pubs/eb-4.txt.
27. Adapted from "TechScribe Writing," *How to Write Instructions* (Sheffield, South Yorkshire, 2004), http://www.techscribe.co.uk/ta/how_to_write_instructions.htm.
28. Excerpted from Gary Roberts, Gary Seldon and Carlotta Roberts, "Human Resources Management" Emerging Business Series, Monograph EB-4. (Washington DC: U.S. Small Business Administration, undated), http://www.sba.gov/library/pubs/eb-4.txt.
29. Allbusiness.com, "Secrets of Effective Employee Training". *Allbusiness.com* (2005). http://www.allbusiness.com/articles/EmploymentHR/1465-33-1817.html
30. Jill Kickul, "Promises Made, Promises Broken: Employee Attraction and Retention in Small Businesses," *Journal of Small Business Management* 39, no. 4 (2001), pp. 320–335.
31. Adapted from Commerce Clearing House, "Building employee involvement," *Business Owners Toolkit* (Riverwoods, IL: Commerce Clearing House, 2005). http://www.toolkit.cch.com/text/P05_7200.asp
32. Alison Stein Wellner, "What Makes Employees Want to Stick Around?" *BusinessWeek* March 2000, 3.20.00. http://www.businessweek.com/smallbiz/ content/mar2000/sb000320a.htm.
33. Elcha Shain Buckman, "Motivating and Retaining Non-Family Employees in a Family-Owned Business." *The UMASS Family Business Center Online Newsletter* (Hadley, MA: The UMASS Family Business Center, 1998). http://www.umass.edu/fambiz/motivate_key_employees.htm
34. *Ibid.*
35. Building Employees' Involvement, on www.toolkit.cch.com.
36. David Newton, "Of One Mind: Keep employees by getting on the same page from the get-go." *Entrepreneur,* August 2003, p. 23. http://www.entrepreneur.com/mag/article/0,1539,309926,00.html
37. Alison Stein Wellner, "What Makes Employees Want to Stick Around?" *BusinessWeek,* March 2000, 3.20.00. http://www.businessweek.com/smallbiz/content/mar2000/sb000320a.htm.
38. Peter L. Allen, "Performance Appraisal Question and Answer Book," *Harvard Management Communication Letter* 6, no. 3 (March 2003), p. 3.
39. BizHelp23.com, "Employee Appraisal." *BizHelp23.com* (Sheffield, UK: BizHelp24.com, 2005). http://www.bizhelp24.com/personal_development/employee_appraisal.shtml
40. Gina Imperato, "How to Give Good Feedback," *Fast Company,* September 17, 1998, p. 144.
41. Allbusiness.com, "Making Performance Appraisals Work," *Allbusiness.com* (2005). http://www.allbusiness.com/articles/content/1383-33-1817.html
42. David G. Javitch, "By setting clear standards and involving employees in the review process, your entire company can benefit from formal appraisals," *Entrepreneur.com,* April 05, 2004. http://www.entrepreneur.com/article/0,4621,314968,00.html.
43. This section is excerpted from an outstanding description of practical compensation management in small businesses which came from Allbusiness.com, "Key compensation components", *Allbusiness.com,* undated, http://www.allbusiness.com/articles/EmploymentHR/794-33-1773.html.
44. Staff of *Family Business,* "The Power of Base Pay," *Inc.,* October 1999, http://www.inc.com/articles/1999/10/19037.html.
45. *Op cit.,* Allbusiness.com, "Key compensation components."
46. *Ibid.*
47. *Ibid.*
48. Renee S. Reid and John S. Adams, "Human Resource Management—a Survey of Practices within Family and Non-Family Firms," *Journal of European Industrial Training* 25, no. 6/7 (2001), pp. 310–320.
49. Many of the key challenges identified here and in subsequent sections come from the classic monograph from the U.S. Small Business Administration, "Challenges in Managing a Family Business," Management and Planning Series, Monograph MP-3, (Washington DC: U.S. Small Business Administration, undated), http://www.sba.gov/library/pubs/mp-3.txt. The text is both excerpted and adapted from that work, which has become the standard for family business consulting, appearing in more than 100 locations on the Internet.
50. *Ibid.*
51. Sandra W. King, George T. Solomon, and Lloyd W. Fernald Jr. "Issues in Growing a Family Business: A Strategic Human Resource Model," *Journal of Small Business Management.* 39, no. 1 (January 2001), pp. 3–13.
52. *Op cit.,* U.S. Small Business Administration, "Challenges in Managing a Family Business."
53. *Ibid.*
54. Nichole L. Torres, "Do You Want to Mix Business with Family or Friends?" *Entrepreneur,* April 2002.
55. Karen E. Spader, "The Good, the Bad & the Ugly of Family Business," *Entrepreneur,* August 12, 2002, http://www.Entrepreneur.com/article/ 0,4621,302389,00.html.
56. Patricia Schiff Estess, "Strictly Business: Taking the Personal Out of Personnel Isn't Easy When You're Talking About Family," *Entrepreneur,* January 2002. p. 118. http://www.entrepreneur.com/article/0.4621,232500,00.html
57. Jeff Wuorio, "How to Fire a Family Member," *Microsoft Small Business Center* (2005). http://www.microsoft.com/smallbusiness/issues/management/employee_relations/how_to_fire_a_family_member.mspx
58. *Op cit.,* Spader.
59. *Op cit.,* Torres.
60. *Op cit.,* Wuorio.
61. *Op cit.,* Spader.
62. *Op cit.,* Estess.
63. *Ibid.*
64. Laura Tiffany, "Family Business Expert Quentin J. Fleming," *Entrepreneur,* April 2, 2001.
65. *Op cit.,* Wuorio.
66. R. Thurik S. Wennekers "Entrepreneurship, Small Business and Economic Growth," *Journal of Small Business and Enterprise Development* 11, no. 1 (March 2004), pp. 140–149. Catherine Armington and Zoltan J. Acs, "Job Creation and Persistence in Services and Manufacturing," *Journal of Evolutionary Economics* 14, no. 3 (July 2004), pp. 309–325.
67. S. Davis, J. Haltiwanger, and S. Schuh, "Small Business and Job Creation: Dissecting the Myth and Reassessing the Facts," *National Bureau of Economic Research Working Paper No. 4492,* October 1993.
68. M. Cardon C. Stevens, "Managing Human Resources in Small Organizations: What Do We know?" *Human Resource Management Review* 14, no. 3 (2004) pp. 295–323. Robert W. Rowden, "The Relationship between Workplace Learning and Job Satisfaction in U.S. Small to Midsize Businesses," *Human Resource Development Quarterly* 13, no. 4 (2002), pp. 407–425.
69. C. Brown, J. Hamilton, and J. Medoff, *Employers Large and Small* (Cambridge, MA: Harvard University Press, 1990). J. S. Hornsby, and D. F. Kuratko, "Human Resource Management in Small Business: Critical Issues for the 1990s," *Journal of Small Business Management,* July 1990, pp. 9–18.
70. Reprinted from Todd Luchik, "Survival of the Fittest", *Winningworkplaces.com,* http://www.winningworkplaces.org/library/success/survival_of_the_fittest.php. Used with permission.

Chapter 20

1. Look at Mark Hendricks, "Stage Right: Make Smarter Management Decisions by Knowing What Stage Your Company's in," *Entrepreneur,* April 1997, http://www.entrepreneur.com/mag/article/0,1539,227098—1-,00.html. The most famous one comes from Larry Greiner (1972), *Harvard Business Review.* Neil C. Churchill and Virginia L. Lewis adapted Greiner's model in "The Five Stages of Small Business Growth," *Harvard Business Review,* May-June 1983. The three-stage simplification follows the idea expressed by Kelin E. Gersick, Ivan Lansberg, Michele Desjardins, and Barbara Dunn, "Stages and Transitions: Managing Change in the Family Business" *Family Business Review,* XII no. 4 (1999), pp. 287–297 http://www.lgassoc.com/library/articles/112-Stages &Transitions.pdf, and in their book. Kelin Gersick, John Davis, Marion McCollum Hampton, and Ivan Lansberg, *Generation to Generation: Life Cycles of the Family Business* (Cambridge: Harvard University Press, 1997).
2. The 7 percent rate comes from Heidi M. Neck, Andrew L. Zacharakis, William D. Bygrave, and Paul D. Reynolds, "Global Entrepreneurship Monitor: National Entrepreneurship Assessment—United States of America," 2002 Executive Report, http://www.gemconsortium.org/download/1061664039492/GEM%20US%202002.pdf. The drop off from those expressing an interest to those taking action comes from J. A. Katz, "Modeling Entrepreneurial Career Progressions: Concepts and Considerations," *Entrepreneurship: Theory & Practice* 19, no. 2 (Winter 1994), pp. 23–40. J. Katz, "Longitudinal Analysis of Entrepreneurial Follow-through," *Journal of Entrepreneurship and Regional Development* 2, no. 1 (1990), pp. 15–25. Paul D. Reynolds, "Who Starts New Firms? Preliminary Explorations of Firms-in-Gestation," *Small Business Economics* 9 (1997), pp. 449–462.
3. Rieva Lesonsky, "It's Never Too Late," *Entrepreneur,* November 2003, http://www.Entrepreneur.com/article/0,4621,311458,00.html. Jacquelyn Lynn, "Don't Be Afraid: Are You a Big Scaredy-Cat? Here's How to Turn Terror into Super-confidence," *Entrepreneur,* June 2000, http://www.Entrepreneur.com/article/0,4621,275016,00.html. Rieva Lesonsky, "What's The Big Idea? Start-up Ideas Are All Around . . . Once You Know Where to Look," *Business Start-Ups,* November 1998, http://www.Entrepreneur.com/article/0,4621,229453,00.html. J. Katz, "Longitudinal Analysis of Entrepreneurial Follow-Through," *Journal of Entrepreneurship and Regional Development* 2, no. 1 (1990), pp. 15–25.
4. Heidi M. Neck, Andrew L. Zacharakis, William D. Bygrave, and Paul D. Reynolds, "Global Entrepreneurship Monitor: National Entrepreneurship Assessment—United States of America," 2002 Executive Report, http://www.kauffman.org/pdf/us_gem_2002.pdf
5. D. A. Shepherd and M. Shanley, *New Venture Strategy* (Newbury Park, CA: Sage, 1998). D. A. Shepherd, E. J. Douglas, and M. Shanley, "New Venture Survival: Ignorance, External Shocks, and Risk Reduction Strategies," *Journal of Business Venturing* 15 (2000), pp. 393–410. H. Robert Dodge, Sam Fullerton, and John E. Robbins, "Stage of the Organizational Life Cycle and Competition as Mediators of Problem Perception for Small Businesses," *Strategic Management Journal* 15, no. 2 (February 1994), pp. 121–135.
6. *Simpson's Contemporary Quotations,* compiled by James B. Simpson, 1988. Quoted by Thomas J. Peters and Robert H. Waterman, *In Search of Excellence* (New York: Harper & Row, 1982), http://www.bartleby.com/63/54/2254.html.
7. Mark Henricks, "Staying Power: Zero Defections Strategy Keeps Customers Coming Back," *Entrepreneur,* July 1997, http://www.Entrepreneur.com/article/0,4621,227415,00.html. Frederick F. Reichheld, *The Loyalty Effect, The Hidden Force Behind Growth, Profits, and Lasting Value* (Cambridge: *Harvard Business School Press,* 1996). Robert C. Blattberg, Gary Getz, and Jacquelyn S. Thomas, *Customer Equity: Building and Managing Relationships as Valuable Assets* (Boston: Harvard Business School Press, 2001). Roland T. Rust and R. L. Oliver, "Should We Delight the Customer," *Journal of The Academy of Marketing* Sciences 28, no.1 (2000), pp. 86–94. Sandy D. Jap, Control Mechanisms and the Relationship Life Cycle: Implications for Safeguarding Specific Investments and Developing Commitment, *Journal of Marketing Research* 37, no. 2 (May 2000), p. 227. F. F. Reichheld and W. E. Sasser, "Zero Defections: Quality Comes to Services," *Harvard Business Review,* 1990, pp. 105–11. R. T. Rust A. J. Zahorik, and T. L. Keiningham, "Return On Quality (ROQ): Making Service Quality Financially Accountable," *Journal of Marketing* 59 (1995), pp. 58–70. Valarie A. Zeithaml, "Service Quality, Profitability, and The Economic Worth of Customers: What We Know and What We Need to Learn," *Academy of Marketing Science Journal* 28, no. 1 (2000), p. 67.
8. Zig Ziglar, *Zig Ziglar's Secrets of Closing the Sale* (Berkley Pub Group, 1985). The ideas came from the long out-of-print Australian series, "10 Sales Cassettes by Dr. Joseph Braysich." Other good sources for this approach include: Kim T. Gordon, "Building Customer Relationships: Increase Your Sales through Better Relationships with Your Existing Customers," *Entrepreneur,* January 01, 2001, http://www.entrepreneur.com/article/0,4621,285279,00.html. Nichole L. Torres, "Marketing Buzz 09/02: Sell Better by Understanding the Six Different Customer Types; How to Respond to Bad Press, *Entrepreneur,* September 2002, http://www.entrepreneur.com/mag/article/0,1539,302387,00.html.
9. D. Guithues-Amrhein and J. A. Katz, "Assessing the Mortality Risk of a Business," *Journal of Enterprising Culture* 7, no. 3 (1999) or http://www.sbaer.uca.edu/Research/1998/ICSB/n004.htm. Joan Stableford, "Business Notes: It's Here: the Great Pumpkin," *Time* 136, no. 21 (November 12, 1990), p. 64. Joan Stableford "For Sun Hill Industries, Success Last Year Was in the Bag," *Fairfield County Business Journal* 22, no 19 (May 27, 1991), p. 10. The pirate pursuit resulted in a legal battle, which was decided in Zinbarg's favor in 1999; see United States Court of Appeals for the Federal Circuit, 98-1498 (Serial No. 08/427,732), in Re Anita Dembiczak and Benson Zinbarg, http://www.law.emory.edu/fedcircuit/apr99/98-1498.wp.html.
10. mereChina, "Fun Chinese Lessons—9: Danger and Opportunity: the Chinese Expression for Crisis," http://www.merechina.com/language/chineselesson9.shtml.
11. Rod P. Burkert, "A Good Deal Depends on Preparation," *Journal of Accountancy* 196, no. 5 (November 2003), pp. 47–52.
12. Thomson Financial, "Thomson Financial Worldwide M&A," 2004, third quarter 2004, http://www.thomson.com/cms/assets/pdfs/financial/league_table/mergers_and_acquisitions/3Q2004/press_releases/3Q04_MA_PR_US_Global.pdf. See also C.J. Prince, "Got Leverage? If You're Ready to Sell, You've Got the Upper Hand. Large Buyout Firms Will Be Looking to Entrepreneurs." *Entrepreneur,* September 2003, http://www. entrepreneur.com/article/0,4621,310248,00.html.
13. The ESOP Association, "ESOP Facts and Figures," 2004, http://www.esopassociation.org/media/media_statistics.asp C. Tawney and J. Levitsky, "Small Enterprise Development as a Strategy for Reducing the Social Cost of Restructuring and the Privatization Process: Public and Private Initiatives," Interdepartmental Action Programme on Privatization, Restructuring and Economic Democracy, Working Paper IPPRED-6, 2000, International Labour Organization (ILO), http://www.ilo.org/public/english/employment/ent/papers/ippred6.htm. G. B. Hansen, "ESOPs in the USA", presentation to the ILO seminar "The Economies in Transition and the Employment Problem: The Role of Cooperatives and Associations," Kiev, Ukraine, 1993.
14. The ESOP Association, "ESOP Facts and Figures," 2004, http://www.esopassociation.org/media/media_statistics.asp
15. Isabelle Le Breton-Miller, Danny Miller, and Lloyd P. Steier, "Toward an Integrative Model of Effective FOB Succession," *Entrepreneurship: Theory & Practice* 28, no. 4 (Summer 2004), pp. 305–328. William S. White, Timothy D. Krinke, and David L. Geller, "Family Business Succession Planning: Devising an Overall Strategy," *Journal of Financial Service Professionals* 58, no. 3 (May 2004), pp. 67–86.
16. Scott Bernard Nelson, "Leave It to Them: Make Sure Your Family Gets What It Needs by Including a Disclaimer Provision in Your Estate Plan," *Entrepreneur,* August 2004, http://www.Entrepreneur.com/ article/0,4621,316380,00.html.
17. Paul DeCeglie, "State of the Estate: What Is Estate Planning and Why Should You Be Doing It Now?" *Entrepreneur Start-Ups,* January 2001, http://www.entrepreneur.com/article/0,4621,284549,00.html.
18. N. Upton and B. Petty, "Funding Options for Transferring the Family-Held Firm: A Comparative Analysis," presented at the 18th annual meeting of the Babson Research Conference, Ghent, Belgium, April 1998. N. Upton and B. Petty, "Venture Capital Funding of Family Business Transition: An Exploratory Analysis," *Proceedings of the United States Association of Small Business and Entrepreneurship,* 1998, pp. 94–101. Neil C. Churchill, and Kenneth J. Hatten, "Non-Market-Based Transfers of Wealth and Power: A Research Framework for Family Businesses," *American Journal of Small Business* 12, no. 2 (Fall 1987), pp. 53–66.
19. N. Upton, and B. Petty, "Funding Options for Transferring the Family-Held Firm: A Comparative Analysis," presented at the 18th annual meeting of the Babson Research Conference, Ghent, Belgium, April 1998.
20. Brian Headd, "Redefining Business Success: Distinguishing between Closure and Failure," *Small Business Economics* 21, no. 1 (2003), pp. 51–61. Timothy Bates and Alfred Nucci, "An Analysis of Small Business Size and Rate of Discontinuance," *Journal of Small Business Management* 27, no. 4 (1989), pp. 1–8. Small Business Administration, U.S. "Small Business Economic Indicators for 2003." (Washington DC: Small Business Administration, August 2004).
21. This approach follows the practical concept pioneered by Dun & Bradstreet in its *Business Failure Reports.* What we call a walkaway was what D&B called a "business discontinuance" and referred to a

business that closed having not left any creditors or legal actions pending. A "business failure" in D&B's language was a firm that closed with unpaid creditors or pending legal actions. These are called *failures* here. The source is Dun & Bradstreet, "Business Failure Record" (Murray Hill, NJ: Dun & Bradstreet, 1998), https://www.dnb.com/newsview/bfr96-97.pdf.
22. Brian Headd, "Redefining Business Success: Distinguishing between Closure and Failure," *Small Business Economics* 21, no. 1 (2003), pp. 51–61.
23. P. Jennings and G. Beaver, "The Performance and Competitive Advantage of Small Firms: A Management Perspective," *International Small Business Journal* 15 (1997), pp. 63–75. Brian Headd, "Redefining Business Success: Distinguishing between Closure and Failure," *Small Business Economics* 21, no. 1 (2003), pp. 51–61. J. Watson, and J. Everett, "Do Small Businesses Have High Failure Rates?" *Journal of Small Business Management* 34, no. 4 (1996), pp. 45–62. J. Watson and J. Everett, "Defining Small Business Failure," *International Small Business Journal* 11, no. 3 (1993), pp. 35–48.
24. Stephen C. Perry, "A Comparison of Failed and Non-failed Small Businesses in the United States: Do Men and Women Use Different Planning and Decision Making Strategies?" *Journal of Developmental Entrepreneurship* 7, no. 4 (December 2002), pp. 415–428. R. M. Hodgetts and D. F. Kuratko, *Effective Small Business Management* (New York: Wiley, 2002). L. Waghorne, "The Cold Hard Facts," *Chartered Accountants Journal of New Zealand* 79, no. 7 (2000), pp. 72–72.
25. Laura Tiffany, "Mail Order: Want to Go Retail but Don't Want to Deal with the Hassles of a Storefront? Follow the Paths Forged by Wards and Sears by Starting a Mail-Order company," *Entrepreneur,* February 22, 2001, http://www.entrepreneur.com/article/0,4621,287061-5,00.html.
26. Experts in management information systems have put in the most work applying CSF approaches to small businesses. For example, see Riyad Eid, Myfanwy Trueman, and Abdel Moneim Ahmed, "A Cross-Industry Review of B2B Critical Success Factors," *Internet Research: Electronic Networking Applications and Policy* 12, no. 2 (2002), pp. 110–123. T. Butler and B. Fitzgerald, "Unpacking the Systems Development Process: An Empirical Application of the CSF Concept in a Research Context," *The Journal of Strategic Information Systems,* 8, no. 4 (1999), pp. 351–371. G. K. Kanji and A. M. Tambi, "Total Quality Management in UK Higher Education Institutions," *Total Quality Management* 10, no. 1 (1999), pp. 129–153.
27. Edward G. Rogoff, Myung-Soo Lee, and Dong-Churl Suh, "Who Done It?" Attributions by entrepreneurs and experts of the factors that cause and impeded small business success. *Journal of Small Business Management* 42, no. 4 (October 2004), pp. 364–376. E. J. Gatewood, K. G. Shaver, J. B. Powers, and W. B. Gartner, "Entrepreneurial Expectancy, Task Effort, and Performance," *Entrepreneurship: Theory & Practice* 27, no. 2 (2002), pp. 187–206. K. G. Shaver, W. B. Gartner, E. Crosby, K. Bakalarova, and E. J. Gatewood, "Attributions about Entrepreneurship: A Framework and Process for Analyzing Reasons for Starting a Business," *Entrepreneurship: Theory & Practice* 26, no. 2 (2001), pp. 5–32.
28. J. J. Chrisman, "The Influence of Outsider-Generated Knowledge Resources on Venture Creation," *Journal of Small Business Management* 37, no. 4 (1999), pp. 42–58. James J. Chrisman and W. Ed McMullan, "A Preliminary Assessment of Outsider Assistance as a Knowledge Resource: The Longer-Term Impact of New Venture Counseling," *Entrepreneurship: Theory & Practice* 24, no. 3 (2000), pp. 37–53. James J. Chrisman and W. Ed McMullan, "Outsider Assistance as a Knowledge Resource for New Venture Survival," *Journal of Small Business Management* 42, no. 3 (2004), pp. 229–244.
29. Devron A. Veasley, "In Depth: Small Business Resource Guide—Business Incubation. Incubators Build Economies, Benefit Communities," *Birmingham Business Journal,* November 8, 2003, http://birmingham. bizjournals.com/birmingham/stories/2003/08/11/focus6.html.
30. A. Charney, and G. Libecap, *Impact of Entrepreneurship Education* (Kansas City, MO: Kauffman Center for Entrepreneurial Leadership, 2000). L. Kolvereid, and O. Moen, "Entrepreneurship among Business Graduates: Does a Major in Entrepreneurship Make a Difference?" *Journal of European Industrial Training* 21, no. 4 (1997), pp. 154–160. W. E. McMullan, and L. M. Gillin, "Entrepreneurship Education: Developing Technological Start-up Entrepreneurs. A Case Study of a Graduate Entrepreneurship Programme at Swinburne University," *Technovation* 18, no. 4 (1998), pp. 275–286. T.V. Menzies, and J. C. Paradi, "Encouraging Technology-Based Ventures: Entrepreneurship Education and Engineering Graduates," *New England Journal of Entrepreneurship* 5, no. 2 (2002), pp. 57–64. T. V. Menzies, and J. C. Paradi, "Entrepreneurship Education and Engineering Students: Career Path and Business Performance," *International Journal of Entrepreneurship and Innovation* 6, no. 2 (2003), pp. 85–96. N. B. Upton, D. L. Sexton, and C. Moore, "Have We Made a Difference? An Examination of Career Activity of Entrepreneurship Majors since 1981" (abstract), *Frontiers of Entrepreneurship Research* 1995 edition (Wellesley, MA: Babson College, 1995), pp. 727–728.
31. Brian Headd, "Redefining Business Success: Distinguishing between Closure and Failure," *Small Business Economics* 21, no. 1 (2003), pp. 51–61. J. Katz, "A Psychosocial Cognitive Model of Employment Status Choice," *Entrepreneurship: Theory & Practice* 16, no. 1 (1992), pp. 29–37.
32. G. N. Chandler and S. H. Hanks, "Founder Competence, the Environment, and Venture Performance," *Entrepreneurship: Theory & Practice* 18, no. 3 (1994), pp. 77–89. R. K. Mitchell, B. Smith, K. W. Seawright, and E. A. Morse, "Cross-Cultural Cognitions and the Venture Creation Decision," *Academy of Management Journal* 43, (2000), pp. 974–993.
33. Robert A. Baron and Gideon D. Markman, "Beyond Social Capital: The Role of Entrepreneurs' Social Competence in Their Financial Success," *Journal of Business Venturing* 18, no. 1 (2003), pp. 41–60.
34. Gerard George, D. Robley Wood Jr., and Raihan Kahn, "Networking Strategy of Boards: Implications for Small and Medium-Sized Enterprises," *Entrepreneurship and Regional Development* 13, no. 3 (2001), pp. 269–285.
35. This is one of the oldest findings in small business research, starting with K. B. Mayer and S. Goldstein, "The First Two Years: Problems of Small Firm Growth and Survival," Washington: Small Business Administration, and continuing through Brian Headd, "Redefining Business Success: Distinguishing between Closure and Failure," *Small Business Economics* 21, no. 1 (2003), pp. 51–61.
36. Brian Headd, "Redefining Business Success: Distinguishing between Closure and Failure," *Small Business Economics* 21, no. 1 (2003), pp. 51–61.
37. Brian Headd, "Redefining Business Success: Distinguishing between Closure and Failure," *Small Business Economics* 21, no. 1 (2003), pp. 51–61.
38. D. A. Shepherd and M. Shanley, *New Venture Strategy* (Newbury Park, CA: Sage, 1998). D. A. Shepherd, E. J. Douglas, and M. Shanley, "New Venture Survival: Ignorance, External Shocks, and Risk Reduction Strategies," *Journal of Business Venturing* 15 (2000), pp. 393–410.
38. Dean A. Shepherd and Evan J. Douglas, *Attracting Equity Investors: Positioning, Preparing and Presenting the Business Plan* (Newbury Park CA: Sage, 1999).
39. Susan A. Sherer and Bill Adams, "Collaborative Commerce: The Role of Intermediaries in e-Collaboration," *Journal of Electronic Commerce Research* 2, no. 2 (2001), pp. 66–77.
40. G. T. Lumpkin and G. G. Dess, "Clarifying the Entrepreneurial Orientation Construct and Linking It to Performance," *Academy of Management Review* 21, no. 1 (1996), pp. 135–172. G. T. Lumpkin and G. G. Dess, "Linking Two Dimensions of Entrepreneurial Orientation to Firm Performance: The Moderating Role of Environment and Industry Life Cycle," *Journal of Business Venturing* 16, no. 5 (2001), pp. 429–451. D. A. Shepherd, and M. Shanley, *New Venture Strategy* (Newbury Park, CA: Sage, 1998).
41. D. A. Shepherd and M. Shanley, *New Venture Strategy* (Newbury Park, CA: Sage, 1998). D. A. Shepherd, E. J. Douglas, and M. Shanley, "New Venture Survival: Ignorance, External Shocks, and Risk Reduction Strategies," *Journal of Business Venturing* 15 (2000), pp. 393–410.
42. Dean A. Shepherd and Evan J. Douglas, *Attracting Equity Investors: Positioning, Preparing and Presenting the Business Plan* (Newbury Park, CA: Sage, 1999.)
43. W. Gibb Dyer, *The Entrepreneurial Experience: Confronting the Career Dilemmas of the Start-up Executive* (San Francisco: Jossey-Bass, 1992) or Dorothy Perrin Moore, *Careerpreneurs: Lesson from Leading Women Entrepreneurs on Building a Career without Boundaries* (Palo Alto, CA: Davies Black, 2000).
44. This approach is called *open-systems theory* or *living systems theory* in the social sciences. Some of the most famous models for studying organizations are rooted in this approach such as Daniel Katz and Robert L. Kahn *The Social Psychology of Organizations* (New York: Wiley, 1978) or William B. Gartner "A Conceptual Framework for Describing the Phenomenon of New Venture Creation," *Academy of Management Review* 10 (1985), pp. 696–706.
45. The latest list comes from home-business gurus Paul Edwards and Sarah Edwards, "The Dark Side, Prepare Yourself for Being Home Based by Understanding the Downside," *Entrepreneur's Be Your Own Boss,* June, http://www.entrepreneur.com/article/0,4621,308968,00.html.
46. Aliza Pilar Sherman, "Teaching by Example," *Entrepreneur,* December 2003, http://www.entrepreneur.com/mag/article/0,1539,311899,00.html.
47. Patricia Schiff Estess, "Gag Order," *Entrepreneur,* September 2000, http://www.entrepreneur.com/article/0,4621,278650,00.html. Quentin Fleming, *Keep the Family Baggage out of the Family Business* (New York: Fireside, 2000). Patricia Schiff Estess, "Close Encounters," *Entrepreneur,* July 1998, http://www.Entrepreneur.com/article/0,4621,228950,00.html.
48. Paul Edwards and Sarah Edwards, "The Dark Side: Prepare Yourself for Being Home Based by Understanding the Downside," *Entrepreneur's Be Your Own Boss,* June 2003, http://www.entrepreneur.com/article/

0,4621,308968,00.html. Paul Edwards and Sara Edwards, *Working from Home* (Los Angeles: Tarcher, 1999).

49. Not surprisingly, there is a lot of disagreement on what exactly constitutes the triple bottom line. For example, for big businesses, the conventional thinking is economic, social, and environmental returns. See European Business Forum /PriceWaterhouseCoopers, "EBF on . . . Sustainable Development," (London: European Business Forum, 2003). http://www.pwc.com/pl/eng/inssol/publ/2003/corp_efb_rap.pdf, or Knowledge @ Wharton, "The Triple Bottom Line: Student Activists Demand More from B-Schools," Wharton School Public Policy and Management website, May 13, 2003. http://knowledge.wharton.upenn.edu/index.cfm?fa=viewfeature&id=773, or John Elkington, "Cannibals with Forks: The Triple Bottom Line of the 21st Century Business (Gabriola Island, BC, Canada: New Society Publishers, 1998). In small businesses, the idea of firm, community, and personal returns is better established, through works such as W. Gibb Dyer, *The Entrepreneurial Experience: Confronting the Career Dilemmas of the Start-up Executive* (San Francisco: Jossey-Bass, 1992) or Dorothy Perrin Moore, *Careerpreneurs: Lesson from Leading Women Entrepreneurs on Building a Career without Boundaries* (Palo Alto, CA: Davies Black, 2000). A very good article on how the triple bottom line operates in family businesses can be found in Robyn Eversole, "Balancing Act: Business and Household in a Small Bolivian City," *Development in Practice* 12, no. 5 (2002), pp. 589–601.

50. Google, Inc., "Amendment No. 9 to Form S-1: Registration Statement, Under The Securities Act of 1933 (Washington, D.C.: US Securities and Exchange Commission, (2004) http://sec.gov/Archives/edgar/data/1288776/000119312504142742/ds1a.htm. Warren Bennis," Warren Bennis: Google's Growth Engine. CIO Insight. June 1, 2004, http://www.cioinsight.com/article2/0,1397,1609425,00.asp. Mary Anne Ostrom and Matt Marshall, "Inside Google: Internet Search Engine's Founders Keep Ideas Rolling and Profits Pouring In," *Mercury News,* May 4, 2003, http://www.madville.com/link.php?id=39525&t=23

Appendix A

1. L. K. Gundry and A. Buchko, *Field Casework: Methods for Consulting to Small and Start-up Businesses* (Thousand Oaks, CA: Sage Publications, 1996).
2. SBI programs are organized today under the umbrella of the Small Business Institute Directors Association, www.sbida.org.
3. Small Business Institute Directors' Association, Small Business Institute® Program Guidelines, 2004, http://www.smallbusinessinstitute.org/guideline.htm.
4. *Op cit.,* Gundry and Buchko.
5. *Ibid.*
6. *Ibid.*
7. *Ibid.*
8. Small Business Institute Director's Association. SBIDA Standards of Ethical Conduct for the SBI Program. Available at http://www.smallbusinessinstitute.org/ethics.htm.
9. B. Elmore, "Best Projects Learning," *Baylor Business Review* 21, no. 1 (Fall 2003), p. 30.
10. T. Auer, "Businesses Win from Student Competition," *Fort Worth Business Press* 13, no. 37 (January 5, 2001), p. 1.
11. *Ibid.*

Appendix B

1. This appendix was developed by Rick Koza of Chadron State College, Chadron, NE, under the direction of Jerome Katz.

2. The kind of project and presentation described here was chosen for a reason. It was not only a project in which the students did good for others, but it was also a project in which the students did well for themselves and their school. In 2004 the Chadron State team won SIFE's national entrepreneurship special competition and placed in the top fifteen in four of the other special competitions. In the last five years the Chadron State College team has placed in the top fifteen in the nation three years in a row.

Appendix C

1. This plan was developed by Yong Xu, a student at California State Polytechnic University—Pomona, under the direction of Professor Susan Peters.

Appendix D

1. Throughout this business plan "Middle Planning Stage" will refer to the time in the planning stage in which the major initial planning has been taken place (i.e., a date has been set, a church or ceremony site selected and booked, and a venue/caterer has been found and contracted) and no other details have been solidified.
2. *Off-peak* describes weddings in slower times; January–April, July–August, and November and December and *peak* describes weddings in busy season; May, June, September, and October.
3. In many cases an event planner will team up with a specific vendor* and will form a contractual agreement with the vendor for discounted services; i.e., if we form a relationship with a florist, we will promise to promote its services first and bring it so much business each year. In turn it will give us its services at a reduced price, which can be passed along to our clients or kept (an agreement that will be detailed in the client contract).
   *We are currently working on establishing a vendor list and making the types of relationships mentioned above
4. Including the paper, binders, and other supplies for client wedding binders.
5. Cash flows and payment are further discussed in section 3.3 Pricing and Payment.
6. The number 11 was taken from data provided by BizMiner—in SIC:7299.0504—wedding consultants. There are 11 firms listed in Des Moines, IA. The number may seem low, and there may be others who do wedding consulting, but they are not listed in this category and therefore are not addressed in the competitive comparison.
7. For sample budget see appendix 8-B (information taken from Denise and Alan Fields, *Bridal Bargains* (Boulder, CO., Windsor Peak Press, 2002), pp. 6–7.
8. We are estimating that each package will average 30 hours of labor.
9. The $10,000 package is based on a $20,000 wedding, our services being 50 percent of the wedding budget.
10. The $70/per additional hour will cover Ms. Evans and the additional consultant. If a third onsite consultant is requested, the client will be billed an additional $30/hour.
11. The 84,994 is an estimated number provided by www.zapdata.com.
12. Information taken from www.bizminer.com. It should be noted that more detailed information about the local Des Moines industry can be purchased from BizMiner for $99.00; however, at this time we are deciding to hold off on the purchase of this information.
13. Taken from a phone interview with, Ann Nola, the director of the Association of Certified Wedding Professional Wedding Consultants.
14. Quote taken from "Eat, Drink and Be Married: Wedding Bells Bring in Big Business for Restaurants," *Westchester County Business Journal* 41, no. 44 (November 4, 2002), p. 19.
15. Article by Karen Benezra and Beckey Ebenkamp, "Alter-Bound, Wallets Open," *Brandweek* 44, no. 20 (May 19, 2003), p. 20.
16. "Wedding Trends," *Florist* 32, no. 12 (May 1999), p. 55.
17. The 7,560 is an estimate: the 2000 census stated that the Iowa population was 5,605,067 and the Des Moines County population was 1,016,315; 1,016,315/5,605,067 = .1813, if based on population an estimated 18 percent of marriages in Iowa were Des Moines County residence .18 × 42,000 = 7,560 estimated marriages in Des Moines County in 2000.
18. Statistics from "Wedding Statistics" pamphlet produced by the *Association of Bridal Consultants,* p. 7.
19. Gerda D. Gallop and Deidra-Ann Parrish, "Wedding Bells Ring Up Big Business," *Black Enterprise*, June 1999, v. 29, 11, p. 56.
20. Details on our promotion through the vendor are discussed in Section 5.2, Sales Strategy.
21. A contract with venues will be prepared by our lawyer and signed by both parties; Emergency Bridal LLC and the venue.
22. Final details about the points system will be arranged at a later date; however, they will average $200 value for 100 points.
23. The details about commissions and discounts will be outlined and agreed upon by Emergency Bridal LLC and the client in the contract, most likely a 50/50 split.

Photo Credits

Chapter 1

page 7 Tom Lankes/ The Austin American-Statesman

page 11 © Wells Fargo

page 18 Anchor Bar & Restaurant

Chapter 2

page 24 Getty Images

page 31 © Derrick A. Bruce/Corbis

page 32 AP Wide World Photo

Chapter 3

page 54 Nick Rowe/ Getty Images/MGH-DIL

page 61 Courtesy Common Dog

page 63 © Stephane Cardinale/Corbis Sygma

page 69 Kate Swan

Chapter 4

page 76 Photo courtesy of Magnetic Poetry

page 80 Traction Plus

page 84 Clif Bar

page 87 Keith Brofsky/ Getty Images/MGH-DIL

Chapter 5

page 114 Dan Murza

page 116 Courtesy Saint Louis University

page 118 AP Wide World Photo

page 120 Courtesy The Pampered Chef

page 122 ebay®

page 124 Courtesy Courtney Hennessey Hopson

Chapter 6

page 136 Courtesy A Pea in the Pod

page 142 Courtesy of NewProductWorks www.newproductworks.com

page 146 Ryan McVay/ Getty Images/MGH-DIL

page 156 Photo provided by Auntie Anne's, Inc.

Chapter 7

page 166 Courtesy EnableMart

page 174 Photo by Jon Perlmutter

page 178 Image provided by Charles Calkins

Chapter 8

page 202 Wake Forest University

Chapter 9

page 230 Digital Vision/ Getty Images

page 240 Photo by Kryptonite®, A registered trademark of Schlage Lock Company

page 244 The Coca-Cola Company

page 254 Courtesy UltraPet

Chapter 10

page 266 Courtesy B*tween Productions, Inc.

page 270 Andrew Resek/ MGH-DIL

page 273 DigitalVision/ Getty Images/ MGH-DIL

page 275 © Royalty-Free/Corbis

page 280 Courtesy 8minutedating.com

page 283 Vermont Teddy Bear Company® www.VermontTeddy-Bear.com

Chapter 11

page 290 McGraw-Hill Companies, Jill Braaten, photographer

page 293 James F. Quinn (www.jamesfquinn.com)

page 297 © ePrinters.com

page 311 © Kelly-Mooney Photography/ Corbis

page 315 Dennis Light/ Light Photographic

Chapter 12

page 328 ZOU QING/ AFP/Getty Images

page 339 © Tom & Dee Ann McCarthy/Corbis

page 340 Bridgestone

Chapter 13

page 354 Mark Gilliland/ Acropolis

Chapter 14

page 392 Be Our Guest, Inc.

page 396 AP/Wide World Photo

page 401 The Baby Einstein Company

Chapter 15

page 430 Courtesy INCELL Corporation, LLC

page 439 Corbis

Chapter 16

page 458 © K. Handke/ zefa/Corbis

page 468 Photo provided courtesy of World Smile Corp. All rights reserved.

page 473 AP Wide World Photo

Chapter 17

page 486 Neil Beer/ Getty Images/MGH-DIL

page 490 Courtesy Dwight Cooper

page 494 Photo courtesy Alienware Corporation

page 495 Uniform Code Council, Inc.

page 498 Photo by Todd Williams, courtesy Huntington Theatre Company

Chapter 18

page 518 Colorstock/ Getty Images

page 523 Business.gov

page 525 Alan Schein Photography/Corbis

page 533 Courtesy Litigation Fairness .org

page 537 Robert Holmes/Corbis

Chapter 19

page 548 Courtesy Jennifer J. Johnson

page 552 © Royalty-Free/Corbis

page 558 © Royalty-Free/ Corbis

page 565 Bill Varie/ Corbis

Chapter 20

page 576 Graeme Teague

page 585 © Royalty-Free/Corbis

page 590 Michael McMyne

Appendix C

page A-23 Nick Cogan

Name and Company Index

C

D

E

H

I

T

X

Y

Z

Subject Index

A

B

D

E

F

G

H

I

J

K

L

M

N

O

P

R